WHERE THE LOCALS EAT

A Guide to the Best Restaurants in America

Compiled by the editors and researchers of
Magellan Press:

*L. Lee Wilson, William B. King,
K. Joy Wood, Carole Cunningham,
Chris Hudson, Rebecca Newton, David Austin,
Kelly Hill-Aronoff, and Warren Wakeland*

MAGELLAN PRESS, INC.
Nashville, Tennessee

Where the Locals Eat: A Guide to the Best Restaurants in America

Compiled by the editors and researchers of Magellan Press:
L. Lee Wilson, William B. King, K. Joy Wood,
Carole Cunningham, Chris Hudson, Rebecca Newton,
David Austin, Kelly Hill-Aronoff, and Warren Wakeland

Published by Magellan Press, Inc., P.O. Box 121075,
Nashville, Tennessee 37212.
Printed in the United States of America.

To order additional copies of *Where the Locals Eat*,
use the order form in the back of the book or
call the publisher at 800/624-5359.
Quantity discounts are available to volume buyers.

Book design by Bruce Gore , Gore Studio, Inc.,
Brentwood, Tennessee.
Cover design by John Robertson, Robertson Design,
Brentwood, Tennessee.
Printed by Malloy Lithographing, Inc.,
Ann Arbor, Michigan.

Library of Congress Catalog Card Number: 96-76447

ISBN: 0-9634403-1-4

Contents

Introduction

It's 6:30. You've had a hard day. Your hotel room is nothing fancy, but it's clean and quiet and the mattress is comfortable. You need to review your notes for your meeting tomorrow, but first you want to eat—after a day during which you had no time for breakfast and only an airline sandwich for lunch, you're famished. But how do you find a decent meal in a city you've never visited before?

Or maybe you're traveling with your children. They ate too much junk food at the theme park and they'd gladly eat pizza again for dinner, but you'd like to find a nice family restaurant where *you* can order something less fattening. There's a phone book in your motel room, but that doesn't tell you what you want to know, which is *Where in this city can I feed two adults and two ravenous kids for under $30.*

Or maybe you want to take your client to lunch. He's old enough to be your father and you think he thinks you're wet behind the ears. You've never been to Boston before, but you don't want *him* to realize that this is your first trip. Where can you take him that will impress him with your *savoir faire* and allow you to close your deal?

Where the Locals Eat is the first book that can answer these questions. There are other restaurant guides, but most of them don't take into account that people travel to cities smaller than New York and Los Angeles. Others are geared more toward the gourmet in search of the ultimate *escargot* experience than the average traveler caught in Detroit overnight. And, whatever they say, those "dining guides" you find in pricey hotel rooms are sometimes no more useful than the Yellow Pages—what a coincidence that every restaurant listed in these slick publications is also the subject of a nice, big ad!

Our researchers spent two years gathering information on the best and most popular restaurants in more than 1,000 American cities. The result of that research is this book. It includes restaurants named as the best in town in local newspaper and magazine readers' polls, by local restaurant critics and editors, and by local business and professional people and field reviewers. None of the restaurants in our directory paid to be included—in fact, the only way to make it into *Where the Locals Eat* is to be recommended by someone who lives in the area and knows which restaurants his or her neighbors like best. We believe that *Where the Locals Eat* is the most reliable restaurant guide on the market—after all, who knows better where to eat in San Jose or Atlanta or Wichita than the people who live there?

A word about the information included in each restaurant listing. We have purposely kept our listings brief. Each contains the name, telephone number, and street address of the recommended restaurant. If the restaurant is in a neighboring town, that town name is also given. (When the town you're visiting is near a state line, you may see a neighboring town listed that is actually in another state.) We figure that knowing what sort of food a restaurant serves, and that people who aren't new to town like it, is just about all a traveler wants to know about any restaurant in our directory except how to get there. For other information about a restaurant, such as its hours of operation or whether it requires reservations, we suggest phoning the restaurant. After all, if you're in Austin, it's a local call to the best steak place in town.

Be sure to look not only at the listings for the town where you're staying, but also at those for nearby cities. *Where the Locals Eat* in Marietta, Georgia may be, sometimes, in restaurants within the sprawl of Atlanta. The reverse situation also occurs. While many suburban communities are large enough to have earned their own listings, the best way to find a good steak near you may be to look at the recommended restaurants in the nearest city, especially if you are visiting a populous area where suburbs of the principal cities have grown to meet each other.

Knowing that our readers would have diverse tastes, we have gathered information on seventy-five different categories of restaurants—restaurants known for everything from their barbecue or burgers to their vegetarian menu or wine list. Because we wer dependent on the recommendations of our local sources and because you just can't find a sports bar good Spanish food or sushi in every town and city, the restaurant listings for most of the cities in our directory include far fewer than seventy-five categories. However, because our sources sometimes told us of really great places to eat and drink that are interesting partly because they are out of the ordinary, in many cities we have included restaurant categories that don't occur elsewhere. Be sure to read carefully the listings for any city you visit to discover excellent sources for both ordinary and extraordinary food.

You'll notice that in most cities, there is more than one "best" restaurant listed for many categories. Again, this is reflective of our research. If our sources named several "best" Italian restaurants, so did we. This is because even though we consider all our sources to be reliable, the opinions of reliable people differ. We also knew that you'd want to know about *all* the best Indian restaurants in Orlando. So we included all the recommendations we gathered. You can decide for yourself if one of several great restaurants outshines the others.

Because our directory is designed to be useful to real people rather than to appeal only to traveling gourmets, we have included in our listings the names of chain restaurants when they were recommended to us as the best restaurants of their sort in a particular town or city. We did this for several reasons. We know that, in some smaller cities, the best burgers in town *are* at Sonic. And we know that sometimes travelers don't want to experiment with dinner—they just want a decent meal at a reasonable price. Chain restaurants were often recommended in more than one category; to avoid repetition and to enable you to easily find the dependable Shoney's or Red Lobster or Cracker Barrel food you're familiar with, we have grouped national chain restaurants in the Standbys listing that follows the other categories for many cities.

We hope you enjoy using **Where the Locals Eat**. Happy trails and *bon appetit!*

Alabama

ANNISTON, AL

Best Atmosphere
Victoria Inn
  1604 Quintard Ave., 205/236-0503
Top of the River
  3220 McClellan Blvd., 205/238-0097

Best Barbecue/Ribs
Betty's Barbecue
  401 S. Quintard Ave., 205/237-1411
Dad's Barbecue
  3101 McClellan Blvd., 205/238-4323
Old Smokehouse Bar-B-Q
  631 S. Quintard Ave., 205/237-5200

Best Cajun/Creole Food
Cajun's
  2900 McClellan Blvd., 205/236-6372

Best Chinese Food
China Luck
  503 Quintard Dr., Oxford, 205/831-5221

Best Dinner
Victoria Inn
  1604 Quintard Ave., 205/236-0503

Best Mexican Food
Los Tres Amigos
  320 S. Quintard Ave., 205/237-4404

Best Pizza
Pizza Inn
  2017 Quintard Ave., 205/236-5671

Best Seafood
Top of the River
  3220 McClellan Blvd., 205/238-0097

Standbys
Sonic Drive-In
  3109 Noble St., 205/236-6796

AUBURN, AL

Best Atmosphere
Legends Bar and Grill
1408 Opelika Rd., 334/826-0712

Best Barbecue/Ribs
Chuck's Bar-B-Que
622 Shug Jordan Pkwy., 334/826-2400
Barbecue House
345 S. College St., 334/826-8277

Best Bottomless Coffee Cup
Auburn Grille
104 N. College St., 334/821-6626

Best Bread
Provino's Italian Restaurant
3903A Pepperell Pkwy., 334/742-0340

Best Brunch
Auburn University Hotel and Center
241 S. College St., 334/821-8200

Best Burgers
Cheeseburger, Cheeseburger
160 N. College St., 334/826-0845
Auburn Grille
104 N. College St., 334/821-6626
Tyler's Restaurant
1478 Opelika Rd., 334/887-5555

Best Business Breakfast
Auburn University Hotel and Center
241 S. College St., 334/821-8200

Best Business Lunch
Ryan's Restaurant and Tavern
1032 Opelika Rd., 334/821-0717

Best Cheap Meal
Auburn Grille
104 N. College St., 334/821-6626

Best Coffeehouse
The Coffee Banque
101 N. College St., 334/887-1005

Best Desserts
The Coffee Banque
101 N. College St., 334/887-1005

Best Diner
Tiger Time Diner
1645 S. College St., 334/826-2000

Best Ice Cream/Yogurt
Dairy Dream
207 S. College St., Greenville, 334/382-5501

Best Italian Food
Denaro's
103 N. College St., 334/821-0349

Standbys
Applebee's
1627 Opelika Rd., 334/887-7747

Chili's
  1447 Opelika Rd., 334/887-9997
Red Lobster
  1805 Opelika Rd., 334/821-4474
Shoney's
  1498 Opelika Rd., 334/826-6224
Subway
  1550 Opelika Rd., 334/821-7835
  108 S. Gay St., 334/821-1029
  186 N. Donahue Dr., 334/826-1716

BESSEMER, AL

Best Restaurant in Town
Bright Star Restaurant
  304 Nineteenth St. N., 205/424-9444

Best Barbecue/Ribs
Bob Sykes Bar-B-Q
  1724 Ninth Ave. N., 205/426-1400

Best Homestyle Food
Hobo Joe's Family Restaurant
  1030 Fourth Ave. N., 205/424-1622

Best Seafood
Bright Star Restaurant
  304 Nineteenth St. N., 205/424-9444

Standbys
Shoney's
  723 Ninth Ave. N., 205/424-4007
Pizza Hut
  829 Eighth Ave. N., 205/426-1204

BIRMINGHAM, AL

Best Restaurant in Town
Highlands Restaurant
  2011 Eleventh Ave. S., 205/939-1400

Best American Food
Fish Market Restaurant
  611 21st St. S., 205/322-3330
  119 Riverchase Village Shopping Ctr., 205/988-9720

Best Atmosphere
Arman's
  2117 Cahaba Park Cir., 205/871-5551

Best Bar
Lou's Pub
  726 29th St. S., 205/322-7005

Best Barbecue/Ribs
Dreamland Bar-B-Que
  1427 Fourteenth Ave. S., 205/933-2133

Best Bread
Arman's
  2117 Cahaba Park Cir., 205/871-5551

Best Breakfast
The Original Pancake House
  1931 Eleventh Ave. S., 205/933-8837

Brunch
ristian Tutwiler's
2001 Park Pl., 205/323-9822

Best Burgers
Heights Cafe
3135 Cahaba Heights Rd., 205/967-3132

Best Business Lunch
Bottega Cafe
2242 Highland Ave. S., 205/933-2001

Best Cajun/Creole Food
Merritt House
2220 Highland Ave. S., 205/933-1200

Best Casual Dining
Magic City Brewery
420 21st St. S., 205/328-2739

Best Cheap Meal
Purple Onion Deli and Grill
1931 Second Ave. N., 205/252-4899

Best Chinese Food
Chop Suey Inn
837 Green Springs Hwy., Homewood, 205/942-9782

Best Coffeehouse
O'Henry's Coffee
2831 Eighteenth St., Homewood, 205/870-1198

Best Continental Food
Bombay Cafe
2839 Seventh Ave. S., 205/322-1930

Best Delicatessen
Vincent's Market
531 Brookwood Village Ctr., 205/871-2800

Best Desserts
Highlands Restaurant
2011 Eleventh Ave. S., 205/939-1400

Best Diner
Crestline Diner
75 Church St., 205/871-7281

Best Family Restaurant
Irondale Cafe
1906 First Ave. N., 205/956-5258

Best French Food
Cafe de France
2612 Lane Park Rd., 205/871-1000

Best Health-Conscious Menu
Golden Temple Natural Grocery
1901 Eleventh Ave. S., 205/933-6333
3309 Lorna Rd., 205/823-7002

Best Homestyle Food
Irondale Cafe
1906 First Ave. N., 205/956-5258

Best Indian Food
Ali Baba
110 Centre at Riverchase, 205/823-2222

Best Italian Food
Ciao Italian Restaurant
2031 Cahaba Rd., Mountain Brook, 205/871-2426

Best Japanese Food
Asahi Japanese Restaurant
444 Cahaba Park Cir., 205/991-5542

Best Late-Night Food
Moneer's Garden Deli and Grill
932 Oxmoor Rd., 205/871-0306

Best Greek/Mediterranean Food
Connie Kanakis' Cafe
3423 Colonnade Pkwy., 205/967-5775

Best Mexican Food
La Paz Mexican Restaurant
99 Euclid Ave., 205/879-2225

Best Middle Eastern Food
Pita Stop Cafe
1106 Twelfth St. S., 205/328-2749

Best Pizza
Cosmo's Pizza
2012 Magnolia Ave. S., 205/930-9971

Best Place to Be "Seen"
Bottega Cafe
2242 Highland Ave. S., 205/933-2001

Best Place to Eat Alone
Pete's Famous Hot Dogs
1925 Second Ave. N., 205/252-2905

Best Place to Eat When Someone Else Is Buying
Arman's
2117 Cahaba Park Cir., 205/871-5551

Best Quick Lunch
The Magic Bagel
3220 Clairmont Ave., 205/326-3354

Best Romantic Dining
Merritt House
2220 Highland Ave. S., 205/933-1200

Best Salad/Salad Bar
Fifth Quarter Steakhouse
195 Vulcan Rd., 205/942-0108

Best Sandwiches
Forest Park Deli and Catering
3811 Clairmont Ave. S., 205/595-5577

Best Schmooze Bar
Highlands Restaurant
2011 Eleventh Ave. S., 205/939-1400

Best Seafood
Fish Market Restaurant
611 21st St. S., 205/322-3330
119 Riverchase Village Shopping Ctr., 205/988-9720

Best Smoke-Free Restaurant
The Anchorage
2826 Eighteenth St. S., 205/870-7760

Best Soul Food
Nelson Brothers Cafe
312 Seventeenth St. N., 205/254-9098

Best Southwestern Food
Arizona Rib Company
217 Lakeshore Pkwy., 205/290-2190

Best Sports Bar
P.T.'s
350 Hollywood Blvd., 205/879-8519

Best Steaks
Michael's
431 Twentieth St. S., 205/322-0419

Best Sushi
Asahi Japanese Restaurant
444 Cahaba Park Cir., 205/991-5542

Best Tea Room
Cobb Lane Restaurant
1 Cobb Lane S., 205/933-0462

Best 24-Hour Restaurant
Moneer's Garden Deli and Grill
932 Oxmoor Rd., 205/871-0306

Best Undiscovered Restaurant
Bro' Chette's Que Bayou
1709 Fourth Ave. N., 205/326-3663

Best Vegetarian Food
Golden Temple Natural Grocery
1901 Eleventh Ave. S., 205/933-6333
3309 Lorna Rd., 205/823-7002

Best Wine Selection
Highlands Restaurant
2011 Eleventh Ave. S., 205/939-1400

Best Other Restaurant
Let's Eat Smoked Meat
2000 High School Rd., 205/491-3059

Standbys
Chuck E. Cheese Pizza
9323 Parkway E., 205/833-8807
500 Old Town Rd., 205/979-3420

DECATUR, AL

Best All-You-Can-Eat Buffet
Formosa Chinese Restaurant
2114 Sixth Ave. SE, 205/350-3300

Best Atmosphere
Court Street Cafe
103 Second St. SW, 205/350-5777
Iron Gate Restaurant
402 Johnston St. SE, 205/350-6795

Best Barbecue/Ribs
B.B. Perrins Beer and BBQ
608 Holly St. NE, 205/355-1045

Big Bob Gibson's Bar-B-Que
  1715 Sixth Ave. SE, 205/350-6969
  2520 Danville Rd. SW, 205/350-0404
Whitt's Barbecue
  2532 Spring Ave. SW, 205/350-2748
  918 Sixth Ave. SE, 205/351-6294

Best Burgers
Court Street Cafe
  103 Second St. SW, 205/350-5777

Best Chinese Food
Formosa Chinese Restaurant
  2114 Sixth Ave. SE, 205/350-3300

Best Coffee
Cafe 113
  113 Grant St. SE, 205/351-1400

Best Desserts
Raymo's Cajun Cuisine
  805 Sixth Ave. SE, 205/309-0005

Best Homestyle Food
Iron Gate Restaurant
  402 Johnston St. SE, 205/350-6795
City Cafe
  101 First Ave. SE, 205/353-9126

Best Ice Cream/Yogurt
Camino Real Mexican Restaurant
  2504 Sixth Ave. SE, 205/353-6727

Best Mexican Food
Camino Real Mexican Restaurant
  2504 Sixth Ave. SE, 205/353-6727

Best Pizza
Mando's Italian Food
  1416 Sixth Ave. SE, 205/355-4430

Best Place to Take the Kids
Camino Real Mexican Restaurant
  2504 Sixth Ave. SE, 205/353-6727

Best Salad/Salad Bar
Court Street Cafe
  103 Second St. SW, 205/350-5777
Iron Gate Restaurant
  402 Johnston St. SE, 205/350-6795
Mando's Italian Food
  1416 Sixth Ave. SE, 205/355-4430

Best Sandwiches
Court Street Cafe
  103 Second St. SW, 205/350-5777

Best Seafood
McCollum's Catfish and Seafood
  Hwy. 24W, 205/353-9321

Best Steaks
Brangus Feed Lot
  1807 Sixth Ave. SE, 205/355-9499

‑Robbins
Sixth Ave. SE, 205/353-1410

DEMOPOLIS, AL

Best Atmosphere
Foscue House
Hwy. 80W, 334/289-2221

Best Breakfast
Camphouse Restaurant
512 Hwy. 80E, 334/289-2312

Best Chinese Food
China Inn Chinese Restaurant
123 W. Washington St., 334/289-4528

Best Dinner
Foscue House
Hwy. 80W, 334/289-2221

Best Family Restaurant
Camphouse Restaurant
512 Hwy. 80E, 334/289-2312
Robert's Family Restaurant
Hwy. 80E, 334/289-1505

Best Homestyle Food
Camphouse Restaurant
512 Hwy. 80E, 334/289-2312

Best Italian Food
Mr. G's Pizza
602 N. Walnut Ave., 334/289-4149

Best Seafood
Ellis V Restaurant
708 Hwy. 80E, 334/289-3446
Red Barn
901 Hwy. 80E, 334/289-0595

Best Steaks
Ellis V Restaurant
708 Hwy. 80E, 334/289-3446
Red Barn
901 Hwy. 80E, 334/289-0595

DOTHAN, AL

Best Burgers
Mrs. Boomer's
224 N. Foster St., 334/793-7810

Best Chinese Food
Chopsticks
1111 W. Troy, 334/677-7664

Best Coffee
Books-A-Million
3489 Ross Clark Circle, 334/712-1341

Best Desserts
Garland House
  200 N. Bell St., 334/793-2043
Old Mill Restaurant
  2501 Murphy Mill Rd., 334/794-8530

Best Homestyle Food
Pat's Diner
  1905 Montgomery Hwy., 334/671-8244

Best Italian Food
Tony's Italian Restaurant
  3803 Ross Clark Circle NW, 334/794-4457

Best Mexican Food
Old Mexican
  2920 Ross Clark Circle, 334/712-1434

Best Pizza
Mama Rosa's Pizza
  3074H Ross Clark Circle SW, 334/794-2252
  2111 Southview Shopping Ctr., 334/793-6868

Best Steaks
Conestoga Steak House
  2429 Montgomery Hwy., 334/794-4445
Old Mill Restaurant
  2501 Murphy Mill Rd., 334/794-8530

Standbys
Waffle House
  2971 Ross Clark Circle SW, 334/792-8389
  1925 E. Main St., 334/794-6406
  3591 Ross Clark Circle NW, 334/793-7739
Shoney's
  3054 Ross Clark Circle SW, 334/792-4415

ENTERPRISE, AL

Best All-You-Can-Eat Buffet
Gran's Home Cooked Buffet
  1032Q Boll Weevil Circle, 334/393-1701

Best Bar
Top's Restaurant and Lounge
  734 Glover Ave., 334/393-2297

Best Barbecue/Ribs
Carolina Bar-B-Que
  608 E. Park Ave., 334/347-1096
Cutt's Restaurant
  417 E. Lee St., 334/347-1110

Best Breakfast
Dottie's Country Kitchen
  925 N. Main St., 334/393-1439

Best Business Lunch
Cutt's Restaurant
  417 E. Lee St., 334/347-1110

Best Chinese Food
Hunan Chinese Restaurant
  1034 Rucker Blvd., 334/393-1417
China Gate Restaurant
  654 Hwy. 84 Bypass, 334/347-2722

Best Desserts
Wildflower Cafe
201 E. Watts St., 334/393-0699

Best Family Restaurant
Gran's Home Cooked Buffet
1032Q Boll Weevil Circle, 334/393-1701

Best Homestyle Food
Cutt's Restaurant
417 E. Lee St., 334/347-1110
Magnolia Room
107 N. Main St., 334/347-0697

Best Italian Food
Italian Villa
Hwy. 123, Newton, 334/299-3533

Best Lunch
Magnolia Room
107 N. Main St., 334/347-0697

Best Mexican Food
Effie's Cantina
913 Rucker Blvd., 334/347-0838

Best Place to Be "Seen"
Cutt's Restaurant
417 E. Lee St., 334/347-1110

Best Regional Food
Cutt's Restaurant
417 E. Lee St., 334/347-1110

Best Salad/Salad Bar
Wildflower Cafe
201 E. Watts St., 334/393-0699

Best Steaks
Western Steer Steakhouse
650 Boll Weevil Circle, 334/347-6556
Indigo Head
1009 Rucker Blvd., 334/393-9566

Best Tea Room
Wildflower Cafe
201 E. Watts St., 334/393-0699

Standbys
Subway
606 Boll Weevil Circle, 334/347-3744

FLORENCE, AL

Best Atmosphere
Renaissance Grille
1 Hightown Pl., 205/718-0092
J.C. Scott's
230 E. Tennessee St., 205/757-3819

Best Barbecue/Ribs
Bunyan's Bar-B-Que
901 W. College St., 205/766-3522

Best Burgers
Calahan's 1877
  219 N. Court St., 205/767-4553
Princeton's Restaurant
  251 Cox Creek Pkwy., 205/766-7163

Best Cajun/Creole Food
Louisiana
  406 N. Montgomery Ave., Sheffield, 205/386-0801

Best Desserts
Court Street Cafe
  116 E. Mobile St., 205/766-6196
  201 N. Seminary St., 205/767-4300

Best Italian Food
Stephano's Little Italy
  218 N. Court St., 205/764-7407

Best Pizza
Stephano's Little Italy
  218 N. Court St., 205/764-7407
The Olive Tree
  1807 Northwood Ave., Sheffield, 205/740-0811

Best Salad/Salad Bar
Dale's Restaurant
  1001 Mitchell Blvd., 205/766-4961

Best Seafood
Renaissance Grille
  1 Hightown Pl., 205/718-0092
J.C. Scott's
  230 E. Tennessee St., 205/757-3819

Best Steaks
Dale's Restaurant
  1001 Mitchell Blvd., 205/766-4961
George's Steak Pit
  1206 S. Jackson Hwy., Sheffield, 205/381-1531

Best View While Dining
Renaissance Grille
  1 Hightown Pl., 205/718-0092

Standbys
Baskin-Robbins
  301 Cox Creek Pkwy., 205/767-2846

GADSDEN, AL

Best American Food
Thee Grill
  135 N. Seventh St., 205/546-7788

Best Bar
Chestnut Station
  410 Chestnut St., 205/546-4229

Best Barbecue/Ribs
Pruitt's
  1617 Rainbow Dr., 205/547-4118

Best Burgers
Magic Burger
  915 Cleveland Ave., 205/538-7350
Rally's Hamburgers
  303 E. Meighan Blvd., 205/547-5773

Best Cheap Meal
Tony's Bar-B-Q
  227 S. Third St., 205/547-0230

Best Chinese Food
Golden China
  957 W. Meighan Blvd., 205/546-9443

Best Diner
Tony's Bar-B-Q
  227 S. Third St., 205/547-0230

Best Happy Hour Snacks
Chestnut Station
  410 Chestnut St., 205/546-4229

Best Homestyle Food
West Gadsden Cafe
  906 Forrest Ave., 205/547-9183

Best Mexican Food
Mi Casita Mexican Restaurant
  209 S. Fourth St., 205/547-9824

Best Place to Be "Seen"
Fuzzy Duck
  231 E. Broad St., 205/546-9149

Best Soul Food
Cunningham's BBQ
  ["Call for directions."], 205/494-0914

Best Undiscovered Restaurant
Cedric's Kitchen
  104 N. College St., 205/492-7664

Standbys
Dairy Queen
  3340 Rainbow Rd., 205/442-0011
Pizza Hut
  607 E. Meighan Blvd., 205/543-2100
  1729 Rainbow Dr., 205/547-5269
Quincy's
  1000 E. Meighan Blvd., 205/492-9200
Red Lobster
  1725 Rainbow Dr., 205/543-2086
Ruby Tuesday
  Gadsden Mall, 1001 Rainbow Dr., 205/543-3900
Ryan's Family Steak House
  127 River Rd., 205/547-3852
Shoney's
  202 E. Meighan Blvd., 205/543-7098
Subway
  445 George Wallace Dr., 205/547-7822

HUNTSVILLE, AL

Best Restaurant in Town
Richard's on the Square
  109 Northside Sq., 205/536-6335

Best American Food
Green Hills Grille
  5100 Sanderson St. NW, 205/837-8282

Best Bar
West End Grill
  6610 Old Madison Pike NW, 205/722-8040

Best Barbecue/Ribs
Green Briar Barbecue
  Hwy. 20, Madison, 205/353-9769

Best Business Lunch
Bubba's
  109 Washington St. NE, 205/534-3133

Best Continental Food
Green Bottle Grill and Bakery
  975 Airport Rd. SW, 205/882-0459

Best Dinner
West End Grill
  6610 Old Madison Pike NW, 205/722-8040

Best French Food
Pho's Cafe and Lounge
  2006 Country Club Ave. NW, 205/533-5001

Best German Food
Cafe Berlin
  505 Airport Rd. SW, 205/880-9920
Ol Heidelberg Cafe
  6125 University Dr. NW, 205/922-0556

Best Homestyle Food
Eunice's Country Kitchen
  1006A Andrew Jackson Way NE, 205/534-9550
Five Points Restaurant
  816 Wellman Ave. NE, 205/536-7356

Best Indian Food
Bombay Cuisine
  420 Jordan Ln. NW, 205/536-3360

Best Italian Food
Fratelli's Italian Restaurant
  4800 Whitesburg Dr. S., 205/650-5944
  501 Jordan Ln. NW, 205/830-1660

Best Japanese Food
Shogun Japanese Steak House
  3780 University Dr. NW, 205/534-3000

Best Lunch
Victoria's Cafe
  7500 Memorial Pkwy. SW, 205/881-0403

Best Mexican Food
Bandito Burrito
  3017 Governors Dr. SW, 205/534-0866

Best Salad/Salad Bar
Victoria's Cafe
7500 Memorial Pkwy. SW, 205/881-0403

Best Sushi
Shogun Japanese Steak House
3780 University Dr. NW, 205/534-3000

JACKSON, AL

Best All-You-Can-Eat Buffet
Rock and Roll Cafe
2704 College Ave., 334/246-5800

Best Barbecue/Ribs
Rock and Roll Cafe
2704 College Ave., 334/246-5800

Best Breakfast
Rock and Roll Cafe
2704 College Ave., 334/246-5800

Best Burgers
Ed's Drive-In
3018 College Ave., 334/246-3054

Best Desserts
Delightful Treats
1916 College Ave., 334/246-3685

Best Family Restaurant
Jackson Seafood
Hwy. 43, 334/246-4441

Best Mexican Food
Nolasco's Mexican and American Restaurant
1204 College Ave., 334/246-6822

Best Sandwiches
Delightful Treats
1916 College Ave., 334/246-3685

Best Seafood
Jackson Seafood
Hwy. 43, 334/246-4441

Best Steaks
Jackson Seafood
Hwy. 43, 334/246-4441

Standbys
Pizza Hut
2123 N. College Ave., 334/246-2402

MOBILE, AL

Best Restaurants in Town
Michael's Midtown Cafe
153 S. Florida St., 334/473-5908
Loretta's Restaurant
19 S. Conception St., 334/432-2200
Lighthouse Restaurant
12495 Padgent Switch, Bayou La Batre, 334/824-2500

Best All-You-Can-Eat Buffet
Hunan Chinese Restaurant
  306 E. Laurel Ave., Foley, 334/943-3909

Best Barbecue/Ribs
Johnny's Smokehouse Restaurant
  3758 Dauphin Island Pkwy., 334/478-8172
Rodger's B-B-Q
  2350 St. Stephens Rd., 334/330-0285
Saucy-Que Barbecue
  1301 Springhill Ave., 334/433-7427

Best Casual Dining
Poppa Rocko's
  Sixth St. at Hwy. 59, Gulf Shores, 334/948-7262
Wolf Bay Lodge
  9050 Pinewood Ave., Elberta, 334/986-7267

Best Cheap Meal
Bangkok Thai Cuisine
  5345 Hwy. 90W, 334/666-7788
Hunan Chinese Restaurant
  306 E. Laurel Ave., Foley, 334/943-3909
Queen G's Cafe
  2518 Old Shell Rd., 334/471-3361
Saucy-Que Barbecue
  1301 Springhill Ave., 334/433-7427

Best Chinese Food
Hunan Chinese Restaurant
  306 E. Laurel Ave., Foley, 334/943-3909

Best Eclectic Menu
Almost Six
  6 1/2 N. Jackson St., 334/438-3447

Best Italian Food
Gambino's Restaurant
  18 Laurel Ave., Fair Hope, 334/928-5444

Best Pizza
Poppa Rocko's
  Sixth St. at Hwy. 59, Gulf Shores, 334/948-7262

Best Quick Lunch
Queen G's Cafe
  2518 Old Shell Rd., 334/471-3361

Best Regional Food
Punta Clara Kitchen
  17111 Scenic Hwy. 98, Point Clear, 334/928-8477

Best Salad/Salad Bar
Lighthouse Restaurant
  12495 Padgent Switch, Bayou La Batre, 334/824-2500

Best Seafood
Bailey's
  10805 Dauphin Island Pkwy., 334/973-1572
The Blue Gill Restaurant and Club
  3775 Battleship Pkwy., Spanish Fort, 334/626-9852
Gambino's Restaurant
  18 Laurel Ave., Fairhope, 334/928-5444
Lighthouse Restaurant
  12495 Padgent Switch, Bayou La Batre, 334/824-2500

A

Wolf Bay Lodge
  9050 Pinewood Ave., Elberta, 334/986-7267

Best Soul Food
Oliver's Restaurant
  Radisson Hotel, 251 Government St., 334/432-8000
Cock of the Walk
  4815 Halls Mill Rd., 334/666-1875

Best Thai Food
Bangkok Thai Cuisine
  5345 Hwy. 90W, 334/666-7788

MONTGOMERY, AL

Best Restaurant in Town
Sahara Restaurant
  511 E. Edgemont Ave., 334/264-9178

Best Breakfast
Farmer's Market Cafe West
  1250 Air Base Blvd., 334/269-2871
  1659 Federal Dr., 334/271-1885
  315 N. McDonough St., 334/262-1970

Best Burgers
Sommer's Place
  7972 Vaughn Rd., 334/279-5401
Joe's Deli
  2960A Zelda Rd., 334/244-0440

Best Business Lunch
Chappy's Deli
  1611 Perry Hill Rd., 334/279-7477

Best Cajun/Creole Food
French Quarter Cafe
  5040 Vaughn Rd., 334/244-1562

Best Chinese Food
Choices Chinese Restaurant
  80 Commerce St., 334/262-0888

Best Greek/Mediterranean Food
Sahara Restaurant
  511 E. Edgemont Ave., 334/264-9178

Best Homestyle Food
Martin's Restaurant
  1796 Carter Hill Rd., 334/265-1767
Down the Street Cafe
  2739 Zelda Rd., 334/279-1009
Shashy's Bakery and Fine Food
  1700 Mulberry St., 334/263-7341

Best Italian Food
Corsino's Italian-American
  911 S. Court St., 334/263-9752

Best Sandwiches
Chappy's Deli
  1611 Perry Hill Rd., 334/279-7477

Best Seafood
Sahara Restaurant
  511 E. Edgemont Ave., 334/264-9178

Best Soul Food
Moses Crawford Catering
700 Columbus St., 334/265-3520

Best Steaks
Green Lantern
5725 Troy Hwy., 334/288-9947

OPELIKA, AL

Best Restaurants in Town
Breeze Way
213 S. Eighth St., 334/749-5167
Venable's
913 S. Railroad Ave., 334/745-0834
The Warehouse Bistro
105C Rocket Ave., 334/745-6353

Best All-You-Can-Eat Buffet
Mister J's Family Steak House
2027 Pepperell Pkwy., 334/749-5741

Best Burgers
Little Ireland's Pub
122 W. Magnolia Ave., 334/821-5634

Best Chinese Food
Rose Chinese Restaurant
2360 Pepperell Pkwy., 334/705-0108

Best Place to Eat When Someone Else Is Buying
The Warehouse Bistro
105C Rocket Ave., 334/745-6353

Best Romantic Dining
Provino's Italian Restaurant
3903A Pepperell Pkwy., 334/742-0340

Best Salad/Salad Bar
Provino's Italian Restaurant
3903A Pepperell Pkwy., 334/742-0340

Best Sandwiches
Mister J's Family Steak House
2027 Pepperell Pkwy., 334/749-5741

Best Steaks
Mister J's Family Steak House
2027 Pepperell Pkwy., 334/749-5741

PHENIX CITY, AL

Best Barbecue/Ribs
Mike and Ed's Bar-B-Q
2001 Crawford Rd., 334/297-1012

Best Breakfast
Tyler's Restaurants
800 Thirteenth St., 334/297-5778

Best Chinese Food
King House
1821 Stadium Dr., 334/480-4009

Best Homestyle Food
C. Argo's
1307 Third Ave., 334/291-1888

Best Lunch
C. Argo's
1307 Third Ave., 334/291-1888

Best Mexican Food
El Vaquero
913 Hwy. 280 Bypass, 334/298-8009

SELMA, AL

Best All-You-Can-Eat Buffet
Jericho Country Fried and Broiled Chicken
2314 Hwy. 80E, 334/872-9204

Best Barbecue/Ribs
Lannie's Bar-B-Q Spot
2115 Minter Ave., 334/874-4478

Best Breakfast
Glass House Restaurant
108 Hwy. 80E, 334/874-9290

Best Chinese Food
China Cook
128 Broad St., 334/872-2778

Best Homestyle Food
Downtowner Restaurant
1114 Selma Ave., 334/875-5933

Best Lunch
Downtowner Restaurant
1114 Selma Ave., 334/875-5933

Best Steaks
Steak Pit
Hwy. 80W, 334/872-3509

TUSCALOOSA, AL

Best Restaurant in Town
Globe Restaurant
430 Main Ave., Northport, 205/391-0949

Best American Food
Kozy's
3510 Loop Rd. E., 205/556-0665

Best Atmosphere
Globe Restaurant
430 Main Ave., Northport, 205/391-0949
Cypress Inn
501 Rice Mine Rd. N., 205/345-6963
Kozy's
3510 Loop Rd. E., 205/556-0665

Best Bar
Kozy's
3510 Loop Rd. E., 205/556-0665

Best Barbecue/Ribs
Dreamland Drive-Inn Bar-B-Que
5535 Fifteenth Ave. E., 205/758-8135

Best Bottomless Coffee Cup
Liberty Cafe
1407 University Blvd., 205/758-1833

Best Bread
Globe Restaurant
430 Main Ave., Northport, 205/391-0949

Best Breakfast
The Waysider
1512 Greensboro Ave., 205/345-8239

Best Burgers
Kwik Snack
1005 University Blvd., 205/752-8783

Best Business Breakfast
The Waysider
1512 Greensboro Ave., 205/345-8239

Best Business Lunch
Fifteenth Street Diner
1036 Fifteenth St., 205/750-8750

Best Casual Dining
City Cafe
408 Main Ave., Northport, 205/758-9171

Best Cheap Meal
City Cafe
408 Main Ave., Northport, 205/758-9171

Best Chinese Food
Trey Yuen Chinese Restaurant
4200 McFarland Blvd. E., 205/752-0088

Best Coffeehouse
Liberty Cafe
1407 University Blvd., 205/758-1833

Best Delicatessen
Subs-N-You
2427 University Blvd., 205/758-0088

Best Desserts
Globe Restaurant
430 Main Ave., Northport, 205/391-0949

Best Diner
Fifteenth Street Diner
1036 Fifteenth St., 205/750-8750

Best Eclectic Menu
Globe Restaurant
430 Main Ave., Northport, 205/391-0949

Best Family Restaurant
Cypress Inn
501 Rice Mine Rd. N., 205/345-6963

Best Fast Food
Chang's Diner
1205 University Blvd., 205/345-2472

Best Health-Conscious Menu
Manna Grocery Natural Gourmet
2300 McFarland Blvd. E., Ste. 12, 205/752-9955

Best Homestyle Food
Mama Jewel's Country Cookin'
5600 McFarland Blvd. E., 205/752-7580

Best Ice Cream/Yogurt
Pure Process Ice Cream
2340 Second St., 205/345-9816

Best Italian Food
Mr. G's Restaurant
908 McFarland Blvd., Northport; 205/339-8505

Best Japanese Food
Benkei Japanese Steak House
1223 McFarland Blvd. NE, 205/759-5300

Best Late-Night Food
Kwik Snack
1005 University Blvd., 205/752-8783

Best Mexican Food
El Pollo Tapatio
1301 McFarland Blvd. E., 205/391-4861

Best Pizza
Globe Restaurant
430 Main Ave., Northport, 205/391-0949
Tut's Place
1400 University Blvd., 205/759-1004

Best Place to Be "Seen"
Globe Restaurant
430 Main Ave., Northport, 205/391-0949

Best Place to Eat Alone
The Liberty Cafe
1407 University Blvd., 205/758-1833

Best Place to Eat When Someone Else Is Buying
Kozy's
3510 Loop Rd. E., 205/556-0665

Best Place to Take the Kids
Baumhover's Wings
500 Harper Lee Dr., 205/556-5658

Best Quick Lunch
City Cafe
408 Main Ave., Northport, 205/758-9171

Best Regional Food
The Cotton Patch
Union Rd., Eutaw, 205/372-4235

Best Romantic Dining
Cypress Inn
501 Rice Mine Rd. N., 205/345-6963

Best Salad/Salad Bar
Subs-N-You
2427 University Blvd., 205/758-0088

Best Sandwiches
The Liberty Cafe
1407 University Blvd., 205/758-1833

Best Schmooze Bar
Globe Restaurant
430 Main Ave., Northport, 205/391-0949

Best Seafood
Cypress Inn
501 Rice Mine Rd. N., 205/345-6963

Best Soul Food
Dreamland Drive-Inn Bar-B-Que
  5535 Fifteenth Ave. E., 205/758-8135

Best Sports Bar
Champs
  320 Paul W. Bryant Dr., 205/752-3200

Best Steaks
Nick's Filet House
  4018 Eutaw Hwy., 205/758-9316

Best Thai Food
Siam House Thai Cuisine
  1306D University Blvd., 205/758-4246

Best 24-Hour Restaurant
Kwik Snack
  1005 University Blvd., 205/752-8783

Best Undiscovered Restaurant
Kozy's
  3510 Loop Rd. E., 205/556-0665

Best Vegetarian Food
Globe Restaurant
  430 Main Ave., Northport, 205/391-0949
Manna Grocery Natural Gourmet
  2300 McFarland Blvd. E., Ste. 12, 205/752-9955

Best Wine Selection
Globe Restaurant
  430 Main Ave., Northport, 205/391-0949
Kozy's
  3510 Loop Rd. E., 205/556-0665

A

Alaska

ANCHORAGE, AK

Best Burgers
Arctic Roadrunner
  2477 Arctic Blvd., 907/279-7311
  5300 Old Seward Hwy., 907/561-1245
O'Brady's Burgers and Brew
  3300 Arctic Blvd., 907/561-7352
  3301 C St., Ste. 101, 907/338-1080
  6901 E. Tudor Rd., 907/338-1080
  800 E. Dimond Blvd., Ste. 159, 907/344-8033
Red Robin
  3401 Penland Pkwy., 907/276-7788
  401 E. Dimond Blvd., 907/522-4321
Phillip's International Inn
  2902 Minnesota Dr., 907/274-3637
  335 Muldoon Rd., 907/338-7606
  3801 Debarr Rd., 907/258-3199
  5121 Arctic Blvd., 907/562-6188
Village Inn
  1130 E. Northern Lights Blvd., 907/279-6012
  720 W. Dimond Blvd., 907/344-0010

Best Pizza
L'Aroma
  3700 Old Stewart Hwy., 907/562-9797
Pizza Olympia
  2809 Spenard Rd., 907/561-5264
Sorrento's
  1011 E. Dimond Blvd., 907/344-9986
  610 E. Fireweed Ln., 907/278-3439

Best Seafood
Elevation 92
  1007 W. Third Ave., 907/279-1578
Sea Galley
  4101 Credit Union Dr., 907/563-3520
Simon and Seafort's
  420 L St., 907/274-3502

Best Sushi
New Sagaya
3700 Old Seward Hwy., 907/561-5173
Tempura Kitchen
3826 Spenard Rd., 907/277-2741

Standbys
Denny's
1231 E. Dimond Blvd., 907/349-2010
1345 Rudakof Cir., 907/333-6776
2900 Denali St., 907/276-0536
3950 Debarr Rd., 907/337-1311

BETHEL, AK

Best All-You-Can-Eat Buffet
Kuskokwim Hotel and City Cafe
751 Third Ave., 907/543-2207

Best Breakfast
Kuskokwim Hotel and City Cafe
751 Third Ave., 907/543-2207

Best Coffee
Alaska Commercial Company
440 Ridgecrest Dr., 907/543-2661

Best Desserts
Diane's Cafe
1220 Hoffman Hwy., 907/543-4305

Best Greek/Mediterranean Food
Dimitri's Restaurant
281 Fourth Ave., 907/543-3434

Best Homestyle Food
Kuskokwim Hotel and City Cafe
751 Third Ave., 907/543-2207

Best Pizza
Brother's Pizza
1725 State Hwy., 907/543-3878

FAIRBANKS, AK

Best Atmosphere
Pike's Landing
4438 Airport Way, 907/479-6500
Two Rivers Lodge Fine Dining
Mile 16.9 Chena Hot Springs Rd., 907/488-6815

Best Breakfast
Sam's Sourdough Cafe
3702 Cameron St., 907/479-0523

Best Burgers
Triggers
900 Noble St., 907/457-8747

Best Chinese Food
Golden Shang Hai
1900 Airport Way, 907/451-1100

Best Coffee
Cookie Jar's Garden Cafe
3415 Airport Way, 907/479-8319

Wolf Run
3360 Wolf Run, 907/458-0636

Best Desserts
Wolf Run
3360 Wolf Run, 907/458-0636

Best Health-Conscious Menu
Cookie Jar's Garden Cafe
3415 Airport Way, 907/479-8319
Whole Earth Grocery and Deli
1157 Deborah Ave., 907/479-2052

Best Homestyle Food
Klondike Lounge and Dining Hall
1347 Bedrock St., 907/479-2224

Best Ice Cream/Yogurt
Hot Licks Homemade Ice Cream
3549 College Rd., 907/479-7813

Best Italian Food
Vallata
2190 Goldstream Rd., 907/455-6600

Best Pizza
Pizza Bella
1694 Airport Way, 907/456-5657

Best Sandwiches
Food Factory
1707 S. Cushman St., 907/452-6348
44 College Rd., 907/452-3313
Wolf Run
3360 Wolf Run, 907/458-0636

Best Seafood
Ivory Jack's
2581 Goldstream Rd., 907/455-6665
Two Rivers Lodge Fine Dining
Mile 16.9 Chena Hot Springs Rd., 907/488-6815

Best Steaks
Ivory Jack's
2581 Goldstream Rd., 907/455-6665
Two Rivers Lodge Fine Dining
Mile 16.9 Chena Hot Springs Rd., 907/488-6815

Best Thai Food
Thai Taste Cuisine
338 Old Steese Hwy., 907/452-7419

JUNEAU, AK

Best Restaurants in Town
The Fiddlehead Restaurant and Bakery
429 W. Willoughby Ave., 907/586-3150
Douglas Cafe
916 Third St., Douglas, 907/364-3307
Summit Restaurant
455 S. Franklin St., 907/586-2050
Hot Bite
Auke Bay Boat Harbor, Auke Bay, 907/790-2483

Best Mexican Food
Armadillo Tex-Mex Cafe
431 S. Franklin St., 907/586-1880

Best Pizza
Giovanni's Restaurant
43989 Sterling Hwy., Soldotna, 907/262-2344
Vito and Nick's
9342 Glacier Hwy., 907/789-7070

SEWARD, AK

Best Atmosphere
Resurrect Art Coffee House
320 Third Ave., 907/224-7161

Best Breakfast
Breeze Inn Motel
1306 Seward Hwy., 907/224-5237

Best Burgers
Apollo Restaurant
229 Fourth Ave., 907/224-3092

Best Chinese Food
Peking Chinese Restaurant
338 Fourth Ave., 907/224-5444

Best Coffee
Resurrect Art Coffee House
320 Third Ave., 907/224-7161

Best Desserts
Ranting Raven Bakery
228 Fourth Ave., 907/224-2228

Best Family Restaurant
Apollo Restaurant
229 Fourth Ave., 907/224-3092

Best Homestyle Food
Mainstreet Cafe
203 Fourth Ave., 907/224-3068

Best Ice Cream/Yogurt
Gordon's In-Home Video
223 Fourth Ave., 907/224-3008

Best Pizza
Apollo Restaurant
229 Fourth Ave., 907/224-3092

Best Place to Take the Kids
Apollo Restaurant
229 Fourth Ave., 907/224-3092

Best Sandwiches
Ray's Waterfront
1316 Fourth Ave., 907/224-5606

Best Seafood
Ray's Waterfront
1316 Fourth Ave., 907/224-5606

Best Steaks
Harbor Dinner Club
220 Fifth Ave., 907/224-3012

WASILLA, AK

Best Asian Restaurant
Peking Garden
500 E. Railroad Ave., 907/376-4919

Best Barbecue/Ribs
JD's Bar-B-Que Pit
1595 E. Parks Hwy., 907/376-1097

Best Breakfast
Windbreak Cafe
2201 E. Parks Hwy., 907/376-4484

Best Brunch
Best Western Lake Lucille Inn
1300 Lake Lucille Dr., 907/376-6199

Best Burgers
Fredeez Diner
Mile 14.5, Old Glen Hwy., Palmer, 907/745-7606

Best Coffee
The Deli
185 E. Parks Hwy., 907/376-2914

Best Delicatessen
The Deli
185 E. Parks Hwy., 907/376-2914

Best Desserts
The Deli
185 E. Parks Hwy., 907/376-2914

Best Dinner
Best Western Lake Lucille Inn
1300 Lake Lucille Dr., 907/376-6199

Best Health-Conscious Menu
Windbreak Cafe
2201 E. Parks Hwy., 907/376-4484

Best Italian Food
Evangelo's Trattoria
Mile 42 Parks Hwy., 907/376-1212

Best Lunch
Windbreak Cafe
2201 E. Parks Hwy., 907/376-4484

Best Mexican Food
Chepo's Fiesta Mexican Restaurant
731 W. Parks Hwy., 907/373-5656

Best Pizza
Evangelo's Trattoria
Mile 42 Parks Hwy., 907/376-1212

Best Romantic Dining
Mat-Su Resort
1850 Bogard Rd., 907/376-3228

Best Salad/Salad Bar
Carrs Quality Centers
565 E. 42 Parks Hwy., 907/376-2421

Best Seafood
Mat-Su Resort
1850 Bogard Rd., 907/376-3228

Best Steaks
Mat-Su Resort
  1850 Bogard Rd., 907/376-3228

Best View While Dining
Mat-Su Resort
  1850 Bogard Rd., 907/376-3228

Standbys
Baskin-Robbins
  591 E. Parks Hwy., 907/373-3131
Subway
  800 Hermon Rd., 907/373-7827

Arizona

BULLHEAD CITY, AZ

Best Chinese Food
China Panda Restaurant
  2164 S. Hwy. 95, 520/763-8899
China Szechuan Restaurant
  1890 S. Hwy. 95, 520/763-2610

Best Italian Food
Joey D's Pizza
  1081 Hwy. 95, 520/754-5300

Best Mexican Food
El Palacio
  1884 S. Hwy. 95, 520/763-2494
Casa Serrano Mexican Restaurant
  5230 Hwy. 95, 520/768-1881
Casa Garcia
  1999 Riviera Blvd., 520/758-8400
  967 Hancock Rd., 520/758-8777

CASA GRANDE, AZ

Best Atmosphere
Paloverde Dining Room
  Francisco Grande Resort, 26000 W. Gila Bend Hwy.,
    520/836-6444

Best Breakfast
Casa Grande Cafe
  301 N. Picacho St., 520/426-1424

Best Brunch
Mr. K's Food and Spirits
  777 N. Pinal Ave., 520/426-3500

Best Burgers
Casa Grande Cafe
  301 N. Picacho St., 520/426-1424

Best Family Restaurant
Ricardo's Mexican Food
  1361 N. Alma School Rd., 520/821-1874

Best Homestyle Food
Mr. K's Food and Spirits
777 N. Pinal Ave., 520/426-3500

Best Mexican Food
Ricardo's Mexican Food
1361 N. Alma School Rd., 520/821-1874

Best Pizza
Dell's Pizza and Sports Bar
1654 N. Pinal Ave., 520/836-2972

Best Southwestern Food
Be Dillon's Cactus Garden
800 N. Park Ave., 520/836-2045

Standbys
Golden Corral Family Steak House
1295 E. Florence Blvd., 520/836-4630
Dairy Queen
211 E. Florence Blvd., 520/836-1935

CHANDLER, AZ

Best Barbecue/Ribs
Tom's BBQ Chicago-Style
2050 N. Alma School Rd., Ste. 35, 602/899-5722

Best Breakfast
J.B.'s Restaurants
600 N. Arizona Ave., 602/963-0512
Marie Callender's
7455 W. Chandler Blvd., 602/961-9673

Best Coffee
Bagel Nosh
985 W. Elliot Rd., 602/814-7608

Best Desserts
Frontier Pie Restaurant
2130 N. Arizona Ave., 602/963-1243
Marie Callender's
7455 W. Chandler Blvd., 602/961-9673

Best French Food
Citrus Cafe
2330 N. Alma School Rd., 602/899-0502

Best Homestyle Food
J.B.'s Restaurants
600 N. Arizona Ave., 602/963-0512
Kountry Kookin'
70 W. Warner Rd., 602/814-7088

Best Ice Cream/Yogurt
Coldstone Creamery
2095 N. Alma School Rd., 602/963-1292
4939 W. Ray Rd., 602/940-0343

Best Italian Food
Rigatony's Authentic Italian Restaurant
1374 N. Arizona Ave., 602/899-1111

Best Mexican Food
Guedo's Taco Shop
71 E. Chandler Blvd., 602/899-7841

Serrano's Mexican Food Restaurants
141 S. Arizona Ave., 602/899-3318

Best Sandwiches
AJ's Cafe
1 S. San Marcos Pl., 602/899-1335

Best Seafood
AJ's Cafe
1 S. San Marcos Pl., 602/899-1335
Chops Classic Steak and Seafood
1371 N. Alma School Rd., 602/899-6735

Best Steaks
Chops Classic Steak and Seafood
1371 N. Alma School Rd., 602/899-6735

Standbys
Chili's
2025 N. Alma School Rd., 602/899-5050
Shoney's
1050 W. Ray Rd., 602/963-0060

FLAGSTAFF, AZ

Best Bar
Buster's Restaurant and Bar
1800 S. Milton Rd., Ste. 111, 520/774-5155

Best Continental Food
Brix
801 S. Milton Rd., 520/779-5117
Kelly's Christmas Tree Restaurant
5200 E. Cortland Blvd., 520/526-0776

Best French Food
Chez Marc Bistro
503 N. Humphreys St., 520/774-1343

Best Mexican Food
Salsa Brava
1800 S. Milton Rd., 520/774-1083

Best Seafood
Buster's Restaurant and Bar
1800 S. Milton Rd., Ste. 111, 520/774-5155

Best Steaks
Black Bart's Steak House Saloon
2760 E. Butler Ave., 520/779-3142

GLENDALE, AZ

Best Barbecue/Ribs
El Paso Barbeque Company
4303 W. Peoria Ave., 602/931-3218

Best Breakfast
Kiss The Cook Restaurant
4915 W. Glendale Ave., 602/939-4663

Best Brunch
The Spicery
7141 N. 59th Ave., 602/937-6534

Best Burgers
Red Robin Restaurant
5830 W. Bell Rd., 602/978-3828

Best Coffee
Java The Hut
5800 W. Peoria Ave., Ste. 102, 602/412-7895

Best Desserts
The Spicery
7141 N. 59th Ave., 602/937-6534

Best Ice Cream/Yogurt
Coldstone Creamery
5850 W. Peoria Ave., 602/487-1707

Best Italian Food
Cucina Tagliani
17045 N. 59th Ave., 602/547-2782
Portofino Ristorante
6020 W. Bell Rd., 602/938-1902

Best Pizza
Bola's Pizza Buffet
6756 W. Camelback Rd., 602/848-7574

Best Seafood
Rosario Ristorante
9250 N. 43rd Ave., 602/931-1810

Best Steaks
Carver's
8172 W. Bell Rd., 602/412-0787

Best Thai Food
Siam Imports Restaurant
5008 W. Northern Ave., Ste. 1, 602/931-2102
Siamese Kitchen
4352 W. Olive, 602/931-3229

Standbys
Outback Steakhouse
5605 W. Bell Rd., 602/547-3236

HOLBROOK, AZ

Best All-You-Can-Eat Buffets
Arizona Country Cafe
I-40 Exit 292, 520/524-2686
R and R Pizza
1002 W. Hopi Dr., 520/524-2888
Jerry's Restaurant
2600 Navajo Blvd., 520/524-2364

Best Burgers
Wayside Drive Inn
1150 W. Hopi Dr., 520/524-3167

Best Cheap Meal
R and R Pizza
1002 W. Hopi Dr., 520/524-2888

Best Chinese Food
Sundown Restaurant
915 W. Hopi Dr., 520/524-3785

Best Family Restaurant
Romo's Cafe
121 W. Hopi Dr., 520/524-2153

Best Health-Conscious Menu
Mesa Grande Italiana
2318 Navajo Blvd., 520/524-6696

Best Homestyle Food
Roadrunner Cafe
1501 Navajo Blvd., 520/524-2787

Best Italian Food
Mesa Grande Italiana
2318 Navajo Blvd., 520/524-6696

Best Mexican Food
Joe and Aggie's Cafe
120 W. Hopi Dr., 520/524-6540
Wayside Drive Inn
1150 W. Hopi Dr., 520/524-3167

Best Place to Take the Kids
R and R Pizza
1002 W. Hopi Dr., 520/524-2888

Best Romantic Dining
Mesa Grande Italiana
2318 Navajo Blvd., 520/524-6696

Best Seafood
Butterfield Stage Company
609 W. Hopi Dr., 520/524-3447
Plainsman Restaurant
1001 W. Hopi Dr., 520/524-3345

Standbys
Denny's
2510 Navajo Blvd., 520/524-2893
Dairy Queen
1001 Navajo Blvd., 520/524-6553

LAKE HAVASU CITY, AZ

Best Restaurants in Town
The Captain's Table
Nautical Inn Resort, 1000 McCulloch Blvd. N.,
520/855-2141
The Pepper Mill Cafe
2187 McCulloch Blvd. N., 520/855-4405

Best American Food
London Arms Pub and Restaurant
422 English Village, 520/855-8782

Best Continental Food
Shugrue's Restaurant Bakery
1425 McCulloch Blvd. S., 520/453-1400

Best German Food
Allee Cafe
1530 El Camino Way, 520/680-1011

Best Mexican Food
Casa de Miguel Mexican Restaurant
1550 Palo Verde Blvd. S., 520/453-1550
El Rio Cantina and Grill
2131 McCulloch Blvd. N., 520/680-0088

Best Seafood
Krystal's Fine Dining
  460 El Camino Dr., 520/453-2999

Best Steaks
Homestead Saloon and Steakhouse
  3465 Maricopa Ave., 520/855-1078

MESA, AZ

Best Appetizers
Native New Yorker
  318 E. Brown Rd., 602/464-4383
  1559 S. Gilbert Rd., 602/892-1010

Best Atmosphere
Landmark Restaurant
  809 W. Main St., 602/962-4652

Best Breakfast
Community Restaurant
  535 N. Country Club Dr., 602/833-3971
  5601 E. Hermosa Vista Dr., 602/832-0640

Best Continental Food
Euro Cafe
  1111 S. Longmore, Ste. 3, 602/962-4224

Best Diner
Community Restaurant
  535 N. Country Club Dr., 602/833-3971
  5601 E. Hermosa Vista Dr., 602/832-0640

Best Dinner
Landmark Restaurant
  809 W. Main St., 602/962-4652

Best German Food
Zurkate
  4815 E. Main St., 602/830-4244

Best Health-Conscious Menu
Landmark Restaurant
  809 W. Main St., 602/962-4652

Best Italian Food
Brunello
  1954 S. Dobson, 602/897-0140

Best Mexican Food
Matta's Restaurant
  932 E. Main St., 602/964-7881

Best Other Ethnic Food
Bavarian Point Restaurant (central European)
  4815 E. Main St., 602/830-0999

Best Salad/Salad Bar
Landmark Restaurant
  809 W. Main St., 602/962-4652

Best Wine Selection
Brunello
  1954 S. Dobson, 602/897-0140

PAGE, AZ

Best Atmosphere
Strombolli's Italian Restaurant
  711 N. Navajo Dr., 520/645-2605

Best Barbecue/Ribs
Ken's Old West
  718 Vista Ave., 520/645-5160

Best Breakfast
M Bar H Cafe
  819 N. Navajo Dr., 520/645-1420

Best Coffee
Beans Gourmet Coffee House
  Page Factory Stores, 520/645-6858

Best Desserts
Sweet Memories
  660 Elm St., 520/645-1678

Best Family Restaurant
Empire House
  107 S. Lake Powell Blvd., 520/645-2406

Best Homestyle Food
Empire House
  107 S. Lake Powell Blvd., 520/645-2406

Best Ice Cream/Yogurt
Sweet Memories
  660 Elm St., 520/645-1678

Best Italian Food
Bella Napoli
  810 N. Navajo Dr., 520/645-2706

Best Mexican Food
Dos Amigos
  608 Elm St., 520/645-3036
Salsa Brava
  1800 S. Milton Rd., Flagstaff, 520/774-1083

Best Outdoor Restaurant
Strombolli's Italian Restaurant
  711 N. Navajo Dr., 520/645-2605

Best Pizza
Strombolli's Italian Restaurant
  711 N. Navajo Dr., 520/645-2605

Best Sandwiches
Sandwich Place
  662 Elm St., 520/645-5267

Best Seafood
Rainbow Room
  Wahweap Resort, 100 Lakeshore Dr., 520/645-2433

Best Steaks
Rainbow Room
  Wahweap Resort, 100 Lakeshore Dr., 520/645-2433

PHOENIX, AZ

Best Restaurants
Christopher's
  2398 E. Camelback, 602/957-3214

Etienne's Different Pointe of View
  Pointe Hilton, 11111 N. Seventh St., 602/863-0912
Top of the Rock
  The Buttes, 2000 Westcourt Way, Tempe,
    602/225-9000
RoxSand
  Biltmore Fashion Shop, 24th St. at Camelback,
    602/381-0444
The Chaparral
  Marriott's Camelback Inn, 5402 E. Lincoln, Paradise
    Valley, 602/948-6644

Best All-You-Can-Eat Buffet
Indian Delhi Palace
  5050 E. McDowell, 602/244-8181

Best American Food
Gabriel's
  Dial Corporate Ctr., 1850 N. Central, 602/207-2070
Eddie's Grill
  4747 N. Seventh St., 602/241-1188
House of Tricks
  114 E. Seventh St., Tempe, 602/968-1114

Best Bars
Pomeroy's
  5551 N. Central St., 602/264-5411
The Monastery
  4114 N. 28th St., 602/840-7510

Best Barbecue/Ribs
Honey Bear's BBQ
  5012 E. Van Buren, 602/273-9148
A and J Chicago Style Barbecue
  6102 B, 16th St., 602/241-7519

Best Bistro
Hops! Bistro and Brewery
  26th at Camelback, 602/468-0500

Best Beer Selection
The Crow's Nest
  4321 N. Scottsdale Rd., Scottsdale, 602/941-0602

Best Breakfast
La Pila
  2020 N. Central Ave., Ste. 150-L, 602/252-7007
Sunlight Family Restaurant
  1910 W. Northern, 602/995-1534
The Original Pancake House
  6840 E. Camelback, Scottsdale, 602/946-4902

Best Brunch
Phoenician Resort
  6000 E. Camelback Rd., 602/941-8200
Marquesa
  Scottsdale Princess Resort, 7575 E. Princess Dr.,
    Scottsdale, 602/585-4848

Best Burger
Harvey's the Wineburger King
  4812 N. Sixteenth St., 602/248-9950
The Chuck Box
  202 E. University, Tempe, 602/968-4712

A

Best Business Lunch
Tom's Tavern and Restaurant
  2 N. Central Ave., 602/257-1688

Best Cafeteria
Palm Grove Food Court
  Dial Corporate Ctr., 1850 N. Central, 602/207-7107

Best Cajun/Creole Food
Baby Kay's Cajun Kitchen
  2119 E. Camelback, 602/955-0011

Best Cheap Meal
Mike's Golden Crust
  15820 N. 35th Ave., 602/938-3383
Eliana's Restaurant
  1627 N. 24th St., 602/225-2925

Best Chinese Food
Big Wong
  1212 E. Northern, 602/943-3835
  616 W. Indian School Rd., 602/277-2870
China Gate
  3033 W. Peoria Ave., 602/944-1982

Best Coffeehouses
Dos Estrellas Coffee House
  Town and Country Shopping Ctr., 20th St. at
    Camelback, 602/957-2236
Coffee Plantation
  Biltmore Fashion Park, 24th St. at Camelback,
    602/5530203
Orbit Espresso
  Uptown Plz., Central at Camelback, 602/265-2354

Best Continental Food
Christo's
  6327 N. Seventh St., 602/264-1784

Best Delicatessens
Beulah's Deli and Market Place
  2022 N. Seventh St., 602/252-5303
JJ's Deli
  1331 E. Northern, 602/997-5555
Tamburino's Deli
  3255 E. Shea, 602/996-6210

Best Desserts
Ricardo's Mexican Food
  2926 N. 24th St., 602/956-5670
Christopher's Bistro
  2398 E. Camelback, 602/957-3214

Best Diner
Five and Diner
  5220 N. Sixteenth St., 602/264-5220

Best Fast Food
Lenny's Burger Shop
  9204 N. Seventh St., 602/997-2349

Best French Food
Citrus Cafe
  2330 N. Alma School, Chandler, 602/899-0502

A

Best German Food
Zur Kate
4815 E. Main, Mesa, 602/830-4244
Bavarian Point
4815 E. Mesa, 602/830-0999

Best Greek/Mediterranean Food
Greekfest
1940 E. Camelback, 602/265-2990
Mike's Golden Crust
15820 N. 35th Ave., 602/938-3383
Nick's Cuisine of Southern Europe
3717 E. Indian School Rd., 602/955-5225

Best Health-Conscious Menu
Saigon Healthy Deli
820 S. Mill, Tempe, 602/967-4199

Best Homestyle Food
Century Pub
1140 E. Washington, 602/257-4447
Mrs. White's Golden Rule Cafe
808 E. Jefferson, 602/262-9256

Best Ice Cream/Yogurt
Bavarian Alps Old World Ice Cream
Biltmore Fashion Park, 24th St. at Camelback,
602/957-8716
Mary Coyle Ice Cream
1335 West Thomas, 602/265-0405

Best Indian Food
India Palace
16842 N. Seventh St., 602/942-4224

Best Italian Food
Christo's
6327 N. Seventh St., 602/264-1784
Tony and Maria's Trattoria and Pizzeria
2814 N. Sixteenth St., 602/266-7173
Nina L'Italian Ristorante
3625 E. Bell Rd., 602/482-6167
Rosario Ristorante
9250 N. 43rd Ave., Glendale, 602/931-1810
Un Bacio Ristorante
4400 N. Scottsdale Rd., Scottsdale, 602/994-0606

Best Japanese Food
Mikado
7111 E. Camelback, Scottsdale, 602/481-9777

Best Korean Food
Korean Restaurant
4214 W. Dunlap, 602/842-0400

Best Kosher Food
Boman's Restaurant and Deli
3731 N. Scottsdale Rd., 602/947-2934
Laura's Kitchen
4818 N. Seventh St., 602/263-9377

Best Late-Night Food
Five and Diner
5220 N. Sixteenth St., 602/264-5220

Nick's Cuisine of Southern Europe
  3717 E. Indian School Rd., 602/955-5225

Best Lunch
Downtown Deli
  130 N. Central, 602/258-3069
New Yorker Family Restaurant
  8002 N. 27th Ave., 602/995-8787
El Chorro Lodge
  5550 E. Lincoln, Paradise Valley, 602/948-5170

Best Mexican Food
La Placita Mexican Restaurant
  4117 N. Sixteenth St., 602/263-0166
Sylvia's La Canasta
  5502 N. Seventh Ave., 602/242-4252
Such Is Life
  3602 N. 24th St., 602/955-7822
Los Dos Molinos
  8646 S. Central, 602/243-9113

Best Middle Eastern Food
Cafe Istanbul
  903 S. Rural, Tempe, 602/731-9499

Best New Restaurants
Oregano's
  3622 N. Scottsdale Rd., Scottsdale, 602/970-1860
Rancho Pinot Grill
  6208 N. Scottsdale Rd., Scottsdale, 602/468-9463

Best Other Ethnic Food
Eliana's Restaurant (Salvadoran)
  1627 N. 24th St., 602/225-2925
Havana Patio Cafe (Cuban)
  4225 E. Camelback, 602/952-1991
  6245 E. Bell Rd., 602/991-1496

Best Outdoor Dining
The Farm at South Mountain
  6106 S. 32nd St., 602/276-6360

Best Pizza
Ray's Pizza
  3414 W. Union Hills Dr., 602/581-1640
Streets of New York
  16838 N. Seventh St., 602/789-7827
  4229 W. Bethany Home Rd., 602/973-2600
  7830 N. Nineteenth Ave., 602/995-5977
  1930 W. Thunderbird Rd., 602/866-7666
  5031 N. 44th St., 602/952-0124

Best Place to Eat When Someone Else Is Buying
Christopher's
  2398 E. Camelback, 602/957-3214

Best Place to Take the Kids
Ed Debevic's Short Orders Deluxe
  2102 E. Highland, 602/956-2760

Best Restaurant Meal Value
Vincent Guerithault on Camelback
  3930 E. Camelback, 602/224-0225

Best Romantic Dining
Top of the Rock
The Buttes, 2000 Westcourt Way, Tempe,
602/225-9000

Best Salad/Salad Bar
Houston's
2425 E. Camelback, 602/957-9700
Cork and Cleaver
5101 N. 44th St., 602/952-0585

Best Sandwiches
J. Edgar's Sandwich Shop
504 E. Roosevelt, 602/252-0351
JJ's Deli
1331 E. Northern, 602/997-5555
Panini
2394 E. Camelback, 602/224-8686

Best Seafood
San Carlos Bay Seafood Restaurant
1901 E. McDowell, 602/340-0892
Palm Court
Scottsdale Conference Resort, 7700 E. McCormick
Pkwy., 602/991-3400

Best Soul Food
Unique Foods and Services
1153 E. Jefferson, 602/257-0701

Best Southwestern Food
Arizona Kitchen
Wigwam Resort, 300 E. Indian School Rd., Litchfield
Park, 602/935-3811
Cafe Terra Cotta
The Borgata, 6166 N. Scottsdale Rd., 602/948-8100

Best Spanish Food
Marquesa
Scottsdale Princess Resort, 7575 E. Princess Dr.,
602/585-4848

Best Sports Bar
Field Goal Bar and Grill
3430 W. Glendale Ave., 602/973-9814

Best Steaks
Rustler's Roost
7777 S. Pointe Parkway W., 602/431-6474

Best Thai Food
Malee's on Main
7131 E. Main St., 602/947-6042
Siamese Kitchen
4352 W. Olive, Glendale, 602/931-3229

Best Vegetarian Food
Supreme Master Ching Hai
4812 N. Seventh Ave., 602/264-3480
Shalimar
616 S. Forest, Tempe, 602/967-8399

Best Vietnamese Food
Pearl of Asia
5025 N. Seventh Ave., 602/265-9818

Best View While Dining
Etienne's Different Pointe of View
  Pointe Hilton, 11111 N. Seventh St., 602/863-0912

A

Best Wine Selection
Christopher's
  2398 E. Camelback, 602/957-3214

Standbys
Applebee's
  2720 W. Bell Rd., 602/789-9449
Chuck E. Cheese Pizza
  8039 N. 35th Ave., 602/973-1945
The Olive Garden
  10223 N. Metro Pkwy. E., 602/943-4573
  2626 N. 75th Ave., 602/849-6533
Perkins
  310 E. Bell Rd., 602/863-1581
Red Lobster
  3507 W. Dunlap Ave., 602/973-7094
  4201 W. Bell Rd., 602/843-1244
  5125 E. Thomas Rd., 602/840-6341
  5301 W. Indian School Rd., 602/245-0135
Ruth's Chris Steak House
  2201 E. Camelback, 602/957-9600
Lone Star Steakhouse
  6003 N. Sixteenth St., 602/248-7827
HomeTown Buffet
  2929 N. 75th Ave., 602/849-8694

PRESCOTT, AZ

Best Restaurant in Town
Murphy's
  201 N. Cortez St., 520/445-4044

Best American Food
Murphy's
  201 N. Cortez St., 520/445-4044
Prescott Resort
  1500 Hwy. 69, 520/776-1666
Pine Cone Inn
  1245 White Spar Rd., 520/445-2970
Hassayampa Inn
  122 E. Gurley St., 520/778-9434
The County Seat
  214 S. Montezuma St., 520/778-9570

Best Italian Food
Panzullo's
  1350 Iron Springs Rd., 520/776-7062

Best Mexican Food
El Chaparral
  628 Miller Valley Rd., 520/445-8447
El Charro Restaurant
  120 N. Montezuma St., 520/445-7130
Pancho's Place
  1459 W. Gurley St., 520/771-9505

A

SCOTTSDALE, AZ

Best Bar
AZ 88
7353 E. Scottsdale Mall, 602/994-5576

Best Bistro
Hops! Bistro and Brewery
7000 E. Camelback, 602/945-4677

Best Breakfast
Original Pancake House
6846 E. Camelback, 602/946-4902
Pierre's Pastry Cafe
7119 E. Shea, Ste. 100, 602/443-2510
Arcadia Farms Catering
7014 E. First Ave., 602/941-5665

Best Brunch
Marquesa
7575 E. Princess Dr., 602/585-4848

Best Cajun/Creole Food
Baby Kay's Cajun Kitchen
7216 E. Shoeman, 602/990-9080

Best Chinese Food
P.F. Chang's Chinese Bistro
7014 E. Camelback Rd., 602/949-2610

Best Indian Food
Indian Cuisine
4228 N. Scottsdale Rd., 602/970-3300

Best Italian Food
Aldo Baldo Ristorante
7014 E. Camelback Rd., 602/994-0062
Un Bacio Ristorante
4400 N. Scottsdale Rd., 602/994-0606

Best Japanese Food
Mikado
7110 E. Camelback Rd., 602/481-9777

Best Kosher Food
Boman's Restaurant Deli
3731 N. Scottsdale Rd., 602/947-2934

Best Seafood
Salt Cellar Restaurant
550 N. Hayden, 602/947-1963

Best Southwestern Food
Z Tejas Grill
7014 E. Camelback Rd., 602/946-4171
Old Town Tortilla Factory
6910 E. Main St., 602/945-4567

Best Spanish Food
Pepin
7363 E. Scottsdale Mall, 602/990-9380

SHOW LOW, AZ

Best All-You-Can-Eat Buffet
JB's Restaurant
480 W. Deuce of Clubs, 520/537-1156

Best Breakfast
Country Kitchen
  201 E. Deuce of Clubs, 520/537-4774

Best Chinese Food
Asia Gardens Restaurant
  59 W. Deuce of Clubs, 520/537-9333

Best Coffee
High in the Pines
  1201 E. Hall, 520/537-1453

Best Desserts
JB's Restaurant
  480 W. Deuce of Clubs, 520/537-1156

Best Family Restaurants
Pat's Place
  981 E. Deuce of Clubs, 520/537-2337
Branding Iron Steak House
  1231 E. Deuce of Clubs, 520/537-5151

Best Homestyle Food
Country Kitchen
  201 E. Deuce of Clubs, 520/537-4774
JB's Restaurant
  480 W. Deuce of Clubs, 520/537-1156

Best Mexican Food
Guayo's
  350 E. Deuce of Clubs, 520/537-9503

Best Pizza
Pat's Place
  981 E. Deuce of Clubs, 520/537-2337

Best Sandwiches
High in the Pines
  1201 E. Hall, 520/537-1453

Best Seafood
Branding Iron Steak House
  1231 E. Deuce of Clubs, 520/537-5151

Best Steaks
Shaffery's
  571 W. Deuce of Clubs, 520/537-4835
Branding Iron Steak House
  1231 E. Deuce of Clubs, 520/537-5151

SIERRA VISTA, AZ

Best Restaurants in Town
Ricardo's Mexican Restaurant
  S. Hwy. 92 at Hereford Rd., 520/378-3220
The Mesquite Tree Restaurant
  6398 S. Hwy. 92, 520/378-2758
J.B.'s
  1697 E. Fry St., 520/459-2040

Best American Food
The Outside Inn
  4907 S. Hwy. 92, 520/378-4645

Best Mexican Food
Ricardo's Mexican Restaurant
  S. Hwy. 92 at Hereford Rd., 520/378-3220

Best Steaks
J.B.'s Bright Spot
10989 E. Hwy. 92, Hereford, 520/366-5203

SUN CITY, AZ

Best American Food
Nancy's Country Cupboard
15400 N. 99th Ave., 602/933-0663
Mercer's Restaurant
9720 W. Peoria Ave., Ste. 101, Peoria, 602/972-0933

Best Chinese Food
Chang Lee Restaurant
13600 N. 99th Ave., 602/974-3601

Best German Food
Ritter's German Chalet
13232 N. 111th Ave., Youngtown, 602/933-6023

Best Italian Food
Lo Perchio's
16901 N. Village Dr. W., 602/583-0600
Cucina Tagliani
17045 N. 59th Ave., Glendale, 602/547-2782

TEMPE, AZ

Best Restaurant in Town
Top of the Rock
2000 W. Westcourt Way, 602/225-9000

Best American Food
Brown Derby Restaurant
4400 S. Rural Rd., 602/345-8223
Radisson Tempe Mission Palms
60 E. Fifth St., 602/894-1400

Best Atmosphere
Monti's La Casa Vieja
3 W. First St., 602/967-7594

Best Breakfast
Coffee Plantation
680 S. Mill Ave., 602/829-7878

Best Burgers
The Chuck Box
202 E. University, 602/968-4712

Best Business Lunch
Tricks
114 E. Seventh St., 602/968-1114

Best Coffee
Coffee Plantation
680 S. Mill Ave., 602/829-7878

Best Continental Food
Top of the Rock
2000 W. Westcourt Way, 602/225-9000

Best Delicatessen
Capistrand's Italian Deli
31 W. Southern Ave., 602/968-0712
655 W. Warner Rd., 602/496-9044

A

Best Dinner
Arches Cafe
Tempe Mission Palms, 60 E. Fifth St., 602/894-1400

Best Family Restaurant
Coco's Restaurant
1717 S. Rural Rd., 602/966-9854
Spaghetti Company
414 S. Mill Ave., 602/966-3848

Best Health-Conscious Menu
Saigon Healthy Deli
820 S. Mill, 602/967-4199
Tricks
114 E. Seventh St., 602/968-1114

Best Homestyle Food
Coco's Restaurant
1717 S. Rural Rd., 602/966-9854

Best Italian Food
Spaghetti Company
414 S. Mill Ave., 602/966-3848

Best Mexican Food
Macayo Mexican Restaurant
300 S. Ash Ave., 602/966-6677

Best Middle Eastern Food
Cafe Istanbul
903 S. Rural, 602/731-9499

Best Pizza
Nello's Pizza
1806 E. Southern Ave., 602/897-2060

Best Place to Eat When Someone Else Is Buying
Top of the Rock
2000 W. Westcourt Way, 602/225-9000

Best Salad/Salad Bar
Brown Derby Restaurant
4400 S. Rural Rd., 602/345-8223

Best Seafood
Rusty Pelican
1606 W. Baseline Rd., 602/345-0972
C-Fu Gourmet
6438 S. McLintock, 602/831-8899

Best Steaks
Monti's La Casa Vieja
3 W. First St., 602/967-7594

TUCSON, AZ

Best Barbecue/Ribs
Rod's K.C. B-B-Que
722 N. Stone Ave., 520/623-0182

Best Burgers
Bum Steer
1910 N. Stone Ave., 520/884-7377

Best Breakfast
Millie's West Pancake Haus
6530 E. Tanque Verde Rd., 520/298-4250

Uncle John's Pancake and Dinner
    6934 E. Tanque Verde Rd., 520/722-5200
Cafe Melange
    6761 E. Tanque Verde Rd., 520/298-2233

Best Brunch
Rincon Market
    2513 E. Sixth St., 520/327-6653
    3150 E. Fort Lowell Rd., 520/321-4567
Canyon Cafe
    Loews Ventana Canyon Resort, 7000 N. Resort Dr.,
        520/299-2020
El Conquistador Resort
    10000 N. Resort Dr., 520/544-1800

Best Cheap Meal
Maya Quetzal
    429 N. Fourth Ave., 520/622-8207

Best Coffee
Rincon Market
    2513 E. Sixth St., 520/327-6653
    3150 E. Fort Lowell Rd., 520/321-4567

Best Delicatessens
Feig's Kosher Foods
    5071 E. Fifth St., 520/325-2255
Jason's Deli
    5420 E. Broadway Blvd., Ste. 260, 520/790-7000
Tony's New York-Style Italian Deli
    6219 E. 22nd St., 520/747-0070

Best Desserts
Coffee Etc.
    2830 N. Campbell Ave., 520/881-8070
    6091 N. Oracle Rd., 520/544-8588
Le Bistro
    2574 N. Campbell Ave., 520/327-3086

Best Diner
Little Anthony's Diner
    7010 E. Broadway Blvd., 520/296-0456

Best Dinner
Mi Nidito Cafe
    1813 S. Fourth Ave., 520/622-5081

Best Greek/Mediterranean Food
Athens on Fourth
    500 N. Fourth Ave., 520/624-6886
Olive Tree Restaurant
    7000 E. Tanque Verde Rd., 520/298-1845

Best Indian Food
India Oven
    2727 N. Campbell Ave., 520/326-8635

Best Italian Food
Boccata Bistro Bar
    5605 E. River Rd., 520/577-9309
Caruso's Restaurant
    434 N. Fourth Ave., 520/624-5765

Best Japanese Food
Sakura Teppan Steak and Sushi
    6534 E. Tanque Verde Rd., 520/298-7777

Japanese Kitchen
  8424 E. Old Spanish Trail, 520/886-4131
Bunbuku
  4520 E. Broadway Blvd., 520/325-6953

Best Late-Night Food
Congress Grill
  100 E. Congress St., 520/623-7621
Coffee Etc.
  2830 N. Campbell Ave., 520/881-8070
  6091 N. Oracle Rd., 520/544-8588
Baggin's Gourmet Sandwiches
  5407 E. Pima St., 520/795-7135
  3755 E. 34th St., 520/790-2403
  6342 N. Oracle Rd., 520/575-8878
  1800 E. Fort Lowell Rd., 520/327-1611
  2741 E. Speedway Blvd., 520/327-4342
  7201 E. Speedway Blvd., 520/290-9383

Best Mexican Food
Mi Nidito Cafe
  1813 S. Fourth Ave., 520/622-5081
El Charro
  311 N. Court Ave., 520/622-5465
El Minuto Cafe
  354 S. Main Ave., 520/882-4145
La Hacienda
  4207 S. Sixth Ave., 520/889-6613
La Parrilla Suiza
  2720 N. Oracle Rd., 520/624-4300
  5602 E. Speedway, 520/747-4838
Cafe Poca Cosa
  88 E. Broadway Blvd., 520/622-6400
Sanchez Burrito
  2530 N. First Ave., 520/622-2092
  615 W. Valencia Rd., 520/741-8538
  1060 N. Craycroft Rd., 520/747-0901
  2526 E. Broadway Blvd., 520/795-3306
  1350 W. Wetmore Rd., 520/887-0955

Best Middle Eastern Food
Tork's Cafe
  1701 N. Country Club Rd., 520/325-3737

Best New Restaurants
Trio Bistro and Bar
  2990 N. Swan Rd., 520/325-3333
City Grill
  6350 E. Tanque Verde Rd., 520/733-1111

Best Other Ethnic Food
La Indidta Restaurant (Mexican/Indian)
  8578 E. Broadway Blvd., 520/886-9191
Seri Melaka (Thai/Malaysian)
  6133 E. Broadway Blvd., 520/747-7810

Best Outdoor Dining
Cafe Terra Cotta
  4310 N. Campbell Ave., 520/577-8181
Blue Willow Restaurant
  2616 N. Campbell Ave., 520/795-8736

A

Wild Johnny's Wagon
  150 N. Main Ave., 520/884-1558

Best Pizza
Magpies Gourmet Pizza
  7315 N. Oracle Rd., 520/297-2712
  605 N. Fourth Ave., 520/628-1661
  4654 E. Speedway Blvd., 520/326-0261
Picurro Pizzeria
  2921 E. Fort Lowell Rd., 520/325-7777
Oven's Restaurant
  4280 N. Campbell Ave., 520/577-9001

Best Romantic Dining
San Remo Ristorante
  2210 N. Indian Ruins Rd., 520/296-9378

Best Seafood
Ye Olde Lantern Restaurant
  1800 N. Oracle Rd., 520/622-6761

Best Spanish Food
Cafe Triana
  2959 N. Swan Rd., 520/881-6611

Best Steaks
OK Corral Catering and Restaurant
  7710 E. Wrightstown Rd., 520/885-2373
The Last Territory Steakhouse
  El Conquistador Resort, 10000 N. Oracle Rd.,
  520/742-7000

YUMA, AZ

Best Restaurant in Town
Hungry Hunter
  2355 S. Fourth Ave., 520/782-3637

Best Bars
Johnny's Other Place
  244 E. Sixteenth St., 520/783-9367
Hungry Hunter
  2355 S. Fourth Ave., 520/782-3637

Best Breakfast
Brownie's Restaurant
  1145 S. Fourth Ave., 520/783-7911
Ligurta Station
  19702 E. Hwy. 80, Wellton, 520/785-4361

Best Brunch
Hungry Hunter
  2355 S. Fourth Ave., 520/782-3637

Best Burgers
Lutes' Casino
  221 S. Main St., 520/782-2192

Best Business Lunch
Panda Restaurant and Lounge
  711 E. 32nd St., 520/341-0323
Famous Sam's Restaurant and Bar
  2052 S. Fourth Ave., 520/783-7267
Crossing Restaurant
  2690 S. Fourth Ave., 520/726-5551

Best Cheap Meal
La Casa Gutierrez
520 S. Orange Ave., 520/782-1402

Best Chinese Food
Mandarin Palace
350 E. 32nd St., 520/344-2805

Best Desserts
Mostly Muffins
2451 W. Sixteenth St., 520/783-7484
1025 W. 24th St., Ste. 16, 520/341-0711
Hungry Hunter
2355 S. Fourth Ave., 520/782-3637

Best Diner
Brownie's Restaurant
1145 S. Fourth Ave., 520/783-7911

Best Family Restaurant
Chateau Basque Restaurant
4340 E. Hwy. 80, 520/341-9776

Best Health-Conscious Menu
Nature's Deli
224 S. Main St., 520/783-3903
692 Marine Corps Air Station, 520/726-2827

Best Homestyle Food
Brownie's Restaurant
1145 S. Fourth Ave., 520/783-7911

Best Italian Food
Bella Vita Restaurant
2755 Fourth Ave., 520/344-3989

Best Late-Night Food
Copper Miner's Kitchen
10800 N. Frontage Rd., 520/342-2110

Best Mexican Food
Chretin's Mexican Food
485 S. Fiftcenth Ave., 520/782-1291

Best Pizza
Bernardo's Pizza
11242 S. Foothills Blvd., 520/342-2034

Best Places to Be "Seen"
Hungry Hunter
2355 S. Fourth Ave., 520/782-3637
Johnny's Other Place
244 E. Sixteenth St., 520/783-9367

Best Place to Eat Alone
Copper Miner's Kitchen
10800 N. Frontage Rd., 520/342-2110

Best Place to Eat When Someone Else Is Buying
Hungry Hunter
2355 S. Fourth Ave., 520/782-3637

Best Place to Take the Kids
Famous Sam's Restaurant and Bar
2052 S. Fourth Ave., 520/783-7267

Arkansas

Best Barbecue/Ribs
Dixie Pig
  701 N. Sixth St., 501/763-4636

Best Breakfast
Sharecropper's
  211 W. Ash St., 501/763-5818

Best Burgers
Burger Broil
  698 N. Sixth St., 501/763-6202

Best Chinese Food
Hong Kong Chinese Steak and Seafood
  829 E. Main St., 501/763-5664
Kowloon Chinese Restaurant
  357 S. Division St., 501/762-2828

Best Desserts
Sharecropper's
  211 W. Ash St., 501/763-5818

Best Family Restaurants
Grecian Steak House
  165 E. State Hwy. 18, 501/763-7550
Sharecropper's
  211 W. Ash St., 501/763-5818

Best Homestyle Food
Sharecropper's
  211 W. Ash St., 501/763-5818

Best Regional Food
Ed's Country Catfish House
  2075 S. Division St., 501/762-2603

Best Steaks
Grecian Steak House
  165 E. State Hwy. 18, 501/763-7550
Harry's
  200 S. First St., 501/763-0443

A

Standbys
Perkins
Hwy. 18 at I-55, 501/763-6797

CONWAY, AR

Best Atmosphere
Place to Eat
808 Front St., 501/327-6858

Best Barbecue/Ribs
J.B.'s Bar-B-Q
Hwy. 65S, 501/327-8304
Shorty's
1101 Harkrider St., 501/329-9213

Best Burgers
Place to Eat
808 Front St., 501/327-6858

Best Desserts
Dixie Cafe
1101 Fendley Dr., 501/327-4777

Best Homestyle Food
Dixie Cafe
1101 Fendley Dr., 501/327-4777

Best Ice Cream/Yogurt
Dixie Cafe
1101 Fendley Dr., 501/327-4777

Best Italian Food
Fazoli's
1100 Hwy. 65N, 501/336-0006

Best Mexican Food
El Chico Restaurant
201 Hwy. 65N, 501/327-6553
Los Amigos Mexican Restaurant
2850 Prince St., 501/329-7919

Best Sandwiches
Place to Eat
808 Front St., 501/327-6858

Best Seafood
Fish House
116 S. Harkrider St., 501/327-9901
Hart's Seafood Restaurant
Hwy. 64 at Hwy. 65, 501/327-7041

Standbys
Pizza Hut
1076 Harkrider St., 501/327-1396
201 Donaghey Ave., 501/450-5981
Pizza Inn
235 Farris Rd., 501/327-1900
724 Oak St., 501/329-3881
Ryan's Family Steak House
1400 Highway 64W, 501/327-7926
Shoney's
11 Faulkner Plz., 501/329-8385
Western Sizzlin
816 First Ave., 501/327-2753

Baskin-Robbins
1035 Hwy. 65N, 501/329-3200

DUMAS, AR

Best Barbecue/Ribs
Hall's BBQ
152 N. Main St., 501/382-4922

Best Breakfast
Delta Inn Restaurant
Hwy. 65S, 501/382-4361

Best Chinese Food
House of Lee Restaurant
350 Twin River Ctr., 501/382-2388

Best Family Restaurant
Dude's Restaurant
Hwy. 65S, 501/382-2879

Best Pizza
Big Banjo Pizza Parlor
Hwy. 65S, 501/382-2880

Best Seafood
Catfish Kitchen
217 N. Hwy. 65, 501/382-4488

Best Steaks
Dude's Restaurant
Hwy. 65S, 501/382-2879

Standbys
Sonic Drive-In
Hwy. 65S, 501/382-2520

ELDORADO, AR

Best Restaurants in Town
Tiger Harry's Diner
117 E. Main St., 501/863-6611
The Brass Ring Dinner Club
1810 Junction City Rd., 501/863-0069

Best Atmosphere
White House Cafe
323 Adams Ave. SE, Camden, 501/836-4663

Best Barbecue/Ribs
Sassy Jones
108 W. Oak St., Montrose, 501/737-2271
Backyard Bar-B-Q
1407 E. Main St., Magnolia, 501/234-7890

Best Catfish
Wood's Place
1173 Washington St. SW, Camden, 501/836-0474

Best Chinese Food
Hunan Chinese Restaurant
1718 N. West Ave., 501/862-7621

Best Homestyle Food
Wood's Place
1173 Washington St. SW, Camden, 501/836-0474

Best Italian Food
La Bella Gourmet Gifts and Deli
   101 E. Main St., 501/862-4335

Best Mexican Food
Tiger Harry's Diner
   117 E. Main St., 501/864-8577

Best Seafood
Catfish Cove
   4414 W. Hillsboro St., 501/862-5814

Best Steaks
White House Cafe
   323 Adams Ave. SE, Camden, 501/836-4663

FAYETTEVILLE, AR

Best Restaurant in Town
Coy's Place
   2908 N. College Ave., 501/442-9664

Best American Food
Kirby's Grill and Bakery
   3722 Front St., 501/443-3900

Best Atmosphere
Cafe Santa Fe and Bar
   25 E. Center St., 501/442-5673
Old Post Office
   1 Center Sq., 501/443-5588
Zachary's Restaurant
   708 N. College Ave., 501/444-7774

Best Barbecue/Ribs
B and B Bar-B-Q
   2227 W. Sixth St., 501/582-3663
   230 S. East St., 501/521-8985

Best Breakfast
Uncle Gaylord's Mountain Cafe
   315 W. Mountain St., 501/444-0605

Best Brunch
Belvedeer's
   3061 N. College Ave., 501/443-7778

Best Burgers
Hoffbrau Steaks
   31 E. Center St., 501/442-4444
Ozark Brewing Company [downstairs]
   430 W. Dickson St., 501/521-2739
Hugo's
   25 1/2 N. Block Ave., 501/521-7585

Best Casual Dining
Ozark Brewing Company [downstairs]
   430 W. Dickson St., 501/521-2739

Best Catfish
The Hush Puppy Catfish Restaurant
   3582 N. Hwy. 112, 501/521-5914

Best Chinese Food
Lin's Chinese Restaurant
   704 N. College Ave., 501/521-2022

A

Best Coffee
The Old Post Office
  1 Center Sq., 501/443-5588

Best Continental Food
Zachary's Restaurant
  708 N. College Ave., 501/444-7774
Ozark Brewing Company [upstairs]
  430 W. Dickson St., 501/521-2739

Best Homestyle Food
Vida Drake's Restaurant
  504 E. Fifteenth St., 501/521-3244

Best Italian Food
Belvedeer's
  3061 N. College Ave., 501/443-7778

Best Mexican Food
La Huerta
  2356 N. College Ave., 501/521-7990
Cafe Santa Fe and Bar
  25 E. Center St., 501/442-5673
Jose's
  324 W. Dickson St., 501/521-0194

Best Pizza
Cable Car Pizza
  1830 N. College Ave., 501/444-7600
Tim's Pizza
  2730 N. College Ave., 501/521-4151
  21 W. Mountain St., 501/ 521-5551

Best Seafood
Powerhouse Seafood
  112 N. University Ave., 501/442-8300
Ozark Brewing Company [upstairs]
  430 W. Dickson St., 501/521-2739

Best Steaks
Coy's Place
  2908 N. College Ave., 501/442-9664
Herman's Ribhouse
  2901 N. College Ave., 501/442-9671
Ozark Brewing Company [upstairs]
  430 W. Dickson St., 501/521-2739

Standbys
Red Lobster
  3885 N. Shiloh Dr., 501/442-2317

FT. SMITH, AR

Best Barbecue/Ribs
Art's Barbeque
  6901 Rogers Ave., 501/452-2550
Jerry Neel's Bar-B-Q
  1823 S. Phoenix St., 501/646-8085

Best Coffee
Guido's
  19 N. Tenth St., 501/785-2110

A

Best Desserts
Dora's Pie Shop
  115 N. Tenth St., Ste. 102, 501/782-0170
Guido's
  19 N. Tenth St., 501/785-2110
Folie A Deux
  2909 Old Greenwood Rd., Ste. 6, 501/648-0041

Best French Food
Folie A Deux
  2909 Old Greenwood Rd., Ste. 6, 501/648-0041

Best German Food
Emmy's German Restaurant
  602 N. Sixteenth St., 501/783-0012

Best Homestyle Food
Calico County Restaurant
  2401 S. 56th St., 501/452-3299

Best Italian Food
Taliano's Italian Restaurant
  201 N. Fourteenth St., 501/785-2292

Best Place to Eat When Someone Else Is Buying
John Q's Fine Dining
  700 Rogers Ave., 501/783-1000

Best Sandwiches
Williamsburg Kitchen
  4120 Rogers Ave., 501/785-0029

Best Seafood
John Q's Fine Dining
  700 Rogers Ave., 501/783-1000
Tommy's Seafood Restaurant
  2428 Midland Blvd., 501/783-9523

Best Steaks
John Q's Fine Dining
  700 Rogers Ave., 501/783-1000
Tommy's Seafood Restaurant
  2428 Midland Blvd., 501/783-9523
Red Barn Steak House
  3716 Newlon Rd., 501/783-4075

HOT SPRINGS, AR

Best Restaurants in Town
Bohemia Restaurant
  417 Park Ave., 501/623-9661
Cajun Boilers
  2806 Albert Pike Rd., 501/767-5695
Coy's Steakhouse
  300 Coy St., 501/321-1414
Miller's Chicken and Steak House
  4723 Central Ave., 501/525-8861
The Hamilton House
  130 Van Lyell Drive, 501/525-2727

Best All-You-Can-Eat Buffet
Buffy's Buffet
3815 Central Ave., 501/525-5793

Best American Food
Johnny's
3413 Central Ave., 501/623-9788
Miller's Chicken and Steak House
4723 Central Ave., 501/525-8861
Mollie's Restaurant
538 W. Grand Ave., 501/623-6582

Best Asian Restaurants
Hunan Oriental Restaurant
5101 Central Ave., 501/525-2053
The Panda
3520 Central Ave., 501/624-5403

Best Atmosphere
The Hamilton House
130 Van Lyell Dr., 501/525-2727

Best Barbecue/Ribs
McClard's Bar-B-Q
505 Albert Pike Rd., 501/624-9586
Stubby's BBQ
3024 Central Ave., 501/624-2484
310 Park Ave., 501/624-2484

Best Breakfast
Colonial Pancake and Waffle House
111 Central Ave., 501/624-9273
Pancake Shop
216 Central Ave., 501/624-9465

Best Brunch
Arlington Fountain and Venetian Restaurant
239 Central Ave., 501/623-7771

Best Burgers
Burgers and More
2800 Albert Pike Rd., 501/767-4601
622 Carpenter Dam Rd., 501/262-2253

Best Catfish
Fish Net Restaurant
Highway 7N, 501/321-1910
Miller's Chicken and Steak House
4723 Central Ave., 501/525-8861

Best Chinese Food
Hunan Oriental Restaurant
5101 Central Ave., 501/525-2053

Best Coffee
Cafe New Orleans
210 Central Ave., 501/624-3200

Best Desserts
Mary's Cafe
1010 Central Ave., 501/624-2988
Mollie's Restaurant
538 W. Grand Ave., 501/623-6582

Best German Food
Brau Haus
  801 Central, 501/624-7866

Best Homestyle Food
Mary's Cafe
  1010 Central Ave., 501/624-2988
Mollie's Restaurant
  538 W. Grand Ave., 501/623-6582

Best Italian Food
Facci's Italian Restaurant
  2910 Central Ave., 501/623-9049
Rocky's Corner
  2600 Central Ave., 501/624-0199
Agostino's Italian Restaurant
  510 Central Ave., 501/624-5500

Best Mexican Food
Acapulco Restaurant
  320 Ouachita Ave., 501/623-8030
La Hacienda Mexican Restaurant
  3836 Central Ave., 501/525-8203
Cafe Santa Fe
  323 Whittington Ave., 501/624-0166

Best Other Ethnic Food
Bohemia Restaurant (Czech/German)
  417 Park Ave., 501/623-9661

Best Pizza
Rocky's Corner
  2600 Central Ave., 501/624-0199
Rod's Pizza Cellar
  3350 Central Ave., 501/624-7637

Best Seafood
Cajun Boilers
  2806 Albert Pike Rd., 501/767-5695
Pirate's Cove Restaurant and Bar
  200 River Heights Terrace, 501/767-8517

Best Steaks
Coy's Steakhouse
  300 Coy St., 501/321-1414
The Hamilton House
  130 Van Lyell Drive, 501/525-2727

Standbys
Red Lobster
  4500 Central Ave., 501/525-7613
Shoney's
  1400 Central Ave., 501/624-4320
Golden Corral Family Steakhouse
  5001 Warden Rd., 501/771-4605

JACKSONVILLE, AR

Best Chinese Food
China Garden
  324 W. Main St., 501/982-2712

Best Homestyle Food
Cody's Cafe
96 Industrial Dr., 501/982-8386

A

Best Seafood
Crooked Hook Catfish
1802 S. Hwy. 161, 501/982-9276

Best Thai Food
Siam Restaurant
1415 W. Main St., 501/982-3651

JONESBORO, AR

Best Restaurants in Town
Dixie Cafe
2406 S. Caraway, 501/932-9400
Oaks Restaurant
3006 S. Caraway Rd., 501/935-2030
The Candlelite Steakhouse
1116 Linwood Dr., Paragould, 501/239-8391
The Galley
1841 E. Highland Dr., 501/933-7300

Best Atmosphere
The Candlelite Steakhouse
1116 Linwood Dr., Paragould, 501/239-8391

Best American Food
Sharecropper's
211 W. Ash St., Blytheville, 501/763-5818

Best Barbecue/Ribs
Couch's Bar-B-Q
5323 E. Nettleton Ave., 501/932-0710
Dixie Pig
701 N. Sixth St., Blytheville, 501/763-4636

Best Burgers
The Hamburger Station
110 E. Main St., Paragould, 501/239-9956

Best Catfish
Catfish Galley
1820 S. Main St., 501/935-1233
1841 E. Highland Ave., 501/933-6955
2113 N. Church St., 501/932-3133

Best Chinese Food
China Garden Restaurant
906 S. Caraway Rd., 501/932-6083

Best Coffee
Kirby's Restaurant
Hwy. 77, Manila, 501/561-4771

Best Desserts
Sharecropper's
211 W. Ash St., Blytheville, 501/763-5818

Best Homestyle Food
Nanna's Kitchen
701 W. Kings Hwy., Paragould, 501/239-2299

Best Italian Food
Pasta Company
2230 S. Caraway Rd., 501/972-4643

A

Piero and Company
314 Union St., 501/933-0034

Best Mexican Food
El Acapulco
1900 E. Highland St., 501/935-6692
Poncho's
2240 S. Caraway St., 501/972-6640

Best Seafood
Kelly's Restaurant
Hwy. 64W, Wynne, 501/238-2616

Standbys
Shoney's
1137 S. Caraway Rd., 501/932-9190

LITTLE ROCK, AR

Best Restaurants in Town
Andre's in Hillcrest
605 Beechwood Ave., 501/666-9191
Cafe St. Moritz
225 E. Markham St., 501/372-0411
Brave New Restaurant
3701 Old Cantrell Rd., 501/663-2677

Best American Food
Bard's Restaurant
1902 N. Grant St., 501/666-9933

Best Atmosphere
Ashley's Restaurant
111 W. Markham St., 501/374-7474
Josephine's
3 Statehouse Plz., 501/375-5000

Best Barbecue/Ribs
Lindsey's Barbecue
203 E. Fourteenth St., 501/374-5901
Dixie Pig
900 W. 35th St., North Little Rock, 501/753-9650
701 N. Sixth St., Blytheville, 501/763-4636
J.R.'s Ribs
1309 Old Forge Dr., 501/224-4004
Sim's Bar-B-Que
1307 Barrow Rd., 501/224-2057
7601 Geyer Springs Rd., 501/562-8844
716 W. 33rd St., 501/372-6868

Best Breakfast
Ozark Mountain Smokehouse
201 Keightly Dr., 501/663-7319

Best Brunch
Victorian Garden
4801C N. Hills Blvd., 501/758-4299

Best Burgers
Backyard Burgers
2821 Kavanaugh Blvd., 501/661-0565
305 N. Shackleford Rd., 501/227-5998
7323 Cantrell Rd., 501/664-1846
824 Broadway St., 501/376-4338

Buffalo Grill
   1611 Rebsamen Park Rd., 501/663-2150

Best Business Lunch
Cafe St. Moritz
   225 E. Markham St., 501/372-0411

Best Casual Dining
Julie's
   110 S. Shackleford Rd., 501/224-4501

Best Catfish
Catfish City
   1817 S. University Ave., 501/663-0552
Cock of the Walk
   7051 Cock of the Walk Lane, North Little Rock,
      501/758-7182
Grampa's Catfish House
   1218 Mission Rd., North Little Rock, 501/758-4654

Best Cheap Meal
Lucky Seven Diner and Catering
   314 E. Sixth St., 501/075-2526

Best Chinese Food
Fu Lin Chinese Restaurant
   200 N. Bowman Rd., 501/225-8989
Forbidden City Chinese Restaurant
   6000 W. Markham St., Ste. 1034, 501/663-9099

Best Coffee
Cafe D'Roma
   2701 Kavanaugh Blvd., 501/663-7397
Wycoff Coffee
   10700 N. Rodney Parham Rd., 501/228-4448

Best Continental Food
Ashley's Restaurant
   111 W. Markham St., 501/374-7474
Cafe St. Moritz
   225 E. Markham St., 501/372-0411
Sixteen Twenty Restaurant
   1620 Market St., 501/221-1620

Best Delicatessen
Cordell's Inc.
   1500 Rebsamen Park Rd., 501/666-5405

Best Desserts
Ashley's Restaurant
   111 W. Markham St., 501/374-7474
Cafe D'Roma
   2701 Kavanaugh Blvd., 501/663-7397

Best Diner
Lucky Seven Diner and Catering
   314 E. Sixth St., 501/375-2526

Best Eclectic Menu
Brave New Restaurant
   3701 Old Cantrell Rd., 501/663-2677

Best French Food
Andre's in Hillcrest
   605 Beechwood Ave., 501/666-9191

A

A

Best Greek/Mediterranean Food
Terrace Restaurant
  301 N. Shackleford Rd., 501/224-1677

Best Homestyle Food
Lucky Seven Diner and Catering
  314 E. Sixth St., 501/375-2526
Bard's Restaurant
  1902 N. Grant St., 501/666-9933
Dixie Cafe
  10700 N. Rodney Parham Rd., 501/224-3728
  8523 Geyer Springs Rd., 501/568-6444
  1220 Rebsamen Park Rd., 501/663-9336
Your Mama's Good Food
  2811 Kavanaugh Blvd., 501/663-6333
  402 Louisiana St., 501/372-1811

Best Indian Food
Star of India
  301 N. Shackleford Rd., 501/227-9900

Best Italian Food
Percito's Italian Kitchen
  1900 E. Broadway St., 501/372-9483
Villa Italian Restaurant
  201 S. Shackleford, 501/219-2244

Best Japanese Food
Shogun Japanese Steakhouse
  2815 Cantrell Rd., 501/666-7070

Best Mexican Food
Tia's Tex-Mex
  225 N. Shackleford Rd., 501/224-9336
  4305 Warden Rd., North Little Rock, 501/753-8675
Juanita's Mexican Cafe and Bar
  1300 S. Main, 501/372-1228

Best Middle Eastern Food
Terrace Restaurant
  301 N. Shackleford Rd., 501/224-1677

Best Pizza
Vino's
  923 W. Seventh St., 501/375-8466
Iriana's Pizza
  103 W. Markham St., 501/374-3656
  400 Bowman Rd., 501/225-2545
Pizza Cafe
  1517 Rebsamen Park Rd., 501/664-6133

Best Place to Be "Seen"
Ashley's Restaurant
  111 W. Markham St., 501/374-7474

Best Place to Eat When Someone Else Is Buying
Ashley's Restaurant
  111 W. Markham St., 501/374-7474

Best Places to Take the Kids
Dixie Cafe
  1220 Rebsamen Park Rd., 501/663-9336
  10700 N. Rodney Parham Rd., 501/224-3728
  8523 Geyer Springs Rd., 501/568-6444

Best Quick Lunch
The Vineyard in the Park
  Ninth at Commerce, 501/372-4000

Best Romantic Dining
Josephine's
  3 Statehouse Plaza, 501/375-5000

Best Salad/Salad Bar
Cafe St. Moritz
  225 E. Markham St., 501/372-0411

Best Sandwiches
Jimmy's Serious Sandwiches
  5116 W. Markham St., 501/666-3354

Best Seafood
Landry's Cajun Wharf
  2400 Cantrell Rd., 501/375-5351
Oyster Bar
  3003 W. Markham St., 501/666-7100

Best Southwestern Food
Tia's Tex-Mex
  225 N. Shackleford Rd., 501/224-9336
Blue Mesa
  1719 Merrill, 501/221-7777

Best Spanish Food
Tapas
  10301 N. Rodney Parham Rd., 501/224-7707

Best Steaks
Sir Loin's Inn
  801 W. 29th St., 501/753-1361
Doe's Eat Place
  1023 W. Markham St., 501/376-1195
Faded Rose Restaurant
  1615 Rebsamen Park Rd., 501/663-9734
  400 N. Bowman Rd., Ste. 28, 501/224-3377
Chuck's Steak House
  3105 Hwy. 25B N., Heber Springs, 501/362-7676

Best Tea Room
Victorian Garden
  4801C N. Hills Blvd., 501/758-4299

Best Vegetarian Food
Cafe St. Moritz
  225 E. Markham St., 501/372-0411

Standbys
Golden Corral Family Steakhouse
  5001 Warden Rd., 501/771-4605
Steak and Ale
  2917 Cantrell Rd., 501/666-7228
The Olive Garden
  10715 N. Rodney Parham Rd., 501/225-7673
Red Lobster
  8407 W. Markham St., 501/224-0940
Outback Steakhouse
  105 Markham Park Dr., 501/221-7655

A

MAGNOLIA, AR

Best Barbecue/Ribs
Backyard Barbeque Company
1407 E. Main St., 501/234-7890

Best Burgers
Burger Blast
1409 E. Main St., 501/234-2034

Best Chinese Food
Royal China
900 E. Main St., 501/234-7719

Best Diner
Beef and Bisquits
417 E. Main St., 501/234-8659

Best Family Restaurants
Marlar's Cafeteria
2116 N. Vine St., 501/234-6900
Miller Cafeteria
2402 N. Vine St., 501/234-2181

Best Homestyle Food
Marlar's Cafeteria
2116 N. Vine St., 501/234-6900

Best Mexican Food
Tiger Harry's Diner
426 E. Main St., 501/234-5125

Best Seafood
Rails
902 E. McKissack St., Waldo, 501/693-2243

Best Steaks
Georgia's Restaurant
2630 Columbia Rd. 15, 501/696-3942

Standbys
Western Sizzlin
1113 E. Main St., 501/234-7910
Dairy Queen
Columbia Shopping Ctr., 501/234-4741
Pizza Inn
915 E. Main St., 501/234-7560

PINE BLUFF, AR

Best Restaurants in Town
Tavern in the Village
2520 West 28th St., 501/534-9013
Tradewinds Restaurant
Hwy. 65N, McGehee, 501/222-4022

Best All-You-Can-Eat Buffet
A Tao Bradley Chinese Wok
921 Main St., 501/535-7722

Best American Food
Arnold's Catfish Place
2122 S. Blake St., 501/536-1834
Jones Cafe
3910 Hwy. 65S, 501/534-6678

Best Asian Restaurant
Tradewinds Restaurant
  Hwy. 65N, McGehee, 501/222-4022

Best Atmosphere
Leon's Catfish and Shrimp Restaurant
  18 Chapel Village, 501/879-3150

Best Bar
Bad Bob's Country Nightclub
  2204 E. Harding Ave., 501/534-9515

Best Barbecue/Ribs
Bar-B-Que Hut
  2203 W. 26th St., 501/536-3801

Best Bread
Sonny's
  128 Main St., 501/534-8887

Best Burgers
Sno-White Grill
  310 E. Fifth St., 501/534-9811

Best Casual Dining
Tommy's Restaurant
  812 Poplar St., 501/534-9622

Best Catfish
Carpenter's
  3510 Hwy., 65S, 501/536-4242

Best Chinese Food
East Winds Chinese Restaurant
  500 Fifth St., 501/535-0108
China Rose Restaurant
  4012 Old Warren Rd., 501/541-0311
Fuh Mei's
  303 W. 31st Ave., 501/536-4500

Best Desserts
Lybrand's Bakery
  2900 S. Hazel St., 501/534-4607
Jones Cafe
  3910 Hwy. 65S, 501/534-6678

Best Homestyle Food
Southern Cook's Kitchen
  3007 S. Olive St., 501/534-0625
Carpenter's
  3510 Hwy., 65S, 501/536-4242

Best Mexican Food
Cow Pen
  Hwy. 82, Lake Village, 501/265-9992

Best Pastries
Jones Cafe
  3910 Hwy. 65S, 501/534-6678

Best Pizza
Big Banjo Pizza Parlor
  1620 Nebraska St., 501/534-3801
  6000 Sheridan Rd., 501/247-3801
  4208 W. 28th St., 501/879-3801
Mazzio's Pizza
  2701 S. Olive St., 501/536-7900

Best Place to Eat When Someone Else Is Buying
Tavern in the Village
    2520 W. 28th Ave., 501/534-9013

Best Quick-Dinner-Before-the-Movie
Corn Dog 7
    2901 Pines Mall Dr., 501/534-9273

Best Sandwiches
Sonny's
    128 S. Main St., 501/534-8887

Best Steaks
Colonial Steak House
    111 W. Eighth Ave., 501/536-3488
Tommy's Restaurant
    812 Poplar St., 501/534-9622
Jones Cafe
    3910 Hwy. 65S, 501/534-6678

Standbys
Bonanza
    2911 Olive St., 501/536-4508

ROGERS, AR

Best Restaurant in Town
Plaza Restaurant and Club
    224 N. Second St., 501/636-9191

Best Asian Restaurant
Aloha Chinese Restaurant
    208 S. Eighth St., 501/631-1781

Best American Food
Cotton Patch Cafe
    1949 W. Walnut St., 501/936-8088

Best Atmosphere
Crumpet Tea Room
    107 W. Elm St., 501/636-7498

Best Bar
Santa Fe Cafe
    117 W. Walnut St., 501/636-4242

Best Barbecue/Ribs
Smokin' Joe's Ribhouse
    803 W. Poplar St., 501/621-0021

Best Brunch
Crumpet Tea Room
    107 W. Elm St., 501/638-7498

Best Burgers
Back Yard Burgers
    1735 W. Walnut St., 501/621-5200

Best Casual Dining
Santa Fe Cafe
    117 W. Walnut St., 501/636-4242
Cotton Patch Cafe
    1949 W. Walnut St., 501/936-8088

Best Catfish
Catfish John's
    447 W. Hudson Rd., 501/631-6908

Best Cheap Meal
Rally's Hamburgers
2205 W. Walnut St., 501/636-1725

Best Diner
Wesner's Grill
117 W. Chestnut St., 501/636-9723

Best Health-Conscious Menu
Aunt Clyde's Bakery
200 W. Poplar St., 501/621-8959

Best Italian Food
Pasta Gardens
200 N. Eighth St., 501/621-9333

Best Mexican Food
Santa Fe Cafe
117 W. Walnut St., 501/636-4242

Best Pizza
Mazzio's Pizza
817 W. Walnut St., 501/636-0003

Best Place to Be "Seen"
Plaza Restaurant and Club
224 N. Second St., 501/636-9191

Best Place to Eat Alone
Hunan Chinese Restaurant
509 S. Eighth St., 501/621-5300

Best Place to Eat When Someone Else Is Buying
Plaza Restaurant and Club
224 N. Second St., 501/636-9191

Best Seafood
Tale of the Trout
4611 W. New Hope Rd., 501/636-0508

Best Tea Room
Crumpet Tea Room
107 W. Elm St., 501/636-7498

Standbys
Ryan's Family Steak House
102 S. 21st St., 501/636-5988
Shoney's
401 S. Eighth St., 501/621-8959
Subway
2301 W. Walnut St., 501/636-6699
Dairy Queen
2325 W. Walnut St., 501/631-6611
TCBY
1307 W. Walnut St., 501/636-7209

RUSSELLVILLE, AR

Best Barbecue/Ribs
Old Post Bar-B-Que
407 S. Arkansas Ave., 501/968-2421

Best Breakfast
Stoby's Depot and Dining Car
405 W. D St., 501/968-3816

Best Burgers
Stoby's Depot and Dining Car
405 W. D St., 501/968-3816

Best Chinese Food
New China
2211 N. Arkansas Ave., 501/968-8881
Tran's Oriental Palace
2621 W. Main St., 501/968-1933

Best Homestyle Food
Zak and Zeke's
1519 S. Arkansas Ave., 501/890-5512

Best Ice Cream/Yogurt
Sugar Creek Shoppe
501 N. Arkansas Ave., 501/968-3878

Best Italian Food
Italian Gardens
3053 E. Main St., 501/967-1707

Best Pizza
Cici's Pizza
3063 E. Main St., 501/967-4432

Best Steaks
Brangus Feed Lot
1509 E. Main St., 501/968-1999

SPRINGDALE, AR

Best Restaurant in Town
Kirby's Grill and Bakery
3722 Front St., Fayetteville, 501/443-3900

Best All-You-Can-Eat Buffet
J.D. China Chinese Restaurant
1466 N. College Ave., Fayetteville, 501/442-5875

Best American Food
Neal's Cafe
Hwy. 71N, 501/751-9996

Best Atmosphere
Old Post Office
1 Center Sq., Fayetteville, 501/443-5588

Best Bar
George's Majestic Lounge
519 W. Dickson St., Fayetteville, 501/442-4226

Best Barbecue/Ribs
Smokin' Joe's Ribhouse
1084 W. Sunset, 501/756-5228
803 W. Poplar St., Rogers, 501/621-0021
Bubba's Barbecue
60 Kings Hwy., Eureka Springs, 501/253-7706

Best Bottomless Coffee Cup
Arsaga's Espresso Cafe
25 N. Block Ave., Fayetteville, 501/443-9801

Best Breakfast
Jerry's Homestyle Cooking
241 N. College Ave., Fayetteville, 501/521-2480

Best Brunch
Uncle Gaylord's Mountain Cafe
  315 W. Mountain St., Fayetteville, 501/444-0605
Tiffany Grille
  Holiday Inn, 1500 S. 48th St., 501/751-8300

Best Burgers
Hugo's
  25 1/2 N. Block Ave., Fayetteville, 501/521-7585

Best Business Breakfast
Tiffany Grille
  Holiday Inn, 1500 S. 48th St., 501/751-8300

Best Business Lunch
Old Post Office
  1 Center Sq., Fayetteville, 501/443-5588

Best Cajun/Creole Food
French Quarter Cafe
  825 Jackson St. SW, Camden, 501/837-1010

Best Casual Dining
Cotton Patch Cafe
  1949 W. Walnut St., Rogers, 501/936-8088

Best Cheap Meal
J.D. China Chinese Restaurant
  1466 N. College Ave., Fayetteville, 501/442-5875

Best Chinese Food
Far East Restaurant
  812 N. Thompson St., 501/756-2460

Best Coffee
Arsaga's Espresso Cafe
  25 N. Block Ave., Fayetteville, 501/443-9801
Spring Street Deli
  82 Spring St., Eureka Springs, 501/253-2111

Best Coffeehouse
Emerald Coast
  412 W. Dickson St., Fayetteville, 501/582-3640

Best Continental Food
Ozark Brewing Company [upstairs]
  430 W. Dickson St., Fayetteville, 501/521-2739
Cottage Inn
  Hwy. 62W, Eureka Springs, 501/253-5282
Plaza Restaurant
  55 Main St., Eureka Springs, 501/253-8866
Blackboard Cafe
  12 Cunningham Rd., Bella Vista, 501/855-0739

Best Delicatessen
Vicenza's
  835 E. Henri de Tonti Blvd., 501/361-9024

Best Desserts
Spring Street Grill and Catering
  101 N. Spring St., 501/751-0323

Best Diner
Wesner's Grill
  117 W. Chestnut, Rogers, 501/636-9723

Best Eclectic Menu
Restaurant on the Corner
248 W. Dickson St., Fayetteville, 501/521-2674

Best Family Restaurant
AQ Chicken House
Hwy. 71B, 501/751-4633

Best Fast Food
Susie Q Malt Shop
612 N. Second St., Rogers, 501/636-1326

Best French Food
Zachary's Restaurant
708 N. College Ave., Fayetteville, 501/444-7774

Best Happy Hour Snacks
Powerhouse Seafood
112 University Ave., Fayetteville, 501/442-8300

Best Health-Conscious Menu
Kirby's Grill and Bakery
3722 Front St., Fayetteville, 501/443-3900

Best Homestyle Food
Monte Ne Inn Chicken
Hwy. 94E, Rogers, 501/636-5511
Neal's Cafe
Hwy. 71N, 501/751-9996

Best Ice Cream/Yogurt
Uncle Gaylord's Mountain Cafe
315 W. Mountain St., Fayetteville, 501/444-0605

Best Italian Food
Belvedeer's
3061 N. College Ave., Fayetteville, 501/443-7778
Mary Maestri's
956 E. Henri de Tonti Blvd., 501/361-2536

Best Late-Night Food
Tony C's Italiano Ristorante
2366 N. College Ave., Fayetteville, 501/442-4433

Best Mexican Food
La Huerta
2356 N. College Ave., Fayetteville, 501/521-7990
Jose's
324 W. Dickson St., Fayetteville, 501/521-0194
Cafe Santa Fe
179 N. Main St., Eureka Springs, 501/253-9617

Best Microbrewery
Ozark Brewing Company
430 W. Dickson St., Fayetteville, 501/521-2739

Best Pastries
Morning Glory's
23 E. Center St., Fayetteville, 501/443-6573

Best Pizza
Cable Car Pizza
1830 N. College Ave., Fayetteville, 501/444-7600

Best Place to Be "Seen"
The Plaza Restaurant and Club
224 N. Second St., Rogers, 501/636-9191

Best Place to Eat Alone
Jim's Razorback Pizza
  University of Arkansas Student Union, Sixth St.,
    Fayetteville, 501/575-7345

Best Place to Eat When Someone Else Is Buying
Old Post Office
  1 Center Sq., Fayetteville, 501/443-5588

Best Place to Take the Kids
AQ Chicken House
  Hwy. 71B, 501/751-4633

Best Quick-Dinner-Before-the-Movie
Hoffbrau Steaks
  31 E. Center St., Fayetteville, 501/442-4444

Best Quick Lunch
Muley's Restaurant and Club
  1 Colt Square Dr., Fayetteville, 501/443-3911

Best Romantic Dining
Fred's Hickory Inn
  1502 N. Walton Blvd., Bentonville, 501/273-3303

Best Salad/Salad Bar
AQ Chicken House
  Hwy. 71B, 501/751-4633

Best Sandwiches
Fatiga's Sub Station
  808 S. Mount Olive St., Siloam Springs, 501/524-6277

Best Schmooze Bar
George's Majestic Lounge
  519 W. Dickson St., Fayetteville, 501/442-4226

Best Seafood
Powerhouse Seafood
  112 N. University Ave., Fayetteville, 501/442-8300

Best Smoke-Free Restaurant
Kirby's Grill and Bakery
  3722 Front St., Fayetteville, 501/443-3900

Best Southwestern Food
Jose's
  324 W. Dickson St., Fayetteville, 501/521-0194

Best Spanish Food
Glasgow's Cafe
  411 SE Walton Blvd., Bentonville, 501/273-9958

Best Sports Bar
Cuckoo's Sports Grill
  965 S. Razorback Rd., Fayetteville, 501/521-5100

Best Steaks
Butcher Block Steak House
  4309 S. Thompson, 501/751-0006

Best Tea Room
Crumpet Tea Room
  107 W. Elm St., Rogers, 501/636-7498

Best Undiscovered Restaurant
J.D. China Chinese Restaurant
  1466 N. College Ave., Fayetteville, 501/442-5875

WEST MEMPHIS, AR

Best Barbecue/Ribs
Slick Willie's
 1100 Ingram Blvd., 501/735-3656

Best Breakfast
Earl's Hot Biscuits
 2005 I-55, 501/735-5380

Best Chinese Food
Fu Gai
 526 E. Broadway St., 501/735-3133

Best Desserts
Granny's Front Porch
 109 S. Worthington Dr., 501/735-9468

Best Homestyle Food
Earl's Hot Biscuits
 2005 I-55, 501/735-5380
Granny's Front Porch
 109 S. Worthington Dr., 501/735-9468

Best Sandwiches
Munchy's
 108 E. Broadway St., 501/735-7358

Standbys
Pizza Hut
 1105 N. Missouri St., 501/735-7607
 190 Shoppingway Blvd., 501/735-3400
Baskin-Robbins
 1806 N. Missouri St., 501/735-1171

California

ANAHEIM, CA

Best Barbecue/Ribs
Chris and Pitt's of Anaheim
601 N. Euclid St., 714/635-2601

Best Breakfast
Mimi's Cafe
1240 E. Euclid St., 714/535-1552

Best Burgers
Angelo's Hamburger
511 S. State College Blvd., 714/533-1401
Chris and Pitt's of Anaheim
601 N. Euclid St., 714/635-2601

Best Casual Dining
Chris and Pitt's of Anaheim
601 N. Euclid St., 714/635-2601

Best Chinese Food
Mandarin Pavillion
1050 W. Valencia, Fullerton, 714/870-7950

Best Continental Food
Mimi's Cafe
1240 E. Euclid St., 714/535-1552

Best Desserts
Marie Callender's
540 N. Euclid St., 714/774-1832
5711 E. La Palma Ave., 714/779-0600

Best Dinner
Mimi's Cafe
1240 E. Euclid St., 714/535-1552

Best Family Restaurant
Marie Callender's
540 N. Euclid St., 714/774-1832
5711 E. La Palma Ave., 714/779-0600

Best Homestyle Food
Marie Callender's
540 N. Euclid St., 714/774-1832
5711 E. La Palma Ave., 714/779-0600

Best Italian Food
Luigi's D'Italia
　801 S. State College Blvd., 714/490-0990
Mama Cozza's
　2170 W. Ball Rd., 714/635-0063

Best Mexican Food
El Torito Restaurant
　2020 E. Ball Rd., 714/956-4880

Best Steaks
Stuart Anderson's Black Angus
　2011 E. La Palma Ave., 714/776-5550

Standbys
HomeTown Buffet
　2190 E. Lincoln, 714/774-6899

ANTIOCH, CA

Best Restaurant in Town
Humphrey's Restaurant
　1 Marina Plaza, 510/778-5800

Best German Food
Margo's Little Bavaria
　71 Sand Creek Rd., Brentwood, 510/634-9131

Best Mexican Food
La Plaza Mexican Restaurant
　2370 Buchanan, 510/754-6556
Taqueria Salsa
　3612 Delta Fair Blvd., 510/778-9281
New Mecca
　328 Railroad Ave., Pittsburg, 510/432-7433

Best Pizza
Skipolini's Pizza
　901 Fitzuren Rd., 510/757-7770

Best Romantic Dining
Grand Island Mansion
　13415 Grand Island Rd., Courtland, 916/775-1705

Best Seafood
Riverview Lodge
　Foot of First St., 510/757-2272

Best Thai Food
Thai Derm Thai Cuisine
　1884 A St., 510/757-8835

Standbys
The Olive Garden
　1195 Century Plaza Blvd., Pittsburg, 510/778-6208

APPLE VALLEY, CA

Best Restaurant in Town
Jeff's Cafe
　21660 Bear Valley Rd., 619/961-8687

Best Continental Food
Honey's
　18564 Hwy. 18, 619/242-4300

Best Homestyle Food
Molly's
   21851 Hwy. 18, 619/240-6130

Best Mexican Food
Estrada's Mexican Cuisine
   18768 Hwy. 18, Ste. 170, 619/242-4952
Las Brisas Restaurant
   13685 John Glenn Rd., 619/240-1051

C

BAKERSFIELD, CA

Best Breakfast
Twenty-Fourth Street Cafe
   1415 24th St., 805/323-8801

Best Brunch
Misty's at the Red Lion
   3100 Camino Del Rio Court, 805/323-7111

Best Burgers
Happy Jack's Hamburgers
   1800 Twentieth St., 805/323-1661

Best Casual Dining
Gatsby's [breakfast and lunch only]
   3113 Chester Ln., 805/323-8347

Best Chinese Food
Peking Palace
   5600 Auburn St., 805/872-9686

Best Fast Food
In-N-Out Burger
   2310 Panama Lane, 800/786-1000

Best German Food
Bit of Germany
   1901 Flower St., 805/325-8874

Best Greek/Mediterranean Food
Goose Loonie's Sports Bar
   1623 Nineteenth St., 805/631-1242

Best Ice Cream/Yogurt
Dewar's Candy Shop
   1120 Eye St., 805/322-0933
Rosemary's Family Creamery
   2733 F St., 805/395-0555
   6401 White Lane, 805/833-8166

Best Indian Food
Taj Mahal Cuisine of India
   5416 California Ave., 805/633-2222

Best Italian Food
Joseph's Italian Restaurant
   3013 F St., 805/322-7710
Sorello Italian
   7800 McNair Court, 805/396-8603
Luigi's
   725 E. 19th St., 805/322-0929

Best Japanese Food
Izumo Sushi
   4412 Ming Ave., 805/398-0608

C

Best Mexican Food
Cactus Valley Cafe
  9517 Rosedale Hwy., 805/588-8440
El Guanaco Restaurant
  807 Baker St., 805/633-2892
El Pueblo
  9705 Main St., Lamont, 805/845-4545
Garcia's Mexican Restaurant
  6051 White Lane, 805/836-2747
Jake's Original Tex-Mex Cafe
  1710 Oak St., 805/322-6380
Taco Fresco
  3701 California Ave., 805/328-0500
La Costa Foods of Mexico
  716 21st St., 805/322-2655
The Red Pepper Restaurant
  2641 Oswell St., 805/871-5787

Best Other Ethnic Food
Noriega Hotel (Basque)
  525 Sumner St., 805/322-8419
Pyrenees Cafe (Basque)
  601 Sumner St., 805/323-0053
The Getaway Cafe (Hawaiian)
  4158 California Ave., 805/327-1378
Cafe Med (Mediterranean)
  5486 California Ave., 805/327-3544

Best Pizza
Sbarro
  2701 Ming Ave., 805/398-9842
  3000 Mall View Rd., 805/871-9844
Trader's Take-N-Bake Pizza
  2660 Oswell St., 805/873-8225
  2301 Brundage Ln., 805/322-2253
  6300 White Ln., 805/398-2253
Jerry's Pizza and Deli
  1817 Chester Ave., 805/633-1000

Best Places to Eat When Someone Else Is Buying
Anton's Airport Bar and Grill
  1229 Skyway Dr., 805/399-3300
The Bistro
  5105 California Ave., 805/323-3905
City Lights by Patrick Beck
  1800 Chester Ave., 805/633-2283
J.C. Scott's
  4001 Auburn St., 805/872-3818
Mama Tosca's Ristorante
  6631 Mins Ave., 805/831-1242
Maxwell's
  5600 Auburn St., 805/872-5171
Tavern By the Green
  6218 Sundale Ave., 805/831-5225

Best Regional Food
Spice Shop Cafe
  3310 Truxton Ave., 805/324-2806

Best Salad/Salad Bar
The Garden Spot
  3320 Truxton Ave., 805/323-3236

Best Wine Selection
Frugatti's Restaurant
  600 Coffee Rd., 805/836-2000

BANNING, CA

Best Restaurants in Town
The Rusty Lantern
  1316 E. Sixth St., Beaumont, 909/845-9000
Jimmy's Casa Figueroa
  1310 E. Sixth St., Beaumont, 909/845-9047

Best Homestyle Food
The Farmhouse
  6261 W. Fifth St., 908/845-2027

Best Italian Food
Guy's Italian Restaurant
  5970 W. Ramsey St., 909/845-9095

BARSTOW, CA

Best Barbecue/Ribs
Slash X Cafe
  28040 Barstow Rd., 619/252-1197

Best Burgers
Peggy Sue's 50's Diner
  35645 Yermo Rd., Yermo, 619/254-3370

Best Family Restaurants
Rosita's Restaurant
  540 W. Main St., 619/256-1058
Peggy Sue's 50's Diner
  35645 Yermo Rd., Yermo, 619/254-3370

Best Homestyle Food
Coco's Restaurant
  1311 E. Main St., 619/256-8992

Best Mexican Food
Plata's Mexican Food
  1521 W. Main St., 619/255-1750
  25569 Main St., 619/253-2449
  36491 Irwin Rd., 619/256-5596
Rosita's Restaurant
  540 W. Main St., 619/256-1058

Best Seafood
Idle Spurs Steak House
  29557 Hwy. 58, 619/256-8888

Best Steaks
Idle Spurs Steak House
  29557 Hwy. 58, 619/256-8888

Standbys
International House of Pancakes
  1441 E. Main St., 619/256-1020

BENICIA, CA

Best Restaurant in Town
Mabel's
635 First St., 707/746-7068

Best Atmosphere
Mabel's
635 First St., 707/746-7068

Best Breakfast
Washington House Deli Cafe
333A First St., 707/745-3364

Best Brunch
Mabel's
635 First St., 707/746-7068
Sardine Can
O Harbor Way, Vallejo, 707/553-9492

Best Casual Dining
Sardine Can
O Harbor Way, Vallejo, 707/553-9492

Best Coffee
Benicia Cafe
714 First St., 707/745-8232

Best Greek/Mediterranean Food
Blandini's
907 First St., 707/747-5263

Best Italian Food
Napoli Pizzeria and Italian Food
124 Tennessee St., Vallejo, 707/644-9270

Best Lunch
Sardine Can
O Harbor Way, Vallejo, 707/553-9492

Best Mexican Food
Sandoval's
640 First St., 707/746-7830
2032 Columbus Pkwy., 707/747-0515

Best Pizza
Napoli Pizzeria and Italian Food
124 Tennessee St., Vallejo, 707/644-9270

Best Salad/Salad Bar
Sardine Can
O Harbor Way, Vallejo, 707/553-9492

Best Seafood
Harbor House Restaurant
23 Harbor Way, Vallejo, 707/642-8984
Sardine Can
O Harbor Way, Vallejo, 707/553-9492

Best Steaks
Harbor House Restaurant
23 Harbor Way, Vallejo, 707/642-8984

Best Thai Food
Sala Thai Restaurant
807 First St., 707/745-4331

BERKELEY, CA

Best Restaurant in Town
Chez Panisse
  1517 Shattuck Ave., 510/548-5525

Best Bagels
Noah's Bagels
  1883 Solano Ave., 510/525-4447
  2344 Telegraph Ave., 510/849-9951
  3170 College Ave., 510/654-0944
Brothers' Bagels
  1281 Gilman St., 510/524-3104
  1469 Shattuck Ave., 510/649-9422

Best Barbecue/Ribs
Flint's Bar-B-Q
  6609 Shattuck Ave., 510/653-0593

Best Beer Selection
Jupiter
  2181 Shattuck Ave., 510/843-8277

Best Breakfast
Rick and Ann's
  2922 Domingo Ave., 510/649-8538
Brick Hut Cafe
  3222 Adeline St., 510/658-5555
Cafe Fanny
  1603 San Pablo Ave., 510/524-5447
Bette's Ocean View Diner
  1807 Fourth St., 510/644-3230

Best Brunch
Bette's Ocean View Diner
  1807 Fourth St., 510/644-3230

Best Burgers
Barney's Gourmet Hamburger
  1591 Solano Ave., 510/526-8185
Fatapple's Restaurant and Bakery
  1346 Martin Luther King Jr. Way, 510/526-2260
  7525 Fairmount Ave., El Cerrito, 510/528-3433

Best Cheap Meal
Fatapple's Restaurant and Bakery
  1346 Martin Luther King Jr. Way, 510/526-2260
  7525 Fairmount Ave., El Cerrito, 510/528-3433

Best Coffee
Peet's Coffee and Tea
  1825 Solano Ave., 510/526-9607
  2124 Vine St., 510/841-0564
  2916 Domingo Ave., 510/843-1434
Caffe Strada
  2300 College Ave., 510/843-5282
Seabreeze Market and Deli
  598 University Ave., 510/486-8119

Best Chinese Food
Long Life Vegi House
  2129 University Ave., 510/845-6072
King Yen
  2995 College Ave., 510/845-1286

Best Delicatessens
Ultra Lucca Delicatessen
  2905 College Ave., 510/849-2701
Saul's Restaurant and Delicatessen
  1475 Shattuck Ave., 510/848-3354

C

Best Desserts
Just Desserts
  1823 Solano Ave., 510/527-7344
  2925 College Ave., 510/841-1600

Best Health-Conscious Menu
O Chamé
  1830 Fourth St., 510/841-8783

Best Ice Cream/Yogurt
Super Stop Market
  747 San Pablo Ave., Albany, 510/525-5575

Best Indian Food
Pasand Madras Cuisine
  2286 Shattuck Ave., 510/549-2559
New Delhi Junction
  2556 Telegraph Ave., 510/486-0477

Best Italian Food
Venezia Cafe
  1799 University Ave., 510/849-4681

Best Japanese Food
Kirala Japanese Restaurant
  2100 Ward St., 510/549-3486

Best Lunch
Gino's Pizza
  2629 Ashby Ave., 510/841-7626
Bette's-To-Go
  1807 Fourth St., 510/548-9494
Chez Panisse
  1517 Shattuck Ave., 510/548-5525

Best Mexican Food
Cactus Taqueria
  1881 Solano Ave., 510/528-1881

Best New Restaurant
Rivoli Restaurant
  1539 Solano Ave., 510/526-2542

Best Other Ethnic Food
The Blue Nile (Ethiopian)
  2525 Telegraph Ave., 510/540-6777
Cambodiana's (Cambodian)
  2156 University Ave., 510/843-4630

Best Outdoor Dining
Chester's Cafe Walnut Square
  1508 Walnut St., 510/849-9995

Best Pizza
Zachary's Chicago Pizza
  1853 Solano Ave., 510/525-5950
  5801 College, 510/655-6385

Best Places to Take the Kids
Fatapple's Restaurant and Bakery
    1346 Martin Luther King Jr. Way, 510/526-2260
    7525 Fairmount Ave., El Cerrito, 510/528-3433
Walker's Pie Shop
    1491 Solano Ave., Albany, 510/525-4647

Best Romantic Dining
Chez Panisse
    1517 Shattuck Ave., 510/548-5525
Skates on the Bay
    100 Seawall Dr., 510/549-1900

Best Sushi
Kirala Restaurant
    2100 Ward St., 510/549-3486

Best Thai Food
Plearn Thai Cuisine No. 2
    2050 University Ave., 510/841-2148
Cha-Am
    1543 Shattuck Ave., 510/848-9664

Best Undiscovered Restaurant
Brick Hut
    3222 Adeline St., 510/658-5555

Best Vegetarian Food
Long Life Vegi House
    2129 University Ave., 510/845-6072
Cafe de La Paz
    1600 Shattuck Ave., 510/843-0662

Standbys
Chevy's
    6 El Cerrito Plaza, El Cerrito, 510/526-2551

BLYTHE, CA

Best Breakfast
Steaks and Cakes
    9026 E. Hobsonway, 619/922-4241

Best Burgers
Jerry's Restaurant
    320 S. Lovekin Blvd., 619/922-9521

Best Coffee
Judy's Restaurant
    9266 E. Hobsonway, 619/922-6015

Best Family Restaurant
Steaks and Cakes
    9026 E. Hobsonway, 619/922-4241

Best Ice Cream/Yogurt
Fosters Old Fashioned Freeze
    540 E. Hobsonway, 619/922-3912

Best Steaks
Steaks and Cakes
    9026 E. Hobsonway, 619/922-4241

Standbys
Sizzler
    1101 W. Hobsonway, 619/922-3808

BUELLTON, CA

Best Restaurant in Town
Mattei's Tavern
  Hwy. 154, Los Olivos, 805/688-4820

Best Seafood
A.J. Spurs Restaurant and Saloon
  350 E. Hwy. 246, 805/686-1655
Buellton Hitching Post
  406 E. Hwy. 246, 805/688-0676
Zaca Creek Restaurant and Saloon
  1297 Hwy. 101, 805/688-2412

Best Steaks
A.J. Spurs Restaurant and Saloon
  350 E. Hwy. 246, 805/686-1655
Buellton Hitching Post
  406 E. Hwy. 246, 805/688-0676
Zaca Creek Restaurant and Saloon
  1297 Hwy. 101, 805/688-2412

BURBANK, CA

Best Burgers
Great Grill
  231 N. Glenoaks Blvd., 818/567-0060
  1909 W. Burbank Blvd., 818/842-9226
  916 W. Magnolia Blvd., 818/841-0066

Best Coffee
Starbucks
  300 N. San Fernando Blvd., 818/567-0630
  4211 Riverside Dr., 818/563-9830
Lancers Coffee Shop
  697 N. Victory Blvd., 818/849-4545
Don's Restaurant and Coffee Shop
  509 S. Glenoaks Blvd., 818/846-9521

Best Desserts
Crocodile Cafe
  201 N. San Fernando Blvd., 818/843-7999
India's Tandoori Restaurant
  662 W. Arrow Hwy., San Dimas, 909/592-7063

Best Homestyle Food
Don's Restaurant and Coffee Shop
  509 S. Glenoaks Blvd., 818/846-9521
Paty's Restaurant
  10001 Riverside Dr., North Hollywood, 818/761-9126

Best Indian Food
India's Tandoori Restaurant
  662 W. Arrow Hwy., San Dimas, 909/592-7063

Best Mexican Food
Bahia Caporales Restaurant
  3821 W. Magnolia Blvd., 818/842-7845

Best Pizza
Pizza Pie
  1700 W. Magnolia Blvd., 818/846-5141

Best Seafood
JP's Lounge
133 N. Hollywood Way, 818/845-1800
Bahia Caporales Restaurant
3821 W. Magnolia Blvd., 818/842-7845

Best Steaks
Smokehouse
4420 Lakeside Dr., 818/845-3731
JP's Lounge
133 N. Hollywood Way, 818/845-1800
Black Angus Restaurant
235 S. First St., 818/848-8880

Standbys
Baskin-Robbins
1201 S. Victory Blvd., 818/843-4651
910 N. San Fernando Blvd., 818/848-3609
4314 W. Magnolia Blvd., 818/843-9169
2400 W. Victory Blvd., 818/845-2050
906 S. Glenoaks Blvd., 818/846-7198
International House of Pancakes
913 N. San Fernando Blvd., 818/842-8622
Ben and Jerry's
164 E. Palm Ave., 818/566-7902

CAMARILLO, CA

Best Coffeehouse
Low Key Bagels
4972 Berduga Way, 805/383-0772

Best Italian Food
Presto Pasta
1701 Daley Dr., 805/383-1583

CARLSBAD, CA

Best Restaurants in Town
The Claim Jumper
5958 Avenida Encinas, 619/431-0889
Neiman's Seagrill American Bar
2978 Carlsbad Blvd., 619/729-4131

Best Bar
Hennessey's Tavern
2777 Roosevelt St., 619/729-6951

Best Breakfast
Kahala Cafe
795 Carlsbad Village Dr., 619/729-5448

Best Brunch
Neiman's Seagrill American Bar
2978 Carlsbad Blvd., 619/729-4131

Best Chinese Food
Golden Garden
2508A El Camino Real, 619/722-8210

Best Coffeehouse
Kafana
3076 Carlsbad Blvd., 619/720-0074

C

Best Desserts
The Claim Jumper
5958 Avenida Encinas, 619/431-0889

Best Italian Food
Tuscany Ristorante-Bar-Cafe
6981 El Camino Real, 619/929-8111
Amedeo's Italian Cafe
2780 State St., 619/729-8799

Best Mexican Food
Fidel's
3003 Carlsbad Blvd., 619/729-0903

Best Other Ethnic Food
Armenian Cafe (Armenian)
3126 Carlsbad Blvd., 619/720-2233

Best Sandwiches
Grand Deli
595 Grand Ave., 619/729-4015

Best Seafood
Fish House Veracruz
417 Carlsbad Village Dr., 619/434-6777

Best Southwestern Food
Coyote Bar and Grill
300 Carlsbad Village Dr., 619/729-4695

Best Sports Bar
Hennessey's Tavern
2777 Roosevelt St., 619/729-6951

CHICO, CA

Best Continental Food
Zephyr's
192 E. Third St., 916/895-1328

Best Desserts
Cory's Sweet Treats and Gallery
230 W. Third St., 916/345-2955

Best Italian Food
Gina Marie's
305 Main St., 916/342-2420
Dancing Noodles Cafe
131 Broadway St., 916/891-1383

Best Mexican Food
La Hacienda Mexican Restaurant
2635 Esplanade, 916/893-8270
Ricardo's Mexican Food
2365 Esplanade, 916/895-9607
La Fonda
243 W. Second St., Ste. 4, 916/345-5289

Best Salad/Salad Bar
Redwood Forest
121 W. Third St., 916/343-4315

Best Restaurant in Town
Red Robin
950 Shaw Ave., 209/299-4500

Best Burgers
Fat Jack's
625 W. Shaw Ave., 209/299-1104
Red Robin
950 Shaw Ave., 209/299-4500

Best Chinese Food
China Buffet
140 W. Shaw Ave., 209/297-9255

Best Italian Food
Il Forno
453 Pollasky Ave., 209/297-4167
Luna Pizzeria
349 Pollasky Ave., 209/299-4141

Best Japanese Food
Japanese Kitchen
711 W. Shaw Ave., Ste. 107, 209/297-1100
Daruma Tei
300 W. Shaw Ave., 209/298-1011

Best Mexican Food
El Quetzal
180 Shaw Ave., 209/298-6271
La Posada
311 Pollasky Ave., 209/298-2211
Sal's Mexican Restaurant
434 Clovis Ave., 209/298-7898

Best Other Ethnic Food
Mediterranean Corner (Armenian)
135 Shaw Ave., 209/297-7801

Best Pizza
Luna Pizzeria
349 Pollasky Ave., 209/299-4141
Popolo's Pizza
200 W. Shaw Ave., 209/276-7600

Best Salad/Salad Bar
Fresh Choice
10 Shaw Ave., 209/297-4272
Grandy's
80 W. Shaw Ave., 209/299-1083

Best Sandwiches
Full O'Bull
632 Fifth St., 209/299-3076

Best Thai Food
Thai Garden
135 W. Shaw Ave., 209/299-0183
Thai House
3185 Willow, 209/292-5774

Standbys
HomeTown Buffet
458 W. Shaw Ave., 209/323-4557

CORONA, CA

Best Barbecue/Ribs
Dan Armadillo Texian Pit BBQ
    784 N. Main St., 909/340-0061

Best Breakfast
Mimi's Cafe
    2230 Griffin Way, 909/734-2073

Best Burgers
Red Robin
    419 N. McKinley St., 909/737-1130

Best Cheap Meal
Carrows Family Restaurant
    12325 Mountain Ave., Chino, 909/627-0271

Best Coffee
Jitters Coffee
    304 N. Main, 909/737-3787

Best Desserts
Mimi's Cafe
    2230 Griffin Way, 909/734-2073

Best Homestyle Food
Mimi's Cafe
    2230 Griffin Way, 909/734-2073

Best Italian Food
Villa Amalfi Ristorante
    1237 W. Sixth St., 909/278-3393
Petrelli's Restaurant
    113 E. Sixth St., 909/734-3003
Pasta Pasta
    1296 Border Ave., 909/371-7874

Best Japanese Food
Misato Restaurant
    261 S. Lincoln Ave., 909/272-2900

Best Mexican Food
Miguel Sonora Style Mexican
    1703 W. Sixth St., 909/371-9299

Best Places to Eat When Someone Else is Buying
Villa Amalfi Ristorante
    1237 W. Sixth St., 909/278-3393
Cask and Cleaver
    12206 Central Ave., Chino, 909/627-6011

Best Salad/Salad Bar
Mimi's Cafe
    2230 Griffin Way, 909/734-2073

Best Sandwiches
Red Robin
    419 N. McKinley St., 909/737-1130

Best Seafood
TB Scott's
    103 N. Lincoln, 909/340-3474
Claim Jumper Restaurant
    380 N. McKinley St., 909/735-6567
Cask and Cleaver
    12206 Central Ave., Chino, 909/627-6011

Best Steaks
TB Scott's
103 N. Lincoln, 909/340-3474
Cask and Cleaver
12206 Central Ave., Chino, 909/627-6011

Standbys
Baskin-Robbins
2210 Griffin Way, 909/272-0357
712 N. Main St., 909/737-6131
1206 Magnolia Ave., 909/734-5592
Chuck E. Cheese Pizza
191 N. McKinley St., 909/279-9903

CORTE MADERA, CA

Best Burgers
Marin Joe's
1585 Casa Buena Dr., 415/924-2081

Best Cheap Meal
Fresh Choice
131 Corte Madera Town Ctr., 415/924-0540

Best Delicatessen
Ultra Lucca Delicatessen
107 Corte Madera Town Ctr., 415/927-4347

Best Health-Conscious Menu
Island Cafe
59 Tamal Vista Blvd., 415/924-6666
Fresh Choice
131 Corte Madera Town Ctr., 415/924-0540

Best Italian Food
Il Fornaio
223 Corte Madera Town Ctr., 415/927-4400

Best Late-Night Food
Marin Joe's
1585 Casa Buena Dr., 415/924-2081

Best Place to Eat Alone
Marin Joe's
1585 Casa Buena Dr., 415/924-2091

Best Seafood
Baby Sal's Seafood Grill
60 Corte Madera Ave., 415/927-0149

COSTA MESA, CA

Best Barbecue/Ribs
Zubie's
1712 Placentia Ave., 714/645-8091

Best Breakfast
Mimi's Cafe
1835F Newport Blvd., 714/722-6722

Best Brunch
Haute Cakes
1807 Westcliff Dr., Newport Beach, 714/642-4114

Best Burgers
Ruby's Diner
3333 Bear St., 714/662-7829

Best Coffee
Starbucks
2801 E. Coast Hwy., Corona Del Mar, 714/675-4416
1128 Irvine Ave., Newport Beach, 714/650-0369
1628 San Miguel Dr., Newport Beach, 714/644-0532

Best Continental Food
Gustaf Anders Restaurant
1651 W. Sunflower Ave., Santa Ana, 714/668-1737

Best Desserts
Five Crowns
3801 E. Coast Hwy., Corona Del Mar, 714/760-0331

Best Health-Conscious Menu
Mother's Market and Kitchen
225 E. Seventeenth St., 714/631-4741

Best Homestyle Food
Marie Callender's
353 E. Seventeenth St., 714/642-0822

Best Ice Cream/Yogurt
Golden Spoon
488 E. Seventeenth St., 714/548-9147
2801 Harbor Blvd., 714/641-7495

Best Italian Food
Antonello Ristorante
1611 W. Sunflower Ave., Santa Ana, 714/751-7153

Best Mexican Food
Avila's El Ranchito
2101 Placentia Ave., 714/645-0209

Best Pizza
Me and Ed's Pizza Parlor
410 E. Seventeenth St., 714/646-7136

Best Place to Take the Kids
Zubie's
1712 Placentia Ave., 714/645-8091

Best Seafood
Crab Cooker
2200 Newport Blvd., Newport Beach, 714/673-0100

Best Steaks
Morton's of Chicago
1661 W. Sunflower, Santa Ana, 714/444-4834
Barn Steak House
2300 Harbor Blvd., Ste. 31, 714/641-9777

Best Thai Food
Bangkok Four Restaurant
3333 Bear St., Ste. 320, 714/540-7661

Best Vegetarian Food
Mother's Market and Kitchen
225 E. Seventeenth St., 714/631-4741

Standbys
Friday's
601 Anton Blvd., 714/540-2227
Haagen-Dazs
3333 Bristol St., 714/754-7752

Best Barbecue/Ribs
Distler's Rafters
  5034 Chiles Rd., 916/756-7970
Mr. B's Bar Grill
  217 E. St., 916/756-3757

Best Breakfast
Baker's Square Restaurant
  255 Second St., 916/756-4190

Best Burgers
Murder Burger
  978 Olive Dr., 916/756-2142

Best Chinese Food
Hing's Restaurant
  707 Second St., 916/756-0666

Best Coffee
Caffino Inc.
  980 Olive Dr., 916/758-0972

Best Desserts
Farmer's Wife
  1260 Lake Blvd., 916/756-1107

Best French Food
La Brioche Restaurant
  129 E. St., 916/756-8676

Best German Food
Sudwerk
  2001 Second St., 916/758-8700

Best Italian Food
Caffe Italia
  1121 Richards Blvd., 916/758-7200

Best Mexican Food
La Esperanza
  200 G St., 916/753-4449
  825 Russell Blvd., 916/757-7579

Best Pizza
Graduate Restaurant
  805 Russell Blvd., 916/758-4723
Woodstock's Pizza
  219 G St., 916/757-2525

Best Sandwiches
Caffe Italia
  1121 Richards Blvd., 916/758-7200
Mustard Seed
  231 G St., 916/758-5750
Togo's Eatery
  715 Second St., 916/753-5330

Best Southwestern Food
Dos Coyotes Border Cafe
  1411 W. Covell Blvd., 916/753-0922

Best Steaks
Buckhorn
  210 Railroad Ave., Winters, 916/795-4503

ndbys
skin-Robbins
640 W. Covell Blvd., 916/753-3931
236 E. St., 916/756-5201

EL CAJON, CA

Best All-You-Can-Eat Buffet
Charlie Brown's
880 Harbor Island Dr., San Diego, 619/291-1805

Best Brunch
Charlie Brown's
880 Harbor Island Dr., San Diego, 619/291-1805

Best Burgers
Rally's Hamburgers
1261 E. Main St., 619/444-3496

Best Business Lunch
Hungry Hunter
402 Fletcher Pkwy., 619/442-0517

Best Cheap Meal
Chinese Village Restaurant
170 Broadway, 619/444-9180

Best Chinese Food
P.F. Chang's
4540 La Jolla Village Dr., 619/458-9007

Best Family Restaurant
Claim Jumper
5500 Grossmont Ctr., La Mesa, 619/469-3927

Best Health-Conscious Menu
Souplantation
Multiple Locations

Best Homestyle Food
Claim Jumper
5500 Grossmont Ctr., La Mesa, 619/469-3927

Best Mexican Food
Antonio's Hacienda
700 N. Johnson Ave., 619/442-9827

Best Romantic Dining
Casa de Pico
2754 Calhoun St., San Diego, 619/296-3267

Best Sandwiches
Patty's Subs
164 E. Main St., 619/588-0878

Best Steaks
Hungry Hunter
402 Fletcher Pkwy., 619/442-0517
Claim Jumper
5500 Grossmont Ctr., La Mesa, 619/469-3927

Best Vegetarian Food
Souplantation
Multiple Locations

Standbys
Sizzler
898 Jackman St., 619/442-0229

Applebee's
107 Fletcher Pkwy., 619/593-3066
Baskin-Robbins
2396 Fletcher Pkwy., 619/462-3870
328 N. Second St., 619/440-3131
The Olive Garden
5500 Grossmont Center Dr., La Mesa, 619/460-7221
3215 Sports Arena Blvd., San Diego, 619/226-2124
3501 Valley Center Dr., San Diego, 619/259-6012
Chuck E. Cheese Pizza
3146 Sports Arena Blvd., San Diego, 619/523-4385
9840 Hibert St., San Diego, 619/578-5860
Red Lobster
8703 Murray Dr., La Mesa, 619/463-4449
8330 Mira Mesa Blvd., San Diego, 619/549-3557
3780 Sports Arena Blvd., San Diego, 619/226-1057

EL CENTRO, CA

Best Restaurant in Town
Barbara Worth Golf Resort and Convention Center
2050 Country Club Dr., 619/356-2806

Best Chinese Food
Lucky Chinese Restaurant
5000 S. Fourth St., 619/352-7680
Ma's Kitchen
290 N. Imperial Ave., 619/352-8713
Airport Garden
1093 Airport Rd., Imperial, 619/355-2838
Imperial Mandarin Restaurant
804 N. Imperial Ave., 619/353-1012
China Palace Restaurant
1075 Adams Ave., 619/353-2798

Best Mexican Food
Mi Casita Restaurant
729 W. Main St., 619/353-8690
El Sombrero Cafe
841 W. Main St., 619/353-8118
Celia's Restaurant
880 N. Imperial Ave., 619/352-4570
Adobe Hacienda
538 E St., Brawley, 619/344-9750

ENCINITAS, CA

Best American Food
Red Robin
294 N. El Camino Real, 619/436-4488
Top O' The Cove
1216 Prospect St., La Jolla, 619/454-7779

Best Bagels
Garden State Bagels
191 N. El Camino Real, 619/942-2435

Best Brunch
Marie Callender's Restaurant
162 S. Rancho Santa Fe Rd., 619/632-0204

Best Cajun/Creole Food
Paradise Grill
1476 Encinitas Blvd., 619/943-9997
Shrimply Delicious
559 First St., 619/944-9172

Best Chinese Food
Golden Bowl Restaurant
1337 Encinitas Blvd., 619/436-8669

Best Coffeehouse
Pannikin Coffee and Tea
510 N. Hwy. 101, 619/436-0033

Best Family Restaurants
Red Robin
294 N. El Camino Real, 619/436-4488
Oscar's
1505 Encinitas Blvd., 619/632-0222

Best French Food
La Bonne Bouffe
471 Encinitas Blvd., 619/436-3081
Chez Henri
1555 Camino Del Mar, Del Mar, 619/793-0067

Best Health-Conscious Menu
Casady's Deli Cafe
284 El Camino Real, 619/436-3663
Ki's Juice Bar
206 Birmingham Dr., Cardiff By The Sea,
619/436-5236

Best Japanese Food
Mr. Sushi
11 N. El Camino Real, 619/944-2800
Sakura Bana Sushi Bar
1031 First St., Ste. 101, 619/942-6414

Best Mexican Food
Tony's Jacal
621 Valley Ave., Solana Beach, 619/755-2274

Best Other Ethnic Food
Khayyam Cuisine (Jordanian/Lebanese)
437 S. Hwy. 101, Solana Beach, 619/755-6343

Best Pizza
Borrelli's Pizza
285 El Camino Real, 619/436-1501

Best Romantic Dining
Elario's Restaurant
7955 La Jolla Shores Dr., Eleventh Fl., La Jolla,
619/459-0541
Jake's Del Mar
1660 Coast Blvd., Del Mar, 619/755-2002

Best Sandwiches
Giovanni's Sandwich Shop
764 First St., 619/753-9614

Best Southwestern Food
Cilantro's
3702 Via De La Valle, Del Mar, 619/259-8777

Best Sports Bar
Yogi's
2005 San Elijo Ave., Cardiff By The Sea, 619/943-9644

Standbys
The Olive Garden
1220 Garden View Rd., 619/634-3070

ESCONDIDO, CA

Best American Food
One Fifty Grand Cafe
150 W. Grand Ave., Escondido, 619/738-6868

Best Atmosphere
Castle Creek Country Club
8797 Circle R Dr., 619/749-2877

Best Breakfast
Champion's Family Restaurant
117 W. Grand Ave., 619/747-0288

Best Chinese Food
China Panda
330 W. Felicita Ave., 619/741-3982

Best Coffeehouse
Metaphor Coffeehouse and Gallery
258 E. Second Ave., 619/489-8890

Best Continental Food
Sirino's Ristorante
113 W. Grand Ave., 619/745-3835

Best Desserts
Metaphor Coffeehouse and Gallery
258 E. Second Ave., 619/489-8890

Best Dinner
Castle Creek Country Club
8797 Circle R Dr., 619/749-2877
One Fifty Grand Cafe
150 W. Grand, 619/738-6868

Best French Food
Sirino's Ristorante
113 W. Grand Ave., 619/745-3835

Best Health-Conscious Menu
Metaphor Coffeehouse and Gallery
258 E. Second Ave., 619/489-8890

Best Homestyle Food
Champion's Family Restaurant
117 W. Grand Ave., 619/747-0288

Best Italian Food
Joe's Italian Dinners
403 W. Grand Ave., 619/489-6835

Best Mexican Food
Cocina Del Charro
525 N. Quince St., 619/745-1382
La Tapatia Restaurant
340 W. Grand Ave., 619/747-8282

Best Pizza
Filippi's Pizza Grotto
114 W. Grand Ave., 619/747-2650

Best Regional Cuisine
One Fifty Grand Cafe
150 W. Grand, 619/738-6868

Best Seafood
Sandcrab Cafe
2229 Micro Pl., 619/480-8990

Best Steaks
Brigantine Restaurant
421 W. Felicita Ave., 619/743-4718

EUREKA, CA

Best Asian Restaurants
Gonsea
2335 Fourth St., 707/444-8899
Hunan Restaurant
2912 E St., 707/444-9241
Samurai
621 Fifth St., 707/442-6802
Smile of Siam
210 Fourth St., 707/442-6999
Tomo Japanese Restaurant
2120 Fourth St., 707/444-3318

Best Breakfast
Chalet House of Omelettes
1935 Fifth St., 707/442-0333
The Cutten Inn Restaurant
3980 Walnut Dr., 707/445-9217
Gill's by the Bay
77 Halibut Ave., 707/442-2554
Loring's Simply the Best
332 Harris St., 707/441-8555
Stanton's Red Barn
2145 Central Ave., McKinleyville, 707/839-3341

Best Burgers
Fresh Freeze
3023 F St., 707/442-6967
Maggie's Burgers
1884 Central Ave., McKinleyville, 707/839-2871
Mike's Drive-Up
637 Broadway St., 707/442-4755
No Brand Burger Stand
989 Milton St., Ferndale, 707/786-9474
Stars
2009 Harrison Ave., 707/445-2061
535 Fifth St., 707/444-3520

Best Coffee
Gold Rush Express
Bayshore Mall, 3300 Broadway St., 707/445-4617
Ramone's Bakery
209 E St., 707/445-2923
2223 Harrison Ave., 707/442-1336
600 F St., Arcata, 707/826-9000

Stanton's Coffee Shop
 1111 Fifth St., 707/442-8141
Stanton's Red Barn
 2145 Central Ave., McKinleyville, 707/839-3341
Udder Place
 2228 Fourth St., 707/442-6487

Best Delicatessens
Deo's Sandwich Shop
 428 Grotto St., 707/445-1111
Enrico's
 1595 Myrtle Ave., 707/442-1771
Hole in the Wall
 1331 Broadway St., 707/443-5362
 590 G St., Arcata, 707/822-7407
Wildberries Marketplace
 747 Thirteenth St., Arcata, 707/822-0095

Best Desserts
Abruzzi
 791 Eighth St., Arcata, 707/826-2345
Adele's Restaurant
 1724 Broadway, 707/445-9777
Bon Boniere Ice Cream Parlor
 215 F St., 707/444-8075
Eureka Baking Company
 3562 Broadway St., 707/445-8997
 502 Henderson St., 707/442-1522
 846 G St., Arcata, 707/826-7578
Larrupin Cafe
 1658 Patricks Point Dr., Trinidad, 707/677-0230
Ramone's Bakery
 209 E St., 707/445-2923
 2223 Harrison Ave., 707/442-1336
 600 F St., Arcata, 707/826-9000

Best Family Restaurants
Adele's
 1724 Broadway, 707/445-9777
Samoa Cookhouse
 Samoa Rd., Samoa, 707/442-1659
Stanton's Coffee Shop
 1111 Fifth St., 707/442-8141
Sweetriver Saloon
 3300 Broadway St., 707/444-9704

Best Health-Conscious Menu
Arcata Co-Op
 811 I St., Arcata, 707/822-5947
Daybreak Cafe
 768 Eighteenth St., Arcata, 707/826-7543
Eureka Natural Foods
 307 Fourth St., 707/442-6325
The Flour Garden
 712 Fifth St., 707/443-1890
Wildberries Marketplace
 747 Thirteenth St., Arcata, 707/822-0095
Wildflower Cafe and Bakery
 1604 G St., Arcata, 707/822-0360

Best Italian Food
Abruzzi
   791 Eighth St., Arcata, 707/826-2345
Mazzotti's Italian Food
   305 F St., 707/445-1912
Parlato's
   320 Main St., Fortuna, 707/725-9961
Roy's
   218 D St., 707/442-4574
Tomaso's
   100 Erickson Ct., Arcata, 707/822-6190

Best Lunch
Adele's Restaurant
   1724 Broadway, 707/445-9777
Bay City Grill
   508 Henderson St., 707/444-9069
Cafe Marina
   601 Startare Dr., 707/443-2233
Gill's by the Bay
   77 Halibut Ave., 707/442-2554
Ron's American Bistro
   521 Fourth St., 707/444-8018
Tomaso's
   100 Erickson Ct., Arcata, 707/822-6190

Best Mexican Food
Cosina Michoacana
   427 V St., 707/443-7840
Jalisco Cafe
   1718 Fourth St., 707/445-9324
Luna's Mexican Restaurant
   1134 Fifth St., 707/445-9162
Luzmilla's Mexican Restaurant
   5000 Valley West Blvd., Arcata, 707/822-5100
Reyes Y Casas Viejas
   1436 Second St., 707/445-4960

Best Pizza
Celestino's Live from New York
   421 Third St., 707/444-8995
Murphy's Take and Bake Pizza
   2015 Central Ave., Arcata, 707/839-8763
   5440 Erickson Way, Arcata, 707/822-9343
   600 F St., Arcata, 707/822-6220
   906 West Ave., 707/442-1499
Pizzeria Pizza
   1604 Fourth St., 707/444-9681
   2850 E St., 707/444-0990
Round Table
   1735 Fourth St.,707/443-3187
   2810 E St., 707/445-3227
   5000 Valley West Blvd., Arcata, 707/822-5158
   600 F St., Arcata, 707/822-3761
Tom's Sourdough Pizza Villa
   1611 Myrtle Ave., 707/443-2728

Best Places to Eat When Someone Else Is Buying
Eureka Inn
   518 Seventh St., 707/442-6441

Folie Douce
  1551 G St., Arcata, 707/822-1042
Hotel Carter
  301 L St., 707/444-8062
Larrupin Cafe
  1658 Patricks Point Rd., Trinidad, 707/677-0230
The Sea Grill
  316 E St., 707/443-7187

Best Romantic Dining
Abruzzi
  791 Eighth St., 707/826-2345
Hotel Carter
  301 L St., 707/444-8062
Larrupin Cafe
  1658 Patricks Point Dr., Trinidad, 707/677-0230
Merryman's
  100 Moonstone Beach Rd., Trinidad, 707/677-3111
The Rib Room
  Eureka Inn, 518 Seventh St., 707/442-6441

Best Seafood
Cafe Marina
  601 Startare Dr., 707/443-2233
Ernie's Briefing Room
  608 A St., 707/442-7146
Seafood Grotto
  605 Broadway St., 707/443-2075
Lazio's
  327 Second St., 707/443-9717
The Sea Grill
  316 E St., 707/443-7187

Best Steaks
The Embers
  4485 Broadway St., 707/443-1807
Geri's Myrtletowne House
  1672 Myrtle Ave., 707/443-8209
O-H's Town House
  206 W. Sixth St., 707/443-4652
Parlato's
  320 Main St., Fortuna, 707/725-9961
Whaler's Inn
  6690 Fields Landing Dr., Field's Landing,
    707/443-6026

FAIRFIELD, CA

Best Bar
Suite 21
  1721 N. Texas St., 707/425-8352

Best Burgers
Dave's Giant Hamburger
  1055 N. Texas St., 707/425-1818
Nations Foodservice
  1955 N. Texas St., 707/425-1800

Best Business Lunch
Strings
  2401C Waterman Blvd., 707/428-3882

Best Chinese Food
Mandarin Restaurant
  219 W. Texas St., 707/428-9736

Best Coffee
Higher Ground Coffee House
  933 Texas, 707/429-0136

Best Desserts
Marie Callender's Restaurant
  1750 Travis Blvd., 707/428-4745

Best Family Restaurant
J.J. North
  1315 Gateway Blvd., 707/428-6000

Best Health-Conscious Menu
Fresh Choice
  1501 The Courtyard, 707/429-2560

Best Homestyle Food
J.J. North
  1315 Gateway Blvd., 707/428-6000

Best Italian Food
String's
  2401C Waterman Blvd., 707/428-3882

Best Mexican Food
Los Gallos Taqueria
  936 Texas St., 707/429-2155

Best Pizza
Scenario's
  1955 W. Texas St., 707/425-1000

Best Place to Be "Seen"
Mullin's
  605 Main St., 707/421-9567

Best Place to Eat Alone
Lyon's Restaurant
  2390 N. Texas St., 707/429-5330

Best Romantic Dining
Fields Landing Cafe
  6720 Fields Landing Dr., 707/441-4930

Best Salad/Salad Bar
Carl Jr.'s Restaurant
  2380 N. Texas St., 707/425-6993
  1401A Travis Blvd., 707/422-9263
Fresh Choice
  1501 The Courtyard, 707/429-2560

Best Steaks
Cattleman's
  I-80 at Curry Rd., Dixon, 916/678-5518

Best Vegetarian Food
Fresh Choice
  1501 The Courtyard, 707/429-2560

Standbys
Baskin-Robbins
  2121 N. Texas St., 707/421-0856

Denny's
29080 Travis Blvd., 707/425-0303
1360 Holiday Ln., 707/422-6511
Chuck E. Cheese Pizza
1027 Oliver Rd., 707/426-4500
Red Lobster
1525 The Courtyard, 707/421-8292

FREMONT, CA

Best American Food
Dina's Family Restaurant
40800 Fremont Blvd., 510/770-1930
Norman's Family Restaurant
4949 Stevenson Blvd., 510/226-7777
Dino's Restaurant
3600 Castro Valley Blvd., Castro Valley, 510/537-1454

Best Breakfast
Mission Pine Cafe
129 Anza St., 510/770-8815

Best Chinese Food
Hong Kong Buffet
41063 Fremont Blvd., 510/656-6908
Fong's Restaurant
3335 Castro Valley Blvd., Castro Valley, 510/581-9707

Best Coffee
Java Bean
2000 Driscoll Rd., 510/656-5517
Joe To Go
40920 Fremont Blvd., 510/659-9555

Best Diner
Norman's Family Restaurant
4949 Stevenson Blvd., 510/226-7777

Best Homestyle Food
Mission Pine Cafe
129 Anza St., 510/770-8815

Best Italian Food
Camilio's Italian Restaurant
40900 Fremont Blvd., 510/657-3027

Best Mexican Food
La Casita Restaurant
41240 Fremont Blvd., 510/657-8602
Mi Pueblo Restaurant
41025A Fremont Blvd., 510/656-8177
Taqueria Los Gallos
39459 Fremont Blvd., 510/770-0526
Pollo Ranchero
39620 Mission Blvd., 510/792-8761

Best Pizza
Mission Pizza
43468 Ellsworth St., 510/651-6858

FRESNO, CA

Best Restaurants in Town
Nicola's
   3705 N. Maroa, 209/224-1660
Daily Planet
   1211 N. Wishon Ave., 209/266-4259
Harland's
   722 W. Shaw Ave., 209/225-7100
Outpost
   1137 N. Chestnut Ave., 209/251-7171

Best Armenian Food
Andre's
   4743 N. Blackstone Ave., 209/229-6353
The Mediterranean
   4631 N St., 209/226-7856
Uncle Paulie's
   2146 Ventura St., 209/233-2146
Zlfred's
   1803 E. Dakota Ave., 209/229-7853
   2344 Tulare St., 209/266-0303

Best Brunch
B.J.'s Kountry Kitchen
   1831 E. Ashlan Ave., 209/229-1036
   4109 E. Ashlan Ave., 209/222-5206
   4325 N. Golden State Blvd., Ste. 102, 209/275-1981
   5673 E. Kings Canyon Rd., 209/456-0256
   6700 N. Cedar Ave., 209/298-5456
Sweet Georgia Brown
   6460 N. Blackstone Ave., 209/431-8700

Best Burgers
Chubby's
   4388 W. Shaw Ave., 209/276-7633
   6451 N. Blackstone Ave., 209/448-9999
Fat Jack's
   3927 N. Blackstone Ave., 209/224-4141
Spoons
   613 E. Shaw Ave., 209/221-6117

Best Casual Dining
Lyon's
   1125 Shaw Ave., Clovis, 209/297-1212
   1746 W. Shaw Ave., 209/432-3806
   4965 N St., 209/224-3566
Wiliker's
   1713 E. Shaw Ave., 209/226-1985

Best Chinese Food
Bow Loy
   1760 W. Bullard Ave., 209/435-0150
Loy Loy
   4360 W. Shaw Ave., 209/277-1688
   6497 N. Blackstone Ave., 209/438-1688
Yen Ching
   467 E. Shaw Ave., 209/222-6223

Best Family Restaurants
Lyon's
   1125 Shaw Ave., Clovis, 209/297-1212

1746 W. Shaw Ave., 209/432-3806
4965 N St., 209/224-3566
Marie Callender's
1781 E. Shaw Ave., 209/224-8434
4239 N. Blackstone Ave., 209/224-1865
Old Spaghetti Factory
2721 Ventura St., 209/442-1066
Spoon's
613 E. Shaw Ave., 209/221-6117

Best French Food
Dine With Us
438 Clovis Ave., 209/297-0783
Harland's
722 W. Shaw Ave., 209/225-7100
La Boulangerie
3234 N. Palm Ave., 209/222-1500
730 W. Shaw Ave., 209/222-0555
Pinchette
1816 Howard Rd., Madera, 209/675-0433

Best Ice Cream/Yogurt
Foster's Freeze
3377 N. Cedar Ave., 209/222-5384
3858 E. Ventura Ave., 209/266-4884
5729 N. Palm Ave., 209/431-5729
753 E. Barstow Ave., 209/227-6522
Skyler's
494 E. Shaw Ave., 209/226-4042
Sugarless Shop
1075 E. Bullard Ave., 209/432-8633

Best Indian Food
Bombay Cuisine
4937 E. Kings Canyon Rd., 209/255-4496
India Sweet and Spice
3209 W. Shaw Ave., 209/225-2824

Best Italian Food
Giulia's
3050 W. Shaw Ave., 209/276-3573
Lucca's
325 N. Gateway Dr., Madera, 209/674-6744
Mike's Pizzeria
3228 N. West Ave., 209/229-2635
Nicola's
2767 W. Shaw Ave., 209/229-1295

Best Japanese Food
Bando-Ya Japanese Cuisine
3050 W. Shaw Ave., 209/275-7535
Dai Ichi
2736 Divisadero St., Ste. 106, 209/266-7843
2745 W. Shaw Ave., 209/224-2243
7058 N. Cedar Ave., 209/297-1110
Kame Sushi House
1089 E. Shaw Ave., 209/226-3701

Best Mexican Food
Acapulco
3966 N. Blackstone Ave., 209/221-6739

El Quetzal
  5731 N. First St., 209/449-8116
El Torro Cafe
  3110 N. Cedar St., 209/225-7724
Javier's
  5680 E. Kings Canyon Rd., 209/252-4511
Sal's Mexican Restaurant
  2839 N. Blackstone Ave., 209/227-1686
  3316 W. Shaw Ave., 209/271-0836

Best Pizza
Aldo's Pizza
  1414 Clovis Ave., 209/298-0801
BC's Pizza
  1056 W. Shaw Ave., 209/224-2224
DaVinci's
  7795 N First St., 209/435-8200
Popolo's Pizza
  2760 W. Shaw Ave., 209/276-7600
  6775 N. Blackstone Ave., 209/276-7600

Best Salad/Salad Bar
Brooks Ranch
  4131 S. Chestnut Ave., 209/485-6951
  4278 W. Ashlan Ave., 209/275-8483
Grandy's
  2340 N. Blackstone Ave., 209/225-9255
  4898 E. Kings Canyon Rd., 209/251-4851
  5180 N. Blackstone Ave., 209/221-8262
Happy Steak
  6759 N. First St., 209/435-3280
  5625 E. Kings Canyon Rd., 209/255-9026
  2345 N. Blackstone Ave., 209/227-0016

Best Sandwiches
Geno's
  1615 E. Ashlan Ave., 209/227-1812
Grape Tray
  5091 N St., 209/226-6828
Packing Shed
  5183 E. Kings Canyon Rd., 209/252-3518
Pat's Blue Ribbon
  389 E. Shaw Ave., 209/227-1949
  5042 N. West Ave., 209/431-3450

Best Seafood
Fresno Grill
  6029 N. Palm Ave., 209/431-4956
Pacific Seafood
  1055 E. Herndon, 209/439-2778
South Sea Grotto
  1418 W. Ashlan Ave., 209/229-4412
Yoshino
  6226 N. Blackstone Ave., 209/431-2205

Best Steaks
Black Angus
  1737 E. Shaw Ave., 209/224-2205
Cask and Cleaver
  2700 W. Shaw Ave., 209/276-1215

Harris Ranch Inn and Restaurant
   I-5 at Hwy. 198, Coalinga, 209/935-0717
Richard's
   1609 E. Belmont Ave., 209/266-4077

Best Thai Food
Bai Tong
   2021 W. Bullard Ave., 209/436-1516
Bangkok Spice
   367 E. Shaw Ave., 209/221-6058
Daruma Tei
   5096 N. West Ave., 209/431-2625

Standbys
Applebee's
   5126 N. Palm Ave., 209/244-6904
HomeTown Buffet
   3744 N. Blackstone Ave., 209/221-0444
Tony Roma's
   2003 W. Bullard Ave., 209/435-7662
Chili's
   7010 N St., 209/432-3711
Sizzler
   125 W. Shaw Ave., 209/299-5845
   3121 W. Shaw Ave., 209/227-1218
   3851 N. Blackstone Ave., 209/229-8355
   4969 N. Kings Canyon Rd., 209/454-0972
   7006 N. Cedar Ave., 209/323-9701
Friday's
   1077 E. Herndon, 209/435-8443
Outback Steakhouse
   2765 W. Shaw Ave., 209/224-1181
Red Lobster
   1460 E. Shaw Ave., 209/221-9495

GILROY, CA

Best Restaurant in Town
O.D.'s Kitchen
   28 Martin St., 408/847-3818

Best Delicatessen
Dunneville Store
   5970 San Felipe Rd., Hollister, 408/636-9191

Best Greek/Mediterranean Food
Station 55 Bar and Grill
   55 Fifth St., 408/847-5555

Best German Food
Harvest Time
   7397 Monterey Hwy., 408/842-7575

Best Homestyle Food
Dunneville Store
   5970 San Felipe Rd., Hollister, 408/636-9191

GLENDALE, CA

Best American Food
Noodles
   215 N. Central Ave., 818/500-8646
Star Cafe
   134 N. Brand Blvd., 818/956-3925

rown Cow
  801 Western Ave., 818/552-5911

Best Breakfast
Porto's Bakery
  315 N. Brand Blvd., 818/956-5996

Best Bar
Jax Bar and Grill
  339 N. Brand Blvd., 818/500-1604

Best Chinese Food
Gourmet 88
  315 S. Brand Blvd., 818/547-9488

Best Coffee
Starbucks
  114 N. Brand Blvd., 818/547-3694
Java City
  134 N. Brand Blvd., 818/956-3925
Brown Cow
  801 Western Ave., 818/552-5911

Best Desserts
Java City
  134 N. Brand Blvd., 818/956-3925

Best Italian Food
Noodles
  215 N. Central Ave., 818/500-8646
Brown Cow
  801 Western Ave., 818/552-5911

Best Steaks
Damon's Steak House
  317 N. Brand Blvd., 818/507-1510

Best Thai Food
Indra Restaurant
  517 S. Verdugo Rd., 818/247-3176

HAYWARD, CA

Best Restaurant in Town
A Street Cafe
  1213 A St., 510/582-2558

Best Breakfast
Val's Burgers
  2115 Kelly St., 510/889-8257

Best Burgers
Val's Burgers
  2115 Kelly St., 510/889-8257

Best Continental Food
A Street Cafe
  1213 A St., 510/582-2558

Best Diner
Val's Burgers
  2115 Kelly St., 510/889-8257

Best Family Restaurant
Vasiliki's
  25202 Hesperian Blvd., 510/785-0184

Best Japanese Food
Ichiban Restaurant
   22560 Foothill Blvd., 510/537-4466

Best Lunch
Pablito's Authentic Mexican
   22800 Mission Blvd., 510/886-6732

Best Mexican Food
La Imperial Restaurant
   948 C St., 510/537-6227
Los Compadres Restaurant
   944 C St., 510/582-1937
Pablito's Authentic Mexican
   22800 Mission Blvd., 510/886-6732

Best Place to Take the Kids
Val's Burgers
   2115 Kelly St., 510/889-8257

Best Salad/Salad Bar
Vasiliki's
   25202 Hesperian Blvd., 510/785-0184

Best Seafood
Hayward Fishery and Restaurant
   1065 C St., 510/537-6410

HEMET, CA

Best Restaurant in Town
Buttons Restaurant
   43271 Florida Ave., 909/927-1144

Best American Food
Falatico's Restaurant
   124 S. Harvard St., 909/652-6851

Best Breakfast
Millie's Country Kitchen
   2020 E. Florida Ave., 909/658-9068

Best Mexican Food
Emilio's Restaurant
   2340 S. San Jacinto Ave., 909/925-3721
Arturo's Restaurant
   117 N. Harvard St., 909/658-0165
   3323 W. Florida Ave., 909/766-7595

Best Chinese Food
Hot Wok
   480L N. State St., San Jacinto, 909/487-0262

LARKSPUR, CA

Best Restaurant in Town
Lark Creek Inn
   234 Magnolia Ave., 415/924-7766

Best American Food
Lark Creek Inn
   234 Magnolia Ave., 415/924-7766

Best Beer Selection
Marin Brewing Company
   1809 Larkspur Landing, 415/461-4677

Best Breakfast
Lark Creek Inn
   234 Magnolia Ave., 415/924-7766

Best Burritos
Roadrunner Burrito
   1813 Larkspur Landing Circle, 415/461-4646

Best Cheap Meal
Good Earth
   2231 Larkspur Landing Circle, 415/461-7322

Best Chinese Food
CJ Chinese Cuisine
   435 Magnolia Ave., 415/924-0717

Best Coffeehouse
Java
   320 Magnolia Ave., 415/ 927-1501

Best Desserts
Pasticerria Rulli
   464 Magnolia Ave., 415/924-7478

Best Eclectic Menu
Left Bank
   117 Throckmorton Ave., 415/388-0741

Best Health-Conscious Menu
Garden of Eatin'
   474 Magnolia Ave., 415/927-7611
Good Earth
   2231 Larkspur Landing Circle, 415/461-7322

Best Japanese Food
Sushi-Ko
   1819 Larkspur Landing Circle, 415/461-8400

Best Late-Night Food
Left Bank
   507 Magnolia Ave., 415/927-3331

Best New Restaurant
Left Bank
   507 Magnolia Ave., 415/927-3331

Best Place to Eat When Someone Else Is Buying
Lark Creek Inn
   234 Magnolia Ave., 415/924-7766
Remillard's
   125 E. Sir Francis Drake Blvd., 415/461-3700

Best Romantic Dining
Remillard's
   125 E. Sir Francis Drake Blvd., 415/461-3700

LOMPOC, CA

Best Restaurant in Town
Sissy's Uptown Cafe
   112 S. I St., 805/735-4877

Best Barbecue/Ribs
The Outpost Restaurant
   1501 E. Ocean Ave., 805/735-1130

Best Burgers
Tom's Educated Burgers
115 E. College Ave., 805/736-9996

Best Breakfast
Tom's Educated Burgers
115 E. College Ave., 805/736-9996

Best Italian Food
La Botte Italian Cuisine
812 N. H St., 805/736-2050

Best Salad/Salad Bar
Tom's Educated Burgers
115 E. College Ave., 805/736-9996

Best Sandwiches
Tom's Educated Burgers
115 E. College Ave., 805/736-9996

Best Seafood
The Jetty Restaurant
304 W. Ocean Ave., 805/735-2400
The Outpost Restaurant
1501 E. Ocean Ave., 805/735-1130

Best Steaks
The Jetty Restaurant
304 W. Ocean Ave., 805/735-2400
The Outpost Restaurant
1501 E. Ocean Ave., 805/735-1130

Best Thai Food
Good Choice Thai Cuisine
920 N. I St., 805/736-7450

LONG BEACH, CA

[After January 1997, the area code for this city will change to 562.]

Best Restaurant in Town
Mustard Seed
5624 Atlantic Ave., 310/422-6090

Best All-You-Can-Eat Buffet
Arnold's Family Restaurant
3925 Atlantic Ave., 310/424-8573

Best Breakfast
Terry's Coffee Shop
4390 Atlantic Ave., 310/427-5979

Best Burgers
Hamburger Henry
4700 E. Second St., 310/433-7070

Best Business Lunch
Simon and Seafort's Fish Chop
340 Golden Shore St., 310/435-2333

Best Casual Dining
Cafe Bixby
3900 Atlantic Ave., 310/427-2233

Best Cheap Meal
Coco's Restaurant
  4750 E. Los Coyotes Diagonal, 310/498-1140
  6405 E. Pacific Coast Hwy., 310/431-6306

Best Coffee
Cafe Chatz
  2300 E. Ocean Blvd., 310/434-5077

Best Continental Food
Papa Jon's
  5006 E. Second St., 310/439-1059

Best Desserts
Grandma's Sugarplums
  4908 E. Second St., 310/439-3363

Best Diners
Babe's Kitchen
  1106 E. Wardlow Rd., 310/427-4897
Cafe Bixby
  3900 Atlantic Ave., 310/427-2233

Best Dinner
Simon and Seafort's Fish Chop
  340 Golden Shore St., 310/435-2333

Best Family Restaurant
Coco's Restaurant
  4750 E. Los Coyotes Diagonal, 310/498-1140
  6405 E. Pacific Coast Hwy., 310/431-6306

Best Health-Conscious Menu
La Salsa Restaurant
  243 Pine Ave., 310/491-1104
Papa Jon's
  5006 E. Second St., 310/439-1059

Best Homestyle Food
Babe's Kitchen
  1106 E. Wardlow Rd., 310/427-4897

Best Italian Food
Andiamo In Citta
  217 Pine Ave., 310/435-1225
Andiamo's Ristorante
  6511 E. Pacific Coast Hwy., 310/493-5529

Best Mexican Food
La Salsa Restaurant
  243 Pine Ave., 310/491-1104
Mi Lupita
  1202 E. Broadway, 310/432-0163
El Ranchito
  5345 Long Beach Rd., 310/428-7348

Best Pizza
Pizza Place
  1431 E. Broadway, 310/432-6000

Best Place to Eat When Someone Else Is Buying
Mustard Seed
  5624 Atlantic Ave., 310/422-6090

Best Place to Take the Kids
Babe's Kitchen
  1106 E. Wardlow Rd., 310/427-4897

Best Salad/Salad Bar
Colonial Buffet
  355 E. First St., 310/590-0220

Best Seafood
Simon and Seafort's Fish Chop
  340 Golden Shore St., 310/435-2333

Best Steaks
Twin Wheels Steak House
  1654 W. Anaheim St., 310/435-4744

LOS ANGELES , CA

Best American Food
Abíquíu
  1413 Fifth St., Santa Monica, 310/395-8611
Vida
  1930 Hillhurst Ave., 213/660-4446
Wolfgang Puck Cafe
  1323 Montana Ave., Santa Monica, 310/393-0290
Eclipse
  8800 Melrose Ave., West Hollywood, 310/724-5959
Gratis
  11658 San Vicente Blvd., Brentwood, 310/571-2345

Best Bagels
Brooklyn Bagel Bakery
  2217 W. Beverly Blvd., 213/413-4114
I and Joy
  1636 Westwood Blvd., 310/474-9001
  713 W. Seventh St., 213/622-5216
  109 N. Fairfax Ave., 213/932-9905
  7361 1/2 W. Sunset Blvd., 213/850-9044
  9227 W. Pico Blvd., 310/858-9094
Noah's New York Bagels
  8919 Santa Monica Blvd., West Hollywood,
    310/289-1795
  200 S. Beverly Dr., Beverly Hills, 310/550-7392

Best Bars
Lava Lounge
  1533 N. LaBrea Ave., Hollywood, 213/876-6612
The Smog Cutter
  864 N. Virgil Ave., Silver Lake, 213/660-4626
Bar Deluxe
  1710 N. Las Palmas Ave., Hollywood, 213/469-1991
Musso and Frank Grill
  6667 Hollywood Blvd., Hollywood, 213/467-7788

Best Barbecue/Ribs
Dr. Hoggly-Woggly's Tyler Texas BBQ
  813 Sepulveda Blvd., Van Nuys, 818/782-2480
The Bear Pit
  10825 Sepulveda Blvd., Mission Hills, 818/365-2509

Best Bread
Breadworks
  7961 W. Third St., 213/930-0047
Il Fornaio Panetteria
  301 N. Beverly Dr., Beverly Hills, 310/550-6355

Best Breakfast
Backburner Cafe
  87 Fourteenth St., Hermosa Beach, 310/372-6973

Best Burgers
Fat Face Fenner's Falloon
  837 Hermosa Ave., Hermosa Beach, 310/376-0996
Johnny Rocket's
  7507 Melrose Ave., Hollywood, 213/651-3361
  10250 Santa Monica Blvd., 310/788-9020
  100 N. La Cienega Blvd., 310/657-6073
  1888 Century Park E., Ste. 224, 310/556-8811
  11677 San Vicente Blvd., 310/447-6565
  10959 Weyburn Ave., 310/824-5656
In-N-Out Burger
  Multiple Locations, 800/786-1000

Best Business Lunch
The Depot
  1250 Cabrillo Ave., Torrance, 310/787-7501

Best Brunch
House of Blues
  8430 Sunset Blvd., West Hollywood, 213/650-0476
Bel Air Hotel
  701 Stone Canyon Rd., 310/472-1211
French Quarter Market
  7985 Santa Monica Blvd., 310/654-0898
Ninety-Fourth Aero Squadron
  2780 Skypark Dr., Torrance, 310/539-6203

Best Cheap Meal
Good Stuff
  Thirteenth at Strand, Hermosa Beach, 310/374-2334
Rosti
  908 S. Barrington Ave., 310/447-8695

Best Chinese Food
Szechwan
  924 N. Sepulveda Blvd., Manhattan Beach,
    310/379-9712
  25229 S. Hawthorne Blvd., Torrance, 310/378-4235
Won Kok Restaurant
  208-210 Alpine St., 213/613-0700
Chin Chin Restaurant
  11740 San Vicente Blvd., 310/826-2525
  8618 W. Sunset Blvd., 310/652-1818
Chinois on Main
  2709 Main St., Santa Monica, 310/392-3037
Panda Inn Chinese Restaurant
  10800 W. Pico Blvd., 310/470-7790

Best Coffee
Coffee Brake
  1507 1/2 S. Robertson Ave., 310/277-6741

Best Coffeehouses
Portfolio Cafe and Gallery
  2300 E. Fourth St., Long Beach, 310/434-2486
Java Man
  157 Pier Ave., Hermosa Beach, 310/379-7209

Starbucks
  Multiple Locations
Highland Grounds
  742 N. Highland Ave., Hollywood, 213/466-1507
Insomnia Cafe
  7286 Beverly Blvd., 213/931-4943

Best Continental Food
Chez Melange
  1718 S. Pacific Coast Hwy., Redondo Beach,
    310/540-9135

Best Delicatessens
Greenblatt's Delicatessen
  8017 Sunset Blvd., Hollywood, 213/656-0606
Bristol Farms
  1570H Rosecrans Ave., Manhattan Beach,
    310/643-5229
Art's Delicatessen and Restaurant
  12224 Ventura Blvd., Studio City, 818/762-1221
Jerry's Famous Deli
  16650 Ventura Blvd., Encino, 818/906-1800
  13181 Mindanao Way, Marina Del Rey, 310/821-6626
Canter's
  419 N. Fairfax Ave., 213/651-2030

Best Desserts
The Cheesecake Factory
  605 N. Harbor Dr., Redondo Beach, 310/376-0466
The Ivy
  113 N. Robertson Blvd., 310/274-8303

Best Eclectic Menu
The Ivy
  113 N. Robertson Blvd., 310/274-8303

Best Family Restaurant
Jerry's Famous Deli
  16650 Ventura Blvd., Encino, 818/906-1800
  13181 Mindanao Way, Marina Del Rey, 310/821-6626

Best Fast Food
Johnny Rocket's
  7507 Melrose Ave., 213/651-3361
  10250 Santa Monica Blvd., 310/788-9020
  100 N. La Cienega Blvd., 310/657-6073
  1888 Century Park E., Ste. 224, 310/556-8811
  11677 San Vicente Blvd., 310/447-6565
  10959 Weyburn Ave., 310/824-5656

Best French Food
Cafe des Artistes
  1534 N. McCadden Pl., 213/461-6889

Best Happy Hour
Bestie's
  1332 Hermosa Ave., Ste. 12, Hermosa Beach,
    310/318-3818

Best Indian Food
Paru's Vegetarian Indian Restaurant
  5140 Sunset Blvd., 213/661-7600
India's Oven
  7231 Beverly Blvd., 213/936-1000

 _ay Cafe
   2113 Santa Monica Blvd., Ste. 205, 310/820-2070
_ay Pit
   3465 W. Sixth St., 213/382-6300
   1815 Hawthorne Blvd., Third Fl., Redondo Beach,
      310/214-0888

Best Italian Food
Brogino's
   2423 Artesia Blvd., PCH, Redondo Beach,
      310/370-4828
Toscana
   11633 San Vicente Blvd., 310/820-2448
Il Pastalo
   400 N. Canon Dr., Beverly Hills, 310/205-5444
Louise's Trattoria
   4500 Los Feliz Blvd., 213/667-0777
   11645 San Vicente Blvd., 310/826-2000
   7505 Melrose Ave., 213/651-3880
   10645 W. Pico Blvd., 310/475-6084
   232 N. Larchmont Blvd., 213/962-9510
Alejo's
   4002 Lincoln Blvd., Marina del Rey, 310/822-0095
   8343 Lincoln Blvd., Westchester, 310/670-6677
Alto Palato
   755 N. La Cienega Blvd., West Hollywood,
      310/657-9271

Best Japanese Food
Mako
   1820 N. Vermont Ave., Los Feliz, 213/660-1211
Benihana of Tokyo
   38 N. La Cienega Blvd., Beverly Hills, 310/655-7311
Matsuhisa
   129 N. La Cienega Blvd., Beverly Hills, 310/659-9639
   8929 Wilshire Blvd., Beverly Hills, 310/289-4925
Yamashiro
   1999 N. Sycamore Ave., 213/466-5125

Best Late-Night Food
Jerry's Famous Deli
   16650 Ventura Blvd., Encino, 818/906-1800
   13181 Mindanao Way, Marina Del Rey, 310/821-6626
Canter's
   419 N. Fairfax Ave., 213/651-2030
Van Go's Ear
   796 Main St., Venice, 310/314-0022
The Original Pantry Cafe
   877 S. Figueroa St., 213/972-9279

Best Mexican Food
Riviera Bar and Grill
   1615 S. Pacific Coast Hwy., Redondo Beach,
      310/540-2501
Tlapazola Grill
   2920 Lincoln Blvd., Santa Monica, 310/392-7292
Paneho's Family Cafe
   12244 W. Pico Blvd., 310/820-9948
Acapulco Mexican Restaurant
   1109 Glendon Ave., 310/208-3884

4444 W. Sunset Blvd., 213/665-5751
3280 Glendale Blvd., 213/663-8275
7038 W. Sunset Blvd., 213/469-5131
El Cholo Restaurant
1121 S. Western Ave., 213/734-2773
La Serenata de Garibaldi
1842 E. First St., 213/265-2887

Best Other Ethnic Food
Rincon Criollo (Cuban)
4361 Sepulveda Blvd., Culver City, 310/391-4478

Best Outdoor Dining
Inn of the Seventh Ray
128 Old Topanga Rd., Topanga, 310/455-1311
Bel Air Hotel
701 Stone Canyon Rd., 310/472-1211
Sidewalk Cafe
1401 Ocean Front Walk, Venice, 310/399-5547

Best Pizza
Mama's Original Pizza and Pasta
2205 Pacific Coast Hwy., Hermosa Beach,
310/376-8486
Numero Uno Pizza, Pasta and More
Multiple Locations
California Pizza Kitchen
330 S. Hope St., 213/626-2616
121 N. La Cienega Blvd., 310/854-6555
1640 S. Sepulveda Blvd., Ste. 200, 310/575-3000
11677 San Vicente Blvd., 310/826-3573
Mr. Damiano's Pizza
1511 1/2 S. Robertson Blvd., 310/475-6751

Best Places to Eat When Someone Else Is Buying
La Rive Gauche
320 Tejon Place, Malaga Cove, Palos Verdes Estates,
310/378-0267
The Ivy
113 N. Robertson Blvd., 310/274-8303
1100 Wall St., 213/746-6124
Michael's Restaurant
6309 E. Washington Blvd., 213/722-5153

Best Romantic Dining
Casablanca
53 Pier Ave., Hermosa Beach, 310/379-4177
Inn of the Seventh Ray
128 Old Topanga Rd., Topanga, 310/455-1311
Yamashiro
1999 N. Sycamore Ave., 213/466-5125

Best Salad/Salad Bar
R.J.'s Restaurant
252 N. Beverly Dr., 310/274-3474

Best Seafood
Lobster Connection
2201 Lincoln Blvd., Venice, 310/822-4062
Captain Kidd's
209 N. Harbor Dr., Redondo Beach, 310/372-7703
Back on the Beach
445 Palisades Beach Rd., Santa Monica, 310/393-8282

adstone's
1000 Universal Center Dr., Universal City,
818/622-3474

Best Soul Food
Roscoe's Chicken and Waffles
5006 W. Pico Blvd., 213/934-4405
106 W. Manchester Ave., 213/752-6211
1514 N. Gower St., 213/466-7453

Best Steaks
Bull Pen
314 Ave. I, Redondo Beach, 310/375-7797
Monty's Steak House
1100 Glendon Ave., 21st Fl., 310/208-8787
Lawry's Primo Rib
100 N. La Cienega Blvd., Beverly Hills, 310/652-2827

Best Sushi
Crazy Fish
9105 W. Olympic Blvd., Beverly Hills, 310/550-8547
Matsuhisa
129 N. La Cienega Blvd., Beverly Hills, 310/659-9639

Best Thai Food
Lumpinee Thai
11020 Vanowen St., North Hollywood, 818/505-0761
Toi on Sunset
7505 1/2 Sunset Blvd., Hollywood, 213/874-8062
Chuam Chin
5644 Hollywood Blvd., Hollywood, 213/464-9805
Thai Thani
1109 S. Pacific Coast Hwy., Redondo Beach,
310/375-7797
Tommy Tang's
7473 Melrose Ave., 213/651-1810

Best 24-Hour Restaurants
Van Go's Ear
796 Main St., Venice, 310/314-0022
The Original Pantry Cafe
877 S. Figueroa St., 213/972-9279

Best Vegetarian Food
Real Food Daily
514 Santa Monica Blvd., Santa Monica, 310/451-7544
A Votre Sante
13016 San Vicente Blvd., 310/395-2500
1025 Abbot Kinney Blvd., Venice, 310/314-1187
345 N. La Brea Ave., 213/857-0412
Follow Your Heart
21825 Sherman Way, Canoga Park, 818/348-3240
Inn of the Seventh Ray
128 Old Topanga Rd., Topanga, 310/455-1311
Vegetable Delight
17823 Chatsworth St., Granada Hills, 818/360-3997

Standbys
Tony Roma's
50 N. La Cienega Blvd., Beverly Hills, 310/659-7427
10850 W. Pico Blvd., 310/470-0737
666 Universal Terrace Pkwy., North Hollywood,
818/777-3939

1000 Universal Center Dr., North Hollywood,
818/763-7662
6300 S. Pacific Coast Hwy., 310/373-0597

MADERA, CA

Best Restaurants in Town
Lucca's Restaurant
325 N. Gateway Dr., 209/674-6744
The Vineyard
605 S. First St., 209/674-0923
Farnesi's Restaurant
2805 W. Kennedy, 209/673-9164
The Vintage House
30338 Twelfth Ave., 209/674-1560
Perko's Cafe
1825 W. Cleveland Ave., 209/675-8020
Eppie's Restaurant
1101 Country Club Dr., 209/674-0368

MARYSVILLE, CA

Best Restaurants in Town
Pasquini's Fine Food and Spirits
6241 Live Oak Blvd., Live Oak, 916/695-3384
Lovey's Landing
3474 N. Meridian Rd., Meridian, 916/696-2449
The Cannery
609 J St., 916/743-3005
The Refuge Restaurant and Lounge
1501 Butte House Rd., Yuba City, 916/673-7620
Lucio's
890 W. Onstott Rd., Yuba City, 916/671-2050
Al's Cafe American
1538 Poole Blvd., Yuba City, 916/674-3213
Ruthie's
229 Clark Ave., Yuba City, 916/674-2611

Best Mexican Food
Casa Lupe
655 Onstott Rd., Yuba City, 916/673-2190

MERCED, CA

Best French Food
Jordan's Chateau
408 W. Main St., 209/384-1607

Best Italian Food
D'Angelo's
350 W. Main St., 209/383-3020

Best Japanese Food
Nagami
2650 W. Sixteenth St., 209/384-1677

Best Seafood
D'Angelo's
350 W. Main St., 209/383-3020

Best Steaks
Pine Cone Bar and Grill
1500 W. Thirteenth St., 209/384-9223

B and G Branding Iron
640 W. Sixteenth St., 209/722-1822
The Ranch
245 W. Sixteenth St., 209/722-7351

Best Thai Food
Star Garden
235 W. Twelfth St., 209/383-5350

MILL VALLEY, CA

Best Restaurant in Town
Buckeye Roadhouse
15 Shoreline Hwy., 415/331-2600

Best Bar
Buckeye Roadhouse
15 Shoreline Hwy., 415/331-2600

Best Brunch
Dipsea Cafe
200 Shoreline Hwy., 415/381-0298
Sam's Anchor Cafe
27 Main St., Belvedere Tiburon, 415/435-4527

Best Burgers
Phyllis' Giant Burgers
72 E. Blithedale Ave., 415/381-5116

Best Cheap Meal
High Tech Burrito
118 Strawberry Village, 415/388-7002

Best Delicatessens
Perry's Delicatessen
246 E. Blithedale Ave., 415/381-0407
La Petite
33 Reed Blvd., 415/381-2336

Best Desserts
True Confections
17 Madrona St., 415/383-3832
Sweet Things
The Cove, 1 Blackfield Dr., Tiburon, 415/388-8583

Best French Food
Guernica
2009 Bridgeway, Sausalito, 415/332-1512

Best Ice Cream/Yogurt
Ultimate Yogurt
214 Strawberry Village, 415/383-4881

Best Indian Food
India Palace
707 Redwood Hwy., 415/388-3350

Best Italian Food
Piazza D'Angelo
22 Miller Ave., 415/388-2185

Best Japanese Food
Sushi to Dai For
869 Fourth St., 415/721-0392

Best Late-Night Food
Buckeye Roadhouse
15 Shoreline Hwy., 415/331-2600

Best Mexican Food
The Cantina
   651 E. Blithedale Ave., 415/381-1070
Guaymas
   5 Main St., Belvedere Tiburon, 415/435-6300

Best Middle Eastern Food
Cairo Cafe
   411 Strawberry Village, 415/389-1101

Best Outdoor Dining
Guaymas
   5 Main St., Belvedere Tiburon, 415/435-6300

Best Pizza
Muzzarella di Bufla
   711 E. Blithedale Ave., 415/381-3972
Round Table Pizza
   50 Belvedere Dr., 415/383-5100

Best Place to Eat When Someone Else Is Buying
El Paseo
   17 Throckmorton Ave., 415/388-0741

Best Romantic Dining
El Paseo
   17 Throckmorton, 415/388-0741
Caprice
   200 Paradise Dr., Belvedere Tiburon, 415/435-3400

Best Seafood
Scoma's
   588 Bridgeway, Sausalito, 415/332-9551

Standbys
Chevy's
   302 Bon Air Center, Marin, 415/461-3203

MODESTO, CA

Best Restaurant in Town
Hazel's Elegant Dining
   513 Twelfth St., 209/578-3463

Best American Food
Farmer's Catfish House
   4937 Beckwith Rd., 209/578-3463

Best Atmosphere
Hazel's Elegant Dining
   513 Twelfth St., 209/578-3463

Best Bar
Mallard's
   1700 McHenry Ave., 209/522-3825
   708 L St., 209/522-1018

Best Barbecue/Ribs
Smoky's Restaurant
   222 McHenry Ave., 209/524-7801

Best Bread
Village Baking Company and Cafe
   1700 McHenry Ave., 209/522-9057

Best Breakfast
Opus 13
   421 McHenry Ave., 209/576-7508

Brunch
Shipyard
7948 Yosemite Blvd., 209/577-3093

Best Burgers
Smoky's Restaurant
222 McHenry Ave., 209/524-7801
Scenic Drive-In
1151 Scenic Dr., 209/522-3536

Best Business Breakfast
Sundial Lodge and Restaurant
808 McHenry Ave., 209/524-4375

Best Business Lunch
Tresetti's World Caffe
927 Eleventh St., 209/572-2990

Best Casual Dining
Benni's
1105 Yosemite Blvd., 209/571-3657

Best Cheap Meal
Noah's Hof Brau
1311 J St., 209/527-1090

Best Coffeehouses
Espresso Caffe
3025D McHenry Ave., 209/571-3337
Deva
1202 J St., 209/572-3382

Best Continental Food
Hazel's Elegant Dining
513 Twelfth St., 209/578-3463

Best Delicatessen
Ferrarese's Deli Restaurant
1161 E. F St., Oakdale, 209/847-2079

Best Desserts
City Hotel and Restaurant
Columbia State Park, Main St., Columbia,
209/532-1479

Best Eclectic Menu
Deja Vu Cafe
825 W. Roseburg Ave., 209/571-3333

Best Fast Food
Teriyaki Chicken Bowl
1725 Prescott Rd., 209/527-6988
1401 Coffee Rd., 209/527-3912
2320 McHenry Ave., 209/578-6738

Best Health-Conscious Menu
The Brighter Side [lunch only]
1125 K St., 209/524-7531

Best Indian Food
India Oven Restaurant
1022 Eleventh St., 209/572-1805
Taste of India
2501 McHenry Ave., 209/529-9000

Best Italian Food
Benni's
1105 Yosemite Blvd., 209/571-3657

Best Mexican Food
La Morenita
    1410 E. Hatch Rd., 209/537-7900
El Ranchito
    3048 Atchison St., Riverbank, 209/869-0196

Best Microbrewery
St. Stan's Brewery Restaurant
    821 L St., 209/524-4782

Best Pastries
Cinnamon Cafe
    330 Needham St., 209/544-3434

Best Place to be "Seen"
Mallard's
    1700 McHenry Ave., 209/522-3825
    708 L St., 209/522-1018

Best Place to Eat When Someone Else Is Buying
Maxi's Restaurant and Lounge
    1150 Ninth St., 209/526-6000

Best Place to Take the Kids
Strings Italian Cafe
    2601 Oakdale Rd., 209/578-9777

Best Quick Lunch
China Gate
    1601 Yosemite Blvd., 209/526-6666

Best Romantic Dining
Hazel's Elegant Dining
    513 Twelfth St., 209/578-3463

Best Salad/Salad Bar
Deva
    1202 J St., 209/572-3382
Fresh Choice Restaurant
    2225 Plaza Pkwy., 209/523-8875

Best Sandwiches
Opus 13
    421 McHenry Ave., 209/527-3450

Best Seafood
Fisherman's Galley
    3008 McHenry Ave., 209/527-3450

Best Southwestern Food
R.J. Sweetwater's
    1029 Ninth St., 209/526-4060

Best Steaks
Marty's Inn
    29030 Hwy. 33, Newman, 209/862-1323

Best Thai Food
Thailand Restaurant
    950 Tenth St., 209/544-0505

Best Undiscovered Restaurant
Bon Appetit
    500 Ninth St., Ste. K-1, 209/526-7000

Best Vegetarian Food
Village Health Food
    1700 McHenry Ave., 209/523-3466

Wine Selection
Appetit Cafe
  00 Ninth St., Ste. K-1, 209/526-7000

andbys
HomeTown Buffet
  1771 Prescott Rd., 209/521-3999

MONTEBELLO, CA

Best Restaurants in Town
Quiet Cannon
  901 Via San Clemente, 213/724-9284
Dal Rae
  9023 Washington Blvd., Pico Rivera, 213/949-2444

Best Bars
Gotham Bar and Grill
  5811 Firestone Blvd., South Gate, 310/806-2224
Mister C's Lounge
  612 W. Whittier Blvd., 213/727-0681

Best Breakfast
Jimmie's Family Restaurant
  701 W. Whittier Blvd., 213/726-7783

Best Brunch
Gotham Bar and Grill
  5811 Firestone Blvd., South Gate, 310/806-2224

Best Burgers
Golden Ox
  902 W. Whittier Blvd., 213/722-2865

Best Business Lunch
Baker's Square Restaurant
  1322 W. Beverly Blvd., 213/722-6324
Quiet Cannon
  901 Via San Clemente, 213/724-9284

Best Casual Dining
Gotham Bar and Grill
  5811 Firestone Blvd., South Gate, 310/806-2224

Best Cheap Meal
Argos Jr. Chicken and Beef Bowl
  1001 W. Whitter Blvd., 213/721-6426

Best Chinese Food
Paul's Kitchen
  1950 S. Atlantic Blvd., Monterey Park, 213/724-1855

Best Desserts
Baker's Square Restaurant
  1322 W. Beverly Blvd., 213/722-6324

Best Diner
Ozzie's
  7780 E. Slauson Ave., 213/726-0300

Best Family Restaurant
Salvatore Pizza and Italian Restaurant
  125 N. Sixth St., 213/727-2803

Best Homestyle Food
Ordonez Mexican Restaurant
  102 1/2 E. Beverly Blvd., 213/728-5263

Best Italian Food
Salvatore Pizza and Italian Restaurant
  125 N. Sixth St., 213/727-2803

Best Late-Night Food
Ordonez Mexican Restaurant
  102 1/2 E. Beverly Blvd., 213/728-5263

Best Mexican Food
Ordonez Mexican Restaurant
  102 1/2 E. Beverly Blvd., 213/728-5263

Best Pizza
Salvatore Pizza and Italian Restaurant
  125 N. Sixth St., 213/727-2803

Best Place to Eat When Someone Else Is Buying
Dal Rae
  9023 Washington Blvd., Pico Rivera, 213/949-2444

Best Romantic Dining
Dal Rae
  9023 Washington Blvd., Pico Rivera, 213/949-2444

Best Salad/Salad Bar
Gotham Bar and Grill
  5811 Firestone Blvd., South Gate, 310/806-2224

Best Sandwiches
BJ's
  3051 W. Seventh St., Los Angeles, 213/386-0928

Best Steaks
Steven's Steak House
  5332 Stevens Pl., Commerce, 213/723-9856

Standbys
Denny's
  2727 Via Campo, 213/722-3424

MONTEREY, CA

Best Restaurants in Town
Rio Grill
  159 Crossroads Blvd., Carmel, 408/625-5436
Sardine Factory
  701 Wave St., 408/373-3775
Fresh Cream
  99 Pacific St., 408/375-9798

Best Bar
Mucky Duck
  479 Alvarado St., 408/655-3031

Best Barbecue/Ribs
Central Texan Barbecue
  10500 Merritt St., Castroville, 408/633-2285

Best Beer Selection
London Bridge Pub
  Fisherman's Wharf, Ste. 2, 408/655-2879
Mucky Duck
  479 Alvarado St., 408/655-3031

Best Bistro
Taste Bistro
  1199 Forest Ave, Pacific Grove, 408/655-0324

121

...st
...nings
...an View Ave., Pacific Grove, 408/372-1125
...kfast Club
...Fremont Blvd., Seaside, 408/394-3238

...Brunch
...rante's
...Marriott Hotel, 350 Calle Principal, 408/649-4234

Best Burgers
Duffy's Tavern
282 High St., 408/372-2565
Del Monte Express
2329 N. Fremont St., 408/655-1941

Best Cheap Meal
Papa Chano's
462 Alvarado St., 408/646-9587

Best Chinese Food
Chef Lee's
2031 North Fremont St., 408/375-9551

Best Clam Chowder
Vivolo's Chowder House
127 Central Ave., Pacific Grove, 408/372-5414

Best Coffeehouses
Morgan's Coffeehouse
498 Washington St., 408/373-5601
Pacific Grove Coffee Roasting Company
510 Lighthouse Ave., Pacific Grove, 408/655-5633

Best French Food
Fresh Cream
100C Heritage Harbor, 99 Pacific St., 408/375-9798

Best Health-Conscious Menu
Tillie Gort's Cafe
111 Central Ave., Pacific Grove, 408/373-0335

Best Italian Food
Vito's
1180A Forest Ave., Pacific Grove, 408/375-3070
Pasta Mia
481 Lighthouse Ave., Pacific Grove, 408/375-7709
Tutto Buono
469 Alvarado St., 408/372-1880

Best Late-Night Food
Peacock Bar and Grill
611 Lighthouse Ave., 408/372-5565

Best Mexican Food
Peppers Mexicali Cafe
170 Forest Ave., Pacific Grove, 408/373-6892

Best Old Favorite Restaurant
Golden Buddha
3678 The Barnyard, Carmel, 408/625-1668

Best Outdoor Dining
The General Store
Fifth at Junipero, Carmel, 408/624-2233

Best Pizza
Allegro Gourmet Pizzeria
   1184 Forest Ave., Pacific Grove, 408/373-5656
   3770 The Barnyard, Carmel, 408/626-5454

Best Place to Eat When Someone Else Is Buying
Fresh Cream
   100C Heritage Harbor, 99 Pacific St., 408/375-9798

Best Restaurant Meal Value
London Bridge Pub
   Fisherman's Wharf, Ste. 2, 408/655-2879

Best Romantic Dining
The Old Bath House
   620 Ocean View Blvd., Pacific Grove, 408/375-5195

Best Salad/Salad Bar
Allegro Gourmet Pizzeria
   1184 Forest Ave., Pacific Grove, 408/373-5656
   3770 The Barnyard, Carmel, 408/626-5454

Best Sandwiches
Bagel Bakery
   Multiple Locations

Best Seafood
Fishwife
   1996 Sunset Dr., Pacific Grove, 408/375-7101
   789 Trinity Ave., Seaside, 408/394-2027

Best Sports Bar
Characters
   350 Calle Principal, 408/647-4023

Best Steaks
Whaling Station
   763 Wave St., 408/373-3778

Best Sushi
Robata Grill
   3658 The Barnyard, Carmel, 408/624-2643

Best Thai Food
Thai Bistro
   55 W. Carmel Valley Rd., Carmel Valley, 408/659-5900
   159 Central Ave., Pacific Grove, 408/372-8700

Best Undiscovered Restaurant
Taste Bistro
   1199 Forest Ave., Pacific Grove, 408/655-0324

Best Vegetarian Food
Tilli Gort's Cafe
   111 Central Ave., Pacific Grove, 408/373-0335

Best Vietnamese Food
Thuy Duong
   1104 Broadway Ave., Seaside, 408/393-9338

Best View While Dining
Pacific's Edge
   Highlands Inn, Hwy. 1, Carmel, 408/624-3801

Best Wine Selection
Rio Grill
   159 Crossroads Blvd., Carmel, 408/625-5436

ctory
ve St., 408/373-3775

ys
.oma's
nicipal Wharf, Ste. 2, 408/655-1401
.kin-Robbins
Multiple Locations

NAPA, CA

Best Breakfast
Old Adobe Restaurant
376 Soscol Ave., 707/255-4310

Best Brunch
Old Adobe Restaurant
376 Soscol Ave., 707/255-4310

Best Burgers
Geezer's Grill and Bar
829 Main St., 707/224-4322
Nation's Hamburgers
1441 Third St., 707/252-8500

Best Chinese Food
Asia Cafe
825 Main St., 707/224-0840

Best Coffee
Napa Valley Coffee Roasting Company
948 Main St., 707/224-2233

Best Desserts
Marie Callender's
1990 Trower Ave., 707/253-7754

Best French Food
Chanterelle Restaurant
804 First St., 707/253-7300
La Boucane
1778 Second St., 707/253-1177

Best Ice Cream/Yogurt
Swensen's Ice Cream
3138 Jefferson St., 707/252-3212

Best Italian Food
Pietro's Pizza Restaurant
999 Trancas St., 707/252-1033
Tra Vigne Restaurant
1050 Charter Oak Ave., St. Helena, 707/963-4444

Best Mexican Food
Red Hen Cantina
5091 Saint Helena Hwy., 707/255-8125

Best Pizza
Pietro's Pizza Restaurant
999 Trancas St., 707/252-1033

Best Seafood
Penguin's
1533 Trancas St., 707/252-4343

Best Restaurants in Town
Bay Wolf Restaurant
  3852 Piedmont Ave., 510/655-6004
Citron
  5484 College Ave., 510/653-5484

Best Asian Restaurant
Uncle Yu's Szechuan
  2005 Crow Canyon Pl., San Ramon, 510/275-1818

Best Bagels
Noah's Bagels
  2060 Mountain Blvd., 510/339-6663
  4240 Hollis St., Emeryville, 510/655-6624
Brothers' Bagels
  4301 Piedmont Ave., 510/654-5211

Best Barbecue/Ribs
Flint's Bar-B-Q
  3114 San Pablo Ave., 510/658-9912
  6672 E. Fourteenth St., 510/569-1312
Doug's Barbecue
  1048 36th St., Emeryville, 510/655-9048

Best Beer Selection
Barclay's Restaurant and Pub
  5940 College Ave., 510/654-1650

Best Breakfast
Country Waffles
  130 Hartz Ave., Danville, 510/838-0651

Best Brunch
Farmers' Market at Jack London Square
  466 Water St., 510/208-4646

Best Burgers
Barney's Gourmet Hamburger
  4162 Piedmont Ave., 510/655-7180
  5819 College Ave., 510/601-0444
Nation's Giant Hamburgers
  Multiple Locations

Best Cheap Meal
Economy Restaurant
  399 Eighth St., 510/832-9886
  2 Theatre Square, Ste. 105, Orinda, 510/254-5290
  202 Sycamore Valley Rd. W., Danville, 510/838-2333

Best Coffee
Peet's Coffee and Tea
  2066 Antioch Court, 510/339-6704
  3258 Lake Shore Ave., 510/832-6761
  4050 Piedmont Ave., 510/655-3228

Best Coffeehouse
Nordstrom Espresso Bar
  Multiple Locations

Best Chinese Food
King Yen
  4080 Piedmont Ave., 510/652-9678

...sens
...catessen and Ravioli Factory
    ...graph Ave., 510/652-7401
    ...ca Delicatessen
    ...elegraph Ave., 510/654-9188
    ...A Piedmont Ave., 510/547-7222
    ...9 La Salle Ave., 510/339-9716

...st Desserts
...ust Desserts
    4001B Piedmont Ave., 510/601-7780

Best Greek/Mediterranean Food
Oliveto Cafe
    5655 College Ave., 510/547-5356

Best Ice Cream/Yogurt
Yogurt Park
    684 Hartz Ave., Danville, 510/838-2243

Best Italian Food
Father Nature's Shed
    172 E. Prospect Ave., Danville, 510/820-3160

Best Korean Food
Sorabol Korean Restaurant
    372 Grand Ave., 510/839-2288
Koryo Restaurant
    4390 Telegraph, 510/652-6007

Best Mexican Food
Cactus Taqueria
    5525 College Ave., 510/547-1305

Best New Restaurant
Battam Bang
    850 Broadway, 510/839-8815

Best Old Favorite Restaurants
Bay Wolf Restaurant
    3852 Piedmont Ave., 510/655-6004
Citron
    5484 College Ave., 510/653-5484

Best Other Ethnic Food
Asmara (African)
    5020 Telegraph Ave., 510/547-5100
Red Sea Restaurant (African)
    5200 Claremont Ave., 510/655-3757

Best Outdoor Dining
Ay Chihuahua Gourmet Latin Food
    6706 San Pablo Ave., 510/655-9799

Best Pizza
Zachary's Chicago Pizza
    5801 College Ave., 510/655-6385

Best Place to Eat When Someone Else Is Buying
Bridges
    44 Church St., Danville, 510/820-7200

Best Romantic Dining
Bridges
    44 Church St., Danville, 510/820-7200

Best Sandwiches
A Sweet Affair
   5345 Clayton Rd., Clayton, 510/672-0936
Togo's Eatery
   Multiple Locations

Best Sports Bar
Tommy T's
   2410 San Ramon Valley Blvd., San Ramon,
   510/743-1500

Best Sushi
Tachibana
   5812 College Ave., 510/654-3668

Best Undiscovered Restaurant
Le Cheval
   1414 Jefferson St., 510/763-8495
   344 Twentieth St., 510/763-3610
   1007 Clay St., 510/763-8495

Best Vegetarian Food
Mudd's Restaurant
   10 Boardwalk, San Ramon, 510/837-9387

Best Vietnamese Food
Le Cheval
   1007 Clay St., 510/763-8495
   344 Twentieth St., 510/763-3610
   1414 Jefferson St., 510/763-8495
Pho 84
   354 Seventeenth St., 510/832-1429
   416 Thirteenth St., 510/832-1499

Standbys
Chevy's
   2400 Mariner Square Dr., Alameda, 510/521-3768

OCEANSIDE, CA

Best All-You-Can-Eat Buffets
Barbecue Bob's Chicken and Ribs
   2810 Thunder Dr., 619/726-9336
Country Harvest Buffet
   2434 Vista Way, 619/966-0344

Best American Food
Barbecue Bob's Chicken and Ribs
   2810 Thunder Dr., 619/726-9336

Best Bagels
Baltimore Bagel Company
   3837 Plaza Dr., 619/726-7700
Garden State Bagels
   1386 Poinsettia Ave., Vista, 619/727-1800

Best Breakfast
Monika's Cafe
   986 E. Vista Way, Vista, 619/598-4223
Wayside Cafe
   507C S. Main Ave., Fallbrook, 619/723-9633

Best Chinese Food
Chin's Szechwan Restaurant
   4140 Oceanside Blvd., 619/631-4808

Best Coffeehouse
Hill Street Coffee House
   524 S. Hill St., 619/966-0985

Best Desserts
Carrow's Restaurant
   936 N. Hill St., 619/722-9435

Best Family Restaurant
Spoons Grill and Bar
   2725 Vista Way, 619/757-7070

Best French Food
Le Bistro
   119 N. Main St., Fallbrook, 619/723-3559

Best Greek/Mediterranean Food
Mykonos Greek and Seafood Restaurant
   258 Harbor Dr. S., 619/757-8757

Best Health-Conscious Menu
Secret Garden
   Fire Mountain Shopping Ctr., 2530R W. Vista Way,
     619/722-3870

Best Italian Food
Vince's Italian Restaurant
   1331 S. Mission Rd., Fallbrook, 619/723-1221

Best Japanese Food
Date Restaurant
   2415 Vista Way, 619/721-0843
Kurando Restaurant
   3815 Mission Ave., 619/754-9343

Best Mexican Food
Roberto's Taco Shop
   1209 S. Hill St., 619/757-2377
Rockin' Baja Lobster
   264 S. Harbor Dr., 619/754-2252

Best Pizza
Sourdough Pizza
   321 E. Alvarado St., Fallbrook, 619/723-3106

Best Sandwiches
Dominick's Sandwiches
   1672 S. Mission Rd., Fallbrook, 619/728-7911

Best Southwestern Food
Spoons Grill and Bar
   2725 Vista Way, 619/757-7070

Best View While Dining
Chart House
   314 Harbor Dr. S., 619/722-1345

Standbys
Pizza Hut
   2028 S. Hill St., 619/433-5215
   2217 S. El Camino Real, 619/433-6391
   2011 Mission Ave., 619/757-5312
   1715 Oceanside Blvd., 619/757-8911

ONTARIO, CA

Best Restaurant in Town
La Cheminee Restaurant
  1133 W. Sixth St., 909/983-7900

Best American Food
Misty's
  Ontario Red Lion Hotel, 222 N. Vineyard Ave.,
    909/983-0909

Best Barbecue/Ribs
Joey's Bar-B-Q
  1964 W. Foothill Blvd., Upland, 909/982-2128
  3689 Riverside Dr., Chino, 909/628-1231
Chuck's Diner
  8890 Eighth St., Rancho Cucamonga, 909/982-5119
The Pit
  8661 Baseline Rd., Rancho Cucamonga, 909/948-5252

Best Breakfast
Molly's Cafe
  230 N. Euclid Ave., 909/391-6907

Best Brunch
Marie Callender's
  2149 E. D St., 909/983-4004
El Torito
  3680 Inland Empire Blvd., 909/944-9102
Hilton
  700 N. Haven Ave., 909/980-0400
Misty's
  Ontario Red Lion Hotel, 222 N. Vineyard Ave.,
    909/983-0909
Sycamore Inn
  8318 Foothill Blvd., Rancho Cucamonga,
    909/982-1104

Best Burgers
Chuck's Diner
  8890 Eighth St., Rancho Cucamonga, 909/982-5119
The Deli
  9671 Foothill at Archibald, Rancho Cucamonga,
    909/989-8122
Final Score
  8411 Foothill Blvd., Rancho Cucamonga,
    909/985-4515

Best Business Lunch
BC Cafe
  701 S. Indian Hill, La Verne, 909/482-1414
Cask and Cleaver
  12206 Central Ave., Chino, 909/627-6011
  8689 Ninth St., Rancho Cucamonga, 909/982-7108
Mimi's Cafe
  370 N. Montana Ave., Upland, 909/982-3038

Best Cajun/Creole Food
Cafe Orleans
  5460 Philadelphia St., Chino, 909/591-4537

129

Best Coffee
The Bookcellar
   9849 Foothill Blvd., Rancho Cucamonga,
      909/948-7966
Chuck's Diner
   8890 Eighth St., Rancho Cucamonga, 909/982-5119
Coffee Klatch
   8916 Foothill Blvd., Rancho Cucamonga,
      909/944-5282
Espresso Yourself
   350 W. Foothill Blvd., Upland, 909/946-0927
Rose's Caffe Luna
   8038 Haven Ave., Rancho Cucamonga, 909/941-9822

Best Chinese Food
Yangtze Restaurant
   126 N. Euclid Ave., 909/986-8941
Panda Inn
   3223 Centre Lake Dr., 909/983-2888
Tokyo Kitchen
   8851 Central Ave., Montclair, 909/625-5588
China Gate
   365 S. Mountain Ave., Upland, 909/982-2449

Best Continental Food
Magic Lamp Inn
   8189 Foothill Blvd., Rancho Cucamonga,
      909/981-8659
Calla Restaurant
   Ontario Hilton, 700 N. Haven Ave., 909/980-0400

Best Delicatessens
The Deli
   9671 Foothill at Archibald, Rancho Cucamonga,
      909/989-8122
Dr. Don's Deli
   296 N. Second Ave., Upland, 909/982-2011
Togo's Eatery
   110B S. Mountain Ave., Upland, 909/982-5445
   7900 Haven Ave., Rancho Cucamonga, 909/944-7888

Best Desserts
Claim Jumper
   12499 Foothill Blvd., Rancho Cucamonga,
      909/899-8022
Marie Callender's
   2149 E. D St., 909/983-4004
Coco's Restaurant
   150 E. Seventh St., Upland, 909/946-2324
   2322 S. Mountain Ave., 909/984-3930
   60 W. Foothill Blvd., Upland, 909/985-9604

Best French Food
La Cheminee Restaurant
   1133 W. Sixth St., 909/983-7900

Best Ice Cream/Yogurt
Goldmine Yogurt
   110A S. Mountain Ave., Upland, 909/946-0623
Penguins Place Frozen Yogurt
   5525 Philadelphia St., Chino, 909/591-2844

Best Italian Food
Rosa's Restaurant
  425 N. Vineyard Ave., 909/391-1971
Vince's Spaghetti
  1206 W. Holt Blvd., 909/986-7074
  8241 Foothill Blvd., Rancho Cucamonga,
    909/981-1003
Cafe Calato
  9640 Center Ave., Ste. 150, Rancho Cucamonga,
    909/948-3671

Best Mexican Food
Juan Pollo
  1702 S. Euclid Ave., 909/988-4888
Zendejas Mexican Restaurant
  2411 S. Vineyard Ave., 909/947-1400
  7945 Vineyard Ave., Rancho Cucamonga,
    909/466-0633
El Gato Gordo
  1241 W. Foothill Blvd., Upland, 909/981-8380
El Torito
  3680 Inland Empire Blvd., 909/944-9102

Best Other Ethnic Food
Centro Basquo (Basque)
  13432 S. Central Ave., Chino, 909/628-9014

Best Pizza
Cafe Calato
  9640 Center Ave., Ste. 150, Rancho Cucamonga,
    909/948-3671
Papa Paul's
  12345 Mountain Ave., Chino, 909/590-0063
Corina's
  670 N. Mountain Ave., Upland, 909/985-0218
Final Score
  8411 Foothill Blvd., Rancho Cucamonga,
    909/985-4515
Sal's Pizza
  6622 Carnelian St., Alto Loma, 909/989-5547
Warehouse Pizza
  2340 D St., La Verne, 909/593-2714

Best Places to Eat When Someone Else Is Buying
Rosa's Restaurant
  425 N. Vineyard Ave., 909/391-1971
Sycamore Inn
  8318 Foothill Blvd., Rancho Cucamonga,
    909/982-1104

Best Salad/Salad Bar
Cask and Cleaver
  12206 Central Ave., Chino, 909/627-6011
  8689 Ninth St., Rancho Cucamonga, 909/982-7108
Souplantation
  8966 Foothill Blvd., Rancho Cucamonga,
    909/980-9690

Best Sandwiches
Marie Callender's
  2149 E. D St., 909/983-4004

Best Seafood
Misty's Restaurant and Lounge
  222 N. Vineyard Ave., 909/983-0909
Cafe Orleans
  5460 Philadelphia-Chino Promenade, Chino,
    909/591-4537
Lord Charley's Grill and Pub
  2035 W. Foothill Blvd., Upland, 909/982-4513

Best Steaks
Misty's Restaurant and Lounge
  222 N. Vineyard Ave., 909/983-0909
Black Angus
  3640 E. Porsche Way, 909/944-6882
  9415 Monte Vista Ave., Montclair, 909/621-4821
Steer and Stein
  8348 Archibald, Rancho Cucamonga, 909/987-4447

Best Sushi
Ken's Japanese Restaurant
  10006 Foothill Blvd., Rancho Cucamonga,
    909/989-3019
Kishi
  320 W. Foothill Blvd., Upland, 909/981-1770
Tokyo Kitchen
  8851 Central Ave., Montclair, 909/625-5588

ORANGE, CA

Best Restaurant in Town
Antoine
  4500 MacArthur Blvd., Newport Beach, 714/476-2001

Best Bread
Il Fornaio
  18051 Von Karman Ave., 714/261-1444

Best Chinese Food
China Palace
  2899 W. Coast Hwy., Newport Beach, 714/631-8031

Best Continental Food
The Ritz
  880 Newport Center Dr., Newport Beach,
    714/720-1800

Best Desserts
The Cheesecake Factory
  Fashion Island, Newport Beach, 714/720-8333

Best French Food
Pascal
  1000 Bristol St. N., Newport Beach, 714/752-0107

Best Indian Food
The Bombay Duck
  229 Ocean Ave., Laguna Beach, 714/497-7303

Best Italian Food
Niccole's Ristorante
  520 Main St., Huntington Beach, 714/960-8091
Rafaello Ristorante
  1998 N. Tustin Ave., 714/283-8230

Rumari Ristorante
  1826 S. Coast Hwy., Laguna Beach, 714/494-0400
Caffe Piemonte
  1835 E. Chapman Ave., 714/532-3296
Antonello
  1611 Sunflower Ave., Santa Ana, 714/751-7153

Best Mexican Food
El Torito Grill
  Fashion Island, Newport Beach, 714/640-2875
  633 Anton Blvd., Costa Mesa, 714/662-0798
  1910 Main St., Irvine, 714/975-1220
Kachina
  222 Forest Ave., Laguna Beach, 714/497-5546

Best New Restaurant
Wofgang Puck Cafe
  South Coast Plz., Costa Mesa, 714/546-9653

Best Other Ethnic Food
Five Feet (Pacific Rim Cuisine)
  328 Glenneyre St., Laguna Beach, 714/497-4955

Best Pizza
California Pizza Kitchen
  Fashion Island, Newport Beach, 714/759-5543
  2957 Michelson Dr., Irvine, 714/975-1585
  Laguna Hills Mall, Laguna Hills, 714/458-9600
  2800 N. Main, Santa Ana, 714/479-0604
Pizza Cucina
  1106 Irvine Blvd., Tustin, 714/669-1599

Best Place To Be "Seen"
Tutto Mare
  Fashion Island, Newport Beach, 714/640-6333

Best Restaurant Meal Value
Bistango
  19100 Von Karman Ave., Irvine, 714/752-5222

Best Salad/Salad Bar
The Atrium Court in Farmer's Market
  Fashion Island, Newport Beach, 714/760-0403

Best Sandwiches
Zov's Bistro and Bakery
  17440 Seventeenth St., Enderle Center, Tustin,
    714/838-8855

Best Seafood
McCormick and Schmick's
  2000 Main St., Irvine, 714/756-0505

Best Traditional Food
Five Crowns
  3801 E. Coast Hwy., Corona Del Mar, 714/760-0331

Best Undiscovered Restaurant
Gustaf Anders
  South Coast Plz. Village, Bear St. side, Santa Ana,
    714/668-1737

Best Vegetarian Food
Mother's Market and Kitchen
  225 E. Seventeenth St., Costa Mesa, 714/548-4279
  19770 Beach Blvd., Huntington Beach, 714/963-6667

Best Wine Selection
Mr. Stox
  1105 E. Katella Ave., Anaheim, 714/634-2994

OXNARD, CA

Best American Food
Marie Callender's
  1600 Ives Ave., 805/487-7437
Mariann's Italian Villa
  301 W. Channel Islands Blvd., 805/985-8663

Best Breakfast
Uncle Herb's Restaurant
  5141 Saviers Rd., 805/488-5515
Coco's Restaurant
  150 W. Vineyard, 805/485-4779

Best Chinese Food
Lao's Garden
  2655 N. Ventura Rd., Port Hueneme, 805/382-8106

Best Coffeehouse
Low Key Bagels
  4972 Berduga Way, Camarillo, 805/383-0772

Best Greek/Mediterranean Food
Greek
  2343 N. Oxnard Blvd., 805/981-1891

Best Homestyle Food
Uncle Herb's Restaurant
  5141 Saviers Rd., 805/488-5515

Best Indian Food
Yasmeen's
  2311 N. Oxnard Blvd., 805/485-3804

Best Italian Food
Armando's Italian Restaurant
  641 S. Ventura Rd., 805/984-4500
Mariann's Italian Villa
  301 W. Channel Islands Blvd., 805/985-8663

Best Seafood
Whale's Tail
  3950 Blue Fin Circle, Channel Islands Harbor,
    805/985-2511

PACIFICA, CA

Best Restaurant in Town
Nick's Rockaway
  100 Rockaway Beach Ave., 415/359-3900

Best Brunch
The Moonraker
  105 Rockaway Beach Ave., 415/359-0303

Best Chinese Food
Tam's
  494 Manor Plaza, 415/359-7575

Best Japanese Food
Kani-Kosen
  580 Crespi St., 415/355-1281

Best Other Ethnic Food
El Zocalo (Salvadoran)
  3230 Mission St., 415/282-2572

PALM SPRINGS, CA

Best American Food
Biga, The California Grill
  Atrium Ctr., 69-930 Hwy. 111, Rancho Mirage,
    619/324-4535
Palomino
  73-101 Hwy. 111, Palm Desert, 619/773-9091
Kaiser Grill
  74225 Hwy. 111, Palm Desert, 619/779-1988

Best Chinese Food
Tsing Tao
  74-040 Hwy. 111, Palm Desert, 619/779-9593
Panda Express
  22451 Antonio Pkwy., Rancho Mirage, 714/459-0978
The Dragon Gate
  44491 Town Center Way, Palm Desert, 619/341-6588
Chen Ling
  787 N. Palm Canyon Dr., 619/322-0039
  69600 Hwy. 111, Rancho Mirage, 619/770-0788
Flower Drum
  424 S. Indian Ave., 619/323-3020

Best Continental Food
Blue Coyote Grill
  445 N. Palm Canyon Dr., 619/327-1196
Players Restaurant at Fantasy Springs Casino
  84-245 Indio Springs Dr., Indio, 619/342-5000
Culstot
  73-111 El Paseo, Palm Desert, 619/340-1000
Doug Arango's
  72-695 Hwy. 111, Ste. A-10, Palm Desert,
    619/341-4120

Best Greasy Spoons
Keedy's Fountain Grill
  73-633 Hwy. 111, Palm Desert, 619/346-6492
Louise's Pantry
  124 S. Palm Canyon Dr., 619/325-5124
  44491 Town Center Way, Palm Desert, 619/346-1315
Vern's
  590 S. Vella Rd., 619/325-3514

Best Ice Cream/Yogurt
Goldmine Yogurt
  42-414 Bob Hope Drive, Rancho Mirage,
    619/568-5540
Penguin's Frozen Yogurt
  333 N. Palm Canyon Dr., Ste. 102, 619/327-6455
Icebird Frozen Yogurt
  72795 Hwy. 111, Ste. 95, Palm Desert, 619/341-8200

Best Italian Food
Trilussa
  123 N. Palm Canyon Dr., 619/323-4255

Tuscany's Ristorante
74855 Country Club Dr., Palm Desert, 619/341-2211

Best Outdoor Dining
Le Vallauris
385 Tahquitz Canyon Way, 619/325-5059
Las Casuelas Nuevas
70050 Hwy. 11, Rancho Mirage, 619/328-8844
Cedar Creek Inn
1555 S. Palm Canyon Dr., 619/325-7300

Best Steaks
LG's Steakhouse
74225 Hwy. 111, Palm Desert, 619/779-9799
Morton's of Chicago
74880 Country Club Dr., Palm Desert, 619/340-6865

Standbys
Ruth's Chris Steak House
Hwy. 111 at Portola Ave., Palm Desert, 619/779-1998

PALMDALE, CA

Best Breakfast
Karen's Kitchen
1003 E. Palmdale Blvd., 805/947-1920
840 W. Palmdale Blvd., 805/947-0550

Best Brunch
Marie Callender's
1649 W. Avenue K, Lancaster, 805/945-6958

Best Burgers
Pete's Burgers
2330 E. Palmdale Blvd., 805/266-0353

Best Cheap Meal
El Pollo Loco
2221 E. Palmdale Blvd., 805/265-1615

Best Chinese Food
Lucky Garden Chinese Restaurant
2542 E. Palmdale Blvd., 805/273-7892

Best Coffee
Westerfield's Coffee Shop
300 W. Palmdale Blvd., 805/273-1200

Best Desserts
Marie Callender's
1649 W. Avenue K, Lancaster, 805/945-6958

Best Italian Food
Eduardo's Italian Restaurant
819 W. Palmdale Blvd., 805/273-0955

Best Late-Night Food
Pete's Burgers
2330 E. Palmdale Blvd., 805/266-0353

Best Mexican Food
El Torreo East
3025 E. Avenue S, 805/266-8496

Best Pizza
Round Table Pizza
1823K E. Palmdale Blvd., 805/947-8944

Cafe Fresco
 42010 N. 50th St. W., Quartz Hill, 805/722-5555

Best Romantic Dining
Forty-Niner Saloon
 31908 Crown Valley Rd., Acton, 805/269-1360

Best Seafood
Forty-Niner Saloon
 31908 Crown Valley Rd., Acton, 805/269-1360

Best Steaks
Forty-Niner Saloon
 31908 Crown Valley Rd., Acton, 805/269-1360

Standbys
Old Country Buffet
 422 W. Avenue P, 805/267-6277
Red Lobster
 1041 W. Avenue P, 805/538-9707
The Olive Garden
 1051 W. Avenue P, 805/266-7927
Sizzler
 853 W. Palmdale Blvd., 805/273-4411
Baskin-Robbins
 1800 E. Palmdale Blvd., 805/273-3331
Subway
 1823 E. Palmdale Blvd., 805/947-3888

PALO ALTO, CA

Best Breakfast
Mike's
 2680 Middlefield Rd., 415/473-6453
Hobee's Restaurant
 67 Town and Country Village, 415/327-4111
 4224 El Camino Real, 415/492-7823

Best Brunch
Mike's
 2680 Middlefield Rd., 415/473-6453

Best Burgers
Marie Callender's
 4710 El Camino Real, Los Altos, 415/941-6989

Best Desserts
Max's Opera Cafe
 711 Stanford Shopping Center, 415/323-6297

Best Health-Conscious Menu
Good Earth Restaurant and Bakery
 185 University Ave., 415/321-9449

Best Homestyle Food
Marie Callender's
 4710 El Camino Real, Los Altos, 415/941-6989

Best Ice Cream/Yogurt
Double Rainbow Gourmet
 520 Ramona St., 415/321-7466

Best Italian Food
Piatti's
 2 Stanford Shopping Center, 415/324-9733

Japanese Food
Restaurant
University Ave., 415/323-9449

st Pizza
urphy's Pizza Take and Bake
2730 Middlefield Rd., 415/328-5200

Best Regional Food
Star's
265 Lytton Ave., 415/321-4466

Best Sandwiches
Simply Sandwiches
2435 Ash St., 415/329-1266

Best Seafood
Fish Market Restaurant
3150 El Camino Real, 415/493-9188

Best Thai Food
Bangkok Cuisine
407 Lytton Ave., 415/322-6533

Best Vegetarian Food
Good Earth Restaurant and Bakery
185 University Ave., 415/321-9449

PASADENA, CA

Best Restaurants in Town
Parkway Grill
510 S. Arroyo Pkwy., 818/795-1001
Sesame Grill
308 E. Huntington Dr., Arcadia, 818/821-0880

Best Atmosphere
Raymond Restaurant
1250 S. Fair Oaks Ave., 818/441-3136
Twin Palms
101 W. Green, 818/577-2567

Best Bar
Barney's Limited
93 W. Colorado Blvd., 818/577-2739

Best Breakfast
Marston's Restaurant
151 E. Walnut St., 818/796-2459

Best Burgers
Crocodile Cafe
140 S. Lake Ave., 818/449-9900

Best Casual Dining
Barney's Limited
93 W. Colorado Blvd., 818/577-2739
Dodsworth Bar and Grill
2 W. Colorado Blvd., 818/578-1344

Best Chinese Food
Grandview Palace
590 S. Fair Oaks Ave., 818/449-0348

Best Coffee
Il Fornaio
24 W. Union, 818/683-8585

Best Continental Food
Raymond Restaurant
1250 S. Fair Oaks Ave., 818/441-3136

Best French Food
Twin Palms
101 W. Green, 818/577-2567

Best Health-Conscious Menu
Good Earth Restaurant
257 N. Rosemead Blvd., 818/351-5488

Best Homestyle Food
Marston's Restaurant
151 E. Walnut St., 818/796-2459

Best Italian Food
Mi Piace Italian Kitchen
25 E. Colorado Blvd., 818/795-3131

Best Lunch
Marston's Restaurant
151 E. Walnut St., 818/796-2459

Best Mexican Food
Acapulco Mexican Restaurant
2936 Colorado Blvd., 818/795-4248
2060 E. Foothill Blvd., 818/449-7273

Best Microbrewery
Crown City Brewery
300 S. Raymond Ave., 818/577-5548

Best Other Ethnic Food
Barneys Limited (British Isles cuisine)
93 W. Colorado Blvd., 818/577-2739
Merida Restaurant (Yucatan Peninsula cuisine)
20 E. Colorado Blvd., 818/792-7371
Rose Tree Cottage (British Isles cuisine)
824 E. California Blvd., 818/793-3337

Best Salad/Salad Bar
Kathleen's Restaurant
595 N. Lake Ave., 818/578-0722

Best Sandwiches
Crown City Brewery
300 S. Raymond Ave., 818/577-5548

Best Seafood
Cameron's Seafood Market
1978 E. Colorado Blvd., 818/793-3474
McCormick and Schmick's
111 N. Los Robles Ave., 818/405-0064

Best Steaks
Beckham Place
77 W. Walnut St., 818/796-3399
Dodsworth Bar and Grill
2 W. Colorado Blvd., 818/578-1344

Best Thai Food
Tommy Tang's
24 W. Colorado Blvd., 818/792-9700

Best Vegetarian Food
Good Earth Restaurant
257 N. Rosemead Blvd., 818/351-5488

PETALUMA, CA

...mestyle Food

   Lakeville St., 707/762-9927

...t Indian Food
...am's Cafe
   122 Kentucky St., 707/765-9775

Best Italian Food
Graziano's
   170 Petaluma Blvd. N., 707/762-5997
Volpi's
   122 Washington St., 707/765-0695
Buona Sera
   148 Kentucky St., 707/763-3333

Best Microbrewery
Dempsey's Ale House
   50 E. Washington St., 707/765-9694

Best Seafood
Little Steamer
   54 Washington Blvd., 707/763-6876

Best Wine Selection
De Schmire Restaurant
   304 Bodega Ave., 707/762-1901

PLEASANTON, CA

Best American Food
Wente Brothers Estate Winery and Restaurant
   5050 Arroyo Rd., 501/447-3696

Best Business Dinner
Wente Brothers Estate Winery and Restaurant
   5050 Arroyo Rd., 501/447-3696

Best Delicatessen
Max's Diner, Bakery and Bar
   2015 Crow Canyon Pl., San Ramon, 510/277-9300

Best Greek/Mediterranean Food
Splendido Restaurant
   4 Embarcadero Ctr., San Francisco, 415/986-3222

Best Health-Conscious Menu
Lark Creek Inn
   234 Magnolia Ave., Larkspur, 415/924-7766

Best Italian Food
Suzio Ristorante Italiano
   20400 Lake Chabot Rd., Castro Valley, 510/733-0788

Best Place to Eat When Someone Else Is Buying
Lark Creek Inn
   234 Magnolia Ave., Larkspur, 415/924-7766

Best Salad/Salad Bar
Sweet Tomatoes
   4501 Hopyard Rd., 510/463-9285

Best Sandwiches
Max's Diner, Bakery and Bar
   2015 Crow Canyon Pl., San Ramon, 510/277-9300

Best Seafood
Hayward Fishery Restaurant
7400 San Ramon Rd., Dublin, 510/828-8882

Best Wine Selection
Wente Brothers Estate Winery and Restaurant
5050 Arroyo Rd., 501/447-3696

C

PORTERVILLE, CA

Best American Food
Palace Hotel Dining Room
22 E. Oak Ave., 209/784-7086

Best Barbecue/Ribs
Oak Pit
615 N. Main St., 209/781-7427

Best Breakfast
Green Valley Cafe
450 W. Olive Ave., 209/783-0747

Best Cheap Meal
Cellar
244 1/2 N. Main St., 209/784-4235

Best Ice Cream/Yogurt
Ginger's Corner Store
1170 W. Henderson Ave., 209/784-6386

Best Italian Food
Rosa's Italian Restaurant
949 W. Henderson Ave., 209/781-6423

Best Mexican Food
El Nuevo Mexicalli
370 N. Main St., 209/781-1742
Mission Restaurant
247 N. Main St., 209/781-8814
El Tapatillo Restaurant
134 E. Orange Ave., 209/781-2115

Best Pizza
Poor Richard's Pizza
205 N. Main St., 209/784-4410

Best Salad/Salad Bar
Palace Hotel Dining Room
22 E. Oak Ave., 209/784-7086

Best Sandwiches
Palace Hotel Dining Room
22 E. Oak Ave., 209/784-7086

Best Seafood
Fish Net
210 N. Main St., 209/784-2226

Best Steaks
Cellar
244 1/2 N. Main St., 209/784-4235
Oak Pit
615 N. Main St., 209/781-7427

REDWOOD CITY, CA

Best Restaurant in Town
The Plantation Deli Cafe
   865 El Camino Real, Menlo Park, 415/854-2327

Best Bar
Los Altos Bar and Grille
   169 Main St., 415/948-4332

Best Brunch
Holiday Inn
   625 El Camino Real, Palo Alto, 415/328-2800

Best Burgers
Donovan's
   1450 Veterans Blvd., 415/361-9702

Best Business Lunch
Dal Baffo European Cuisine
   878 Santa Cruz Ave., Menlo Park, 415/325-1588

Best Chinese Food
Speedy's Broasted Chicken
   756 Woodside Rd., 415/369-3767

Best Family Restaurant
Fifth Quarter Pizza
   976 Woodside Rd., 415/369-2686

Best French Food
Dante's on Woodside
   1515 Woodside Rd., 415/363-0949

Best Health-Conscious Menu
Fresh Choice
   600 Santa Cruz Ave., Menlo Park, 415/323-4061
   379 Stanford Shopping Ctr., Palo Alto, 415/322-6995
   1952 El Camino Real, San Mateo, 415/341-8498

Best Italian Food
Messina's Italian Restaurant
   542 El Camino Real, 415/593-9116
Piacere Restaurant
   727 Laurel St., San Carlos, 415/592-3536
Lucia's
   1725 Woodside Rd., 415/365-3812

Best Late-Night Food
Charlie Brown's
   451 Seaport Ct., 415/364-2848

Best Mexican Food
La Azteca
   1531 Main St., 415/368-3486

Best Pizza
Round Table Pizza
   128 Woodside Plz., 415/365-2770
   1483 Broadway St., 415/365-7226

Best Place to Eat Alone
Happi House Restaurant
   30 Woodside Rd., 415/368-3306

Best Salad/Salad Bar
Fresh Choice
   600 Santa Cruz Ave., Menlo Park, 415/323-4061

379 Stanford Shopping Ctr., Palo Alto, 415/322-6995
1952 El Camino Real, San Mateo, 415/341-8498

Best Sandwiches
Erik's Deli Cafe
400C Walnut St., 415/364-1717

Best Seafood
Scott's Seafood Grill and Bar
2300 E. Bayshore Rd., Palo Alto, 415/856-1046

Best Sports Bar
Sneakers Pub and Grill
1163 San Carlos Ave., 415/802-0177

Standbys
Baskin-Robbins
2107 Roosevelt Ave., 415/365-0331
Sizzler
1011 Veterans Blvd., 415/368-1904

RICHMOND, CA

Best Barbecue/Ribs
Ernie Foods Bar-B-Q
2401 MacDonald Ave., 510/237-2346

Best Breakfast
Baker's Square Restaurant
12323 San Pablo Ave., 510/232-6350

Best Brunch
Hotel Mac Restaurant
50 Washington Ave., 510/233-0576

Best Burgers
Nation's Foodservice
1100 23rd St., 510/234-1445

Best Coffee
Rosemary Bakery
101 Park Pl., 510/234-2384
Bear Claw Bakery
2340 San Pablo Ave., Pinole, 510/724-3105

Best Desserts
Salute
1900 Esplanade, 510/215-0803
Hotel Mac Restaurant
50 Washington Ave., 510/233-0576

Best Italian Food
Angelo's Poultry and Deli
12025 San Pablo Ave., 510/234-2485
Salute
1900 Esplanade, 510/215-0803

Best Korean Food
Cafe Annie
130 Washington Ave., 510/237-7585

Best Regional Food
Hidden City Cafe
109 Park Pl., 510/232-9738

Best Sandwiches
Angelo's Poultry and Deli
12025 San Pablo Ave., 510/234-2485

Cafe Annie
130 Washington Ave., 510/237-7585

Best Seafood
Salute
1900 Esplanade, 510/215-0803
Hotel Mac Restaurant
50 Washington Ave., 510/233-0576

Best Steaks
Hotel Mac Restaurant
50 Washington Ave., 510/233-0576

RIDGECREST, CA

Best Chinese Food
China Garden
206 S. China Lake Blvd., 619/375-3533

Best Coffeehouse
Casa Java
972 N. Norma St., 619/446-9161

Best Mexican Food
La Fiesta Sandwiches and Things
119 N. China Lake Blvd., 619/375-5901
Santa Fe Grill
901 N. Heritage Dr., 619/446-5404

Best Sandwiches
Blimpie's
1028 N. Norma St., 619/446-6969

RIVERSIDE, CA

Best American Food
Brittany's
12125 Day St., Canyon Springs Plz., Moreno Valley,
909/885-9177
CJ's Restaurant
Holiday Inn, 3400 Market St., 909/784-8000
Casual Elegance
26848 Hwy. 189, Aqua Fria, San Bernadino National
Forest, 909/337-8932
Coachman Dinner House
1805 University Ave., 909/788-0310
Creola's Restaurant
1015 Alessandro Blvd., 909/653-8150
Mission Inn
3649 Seventh St., 909/784-0300
Mrs. Knott's
12625 Frederick St., Moreno Valley, 909/697-4480
New York Deli
12190 Perris Blvd., Moreno Valley, 909/924-4910
Riverside Brewing Company
3397 Seventh St., 909/784-2739
Sire Bar and Grill
10909 Magnolia Ave., 909/358-0570
Steer Grill
2395 Hamner Ave., Norco, 909/734-5441

Best Burgers
In-N-Out Burger
Multiple Locations

Best Cajun/Creole Food
Crescent City Creole
  5250 Arlington Ave., 909/351-6934

Best Desserts
Coco's Restaurant
  309 E. Foothill Blvd., Pomona, 909/596-5909

Best Indian Food
Bengal Kitchen
  3375 Iowa Ave., 909/784-3811

Best Italian Food
Marino's Pasta House
  31361 Riverside Dr., Lake Elsinore, 909/674-5657
Villa Amalfi
  1237 W. Sixth St., Corona, 909/278-3393
Rillo's Restaurant
  510 E. Foothill Blvd., Pomona, 909/621-4954

Best Japanese Food
Akina Sushi-Teppan
  195 E. Alessandro Blvd., 909/789 2621
Matsuri Japanese Restaurant
  25100E Alessandro Blvd., Moreno Valley,
    909/247-0767

Best Mexican Food
Amapola Cafe
  23750 Alessandro Blvd., Moreno Valley, 909/653-8464
The Live Oak Inn
  21700 Temescal Canyon Rd., Corona, 909/277-0605
Tempio del Sol
  1365 University Ave., 909/682-6562
Zacatecas Cafe
  2472 University Ave., 909/683-3939

Best Other Ethnic Food
Banig Restaurant (Filipino)
  23962 Alessandro Blvd., Moreno Valley, 909/653-5268
Nipa Hut (Filipino)
  14420 Elsworth St., Moreno Valley, 909/653-1729

Best Place to Eat When Someone Else Is Buying
Rillo's Restaurant
  510 E. Foothill Blvd., Pomona, 909/621-4954

Best Thai Food
Pattaya Palace
  24050 Alessandro Blvd., Ste. 8, Moreno Valley,
    909/242-3189
River Kwai Thai Cuisine
  22920 Alessandro Blvd., Moreno Valley, 909/656-3355
Thai Ice Tea
  7207F Arlington Ave., 909/687-2270

SACRAMENTO, CA

Best Restaurants in Town
Harlow's Bar and Restaurant
  2708 J St., 916/441-4693
Lemon Grass Restaurant
  601 Monroe St., 916/486-4891

Paragary's Bar and Oven
  1401 28th St., 916/457-5737
  2384 Fair Oaks Blvd., 916/485-7100
Ristorante Piatti
  569 Pavilions Ln., 916/649-8885

Best Barbecue/Ribs
Great Wall Bar-B-Q
  1537 Howe Ave., 916/925-5347
Texas Bar-B-Que
  180 Otto Circle, 916/424-3520

Best Breakfast
Cafe Bernardo
  2726 Capitol Ave., 916/443-1180
Fox and Goose
  1001 R St., 916/443-8825
Lucky Cafe
  1111 21st St., 916/442-9620
Land Park Grill
  1517 Broadway, 916/552-2893

Best Brunch
Ciao-Yama
  Hyatt Regency Hotel, 1209 L St., 916/443-1234
Maxi's: An American Cafe
  Red Lion Hotel, 2001 Point West Way, 916/929-8855
Pilothouse Restaurant [on the Delta King]
  1000 Front St., 916/441-4440
The Palm Court
  Radisson Hotel, 500 Leisure Ln., 916/922-2020

Best Burgers
Ford's Real Hamburgers
  1948 Sutterville Rd., 916/452-6979
Murder Burger
  978 Olwe Dr., 916/756-2142
Willie's Burgers and Chiliburgers
  2415 Sixteenth St., 916/444-2006

Best Business Lunch
Delta King
  1000 Front St., 916/441-4440
Land Park Grill
  1517 Broadway, 916/552-2893
Paragary's Bar and Oven
  1401 28th St., 916/457-5737
  2384 Fair Oaks Blvd., 916/485-7100

Best Cheap Meal
Pescado's
  2801 P St., 916/452-7237
Taqueria Taco Loco
  2326 J St., 916/447-0711

Best Chinese Food
Chinois City Cafe
  12251 Folsom Blvd., Rancho Cordova, 916/351-1949
Frank Fat's
  806 L St., 916/442-7092
Hoi Sing Chinese Sea Food Restaurant
  7007 S. Land Park Dr., 916/392-9630

C

Tea Cup Cafe
  1614 21st St., 916/448-6212
Great Wall Mongolian Bar-B-Q
  1537 Howe Ave., 916/925-7813
  4314 Florin Rd., 916/427-8888
Luau Garden
  1890 Arden Way, 916/929-3690

Best Coffeehouses
Java City
  Multiple Locations
La Bou
  Multiple Locations
Lyon's
  Multiple Locations
Delta of Venus
  122 B St., Davis, 916/753-8639

Best Delicatessens
Corti Brothers
  5810 Folsom Blvd., 916/736-3800
Togo's Eatery
  Multiple Locations

Best Desserts
European Bakery: Caffe Ettore
  2376 Fair Oaks Blvd., 916/482-0708
Leatherby's Family Creamery
  2333A Arden Way, 916/920-8382
Rick's Dessert Diner
  2322 K St., 916/444-0969

Best Diners
Artie's Star-Lite Fountain
  3839 J St., 916/454-4555
Huey's Diner
  2100 Arden Way, 916/929-1950

Best French Food
Aldo's
  2914 Pasatiempo Ln., 916/483-5031
Cafe La Salle
  1028 Second St., 916/442-4775
La Boheme
  1001 K St., 916/443-7336

Best Happy Hour Snacks
Bobby McGee's
  5623 Sunrise Blvd., Citrus Heights, 916/966-1364
El Torito Restaurant and Cantina
  1212 Howe Ave., 916/924-1000
  1598 Arden Way, 916/927-0071
Peppermill Restaurant and Lounge
  1500 Arden Way, 916/929-4014

Best Homestyle Food
Good Earth Restaurant
  2024 Arden Way, 916/920-5544
Lucky Cafe
  1111 21st Ave., 916/442-9620
Sam's Kosher-Style Restaurant and Deli
  8121 Greenback Ln., Fair Oaks, 916/726-7267

Silva's Sheldon Inn
9000 Grant Line Rd., Elkgrove, 916/686-8330

Best Ice Cream/Yogurt
Leatherby's Family Creamery
2333A Arden Way, 916/920-8382

Best Italian Food
Amerigo
2000 Capital Ave., 916/442-8119
Biba
2801 Capital Ave., 916/455-2422
Old Spaghetti Factory
1910 J St., 916/443-2862

Best Japanese Food
Fuji
2422 Thirteenth St., 916/446-4135
Hana Tsubaki
5006 J St., 916/456-2849
Mikuni Japanese Restaurant
4323 Hazel Ave., Fair Oaks, 916/961-2112

Best Mexican Food
Carmelita's Mexican Restaurant
4071 Howard St., Fair Oaks, 916/961-3327
1234 Howe Ave., 916/923-6574
1369 Garden Hwy., 916/649-0390
7778 La Mancha Way, 916/688-8455
Ernesto's Mexican Food
1901 Sixteenth St., 916/441-5850
El Novillero
4216 Franklin Blvd., 916/456-4287
El Torito Mexican Restaurant and Cantina
1212 Howe Ave., 916/924-1000
1598 Arden Way, 916/927-0071

Best New Restaurants
Bravo
2333 Fair Oaks Blvd., 916/568-0494
Cafe Bernardo
2726 Capitol Ave., 916/443-1180
Il Fornaio Gastronomia
400 Capitol Mall, 916/446-4100

Best Outdoor Dining
Delta King
1000 Front St., 916/441-4440
Tower International Cafe
1518 Broadway, 916/441-0222
Bernice's Cookery
5132 Arden Way, Carmichael, 916/484-6632
Jammin' Salmon
1801 Garden Hwy., 916/929-6232

Best Pizza
Original Pete's Pizza
Multiple Locations
Paragary's Bar and Oven
1401 28th St., 916/457-5737
2384 Fair Oaks Blvd., 916/485-7100
Zelda's Original Gourmet Pizza
1415 21st St., 916/447-1400

Best Places to Eat When Someone Else Is Buying
Biba Restaurant
  2801 Capitol Ave., 916/455-2422
Firehouse
  1112 Second St., 916/442-4772
Morton's of Chicago
  521 L St., 916/442-5091

Best Romantic Dining
Aldo's Restaurant
  2673 El Paseo Ln., 916/483-5031
  2914 Pasatiempo Ln., 916/483-5031
John Q's
  300 J St., 916/446-0100
Mace's Restaurant
  501 Pavilions Ln., 916/922-0222
Cliff House of Folsom
  9900 Greenback Ln., Folsom, 916/989-9243
Delta King
  1000 Front St., 916/441-4440
Slocum House
  7992 California Ave., Fair Oaks, 916/961-7211

Best Salad/Salad Bar
Eat Your Vegetables
  1841 Howe Ave., 916/922-8413
Fresh Choice
  1689 Arden Way, 916/649-3839
  535 Howe Ave., 916/649-8046

Best Seafood
The Fish Restaurant
  2310 Fair Oaks Blvd., 916/927-3474
Scott's Seafood Grill and Bar
  545 Monroe St., 916/489-1822
Delta King
  1000 Front St., 916/441-4440

Best Steaks
Fulton's Prime Rib
  900 Second St., 916/444-9641
Morton's of Chicago
  521 L St., 916/442-5091
Stuart Anderson's Black Angus
  1625 Watt Ave., 916/973-1901
  6601 Florin Rd., 916/381-4900
Cattlemen's
  12409 Folsom Blvd., Rancho Cordova, 916/985-3030
  2000 Taylor Rd., Roseville, 916/782-5587

Best Sushi
Fuji
  2422 Thirteenth St., 916/446-4135
Shige Sushi
  1608 Howe Ave., 916/929-1184
Sushi-Sei Japanese Restaurant
  2372 Fair Oaks Blvd., 916/971-1222

Best Thai Food
Lemon Grass
  601 Monroe St., 916/486-4891

Siam
5100 Franklin Blvd., 916/452-8382
Thai Palms
943 Howe Ave., 916/929-5915
Sorn Daeng Buffet and Cuisine
1537 Howe Ave., 916/929-8470

Best View While Dining
Crawdad's River Cantina
1375 Garden Hwy., 916/929-2268
Jammin' Salmon
1801 Garden Hwy., 916/929-6232
Pilothouse Restaurant [on the Delta King]
1000 Front St., 916/441-4440

Best Vegetarian Food
Eat Your Vegetables
1841 Howe Ave., 916/922-8413
Fresh Choice
1689 Arden Way, 916/649-3839
535 Howe Ave., 916/649-8046
Mum's Vegetarian
2968 Freeport Blvd., 916/444-3015

Best Wine Selection
Aldo's Restaurant
2673 El Paseo Ln., 916/483-5031
2914 Pasatiempo Ln., 916/483-5031
Biba
2801 Capitol Ave., 916/455-2422
Mace's Restaurant
501 Pavilions Ln., 916/922-0222
Terrace Grill
544 Pavilions Ln., 916/920-3800

Standbys
Chevy's
1234 Howe Ave., 916/923-6574
1369 Garden Hwy., 916/649-0390
7778 La Mancha Way, 916/688-8455

SALINAS, CA

Best American Food
Giant Artichoke Restaurant
11261 Merritt St., Castroville, 408/633-3204

Best Atmosphere
Steinbeck House
132 Central Ave., 408/424-2735
La Scuola
10700 Merritt St., Castroville, 408/633-2111

Best Barbecue/Ribs
Big Joe's BBQ
1104 S. Main St., 408/422-4213

Best Dinner
Steinbeck House
132 Central Ave., 408/424-2735
La Scuola
10700 Merritt St., Castroville, 408/633-2111

Best Homestyle Food
Steinbeck House
132 Central Ave., 408/424-2735

Best Italian Food
La Scuola
10700 Merritt St., Castroville, 408/633-2111

C

Best Mexican Food
Chapala Restaurant
438 Salinas St., 408/757-4959
Cozumel Mexican Restaurant
1447 N. Main St., 408/442-2854
El Charrito Taqueria and Grill
607 N. Sanborn Rd., 408/424-4092
El Pollo Dorado
701 E. Alisal St., 408/424-5444
Gutierrez and Rico Drive-In
61 Sherwood Dr., 408/424-8382
Mi Tierra Restaurant
18 E. Gabilan St., 408/422-4631

Best Restaurant Meal Value
Steinbeck House
132 Central Ave., 408/424-2735

Best Seafood
Fishwife Seafood Restaurant
1996 1/2 Sunset Dr., Pacific Grove, 408/375-7107

SAN ANSELMO, CA

Best Chinese Food
Maylee's Chinese Restaurant
115 San Anselmo Ave., 415/455-9988

Best Eclectic Menu
Comforts
337 San Anselmo Ave., 415/454-6790

Best Health-Conscious Menu
Comforts
337 San Anselmo Ave., 415/454-6790

Best Mexican Food
Las Camelias
912 Lincoln Ave., 415/453-5850

Best New Restaurant
New Moon Cafe
706 San Anselmo Ave., 415/459-4151

Best Pizza
Lococo's
638 San Anselmo Ave., 415/453-123

Best Place to Eat Alone
Bubba's Diner
566 San Anselmo Ave., 415/459-6862

Best Thai Food
Orchid
726 San Anselmo Ave., 415/457-9470

Standbys
TCBY
754 Sir Francis Drake Blvd., 415/453-6525

SAN BERNARDINO, CA

Best American Food
Clara's
101 E. Redlands Blvd., 909/335-1466
Bobby Ray's Bar-B-Que
1657 Baseline St., 619/324-4535
Greensleeves
220 N. Orange St., Redlands, 909/792-6969

Best Bagels
Bagel Peddler
1150 Brookside Ave., 909/792-1399

Best Bar
Celebrities
3993 N. Sierra Way, 909/882-9144

Best Breakfast
D.J. Coffee Shop
265 E. 40th St., 909/882-3917
Bagel Peddler
1150 Brookside Ave., 909/792-1399

Best Burgers
Celebrities
3993 N. Sierra Way, 909/882-9144

Best Business Lunch
Bon Appetito Restaurant
246 E. Base Line St., 909/884-5054
Isabella's
201 N. E St., 909/884-2534

Best Continental Food
Clara's
101 E. Redlands Blvd., Redlands, 909/335-1466
The Wild Rabbit
1502 Barton Rd., Redlands, 909/793-2038

Best Dinner
Clara's
101 E. Redlands Blvd., 909/335-1466

Best French Food
Le Rendezvous Restaurant
4775 N. Sierra Way, 909/883-1231
Gigi et Jean
1001 Park Ave., Redlands, 909/793-3714

Best German Food
Gazzolo's European Restaurant and Deli
132 E. Highland Ave., 909/886-3213

Best Homestyle Food
Celebrities
3993 N. Sierra Way, 909/882-9144

Best Ice Cream/Yogurt
Fosdick's Grinders and Ice Cream
3970 N. Sierra Way, 909/882-0523

Best Italian Food
Alfredo's Pizza and Restaurant
251 W. Base Line St., 909/885-0218
Bambino's Restaurant
27208 E. Baseline, Highland, 909/864-6292

Isabella's Ristorante Italiano
201 N. E St., 909/884-2534

Best Mexican Food
Nena's Restaurant
642 N. D St., 909/885-4161
Rosa Maria Drive-In
4202 N. Sierra Way, 909/881-1731
Su Casa
1566 E. Highland Ave., 909/883-4640

Best Middle Eastern Food
Caprice Cafe
104 E. State St., Redlands, 909/793-8787

Best Other Ethnic Food
Bambino's (Argentinian)
27208 Base Line St., Highland, 909/864-6292

Best Pizza
Alfredo's Pizza and Restaurant
251 W. Base Line St., 909/885-0218

Best Sandwiches
Fosdick's Grinders and Ice Cream
3970 N. Sierra Way, 909/882-0523

Best Steaks
Black Angus Restaurant
290 E. Hospitality Ln., 909/885-7551

SAN CLEMENTE, CA

Best Restaurant in Town
Bootlegger
11 Avenida Palizada, 714/366-6700

Best American Food
Antoine's Cafe
218 S. El Camino Real, 714/492-1763

Best Chinese Food
New Mandarin Garden
111 W. Avenida Palizada, 714/492-7432
Eastern Wind
201 N. El Camino Real, 714/492-3008

Best French Food
Etienne's French Restaurant
215 S. El Camino Real, 714/492-7263

Best Mexican Food
El Mirador
301 N. El Camino Rd., 714/366-0855

Best Seafood
The Fisherman
611 Avenida Victoria, 714/498-6390

Best Thai Food
Mongkut Thai
212 Avenida Del Mar, 714/492-3871

SAN DIEGO, CA

Best Restaurants in Town
Lamont Street Grill
4445 Lamont St., 619/270-3060

Top O' the Cove
    1216 Prospect St., 619/233-5757
Brigantine Restaurant
    2444 San Diego Ave., 619/298-9840
    2725 Shelter Island Dr., 619/224-2871
    3990 Old Town Ave., Ste. 207C, 619/299-5804
Belgian Lion
    2265 Bacon St., 619/223-2700
Mille Fleurs
    6009 Paseo Delicias Rancho, Santa Fe, 619/756-3085

Best American Food
Bread Basket
    1471 E. Plaza Blvd., 619/474-1821
    1347 Tavern Rd., 619/445-0706

Best Atmosphere
Corvette Diner Bar and Grill
    3946 Fifth Ave., 619/542-1001

Best Bars
Piatti
    2182 Avenita de La Playa, La Jolla, 619/454-1589
Triangles
    4370 La Jolla Village Dr., 619/453-6650
The Whaling Bar at La Valencia
    1132 Prospect St., La Jolla, 619/454-0771
Karl Strauss Brewery Gardens
    9675 Scranton Rd., 619/587-2739
    1167 Columbia St., 619/234-2739

Best Barbecue/Ribs
Kansas City Barbecue
    610 W. Market, 619/231-9680
Buffalo Joe's
    600 Fifth Ave., 619/236-1616

Best Breakfast
Hob Nob Hill
    2271 First Ave., 619/239-8176
La Valencia
    1132 Prospect St., La Jolla, 619/454-0771
Harry's La Jolla
    7545 Girard Ave., La Jolla, 619/454-7381
Original Pancake House
    3906 Convoy St., Clairemont, 619/565-1740

Best Brunch
The Grill
    Wyndham Hotel, 402 W. Broadway, 619/239-4500
Rancho Valencia
    5921 Valencia Circle, Rancho Santa Fe, 619/756-3645
Catamaran
    Hilton Hotel, 1775 E. Mission Bay Dr., 619/276-4010

Best Burgers
Grant Grill
    326 Broadway, 619/239-6806
Bully's
    2401 Camino Del Rio S., 619/291-2665
T-Bird Diner
    601 N. Broadway, Escondido, 619/480-2473

Best Business Lunch
Cindy Black's
5721 La Jolla Blvd., La Jolla, 619/456-6299
University Club
750 B St., 34th Fl., 619/234-5200
Dakota Grill and Spirits
901 Fifth Ave., 619/234-5554
Rainwater's on Kettner
1202 Kettner Blvd., 619/233-5757

Best Cheap Meal
The Bread Basket
1471 E. Plaza Blvd., 619/474-1821
1347 Tavern Rd., 619/445-0706
Come On In
1030 Torrey Pines Rd., 619/551-1063
Lorna's
3945 Governor Dr., 619/452-0661
Osteria Panevino
722 Fifth Ave., 619/595-7959

Best Chinese Food
Emerald Chinese Seafood
3709 Convoy St., Ste. 101, 619/565-6888
Ming's Court
12750 Carmel Country Rd., 619/793-2933
Fortune Cookie
16425 Bernardo Center Dr., 619/451-8958
Mandarin House
2604 Fifth Ave., 619/232-1101
Panda Inn
506 Horton Plaza, 619/233-7800

Best Coffeehouses
Pannikin
7467 Girard Ave., La Jolla, 619/454-5453
XpreZZo's
15717 Bernardo Hts. Pkwy., Rancho Bernardo,
619/485-8055
Wall Street Cafe
1044 Wall St., La Jolla, 619/551-1044

Best Delicatessens
D.Z. Akin's
6930 Alvarado Rd., 619/265-0218
Samson's
501 W. Broadway, 619/232-2340
Submarina
3225 Sports Arena Blvd., 619/523-1053
12396 World Trade Dr., Ste. 214, 619/675-0155

Best Desserts
El Bizcocho
17550 Bernardo Oaks Dr., 619/487-1611
Cafe Pacifica
2414 San Diego Ave., Old Town, 619/291-6666
Karen Krasne's Extraordinary Desserts
2929 Fifth Ave., 619/294-7001
D.Z. Akin's
6930 Alvarado Rd., 619/265-0218

C

Sweetlips
8980 University Center Ln., 619/587-4600

Best Diner
Chicken Pie Diner
14727 Pomerado Rd., 619/748-2445

Best Eclectic Menu
Marrakesh Restaurant
756 Fifth Ave., 619/231-8353

Best French Food
Mille Fleurs
6009 Paseo Delicias, Rancho Santa Fe, 619/756-3085
Cindy Black's
5721 La Jolla Blvd., La Jolla, 619/456-6299

Best German Food
Kaiserhof
2253 Sunset Cliffs Blvd., 619/224-0606
Alpine Haus
2282 Carmel Valley Rd., Del Mar, 619/259-2006
Ingrid's
1520 Garnet Ave., 619/270-4250
House of Munich Restaurant
230 Third Ave., Chula Vista, 619/426-5172

Best Greek/Mediterranean Food
Aladdin
5420 Claremont Mesa Blvd., 619/573-0000
Athens Market
Senator Hotel, 109 W. F St., 619/234-1955
Aesop's Tables
Costa Verde Center, 8650 Genesee, La Jolla,
619/455-1535

Best Health-Conscious Menu
Greek Corner Restaurant
5841 El Cajon Blvd., 619/287-3303
13185 Black Mountain Rd., 619/484-9197
Daily's Restaurant
8915 Towne Centre Dr., 619/453-1112
Kung Food Vegetarian Restaurant
2949 Fifth Ave., 619/298-7302

Best Homestyle Food
The Bread Basket
1471 E. Plaza Blvd., 619/474-1821
1347 Tavern Rd., 619/445-0706

Best Indian Food
Ashoka Cuisine of India
8008 Girard Ave., Second Fl., La Jolla, 619/454-6263
Passage to India
13185 Black Mountain Rd., 619/484-9688
Star of India
1492 N. Harbor Dr., 619/234-9153
423 F St., 619/544-9891

Best Italian Food
La Strada
702 Fifth Ave., 619/239-3400
Salvatore's Cucina Italiana
750 Front St., 619/544-1865

Fio's Cucina Italiana
    801 Fifth Ave., 619/234-3467

Best Japanese Food
Nobu
    315 S. Hwy. 101, 619/755-7787
Samurai
    979 Lomas Santa Fe Dr., Solana Beach, 619/481-0032
Cafe Japengo
    3787 La Jolla Village Dr., 619/450-3355

Best Late-Night Food
Dobson's
    956 Broadway Circle, 619/231-6771
Croce's
    802 Fifth Ave., 619/233-4355
Saska's
    3768 Mission Blvd., 619/488-7311

Best Mexican Food
La Fonda Roberto's
    300 Third Ave., Chula Vista, 619/585-3017
Casa de Bandini
    2660 Calhoun St., 619/297-8211
Old Town Mexican Cafe
    2489 San Diego Ave., 619/297-4330
Marietta's Restaurant
    1746 E. Main St., El Cajon, 619/442-6671
    8949 La Mesa Blvd., La Mesa, 619/462-3500
    1020 W. San Marcos Blvd., San Marcos, 619/752-1765
    8915 Carlton Hills Blvd., Santee, 619/449-2365

Best Microbrewery
Hops! Bistro and Brewery
    University Town Center Mall, 4545 La Jolla
        Village Dr., Ste. E-25, La Jolla, 619/587-6677
La Jolla Brewing Company
    7536 Fay Ave., 619/456-2739
Brewski's Gaslamp Pub, Bistro and Brewery
    310 Fifth Ave., La Jolla, 619/231-7700
Karl Strauss' Old Columbia Brewery and Grill
    1157 Columbia St., La Jolla, 619/234-2739

Best Middle Eastern Food
Marrakesh Restaurant
    756 Fifth Ave., 619/231-8353

Best New Restaurants
Bella Luna
    748 Fifth Ave., 619/239-3222
Come On In
    1030 Torrey Pines Rd., La Jolla, 619/551-1063
Jasmine
    4609 Convoy St., 619/268-0888
Dakota Grill and Spirits
    901 Fifth Ave., 619/234-5554
Trattoria Acqua
    1298 Prospect, La Jolla, 619/454-0709

Best Outdoor Dining
Jake's Del Mar
    1660 Coast Blvd., Del Mar, 619/755-2002

Osteria Panevino
  722 Fifth Ave., 619/595-7959
George's Terrace
  1250 Prospect St., La Jolla, 619/454-4244

Best Pizza
Sammy's California Woodfired Pizza
  702 Pearl St., La Jolla, 619/456-5222
Pizza Nova
  5120 N. Harbor Dr., 619/226-0268
  8650 Genesee Ave., 619/458-9525
Oscar's
  12045 Carmel Mountain Rd., 619/592-0222

Best Places to Eat When Someone Else Is Buying
Mille Fleurs
  6009 Paseo Delicias, Rancho Santa Fe, 619/756-3085
Marius
  Le Meridian Hotel, 2000 Second St., Coronado,
    619/435-3000
George's at the Cove
  1250 Prospect St., La Jolla, 619/454-4244
Crab Catcher
  1298 Prospect St., 619/454-9587

Best Places to Take the Kids
Casa de Bandini
  2660 Calhoun St., 619/297-8211
Corvette Diner Bar and Grill
  3946 Fifth Ave., 619/542-1001
Hard Rock Cafe
  909 Prospect St., La Jolla, 619/454-5101

Best Quick-Dinner-Before-the-Movie
Chicken Pie Diner
  14727 Pomerado Rd., 619/748-2445

Best Romantic Dining
Mille Fleurs
  6009 Paseo Delicias, Rancho Santa Fe, 619/756-3085
The Sky Room at La Valencia
  1132 Prospect St., La Jolla, 619/454-0771
Top o' The Cove
  1216 Prospect St., La Jolla, 619/454-7779
Marine Room
  2000 Spindrift Dr., La Jolla, 619/459-7222
Lamont Street Grill
  4445 Lamont St., 619/270-3060

Best Salad/Salad Bar
Souplantation
  8105 Mira Mesa Blvd., 619/566-1172
  6171 Mission Gorge Rd., 619/280-7087
  3960 Westpoint Loma Blvd., 619/222-7404

Best Sandwiches
Submarina
  3225 Sports Arena Blvd., 619/523-1053
  12396 World Trade Dr., Ste. 214, 619/675-0155

Best Schmooze Bar
Banx
  2828 Camino Del Rio S., 619/299-6666

Best Seafood
Point Loma Seafoods
2805 Emerson St., 619/223-1109
Top of the Market
750 N. Harbor Dr., 619/232-3474
Anthony's
555 Harbor Ln., 619/232-2933
1360 N. Harbor Dr., 619/232-5103
The Fish Market
750 N. Harbor Dr., 619/232-3474
Crab Catcher
1298 Prospect St., 619/454-9587

Best Southwestern Food
Marietta's
1746 E. Main St., El Cajon, 619/442-6671
8949 La Mesa Blvd., La Mesa, 619/462-3500
1020 W. San Marcos Blvd., San Marcos, 619/752-1765
8915 Carlton Hills Blvd., Santee, 619/449-2365

Best Spanish Food
La Gran Tapa
611 B St., 619/234-8272
Tapas Picasso
3923 Fourth Ave., 619/294-3061
Cafe Sevilla
555 Fourth Ave., 619/233-5979

Best Sports Bars
La Jolla Brewing Company
7536 Fay Ave., 619/456-2739
Trophy's Sports Grill
7510 Hazard Center Dr., Ste. 215, 619/286-9600
Sports Cafe
15817 Bernardo Center Dr., 619/487-0224

Best Steaks
Kelly's
Town and Country Hotel, 500 Hotel Circle N.,
619/291-7131
Rainwater's on Kettner
1202 Kettner Blvd., 619/233-5757
Chart House
2760 Shelter Island Dr., 619/22-2216
525 E. Harbor Dr., 619/233-7391

Best Sushi
Cafe Japengo
3787 La Jolla Village Dr., 619/450-3355
Sushi Ota
4529 Mission Bay Dr., 619/270-5670
The Fish Market
750 N. Harbor Dr., 619/232-3474

Best Thai Food
Saffron
3731 India St., 619/574-0177
Thai Spices Cafe
3810 Valley Center Dr., Del Mar, 619/259-0889
Taste of Thai
527 University Ave., 619/291-7525

C

Best Undiscovered Restaurant
The Bread Basket
 1471 E. Plaza Blvd., 619/474-1821
 1347 Tavern Rd., 619/445-0706

Best Vegetarian Food
Kung Food
 2949 Fifth Ave., 619/298-7302
Monsoon
 3975 Fifth Ave., 619/298-3155

Best View While Dining
George's at the Cove
 1250 Prospect St., La Jolla, 619/454-4244
Top o' the Cove
 1216 Prospect St., La Jolla, 619/454-7779
Mr. A's
 2550 Fifth Ave., 619/239-1377

Best Wine Selection
The WineSellar and Brasserie
 9550 Waples St., Ste. 115, 619/450-9576
Elario's Restaurant
 7955 La Jolla Shores Dr., Eleventh Fl., 619/459-0541
Marius
 Le Meridian Hotel, 2000 Second St., Coronado,
  619/435-3000

SAN FRANCISCO, CA

Best Restaurants in Town
Alain Rondelli
 126 Clement St., 415/387-0408
Postrio Restaurant
 545 Post St., 415/776-7825

Best American Food
Stars Restaurant
 555 Golden Gate Ave., 415/861-4344
 150 Redwood St., 415/431-2716

Best Atmosphere
Kan Zaman
 1793 Haight, 415/751-9656

Best Beer Selection
Jack's
 Multiple Locations

Best Bistro
Fringale
 570 Fourth St., 415/543-0573

Best Breakfast
Mama's Girl
 1701 Stockton St., 415/362-6421
Kate's Kitchen
 471 Haight, 415/626-3984
Campton Place Restaurant
 340 Stockton St., 415/955-5555

Best Brunch
Kate's Kitchen
 471 Haight, 415/626-3984

The Ritz-Carlton
   600 Stockton St., 415/296-7465

Best Burgers
Barney's Hamburgers
   4138 24th St., 415/282-7770
Hamburger Mary's
   1582 Folsom, 415/626-1985

Best Cheap Meal
Ti Couz Creperie
   3108 Sixteenth St., 415/252-7373
Cafe O'Shea's
   3854 Geary Blvd., 415/379-9077
Caffe Delle Stelle
   330 Gough St., 415/252-1110
Timo's
   842 Valencia St., 415/647-0558
Baker Street Bistro
   2953 Baker St., 415/931-1475

Best Chinese Food
House of Nanking
   919 Kearny, 415/421-1429
Hong Kong Flower Lounge Restaurant
   5322 Geary Blvd., 415/668-8998
Wu Kong Restaurant
   101 Spear St., 415/957-9300
Yank Sing Restaurant
   427 Battery St., 415/781-1111
   49 Stevenson St., 415/541-4949
Tommy Toy's Haute Cuisine
   655 Montgomery St., 415/397-4888

Best Coffee
Peet's Coffee and Tea
   2139 Polk, 415/474-1871
   2156 Chestnut, 415/931-8302
   2257 Market, 415/626-6416
   3419 California, 415/221-8506
   54 West Portal Ave., 415/731-0375

Best Coffeehouse
Horse Shoe Coffee House
   566 Haight, 415/626-8852

Best Desserts
Boulevard
   1 Mission St., 415/543-6084
Just Desserts
   248 Church, 415/626-5774
   3 Embarcadero Center, 415/421-1609
   3735 Buchanan, 415/922-8675
   836 Irving, 415/681-1277

Best Diner
Mel's Drive-In
   2165 Lombard, 415/921-3039
   3355 Geary, 415/387-2244

Best French Food
Masa's Restaurant
   648 Bush St., 415/989-7154

Fringale
570 Fourth St., 415/543-0573
Fleur de Lys
777 Sutter St., 415/673-7779
La Folie
2316 Polk St., 415/776-5577

Best German Food
Speckmann's
1550 Church, 415/282-6850

Best Greek/Mediterranean Food
Square One Restaurant
190 Pacific Ave., 415/788-1110
LuLu
816 Folsom St., 415/495-5775
Splendido Restaurant
4 Embarcadero Ctr., 415/986-3222
Asimakopoulos Cafe
288 Connecticut St., 415/552-8789
Stoyanof's Restaurant
1240 Ninth Ave., 415/664-3664
The Helmand
430 Broadway, 415/362-0641
YaYa Restaurant
1220 Ninth Ave., 415/566-6966

Best Health-Conscious Menu
O'Chame
1830 Fourth St., Berkeley, 510/841-8783

Best Ice Cream/Yogurt
Pure T Ice Cream
2238 Polk St., 415/441-7878
St. Francis Fountain and Candy
2801 24th St., 415/826-4200

Best Indian Food
Gaylord India Restaurant
900 N. Point St., 415/771-8822
275 Battery St., Ste. 1, 415/397-7775
Zante Pizza and Indian Cuisine
3489 Mission, 415/821-3949
North India Restaurant
3131 Webster St., 415/931-1556
Kuleto's Restaurant
221 Powell St., 415/397-7720
Maharani
1122 Post St., 415/775-1988

Best Italian Food
Il Fornaio
1265 Battery St., 415/986-0100
Buca Giovanni
800 Greenwich St., 415/776-7766
Caffe Macaroni
59 Columbus, 415/956-9737
Pane e Vino Restaurant
3011 Steiner St., 415/346-2111

Best Japanese Food
Kabuto Sushi
5116 Geary Blvd., 415/752-5652

Kyo-Ya Restaurant
  2 New Montgomery St., 415/392-8600
Yoshida-Ya Japanese Restaurant
  2909 Webster St., 415/346-3431
Ebisu Restaurant
  1283 Ninth Ave., 415/566-1770

Best Korean Food
Korea House
  1640 Post Rd., 415/563-1388

Best Late-Night Food
Sparky's Diner
  242 Church, 415/626-8666

Best Lunch
Barney's Hamburgers
  4138 24th St., 415/282-7770
Zuni Cafe
  1658 Market St., 415/552-2522

Best Mexican Food
Cafe Marimba
  2317 Chestnut St., 415/776-1506
Guaymas
  5 Main St., Tiburon, 415/435-6300

Best New Restaurants
Firefly
  4288 24th St., 415/821-7652
Kate's Kitchen
  471 Haight, 415/626-3984
Boulevard
  1 Mission St., 415/543-6084
LuLu
  816 Folsom St., 415/495-5775
One Market Restaurant
  1 Market St., 415/777-5577
Bistro M
  55 Fifth St., 415/543-5554
French Laundry Restaurant
  6640 Washington St., Yountville, 707/944-2380
Catahoula Restaurant and Bar
  1457 Lincoln Ave., Calistoga, 707/942-2275
L'Amie Donia
  530 Bryant St., Palo Alto, 415/323-7614

Best Other Ethnic Food
Blue Nile (African)
  2525 Telegraph, Berkeley, 510/540-6777
Rasselas Ethiopian Cuisine (Ethiopian)
  2801 California St., 415/567-5010
Masawa (African)
  1538 Haight, 415/621-4129
Angkor Wat Cambodian Restaurant (Cambodian)
  4217 Geary Blvd., 415/221-7887
Phnom Penh Cambodian Restaurant (Cambodian)
  631 Larkin St., 415/775-5979
Bahia Brazilian Restaurant (Brazilian)
  41 Franklin St., 415/626-3306
Cha Cha Cha Cafe (Central/South American)
  1801 Haight St., 415/386-5758

Miss Pearl's Jam House (Central/South American)
601 Eddy St., 415/775-5267
Geva's Caribbean Cuisine (Central/South American)
482 Hayes St., 415/863-1220

Best Pizza
North Beach Pizza
1499 Grant, 415/433-2444
1310 Grant, 415/433-2444
3054 Taraval, 415/242-1900
4787 Mission, 415/586-1400
800 Stanyan, 415/751-2300

Best Place to Eat Alone
China Moon Cafe
639 Post St., 415/775-4789

Best Place to Take the Kids
L'Osteria del Forno
519 Columbus Ave., 415/982-1124

Best Seafood
PJ's Oyster Bed
737 Irving, 415/566-7775
Aqua
252 California St., 415/956-9662
Hayes Street Grill
324 Hayes St., 415/863-5545

Best Steaks
Harris' Restaurant
2100 Van Ness Ave., 415/673-1888
Izzy's Steak and Chop House
3349 Steiner St., 415/563-0487

Best Sushi
Samurai Nippon Sushi Bar
2365 Chestnut St., 415/346-9399

Best Tea Rooms
The Ritz-Carlton
600 Stockton St., 415/296-7465
Sheraton Palace
2 New Montgomery St., 415/392-8600
Westin St. Francis Hotel
335 Powell St., 415/397-7000

Best Thai Food
Khan Toke Thai House
5937 Geary, 415/668-6654
Manora's Thai Cuisine
3226 Mission St., 415/550-0856
Royal Thai Restaurant
951 Clement St., 415/386-1795

Best Undiscovered Restaurants
Cafe Pescatore
2455 Mason St., 415/561-1111
Cafe Tiramisu
28 Belden Pl., 415/421-7044
Caffe Macaroni
59 Columbus, 415/956-9737
Eliza Restaurant
205 Oak St., 415/621-4819

Embarko
  100 Brannan St., 415/495-2021
Jack's Restaurant
  615 Sacramento St., 415/421-7355
Splendido Restaurant
  4 Embarcadero Ctr., 415/986-3222
Tadich Grill
  240 California St., 415/391-2373
Washington Square Bar and Grill
  1707 Powell St., 415/982-8123

Best Vegetarian Food
Greens
  Fort Mason Center, Bldg. A, Marina at Buchanan,
    415/771-6222
Millennium
  246 McAllister St., 415/487-9800

Best Vietnamese Food
Tu Lan
  8 Sixth St., 415/626-0927
Emerald Garden Restaurant
  1550 California St., 415/673-1155
New Golden Turtle Restaurant
  308 Fifth Ave., 415/221-5285
  2211 Van Ness Ave., 415/441-4419

Best Wine Selection
Masa's Restaurant
  648 Bush St., 415/989-7154
One Market Restaurant
  1 Market St., 415/777-5577
Square One Restaurant
  190 Pacific Ave., 415/788-1110

Standbys
Chevy's
  2 Embarcadero Ctr., 415/391-2323
  631 Howard St., Ste. 400, 415/546-1200
  150 Fourth St., 415/543-8060

SAN JOSE, CA

Best All-You-Can-Eat Buffet
Soong Soong
  3680C Stevens Creek Blvd., 408/249-2272

Best Bars
Live
  150 S. First St., 408/294-5483
Drying Shed
  402 Toyon Ave., 408/272-1512
Blue Chalk Cafe
  630 Ramona St., Palo Alto, 415/326-1020
Britannia Arms
  5027 Almaden Expwy., Almaden, 408/266-0550
  1087 Saratoga-Sunnyvale Rd., Cupertino,
    408/252-7262
Paul and Eddie's
  10014 Peninsula Ave., Cupertino, 408/252-2226
The Black Watch
  141 1/2 N. Santa Cruz Ave., Los Gatos, 408/354-2200

Best Beer Selection
Tied House Cafe and Brewery
65 N. San Pedro St., 408/295-2739
954 Villa St., Mountain View, 415/965-2739

Best Breakfast
Hobee's Restaurant
920 Town and Country Village, 408/244-5212

Best Burgers
Kirk's Steakburgers
1330 Saratoga-Sunnyvale Rd., 408/446-2988

Best Cheap Meal
Old Spaghetti Factory
51 N. San Pedro St., 408/288-7488

Best Chinese Food
Blue Sky Chinese Restaurant
2028 S. Winchester Blvd., Campbell, 408/378-0424

Best Coffee
Starbucks
1696 S. Bascom Ave., Campbell, 408/371-6703

Best Delicatessen
Erik's DeliCafe
5705 Cottle Rd., 408/365-1515
4611 Almaden Expwy., 408/265-1818
1120 Branham Ln., 408/265-1818

Best Desserts
Max's Opera Cafe
711 Stanford Shopping Center, Palo Alto,
415/323-6297

Best French Food
Rue de Paris
19 N. Market St., 408/298-0704

Best Indian Food
Pasand Madras Cuisine
3701 El Camino Real, Santa Clara, 408/241-5150
Royal Taj
5155 Stevens Creek Blvd., Santa Clara, 408/248-1365
1350 Camden Ave., Campbell, 408/559-6801

Best Italian Food
Florentine Italian Foods
745 S. Winchester Blvd., 408/243-4040
1070 Commercial St., Ste. 107, 408/452-0170
1057 Blossom Hill Rd., 408/723-3211
285 Richfield Dr., 408/246-5656

Best Japanese Food
Miyake
10650 S. De Anza Blvd., Cupertino, 408/253-2668

Best Mexican Food
Aqui Mex-Grill
1145 Lincoln Ave., 408/995-0381
Ernesto's
14101 Winchester Blvd., Los Gatos, 408/374-3522

Best Microbrewery
Tied House Cafe and Brewery
65 N. San Pedro St., 408/295-2739
954 Villa St., Mountain View, 415/965-2739

Best New Restaurant
Bella Mia
58 S. First St., 408/280-1993

Best Romantic Dining
La Fondue
14510 Big Basin Way, Saratoga, 408/867-3332

Best Sports Bar
Live
150 S. First St., 408/294-5483

Best Steaks
Stuart Anderson's Black Angus
1011 Blossom Hill Rd., 408/266-6602
380 Kiely Blvd., 408/261-6900

Best Thai Food
Thepthai
23 N. Market St., 408/292-7515

Best Vegetarian Food
White Lotus
80 N. Market St., 408/977-0540

Best Vietnamese Food
Golden Chopsticks
1765 S. Winchester Blvd., Campbell, 408/370-6610

Best Wine Selection
Plumed Horse
14555 Big Basin Way, Saratoga, 408/867-4711

Standbys
Chevy's
5305 Almaden Expwy., 408/266-1815
550 S. Winchester Blvd., 408/241-0158
204 S. Matida Ave., Sunnydale, 408/737-7395

SAN LEANDRO, CA

Best All-You-Can-Eat Buffet
Harry's Hofbrau
14900 E. Fourteenth St., 510/357-1707

Best American Food
Cornerstone Cafe
600 Dutton Ave., 510/562-2535

Best Bagels
Everybody's Bagel
1099 MacArthur Blvd., 510/430-8700

Best Barbecue/Ribs
Emil Villa's Hickory Pit
1800 E. Fourteenth St., 510/357-2780

Best Breakfast
Sabino's Coffee
1273 MacArthur Blvd., 510/357-5282

Best Casual Dining
Cornerstone Cafe
600 Dutton Ave., 510/562-2535

Best Chinese Food
Lucky's Chinese Restaurant
  1456 E. Fourteenth St., 510/351-8131

Best Family Restaurant
Harry's Hofbrau
  14900 E. Fourteenth St., 510/357-1707

Best French Food
Le Gourmet French Restaurant
  635 E. Fourteenth St., 510/635-8260

Best Italian Food
Strizzi's Restaurant
  1376 E. Fourteenth St., 510/483-4883

Standbys
Chevy's
  312 Bay Fair Mall, 510/276-0962

SAN LUIS OBISPO, CA

Best Restaurants in Town
Eighteen Sixty-Five
  1865 Monterey St., 805/544-1865
Ian McPhee's Grille
  416 Main St., Templeton, 805/434-3204
Robin's on Burton
  4095 Burton Dr., Cambria, 805/927-5007
Benvenuti
  40 Marsh St., 805/541-5393

Best All-You-Can-Eat Buffets
China Bowl and Kyoto
  685 Higuera St., 805/546-9700
Fresh Choice
  Downtown Centre, 876 Marsh St., 805/543-0943

Best Bagels
Bagel Basement
  673 Higuera St., 805/544-5785
Bagel Cafe
  6551 Trigo Rd., Isla Vista, 805/685-7114
Boston Bagel
  1127 Broad St., 805/541-5134

Best Breakfast
Big Sky Cafe
  1121 Broadway, 805/545-5401
Hobee's Restaurant
  1443 Calle Joaquin, 805/549-9186
Margie's Diner
  1575 Calle Joaquin, 805/541-2940

Best Brunch
Sea Cliffs Restaurant
  2757 Shell Beach Rd., Shell Beach, 805/773-3555
The Old Custom House
  324 Front St., Avila Beach, 805/595-7555
Sea Venture
  100 Ocean View Ave., Pismo Beach, 805/773-3463

Best Burgers
Garland's Hamburgers
  1090 Price St., Pismo Beach, 805/773-3376

Hudson's Grill
   1005 Monterey St., 805/541-5999
Scrubby and Lloyd's Cafe
   1136 Carmel St., 805/543-5885

Best Chinese Food
Golden China
   1085 Higuera St., 805/543-7354
   675 Higuera St., 805/543-7576
   7425 El Camino Real, Atascadero, 805/466-1828

Best Coffee
Linnaea's Cafe
   1110 Garden St., 805/541-5888
Nectar of the Bean
   940 Chorro St., 805/545-0870
Starbucks
   Downtown Centre, 876 Marsh St., 805/547-0465

Best Coffeehouses
Coffee Merchant
   1065 Higuera St., 805/543-6701
Linnaea's Cafe
   1110 Garden St., 805/541-5888

Best Delicatessens
Ben Franklin's Sandwich Company
   313 Higuera St., 805/544-4948
Cisco's
   778G Higuera St., 805/543-5555
   594 California Blvd., 805/543-3334
Gus' Grocery
   1683 Osos St., 805/543-8684

Best Desserts
Linn's Fruit Bin
   1141 Chorro St., 805/546-8444
Madonna Inn
   100 Madonna Rd., 805/543-3000

Best Health-Conscious Menu
Big Sky Cafe
   1121 Broadway, 805/545-5401
Fresh Choice
   Downtown Centre, 876 Marsh St., 805/543-0943
Hobee's Restaurant
   1443 Calle Joaquin, 805/549-9186

Best Ice Cream/Yogurt
Burnardo'z Candy and Ice Cream
   750 Grand Ave., Grover Beach, 805/481-7784
SLO Maid Ice Cream
   728 Higuera St., 805/541-3117
Country Culture Yogurt Bar
   746 Higuera St., 805/544-9007
Froggie's Frozen Yogurt
   578 California Blvd., 805/546-8181
The Yogurt Station
   890 Foothill Blvd., 805/544-2104

Best Italian Food
Buona Tavola
   1037 Monterey St., 805/545-8000

Cafe Roma
  1819 Osos St., 805/541-6800
Rosa's Italian Restaurant
  491 Price St., Pismo Beach, 805/773-0551

Best Late-Night Food
Fat Cats
  480 Front St., Avila Beach, 805/595-7715
Hudson's Grill
  1005 Monterey St., 805/541-5999

Best Mexican Food
Izzy Ortega's Mexican Restaurant
  1850 Monterey St., 805/543-3333
Pepe Delgado's Mexican Restaurant
  1601 Monterey St., 805/544-6660
Pete's Southside Cafe
  1815 Osos St., 805/549-8133

Best New Restaurants
Big Sky Cafe
  1121 Broadway, 805/545-5401
Mother's Tavern
  725 Higuera St., 805/541-8733

Best Outdoor Dining
Cisco's
  778G Higuera St., 805/543-5555
  594 California Blvd., 805/543-3334
The Old Custom House
  324 Front St., Avila Beach, 805/595-7555
Pete's Southside Cafe
  1815 Osos St., 805/549-8133

Best Pizza
Upper Crust
  785 Foothill Blvd., 805/542-0400
Woodstock's Pizza Parlor
  1000 Higuera St., 805/541-4420

Best Places to Take the Kids
Apple Farm Restaurant
  2015 Monterey St., 805/544-6100
F. McClintock's Saloon and Dining
  686 Higuera St., 805/541-0686

Best Romantic Restaurants
Buona Tavola
  1037 Monterey St., 805/545-8000
Cafe Roma
  1819 Osos St., 805/541-6800
Gardens of Avila
  1215 Avila Beach Dr., 805/595-7365

Best Seafood
Great American Fish Company
  1185 Embarcadero, Morro Bay, 805/772-4407
Olde Port Inn Restaurant
  Port San Luis Pier 3, Avila Beach, 805/595-2515
Simply Shrimp
  570 Higuera St., 805/542-0237

Best Steaks
A.J. Spur's Saloon and Dining Hall
  508 Main St., Templeton, 805/434-2700
F. McClintock's Saloon and Dining
  686 Higuera St., 805/541-0686
This Old House
  740 W. Foothill Blvd., 805/543-2690

Best Wine Selection
Benvenuti
  40 Marsh St., 805/541-5393
Buona Tavola
  1037 Monterey St., 805/545-8000
Rosa's Italian Restaurant
  491 Price St., Pismo Beach, 805/773-0551

SAN MARCOS, CA

Best American Food
Quails Inn Dinnerhouse
  1035 La Bonita Dr., 619/744-2445

Best Bar
Camelot Inn
  887 W. San Marcos Blvd., 619/744-1332

Best Burgers
George's Burgers
  122 N. Las Poisas Rd., 619/744-0164

Best Cajun/Creole Food
Cajun Connection
  740 Nordahl Rd., Ste. 114, 619/741-5680

Best Greek/Mediterranean Food
Grecian Gardens
  1020 W. San Marcos Blvd., 619/744-3790

Best Health-Conscious Menu
Panda Garden
  748 S. Rancho Santa Fe Rd., 619/727-2322

Best Italian Food
Bruno's Italian Restaurant
  1020 W. San Marcos Blvd., 619/744-7700

Best Japanese Food
Katsu Seafood and Steak House
  1020 W. San Marcos Blvd., 619/744-7156

Best Mexican Food
Rockin' Baja Lobster
  1020 W. San Marcos Blvd., 619/744-7550

Best Microbrewery
San Marcos Brewery
  1080 San Marcos Blvd., 619/471-0050

Best Sandwiches
Sub Marina
  997 W. San Marcos Blvd., 619/471-7707

Best Seafood
Fish House Veracruz
  1020 W. San Marcos Blvd., 619/744-8000

SAN MATEO, CA

Best Breakfast
First Watch
  201 Second Ave., 415/342-2356
Stacks
  361 California Dr., Burlingame, 415/579-1384

Best Coffee
Noah's Bagels
  50 E. Fourth Ave., 415/347-2364
Starbucks
  1160 Burlingame Ave., Burlingame, 415/348-5138
Pete's
  1309 Burlingame Ave., Burlingame, 415/548-0494

Best Desserts
Capellini Ristorante
  310 Baldwin Ave., 415/348-2296
Max's Opera Cafe
  1250 Bayshore Hwy., Burlingame, 415/342-6297

Best Italian Food
Bella Mangiata Caffe
  233 Baldwin Ave., 415/343-2404
Luceti's on 25th Avenue
  109 W. 25th Ave., 415/574-1256
Capellini Ristorante
  310 Baldwin Ave., 415/348-2296

Best Pizza
Amici's East Coast Pizzeria
  69 E. Third Ave., 415/342-9392
Jack's Pizza
  770 Polhemus Rd., 415/574-2233
  212 Second Ave., 415/343-9229

Best Regional Food
Buffalo Grill
  66 31st Ave., 415/358-8777

Best Seafood
Clamhouse San Mateo
  33 W. 25th Ave., 415/571-1846

Best Steaks
Barley Hops
  201 S. B St., 415/348-7808

Best Thai Food
Bow Thai Cafe
  43 S. B St., 415/340-8424
Nipa-Pon
  121 W. 25th Ave., 415/578-9211

Best Vegetarian Food
World Wrapps
  1318 Burlingame Ave., Burlingame, 415/342-9777

Standbys
Friday's
  3101 S. El Camino, 415/570-4629

SAN RAFAEL, CA

Best Bagels
Marin Bagel Company
1560 Fourth St., 415/457-8127

Best Beer Selection
Pacific Tap and Grill
812 Fourth St., 415/457-9711

Best Bread
Bordenave's
1512 Fourth St., 415/453-2957

Best Brunch
Half Day Cafe
848 College Ave., Kentfield, 415/459-0291

Best Burgers
Phyllis' Giant Burgers
2202 Fourth St., 415/456-0866

Best Cheap Meal
High Tech Burrito
2042 Fourth St., 415/485-0214
942 Diablo Ave., Novato, 415/897-8083

Best Chinese Food
Pier 6
1559 Fourth St., 415/457-1733

Best Delicatessens
Belli-Deli
1304 2nd St., 415/456-2626
Art and Larry's Restaurant-Deli
1242 Fourth St., 415/457-3354

Best French Food
La Petite Auberge
704 Fourth St., 415/456-5808

Best Health-Conscious Menu
Milly's
1613 Fourth St., 415/459-1601

Best Ice Cream/Yogurt
Double Rainbow
860 Fourth St., 415/457-0803
112 Vintage Way, Novato, 415/898-8500

Best Indian Food
Pasand Madras Cuisine
802 B St., 415/456-6099
India Village
555 Francisco Blvd. W., 415/456-2411

Best Italian Food
Salute
706 Third St., 415/453-7596
Ristorante Dalecio
340 Ignacio Blvd., Novato, 415/883-0960

Best Japanese Food
Kamikaze Sushi Bar
223 Third St., 415/457-6776

Best Mexican Food
Pancho Villa's
  1625 Sir Francis Drake Blvd., Fairfax, 415/459-9606

Best Pizza
Redboy Pizzeria
  1115 Fourth St., 415/454-3131
Stefano's Pizzeria
  3815 Redwood Hwy., 415/491-1900
Mulberry Street Pizza
  101 Smith Ranch Rd., 415/472-7272
Round Table Pizza
  186 Northgate One, 415/472-3232
Lococo's
  631 Del Granado Rd., Terra Linda, 415/472-3323

Best Thai Food
Anita's Kitchen
  534 Fourth St., 415/454-2626
My Thai
  1230 Fourth St., 415/459-4455

SANTA ANA, CA

Best Breakfast
Pop's Cafe
  112 E. Ninth, 714/543-2772

Best Burgers
Knowl-Wood Restaurant
  2107 E. Seventeenth St., 714/541-0555
Mos Food Service
  1504 W. Edinger Ave., 714/540-9673

Best Casual Dining
Knowl-Wood Restaurant
  2107 E. Seventeenth St., 714/541-0555

Best Desserts
Mrs. Gooch's
  14945 Holt Ave., Tustin, 714/731-3400
Cookie Creations
  4250Q Barranca Pkwy., Irvine, 714/857-9267

Best Health-Conscious Menu
Mrs. Gooch's
  14945 Holt Ave., Tustin, 714/731-3400

Best Indian Food
Niki's Tandoori Express
  3705 S. Bristol St., 714/850-0595
  2031 E. First St., 714/542-2969

Best Italian Food
Luigi D'Italia
  1287 E. Lincoln Ave., Anaheim, 714/533-1300
  801 S. State College Blvd., 714/490-0990
Antonello
  1611 Sunflower Ave., 714/751-7153

Best Mexican Food
El Torito Grill
  1910 Main St., Irvine, 714/975-1220

Best Pizza
California Pizza Kitchen
  2800 N. Main, 714/479-0604

Best Restaurant Meal Value
Bistango
  19100 Von Karman Ave., Irvine, 714/752-5222

Best Salad/Salad Bar
Mrs. Gooch's
  14945 Holt Ave., Tustin, 714/731-3400

Best Seafood
King Neptune Sea Foods
  17115 Pacific Coast Hwy., Sunset Beach,
    310/592-4878
McCormick and Schmick's
  2000 Main St., Irvine, 714/756-0505

Best Undiscovered Restaurant
Gustaf Anders
  South Coast Plz., Village at Bear St. at Sunflower
    Ave., 714/668-1737

SANTA BARBARA, CA

Best Restaurant in Town
Palace Cafe
  8 E. Cota St., 805/966-3133

Best Barbecue/Ribs
Woody's
  229 W. Montecito St., 805/963-9326
  5112 Hollister Ave., 805/967-3775

Best Beer Selection
Trader Joe's
  29 South Milpas St., 805/564-7878

Best Breakfast
Esau's
  403 State St., 805/965-4416

Best Brunch
Four Seasons Bilmore Hotel
  1260 Channel Dr., 805/969-2261

Best Burgers
Chubbie's
  1027 State St., 805/965-6004

Best Cajun/Creole Food
Palace Cafe
  8 E. Cota St., 805/966-3133

Best Cheap Meal
Fresh Choice
  740 State St., 805/965-6599

Best Chinese Food
China Castle
  1202 Chapala St., 805/965-9219

Best Coffeehouses
S.B. Roasting Company
  321 Motor Way, 805/962-0320
Coffee Cat
  1201 Anacapa St., 805/962-7164

3615 State St., 805/569-8868
888 Embarcadero Del Norte, 805/685-5138

Best Delicatessen
Italian-Greek Deli
636 State St., 805/962-6815

Best French Food
Mousse Odile
18 E. Cota St., 805/962-5393

Best Health-Conscious Menu
The Natural Cafe
508 State St., 805/962-9494

Best Ice Cream/Yogurt
McConnell's
835 E. Canon Perdido St., 805/965-3764
201 W. Mission St., 805/569-2323
1213 State St., 805/965-5400
Penguin's
935 State St., 805/965-0255

Best Indian Food
Paul Bhalla's Cuisine of India
1311 State St., 805/966-2733

Best Italian Food
Palazzio Trattoria
1511 Coast Village Rd., 805/969-8565

Best Japanese Food
Azuma
24 W. Figueroa St., 805/966-2139

Best Lunch
Natural Cafe
508 State St., 805/962-9494

Best Mexican Food
La Super Rica Taqueria
622 N. Milpas St., 805/963-4940

Best Neighborhood Bar
Mel's
6 W. De La Guerra St., 805/963-2211

Best New Restaurants
Rio Bravo
202 State St., 805/966-1561
Roy
7 W. Carrillo St., 805/966-5636

Best Outdoor Dining
Earthling Bookstore Cafe
1137 State St., 805/564-6096
Paradise Cafe
702 Anacapa St., 805/962-4416

Best Pizza
Giovanni's
6583 Pardall Rd., Isla Vista, 805/968-2254
3020 State St., 805/682-3621
1187 Coast Village Rd., Montecito, 805/969-1277
5003 Carpinteria Ave., Carpinteria, 805/684-8288

Best Place to Be "Seen"
Brophy Brothers
  Breakwater at the Harbor, 805/966-4418

Best Places to Eat When Someone Else Is Buying
Downey's
  1305 State St., 805/966-5006
The Wine Cask
  813 Anacapa St., 805/966-9463
El Encanto Hotel and Villas
  1900 Lasuen Rd., 805/687-5000
The Stonehouse
  900 San Ysidro Ln., 805/969-5046
Four Seasons Biltmore Hotel
  1260 Channel Dr., 805/969-2261

Best Place to Eat Alone
Sojourner Cafe
  134 E. Canon Perdido St., 805/965-7922

Best Romantic Dining
El Encanto
  1900 Lasuen Rd., 805/687-5000

Best Seafood
Brophy's
  Breakwater at the Harbor, 805/966-4418

Best Steaks
Chuck's of Hawaii
  3888 State St., 805/687-4414

Best Sushi
Arigato
  Victoria Court, 11 W. Victoria St., 805/965-6074

Best Thai Food
Your Place
  22 N. Milpas St., 805/966-5151

SANTA CLARITA, CA

Best Restaurant in Town
Pasta Grill
  23254 Lyons Ave., 805/255-3241

Best American Food
Tip's Restaurant
  24737 Pico Canyon Rd., 805/259-1777

Best Asian Restaurant
Grand Panda
  23802 Lyons Ave., Newhall, 805/253-1898

Best Atmosphere
Backwoods Inn
  17846 Sierra Hwy., Canyon Country, 805/252-5522

Best Bar
Santa Clarita Brewing Company
  20655 Soledad Canyon Rd., 805/298-5676

Best Barbecue/Ribs
Pit BBQ Restaurant
  26057 Bouquet Canyon Rd., Saugus, 805/253-0115

Best Bottomless Coffee Cup
Tip's Restaurant
  24737 Pico Canyon Rd., 805/259-1777

Best Bread
Chi Chi's Pizza
  23043 Soledad Canyon Rd., Saugus, 805/259-4040

Best Breakfast
Way Station Coffee Shop
  24377 Fernando Rd., Newhall, 805/255-0222

Best Brunch
El Chaparral Mexican Restaurant
  19132 Soledad Canyon Rd., Canyon Country,
    805/252-5599

Best Burgers
Cuzzin's Burgers
  19318 Soledad Canyon Rd., Canyon Country,
    805/298-4200

Best Business Breakfast
Coco's Restaurant
  16526 Soledad Canyon Rd., Canyon Country,
    805/251-7725

Best Casual Dining
Caruso's II
  18340 Sierra Hwy., Canyon Country, 805/251-8450

Best Cheap Meal
Pit BBQ Restaurant
  26057 Bouquet Canyon Rd., Saugus, 805/253-0115

Best Chinese Food
Grand Panda
  23802 Lyons Ave., Newhall, 805/253-1898

Best Coffeehouse
Mitch's Java and Jazz
  22722 Lyons Ave., Newhall, 805/254-7500

Best Continental Food
Gerard's Fine Dining
  23329 Lyons Ave., Valencia, 805/253-0995

Best Delicatessen
That's Italian Deli
  27540 Sierra Hwy., Canyon Country, 805/298-3663

Best Desserts
Le Chene French Cuisine
  12625 Sierra Hwy., Saugus, 805/251-4315
Kendalls Cuisine and Catering
  22942 Lyons Ave., Newhall, 805/259-6001

Best Diner
Way Station Coffee Shop
  24377 Fernando Rd., Newhall, 805/255-0222

Best Eclectic Menu
Way Station Coffee Shop
  24377 Fernando Rd., Newhall, 805/255-0222

Best Family Restaurant
Country Burgers
  27125 Sierra Hwy., 805/298-4898

Best French Food
Le Chene French Cuisine
  12625 Sierra Hwy., Saugus, 805/251-4315

Best German Food
German Place Deli
  23115 Lyons Ave., Newhall, 805/255-9790

Best Happy Hour Snacks
Don Cuco's Restaurant
  24130 Lyons Ave., Newhall, 805/254-4874

Best Health-Conscious Menu
Nature's Harvest
  25067 Peachland Ave., Newhall, 805/259-0807
  19366 Soledad Canyon Rd., Canyon Country,
    805/252-6744

Best Homestyle Food
Saugus Cafe
  25861 San Fernando Rd., Saugus, 805/259-7886

Best Indian Food
Tandoori Grill
  23360 W. Valencia Blvd., 805/288-1200

Best Italian Food
L'Italiano
  28200 Bouquet Canyon Rd., Saugus, 805/296-1200

Best Japanese Food
Kotobuki Restaurant
  27665 Bouquet Canyon Rd., Saugus, 805/296-1353

Best Late-Night Food
Tip's Restaurant
  24737 Pico Canyon Rd., 805/259-1777

Best Mexican Food
Don Cuco's Restaurant
  24130 Lyons Ave., Newhall, 805/254-4874

Best Microbrewery
Santa Clarita Brewing Company
  20655 Soledad Canyon Rd., 805/298-5676

Best Other Ethnic Food
Pasta Grill (Italian/Argentinian)
  23254 Lyons Ave., 805/255-3241

Best Pastries
Kendall's Cuisine and Catering
  22942 Lyons Ave., Newhall, 805/259-6001

Best Pizza
Pauli's
  23360 Valencia Blvd., 805/259-3220
Round Table Pizza
  26524 Bouquet Canyon Rd., Saugus, 805/297-3556

Best Place to Eat When Someone Else Is Buying
Sisley Italian Kitchen
  24201 Valencia Blvd., 805/287-4444

Best Quick-Dinner-Before-the-Movie
Pauli's
  23360 Valencia Blvd., 805/259-3220

Best Quick Lunch
Chuy's Mesquite Broiler Restaurant
   25289 The Old Rd., Newhall, 805/288-1022

Best Romantic Dining
Le Chene French Cuisine
   12625 Sierra Hwy., Saugus, 805/251-4315
L'Italiano
   28200 Bouquet Canyon Rd., Saugus, 805/296-1200

Best Salad/Salad Bar
Hughes Market
   19340 Soledad Canyon Rd., 805/252-6226
Nature's Harvest
   25067 Peachland Ave., Newhall, 805/259-0807
   19366 Soledad Canyon Rd., Canyon Country,
      805/252-6744

Best Sandwiches
Final Score Food and Beverage
   23942 Lyons Ave., Newhall, 805/254-6557

Best Schmooze Bar
Hamburger Hamlet
   27430 The Old Rd., Valencia, 805/253-0888

Best Southwestern Food
El Torito
   27510 The Old Rd., Valencia, 805/254-2994

Best Spanish Food
El Mas Cafe
   24367 San Fernando Rd., Newhall, 805/253-0609

Best Sports Bar
Prime Tyme
   27125 N. Sierra, 805/251-8554

Best Steaks
Backwoods Inn
   17846 Sierra Hwy., Canyon Country, 805/252-5522

Best Sushi
Light and Healthy Sushi Bar
   23546 Lyons Ave., Newhall, 805/255-1921

Best Tea Room
A Touch of Class
   25914 McBean Pkwy., Valencia, 805/259-1625

Best Thai Food
Thai Dishes
   23328 Valencia Blvd., Valencia, 805/253-3663

Best 24-Hour Restaurant
Saugus Cafe
   25861 San Fernando Rd., Saugus, 805/259-7886

Best Undiscovered Restaurant
La Cocina Bar and Grill
   28022 N. Deco Canyon Rd., Saugus, 805/297-4546

Best Vegetarian Food
Nature's Harvest
   25067 Peachland Ave., Newhall, 805/259-0807
   19366 Soledad Canyon Rd., Canyon Country,
      805/252-6744

Best Wine Selection
Le Chene French Cuisine
12625 Sierra Hwy., Saugus, 805/251-4315

SANTA CRUZ, CA

Best Restaurant in Town
India Joze Restaurant and Bakery
1001 Center St., 408/427-3554

Best Beer Selection
Ninety-Nine Bottles of Beer on the Wall Beer Pub
104 Walnut Ave., 408/459-9999
Seabright Brewery
519 Seabright Ave., 408/426-2739
The Catalyst
1011 Pacific Ave., 408/423-1336

Best Bread
Alfaro's Cafe and Bakery
920 Pacific Ave., 408/426-9240
Kelly's French Pastry
1547 Pacific Ave., 408/423-9059
7486 Soquel Dr., Aptos, 408/662-2911

Best Breakfast
Zachary's Restaurant
819 Pacific Ave., 408/427-0646
Linda's Seabreeze Cafe
542 Seabright Ave., 408/427-9713
Walnut Avenue Cafe
106 Walnut Ave., 408/457-2307

Best Burgers
Carpo's
2400 Porter St., Soquel, 408/476-6260
Pontiac Grill
429 Front St., 408/427-2290
Jack's Hamburgers
202 Lincoln St., 408/423-4421

Best Cheap Meal
Taqueria Vallarta
608 Soquel Ave., 408/457-8226
Crow's Nest
2218 E. Cliff Dr., 408/476-4560
Marcelo's the Restaurant
1520 Mission St., 408/423-2845

Best Coffee
Coffee Roasting Company
1330 Pacific Ave., 408/459-0100
Espresso Royale Caffe
1545 Pacific Ave., 408/429-9804

Best Coffeehouses
Jahva House
120 Union St., 408/459-9876
Espresso Royale Caffe
1545 Pacific Ave., 408/429-9804
Cafe Pergolesi
418 Cedar St., 408/426-1775

Best Desserts
Cafe Bittersweet
2332 Mission St., 408/423-9999
India Joze Restaurant and Bakery
1001 Center St., 408/427-3554
Kelly's French Pastry
1547 Pacific Ave., 408/423-9059
7486 Soquel Dr., Aptos, 408/662-2911

Best Health-Conscious Menu
Aragona's
2591 Main St., Soquel, 408/462-5100
Fresh Choice Restaurant
3555 Clares St., Capitola, 408/479-9873
Dharma's Restaurant
4250 Capitola Rd., Capitola, 408/462-1717

Best Ice Cream/Yogurt
Yogurt Delite
1306 Mission St., 408/429-6400
1420 41st Ave., Capitola, 408/462-9393
Polar Bear Ice Cream
1224 Soquel Ave., 408/425-5188
Donatello's Gelato
113 Walnut Ave., 408/425-1108

Best Late-Night Food
The Crepe Place
1134 Soquel Ave., 408/429-6994
Saturn Cafe
1230 Mission St., 408/429-8505
Pontiac Grill
429 Front St., 408/427-2290

Best Mexican Food
Taqueria
608 Soquel Ave., 408/457-8226
Tucson Taqueria
218 Mount Hermon Rd., Scotts Valley, 408/439-8470
Rosa's Rosticeria
439 Lake Ave., 408/479-3536

Best Microbreweries
Brewing Company/Front Street Pub
516 Front St., 408/429-8838
Seabright Brewery
519 Seabright Ave., 408/426-2739
Live Soup Brewery and Cafe
1602 Ocean St., 408/458-3461

Best New Restaurants
Papa's Church
415 Seabright Ave., 408/426-5558
Marcelo's the Restaurant
1520 Mission St., 408/423-2845
Jammin' Fish
303 Potrero St. at the Old Sash Mill, 408/425-0884
Vertigo
703 Pacific Ave., 408/459-6605

Best Outdoor Dining
Crow's Nest Restaurant
2218 E. Cliff Dr., 408/476-4560

The Crepe Place
 1134 Soquel Ave., 408/429-6994
Seabright Brewery
 519 Seabright Ave., 408/426-2739

Best Pizza
Tony and Alba's Pizza
 817 Soquel Ave., 408/425-8669
 1501 41st Ave., Capitola, 408/475-4450
Pleasure Pizza
 4000 Portola St., 408/475-4009
Pizza My Heart
 1116 Pacific Ave., 408/426-2511
 209 Esplanade, Capitola, 408/475-5714
 5401 Scotts Valley Dr., Scotts Valley, 408/439-0880

Best Places to Eat When Someone Else Is Buying
Shadowbrook Restaurant
 1750 Wharf St., Capitola, 408/475-1511
Casablanca
 101 Main St., 408/426-9063
Chaminade
 1 Chaminade Ln., 408/475-5600

Best Romantic Dining
Shadowbrook Restaurant
 1750 Wharf St., Capitola, 408/475-1511
Casablanca Restaurant
 101 Main St., 408/426-9063
Gabriella Cafe
 910 Cedar St., 408/457-1677

Best Sandwiches
Togo's Eatery
 1315 Pacific Ave., 408/426-8441
 425 Barson St., 408/423-7330
 1550 41st Ave., Capitola, 408/476-7330
 266 Mount Hermon Rd., Scotts Valley, 408/438-0742
Erik's DeliCafe
 712 Front St., 408/425-5353
 1664 Soquel Ave., 408/458-1414
 102 Rancho Del Mar Shopping Center, Aptos,
  408/688-5656
 1601 41st Ave., Capitola, 408/475-4646
 222 Mount Hermon Rd., Scotts Valley, 408/438-4646
Zoccoli's Delicatessen
 1534 Pacific Ave., 408/423-1711

Best Vegetarian Food
Dharma's Restaurant
 4250 Capitola Rd., Capitola, 408/462-1717
India Joze Restaurant and Bakery
 1001 Center St., 408/427-3554
Malabar Cafe
 1116 Soquel Ave., 408/423-7906

Best View While Dining
Chaminade
 1 Chaminade Ln., 408/475-5600
Crow's Nest Restaurant
 2218 E. Cliff Dr., 408/476-4560

Casablanca Restaurant
101 Main St., 408/426-9063

Best Wine Selection
Pearl Alley Bistro
110 Pearl Alley, 408/429-8070
Theo's French Restaurant
3101 N. Main St., Soquel, 408/462-3657
Balzac Bistro
112 Capitola Ave., Capitola, 408/476-5035

SANTA MARIA, CA

Best Restaurants in Town
Central City Broiler
1520 N. Broadway, 805/922-3700
Santa Maria Inn
801 S. Broadway, 805/928-7777

Best American Food
Far Western Tavern
899 Guadalupe St., 805/343-2211

Best Homestyle Food
Jack's
156 S. Broadway, 805/937-1871

Best Italian Food
Marianne's
800 S. Broadway, 805/347-2737

Best Seafood
Jetty Restaurant
135 E. Foster Rd., 805/937-5144

Best Steaks
Shaw's
714 S. Broadway, 805/925-5862

SANTA ROSA, CA

Best Restaurants in Town
Tra Vigne
1050 Charter Oak, St. Helena, 707/963-4444
Mustard's Grill
7399 St. Helena Hwy., Napa, 707/944-2424
Sonoma Piatti
405 First St., Sonoma, 707/996-2351
John Ash and Company
4330 Barnes Rd., 707/527-7687

Best Bagels
Sonoma Valley Bagel Company
2310 Mendocino Ave., 707/542-7568

Best Beer Selection
The English Rose
2024 Armory Dr., 707/544-7673

Best Breakfast
Omelette Express
112 Fourth St., 707/525-1690

Best Brunch
Omelette Express
112 Fourth St., 707/525-1690

Best Burgers
Rocco's
  12750 Bodega Hwy., Freestone, 707/823-7765

Best Cheap Meal
East West Cafe
  128 N. Main St., Sebastopol, 707/829-2822

Best Chinese Food
Gary Chu's
  611 Fifth St., 707/526-5840

Best Coffeehouse
A'Roma Roasters
  95 Fifth St., 707/576-7765

Best Delicatessen
Traverso's
  Third St. at B St., 707/542-2530

Best Desserts
Michelle Marie's Patisserie
  2404 Magowan, 707/575-1214

Best French Food
La Gare
  208 Wilson St., 707/528-4355

Best German Food
Cafe Europe
  65 Brookwood Ave., 707/526-2200

Best Ice Cream/Yogurt
Swensen's
  630 Third St., 707/526-1744

Best Indian Food
Sizzling Tandoor
  409 Mendocino Ave., 707/579-5999

Best Italian Food
Italian Affair
  1612 Terrace Way, 707/528-4336
Checkers
  523 Fourth St., 707/578-4000

Best Japanese Food
Sushi Hana
  6930 Burnett St., Sebastopol, 707/823-3778

Best Microbrewery
Santa Rosa Brewing Company
  458 B St., 707/544-4677

Best New Restaurant
Western Caffe
  10 Fourth St., 707/525-8165

Best Outdoor Dining
Topolos at Russian River Vineyards
  5700 Gravenstein Hwy. N., Forestville, 707/887-1575

Best Pizza
La Vera
  629 Fourth St., 707/575-1113

Best Place to Eat When Someone Else Is Buying
John Ash and Company
  4330 Barnes Rd., 707/527-7687

Best Romantic Dining
La Gare
  208 Wilson St., 707/528-4355

Best Seafood
Lucas Wharf
  595 Hwy. 1, Bodega Bay, 707/875-3522

Best Thai Food
Thai House
525 Fourth St., 707/526-3939

Best Vegetarian Food
East West Cafe
  128 N. Main St., Sebastopol, 707/829-2822

Best Wine Selection
Gaffney's Wine Bar
  404 Mendocino Ave., 707/542-8463
Traverso's
  Third St. at B St., 707/542-2530

Standbys
Chevy's
  24 Fourth St., 707/571-1082

SANTEE, CA

Best Breakfast
Omelette Factory
  7941 Mission Gorge Rd., 619/596-9686

Best Desserts
D.Z. Akin's
  6930 Alvarado Rd., San Diego, 619/265-0218

Best Romantic Dining
Humphrey's
  2241 Shelter Island Dr., San Diego, 619/224-3577

Best Salad/Salad Bar
Souplantation
  3960 W. Point Loma Blvd., San Diego, 619/222-7404
  6171 Mission Gorge Rd., San Diego, 619/280-7087
  8105 Mira Mesa Blvd., San Diego, 619/566-1172
  17210 Bernardo Center Dr., San Diego, 619/675-3353

Best Seafood
Fish Merchant
  7005 Navajo Rd., San Diego, 619/462-3811

Best Sports Bar
Trophy's Sports Grill
  5500 Grossmont Center Dr., La Mesa, 619/698-2900

Standbys
HomeTown Buffet
  275 Town Center Pkwy., 619/562-1555

SIMI VALLEY, CA

Best Restaurant in Town
Ciao Restaurant
  1627 E. Los Angeles Ave., 805/522-1049

Best Barbecue/Ribs
Red's BBQ and Grillery
  2892 Cochran St., 805/581-9076

Best Breakfast
Eggs and Things
  2955 Cochran St., 805/527-0055

Best Burgers
Del Taco
  2990 Cochran St., 805/583-3717
Hudson's Grill
  2900 Cochran St., 805/581-1740

Best Business Lunch
Siam Cuisine
  1960 Sequoia Ave., 805/581-5526

Best Continental Food
Ciao Restaurant
  1627 E. Los Angeles Ave., 805/522-1049

Best Greek/Mediterranean Food
It's Greek To Me
  2375 Sycamore Dr., 805/527-5316

Best Italian Food
Paul's Italian Villa
  1951 Erringer Rd., 805/526-5360
Giovanni's Italian Kitchen
  4210 E. Los Angeles Ave., 805/582-2375

Best Japanese Food
Ken of Japan
  4340 Cochran St., 805/527-6490

Best Mexican Food
Carrillo's Mexican Deli
  2836 Cochran St., 805/522-8939
Tico's Taco
  2090 First St., 805/527-6456

Best Pizza
Paul's Italian Villa
  1951 Erringer Rd., 805/526-5360

Best Place to Eat When Someone Else Is Buying
Ciao Restaurant
  1627 E. Los Angeles Ave., 805/522-1049

Best Steaks
Maverick's
  5225 Cochran St., 805/527-8730

Best Thai Restaurant
Siam Cuisine
  1960 Sequoia Ave., 805/581-5526

STOCKTON, CA

Best Restaurants in Town
Isadore's
  680 N. Main St., Manteca, 209/825-4300
Strings
  1125 S. Main, Manteca, 209/823-9777
Albert's Restaurant
  8103 Hwy. 99N, 209/476-1763

Best American Food
Farmer's Table
  1185 N. Main St., Manteca, 209/823-7777

Best Breakfast
Hoosier Inn
1537 N. Wilson Ln., 209/463-0271

Best Business Lunch
Eureka
445 W. Weber, 209/462-2996

Best Casual Dining
Eldorado Brewing
171 W. Adams, 209/948-2537

Best Chinese Food
Yen Ching Restaurant
6511 Pacific Ave., 209/473-9813
Dave Wong's Chinese Cuisine
5620 N. Pershing Ave., 209/951-4150

Best Continental Food
Albert's Restaurant
8103 Hwy. 99N, 209/476-1763
Le Bistro
3121 W. Benjamin Holt Dr., 209/951-0885

Best Dinner
Le Bistro
3121 W. Benjamin Holt Dr., 209/951-0885

Best French Food
Le Bistro
3121 W. Benjamin Holt Dr., 209/951-0885

Best Greek/Mediterranean Food
Papapavlo's Gourmet Greek Cafe
7555 Pacific Ave., 209/477-6855

Best Homestyle Food
Hoosier Inn
1537 N. Wilson Ln., 209/463-0271

Best Italian Food
Strings
1125 S. Main, Manteca, 209/823-9777
Estasi
296 Lincoln Ctr., 209/951-3311
Ristorante Primavera
856 W. Benjamin Holt Dr., 209/477-6128

Best Lunch
Eldorado Brewing
171 W. Adams, 209/948-2537

Best Mexican Food
Santiago's Cocina Mexicana
222 Lincoln Ctr., 209/478-6444

Best Microbrewery
Eldorado Brewing
171 W. Adams, 209/948-2537

Best Salad/Salad Bar
Eldorado Brewing
171 W. Adams, 209/948-2537

Best Seafood
Bud's Seafood Grill
314 Lincoln Ctr., 209/956-0270

Best American Food
Temet Grill
44501 Rainbow Canyon Rd., 909/694-1000

Best Chinese Food
Little Chung King
27371 Jefferson Ave., 909/699-1234

Best Coffee
Rio De Java
26459 Ynez Rd., 909/699-8082

Best Desserts
Katie McGuire's Pie Shoppe
27495 Ynez Rd., 909/676-9194

Best Ice Cream/Yogurt
Sweet Bean
30590 Rancho California Rd., 909/699-8443

Best Italian Food
Pasquale's
27315 Jefferson St., 909/699-4428
Scarcella's
27485 Ynez Rd., 909/676-5450
Vera's Italian Restaurant
27326 Jefferson Ave., Ste. 17, 909/676-6474

Best Mexican Food
Rosa's Cantina
28636 Front St., 909/695-2428

Best Pizza
Filippi's Pizza Grado
27309 Jefferson Ave., 909/699-8900

Best Regional Food
Cafe Champagne
32575 Rancho California Rd., 909/699-0088

Best Sandwiches
Euro-Deli
28860 Front St., 909/695-0201

Best Seafood
Fish Exchange
24910 Washington Ave., Murrieta, 909/677-9449
Pirates of the Caribbean
41925 Third St., 909/695-1405
Cafe Champagne
32575 Rancho California Rd., 909/699-0088

Best Steaks
Black Angus
27735 Ynez Rd., 909/699-8000
Cafe Champagne
32575 Rancho California Rd., 909/699-0088
Hungry Hunter
27600 Jefferson Ave., 909/694-1475

Standbys
Tony Roma's
27464 Jefferson Ave., 909/676-7662

THOUSAND OAKS, CA

Best Atmosphere
Boccaccio's Restaurant
   32123 Lindero Canyon Rd., Westlake Village,
      818/889-8300

Best Breakfast
Dupar's
   75 W. Thousand Oaks Blvd., 818/373-8785
Mimi's Cafe
   19710 Nordhoff Pl., Chatsworth, 818/717-8334

Best Burgers
Marcello Ristorante
   140 W. Hillcrest Dr., Ste. 107, 805/371-4367
Mimi's Cafe
   19710 Nordhoff Pl., Chatsworth, 818/717-8334

Best Chinese Food
Hunan Chinese Restaurant
   1352 N. Moorpark Rd., 805/371-0075

Best Coffee
Starbucks
   33 N. Moorpark Rd., 818/381-1848

Best Continental Food
Boccaccio's Restaurant
   32123 Lindero Canyon Rd., Westlake Village,
      818/889-8300

Best Desserts
Baker's Square Restaurant
   3887 E. Thousand Oaks Blvd., Westlake Village,
      805/496-7437
Coco's Bakery Restaurant
   55 Rolling Oaks Dr., 805/379-3939

Best French Food
The Rendezvous
   1282 Newbury Rd., 818/498-1019

Best Italian Food
Tuscany Il Ristorante
   968 S. Westlake Blvd., Ste. 4, 818/880-5642
Allegro Italian Restaurant
   579A N. Ventu Park Rd., Newbury Park, 805/499-6767

Best Restaurant Meal Value
Los Robos Inn
   299 S. Moorpark Rd., 818/495-0431

Best Romantic Dining
Boccaccio's Restaurant
   32123 Lindero Canyon Rd., Westlake Village,
      818/889-8300

Best Salad/Salad Bar
Los Robos Inn
   299 S. Moorpark Rd., 818/495-0431

Best Sandwiches
Roxy's Famous Deli
   1345 E. Thousand Oaks Blvd., 805/379-6767

Oak Tree Restaurant
   3955 E. Thousand Oaks Blvd., Westlake Village,
      818/991-8454
Plug Nickel Restaurant
   717 Lakefield Rd., Ste. 1, Westlake Village,
      805/495-3469

Best Seafood
Fins Seafood Grill
   982 S. Westlake Blvd., Ste. 8, Westlake Village,
      805/494-6494

Best Steaks
Black Angus Restaurant
   139 W. Thousand Oaks Blvd., 805/497-0757
Hungry Hunter
   487 N. Moorpark Rd., 805/497-3925

Best View While Dining
Boccaccio's Restaurant
   32123 Lindero Canyon Rd., Westlake Village,
      818/889-8300

Standbys
International House of Pancakes
   5031 Kanan Rd., Agoura Hills, 818/991-4957
Tony Roma's
   30105 Agoura Rd., Agoura Hills, 818/889-0025
Baskin-Robbins
   324 N. Moorpark Rd., 805/495-3144

TORRANCE, CA

Best Restaurants in Town
La Rive Gauche
   320 Tejon Pl., Palos Verdes Estates, 310/378-0267
Chez Melange
   1718 S. Pacific Coast Hwy., 310/540-9135

Best American Food
Depot Inc.
   1250 Cabrillo Ave., 310/787-7501

Best Barbecue/Ribs
Chicago Ribs
   1410 S. Pacific Coast Hwy., 310/316-7427

Best Breakfast
Cimarron Cafe
   5160 W. 190th St., 310/371-6007
Torrance Bakery and Party Center
   1341 El Prado Ave., 310/787-7501

Best Brunch
Torrance Bakery and Party Center
   1341 El Prado Ave., 310/787-7501

Best Burgers
Snax Home-Original Superburger
   4535 Sepulveda Blvd., 310/316-6631

Best Business Lunch
Misto Caffe and Bakery
   24558 Hawthorne Blvd., 310/375-3608

Cheesecake Factory
605 N. Harbor Dr., Redondo Beach, 310/376-0466
The Depot
1250 Cabrillo Ave., 310/787-7501

Best Casual Dining
Grunions Sports Bar and Grill
1501 N. Sepulveda Blvd., Manhattan Beach,
310/545-9910
Misto Caffe and Bakery
24558 Hawthorne Blvd., 310/375-3608

Best Chinese Food
Szechwan
25229 S. Hawthorne Blvd., 310/378-4235

Best Continental Food
Depot Inc.
1250 Cabrillo Ave., 310/787-7501

Best Desserts
Cheesecake Factory
605 N. Harbor Dr., Redondo Beach, 310/376-0466

Best Dinner
Depot Inc.
1250 Cabrillo Ave., 310/787-7501

Best Family Restaurants
Carrows Restaurant
20535 Hawthorne Blvd., 310/371-6444
Vince's Spaghetti Restaurant
23609 Hawthorne Blvd., 310/375-1455

Best French Food
La Rive Gauche
320 Tejon Pl., Palos Verdes Estates, 310/378-0267

Best Health-Conscious Menu
La Salsa
24223 Crenshaw Blvd., 310/326-1444

Best Italian Food
Vince's Spaghetti Restaurant
23609 Hawthorne Blvd., 310/375-1455

Best Japanese Food
Kanda
23305 Hawthorne Blvd., 310/378-6699

Best Lunch
Manhattan Coolers
309 Manhattan Beach Blvd., Manhattan Beach,
310/546-7344

Best Mexican Food
El Torito Restaurant
23225 Hawthorne Blvd., 310/378-0331
La Salsa
24223 Crenshaw Blvd., 310/326-1444

Best Other Ethnic Food
Descanso (Caribbean)
705 Pier Ave., Hermosa Beach, 310/379-7997
Barnabey's Hotel and Restaurant (British)
3501 N. Sepulveda Blvd., Manhattan Beach,
310/545-5693

El Pollo Inka (Peruvian)
23705 Hawthorne Blvd., 310/373-0062

Best Regional Food
Chez Melange
1718 S. Pacific Coast Hwy., 310/540-9135

Best Salad/Salad Bar
Manhattan Coolers
309 Manhattan Beach Blvd., Manhattan Beach, 310/546-7344
Misto Caffe and Bakery
24558 Hawthorne Blvd., 310/375-3608

Best Sandwiches
Manhattan Coolers
309 Manhattan Beach Blvd., Manhattan Beach, 310/546-7344

Best Seafood
Descanso
705 Pier Ave., Hermosa Beach, 310/379-7997

Best Sports Bar
Grunion's Sports Bar and Grill
1501 N. Sepulveda Blvd., Manhattan Beach, 310/545-9910

TRACY, CA

Best Chinese Food
Mandarin Villa Restaurant
2501 Tracy Blvd., 209/836-1818

Best Italian Food
Fabio's
88 W. Tenth St., 209/836-2012

Best Mexican Food
Casa Nachos Family Mexican
2321 Tracy Blvd., 209/835-9402

Best Microbrewery
Central Station Ale House
714 Central, 209/832-1690

TULARE, CA

Best Bar
Papa Joe's Place
424 N. N St., 209/686-5472

Best Breakfast
V's
210 E. Tulare, 209/684-1264

Best Burgers
Nielson's Restaurant
137 S. M St., 209/688-8563
Monty's Walk-Up Drive-In
700 W. Inyo Ave., 209/686-3491

Best Chinese Food
Jean Jean Chinese Restaurant
72 N. Tower Sq., 209/688-1818
Rice Bowl
300 W. Inyo Ave., 209/686-5634

Best Coffee
Hazel's Kitchen
   237 N. L St., 209/685-0455
Java Villa
   1237 N. Cherry St., 209/688-5282

Best Family Restaurant
Nielson's Restaurant
   137 S. M St., 209/688-8563

Best Homestyle Food
Apple Annie's
   1165 N. Blackstone St., 209/686-3411

Best Italian Food
Rosa's Italian Restaurant
   1351 E. Tulare Ave., 209/686-3938

Best Mexican Food
Ricardo's Mexican
   262 E. Cross Ave., 209/688-6782
Vejar's Mexican Restaurant
   533 E. Cross Ave., 209/688-0279
   1293 S. K St., 209/688-0355
Papa Joe's Place
   424 N. N St., 209/686-5472

Best Pizza
VIP Pizza
   449 E. Pine St., Exeter, 209/592-5170

Best Sandwiches
Nielson's Restaurant
   137 S. M St., 209/688-8563
Hazel's Kitchen
   237 N. L St., 209/685-0455

Best Steaks
Apple Annie's
   1165 N. Blackstone St., 209/686-3411

Standbys
Baskin-Robbins
   1297 N. Cherry St., 209/688-7031

TURLOCK, CA

Best Chinese Food
Golden Hour Restaurant
   415 E. Main St., 209/634-8677

Best Homestyle Food
Latif's Restaurant
   111 N. Golden State Blvd., 209/634-5351

Best Italian Food
Angelini's Italian Restaurant
   2251 Geer Rd., 209/667-6644

Best Mexican Food
El Jardin
   409 E. Olive St., 209/632-0932

Best Outdoor Dining
La Creme Restaurant
   310 E. Main St., 209/667-2293

Best Regional Food
La Creme Restaurant
  310 E. Main St., 209/667-2293

Best Steaks
Trax Bar and Grill
  10 E. Main St., 209/668-8729

VACAVILLE, CA

Best Restaurant in Town
Main 627
  627 Main St., Suisun City, 707/428-6270

Best All-You-Can-Eat Buffet
J.J. North's
  1315 Gateway Blvd., 707/428-6000

Best Bar
T.J.'s Tavern
  554 Main St., 707/448-9993

Best Breakfast
Coffee Tree
  100 Nut Tree Rd., 707/448-8435

Best Brunch
Merchant and Main Grill and Bar
  349 Merchant St., 707/446-0368

Best Casual Dining
Garlic Grill
  1031 Helen Power Dr., 707/447-8979

Best Cheap Meal
Favela's Taqueria
  2040 Harbison Dr., 707/447-1120

Best Chinese Food
China House Restaurant
  513 Main St., 707/446-8068

Best Coffee
Starbucks
  1031 Helen Power Rd., Ste. D-100, 707/447-9668

Best Desserts
Merchant and Main Grill and Bar
  349 Merchant St., 707/446-0368

Best Diner
Chubby's
  1989 Peabody Rd., 707/446-9640
  2091 Harbison Dr., 707/451-2954

Best Health-Conscious Menu
Fresh Choice
  1001 Helen Power Dr., 707/446-1056

Best Homestyle Food
Marie Callender's
  1750 Travis Blvd., Fairfield, 707/428-4745

Best Ice Cream/Yogurt
Colleen's Creamery
  713 Second St., Davis, 916/753-0802

Best Italian Food
Fusilli Ristorante
  620 Jackson St., Fairfield, 707/428-4211

195

Best Late-Night Food
Lyon's Restaurant
909 Merchant St., 707/447-4600

Best Mexican Food
Pelayo's Mexican Dining
1160 E. Monte Vista Ave., 707/449-9365

Best Pizza
Pepperoni's Pizza
700 Merchant St., 707/451-0370

Best Place to be "Seen"
County Grill
811 Texas St., Fairfield, 707/434-8090

Best Place to Eat Alone
Coffee Tree
100 Nut Tree Rd., 707/448-8435

Best Place to Eat When Someone Else Is Buying
Buckhorn
210 Railroad Ave., Winters, 916/795-4503

Best Romantic Dining
Main 627
627 Main St., Suisun City, 707/428-6270

Best Salad/Salad Bar
Fresh Choice
1501 The Courtyard, Fairfield, 707/429-2560

Best Sandwiches
Tortellini Originali
5139 Quinn Rd., 707/453-1514

Best Steaks
Buckhorn
210 Railroad Ave., Winters, 916/795-4503

Best Vegetarian Food
Favela's Taqueria
2040 Harbison Dr., 707/447-1120

Standbys
Applebee's
160 Nut Tree Pkwy., 707/452-1167
Chili's
2001 Harbison Dr., 707/449-8072

VALLEJO, CA

Best Restaurant in Town
Mabel's
635 First St., Benicia, 707/746-7068

Best Atmosphere
Mabel's
635 First St., Benicia, 707/746-7068

Best Breakfast
Washington House Deli Cafe
333A First St., Benicia, 707/745-3364
Joy of Eating
1828 Springs Rd., 707/644-5315
Country Waffle
1601 Marine World Pkwy., 510/552-6940

Best Brunch
Mabel's
635 First St., Benicia, 707/746-7068
Sardine Can
O Harbor Way, 707/553-9492

Best Casual Dining
Sardine Can
O Harbor Way, 707/553-9492

Best Chinese Food
Szechuan Chinese Cuisine
2079 Solano Ave., 707/554-4657
Yet Wah
20050 San Pablo Ave., Crockett, 510/787-3011

Best Coffee
Benicia Cafe
714 First St., Benicia, 707/745-8232
Buttercup Kitchen
2387 N. Main St., Walnut Creek, 510/938-2270

Best Eclectic Menu
Breakfast Break
301 Georgia St., 707/644-6421

Best French Food
Suzanne's
301 Georgia, 510/649-1840

Best Greek/Mediterranean Food
Blandini's
907 First St., Benicia, 707/747-5263

Best Italian Food
Napoli Pizzeria and Italian Food
124 Tennessee St., 707/644-9270

Best Lunch
Sardine Can
O Harbor Way, 707/553-9492

Best Mexican Food
Sandoval's
640 First St., Benicia, 707/746-7830
2032 Columbus Pkwy., Benicia, 707/747-0515

Best Pizza
Napoli Pizzeria and Italian Food
124 Tennessee St., 707/644-9270

Best Salad/Salad Bar
Sardine Can
O Harbor Way, 707/553-9492

Best Seafood
Harbor House Restaurant
23 Harbor Way, 707/642-8984
Sardine Can
O Harbor Way, 707/553-9492

Best Steaks
Harbor House Restaurant
23 Harbor Way, 707/642-8984
Black Angus Restaurant
124 Plaza Dr., 707/647-0595

Best Thai Food
Sala Thai Restaurant
807 First St., Benicia, 707/745-4331

Standbys
Chevy's
157 Plaza Dr., 707/644-1373

VENTURA, CA

Best American Food
Sportsman Restaurant and Lounge
53 S. California St., 805/643-2851
Pierpont Inn
550 San Jon Rd., 805/653-6144

Best Atmosphere
Pierpont Inn
550 San Jon Rd., 805/653-6144

Best Bar
Bombay Bar and Grill
143 S. California St., 805/643-4404

Best Barbecue/Ribs
Rib Tickler
11012 Violeta, 805/6478-7427

Best Breakfast
Vagabond Coffee Shop
760 E. Thompson Blvd., 805/643-1390
Cottage Cafe
1907 E. Thompson Blvd., 805/643-1231

Best Chinese Food
Golden China Restaurant
1105 S. Seaward Ave., 805/652-0688

Best Diner
Busy Bee Cafe
478 E. Main St., 805/643-4864

Best Dinner
Alexander's
1050 Schooner Dr., 805/658-2000

Best Family Restaurant
Sixty-Six California
66 S. California, 805/648-2266

Best Italian Food
Ferraro's Italian Restaurant
2788 E. Main St., 805/648-7270

Best Lunch
Casa de Soria
1961 E. Thompson Blvd., 805/648-2083
Alexander's
1050 Schooner Dr., 805/658-2000

Best Mexican Food
Casa de Soria
1961 E. Thompson Blvd., 805/648-2083
Familia Diaz
245 S. Tenth St., Santa Paula, 805/525-2813
Yolanda's Mexican Restaurant
2753 E. Main St., 805/643-2700

Best Pizza
Beachside Pizzeria
 1141 S. Seaward Ave., 805/648-7858

Best Sandwiches
Sixty-Six California
 66 S. California, 805/648-2266

Best Seafood
Palms
 701 Linden Ave., 805/684-3811
Sportsman Restaurant and Lounge
 53 S. California St., 805/643-2851
Alexander's
 1050 Schooner Dr., 805/658-2000

Best Steaks
Palms
 701 Linden Ave., 805/684-3811
Tony's Steak and Sea Food
 2009 E. Thompson Blvd., 805/643-3322

VICTORVILLE, CA

Best Breakfast
Mollie's Kountry Kitchen
 15775 Mojave Dr., 619/241-4900

Best Burgers
Jason's Hamburgers
 14876 Bear Valley Rd., 619/241-8858

Best Casual Dining
The Bum Steer
 23323 Hwy. 18, Apple Valley, 619/247-1336
The Cocky Bull Ribhouse and Hall
 14180 Hwy. 395, 619/241-2855

Best Cheap Meal
Jason's Hamburgers
 14876 Bear Valley Rd., 619/241-8858
Mollie's Kountry Kitchen
 15775 Mojave Dr., 619/241-4900

Best Chinese Food
Chateau Chang Restaurant
 15425 Anacapa Rd., 619/241-3040

Best Desserts
Marie Callender's
 12180 Mariposa Rd., 619/241-6973

Best Family Restaurant
Mollie's Kountry Kitchen
 15775 Mojave Dr., 619/241-4900

Best French Food
Pagano's Restaurant
 14747 Bear Valley Rd., Hesperia, 619/948-4880

Best Homestyle Food
Mollie's Kountry Kitchen
 15775 Mojave Dr., 619/241-4900

Best Italian Food
Pagano's Restaurant
 14747 Bear Valley Rd., Hesperia, 619/948-4880

Best Mexican Food
Estrada's Mexican Cuisine
18768 Hwy. 18, Ste. 170, Apple Valley, 619/242-4952
John's Pizza Pasta Parlor
15010 Circle Dr., 619/243-3801

Best Place to Eat When Someone Else Is Buying
Pagano's Restaurant
14747 Bear Valley Rd., Hesperia, 619/948-4880

Best Places to Take the Kids
Cask and Cleaver
13885 Park Ave., 619/241-7318
Steer and Stein
12224 Mariposa Rd., 619/241-0775

Best Romantic Dining
Pagano's Restaurant
14747 Bear Valley Rd., Hesperia, 619/948-4880
Honey French Country Restaurant
18564 Hwy. 18, 619/242-4300

Best Steaks
The Bum Steer
23323 Hwy. 18, Apple Valley, 619/247-1336

Standbys
HomeTown Buffet
14689 Valley Center Dr., 619/241-3311
Baskin-Robbins
14558 Seventh St., 619/245-3131
17100 Bear Valley Rd., 619/245-6550
The Olive Garden
12330 Amargosa Rd., 619/245-8100

VISALIA, CA

Best All-You-Can-Eat Buffet
Gumbo Chinese Buffet Restaurant
101 W. Main St., 209/732-4263

Best Bars
Vintage Press Restaurant
216 N. Willis St., 209/733-3033
Michael's on Main
123 W. Main St., 209/635-2686

Best Barbecue/Ribs
Tour's Mesquite Grill
3730 S. Mooney Blvd., 209/635-8687
Breenie's
314 W. Main St., 209/741-1466

Best Breakfast
Valhalla Restaurant
314 W. Center Ave., 209/627-2113

Best Burgers
Checkers
401 W. Acequia Ave., 209/733-4227

Best Business Lunch
Michael's on Main
123 W. Main St., 209/635-2686

Cafe 225
225 W. Main St., 209/733-2967

Best Cheap Meal
A and W Family Restaurant
2611 S. Mooney Blvd., 209/733-4445
301 N. Willis St., 209/625-1513

Best Chinese Food
Lum-Lum's
417 E. Center Ave., 209/733-5292

Best Coffee
Java Jungle Espresso Bar
208 W. Main St., 209/732-5282
Visalia Coffee Company
2933 S. Mooney Blvd., 209/732-6333
The Fox Den
214 W. Main St., 209/635-4265

Best Desserts
Vintage Press Restaurant
216 N. Willis St., 209/733-3033
Michael's on Main
123 W. Main St., 209/635-2686

Best Diner
Main Street Diner
127 W. Main St., 209/739-1822

Best Family Restaurants
Shagnasty's Big Play Cafe
210 W. Center Ave., 209/625-8910
Apline Station
1800 W. Mineral King Ave., 209/627-2643

Best Health-Conscious Menu
Watson's Veggie Garden
615 W. Main St., 209/635-7355

Best Homestyle Food
Valhalla Restaurant
314 W. Center Ave., 209/627-2113

Best Ice Cream/Yogurt
Alpine Station
1800 W. Mineral King Ave., 209/627-2643

Best Italian Food
Little Italy Italian Restaurant
303 W. Main St., 209/734-2906

Best Mexican Food
Las Palmas Restaurant
309 E. Main St., 209/734-5405

Best Pizza
Coastal Pizza
106 S. Locust St., 209/733-4210

Best Place to Be "Seen"
Vintage Press Restaurant
216 N. Willis St., 209/733-3033

Best Place to Eat Alone
Bulene's Restaurant
208 W. Main St., 209/739-8136

Best Places to Eat When Someone Else Is Buying
Vintage Press Restaurant
216 N. Willis St., 209/733-3033
Avalon Cafe 112
1800 W. Mineral King Ave., 209/627-2643

Best Place to Take the Kids
Alpine Station
1800 W. Mineral King Ave., 209/627-2643

Best Romantic Dining
Vintage Press Restaurant
216 N. Willis St., 209/733-3033
Michael's on Main
123 W. Main St., 209/635-2686
Bulene's Restaurant
208 W. Main St., 209/739-8136

Best Sandwiches
Picnic Sandwich Shop
114 W. Main St., 209/734-1847

Best Seafood
Bulene's Restaurant
208 W. Main St., 209/739-8136

Best Steaks
The Double L Steakhouse
401E E. Center Ave., 209/627-1126

Best Tea Rooms
The Fox Den
214 W. Main St., 209/635-4265
Ben Maddox House Bed and Breakfast
601 N. Encina, 209/739-0721

WALNUT CREEK, CA

Best Restaurant in Town
Spiedini Northern Italian Restaurant
101 Ygnacio Valley Rd., 510/939-2100

Best Asian Restaurant
Uncle Yu's Szechuan
999 Oak Hill Rd., Lafayette, 510/283-1688

Best Bagels
The Bagel King
1686 Locust St., 510/938-5464
1701 Willow Pass Rd., Concord, 510/686-4212

Best Bar
Crogan's Bar and Grill
1387 Locust St., 510/933-7800

Best Breakfast
Millie's Kitchen
1018 Oak Hill Rd., Lafayette, 510/283-2397

Best Brunch
Duck Club Restaurant
The Lafayette Park Hotel, 3287 Mt. Diablo Blvd.,
Lafayette, 510/283-7108

Best Coffee
Peet's Coffee and Tea
1343 Locust St., 510/933-9580

Best Coffeehouses
Starbucks
   3547A Mt. Diablo Blvd., Lafayette, 510/284-5811
   1146 Broadway Plz., 510/937-1377
Peet's Coffee and Tea
   1343 Locust St., 510/933-9580

Best Delicatessen
Genova Delicatessen
   1105 S. California Blvd., 510/939-3838

Best French Food
La Cigale
   2195 N. Broadway, 510/937-8800
Le Marquis
   3524 Mt. Diablo Blvd., Lafayette, 510/284-4422

Best Ice Cream/Yogurt
Yogurt Park
   1499 N. California Blvd., 510/937-2569
   80 Broadway Ln., 510/944-4748

Best Italian Food
Spiedini Northern Italian Ristorante
   101 Ygnacio Valley Rd., 510/939-2100

Best Regional Food
High Tech Burrito
   1815 Ygnacio Valley Blvd., 510/938-3888
California Cafe
   1540 N. California Blvd., 510/938-9977

Best Sandwiches
A Sweet Affair
   1815 Ygnacio Valley Rd., 510/944-1910

Best Seafood
Scott's Seafood Grill and Bar
   1333 N. California Blvd., 510/934-1300
   2 Broadway, 510/444-3456

Best Vegetarian Food
Fresh Choice Restaurant
   486 Sunvalley Mall, Concord, 510/671-7222
   1275 S. Main St., 510/938-1529
   2453 Stoneridge Mall Rd., Pleasanton, 510/734-8186

Best Wine Selection
Prima Trattoria e Negozio di Vini
   1522 N. Main St., 510/935-7780

Standbys
Chevy's
   5877 Owens Dr., Pleasanton, 510/416-0451
   650 Ellinwood Way, Pleasant Hill, 510/685-6651

WATSONVILLE, CA

Best Restaurants in Town
Green Valley Grill
   40 Penny Ln., 408/728-0644
Palapas Restaurant and Cantina
   21 Seascape Village, Aptos, 408/662-9000
Seacliff Inn
   7500 Old Dominion Ct., Aptos, 408/688-7300

Shadowbrook Restaurant
1750 Wharf Rd., Capitola, 408/475-1511
The Villager
1032 E. Lake Ave., 408/722-5200

Best Chinese Food
Bamboo Garden
1012 E. Lake Ave., 408/724-1486

Best Italian Food
Anna Maria's Italian Restaurant
640 Eaton St., Santa Cruz, 408/458-9534

Best Mexican Food
Jalisco Restaurant
618 Main St., 408/728-9080
Zuniga's Mexican Food
100 Aviation Way, 408/724-5788
Crow's Nest Restaurant
2218 E. Cliff Dr., Santa Cruz, 408/476-4560

WEST COVINA, CA

Best Restaurants in Town
Marty's Charbroiler
510 S. Glendora Ave., Covina, 818/338-8814
Northwood's Inn of Covina
540 N. Azusa Ave., Covina, 818/331-7444

Best American Food
National Sports Grill and Bar
5970 Orangethorpe Ave., Buena Park, 714/523-0803

Best Asian Restaurants
Shanghai Chinese Restaurant
316 N. Azusa Ave., Covina, 818/966-1890
Restaurant Hayakawa
750 Terrado Plz., Covina, 818/332-8288
Sakura of Tokyo
533 S. Glendora Ave., 818/960-7155

Best Business Lunch
Cask and Cleaver
125 Village Ct., San Dimas, 909/592-1646

Best Continental Food
Walter's Restaurant
308 N. Yale Ave., Claremont, 909/624-4914

Best Delicatessens
Danny's Kosher Pickle Restaurant
402 N. Azusa Ave., Covina, 818/339-1373
Greene's Delicatessen and Restaurant
1025 W. Foothill Blvd., Claremont, 909/626-8802

Best Desserts
Marie Callender's
1030 W. Foothill Blvd., Claremont, 909/621-3985
Some Crust Bakery
119 Yale Ave., Claremont, 909/621-9772

Best Ice Cream/Yogurt
21 Choices
328 S. Indian Hill Blvd., Claremont, 909/621-7175

Best Italian Food
Giovanni Restaurant
  143 N. Citrus Ave., Covina, 818/332-9539
Aruffo's
  126 Yale Ave., Claremont, 909/624-9624

Best Mexican Food
Zendejas
  665 W. Arrow Hwy., San Dimas, 909/592-6762

Best Salad/Salad Bar
Cask and Cleaver
  125 Village Ct., San Dimas, 909/592-1646
Pinnacle Peak
  269 W. Foothill Blvd., San Dimas, 909/599-5312

Best Seafood
Shrimp House
  962 W. Foothill Blvd., Claremont, 909/621-6805

Best Steaks
Derby East
  545 W. Alosta Ave., Glendova, 818/914-2977

Standbys
Chevy's
  1200W West Covina Pkwy., 818/851-9400

WHITTIER, CA

Best Breakfast
Spire's Restaurant
  10140 Carmenita Rd., 562/941-5673
Mimi's Cafe
  15436 Whittier Blvd., 562/947-0339

Best Burgers
Carl's Jr. Restaurant
  13157 Telegraph Rd., 562/941-0548
  16105 Valley View Ave., 562/404-0704

Best Business Lunch
Mimi's Cafe
  15436 Whittier Blvd., 562/947-0339

Best Chinese Food
Mandarin Inn
  10120 S. Carmenita Rd., Santa Fe Springs,
    562/946-4539

Best Desserts
Mimi's Cafe
  15436 Whittier Blvd., 562/947-0339

Best Family Restaurant
Baker's Square Restaurant
  16255 Whittier Blvd., 562/943-6756

Best Health-Conscious Menu
Mimi's Cafe
  15436 Whittier Blvd., 562/947-0339

Best Homestyle Food
Marie Callender's
  12402 Washington Blvd., 562/693-2724
  9829 La Serna Dr., 562/945-3471

Best Mexican Food
Green Burrito
  8536 Norwalk Blvd., 562/699-9143

Best Pizza
Pizza Mania
  13547 Telegraph Rd., 562/944-8803

Best Place to Be "Seen"
Acapulco Mexican Restaurant
  13473 E. Telegraph Rd., Santa Fe Springs,
    562/946-7577

Best Steaks
Stuart Anderson's Black Angus Steakhouse
  15500 E. Whittier Blvd., 562/947-2200

Best Tea Room
Mimi's Cafe
  15436 Whittier Blvd., 562/947-0339

Standbys
The Olive Garden
  13500 Whittier Blvd., 562/693-5999
Red Lobster
  13580 Whittier Blvd., 562/698-0116

WOODLAND, CA

Best American Food
Morrison's Upstairs
  428 1/2 First St., 916/666-6176
Gorman's Restaurant
  37380 Sacramento, Yolo, 916/662-6889

Best Italian Food
Pheasant Club
  2525 Jefferson Blvd., West Sacramento, 916/371-9530

Best Mexican Food
El Charro
  306 Sixth St., 916/662-3804

Best Steaks
Buckhorn
  210 Railroad Ave., Winters, 916/795-4503

Colorado

Best Atmosphere
Hideaway Steakhouse
1212 Eighth St., 719/589-4444

Best Bar
Cattails Bar and Grill
6615 N. River Rd., 719/589-4655

Best Burgers
A and W
2061 Main St., 719/589-4562

Best Chinese Food
Hunan Chinese Restaurant
419 Main St., 719/589-9002

Best Eclectic Menu
Cafe Maya
529 Main St., 719/589-6175

Best Health-Conscious Menu
Lara's Soft Spoken Restaurant
801 State Ave., 719/589-6769
Cafe Maya
529 Main St., 719/589-6175

Best Pizza
Pizza Den
1419 Main St., 719/589-3039

Best Sandwiches
St. Ives A Pub and Eatery
719 Main St., 719/589-0711

Best Seafood
Hideaway Steakhouse
1212 Eighth St., 719/589-4444

Best Steaks
St. Ives, A Pub and Eatery
719 Main St., 719/589-0711

Standbys
Dairy Queen
400 Main St., 719/589-3937

BOULDER, CO

Best All-You-Can-Eat Buffet
Salad Company
  2595 Canyon Blvd., 303/447-8272

Best Asian Restaurant
Young's Place on the Hill
  1083 Fourteenth St., 303/447-9837

Best Bagels
Moe's Broadway Bagels
  2650 Broadway St., 303/444-3252

Best Brunch
Broker Inn
  555 30th St., 303/449-1752
Greenbriar
  8735 N. Foothills Hwy., 303/440-7979
Lucille's
  2124 Fourteenth St., 303/442-4743

Best Burgers
Dark Horse
  2922 Baseline Rd., 510/442-8162
Red Robin
  2580 Arapahoe Ave., 303/442-0320
Tom's Tavern
  1047 Pearl St., 303/442-9363

Best Chinese Food
First Wok
  1718 Broadway St., 303/444-8886
Hunan Garden
  949 Walnut St., 303/442-2772
Orchid Pavilion
  1050 Walnut St., 303/449-4353

Best Coffeehouses
Bookend Cafe
  1115 Pearl St., 303/440-6699
Brewing Market
  1918 Thirteenth St., 303/443-2098
Peaberry
  2721 Arapahoe Ave., 303/449-4111
  947 Pearl St., 303/449-9646
Starbucks
  1402 Broadway St., 303/442-9199
  3033 Arapahoe Ave., 303/440-5090
Trident Cafe
  940 Pearl St., 303/443-3133

Best Delicatessens
Deli Zone
  2900 Valmont Rd., 303/447-9349
On the Hill
  1091 Thirteenth St., 303/449-6952
New York Deli
  1117 Pearl St., 303/449-5161
Salvaggio's Italian Deli
  2655 Pearl St., 303/938-1981

c

Best Desserts
The Cork
   3295 30th St., 303/443-9505
Pour La France
   1001 Pearl St., 303/449-3929
Zolo
   2525 Arapahoe Ave., 303/449-0444

Best Happy Hour Snacks
Piccolo's
   1101 Walnut St., 303/444-3532

Best Ice Cream/Yogurt
Ice Cream
   1964 Thirteenth St., 303/444-6624
Josh and John's
   1111 Thirteenth St., 303/440-9310

Best Indian Food
MijBani Indian Restaurant
   2005 Eighteenth St., 303/442-7000

Best Japanese Food
Sushi Tora
   2014 Tenth St., 303/444-2280
Sushi Zanmai
   1221 Spruce St., 303/449-1752

Best Korean Food
Korea House
   2750 Glenwood, 303/449-1657

Best Mexican Food
Juanita's
   1043 Pearl St., 303/449-5273
Zolo Grill
   2525 Arapahoe Ave., 303/449-0444

Best Microbreweries
Mountain Sun Pub and Brewery
   1535 Pearl St., 303/546-0886
Oasis Brewery and Restaurant
   1095 Canyon Blvd., 303/449-0363
Walnut Brewery
   1123 Walnut St., 303/447-1345

Best Other Ethnic Food
Narayan's Nepal Restaurant (Nepalese)
   921 Pearl St., 303/447-2816

Best Outdoor Dining
Chautauqua Dining Hall
   900 Baseline Rd., 303/442-3282
West End Tavern
   926 Pearl St., 303/444-3535

Best Pizza
Fourteenth Street Bar and Grill
   1400 Pearl St., 303/444-5854
Abo's
   2761 Iris Ave., 303/443-1921
Beau Jo's
   1600 28th St., 303/444-5135
Jalino's
   1647 Arapahoe Ave., 303/443-6300

Nick and Willy's
4800 Baseline Rd., 303/499-9898
801 Pearl St., 303/444-9898
Old Chicago
1102 Pearl St., 303/443-5031

Best Place to Eat When Someone Else Is Buying
Flagstaff House
1138 Flagstaff Dr., 303/442-4640

Best Place to Take the Kids
Red Robin
2580 Arapahoe Ave., 303/442-0320

Best Quick Lunch
Alfalfa's
1651 Broadway St., 303/442-0909
Pressto
3960 Broadway St., 303/444-0780
Quizno's
1136 Pearl St., 303/449-3366
2875 Pearl St., 303/444-6744
601E S. Broadway St., 303/494-5360
6525 Gunpark Dr., 303/530-4920

Best Romantic Dining
Cork
3295 30th St., 303/443-9505
European Cafe
2460 Arapahoe Ave., 303/938-8250
Flagstaff House
1138 Flagstaff Dr., 303/442-4640
Greenbriar
8735 N. Foothills Hwy., 303/440-7979
John's Restaurant
2328 Pearl St., 303/444-5232
Q's
2115 Thirteenth St., 303/442-4880

Best Salad/Salad Bar
Alfalfa's
6151 Broadway St., 303/442-0909
Salad Company
2595 Canyon Blvd., 303/447-8272
Healthy Habits
4760 Baseline Rd., 303/494-9177

Best Sandwiches
Alfalfa's
6151 Broadway St., 303/442-0909
New York Deli
1117 Pearl St., 303/449-5161
Pressto
3960 Broadway St., 303/444-0780
Quizno's
1136 Pearl St., 303/449-3366
2875 Pearl St., 303/444-6744
601E S. Broadway St, 303/494-5360
6525 Gunpark Dr., 303/530-4920

Best Thai Food
Sawaddee
1401 Pearl St., 303/447-3321

Siamese Plate
  1575 Folsom St., 303/447-9718

Best Vegetarian Food
Creative Vegetarian Cafe
  1837 Pearl St., 303/449-1952
Harvest Restaurant
  1738 Pearl St., 303/449-6223
Masala's Creekside Cafe
  2111 30th St., 303/447-1776
MijBani Indian Restaurant
  2005 Eighteenth St., 303/442-7000
Rudi's
  4720 Table Mesa Dr., 303/494-5858
Turley's
  2350 Arapahoe Ave., 303/442-2800

Best Vietnamese Food
Chez Thuy
  2655 28th St., 303/442-1700
Viet Hoa
  2015 Broadway St., 303/440-4745

Standbys
Haagen-Dazs
  1148 Pearl St., 303/443-9032
TCBY
  2430 Arapahoe Ave., 303/939-8289

COLORADO SPRINGS, CO

Best Restaurants in Town
Peppertree Restaurant
  888 W. Moreno Ave., 719/471-4888
Broadmoore Hotel
  1 Lake Ave., 719/577-5733

Best American Food
Beckett's Brewhouse and Restaurant
  128 S. Tejon St., 719/633-3230

Best Appetizers
Judge Baldwin's Brewing Company
  4 S. Cascade Ave., 719/473-5600

Best Bagels
Lots A' Bagels
  445 E. Cheyenne Mountain Blvd., 719/540-9096
  8041 N. Academy Blvd., 719/522-1225
  1025 N. Academy Blvd., 719/591-1104

Best Barbecue/Ribs
B.F. Goodribs
  319 N. Chelton Rd., 719/597-7400

Best Breakfast
Olive Branch Restaurant
  333 N. Tejon St., 719/475-1199
  2140 Vickers Dr., 719/593-9522

Best Casual Dining
Bambino's Pizzeria/Italian
  3661A Star Ranch Rd., 719/576-7600
  2514 W. Colorado Ave., 719/635-1212

2849 E. Platte Ave., 719/630-8121
4737 N. Academy Blvd., 719/590-7070

Best Continental Food
Briarhurst Manor
404 Manitou Ave., Manitou Springs, 719/685-1864

Best Delicatessen
Bell's Deli
154 E. Cheyenne Mountain Blvd., 719/576-8633

Best Desserts
Bell's Deli
154 E. Cheyenne Mountain Blvd., 719/576-8633

Best French Food
La Petit Maison
1015 W. Colorado Ave., 719/632-4887

Best German Food
Edelweiss Restaurant
34 E. Ramona Ave., 719/633-2220

Best Health-Conscious Menu
Adams Mountain Cafe
733 Manitou Ave., Manitou Springs, 719/685-1430

Best Italian Food
Panino's
604 N. Tejon St., 719/635-7452
1732 S. Eighth St., 719/635-1188
Luigi's Restaurant
947 S. Tejon St., 719/632-0700
Bambino's Pizzeria/Italian
3661A Star Ranch Rd., 719/576-7600
2514 W. Colorado Ave., 719/635-1212
2849 E. Platte Ave., 719/630-8121
4737 N. Academy Blvd., 719/590-7070

Best Lunch
Beckett's Brewhouse and Restaurant
128 S. Tejon St., 719/633-3230

Best Mexican Food
Jose Muldoon's
222 N. Tejon St., 719/636-2311
Pepe's Restaurante and Cantina
2427 N. Academy Blvd., 719/574-5801

Best Microbreweries
Judge Baldwin's Brewing Company
4 S. Cascade Ave., 719/473-5600
Phantom Canyon Brewing Company
2 E. Pikes Peak Ave., 719/635-2800
Beckett's Brewhouse and Restaurant
128 S. Tejon St., 719/633-3230

Best Other Ethnic Food
Mataam Fez Moroccan Restaurant (Moroccan)
3625 W. Colorado Ave., 719/634-2101

Best Pizza
Old Chicago Pasta Pizza and Beer
118 N. Tejon St., 719/634-8812
7115 Commerce Center Dr., 719/593-7678

Best Place to Eat When Someone Else Is Buying
Broadmoore Hotel
1 Lake Ave., 719/577-5733

Best Sandwiches
Bell's Deli
154 E. Cheyenne Mountain Blvd., 719/576-8633
Ritz Grille
15 S. Tejon St., 719/635-8484

Best Seafood
Hatch Cover Restaurant
252 E. Cheyenne Mountain Blvd., 719/576-5223

DENVER, CO

Best Restaurants in Town
Strings
1700 Humboldt St., 303/831-7310
Briarwood Inn
1630 Eighth St., Golden, 303/279-3121
Flagstaff House
1138 Flagstaff Dr., 303/442-4640

Best All-You-Can-Eat Buffet
Alfalfa's
900 E. Eleventh Ave., 303/832-7701
5910 S. University Blvd., Littleton, 303/798-9699
865 S. Colorado Blvd., 303/733-2105

Best American Food
Old Fort Restaurant and Lounge
1409 Barlow Rd., Ft. Morgan, 303/867-9481
Marvin Gardens
2223 S. Monaco Pkwy., 303/756-8230
Black-Eyed Pea
3480 S. Galena St., 303/337-0778

Best Bagels
Finster Brother's Bagel Bakery and Cafe
5709 E. Colfax Ave., 303/377-2088
8100 S. Quebec St., Englewood, 303/740-7277

Best Barbecue/Ribs
Sam Taylor's Barbecue at City Park
2500 York St., 303/295-2095
Bennett's
1201 Sixteenth St., 303/893-3399
3700 Peoria St., 303/375-0339
County Line
8351 South Park Ln., Littleton, 303/797-3727

Best Breakfast
Fratelli's Italian Restaurant
1200 E. Hampden Ave., Englewood, 303/761-4771
Chef Zorba's Cuisine
2630 E. Twelfth Ave., 303/321-0091
Simm's Landing
11911 W. Sixth Ave., Golden, 303/237-0465
Fresh Fish Company
7800 E. Hampden Ave., 303/740-9556

Best Brunch
Marina Landing
  8101 E. Belleview Ave., 303/770-4741
Boulder Broker Inn
  555 30th St., Boulder, 303/444-3330
Grand Slam Sports Cafe
  810 S. Wadsworth Blvd., Lakewood, 303/922-3400
Tuscany
  Loews Giorgio Hotel, 4150 E. Mississippi Ave.,
    Glendale, 303/782-9300
Simm's Landing
  11911 W. Sixth Ave., Golden, 303/237-0465
Fresh Fish Company
  7800 E. Hampden Ave., 303/740-9556

Best Burgers
Cherry Cricket
  2641 E. Second Ave., 303/322-7666
Good Times
  808 E. Colfax Ave., 303/830-8060
  6151 E. Colfax Ave., 303/322-6339
  1300 S. Colorado Blvd., 303/782-9223
Red Robin
  3333 S. Wadsworth Blvd., 303/989-8448

Best Business Lunch
The Augusta at Westin Hotel Tabor Center
  1672 Lawrence St., 303/572-9100
Ocean Fresh Grill
  4151 E. County Line Rd., 303/770-7722

Best Cheap Meal
Lim's Mongolian BBQ
  1530 Blake St., 303/893-1158

Best Chinese Food
Jade Garden
  5120 E. Arapahoe Rd., Littleton, 303/770-5188
China Terrace
  1512 Larimer St., 303/592-1032
Imperial Chinese Seafood
  431 S. Broadway, 303/698-2800

Best Coffee
Pizza Colore Cafe
  1512 Larimer St., Ste. 12R, 303/534-6844
Starbucks
  2701 E. Third Ave., 303/331-9910
  1401 Larimer St., 303/446-8534
  200 Fillmore St., 303/388-7656
  7777 E. Hampden Ave., 303/695-8853
Peaberry
  4785 Elati St., 303/741-4111
  1685 S. Colorado Blvd., 303/756-4111
  1201 Sixteenth St., 303/595-4111
  3031 E. Second Ave., 303/322-4111
The Market
  1445 Larimer St., 303/534-5140

Best Coffeehouses
Trident Booksellers Inc.
  940 Pearl St., Boulder, 303/443-3133

Caffe Mars
  1425 Pearl St., Boulder, 303/938-1750

Best Desserts
Zolo Grill
  2525 Arapahoe Ave., Boulder, 303/449-0444
Marie Callender's
  3535 S. Yosemite St., 303/779-0216
Le Delice
  250 Steele St., 303/331-0972

Best French Food
Le Central
  112 E. Eighth Ave., 303/863-9094
Tante Louise
  4900 E. Colfax Ave., 303/355-4488
The Normandy
  1515 Madison St., 303/321-3312

Best Greek/Mediterranean Food
The Mediterranean Restaurant
  1002 Walnut St., Boulder, 303/444-5335
Yanni's
  2223 S. Monaco Pkwy., 303/692-0404
Central 1
  300 S. Pearl St., 303/778-6675
Mataam Fez
  4609 E. Colfax Ave., 303/399-9282

Best Happy Hour Snacks
Gate 12
  2301 Blake St., 303/292-2212

Best Ice Cream/Yogurt
Cucina Leone
  763 S. University Blvd., 303/722-5466

Best Italian Food
Grisanti's
  4100 E. Mexico Ave., 303/782-5170
Josephina's
  1433 Larimer St., 303/623-0166
  1035 E. Seventeenth Ave., 303/860-8011
  7777 E. Hampden Ave., 303/750-4422

Best Japanese Food
Mori
  2019 Market St., 303/298-1864
Sushi Den
  1487 S. Pearl St., 303/777-0826
Gasho of Japan
  5071C S. Syracuse St., 303/773-3277
Benihana
  3295 S. Tamarac Dr., 303/750-0200

Best Korean Food
Silla
  3005 S. Peoria St., Aurora, 303/338-5070

Best Late-Night Food
Pasquini's Pizzeria and Blu Luna Room
  1310 S. Broadway, 303/744-0917
Chives American Bistro
  1120 E. Sixth Ave., 303/722-3800

C

Best Mexican Food
La Cueva
   9742 E. Colfax Ave., Aurora, 303/367-1422
Blue Bonnet
   457 S. Broadway, 303/778-0147
Chez Jose
   3027 E. Second Ave., 303/322-9160

Best Middle Eastern Food
Jerusalem
   1890 E. Evans Ave., 303/777-8828

Best Neighborhood Restaurant
RosaLinda's Mexican Cafe
   2005 W. 33rd Ave., 303/455-0608

Best Outdoor Dining
La Coupole Cafe
   2191 Arapahoe St., 303/297-2288
Rock Bottom Brewery
   1001 Sixteenth St., 303/534-7616

Best Salad/Salad Bar
Healthy Habits
   4760 Baseline Rd., 303/494-9177
   865 S. Colorado Blvd., 303/733-2105
   14195 W. Colfax Ave., Golden, 303/277-9293
   7418 S. University Blvd., Littleton, 303/740-7044
Denver Salad Company
   14201 E. Public Market Dr., Aurora, 303/750-1339
   2700 S. Colorado Blvd., 303/691-2050
   102 Inverness Terrace E., Englewood, 303/790-7706
   2010 E. County Line Rd., Littleton, 303/798-3453
Coos Bay Bistro
   2076 S. University Blvd., 303/744-3591

Best Sandwiches
Old-Fashioned Italian Deli
   395 W. Littleton Blvd., Littleton, 303/794-1402

Best Seafood
Fresh Fish Company
   7800 E. Hampden Ave., 303/740-9556
McCormick's
   1659 Wazee, 303/825-1107

Best Steaks
Luke's
   4990 Kipling St., 303/422-3300
Morton's of Chicago
   900 Aurora Pkwy., 303/825-3353
Aurora Summit
   2700 S. Havana St., Aurora, 303/751-2112
Black Angus
   1295 Cortez St., 303/426-6010

Best Sushi
Sushi Den
   1487 S. Pearl St., 303/777-0826
Mori
   2019 Market St., 303/298-1864
Kobe An
   85 S. Union Blvd., Lakewood, 303/989-5907

Best Thai Food
Taste of Thailand
  504 E. Hampden Ave., Englewood, 303/762-9112

Best Vegetarian Food
Porter Memorial Hospital Cafeteria
  2525 S. Downing St., 303/778-1955
Masala's International Creekside Cafe
  2111 30th St., Boulder, 303/447-1776
Healthy Habits
  865 S. Colorado Blvd., 303/733-2105
Harvest
  430 S. Colorado Blvd., 303/399-6652
  3900 E. Mexico Ave., Ste. 740, 303/753-0114
Greens Cafe
  1469 S. Pearl St., 303/744-1940

Best Vietnamese Food
New Saigon
  630 S. Federal Blvd., 303/936-4954
Little Saigon
  201 Steele St., Ste. 3C, 303/333-4569
T-Wa Inn
  555 S. Federal Blvd., 303/922-4584
New Orient
  10203 E. Iliff Ave., 303/751-1288

Best Wine Selection
Napa Cafe
  2033 E. Colfax Ave., 303/377-6869
Flagstaff House
  1138 Flagstaff Dr., 303/442-4640

Standbys
Tony Roma's
  12161 E. Iliff Ave., Aurora, 303/750-1212
The Olive Garden
  2390 S. Havana St., Aurora, 303/745-9945
  3905 S. College Ave., Ft. Collins, 303/225-3803
  5380 S. Wadsworth Blvd., Littleton, 303/978-0444
  2520 E. County Line Rd., Littleton, 303/843-9822
  5551 W. 88th Ave., Westminster, 303/650-0889
Sizzler
  2440 Hwy. 6 at Hwy. 50, Grand Junction,
    303/245-2849
  7961 S. Broadway, Littleton, 303/798-0355
  7900 W. Quincy Ave., Littleton, 303/972-0806
  601 S. Main St., Longmont, 303/772-8457

DURANGO, CO

Best Bar
AJ's Grill and Sports Bar
  128 E. Sixth St., 970/247-5085
Farquharts-Pizza Mia
  725 Main Ave., 970/247-5442
  1 Skier Pl., 970/247-9000

Best Brunch
Edgewater Restaurant and Lounge
  501 Camino Del Rio, 970/259-6582

Best Burgers
Olde Tymer's Cafe
  1000 Main Ave., 970/259-2990

Best Chinese Food
Golden Dragon Restaurant
  992 Main Ave., 970/259-0956

Best Coffee
Steaming Bean Coffee Company
  915 Main Ave., 970/385-7901
Durango Coffee Company
  730 Main Ave., 970/259-2059

Best Desserts
Carver's Bakery Cafe
  1022 Main Ave., 970/259-2545
Le Rendezvous Swiss Bakery
  750 Main Ave., 970/385-5685

Best Family Restaurants
Carver's Bakery Cafe
  1022 Main Ave., 970/259-2545
Lori's Family Dining
  2653 Main Ave., 970/247-1224

Best Ice Cream/Yogurt
Durango Country Creamery
  600 Main Ave., 970/247-8111

Best Italian Food
Ariano's Italian Restaurant
  150 E. Sixth St., 970/247-1510

Best Mexican Food
Francisco's Restaurante
  619 Main Ave., 970/247-4098
Gazpacho New Mexican Restaurant
  431 E. Second Ave., 970/259-9494

Best Pizza
Pronto Pizza and Pasta
  160 E. Sixth St., 970/247-1510
A'Roma Restaurant and Tavern
  2659 Main Ave., 970/259-0188

Best Salad/Salad Bar
Red Snapper
  144 E. Ninth St., 970/259-3417

Best Sandwiches
Mr. Rosewater's Deli
  552 Main Ave., 970/247-8788

Best Seafood
Ore House
  147 E. Sixth St., 970/247-5707

Best Steaks
Palace Grill
  501B Main Ave., 970/247-2018
Sweeney's
  1644 County Rd. 203, 970/247-5236

Best Vegetarian Food
Durango's Meeting Place
  666 E. Sixth Ave., 970/247-5322

Best View While Dining
Sweeney's
  1644 County Rd. 203, 970/247-5236

FT. COLLINS, CO

Best Atmosphere
Nico's Catacombs
  115 S. College Ave., 970/482-6426

Best Breakfast
Cafe Bluebird
  524 W. Laurel St., 970/484-7755
Rainbow Limited
  212 W. Laurel St., 970/221-2664
Silver Grill Cafe
  218 Walnut St., 970/484-4656

Best Coffee
Deja Vu Coffeehouse
  646 1/2 S. College Ave., 970/221-3243
Starry Night Coffee Company
  112 S. College Ave., 970/493-3039

Best Desserts
Pour La France Bakery and Cafe
  100 W. Mountain Ave., 970/482-9868

Best Homestyle Food
Black-Eyed Pea
  4312 S. College Ave., 970/226-6661

Best Ice Cream/Yogurt
Walrus Ice Cream
  125 W. Mountain Ave., 970/482-5919

Best Italian Food
Canino's Italian Restaurant
  613 S. College Ave., 970/493-7205

Best Mexican Food
Armadillo
  354 Walnut St., 970/492-4440
Gonzalo's Restaurant
  172 N. College Ave., 970/493-2002

Best Pizza
Cozzola's Pizza
  241 Linden St., 970/482-3557

Best Places to Eat When Someone Else Is Buying
Cuisine Cuisine
  130 S. Mason St., 970/221-0399
Matthew and Company
  1204 S. College Ave., 970/221-1343

Best Romantic Dining
Canino's Italian Restaurant
  613 S. College Ave., 970/493-7205

Best Sandwiches
Avogadro's Number
  605 S. Mason St., 970/493-5555
Pickle Barrel
  122 W. Laurel St., 970/484-0235

Best Seafood
Pelican Fish
3512 S. Mason St., 970/226-1522

Best Vegetarian Food
Rainbow Limited
212 W. Laurel St., 970/221-2664

Best Vietnamese Food
Saigon 17
146 N. College Ave., 970/484-7255

GLENWOOD SPRINGS, CO

Best American Food
Rivers
2525 S. Grand Ave., 970/928-8813

Best Atmosphere
Hotel Colorado
526 Pine St., 970/945-6511

Best Barbecue/Ribs
Smokin' Willies
101 W. Sixth St., 970/945-2479

Best Breakfast
Daily Bread Cafe and Bakery
729 Grand Ave., 970/945-6253

Best Brunch
Hotel Colorado
526 Pine St., 970/945-6511

Best Burgers
Charcoalburger Drive In
51659 Hwy. 6 at 24, 970/945-6652

Best Chinese Food
May Palace
820 Grand Ave., 970/945-0472

Best Desserts
Daily Bread Cafe and Bakery
729 Grand Ave., 970/945-6253

Best Family Restaurant
Italian Underground
715 Grand Ave., 970/945-6422

Best Italian Food
Italian Underground
715 Grand Ave., 970/945-6422

Best Mexican Food
Dos Hombres Restaurant
51783 Hwy. 6 at 24, 970/928-0490
Los Desperados
55 Mel Rey Rd., 970/945-6878

Best Pizza
Italian Underground
715 Grand Ave., 970/945-6422

Best Seafood
Rivers
2525 S. Grand Ave., 970/928-8813

Standbys
Baskin-Robbins
  1105 Grand Ave., 970/945-7338

GREELEY, CO

Best Restaurants in Town
Potato Brumbaugh's
  2400 Seventeenth St., 970/356-6340
The Egg and I
  3830 Tenth St., 970/353-7737
Fat Albert's
  1717 23rd Ave., 970/356-1999

Best All-You-Can-Eat Buffet
Salad and Pasta Company
  2140 35th Ave., 970/330-2766

Best Asian Restaurants
Hunan
  2028 35th Ave., 970/330-0755
Canton Garden
  1330 Eighth Ave., 970/353-7314
Jade Palace
  3605 Tenth St., 970/356-3388

Best Bars
Jackson's Hole
  2100 35th Ave., 970/330-3400
Smiling Moose
  2501 Eleventh Ave., 970/356-7010
Fat Albert's
  1717 23rd Ave., 970/356-1999
The Gambler
  618 25th Ave., 970/351-7575
Lucky Star
  33131 Hwy. 85, Lucerne, 970/351-8000
Bruce's Bar
  345 First St., Severence, 970/686-2320

Best Breakfast
The Egg and I
  3830 Tenth St., 970/353-7737
The Kitchen
  905 Sixteenth St., 970/351-7396

Best Burgers
JB's
  2501 Eighth Ave., 970/352-3202
Jackson's Hole
  2100 35th Ave., 970/330-3400
Neighborhood Grill
  3820 Tenth St., 970/353-4449
  3000 23rd Ave., 970/356-4449
  1630 25th Ave., 970/352-4099

Best Coffee
Margie's Java Joint
  931 Sixteenth St., 970/356-6364
Village Inn
  2729 Eighth Ave., 970/353-5187
  921 30th Ave., 970/356-5449

Best Desserts
Fat Albert's
  1717 23rd Ave., 970/356-1999
Potato Brumbaugh's
  2400 Seventeenth St., 970/356-6340

Best Happy Hour Snacks
Smiling Moose
  2501 Eleventh Ave., 970/356-7010
Jackson's Hole
  2100 35th Ave., 970/330-3400
Pepe O'Toole's
  2726 Eleventh Street Rd., 970/353-5950
Old Chicago
  2349 W. 29th St., 970/330-1116

Best Italian Food
Cable's End
  3780 Tenth St., 970/356-4847
Roma
  728 Sixteenth St., 970/352-9511
Old Chicago
  2349 W. 29th St., 970/330-1116

Best Mexican Food
Farmer's Inn
  109 S. Third St., La Salle, 970/284-6100
Armadillo
  111 S. First St., La Salle, 970/284-5565
Alberto's
  2525 Tenth St., 970/356-1417

Best Pizza
Old Chicago
  2349 W. 29th St., 970/330-1116
Roma
  728 Sixteenth St., 970/352-9511

Best Places to Eat When Someone Else Is Buying
Potato Brumbaugh's
  2400 Seventeenth St., 970/356-6340
The Egg and I
  3830 Tenth St., 970/353-7737
Rafferty's
  5990 Tenth St., 970/352-1664

Best Restaurant Meal Value
The Egg and I
  3830 Tenth St., 970/353-7737

Best Romantic Dining
Potato Brumbaugh's
  2400 Seventeenth St., 970/356-6340
Fat Albert's
  1717 23rd Ave., 970/356-1999
Ebony Room
  3313 Eleventh Ave., Evans, 970/339-5241

Best Salad/Salad Bar
Salad and Pasta Company
  2140 35th Ave., 970/330-2766

Best Sandwiches
Fat Albert's
   1717 23rd Ave., 970/356-1999
The Egg and I
   3830 Tenth St., 970/353-7737
Neighborhood Grill
   3820 Tenth St., 970/353-4449
   3000 23rd Ave., 970/356-4449
   1630 25th Ave., 970/352-4099

Best Seafood
New Plantation
   3520 Eleventh Ave., Evans, 970/330-7903
Potato Brumbaugh's
   2400 Seventeenth St., 970/356-6340

Best Sports Bars
Jackson's Hole
   2100 35th Ave., 970/330-3400
Old Chicago
   2349 W. 29th St., 970/330-1116
The Dugout
   2509 Eleventh Ave., 970/356-8739

Best Steaks
Ebony Room
   3313 Eleventh Ave., Evans, 970/339-5241
Potato Brumbaugh's
   2400 Seventeenth St., 970/356-6340
Rafferty's
   5990 Tenth St., 970/352-1664

Best Vegetarian Food
Salad and Pasta Company
   2140 35th Ave., 970/330-2766
The Egg and I
   3830 Tenth St., 970/353-7737
Old Chicago
   2349 W. 29th St., 970/330-1116

Standbys
Western Sizzlin
   3033 Eighth Ave., 970/351-7000
Golden Corral Family Steakhouse
   3035 23rd Ave., 970/330-1014
Denny's
   2319 Eighth Ave., 970/351-6644
Perkins
   2297 Greeley Mall, 970/352-9251
Pizza Hut
   2439 W. Tenth St., 970/356-6736
   2523 Eighth Ave., 970/352-8981
Red Lobster
   2885 23rd Ave., 970/330-6200

LAMAR, CO

Best All-You-Can-Eat Buffet
Ranchers Restaurant
   Lamar Truck Plaza, 33110 County Rd. 7,
   719/336-3445

Best Atmosphere
Cow Palace Inn
1301 N. Main St., 719/336-7753

Best Barbecue/Ribs
Hickory House
1113 N. Main St., 719/336-5018

Best Breakfast
Ranchers Restaurant
Lamar Truck Plaza, 33110 County Rd. 7,
719/336-3445

Best Burgers
BJ's Burger and Beverage
1510 S. Main St., 719/336-5386

Best Chinese Food
Green Garden
601 E. Olive St., 719/336-3264

Best Coffee
Ranchers Restaurant
Lamar Truck Plaza, 33110 County Rd. 7,
719/336-3445

Best Family Restaurant
Blackwell Station
1301 S. Main St., 719/336-7575

Best Ice Cream/Yogurt
BJ's Burger and Beverage
1510 S. Main St., 719/336-5386

Best Mexican Food
The Main Cafe
114 S. Main St., 719/336-5736

Best Salad/Salad Bar
Ranchers Restaurant
Lamar Truck Plaza, 33110 County Rd. 7,
719/336-3445

Best Steaks
Blackwell Station
1301 S. Main St., 719/336-7575

Standbys
Pizza Hut
610 N. Main St., 719/336-7300

LOVELAND, CO

Best Atmosphere
Parsonage Restaurant
405 E. Fifth St., 970/962-9700

Best Breakfast
Egg and I
2525 N. Lincoln Ave., 970/635-0050
Heartland Cafe
301 E. Fourth St., 970/669-7774

Best Business Lunch
Summit Restaurant
3208 W. Eisenhower Blvd., 970/669-6648

Best Chinese Food
China Dragon
　1525 W. Eisenhower Blvd., 970/663-3734

Best Coffee
Coffee Bean
　444 N. Lincoln Ave., 970/663-1144
Black Cup
　4527 W. Eisenhower Blvd., 970/663-0795
Boyer's Coffee Emporium
　257D E. 29th St., 970/593-0635

Best Continental Food
Parsonage Restaurant
　405 E. Fifth St., 970/962-9700

Best Desserts
Schmidt's Bakery and Deli
　2248 W. First St., 970/667-9811

Best Health-Conscious Menu
Peaks Cafe
　425 E. Fourth St., 970/669-6158
Cabin Country Natural Foods
　248 E. Fourth St., 970/669-9280

Best Ice Cream/Yogurt
Peaks Cafe
　425 E. Fourth St., 970/669-6158

Best Mexican Food
Adelita's Fine Mexican Food
　414 E. Sixth St., 970/669-9577
Juan's Cantina
　128 E. Fourth St., 970/593-9197

Best Pizza
Justine's Pizza
　1906 W. Eisenhower Blvd., 970/667-8808

Best Sandwiches
Colorado Grill
　106 E. 29th St., 970/663-5698
　2225 W. Eisenhower Blvd., 970/669-7377

Best Seafood
Black Steer
　436 N. Lincoln Ave., 970/667-6679
Summit Restaurant
　3208 W. Eisenhower Blvd., 970/669-6648

Best Southwestern Food
Cactus Grille
　125 E. Fourth St., 970/663-4500

Best Steaks
Black Steer
　436 N. Lincoln Ave., 970/667-6679

MONTROSE, CO

Best Bar
JJ's Restaurant
　613 E. Main St., 970/249-5349

Best Breakfast
Starvin' Arvin's
  1320 Hwy. 550, 970/249-7787

Best Burgers
Backwoods Inn
  103 Rose Ln., 970/249-1961

Best Coffee
Mocha Joe's
  833 S. Townsend Ave., 970/240-1808
Mountain Valley Booksellers and Coffee Shop
  328 E. Main St., 970/249-1841

Best Desserts
Red Barn Restaurant
  1413 E. Main St., 970/249-8100

Best Family Restaurants
Backwoods Inn
  103 Rose Ln., 970/249-1961
Red Barn Restaurant
  1413 E. Main St., 970/249-8100

Best Italian Food
Sicily's Italian Restaurant
  1135 E. Main St., 970/240-9199

Best Mexican Food
El Sombrero
  82 Rose Ln., 970/249-0217

Best Pizza
Sicily's Italian Restaurant
  1135 E. Main St., 970/240-9199

Best Sandwiches
Backstreet Bagel Shop
  192 S. Townsend Ave., 970/240-3675

Best Steaks
Backwoods Inn
  103 Rose Ln., 970/249-1961
Red Barn Restaurant
  1413 E. Main St., 970/249-8100

Standbys
Dairy Queen
  1001 S. Townsend Ave., 970/249-8291
Baskin-Robbins
  300 S. Sixth St., 970/249-1991

PUEBLO, CO

Best Restaurants in Town
La Renaissance
  217 E. Routt Ave., 719/543-6367
La Tranica's
  1143 E. Abriendo Ave., 719/542-1113

Best All-You-Can-Eat Buffet
Country Buffet
  3020 Hart Rd., 719/545-3502

Best Bars
Irish Pub and Grille
  108 W. Third St., 719/542-9974

Gold Dust Saloon
130 S. Union Ave., 719/545-0741

Best Breakfast
Pantry Restaurant
109 E. Abriendo Ave., 719/543-8072

Best Brunch
Pueblo West Inn
201 S. McCulloch Blvd., 719/547-2111

Best Burgers
Star Bar and Lunch
300 Spring St., 719/542-9718
Gold Dust Saloon
130 S. Union Ave., 719/545-0741

Best Business Lunch
Ianne's B Street Cafe
121 W. B St., 719/583-9239

Best Casual Dining
Cafe Del Rio
5200 Nature Center Rd., 719/545-1009

Best Cheap Meal
Pinon Restaurant Stop
4803 N. I-25, 719/545-3990

Best Chinese Food
Orient Express Cafe
629 N. Main St., 719/542-4442
Mandarin Chinese Restaurant
240 W. 29th St., 719/542-5151

Best Coffee
The Lamplight
126 S. Union Ave., 719/542-4010

Best Desserts
Magpie's
229 S. Union Ave., 719/542-5522

Best Diner
The Drugstore
112 W. Second St., 719/542-5528

Best Family Restaurant
Black-Eyed Pea
801 W. Hwy. 50, 719/583-9544

Best French Food
Le Petit Chablis
512 Royal Gorge Blvd., Canon City, 719/269-3333

Best Health-Conscious Menu
Magpie's
229 S. Union Ave., 719/542-5522

Best Homestyle Food
Pantry Restaurant
109 E. Abriendo Ave., 719/543-8072

Best Italian Food
La Tranica's
1143 E. Abriendo Ave., 719/542-1113
Ianne's Whiskey Ridge
4333 Thatcher Ave., 719/564-8551

227

Best Late-Night Food
Patti's Restaurant
  241 S. Santa Fe Ave., 719/543-2371

Best Mexican Food
Mill Stop
  317 Bay State Ave., 719/564-0407
Grand Prix Restaurant and Lounge
  615 E. Mesa Ave., 719/542-9825

Best Pizza
Do Drop Inn
  1201 S. Santa Fe Ave., 719/542-0818

Best Place to Be "Seen"
Ianne's B Street Cafe
  121 W. B St., 719/583-9239

Best Place to Eat Alone
Magpie's
  229 S. Union Ave., 719/542-5522

Best Place to Eat When Someone Else Is Buying
Lindy's at Rosemount
  419 W. Fourteenth St., 719/544-9593

Best Place to Take the Kids
Peter Piper Pizza
  160 W. 29th St., 719/544-9593

Best Romantic Dining
Park East Restaurant
  720 Goodnight Ave., 719/561-8707

Best Sandwiches
Pagano's
  3416 W. Northern Ave., 719/566-0067
All Seasons Gourmet Deli Cafe
  2800 N. Elizabeth St., 719/543-5060

Best Steaks
Mozart's Lounge
  1120 N. Main St., 719/542-9662

Best Tea Room
Tivoli's
  325 S. Union Ave., 719/545-1448

Best Other Restaurant
Gaetaun's Restaurant
  910 W. Hwy. 50, 719/546-0949

Standbys
Baskin-Robbins
  3016 W. Northern Ave., 719/561-8969
  3407 Dillon Dr., 719/544-9711
  116 Bonforte Blvd., 719/542-8666
Red Lobster
  3306 N. Elizabeth St., 719/544-1000

STEAMBOAT SPRINGS, CO

Best Barbecue/Ribs
Double Z Bar and Bar BQ
  1124 Yampa St., 970/879-0890

Best Breakfast
The Shack Cafe
  740 Lincoln Ave., 970/879-9975

Best Chinese Food
Canton Chinese Restaurant
  720 Lincoln Ave., 970/879-4480

Best Coffee
Mocha Molly's
  635 S. Lincoln Ave., 970/879-0587

Best Coffeehouse
Off The Beaten Path Bookstore
  56 Seventh St., 970/879-6830

Best Continental Food
Ore House at the Pine Grove
  1465 Pine Grove Rd., 970/879-1190

Best Family Restaurant
Ore House at the Pine Grove
  1465 Pine Grove Rd., 970/879-1190

Best Ice Cream/Yogurt
Banana Boat
  845 Lincoln Ave., 970/879-7424

Best Mexican Food
La Montana Mexican Restaurant
  2500 Village Dr., 970/879-5800

Best Microbrewery
Steamboat Brewery and Tavern
  435 Lincoln Ave., 970/879-2233

Best Places to Take the Kids
Old Town Pub and Restaurant
  600 S. Lincoln Ave., 970/879-2101
Ore House at the Pine Grove
  1465 Pine Grove Rd., 970/879-1190

Best Seafood
Coral Grill
  Anglers Dr., 970/879-6858

Best Steaks
Old West Steak House
  1104 Lincoln Ave., 970/879-1441

Best View While Dining
Hazie's
  2305 Mount Werner Cir., 970/879-6111

STERLING, CO

Best Atmosphere
China Garden Restaurant
  126 W. Main St., 970/522-1137

Best Breakfast
TJ Bummer's Kitchen
  203 Broadway St., 970/522-8397
Village Inn
  203 N. Fourth Ave., 970/522-4882

Best Burgers
TJ Bummer's Kitchen
203 Broadway St., 970/522-8397

Best Chinese Food
China Garden Restaurant
126 W. Main St., 970/522-1137

Best Desserts
Village Inn
203 N. Fourth Ave., 970/522-4882

Best Homestyle Food
TJ Bummer's Kitchen
203 Broadway St., 970/522-8397

Best Mexican Food
Cocina Alvarado
715 W. Main St., 970/522-8884
Momma Conde's
100 Broadway St., 970/522-0802

Best Seafood
TJ Bummer's Kitchen
203 Broadway St., 970/522-8397

Best Steaks
TJ Bummer's Kitchen
203 Broadway St., 970/522-8397
Steak House
I-76 at I-63 Interchange, Atwood, 970/522-7088

Standbys
Pizza Hut
224 W. Main St., 970/522-7363

VAIL, CO

Best American Food
Hong Kong Cafe
227 Wall St., 970/476-1818

Best Breakfast
The Daily Grind
288 Bridge St., 970/476-5856

Best Coffee
The Daily Grind
288 Bridge St., 970/476-5856

Best Desserts
Villager Restaurant and Bar
100 E. Meadow Dr., 970/476-8683

Best Italian Food
Sweet Basil
193 Gore Creek Dr., 970/476-0125

Best Pizza
Pazzo's Pizzeria
122 E. Meadow Dr., 970/476-9026

Best Place to Take the Kids
The Bully Ranch
20 Vail Rd., 970/476-5656

Best Seafood
Louie's Restaurant
  227 Wall St., 970/479-9008
Montauk Seafood Grill
  549 W. Lionshead Mall, 970/476-2601

Best Steaks
Red Lion
  304 Bridge St., 970/476-7676

Best Thai Food
Siamese Orchid
  12 S. Frontage Rd. W., 970/476-9417

C

Connecticut

Best Restaurant in Town
Wellington's Market Restaurant
2521 Main St., 203/335-9431

Best Bar
Black Rock Castle
2895 Fairfield Ave., 203/336-3990

Best Breakfast
Frankie's Diner
1660 Barnum Ave., 203/334-8971

Best Business Lunch
Ralph and Rich's
121 Wall St., 203/366-3597

Best Casual Dining
Kossuth Club
2931 Fairfield Ave., 203/335-7877

Best Continental Food
Ralph and Rich's
121 Wall St., 203/366-3597

Best Delicatessen
Corporate Deli
130 John St., 203/576-1116

Best Diners
Frankie's Diner
1660 Barnum Ave., 203/334-8971
New Colony Diner Bridgeport
2321 Main St., 203/367-1217

Best Family Restaurant
Jennie's Family Restaurant
4107 Main St., 203/374-8224

Best Health-Conscious Menu
Marisa's Ristorante
1084 Madison Ave., 203/333-8047

Best Italian Food
La Scogliera Restaurant
697 Madison Ave., 203/333-0673

nnie's Family Restaurant
4107 Main St., 203/374-8224
Marisa's Ristorante
1084 Madison Ave., 203/333-8047

Best Mexican Food
Taco Loco
3170 Fairfield Ave., 203/335-8228

Best Other Ethnic Food
Omanel Restaurant (Portuguese)
1909 Main St., 203/335-1676
Black Rock Castle (Irish)
2895 Fairfield Ave., 203/336-3990
Kossuth Club (Hungarian)
2931 Fairfield Ave., 203/335-7877
Minabela Restaurant (Portuguese/Italian)
1282 North Ave., 203/384-1159

Best Pizza
Famous Pizza House
430 Park Ave., 203/333-8173
Jennie's Family Restaurant
4107 Main St., 203/374-8224

Best Sandwiches
Corporate Deli
130 John St., 203/576-1116

Best Seafood
Seascape Restaurant
14 Beach Dr., 203/375-1332

Best Thai Food
King and I
545 Broadbridge Rd., 203/374-2081

DANBURY, CT

Best Restaurant in Town
Ondine Restaurant
69 Pembroke Rd., 203/746-4900

Best American Food
Poor Henry
65 Bank St., New Milford, 203/355-2274

Best Appetizers
Tuxedo Junction
2 Ives St., 203/748-2561

Best Atmosphere
Stonehenge Inn
1 Stonehenge Rd., Ridgefield, 203/438-6511

Best Breakfast
JK's
122 South St., 203/743-4004
Station Break
1 Depot Pl., Bethel, 203/790-1577

Best Casual Dining
Tuxedo Junction
2 Ives St., 203/748-2561

Best Chinese Food
Panda West
 93 Mill Plain Rd., 203/730-8888

Best Coffee
Seattle Espresso
 262 Main St., 203/748-6618

Best Dinner
Stonehenge Inn
 1 Stonehenge Rd., Ridgefield, 203/438-6511

Best French Food
Ondine Restaurant
 69 Pembroke Rd., 203/746-4900

Best Italian Food
Bentley's Restaurant
 1 Division St., 203/778-3637
Ciao Cafe
 2B Ives St., 203/791-0404

Best Middle Eastern Food
Hannah's
 72 Lake Ave., 203/748-5713

Best Other Ethnic Food
Goulash Place (Hungarian)
 42 Highland Ave., 203/744-1971
O'Faia Restaurant (Portuguese)
 195 Main St., 203/791-2208

Best Pastries
Station Break
 1 Depot Pl., Bethel, 203/790-1577
Alpine Pastry Hut
 109 Federal Rd., 203/748-0060

Best Sandwiches
Tuxedo Junction
 2 Ives St., 203/748-2561

Best Seafood
Down the Hatch Restaurant
 292 Candlewood Lake Rd., Brookfield, 203/775-6635

Best Southwestern Food
Two Steps
 5 Ives St., 203/794-0032

Best Steaks
Chuck's Steak House
 20 Segar St., 203/748-6688
Kabuki Japanese Steak House
 39 Lake Ave. Exit, 203/744-6885

FAIRFIELD, CT

Best American Food
Sonoma California Grill
 2600 Post Rd., 203/255-2399

Best Atmosphere
Centro Ristorante and Bar
 1435 Post Rd., 203/255-1210

Best Breakfast
Duchess Drive-In
625 Post Rd., 203/259-4874
Firehouse Deli
22 Reef Rd., 203/255-5527

Best Brunch
Sidetracks Restaurant
2070 Post Rd., 203/254-3606

Best Burgers
Duchess Drive-In
625 Post Rd., 203/259-4874
Rattlesnake Grill
55 Miller St., 203/259-9987
Tommy's
1418 Post Rd., 203/254-1478

Best Chinese Food
Hunan Pavillion
80 Post Rd., 203/254-3444

Best Coffee
P. Gordon Coffee Roaster
1740 Post Rd., 203/254-2034

Best Desserts
Firehouse Deli
22 Reef Rd., 203/255-5527

Best Health-Conscious Menu
Sprouts Natural Foods Market and Cafe
2057 Black Rock Turnpike, 203/333-3455

Best Ice Cream/Yogurt
Carvel
1838 Black Rock Turnpike, 203/384-2253
562 Post Rd., 203/259-1315

Best Italian Food
Centro Ristorante and Bar
1435 Post Rd., 203/255-1210

Best Japanese Food
Mako of Japan
941 Black Rock Turnpike, 203/367-5319

Best Other Ethnic Food
Pearl of Budapest (Hungarian)
57 Unquowa Rd., 203/259-4777
Nazar's Turkish Cuisine (Turkish)
1253 Post Rd., 203/256-8893

Best Pizza
Spazzi
1229 Post Rd., 203/256-1629
Uno Chicago Bar and Grill
2320 Black Rock Turnpike, 203/372-2909

Best Sandwiches
Firehouse Deli
22 Reef Rd., 203/255-5527
Gold's Delicatessen
873 Post Rd., 203/259-2233
Maggie's Pantry
1891 Post Rd., 203/255-1579

Best American Food
Thataway Cafe
  409 Greenwich Ave., 203/622-0947
Boxing Cat Grill
  1392 E. Putnam Ave., Old Greenwich, 203/698-1995

Best Burgers
Manero's
  559 Steamboat Rd., 203/869-0049

Best French Food
Jean Louis Restaurant
  61 Lewis St., 203/622-8450
Le Figaro Bistro De Paris
  372 Greenwich Ave., 203/622-0018
Bertrand
  253 Greenwich St., 203/661-4459

Best Health-Conscious Menu
Greenwich Health Mart
  30 Greenwich Ave., 203/869-9658

Best Italian Food
Terra Ristorante Italiano
  156 Greenwich Ave., 203/629-5222
Valbella
  1309 E. Putnam Ave., Old Greenwich, 203/637-1155

Best Pizza
Arcuri's Pizza and Salads
  226 E. Putnam Ave., 203/869-6999
Mare E. Monte Ristorante
  235 Greenwich Ave., 203/661-5831

Best Salad/Salad Bar
Thataway Cafe
  409 Greenwich Ave., 203/622-0947

Best Sandwiches
Greenwich Health Mart
  30 Greenwich Ave., 203/869-9658
Gourmet Galley
  100 Greenwich Ave., 203/869-9617
Thataway Cafe
  409 Greenwich Ave., 203/622-0947

Best Seafood
Mare E. Monte Ristorante
  235 Greenwich Ave., 203/661-5831
Fjord Fisheries
  137 River Rd., 203/661-5006

Best Southwestern Food
Boxcar Cantina
  44 Old Field Point Rd., 203/661-4774

Best Steaks
Manero's
  559 Steamboat Rd., 203/869-0049

Standbys
Baskin-Robbins
  89 Greenwich Ave., 203/869-4098

237

,en-Dazs
4E Greenwich Ave., 203/629-8000

HARTFORD, CT

Best Restaurant in Town
Carbone's Ristorante
588 Franklin Ave., 860/296-9646

Best American Food
Avon Old Farms Inn
1 Nod Rd., Avon, 860/677-2818

Best Brunch
Avon Old Farms Inn
1 Nod Rd., Avon, 860/677-2818

Best Business Lunch
Max on Main
205 Main St., 860/522-2530

Best Chinese Food
Panda Inn Chinese Restaurant
964 Farmington Ave., West Hartford, 860/233-5384
Butterfly
831 Farmington Ave., West Hartford, 860/236-2816

Best Continental Food
Ann Howard's Apricots
1593 Farmington Ave., Farmington, 860/673-5405

Best Delicatessen
Top Nosh New York Style Deli and Bakery
29 S. Main St., West Hartford, 860/521-7110

Best Desserts
Ann Howard's Apricots
1593 Farmington Ave., Farmington, 860/673-5405

Best Family Restaurant
Spaghetti Warehouse
45 Bartholomew Ave., 860/951-1680

Best German Food
Edelweiss Restaurant
980 Farmington Ave., West Hartford, 860/236-3096

Best Greek/Mediterranean Food
Tapa's Restaurant
1150 New Britain Ave., West Hartford, 860/521-4609

Best Happy Hour Snacks
The Whitman
1125 Farmington Ave., Farmington, 860/678-9217

Best Italian Food
Carbone's Ristorante
588 Franklin Ave., 860/296-9646
Di Fiore Ristorante
395 Franklin Ave., 860/296-2123

Best Japanese Food
Fuji Japanese Restaurant
1144 New Britain Ave., West Hartford, 860/232-1732

Best Mexican Food
Margarita's
144 Albany Turnpike, Canton, 860/693-8237

Best Other Ethnic Food
Casa Lisboa (Portuguese)
    1911 Park St., 860/233-3184
Shish-Kebab House (Afghan)
    360 Franklin Ave., 860/296-0301

Best Pizza
First and Last Tavern
    939 Maple Ave., 860/956-6000

Best Place to Eat When Someone Else Is Buying
Carbone's Ristorante
    588 Franklin Ave., 860/296-9646

Best Sandwiches
Congress Rotisserie
    7 Maple Ave., 860/560-1965
    274 Farmington Ave., 860/278-7711
    280 Trumbull St., 860/525-5141

Best Seafood
Capitol Fish House
    391 Main St., 860/724-3370

Best Soul Food
Hal's Aquarius Restaurant
    2790 Main St., 860/247-0453

Best Spanish Food
Costa Del Sol Restaurante
    901 Wethersfield Ave., 860/296-1714

Best Thai Food
Lemon Grass Restaurant
    7 S. Main St., West Hartford, 860/233-4405

Best Vietnamese Food
Truc Orient Express
    735 Wethersfield Ave., 860/296-2818

MANCHESTER, CT

Best Barbecue/Ribs
Heavenly Hog
    520 Center St., 860/649-1212

Best Breakfast
Fani's Kitchen
    1015 Main St., 860/643-2603

Best Burgers
Shady Glen Dairy Stores
    360 Middle Turnpike W., 860/643-0511

Best Chinese Food
Golden Dragon Restaurant
    1131U Tolland Turnpike, 860/645-0300
House of Chung
    363 Broad St., 860/649-4958

Best French Food
Cavey's Restaurant
    45 E. Center St., 860/643-2751

Best Ice Cream/Yogurt
Shady Glen Dairy Stores
    360 Middle Turnpike W., 860/643-0511

dian Food
ay Raj Mahal
 Main St., 860/646-5330

t Italian Food
allis' Italia Ristorante
706 Hartford Rd., 860/647-1500

Best Pizza
Pizzeria Uno
180 Deming Rd., 860/648-2238
Sarantino's
238 N. Main St., 860/646-0836

Best Romantic Dining
Cavey's Restaurant
43 E. Center St., 860/643-2751

Best Sandwiches
Shady Glen Dairy Stores
360 Middle Turnpike W., 860/643-0511

Best Steaks
Willie's Steak House
444 Center St., 860/649-5271

Best Vegetarian Food
Bombay Rajnahal
836 Main St., 860/646-5330

Standbys
Friendly's
1155 Tolland Turnpike, 860/649-5563
435 Main St., 860/649-7738

MERIDEN, CT

Best Restaurant in Town
Hawthorne Inn
2387 Wilbur Cross Hwy., Berlin, 203/828-4181

Best American Food
Yankee Silversmith Inn
1086 N. Colony Rd., Wallingford, 203/269-5444
Fareways Restaurant
688 Westfield Rd., 203/237-3030

Best Atmosphere
Huxley's Cafe
1231 E. Main St., 203/237-4087

Best Breakfast
Mike and Dee's Dinette
85 W. Main St., 203/630-1331
Justin Tyme Diner
31 Colony Pl., 203/238-3301
Huxley's Cafe
1231 E. Main St., 203/237-4087
Neptune House Restaurant
1086 N. Colony Rd., Wallingford, 203/269-9317
Fischer's Fine Food
21 Colony Pl., 203/235-1221

Best Chinese Food
King's Garden
1231 E. Main St., 203/630-2188

Wa Wah Kitchen
  98 State St., 203/238-2100

Best Continental Food
San Souci
  2003 N. Broad St., 203/639-1777

Best Diners
Mike and Dee's Dinette
  85 W. Main St., 203/630-1331
Justin Tyme Diner
  31 Colony Pl., 203/238-3301

Best Dinner
Neptune House Restaurant
  1086 N. Colony Rd., Wallingford, 203/269-9317

Best Italian Food
Lido's Italian Foods
  361 Liberty St., 203/634-3959

Best Lunch
Huxley's Cafe
  1231 E. Main St., 203/237-4087

Best Pizza
Lido's Italian Foods
  361 Liberty St., 203/634-3959
Zorba's Pizza
  1257 E. Main St., 203/238-2077

Best Sandwiches
Goldilocks
  612 E. Main St., 203/237-4087
Huxley's Cafe
  1231 E. Main St., 203/237-4087

Best Seafood
Sand Dollar
  90041 Meriden/Waterbury Turnpike, Southington,
    860/621-6456
Hawthorne Inn
  2387 Wilbur Cross Hwy., Berlin, 203/828-4181

Best Steaks
Hawthorne Inn
  2387 Wilbur Cross Hwy., Berlin, 203/828-4181
Jacoby's Restaurant
  1388 E. Main St., 203/634-3222

MIDDLETOWN, CT

Best American Food
Eli Cannon's
  695 Main St., 860/344-0222

Best Breakfast
O'Rourke's Diner
  728 Main St., 860/346-6101

Best Brunch
O'Rourke's Diner
  728 Main St., 860/346-6101

Best Indian Food
Taj of India
  170 Main St., 860/346-2050

Best Mexican Food
Coyote Blue Tex Mex Cafe
  1960 Saybrook Rd., 860/354-2403

Best Other Ethnic Food
Fiasco (California cuisine)
  98 Washington St., 860/344-0222

MILFORD, CT

Best Barbecue/Ribs
Bar-B-Q Restaurant
  591 Boston Post Rd., 203/874-5653

Best Burgers
Bennigan's
  290 Old Gate Ln., 203/877-1903

Best Coffee
Jittermug
  554 Boston Post Rd., 203/874-3853
Elfie's
  58 River St., 203/878-8393

Best Ice Cream/Yogurt
Carvel
  1081 Bridgeport Ave., 203/874-1427
  866 Boston Post Rd., 203/874-5498

Best Italian Food
Gusto's Restaurant
  255 Boston Post Rd., 203/876-7464
Gabriele Restaurant and Pizza
  326 Boston Post Rd., Orange, 203/799-2633
Pasta Fair Restaurant
  262 Boston Post Rd., Orange, 203/799-9601

Best Mexican Food
El Torero Mexican Restaurant
  1698 Boston Post Rd., 203/878-7734

Best Pastries
Elfie's
  58 River St., 203/878-8393

Best Pizza
Bella Napoli Pizza
  864 Boston Post Rd., 203/877-1102
Bertucci's
  550 Boston Post Rd., 203/799-6828
Gabriele Restaurant and Pizza
  326 Boston Post Rd., Orange, 203/799-2633

Best Place to Eat When Someone Else Is Buying
Elfie's
  58 River St., 203/878-8393

Best Sandwiches
Bennigan's
  290 Old Gate Ln., 203/877-1903
Gabriele Restaurant and Pizza
  326 Boston Post Rd., Orange, 203/799-2633
Elfie's
  58 River St., 203/878-8393

Best Seafood
Captain's Galley
258 Broad St., 203/877-9497
The Gathering
989 Boston Post Rd., 203/878-6537
Scribner's
31 Village Rd., 203/878-7019

Best Steaks
The Gathering
989 Boston Post Rd., 203/878-6537
Indian River Steak and Seafood
471 New Haven Ave., 203/874-4624

Standbys
Howard Johnson
1040 Boston Post Rd., 203/874-1575

NAUGATUCK, CT

Best Restaurant in Town
Milestone Inn
18 Neumann St., 203/723-6693

Best Breakfast
Coddington's on Meadow
262 Meadow St., 203/729-6551

Best Casual Dining
Old Corner Cafe
178 N. Main St., Union City, 203/729-8087

Best Chinese Food
Hunan Pearl Restaurant
Mountain View Plz., 203/729-8281

Best Homestyle Food
Coddington's on Meadow
262 Meadow St., 203/729-6551

Best Italian Food
Casa Nuova
1 S. Main St., 203/723-4212

Best Lunch
Coddington's on Meadow
262 Meadow St., 203/729-6551

Best Pizza
American Pie Pizza and Restaurant
500 S. Main St., 203/723-8661

NEW BRITAIN, CT

Best American Food
Angelico's Cafe
542 E. Main St., 860/224-3811

Best Breakfast
Guy's Place
224 S. Main St., 860/224-7883

Best Burgers
Angelico's Cafe
542 E. Main St., 860/224-3811

t Chinese Food
at Taste
597 W. Main St., 860/827-8988

Best German Food
East Side Restaurant
131 Dwight St., 860/223-1188

Best Health-Conscious Menu
Good Times Deli
298 Main St., 860/225-2233

Best Ice Cream/Yogurt
Guida's Milk Bar
975 Farmington Ave., 860/224-2404

Best Other Ethnic Food
Guy's Place (French Canadian)
224 S. Main St., 860/224-7883
Fatherland Restaurant (Polish)
450 S. Main St., 860/224-3345

Best Pizza
Paradise Pizza
10 East St., 860/827-8123
Bella Via
66 W. Main St., 860/222-4447
Teresa's Restaurant
356 S. Main St., 860/229-0710

Best Sandwiches
Good Times Deli
298 Main St., 860/225-2233

Best Steaks
Angelico's Cafe
542 E. Main St., 860/224-3811

Standbys
Friendly's
272 W. Main St., 860/225-2457

NEW HAVEN, CT

Best Restaurant in Town
Five Hundred Blake Street Cafe
500 Blake St., 203/387-0500

Best Barbecue/Ribs
The Rib House
16 Main St., East Haven, 203/468-6695

Best Brunch
Five Hundred Blake Street Cafe
500 Blake St., 203/387-0500

Best Business Lunch
Bruxelles Brasserie and Bar
220 College St., 203/777-7752

Best Chinese Food
China Pavilion
185 Boston Post Rd., Orange, 203/795-3555

Best Continental Food
Riviera Cafe
3 Linden Ave., Branford, 203/481-7011

Best Family Restaurant
The Amber Restaurant
132 Middletown Ave., North Haven, 203/239-4072

Best French Food
Union League Cafe
1032 Chapel St., 203/562-4299

Best Happy Hour Snacks
Five Hundred Blake Street Cafe
500 Blake St., 203/387-0500

Best Indian Food
India Palace
65 Howe St., 203/776-9010

Best Italian Food
Gennaro's Ristorante D'Amalfi
937 State St., 203/777-5490

Best Japanese Food
Akasaka
1450 Whalley Ave., 203/387-4898

Best Mexican Food
Su Casa
400 E. Main St., Branford, 203/481-5001

Best New Restaurant
Le Petit Cafe
225 Montowese St., Branford, 203/483-9791

Best Pizza
Frank Pepe Pizzeria
157 Wooster St., 203/865-5762
Sally's Pizza
237 Wooster St., 203/624-5271

Best Restaurant Meal Value
Captain's Galley
19 Beach St., West Haven, 203/932-1811

Best Romantic Dining
Riviera Cafe
3 Linden Ave., Branford, 203/481-7011

Best Sandwiches
Humphrey's East
175 Humphrey St., 203/782-1506

Best Steaks
Chart House
100 S. Water St., 203/787-3466

NEW LONDON, CT

Best Barbecue/Ribs
Russell's Ribs
214 Rte. 12, Groton, 860/445-8849

Best Breakfast
Restaurant Bravo Bravo
The Whaler's Inn, 20 E. Main St., Mystic,
860/536-3228
Noah's Restaurant
113 Water St., Stonington, 860/535-3925
Bee and Thistle Inn
100 Lyme St., Old Lyme, 860/434-1667

Best Chinese Food
Hook City
, Captains Walk, 860/442-6970

Best Continental Food
Foodtide Restaurant
Rte. 1 at Hwy. 27, Mystic, 860/536-8140

Best Desserts
Bee and Thistle Inn
100 Lyme St., Old Lyme, 860/434-1667

Best French Food
Harbor View
60 Water St., Stonington, 860/535-2720

Best Happy Hour Snacks
Cherrystones
218 Shore Dr., Old Lyme, 860/434-1721

Best Indian Food
India Mahal
203 Gold Star Hwy., Groton, 860/446-9363

Best Italian Food
Gondolier
92 Huntington St., 860/447-1781
Restaurant Bravo Bravo
The Whaler's Inn, 20 E. Main St., Mystic,
860/536-3228

Best Lunch
Harbor View Restaurant
60 Water St., Stonington, 860/535-2720

Best Mexican Food
Margaritas
12 Water St., Mystic, 860/536-4589

Best Pizza
Recovery Room Cafe
445 Ocean Ave., 860/443-2619
Paul's Pasta
223 Thames St., Groton, 860/445-5276

Best Romantic Dining
Bee and Thistle Inn
100 Lyme St., Old Lyme, 860/434-1667

Best Sandwiches
Two Sisters Deli
4 Pearl St., Mystic, 860/536-1244

Best Seafood
Floodtide Restaurant
Rte. 1 at Hwy. 27, Mystic, 860/536-8140
Abbott's Lobster in the Rough
117 Pearl St., Noank, 860/536-7719

Best Steaks
Ye Olde Tavern
345 Bank St., 860/442-0353
Chuck's Steakhouse
250 Pequot Ave., 860/443-1323
Steak Loft
I-95, Exit 90, Mystic, 860/536-2661

NORWALK, CT

Best Restaurant in Town
New England Brew Company
  13 Marshall St., 203/866-1339

Best American Food
Three Bears
  Rte. 33, Westport, 203/227-7219

Best Barbecue/Ribs
Cogburn's, The Place For Ribs
  16 River St., 203/866-2112

Best Breakfast
Penny's Diner and Restaurant
  212 East Ave., 203/852-0326
Silvermine Tavern
  194 Perry Ave., 203/847-4558

Best Burgers
Bobby Valentine's Sports Gallery
  280 Connecticut Ave., 203/854-9300

Best Chinese Food
Panda Pavilion
  1300 Post Rd. E., Westport, 203/255-3988

Best Continental Food
Restaurant Zanghi
  2 Post Rd. W., Westport, 203/221-7572

Best Desserts
Le Chambord
  1572 Post Rd. E., Westport, 203/255-2654

Best Diner
Silvermine Tavern
  194 Perry Ave., 203/847-4558

Best Family Restaurant
Brock's Restaurant
  606 Main Ave., 203/853-3663

Best French Food
La Provence
  86 Washington Ave., 203/855-8958
Le Chambord
  1572 Post Rd. E., Westport, 203/255-2654

Best Italian Food
Apulia Italian Restaurant
  70 N. Main St., 203/852-1168
Maria's Trattoria
  172 Main St., 203/847-5166
Arturo's
  426 Main Ave., 203/845-0808
Via Sforza Trattoria Pizzeria
  250 Westport Ave., 203/846-1116

Best Japanese Food
Sakura
  680 Post Rd. E., Westport, 203/222-0802
Plum Tree Japanese Restaurant
  70 Main St., New Canaan, 203/966-8050

C

Best Microbrewery
New England Brew Company
13 Marshall St., 203/866-1339

Best Other Ethnic Food
Brock's Restaurant (Irish)
606 Main Ave., 203/853-3663

Best Pizza
Sunrise Pizza Cafe
211 Liberty Sq., 203/838-0166
Bertucci's Brick Oven Pizzeria
833 Post Rd. E., Westport, 203/454-1559

Best Restaurant Meal Value
Mario's
36 Railroad Pl., Westport, 203/226-0308

Best Romantic Dining
Cobb's Mill Inn
12 Weston Rd., Weston, 203/227-7221

Best Salad/Salad Bar
Brock's Restaurant
606 Main Ave., 203/853-3663

Best Seafood
Skipper's Restaurant
Beach Rd., 203/838-2211
Allen's Clam and Lobster House
191 Hillspoint Rd., Westport, 203/226-4411

Best Spanish Food
Meson Galicia
10 Wall St., 203/866-8800

Best Steaks
Eric and Michael's Steak House
205 Wilton Town Green, Wilton, 203/834-2000

NORWICH, CT

Best Restaurant in Town
Yantic River Inn
270 W. Town St., Yantic, 860/887-2440

Best American Food
Modesto's Restaurant
10 Rte. 32, North Franklin, 860/887-7755

Best Atmosphere
The Liberty Tree
1 Market St., 860/886-4465

Best Breakfast
Olde Tymes Restaurant
360 W. Main St., 860/887-6865

Best Chinese Food
Phoenix Chinese Restaurant
595 W. Main St., 860/889-8868
Pagoda Chinese Restaurant
47 Town St., 860/887-7500

Best Coffee
The Liberty Tree
1 Market St., 860/886-4465

Best Family Restaurant
Yantic River Inn
  270 W. Town St., Yantic, 860/887-2440

Best Greek/Mediterranean Food
Olympic Pizza Restaurant
  372 W. Main St., 860/887-0196

C

Best Outdoor Dining
Americus on the Wharf
  1 American Wharf, 860/887-8555

Best Pizza
Olympic Pizza Restaurant
  372 W. Main St., 860/887-0196

Best Sandwiches
The Liberty Tree
  1 Market St., 860/886-4465

Best Seafood
Americus on the Wharf
  1 American Wharf, 860/887-8555

PUTNAM, CT

Best All-You-Can-Eat Buffets
J.D. Cooper's
  146 Park Rd., 860/928-0501
Vernon Stiles Inn
  Rte. 193, Thompson, 860/923-9571

Best American Food
Golden Lamb Buttery
  469 Bush Hill Rd., Brooklyn, 860/774-4423

Best Atmosphere
Vernon Stiles Inn
  Rte. 193, Thompson, 860/923-9571

Best Bistro
Vine Bistro
  85 Main St., 860/928-1660

Best Breakfast
Marketplace
  319 Kennedy Dr., 860/928-3346

Best Brunch
Vernon Stiles Inn
  Rte. 193, Thompson, 860/923-9571
Inn at Woodstock Hill
  94 Plaine Hill Rd., Woodstock, 860/928-0528

Best Chinese Food
Jade Garden II
  237 Kennedy Dr., 860/928-5351

Best Coffeehouse
Vanilla Bean Cafe
  450 Deerfield Rd., Pomfret, 860/928-1562

Best Desserts
Vine Bistro
  85 Main St., 860/928-1660
Golden Lamb Buttery
  469 Bush Hill Rd., Brooklyn, 860/774-4423

Best Family Restaurants
Mediterranean Family Restaurant
753 Hartford Pike, Dayville, 860/774-7666
Jason's Restaurant
274 Riverside Dr., Thompson, 860/923-2908
Golden Greek Restaurant
474 Putnam Turnpike, Killingly, 860/774-0167

Best Happy Hour Snacks
J. D. Cooper's
146 Park Rd., 860/928 0501

Best Ice Cream/Yogurt
We-Li-Kit Cider Mill
Rte. 97, Abington, 860/974-1095

Best Italian Food
Vine Bistro
85 Main St., 860/928-1660

Best Pizza
Someplace Special
58 Main St., 860/928-2884

Best Restaurant Meal Value
Golden Greek Restaurant
474 Putnam Turnpike, Killingly, 860/774-0167

Best Romantic Dining
Golden Lamb Buttery
469 Bush Hill Rd., Brooklyn, 860/774-4423

Best Sandwiches
Vanilla Bean Cafe
450 Deerfield Rd., Pomfret, 860/928-1562

Best Seafood
Inn at Woodstock Hill
94 Plaine Hill Rd., Woodstock, 860/928-0528

Best Steaks
J.D. Cooper's
146 Park Rd., 860/928-0501

STAMFORD, CT

Best Restaurant in Town
Amadeus
201 Summer St., 203/348-7775

Best Continental Food
Amadeus
201 Summer St., 203/348-7775

Best German Food
The European Chef
83 Bedford St., 203/325-0789

Best Happy Hour Snacks
Hacienda Don Emilio
222 Summer St., 203/324-0577

Best Indian Food
Meera
227 Summer St., 203/496-9916

Best Italian Food
Papa Jo's Restaurant
  1973 Post Rd., Darien, 213/655-1330

Best Mexican Food
Hacienda Don Emilio
  222 Summer St., 203/324-0577

Best Pizza
Hope Pizza Restaurant
  230 Hope St., 203/325-0660

Best Seafood
Crab Shell
  46 Southfield Ave., 203/967-7229

Best Spanish Food
Fonda La Paloma
  531 Boston Post Rd., Cos Cob, 203/661-9395

Best Sports Bar
Bobby Valentine's Sports
  225 Main St., 203/661-9395

TORRINGTON, CT

Best Restaurants in Town
Venetian Restaurant
  52 E. Main St., 860/489-8592
West Street Grill
  43 West St., Litchfield, 860/567-3885

Best American Food
Hilltop Inn
  1057 Torringford St., 860/482-3326
West Street Grill
  43 West St., Litchfield, 860/567-3885

Best Coffeehouse
Talk to the Town
  77 Main St., 860/489-9627

Best Desserts
West Street Grill
  43 West St., Litchfield, 860/567-3885

Best Diner
Central Lunch
  31 Hungerford St., 860/496-0297

Best Dinner
Hilltop Inn
  1057 Torringford St., 860/482-3326

Best Italian Food
Venetian Restaurant
  52 E. Main St., 860/489-8592

Best Late-Night Dining
Twin Colony Diner
  417 E. Elm St., 860/482-5346

Best Mexican Food
La Tienda Cafe
  Rte. 202, Litchfield, 860/567-8778

Best Pizza
Paisano's Restaurant
  236 N. Elm St., 860/496-9777
Berkshire Cafe
  71 Albert St., 860/489-0600

Best Restaurant Meal Value
Central Lunch
  31 Hungerford St., 860/496-0297
Aspen Garden
  51 West St., Litchfield, 860/379-1094

Best Sandwiches
West Street Grill
  43 West St., Litchfield, 860/567-3885

Best Seafood
The Tributary
  19 Rowley St., Winsted, 860/379-7679

VERNON, CT

Best Barbecue/Ribs
Little Mark's Big BBQ
  226 Talcottville Rd., 860/872-1410

Best Chinese Food
Panda Palace
  519 Talcottville Rd., 860/872-1977

Best Sandwiches
Rein's New York Style Deli
  435 Hartford Turnpike, 860/875-1344

Best Seafood
Valley Fish Market and Restaurant
  80 West Rd., Ellington, 860/872-9659

WATERBURY, CT

Best American Food
Hill's
  17 Clough Rd., 203/755-1331

Best Bagels
Bagel-Mania
  464 Reidville Dr., 203/573-9473

Best Barbecue/Ribs
Big Daddy's Rib Shack
  1351 N. Main St., 203/753-0505

Best Breakfast
Leo's Restaurant
  900 Straits Turnpike, Middlebury, 203/598-0166

Best Burgers
Morcey's
  572 Watertown Ave., 203/574-9175

Best Chinese Food
Golden Palace
  544 Straits Turnpike, Watertown, 203/274-6770

Best Delicatessen
Ann's Deli
  1622 Baldwin St., 203/575-9051

Best Desserts
Pie Plate
    835 Wolcott St., 203/757-8555

Best Happy Hour Snacks
Heminway's
    545 Main St., Watertown, 203/274-5439

Best Ice Cream/Yogurt
Big Dipper Ice Cream Parlour
    91 Waterbury Rd., Prospect, 203/758-3200

Best Italian Food
San Marino Restaurant
    111 Thomaston Ave., 203/755-1148
Diorio
    231 Bank St., Waterbury, 203/754-5111

Best Other Ethnic Food
Lisboa Restaurante (Portuguese)
    19 Lafayette St., 203/754-0789

Best Pizza
Bacco's
    1230 Thomaston Ave., 203/755-1173

Best Romantic Dining
Cafe 457
    457 W. Main St., 203/574-4507

Best Seafood
Seafood Peddler
    689 Wolcott St., 203/597-9466

Best Steaks
The Olive Tree Restaurant
    20 Sherman Hill Rd., Woodbury, 203/263-4555

WILLIMANTIC, CT

Best All-You-Can-Eat Buffet
Homestead Restaurant
    50 Higgins Hwy., Mansfield Center, 860/456-2240

Best Breakfast
Bud's Coffee Nook
    69 Church St., 860/423-4373
Gil's Restaurant
    725 Main St., 860/423-0062

Best Burgers
Main Street Cafe
    877 Main St., 860/423-6777

Best Family Restaurant
Angellino's Restaurant
    135A Storrs Rd., Mansfield Center, 860/450-7071

Best Homestyle Food
Homestead Restaurant
    50 Higgins Hwy., Mansfield Center, 860/456-2240

Best Ice Cream/Yogurt
Dairy Bar
    University of Connecticut, 478 Valley St.,
        860/423-4491

Best Italian Food
Angellino's Restaurant
  135A Storrs Rd., Mansfield Center, 860/450-7071
Tony's Pizza and Restaurant
  117 Main St., 860/423-7717

Best Mexican Food
Chuck's and Margarita's
  Rte. 32, Mansfield Center, 860/429-1900

Best Pizza
Alexandra's Family Restaurant
  1310 Main St., 860/423-5407
Tony's Pizza and Restaurant
  117 Main St., 860/423-7717

Best Place to Take the Kids
Main Street Cafe
  877 Main St., 860/423-6777

Best Seafood
Mulberry Tree
  28 North St., 860/423-0299
Husky Blues
  1254 Storrs Rd., Mansfield, 860/429-2587

Best Steaks
Husky Blues
  1254 Storrs Rd., Mansfield, 860/429-2587
Chuck's and Margarita's
  Rte. 32, Mansfield, 860/429-1900

Delaware

Best Restaurant in Town
Paradiso Restaurant
115B E. Lebanon Rd., 302/697-3055

Best Bagels
Bagel Corner
178 N. DuPont Hwy., 302/678-3211

Best Barbecue/Ribs
Where Pigs Fly
617 E. Lockerman St., 302/678-0586
Bull on the Beach
3072 Dover Mall, 302/736-0337

Best Brunch
Blue Coat Inn
800 N. State St., 302/674-1776
Captain John's Restaurant
518 S. Bay Rd., 302/678-8166
Air Transport Command
143 N. DuPont Hwy., 302/328-3527

Best Chinese Food
Sing House Chinese Restaurant
45 Greentree Dr., 302/678-4844

Best Delicatessen
Bradford Street Cafe
150 S. Bradford St., 302/736-6200

Best Desserts
Bradford Street Cafe
150 S. Bradford St., 302/736-6200
Paradiso Restaurant
115B E. Lebanon Rd., 302/697-3055
Kirby and Holloway Restaurant
656 N. DuPont Hwy., 302/734-7133

Best Family Restaurant
Where Pigs Fly
617 E. Lockerman St. at Hwy. 13, 302/678-0586

Best Italian Food
Attilio's
   Rodney Village Shopping Ctr., 302/674-8700

Best Japanese Food
Hibachi Japanese Steak House
   691 N. DuPont Hwy., 302/734-5900

Best Mexican Food
El Sombrero Mexican Restaurant
   655 N. DuPont Hwy., 302/678-9445
La Tolteca Restaurant
   245 S. DuPont Hwy., 302/734-3444

D

Best Pizza
Grotto Pizza
   Multiple Locations

Best Place to Take Guests
Blue Coat Inn
   800 N. State St., 302/674-1776

Best Romantic Dining
Paradiso Ristorante
   Rte. 10 Plaza, 1151 E. Lebanon Rd., 302/697-3055

Best Salad/Salad Bar
Kathy's Kitchen
   1819 S. DuPont Hwy., 302/734-4111
Captain John's Restaurant
   518 Bay Rd., 302/678-8166

Best Seafood
Shuckers Pier 13
   889 N. DuPont Hwy., 302/674-1190

Standbys
Lone Star Steakhouse
   365 N. DuPont Hwy., 302/736-5836
Bob Evans
   1650 N. DuPont Hwy., 302/678-5042
   947 N. DuPont Hwy., Milford, 302/424-4771
The Olive Garden
   263 N. DuPont Hwy., 302/734-5837
Chi Chi's
   293 N. DuPont Hwy., 302/674-5902

MILFORD, DE

Best Restaurants in Town
Banking House Inn
   112 NW Front St., 302/422-5708
Southern Grille
   Hwy. 113 at Delaware Rte. 16, Ellendale,
      302/422-6765

Best Atmosphere
Banking House Inn
   112 NW Front St., 302/422-5708

Best Bagels
J and F Bagels
   917 N. Dupont Hwy., 302/424-0708

Best Breakfast
Milford Diner
  Walnut St. at Dupont Blvd., 302/422-6111
J and F Bagels
  917 N. Dupont Hwy., 302/424-0708
Second Cup
  1 N. Walnut St., 302/424-2287

Best Brunch
Second Cup
  1 N. Walnut St., 302/424-2287

Best Burgers
Library Square Cafe
  227 N. Rehoboth Blvd., 302/424-0515

Best Chinese Food
Shang Hai
  113 N. Walnut St., 302/422-2270

Best Coffee
Second Cup
  1 N. Walnut St., 302/424-2287

Best Desserts
Second Cup
  1 N. Walnut St., 302/424-2287
Southern Grill
  Rte. 113 at Rte. 16, Ellendale, 302/422-6765

Best Diner
Milford Diner
  Walnut St. at Dupont Blvd., 302/422-6111

Best Italian Food
Library Square Cafe
  227 N. Rehoboth Blvd., 302/424-0515
Attilio's
  664 Milford Plaza, 302/422-2730

Best Pizza
Attilio's
  664 Milford Plz., 302/422-2730

Best Romantic Dining
Sail Loft Restaurant
  Rte. 113, 302/422-5858

Best Steaks
Geyer's Restaurant
  556 S. Dupont Blvd., 302/422-5327
Sail Loft Restaurant
  Rte. 113, 302/422-5858
Southern Grille
  Hwy. 113 at Delaware Rte. 16, Ellendale,
    302/422-6765

Best Vegetarian Food
Library Square Cafe
  227 N. Rehoboth Blvd., 302/424-0515

Standbys
Bonanza
  654A N. Dupont Blvd., 302/422-2723

NEW CASTLE, DE

Best American Food
Air Trans Command Restaurant
143 N. DuPont Hwy., 302/328-3527
Arsenal on the Green
30 Market St., 302/328-1290

Best Bar
The Green Frog
114 Delaware St., 302/322-1844

Best Breakfast
Cellar Gourmet
208 Delaware St., 302/323-0999

Best Casual Dining
The Green Frog
114 Delaware St., 302/322-1844

Best Delicatessen
Arner's Family Restaurant
215 N. DuPont Hwy., 302/322-3279

Best Desserts
Arner's Family Restaurant
215 N. DuPont Hwy., 302/322-3279

Best Family Restaurant
Arner's Family Restaurant
215 N. DuPont Hwy., 302/322-3279

Best Indian Food
Casablanca Restaurant
4010 N. DuPont Hwy., 302/652-5344

Best Pizza
Portofino Pizza and Restaurant
730 Ferry Cut-Off St., 302/322-3330

Best Romantic Dining
Air Trans Command Restaurant
143 N. DuPont Hwy., 302/328-3527

Best Salad/Salad Bar
Arner's Family Restaurant
215 DuPont Hwy., 302/322-3279

Best Seafood
Alex's Seafood Restaurant
110 N. DuPont Hwy., 302/328-5666
Arsenal on the Green
30 Market St., 302/328-1290

Best Steaks
Lone Star Steakhouse and Saloon
113 S. DuPont Hwy., 302/322-3854
Arsenal on the Green
30 Market St., 302/328-1290

Standbys
Sizzler
800 N. DuPont Hwy., 302/322-1428

NEWARK, DE

Best Brunch
Alyson's
16 Marrows Rd., 302/368-4545
Deer Park
108 W. Main St., 302/731-5315

Best Burgers
Jake's Hamburgers
1100 Ogletown Rd., 302/737-1118

Best Chinese Food
Wing Wah
Chestnut Hill Plz., 302/738-7681
Wok's
132 Sunset Blvd., Hares Corner, 302/328-6833

Best Diner
Jude's Diner
137 E. Main St., 302/368-8338

Best Family Restaurants
Beeches
748 E. Chestnut Hill Rd., 302/292-2700
Michael's Restaurant
1000 Churchman's Rd., 302/368-4230
Oliver's Holiday Inn
1203 Christiana Rd., 302/737-2899
Pappy's Family Restaurant
Midway Shopping Ctr., Kirkwood Hwy., 302/998-0123

Best Indian Food
Taste of India Restaurant
2628 Capitol Trail, 302/737-9483

Best Korean Food
Korean Barbecue and Sushi Bar
Liberty Plaza, 3602 Kirkwood Hwy., 302/455-9100

Best Mexican Food
El Sombrero
160 Elkton Rd., 302/738-0808
Santa Fe Bar and Grill
University Plz., Delaware Rte. 73, 302/738-0758

Best Outdoor Dining
Klondike Kate's
158 E. Main St., 302/737-6100

Best Pizza
Pappy's Family Restaurant
Midway Shopping Ctr., Kirkwood Hwy., 302/998-0123

Best Restaurant Meal Value
Alyson's Restaurant
16 Marrows Rd., 302/368-4545

Best Romantic Dining
Bourbon Street Cafe
Kirkwood Sq., Kirkwood Hwy., 302/633-1944
Mirage
100 Elkton Rd., 302/453-1711

Best Sandwiches
Daffy Deli
111 Elkton Rd., 302/737-8848

259

Jake's Hamburgers
  1100 Ogletown Rd., 302/737-1118

Best Vegetarian Food
Ninety East Main Street
  90 E. Main St., 302/368-9040

Best Vietnamese Food
Saigon Vietnam Restaurant
  2938 Ogletown Rd., 302/737-1590

D

REHOBOTH BEACH, DE

Best Restaurant in Town
La La Land
  22 Wilmington Ave., 302/227-3887

Best Barbecue/Ribs
Bull on the Beach
  201 Boardwalk, 302/226-3015
JR's, The Place for Ribs
  Rte. 1, 302/227-1777

Best Beer Selection
Rose and Crown Restaurant and Pub
  108 Second St., Lewes, 302/645-2373

Best Breakfast
Starboard Restaurant
  2009 Hwy. 1, Dewey Beach, 302/227-4600

Best Brunch
Victoria's
  2 Olive Ave., 302/227-0615
Sea Horse Restaurant
  330 Rehoboth Ave., 302/227-7451
Rusty Rudder Restaurant
  113 Dickinson St., Dewey Beach, 302/227-3888

Best Burgers
Starboard Restaurant
  2009 Hwy. 1, Dewey Beach, 302/227-4600
Rose and Crown Restaurant and Pub
  108 Second St., Lewes, 302/645-2373
Col. Mustard's Phat Burgers
  1904 Dewey Beach, Hwy. 1, Dewey Beach,
    302/227-1550

Best Cajun/Creole Food
Sydney's, the Blues and Jazz Place
  25 Christian St., 302/227-1339

Best Desserts
Back Porch Cafe
  59 Rehoboth Ave., 302/227-3674
Blue Moon Restaurant
  35 Baltimore Ave., 302/227-6515

Best Family Restaurant
The Roadhouse Steak Joint
  Hwy. 1, 302/645-8273

Best Ice Cream/Yogurt
King's Homemade Ice Cream
  201 Second St., Lewes, 302/645-9425

Ice Cream Store
　Rehoboth Ave. at Boardwalk, 302/227-4609
The Market Place
　Rte. 1, Ste. 10, 302/226-0690

Best Middle Eastern Food
Camel's Hump
　21 Baltimore Ave., 302/227-0947

Best Outdoor Dining
Obie's by the Sea
　Boardwalk at Olive Ave., 302/227-6261
Rusty Rudder Restaurant
　113 Dickinson St., Dewey Beach, 302/227-3888
Starboard Restaurant
　2009 Hwy. 1, Dewey Beach, 302/227-4600

Best Pizza
Nicola Pizza
　8 N. First St., 302/227-6211

Best Salad/Salad Bar
Rusty Rudder Restaurant
　113 Dickinson St., Dewey Beach, 302/227-3888
Fran O'Brien's Beach House
　59 Lake Avenue, 302/227-6121

Best Sandwiches
Al Casapulla's Italian Deli
　Shoppes of Millville, Rte. 26, Bethany Beach,
　　302/539-5488

Best Seafood
Taylor's Seashore Restaurant
　51 Wilmington Ave., 302/227-5685

Best Southwestern Food
Sedona Restaurant and Bar
　26 Pennsylvania Ave., Bethany Beach, 302/539-1200

SEAFORD, DE

Best Restaurant in Town
Bon Appetit
　312 High St., 302/629-3700

Best Atmosphere
Flagship Restaurant
　920 Concord Rd., 302/629-9767

Best Breakfast
Dillard's Restaurant
　501 N. Dual Hwy., 302/629-4814

Best Burgers
Dillard's Restaurant
　501 N. Dual Hwy., 302/629-4814

Best Desserts
Jimmy's Grille
　Rte. 1, Bridgeville, 302/337-7575

Best Family Restaurants
Dillard's Restaurant
　501 N. Dual Hwy., 302/629-4814
Jimmy's Grille
　Rte. 1, Bridgeville, 302/337-7575

Best Homestyle Food
Dillard's Restaurant
  501 N. Dual Hwy., 302/629-4814

Best Pizza
Pizza King
  300 W. Stein Hwy., 302/629-6003

Best Sandwiches
Bon Appetit
  312 High St., 302/629-3700
Dairy Bar and Restaurant
  511 King St., 302/629-9403

Best Steaks
Flagship Restaurant
  920 Concord Rd., 302/629-9767

Standbys
Friendly's
  Rte. 13, 302/629-6090

WILMINGTON, DE

Best Restaurants in Town
Harry's Savoy Grill
  2020 Naamans Rd., Brandywine Hundred,
    302/475-3000
Columbus Inn
  2216 Pennsylvania Ave., 302/571-1492
Green Room
  Hotel DuPont, 100 W. Eleventh St., 302/594-3154
Griglia Toscana
  1412 N. DuPont St., 302/654-8001
Back Burner
  Old Lancaster Pike at Mill Creek Rd., Hockessin,
    302/239-2314

Best American Food
Columbus Inn
  2216 Pennsylvania Ave., 302/571-1492
Harry's Savoy Grill
  2020 Naamans Rd., Brandywine Hundred,
    302/475-3000

Best Barbecue/Ribs
Back Burner
  Old Lancaster Pike at Mill Creek Rd., Hockessin,
    302/239-2314
Lewes Crab House
  Henlopen Rd. at Savannah Rd., 302/645-1722

Best Beer Selection
Bottlecaps Bar and Restaurant
  216 W. Ninth St., 302/427-9119
Stanley's Tavern
  2038 Foulk Rd., 302/475-1887

Best Breakfast
Post House Restaurant
  4303 N. Market St., 302/764-1248
  105 N. Union St., 302/654-4414
Alyson's Restaurant
  714 Greenbank Rd., 302/998-8853

Best Brunch
Bourbon Street Cafe
105 Kirkwood Sq., 302/633-1944
Alyson's
Kirkwood Hwy. at Greenbank Rd., 302/998-8853
Green Room
Hotel DuPont, 100 W. Eleventh St., 302/594-3154

Best Burgers
Charcoal Pit
5200 Pike Creek Blvd., 302/999-7483
2600 Concord Pike, 302/478-2165
Fox Run Shopping Ctr., Bear, 302/834-8000

Best Business Lunch
Tiffin
1208 N. Market St., 302/571-1133
Brandywine Room
Hotel DuPont, 100 W. Eleventh St., 302/594-3156

Best Chinese Food
China Royal
Plaza III Shopping Ctr., Marsh Rd., Brandywine
Hundred, 302/475-3686
The Crownery
228 Lantana Dr., Hockessin, 302/239-3825
Tri-State Mall, Claymont, 302/798-6638
Imperial Inn
Concord Pike at Silverside Rd., Talleyville,
302/478-7600
Tung Yan
3007 Concord Pike, Talleyville, 302/478-0660

Best Coffeehouses
BREW-haha!
1802 Marsh Rd., 302/529-1125
Il Fornaio Bakery Cafe
1602 Delaware Ave., 302/888-0148

Best Delicatessens
Capriotti's Sandwich Shop
510 N. Union St., 302/571-8929
2124 Silverside Rd., 302/479-9818
Casapulla's North Steak and Sub
514 Philip St. at Junction St., 302/994-5934
2707 Concord Pike, 302/477-0221

Best Desserts
Charcoal Pit
5200 Pike Creek Blvd., 302/999-7483
2600 Concord Pike, 302/478-2165
Fox Run Shopping Ctr., Bear, 302/834-8000
Brandywine Room
Hotel DuPont, 100 W. Eleventh St., 302/594-3156

Best Diner
The Hop Diner
4542 Kirkwood Hwy., 302/633-1955

Best Family Restaurants
Charcoal Pit
5200 Pike Creek Blvd., 302/999-7483
2600 Concord Pike, 302/478-2165
Fox Run Shopping Ctr., Bear, 302/834-8000

Alyson's Restaurant
714 Greenbank Rd., 302/998-8853
Wing Wah Chinese Restaurant
3901 Concord Pike, Talleyville, 302/478-9500
Mrs. Robino's Restaurant
520 N. Union St., 302/652-9223

Best German Food
Edda's Delicatessen
12A Trolley Square, 302/658-3361

Best Greek/Mediterranean Food
Tarabico's
808 N. Union St., 302/654-9780

Best Ice Cream/Yogurt
Temptations
2900 Concord Pike, 302/478-9094
11A Trolley Sq., 302/429-9162

Best Indian Food
India Palace
101 N. Maryland Ave., 302/655-8772

Best Italian Food
Toscana
1402 N. DuPont St., 302/655-8600
Robino's Restaurant
520 N. Union St., 302/652-9223
Griglia Toscana
1412 N. DuPont St., 302/654-8001
Ristorante Trevi
3100 Naamans Rd., Brandywine Hundred,
302/478-7434
Piccolo Mondo
Talleyville Towne Shoppes, 3604 Silverside Rd.,
Talleyville, 302/478-9028
Vincente's Restaurant
1836 W. Fourth St., 302/625-5142

Best Japanese Food
Hibachi Japanese Steak House
5607 Concord Pike, 302/477-0194
Utage Japanese Restaurant
Independence Mall, 1601 Concord Pike, Brandywine
Hundred, 302/652-1230

Best Mexican Food
La Tolteca Restaurant
4701 Concord Pike, Brandywine Hundred,
302/477-0433
Coyote Cafe
1801 Lancaster Ave., 302/652-1377
El Huracan
1314 Washington St., 302/888-1051

Best Neighborhood Pub
Stanley's Tavern
2038 Foulk Rd., 302/475-1887
O'Friel's Irish Pub
600 Delaware Ave., 302/654-9952

Best Outdoor Dining
Kid Shelleen's
1801 W. Fourteenth St., 302/658-4600

Best Pizza
Cafe Riviera
4737 Concord Pike, 302/478-8288
Gerardo's
114 N. Union, 302/658-0569
111 W. 8th St., 302/658-1225
Pala's Cafe
701 N. Union St., 302/658-2346
Grotto Pizza
2311 Concord Pike, 302/888-2222
303 Rocky Run Pkwy., Brandywine Commons,
302/479-8300
Pizza by Elizabeth
4019A Kennett Pike, 302/654-4478

Best Places to Eat When Someone Else Is Buying
Green Room
Hotel DuPont, 100 W. Eleventh St., 302/594-3154
Dilworthtown Inn
Old Wilmington Pike at Brinton Bridge Rd., West
Chester, 610/399-1390

Best Regional Food
Fox Point Grill
321 E. Lea Blvd., 302/762-5655

Best Restaurant Meal Value
Alyson's Restaurant
714 Greenbank Rd., 302/998-8853
Caffe Bellisimo Seafood
3421 Kirkwood Hwy., 302/994-9200

Best Romantic Dining
Columbus Inn
2216 Pennsylvania Ave., 302/571-1492
Mendenhall Inn
Kennett Pike, Mendenhall, 610/388-1181
Green Room
Hotel DuPont, 100 W. Eleventh St., 302/594-3154
Dilworthtown Inn
Old Wilmington Pike at Brinton Bridge Rd., West
Chester, 610/399-1390
Harry's Savoy Grill
2020 Naamans Rd. N., Brandywine Hundred,
302/475-3000

Best Salad/Salad Bar
Alyson's Restaurant
714 Greenbank Rd., 302/998-8853
Stanley's Restaurant and Tavern
2038 Foulk Rd., 302/475-1887

Best Sandwiches
Borgia's Subs and Steaks
414 N. Union St., 302/654-5061
Glasgow Deli
5916 Kirkwood Hwy., 302/994-2700

Talkin' Turkey
907 Shipley St., 302/428-0665

Best Seafood
DiNardo's Restaurant
405 N. Lincoln St., 302/656-3685
Feby's Fishery
3701 Lancaster Pike, 302/998-9501

Best Steaks
Walter's Steakhouse and Saloon
802 N. Union St., 302/652-6780
Harry's Savoy Grill
2020 Naamans Rd., Brandywine Hundred,
302/475-3000
Constantinou's House of Beef
1616 Delaware Ave., 302/652-0653

Best Thai Food
Bangkok House Restaurant
104 N. Union St., 302/654-8555
Pan Tai
837 N. Union St., 302/652-6633

Best Vegetarian Food
Indian Paradise Restaurant
1710A Newport Gap Pike, 302/999-0855

Best Wine Selection
Green Room
Hotel DuPont, 100 W. Eleventh St., 302/594-3154
Dilworthtown Inn
Old Wilmington Pike at Brinton Bridge Rd., West
Chester, 610/399-1390

Florida

BELLE GLADE, FL

Best All-You-Can-Eat Buffet
Drawbridge
  3300 E. Lake Rd., 561/992-9370

Best Barbecue/Ribs
Fat Boy's Bar-B-Q
  255 Hwy. 27N, South Bay, 561/996-5554

Best Burgers
Dino's Pizza Restaurant
  1100 N. Main St., 561/996-1901

Best Chinese Food
Bob Yee Chinese Food
  531 S. Main St., 561/996-1903

Best Homestyle Food
Kountry Kitchen
  1525 NW Avenue L, 561/996-0284

Best Pizza
Dino's Pizza Restaurant
  1100 N. Main St., 561/996-1901

Best Seafood
Drawbridge
  3300 E. Lake Rd., 561/992-9370

Best Steaks
Drawbridge
  3300 E. Lake Rd., 561/992-9370

BOCA RATON, FL

Best American Food
Carson's
  5798 N. Federal Hwy., 561/995-2500
Max's Grille
  Mizner Park, 404 Plaza Real, 561/368-0080
Maxwell's Chophouse
  501 E. Palmetto Park Rd., 561/347-7077
Pete's
  7940 Glades Rd., 561/487-1600

Sweetwater
  Glades Plaza, 2200 W. Glades Rd., 561/368-7427
Wilt Chamberlain's
  Somerset Shoppes, 8903 Glades Rd., 561/488-8881

Best Asian Restaurant
Pine Garden
  1668 N. Federal Hwy., 561/395-7534

Best Bagels
Bagels With
  5580 N. Federal Hwy., 561/997-7108
  3013 Yamato Rd., 561/997-9911
Flakowitz Bagel Inn
  1999 N. Federal Hwy., 561/368-0666
Offerdahl's Bagel Gourmet
  10 E. Palmetto Park Rd., 561/368-4088

Best Chinese Food
Peking
  Fifth Avenue Shops, 2300 N. Federal Hwy.,
    561/392-0666

Best Continental Food
Bistro L'Europe
  Mizner Park, 346 Plaza Real, 561/368-4488
Cafe Gloria
  855 S. Federal Hwy., 561/338-9692
Gazebo Cafe
  4199 N. Federal Hwy., 561/395-6033
La Finestra
  171 E. Palmetto Park Rd., 561/392-1838
Rabelais
  461 E. Palmetto Park Rd., 561/347-7444

Best French Food
Auberge Le Grillon
  6900 N. Federal Hwy., 561/997-6888
La Veille Maison
  770 E. Palmetto Park Rd., 561/391-6701
Marcel's
  1 S. Ocean Blvd., 561/362-9911

Best Italian Food
Addison's Flavors of Italy
  2 E. Camino Real, 561/391-9800
Arturo's Ristorante
  6750 N. Federal Hwy., 561/997-7373
Arturo's Trattoria Romano
  499 E. Palmetto Park Rd., 561/393-6715
Baci
  Mizner Park, 344 Plaza Real, 561/362-8500
Basil Garden
  5837 N. Federal Hwy., 561/994-2554
Buona Sera
  499 S. Federal Hwy., 561/338-8780
Culinaria Gourmet Cafe
  7400 N. Federal Hwy., 561/994-4300
La Trattoria
  Village Corner Stores, 6060 SW Eighteenth St.,
    561/750-1296

Maxaluna Tuscan Grill
  Boca Center, 5050 Town Center Circle, 561/391-7177
Marianne's
  169 NE Fourth Ave., Delray Beach, 561/278-3349
Max's Grill
  Mizner Park, 404 Plaza Real, 561/368-0080
Prezzo
  7820 Glades Rd., 561/451-2800
Renzo's of Boca
  5999 N. Federal Hwy., 561/994-3495
Roboli Restaurante Italiano
  2901 Clint Moore Rd., 561/995-9940
Vito's
  Regency Court at Woodfield, 3013 Yamato Rd.,
    561/995-0800

Best Japanese Food
Fuji Japanese Restaurant
  Palms Plz., 21191 Powerline Rd., 561/392-8778

Best New Restaurants
Angelique's
  1840 N. Dixie Hwy., 561/368-7270
Carson's
  5798 N. Federal Hwy., 561/995-2500
Cheesecake Factory
  5530 Glades Rd., 561/393-0344
Splendid Blendids Cafe
  432 E. Atlantic Ave., 561/265-1035
Rancho Deluxe
  8825 Glades Rd., 561/852-5557

Best Other Ethnic Food
Caribbean Grill (Cuban)
  1332 NW Second Ave., 561/362-0161
Cuban Cafe (Cuban)
  3350 NW Boca Raton Blvd., 561/750-8860

Best Pizza
California Pizza Kitchen
  2006 Executive Center Circle NW, 561/241-2664

Best Place to Take the Kids
Boomer's
  2001 Tenth Ave. N., Lake Worth, 561/582-1944

Best Seafood
Muers
  6450 N. Federal Hwy., 561/997-6688
Nick's Italian Fishery
  1 Boca Pl., 561/994-2201

Best Southwestern Food
Baja Cafe/Cantina
  2399 N. Federal Hwy., 561/391-5300

Best Thai Food
Siam Garden
  Oaks Plz., 680 Glades Rd., 561/368-9013
Uncle Tai's
  Boca Center, Military Trail, 561/368-8806

Best Vietnamese Food
La Truc Vietnamese Restaurant
  299 E. Palmetto Park Rd., 561/392-4568

BRADENTON, FL

Best Restaurant in Town
Euphemia Haye Restaurant
  5540 Gulf of Mexico Dr., Longboat Key, 941/383-3633

Best Bar
Duffy's Tavern
  3901 Gulf Dr. N., Bradenton Beach, 941/778-2501

Best Barbecue/Ribs
J and J Bar-B-Que
  2620 Ninth St. W., 941/746-6683
Sonny's Real Pit Bar-B-Q
  6515 Fourteenth St. W., 941/753-3993

Best Breakfast
Jean's Restaurant
  3513 Cortez Rd. W., 941/753-5529
Peach's Restaurant
  3201 Manatee Ave. W., 941/747-2894
  5702 44th Ave. W., 941/794-5140
Cafe on the Beach
  4000 Gulf Dr. N., Bradenton Beach, 941/778-0784
Gulf Drive Cafe
  900 Gulf Dr. N., Bradenton Beach, 941/778-1919

Best Burgers
Duffy's Tavern
  3901 Gulf Dr. N., Bradenton Beach, 941/778-2501

Best Chinese Food
Panda Garden Restaurant
  3240 Fourteenth St. W., 941/747-0201

Best Desserts
Euphemia Haye Restaurant
  5540 Gulf of Mexico Dr., Longboat Key, 941/383-3633

Best Homestyle Food
Al-Jan's
  6650 Cortez Rd. W., 941/794-5150
Peach's Restaurant
  3201 Manatee Ave. W., 941/747-2894
  5702 44th Ave. W., 941/794-5140
Jean's Restaurant
  3513 Cortez Rd. W., 941/753-5529

Best Italian Food
Demetrio's Pizza House
  1720 Cortez Rd. W., 941/758-6478

Best Lunch
Council's Bradenton Recreation
  536 Twelfth St. W., 941/746-8350

Best Other Ethnic Food
Miller's Dutch Kitchen (Amish)
  3401 Fourteenth St. W., 941/746-8253

Best Sandwiches
Council's Bradenton Recreation
536 Twelfth St. W., 941/746-8350
Rotten Ralph's Restaurant
902 Bay Blvd. S., Anna Maria, 941/778-3953

Best Seafood
Leverock's Seafood House
12320 Manatee Ave. W., 941/794-8900
Euphemia Haye Restaurant
5540 Gulf of Mexico Dr., Longboat Key, 941/383-3633
Pier Restaurant
1200 First Ave. W., 941/748-8087
Seafood Shack
4110 127th St. W., Cortez, 941/794-1235

F

BROOKSVILLE, FL

Best Barbecue/Ribs
Florida Boy's Barbeque
915 W. Jefferson St., 352/796-6333

Best Bistro
Michael's Bistro
2410 Commercial Way, 352/683-8420

Best Breakfast
Robby's Pancake House
8274 River Country Dr., 352/596-6699

Best Chinese Food
Rose Garden
7391 Commercial Way, 352/597-3434

Best Homestyle Food
Country Kitchen
20020 Cortez Blvd., 352/796-2041

Best Italian Food
Sorrento's Restaurant
5526 Commercial Way, 352/596-5383

Best Pizza
Five Star Pizza
31156 Cortez Blvd., 352/799-3787
Besta-One Pizzeria and Restaurant
8405 Northcliffe Blvd., 352/688-5555

Best Seafood
Zip's Italian Steakhouse
11738 Broad St., 352/799-8985

Best Steaks
Pier 688 Restaurant
1177 S. Broad St., 352/799-5200

CAPE CORAL, FL

Best Barbecue/Ribs
Santa Fe Barbecue and Steakhouse
4400 Hancock Bridge Pkwy., North Ft. Meyers,
941/656-5002

Best Breakfast
Cape Cafe
910 Cape Coral Pkwy. E., 941/549-4001

Jimbo's Restaurant
1604 SE 46th St., 941/549-1818

Best Burgers
Cape Crab House
2301 Del Prado Blvd. S., 941/574-2722
Jimbo's Restaurant
1604 SE 46th St., 941/549-1818

Best Desserts
New England Mooring
1326 SW Sixteenth Pl., 941/772-9900

Best Homestyle Food
Jimbo's Restaurant
1604 SE 46th St., 941/549-1818

Best Sandwiches
Englund's Deli II
125 Del Prado Blvd. N., 941/458-0183
Palate Pleasers Cafe and Pub
3512 Del Prado Blvd., 941/945-6333

Best Seafood
Cape Crab House
2301 Del Prado Blvd. S., 941/574-2722
New England Mooring
1326 SW Sixteenth Pl., 941/772-9900

Best Steaks
Bubba's Road House and Saloon
1719 Cape Coral Pkwy. E., 941/540-0400
Santa Fe Barbecue and Steakhouse
4400 Hancock Bridge Pkwy., North Ft. Meyers,
941/656-5002
Cape Crab House
2301 Del Prado Blvd. S., 941/574-2722

Best Thai Food
Siam Hut Thai Food
1873 Del Prado Blvd. S., 941/772-3131

Best View While Dining
Mariners Inn Grog and Galley
3448 Marina Town Ln., North Ft. Meyers,
941/997-8300

CLEARWATER, FL

Best All-You-Can-Eat Buffet
The Crystal Room at K-Lynn's Banquet Hall
1106 Overcash Dr., Dunedin, 813/734-3767

Best Appetizers
Hub Cap Bar and Grill
13225 N. 66th St., Largo, 813/531-9865

Best Barbecue/Ribs
Hickory Smoke House Bar-B-Que
6769 Hwy. 19N, Pinellas Park, 813/525-0948

Best Beer Selection
The Oak Barrel
1901 N. Thirteenth St., Ybor City, 813/247-1164

Best Breakfast
Frog Pond
 16909 Gulf Blvd., North Redington Beach,
  813/384-4803

Best French Food
Cafe Largo
 12551 Indian Rocks Beach, Largo, 813/596-6282

Best Greek/Mediterranean Food
Hellas
 784 Dodecanese Blvd., Tarpon Springs, 813/934-8400

Best Mexican Food
Carambas
 1842 Drew St., 813/446-7469

Best Seafood
Clearwater Beach Seafoods
 37 Causeway Blvd., 813/442-2163
Guppy's
 1701 Gulf Blvd., Indian Rocks Beach, 813/593-2032

Best Spanish Food
Tio Pepe Restaurant
 2930 Gulf To Bay Blvd., 813/799-3082

Best Sushi
Kiku Japanese Restaurant
 13505 Icot Blvd., 813/532-9559

Best Vietnamese Food
East Wind
 6139 Parks Blvd., Pinellas Park, 813/541-6377

CORAL SPRINGS, FL

Best American Food
Dan Marino's Town Tavern
 901 University Dr., 954/341-4658

Best Barbecue/Ribs
Bobby Rubino's Place for Ribs
 6001 N. Kimberly Blvd., Pompano Beach,
  954/971-4740
 2501 N. Federal Hwy., Pompano Beach, 954/781-7550

Best Casual Dining
McDivitt's
 3011 Rock Island Rd., 954/753-3500

Best Family Restaurant
Morrison's Cafeteria
 9025 N. Atlantic Blvd., 954/753-4441

Best Lunch
Borders Bookstore
 700 University Dr., 954/340-3307

Best Microbrewery
Hops
 2600 University Dr., 954/340-3868

Best Steaks
Dan Marino's Town Tavern
 901 University Dr., 954/341-4658

andbys
he Olive Garden
  1555 University Dr., 954/344-5226

DAYTONA BEACH, FL

Best Barbecue/Ribs
Gator Rib House
  456 S. Martin Luther King Jr. Blvd., 904/248-0030

Best Breakfast
Aunt Catfish's On The River
  4009 Halifax Dr., 904/767-4768

Best Burgers
The Ave
  585 Dr. Mary McLeod Bethune Blvd., 904/238-5592

Best Coffee
Java Lava
  550 Seabreeze Blvd., 904/257-0599
Cafe Bravo
  176 N. Beach St., 904/252-7747

Best Health-Conscious Menu
Rosemary's Garden Restaurant
  670 S. Yonge St., Ormond Beach, 904/677-5363

Best Homestyle Food
Aunt Catfish's On The River
  4009 Halifax Dr., 904/767-4768

Best Ice Cream/Yogurt
Flamingo Homemade Ice Cream
  559 N. Beach St., 904/255-8090

Best Mexican Food
Rio Bravo
  1735 International Speedway Blvd., 904/255-6500

Best Other Ethnic Food
Tropical Gourmet (Caribbean)
  1420 Mason Ave., 904/274-4450

Best Pizza
Pantheon Pizza
  505 White St., 904/258-7180

Best Salad/Salad Bar
Rosemary's Garden Restaurant
  670 S. Yonge St., Ormond Beach, 904/677-5363

Best Sandwiches
Bopper's Sandwich Emporium
  137 W. International Speedway Blvd., 904/253-3778

Best Seafood
Park's Seafood Restaurant
  951 N. Ceach St., 904/258-7272
Top Of Daytona Restaurant
  2625 S. Atlantic Ave., 904/767-5791

Best Steaks
Top Of Daytona Restaurant
  2625 S. Atlantic Ave., 904/767-5791
Webber's Penn Jersey Bar
  2017 S. Ridgewood Ave., 904/761-5982

Best Vegetarian Food
Rosemary's Garden Restaurant
670 S. Yonge St., Ormond Beach, 904/677-5363

Standbys
Quincy's
1031 Dunlawton Ave., 904/756-3908
145 N. Nova Rd., 904/258-0547
Shoney's
2558 N. Atlantic Ave., 904/673-4288
2725 W. International Speedway Blvd., 904/255-9054

DEERFIELD BEACH, FL

F

Best Restaurant in Town
Brooks Restaurant
500 S. Federal Hwy., 954/427-9302

Best All-You-Can-Buffet
George's Place, A Family Restaurant
699 S. Federal Hwy., 954/428-7464

Best American Food
Cove Restaurant and Lounge
1755 SE Third Ct., 954/421-9272

Best Atmosphere
Cove Restaurant and Lounge
1755 SE Third Ct., 954/421-9272

Best Chinese Food
Hong Kong Chinese Takeout
206 N. Federal Hwy., 954/421-3126

Best Diner
Olympia Flame Diner
80 S. Federal Hwy., 954/480-8402

Best Family Restaurant
George's Place, A Family Restaurant
699 S. Federal Hwy., 954/428-7464

Best French Food
Brooks Restaurant
500 S. Federal Hwy., 954/427-9302
Le Val de Loire
1576 SE Third Ct., 954/427-5354
Cafe Claude
1544 SE Third Ct., 954/421-7337

Best Greek/Mediterranean Food
Olympia Flame Diner
80 S. Federal Hwy., 954/480-8402

Best Italian Food
Brusco Italian Restaurant
1380 S. Federal Hwy., 954/428-2676
Carafiello's Restaurant
949 S. Federal Hwy., 954/421-2481

Best Place to Eat When Someone Else Is Buying
Brooks Restaurant
500 S. Federal Hwy., 954/427-9302

Standbys
International House of Pancakes
516 S. Federal Hwy., 954/481-8338

DUNEDIN, FL

Best Restaurant in Town
Bon Appetit
148 Marina Plz., 813/733-2151

Best American Food
Jesse's Dockside
345 Causeway Blvd., 813/736-2611

Best Atmosphere
Sea Sea Rider's
221 Main St., 813/734-1445

Best Breakfast
Kelly's For Just About Anything
319 Main St., 813/736-5274

Best Casual Dining
Sea Sea Rider's
221 Main St., 813/734-1445

Best Family Restaurants
Iris Family Restaurant
234 Douglas Ave., 813/734-0779
Corner House Family Restaurant
2836 Alternate 19, 813/786-3736

Best Homestyle Food
Iris Family Restaurant
234 Douglas Ave., 813/734-0779
Corner House Family Restaurant
2836 Alternate 19, 813/786-3736

Best Other Ethnic Food
Flanagans Hunt Irish Pub (Irish)
465 Main St., 813/736-4994

Best Seafood
Bon Appetit
148 Marina Plz., 813/733-2151
Jesse's Dockside
345 Causeway Blvd., 813/736-2611

FT. LAUDERDALE, FL

Best Restaurant in Town
Cafe Arugula
3150 N. Federal Hwy., Lighthouse Point,
954/785-7732

Best Business Lunch
Cave's Restaurant
2205 N. Federal Hwy., 954/561-4622

Best Cheap Meal
Shells Restaurant
2019 N. University Dr., 954/749-0557

Best Chinese Food
Mai Kai Restaurant and Catering
3599 N. Federal Hwy., 954/563-3272

Best French Food
Left Bank
214 SE Sixth Ave., 954/462-5376

Best Indian Food
Punjab Indian Restaurant
    5975 N. Federal Hwy., Ste. 103, 954/491-6710

Best Italian Food
Mario's East
    1313 E. Las Olas Blvd., 954/523-4990

Best Mexican Food
Carlos and Pepe's
    1302 SE Seventeenth St., 954/467-7192

Best New Restaurants
Indochine
    8916 State Rd. 84, Davie, 954/452-8502
Kong Wah
    2640 S. State Rd. 7, Miramar, 954/962-8050
L'Aventure Restaurant Francais
    3322 E. Atlantic Blvd., Pompano Beach, 954/941-1724
Le Bistro
    4626 N. Federal Hwy., Lighthouse Point,
        954/946-9240

Best Other Ethnic Food
La Bamba (Cuban)
    5552 W. Oakland Park Blvd., 954/735-1891

Best Romantic Dining
Cafe Arugula
    3150 N. Federal Hwy., Lighthouse Point,
        954/785-7732
Le Dome
    333 Sunset Dr., 954/463-3303

Best Seafood
Fifteenth Street Fisheries
    1900 SE Fifteenth St., 954/763-2777

Best Thai Food
Thai Spice
    1514 E. Commercial Blvd., 954/771-4335

FT. MYERS, FL

Best Restaurants in Town
The Veranda
    2121 Second St., 941/332-2065
Melanie's Restaurant
    2534 Fowler St., 941/334-3139
Mucky Duck
    2500 Estero Blvd., Ft. Myers Beach, 941/463-5519

Best Atmosphere
The Veranda
    2121 Second St., 941/332-2065

Best Barbecue/Ribs
Rib City Grill
    12575 S. Cleveland Ave., 941/278-1300

Best Chinese Food
Brass Phoenix
    16520 Tamiami Trail, 941/489-4242

Best Continental Food
The Veranda
2121 Second St., 941/332-2065

Best Desserts
The Bubble Room
15001 Captiva Dr., Captiva, 941/472-5558

Best French Food
Peter's La Cuisine
2224 Bay St., 941/332-2228

Best German Food
Tannengarten
3724 Del Prado Blvd. S., Cape Coral, 941/549-1300

Best Italian Food
Dario's Restaurant and Lounge
1805 Del Prado Blvd., Cape Coral, 941/574-7798

Best Japanese Food
Yokahama
4650 Cleveland Ave. S., 941/936-4007

Best Mexican Food
Iguana Mia
1027 Cape Coral Pkwy., Cape Coral, 941/945-7755

Best Outdoor Dining
Anthony's on the Gulf
3040 Estero Blvd., Ft. Myers Beach, 941/463-2600

Best Seafood
Prawn Broker Restaurant and Lounge
13451 McGregor Blvd., 941/489-2226

Best Thai Food
Thai Gardens
7091 College Pkwy., 941/275-0999

Best Wine Selection
Peter's La Cuisine
2224 Bay St., 941/332-2228

FT. PIERCE, FL

Best Bar
Tiki Bar and Restaurant
1 Avenue A, 561/467-1188

Best Barbecue/Ribs
Norris's Famous Place For Ribs
3080 N. Hwy. 1, 561/464-4000

Best Breakfast
Captain's Galley
825 N. Indian River Dr., 561/466-8495
Crystal's Restaurant
127 S. Second St., 561/461-9550
Galley Grille
927 N. Hwy. 1, 561/468-2081

Best Brunch
Christopher's
1420 SE Westmoreland Blvd., Port St. Lucie,
561/335-0800

Best Burgers
Billy's Bar and Grill
4810 S. Hwy. 1, 561/460-1411

Best Chinese Food
Peking Chinese Restaurant
1012 S. Hwy. 1, 561/464-5960

Best Continental Food
Eleven Maple Street
3224 NE Maple Ave., Jensen Beach, 561/334-7714
Country Place
1205 NE State Rd. 707, Jensen Beach, 561/334-4563

Best Diners
Bel Air Diner
2825 Peters Rd., 561/465-5218
Crystal's Restaurant
127 S. Second St., 561/461-9550

Best Family Restaurant
Johnny's Corner Family Restaurant
7180 S. Hwy. 1, 561/878-2686

Best French Food
Le Brittany
897 E. Prima Vista Blvd., Port St. Lucie, 561/871-2231

Best Health-Conscious Menu
Lee's Sub and Salad Shop
850 S. 21st St., 561/466-4243

Best Homestyle Food
Johnny's Corner Family Restaurant
7180 S. Hwy. 1, 561/878-2686

Best Ice Cream/Yogurt
Bresler's Ice Cream and Yogurt
4420 Okeechobee Rd., 561/466-9490

Best Italian Food
Da Vinci's Restaurant
6692 S. Federal Hwy., Port St. Lucie, 561/466-9331

Best Mexican Food
Enriqo's Mexican Kitchen
3215 S. Hwy. 1, 561/465-1608
Casa Stefano
10786 S. Federal Hwy., Port St. Lucie, 561/335-3616
Guadalajara Mexican Food
221 Orange Ave., 561/489-2403

Best Pizza
Luna Italian Restaurant
49 SW Flagler Ave., Stuart, 561/288-0550

Best Places to Eat When Someone Else Is Buying
Mangrove Mattie's
1640 Seaway Dr., 561/466-1044
Eleven Maple Street
3224 NE Maple Ave., Jensen Beach, 561/334-7714
Country Place
1205 NE State Rd. 707, Jensen Beach, 561/334-4563

Best Romantic Dining
Toucan's Top Of The Dock
201 Fisherman's Wharf, 561/465-1334

F

Best Salad/Salad Bar
Gentleman Jim's
1651 SE Federal Hwy., Stuart, 561/287-1250

Best Sandwiches
Sottini's Sub Shop
3211 Orange Ave., 561/461-0077

Best Seafood
Galley Grille
927 N. Hwy. 1, 561/468-2081
Oceans Village Restaurant
2400 S. Ocean Dr., 561/465-4200
Theo Thudpucker's Raw Bar
2025 Seaway Dr., 561/465-1078

Best Steaks
Galley Grille
927 N. Hwy. 1, 561/468-2081
Norris's Famous Place For Ribs
3080 N. Hwy. 1, 561/464-4000
Oceans Village Restaurant
2400 S. Ocean Dr., 561/465-4200

Standbys
Denny's
2625 Hwy. 1, 561/465-6340
6501 Darter Ct., 561/466-0903
Dunkin' Donuts
2315 Okeechobee Rd., 561/460-1366
Po Folks
2301 S. Hwy. 1, 561/465-5001

FT. WALTON BEACH, FL

Best Restaurants in Town
Criolla's
Hwy. 30A, Santa Rosa Beach, 904/267-1267
Bud-n-Alley's
Hwy. 30A, Seaside, 904/231-5900

Best Continental Food
Marina Cafe
404 Hwy. 98E, 904/837-7960

Best Italian Food
Guglielmo's Ristorante and Lounge
573 Santa Rosa Blvd., 904/664-5408

GAINESVILLE, FL

Best Barbecue/Ribs
David's Real Pit Bar-B-Que
5121A NW 39th Ave., 352/373-2002

Best Breakfast
Forty-Third Street Deli and Breakfast House
4401 NW 25th Pl., 352/373-2927

Best Burgers
Snuffy's Islander Cafe
1017 W. University Ave., 352/376-8899

Best Chinese Food
Mr. Han's Restaurant
6944 NW Tenth Pl., Ste. 1, 352/331-6400

Best Health-Conscious Menu
Mill Bakery Eatery Brewery
    6791 W. Newberry Rd., 352/331-0110

Best Ice Cream/Yogurt
Doug's Dairy Twirl
    2117 NW Sixth St., 352/376-7154

Best Italian Food
Amelia's Italian Cuisine
    235 S. Main St., 352/373-1919
Ruscito's Italian Restaurant
    521 NE 23rd Ave., 352/373-0192

Best Mexican Food
Ashley's Mexican and American Restaurant
    3236 SW 35th Blvd., 352/375-4064
El Indio
    407 NW Thirteenth St., 352/377-5828
    5011 NW 34th St., 352/374-8647

Best Pizza
Pizza Palace
    608 NW Thirteenth St., 352/372-1546

Best Sandwiches
Forty-Third Street Deli and Breakfast House
    4401 NW 25th Pl., 352/373-2927

Best Seafood
Harry's Seafood Bar and Grille
    110 SE First St., 352/372-1555

Best Steaks
Steak and Pasta Works
    372 NW Thirteenth St., 352/377-2782

Best Thai Food
Tim's Thai Restaurant
    501 NW 23rd Ave., 352/372-5424

Standbys
Cracker Barrel
    4001 SW 43rd St., 352/375-2424
Outback Steakhouse
    3536 SW Archer Rd., 352/373-9499

HALLANDALE, FL

Best Bar
Flanagan's Seafood Bar and Grill
    4 N. Federal Hwy., 954/458-2566

Best Casual Dining
Flanagan's Seafood Bar and Grill
    4 N. Federal Hwy., 954/458-2566

Best Chinese Food
Mott Street Chinese Restaurant
    1295 E. Hallandale Beach Blvd., 954/456-7555

Best Diner
Nick's Restaurant
    105 E. Hallandale Beach Blvd., 954/458-0363

Best Italian Food
Manero's Steak House
    2600 E. Hallandale Beach Blvd., 954/456-1000

Best Japanese Food
Koto Japanese Restaurant
  1111 E. Hallandale Beach Blvd., 954/457-0078

Best Lunch
Miami Subs
  116 W. Hallandale Beach Blvd., 954/454-4488

Best Sandwiches
Miami Subs
  116 W. Hallandale Beach Blvd., 954/454-4488

Best 24-Hour Restaurant
Nick's Restaurant
  105 E. Hallandale Beach Blvd., 954/458-0363

Standbys
Tony Roma's
  606 E. Hallandale Beach Blvd., 954/454-7427

HOLLYWOOD, FL

Best Restaurant in Town
Martha's Restaurant
  6024 N. Ocean Dr., 954/923-5444

Best Atmosphere
Martha's Restaurant
  6024 N. Ocean Dr., 954/923-5444

Best Barbecue/Ribs
Sonny's Real Pit Bar-B-Q
  2100 S. State Rd. 7, 954/987-2336

Best German Food
Bavarian Village Restaurant
  1401 N. Federal Hwy., 954/922-7321

Best Seafood
Martha's Restaurant
  6024 N. Ocean Dr., 954/923-5444

Best Steaks
Roadhouse Grill
  3300 E. Commercial Blvd., Ft. Lauderdale,
    954/772-3777
  1900 S. University Dr., Ft. Lauderdale, 954/370-3044

Standbys
The Olive Garden
  4500 Hollywood Blvd., 954/966-9553

HOMESTEAD, FL

Best Barbecue/Ribs
Shiver's Bar-B-Q
  28001 S. Dixie Hwy., 305/248-2272

Best Casual Dining
Potlikker's Restaurant
  591 Washington Ave., 305/248-0835

Best Chinese Food
Canton Chinese Restaurant
  1657 NE Eighth St., 305/248-9956

Best Homestyle Food
Potlikker's Restaurant
  591 Washington Ave., 305/248-0835

Best Italian Food
Capri Restaurant
935 N. Krome Ave., Florida City, 305/247-1542

Best Lunch
Shiver's Bar-B-Q
28001 S. Dixie Hwy., 305/248-2272

Best Seafood
The Mutineer
11 SE First, Florida City, 305/245-3377

Best Steaks
Capri Restaurant
935 N. Krome Ave., Florida City, 305/247-1542

F

JACKSONVILLE, FL

Best American Food
Beech Street Grill
801 Beech St., Fernandina Beach, 904/277-3662
Old City House
115 Cordova St., St. Augustine, 904/826-0781

Best Barbecue/Ribs
Bono's Pit Bar-B-Q
Multiple Locations
Homestead Restaurant
1712 Beach Blvd., Jacksonville Beach, 904/249-5240

Best Breakfast
Metro Diner
3302 Hendricks Ave., 904/398-3701
Beach Hut Cafe
1281 S. Third St., 904/249-3516

Best Brunch
Juliette's
Omni Jacksonville Hotel, 245 W. Water St.,
904/355-6664

Best Casual Dining
Gypsy Cab Company
828 Anastasia Blvd., St. Augustine, 904/824-8244

Best Cheap Meal
Slider's Cafe
9810 Baymeadows Rd., 904/645-7777

Best Coffee
Biscotti's
3556 St. John's Ave., 904/387-2060

Best Continental Food
The Grill and Cafe
Ritz-Carlton, 4745 Amelia Island Pkwy., Amelia
Island, 904/277-1100
Horizons Restaurant
802 Ash St., Fernandina Beach, 904/321-2430

Best Desserts
Cafe Carmon
1986 San Marco Blvd., 904/399-4488

Best French Food
La Parisienne
60 Hypolita St., St. Augustine, 904/829-0055

Best Italian Food
La Cena Ristorante
  6271 St. Augustine Rd., 904/737-5350

Best Lunch
European Street Restaurant
  9501 Arlington Expwy., 904/725-8992
  2753 Park St., 904/384-9999

Best Microbrewery
River City Brewing Company
  835 Museum Circle, 904/398-2299

Best New Restaurants
Rio Bravo Cantina
  8520 Bay Meadows Rd., 904/739-3601
Island Grill
  981 N. First St., Jacksonville Beach, 904/241-1881

Best Other Ethnic Food
A 1A Ale Works (Caribbean)
  1 King St., St. Augustine, 904/829-2977

Best Place to Eat When Someone Else Is Buying
Matanzas Bay Cafe
  12 Avenida Menendez, St. Augustine, 904/829-8141

Best Romantic Dining
The Hilltop
  2030 Wells Rd., Orange Park, 904/279-5959
West River
  1711 Edgewood Ave. S., 904/389-4171
The Augustine Room
  Marriott Sawgrass, 1000 TPC Blvd., 904/285-7777

Best Salad/Salad Bar
Silver Spoon Bar and Grill
  2 E. Independent Dr., Ste. 2, 904/353-4503

Best Seafood
Dolphin Depot
  704 N. First St., Jacksonville Beach, 904/270-1424
Ragtime Tavern and Seafood Grill
  207 Atlantic Blvd., Atlantic Beach, 904/241-7877

Best Undiscovered Restaurant
Dolphin Depot
  704 N. First St., Jacksonville Beach, 904/270-1424

Best Wine Selection
Wine Cellar
  1314 Prudential Dr., 904/398-8989

Standbys
Outback Steakhouse
  9400 Atlantic Blvd., 904/720-1818
  9773 San Jose Blvd., 904/268-4329

KEY LARGO, FL

Best Barbecue/Ribs
B.J.'s Bar BQ
  102570 Overseas Hwy., 305/451-0900

Best Brunch
Cheeca Lodge
  81081 Overseas Hwy., Islamorada, 305/664-4651

Gus' Grille
  Marriott Hotel, 103800 Overseas Hwy., 305/453-0066

Best Business Lunch
Gus' Grille
  Marriott Hotel, 103800 Overseas Hwy., 305/453-0066

Best Japanese Food
Makoto Japanese Restaurant
  99470 Hwy. 1, 305/451-7083
Papa Joe's Landmark Restaurant
  Hwy. 1, Islamorada, 305/664-8756

Best Pizza
Gus' Grille
  Marriott Hotel, 103800 Overseas Hwy., 305/453-0066

F

KEY WEST, FL

Best Breakfast
Camille's Restaurant
  703 1/2 Duval St., 305/296-4811

Best Chinese Food
Dynasty Chinese Restaurant
  918 Duval St., 305/294-2943

Best Continental Food
Bagatelle
  115 Duval St., 305/296-6609

Best Diner
Harpoon Harry's
  832 Caroline St., 305/294-8744

Best French Food
Cafe Des Artistes
  1007 Simonton St., 305/294-7100

Best Homestyle Food
Camille's Restaurant
  703 1/2 Duval St., 305/296-4811

Best Italian Food
La Trattoria Venezia
  524 Duval St., 305/296-1075

Best Seafood
Quay Restaurant
  12 Duval St., 305/294-4446
Martha's
  3591 S. Roosevelt Blvd., 305/294-3466

Best Sports Bar
P.T.'s Late Night Bar and Grill
  920 Caroline St., 305/296-4245

Best Steaks
Pepe's Cafe
  806 Caroline St., 305/294-7192

LAKELAND, FL

Best Atmosphere
Palm Court
  819 S. Florida Ave., 941/682-4140

F

Best Barbecue/Ribs
Brothers Bar-B-Q
1046 Martin Luther King Jr. Ave., 941/688-5303
Jaybird's Bar-B-Q
6120 Hwy. 98N, 941/858-1970
Jimbo's Pit Bar-B-Q
1215 Memorial Blvd., 941/683-3777

Best Breakfast
Dale's Kitchen
223 N. Wabash Ave., 941/683-3702
Reececliff Restaurant
940 S. Florida Ave., 941/686-6661

Best Burgers
Fat Jack's Deli and Pub
2940 S. Florida Ave., 941/687-0262
Reececliff Restaurant
940 S. Florida Ave., 941/686-6661

Best Desserts
Palm Court
819 S. Florida Ave., 941/682-4140
Strollo's Cucina
1295 E. Main St., 941/686-1295

Best Homestyle Food
Brothers Bar-B-Q
1046 Martin Luther King Jr. Ave., 941/688-5303

Best Italian Food
CDB Pizza and Italian Restaurant
804 E. Memorial Blvd., 941/688-6444
Strollo's Cucina
1295 E. Main St., 941/686-1295
Palm Court
819 S. Florida Ave., 941/682-4140

Best Other Ethnic Food
El Coqui Restaurant (Puerto Rican)
4417 S. Florida Ave., 941/648-4374

Best Sandwiches
Fat Jack's Deli and Pub
2940 S. Florida Ave., 941/687-0262
Deli Delicacies
4110 S. Florida Ave., 941/644-3363

Best Seafood
Catfish Country Restaurant
2400 E. F. Griffin Rd., Bartow, 941/646-6767

Best Steaks
Texas Cattle Company
735 E. Main St., 941/686-1434
Farmer Jones Red Barn House
6150 New Tampa Hwy., 941/686-2754

Best Thai Food
King and I
304 E. Lemon St., 941/682-2525

Standbys
Chuck E. Cheese Pizza
  3558 Hwy. 98N, 941/853-8668
Baskin-Robbins
  2106 S. Florida Ave., 941/688-4168

MELBOURNE, FL

Best Barbecue/Ribs
Woody's Bar-B-Que
  2227 W. New Haven Ave., 407/951-9163

Best Breakfast
Sue's Wrangler
  914 W. New Haven Ave., 407/984-0770

Best Chinese Food
China Coast Restaurant
  2355 W. New Haven, 407/952-2290

Best Homestyle Food
Ethel and Fred's Restaurant
  3016 W. New Haven Ave., 407/725-6855
Sue's Wrangler
  914 W. New Haven Ave., 407/984-0770

Best Italian Food
Paolo's Italian Kitchen
  476 Ballard Dr., 407/259-2089
Dove Restaurant
  1790 A1A Hwy., Satellite Beach, 407/777-5817

Best Pizza
Leaning Tower of Pizza
  681 N. Wickham Rd., 407/259-6100

Best Sandwiches
Doubles Hoagies
  1897 S. Patrick Dr., 407/773-5341
  575 S. Wickham Rd., 407/676-6945
Don's Famous Hoagies
  784 S. Apollo Blvd., 407/676-7030

Best Seafood
Bone Fish Willy's
  2459B Pineapple Ave., 407/255-0735
Rooney's
  2641 Palm Bay Rd. NE, Palm Bay, 407/724-8520
Jack Baker's Lobster Shanty
  2200 S. Orlando Ave., 407/783-1350
Shells Restaurant
  1490 W. New Haven Ave., 407/722-1122

Best Steaks
Durango Steak House
  6765 N. Wickham Rd., 407/259-2955

Standbys
Chili's
  955 N. Wickham Rd., 407/757-9449
Cracker Barrel
  8400 N. Wickham Rd., 407/242-0350
Baskin-Robbins
  2330 N. Wickham Rd., 407/253-2280

MIAMI, FL

Best Restaurants in Town
Caffe Abbracci
318 Aragon Ave., Coral Gables, 305/441-0700
Norman's
21 Almeria Ave., Coral Gables, 305/446-6767
Mark's Place
2286 NE 123rd St., North Miami, 305/893-6888
Grand Cafe
2669 S. Bayshore Dr., Coconut Grove, 305/858-9600
Marco's
3339 Virginia St., Coconut Grove, 305/444-5333
Pacific Time
915 Lincoln Rd., Miami Beach, 305/534-5979
Paparazzi Ristorante and Nightclub
940 Ocean Dr., Miami Beach, 305/531-3500

Best Barbecue/Ribs
People's Barbecue
402 NW Eighth St., 305/374-5874
The Pit Bar-B-Q
16400 SW Eighth St., West Dade, 305/226-2272
Shorty's Bar-B-Q
9200 S. Dixie Hwy., Kendall, 305/670-7732
5989 S. University Dr., Davie, 305/944-0348
115755 SW 40th St., 305/227-3196
Midtown BBQ
1772 NW 79th St., North Dade, 305/836-4142

Best Brunch
The Biltmore Hotel
1200 Anastasia Ave., Coral Gables, 305/445-1926

Best Business Lunch
Restaurant Le Pavillon
Hotel Inter-Continental, 100 Chopin Plaza,
305/372-4494
Christy's Restaurant
3101 Ponce De Leon Blvd., Coral Gables,
305/446-1400

Best Cheap Meal
Nick's
300 Alton Rd., Miami Beach, 305/673-3444

Best Chinese Food
Canton Chinese Restaurant
2614 Ponce De Leon Blvd., Coral Gables,
305/448-3736
9796 SW Eighth St., 305/226-8032
17082 Collins Ave., 305/949-7777
14487 S. Dixie Hwy., King's Bay, 305/255-5115
Christine Lee's Gaslight
8401 Collins Ave., Miami Beach, 305/931-7700
Chrysanthemum
1256 Washington Ave., Miami Beach, 305/531-5656

Best Coffeehouse
Aurora
1205 Seventeenth St., Miami Beach, 305/534-1744

Best Delicatessens
Arnie and Richie's
    525 41st St., Miami Beach, 305/531-7691
The Villa Deli
    1608 Alton Rd., Miami Beach, 305/538-4552

Best Desserts
Cheesecake Factory
    3015 Grand Ave. (in CoCoWalk), Coconut Grove,
        305/447-9898
Mark's Place
    2286 NE 123rd St., North Miami, 305/893-6888

Best Diner
Il Piccolo Diner
    2112 NE 123rd St., North Miami, 305/893-6538

Best French Food
The Bistro
    2611 Ponce de Leon Blvd., Coral Gables,
        305/442-9671
Didier's
    2530 Ponce de Leon Blvd., Coral Gables,
        305/567-2444
Le Festival
    2120 Salzedo St., Coral Gables, 305/442-8545

Best German Food
Treffpunkt Biergarten
    18090 Collins Ave., North Miami Beach, 305/933-3942

Best Greek/Mediterranean Food
Vakhos
    1915 Ponce de Leon Blvd., Coral Gables,
        305/444-8444

Best Health-Conscious Menu
Unicorn Village Market and Restaurant
    3565 NE 207th St., Aventura, 305/933-8829

Best Ice Cream/Yogurt
DasGUTTyogurt
    10793 Biscayne Blvd., Northeast Dade, 305/893-9550
The Frieze
    1626 Michigan Ave., Miami Beach, 305/538-0207

Best Indian Food
Darbar
    276 Alhambra Circle, Coral Gables, 305/448-9691
Kebab Indian Restaurant
    514 NE 167th St., North Miami Beach, 305/940-6309
House of India
    22 Merrick Way, Coral Gables, 305/444-2348

Best Italian Food
Caffe Abbracci
    318 Aragon Ave., Coral Gables, 305/441-0700
Caffe CJ
    65 Merrick Way, Coral Gables, 305/445-1200
Oggie Caffe and Deli
    1740 79th Street Causeway, Miami Beach,
        305/866-1238

Prezzo
18831 Biscayne Blvd., 305/933-9004
8888 SW 136th St., 305/234-1010
Sport Cafe
538 Washington Ave., Miami Beach, 305/674-9700

Best Japanese Food
Akashi Japanese Restaurant
5830 S. Dixie Hwy., South Miami, 305/665-6261
Benihana
8727 S. Dixie Hwy., 305/665-0044

Best Late-Night Food
San Loco
235 Fourteenth St., Miami Beach, 305/538-3009
Versailles
3555 SW Eighth St., 305/444-0240
David's Coffee Shop
1058 Collins Ave., Miami Beach, 305/534-8736

Best Mexican Food
Chilango's Mexican Grill
5859 SW 73rd St., South Miami, 305/663-9333
El Torito
10633 NW Twelfth St., 305/591-0671
Senor Frog's
3008 Grand Ave., 305/448-0999

Best Middle Eastern Food
Palace Cuisine
9537 S. Dixie Hwy., Kendall, 305/662-1113

Best New Restaurants
Cafe Del Sol
1601 Biscayne Blvd., 305/374-0000
Max's South Beach
764 Washington Ave., 305/573-0658
Chef Allen's
19088 NE 29th Ave., North Miami Beach,
305/935-2900
The Big Tomato
12447 S. Dixie Hwy., South Miami, 305/233-3344
Norma's on the Beach!
646 Lincoln Rd., Miami Beach, 305/532-2809
Nemo
100 Collins Ave., Miami Beach, 305/532-4550

Best Other Ethnic Food
World Resources (multicultural cuisine)
719 Lincoln Rd., Miami Beach, 305/534-9095
Rincon Argentino (Argentinian)
3650 Coral Way, 305/444-2494
Exquisito Restaurant (Cuban)
1510 SW Eighth St., 305/643-0227
Yuca Restaurant (Cuban)
177 Giralda Ave., Coral Gables, 305/444-4448
Shabeen Restaurant (Caribbean)
1200 Collins Ave., Miami Beach, 305/931-7700
Chez Moy (Haitian)
1 NW 54th St., 305/757-5056

Vatapa (Brazilian)
   2415 Ponce de Leon Blvd., Coral Gables,
     305/461-5669
Granny B's Kitchen (Caribbean)
   1700 NW 183rd St., North Dade, 305/624-8878
Mango's Tropical Cafe (Caribbean)
   900 Ocean Dr., Miami Beach, 305/673-4422
Norma's on the Beach! (Caribbean)
   646 Lincoln Rd., Miami Beach, 305/532-2809
Yambo (Nicaraguan)
   1643 SW First St., 305/642-6616
Restaurant Atlacatl (Salvadoran)
   2273 NW Seventh St., 305/643-2545

Best Outdoor Dining
News Cafe
   800 Ocean Dr., Miami Beach, 305/538-6397
Van Dyke Cafe
   846 Lincoln Rd., Miami Beach, 305/534-3600

Best Pizza
Casola's Pizza
   2437 SW Seventeenth Ave., 305/858-0090
Mark's Place
   2286 NE 123rd St., North Miami, 305/893-6888
Au Natural Gourmet Pizza
   1427 Alton Rd., Miami Beach, 305/531-0666

Best Places to Eat When Someone Else Is Buying
The Forge
   432 41st St., Miami Beach, 305/538-8533
Mark's Place
   2286 NE 123rd St., North Miami, 305/893-6888

Best Romantic Dining
Didier's
   2530 Ponce de Leon Blvd., Coral Gables,
     305/567-2444
The Forge
   432 41st St., Miami Beach, 305/538-8533
Caffe Abbracci
   318 Aragon Ave., Coral Gables, 305/441-0700

Best Seafood
Fishbone Grille
   650 S. Miami Ave., 305/530-1915
Joe's Stone Crab
   227 Biscayne St., Miami Beach, 305/673-0365

Best Spanish Food
Casa Juancho
   2436 SW Eighth St., 305/642-2452
Las Rias Gallegas
   804 Ponce de Leon Blvd., Coral Gables, 305/442-9058

Best Steaks
Linda B. Steak House
   320 Crandon Blvd., Key Biscayne, 305/361-1111
Los Ranchos of Bayside
   401 Biscayne Blvd., 305/375-0666

F

Best Thai Food
Thai House
  1137 Washington Ave., Miami Beach, 305/531-4841
Thai Tony
  890 Washington Ave., Miami Beach, 305/538-8424

Best Vegetarian Food
Here Comes the Sun
  2188 NE 123rd St., North Miami, 305/893-5711
Neal's
  2570 NE Miami Gardens Dr., Adventura,
    305/936-8333
Juices and More
  1315 Ponce de Leon Blvd., Coral Gables,
    305/461-1262

Best Vietnamese Food
Hy-Vong
  3458 SW Eighth St., 305/446-3674

Best Wine Selection
The Forge
  432 41st St., Miami Beach, 305/538-8533
Grand Cafe
  2669 S. Bayshore Dr., Coconut Grove, 305/858-9600

NAPLES, FL

Best All-You-Can-Eat Buffets
Grouper House
  396 Goodlette Rd. S., 941/263-4900
Pippin's Restaurant
  1390 Ninth St. N., 941/261-6662

Best Atmosphere
St. George and The Dragon
  936 Fifth Ave. S., 941/262-6546

Best Barbecue/Ribs
Michelbob's
  869 103rd Ave. N., 941/594-7675
  371 Airport Pulling Rd. N., 941/643-2877

Best Breakfast
First Watch Restaurant
  1400 Gulf Shore Blvd. S., 941/434-0005

Best Burgers
Lindburgers
  330 Ninth St. S., 941/262-1127

Best Desserts
Truffles
  1300 Third St. S., 941/262-5500

Best Family Restaurant
Pippin's Restaurant
  1390 Ninth St. N., 941/261-6662

Best French Food
Chardonnay Restaurant
  2331 Tamiami Trail N., 941/261-1744
Sign Of The Vine Restaurant
  980 Solano Rd., 941/261-6745

Best Ice Cream/Yogurt
Tropic Chill
   493 Goodlette Rd. N., 941/262-8339

Best Italian Food
Frascatti's Italian Restaurant
   1258 Airport Pulling Rd. N., 941/643-5709
Il Posto Cafe
   1170 Third St. S., 941/261-8650
Antonia's
   2327 County Rd. 951, 941/455-2000

Best Place to Eat When Someone Else Is Buying
Casablanca Restaurant
   3078 Tamiami Trail N., 941/261-8779

F

Best Sandwiches
Tropic Chill
   493 Goodlette Rd. N., 941/262-8339

Best Seafood
Grouper House
   396 Goodlette Rd. S., 941/263-4900
Riverwalk Fish and Ale House
   1200 Fifth Ave. S., 941/263-2734
St. George and The Dragon
   936 Fifth Ave. S., 941/262-6546

Best Steaks
St. George and The Dragon
   936 Fifth Ave. S., 941/262-6546
Riverwalk Fish and Ale House
   1200 Fifth Ave. S., 941/263-2734

Best Thai Food
Bangkok Cuisine
   572 Ninth St. N., 941/261-5900

Standbys
Ben and Jerry's
   4320 Gulf Shore Blvd. N., 941/434-5850

OCALA, FL

Best Restaurant in Town
Fiddlestix Steak Pit and Tavern
   1016 SE Third Ave., 352/629-8000

Best American Food
Carmichael's Restaurant
   3105 NE Silver Springs Blvd., 352/622-3636

Best Atmosphere
Petite Jardin
   2209 E. Silver Springs Blvd., 352/351-4140

Best Bar
Dooley's Eating and Drinking
   3305 NE Silver Springs Blvd., 352/629-2740

Best Barbecue/Ribs
Sonny's Real Pit Bar-B-Q
   1845 SW College Rd., 352/629-2663
   4102 E. Silver Springs Blvd., 352/236-1012

Best Bread
Carmichael's Restaurant
3105 NE Silver Springs Blvd., 352/622-3636

Best Brunch
Ocala Hilton
3600 SW 36th Ave., 352/854-1400

Best Burgers
Miami Subs
3358-100 SW College Rd., 352/237-1499

Best Chinese Food
Mandarin House
2436 E. Silver Springs Blvd., 352/732-3077

Best Continental Food
Carmichael's Restaurant
3105 NE Silver Springs Blvd., 352/622-3636

Best Diner
Wayne's Brick City Cafe
26 S. Magnolia Ave., 352/629-4700

Best French Food
Petite Jardin
2209 E. Silver Springs Blvd., 352/351-4140

Best German Food
German Kitchen
5340 E. Silver Springs Blvd., 352/236-3055

Best Greek/Mediterranean Food
Laki's Greek Restaurant
1605 SE Magnolia Ext., 352/351-2550

Best Japanese Food
The Wokery I
2701 SW College Rd., Ste. 309, 352/873-3222
The Wokery II
2019 E. Silver Springs Blvd., Ste. 102, 352/622-6655

Best Mexican Food
El Toreo
3790 NE Silver Springs Blvd., 352/694-1401

Best Pizza
Abio's Italian Restaurant
Plaza 200, 2377 SW College Rd., 352/629-4886

Best Place to Be "Seen"
Fiddlestix Steak Pit and Tavern
1016 SE Third Ave., 352/629-8000

Best Quick Lunch
Wayne's Brick City Cafe
26 S. Magnolia Ave., 352/629-4700

Best Romantic Dining
Petite Jardin
2209 E. Silver Springs Blvd., 352/351-4140

Best Salad/Salad Bar
Holiday House
4011 E. Silver Springs Blvd., 352/236-3014

Best Sandwiches
Charley Horse Restaurant
2426 E. Silver Springs Blvd., 352/622-4050

Best Seafood
Sam's St. John's Seafood
    7119 N. Hwy. 441, 352/622-2927

Best Southwestern Food
Lone Star Saloon
    3410 SW College Rd., 352/873-1133

Best Spanish Food
Latinos Y Mas
    2030 S. Pine Ave., 352/622-4777

Best Sports Bar
Ocala Ale House
    305 SE Seventeenth St., 352/620-8989

Best Sushi
Kotobuki Japanese Steak House
    2463 SW 27th Ave., 352/629-6649

Best Wine Selection
Petite Jardin
    2209 E. Silver Springs Blvd., 352/351-4140

F

ORLANDO, FL

Best American Food
Pebbles
    2110 E. State Rd. 434, Longwood, 407/774-7111
    2516 Aloma Ave., Winter Park, 407/678-7001
    12551 State Rd. 535, 407/827-1111
    17 W. Church St., 407/839-0892

Best Barbecue/Ribs
Bubbalou's Bodacious BBQ
    1471 Lee Rd., Winter Park, 407/628-1212

Best Chinese Food
China Coast
    7500 International Dr., 407/351-9776
    7373 W. Colonial Dr., 407/297-8100

Best Continental Food
Maison and Jardin
    430 Wymore Rd., Altamonte Springs, 407/862-4410

Best French Food
Le Coq Au Vin
    4800 South Orange Ave., 407/851-6980

Best Greek/Mediterranean Food
Olympia
    8505 East Colonial Dr., 407/273-7836

Best Indian Food
Far Pavilion
    474 West State Rd, Altamonte Springs, 407/682-4711

Best Italian Food
Enzo's Restaurant on the Lake
    1130 S. Hwy. 17-92, Longwood, 407/834-9872

Best Japanese Food
Kobe Japanese Steakhouse and Sushi Bar
    2110 E. Colonial Dr., 407/895-6868
    8460 Palm Pkwy., 407/239-1119

Best Mexican Food
Amigos
  120 N. Westmonte Dr., Altamonte Springs,
    407/774-4334

Best Middle Eastern Food
Phoenician
  7600 Dr. Phillips Blvd., 407/354-1001

Best New Restaurant
Le Provence
  50 East Pine St., 407/843-1320

Best Other Ethnic Food
Numero Uno (Cuban)
  2499 South Orange Ave., 407/841-3840
All Nations (Caribbean)
  115 East State Rd., Fern Park, 407/332-9577

Best Seafood
Straub's Fine Seafood
  512 E. Altamonte Dr., Altamonte Springs,
    407/831-2250
  5101 E. Colonial Dr., 407/273-9330

Best Thai Food
Siam Orchid
  7575 Republic Dr., 407/351-0821

Standbys
Outback Steakhouse
  1301 Florida Mall Ave., 407/240-6857
  990 N. State Rd. 434, Altamonte Springs,
    407/862-1050

PANAMA CITY, FL

Best Breakfast
Dock at Jr.'s, Eat at Joe's
  112A E. Third Ct., 904/763-6442

Best Brunch
Hawk's Nest Restaurant
  123 E. Beach Dr., 904/872-1333

Best Continental Food
Terrace Restaurant
  13741 Emerald Coast Pkwy., Sea Grove, 904/231-5202

Best Desserts
Cheese Barn
  440 Grace Ave., 904/769-3892

Best Diner
Taxi's Diner
  3101 W. 23rd St., 904/763-5025

Best Homestyle Food
Dock at Jr.'s, Eat at Joe's
  112A E. Third Ct., 904/763-6442

Best Japanese Food
Mikato at the Beach
  7724 Front, Panama City Beach, 904/235-1338

Best Lunch
Taxi's Diner
 3101 W. 23rd St., 904/763-5025

Best Seafood
Harbour House Restaurant
 3001 W. Tenth St., 904/785-9053
Captain Anderson's Restaurant
 5551 N. Lagoon Dr., 904/234-2225

Best Steaks
Mikato at the Beach
 7724 Front, Panama City Beach, 904/235-1338

F

PENSACOLA, FL

Best All-You-Can-Eat Buffet
Montana's Bar-B-Q and Seafood
 7813 N. Davis Hwy., 904/477-1313

Best Atmosphere
McGuire's Irish Pub and Brewery
 600 E. Gregory St., 904/433-6789

Best Bar
McGuire's Irish Pub and Brewery
 600 E. Gregory St., 904/433-6789

Best Barbecue/Ribs
Billy Bob's Barbeque
 6403 N. Ninth Ave., 904/484-5480
Roger's Barbecue
 4908 N. Davis Hwy., 904/478-7864
King's Bar-B-Q
 2120 N. Palafox St., 904/433-4479
Montana's Bar-B-Q and Seafood
 7813 N. Davis Hwy., 904/477-1313

Best Breakfast
Coffee Cup Restaurant
 520 E. Cervantes St., 904/432-7060

Best Burgers
McGuire's Irish Pub and Brewery
 600 E. Gregory St., 904/433-6789

Best Coffee
Bean and Leaf Coffeehouse
 4350 Bayou Blvd., 904/477-7469
Books-A-Million
 6235 N. Davis Hwy., 904/478-4849

Best Desserts
Chan's Saloon and Eatery
 7000 Plantation Rd., 904/477-9961
Jubilee Restaurant and Cafe
 500 Quietwater Beach Rd., Gulf Breeze, 904/934-3108
Napoleon Bakery
 101 S. Jefferson St., 904/434-9701

Best Family Restaurant
Montana's Bar-B-Q and Seafood
 7813 N. Davis Hwy., 904/477-1313

Best French Food
Jamie's French Restaurant
424 E. Zarragossa St., 904/434-2911

Best Greek/Mediterranean Food
Georgio's Pizza
3000 E. Cervantes St., 904/432-5996

Best Homestyle Food
H and O Cafe
301 E. Gonzalez St., 904/432-1991
Hopkins Boarding House
900 N. Spring St., 904/438-3979

Best Ice Cream/Yogurt
Jubilee Restaurant and Cafe
500 Quietwater Beach Rd., Gulf Breeze, 904/934-3108

Best Italian Food
Marchelo's Italian Restaurant
620 S. Navy Blvd., 904/456-5200

Best Japanese Food
Yamato
131 N. New Warrington Rd., 904/453-3461

Best Pizza
Fournaris Brothers Restaurant
1015 N. Ninth Ave., 904/432-0629
Georgio's Pizza
3000 E. Cervantes St., 904/432-5996
Marchelo's Italian Restaurant
620 S. Navy Blvd., 904/456-5200
Godfather's Pizza
4479 Mobile Hwy., 904/455-5438
6847 N. Ninth Ave., 904/484-9900

Best Sandwiches
McGuire's Irish Pub and Brewery
600 E. Gregory St., 904/433-6789
Napoleon Bakery
101 S. Jefferson St., 904/434-9701
New Yorker Deli
3001 E. Cervantes St., 904/469-0029

Best Seafood
Chan's Saloon and Eatery
7000 Plantation Rd., 904/477-9961
Oscar's Restaurant
2805 W. Cervantes St., 904/432-8388
Chet's Food Restaurant
3708 W. Navy Blvd., 904/456-0165
Boy On A Dolphin Restaurant
400 Pensacola Beach Blvd., Gulf Breeze,
904/932-7954
Flounder's Chowder and Ale House
800 Quietwater Beach Rd., Gulf Breeze, 904/932-2003
Jubilee Restaurant and Cafe
500 Quietwater Beach Rd., Gulf Breeze, 904/934-3108
Cock of the Walk
550 Scenic Hwy., 904/432-6766
Skopelos Seafood and Steak
670 Scenic Hwy., 904/432-6565

Best Steaks
McGuire's Irish Pub and Brewery
  600 E. Gregory St., 904/433-6789
Skopelos Seafood and Steak
  670 Scenic Hwy., 904/432-6565
Mesquite Charlie's
  5901 N. W St., 904/434-0498

PORT CHARLOTTE, FL

Best Restaurant in Town
Zito's Restaurant
  24100 Rampant Rd., 941/625-4900

F

Best Italian Food
Mama Nunzia Ristorante
  1975 Tamiami Trail, Punta Gorda, 941/575-7575

Best Seafood
Salty's Harborside Restaurant
  5000 Burnt Store Rd. N., 941/639-3650

Best Steaks
Zito's Restaurant
  24100 Rampant Rd., 941/625-4900

Standbys
Chili's
  1471 Tamiami Trail, 941/255-0058
The Olive Garden
  1341 Tamiami Trail, 941/625-8807

ST. PETERSBURG, FL

Best American Food
Harvey's Fourth Street Grill
  3121 Fourth St. N., 813/821-6516

Best Barbecue/Ribs
Big Tim's Bar-B-Q
  530 34th St. S., 813/327-7388

Best Brunch
Cosmic Cafe
  1393 Pasadena Ave., St. Petersburg Beach,
  813/384-4803
Harvey's Fourth Street Grill
  3121 Fourth St. N., 813/821-6516

Best Burgers
Big Apple Bistro North
  11270 Fourth St. N., 813/576-3326

Best Casual Dining
Harvey's Fourth Street Grill
  3121 Fourth St. N., 813/821-6516

Best Cheap Meal
Family Kitchen Restaurant
  2339 Ninth St. N., 813/822-8500

Best Family Restaurant
Family Kitchen Restaurant
  2339 Ninth St. N., 813/822-8500

Best Fast Food
Coney Island Sandwich Shop
  250 Ninth St. N., 813/822-4493

Best German Food
Der Eisenhut
  357 Corey Ave., 813/367-6495

Best Homestyle Food
Atwater's Cafeteria
  895 22nd Ave. S., 813/823-7018
Skyway Jack's Restaurant
  6701 34th St. S., 813/866-3217

Best Italian Food
C.D. Roma's
  1280 66th St. N., 813/344-3837

Best Japanese Food
Arigato Japanese Steak House
  3600 66th St. N., 813/343-5200

Best New Restaurant
The Steak Joint
  4871 Park St., 813/545-9481

Best Other Ethnic Food
Saffron's Caribbean Cuisine (Caribbean)
  537 Central Ave., 813/898-9200

Best Sandwiches
Williams Submarine Sandwich
  3801 Tyrone Blvd. N., 813/347-9497

Best Soul Food
Atwater's Cafeteria
  895 22nd Ave. S., 813/823-7018

Best Sports Bar
Bleachers
  10478 Roosevelt Blvd., 813/576-2216

Best Steaks
The Steak Joint
  4871 Park St., 813/545-9481
Arigato Japanese Steak House
  3600 66th St. N., 813/343-5200
Keystone Club
  320 Fourth St. N., 813/822-6600

SANFORD, FL

Best Restaurant in Town
Sanford Landing
  Marina Hotel, 530 N. Palmetto, 407/323-1910

Best Atmosphere
Sanford Landing
  Marina Hotel, 530 N. Palmetto, 407/323-1910

Best Breakfast
Colonial Room Restaurant
  115 E. First St., 407/323-2999

Best Chinese Food
China King
  2508 S. French Ave., 407/323-6166

Best Homestyle Food
M and M Sandwich Shop and Deli
    205 S. Spring Garden Ave., De Land, 561/734-9663
Colonial Room Restaurant
    115 E. First St., 407/323-2999

Best View
Sanford Landing at the Marina Hotel
    530 N. Palmetto, 407/323-1910

Standbys
Denny's
    3771 S. Orlando Dr., 407/321-6306
The Olive Garden
    300 W. State Rd. 436, Altamonte Springs,
        407/862-0378

F

SARASOTA, FL

Best American Food
Ophelia's Restaurant
    9105 Midnight Pass Rd., 941/349-2212
Patrick's Restaurant
    1442 Main St., 941/952-1170

Best Atmosphere
Alley Cat Cafe
    1558 Fourth St., 941/954-1228

Best Bars
Patrick's Restaurant
    1442 Main St., 941/952-1170
Stock Yard Steakhouse
    4041 Cattlemen Rd., 941/378-9699

Best Breakfast
Chef Paul's
    1603 N. Tamiami Trail, 941/365-5976
Mel-O-Dee Restaurant
    4685 N. Tamiami Trail, 941/355-5768
First Watch Restaurant
    8383 S. Tamiami Trail, 941/923-6754

Best Burgers
Stock Yard Steakhouse
    4041 Cattlemen Rd., 941/378-9699

Best Business Lunch
Michael's On East
    1212 S. East Ave., 941/366-0007

Best Casual Dining
Patrick's Restaurant
    1442 Main St., 941/952-1170

Best Continental Food
Cafe L'Europe
    431 Saint Armands Circle, 941/388-4415
Alley Cat Cafe
    1558 Fourth St., 941/954-1228

Best Desserts
Yoder's Restaurant
    3434 Bahia Vista St., 941/955-7771

Best Diner
Mel-O-Dee Restaurant
4685 N. Tamiami Trail, 941/355-5768

Best Dinner
Coasters of Sarasota
1500 Stickney Point Rd., 941/923-4848

Best Family Restaurant
Yoder's Restaurant
3434 Bahia Vista St., 941/955-7771

Best French Food
Chez Sylvie's Restaurant
1526 Main St., 941/953-3232

Best Homestyle Food
Sommers Family Kitchen
1766 Main St., 941/366-7273

Best Italian Food
Nick's Italian Restaurant
230 Sarasota Quay, 941/954-3839

Best Mexican Food
El Adobe
4023 S. Tamiami Trail, 941/921-7576
Two Senoritas
1355 Main St., 941/366-1618

Best Other Ethnic Food
Sommers Family Kitchen (Amish)
1766 Main St., 941/366-7273
Yoder's Restaurant (Amish)
3434 Bahia Vista St., 941/955-7771

Best Place to Eat When Someone Else Is Buying
Jack's Chop House
214 Sarasota Quay, 941/951-2467

Best Sandwiches
Patrick's Restaurant
1442 Main St., 941/952-1170

Best Seafood
Coasters of Sarasota
1500 Stickney Point Rd., 941/923-4848

Best Steaks
Joto Japanese Steak House
7971 N. Tamiami Trail, 941/351-4677

Best Thai Food
Siam Orchid
4141 S. Tamiami Trail, 941/923-7447

Best View While Dining
Coasters of Sarasota
1500 Stickney Point Rd., 941/923-4848

TALLAHASSEE, FL

Best Restaurant in Town
Anthony's Italian Restaurant
1950 Thomasville Rd., 904/224-1447

Best All-You-Can-Eat Buffet
Kitcho Japanese Restaurant
  1415 Timberlane Rd., 904/893-7686

Best Atmosphere
Chez Pierre Restaurant
  115 N. Adams St., 904/222-0936

Best Barbecue/Ribs
Jim and Milt's Bar-B-Q
  1923 W. Pensacola St., 904/576-3998

Best Breakfast
Bagel Peddler's New York Deli
  1400 Village Square Blvd., 904/668-2345
Cross Creek Restaurant
  6725 Mahan Dr., 904/877-4130

Best Chinese Food
Lucy Ho's Oriental Court
  1700 Halstead Blvd., Ste. 5, 904/893-4112

Best Continental Food
Anthony's Italian Restaurant
  1950 Thomasville Rd., 904/224-1447
Grand Old House
  502 S. Broad St., Thomasville, 912/227-0108

Best Delicatessen
Hopkins Eatery
  1415 Market St., 904/668-0311
  1840 N. Monroe St., 904/386-4258

Best Desserts
Chez Pierre Restaurant
  115 N. Adams St., 904/222-0936

Best Dinner
Chez Pierre Restaurant
  115 N. Adams St., 904/222-0936
Mustard Tree
  1415 Timberlane Rd., 904/893-8733

Best French Food
Chez Pierre Restaurant
  115 N. Adams St., 904/222-0936

Best Health-Conscious Menu
Hopkins Eatery
  1415 Market St., 904/668-0311
  1840 N. Monroe St., 904/386-4258

Best Italian Food
Anthony's Italian Restaurant
  1950 Thomasville Rd., 904/224-1447
East Side Mario's
  2576 N. Monroe St., 904/385-1774

Best Japanese Food
Kitcho Japanese Restaurant
  1415 Timberlane Rd., 904/893-7686
Lucy Ho's Oriental Court
  1700 Halstead Blvd., Ste. 5, 904/893-4112

Best Lunch
Chez Pierre Restaurant
  115 N. Adams St., 904/222-0936

F

Food Glorious Food
106 E. College Ave., 904/222-5232
Hopkins Eatery
1415 Market St., 904/668-0311
1840 N. Monroe St., 904/386-4258
Melissa's
134 S. Madison St., Thomasville, 912/228-9844

Best Mexican Food
La Fiesta Mexican Restaurant
911 Apalachee Pkwy., 904/656-3392

F

Best Romantic Dining
Melting Pot Restaurant
1832 N. Monroe St., 904/386-7440

Best Salad/Salad Bar
Food Glorious Food
106 E. College Ave., 904/222-5232

Best Seafood
Wharf Seafood Restaurant
4141 Apalachee Pkwy., 904/656-2332

Best Steaks
Texas Steak House
3212 Apalachee Pkwy., 904/877-2986

Best Sushi
Kitcho Japanese Restaurant
1415 Timberlane Rd., 904/893-7686

TAMPA, FL

Best Restaurants in Town
Bern's Steak House
1208 S. Howard Ave., 813/251-2421
Mise En Place
442 W. Kennedy Blvd., 813/254-5373

Best American Food
Mise En Place
442 W. Kennedy Blvd., 813/254-5373
Next City Grill
2902 W. Kennedy Blvd., 813/879-1990

Best Bar
Four Green Fields
205 W. Platt St., 813/254-4444

Best Business Lunch
Oystercatcher's
6200 W. Courtney Campbell Causeway, 813/281-9116

Best Cajun/Creole Food
Cafe Creole and New Orleans Bar
1330 E. Ninth Ave., 813/247-6283

Best Cheap Meal
Lauro Ristorante Italiano
3915 Henderson Blvd., 813/281-2100

Best Coffee
Bean There
3203 Bay to Bay Blvd., 813/837-7022

Best Desserts
Bern's Steak House
1208 S. Howard Ave., 813/251-2421
Village Inn
8602 N. Dale Mabry Hwy., 813/935-6342
7011 W. Hillsborough Ave., 813/884-5292
215 N. Dale Mabry Hwy., 813/877-2617
11302 N. 30th St., 813/977-7925

Best Indian Food
Bombay Masala
4023 W. Waters Ave., Tampa, 813/880-7511

Best Italian Food
Cafe Italia
3215 S. MacDill Ave., 813/831-0600
Armani's
6200 W. Courtney Campbell Causeway, 813/281-9165
Caffe Paradiso
4205 S. MacDill Ave., 813/835-6622
Fresco
3333 Westshore Blvd., 813/839-3933
Lauro Ristorante Italiano
3915 Henderson Blvd., 813/281-2100

Best Japanese Food
Arigato Japanese Steak House
13755 N. Dale Mabry Hwy., 813/960-5050

Best Korean Food
Sam Oh Jung
602 N. Dale Mabry Hwy., 813/871-3233

Best Microbrewery
Hops Grill and Bar
14303 N. Dale Mabry Hwy., 813/264-0522
327 N. Dale Mabry Hwy., 813/871-3600
3030 N. Rocky Point Dr. W., 813/282-9350

Best Middle Eastern Food
Amtranik's Middle Eastern Bakery
5710 E. Fowler Ave., 813/988-3737

Best Other Ethnic Food
El Sol De Cuba (Cuban)
3101 N. Armenia Ave., 813/872-9880
Ibex Restaurant (Ethiopian)
1005 N. MacDill Ave., 813/876-3890

Best Outdoor Dining
Selena's Catering
1623 W. Snow Ave., 813/251-2116

Best Pizza
Windy City Pizza
12908 N. Dale Mabry Hwy., 813/960-1400

Best Romantic Dining
Cafe Italia
3215 S. MacDill Ave., 813/831-0600

Best Salad/Salad Bar
Sweet Tomatoes
14703 N. Dale Mabry Hwy., 813/960-5220

F

Best Seafood
Fetishes
6690 Gulf Blvd., St. Petersburg, 813/363-3700
Bern's Steak House
1208 S. Howard Ave., 813/251-2421

Best Steaks
Arigato Japanese Steak House
13755 N. Dale Mabry Hwy., 813/960-5050
Bern's Steak House
1208 S. Howard Ave., 813/251-2421

Best Vegetarian Food
NK Cafe
4100 W. Kennedy Blvd., 813/287-1385

Best View While Dining
Armani's
6200 W. Courtney Campbell Causeway, 813/281-9165

Best Wine Selection
Bern's Steak House
1208 S. Howard Ave., 813/251-2421

Standbys
Waffle House
922 E. Fowler Ave., 813/971-0252
6502 N. Hwy. 301, 813/621-2227
9112 N. Florida Ave., 813/932-9760
5001 E. Twentieth Ave., 813/626-9493
509 N. Westshore Blvd., 813/287-8875
2502 N. Dale Mabry Hwy., 813/872-7151

TITUSVILLE, FL

Best Barbecue/Ribs
Paul's Smokehouse
3665 S. Washington Ave., 407/267-3663

Best Breakfast
Village Inn
2925 S. Washington Ave., 407/267-6611
New York-New York
3434 S. Washington Ave., 407/264-2585

Best Brunch
Royal Oak Resort and Golf Club
2150 Country Club Dr., 407/268-2150

Best Burgers
Moon Light Drive-In
1515 S. Washington Ave., 407/267-8222

Best Coffee
New York-New York
3434 S. Washington Ave., 407/264-2585

Best Italian Food
Lorenzo's Italian Cuisine
3350 S. Hwy. 1, 407/269-0202

Best Seafood
Dixie Crossroads
1475 Garden St., 407/268-5000
Steamer's
801 Marina Rd., 407/269-1012

WEST PALM BEACH, FL

Best American Food
Dontee's 1
  620 Belvedere Rd., 561/655-6001

Best Barbecue/Ribs
Park Avenue BBQ and Grill
  2401 N. Dixie Hwy., Lake Worth, 561/586-7427

Best Breakfast
Chuck and Harold's
  207 Royal Poinciana Way, Palm Beach, 561/659-1440
Tiesta's Restaurant
  221 Royal Poinciana Way, Palm Beach, 561/832-0992

Best Brunch
The Breakers Hotel
  1 S. County Rd., Palm Beach, 561/655-6611

Best Burgers
Dontee's 1
  620 Belvedere Rd., 561/655-6001

Best Business Lunch
Arugula Grill
  222 Lakeview Dr., 561/833-3308
Casablanca Cafe American
  101 N. County Rd., 561/655-1115
Dontee's 1
  620 Belvedere Rd., 561/655-6001
Pollo Tropical
  2611 Okeechobee Blvd., 561/688-0578

Best Casual Dining
Basil's Neighborhood Cafe
  771 Village Blvd., 561/687-3801

Best Dinner
The Breakers Hotel
  1 S. County Rd., Palm Beach, 561/655-6611

Best French Food
Chez Jean Pierre
  520 S. Dixie Hwy., 561/586-9579

Best Greek/Mediterranean Food
Casablanca Cafe American
  101 N. County Rd., 561/655-1115

Best Italian Food
Malsoris Pizza and Restaurant
  523 Clematis St., 561/835-8522
Seven Brothers Gourmet Pizza
  116 N. Dixie Hwy., 561/832-4300
Four Brothers Italian Restaurant
  2495 Tenth Ave. N., Lake Worth, 561/969-6046
Amici Restaurant
  288 S. County Rd., Palm Beach, 561/832-0201

Best Japanese Food
Sagami Japanese Restaurant
  871 Village Blvd., 561/683-4600

Best Lunch
Jupiter Crab Company
  181 S. Ocean Ave., 561/840-7464

F

307

Dontee's 1
620 Belvedere Rd., 561/655-6001

Best Mexican Food
Margarita Y Amigas
2030 Palm Beach Lakes Blvd., 561/684-7788
La Taqueria
419 Clematis St., 561/655-5450

Best Other Ethnic Food
Havana Restaurant (Cuban)
6803 S. Dixie Hwy., 561/547-9799
Bahama Mama's Conch and Ribs (Caribbean)
4800 Broadway, 561/881-4451
Aruba Beach Cafe (Caribbean)
1 E. Commercial Blvd., Ft. Lauderdale, 305/776-0001

Best Pizza
Zuccarelli
1939 N. Military Trail, 561/686-7739
Basil's Neighborhood Cafe
771 Village Blvd., 561/687-3801

Best Romantic Dining
Riggins Crab House
607 Ridge Rd., Lantana, 561/586-3000

Best Salad/Salad Bar
Basil's Neighborhood Cafe
771 Village Blvd., 561/687-3801

Best Seafood
The Breakers Hotel
1 S. County Rd., Palm Beach, 561/655-6611
Bimini Bay Cafe
104 Clematis St., 561/833-9554
Jupiter Crab Company
181 S. Ocean Ave., 561/840-7464
Bridge Cafe
1555 Palm Beach Lakes Blvd., 561/478-9942

Best Southwestern Food
Arugula Grill
222 Lakeview Ave., 561/833-3308

Best Steaks
Morton's of Chicago
777 S. Flagler Dr., 561/835-9664
Raindancer Steak House
2300 Palm Beach Lakes Blvd., 561/684-2810

Best Thai Food
Bangkok House
1847 N. Military Trail, 561/697-4704
2062 Palm Beach Lakes Blvd., 561/471-7711

WINTER HAVEN, FL

Best Restaurant in Town
Christy's Sundown Restaurant
1100 Third St. SW, 941/293-0069

Best Barbecue/Ribs
Sonny's Bar-B-Q
4600 Recker Hwy., 941/293-4744

Fat Boy's Bar-B-Q
  3000 Cypress Gardens Rd., 941/324-1537

Best Breakfast
Cypress Cafe
  3055 Cypress Gardens Rd. SE, 941/324-6385

Best Burgers
Andy's Drive-In Restaurant
  703 Third St. SW, 941/293-0019

Best Seafood
Harbor Side
  2435 Seventh St. SW, 941/293-7070
Harry's Old Place
  3751 Cypress Gardens Rd. SE, 941/324-0301

Best Steaks
Christy's Sundown Restaurant
  1100 Third St. SW, 941/293-0069

Standbys
The Olive Garden
  406 Cypress Gardens Blvd. SE, 941/294-6641

Georgia

ALBANY, GA

Best All-You-Can-Eat Buffets
Gargano's East
  1710 E. Oglethorpe Blvd., 912/432-0241
Pearly's
  814 N. Slappey Blvd., 912/432-0141

Best Barbecue/Ribs
B and B Bar-B-Que
  1001 Radium Springs Rd., 912/436-5911
Gus' Barbecue
  2347 Dawson Rd., 912/883-2404

Best Burgers
Sonny's Real Pit Bar-B-Q
  1900 N. Slappey Blvd., 912/888-6023

Best Chinese Food
China Palace
  301 E. Oglethorpe Blvd., 912/883-2084
House of China Restaurant
  1514 N. Slappey Blvd., 912/432-1001
  2526 Dawson Rd., 912/883-7156
Hunan Chinese Restaurant
  2413 Dawson Rd., 912/436-9261

Best Coffee
Pat's French Press
  2610 Dawson Rd., 912/889-9045

Best Desserts
Mattie's Bakery and Bistro
  1116 W. Broad Ave., 912/431-3180
Cakery
  1003 N. Slappey Blvd., 912/436-6686

Best Homestyle Food
Aunt Fannie's Checkered Apron
  826 Byron Rd., 912/888-8416

Best Ice Cream/Yogurt
Cakery
  1003 N. Slappey Blvd., 912/436-6686

Best Italian Food
Gargano's East
1710 E. Oglethorpe Blvd., 912/432-0241

Best Japanese Food
Mikata Japanese Steakhouse
2610 Dawson Rd., 912/435-3516

Best Mexican Food
El Maya Mexican Restaurant
2800 Old Dawson Rd., 912/434-1566
106 N. Slappey Blvd., 912/889-9712
Zapata's
2621 Dawson Rd., 912/432-9698

Best Pizza
Gargano's East
1710 E. Oglethorpe Blvd., 912/432-0241
Moma's Family Favorite U Bake
2603 Stuart Ave., 912/883-2508

Best Salad/Salad Bar
Yesterday's Ole Time Saloon
2601 Dawson Rd., 912/883-7543

Best Sandwiches
Cookie Shoppe
115 N. Jackson St., 912/883-3327
Ye Olde World Sandwich Shoppe
100 N. Washington St., Ste. 2, 912/436-6496

Best Seafood
Blackbeard's Family Restaurant
1009 Radium Springs Rd., 912/888-5041

Best Steaks
Austin's Cattle Company
101 N. Slappey Blvd., 912/889-0699
Texas Star
1111 Dawson, 912/888-7797

Standbys
Red Lobster
2403 N. Slappey Blvd., 912/439-8857
Shoney's
1812 E. Oglethorpe Blvd., 912/435-0680
1108 W. Broad Ave., 912/435-1396
Dairy Queen
1804 E. Oglethorpe Blvd., 912/432-6339
TCBY
2416 Dawson Rd., 912/883-7143

ATHENS, GA

Best Restaurants in Town
East West Bistro
351 E. Broad St., 706/546-9378
The Grill
171 College Ave., 706/543-4770

Best All-You-Can-Eat Buffet
Pinecrest Lodge
1 Pinecrest Lodge Rd., 706/353-2606

Best Barbecue/Ribs
Sonny's Bar-B-Que
  3755 Atlanta Hwy., 706/546-0385

Best Burgers
The Grill
  171 College Ave., 706/543-4770

Best Cajun/Creole Food
Harry Bissett's Restaurant
  279 E. Broad St., 706/353-7065

Best Eclectic Menu
The Last Resort Grill
  184 W. Clayton St., 706/549-0810

Best Italian Food
DePalma's Italian Cafe
  401 E. Broad St., 706/354-6966
  1965 Barnett Shoals Rd., 706/369-0085

Best Mexican Food
Compadre's
  320 E. Clayton St., 706/546-0190

Best Pizza
Rocky's Pizzeria
  233 E. Clayton St., 706/353-0000
DaVinci's Pizza-in-a-Pan
  1065 Baxter St., 706/353-1065

Best Steaks
T-Bones Steak House and Saloon
  1061 Baxter St., 706/548-8702

Best Vegetarian Food
The Bluebird Cafe
  493 E. Clayton St., 706/549-3663
Guaranteed
  167 E. Broad St., 706/208-0962
The Grit
  199 Prince Ave., 706/543-4770

ATLANTA, GA

Best Restaurants in Town
The Dining Room
  Ritz-Carlton, 3434 Peachtree Rd. NE, Buckhead,
    404/237-2700
Pano's and Paul's
  1232 W. Paces Ferry Rd., 404/261-3662

Best Barbecue/Ribs
Bar-B-Que At Its Best By Sonny's
  6869 Peachtree Industrial Blvd., 404/447-6616
Dusty's Barbecue Restaurant
  1815 Briarcliff Rd. NE, 404/320-6264
Rib Ranch
  25 Irby Ave. NW, 404/233-7644
Fat Matt's Rib Shack
  1811 Piedmont Ave. NE, 404/607-1622
Jilly's, The Place For Ribs
  2647 Cobb Pkwy. NW, 404/952-7437

Best Beer Selection
Taco Mac
771 Cherokee Ave. SE, 404/624-4641
2120 Johnson Ferry Rd. NE, 404/454-7676
1006 N. Highland Ave. NE, 404/873-6529
5830 Roswell Rd. NE, 404/257-0735
Three Dollar Cafe
8595 Roswell Rd., 404/992-5011
3002 Peachtree Rd. NW, 404/266-8667

Best Bistro
Partners
1399 N. Highland Ave., 404/876-8104

Best Breakfast
Java Jive
790 Ponce De Leon Ave., 404/876-6161

Best Brunch
Indigo Coastal Grill
1397 N. Highland Ave., 404/876-0676
Ray's on the River
6700 Powers Ferry Rd. NW, 404/955-1187
Le Peep Restaurant
233 Peachtree St. NE, 404/688-3782
2484 Briarcliff Rd. NE, 404/325-7069

Best Burgers
Carey's
1021 Cobb Pkwy., Marietta, 404/422-8042
The Varsity
61 North Ave. NW, 404/881-1706

Best Business Lunch
Delectables
Atlanta Fulton Public Library, 1 Margaret Mitchell
Sq., 404/681-2909
Kudzu Cafe
3215 Peachtree Rd. NE, 404/262-0661

Best Cajun/Creole Food
New Orleans Cafe
7887 Roswell Rd., Dunwoody, 404/396-9665
French Quarter Food Shop
923 Peachtree St. NE, 404/875-2489
A Taste of New Orleans
889 W. Peachtree St. NE, 404/874-5535

Best Casual Dining
Buckhead Diner
3073 Piedmont Rd., 404/262-3336

Best Cheap Meal
Cafe Diem
642 N. Highland Ave. 404/607-7008
Eats
600 Ponce De Leon Ave., 404/888-9149
El Taco Veloz
5084 Buford Hwy., 404/936-9094
925 Windy Hill Rd., 404/432-8800
Grecian Gyro Restaurant
855 Virginia Ave., 404/762-1627

La Fonda Latina
  1150 Euclid Ave. NE, 404/577-8317
  2813 Peachtree Rd. NE, 404/816-8311
Madras Cafe
  Williamsburg Village, 3086 Briarcliff Rd.,
    404/320-7120
Heath's Cascade Grocery and Restaurant
  787 Cascade Ave., 404/755-0543
Oasis Cafe
  1799 Briarcliff Rd. NE, 404/876-0003
  752 Ponce De Leon Ave. NE, 404/881-0815
Sundown Cafe
  2165 Cheshire Bridge Rd., 404/321-1118
Thelma's Kitchen
  190 Luckie St., 404/688-5855
Vortex
  1041 W. Peachtree St., 404/875-1667

Best Chinese Food
Chopstix
  4279 Roswell Rd., 404/255-4868
Little Szechuan
  5091 Buford Hwy., Doraville, 404/451-0192
Golden Buddha
  2055 Beaver Ruin Rd., 404/448-3377
  1905 Clairmont Rd., 404/633-5252
  3200 Buford Hwy., 404/497-1954
  3610 Thompson Bridge Rd., 404/534-0767
Honto Restaurant
  3295 Chamblee Dunwoody Rd., Chamblee,
    404/458-8088

Best Coffeehouses
Cafe Intermezzo
  1845 Peachtree Rd. NE, 404/355-0411
  4505 Ashford Dunwoody Rd. NE, 404/396-1344
  333 Sandy Springs Circle NE, 404/250-0063
Caffeind's
  3095 Peachtree Rd. NE, 404/262-7774
Aurora Coffee
  230 Peachtree St. NW, 404/524-1515
  992 N. Highland Ave. NE, 404/892-7158

Best Continental Food
Pano's and Paul's
  1232 W. Paces Ferry Rd., 404/261-3662
The Hedgerose Heights Inn
  490 E. Paces Ferry Rd., 404/233-7673

Best Delicatessens
Snack and Shop
  3515 Northside Pkwy., 404/261-4737
St. Charles Deli
  2470 Briarcliff Rd. NE, 404/636-5201
Harry's Farmers Market
  2025 Satellite Pt. NW, Norcross, 404/416-6900
  70 Powers Ferry Rd., Marietta, 404/578-4400
  1180 Upper Hembree Rd., Alpharetta, 404/664-6300
Bagelicious of Buckhead
  3722 Roswell Rd. NE, Ste. 6, 404/816-0550

Best Desserts
Cafe Intermezzo
   1845 Peachtree Rd. NE, 404/355-0411
   4505 Ashford Dunwoody Rd. NE, 404/396-1344
   333 Sandy Springs Circle NE, 404/250-0063
The Dessert Place
   279 E. Paces Ferry Rd., 404/233-2331
   1000 Virginia Ave. NE, 404/892-8921

Best Dim Sum
Honto Restaurant
   3295 Chamblee Dunwoody Rd., Chamblee,
     404/458-8088
Bamboo Luau's Chinatown
   2269 Cheshire Bridge Rd. NE, 404/636-9131

Best Diners
Buckhead Diner
   3073 Piedmont Rd. NE, 404/262-3336
Landmark Cafe
   22 Main St., Grantville, 404/583-2599

Best Eclectic Menu
Lox Around the Clock
   285 E. Paces Ferry Rd., 404/365-0422

Best Family Restaurant
Dominick's
   95 S. Peachtree St., Norcross, 404/449-1611

Best French Food
Toulouse
   2293B Peachtree Rd., 404/351-9533
Violette Restaurant
   2948 Clairmont Rd. NE, 404/633-3323
Petite Auberge Restaurant
   2935 N. Druid Hills Rd. NE, 404/634-6268
Ciboulette Restaurant
   1529 Piedmont Ave. NE, 404/874-7600
Brasserie Le Coze
   3393 Peachtree Rd., 404/266-1440

Best Health-Conscious Menu
Rainbow Restaurant
   2118 N. Decatur Rd., 404/633-3538

Best Homestyle Food
Heath's Cascade Groceries
   787 Cascade Ave., 404/755-0543

Best Ice Cream/Yogurt
Jake's
   931 Monroe Dr., 404/874-0418
Gorin's Homemade Ice Cream
   1043 Ponce De Leon Ave. NE, 404/875-3795
   2903 N. Druid Hills Rd. NE, 404/634-7042

Best Indian Food
Haveli Indian Cuisine
   2706 Cobb Pkwy., Smyrna, 404/955-4525
Touch of India Tandoori
   2065 Piedmont Rd. NE, 404/876-7775

Best Italian Food
La Grotta
  2637 Peachtree Rd., 404/231-1368
Provino's
  4387 Roswell Rd. NE, 404/256-4300

Best Japanese Food
Shiki
  1492 Pleasant Hill Rd., Duluth, 404/279-0097
Kobe Steaks
  5600 Roswell Rd. NE, N320, 404/256-1173
Benihana of Tokyo
  229 Peachtree St. NE, 404/522-9627
  2143 Peachtree Rd. NE, 404/355-8565

Best Korean Food
Chosun Ok
  5865 Buford Hwy., 770/452-1821

Best Late-Night Food
R. Thomas Deluxe Grill
  1812 Peachtree Rd. NW, 404/872-2942
Majestic Food Shops
  1031 Ponce De Leon Ave. NE, 404/875-0276

Best Lunch
Chef's Cafe
  2115 Piedmont Rd., 404/872-2284
Bella Cucina
  55 Bennett St., 404/350-0024

Best Mexican Food
Nuevo Laredo Cantina
  1495 Chattahoochee Ave., 404/352-9009
Rio Bravo
  3172 Roswell Rd. NE, 404/262-7431
El Toro
  3186 Marjan Dr., 404/451-3414
Las Americas Mexican Taqueria
  3652 Shallowford Rd., Doraville, 404/458-7062

Best Other Ethnic Food
Imperial Fez Moroccan Restaurant (Moroccan)
  2285 Peachtree Rd. NE, 404/351-0870
Malaysian Restaurant (Malaysian)
  5945 Jimmy Carter Blvd., 404/368-8368
Mambo Restaurante Cubano (Cuban)
  1402 N. Highland Ave., 404/876-2626
Coco Loco (Cuban)
  2625 Piedmont Rd. NE, Ste. 640, 404/364-0212
Bridgetown Grill (Caribbean)
  689 Peachtree St. NE, 404/873-5361
  1156 Euclid Ave. NE, 404/653-0110
  7285 Roswell Rd. NE, 404/394-1575

Best Pizza
California Pizza Kitchen
  4600 Ashford Dunwoody Rd., 404/393-0390
  181 Fourteenth St. NE, 404/892-4220
  3393 Peachtree Rd. NE, 404/262-9221
Fellini's Pasta
  4427 Roswell Rd. NE, 404/303-8201

Rocky's Brick Oven Pizzeria
1770 Peachtree St. NW, 404/876-1111
Pizza by Tomaselli
365 Par Mell Rd., Marietta, 404/438-1819

Best Places to Eat When Someone Else Is Buying
Pano's and Paul's
1232 W. Paces Ferry Rd. NW, 404/261-3662
The Dining Room
Ritz-Carlton, 3434 Peachtree Rd. NE, Buckhead,
404/237-2700

Best Regional Food
Horseradish Grill
4320 Powers Ferry Rd., 404/255-7277
1848 House
780 S. Cobb Dr., Marietta, 404/428-1848
Colonnade Restaurant
1879 Cheshire Bridge Rd. NE, 404/874-5642
Mary Mac's Tea Room
224 Ponce De Leon Ave. NE, 404/875-4337

Best Romantic Dining
Ray's on the River
6700 Powers Ferry Rd. NW, 404/955-1187
Imperial Fez
2285 Peachtree Rd., 404/351-0870
Bacchanalia
3125 Piedmont Rd., 404/365-0410

Best Salad/Salad Bar
Lettuce Souprise You
1109 Cumberland Mall NW, 404/438-2288
3525 Mall Blvd., 404/418-9969
1475 Holcomb Bridge Rd., 404/642-1601
3200 Professional Pkwy. NW, 404/955-3999
2470 Briarcliff Rd. NE, 404/636-8549
245 Pharr Rd. NE, 404/841-9583
595 Piedmont Ave. N., 404/874-4998
5975 Roswell Rd. NE, 404/250-0304
Houston's
3321 Lenox Rd. NE, 404/237-7534

Best Sandwiches
Pain De Lyon
2625 Piedmont Rd., 404/814-0827
Monterey Jack's Sandwich Company
3330 Piedmont Rd. NE, 404/233-8020

Best Seafood
Atlanta Fish Market
265 Pharr Rd. NE, 404/262-3165

Best Soul Food
Heath's Cascade Grocery and Restaurant
787 Cascade Ave., 404/755-0543

Best Southwestern Food
Sundown Cafe
2165 Cheshire Bridge Rd., 404/321-1118

Best Steaks
The Palm
Swissotel, 3391 Peachtree Rd., 404/814-1955

Houston's
   3321 Lenox Rd. NE, 404/237-7534
   2166 Peachtree St. NW, 404/351-2442
   3539 Northside Pkwy. NW, 404/262-7130
Bone's Steak and Seafood
   3130 Piedmont Rd. NE, 404/237-2663
Chops Meats Fish Spirits
   70 W. Paces Ferry Rd. NW, 404/262-2675

Best Thai Food
Thai Chilli
   2169 Briarcliff Rd., 404/315-6750
Annie's Thai Castle
   3195 Roswell Rd., 404/264-9546
Surin of Thailand
   810 N. Highland Ave. NE, 404/892-7789
My Thai Restaurant
   1248 Clairmont Rd., 404/636-4280

Best Vegetarian Food
Cafe Sunflower
   5975 Roswell Rd., Sandy Springs, 404/256-1675
Eat Your Vegetables Cafe
   438 Moreland Ave. NE, 404/523-2671
Atlantis Natural Foods and Cafe
   2488 Mount Vernon Rd., Dunwoody, 404/393-1297
Homage
   Little Five Points, 1174 Euclid Ave., 404/522-7471
Fellini's Pasta
   4427 Roswell Rd. NE, 404/303-8201
Mellow Mushroom
   1715 Howell Mill Rd. NW, 404/350-0501
   1679 La Vis, 404/325-0330
   931 Monroe Dr. NE, 404/874-2291
   30 Pharr Rd. NW, Buckhead, 404/233-3443
   6218 Roswell Rd. NE, 404/252-5560

Best Vietnamese Food
Bien Thuy
   5095 Buford Hwy., Doraville, 404/454-9046
Cha Gio
   966 Peachtree St. NE, 404/885-9387

Best Wine Selection
Toulouse
   2293B Peachtree Rd., 404/351-9533
Aldo's Italian Restaurant
   6690 Roswell Rd. NE, 404/252-4832
RJ's
   870 N. Highland Ave., 404/875-7775
Azalea
   3167 Peachtree Rd. NE, 404/237-9939

Standbys
Old Country Buffet
   3371 Buford Hwy. NE, 404/321-6107
Fuddruckers
   240 Perimeter Center Pkwy. NE, 404/399-6641
Baskin-Robbins
   3754 Roswell Rd. NE, 404/814-1161
   1000 Cumberland Mall NW, 404/432-7442

Ben and Jerry's
    5920 Roswell Rd. NE, 404/255-3528
TCBY
    2484 Briarcliff Rd. NE, 404/325-8736
    4920 Roswell Rd. NE, 404/252-7437
    6049 Sandy Springs Circle NE, 404/255-7006
The Olive Garden
    6317 Roswell Rd. NE, 404/851-9070
Shoney's
    320 Tri-County Plaza, Cumming, 404/887-9657
    3529 Main St., College Park, 404/767-4343
    5551 Mableton Pkwy., Mableton, 404/941-8539
Ruby Tuesday
    Perimeter Mall, 4400 Ashford Dunwoody Rd. NE,
        404/394-6559
    2090 Dunwoody Club Dr., Orchard Park,
        404/512-0343
Red Lobster
    5350 Old National Hwy., 404/761-5271
Steak and Ale
    2775 Spring Rd. NW, 404/952-3367
Longhorn Steaks
    2151 Peachtree Rd. NE, 404/351-6086
    5403 Old National Hwy., 404/761-8018
    6390 Roswell Rd. NE, 404/843-1215
    2973 Cobb Pkwy. NW, 404/859-0341
Outback Steakhouse
    2145 Lavista Rd. NE, 404/636-5110
    3565 Austell Rd., Marietta, 404/433-0086
    4800 Lawrenceville Hwy. NW, Lilburn, 404/381-7744

AUGUSTA, GA

Best Breakfast
Duke Restaurant
    1920 Walton Way, 706/736-6879

Best Cajun/Creole Food
Cafe du Teau
    1855 Central Ave., 706/733-3505
The French Market Grille
    425 Highland Ave., 706/737-4865

Best Cheap Meal
Al's Family Restaurant
    611 Atomic Rd., North Augusta, 803/278-3140

Best Italian Food
Luigi's Restaurant
    590 Broad St., 706/722-4056

BRUNSWICK, GA

Best Atmosphere
Blanche's Courtyard Restaurant
    440 Ocean Blvd., St. Simons Island, 912/638-3030

Best Bar
Brogen's
    200 Pier Aly, St. Simons Island, 912/638-1660

Best Barbecue/Ribs
Twin Oaks Drive-In
  2618 Norwich St., 912/265-3131

Best Breakfast
Dressner's Village Cafe
  223 Mallory St., St. Simons Island, 912/634-1217

Best Casual Dining
Captain's Table
  146 Darien Hwy., 912/265-2549

Best Chinese Food
New China Restaurant
  3202 Glynn Ave., 912/265-6722

Best Delicatessen
Salvador's Delicatessen
  3015 Norwich St., 912/265-7582
  205 Gloucester St., 912/264-1543

Best Ice Cream/Yogurt
Clifton's
  214 Mallory St., St. Simons Island, 912/638-1862

Best Italian Food
Allegro
  2465 Demere Rd., St. Simons Island, 912/638-7097

Best Mexican Food
El Potro Mexican Restaurant
  2806 Cypress Mill Rd., 912/264-1619

Best Sandwiches
Grapevine Cafe
  1519 Newcastle St., 912/265-0115

Best Seafood
Jinright's Seafood House
  2815 Glynn Ave., 912/267-1590
Crab Trap
  1209 Ocean Blvd., St. Simons Island, 912/638-3552
Crabdaddy's Seafood Bar
  1219 Ocean Blvd., St. Simons Island, 912/634-1120

Best Steaks
Bennie's Red Barn
  Frederica Rd., St. Simons Island, 912/638-2844

COLUMBUS, GA

Best Restaurant in Town
Bludau's Goetchius House
  405 Broadway, 706/324-4863

Best American Food
Speakeasy Pub
  3123 Mercury Dr., 706/561-0411
W.D. Crowley's Restaurant
  3111 Manchester Expwy., 706/324-3463

Best Atmosphere
Bludau's Goetchius House
  405 Broadway, 706/324-4863
McKinley's
  2042A Auburn Ave., 706/563-4488

Best Barbecue/Ribs
Country's Barbecue
   3137 Mercury Dr., 706/563-7604
   6298 Hamilton Rd., 706/660-1415
   1329 Broadway, 706/596-8910

Best Breakfast
Gabby's 24-Hour Diner
   5753 Milgen Rd., 706/568-4435
   5915 Hamilton Rd., 706/323-2226
Brewery Company
   1009 Broadway, 706/323-2739

Best Casual Dining
Speakeasy Pub
   3123 Mercury Dr., 706/561-0411
Tavern on the Square
   14 Eleventh St., 706/324-2238
W.D. Crowley's Restaurant
   3111 Manchester Expwy., 706/324-3463

Best Continental Food
Bludau's Goetchius House
   405 Broadway, 706/324-4863

Best Desserts
Minni's Uptown Restaurant
   104 Eighth St., 706/322-2766

Best Diner
Gabby's 24-Hour Diner
   5753 Milgen Rd., 706/568-4435
   5915 Hamilton Rd., 706/323-2226

Best Dinner
Olive Branch Cafe
   1024 Broadway, 706/322-7410
McKinley's
   2042A Auburn Ave., 706/563-4488

Best Family Dining
Speakeasy Pub
   3123 Mercury Dr., 706/561-0411
Country's Barbecue
   3137 Mercury Dr., 706/563-7604
   6298 Hamilton Rd., 706/660-1415
   1329 Broadway, 706/596-8910

Best German Food
Amadeus
   7747 Macon Rd., 706/563-7427

Best Homestyle Food
Minni's Uptown Restaurant
   104 Eighth St., 706/322-2766

Best Italian Food
Olive Branch Cafe
   1024 Broadway, 706/322-7410

Best Japanese Food
Mikata Japanese Steakhouse
   5300 Sidney-Simons, 706/327-5100

Best Mexican Food
El Vaquero Mexican Restaurante
  3135 Cross Country Plz., 706/569-1420

Best Place to Eat When Someone Else Is Buying
Bludau's Goetchius House
  405 Broadway, 706/324-4863

Best Sandwiches
W.D. Crowley's Restaurant
  3111 Manchester Expwy., 706/324-3463
Brewery Company
  1009 Broadway, 706/323-2739

Best Steaks
W.D. Crowley's Restaurant
  3111 Manchester Expwy., 706/324-3463
Mikata Japanese Steakhouse
  5300 Sidney-Simons, 706/327-5100

G

DALTON, GA

Best Restaurants in Town
Oakwood Cafc
  201 W. Cuyler St., 706/278-4421
Dalton Depot Restaurant
  110 Depot St., 706/226-3160
Taste of It All Cafe
  2305 Chatsworth Hwy., 706/278-5856
Powell's Country Kitchen
  116 W. King St., 706/278-1545

Best Italian Food
Flammini's Cafe Italia
  1205 W. Walnut Ave., 706/226-0667

GRIFFIN, GA

Best Barbecue/Ribs
Southern Pit Bar-B-Que
  2964 N. Expressway, 404/229-5887

Best Breakfast
Anderson's Cafeteria
  814 W. Taylor St., 404/227-2962
Marion's Country Kitchen
  133 N. Hill St., 404/229-1860

Best Burgers
Jasmine's
  315 W. Soloman St., 404/227-1155

Best Homestyle Food
Anderson's Cafeteria
  814 W. Taylor St., 404/227-2962
Marion's Country Kitchen
  133 N. Hill St., 404/229-1860

Best Sandwiches
Jasmine's
  315 W. Soloman St., 404/227-1155

Best Seafood
Yasin's Fish Supreme
  3541 Martin Luther King Jr. Dr. NW, Atlanta,
    404/696-3277

387 Cleveland Ave. SW, Atlanta, 404/559-0336
5340 Old National Hwy., Atlanta, 404/765-9823
736 Ponce de Leon Ave. NE, Atlanta, 404/873-9971

Best Steaks
Manhattan's Restaurant
1707 N. Expressway, 404/228-5442

LA GRANGE, GA

Best American Food
The Lemon Tree
200 S. Morgan, 706/882-5382
Spring House Inn
1 Youngs Mill Rd., 706/812-1546

Best Bar
Knickers Restaurant
1510 Lafayette Pkwy., 706/882-3873

Best Breakfast
Charlie Joseph's
128 Bull St., 706/884-5416
2238 Westpoint Rd., 706/884-0379
Tyler's Restauarant
401 Vernon St., 706/884-4158

Best Dinner
Knickers Restaurant
1510 Lafayette Pkwy., 706/882-3873

Best Homestyle Food
Jimmy's
120 Main St., 706/845-0406

Best Italian Food
Hogan's Hero's Too
306 Cherry St., 706/882-3354

Best Lunch
The Lemon Tree
200 S. Morgan, 706/882-5382

Best Mexican Food
Los Nopales Mexican Restaurant
1014 Hogansville Rd., 706/883-8547

Best Sandwiches
Hogan's Hero's Too
306 Cherry St., 706/882-3354

Best Steaks
Spring House Inn
1 Youngs Mill Rd., 706/812-1546

MACON, GA

Best Restaurant in Town
Natalia's
2720 Riverside Dr., 912/741-1380

Best All-You-Can-Eat Buffet
S and S Cafeteria
2626 Riverside Dr., 912/746-9406
3724 Eisenhower Pkwy., 912/788-5913

Best Barbecue/Ribs
Fincher's Barbecue
   3057 Columbus Rd., 912/742-2220
   3947 Houston Ave., 912/788-1900
   891 Gray Hwy., 912/743-5866
Satterfield's
   120 New St., 912/742-0352
   3267 Vineville Ave., 912/477-1019

Best Breakfast
H and H Restaurant
   807 Forsyth St., 912/742-9810

Best Burgers
Grey Goose Players Club
   4524 Forsyth Rd., 912/471-0987
Polly's Corner Cafe
   6351 Zebulon Rd., 912/757-9926

Best Casual Dining
Hotlanta Wings
   3485 Mercer University Dr., 912/742-8090

Best Chinese Food
Golden Palace
   172 Tom Hill Sr. Blvd., 912/471-0732
Hong Kong Express
   610 North Ave., 912/745-7975
   593 Zebulon Rd., 912/471-0979

Best Dinner
Natalia's
   2720 Riverside Dr., 912/741-1380

Best Homestyle Food
H and H Restaurant
   807 Forsyth St., 912/742-9810
Len Berg's Carryout Meal
   2395 Ingleside Ave., 912/743-7011
   240 Post Office Alley, 912/742-9255

Best Italian Food
Naples on Forsyth
   4524 Forsyth Rd., 912/471-7017
Natalia's
   2720 Riverside Dr., 912/741-1380

Best Lunch
Between the Bread Cafe
   2720 Riverside Dr., 912/743-3999
Hong Kong Express
   610 North Ave., 912/745-7975
   593 Zebulon Rd., 912/471-0979
H and H Restaurant
   807 Forsyth St., 912/742-9810
Len Berg's Carryout Meal
   2395 Ingleside Ave., 912/743-7011
   240 Post Office Alley, 912/742-9255
Sid's Sandwich Shop
   336 Second St., 912/746-1772
   1510 Forsyth St., 912/746-2772

G

Best Mexican Food
El Sombrero
3670 Eisenhower Pkwy., 912/781-1546
610 North Ave., 912/750-8159

Best Pizza
Ingleside Village Pizza
2396 Ingleside Ave., 912/750-8488

Best Salad/Salad Bar
Grey Goose Players Club
4524 Forsyth Rd., 912/471-0987

Best Sandwiches
Between the Bread Cafe
2720 Riverside Dr., 912/743-3999
Sid's Sandwich Shop
336 Second St., 912/746-1772
1510 Forsyth St., 912/746-2772

Best Seafood
Green Jacket Restaurant
325 Fifth St., 912/746-4680
Harbor Pointe Restaurant
6420 Moseley Dixon Rd., 912/471-0393
Jim Shaw's Restaurant
3040 Vineville Ave., 912/746-3697
Polly's Corner Cafe
6351 Zebulon Rd., 912/757-9926

Best Steaks
Green Jacket Restaurant
325 Fifth St., 912/746-4680
Mikata Japanese Steakhouse
2972 Riverside Dr., 912/471-7573

Best Thai Food
Bangkok Express
3311 Pio Nono Ave., 912/788-6848

Best Vegetarian Food
Hong Kong Express
610 North Ave., 912/745-7975
593 Zebulon Rd., 912/471-0979

MARIETTA, GA

Best Restaurants in Town
Eighteen Forty-Eight House Restaurant
780 S. Cobb Dr., 404/428-1848
Shilling's on the Square
19 N. Park Sq., 404/428-9520
Jimmy's on the Square
164 Roswell St., 404/428-5627

ROME, GA

Best Chinese Food
Happy Family Chinese Restaurant
2004 Shorter Ave., 706/234-6888

Best Delicatessen
Schroeder's New Deli
406 Broad St., 706/234-4613

Best Italian Food
The Gondolier Pizza Italian Restaurant
  152 Shorter Ave., 706/291-8080

Best Mexican Food
El Zarape Mexican Restaurant
  429 Broad St., 706/295-5330

ROSWELL, GA

Best American Food
Slocum's of Roswell
  8849 Roswell Rd., 404/587-3022

Best Homestyle Food
Lickskillet Farm Restaurant
  1380 Old Roswell Rd., 404/475-6484

Best Italian Food
La Grotta Italian Restaurant
  4355 Ashford Dunwoody Rd. NE, 404/395-9925

Best Japanese Food
Gojinka Japanese Restaurant
  6241 Peachtree Industrial Blvd., 404/458-0558

Best Kosher Food
Bagelicious
  2500 Old Alabama Rd., 404/998-3401

Best Other Ethnic Food
Janousek's Restaurant (Czech)
  1475 Holcomb Bridge Rd., 404/587-2075

Best Pizza
Mellow Mushroom Pizza Bakers
  1570 Holcomb Bridge Rd., 404/998-8260

Standbys
Ryan's Family Steak House
  100 Mansell Pl., 404/664-9512

SAVANNAH, GA

Best Restaurant in Town
Il Pasticcio
  2 E. Broughton St., 912/231-8888

Best American Food
Skyler's
  225 E. Bay St., 912/232-3955

Best Atmosphere
Il Pasticcio
  2 E. Broughton St., 912/231-8888

Best Bar
Crystal Beer Parlor
  301 W. Jones St., 912/232-1153

Best Barbecue/Ribs
Johnny Harris Restaurant
  1651 E. Victory Dr., 912/354-7810

Best Breakfast
Bakery
  18 W. State St., 912/232-5748

Best Burgers
Crystal Beer Parlor
 301 W. Jones St., 912/232-1153

Best Business Lunch
Broughton Street Firehouse
 420 E. Broughton St., 912/233-1353
Sam Fink's Deli
 11 W. Liberty St., 912/236-3354

Best Casual Dining
Skyler's
 225 E. Bay St., 912/232-3955
Clary's Cafe
 404 Abercorn St., 912/233-0402
Crystal Beer Parlor
 301 W. Jones St., 912/232-1153

Best Coffee
Bakery
 18 W. State St., 912/232-5748

Best Diner
Clary's Cafe
 404 Abercorn St., 912/233-0402

Best Dinner
Shrimp Factory
 313 E. River St., 912/236-4229

Best Family Restaurant
Mrs. L.H. Wilkes' House
 107 Jones, 912/232-5997

Best Homestyle Food
Mrs. L.H. Wilkes' House
 107 Jones, 912/232-5997
Johnny Harris Restaurant
 1651 E. Victory Dr., 912/354-7810

Best Italian Food
Semolina's
 550 Abercorn St., 912/353-9335
Il Pasticcio
 2 E. Broughton St., 912/231-8888

Best Lunch
Clary's Cafe
 404 Abercorn St., 912/233-0402

Best Mexican Food
Pepe's
 325 E. Bay, 912/236-0530

Best Sandwiches
Broughton Street Firehouse
 420 E. Broughton St., 912/233-1353
Sam Fink's Deli
 11 W. Liberty St., 912/236-3354

Best Seafood
Shrimp Factory
 313 E. River St., 912/236-4229
Williams Seafood Restaurant
 8101 Hwy. 80E, 912/897-2219

STATESBORO, GA

Best Family Restaurant
Beaver House
121 S. Main St., 912/764-2821

Best Health-Conscious Menu
Health Attack Cafe and Yogurt
8 Gentilly Sq., 912/764-7858

Best Mexican Food
El-Sombrero Restaurant
406 Fair Rd., 912/764-9828

Best Pizza
Holiday Pizza
406 Fair Rd., 912/764-7669
Mellow Mushroom
6 University Plz., 912/681-8788

Standbys
Baskin-Robbins
606 Fair Rd., 912/681-1227

THOMASVILLE, GA

Best Restaurants in Town
The Plaza Restaurant
217 S. Broad St., 912/226-5153
George's and Louie's Seafood
217 Remington Ave., 912/226-1218
Mom and Dad's Italian Restaurant
1800 Smith Ave., 912/226-6265

Best Barbecue/Ribs
Fallin's Real Pit Bar-B-Que
2250 E. Pinetree Blvd., 912/228-1071

Best Chinese Food
Golden Gate Chinese Restaurant
501 Hwy. 19S, 912/228-1070

VALDOSTA, GA

Best Restaurants in Town
J.P. Mulldoon's Restaurant
1405 Gornto Rd., 912/247-6677
Willy Hofbrau
2325 N. Ashley St., 912/247-0611
Big O's Country Buffet
2801 N. Ashley St., 912/242-0863

WARNER ROBINS, GA

Best Restaurant in Town
Richard's Restaurant
604 Russell Pkwy., 912/922-1547

Best Barbecue/Ribs
Sonny's Bar BQ
811 Russell Pkwy., 912/929-3333

Best Chinese Food
China Palace
306 Russell Pkwy., 912/923-8263

329

Top Wok
1244 Watson Blvd., 912/929-4655

Best Mexican Food
Gregg's Mexican Restaurant
115 Russell Pkwy., 912/929-1756
Casa Maria Mexican Restaurant
1855 Watson Blvd., 912/328-1906

Best Steaks
Montana Steak House
2212 Watson Blvd., 912/929-9555

Standbys
Applebee's
314 Russell Pkwy., 912/922-3838

WAYCROSS, GA

Best All-You-Can-Eat Buffets
Adolph's
410 Plant Ave., 912/283-1766
Holiday Inn
1725 Memorial Dr., 912/283-4170

Best Barbecue/Ribs
Pig
768 State St., 912/283-4875
B and E Bar-B-Q
2403 Plant Ave., 912/283-3516

Best Burgers
Jerry J's
1404 Plant Ave., 912/287-1303
1809 Reynolds St., 912/285-3657

Best Chinese Food
Wong's Palace Restaurant
903 Knight Ave., 912/285-8747

Best Coffee
Huddle House
1010 Memorial Dr., 912/283-0915

Best Mexican Food
El Potro Mexican Restaurant
1506 Memorial Dr., 912/285-2855

Best Sandwiches
Downtown Sandwich Shoppe
417 Tebeau St., 912/285-8476
Michael's Deli
910 Memorial Dr., 912/283-3724

Best Steaks
Whitfield's
514 May St., 912/285-9027

Standbys
Dairy Queen
120 Screven Ave., 912/283-6590
Pizza Hut
1110 Plant Ave., 912/285-7320
1768 Memorial Dr., 912/285-8927
Shoney's
1900 Memorial Dr., 912/285-7131

Hawaii

HONOLULU, HI

Best Restaurants in Town
Thirty-Six Sixty on the Rise
  3660 Waialae Ave., 808/737-1177
Kua Aina Sandwich
  66-214 Kamehameha Hwy., 808/637-6067
Maile Restaurant
  5000 Kahala Ave., 808/734-2211
Roy's Restaurant
  6600 Kalanianaole Hwy., 808/396-7697
A Pacific Cafe
  4-831 Kuhio Hwy., Ste. 220, Kapaa, 808/822-3791
The Bull Shed
  796 Kuhio Hwy., Kapaa, 808/822-3791
Canoe House
  Mauna Lani Bay Hotel, 68-1400 Mauna Lani Dr.,
    Kohala Coast, 808/885-6622
Gaylord's
  3-2087 Kaumualii Hwy., Lihue, 808/245-9593
Merriman's
  Opela Plaza Kawaihae Rd., 808/885-6822

Best Bars
Row Bar
  500 Ala Moana Blvd., 808/528-2345
Ryan's
  1200 Ala Moana Blvd., 808/591-9132
Studebaker's
  500A Ala Moana Blvd., 808/528-9888

Best Brunch
Hala Terrace
  5000 Kahala Ave., 808/734-2211
John Dominis
  43 Ahui St., 808/523-0955
Orchids
  2199 Kalia Rd., 808/923-2311

Best Burgers
W and M Bar-B-Q Burger
  3104 Waialae Ave., 808/734-3350

Best Business Lunch
Byron II Steak House
  1450 Ala Moana Blvd., 808/949-8855
Horatio's
  1050 Ala Moana Blvd., 808/591-2005
Sunset Grill
  500 Ala Moana Blvd., Ste. 1A, 808/521-4409

Best Chinese Food
Golden Dragon
  2005 Kalia Rd., 808/946-5336
Hee Hing
  449 Kapahulu Ave., 808/735-5544
Maple Garden
  909 Isenberg St., 808/941-6641

Best Coffee
Lion Coffee
  831 Queen St., 808/591-2479

Best Coffeehouses
Coffee Manoa
  2752 E. Manoa Rd., 808/988-5113
Coffee Talk
  1152 Koko Head Ave., 808/737-7444
Espresso Bravissimo
  4211 Waialae Ave., 808/737-6574

Best Italian Food
Andrew's Restaurant
  1200 Ala Moana Blvd., 808/591-8677
Auntie Pasto's
  1099 S. Beretania St., 808/523-8855
Matteo's Italian Restaurant
  364 Seaside Ave., 808/922-5551
Salerno Italian Restaurant
  1960 Kapiolani Blvd., Ste. 204, 808/946-3299
Verbano Italiano Ristorante
  3571 Waialae Ave., Ste. 101, 808/735-1777

Best Japanese Food
Kyo-Ya
  2057 Kalakaua Ave., 808/947-3911
Tanaka of Tokyo
  131 Kaiulani Ave., Third Fl., 808/922-4233
  1777 Ala Moana Blvd., 808/945-3443
  2250 Kalakaua Ave., Fourth Fl., 808/922-4702
Yanagi Sushi
  762 Kapiolani Blvd., 808/537-1525

Best Korean Food
Kim Chee
  1040 S. King St., 808/536-1426
  3569 Waialae Ave., 808/737-0006
Sorabol
  805 Ke'eaumoku St., 808/947-3113
Yummy Korean Bar-B-Q
  7192 Kalanianaole Hwy., 808/395-4888
  801 Kaheka St., 808/942-0288

Best Mexican Restaurant
Compadres Mexican Bar and Grill
  1200 Ala Moana Blvd., Ste. 3, 808/523-1307

La Bamba
  847 Kapahulu Ave., 808/737-1956
Quintero's
  1102 Piikoi St., 808/593-1561

Best New Restaurants
Beau Soleil
  3184 Waialae Ave., 808/732-0967
Cascada
  440 Olohana St., 808/943-0202
Kahala Moon Cafe
  4614 Kilauea Ave., 808/732-7777
Tulips
  5730 Kalanianaole Hwy., 808/377-8854

Best Other Ethnic Food
Elena's (Filipino)
  2153 N. King St., 808/845-0340
Jo-Ni's of Hawai'i (Filipino)
  1450 Ala Moana Blvd., 808/945-7733
Mabuhay (Filipino)
  1049 River St., 808/545-1956

Best Pizza
California Pizza Kitchen
  98-1005 Moanalua Rd., Ste. 554, Aiea, 808/487-7741
  4211 Waialae Ave., 808/737-9446

Best Places to Eat When Someone Else Is Buying
The Bali
  2005 Kalia Rd., 808/941-2254
La Mer
  2199 Kalie Rd., 808/941-2254
Maile Restaurant
  5000 Kahala Ave., 808/734-2211
Roy's Restaurant
  6600 Kalanianaole Hwy., 808/396-7697

Best Regional Food
Thirty-Six Sixty on the Rise
  3660 Waialae Ave., 808/737-1177
Roy's Restaurant
  6600 Kalanianaole Hwy., 808/396-7697
Sam Choy's
  73-5576 Kauhola St., Ste. 1, 808/326-1545

Best Restaurant Meal Value
Auntie Pasto's
  1099 S. Beretania St., 808/523-8855
Swiss Inn
  5730 Kalanianaole Hwy., 808/377-5447
Tripton's American Cafe
  449 Kapahulu Ave., Ste. 2, 808/737-3819

Best Sandwiches
Ba-Le Sandwich Shop
  Multiple Locations

Best Seafood
Horatio's
  Ward Warehouse, 808/591-2005

Nick's Fishmarket
  Waikiki Gateway Hotel, 2070 Kalakaua Ave.,
    808/955-6333
John Dominis
  43 Ahvi St., 808/523-0955
Orson's
  1050 Ala Moana Blvd., Ste. 2, 808/591-8681

Best Steaks
Buzz's Original Steak House
  98-751 Kuahao Pl., Oahu, 808/487-6465
Hy's Steak House
  2440 Kuhio Ave., 808/922-5555

Best Thai Food
Keo's Thai Cuisine
  1200 Ala Moana Blvd., 808/596-0020
  1486 S. King St., 808/947-9988
  625 Kapahulu Ave., 808/737-8240
Siam Orchid Thai Restaurant
  1614 Kona St., 808/955-6161
Singha Thai Cuisine
  1910 Ala Moana Blvd., 808/941-2898

Best Vietnamese Food
A Little Bit of Saigon
  1160 Maunakea St., 808/528-3663
Diem Vietnamese
  2633 S. King St., 808/941-8657
Hale Vietnam
  1140 Twelfth Ave., 808/735-7581

Best Wine Selection
Maile Restaurant
  5000 Kahala Ave., 808/734-2211
Matteo's Italian Restaurant
  364 Seaside Ave., 808/922-5551

Standbys
Ruth's Chris Steak House
  500 Ala Moana Blvd., Ste. 6C, 808/599-3860

KAHULUI, HI

Best All-You-Can-Eat Buffet
Maui Beach Hotel
  170 W. Kaahumanu Ave., 808/877-0051

Best American Food
Koho Grill and Bar
  275 W. Kaahumanu Ave., 808/877-5588

Best Atmosphere
Chart House
  500 N. Puuene Ave., 808/877-2476

Best Barbecue/Ribs
S.W. Bar-B-Q
  Maui Mall Shopping Center, 808/877-0706

Best Brunch
Maui Beach Hotel
  170 W. Kaahumanu Ave., 808/877-0051

Best Burgers
Cupie's Drive-In
134 W. Kaahumanu Ave., 808/877-3055

Best Cheap Meal
S.W. Bar-B-Q
Maui Mall Shopping Center, 808/877-0706

Best Chinese Food
Ming Yuen Chinese Restaurant
162 Alamaha St., 808/871-7787

Best Coffee
Coffee Store
275 W. Kaahumanu Ave., 808/871-6860
Azeka Place II Shopping Center, 808/875-4244
Sir Wilfred's
Lahaina Cannery Mall, 808/667-1941

Best Family Restaurant
Koho Grill and Bar
275 W. Kaahumanu Ave., 808/877-5588

Best Italian Food
Luigi's Pasta Pizzeria
426 Maui Mall, 808/877-3761

Best Japanese Food
Maui Palms Hotel
170 W. Kaahumanu Ave., 808/877-0071

Best Sandwiches
Marco's Grill and Deli
444 Hana Hwy., 808/877-4446

Best Seafood
Chart House
500 N. Puuene Ave., 808/877-2476

Best View While Dining
Chart House
500 N. Puuene Ave., 808/877-2476

H

KAILUA KONA, HI

Best Restaurants in Town
Sam Choy's
73-5576 Kauhola St., Ste. 1, Kailua Kona,
808/326-1545
Old World Bistro
20 Kainehe St., 808/261-1987
Edward's at the Terrace
78-261 Manukai St., 808/322-1434
Palm Cafe
75-5819 Alii Dr., 808/329-7765

Best French Food
La Bourgogne French Restaurant
Kuakini Plaza S., 808/329-6711

Best Regional Food
Ocean View Inn
75-5683 Alii Dr., 808/329-9998

KANEOHE, HI

Best Breakfast
Koa House
46-126 Kahuhipa St., 808/235-5772

Best Chinese Food
Kin Wah Chop Suey
45-588 Kamehameha Hwy., 808/247-4812

Best Italian Food
Satino Ristorante Italiano
46-138A Kahuhipa St., 808/236-0062

Best Steaks
Chart House of Haiku Gardens
46-336 Haiku Rd., 808/247-6671

Best Sushi
Kozo Sushi
45-480 Kaneohe Bay Dr., 808/235-8881

Best Vietnamese Food
Ba-Le Sandwich Shop
45-1117 Kamehameha Hwy., Ste. 102, 808/247-7111

MAUI, HI

Best Restaurants in Town
Avalon
844 Front St., Lahaina, 808/667-5559
David Paul's Lahaina Grill
127 Lahainaluna Rd., Lahaina, 808/667-5117
Mama's Fish House
799 Poho Pl., Paia, 808/579-8488

WAILUKU, HI

Best Atmosphere
Saeng's Thai Cuisine
2119 W. Vineyard St., 808/244-1567

Best Barbecue/Ribs
Lone Star Cookout
1234 Lower Main St., 808/242-6616

Best Breakfast
Chums Family Restaurant
1900 Main St., 808/244-1000

Best Coffee
Cafe Kup A Kuppa
79 Church St., 808/244-0500

Best Desserts
Chums Family Restaurant
1900 Main St., 808/244-1000

Best Health-Conscious Menu
Cafe Kup A Kuppa
79 Church St., 808/244-0500

Best Mexican Food
Ramon's
2102 Vineyard Ave., 808/244-7243

Best Thai Food
Saeng's Thai Cuisine
  2119 W. Vineyard St., 808/244-1567

Best Vietnamese Food
A Touch of Saigon
  1246 Lower Main St., 808/244-7845

H

Idaho

Best Brunch
Murphy's Seafood Bar and Grill
  1555 Broadway Ave., 208/344-3691
Red Lion Riverside
  2900 Chinden Blvd., 208/343-1871
Downtowner
  477 Shoup Ave., Ste. 103, 208/524-2524
Cristina's Bakery and Coffee Bar
  504 Main St., 208/385-0133

Best Business Lunch
Angell's Bar and Grill
  999 Main St., 208/342-4900
Noodle's Pizza Pasta Pizzazz
  601 Main St., 208/342-9300
  134 N. Milwaukee St., 208/322-8300

Best Coffeehouses
Moxie Java
  Multiple Locations
Cafe Soho
  6932 W. State St., 208/853-4641

Best Pizza
Flying Pie
  6508 Fairview Ave., 208/376-3454
  1016 Broadway Ave., 208/384-0000
  4320 W. State St., 208/345-8585
Chicago Connection Pizza
  3504 W. State St., 208/345-3278
  3931 Overland Rd., 208/344-6838
  7070 Fairview Ave., 208/377-5551
  7766 Lemhi St., 208/323-1231
  10668 Overland Rd., 208/323-0216
Lucky 13
  1602 N. Thirteenth St., 208/344-6967

Best Places to Take the Kids
Red Robin
  211 W. Parkcenter Blvd., 208/344-7471
  267 N. Milwaukee St., 208/323-0023

Noodle's Pizza Pasta Pizzazz
  601 Main St., 208/342-9300
  134 N. Milwaukee St., 208/322-8300

Standbys
Chili's
  7997 Franklin Rd., 208/327-0088
  960 Broadway Ave., 208/389-7848
Chuck E. Cheese Pizza
  6255 Fairview Ave., 208/322-1833

COEUR D'ALENE, ID

Best Restaurants in Town
Beverly's Restaurant
  Coeur d'Alene Resort, Second St. at Front St.,
    208/765-4000
Cedars Floating Restaurant
  Blackwell Island, 208/664-2922
Chef In The Forest
  7900 E. Hauser Lake Rd., Post Falls, 208/773-3654
Jimmy D's
  320 E. Sherman Ave., 208/664-9774
Tomato Street
  221 W. Appleway Ave., 208/667-5000

IDAHO FALLS, ID

Best Restaurant in Town
Hawg Smoke Cafe
  475 Northgate Mile, 208/523-4804

Best American Food
The Sandpiper
  750 Lindsay Blvd., 208/524-3344

Best Mexican Food
Mama Inez
  344 Park Ave., 208/525-8968
The Snake Bite
  425 River Pkwy., 208/525-2522

Best Sandwiches
Pap Kelsey's Pizza and Subs
  2285 E. Seventeenth St., 208/523-3136

Best Steaks
Jake's
  851 Lindsay Blvd., 208/524-5240

LEWISTON, ID

Best Breakfast
Panhandler Pies
  1407 Main St., 208/746-0010
Waffles and More
  1421 Main St., 208/743-5189

Best Burgers
Effie's Tavern
  1120 Main St., 208/746-1889

Best Coffee
Il Espresso
  Myklebust's, 609 Main St., 208/746-0429

Best Desserts
Panhandler Pies
1407 Main St., 208/746-0010

Best Mexican Food
El Sombrero Mexican Restaurant
629 Bryden Ave., 208/746-0658

Best Place to Eat When Someone Else Is Buying
Jonathan's
301 D St., 208/746-3438

Best Seafood
Jonathan's
301 D St., 208/746-3438

Best Steaks
Bojack's Broiler Pit
311 Main St., 208/746-9532

Standbys
Baskin-Robbins
1430 21st St., 208/746-1482

MOSCOW, ID

Best Restaurants in Town
The Broiler
Best Western University Inn, 1516 Pullman Rd.,
208/882-0550
The Seasons
215 SE Paradise St., Pullman, 509/334-1410

Best American Food
The Nobby Inn
501 S. Main St., 208/882-2932

Best Desserts
The Nobby Inn
501 S. Main St., 208/882-2932

NAMPA, ID

Best Restaurant
O'Callahan's
1401 Shilo Dr., 208/465-5908

Best American Food
Little Kitchen Restaurant
1224 First St. S., 208/467-9677
O'Callahan's
1401 Shilo Dr., 208/465-5908
Generations
112 Third St. S., 208/467-4941

Best Breakfast
The Koffee Pot
1730 Garrity Blvd., 208/466-2979

Best Chinese Food
Hong Kong Restaurant
117 Twelfth Ave. S., 208/466-1244

Best Seafood
O'Callahan's
1401 Shilo Dr., 208/465-5908

est Steaks
Generations
  112 Third St. S., 208/467-4941

POCATELLO, ID

Best Restaurants in Town
Blue Ribbon Restaurant
  2036 Thunderbolt St., 208/233-8002
Continental Bistro
  140 S. Main St., 208/233-4433
Sandpiper
  1400 Bench Rd., 208/233-1000
Wagon Wheel Inn
  2720 Bannock Hwy., 208/232-9850
Whistle Stop
  200 S. Main St., 208/233-1037

Best Seafood
Remo's Steak-Seafood-Pasta
  160 W. Cedar, 208/233-1710

Best Steaks
Remo's Steak-Seafood-Pasta
  160 W. Cedar, 208/233-1710

SALMON, ID

Best Restaurant in Town
Shady Nook Restaurant and Lounge
  Hwy. 93N, 208/756-4182

Best Barbecue/Ribs
North Fork Cafe
  Hwy. 93N, 208/865-2412
Lewis and Clark Cafe
  Hwy. 93, 208/865-2244

Best Breakfast
Salmon River Coffee Shop
  606 Main St., 208/756-3521

Best Burgers
A and W
  609 Hwy. 93N, 208/756-3630
Savage Circle
  1111 Main St., 208/756-3458
Twenty-Eight Supper Club
  Hwy. 28, 208/756-2804

Best Coffee
Salmon River Coffee Shop
  606 Main St., 208/756-3521

Best Mexican Food
Broken Arrow
  Hwy. 93N, 208/865-2241

Best Pizza
Garbonzo's Pizza
  Hwy. 28, 208/756-4565
Last Chance Pizza
  605 Lena St., 208/756-4559

Best Place to Take the Kids
Savage Circle
  1111 Main St., 208/756-3458

Best Sandwiches
Starr's Meats
  1100 Main St., 208/756-6525

Best Seafood
Salmon River Coffee Shop
  606 Main St., 208/756-3521

Best Steaks
Twenty-Eight Supper Club
  Hwy. 28, 208/756-2804

Standbys
Subway
  179 Green Acres Ln., 208/983-0090

TWIN FALLS, ID

Best Restaurants in Town
Jaker's
  1564 Blue Lakes Blvd. N., 208/733-8400
Rock Creek
  200 Addison Ave. W., 208/734-4154
The Sandpiper Restaurant
  1309 Blue Lakes Blvd. N., 208/734-7000
The Metropolis Bakery and Cafe
  125 Main Ave. E., 208/734-4457

Best Breakfast
Buffalo Cafe
  218 Fourth Ave. N., 208/734-0271

Best Pizza
Louie's Pizza
  331 Leadville Ave. N., Ketchum, 208/726-7775

Illinois

ALTON, IL

Best American Food
Joshua's Restaurant
  1900 E. Homer Adams Pkwy., 618/465-0886

Best Breakfast
Boyd's Sandwich Shop
  2427 College Ave., 618/465-9726

Best Burgers
Boyd's Sandwich Shop
  2427 College Ave., 618/465-9726
Midtown Restaurant
  1026 E. Seventh St., 618/465-1321

Best Coffee
A Taste of Class
  210 Market St., 618/465-7507

Best Desserts
Old Post Office Mall
  300 Alby, 618/462-8204
My Just Desserts
  31 E. Broadway, 618/462-5881

Best Health-Conscious Menu
Midtown Restaurant
  1026 E. Seventh St., 618/465-1321

Best Homestyle Food
Boyd's Sandwich Shop
  2427 College Ave., 618/465-9726

Best Ice Cream/Yogurt
Kerr's Drug Store
  2512 College Ave., 618/465-5631

Best Italian Food
Moonlight Restaurant
  3400 Fosterburg Rd., 618/462-4620
Tony's Restaurant
  312 Piasa St., 618/462-8384

Best Pizza
Tony's Restaurant
312 Piasa St., 618/462-8384

Best Salad/Salad Bar
Old Post Office Mall
300 Alby, 618/462-8204
Midtown Restaurant
1026 E. Seventh St., 618/465-1321

Best Sandwiches
Old Post Office Mall
300 Alby, 618/462-8204

Best Steaks
Riverwalk Steakhouse
201 W. Third St., 618/465-0804

Best Tea Room
Franklin House
202 State St., 618/463-1078

ARLINGTON HEIGHTS, IL

Best Breakfast
Walker Brothers Pancake House
825 W. Dundee Rd., 847/392-6600
Egg Harbor
140 E. Wing St., 847/253-4363

Best Burgers
Assembly
2570 Hassell Rd., Hoffman Estates, 847/843-3993

Best Chinese Food
Yen-Yen Restaurant
4226 N. Arlington Heights Rd., 847/259-3400

Best Desserts
Le Titi de Paris
1015 W. Dundee Rd., 847/506-0222
Hob Nob Restaurant
4419 Northwest Hwy., Crystal Lake, 815/459-7234

Best French Food
Le Titi de Paris
1015 W. Dundee Rd., 847/506-0222

Best Health-Conscious Menu
Chowpatti Vegetarian Restaurant
1035 Arlington Heights Rd., 847/640-9554

Best Ice Cream/Yogurt
Swensen's Ice Cream
445 E. Palatine Rd., 847/259-8787

Best Japanese Food
Rokbonki Japanese Steak House
876 W. Dundee Rd., 847/506-1212

Best Pizza
Tortorice's Pizzeria
1735 E. Central Rd., 847/437-7668

Best Place to Take the Kids
Barnaby's
933 W. Rand Rd., 847/394-5270

Best Sandwiches
Portillo's Hot Dogs
  806 W. Dundee Rd., 847/870-0870

Best Seafood
Chin's Restaurant
  10 E. Miner St., 847/255-9080
Rusty Pelican
  10 E. Algonquin Rd., 847/228-0040

Best Steaks
Wellington
  2121 S. Arlington Heights Rd., 847/439-6610

Best Vegetarian Food
Chowpatti Vegetarian Restaurant
  1035 Arlington Heights Rd., 847/640-9554

Best Wine Selection
Sage's
  75 W. Algonquin Rd., 847/593-6200

Standbys
The Olive Garden
  630 E. Rand Rd., 847/818-8821

AURORA, IL

Best All-You-Can-Eat Buffet
Hollywood Casino Aurora
  49 W. Galena Blvd., 847/801-7000

Best American Food
Hollywood Casino Aurora
  49 W. Galena Blvd., 847/801-7000

Best Breakfast
Aurora Pancake House
  321 N. Lake St., 847/859-1122
Jeffery Killabrew's Pub and Eatery
  7 S. Stolp Ave., 847/897-0100
Harner's Bakery Restaurant
  10 W. State St., North Aurora, 847/892-4400
Hollywood Casino Aurora
  49 W. Galena Blvd., 847/801-7000

Best Burgers
Office
  746 S. Lincoln Ave., 847/896-5510

Best Business Lunch
Tavern on the Fox
  24 N. Broadway, 847/896-6667

Best Family Restaurant
Nikarry's Restaurant
  1055 N. Lake St., 847/264-1500

Best Homestyle Food
Jeffery Killabrew's Pub and Eatery
  7 S. Stolp Ave., 847/897-0100

Best Italian Food
Luciano's
  77 S. Stolp Ave., 847/892-1070

Best Lunch
Jeffery Killabrew's Pub and Eatery
7 S. Stolp Ave., 847/897-0100

Best Mexican Food
La Cabana Restaurant
835 S. River St., 847/859-8885

Best Pizza
Nancy's Pizza
849 N. Lake St., 847/897-8000

Best Seafood
Fisherman's Inn
43W 901 Main Street Rd., 847/365-6265

Best Steaks
Fisherman's Inn
43W 901 Main Street Rd., 847/365-6265
Hi-Way Lounge and Steakhouse
1518 E. New York St., 847/820-8222

Best View While Dining
Fisherman's Inn
43W 901 Main Street Rd., 847/365-6265

BELLEVILLE, IL

Best American Food
Fischer's Restaurant
2100 W. Main St., 618/233-1131

Best Barbecue/Ribs
Hickory Hut
1030 Freeburg Ave., 618/277-7138

Best Breakfast
The Shrine Restaurant
9500 W. State Rte. 15, 618/397-6700
Imperial Restaurant
200 W. Main St., 618/235-5875

Best Burgers
Shenanigan's
15 N. 64th St., 618/398-6979
Rally's Hamburgers
1105 S. Illinois St., 618/236-2003

Best Coffee
Rebo's
7410 Westchester Dr., 618/398-3255

Best Desserts
Pie Pantry
301 E. Main St., 618/277-4140

Best Homestyle Food
Pie Pantry
301 E. Main St., 618/277-4140

Best Ice Cream/Yogurt
White Cottage
102 Lebanon Ave., 618/234-1120

Best Italian Food
Viviano's Italian Restaurant
6A Wade Sq., 618/235-1558

Best Mexican Food
Casa Gallardo Mexican Restaurant
  6600 N. Illinois St., Fairview Heights, 618/632-4404

Best Pizza
Wolf's Den
  211 N. Main St., Freeburg, 618/539-5829

Best Seafood
Stockpot Cafe
  310 E. Main St., 618/277-2723

Best Steaks
BarbWire's
  4204 W. Main St., 618/234-3303
Andrea's
  68050 Collinsville Rd., O'Fallon, 618/632-4866

Standbys
Red Lobster
  6118 N. Illinois St., Fairview Heights, 618/632-7558

BLOOMINGTON, IL

Best Burgers
Bennigan's
  115 Veterans Pkwy., Normal, 309/454-5577

Best Chinese Food
Tien Tsin Mandarin Chinese
  1500 E. Empire St., 309/663-9361
Dragon Palace Chinese Restaurant
  1407 N. Veterans Pkwy., 309/663-1388

Best Coffee
Coffee World Coffeehouse
  114 E. Beaufort St., Normal, 309/452-6774

Best Family Restaurant
Ozark House
  704 McGregor St., 309/827-3900

Best German Food
Bayern Stube
  209 N. Sangamon Ave., Gibson City, 217/784-8304

Best Italian Food
Paparazzi
  4315 N. Voss St., Peoria Heights, 309/682-5205

Best Late-Night Food
Sonoma Cucina
  1603B Morrissey Dr., 309/664-0044

Best Mexican Food
Delgado's Mexican Food and Drink
  201 Landmark Dr., Normal, 309/454-4747

Best Pizza
Sonoma Cucina
  1603B Morrissey Dr., 309/664-0044

Best Place to Take the Kids
Ozark House
  704 McGregor St., 309/827-3900

Best Romantic Dining
Juner's Chateau
    1601 Juner Dr., 309/662-2020

Best Sandwiches
Bennigan's
    115 Veterans Pkwy., Normal, 309/454-5577

Best Seafood
Phil's Bar and Grill
    401 N. Veterans Pkwy., 309/662-9637

Best Steaks
Mountain Jack's
    607 S. El Dorado St., 309/663-5998

Standbys
Old Country Buffet
    301 S. Veterans Pkwy., Normal, 309/454-6755
The Olive Garden
    1701 E. Empire St., 309/663-7375

CARBONDALE, IL

Best Bar
Hangar 9
    511 S. Illinois Ave., 618/549-0511

Best Burgers
Rally's Hamburgers
    709 S. Illinois Ave., 618/549-7882

Best Cheap Meal
El Bajio
    1010 E. Main St., 618/529-1648

Best Chinese Food
Hunan Village
    710 E. Main St., 618/529-1108

Best Coffee
Melange
    607 S. Illinois Ave., 618/549-9161

Best Desserts
Murphy's Bar and Grill
    501 E. Walnut St., 618/457-5544

Best Diner
Johnny's 50s and 60s Cafe
    206 S. Wall St., 618/549-6930

Best Family Restaurants
Italian Village
    405 S. Washington St., 618/457-0212
Mugsy McGuire's
    1620 W. Main St., 618/457-6847

Best Homestyle Food
Murphy's Bar and Grill
    501 E. Walnut St., 618/457-5544

Best Italian Food
Pasta House Company
    1245 E. Main St., 618/457-5545

Best Late-Night Food
Sam's Cafe
521 S. Illinois Ave., 618/549-2234

Best Mexican Food
El Bajio
1010 E. Main St., 618/529-1648

Best Pizza
Pagliai's Pizza and Pasta
515 S. Illinois Ave., 618/457-0321
Quatro's Deep Pan Pizza
220 W. Freeman St., 618/549-5326
La Roma's Pizza
515 1/2 S. Illinois Ave., 618/529-1344

Best Place to Eat Alone
Kahala Gardens
1901 Murdale Shopping Ctr., 618/529-2813

Best Place to Eat When Someone Else Is Buying
Mugsy McGuire's
1620 W. Main St., 618/457-6847

Best Place to Take the Kids
Italian Village
405 S. Washington St., 618/457-0212

Best Salad/Salad Bar
Murphy's Bar and Grill
501 E. Walnut St., 618/457-5544

Best Sandwiches
Jimmy John's Gourmet Sub Shop
701A S. Illinois Ave., 618/549-3334

Best Steaks
Murphy's Bar and Grill
501 E. Walnut St., 618/457-5544

Standbys
Denny's
1915 W. Sycamore St., 618/457-7196
Baskin-Robbins
1709 W. Main St., 618/549-5432

CHAMPAIGN, IL

Best American Food
Silver Creek
402 N. Race St., Urbana, 217/328-3402
Top of the Inn
302 E. John St., 217/384-7171

Best Asian Restaurant
Asiana
408 E. Green St., 217/398-3344

Best Breakfast
Cafe Kopi
109 N. Walnut St., 217/359-4266
Original Pancake House
1909 W. Springfield Ave., 217/352-8866

Best Burgers
Vriner's
55 E. Main, 217/359-5408

Best Cajun/Creole Food
City of New Orleans
 116 N. Chestnut St., 217/359-2489

Best Chinese Food
First Wok
 1805 S. Philo, Urbana, 217/344-4500

Best Coffee
Cafe Kopi
 109 N. Walnut St., 217/359-4266

Best Diner
Silver Creek
 402 N. Race St., Urbana, 217/328-3402

Best Dinner
Top of the Inn
 302 E. John St., 217/384-7171

Best Ice Cream/Yogurt
Vriner's
 55 E. Main, 217/359-5408

Best Italian Food
Great Impasta
 132 W. Church St., 217/359-7377

Best Japanese Food
Miko Steak House
 407 W. University Ave., Urbana, 217/367-0822

Best Pizza
Papa Del's Pizza
 206 E. Green St., 217/359-7700

Best Sandwiches
Vriner's
 55 E. Main, 217/359-5408

Best Steaks
Prime Room
 1501 S. Neil, 217/352-8178

Best Thai Food
Miko Steak House
 407 W. University Ave., 217/367-0822

Best View While Dining
Top of the Inn
 302 E. John St., 217/384-7171

CHICAGO, IL

Best Restaurants
Ambria
 2300 N. Lincoln Park West, 312/472-5959
Everest
 440 S. La Salle, 312/663-8920
Ritz-Carlton Dining Room
 160 E. Pearson St., 312/266-1000
Cuisines
 Stouffer Riviere Hotel, 1 Wacker Dr., 312/372-7200
Cafe Spiaggia
 980 N. Michigan Ave., 312/280-2764

Coco Pazzo
300 W. Hubbard, 312/836-0900

Best American Food
The Blackhawk Lodge
41 E. Superior, 312/280-4080
Farrago
733 N. Wells, Old Town, 312/951-7350
Gypsy Restaurant and Wine Bar
215 E. Ohio, 312/644-9779
Mrs. Park's Tavern
Guest Quarters Suite Hotel, First Fl., 312/944-4414
Prairie
550 S. Dearborn, 312/663-1143

Best Bagels
Jacobs Brothers
58 E. Randolph, 312/368-1181
50 E. Chicago, 312/664-0026
53 W. Jackson, 312/922-2245

Best Bar
Jimmy's Woodlawn Tap and Liquor Store
1172 E. 55th, 312/643-5516

Best Barbecue/Ribs
Carson's Place for Ribs
5970 N. Ridge Ave., 312/271-4000
612 N. Wells St., 312/280-9200
Gale Street Inn
4914 N. Milwaukee Ave., 312/725-1300
906 Diamond Lake Rd., Mundelein, 847/566-1090
Bones
7110 N. Lincoln Ave., Lincolnwood, 847/677-3350
Nite and Gale
346 Waukegan Ave., Highwood, 847/432-9744
Brandt's - The Little Cafe
807 W. Baldwin Rd., Palatine, 847/359-6373

Best Beer Selection
Quencher's Saloon
2401 N. Western, 312/276-9730
Mickey Finn's Brewery
412 N. Milwaukee Ave., Libertyville, 847/362-6688
Goose Island Brewery
1800 N. Clybourn Ave., 312/915-0071
Village Tap
2055 W. Roscoe, 312/883-0817

Best Breakfast
Ann Sather's
5207 N. Clark St., 312/271-6677
929 W. Belmont Ave., 312/348-2378
1329 E. 57th St., 312/947-9323
Tim and Becky's
1500 W. Division, 312/227-3490
Walker Brothers Pancake House
200 Marriott Dr., Lincolnshire, 847/634-2220
Egg Harbor
210 S. Cook St., Barrington, 847/304-4033
221 Town Sq., Wheaton, 708/510-1344

512 N. Western Ave., Lake Forest, 847/295-3449
777 N. York Rd., Hinsdale, 708/920-1344
Omega Restaurant
9100 W. Golf Rd., Niles, 847/296-7777
Gladys' Luncheonette
4527 S. Indiana, 312/548-6848

Best Brunch
Deerpath Inn
255 E. Illinois Rd., Lake Forest, 847/234-2280
Celebrity Cafe
Hotel Nikko Chicago, 320 N. Dearborn St.,
312/744-1900
Allgauer's Fireside Restaurant
3003 Corporate West Dr., Lisle, 708/505-0700

Best Burgers
Hackney's
123rd at Rte. 45, Palos Park, 708/448-8300
Hamburger Hamlet
1000 Lakeview Pkwy., Vernon Hills, 847/918-0505
1024 N. Rush St., 312/649-6600
51 Town Sq., Wheaton, 708/510-8350
Brandt's - The Little Cafe
807 W. Baldwin Rd., Palatine, 847/359-6373
Ed Debevic's
660 Lake Cook Rd., Deerfield, 847/945-3242
640 N. Wells St., 312/664-1707

Best Business Lunch
Vivere
71 W. Monroe St., 312/332-4040
Tuscany
1425 W. 22nd St., Oak Brook, 708/990-1993
The Silk Mandarin
4 E. Phillip Rd., Vernon Hills, 847/680-1760

Best Chinese Food
The Silk Mandarin
4 E. Phillip Rd., Vernon Hills, 847/680-1760
Heng Wing
121 W. Palatine Rd., Palatine, 847/358-3061
Emperor's Choice
238 S. Wentworth, 312/225-8800
Triple Crown Chinese Seafood Restaurant
211 W. 22nd Pl., 312/791-0788
Mars Restaurant
3124 N. Broadway, 312/404-1600
Furama
2828 S. Wentworth Ave., 312/225-6888

Best Coffee
Starbucks
617 W. Diversey, 312/880-5172
227 W. Monroe St., 312/346-4360
2200 N. Halsted St., 312/935-2622
105 W. Adams, 312/855-0099
1001 W. Armitage Ave., 528-1340
Brewster's
171 N. Clark St., 312/759-2811

Borders
    Michigan Ave. at Pearson St., 312/573-0564

Best Continental Food
Entre Nous
    Fairmont Hotel at Grant Park, 200 N. Columbus Dr.,
        312/565-7997

Best Delicatessens
Max and Benny's
    2301 N. Clark St., 312/281-9100
Ada's Famous Restaurant and Deli
    405 Lake Cook Rd., Deerfield, 847/564-4446
D.B. Kaplan's
    845 N. Michigan Ave., 312/280-2700
Frances' Restaurant and Deli
    2552 N. Clark, 312/248-4580
Harrie's Delicatessen and Restaurant
    317 Park Ave., Glencoe, 847/835-1000

Best Desserts
My Place For ?
    7545 N. Clark St., 312/262-5767
Lutz Continental Cafe
    2458 W. Montrose Ave., 312/478-7785
Jackie's
    2478 N. Lincoln Ave., 312/880-0003
Tallgrass's
    1006 S. State, Lockport, 815/838-5566

Best Family Restaurants
Gocky's Pancake House
    305 S. Waukegan Rd., Lake Bluff, 847/726-2253
Ed Debevic's
    640 N. Wells St., 312/664-1707
    660 Lake Cook Rd., Deerfield, 847/945-3242
Maggiano's Little Italy
    240 Oakbrook Ctr., Oak Brook, 708/368-0300

Best French Food
Froggy's French Cafe
    306 Green Bay Rd., Highwood, 847/433-7080
Ambria
    2300 N. Lincoln Park West, 312/472-5959
Everest
    440 S. La Salle, 312/663-8920
Kiki's Bistro
    900 N. Franklin, 312/335-5454
Le Bouchon
    1958 N. Damen, 312/862-6600
Marche
    830 W. Randolph, 312/226-8399
Un Grand Cafe
    2300 N. Lincoln Park W., 312/348-8886

Best German Food
Black Forest Chalet
    8840 Waukegan Rd., Morton Grove, 847/965-6830
The Berghoff
    17 W. Adams St., 312/427-3170
Zum Deutschen Eck
    2924 N. Southport Ave., 312/525-8389

Schulien's Restaurant and Saloon
2100 W. Irving Park Rd., 312/478-2106

Best Greek/Mediterranean Food
Greek Islands
200 S. Halsted St., 312/782-9855
Santorini
138 S. Halsted, 312/829-8820
Papagus Greek Taverna
620 N. State St., 312/642-8450
Rodity's Restaurant
222 S. Halsted St., 312/454-0800
Cuisines
Stouffer Riviere Hotel, 1 Wacker Dr., 312/372-7200

Best Health-Conscious Menu
Seasons
120 E. Delaware Pl., 312/280-8800
Heartland Cafe
7000 N. Glenwood Ave., 312/465-8005
Ritz-Carlton Dining Room
160 E. Pearson St., 312/266-1000

Best Homestyle Food
Ann Sather's
5207 N. Clark St., 312/271-6677
929 W. Belmont Ave., 312/348-2378
1329 E. 57th St., 312/947-9323

Best Indian Food
Moti Mahal
1031 W. Belmont, 312/348-4392
2525 W. Devon, 312/262-2080
Udupi Palace
2543 W. Devon, 312/338-2152
Bukhara
2 E. Ontario, 312/943-0188
Klay Oven
414 N. Orleans, 312/527-3999

Best Italian Food
Stefani's
1418 W. Fullerton Ave., 312/348-0111
Del Rio
228 Green Bay Rd., Highwood, 847/432-4608
Gilardi's Restaurant
23397 Hwy. 45N, Vernon Hills, 847/634-1811
Cafe Angelo
225 N. Wacker, 312/332-3370
Cafe Spiaggia
980 N. Michigan Ave., 312/280-2764
Coco Pazzo
300 W. Hubbard, 312/836-0900
Scoozi!
410 W. Huron, 312/943-5900
Original Rosebud Cafe
1500 W. Taylor, 312/942-1117

Best Japanese Food
Daruma Japanese Restaurant
1823 W. Golf Rd., Schaumburg, 847/310-8877

The Kampai
2330 S. Elmhurst Rd., Mt. Prospect, 708/640-6700
Ron of Japan
230 E. Ontario St., 312/644-6500
Tsukasa of Tokyo
700 Milwaukee Ave., Vernon Hills, 847/816-8770

Best Late-Night Food
Jack's
800 N. Michigan Ave., 312/280-2230
Bella Vista
1001 W. Belmont Ave., 312/404-1658
Riptide
1745 W. Armitage, 312/278-7317
Cafe Iberico
739 N. La Salle, 312/573-1510

Best Lunch
Big Bowl Cafe
159 1/2 W. Erie, 312/787-8297
Caffe Baci
231 La Salle, 312/629-2224
Foodlife
Water Tower Place, 835 N. Michigan, 312/335-3663
Mity Nice Grill
835 N. Michigan Ave., 312/335-4745
Nick and Tony's
1 E. Wacker, 312/467-9449
Reza's
432 W. Ontario, 312/664-4500
Wishbone Restaurant and Cafeteria
1001 W. Washington, 312/850-2663

Best Mexican Food
Hat Dance
325 W. Huron St., 312/649-0066
Lindo Mexico
830 Sheridan Rd., Highwood, 847/432-6734
8990 N. Milwaukee Ave., Niles, 847/296-2540
El Barrio
1122 Diamond Lake Rd., Mundelein, 847/566-0475
Topolobampo and Frontera Grill
445 N. Clark St., 312/661-1434
Las Tres Hermanas
329 Waukegan Ave., Highwood, 847/432-0774
Blue Mesa
1729 N. Halsted, 312/944-5990

Best Other Ethnic Food
Healthy Food (Eastern European)
3236 S. Halsted, 312/326-2724
Little Bucharest (Eastern European)
3001 N. Ashland, 312/929-8640
Busy Bee (Polish-American)
1540 N. Damen, 312/772-4433
Bossa Nova (international tapas)
1960 N. Clybourn Ave., 312/248-4800

Best Pizza
Bacino's
2204 N. Lincoln Ave., 312/472-7400

75 E. Wacker Dr., 312/263-0070
1504 N. Naper Blvd., Naperville, 708/505-0600
15256 La Grange Rd., Orland Park, 708/403-3535
California Pizza Kitchen
303 W. Erie St., 312/573-0400
414 N. Orleans St., 312/222-9030
835 N. Michigan Ave., Seventh Fl., 312/787-7300
551 Oakbrook Ctr., Oak Brook, 708/571-7800
Gino's East
160 E. Superior St., 312/943-1124
1321 Golf Rd., Rolling Meadows, 847/364-6644
9751 W. Higgins Rd., Rosemont, 847/698-4949
1590 E. Main St., St. Charles, 708/513-1311
The Silo
625 Rockland Rd., Lake Bluff, 847/234-6660

Best Places to Take the Kids
Ed Debevic's
660 Lake Cook Rd., Deerfield, 847/945-3242
640 N. Wells St., 312/664-1707
Barnaby's
2832 W. Touhy Ave., 312/973-4550
7950 N. Caldwell Ave., Niles, 847/967-8600
134 W. Golf Rd., Schaumburg, 847/882-3220

Best Romantic Dining
La Boheme
566 Chestnut St., Winnetka, 847/446-4600
The Pump Room
1301 N. State Pkwy., 312/266-0360
6908 W. 111th St., Worth, 708/448-8542

Best Salad/Salad Bar
Corosh
1072 N. Milwaukee, 312/235-0600
R.J. Grunt's
2056 N. Lincoln Park W., 312/929-5363
Chicago Claim Company
900 N. Michigan, Sixth Fl., 312/787-5757

Best Seafood
Bob Chinn's Crab House
393 S. Milwaukee Ave., 708/520-3633
My Place For ?
7545 N. Clark St., 312/262-5767
Dover Straits
1149 W. Golf Rd., Hoffman Estates, 847/884-3900
Rte. 45 at Hwy. 83, Mundelein, 847/949-1550
Carmine's Clamhouse
1043 N. Rush, 312/988-7676
Shaw's Blue Crab Lounge
660 Lake Cook Rd., Deerfield, 847/948-1020

Best Soul Food
Army and Lou's
422 E. 75th St. near Martin Luther King Jr. Dr.,
312/483-3100

Best Steaks
Gibson's Steakhouse
1028 N. Rush, 312/266-8999

Morton's of Chicago
  350 W. Hubbard St., 312/923-0030
  1050 N. State St., 312/266-4820
  9525 Bryn Mawr Ave., Rosemont, 847/678-5155
  1 Westbrook Corporate Ctr., Westchester,
    708/562-7000
Eli's The Place For Steak
  215 E. Chicago Ave., 312/642-1393
Myron and Phil's
  3900 W. Devon, Lincolnwood, 847/677-6663
Chicago Chop House
  60 W. Ontario, 312/787-7100
Gene and Georgetti
  500 N. Franklin, 312/527-3718

Best Tea Room
Drake Hotel
  140 E. Walton St., 312/787-2200
Marshall Field's Walnut Room
  111 N. State St., 312/781-3697
Cafe Selmarie
  2327 W. Giddings St., 312/989-5595

Best Thai Food
Arun's
  4156 N. Kedzie, 312/539-1909
Pasteur Cafe
  45 E. Chicago Ave., 312/587-9992
Star of Siam
  11 E. Illinois, 312/670-0100
Thai Borrahn Siam
  247 E. Ontario, 312/642-1385
Roong Petch
  1828 W. Montrose, 312/989-0818
P.S. Bangkok
  3345 N. Clark St., 312/871-7777

Best Vegetarian Food
Ethio Cafe
  3462 N. Clark, 312/929-8300
Hatsuhana
  160 E. Ontario, 312/280-8287
Il Rospo Verdi
  1142 N. Milwaukee, 312/342-0565
Heartland Cafe
  7000 N. Glenwood Ave., 312/465-8005
Chicago Diner
  3411 N. Halsted, 312/935-6696
Eat Your Hearts Out!
  1835 W. North Ave., 312/235-6361
Jane's
  1655 W. Cortland St., 312/862-5263

Best Vietnamese Food
Thai Binh
  1113 W. Argyle St., 312/728-0283

Best View While Dining
Seasons
  120 E. Delaware Pl., 312/280-8800

The Signature Room at the 95th
John Hancock Ctr., 875 N. Michigan Ave.,
312/787-9596

Best Wine Selection
Entre Nous
Fairmont Hotel at Grant Park, 200 N. Columbus Dr.,
312/565-7997

CHICAGO HEIGHTS, IL

Best Barbecue/Ribs
Princess Cafe
502 S. Dixie Hwy., Beecher, 708/946-3141
Enzo's Restaurant
1710 Chicago Rd., 708/754-7040
Glenwood Oaks Restaurant
106 N. Main St., Glenwood, 708/758-4400

Best Breakfast
Looking Glass Restaurant
1425 Western Ave., 708/747-7970
Egg and I
222 Dixie Hwy., 708/754-0909
Harry's Old Town Restaurant
1390 Main St., Crete, 708/672-8766

Best Burgers
Big Boy's
405 W. Fourteenth St., 708/481-3369

Best Chinese Food
Liang's Garden Restaurant
480 W. Lincoln Hwy., 708/481-5438

Best Homestyle Food
Mama Mary's
96 E. 24th St., 708/754-1147

Best Ice Cream/Yogurt
Buckets
2601 Chicago Rd., 708/754-0253

Best Italian Food
Tivoli
19600 Glenwood Rd., 708/755-7411
La Pergola Restaurant
525 Dixie Hwy., 708/756-2327
Carlo Lorenzetti
560 W. Fourteenth St., 708/747-9480

Best Mexican Food
L.A. Cafe
22325 Governor's Hwy., Richton Park, 708/747-4440
Coco's Tacos
2617 Chicago Rd., 708/754-5940

Best Pizza
Nino's Pizza
203 156th Pl., Calumet City, 708/862-5555

Best Salad/Salad Bar
Carlo Lorenzetti
560 W. Fourteenth St., 708/747-9480

Best Sandwiches
Gabe's Place
9 E. Main St., Glenwood, 708/757-7171
Enrico's
427 N. La Grange Rd., Frankfort, 815/469-4187
106 W. Saint Francis Rd., Frankfort, 815/469-1000

Best Steaks
Princess Cafe
502 S. Dixie Hwy., Beecher, 708/946-3141
Glenwood Oaks Restaurant
106 N. Main St., Glenwood, 708/758-4400

DANVILLE, IL

Best Bar
O'Leary's Pub
510 N. Gilbert St., 217/442-1485

Best Barbecue/Ribs
Bud's
504 N. Bowman Ave., 217/442-0614
Kag's Bar-B-Q
612 1/2 E. Seminary St., 217/442-9679

Best Breakfast
Cahill's Family Restaurant
334 N. Gilbert St., 217/442-3992
Danville Family Restaurant
515 N. Vermillion St., 217/431-6044

Best Burgers
Moonglow
Rural Route 5, 217/442-9519
Gross's Burgers
25 Henderson St., 217/442-8848

Best Business Lunch
Deluxe Restaurant
21 W. North St., 217/442-0685
Regina's Kitchen
34 N. Vermillion St., 217/446-3354

Best Chinese Food
Great Wall
2 E. Main St., 217/443-2888

Best Coffee
Java Hut
1419 Bowman Ave., 217/477-1033

Best Desserts
Deluxe Restaurant
21 W. North St., 217/442-0685
Regina's Kitchen
34 N. Vermillion St., 217/446-3354

Best Greek/Mediterranean Food
Deluxe Restaurant
21 W. North St., 217/442-0685

Best Ice Cream/Yogurt
Custard Cup
2507 N. Vermillion St., 217/443-0221

Best Mexican Food
Buen Apetito
   3 E. Woodbury St., 217/442-6086
Mi Casa
   129 N. Vermillion St., 217/446-9856

Best Seafood
O'Leary's Pub
   510 N. Gilbert St., 217/442-1485

Best Steaks
O'Leary's Pub
   510 N. Gilbert St., 217/442-1485
Beef House
   I-74 at Rte. 63, Covington, 317/793-3947
Maple Corner Restaurant
   1126 Liberty St., Covington, 317/793-2224

DECATUR, IL

Best Bar
Lock, Stock and Barrel
   129 S. Oakland Ave., 217/429-7411

Best Brunch
Central Park West
   170 Merchant St., 217/429-0669

Best Burgers
Krekel's Custard
   801 E. Wood St., 217/429-1122
   1355 N. State Rte. 48, 217/362-0121
   3727 N. Woodford St., 217/875-4044

Best Business Lunch
Robbie's
   122 N. Merchant St., 217/423-0448

Best Casual Dining
Central Park West
   170 Merchant St., 217/429-0669

Best Cheap Meal
Carlos O'Kelley's Mexican Cafe
   2930 N. Main St., 217/877-0967

Best Chinese Food
First Wok
   702 Keokuk St., Lincoln, 217/732-7862

Best Health-Conscious Menu
Marcia's Waterfront
   2301 E. Lakeshore Dr., 217/422-7202
Felice's Italian Restaurant
   2880 N. Oakland Ave., 217/872-0303

Best Late-Night Food
Blue Mill
   1099 W. Wood St., 217/423-7717

Best Mexican Food
Carlos O'Kelley's Mexican Cafe
   2930 N. Main St., 217/877-0967

Best Pizza
Godfather's Pizza
   201 S. Nelson Blvd., 217/429-2240
   1590 E. Pershing Rd., 217/875-7000

Best Place to Be "Seen"
Robbie's
122 N. Merchant St., 217/423-0448

Best Place to Eat Alone
Marcia's Waterfront
2301 E. Lakeshore Dr., 217/422-7202

Best Place to Eat When Someone Else Is Buying
Central Park West
170 Merchant St., 217/429-0669

Best Romantic Dining
Central Park West
170 Merchant St., 217/429-0669

Best Salad/Salad Bar
Marcia's Waterfront
2301 E. Lakeshore Dr., 217/422-7202

Best Sandwiches
Central Park West
170 Merchant St., 217/429-0669

Best Steaks
Stoney's
120 Main St., Dalton City, 217/874-2213

Standbys
Bonanza
371 W. First Dr., 217/423-0082
1987 E. Pershing Rd., 217/877-3349
Bob Evans
3020 N. Water St., 217/875-4577
Applebee's
1275 S. 51st St., 217/875-0281
Baskin-Robbins
3160 N. Water St., 217/877-5306
Hickory Point Mall, Ste. 43, 217/875-2842
Red Lobster
1280 E. Pershing Rd., 217/875-1610

DES PLAINES, IL

Best American Food
Fountain Blue Restaurant
2300 Mannheim Rd., 847/298-3636

Best Breakfast
Grandma Sally's Waffle House
1145 Elmhurst Rd., 847/364-0883

Best Coffee
Java Junction
605 Lee St., 847/298-2828

Best Continental Food
Cafe La Cave
2777 Mannheim Rd., 847/827-7818

Best Dinner and Dancing
Knickers
1050 E. Oakton St., 847/299-0011

Best French Food
Cafe La Cave
2777 Mannheim Rd., 847/827-7818

Best Greek/Mediterranean Food
Mykonos
8660 W. Golf Rd., 847/296-6777

Best Ice Cream/Yogurt
Sugar Bowl Sweet Shop and Restaurant
1949 Miner St., 847/824-7380

Best Italian Food
Giuseppe's La Cantina
1062 Lee St., 847/824-4230
Little Villa Restaurant
660 N. Wolf Rd., 847/296-7763

Best Pizza
Giuseppe's La Cantina
1062 Lee St., 847/824-4230

Best Places to Take the Kids
Barnaby's
636 E. Touhy Ave., 847/297-8866
Choo-Choo Restaurant
600 Lee St., 847/298-5949

Best Salad/Salad Bar
Black Ram
1414 E. Oakton St., 847/824-1227

Best Seafood
Black Ram
1414 E. Oakton St., 847/824-1227
Crab and Things
1249 Elmhurst Rd., 847/437-1595
Knickers
1050 E. Oakton St., 847/299-0011
Don's Dock
1220 E. Northwest Hwy., 847/827-1817

Best Steaks
Black Ram
1414 E. Oakton St., 847/824-1227
Knickers
1050 E. Oakton St., 847/299-0011

DOWNERS GROVE, IL

Best Breakfast
Omega Restaurant
1300 Ogden Ave., 630/963-0300

Best Desserts
Omega Restaurant
1300 Ogden Ave., 630/963-0300

Best Family Restaurant
Steven's Restaurant
2001 63rd St., 630/810-9812

Best Late-Night Food
Omega Restaurant
1300 Ogden Ave., 630/963-0300

Best Pizza
Papa Passero's
6326 S. Cass Ave., Westmont, 630/963-7660
Aurelio's Pizza
1002 Warren Ave., 630/810-0097

Best Place to Take the Kids
Omega Restaurant
1300 Ogden Ave., 630/963-0300

Best Sandwiches
Teddy's Red Hots
6310 Main St., 630/968-8444

Best Steaks
Lone Star Steakhouse
6250 Main St., 630/852-7037

Standbys
The Olive Garden
1211 Butterfield Rd., 630/852-4224
Bob Evans
1400 E. Ogden Ave., Naperville, 630/355-0877
Baskin-Robbins
601 Ogden Ave., 630/960-0789
6313 Woodward Ave., 630/963-2142

EFFINGHAM, IL

Best All-You-Can-Eat Buffet
Ethridge's Restaurant
2102 S. Banker St., 217/347-5159

Best Atmosphere
Old Grey Dog Bar and Grill
303 E. Fayette Ave., 217/342-2035

Best Barbecue/Ribs
Stix
1310 N. Keller, 217/347-2222

Best Brunch
Thelma's
Ramada Inn, N. Rte. 32 at Rte. 33, 217/342-2131

Best Burgers
Cruiser's
806 E. Fayette St., 217/342-3760

Best Cheap Meal
China Buffet
1500 W. Fayette St., 217/342-3188

Best Chinese Food
Golden China
1603 W. Fayette Ave., 217/342-2412

Best Coffee
Niemerg's Steak House
1410 W. Fayette St., 217/342-3921

Best Desserts
Rexroat's Distinctive Dining
221 W. Jefferson Ave., 217/347-5831
Thelma's
Ramada Inn, N. Rte. 32 at Rte. 33, 217/342-2131

Best Family Restaurants
Trailways Restaurant
N. Rte. 45, 217/342-2680
Niemerg's Steak House
1410 W. Fayette St., 217/342-3921

Best Mexican Food
El Rancherito
1313 N. Keller Dr., 217/342-4753

Best Pizza
Pizza Man
604 W. Jefferson St., 217/347-7766

Best Place to Take the Kids
Niemerg's Steak House
1410 W. Fayette St., 217/342-3921

Best Salad/Salad Bar
Niemerg's Steak House
1410 W. Fayette St., 217/342-3921

Best Sandwiches
Old Grey Dog Bar and Grill
303 E. Fayette Ave., 217/342-2035
Deb's Wings and Subs
3002 Four Seasons Dr., 217/536-9464

Best Seafood
Rexroat's Distinctive Dining
221 W. Jefferson Ave., 217/347-5831

Best Steaks
Rexroat's Distinctive Dining
221 W. Jefferson Ave., 217/347-5831

Standbys
Dairy Queen
1411 S. Banker St., 217/342-9432

ELGIN, IL

Best Breakfast
Paul's Family Restaurant
1300 Lawrence Ave., 847/695-8687

Best Burgers
Leitner's Hamburgers
992 Saint Charles St., 847/742-8380

Best Chinese Food
Green Jade Restaurant
10 Tyler Creek Plz., 847/888-8010

Best Desserts
Al's Cafe and Creamery
43 Fountain Square Plz., 847/742-1180

Best Family Restaurant
Paul's Family Restaurant
1300 Lawrence Ave., 847/695-8687

Best German Food
Dieterle's Restaurant
550 S. McLean Blvd., 847/697-7311

Best Ice Cream/Yogurt
Al's Cafe and Creamery
  43 Fountain Square Plz., 847/742-1180
Colonial Ice Cream Restaurant
  600 S. McLean Blvd., 847/888-3939

Best Italian Food
Facaccia's Restaurant
  50 N. Spring St., 847/695-4495

Best Pizza
Geno Nottolini's
  1061 N. Liberty St., 847/888-4884

Standbys
Ponderosa
  1568 Larkin Ave., 847/741-2250
Friday's
  101 Southwestern Ave., 847/836-8443
The Olive Garden
  800 N. Eighth St., 847/428-1981
Red Lobster
  701 Springhill Ring Rd., 847/428-0820

ELMHURST, IL

Best All-You-Can-Eat Buffet
Tree Town Buffet
  1042 S. York Rd., 630/279-8994

Best Barbecue/Ribs
Dixie Ribs
  683 N. York St., 630/617-9933

Best Breakfast
Our Kitchen
  363 W. Lake St., 630/279-3738
Rainbow Restaurant
  233 N. York St., 630/833-0556

Best Burgers
Crossroads of Ivanhoe
  20915 W. Park St., Mundelein, 630/949-9009
Silverado Grill
  447 Spring Rd., 630/833-1602
Elmhurst Public House
  683 W. Saint Charles Rd., 630/834-8989

Best Chinese Food
Red Dragon
  117 W. First St., 630/832-8326

Best Desserts
Zealous
  174 N. York St., 630/834-9300
Melting Pot
  Summit Ave. at Roosevelt Rd., Oakford Terrace,
    630/495-5778

Best Ice Cream/Yogurt
Fresco's Ice Cream Cafe
  Elmhurst City Center, 630/834-3333
Yummy Armadillo Ice Cream Shop
  489A Spring Rd., 630/530-9866

Best Italian Food
Angelo's Pizza and Restaurant
  3026 W. Montrose Ave., 630/539-0111

Best Mexican Food
Cafe Las Bellas Artes
  112 W. Park Ave., 630/530-7725

Best Pizza
Two Brothers From Italy
  128 W. Park Ave., 630/833-0414
Roberto's Family Restaurant
  3352 147th St., Midlothian, 630/385-9109

Best Steaks
Steven's Steak House
  476 N. York St., 630/834-6611

EVANSTON, IL

Best Barbecue/Ribs
Hecky's Barbecue
  1902 Green Bay Rd., 847/492-1182
Merle's No. 1 Barbecue
  1727 Benson Ave., 847/475-7766

Best Breakfast
Sarkis' Cafe
  2632 Grosse Point Rd., 847/328-9703

Best Chinese Food
Pine Yard
  924 Church St., 847/475-4940

Best Coffee
Bean Counter Cafe
  1932 Central St., 847/332-1116

Best Desserts
Verdi and Puccini Opera Cafe
  1458 Sherman Ave., 847/332-2742

Best Health-Conscious Menu
Blind Faith Cafe
  525 Dempster St., 847/328-6875

Best Italian Food
Va Pensiero
  1566 Oak Ave., 847/475-7779

Best Japanese Food
Daruma Japanese Restaurant
  2901 Central St., 847/864-6633
Kuni's
  511 Main St., 847/328-2004

Best Mexican Food
Las Palmas
  1642 Maple Ave., 847/328-2555

Best Seafood
Oceanique
  505 Main St., 847/864-3435

Best Vegetarian Food
Blind Faith Cafe
  525 Dempster, 847/328-6875
Wild Asparagus
  1709 Benson Ave., 847/866-8181

FREEPORT, IL

Best Atmosphere
Cannova's Pizza
  1101 W. Empire St., 815/233-0032

Best Breakfast
Spring Grove Family Restaurant
  1521 S. West Ave., 815/233-3181

Best Cheap Meal
Spring Grove Family Restaurant
  1521 S. West Ave., 815/233-3181

Best Chinese Food
Imperial Palace Chinese Restaurant
  1735 S. Ihm Blvd., 815/233-5944

Best Delicatessen
Garden Deli
  1264 W. Galena Ave., 815/235-3913

Best Desserts
Club Esquire
  1121 W. Empire St., 815/235-7404

Best Family Restaurant
Spring Grove Family Restaurant
  1521 S. West Ave., 815/233-3181

Best Greek/Mediterranean Food
Club Esquire
  1121 W. Empire St., 815/235-7404

Best Homestyle Food
Spring Grove Family Restaurant
  1521 S. West Ave., 815/233-3181

Best Italian Food
Cannova's Pizza
  1101 W. Empire St., 815/233-0032
Mama Cimino's Pizzeria
  1713 Southwest Ave., 815/235-3545

Best Pizza
Cannova's Pizza
  1101 W. Empire St., 815/233-0032
Mama Cimino's Pizzeria
  1713 Southwest Ave., 815/235-3545

Best Sandwiches
Garden Deli
  1264 W. Galena Ave., 815/235-3913

Best Seafood
Club Esquire
  1121 W. Empire St., 815/235-7404

Best Steaks
Club Esquire
  1121 W. Empire St., 815/235-7404

Standbys
Dairy Queen
651 W. South St., 815/232-1235

GALESBURG, IL

Best Restaurants in Town
Grady's 2100 Club
2100 Grand Ave., 309/342-6414
Cerar's Barnstormer Restaurant
1201 W. Broadway Ave., Monmouth, 309/734-9494
Landmark Cafe and Creperie
62 S. Seminary St., 309/343-5376
Jumer's Continental Inn
I-74 at E. Main St., 309/343-7151

Best Mexican Food
John's Taco Hide Out
1256 W. Berrien St., 309/343-5610

Best Steaks
The Steak House
951 N. Henderson St., 309/343-9994

GLENVIEW, IL

Best Beer Selection
Glenview House
1843 Glenview Rd., 847/724-7999

Best Breakfast
Walker Brothers Pancake House
1615 Waukegan Rd., 847/724-0220
Egg Harbor
2853 Pfingsten Rd., 847/559-9905

Best Burgers
Hackney's
1241 Harms Rd., 847/724-5577
1514 E. Lake Ave., 847/724-7171
Hamburger Hamlet
1432 Waukegan Rd., 847/998-6900

Best Business Lunch
Lucci's Pasta Facce
601 N. Milwaukee, 847/729-2268

Best Delicatessen
Max and Benny's
2749 Pfingsten Rd., 847/272-9490

Best Family Restaurant
Hackney's
1241 Harms Rd., 847/724-5577
1514 E. Lake Ave., 847/724-7171

Best Italian Food
Lucci's Pasta Facce
601 N. Milwaukee, 847/729-2268

Best Mexican Food
Las Palmas
1401 Waukegan Rd., 847/998-8700

Best Romantic Dining
Lucci's Pasta Facce
601 N. Milwaukee, 847/729-2268

HIGHLAND PARK, IL

Best Coffee
Carlo's
429 Temple Ave., 847/432-0770

Best Desserts
Carlo's
429 Temple Ave., 847/432-0770

Best French Food
Ravinia Bistro
581 Roger Williams Ave., 847/432-1033
Carlo's
429 Temple Ave., 847/432-0770

Best Health-Conscious Menu
Ravinia Bistro
581 Roger Williams Ave., 847/432-1033

Best Romantic Dining
Carlo's
429 Temple Ave., 847/432-0770
Ravinia Bistro
581 Roger Williams Ave., 847/432-1033

Best Steaks
Morton's of Chicago
1876 First St., 847/432-3484

Best Wine Selection
Ravinia Bistro
581 Roger Williams Ave., 847/432-1033

JOLIET, IL

Best Restaurant in Town
Al's Steak House
1990 W. Jefferson St., 815/725-2388

Best Bar
W.C. Flicks of Shorewood
700 W. Jefferson St., Shorewood, 815/725-7773

Best Brunch
Al's Steak House
1990 W. Jefferson St., 815/725-2388

Best Burgers
Heroes and Legends Original Bar
2400 W. Jefferson St., 815/725-1113

Best Business Lunch
Earl's Cafe
1987 W. Jefferson St., 815/729-1971

Best Casual Dining
Diamond's Family Restaurant
3000 Plainfield Rd., 815/436-1070

Best Cheap Meal
Diamond's Family Restaurant
3000 Plainfield Rd., 815/436-1070

Best Chinese Food
Dragon Light Restaurant
   1809 N. Larkin Ave., Shorewood, 815/725-1006

Best Coffee
Bakers Square Restaurant
   2211 W. Jefferson St., 815/729-1531

Best Diner
Steak and Shake Restaurant
   2675 Plainfield Rd., 815/439-9145

Best Family Restaurant
Diamond's Family Restaurant
   3000 Plainfield Rd., 815/436-1070

Best Homestyle Food
Diamond's Family Restaurant
   3000 Plainfield Rd., 815/436-1070

Best Ice Cream/Yogurt
Creamy Delight
   920 N. Broadway, 815/723-5298

Best Italian Food
Earl's Cafe
   1987 W. Jefferson St., 815/729-1971

Best Late-Night Food
Diamond's Family Restaurant
   3000 Plainfield Rd., 815/436-1070

Best Mexican Food
Los Primos
   2219 W. Jefferson St., 815/744-5144

Best Pizza
Maurie's Table Inc.
   2360 Glenwood Ave., 815/744-2619

Best Places to Be "Seen"
Earl's Cafe
   1987 W. Jefferson St., 815/729-1971
Al's Steak House
   1990 W. Jefferson St., 815/725-2388

Best Place to Eat Alone
Bakers Square Restaurant
   2211 W. Jefferson St., 815/729-1531

Best Place to Eat When Someone Else Is Buying
Al's Steak House
   1990 W. Jefferson St., 815/725-2388

Best Place to Take the Kids
Diamond's Family Restaurant
   3000 Plainfield Rd., 815/436-1070

Best Romantic Dining
Earl's Cafe
   1987 W. Jefferson St., 815/729-1971

Best Salad/Salad Bar
Rockwell Inn
   2400 W. Rte. 6, Morris, 815/942-6224

Best Sandwiches
Merichka's
   604 Theodore St., 815/723-9371

Best Seafood
Syl's Restaurant and Lounge
   829 Moen Ave., 815/725-1977

Best Steaks
Syl's Restaurant and Lounge
   829 Moen Ave., 815/725-1977

Best Vegetarian Food
Bakers Square Restaurant
   2211 W. Jefferson St., 815/729-1531

Standbys
Old Country Buffet
   2450 W. Jefferson St., 815/744-3904
Cracker Barrel
   1511 Riverboat Ctr., 815/744-0985

LAKE ZURICH, IL

Best Beer Selection
The Great Kahn
   139 S. Rand Ave., 847/550-9622

Best Bistro
D and J Bistro
   466 S. Rand Rd., 847/438-8001

Best Burgers
Hackney's
   880 N. Old Rand Rd., 847/537-4141

Best Business Lunch
The Great Kahn
   139 S. Rand Ave., 847/550-9622

Best Cheap Meal
The Great Kahn
   139 S. Rand Ave., 847/550-9622

Best Family Restaurant
Hackney's
   880 N. Old Rand Rd., 847/537-4141

Best French Food
D and J Bistro
   466 S. Rand St., 847/438-8001

Best German Food
Fritzl's
   900 Ravinia Terrace, 847/540-8844

Best Japanese Food
The Great Kahn
   139 S. Rand Ave., 847/550-9622

Best Mexican Food
Lindo Mexico
   35 N. Old Rand Rd., 847/438-3770

Best Other Ethnic Food
Julio's Latin Cafe (Latin American)
   95 S. Rand St., 847/438-3484

Best Salad/Salad Bar
D and J Bistro
   466 S. Rand St., 847/438-8001

Best Vegetarian Food
The Great Kahn
139 S. Rand Ave., 847/550-9622

LOMBARD, IL

Best Barbecue/Ribs
Carson's Place for Ribs
400 E. Roosevelt Rd., 630/627-4300

Best Bistro
Bistro Banlieue
44 Yorktown Convenience Ctr., Highland Ave. at
Butte, 630/629-6560

Best Greek/Mediterranean Food
Greek Islands Restaurant West
300 E. 22nd St., 630/932-4545

Best Ice Cream/Yogurt
Bresler's
154 Yorktown Shopping Center, 630/620-7253
Cock Robin Ice Cream
396 E. Saint Charles Rd., 630/495-9777

Best Italian Food
Lorica Ristorante
229 W. Saint Charles Rd., 630/495-0470

Best Japanese Food
Benihana of Tokyo
747 E. Butterfield Rd., 630/571-4440

Best Seafood
Terrace Restaurant
315 E. North Ave., 630/629-9500
Casey's Restaurant
415 E. North Ave., 630/932-4777

Standbys
Outback Steakhouse
100 E. Roosevelt Rd., 630/530-0005

MOLINE, IL

Best Barbecue/Ribs
RJ Boar's
4110 Blackhawk Rd., Rock Island, 309/786-0667
Jim's Rib Haven
1600 Tenth St., East Moline, 309/752-1240

Best Breakfast
Village Inn
560 Seventeenth Ave., 309/764-9222
2122 53rd St., 309/797-5556

Best Business Lunch
Duck City Delicatessen
115 E. Third St., Davenport, 319/322-3825

Best Casual Dining
Dock Steak Seafood Spirits
125 S. Perry St., Davenport, 319/322-5331
Duck City Delicatessen
115 E. Third St., Davenport, 319/322-3825

Best Coffee
Peabody's Espresso
 1603 Fifth Ave., 309/764-5282

Best Desserts
Lagomarcino's Confectionary
 1422 Fifth Ave., 309/764-9548

Best French Food
C'est Michele
 1514 Fifth Ave., 309/762-0585

Best Ice Cream/Yogurt
Whitey's Ice Cream
 2525 41st St., 309/762-4548

Best Mexican Food
Rudy's Tacos
 1518 Sixteenth St., 309/762-3293

Best Pizza
Happy Joe's Pizza and Ice Cream
 2041 Sixteenth St., 309/764-3388

Best Sandwiches
Lagomarcino's Confectionary
 1422 Fifth Ave., 309/764-9548

Best Seafood
Dock Steak Seafood Spirits
 125 S. Perry St., Davenport, 319/322-5331
Sky Line Inn
 2621 Airport Rd., 309/764-9128
Harold's on the Rock
 2600 N. Shore Dr., 309/764-4813
Captain's Table
 4801 River Dr., 309/797-9222

Best Steaks
Captain's Table
 4801 River Dr., 309/797-9222
Sky Line Inn
 2621 Airport Rd., 309/764-9128
Harold's on the Rock
 2600 N. Shore Dr., 309/764-4813

Best Vietnamese Food
Le Mekong Vietnamese Cuisine
 1606 Fifth Ave., 309/797-3709

I

NAPERVILLE, IL

Best Breakfast
Grandma Sally's Waffle House
 450 E. Ogden Ave., 630/355-7771

Best Brunch
Algar's
 3003 Corporate West Dr., 630/505-0900

Best Burgers
Lantern
 8 W. Chicago Ave., 630/355-7099

Best Chinese Food
New China Chef Restaurant
614 E. Ogden Ave., 630/717-1199

Best Coffee
Starbucks
1163 E. Ogden Ave., 630/355-5884
42 W. Jefferson Ave., 630/778-8614
Green Mountain Coffee Roasters
131 W. Jefferson Ave., 630/355-6444

Best Continental Food
Washington Square Restaurant
218 S. Washington St., 630/357-3462

Best French Food
Montparnasse Restaurant
200 E. Fifth Ave., 630/961-8203

Best Ice Cream/Yogurt
Colonial Ice Cream
8 W. Gartner Rd., 630/420-7722

Best Italian Food
Cafe Buonaro's
300 E. Fifth Ave., 630/717-0006
Garardo's Cafe
1021 W. Ogden Ave., 630/369-6100
Sorella Di Francesca
18 W. Jefferson Ave., 630/961-2706

Best Mexican Food
Potter's Place
29 W. Jefferson Ave., 630/355-9165

Best Pizza
Lou Malnati's Pizzeria
131 W. Jefferson Ave., 630/717-0700

Best Place to Eat When Someone Else Is Buying
Washington Square Restaurant
218 S. Washington St., 630/357-3462

Best Sandwiches
Rocco's Pizza
931 W. 75th St., Ste. 119, 630/369-8899

Best Seafood
Washington Square Restaurant
218 S. Washington St., 630/357-3462
Chinn's 34
3011 Ogden Ave., Lisle, 630/637-1777

Best Steaks
Washington Square Restaurant
218 S. Washington St., 630/357-3462

NORTHBROOK, IL

Best Brunch
Allgauer's Fireside Restaurant
2855 Milwaukee Ave., 847/480-7500

Best Burgers
Charlie Beinlich's
On Skokie Blvd. across from Edens Theatres [no
phone]

Best Business Lunch
Ceiling Zero
500 Anthony Trail, 847/272-8111

Best Italian Food
Trattoria Oliverii
1358 Shermer Ave., 847/559-8785

Best Japanese Food
Ron of Japan
633 Skokie Blvd., 847/564-5900

Best Late-Night Food
The Prime Minister
3355 Milwaukee Ave., 847/296-4423

Best Place to Take the Kids
Barnaby's
960 Skokie Blvd., 847/498-3900

Best Steaks
The Prime Minister
3355 Milwaukee Ave., 847/296-4423

I

PEKIN, IL

Best Bar
Yesterday's Bar and Grill
363 Court St., 309/346-3255

Best Burgers
Ernie's Family Restaurant
613 Derby St., 309/353-8109

Best Homestyle Food
Ernie's Family Restaurant
613 Derby St., 309/353-8109

Best Mexican Food
Margarita's
121 S. Second, 309/353-8226

Best Pizza
Godfather's Pizza
2111 Court St., 309/347-3135

Best Place to Eat When Someone Else Is Buying
The Summit
1620 Summit Dr., 309/347-4154

Best Sandwiches
Larkin's Home Bakery
1526 N. Eighth St., 309/353-2414

Best Steaks
The Summit
1620 Summit Dr., 309/347-4154
Lum's Restaurant
3500 Court St., 309/347-4847
Normandy Club
1703 S. Second St., 309/346-3803

Standbys
Pizza Hut
2925 Court St., 309/347-5596

PEORIA, IL

Best American Food
Carnegie's Restaurant
  501 Main St., 309/637-6500
Stephanie's Restaurant
  1825 N. Knoxville Ave., 309/682-7300
Chateau on the Lake
  901 Chateau Dr., Pekin, 309/382-3414

Best Atmosphere
Jumer's Castle Lodge
  117 N. Western Ave., 309/673-8181

Best Barbecue/Ribs
Big John's North
  7805 N. University St., 309/693-7800

Best Beer Selection
Hofbrau Restaurant
  2210 NE Jefferson Ave., 309/686-9739

Best Breakfast
Busy Bee Snack Shop
  414 1/2 Hamilton Blvd., 309/674-8782
Doc's Mt. Hawley Inn
  8412 N. Knoxville Ave., 309/691-3122
Joe's International Deli
  425 Hamilton Blvd., 309/637-3354

Best Brunch
O'Leary's
  3300 W. Willow Knolls Dr., 309/692-9030

Best Cajun/Creole Food
Alligator Bar and Grill
  308 Walnut, 309/673-5244

Best Chinese Food
China Gate Express
  4100 W. Willow Knolls Dr., 309/692-6503

Best Coffee
Mocha Joe's Beanery
  4700 N. University St., 309/689-9800

Best German Food
Hofbrau Restaurant
  2210 NE Jefferson Ave., 309/686-9739

Best Italian Food
Agatucci's Restaurant
  2607 N. University St., 309/688-8200
Avanti's Italian Restaurant
  1301 W. Main St., 309/674-4923
  4711 N. Rockwood Dr., 309/688-6565
Capponi's Restaurant
  302 N. Main St., Toluca, 815/452-2343
Mona's Italian Foods
  202 N. Main St., Toluca, 815/452-2303
Paparazzi
  4315 W. Voss Ave., Peoria Heights, 309/682-5205

Best Other Ethnic Food
Haddad's (Lebanese)
  1024 W. Main, 309/672-5339

Best Sandwiches
Silly Joe's [cart]
  Illinois Antique Ctr., 308 SW Commercial,
  309/673-3354

Best Steaks
Jim's Downtown Steak House
  110 SW Jefferson Ave., 309/673-5300
Lariat Club
  2232 W. Glen Ave., 309/691-4731

QUINCY, IL

Best Bar
Lakeview Restaurant and Patio
  4300 Broadway, 217/222-9661

Best Barbecue/Ribs
Patio
  133 S. Fourth St., 217/222-1281

Best Breakfast
Village Inn
  200 N. 36th St., 217/228-1817
Sprout's Inn
  2814 N. Twelfth St., 217/223-6294

Best Burgers
Artie's Scoreboard
  234 S. Eighth St., 217/222-3793
Lakeview Restaurant and Patio
  4300 Broadway, 217/222-9661

Best Coffee
CJ's
  234 N. Twelfth St., 217/223-3333
Pampered Palate
  4 W. State St. at Eighth St., 217/224-0025

Best Desserts
Village Inn
  200 N. 36th St., 217/228-1817
Sprout's Inn
  2814 N. Twelfth St., 217/223-6294

Best Homestyle Food
Sprout's Inn
  2814 N. Twelfth St., 217/223-6294
Stipp's Restaurant
  1130 S. Sixth St., 217/223-1212

Best Ice Cream/Yogurt
Deter's Dairy Farms
  4801 State St., 217/223-5484

Best Mexican Food
Gem City Pizzeria
  1801 State St., 217/228-0550

Best Pizza
Tower of Pizza
  1221 Broadway, 217/224-6030

Best Sandwiches
Maid Rite
   507 N. Twelfth St., 217/222-9767
   3120 Broadway, 217/224-5622
River House
   238 N. Front St., 217/224-6888

Best Seafood
Tony's Old Place
   810 Hampshire St., 217/224-4800

Best Steaks
Lakeview Restaurant and Patio
   4300 Broadway, 217/222-9661
Patio
   133 S. Fourth St., 217/222-1281

ROBINSON, IL

Best Barbecue/Ribs
Poor Little Mikey's
   508 S. Cross St., 618/546-5212

Best Breakfast
Judy's Cafe
   108 E. Main St., 618/544-8864

Best Chinese Food
Yen Ching Mandarin Restaurant
   507 N. Jackson St., 618/546-1307

Best Coffee
Judy's Cafe
   108 E. Main St., 618/544-8864

Best Desserts
Studio Cafe
   206 N. Cross St., 618/544-3732

Best Italian Food
Joe's Italian Food and Pizza
   1111 E. Main St., 618/544-8212

Best Pizza
Joe's Italian Food and Pizza
   1111 E. Main St., 618/544-8212

Standbys
Dairy Queen
   1105 E. Main St., 618/544-7410

ROCK ISLAND, IL

Best Atmosphere
Charlie's Pizza
   1407 30th St., 309/786-0911

Best Barbecue/Ribs
Jim's Rib Haven
   531 24th Ave., 309/786-8084

Best Breakfast
Fourteenth Avenue Waffle Shop
   4128 Fourteenth Ave., 309/788-4181
Bigsby's Bagels
   140 Eighteenth Ave., 309/788-6610

Best Burgers
Hunter's Club
2107 Fourth Ave., 309/786-9880

Best Family Restaurant
Charlie's Pizza
1407 30th St., 309/786-0911

Best Homestyle Food
Aunt Bea's Cafe
2429 Ninth, 309/793-0905

Best Ice Cream/Yogurt
Whitey's Ice Cream
2516 Eighteenth Ave., 309/788-5948

Best Microbrewery
Blue Cat Brew Pub
113 Eighteenth Ave., 309/788-8247

Best Pizza
Charlie's Pizza
1407 30th St., 309/786-0911
Original Huckleberry's Pizza
223 Eighteenth Ave., 309/786-1122

Best Sandwiches
Hunter's Club
2107 Fourth Ave., 309/786-9880

Best Soul Food
Aunt Bea's Cafe
2429 Ninth, 309/793-0905

Best Steaks
O'Melia's Supper Club
2900 Blackhawk Rd., 309/788-5635

Best View While Dining
Skarfi's
134 Ninteenth Ave., Moline, 309/797-7992

ROCKFORD, IL

Best Atmosphere
Beef-A-Roo
6116 N. Second St., Loves Park, 815/633-6585
6380 E. Riverside Blvd., Loves Park, 815/877-5610

Best Bar
The Olympic Tavern
2327 N. Main St., 815/962-8758

Best Barbecue/Ribs
Box's Bar-B-Q
815 Marchesano Dr., 815/962-9629

Best Breakfast
Stockholm Inn
1422 Twentieth St., 815/397-3534

Best Brunch
Cliffbreaker's
700 W. Riverside, 815/282-3033

Best Burgers
Mary's Kitchen
2515 S. Main St., 815/965-8838

Best Coffee
Capri Italian Restaurant
 313 E. State St., 815/965-6341
Mary's Market
 1659 N. Alpine Rd., 815/394-0765
 308 W. State St., 815/968-8787
 4431 E. State St., 815/397-7291

Best Diner
The Huddle
 1100 N. State St., Belvidere, 815/544-9214

Best Italian Food
Lino's
 5611 E. State St., 815/397-2077

Best Mexican Restaurant
Ricardo's Mexican Restaurant
 5855 E. State St., 815/397-8355

Best New Restaurants
A Moveable Feast
 1608 N. Alpine Rd., 815/227-0102
Ricardo's Mexican Restaurant
 5855 E. State St., 815/397-8355

Best Pizza
Giordano's Restaurant and Pizzeria
 333 N. Mulford Rd., 815/398-5700
Sam's Pizza
 2134 Charles St., 815/398-5952
Lino's
 5611 E. State St., 815/397-2077
Franchesco's
 2404 N. Perryville Rd., 815/332-4992

Best Place to Eat When Someone Else Is Buying
Lucerne's Fondue and Spirits
 845 N. Church St., 815/968-2665

Best Salad/Salad Bar
Mary's Market
 1659 N. Alpine Rd., 815/394-0765
 308 W. State St., 815/968-8787
 4431 E. State St., 815/397-7291

Best Sandwiches
Mary's Market
 1659 N. Alpine Rd., 815/394-0765
 308 W. State St., 815/968-8787
 4431 E. State St., 815/397-7291

Best Seafood
St. James Envoy
 4 SE Airport Circle, 815/965-5577
Michael's
 601 N. Perryville Rd., 815/226-8286
Cliffbreaker's
 700 W. Riverside, 815/282-3033

Best Steaks
Tumbleweed Mexican Food and Mesquite Grill
 5494 E. State St., 815/227-0192
Michael's
 601 N. Perryville Rd., 815/226-8286

Standbys
Baskin-Robbins
   3600 N. Main St., 815/877-7017
   1710 Rural St., 815/226-1690
   4224 Newburg Rd., 815/397-6598
   2579 N. Mulford Rd., 815/877-8646
   3134 Eleventh St., 815/398-2535

SKOKIE, IL

Best Barbecue/Ribs
Carson's Place for Ribs
   8617 Niles Center Rd., 847/275-3499

Best Delicatessens
Bagel Restaurant and Deli
   50 Old Orchard Shopping Ctr., 847/677-0100
Barnum and Bagel
   4700 Dempster St., 847/676-4466

Best Health-Conscious Menu
Slice of Life
   4120 Dempster St., 847/674-2021

Best Pizza
Gino's East
   3517 Dempster St., 847/982-9401

Best Salad/Salad Bar
Sasha's Cafe
   9599 Skokie Blvd., 847/675-3300

Best Seafood
Don's Fishmarket
   9335 Skokie Blvd., 847/677-3424

Best Vegetarian Food
Slice of Life
   4120 Dempster St., 847/674-2021

SPRINGFIELD, IL

Best Bagels
Big Apple Bagels
   2347 W. Monroe, 217/787-0505

Best Barbecue/Ribs
Popeye's
   1100 S. Eighteenth St., 217/522-0386

Best Coffee
Espress-OH! Gourmet Cafe
   2769 S. Veterans, 217/787-6381

Best Desserts
George Warburton's Food and Drink
   Rte. 3, Petersburg, 217/632-7878

Best Italian Food
Saputo's
   801 E. Monroe, 217/544-2523

Best Late-Night Food
Mr. Ted's Grill
   926 W. Jefferson, 217/525-8368

Best Mexican Food
Cancun
2849 S. Sixth, Southern View, 217/753-0088

Best Pizza
Joe's Italian Pizza
1552 W. Jefferson, 217/787-6005

Best Romantic Dining
Stagecoach Inn
Rte. 125, Pleasant Plains, 217/626-1132

Best Thai Food
Magic Kitchen Thai Restaurant
4112 Peoria Rd., 217/525-2230

WATERLOO, IL

Best Bars
Greenfield's Lounge
127 N. Main St., Columbia, 618/281-9989
Columbia City Saloon Bar
1101 Valmeyer Rd., Columbia, 618/281-6410
Wartburg Inn
5831 Maeystown Rd., 618/939-8981

Best Breakfast
Hoefft's Village Inn
1026 Main St., Maeystown, 618/458-6425

Best Burgers
Sports Page Inn
2635 Old State Rte. 3, East Carondelet, 618/286-5628

Best Casual Dining
Greenfield's Lounge
127 N. Main St., Columbia, 618/281-9989

Best Chinese Food
Mr. Chiu Restaurant
1260 Columbia Ctr., Columbia, 618/281-6030

Best Coffee
Courthouse Espresso Cafe
219 S. Main St., 618/939-5995
Book Nook and Beanery
123 S. Main St., Columbia, 618/281-6010

Best Family Restaurants
Dreamland Palace
3043 State Rte. 156, 618/939-9922
Lantern Restaurant
230 N. Main St., Columbia, 618/281-7312
Lincoln Trail Restaurant
108 N. Market St., 618/939-7310

Best Italian Food
Joe Boccardi's Ristorante
117 S. Main St., Columbia, 618/281-6700
Tripoli Italian Restaurant
1280 Columbia Ctr., Columbia, 618/281-7400

Best Lunch
JV's
117 N. Main St., 618/939-7127

Best Pizza
Vito's
  114 W. Mill St., 618/939-9939

Best Sandwiches
Tripoli Italian Restaurant
  1280 Columbia Ctr., Columbia, 618/281-7400

Standbys
Dairy Queen
  512 S. Market St., 618/939-8801
Subway
  124 W. Mill St., 618/939-4848

WAUKEGAN, IL

Best Restaurant in Town
Parkway Restaurant
  3035 Belvidere Rd., 847/336-0222

Best Bar
Midlane Country Club
  14565 W. Yorkhouse Rd., Wadsworth, 847/360-0550

Best Desserts
Parkway Restaurant
  3035 Belvidere Rd., 847/336-0222

Best Mexican Food
Pepe's Mexican Restaurant
  760 N. Green Bay Rd., 847/244-7887

Best Place to Eat When Someone Else Is Buying
Dover Straits
  Rte. 45 at Hwy. 83, Mundelein, 847/949-1550

Best Romantic Dining
Parkway Restaurant
  3035 Belvidere Rd., 847/336-0222

Best Sandwiches
Midlane Country Club
  14565 W. Yorkhouse Rd., Wadsworth, 847/360-0550

Best Seafood
Dover Straits
  Rte. 45 at Hwy. 83, Mundelein, 847/949-1550

Standbys
Chili's
  5435 Touhy Ave., Skokie, 847/679-1425
Ruby Tuesday
  307 Hawthorn Ct., Vernon Hills, 847/816-0227

WHEELING, IL

Best Burgers
Hackney's
  241 Milwaukee Ave., 847/537-2100

Best Business Lunch
Harry Caray's
  933 N. Milwaukee Ave., 847/537-2827

Best Desserts
Le Francais
  269 S. Milwaukee Ave., 847/541-7470

Best Family Restaurant
Hackney's
241 Milwaukee Ave., 847/537-2100

Best French Food
Le Francais
269 S. Milwaukee Ave., 847/541-7470

Best German Food
Hans' Bavarian Lodge
931 N. Milwaukee Ave., 847/537-4141

Best Salad/Salad Bar
Don Roth's
612 N. Milwaukee Ave., 847/537-5800

Best Steaks
The Weber Grill Restaurant
920 N. Milwaukee Ave., 847/215-0996

Best Wine Selection
Le Francais
269 Milwaukee Ave., 847/541-7470

WILMETTE, IL

Best Breakfast
Walker Brothers
153 Green Bay Rd., 847/251-6000

Best Burgers
Old Ouilmette Depot
1139 Wilmette Ave., 847/256-0771

Best Chinese Food
Tsing Tao Mandarin Chinese Restaurant
537 Green Bay Rd., 847/251-7760

Best Coffee
Marie's Restaurant
415 Fourth St., 847/251-1636
Ridgeview Restaurant
827 Ridge Rd., 847/251-2770

Best French Food
Betise
1515 Sheridan Rd., 847/853-1711

Best Homestyle Food
Butt'ry
1137 Greenleaf Ave., 847/256-1133

Best Ice Cream/Yogurt
Homer's Ice Cream
1237 Green Bay Rd., 847/251-0477

Best Italian Food
Convito Italiano
1515 Sheridan Rd., 847/251-3654
Red Noodle
804 E. Rollins Rd., 847/223-7010

Best Salad/Salad Bar
C.J. Arthur's
1168 Wilmette Ave., 847/256-8870
A La Carte
111 Green Bay Rd., 847/256-4102

Best Sandwiches
Butt'ry
    1137 Greenleaf Ave., 847/256-1133
C.J. Arthur's
    1168 Wilmette Ave., 847/256-8870
A La Carte
    111 Green Bay Rd., 847/256-4102

Best Steaks
Betise
    1515 Sheridan Rd., 847/853-1711

I

Indiana

I

Best Restaurant in Town
Pendleton House
  118 N. Pendleton Ave., Pendleton, 317/778-8061

Best Bar
Elliott's Downtown
  709 Main St., 317/640-0150

Best Brunch
Springfield's
  5920 Scatterfield Rd., 317/644-2581

Best Burgers
Madewell Food and Ice Cream
  2326 Columbus Ave., 317/649-8918

Best Cheap Meal
Fazoli's
  4410 Scatterfield Rd., 317/622-9163

Best Chinese Food
Magic Wok
  817 S. State Rd. 9, 317/643-7000

Best Diner
Post Restaurant
  State Rd. 967, Pendleton, 317/778-4651

Best Ice Cream/Yogurt
Madewell Food and Ice Cream
  2326 Columbus Ave., 317/649-8918

Best Italian Food
Fazoli's
  4410 Scatterfield Rd., 317/622-9163

Best Late-Night Food
Steak and Shake Restaurant
  5825 Scatterfield Rd., 317/622-9367

Best Mexican Food
Tio's Restaurant
  2902 Broadway St., 317/649-5655

Best Middle Eastern Food
Nile Restaurant
  723 E. Eighth St., 317/640-9028

Best Pizza
Noble Roman's
  265 State Rd. 9N, 317/643-0038
  5713 Scatterfield Rd., 317/643-6506

Best Place to Be "Seen"
Elliott's Downtown
  709 Main St., 317/640-0150

Best Place to Eat When Someone Else Is Buying
Pendleton House
  118 N. Pendleton, Pendleton, 317/778-8061

Best Romantic Dining
Pendleton House
  118 N. Pendleton, Pendleton, 317/778-8061

Standbys
Old Country Buffet
  5567 Scatterfield Rd., 317/641-1860
Cracker Barrel
  2012 E. 59th St., 317/642-6424
Applebee's
  1922 E. 53rd St., 317/642-7763
Red Lobster
  5806 Scatterfield Rd., 317/643-7663
Ponderosa
  2006 State Rd. 109S, 317/642-2720

BLOOMINGTON, IN

Best Restaurant in Town
Michael's Uptown Cafe and Bakery
  102 E. Kirkwood Ave., 812/339-0900

Best Bars
Nick's English Hut
  423 E. Kirkwood Ave., 812/332-4040
Second Story Nightclub
  201 S. College Ave., 812/336-2582
Irish Lion
  212 W. Kirkwood Ave., 812/336-9076

Best Breakfast
Runcible Spoon Cafe and Restaurant
  412 E. Sixth St., 812/334-3997
Village Deli
  409 E. Kirkwood Ave., 812/336-2303
Michael's Uptown Cafe and Bakery
  102 E. Kirkwood Ave., 812/339-0900

Best Brunch
The Tudor Room
  Indiana University, 900 W. Seventh St., 812/855-1620
Runcible Spoon Cafe and Restaurant
  412 E. Sixth St., 812/334-3997
Michael's Uptown Cafe and Bakery
  102 E. Kirkwood Ave., 812/339-0900

Best Burgers
The Trojan Horse
  100 E. Kirkwood Ave., 812/332-1101
Opie Taylor's Burger Works
  212 N. Walnut St., 812/333-7287
Mustard's
  300 College Mall Rd., Ste. 511, 812/334-3344

Best Business Lunch
Malibu Grill
  106 N. Walnut St., 812/332-4334

Best Casual Dining
White River Cafe and Coffee
  910 N. College Ave., 812/330-1212

Best Cheap Meal
Laughing Planet
  322 E. Kirkwood Ave., 812/323-2233
Runcible Spoon Cafe and Restaurant
  412 E. Sixth St., 812/334-3997

Best Chinese Food
Lung Cheung Restaurant
  119 S. College Ave., 812/332-2283
Wok
  430 E. Kirkwood Ave., Second Fl., 812/339-4296
Leofoo Chinese Cuisine
  110 N. Walnut St., 812/333-4474
Phoenix Dumpling
  307 E. Third St., 812/333-5262

Best Coffee
The Daily Grind
  430 E. Kirkwood Ave., Ste. 4, 812/339-6038
  919 S. College Mall Rd., 812/339-2253
  301 E. Third St., 812/333-2326
Runcible Spoon Cafe and Restaurant
  412 E. Sixth St., 812/334-3997

Best Desserts
Tina's Carryout and Cuisine
  309 E. Third St., 812/332-0464
Runcible Spoon Cafe and Restaurant
  412 E. Sixth St., 812/334-3997
Encore Cafe
  316 W. Sixth St., 812/333-7312

Best Diner
Walnut Street Cafe
  1500 S. Walnut St., 812/333-4812

Best Family Restaurant
Encore Cafe
  316 W. Sixth St., 812/333-7312

Best French Food
Le Petit Cafe
  308 W. Sixth St., 812/334-9747

Best Health-Conscious Menu
Lennie's Restaurant
  1795 E. Tenth St., 812/323-2112

Best Homestyle Food
Ladyman's Cafe
122 E. Kirkwood Ave., 812/336-5557

Best Ice Cream/Yogurt
White Mountain Ice Creamery
107 N. Dunn St., 812/333-8975

Best Italian Food
Puccini's International Restaurant
420 E. Fourth St., 812/333-5522

Best Late-Night Food
Crazy Horse Food and Beverage
214 W. Kirkwood Ave., 812/336-8877

Best Mexican Food
La Charreada
1720 N. Walnut St., 812/332-2343

Best Other Ethnic Food
Snow Lion (Tibetan)
113 S. Grant St., 812/336-0835

Best Pizza
Mother Bear's Pizza
1402 N. Walnut St., 812/332-6812
1428 E. Third St., 812/332-4495
6840 Lake Plaza Dr., 812/849-8220
Rockit's Famous Pizza
222 N. Walnut St., 812/336-7625
Lennie's Restaurant
1795 E. Tenth St., 812/323-2112

Best Place to Be "Seen"
Michael's Uptown Cafe and Bakery
102 E. Kirkwood Ave., 812/339-0900

Best Place to Eat Alone
The Irish Lion
212 W. Kirkwood Ave., 812/336-9076

Best Places to Eat When Someone Else Is Buying
Janko's Little Zagreb
223 W. Sixth St., 812/332-0694
Michael's Uptown Cafe and Bakery
102 E. Kirkwood Ave., 812/339-0900
Positively Fourth Street
111 W. Fourth St., 812/323-1055

Best Place to Take the Kids
Leslie's Italian Villa
206 N. Walnut St., 812/336-5822

Best Romantic Dining
Chapman's Restaurant
300 S. State Rd. 446, 812/337-9999
Positively Fourth Street
111 W. Fourth St., 812/323-1055
Siam House
430 E. Fourth St., 812/331-1233

Best Salad/Salad Bar
Inn of the Four Winds
9301 Fairfax Rd., 812/824-9904

Lennie's Restaurant
1795 E. Tenth St., 812/323-2112
Encore Cafe
316 W. Sixth St., 812/333-7312

Best Sandwiches
Macri's Deli
1221 S. College Mall Rd., 812/333-0606
Dagwood's Deli-Sub Shop
116 1/2 S. Indiana Ave., 812/333-3000
Village Deli
409 E. Kirkwood Ave., 812/336-2303

Best Seafood
Mikado Japanese Restaurant
895 S. College Mall Rd., 812/333-1950

Best Steaks
Janko's Little Zagreb
223 W. Sixth St., 812/332-0694

Best Tea Room
Casablanca
402 E. Fourth St., 812/335-9094

Best Thai Food
Siam House
430 E. Fourth St., 812/331-1233

Best Vegetarian Food
Ekimae Japanese Restaurant
825 N. Walnut St., 812/334-1661
Positively Fourth Street
111 W. Fourth St., 812/323-1055
Siam House
430 E. Fourth St., 812/331-1233

Best Wine Selection
Michael's Uptown Cafe and Bakery
102 E. Kirkwood Ave., 812/339-0900
Positively Fourth Street
111 W. Fourth St., 812/323-1055

Standbys
Ryan's Family Steak House
4400 E. Third St., 812/331-1187
Ben and Jerry's
413 E. Kirkwood, 812/333-5136

COLUMBUS, IN

Best Atmosphere
Zaharako's
329 Washington St., 812/379-9329

Best Burgers
Lucas Brothers Sandwich Shop
1842 Indiana Ave., 812/376-7010

Best Casual Dining
Grindstone Charley's
2607 Central Ave., 812/372-2532

Best Eclectic Menu
Zaharako's
329 Washington St., 812/379-9329

Best Pizza
Noble Roman's
2995 N. National Rd., 812/376-9438
4140 W. Jonathan Moore Pike, 812/342-4477

Best Place to Eat When Someone Else Is Buying
Weinantz Food and Spirits
State Rd. 46W, 812/379-2323

Best Seafood
Peter's Bay Restaurant
310 Commons Mall, 812/372-2270

Best Southwestern Food
La Bomba's Tex-Mexican Restaurant
2326 25th St., 812/379-1234

Best Steaks
Ribeye Steak and Ribs
2506 25th St., 812/376-6410
Sirloin Stockade
3114 N. National Rd., 812/378-3867

Standbys
Bob Evans
221 Carrie Ln., 812/378-0442
Baskin-Robbins
2610 25th St., 812/376-7211

CROWN POINT, IN

Best Atmosphere
Valentino's Ice Cream
Courthouse Cafe, 219/663-4812

Best Breakfast
Schoop's Hamburgers
1124 N. Main St., 219/663-2288
Twelve Islands
114 S. Main St., First Fl., 219/663-5070

Best Brunch
Bon Appetit
302 S. Main St., 219/663-6363

Best Burgers
Schoop's Hamburgers
1124 N. Main St., 219/663-2288

Best Chinese Food
Twin Happiness Chinese Restaurant
1188 N. Main St., 219/663-4433

Best Coffee
Chocolate Cafe
192 W. Joliet St., 219/662-9667

Best Delicatessen
Pap's Deli
119 W. Joliet St., 219/663-9745

Best Desserts
Chocolate Cafe
192 W. Joliet St., 219/662-9667

Best Family Restaurants
Bronko's
1244 N. Main St., 219/662-0145

Twelve Islands
  114 S. Main St., First Fl., 219/663-5070

Best Homestyle Food
Crown Kitchen
  111 N. Main St., 219/663-7466

Best Ice Cream/Yogurt
Valentino's Ice Cream
  Courthouse Cafe, 219/663-4812

Best Mexican Food
Fiesta Mexico
  1 N. Court St., 219/663-5890

Best Pizza
Chicago's Restaurant and Lounge
  109 W. Joliet St., 219/663-6040

Best Place to Take the Kids
Celebration Station
  8121 Georgia St., Merrillville, 219/769-7672

Best Restaurant Meal Value
Truffles
  400 N. Main St., 219/662-7764

Best Seafood
Chicago's Restaurant and Lounge
  109 W. Joliet St., 219/663-6040

Best Steaks
Chicago's Restaurant and Lounge
  109 W. Joliet St., 219/663-6040

Standbys
Ponderosa
  1498 N. Main St., 219/662-1369

EVANSVILLE, IN

Best Restaurant in Town
The Sunset Dining Room
  Bernie Little's Riverhouse, 20 Walnut St.,
    812/425-6500

Best American Food
Jungle Mornings
  416 Main, 812/425-5282
Greeley's
  100 NW Second St., 812/425-5553

Best Bars
Jacob's Pub and Restaurant
  4428 N. First Ave., 812/423-0050
Bockelman's Restaurant
  4001 Big Cynthiana Rd., 812/963-9017

Best Barbecue/Ribs
Shyler's Bar-B-Q
  324 S. Green River Rd., 812/476-4599

Best Breakfast
Merry-Go-Round Restaurant
  2101 Hwy. 41N, 812/423-6388
  5115 Monroe Ave., 812/479-6388

Pie Pan
905 N. Park Dr., 812/425-2261
4301 Vogel Rd., 812/477-8800

Best Business Lunch
TK Pepper's Restaurant
217 Main St., 812/422-2555

Best Casual Dining
Bockelman's Restaurant
4001 Big Cynthiana Rd., 812/963-9017
Jacob's Pub and Restaurant
4428 N. First Ave., 812/423-0050

Best Chinese Food
Canton Inn Restaurant
915 N. Park Dr., 812/428-6611
Shing-Lee Chinese Restaurant
215 Main St., 812/464-2769

Best Delicatessen
Bits and Bytes
216 NW Fourth St., 812/423-5113

Best Dinner
Greeley's
100 NW Second St., 812/425-5553
Haub Steak House
Main St., Haubstadt, 812/768-6462

Best Family Restaurants
Bockelman's Restaurant
4001 Big Cynthiana Rd., 812/963-9017
Wolf's Bar-B-Q Restaurant
6600 N. First Ave., 812/424-8891
1414 E. Columbia St., 812/423-3599

Best Homestyle Food
Jojo's Family Restaurant
3901 Hwy. 41N, 812/425-1486

Best Italian Food
Crazy Tomato Italian
500 S. Greenriver, 812/474-9977

Best Lunch
Emge's Deli
206 Main, 812/422-3026

Best Mexican Food
Los Bravos Mexican Restaurant
640 S. Green River Rd., 812/474-9078
900 W. Buena Vista Rd., 812/424-4101

Best Sandwiches
Bits and Bytes
216 NW Fourth St., 812/423-5113

Best Steaks
F's Steak House
125 SE Fourth St., 812/422-6788
The Sunset Dining Room
Bernie Little's Riverhouse, 20 Walnut St.,
812/425-6500
Haub Steak House
Main St., Haubstadt, 812/768-6462

FT. WAYNE, IN

Best Restaurant in Town
Cafe Johnell
2529 S. Calhoun St., 219/456-1939

Best American Food
Triangle Park
3010 Trier Rd., 219/482-4342
Back 40 Junction
1011 Thirteenth St., Decatur, 219/724-3355

Best Bars
Munchie Emporium
1109 Taylor St., 219/424-6883
Triangle Park
3010 Trier Rd., 219/482-4342
Park Place Grill
200 E. Main St., 219/420-7275

Best Breakfast
ATZ Ice Cream Shoppe
3235 N. Anthony Blvd., 219/483-3213
211 E. Tillman Rd., 219/447-2121
3235 N. Anthony St., 219/482-2979

Best Business Lunch
Don Hall's Old Gas House
305 E. Superior St., 219/426-3411
Park Place Grill
200 E. Main St., 219/420-7275

Best Chinese Food
House of Hunan
5626 Coldwater Rd., 219/482-9402

Best Dinner
Casa D'Angelo
3402 Fairfield Ave., 219/745-7200
4111 Parnell Ave., 219/483-0202

Best Family Restaurants
Richards Restaurant
2912 Getz Rd., 219/432-0913
629 E. Paulding Rd., 219/745-7432
717 W. Washington Center Rd., 219/489-4279
Zoli's Family Restaurant
2426 Broadway, 219/745-2740
Back 40 Junction
1011 Thirteenth St., Decatur, 219/724-3355

Best French Food
Cafe Johnell
2529 S. Calhoun St., 219/456-1939

Best Homestyle Food
Zoli's Family Restaurant
2426 Broadway, 219/745-2740

Best Italian Food
Casa D'Angelo
3402 Fairfield Ave., 219/745-7200
4111 Parnell Ave., 219/483-0202

I

Best Mexican Food
El Azteca
  535 E. State Blvd., 219/482-2172

Best Other Ethnic Food
Zoli's Family Restaurant (Hungarian)
  2426 Broadway, 219/745-2740

Best Pizza
Munchie Emporium
  1109 Taylor St., 219/424-6883

Best Place to Take the Kids
Richard's Restaurant
  2912 Getz Rd., 219/432-0913
  629 E. Paulding Rd., 219/745-7432
  717 W. Washington Center Rd., 219/489-4279

Best Salad/Salad Bar
Munchie Emporium
  1109 Taylor St., 219/424-6883

Best Sandwiches
Munchie Emporium
  1109 Taylor St., 219/424-6883

Best Seafood
Chappell's Number Two
  3311 N. Anthony Blvd., 219/456-9652
  2723 Broadway, 219/456-9652

Best Steaks
Chappell's Number Two
  3311 N. Anthony Blvd., 219/456-9652
  2723 Broadway, 219/456-9652

GARY, IN

Best Restaurant in Town
Chez Criton
  1700 Grant, 219/944-0775

Best American Food
Purple Steer
  1402 Indianapolis Blvd., Whiting, 219/659-3950
L.L. Coney Island
  1744 Broadway, 219/882-2287
Chez Criton
  1700 Grant, 219/944-0775

Best Breakfast
Big Wheel Restaurant
  6140 Melton Rd., 219/938-3516

Best Burgers
That's-A-Burger
  4123 Broadway, 219/887-8859

Best Chinese Food
Ming Ling
  566 S. Lake St., 219/938-6617

Best Dinner
Freddy's Steakhouse
  6442 Kennedy Ave., Hammond, 219/844-1500

Best French Food
Chez Criton
1700 Grant, 219/944-0775

Best Homestyle Food
Big Wheel Restaurant
6140 Melton Rd., 219/938-3516

Best Mexican Food
Pepe's Mexican Restaurant
6400 Melton Rd., 219/938-0777

Best Romantic Dining
Purple Steer
1402 Indianapolis Blvd., Whiting, 219/659-3950

Best Seafood
Ray's Shrimp House
4499 W. Fifth Ave., 219/944-8545
3770 Grant St., 219/884-5707

Best Steaks
Freddy's Steakhouse
6442 Kennedy Ave., Hammond, 219/844-1500

Standbys
Friday's
2487 80th Ave., Maryville, 219/942-1845
The Olive Garden
1900 South Lake Mall, 219/769-2479

INDIANAPOLIS, IN

Best Restaurants in Town
Something Different
2411 E. 65th St., 317/257-7973
Majestic
47 S. Pennsylvania, 317/636-5418
Restaurant at the Canterbury
123 S. Illinois St., 317/634-3000
Keystone Grill
8650 Keystone Crossing, 317/848-5202
Malibu Grill
4503 E. 82nd St., 317/845-4334
Peter's Restaurant and Bar
8505 Keystone Crossing, 317/465-1155
Johnson County Line
1265 N. Madison Ave., Greenwood, 317/887-0404

Best All-You-Can Eat Buffet
Heritage House
4990 Hwy. 31S, 317/783-9388
6000 E. 21st St., 317/356-2148

Best Bagels
Shapiro's Deli
2370 W. 86th St., 317/872-7255
Bagel King/Harlan Bakeries
7768 Zionsville Rd., 317/876-1400
Baranca's Bagels
11854 Allisonville Rd., 317/577-1552

Best Bars
Ale Emporium
  8617 Allisonville Rd., 317/842-1333
  2650 Lake Circle Dr., 317/879-1212
Broad Ripple Brew Pub
  840 E. 65th St., 317/253-2739
Daddy Jack's
  9419 N. Meridian St., 317/843-1609

Best Barbecue/Ribs
Odie's Pit Bar B Que
  6825 Graham Rd., 317/849-6901
King Ribs Bar-B-Q
  4130 N. Keystone Ave., 317/543-0841
  2660 Lafayette, 317/488-0223
  5610 Georgetown Rd., 317/291-2695
Babyback's
  39 W. Jackson St., 317/321-1035
Zeb's
  2379 E. 38th St., 317/925-5263
Pa and Ma's
  974 W. 27th St., 317/924-3698
Mountain Jack's
  3650 W. 86th St., 317/872-4500
  6901 W. 38th St., 317/329-6929

Best Beer Selection
Union Jack Pub
  6225 W. 25th St., 317/243-3300
Shallos Antique Restaurant
  8811 Hardegan St., Ste. 1B, 317/882-7997

Best Breakfast
Le Peep
  301 N. Illinois St., 317/237-3447
  8255 Craig St., Ste. 102, 317/576-0433
Original Pancake House
  121 W. Louisiana St., 317/266-0304
  1518 W. 86th St., 317/872-0022
Cafe Patachou
  4911 N. Pennsylvania St., 317/925-2823

Best Brunch
The Porch
  1 S. Capitol Ave., 317/632-1234
Waterson's
  8787 Keystone Crossing, 317/846-2700

Best Burgers
Flakey Jake's
  7975 E. Washington St., 317/359-1456
  6530 E. 82nd St., 317/841-0274
Max and Erma's
  8930 Wesleyan Rd., 317/872-2300
  5899 E. 86th St., 317/841-1411
  8817 Hwy. 31S, 317/882-4477

Best Business Lunch
Daddy Jack's Restaurant and Bar
  9419 N. Meridian St., 317/843-1609

Best Cafeterias
Laughner's Cafeteria
  4004 S. East St., 317/783-2907
  20 N. Franklin Rd., 317/356-3388
  5206 W. 38th St., 317/293-4572
  4030 Hwy. 31S, 317/787-3745
  1616 E. 86th St., 317/846-1112
Gray Brothers Cafeteria
  555 S. Indiana St., Mooresville, 317/831-5614
Jonathan Byrd's Cafeteria
  100 Byrd Way, Greenwood, 317/881-8888

Best Cajun/Creole Food
Jazz Cooker
  925 Westfield Blvd., 317/253-2883
New Orleans House
  8845 Township Line Rd., 317/872-9670

Best Cheap Meal
Shapiro's Delicatessen
  808 S. Meridian St., 317/872-7255
  3944 E. 82nd St., 317/842-4028
  1508 W. 86th St., 317/875-9223
Old Spaghetti Factory
  210 S. Meridian St., 317/635-6325
Kory's Restaurant
  1850 E. 62nd St., 317/251-2252

Best Chinese Food
Forbidden City
  2606 E. 65th St., 317/257-7388
  3837 N. High School Rd., 317/298-3588
  3517 W. 86th St., 317/872-2888
Broad Ripple Chinese
  840 Broad Ripple Ave., 317/259-1688
Yen Ching
  1300 E. 86th St., 317/844-1910
  8512 Washington St., 317/889-3270

Best Coffee
Houlihan's Old Place
  6101 N. Keystone Ave., 317/257-3285
Espresso Yourself
  1460 W. 86th St., 317/872-6055

Best Coffeehouses
The Abbey Coffeehouse
  771 Massachusetts Ave., 317/269-8426
Coffee Zon's Courtyard
  137 E. Ohio St., 317/684-0432
Village Idiot
  6360 Guilford Ave., 317/257-5556
Cath Inc.
  222 E. Market St., Ste. 1, 317/634-0600
  126 N. Delaware St., 317/685-0600
  705 E. 54th St., 317/255-1075

Best Delicatessens
Shapiro's Deli
  2370 W. 86th St., 317/ 872-7255

D'Amico's Deli and Bagel
6311 Guilford Ave., 317/475-1209
9546 Allisonville Rd., Ste. 138, 317/845-5460
Weiss Deli
32 E. Washington St., 317/631-0240
IKA's Delicatessen
8255 Craig, Ste. 128, Castleton, 317/595-9400

Best Desserts
Renee's French Restaurant
839 E. Westfield Blvd., 317/251-4142
Baker's Square
3802 E. 82nd St., 317/578-0280
6915 W. 38th St., Eagle Creek, 317/297-8176

Best French Food
Renee's
839 E. Westfield Blvd., 317/251-4142
Chante Clair
2501 S. High School Rd., 317/243-1040
Chez Jean
8821 S. State Rd. 67, 317/831-0870

Best German Food
Rathskeller
401 E. Michigan St., 317/636-0396
Gisela's Kaffeekranzchen
112 S. Main St., 317/873-5523
Heidelberg Cafe
7625 Pendleton Pike, 317/547-1230

Best Greek/Mediterranean Food
Kory's Restaurant
1850 E. 62nd St., 317/251-2252
Hellas Cafe
8501 Westfield Blvd., 317/257-6211
Acropolis
1625 E. Southport Rd., 317/787-8883

Best Homestyle Food
Hollyhock Hill
8110 N. College Ave., 317/251-2294
Dodd's Townhouse
5694 N. Meridian St., 317/257-1872
The Eller House
7050 E. 116th St., 317/849-2299

Best Ice Cream/Yogurt
Nick's Sweet Retreat
920 Broad Ripple Ave., 317/251-8379
J.D. Cream's
326 E. Vermont St., 317/237-0363

Best Indian Food
India Garden
830 Broad Ripple Ave., 317/253-6060
Star of India
1043 Broad Ripple Ave., 317/465-1100

Best Italian Food
Bravo!
8651 Castle Creek Pkwy., 317/577-2211

Milano Inn
231S College Ave., 317/638-7706
Iaria's
317 S. College Ave., 317/638-7706
Arturo's Ristorante Italiano
2727 E. 86th St., Ste. 232, 317/257-4806

Best Japanese Food
Benihana of Tokyo
8830 Keystone Crossing, 317/846-2495
Ginza Japanese Steakhouse
5380 W. 28th St., 317/298-3838

Best Late-Night Food
Rock Lobster
820 Broad Ripple Ave., 317/257-9001

Best Mexican Food
Don Pablo's Mexican Kitchen
3824 E 82nd St., 317/576-0819
6929 E. 38th St., 317/293-2178
8150 Hwy. 31S, 317/888-0363
Cantina del Rio
6220 Castleway Dr., 317/842-3711
El Sol de Tala Mexican Restaurante Y Cantina
2444 E. Washington St., 317/635-8252

Best Outdoor Dining
Rick's Cafe Boatyard
4100 Dandy Trail, 317/290-9300

Best Pizza
Bazbeaux Pizza
832 E. Westfield Blvd., 317/255-5711
334 Massachusetts Ave., 317/636-7662
Puccini's Smiling Teeth Pizza and Pasta
3944 E. 82nd St., 317/842-4028
1508 W. 86th St., 317/875-9223
Enzo
222 E. Market St., 317/266-0498
29 E. McCarty St., 317/638-0337
8701 Keystone Crossing, 317/846-9332
39 Jackson Pl., Floor C, 317/635-1144

Best Places to Eat When Someone Else Is Buying
Keystone Grill
8650 Keystone Crossing, 317/848-5202
The Glass Chimney
12901 Old Meridian St., Carmel, 317/844-0921
Something Different
2411 E. 65th St., 317/257-7973

Best Places to Take the Kids
Max and Erma's
8930 Wesleyan Rd., 317/872-2300
5899 E. 86th St., 317/841-1411
8817 Hwy. 31S, 317/882-4477
Arni's
3443 W. 86th St., 317/875-7034
Hollyhock Hill
8110 N. College Ave., 317/251-2294

Best Romantic Dining
Chanteclair Sur Le Toit
  2501 S. High School Rd., Fifth Fl., 317/243-1040
Restaurant at the Canterbury
  123 S. Illinois St., 317/634-3000

Best Sandwiches
Shapiro's Deli
  2370 W. 86th St., 317/872-7255
Flakey Jake's
  7975 E. Washington St., 317/359-1456
  6530 E. 82nd St., 317/841-0274
Brother Juniper's
  150 E. Sixteenth St., Ste. 1, 317/924-9529
  339 Massachusetts Ave., 317/636-3115

Best Seafood
Kona Jack's Fish Market and Oyster Bar
  9413 N. Meridian St., 317/843-2600
Fisherman's Dock
  3451 W. 86th St., 317/876-3474

Best Soul Food
Lauren's Southern Soul
  2172 E. 54th St., 317/255-3554
Zeb's Bar-B-Q
  2379 E. 38th St., 317/925-5263
Pa and Ma's
  974 W. 27th St., 317/924-3698
Big Mama's
  2356 N. Sherman Dr., 317/547-6262

Best Steaks
St. Elmo Steak House
  127 S. Illinois St., 317/365-0636
Broad Ripple Steakhouse
  929 E. Westfield Blvd., 317/253-8101
Del Frisco's
  3 E. Market St., 317/687-8888
  1365 E. 86th St., 317/251-0222

Best Sushi
Sakura
  7201 N. Keystone, 317/259-4171
Sansui Japanese Restaurant
  1329 S. Range Line Rd., 317/848-9050

Best Thai Food
Bangkok
  7269 N. Keystone Ave., 317/255-7799

Best Vegetarian Food
Nature's Pantry
  3000 N. Meridian St., 317/926-8439
Brother Juniper's
  150 E. Sixteenth St., Ste. 1, 317/924-9529
  339 Massachusetts Ave., 317/636-3115

Best Wine Selection
Corner Wine Bar
  6331 Guilford Ave., 317/255-5159
Schaffer's
  6125 Hillside Ave., 317/253-1404

The Glass Chimney
  12901 Old Meridian St., 317/844-0921

Standbys
Bob Evans
  Multiple Locations
Cracker Barrel
  4350 E. Southport Rd., 317/784-7691
  3840 Eagle View Dr., 317/298-8908
  2340 Post Dr., 317/897-1042
Friday's
  3502 E. 86th St., 317/844-3355
  12117 E. 75th St., 317/335-2567
  501 W. Washington St., 317/685-8443
The Olive Garden
  6130 E. 82nd St., 317/842-6321
  5515 W. 38th St., 317/293-4725
  8155 E. Washington St., 317/895-0800
  8840 Signature Dr., 317/876-1024
Outback Steakhouse
  4624 W. 38th St., 317/291-2663
  7525 Hwy. 31S, 317/881-6283
  3454 W. 86th St., 317/872-4329
  5771 E. 86th St., 317/842-6283
Red Lobster
  5520 W. 38th St., 317/293-3953
  1752 N. Shadeland Ave., 317/352-1679
  690 E. Thompson Rd., 317/786-9201
  6410 E. 82nd St., 317/842-8871
  8846 Signature Dr., 317/876-1101
Ryan's Family Steak House
  8180 Hwy. 31S, 317/881-1156
  6515 N. Keystone Ave., 317/257-9098
  3560 Lafayette Rd., 317/293-8760
  655 N. Shadeland Ave., 317/359-7747
Shoney's
  5613 W. 38th St., 317/298-9708
  7803 E. Washington St., 317/357-5476
  6225 W. Washington St., 317/243-7646
  5010 S. East St., 317/782-9292
  9150 N. Michigan Rd., 317/875-0983
Steak and Ale
  9333 Haver Way, 317/848-1772
  7020 E. 21st St., 317/352-1284
  4302 S. East St., 317/784-2479
  4830 W. 38th St., 317/298-4400
Ben and Jerry's
  1437 E. 86th St., 317/253-9880
  2662 Lake Circle Dr., 317/879-8025
Chuck E. Cheese Pizza
  4910 W. 38th St., 317/299-2544
  8109 E. Washington St., 317/897-2751
Ruth's Chris Steak House
  96th at Keystone, 317/844-1155
Lone Star Steakhouse
  3902 E. 82nd St., 317/594-0050
  8820 Hwy. 31S, 317/882-0413
  10087 E. Washington St., 317/899-3780
  5116 W. 38th St., 317/293-9095

...d Country Buffet
  4873 W. 38th St., 317/293-3409
  6342 E. 82nd St., 317/595-9082
  7783 E. Washington St., 317/356-9236
  4200 S. East St., 317/781-0163

JEFFERSONVILLE, IN

Best Desserts
Jenny Lynn Tea Room
  249 Spring St., 812/283-4832

Best Homestyle Food
Ann's on The River
  149 Spring St., 812/284-2667

Best Italian Food
Parrella's Italian Restaurant
  214 W. Court Ave., 812/283-7933

Best Pizza
Rocky's Sub Pub
  1207 E. Market St., 812/282-3844

Best Sandwiches
Rocky's Sub Pub
  1207 E. Market St., 812/282-3844
Jenny Lynn Tea Room
  249 Spring St., 812/283-4832

Best Seafood
Towboat Annie's
  707 W. Riverside, 812/282-2368

Best Steaks
Frank's Steak House
  520 W. Seventh St., 812/283-3383

KOKOMO, IN

Best Burgers
Sycamore Grill
  113 W. Sycamore, 317/457-2220

Best Chinese Food
Chinese Gourmet
  242 E. Southway Blvd., 317/453-0292

Best German Food
Pumpernickel
  1906 S. Elizabeth, 317/868-7453

Best Ice Cream/Yogurt
Freshens Premium Yogurt
  1826 E. Boulevard, 317/452-9478
Kokomo Frozen Custard
  3107 S. Webster St., 317/453-2482
Del's Ice Cream and Yogurt
  1233 1/2 Reed St., 317/452-3440

Best Italian Food
Fazoli's
  622 S. Reed Rd., 317/868-2538
Martino's Italian Villa
  1929 N. Washington St., 317/457-6621

Best Mexican Food
Hacienda Mexican Restaurant
  2006 S. Plate St., 317/452-8231

Best Pizza
Noble Roman's
  649 N. Dixon Rd., 317/457-9311
  1427 S. Reed Rd., 317/459-0781

Best Sandwiches
Pumpernickel
  1906 S. Elizabeth, 317/868-7453

Best View While Dining
Country Cook-Inn
  Hwy. 1100E at Hwy. 180S, Greentown, 317/628-7676

LA PORTE, IN

Best All-You-Can-Eat Buffet
Miller's Home Cafe
  110 E. Michigan St., New Carlisle, 219/654-3431

Best Breakfast
Christo's Family Dining
  1462 W. State Rd. 2, 219/326-1644
Round the Clock Restaurant
  219 Pine Lake Ave., 219/326-5817
Louie's Cafe
  920 Lincolnway, 219/326-9686

Best Brunch
Tangerine
  601 Michigan Ave., 219/326-8000

Best Burgers
Dick's Bar
  912 Lincolnway, 219/326-9702

Best Coffee
Temple News Agency
  816 Jefferson Ave., 219/362-2676

Best Desserts
Ole's Meat, Fish and Liquor
  502 State St., 219/362-8270
Tangerine
  601 Michigan Ave., 219/326-8000

Best Homestyle Food
Miller's Home Cafe
  110 E. Michigan St., New Carlisle, 219/654-3431

Best Ice Cream/Yogurt
Temple News Agency
  816 Jefferson Ave., 219/362-2676

Best Pizza
Mancino's
  41 Pine Lake Ave., 219/362-9032
Albano's Pizza
  325 J St., 219/325-3331

Best Place to Eat When Someone Else Is Buying
Tangerine
  601 Michigan Ave., 219/326-8000

st Sandwiches
diana Deli and Catering Company
805 Indiana Ave., 219/324-3383

Best Seafood
Kelsey's Steak House
304 Detroit St., 219/325-0000
Tangerine
601 Michigan Ave., 219/326-8000
Ole's Meat, Fish and Liquor
502 State St., 219/362-8270

Best Steaks
Kelsey's Steak House
304 Detroit St., 219/325-0000
Tangerine
601 Michigan Ave., 219/326-8000

LAFAYETTE, IN

Best All-You-Can-Eat Buffet
Sirloin Stockade
4023 State Rd. 26E, 317/448-4210

Best Bar
The Other Pub
3000 S. Ninth St., 317/474-9527

Best Breakfast
Four Boys Manner
1201 Teal Rd., 317/474-6675

Best Burgers
Steak 'N Shake Restaurant
2 Sagamore Pkwy. N., 317/447-6091

Best Business Lunch
Sarge Oak on the Alley
721 Main St., 317/742-5230

Best Casual Dining
The Other Pub
3000 S. Ninth St., 317/474-9527

Best Cheap Meal
Hacienda Mexican Restaurant
112 N. Third St., 317/423-2347

Best Desserts
Jane's Gourmet Deli and Catering
524 N. Fourth St., 317/742-5000

Best Family Restaurant
Arni's
2323 Wallace Ave., 317/447-9436
2200 Elmwood Ave., 317/447-1108

Best Homestyle Food
Sirloin Stockade
4023 State Rd. 26E, 317/448-4210

Best Italian Food
Spaghetti Shop
1947 Elmwood Ave., 317/447-4177

Best Late-Night Food
The Other Pub
3000 S. Ninth St., 317/474-9527

Best Mexican Food
Don Pablo's Mexican Restaurant
50 N. Creasy, 317/449-0511

Best Pizza
Noble Roman's
2919 Sagamore Pkwy. S., 317/447-6905

Best Place to Be "Seen"
The Other Pub
3000 S. Ninth St., 317/474-9527

Best Place to Eat When Someone Else Is Buying
Sarge Oak on the Alley
721 Main St., 317/742-5230

Best Romantic Dining
Patout's
3614 State Rd. 38E, 317/447-5400

Best Salad/Salad Bar
Sergeant Preston's of the North
6 N. Second St., 317/742-7378

Best Sandwiches
The Other Pub
3000 S. Ninth St., 317/474-9527

Best Seafood
Patout's
3614 State Rd. 38E, 317/447-5400

Best Steaks
Sarge Oak on the Alley
721 Main St., 317/742-5230

MARION, IN

Best Atmosphere
Brassery Restaurant
501 E. Fourth St., 317/668-8801
Erma's Restaurant
1197 N. Washington St., 317/668-7680

Best Barbecue/Ribs
King Gyros
1305 W. Kem Rd., 317/662-2666

Best Breakfast
Jim Dandy Restaurant
1229 N. Baldwin Ave., 317/664-6702

Best Brunch
Brassery Restaurant
501 E. Fourth St., 317/668-8801
Marion Cafeteria
201 W. Third St., 317/664-2443

Best Burgers
Myers Drive-In
938 S. Washington St., 317/664-9736

Best Chinese Food
Main Moon
3316 S. Western Ave., 317/662-0503

Desserts
ntown Deli
01 W. Third St., 317/664-2443
ng Gyros
1305 W. Kem Rd., 317/662-2666

Best Health-Conscious Menu
Marion Cafeteria
201 W. Third St., 317/664-2443

Best Homestyle Food
Marketplace Restaurant
428 S. Washington St., 317/668-7004

Best Ice Cream/Yogurt
Ivanhoe's Drive-In
914 S. Main St., Upland, 317/998-7261

Best Pizza
Noble Roman's
1414 W. Kem Rd., 317/662-9941
Pizza King
1212 N. Baldwin Ave., 317/664-0523
3404 S. Adams St., 317/674-6966

Best Place to Take the Kids
Ivanhoe's Drive-In
914 S. Main St., Upland, 317/998-7261

Best Sandwiches
Downtown Deli
201 W. Third St., 317/664-2443
King Gyros
1305 W. Kem Rd., 317/662-2666

Best Seafood
Brassery Restaurant
501 E. Fourth St., 317/668-8801
Erma's Restaurant
1197 N. Washington St., 317/668-7680

Best Soul Food
Marketplace Restaurant
428 S. Washington St., 317/668-7004

Best Steaks
Icehouse
1412 W. Kem Rd., 317/664-6646
Malone's
515 N. Washington St., 317/668-8722

MICHIGAN CITY, IN

Best Breakfast
Minos Family Restaurant
Hwy. 421 at Hwy. 400N, 219/874-6688
Schoop's Hamburgers
4105 Franklin St., 219/872-0170

Best Burgers
Swing Belly's
103 S. Lake Ave., 219/874-5718
Rose Bowl Lanes
2309 Franklin St., 219/874-5935

Best Chinese Food
Fortune House
312 W. Rte. 20, 219/872-6664
Panda Restaurant
3801 Franklin St., 219/872-7566

Best Homestyle Food
Miller's Home Cafe
110 E. Michigan St., New Carlisle, 219/654-3431

Best Italian Food
Rodini Restaurant
4125 Franklin St., 219/879-7388

Best Pizza
Albano's Villa
1612 Franklin St., 219/872-0571

Best Sandwiches
Fifth Street Deli
431 Washington St., 219/872-5204

Best Steaks
Rodini Restaurant
4125 Franklin St., 219/879-7388

Standbys
Red Lobster
4353 Franklin St., 219/879-1328
Shoney's
4600 Franklin St., 219/873-1024

MUNCIE, IN

Best Burgers
Rally's
400 S. Madison St., 317/282-4732
220 E. McGalliard Rd., 317/286-0350

Best Business Lunch
Radisson Hotel
420 S. High St., 317/741-7777

Best Chinese Food
Szechuan Garden
1312 W. McGalliard Rd., 317/289-8007

Best Late-Night Food
Pizza King
Multiple Locations

Best Mexican Food
La Hacienda Mexican Restaurant
2620 S. Madison St., 317/289-0909

Best Pizza
Noble Roman's
3001 N. Oakwood Ave., 317/284-0999

Best Place to Be "Seen"
Radisson Hotel
420 S. High St., 317/741-7777

Best Salad/Salad Bar
Flamingo
1930 W. Kilgore Ave., 317/288-5077

...
...ockade
...w. Hessler Rd., 317/287-9051

...ys
...ountry Buffet
...0 E. McGalliard Rd., 317/288-5562
...rger King
2710 N. Wheeling Ave., 317/289-4095
810 E. McGalliard Rd., 317/282-6557
Ponderosa
2401 S. Madison St., 317/289-2297
3100 N. Oakwood Ave., 317/289-6069
Dairy Queen
640 N. Walnut St., 317/289-9211
2800 S. Madison St., 317/289-0066
The Olive Garden
304 W. McGalliard Rd., 317/287-0450
Red Lobster
223 W. McGalliard Rd., 317/288-6768

NEW ALBANY, IN

Best Barbecue/Ribs
Sloppy's Enterprises
3316 Grant Mine Rd., 812/945-5586

Best Burgers
Ranch House
2612B Charlestown Rd., 812/944-9199

Best Mexican Food
Tumbleweed
2005 State St., 812/945-0177
1638 Slate Run Rd., 812/945-9333

Best Pizza
Hoosier Pizza
132 E. Market, 812/948-2229

Best Sandwiches
Mancino
330 Grant Mine Rd., 812/949-7777

Best Southwestern Food
Tumbleweed
2005 State St., 812/945-0177
1638 Slate Run Rd., 812/945-9333

Best Steaks
Texas Roadhouse
701 E. State Rd. 131, Clarksville, 812/280-1103

RICHMOND, IN

Best Barbecue/Ribs
Damon's
4700 National Rd. E., 317/962-5555

Best Breakfast
Olde Richmond Inn
138 S. Fifth St., 317/962-2247

Best Brunch
Olde Richmond Inn
138 S. Fifth St., 317/962-2247

Best Burgers
Circus Shoppe
820 Promenade, 317/962-4441

Best Chinese Food
Jade Palace Chinese Restaurant
4340 National Rd. E., 317/935-4575

Best Coffee
Anything Goes
704 Promenade, 317/966-4637

Best Health-Conscious Menu
MCL Richmond Cafeteria
3801 E. Main St., 317/966-2939

Best Italian Food
Fazoli's
4711 National Rd. E., 317/935-6219

Best Mexican Food
Pedro's Mexican Restaurant
540 W. Eaton Pike, 317/966-1330

Best Pizza
Clara's Pizza King
203 W. Main St., 317/966-1541

Best Sandwiches
Court Cafe
211 S. Fifth St., 317/962-0359

Best Steaks
Country Rib Eye Steakhouse
725 Progress Dr., 317/966-4902

Standbys
Bob Evans
401 Commerce Dr., 317/966-7740
Cracker Barrel
6050 National Rd. E., 317/935-0881

SOUTH BEND, IN

Best All-You-Can-Eat Buffet
Bennett's Buffet
120 Dixie Way N., 219/727-7644

Best American Food
La Salle Grill
115 W. Colfax Ave., 219/288-1155
Tippecanoe Place Restaurant
620 W. Washington St., 219/234-9077

Best Bar
Heartland Texas Barbecue
222 S. Michigan St., 219/234-5200

Best Barbecue/Ribs
Heartland Texas Barbecue
222 S. Michigan St., 219/234-5200

Best Breakfast
Morse Inn
Notre Dame University, 219/631-2000

e Place Restaurant
Washington St., 219/234-9077

rgers
e Doon Ice Cream Corp.
19 S. Michigan St., 219/288-0112
030 Lincoln Way W., 219/234-5995
52446 Dixie Way N., 219/272-2500

Best Casual Dining
Emporium
121 S. Nile, 219/234-9000

Best Continental Food
Tippecanoe Place Restaurant
620 W. Washington St., 219/234-9077

Best Delicatessen
Macri's Milano Inn Pizza
61021 Hwy. 31, 219/291-4308

Best Dinner
Emporium
121 S. Nile, 219/234-9000

Best Fast Food
Bonnie Doon Ice Cream Corp.
1619 S. Michigan St., 219/288-0112
3030 Lincoln Way W., 219/234-5995
52446 Dixie Way N., 219/272-2500

Best German Food
Hans Haus
2803 S. Michigan St., 219/291-5522

Best Mexican Food
Hacienda Mexican Restaurant
1224 Scottsdale Mall, 219/291-2566
1501 N. Ironwood Dr., 219/272-5922
3302 Mishawaka Ave., 219/234-3700

Best Pizza
Edwardo's Natural Pizza
235 S. Michigan St., 219/233-1000
Macri's Milano Inn Pizza
61021 Hwy. 31, 219/291-4308

Best Soul Food
Franny's Restaurant
416 S. Main St., 219/232-2165

Best Steaks
Emporium
121 S. Nile, 219/234-9000
Morse Inn
Notre Dame University, 219/631-2000

TERRE HAUTE, IN

Best Bars
Ballyhoo Pizza King
900 Chestnut St., 812/232-3939
2405 Poplar St., 812/232-3423

The Terminal
820 Wabash Ave., 812/232-8480
Larry Byrd's Boston Connection
555 S. Third St., 812/235-3333

Best Brunch
Marriott Hotel
St. Mary of the Woods College, St. Mary's Rd.,
812/535-4285

Best Burgers
Bohannon's
1728 Wabash Ave., 812/234-2638
2961 S. Seventh St., 812/232-9305

Best Business Lunch
Larry Byrd's Boston Connection
555 S. Third St., 812/235-3333

Best Chinese Food
Peking Chinese Restaurant
2828 S. Third St., 812/232-0665

Best Homestyle Food
Gran-Ma Joy's
3631 Wabash Ave., 812/232-6598

Best Italian Food
Louise's Restaurant
1849 S. Third St., 812/232-4989

Best Mexican Food
Cancun Mexican Restaurant
3495 S. Fourth St., 812/232-4347

Best Place to Be "Seen"
Garfield's Restaurant
201 W. Division St., Evansville, 812/421-1171

Best Place to Eat When Someone Else Is Buying
Runyon's Black Angus
502 S. Third St., 812/235-5549

Best Romantic Dining
Pino's Il Sonetto
4234 S. Seventh St., 812/299-9255

Best Salad/Salad Bar
Western Rib-Eye Restaurant
100 S. Fruitridge Ave., 812/232-5591

Best Sandwiches
Candy's Deli Corner
3030 S. Seventh St., 812/234-0222

Best Steaks
Runyon's Black Angus
502 S. Third St., 812/235-5549

Best Tea Room
Beaver House
1430 S. 25th St., 812/232-8992

Standbys
Ponderosa
3401 S. Hwy. 41, 812/232-6260
2301 Wabash Ave., 812/235-1243

Denny's
   3442 Hwy. 41, 812/235-5739
   233 S. Third St., 812/234-0699
Applebee's
   2506 S. Third St., 812/232-2661
Taco Bell
   3636 S. Hwy. 41, 812/234-5455
   3132 Wabash Ave., 812/234-4307
   2105 Lafayette Ave., 812/466-6875
Chi Chi's
   3830 S. Hwy. 41, 812/234-2248
Baskin-Robbins
   3801 Wabash Ave., 812/232-5200
   428 Wabash Ave., 812/232-5825
Pizza Hut
   2400 S. Third St., 812/232-3462
   3401 S. Hwy. 41, 812/232-7147
   3040 Wabash Ave., 812/232-6231
   2001 Lafayette Ave., 812/466-6868
Red Lobster
   3407 S. Hwy. 41, 812/234-7727

VALPARAISO, IN

Best Barbecue/Ribs
Wagner's Too
   597 W. Hwy. 30, 219/759-6334

Best Breakfast
Schoop's Hamburgers
   2816 Calumet Ave., 219/464-2996
Round the Clock Restaurant
   217 E. Lincolnway, 219/462-6339
Big Wheel Restaurant
   902 Lincolnway, 219/462-4169

Best Chinese Food
China House
   120 E. Lincolnway, 219/462-5788

Best Coffee
Coffee and Tea Market
   157 Lincolnway, 219/462-7265

Best Homestyle Food
Strongbow Inn
   2405 Hwy. 30, 219/462-5121
Birky's Cafe
   205 S. Main St., Kouts, 219/766-3851

Best Italian Food
Fazoli's
   2809 Calumet Ave., 219/531-0001
Billy Jack's Cafe and Grill
   2904 Calumet Ave., 219/477-3797

Best Pizza
Giggles Pizza
   1901 Calumet Ave., 219/462-9945

Best Salad/Salad Bar
Billy Jack's Cafe and Grill
   2904 Calumet Ave., 219/477-3797

Best Sandwiches
D'Ouevres by Dottie
  21 E. Lincolnway, 219/462-1416

Best Seafood
Clayton's
  66 W. Lincolnway, 219/531-0612

Best Southwestern Food
Billy Jack's Cafe and Grill
  2904 Calumet Ave., 219/477-3797

Best Steaks
Kelsey's Steak House
  1905 Northland Dr., 219/465-4022

VINCENNES, IN

Best All-You-Can-Eat Buffet
Executive Inn
  1 Executive Blvd., 812/886-5000

Best Barbecue/Ribs
Oink's Gourmet BBQ
  1003 Main St., 812/882-3311

Best Burgers
Market Restaurant and Pub
  106 St. Honore Pl., 812/886-5201

Best Chinese Food
Hong Kong Restaurant
  2447 N. Sixth St., 812/882-0508
Marone's Formosa Gardens
  101 N. Second St., 812/882-0460

Best Ice Cream/Yogurt
Lic's Ice Cream and Sandwich Shop
  2815 N. Sixth St., 812/882-3526

Best Pizza
Bill Bobe's Pizzeria
  1651 N. Sixth St., 812/882-2992

Best Sandwiches
Market Restaurant and Pub
  106 St. Honore Pl., 812/886-5201

Standbys
Ponderosa
  2625 Hart St., 812/882-9469

WARSAW, IN

Best Breakfast
American Table Restaurant
  3575 Lake City Hwy., 219/267-8171
Richard's Restaurant
  975 Anchorage Rd., 219/267-3244

Best Cajun/Creole Food
Orion's Restaurant
  1700 Rozella Rd., 219/269-9100

Best Desserts
Mosaic
  115 S. Buffalo St., 219/269-5080

Best Pizza
Gordy's Sub Pub
   321 S. Buffalo St., 219/269-6963

Best Place to Eat When Someone Else Is Buying
Mosaic
   115 S. Buffalo St., 219/269-5080

Best Salad/Salad Bar
Mosaic
   115 S. Buffalo St., 219/269-5080

Best Sandwiches
Barbee Hotel Bar and Grill
   3620 N. Barbee Rd., 219/834-2984
Gordy's Sub Pub
   321 S. Buffalo St., 219/269-6963

Best Seafood
Barbee Hotel Bar and Grill
   3620 N. Barbee Rd., 219/834-2984
Wolfgang's Restaurant
   617 S. Buffalo St., 219/269-6678
Mosaic
   115 S. Buffalo St., 219/269-5080

Best Steaks
Barbee Hotel Bar and Grill
   3620 N. Barbee Rd., 219/834-2984
Wolfgang's Restaurant
   617 S. Buffalo St., 219/269-6678
City Limits
   1535 N. Detroit St., 219/269-3875

Iowa

AMES, IA

Best American Food
Aunt Maude's
547 Main St., 515/233-4136

Best Barbecue/Ribs
Battle's Bar-B-Q
112 Hayward Ave., 515/292-1670

Best Homestyle Food
Ivy's Garden Cafe
517 Grand Ave., 515/232-0275

Best Italian Food
Lucullan's Restaurant
400 Main St., 515/232-8484

Best Japanese Food
The Mikado
320 S. Sixteenth St., 515/232-6418

Best Mexican Food
O'Malley and McGee's Cafe
716 S. Duff Ave., 515/232-0007

Best Steaks
Hickory Park
121 S. Sixth St., 515/232-8940
The Broiler
6008 W. Lincoln Way, 515/292-2516
The Open Flame Steak and Lounge
Main St., Gilbert, 515/232-9745

BURLINGTON, IA

Best Barbecue/Ribs
Dillon's Real Pit Barbeque
2107 N. Roosevelt Ave., 319/752-4263

Best Breakfast
J.J. Maguire's Restaurant
3001 Winegard Dr., 319/753-2291

Best Burgers
J.J. Maguire's Restaurant
3001 Winegard Dr., 319/753-2291

Best Chinese Food
Great Wall
  3103 Kirkwood St., 319/753-6788

Best Homestyle Food
Pantry Restaurant
  325 Angular St., 319/753-1593

Best Ice Cream/Yogurt
Bridgeman's Restaurant
  1414 N. Roosevelt, 319/752-8541

Best Mexican Food
Carlos O'Kelley's
  321 N. Roosevelt, 319/753-9800

Best Sandwiches
Big Muddy's
  710 N. Front St., 319/753-1699
Pantry Restaurant
  325 Angular St., 319/753-1593

Best Steaks
Big Muddy's
  710 N. Front St., 319/753-1699
J.J. Maguire's Restaurant
  3001 Winegard Dr., 319/753-2291

CEDAR RAPIDS, IA

Best Burgers
Ragtop Diner
  240 Classic Car Ct. SW, 319/366-6070

Best Business Lunch
Ashley's Restaurant
  201 Third Ave. SE, Ste. 50, 319/364-2509

Best Casual Dining
Ragtop Diner
  240 Classic Car Ct. SW, 319/366-6070

Best Cheap Meal
Zio Johno's Spaghetti House
  1125 First Ave. SE, 319/362-9667
  4640 First Ave. NE, 319/393-5900
  355 Edgewood Rd. NW, 319/396-1700

Best Chinese Food
Pei's Mandarin Restaurant
  3287 Sixth St. SW, 319/362-6165

Best Delicatessen
Ashley's Restaurant
  201 Third Ave. SE, Ste. 50, 319/364-2509

Best Family Restaurant
Zio Johno's Spaghetti House
  1125 First Ave. SE, 319/362-9667
  4640 First Ave. NE, 319/393-5900
  355 Edgewood Rd. NW, 319/396-1700

Best German Food
Brick Haus Restaurant
  118 First St., Amana, 319/622-3278
Colony Inn
  Main St., Amana, 319/622-6270

Ox Yoke Inn
  Main St., Amana, 319/622-3441

Best Italian Food
Isabel's Italian Grill
  715 First Ave. SW, 319/363-7344
Zio Johno's Spaghetti House
  1125 First Ave. SE, 319/362-9667
  4640 First Ave. NE, 319/393-5900
  355 Edgewood Rd. NW, 319/396-1700

Best Mexican Food
Papa Juan's Mexican Restaurant
  5505 Center Point Rd. NE, 319/393-0258

Best Place to Take the Kids
Zio Johno's Spaghetti House
  1125 First Ave. SE, 319/362-9667
  4640 First Ave. NE, 319/393-5900
  355 Edgewood Rd. NW, 319/396-1700

Best Salad/Salad Bar
Ashley's Restaurant
  201 Third Ave. SE, Ste. 50, 319/364-2509

Best Sandwiches
Flamingo Pizza Palace
  1211 Ellis Blvd. NW, 319/364-9926

Best Seafood
Winifred's
  3847 First Ave. SE, 319/364-6125

Best Steaks
Amalgamated Spirit and Provisions
  3320 Southgate Ct. SW, 319/363-2031
  4401 First Ave. SE, 319/393-9727
Winifred's
  3847 First Ave. SE, 319/364-6125

Standbys
Ryan's Family Steak House
  230 Collins Rd. NE, 319/377-9722

CLINTON, IA

Best Restaurants in Town
Rastelli's
  238 Main Ave., 319/242-7441
Holiday Harry's
  226 Fifth Ave. S., 319/243-5736
The Frontier Motor Inn Restaurant
  2300 Lincoln Way, 319/242-7112
The Unicorn
  1004 N. Second St., 319/242-7355
McKinley Street Taverne
  2301 McKinley St., 319/242-3134

Best Chinese Food
Yen Ching Restaurant
  1105 N. Second St., 319/242-6422

COUNCIL BLUFFS, IA

Best Restaurant in Town
Pizza King
 1101 N. Broadway, 712/323-4911

Best All-You-Can-Eat Buffet
Best Western Inn
 2216 27th Ave., 712/322-3150

Best American Food
Gallagher's Restaurant
 10730 Pacific St., 402/393-1421

Best Breakfast
Hy Vee Food Store
 1706 N. Sixteenth St., 712/328-9792
 1745 Madison Ave., 712/322-9260

Best Business Lunch
Bleu Ox West
 3549 W. Broadway, 712/323-6848

Best Casual Dining
Christy Creme
 2733 N. Broadway, 712/322-2778

Best Chinese Food
Royal China Restaurant
 9006 Maple St., 402/571-6910

Best Desserts
Village Inn
 2935 W. Broadway, 712/328-7377
 1131 N. Broadway, 712/328-8212

Best Health-Conscious Menu
Barn'rds Old Fashioned Roast Beef
 623 W. Broadway, 712/323-3278

Best Homestyle Food
Iowa Feed and Grain
 I-29 at Honey Creek Rd., Crescent, 712/545-3190

Best Italian Food
Mister C's Steakhouse
 5319 N. 30th St., Omaha, 402/451-1998

Best Mexican Food
Romeo's
 1821 W. Broadway, 712/323-0042

Best Place to Take the Kids
Royal Fork Buffet
 1751 Madison Ave., 712/323-3398

Best Salad/Salad Bar
Club 64
 701 McKenzie Ave., 712/323-6464

Best Seafood
Gurney's Restaurant
 229 S. Sixth St., Missouri Valley, 712/642-2580

Best Tea Room
Garden Cafe
 1707 Madison Ave., 712/322-2233

Standbys
Little Caesar's
 1824 W. Broadway, 712/325-1030

DAVENPORT, IA

Best Restaurant in Town
Kernan's Riverview Restaurant
 333 River Dr., Princeton, 319/289-5137

Best American Food
Ross' Restaurant
 430 Fourteenth St., Bettendorf, 319/355-7573
Kernan's Riverview Restaurant
 333 River Dr., Princeton, 319/289-5137

Best Bar
Pat McGuire's Irish Cafe
 3333 N. Harrison St., 319/386-0090

Best Breakfast
Harlan's Fine Foods
 3923 W. Kimberly Rd., 319/391-5560

Best Burgers
Pat McGuire's Irish Cafe
 3333 N. Harrison St., 319/386-0090

Best Business Lunch
Pat McGuire's Irish Cafe
 3333 N. Harrison St., 319/386-0090
Ross' Restaurant
 430 Fourteenth St., Bettendorf, 319/355-7573

Best Homestyle Food
Harlan's Fine Foods
 3923 W. Kimberly Rd., 319/391-5560

Best Italian Food
Lunardi's Supermarkets
 102 E. Kimberly Rd., 319/388-0001

Best Mexican Food
Rudy's Tacos
 326 Cedar St., 319/322-0662
 2214 E. Eleventh St., 319/322-0668
 4334 N. Brady St., 319/386-2475

Best Pizza
Dudley's Davenport Pizza
 1720 E. Kimberly Rd., 319/359-4411
Happy Joe's Pizza and Ice Cream
 2630 Rockingham Rd., 319/324-0477
 1414 W. Locust St., 319/324-5656
 201 E. 50th St., 319/386-1766
 320 W. Kimberly Rd., 319/386-5415

Best Salad/Salad Bar
Happy Joe's Pizza and Ice Cream
 2630 Rockingham Rd., 319/324-0477
 1414 W. Locust St., 319/324-5656
 201 E. 50th St., 319/386-1766
 320 W. Kimberly Rd., 319/386-5415

Best Sandwiches
Dudley's Davenport Pizza
   1720 E. Kimberly Rd., 319/359-4411

Best Seafood
Dock Steak Seafood Spirits
   125 S. Perry St., 319/322-5331
Captain's Table
   4801 River Dr., Moline, 309/797-9222
Kernan's Riverview Restaurant
   333 River Dr., Princeton, 319/289-5137

Best Steaks
Captain's Table
   4801 River Dr., Moline, 309/797-9222

DES MOINES, IA

Best American Food
Christopher's Clothiers
   2816 Beaver Ave., 515/274-3694
Champion Sports
   I-35 at First St., 515/964-1717
Eighth Street Seafood Bar and Grill
   1261 Eighth St., West Des Moines, 515/223-8808
Greenbriar Restaurant and Bar
   5810 Merle Hay Rd., 515/253-0124

Best Atmosphere
Greenbriar Restaurant and Bar
   5810 Merle Hay Rd., 515/253-0124

Best Breakfast
Boswell's Select Foods
   1409 Martin Luther King Jr. Pkwy., 515/243-9518
Drake Diner
   1111 25th St., 515/277-1111

Best Burgers
Stella's Blue Sky Diner
   400 Locust St., 515/246-1953

Best Business Lunch
Stella's Blue Sky Diner
   400 Locust St., 515/246-1953
Jimmy's American Cafe
   1238 Eighth St., West Des Moines, 515/224-1212

Best Casual Dining
Chicago Speakeasy
   1520 Euclid Ave., 515/243-3141

Best Diner
Drake Diner
   1111 25th St., 515/277-1111

Best Dinner
Iowa Beef Steak House
   1201 E. Euclid Ave., 515/262-1138
Greenbriar Restaurant and Bar
   5810 Merle Hay Rd., 515/253-0124

Best Family Restaurant
Iowa Machine Shed Restaurant
   11151 Hickman Rd., Urbandale, 515/270-6818

Best Homestyle Food
Boswell's Select Foods
   1409 Martin Luther King Jr. Pkwy., 515/243-9518
Iowa Machine Shed Restaurant
   11151 Hickman Rd., Urbandale, 515/270-6818

Best Italian Food
Christopher's Clothiers
   2816 Beaver Ave., 515/274-3694
Riccelli's Restaurant
   3803 Indianola Ave., 515/288-7755
Cosi Cucina Italian Grill
   1975 NW 86th St., 515/278-8148
Noah's Ark Restaurant and Lounge
   2400 Ingersoll Ave., 515/288-2246

Best Mexican Food
Nacho Mammas
   216 Court Ave., 515/280-6262

Best Pizza
Orlondo's Italian Restaurant
   3835 University Ave., 515/277-3600
Tavern
   205 Fifth St., West Des Moines, 515/255-9827

Best Salad/Salad Bar
Stella's Blue Sky Diner
   400 Locust St., 515/246-1953
Chicago Speakeasy
   1520 Euclid Ave., 515/243-3141

Best Seafood
Pier
   4555 Fleur Dr., 515/285-6996
Eighth Street Seafood Bar and Grill
   1261 Eighth St., West Des Moines, 515/223-8808

Best Steaks
Christopher's
   2816 Beaver Ave., 515/274-3694
Iowa Beef Steak House
   1201 E. Euclid Ave., 515/262-1138
Duffy's Bar and Grill
   I-35 at First St., 515/964-1717

DUBUQUE, IA

Best All-You-Can-Eat Buffet
Bishop's Cafeteria
   555 John F. Kennedy Rd., 319/588-2031

Best Bars
Circle Saloon
   806 Pleasant St., La Motte, 319/773-2352
3100 Club
   Midway Hotel, 3100 Dodge St., 319/557-8900

Best Breakfast
Timmerman's
   7777 Timmerman Dr., East Dubuque, 815/747-3181

Best Brunch
Timmerman's
   7777 Timmerman Dr., East Dubuque, 815/747-3181

Best Burgers
Dubuque Mining Company
  555 John F. Kennedy Rd., 319/557-1729
West Dubuque Tap
  1701 Ashbury St., 319/556-9647

Best Business Lunch
Tollbridge Inn
  2800 Rhomberg Ave., 319/556-5566

Best Casual Dining
Mario's Pizza and Restaurant
  1298 Main St., 319/556-9424
Papa Sarducci's
  1895 John F. Kennedy Rd., 319/583-1371
The Shot Tower Inn
  395 W. Ninth St., 319/582-7057

Best Cheap Meal
Papa Sarducci's
  1895 John F. Kennedy Rd., 319/583-1371

Best Chinese Food
Yen Ching Restaurant
  926 Main St., 319/556-2574
House of China
  801 Main St., 319/582-7565

Best Coffee
Take Five
  371 Bluff St., 319/557-2506
The Last Drop Java Joint
  1120 University Ave., 319/583-1577

Best Diners
Beanie's Cafe
  1400 Central Ave., 319/557-9533
Dottie's Cafe
  504 Central Ave., 319/556-9617

Best Family Restaurants
Papa Sarducci's
  1895 John F. Kennedy Rd., 319/583-1371
The Shot Tower Inn
  395 W. Ninth St., 319/582-7057

Best Homestyle Food
Dottie's Cafe
  504 Central Ave., 319/556-9617
Busy Bee Cafe
  1958 Central Ave., 319/583-1567
West Dubuque Tap
  1701 Ashbury St., 319/556-9647

Best Ice Cream/Yogurt
Happy Joe's Pizza and Ice Cream
  855 Century Dr., 319/556-0820
  1099 University Ave., 319/556-0823
Yogurt D'Lite Coffee Shop
  469 Bluff St., 319/557-8825

Best Italian Food
Mario's Pizza and Restaurant
  1298 Main St., 319/556-9424

Papa Sarducci's
1895 John F. Kennedy Rd., 319/583-1371
Pasta O'Shea's
395 W. Ninth St., 319/582-7057

Best Mexican Food
The Silver Dollar Cantina
342 Main St., 319/556-9327

Best Pizza
Happy Joe's Pizza and Ice Cream
855 Century Dr., 319/556-0820
1099 University Ave., 319/556-0823

Best Place to Eat Alone
Pasta O'Shea's
395 W. Ninth St., 319/582-7057

Best Places to Eat When Someone Else Is Buying
Tollbridge Inn
2800 Rhomberg Ave., 319/556-5566
Timmerman's
7777 Timmerman Dr., East Dubuque, 815/747-3181

Best Places to Take the Kids
Shot Tower Inn
395 W. Ninth St., 319/582-7057
Papa Sarducci's
1895 John F. Kennedy Rd., 319/583-1371

Best Romantic Dining
Mario's Pizza and Restaurant
1298 Main St., 319/556-9424
Tollbridge Inn
2800 Rhomberg Ave., 319/556-5566

Best Salad/Salad Bar
Hoffman House Restaurant
3100 Dodge St., 319/557-8900

Best Sandwiches
Dubuque Mining Company
555 John F. Kennedy Rd., 319/557-1729

Best Southwestern Food
Laredo's
225 W. Sixth St., 319/582-3294

Best Steaks
Tollbridge Inn
2800 Rhomberg Ave., 319/556-5566
Morocco
1413 Rockdale Rd., 319/582-2947

Best Tea Room
Heirloom Treasures and Tea Room
411 Bluff St., 319/557-8072

Standbys
Ponderosa
2035 John F. Kennedy Rd., 319/556-5543
Ground Round
50 John F. Kennedy Rd., 319/556-3540

FT. DODGE, IA

Best Restaurants in Town
Marvin Gardens
809 Central Ave., 515/955-5333
The Sports Page Bar and Grill
2707 N. Fifteenth St., 515/955-1890

Best American Food
Colonial Inn
1306 A St., 515/576-5757
Hickory House
3022 Fifth Ave. S., 515/955-2722

Best Brunch
Colonial Inn
1306 A St., 515/576-5757

Best Chinese Food
Ching Dow
21 S. Twelfth St., 515/576-3838
Won Ton Inn
425 Second Ave. S., 515/573-5929

Best Desserts
Bloomer's on Central
900 Central Ave., 515/955-2221

Best Sandwiches
Bloomer's on Central
900 Central Ave., 515/955-2221

IOWA CITY, IA

Best Restaurant in Town
House of Lords Restaurant
704 First Ave., Coralville, 319/351-0400

Best Bar
Wig and Pen
1220 Hwy. 6W, 319/354-2767

Best Breakfast
J.C.'s Cafe
1910 S. Gilbert St., 319/351-2756

Best Burgers
Flannigan's Bar and Grill
501 First Ave., Coralville, 319/351-1904

Best Business Lunch
Season's Best Restaurant and Bar
325 E. Washington St., Ste. 15, 319/337-2378

Best Casual Dining
The Mill Restaurant
120 E. Burlington St., 319/351-9529

Best Cheap Meal
Hawk I Feed and Relay
903 First Ave., Coralville, 319/354-3335

Best Chinese Food
Hunan Restaurant
118 Second St., Coralville, 319/338-8885

Best Desserts
Season's Best Restaurant and Bar
325 E. Washington St., Ste. 15, 319/337-2378

Best Diner
Hamburg Inn
214 N. Linn St., 319/337-5512

Best Family Restaurant
Country Kitchen
1402 S. Gilbert St., 319/337-7696

Best Homestyle Food
Hawk I Feed and Relay
903 First Ave., Coralville, 319/354-3335

Best Italian Food
Brown Bottle
115 E. Washington St., 319/351-6704
Givanni's
109 E. College St., 319/338-5967

Best Late-Night Food
Village Inn
9 Sturgis Corner Dr., 319/351-1094

Best Mexican Food
Carlos O'Kelley's
1411 Waterfront Dr., 319/354-5800

Best Pizza
The Sanctuary Restaurant and Pub
405 S. Gilbert St., 319/351-5692
The Mill Restaurant
120 E. Burlington St., 319/351-9529

Best Place to Be "Seen"
Mondo's Tomato Pie
516 Second St., Coralville, 319/337-3000

Best Place to Eat Alone
Bushnell's Turtle
127 E. College St., 319/351-5536

Best Place to Eat When Someone Else Is Buying
Highlander Inn Restaurant
2525 N. Dodge St., 319/354-2000

Best Romantic Dining
Iowa River Power Company
501 First Ave., Coralville, 319/351-1904

Best Sandwiches
Slugger's Sports Bar and Grill
303 Second St., 319/354-4459

Best Steaks
Lark Supper Club
Hwy. 6W, Tiffin, 319/645-2461

Best Vegetarian Food
Masala Indian Vegetarian Cuisine
9 S. Dubuque St., 319/338-6199

Best Other Restaurants
Vito's
118 E. College St., 319/338-1393

Bruegger's Bagel Bakery
225 Iowa Ave., 319/354-5343
715 S. Riverside Dr., 319/337-6795

Standbys
Golden Corral Family Steak House
621 S. Riverside Dr., 319/354-2991
Red Lobster
163 Collins Rd. NE, Cedar Rapids, 319/395-0450

LE MARS, IA

Best All-You-Can-Eat Buffet
King Sea Chinese Restaurant
630 Eighth Ave. SW, 712/546-1666

Best Chinese Food
King Sea Chinese Restaurant
630 Eighth Ave. SW, 712/546-1666

Best Family Restaurants
East Side Restaurant
125 Plymouth St. NE, 712/546-4406
Pantry Cafe
15 First St. NE, 712/546-6800

Best Pizza
Godfather's Pizza
Hwy. 75S, 712/546-4159

Best Place to Take the Kids
Bob's Drive-In
Hwy. 75S, 712/546-5445

Best Sandwiches
Susie's Deli
Hwy. 75S at Fourth Ave., 712/546-9555

Best Steaks
Archie's Waeside
224 Fourth Ave. NE, 712/546-7011
Depot Steakhouse and Lounge
45 Third Ave. NE, 712/546-5918

MARSHALLTOWN, IA

Best Breakfast
Cecil's Cafe
Hwy. 30 at Hwy. 14, 515/753-9796

Best Burgers
Maid Rite
106 S. Third Ave., 515/753-9684

Best Coffee
Muddy Waters
14 W. Main, 515/754-9082

Best Homestyle Food
Country Kitchen
2003 S. Center St., 515/752-7363

Best Mexican Food
Taco John's
907 S. Center St., 515/753-6211

Best Pizza
Zeno's Pizza
109 E. Main St., 515/752-1245

Best Sandwiches
Maid Rite
106 S. Third Ave., 515/753-9684

Best Steaks
Rube's Lounge's Supper Club
501 Elm St., Montour, 515/492-6222
Jax Supper Club
903 W. Lincoln Way, 515/752-7711

MASON CITY, IA

Best Barbecue/Ribs
Bill's Bar-B-Q
215 S. Madison Ave., 515/424-4944

Best Breakfast
Country Kitchen
Willowbrook Plz., 515/423-4000

Best Chinese Food
Best of China
2751 Fourth St. SW, 515/424-5315

Best Coffee
Cupper's
11 Second St. NE, 515/424-5616

Best Homestyle Food
Checkered Flag Cafe
1327 N. Federal Ave., 515/423-8888

Best Ice Cream/Yogurt
Birdsall Ice Cream
518 N. Federal Ave., 515/423-5365
100 S. Federal Ave., 515/424-5445

Best Mexican Food
Pastime Gardens
404 S. Madison, 515/423-8896

Best Sandwiches
Bagel Depot
124 Fourth St. SW, 515/424-0100
Hungry Mind
16 S. Commercial Alley, 515/423-0121

Best Seafood
Max Sea's
1828 S. Taft, 515/424-0438
Prime and Wine
3000 Fourth St. SW, 515/424-8153

Best Steaks
Prime and Wine
3000 Fourth St. SW, 515/424-8153

MUSCATINE, IA

Best Restaurant in Town
Hotel Muscatine
101 W. Mississippi Dr., 319/263-8231

Best Mexican Food
El Charro Restaurant and Tavern
209 N. Todds Ferry Rd., 319/725-4242

Best Seafood
The Catfish Place
425 Main St., Nichols, 319/723-4330

Best 24-Hour Restaurant
The Sports Page Bar and Grill
2707 N. Fifteenth St., 515/955-1890

OTTUMWA, IA

Best All-You-Can-Eat Buffet
Sirloin Stockade
2645 Northgate Dr., 515/682-8731

Best Barbecue/Ribs
Carl's Barbeque Pit
708 E. Main St., 515/682-3828

Best Breakfast
Country Kitchen
1107 N. Quincy Ave., 515/682-0776

Best Chinese Food
Ching Dow Restaurant
704 Richmond Ave., 515/683-3133

Best Family Restaurants
Greenbriar
1207 N. Jefferson St., 515/682-8147
Stanley's Restaurant
345 Richmond Ave., 515/682-1213

Best Homestyle Food
Canteen Lunch in the Alley
112 E. Second St., 515/682-5320
Ellis Tenderloins and Ice Cream
233 N. Sheridan Ave., 515/683-1105
Maid Rite
107 N. Market St., 515/682-7385
1110 N. Quincy Ave., 515/684-8823

Best Mexican Food
Fiesta Cantina
2519 Northgate St., 515/682-8541

Best Pizza
Happy Joe's Pizza and Ice Cream
315 Church St., 515/682-0125
Breadeaux Pisa
401 E. Main St., 515/684-4617

Best Places to Take the Kids
Happy Joe's Pizza and Ice Cream
315 Church St., 515/682-0125
Breadeaux Pisa
401 E. Main St., 515/684-4617
Sirloin Stockade
2645 Northgate Dr., 515/682-8731
Stanley's Restaurant
345 Richmond Ave., 515/682-1213

Best Salad/Salad Bar
Sirloin Stockade
  2645 Northgate Dr., 515/682-8731

Best Seafood
Fisherman's Bay
  221 N. Wapello St., 515/682-6325

Best Thai Food
Wang's Chinese Kitchen
  121 N. Market St., Oskaloosa, 515/673-7777

Standbys
Baskin-Robbins
  619 Pennsylvania Ave., 515/682-7922
  1110 N. Quincy Ave., 515/682-6131

RED OAK, IA

Best All-You-Can-Eat Buffet
Red Coach Inn
  N. Hwy. 34, 712/623-4864

Best Breakfast
JD Cafe
  709 N. Broadway St., 712/623-9600
Reed Street Cafe
  311 Reed St., 712/623-4322

Best Chinese Food
China Gate
  1402 W. Sheridan Ave., Shenandoah, 712/246-4150

Best Mexican Food
Taco Tico
  900 Senate Ave., 712/623-2012

Best Pizza
Breadeaux Pisa
  308 Coolbaugh St., 712/623-5488

Best Salad/Salad Bar
Red Coach Inn
  N. Hwy. 34, 712/623-4864

Best Steaks
Johnny's Steak House
  101 Broadway, 712/623-3136
Red Lion Pizza and Steak House
  203 Coolbaugh St., 712/623-9545

Standbys
Dairy Queen
  805 N. Broadway St., 712/623-4514

SIOUX CITY, IA

Best All-You-Can-Eat Buffet
Eastgate
  5900 E. Gordon Dr., 712/276-5126

Best Bar
The Marina Inn
  Fourth at B St., 402/494-4000

Best Breakfast
Dizzy's Diner
  620 S. Louis Blvd., 712/258-4727

Best Burgers
Dizzy's Diner
620 S. Louis Blvd., 712/258-4727

Best Business Lunch
First Edition
416 Jackson St., 712/277-3200

Best Chinese Food
King Sea Chinese Restaurant
512 Fifth St., 712/255-0222
Hunan Palace
4280 Sergeant Rd., 712/274-2336

Best Coffee
Espresso Cafe
4280 Sergeant Rd., 712/274-7122

Best Diner
Dizzy's Diner
620 S. Louis Blvd., 712/258-4727

Best Family Restaurants
Harvey's
5307 Military Rd., 712/233-1337
Green Gables
1800 Pierce St., 712/258-4246

Best Place to Be "Seen"
The Marina Inn
Fourth at B St., 402/494-4000

Best Salad/Salad Bar
John's Steak House
1100 Steuben St., 712/277-4403
Theo's Steak House
1911 Hwy. 20, Lawton, 712/944-5731

Best Vegetarian Food
Minerva's
2901 Hamilton Blvd., 712/252-1012

Standbys
Applebee's
1700 Hamilton Dr., 712/233-2226
4555 Southern Hills Dr., 712/276-2226
TCBY
2129 Hamilton Blvd., 712/252-2730
4289 Sergeant Rd., 712/274-7484
Domino's Pizza
4021 Floyd Blvd., 712/239-1100

STORM LAKE, IA

Best All-You-Can-Eat Buffet
Ken-A-Bob Buffet
606 Flindt Dr., 712/732-2091

Best Breakfast
Lakeshore Cafe
1520 Lake Ave., 712/732-9800
Country Kitchen
Hwy. 71N, 712/732-9920

Best Burgers
Embers
723 Lake Ave., 712/732-9887
Boz-Wellz
507 Erie St., 712/732-3616

Best Chinese Food
China House
624 W. Milwaukee Ave., 712/732-1676
Yen Ching Palace
1411 E. Lakeshore Dr., 712/732-1081

Best Coffee
Flying Pig Cafe
617 Lake Ave., 712/732-5636

Best Desserts
Flying Pig Cafe
617 Lake Ave., 712/732-5636

Best Homestyle Food
Pantry
505 Lake Ave., 712/732-3240
Villager Restaurant
421 Flindt Dr., 712/732-2372

Best Pizza
Godfather's Pizza
Hwy. 7 at 71, 712/732-2965
Honey-Kissed Pizza
116 W. Milwaukee Ave., 712/732-2222

Best Steaks
Baker's Court
1605 W. Milwaukee Ave., 712/732-6298
Boat House
502 Lake Ave., 712/732-1462

Standbys
Dairy Queen
820 Flindt Dr., 712/732-6290
Subway
1125 N. Lake Ave., 712/732-5215

WATERLOO, IA

Best Restaurant in Town
Victoria's by the Park
323 W. Second St., Cedar Falls, 319/266-4725

Best American Food
Tally's
4214 University Ave., Cedar Falls, 319/268-1655

Best Atmosphere
Victoria's by the Park
323 W. Second St., Cedar Falls, 319/266-4725

Best Bar
Green Streets
Holiday Inn, 5826 University Ave., 319/277-2230

Best Breakfast
Joe's Country Grill
4117 University Ave., Cedar Falls, 319/277-8785

Best Burgers
Danny's Diner
  1525 W. First St., Cedar Falls, 319/266-1462

Best Business Lunch
Mrs. Beasley and Friends Too
  501 Sycamore St., 319/232-8429
Tally's
  4214 University Ave., Cedar Falls, 319/268-1655

Best Chinese Food
Golden China Restaurant
  2046 E. Ridgeway Ave., 319/232-3928
Yen Ching
  107 Commercial St., 319/236-5005

Best Diner
Garfield's Cafe and Catering
  2820 Falls Ave., 319/291-6742

Best Dinner
Brown Bottle
  209 W. Fifth St., 319/232-3014

Best Fast Food
Danny's Diner
  1525 W. First St., Cedar Falls, 319/266-1462

Best Homestyle Food
Joe's Country Grill
  4117 University Ave., Cedar Falls, 319/277-8785

Best Italian Food
Brown Bottle
  209 W. Fifth St., 319/232-3014

Best Lunch
Garfield's Cafe and Catering
  2820 Falls Ave., 319/291-6742
Green Streets
  Holiday Inn, 5826 University Ave., 319/277-2230

Best Seafood
Olde Broome Factory Restaurant
  110 N. Main St., Cedar Falls, 319/268-0877

Best Steaks
Olde Broome Factory Restaurant
  110 N. Main St., Cedar Falls, 319/268-0877

Best Tea Room
Mrs. Beasley and Friends Too
  501 Sycamore St., 319/232-8429

Best View While Dining
Olde Broome Factory Restaurant
  110 N. Main St., Cedar Falls, 319/268-0877

Standbys
The Olive Garden
  1315 E. San Marnan, 319/235-6494

Kansas

Best All-You-Can-Eat Buffets
Sirloin Stockade
    1855 S. Range Ave., 913/462-7178
Deep Rock Cafe
    1170 S. Range Ave., 913/462-8806

Best Breakfast
Ramada Inn Restaurant
    1950 S. Range Ave., 913/462-3933
Village Inn
    2215 S. Range Ave., 913/462-6683

Best Burgers
A and W
    965 E. Fourth St., 913/462-3033

Best Chinese Food
Big Wong Restaurant
    1745 W. Fourth St., 913/462-7722

Best Family Restaurant
Deep Rock Cafe
    1170 S. Range Ave., 913/462-8806

Best Homestyle Food
Bourquin's Farm Market Company
    155 E. Willow St., 913/462-3300
Deep Rock Cafe
    1170 S. Range Ave., 913/462-8806

Best Pizza
Gambino's Pizza
    485 N. Franklin Ave., 913/462-3347

Best Steaks
Sirloin Stockade
    1855 S. Range Ave., 913/462-7178

Standbys
Dairy Queen
    1100 W. Fourth St., 913/462-6364
Pizza Hut
    980 S. Range Ave., 913/462-6211
    1950 S. Range Ave., 913/462-3933

K

Long John Silver's
855 Davis Ave., 913/462-2044

DODGE CITY, KS

Best Restaurants in Town
Cafe Potpourri
100 Military Ave., 316/225-0477
Cafe Latte
614 N. Second Ave., 316/227-6120

Best American Food
Westside Grill
2001 W. Wyatt Earp Blvd., 316/225-3100
Peppercorn's Bar and Grill
1301 W. Wyatt Earp Blvd., 316/225-2335

Best Asian Restaurants
Saigon Market
1202 E. Wyatt Earp Blvd., 316/225-9099
Silver Spur Club
1510 W. Wyatt Earp Blvd., 316/225-9362

Best Mexican Food
El Charro Restaurant
1209 W. Wyatt Earp Blvd., 316/225-0371
Casa Alvarez
1701 W. Wyatt Earp Blvd., 316/225-7164
Costa Azul
208 S. Second St., 316/227-2448

Best Steaks
Silver Spur Club
1510 W. Wyatt Earp Blvd., 316/225-9362

EMPORIA, KS

Best Restaurants in Town
Chicken House Cafe
Hwy. 99, Olpe, 316/475-3386
Love's
101 Commercial St., Hartford, 316/392-5548

Best American Food
Coach's Restaurant and Bar
1408 Industrial Rd., 316/343-6362

Best Chinese Food
House of Ma
1404 Industrial Rd., 316/342-3433

Best Mexican Food
El Palenque Cafe
315 Commercial St., 316/342-0200

Best Steaks
Lujan's Waterworks
402 Merchant St., 316/343-9980

GARDEN CITY, KS

Best Restaurants in Town
Southland Country Club
77 Grand View, 316/275-2117

Wheat Lands
1521 E. Fulton St., 316/275-9794

Best Chinese Food
Golden Dragon Restaurant
519 W. Mary St., Ste. 111, 316/275-8661

Best Mexican Food
Casa Alvarez
1109 College Dr., 316/275-5494

Best Steaks
Grain Bin Supper Club
1301 E. Fulton St., 316/275-5954

HAYS, KS

Best All-You-Can-Eat Buffets
Holiday Inn
3603 Vine St., 913/625-7371
Vagabond
2524 Vine St., 913/625-5914

Best Barbecue/Ribs
Richard's
1101 Elm, 913/628-8505

Best Breakfast
Village Inn
3402 Vine St., 913/628-1938

Best Chinese Food
China Garden Restaurant
2503 Vine St., 913/628-2280
Quan's Chinese Restaurant
2520 Vine St., 913/628-1238

Best Desserts
Rooftops Restaurant and Bar
1200 Main St., Ste. 6, 913/628-8631

Best Family Restaurants
Al's Chickenette
700 Vine St., 913/625-7414
Pheasant Run
3201 Vine St., 913/628-1044

Best Mexican Food
Gutierrez Mexican Restaurant
1106 E. 27th St., 913/625-4402
Taco Shop
333 W. Eighth St., 913/625-7114

Best Pizza
Lomato's Pizza
107 W. Fourth St., 913/623-2888
Augustino's Pizza Palette
2405 Vine St., 913/628-2222

Best Steaks
Rooftops Restaurant and Bar
1200 Main St., Ste. 6, 913/628-8631

Standbys
Subway
1211 Vine St., 913/625-7171

K

HUTCHINSON, KS

Best Barbecue/Ribs
Roy's Hickory Pit BBQ
  1018 W. Fifth Ave., 316/663-7421

Best Homestyle Food
The Dutch Kitchen
  6803 W. State Rd. 61, 316/662-2554
Mom's Cafe
  507 N. Main St., 316/662-1543

Best Italian Food
Tommassi Italian Restaurant
  17 E. Second Ave., 316/663-9633

Best Mexican Food
The Anchor Inn
  128 S. Main St., 316/669-9633

Best Other Ethnic Food
The Carriage Crossing (Amish)
  10002 S. Yoder Rd., Yoder, 316/465-3612

Best Steaks
Sampler's
  6311 N. Kansas Rte. 61, 316/662-7736
Prime Thyme
  2803 N. Main St., 316/663-8037
The Airport Steakhouse
  1100 Airport Rd., 316/662-4281

INDEPENDENCE, KS

Best All-You-Can-Eat Buffets
Kinsey's Restaurant
  1921 W. Main St., 316/331-2141
Applewood's
  120 W. Laurel, 316/331-7960

Best Barbecue/Ribs
Chubby's Smoke House and Lounge
  1721 N. Penn Ave., 316/331-2450

Best Breakfast
Eggbert's International
  1724 W. Main St., 316/331-0520

Best Burgers
Eggbert's International
  1724 W. Main St., 316/331-0520
Kinsey's Restaurant
  1921 W. Main St., 316/331-2141

Best Chinese Food
Great China Restaurant
  2001 W. Main St., 316/331-0060

Best Desserts
Applewood's
  120 W. Laurel, 316/331-7960

Best Diner
Eggbert's International
  1724 W. Main St., 316/331-0520

Best Family Restaurant
Kinsey's Restaurant
  1921 W. Main St., 316/331-2141

Best Homestyle Food
Kinsey's Restaurant
  1921 W. Main St., 316/331-2141

Best Ice Cream/Yogurt
Braum's Ice Cream and Dairy
  1415 N. Pennsylvania Ave., 316/331-1973

Best Mexican Food
Ortega's
  1100 E. Main St., 316/331-3027

Best Pizza
Big Cheese Pizza
  103 E. Main St., 316/331-2330

Best Places to Take the Kids
Big Cheese Pizza
  103 E. Main St., 316/331-2330
Chubby's Smoke House and Lounge
  1721 N. Penn Ave., 316/331-2450

Best Salad/Salad Bar
Applewood's
  120 W. Laurel, 316/331-7960

Best Sandwiches
Chubby's Smoke House and Lounge
  1721 N. Penn Ave., 316/331-2450

Best Steaks
Applewood's
  120 W. Laurel, 316/331-7960

JUNCTION CITY, KS

Best All-You-Can-Eat Buffet
Sirloin Stockade
  1029 S. Washington St., 913/238-1817

Best Barbecue/Ribs
Chubby's
  203 S. Washington St., 913/762-2773

Best Breakfast
Stacy's Restaurant
  118 W. Flint Hills Blvd., 913/238-3039

Best Chinese Food
Peking Chinese Restaurant
  836 S. Washington St., 913/238-2336

Best German Food
Gasthaus Erika's
  610 N. Washington St., 913/762-6414

Best Homestyle Food
Stacy's Restaurant
  118 W. Flint Hills Blvd., 913/238-3039

Best Mexican Food
Pinata Mexican Restaurant
  322 W. Sixth St., 913/238-7346

441

Best Steaks
Sirloin Stockade
  1029 S. Washington St., 913/238-1817

Standbys
Baskin-Robbins
  1012 W. Sixth St., 913/762-4655

KANSAS CITY, KS

Best Barbecue/Ribs
Gates and Sons Bar-B-Q
  411 Swope Pkwy., Kansas City, MO, 816/921-0409

Best Breakfast
Fritz's Union Station
  250 N. Eighteenth St., 913/281-2777

Best Burgers
Winstead's
  6260 NW Barry Rd., Kansas City, MO, 816/587-7333
  101 Brush Creek Blvd., Kansas City, MO, 816/753-2244
  1628 Burlington St., Kansas City, MO, 816/842-5952
  4717 Grand Ave., Kansas City, MO, 816/931-2250
  1200 Main St., Kansas City, MO, 816/221-3339
  8725 State Line Rd., Kansas City, MO, 816/363-5937
Loretta's Cafe
  838 Minnesota Ave., 913/371-9175
Fritz's Union Station
  250 N. Eighteenth St., 913/281-2777

Best Delicatessens
Sophie's Catering and Deli
  553 Central Ave., 913/371-9454
Gino Deli
  901 N. Seventh St., 913/342-8225

Best Dinner
Mrs. Peters Chicken Dinners
  4960 State Ave., 913/287-7711

Best Fast Food
Fritz's Union Station
  250 N. Eighteenth St., 913/281-2777

Best Homestyle Food
Loretta's Cafe
  838 Minnesota Ave., 913/371-9175
Mrs. Peters Chicken Dinners
  4960 State Ave., 913/287-7711

Best Italian Food
Figlio Italian Restaurant
  209 W. 46th Terrace, Kansas City, MO, 816/561-0505

Best Japanese Food
Gojo Japanese Steak House
  4163 Broadway St., Kansas City, MO, 816/561-2501

Best Lunch
Jennie's Restaurant
  402 N. Fifth St., 913/621-4222
Loretta's Cafe
  838 Minnesota Ave., 913/371-9175

K

Best Mexican Food
Manny's Restaurante Mexicano
 207 Southwest Blvd., Kansas City, MO, 816/474-7696
Casa De Tacos
 1817 Park Dr., 913/342-6226

Best Sandwiches
Jennie's Restaurant
 402 N. Fifth St., 913/621-4222
Gino Deli
 901 N. Seventh St., 913/342-8225

Best Steaks
Gojo Japanese Steak House
 4163 Broadway St., Kansas City, MO, 816/561-2501
Frontier Restaurant
 9338 State Ave., 913/788-9159

LAWRENCE, KS

Best Restaurant in Town
Fifi's Restaurant
 925 Iowa St., 913/841-7226

Best Bar
Free State Brewing Company
 636 Massachusetts St., 913/843-4555

Best Breakfast
Village Inn Pancake House
 821 Iowa St., 913/842-3251

Best Burgers
Johnny's Tavern
 401 N. Second St., 913/842-0377

Best Chinese Food
Panda Garden
 1500 W. Sixth St., 913/843-4312
Royal Peking
 711 W. 23rd St., 913/841-4599

Best Family Restaurants
Old Chicago
 2329 S. Iowa St., 913/841-4124
Village Inn Pancake House
 821 Iowa St., 913/842-3251

Best Mexican Food
Carlos O'Kelly's Mexican Cafe
 707 W. 23rd St., 913/832-0550
Pancho's Mexican Restaurant
 711 W. 23rd St., 913/843-4044

Best Pizza
Old Chicago
 2329 S. Iowa St., 913/841-4124
Teller's
 746 Massachusetts St., 913/843-4111

Best Place to Eat Alone
Sirloin Stockade
 1015 Iowa St., 913/749-3005

K

Best Places to Eat When Someone Else Is Buying
Fifi's Restaurant
   925 Iowa St., 913/841-7226
Village Inn Pancake House
   821 Iowa St., 913/842-3251

Best Sandwiches
Paradise Cafe
   728 Massachusetts St., 913/842-5199

Best Steaks
Mr. Steak
   920 W. 23rd St., 913/841-3454
Sirloin Stockade
   1015 Iowa St., 913/749-3005

Best Other Restaurants
Mad Greek Restaurant
   907 Main St., 913/843-2441
Eldridge Hotel
   701 Massachusetts St., 913/749-5011

LEAVENWORTH, KS

K

Best Restaurant in Town
Pullman Place
   232 Cherokee St., 913/682-8658

Best Italian Food
Mama Mia's Pizza
   402 S. Twentieth St., 913/682-2131

Best Mexican Food
El Sambre Restaurant
   781 Shawnee St., 913/682-3200

LIBERAL, KS

Best Barbecue/Ribs
King's Pit Bar BQ
   355 E. Pancake Blvd., 316/624-2451

Best Breakfast
Golden Derrick Restaurant
   1115 N. Kansas Ave., 316/624-1101

Best Chinese Food
Hong Kong Restaurant
   802 Hwy. 54E, 316/624-7012

Best Coffee
Golden Derrick Restaurant
   1115 N. Kansas Ave., 316/624-1101

Best Homestyle Food
Dean's Family Restaurant
   339 E. Pancake Blvd., 316/624-1875
Golden Derrick Restaurant
   1115 N. Kansas Ave., 316/624-1101

Best Mexican Food
Casa Alvarez
   1010 S. Kansas Ave., 316/624-5205

Best Steaks
Bramleau's Grill
   Hwy. 54E, 316/624-0133

MANHATTAN, KS

Best Barbecue/Ribs
Texas Star Cafe
  606 N. Twelfth St., 913/537-9077
Calico Inn
  105 S. Broadway, Riley, 913/485-2622

Best Brunch
Holiday Inn, Scampi's
  530 Richards Dr., 913/539-5311

Best Burgers
Fish Bowl
  105 N. Third St., 913/776-8979

Best Cajun/Creole Food
Hibachi Hut
  608 N. Twelfth St., 913/539-9393

Best Chinese Food
Hunan Chinese Restaurant
  1304 Westloop Pl., 913/539-8888
Yen Ching Chinese Restaurant
  1005 N. Seth Child Rd., 913/776-2020

Best Coffee
Espresso Royale
  616 N. Manhattan Ave., 913/537-2345

Best Desserts
Harry's Uptown Supper Club
  418 Poyntz Ave., 913/537-1300

Best Family Restaurant
Village Inn
  204 Tuttle Creek Blvd., 913/537-3776

Best Health-Conscious Menu
Texas Star Cafe
  606 N. Twelfth St., 913/537-9077

Best Homestyle Food
Calico Inn
  105 S. Broadway, Riley, 913/485-2622

Best Mexican Food
Texas Star Cafe
  606 N. Twelfth St., 913/537-9077

Best Pizza
Pyramid Pizza
  1130 Moro St., 913/539-4888

Best Steaks
Harry's Uptown Supper Club
  418 Poyntz Ave., 913/537-1300
Little Apple Brewing Company
  1110 Westloop Pl., 913/539-5500

K

OLATHE, KS

Best Bar
Austin's
  2103 E. 151st St., 913/829-2106

Best Breakfast
First Watch
  4117 W. 83rd St., Shawnee Mission, 913/649-8875
  7305 W. 95th St., 913/383-2904
  9916 College Blvd., 913/339-6686

Best Burgers
Austin's
  2103 E. 151st St., 913/829-2106
Back Yard Burgers
  124 N. Claiborne Rd., 913/780-4114

Best Business Lunch
Ambrosia's
  Holiday Inn, 101 W. 151st St., 913/829-4000

Best Casual Dining
Austin's
  2103 E. 151st St., 913/829-2106

Best Chinese Food
Golden Bowl Restaurant
  1808 E. Santa Fe St., 913/829-3435

Best Coffee
Cinnamon's Deli
  2097 E. Santa Fe St., 913/782-7887
Christian Book and Gift Shoppe
  1229 E. Santa Fe St., 913/764-1752

Best Desserts
Britni's Cafe and Catering
  100 E. Park St., 913/780-0878

Best Diner
West Side Diner
  117 S. Kansas Ave., 913/780-6611

Best Family Restaurant
Kansas Machine Shed Restaurant
  12080 S. Stringline Rd., 913/780-2697

Best Ice Cream/Yogurt
Maggie Moo's
  9218 Metcalf Ave., Overland Park, 913/642-7888

Best Italian Food
Pizzetti's Pizza
  2018 E. Santa Fe St., 913/764-9300

Best Mexican Food
Cocina de Mino
  13515 S. Mur Len Rd., 913/829-8874

Best Pizza
Pizzetti's Pizza
  2018 E. Santa Fe St., 913/764-9300

Best Place to Eat Alone
Cinnamon's Deli
  2097 E. Santa Fe St., 913/782-7887

Best Place to Eat When Someone Else Is Buying
Houston's
  7111 W. 95th St., Shawnee Mission, 913/642-0630

Best Place to Take the Kids
Kansas Machine Shed Restaurant
  12080 S. Stringline Rd., 913/780-2697

Best Salad/Salad Bar
Jasper's
  405 W. 75th St., Kansas City, 816/363-3003

Best Sandwiches
Cinnamon's Deli
  2097 E. Santa Fe St., 913/782-7887

Best Tea Room
Britni's Cafe and Catering
  100 E. Park St., 913/780-0878

Standbys
Ponderosa
  1109 E. Santa Fe St., 913/782-8497
Perkins
  1828 E. Santa Fe St., 913/764-7288
Applebee's
  13505 S. Mur Len Rd., 913/764-5533
Cracker Barrel
  12101 Stringline Rd., 913/780-9108

K

SALINA, KS

Best Restaurants in Town
The Scheme Restaurant
  123 N. Seventh St., 913/823-5125
The Coffee Gallery
  104 S. Fifth St., 913/823-5093
The Brookville Hotel
  204 Perry St., Brookville, 913/225-6666

Best Burgers
The Cozy Inn
  108 N. Seventh St., 913/825-9407

Standbys
Applebee's
  2875 S. Ninth St., 913/827-8385

SHAWNEE MISSION, KS

Best Barbecue/Ribs
Board Room Bar-B-Q
  9600 Antioch Rd., 913/642-6273
K.C. Masterpiece Barbecue
  10985 Metcalf Ave., 913/345-1199

Best Breakfast
First Watch
  4117 W. 83rd St., 913/649-8875
  7305 W. 95th St., 913/383-2904
  9916 College Blvd., 913/339-6686
Le Peep Restaurant
  7218 College Blvd., 913/661-9441

Best Brunch
First Watch
  4117 W. 83rd St., 913/649-8875
  7305 W. 95th St., 913/383-2904
  9916 College Blvd., 913/339-6686

Forks In The Air
11942 Roe Ave., 913/345-9110
Le Peep Restaurant
7218 College Blvd., 913/661-9441

Best Burgers
Houston's Restaurant
7111 W. 95th St., 913/642-0630
Talk of the Town Grill and Bar
11922 W. 119th St., 913/661-9922
Dick Clark's American Bandstand Grill
10975 Metcalf Ave., 913/457-1600

Best Coffee
Mildred's
7921 Santa Fe Dr., 913/341-0301
One Hundred and One Bean Company
9220 Metcalf Ave., 913/642-3267

Best Homestyle Food
Black-Eyed Pea
11836 W. 95th St., 913/599-3222
11900 Shawnee Mission Pkwy., 913/962-0900

Best Ice Cream/Yogurt
Maggie Moo's Creamery
12014 College Blvd., 913/339-9009
4308 W. 119th St., 913/338-1428
6471 Quivira Rd., 913/268-8500
7628 State Line Rd., 913/649-0979

Best Mexican Food
Jalapeno's Mexican Restaurant
7729 W. 151st St., 913/681-3555
La Cocina Del Puerco
9097 Metcalf Ave., 913/341-2800
Jose Pepper's
10316 Metcalf Ave., 913/341-5673

Best Microbrewery
Rock Bottom Brewery
11721 Metcalf Ave., 913/663-2422

Best Sandwiches
Bagel and Bagel
4949 W. 119th St., 913/338-2080
5200 W. 94th Ter., 913/663-2080
7960 Lee Blvd., 913/341-2080

Best Seafood
J. Alexander's
11471 Metcalf Ave., 913/469-1995

Best Southwestern Food
Coyote Grill
4843 Johnson Dr., 913/362-3333

Best Steaks
Houston's Restaurant
7111 W. 95th St., 913/642-0630
J. Alexander's
11471 Metcalf Ave., 913/469-1995
Martini's Restaurant
11723 Roe Ave., 913/451-4515

TOPEKA, KS

Best American Food
Pore Richard's
705 S. Kansas Ave., 913/233-4276

Best Breakfast
Kozy Kitchen
315 SE 29th St., 913/267-6128

Best Burgers
Prize Package Store
1420 SE Sixth Ave., 913/232-5764

Best Business Lunch
Pore Richard's
705 S. Kansas Ave., 913/233-4276

Best Chinese Food
Great Wall Chinese Restaurant
1336 SW Seventeenth St., 913/234-1060

Best Dinner
Paisano's Italian Ristorante
104 SW Fifth St., 913/357-7084
4043 SW Tenth Ave., 913/273-1011
435 S. Kansas Ave., 913/357-6545

Best Homestyle Food
Kozy Kitchen
315 SE 29th St., 913/267-6128
Byrd's Nest Restaurant
921 S. Kansas Ave., 913/232-6239

Best Italian Food
Pappas' Eatery and Pub
926 S. Kansas Ave., 913/232-6161

Best Japanese Food
Kobe Steak House of Japan
5331 SW 22nd Pl., 913/272-6633

Best Salad/Salad Bar
Kozy Kitchen
315 SE 29th St., 913/267-6128
Willie C's
2047 SW Topeka Blvd., 913/232-8080

Best Sandwiches
Corner Pocket Carryout
623 SW Sixth Ave., 913/232-5522
Willie C's
2047 SW Topeka Blvd., 913/232-8080

Best Steaks
Kobe Steak House of Japan
5331 SW 22nd Pl., 913/272-6633
Willie C's
2047 SW Topeka Blvd., 913/232-8080

WICHITA, KS

Best American Food
Old Mill Tasty Shop
604 E. Douglas Ave., 316/264-6500

Best Asian Restaurant
Asia Chinese Restaurant
509 N. Hillside St., 316/688-5511

Best Barbecue/Ribs
Miller's Bar B Que
4788 E. Thirteenth St. N., 316/684-8080

Best Breakfast
Willie C's Cafe and Bar
7525 E. Douglas Ave., 316/686-0753
1320 E. Kellogg Dr., 316/262-3424
656 S. West St., 316/942-4077

Best Burgers
Dine-In Roses
104 S. Emporia, 316/267-8033

Best Chinese Food
Kwan Wah
7700 E. Kellogg Dr., 316/686-8396
795 N. West St., 316/945-5484
945 S. Oliver St., 316/682-1081
4600 W. Kellogg Dr., 316/945-8099

Best Delicatessen
Piccadilly Market
7728 E. Central Ave., 316/681-1100

Best Desserts
Dine-In Roses
104 S. Emporia, 316/267-8033

Best Diners
Old Mill Tasty Shop
604 E. Douglas Ave., 316/264-6500
Rock Island Cafe
725 E. Douglas Ave., 316/263-1616

Best Fast Food
Artichoke Sandwich Bar
811 N. Broadway St., 316/263-9164

Best Greek/Mediterranean Food
Piccadilly Market
7728 E. Central Ave., 316/681-1100

Best Homestyle Food
Dine-In Roses
104 S. Emporia, 316/267-8033

Best Italian Food
Angelo's Italian Foods
3105 E. Harry St., 316/682-1473
Savute's Italian Ristorante
3303 N. Broadway St., 316/838-0455

Best Pizza
Piccadilly Market
7728 E. Central Ave., 316/681-1100

Best Salad/Salad Bar
Piccadilly Market
7728 E. Central Ave., 316/681-1100

Best Sandwiches
Old Mill Tasty Shop
  604 E. Douglas Ave., 316/264-6500
Artichoke Sandwich Bar
  811 N. Broadway St., 316/263-9164

Best Steaks
Doc's Steak House
  1515 N. Broadway St., 316/264-4735
Savute's Italian Ristorante
  3303 N. Broadway St., 316/838-0455

K

Kentucky

Best Barbecue/Ribs
Damon's
  500 Winchester Ave., 606/325-8929

Best Breakfast
Tudor's Biscuit World
  3000 Winchester Ave., 606/324-7744

Best Casual Dining
Damon's
  500 Winchester Ave., 606/325-8929

Best Homestyle Food
Chimney Corner Tea Room
  1624 Carter Ave., 606/324-3300

Best Italian Food
Italian Oven
  500 Winchester Ave., 606/324-6622

Best Steaks
Columbia Steak House
  1290 Montgomery Ave., 606/329-1012

Best Restaurant in Town
Boone Tavern Hotel
  Boone Tavern Hotel, Main and Prospect St.,
    606/986-9358

Best Breakfast
Dinner Bell Restaurant
  I-75 Plaza, 606/986-2777

Best Coffee
Berea Coffee and Tea Company
  124 Main St., 606/986-7656

Best Family Restaurant
Columbia's Steak House
  I-75 Interchange Exit 76, 606/986-3639

Best Homestyle Food
Dinner Bell Restaurant
  I-75 Plaza, 606/986-2777

K

453

Best Pizza
Papaleno's Restaurant
    108 Center St., 606/986-4497

Best Sandwiches
Papaleno's Restaurant
    108 Center St., 606/986-4497

Best Steaks
Columbia's Steak House
    I-75 Interchange Exit 76, 606/986-3639

Standbys
Dairy Queen
    131 Clay Dr., 606/986-2535
    200 Brenwood Dr., 606/986-9110

BOWLING GREEN, KY

Best Restaurant in Town
Four Forty Main Restaurant and Bar
    440 E. Main St., 502/793-0450

Best Business Lunch
Four Forty Main Restaurant and Bar
    440 E. Main St., 502/793-0450

Best Chinese Food
Beijing Restaurant
    1951 Scottsville Rd., 502/842-2288

Best Homestyle Food
Judy's Castle
    1302 31W Bypass, 502/842-8736
Teresa's Restaurant
    430 Center St., 502/782-6540

Best Mexican Food
Puerto Vallarta Mexican Restaurant
    1632 31W Bypass, 502/796-3842

Best Sandwiches
Cambridge Market and Cafe
    830 Fairview Ave., 502/782-9367

Best Seafood
Mariah's
    801 State St., 502/842-6878

Best Thai Food
Oulay's Oriental Restaurant
    2945 Scottsville Rd., 502/781-2751

COVINGTON, KY

Best American Food
Coach and Four Restaurant
    214 Scott St., 606/431-6700

Best Barbecue/Ribs
Walt's Hitching Post
    3300 Madison Pike, 606/331-0494

Best Chinese Food
First Wok
    3180 Dixie Hwy., 606/344-8885

K

Best Homestyle Food
Anchor Grill
   438 Pike St., 606/431-9498

Best Mexican Food
Montoya's
   2507 Chelsea Dr., 606/341-0707

Best Seafood
Mike Fink Restaurant
   Foot of Greenup St., 606/261-4212

ELIZABETHTOWN, KY

Best All-You-Can-Eat Buffet
Whistle Stop
   216 E. Main St., Glendale, 502/369-8586

Best Chinese Food
Green Bamboo Restaurant
   902 N. Dixie Ave., 502/769-3457

Best Desserts
Whistle Stop
   216 E. Main St., Glendale, 502/369-8586

Best Pizza
Pasquale's Pizza
   B-2 Helmwood Plz., 502/765-6651

Best Seafood
Stone Hearth
   1001 N. Mulberry St., 502/765-4898

Best Steaks
Whistle Stop
   216 E. Main St., Glendale, 502/369-8586

Standbys
Baskin-Robbins
   910 N. Dixie Ave., 502/765-5955
Cracker Barrel
   1047 Executive Dr., 502/765-5525
Po' Folks
   1009 N. Dixie Hwy., 502/765-5100
Shoney's
   1046 Executive Dr., 502/765-7077
Subway
   1705 N. Dixie Hwy., 502/737-8336
   928 N. Mulberry St., 502/737-7336

FT. KNOX, KY

Best Restaurant in Town
Stone Hearth
   1001 N. Mulberry St., Elizabethtown, 502/765-4898

Best Atmosphere
Doe Run Inn
   500 Doe Run Hotel Rd., Brandenburg, 502/422-2982

Best Bread
Depot Restaurant
   201 E. Main St., Glendale, 502/369-6000

K

Best Homestyle Food
Doe Run Inn
   500 Doe Run Hotel Rd., Brandenburg, 502/422-2982
Back Home
   251 W. Dixie Ave., Elizabethtown, 502/769-2800
Whistle Stop
   216 E. Main St., Glendale, 502/369-6000

Best Italian Food
Gallotta's Italian Restaurant
   Anderson Family Ctr., 7959 Wilson Rd., 502/942-7417

Best View While Dining
Otter Creek Restaurant
   Otter Creek Park, 850 Otter Creek Park Rd.,
     Brandenburg, 502/942-8686

FRANKFORT, KY

Best American Food
Bullfrog's Restaurant
   243 W. Broadway St., 502/875-0090

Best Burgers
Cliffside Restaurant
   Lawrenceburg Rd., 502/223-3173

Best Lunch
Pot Belly Deli
   120 Brighton Park Blvd., 502/695-8494

Best Mexican Food
Aranda's
   193 Versailles Rd., 502/695-4002

Best Seafood
Jim's Seafood
   950 Wilkinson Blvd., 502/223-7448

Best Thai Food
Smile of Siam
   19 Century Plz. S., 502/227-9934

HAZARD, KY

Best Burgers
Day's Dairy Bar
   1416 N. Main St., 606/439-5105

Best Chinese Food
Peking Chinese Restaurant
   446 Main St., 606/439-5001

Best Ice Cream/Yogurt
Day's Dairy Bar
   1416 N. Main St., 606/439-5105

Best Salad/Salad Bar
Cliff Hagan's Rib Eye
   Grand Vue Plaza, 606/439-3739
La Citadelle
   651 Skyline Dr., 606/436-2126

Best Seafood
Cliff Hagan's Rib Eye
   Grand Vue Plaza, 606/439-3739

La Citadelle
651 Skyline Dr., 606/436-2126

Best Steaks
Cliff Hagan's Rib Eye
Grand Vue Plaza, 606/439-3739
La Citadelle
651 Skyline Dr., 606/436-2126

Best View While Dining
La Citadelle
651 Skyline Dr., 606/436-2126

Standbys
Denny's
200 Morton Blvd., 606/436-2037
Pizza Hut
125 E. Main St., 606/439-5886
Rural Route 1, 606/439-5891
Ponderosa
308 Morton Blvd., 606/439-1525
Shoney's
106 Black Gold Ct., 606/439-1770
Subway
218 Village Ln., 606/439-0841

K

HENDERSON, KY

Best Restaurant in Town
The Mill
526 S. Main, 502/826-8012

Best American Food
The Mill
526 S. Main, 502/826-8012

Best Barbecue/Ribs
Ralph's Hickory Pit
739 N. Green St., 502/826-5656

Best Breakfast
Downtown Diner
122 First St., 502/827-9671

Best Brunch
Mezzaluna
104 N. Water, 502/826-9401

Best Chinese Food
Hunan Chinese Restaurant
1765 S. Green St., 502/827-2229

Best Coffee
Planter's Coffeehouse
130 N. Main, 502/830-0927

Best Homestyle Food
Downtown Diner
122 First St., 502/827-9671

Best Mexican Food
Los Toribo's
1739 S. Green, 502/831-2367

Best Salad/Salad Bar
Mezzaluna
104 N. Water, 502/826-9401

HOPKINSVILLE, KY

Best American Food
Bartholomew's
914 S. Main St., 502/886-5768
J's on Main
1004 S. Main, 502/885-2896

Best Barbecue/Ribs
Barbecue Shack
41S, Pembroke, 502/475-4844

Best Breakfast
Roundie's Restaurant
115 E. First St., 502/886-4240

Best Burgers
Ferrell's Snappy Service
1001 S. Main St., 502/886-1445

Best Desserts
Owen's Delicatessen
206 North Dr., 502/886-2022

Best Homestyle Food
Owen's Delicatessen
206 North Dr., 502/886-2022

Best Seafood
Bartholomew's
914 S. Main St., 502/886-5768

Best Steaks
Charlie's Steakhouse
Hwy. 41A, Oak Grove, 502/439-4592

LEXINGTON, KY

Best Restaurant in Town
A La Lucie
159 N. Limestone St., 606/252-5277

Best American Food
Coach House
855 S. Broadway St., 606/252-7777
Roy and Nadine's
3775 Harrodsburg Rd., 606/223-0797
Merrick Inn
3380 Tates Creek Rd., 606/269-5417

Best Bar
Buffalo and Dad's
805 N. Broadway, 606/252-7602

Best Barbecue/Ribs
Billy's Hickory Pit Bar-B-Q
101 Cochran Rd., 606/269-9593

Best Burgers
Linus Irish Pub and Grill
388 Woodland Ave., 606/255-6614
Buffalo and Dad's
805 N. Broadway, 606/252-7602

Best Business Lunch
De Sha's Grille and Bar
101 N. Broadway St., 606/259-3771

Ramsey's Diner
  4053 Tates Creek Rd., 606/271-2638
  496 E. High St., 606/259-2708

Best Casual Dining
Linus Irish Pub and Grill
  388 Woodland Ave., 606/255-6614
Lexington City Brewery
  1050 S. Broadway, 606/259-2739

Best Continental Food
A La Lucie
  159 N. Limestone St., 606/252-5277

Best Diner
Ramsey's Diner
  4053 Tates Creek Rd., 606/271-2638
  496 E. High St., 606/259-2708

Best Dinner
Coach House
  855 S. Broadway St., 606/252-7777

Best Homestyle Food
Ramsey's Diner
  4053 Tates Creek Rd., 606/271-2638
  496 E. High St., 606/259-2708

Best Italian Food
Lexitalia Ristorante
  1765 Alexandria Dr., 606/277-1116

Best Mexican Food
Don Pablo's Mexican Restaurant
  3737 Nicholasville Rd., 606/271-7094

Best Microbrewery
Lexington City Brewery
  1050 S. Broadway, 606/259-2739

Best Outdoor Dining
Merrick Inn
  3380 Tates Creek Rd., 606/269-5417

Best Salad/Salad Bar
Cliff Hagan's Ribeye
  941 Winchester Rd., 606/253-0750

Best Southwestern Food
Ed and Fred's Desert Moon
  249 E. Main St., 606/231-1161
Roy and Nadine's
  3775 Harrodsburg Rd., 606/223-0797

Best Steaks
Cliff Hagan's Ribeye
  941 Winchester Rd., 606/253-0750

LOUISVILLE, KY

Best Restaurant in Town
Allo Spiedo
  2309 Frankfort Ave., 502/895-4878

Best Asian Restaurants
Cafe Mimosa
  1216 Bardstown Rd., 502/458-2233

Shogun
9026 Taylorsville Rd., 502/499-5700
Thai-Siam
3002 1/2 Bardstown Rd., 502/458-6871
Sesame
9409 Shelbyville Rd., 502/339-7000

Best Barbecue/Ribs
Mark's Feed Store
11422 Shelbyville Rd., Middletown, 502/244-0140
Gib's
2224 Dundee Rd., 502/451-5154
Rib Tavern
4157 Bardstown Rd., 502/499-1515
Vince Staten's Old Time Barbecue
9219 Hwy. 42, 502/228-7427
Bibby's
3812 Bardstown Rd., 502/451-2122

Best Bistros
Baxter Station Bar and Grill
1201 Payne St., 502/584-1635
Bobby J's
3220 Frankfort Ave., 502/899-7142
Bristol Bar and Grille
1321 Bardstown Rd., 502/456-1702
Deitrich's
2862 Frankfort Ave., 502/897-6076
Uptown Cafe
1624 Bardstown Rd., 502/458-4212

Best Breakfast
Lynn's Paradise Cafe
2206 Frankfort Ave., St. Matthews, 502/896-2585

Best Cafeterias
Morrison's
133 S. Hurstbourne Pkwy., 502/423-1733
4801 Outer Loop, 502/964-5756
Blue Boar
3008 Bardstown Rd., 502/458-7262
106 Bauer Ave., 502/899-3030
7900 Shelbyville Rd., 502/426-3310
802 Eastern Pkwy., 502/634-1052
Colonnade
455 S. Fourth Ave., Ste.120, 502/584-6846
Jay's
504 S. Eighteenth St., 502/538-2534
Miller's
429 S. Second St., 502/582-9135

Best Chinese Food
Asian Pearl
2060 S. Hurstbourne Pkwy., 502/495-6800
August Moon
2296 Lexington Rd., 502/456-6569
Sichuan Garden
9850 Linn Station Rd., 502/426-6767
Emperor of China
6100 Dutchmans Ln., Ste. 210, 502/426-1717
2249 Hikes Ln., 502/451-2500

Best Coffeehouses
Twice Told
  1604 Bardstown Rd., 502/456-0507
John Conti
  4023 Bardstown Rd., 502/499-8602
Highland Grounds
  919 Baxter Ave., 502/459-6478

Best Continental Food
Two Eleven Clover Lane
  The Colony Center, 211 Clover Ln., 502/896-9570

Best Delicatessens
Stevens and Stevens
  1114 Bardstown Rd., 502/584-3354
La Peche
  1147 Bardstown Rd., 502/451-0377
Karem Deeb Liquors and Deli
  2228 Taylorsville Rd., 502/458-1668
Wall Street Deli
  400 W. Market St., 502/585-4202

Best Desserts
Sweet Surrender
  2311 Frankfort Ave., 502/896-0519
Queen of Tarts
  1649 Cowling Ave., 502/473-0735
Cafe Metro
  1700 Bardstown Rd., 502/458-4830
La Peche
  1147 Bardstown Rd., 502/451-0377
Lilly's
  1147 Bardstown Rd., 502/451-0447

K

Best Family Restaurants
KT's
  2300 Lexington Rd., 502/458-8888
W.W. Cousins
  2101 S. Hurstbourne Pkwy., 502/896-8881
Austin's
  4950 Hwy. 42, 502/423-1990

Best German Food
Gasthaus
  4818 Brownsboro Center, 502/899-7177

Best Greek/Mediterranean Food
Pita Delights
  1015 Barret Ave., 502/583-2926

Best Homestyle Food
Lynn's Paradise Cafe
  984 Barret Ave., 502/583-3447
Mr. Thompson's Old Recipe Style Barbecue
  30th St. at River Park Dr., 502/778-1700
Pat's Steak House
  2437 Brownsboro Rd., 502/893-2062

Best Italian Food
Bravo's
  600 W. Main St., 502/568-2222
Cafe Marcella
  12004 Shelbyville Rd., 502/245-4800

Mama Grisanti
  3938 Dupont Circle., 502/893-0141
Fred Grisanti
  10212 Taylorsville Rd., Jeffersontown, 502/267-0050
Romano's Macaroni Grill
  401 S. Hurstbourne Pkwy., 502/423-9220
Vincenzo's
  150 S. Fifth St., 502/580-1350
Porcini
  2730 Frankfort Ave., St. Matthews, 502/894-8686

Best Korean Food
A Little Bit of Seoul
  2206 Frankfort Ave., 502/894-9807
Koreana
  5009 Preston Hwy., 502/966-2115

Best Mexican Food
Tumbleweed Mexican Cafe
  12975 Shelbyville Rd., 502/245-2113
  7900 Shelbyville Rd., 502/339-8411
La Cazuela
  7707 Preston Hwy., 502/966-2828
El Caporal
  2209 Meadow Dr., 502/473-7840
Chico's
  2945 Richland Ave., 502/452-2479

Best New Restaurants
Shariat's
  2901 Brownsboro Rd., 502/899-7878
Bobby J's
  3220 Frankfort Ave., Franklin, 502/899-7142
The Irish Rover
  2319 Frankfort Ave., 502/899-3544
Bluegrass Brewing Company
  3929 Shelbyville Rd., St. Matthews, 502/899-7070
Asiatique
  106 Sears Ave., 502/899-3578
Club Grotto
  2222 S. Ninth St., 502/637-9280
Romano's Macaroni Grill
  401 S. Hurstbourne Pkwy., 502/423-9220

Best Other Ethnic Food
Cafe Kilimanjaro (Caribbean/South American)
  649 Fourth Ave. on Theatre Sq., 502/583-4332
Mo Flav (Caribbean/South American)
  3334 Frankfort Ave., 502/899-5555
De La Torre's (Spanish/Mediterranean)
  1606 Bardstown Rd., 502/456-4955

Best Places to Eat When Someone Else Is Buying
The English Grill
  The Brown Hotel, Fourth Ave. at Broadway,
    502/583-1234
Equus
  122 Sears Ave., 502/897-9721
The Inn on Spring
  348 Spring St., Jeffersonville, 812/284-5545

Jack Fry's
   1007 Bardstown Rd., 502/452-9244
The Oakroom
   The Seelbach Hotel, 500 S. Fourth Ave., 502/585-3200
Timothy's
   826 E. Broadway, 502/561-0880
Lilly's
   1147 Bardstown Rd., 502/451-0447
Vincenzo's
   150 S. Fifth St., 502/580-1350
Cafe Metro
   1700 Bardstown Rd., 502/458-4830
Le Relais
   Taylorsville Rd. at Bowman Field, 502/451-9020

Best Romantic Dining
Terrace
   6100 Dutchmans Ln., Ste.16, 502/456-4444
Vincenzo's
   150 S. Fifth St., 502/580-1350
Le Relais
   Taylorsville Rd. at Bowman Field, 502/451-9020
Lilly's
   1147 Bardstown Rd., 502/451-0447
Cafe Metro
   1700 Bardstown Rd., 502/458-4830

Best Salad/Salad Bar
Melrose Inn
   13306 Hwy. 42, Prospect, 502/228-1461

Best Sandwiches
Stevens and Stevens
   1114 Bardstown Rd., 502/584-3354
Bluegrass Brewing Company
   3929 Shelbyville Rd., 502/899-7070
Another Place
   1514 Bardstown Rd., 502/458-8141
Karem Deeb
   2228 Taylorsville Rd., 502/458-1668
J.P. Kayrouz
   130 St. Matthews Ave., St. Matthews, 502/897-9300

Best Southwestern Food
Alameda
   1381 Bardstown Rd., 502/459-6300
Baja Bay
   1801 Bardstown Rd., 502/459-6398
Chico's
   3003 Breckenridge Ln., 502/452-2479
Mexico Tipico
   6517 Dixie Hwy., 502/933-9523

Best Steaks
Pat's Steak House
   2437 Brownsboro Rd., St. Matthews, 502/893-2062
Del Frisco's
   4107 Oechsli Ave., 502/897-7077
John E's
   3708 Bardstown Rd., 502/456-1111

K

Dillon's
  2101 S. Hurstbourne Pkwy., 502/499-7106

Best Vegetarian Food
Lynn's Paradise Cafe
  2206 Frankfort Ave., St. Matthews, 502/896-2585
Rainbow Blossom
  12401 Shelbyville Rd., 502/244-2022
Shariat's
  2901 Brownsboro Rd., 502/899-7878
Twice Told
  1604 Bardstown Rd., 502/456-0507
Thai Siam
  3002 1/2 Bardstown Rd., 502/458-6871

Best Vietnamese Food
Vietnam Kitchen
  Iroquois Manor Shopping Ctr., 5339 Mitscher Ave.,
  502/363-5154

Standbys
Cracker Barrel
  1401 Kentucky Mills Dr., Jeffersontown, 502/266-8895
Denny's
  434 Eastern Pkwy., 502/636-2538
  3618 Bardstown Rd., 502/459-1444
  337 Whittington Pkwy., 502/423-0489
Bob Evans
  9797 Blairwood Rd., 502/423-0236
  4620 Preston Hwy., 502/361-8161
  1463 Gardiner Ln., 502/456-2636
Waffle House
  4706 Preston Hwy., 502/968-7697
  3347 Fern Valley Rd., 502/968-8090
  4318 Bishop Ln., 502/458-6434
  1203 S. Hurstbourne Pkwy., 502/425-6580
Outback Steakhouse
  12717 Shelbyville Rd., 502/245-2158
Ryan's Family Steak House
  4117 Browns Ln., 502/458-8665
  5338 Bardstown Rd., 502/491-1088
Chi Chi's
  10200 Linn Station Rd., 502/426-3900
  3664 Bardstown Rd., 502/456-1115

MADISONVILLE, KY

Best Barbecue/Ribs
Cody's Restaurant
  50 Chelsea Dr., 502/825-1949

Best Burgers
Ferrell's Snappy Service
  112 N. Main St., 502/821-7515

Best Chinese Food
China Garden Restaurant
  851 S. Main St., 502/821-1617

Best Coffee
Khaldi's Koffee
  11 W. Center St., 502/825-4905

Best Homestyle Food
Country Cupboards
581 McCoy Ave., 502/821-6652

Best Italian Food
Di Fabio's Casa Pela
17 W. Center St., 502/825-1900

Best Sandwiches
Dobie's Deli
1041 W. Noel Ave., 502/821-9460

Best Steaks
Bartholomew's Fine Foods
51 S. Main St., 502/821-1061

MAYSVILLE, KY

Best Restaurant in Town
Gourmet Garden
13 W. Second St., 606/564-0180

Best Breakfast
Victorian
Ramada Inn, 484 Moody Dr., 606/564-6793

Best Burgers
De Sha's Restaurant
1166 Hwy. 68, 606/564-9275

Best Chinese Food
China Pearl Restaurant
1545 Hwy. 68, 606/759-5959
Asian Garden
1152 Hwy. 68, 606/564-8889

Best Homestyle Food
Ole Country Inn
Main St., Germantown, 606/728-2912

Best Italian Food
Pasquale's Pizza
Hwy. 68, 606/564-4039

Best Salad/Salad Bar
Pasquale's Pizza
Hwy. 68, 606/564-4039

Best Sandwiches
De Sha's Restaurant
1166 Hwy. 68, 606/564-9275

Best Seafood
De Sha's Restaurant
1166 Hwy. 68, 606/564-9275
Loose Leaf
545 Tucker Dr., 606/759-5323

Best Steaks
De Sha's Restaurant
1166 Hwy. 68, 606/564-9275
Loose Leaf
545 Tucker Dr., 606/759-5323

Standbys
Golden Corral Family Steak House
890 Hwy. 68, 606/564-3831

K

465

Shoney's
603 Martin Luther King Hwy., 606/759-5075
Pizza Hut
1408 Hwy. 68, 606/564-9488

MOREHEAD, KY

Best All-You-Can-Eat Buffet
Iris Cafe
Holiday Inn, 1698 Flemingsburg Rd., 606/784-7591

Best Chinese Food
China House Chinese Restaurant
228 Morehead Plz., 606/784-2388

Best Coffee
Jerry's Restaurant
512 E. Main St., 606/784-7562

Best Desserts
Dixie Grill
172 E. Main St., 606/784-9051

Best Homestyle Food
Dixie Grill
172 E. Main St., 606/784-9051

Best Italian Food
Fazoli's Restaurant
900 S. Main St., Nicholasville, 606/885-3580

Best Pizza
Pasquale's Pizza
182 E. Main St., 606/784-9111

Best Place to Take the Kids
Mr. Gatti's Pizza
520 E. Main St., 606/784-6637

Best Steaks
Cutter's Roadhouse
140 Trademoore Ctr., 606/783-1153

Standbys
Dairy Queen
1125 E. Main St., 606/784-5205
Pizza Hut
333 Flemingsburg Rd., 606/784-8654
212 Morehead Plz., 606/784-8844
Shoney's
1617 Flemingsburg Rd., 606/784-2286

OWENSBORO, KY

Best Restaurant in Town
Campbell Club
521 Frederica St., 502/684-4249

Best All-You-Can-Eat Buffet
Moonlite Bar-B-Que Inn
2840 W. Parrish Ave., 502/684-8143

Best Bar
Martin's
622 1/2 E. Second St., 502/684-3306

Best Breakfast
Patio Room
Ramada Inn, 1 Executive Blvd., 502/926-8000

Best Brunch
Colby's
202 W. Third St., 502/685-4239

Best Burgers
Eight-Ball Restaurant
1846 Triplett St., 502/683-3693

Best Business Lunch
Trotters Restaurant
1100 Walnut St., 502/685-2771

Best Cheap Meal
Jay Dee's Restaurant
1420 Breckenridge St., 502/683-9419

Best Chinese Food
House of Hunan
2845 W. Parrish Ave., 502/683-6267

Best Coffee
Santa Fe Cafe
1035 Frederica St., 502/688-0260

Best Desserts
Pastalotta Cafe
120 W. Second St., 502/684-3752

Best Diner
Jack and Jenny's Diner
201 E. Ninth St., 502/685-0226

Best Homestyle Food
Jay Dee's Restaurant
1420 Breckenridge St., 502/683-9419

Best Italian Food
Pastalotta Cafe
120 W. Second St., 502/684-3752

Best Mexican Food
Los Toribas
34 E. Fourth St., 502/683-8361

Best Place to Be "Seen"
Colby's
202 W. Third St., 502/685-4239

Best Place to Eat When Someone Else Is Buying
Briar Patch
2760 Veach Rd., 502/685-3329

Best Romantic Dining
Campbell Club
521 Frederica St., 502/684-4249

Best Salad/Salad Bar
Pinocchio's Restaurant
109 Frederica St., 502/684-3220

Best Sandwiches
Colby's Deli and Cafe
401 Frederica St., 502/684-2495

K

467

Best Steaks
Briar Patch
  2760 Veach Rd., 502/685-3329

Standbys
Applebee's
  5120 Frederica St., 502/926-3472
Subway
  3124 Hwy. 54, 502/686-1893
  3333 Frederica St., 502/684-2672
  2425 W. Parrish Ave., 502/686-7115
Domino's
  1003 Burlew Blvd., 502/683-8777
  3333 Frederica St., 502/926-6400
Chi Chi's
  4820 Frederica St., 502/683-4455

PADUCAH, KY

Best Barbecue/Ribs
Starnes Bar-B-Q
  1008 Joe Clifton Dr., 502/444-9555

Best Breakfast
Skin Head's Restaurant
  1020 S. 21st St., 502/442-6471

Best Burgers
Downtown Diner
  308 Broadway St., 502/443-1288

Best Chinese Food
Double Happiness
  3794 Hinkleville, 502/443-5010

Best Homestyle Food
Little Castle Restaurant
  1008 Jefferson St., 502/442-1979

Best Italian Food
Cynthia's Ristorante
  127 S. Second St., 502/443-3319

Best Lunch
Hillbilly Cooker
  2530 Jackson St., 502/443-8748

Best Pizza
Parlor
  3033 Lone Oak Rd., 502/554-3707

Best Seafood
Whaler's Catch Restaurant
  306 N. Thirteenth St., 502/444-7701

Best Steaks
Jeremiah's
  225 Broadway St., 502/443-3991

RICHMOND, KY

Best Bar
Madison Garden
  152 N. Madison Ave., 606/623-9720

Best Breakfast
Early Bird Restaurant
　1417 E. Main St., 606/624-1649

Best Burgers
Jet Drive-In
　613 Big Hill Ave., 606/624-2018

Best Business Lunch
Madison Garden
　152 N. Madison Ave., 606/623-9720

Best Chinese Food
Tsing Tao Restaurant
　300 W. Main St., 606/624-0133

Best Mexican Food
Paco's Mexican Restaurant
　124 S. First St., 606/623-0021

K

Louisiana

Best Restaurant in Town
Mariner's Seafood and Steak House
  Hwy. 1 Bypass, 318/357-1220

Best Bar
Mirror Room
  Bentley Hotel, 200 DeSoto St., 318/448-9600

Best Breakfast
Pitt Grill Restaurant
  2360 S. MacArthur Dr., 318/442-9675

Best Brunch
Mirror Room
  Bentley Hotel, 200 DeSoto St., 318/448-9600

Best Burgers
Speedy Bee's
  2705 Shreveport Hwy., Pineville, 318/640-9755

Best Business Lunch
Tobe's
  Ramada Inn, 2211 N. MacArthur Dr., 318/443-2561

Best Casual Dining
Tunk's Cypress Inn Restaurant
  Louisiana Hwy. 28W, 318/487-4014

Best Cheap Meal
Red Kettle Grill
  3746 S. MacArthur Dr., 318/445-6642

Best Chinese Food
Oriental Wok
  6 N. Bolton Ave., 318/448-8247

Best Coffee
Coffee Unlimited
  5820 Jackson St., 318/445-7451

Best Desserts
Lee J's Restaurant
  208 Main St., Pineville, 318/443-8789

Best Diner
Delia's Family Dining
1106 Main St., Pineville, 318/443-8789

Best Health-Conscious Menu
Bless Your Hearts
959 MacArthur Dr., 318/443-6966

Best Homestyle Food
Delia's Family Dining
1106 Main St., Pineville, 318/443-8789

Best Italian Food
Suburban Garden
3322 Jackson St., 318/442-6974

Best Late-Night Food
Ann's Coffee Shoppe
2314 N. MacArthur Dr., 318/448-9073

Best Mexican Food
Julia's Mexican Restaurant
2204 Worley Dr., 318/445-2405

Best Pizza
B.J. Pizza
902 Versailles Dr., 318/448-4104

Best Place to Be "Seen"
Bentley Room
Bentley Hotel, 200 DeSoto St., 318/448-9600

Best Place to Eat Alone
Piccadilly Cafeteria
1400 MacArthur Dr., 318/445-0209
3451 Masonic Dr., 318/445-9574

Best Places to Eat When Someone Else Is Buying
Gray Fox Inn
5521 Jackson St. Ext., 318/487-8333
Bentley Room
Bentley Hotel, 200 Desoto St., 318/448-9600

Best Romantic Dining
Mariners Seafood and Steak House
Hwy. 1 Bypass, 318/357-1220

Best Sandwiches
Critics' Choice
415 Murray St., 318/442-3333
5208 Rue Verdun, 318/445-1680

Best Seafood
Cajun Landing
2728 N. MacArthur Dr., 318/487-4912

Best Steaks
Mariners Seafood and Steak House
Hwy. 1 Bypass, 318/357-1220

Best Vegetarian Food
Bless Your Heart
959 MacArthur Dr., 318/443-6966

Best Other Restaurant
Lee J's Restaurant
208 Main St., Pineville, 318/487-4628

Standbys
Baskin-Robbins
  4726 Jackson St. Ext., 318/473-8217
Chuck E. Cheese Pizza
  1725 Metro Dr., 318/445-9843
Ryan's Family Steak House
  3024 N. MacArthur Dr., 318/445-8796
Shoney's
  16 MacArthur Dr., 318/443-0432

BATON ROUGE, LA

Best Restaurants in Town
Chalet Brandt
  7655 Old Hammond Hwy., 504/927-6040
Giamanco's
  4624 Government St., 504/928-5045
Mansur's
  3044 College Dr., 504/923-3366
Joe's Dreyfus Store Restaurant
  Hwy. 77, Livonia, 504/637-2625
Lafitte's Landing
  10275 Louisiana 70 Access St., Donaldsonville,
    504/473-1232
Middendorf's
  Off Hwy. 51, Manchac, 504/386-6666

Best American Food
Copeland's of New Orleans
  4957 Essen Ln., 504/769-1800
Piccadilly Cafeteria
  3164 Government St., 504/293-9440
  3232 S. Sherwood Forest Blvd., 504/293-9440
  7169 Florida Blvd., 504/924-6535

Best Barbecue/Ribs
Podnuh's Bar-B-Q
  2648 S. Sherwood Forest Blvd., 504/295-7056
  5565 Essen Ln., 504/769-6617
  7026 Florida Blvd., 504/926-3341
Sonny's Real Pit Bar-B-Q
  12475 Florida Blvd., 504/272-5028
TJ Ribs
  2324 S. Acadian Thruway, 504/383-7427

Best Cajun/Creole Food
The Factory
  3130 College Dr., 504/924-6735
Juban's
  3739 Perkins Rd., 504/346-8422
Mansur's
  3044 College Dr., 504/923-3366
Ralph and Kacoo's
  7110 Airline Hwy., 504/356-2361
  6110 Bluebonnet Blvd., 504/766-2113

Best Casual Dining
Superior Grill
  5435 Government St., 504/927-2022

L

473

Best Chinese Food
Bamboo Garden
  5207 Essen Ln., 504/769-2877
Hunan Chinese Restaurant
  4215 S. Sherwood Forest Blvd., 504/291-6868
Taste of China
  9716 Airline Hwy., 504/928-9911

Best Continental Food
Chalet Brandt
  7655 Old Hammond Hwy., 504/927-6040
DaJoNel's
  7327 Jefferson Hwy., 504/924-7537
Maison LaCour
  11025 N. Harrells Ferry Rd., 504/275-3755

Best Greek/Mediterranean Food
Zorba's Greek Place
  9990 Perkins Rd., 504/769-8833

Best Italian Food
Cippriani's
  4550 Concord Ave., 504/924-3930
Giamanco's
  4624 Government St., 504/928-5045
Gino's
  4542 Bennington Ave., 504/927-7156
Louie's Cafe
  1058 North Blvd., 504/336-1745
  209 W. State St., 504/346-8221

Best Mexican Food
Mamacita's Restaurant and Cantina
  7524 Bluebonnet Blvd., 504/769-3850
Ninfa's Mexican Restaurant
  4738 Constitution Ave., 504/924-0377
Superior Grill
  5435 Government St., 504/927-2022

Best Other Ethnic Food
Arzi's Ethnic Cafe (Lebanese)
  4625 S. Sherwood Forest Blvd., 504/293-2999
Serop's (Lebanese)
  4065 Government St., 504/383-3658

Best Places to Eat When Someone Else Is Buying
Juban's Restaurant
  3739 Perkins Rd., 504/346-8422
Warehouse Restaurant
  12328 S. Choctaw Dr., 504/272-1067

Best Salad/Salad Bar
Ralph and Kacoo's
  7110 Airline Hwy., 504/356-2361

Best Sandwiches
George's
  2943 Perkins Rd., 504/343-2363

Best Seafood
Don's Seafood
  6823 Airline Hwy., 504/357-0601
Mike Anderson's Seafood
  1031 W. Lee Dr., 504/766-7823

Ralph and Kacoo's
6110 Bluebonnet Blvd., 504/766-2113
7110 Airline Hwy., 504/356-2361

Best Steaks
The Place
5255 Florida Blvd., 504/924-5069

Standbys
Chili's
4550 Constitution Ave., 504/927-6040
Denny's
2313 S. Sherwood Forest Blvd., 504/275-3441
2323 S. Acadian Thruway, 504/343-7045
Outback Steakhouse
2415 S. Acadian Thruway, 504/927-9488
Ruth's Chris Steak House
4836 Constitution Ave., 504/925-0163

CHALMETTE, LA

Best Barbecue/Ribs
Luther's Barbeque
8740 W. Judge Perez Dr., 504/277-8167

Best Breakfast
Breakfast Club
2200 Paris Rd., 504/279-7364

Best Italian Food
Rocky and Carlo Restaurant and Bar
613 W. Saint Bernard Hwy., 504/279-8323

Best Place to Eat When Someone Else Is Buying
Jean Lafitte
3220 Jean Lafitte Pkwy., 504/279-7437

Best Salad/Salad Bar
Marina Wharf Seafood Restaurant
5353 Paris Rd., 504/277-8215

Best Seafood
Bubba John's Seafood Restaurant
9212 W. Judge Perez Dr., 504/279-1589
Par 3 Restaurant
1530 E. Judge Perez Dr., 504/279-9114
Marina Wharf Seafood Restaurant
5353 Paris Rd., 504/277-8215

Best Steaks
Marina Wharf Seafood Restaurant
5353 Paris Rd., 504/277-8215
Rocky and Carlo Restaurant and Bar
613 W. Saint Bernard Hwy., 504/279-8323

Standbys
Shoney's
8350 W. Judge Perez Dr., 504/277-5758
Baskin-Robbins
1515 E. Judge Perez Dr., 504/271-3107

HOUMA, LA

Best Breakfast
A-Bear's Restaurant
809 Bayou Black Dr., 504/872-6303

Best Cheap Meal
Lunch Basket
649 E. Main St., 504/876-7420

Best Desserts
Your Just Desserts
2731 W. Main St., 504/851-3336

Best Ice Cream/Yogurt
Scarlett Scoop Ice Cream
300 Barrow St., 504/872-5114

Best Mexican Food
Cuco's Border Cafe
3038 W. Park Ave., 504/868-0800
La Casa Del Sol Fine Mexican Restaurant
101 Monarch Dr., 504/872-3474

Best Sandwiches
Lunch Basket
649 E. Main St., 504/876-7420

Best Seafood
Dave's Cajun Kitchen
2433 W. Main St., 504/868-3870
Saphr's Seafood Restaurant
52 Hwy. 90W, Des Allemands, 504/758-1602

Best Steaks
Tropical Breeze Restaurant
2105 Grand Caillou Rd., 504/873-0012

LAFAYETTE, LA

Best Restaurants in Town
Cafe Vermilionville
1304 W. Pinhook Rd., 318/237-0100
Randall's
2320 Kaliste Saloom, 318/981-7080
Blair House Restaurant
1316 Surrey St., 318/234-0357

Best Bar
Charley G's
3809 Ambassador Caffery Pkwy., 318/981-0108

Best Breakfast
Bayou Bistro
Best Western Hotel, 1801 W. Pinhook Rd., Acadiana,
318/233-8120

Best Brunch
Cafe Jardin
Hilton Hotel, 521 Pinhook Rd., 318/235-6111

Best Burgers
Bun's
1406 Surrey St., 318/232-0979
105 St. Landry St., 318/232-3287

Best Business Lunch
City Club of Lafayette
   600 Jefferson St., Ste. 1600, 318/266-2250

Best Casual Dining
A La Carte Restaurant
   301 Heymann Blvd., 318/235-8493
La Fonda's
   3809 Johnston St., 318/984-5630
Riverside Inn
   Tubing Rd., 318/235-8559

Best Cheap Meal
La Fonda
   3809 Johnston St., 318/984-5630

Best Chinese Food
Kim's Chinese and Seafood Restaurant
   1523 N. Bertrand Dr., 318/235-7874

Best Coffee
Anjo's Bakery
   1507A Kaliste Saloom Rd., 318/989-1977

Best Desserts
A La Carte Restaurant
   301 Heymann Blvd., 318/235-8493

Best Diner
Hub City Diner
   1412 S. College Rd., 318/235-5683

Best Family Restaurant
Don's Seafood Hut
   4309 Johnston Rd., 318/981-1141

Best Health-Conscious Menu
Red Lerille's Health Club
   301 Doucet Rd., 318/984-7738

Best Homestyle Food
T-Coon's
   740 Jefferson St., 318/232-3803

Best Ice Cream/Yogurt
Copeland's
   3804 Ambassador Caffery Pkwy., 318/984-7797

Best Italian Food
iMonelli Italian Restaurant
   4017 Johnston St., 318/989-9291

Best Late-Night Food
Hub City Diner
   1412 S. College Rd., 318/235-5683

Best Mexican Food
Ninfa's Mexican Restaurant
   3551 Ambassador Caffery Pkwy., 318/988-2333

Best Pizza
Louisiana Pizza Kitchen
   1926 W. Pinhook Rd., 318/237-5800

Best Place to Be "Seen"
Charley G's
   3809 Ambassador Caffery Pkwy., 318/981-0108

L

Best Place to Eat Alone
Dwyer's Cafe
323 Jefferson Blvd., 318/235-9364

Best Place to Eat When Someone Else Is Buying
Cafe Vermilionville
1304 W. Pinhook Rd., 318/237-0100

Best Romantic Dining
iMonelli Italian Restaurant
4017 Johnston St., 318/989-9291

Best Sandwiches
Old Tyme Grocery
218 W. Saint Mary Blvd., 318/235-8165
Chris' Po-Boys
1900 W. Pinhook Rd., 318/234-6333
631 Jefferson St., 318/234-1696
1941 Moss St., 318/237-1095
3304 Johnston St., 318/981-5073

Best Seafood
Prejean's Restaurant
3480 Hwy. 67N, 318/896-3247

Best Vegetarian Food
Baracca's Italian Grill
3502 Ambassador Caffery Pkwy., 318/988-6119

Best Other Restaurant
Edie's Restaurant
1895 W. Pinhook Rd., 318/234-2485

Standbys
Ruth's Chris Steak House
507 W. Pinhook Rd., 318/237-6123
Ryan's Family Steak House
3252 Ambassador Caffery Pkwy., 318/989-8028

LAKE CHARLES, LA

Best Bar
Toucan on the Bayou
1103 W. Prien Lake Rd., 318/477-3337

Best Breakfast
Pitt Grill
928 Shady Ln., 318/478-4166

Best Business Lunch
Jean Lafitte Inn
501 W. College St., 318/474-2730

Best Casual Dining
Darrell's
119 W. College St., 318/474-3651
Piccadilly Classic American
316 W. Prien Lake Rd., 318/477-7010

Best Family Restaurant
Mr. Gatti's Pizza
3522 Ryan St., 318/474-6625

Best French Food
Pat's of Henderson
1500 Siebarth Dr., 318/439-6618

Best Homestyle Food
Pitt Grill
  928 Shady Ln., 318/478-4166

Best Italian Food
Italian Villa
  3716 Ryan St., 318/477-8376
Tony's Pizza and Restaurant
  335 W. Prien Lake Rd., 318/477-1611

Best Late-Night Food
Pitt Grill
  928 Shady Ln., 318/478-4166

Best Mexican Food
Pepper's
  545 W. Prien Lake Rd., 318/474-9869
Casa Manana Mexican Restaurant
  2510 Ryan St., 318/433-4112

Best Pizza
Tony's Pizza and Restaurant
  335 W. Prien Lake Rd., 318/477-1611
Mr. Gatti's Pizza
  3522 Ryan St., 318/474-6625

Best Place to Be "Seen"
Pat's of Henderson
  1500 Siebarth Dr., 318/439-6618

Best Place to Eat When Someone Else Is Buying
Hunter's Harlequin Steaks
  1717 Hwy. 14, 318/439-2780

Best Place to Take the Kids
Mr. Gatti's Pizza
  3522 Ryan St., 318/474-6625

Best Romantic Dining
Hunter's Harlequin Steaks
  1717 Hwy. 14, 318/439-2780

Best Sandwiches
Darrell's
  119 W. College St., 318/474-3651

Best Seafood
Mr. D's on the Bayou
  3205 Common St., 318/433-9652

Best Steaks
Hunter's Harlequin Steaks
  1717 Hwy. 14, 318/439-2780

Best Other Restaurant
Schillileagh's Restaurant Bar
  1016 E. Prien Lake Rd., 318/478-4125

Standbys
Baskin-Robbins
  149 W. Prien Lake Rd., 318/478-6869
Ryan's Family Steak House
  4051 Ryan St., 318/477-2107

L

MINDEN, LA

Best Barbecue/Ribs
Neta's Drive-In
1433 Shreveport Rd., 318/377-5675

Best Burgers
Hamburger Happiness
Hwy. 80, 318/371-0609

Best Chinese Food
China Town Restaurant
712 Homer Rd., 318/377-7121

Best Coffee
Lisa Ellen's Cafe Cakes and Catering
515 Main St., 318/377-2881

Best Desserts
Lisa Ellen's Cafe Cakes and Catering
515 Main St., 318/377-2881

Best Seafood
Earl's Bayou Inn
1 Dorcheat St., 318/371-0287

Standbys
Dairy Queen
1105 Shreveport Rd., 318/371-1400
Golden Corral Family Steak House
121 Homer Rd., 318/377-1208
Pizza Hut
930 Homer Rd., 318/371-1240

MONROE, LA

Best Restaurants in Town
The Atrium Grille
2001 Louisville Ave., 318/325-0641
New Orleans East
300 Washington St., 318/323-8996
Warehouse No. 1 Restaurant
1 Olive St., 318/322-1340
Chateau
2007 Louisville Ave., 318/325-0384

Best Barbecue/Ribs
Podnuh's Bar-B-Q
1810 Louisville Ave., 318/325-4261
1510 Hwy. 165 Bypass, 318/325-8747
2021 Hudson Ln., 318/387-7684

Best Beer Selection
Trenton Street Bar
207 Trenton St., West Monroe, 318/387-2157

Best Brunch
The Atrium Grille
2001 Louisville Ave., 318/325-0641

Best Burgers
Melvyn's Restaurant
2000 N. Eighteenth St., 318/325-2055

Best Cafeteria
Piccadilly Classic American
2203 Louisville Ave., 318/325-5414

Best Cajun/Creole Food
Cormier's Cajun Restaurant
  1205 Forsythe Ave., 318/322-0414
Captain Avery Louisiana Restaurant
  1500 Hwy. 165N, 318/345-0100

Best Catfish
Joe Bob's
  1100 Bayou Darbonne Dr., West Monroe,
    318/396-1818

Best Chinese Food
Peking Chinese Restaurant
  903 N. Fourth St., 318/361-0231

Best Coffeehouse
The Coffee Bean
  1420 Eighteenth St., 318/324-9114

Best Desserts
Not Just Pie
  2117 Forsythe Ave., 318/322-9928

Best Homestyle Food
Kitchen Restaurant
  202 S. Sixth St., 318/322-4224

Best Italian Food
Genusa's Italian Restaurant
  815 Park Ave., 318/387-3083
Cascio's Italian and Cajun
  305 Finks Hideaway, 318/345-4536

Best Mexican Food
Rio Cafe
  3211 Hwy. 165, 318/324-0500

Best Pizza
Johnny's Pizza House
  50 Old Sterling Rd., 318/343-2992
  801 S. Second St., 318/323-4458
  1126 Hwy. 139, 318/345-0540
  1707 McKeen Pl., 318/387-8668
  3812 Desiard St., 318/343-1835

Best Salad/Salad Bar
Monroe's Steak House
  1301 N. Nineteenth St., 318/387-0908

Best Sandwiches
Ray's Pe Ge
  8209 Desiard St., 318/343-0710

Best Seafood
Captain Avery Seafood Restaurant
  1500 Hwy. 165N, 318/345-0100
Mohawk Tavern Seafood Restaurant
  704 Louisville Ave., 318/322-5481
Joe Bob's
  1100 Bayou Darbonne Dr., West Monroe,
    318/396-1818

Best Steaks
Monroe's Steak House
  1301 N. Nineteenth St., 318/387-0908

L

Best Wine Selection
Genusa's Italian Restaurant
  815 Park Ave., 318/387-3083

Standbys
Outback Steakhouse
  305 Constitution Dr., 318/387-6700
Shoney's
  3210 Desiard St., 318/323-0219

MORGAN CITY, LA

Best Breakfast
Holiday Inn Restaurant
  520 Roderick St., 504/385-2200
Manny's Restaurant and Grill
  7027 Hwy. 90E, 504/384-2359

Best Brunch
Holiday Inn Restaurant
  520 Roderick St., 504/385-2200

Best Chinese Food
Formosa Gardens
  7545 Hwy. 90E, 504/384-9436

Best Ice Cream/Yogurt
Tastee Freez
  7708 Hwy. 90E, 504/384-1284

Best Mexican Food
Tampico Restaurant
  1025 N. Victor II Blvd., 504/385-2784
  1425 Hwy. 90W, 504/395-2859

Best Seafood
Landry's Seafood Inn
  6509 Hwy. 90E, 504/385-2285
Pat and Carolyn's Seafood Inn
  6701 Hwy. 90E, 504/384-8550
Rita Mae's Kitchen
  711 Federal Ave., 504/384-3550

Standbys
Pizza Hut
  609 Brachear Ave., 504/385-3661
  7244 Hwy. 90E, 504/384-6660
Shoney's
  1011 Greenwood St., 504/384-5767
Subway
  7552 1/2 Hwy. 90E, 504/385-1180

NEW IBERIA, LA

Best Burgers
Duffy's Diner
  929 Parkview Dr., 318/365-8577
  1120 Center St., 318/365-2326
Lil's Kitchen
  521 Main St., Jeanerette, 318/276-9600
Freez-O
  1215 Center St., 318/369-9391

Best Homestyle Food
Lil's Kitchen
   521 Main St., Jeanerette, 318/276-9600

Best Mexican Food
Tampico Restaurant
   602 W. Admiral Doyle Dr., 318/365-9547

Best Seafood
Patio Restaurant
   105 N. Main St., Loreauville, 318/229-8281
Yellow Bowl Restaurant
   19466 Hwy. 182W, Jeanerette, 318/276-5512
Landry's Seafood Restaurants
   20371 Hwy. 90, Jeanerette, 318/276-4857

Standbys
Mr. Gatti's Pizza
   929 E. Admiral Doyle Dr., 318/365-7359
Pizza Hut
   635 E. Admiral Doyle Dr., 318/364-1176
Baskin-Robbins
   1104 E. Main St., 318/367-3531

NEW ORLEANS, LA

Best Restaurants in Town
Commander's Palace
   1427 Washington Ave., 504/891-4466
Bayona
   430 Dauphine St., 504/525-4455
Brigtsen's
   723 Dante St., 504/861-7610
Emeril's
   800 Tchoupitoulas St., 504/528-9393
Gautreau's
   1728 Soniat St., 504/899-7397
Grill Room
   Windsor Court, 300 Gravier St., 504/522-1992
La Provence
   I-90 between Mandeville and Lacombe, 504/626-7662
Mike's on the Avenue
   628 St. Charles Ave., 504/523-1709
Peristyle
   1041 Dumaine St., 504/593-9535

Best All-You-Can-Eat Buffet
Court of the Two Sisters
   613 Royal St., 504/522-7261

Best Atmosphere
Bacco
   310 Chartres St., Metairie, 504/522-2426
Commander's Palace
   1427 Washington Ave., 504/891-4466

Best Barbecue/Ribs
Tipton County Tennessee Pit
   5538 Magazine St., 504/899-9626
Stonebreaker's
   2700 Edenborn Ave., Metairie, 504/456-7427

Corky's Bar-B-Q
  4243 Veterans Memorial Blvd., Metairie,
    504/887-5000

Best Bread
La Madeleine
  547 Saint Ann St., 504/568-9950
  601 S. Carrollton Ave., 504/861-8661

Best Breakfast
Camellia Grill
  626 S. Carrollton Ave., 504/866-9573
Bluebird Cafe
  3625 Prytania St., 504/895-7166

Best Brunch
Commander's Palace
  1427 Washington Ave., 504/891-4466

Best Burgers
Port of Call
  838 Esplanade Ave., 504/523-0120
Camellia Grill
  626 S. Carrollton Ave., 504/866-9573

Best Business Lunch
Mr. B's
  201 Royal St., 504/523-2078

Best Cajun/Creole Food
Mike Anderson's Seafood Restaurant
  215 Bourbon St., 504/524-3884
Prudhomme's Cajun Cafe
  4676 NE Evangeline Thruway, Carencro,
    318/896-1026
Copeland's
  4338 Saint Charles Ave., 504/897-6465
Praline Connection
  542 Frenchmen St., 504/943-3934
  630 Mandeville St., 504/947-4558
Mother's
  401 Poydras, 504/523-9656

Best Casual Dining
Lea's
  1810 Hwy. 71S, Lecompte, 318/776-5178
Copeland's
  4338 Saint Charles Ave., 504/897-6465
Palace Cafe
  605 Canal St., 504/523-1661

Best Chinese Food
Five Happiness
  3605 S. Carrollton Ave., 504/482-3935
Trey Yuen Cuisine of China
  2100 N. Morrison Blvd., Hammond, 504/345-6789

Best Coffeehouse
P. J.'s
  24 McAlister Dr., 504/865-5705

Best Desserts
Commander's Palace
  1427 Washington Ave., 504/891-4466

Camellia Grill
626 S. Carrollton Ave., 504/866-9573
Caribbean Room
Ponchartrain Hotel, 2031 Saint Charles Ave.,
504/524-0581

Best French Food
Louis XVI
730 Bienville St., 504/581-7000

Best Greek/Mediterranean Food
Little Greek
619 Pink St., Metairie, 504/831-9470

Best Gumbo
The Gumbo Shop
5900 S. Front St., 504/899-2460
Mr. B's
201 Royal St., 504/523-2078

Best Health-Conscious Menu
Whole Foods Market
3135 Esplanade Ave., 504/943-1626

Best Indian Food
Tandoor
3000 Severn Ave., Metairie, 504/887-7414
Taj Mahal
923C Metairie Rd., 504/836-6859

Best Italian Food
Bacco
310 Charles St., Metairie, 504/522-2426
Semolina
3242 Magazine St., 504/895-4260
5080 Pontchartrain Blvd., 504/486-5581

Best Japanese Food
Shogun
2325 Veterans Memorial Blvd., 504/833-7477

Best Late-Night Food
Camellia Grill
626 S. Carrollton Ave., 504/866-9573

Best Mexican Food
Vaquero's
4938 Prytania St., 504/891-6441

Best Neighborhood Restaurant
Mandina's
3800 Canal St., 504/482-9179

Best New Restaurant
NOLA
534 Saint Louis St., 504/522-6652

Best Pizza
Pizza Roma
4840 Bienville St., 504/483-9949
Louisiana Pizza Kitchen
2800 Esplanade Ave., 504/488-2800
95 French Market Pl., 504/522-9500
Cafe Roma
1901 Sophie Wright Pl., 504/524-2419

L

New York Pizza
5201 Magazine St., 504/891-2376
208 N. Carrollton Ave., 504/482-2376

Best Places to Eat When Someone Else Is Buying
Commander's Palace
1427 Washington Ave., 504/891-4466
La Provence Restaurant
I-90 between Mandeville and Lacombe, 504/626-7662

Best Salad/Salad Bar
Ralph and Kacoo's
6110 Bluebonnet Blvd., 504/766-2113
Louisiana Pizza Kitchen
2800 Esplanade Ave., 504/488-2800
95 French Market Pl., 504/522-9500
Houston's
1755 Saint Charles Ave., 504/524-1578
Semolina
3242 Magazine St., 504/895-4260
5080 Pontchartrain Blvd., 504/486-5581

Best Sandwiches
Maspero's
440 Chartres St., 504/527-8990
Mother's
401 Poydras St., 504/523-9656
Acme Oyster and Seafood House
724 Iberville St., 504/522-5973
Louisiana Seafood Exchange
4418 Downman Rd., 504/245-1661

Best Seafood
Palace Cafe
605 Canal St., 504/523-1661
Franky and Johnny's
321 Arabella St., 504/899-9146
Deanie's
1713 Lake Avenue, Metairie, 504/831-4141
1016 Annunciation St., 504/561-9251
Mr. B's
201 Royal St., 504/523-2078
Pascal's Manale
1838 Napoleon Ave., 504/895-4877
Mosca's
4137 Hwy. 90W, Avondale, 504/436-9942
Mandina's
3800 Canal St., 504/482-9179
Copeland's
4338 Saint Charles Ave., 504/897-6465
Acme Oyster and Seafood House
724 Iberville St., 504/522-5973
Charley G's
111 Veterans Memorial Blvd., Second Fl., Metairie,
504/837-6408
Gumbo Shop
630 Saint Peter St., 504/525-1486

Best Soul Food
Praline Connection
542 Frenchmen St., 504/943-3934

630 Mandeville St., 504/947-4558
901 S. Peters St., 504/523-3973

Best Thai Food
Bangkok Cuisine
4137 S. Carrollton Ave., 504/482-3606

Best View While Dining
Bella Luna
914 N. Peters St., 504/529-1583

Best Wine Selection
Commander's Palace
1427 Washington Ave., 504/891-4466

Standbys
Ruth's Chris Steak House
711 N. Broad St., 504/486-0810

RUSTON, LA

Best Burgers
Trenton Street Cafe
201 N. Trenton St., 318/251-2103

Best Delicatessen
Sundown
111 E. Park Ave., 318/255-8028

Best Italian Food
Anthony's Pasta and Seafood
109 N. Trenton St., 318/255-9000

Best Mexican Food
Nicky's
2803 S. Service Rd. W., 318/255-5012

Best Soul Food
Sarah's Kitchen
607 Lee Ave., 318/255-1726

SHREVEPORT, LA

Best Restaurant in Town
Monsieur Patou-French Restaurant
855 Pierremont Rd., 318/868-9822

Best American Food
Village Grille
1313 Louisiana Ave., 318/424-2874

Best Barbecue/Ribs
Podnuh's Bar-B-Q
1146 Shreveport Barksdale Hwy., 318/869-3371
1915 N. Market St., 318/222-7480
8995 Mansfield Rd., 318/688-0818

Best Breakfast
Grandy's Restaurant
6605 Youree Dr., 318/797-0316
6811 Pines Rd., 318/687-0718

Best Business Lunch
Superior Bar and Grill
1014 Pierremont Rd., 318/869-2500
6123 Line Ave., 318/869-3243

Best Cajun/Creole Food
Pete Harris Cafe
1355 Milam St., 318/425-4277

Best Chinese Food
Ming Garden Restaurant
1250 Shreveport Barksdale Hwy., 318/861-2741

Best Continental Food
Village Grille
1313 Louisiana Ave., 318/424-2874

Best Dinner
Superior Bar and Grill
1014 Pierremont Rd., 318/869-2500
6123 Line Ave., 318/869-3243

Best French Food
Monsieur Patou-French Restaurant
855 Pierremont Rd., 318/868-9822

Best Homestyle Food
M and P Superior Kitchen
3530 Jewella Ave., 318/636-0633

Best Italian Food
Monjuni's Italian Cafe and Grocery
1315 Louisiana Ave., 318/227-0847
Rosati's
502 E. Kings Hwy., 318/868-5435

Best Mexican Food
Superior Bar and Grill
1014 Pierremont Rd., 318/869-2500
6123 Line Ave., 318/869-3243

Best Places to Eat When Someone Else Is Buying
Village Grille
1313 Louisiana Ave., 318/424-2874
Monsieur Patout
855 Pierremont Rd., 318/868-9822

Best Seafood
Ralph and Kacoo's
1700 Old Minden Rd., 318/747-6660

Best Soul Food
Pete Harris Cafe
1355 Milam St., 318/425-4277

SLIDELL, LA

Best Restaurant in Town
La Provence Restaurant
I-90 between Mandeville and Lacombe, 504/626-7662

Best American Food
Southside Cafe
3154 Pontchartrain Dr., 504/643-6133
Annabelle's by the Sea
4820 Pontchartrain Dr., 504/646-0021

Best Italian Food
Salvaggio's
4416 Pontchartrain Dr., 504/641-8360

Best Seafood
Boiling Point
  2998 Pontchartrain Dr., 504/641-5551
Young's Restaurant
  850 Robert Blvd., 504/643-9331

SULPHUR, LA

Best Asian Restaurants
Hong Kong Restaurant
  2009 S. Ruth St., 318/527-3804
China King
  1707 Maplewood Dr., 318/625-5358

Best Cajun/Creole Food
Cajun Charlie's Restaurant
  202 Henning Dr., 318/527-9044
Boiling Point
  1730 N. Arizona St., 318/625-9282

Best Seafood
Richard's Boudin and Seafood
  2250 E. Napoleon St., 318/625-8474

L

Maine

Best American Food
Senator Restaurant
   284 Outer Western Ave., 207/622-0320
The A-1 Diner
   3 Bridge St., Gardiner, 207/582-4804

Best Atmosphere
Senator Restaurant
   284 Outer Western Ave., 207/622-0320

M

Best Brunch
Senator Restaurant
   284 Outer Western Ave., 207/622-0320

Best Chinese Food
Hong Kong Isle Restaurant
   208 Western Ave., 207/623-8878

Best Coffee
Java Joe's
   287 Water St., 207/622-1110

Best Eclectic Menu
Slate's Restaurant
   167 Water St., Hallowell, 207/622-9575

Best Family Restaurant
Mike's Restaurant
   15 Bangor St., 207/622-3221

Best Italian Food
Ardito's Family Restaurant
   Augusta Airport, Winthrop St., 207/623-2044

Best Mexican Food
Margarita's Mexican Restaurant
   390 Western Ave., 207/622-7874

Best Other Ethnic Food
River Cafe (Lebanese)
   119 Water St., Hallowell, 207/622-2190

Best Pizza
Pat's Pizza
   292 State St., 207/623-1748

Best Sandwiches
Java Joe's
  287 Water St., 207/622-1110

Best Steaks
Mike's Restaurant
  15 Bangor St., 207/622-3221

Standbys
Friendly's
  48 Western Ave., 207/622-5831
Ground Round
  110 Community Dr., 207/623-0022

BANGOR, ME

Best Restaurants in Town
Governor's Restaurant
  643 Broadway, 207/947-3113
Dysart's Service
  Coldbrook Rd., 207/942-4878

Best Breakfast
Dysart's Service
  Coldbrook Rd., 207/942-4878

Best Diner
Dysart's Service
  Coldbrook Rd., 207/942-4878

Best Dinner
Governor's Restaurant
  643 Broadway, 207/947-3113
Captain Nick's
  1165 Union St., 207/942-6444

Best Microbrewery
Sea Dog Pub
  26 Front St., 207/947-8004

Best Seafood
Captain Nick's
  1165 Union St., 207/942-6444
Pilot's Grill
  1528 Hammond St., 207/942-6325

Best Steaks
Pilot's Grill
  1528 Hammond St., 207/942-6325

BIDDEFORD, ME

Best Restaurants in Town
Alex's Pizza
  91 Alfred St., 207/283-0002
Village Inn Family Restaurant
  213 Saco Ave., Old Orchard Beach, 207/934-7370

Best Breakfast
Jonesy's Restaurant
  273 Main St., 207/282-6406

Best Chinese Food
Happy Dragon Chinese
  115 Main St., 207/282-0440

Best Dinner
Dan's Restaurant
   106 Elm St., 207/284-5970

Best Homestyle Food
Dan's Restaurant
   106 Elm St., 207/284-5970

Best Italian Food
George's Cash and Carry
   44 Alfred St., 207/282-7479

Best Pizza
Alex's Pizza
   91 Alfred St., 207/283-0002

Best Sandwiches
George's Cash and Carry
   44 Alfred St., 207/282-7479

Best Seafood
Wonderbar Restaurant
   12 Washington St., 207/282-9926
Dry Dock
   631A Elm St., 207/282-3775

Best Sports Bar
Shelly's
   12 Lincoln St., 207/284-9283

Best Steaks
Wonderbar Restaurant
   12 Washington St., 207/282-9926

M

LEWISTON, ME

Best All-You-Can-Eat Buffet
Jungle Jim's Restaurant
   729 Main St., 207/783-4900

Best Atmosphere
Eli's
   Rte. 117, Turner, 207/224-7090
Sedgley Place
   Sedgley Rd., Greene, 207/946-5990

Best Breakfast
Bagels and Things
   213 Center St., Auburn, 207/782-4426
Mister Bagel
   336 Center St., Auburn, 207/777-7007

Best Burgers
Gipper's Sports Grill
   120 Center St., Auburn, 207/786-0715

Best Chinese Food
Chopsticks Restaurant
   37 Park St., 207/783-6300

Best Coffee
Austin's Fine Wines and Foods
   78 Main St., Auburn, 207/783-6312
Nothing But the Blues Cafe
   81 College St., 207/784-6493

Best Desserts
Marois Restaurant
249 Lisbon St., 207/782-9055
Austin's Fine Wines and Foods
78 Main St., Auburn, 207/783-6312

Best Family Restaurant
Village Inn
165 High St., Auburn, 207/782-7796

Best Homestyle Food
Fran's Place
1384 Lisbon St., 207/786-0667

Best Ice Cream/Yogurt
Cote's Old Fashioned Ice Cream
229 Center St., Auburn, 207/783-7177
585 College Rd., 207/784-7745
688 Main St., 207/786-2048

Best Mexican Food
Margarita's
838 Lisbon St., 207/782-6036

Best Pizza
George's Pizza
563 Center St., Auburn, 207/782-7141

Best Place to Eat When Someone Else Is Buying
Seasons Cafe
157 Main St., 207/782-5054

Best Seafood
Village Inn
165 High St., Auburn, 207/782-7796

PORTLAND, ME

Best Atmosphere
G'vanni's
37 Wharf St., 207/775-9061
Cafe Always
47 Middle St., 207/774-9399

Best Barbecue/Ribs
Uncle Billy's Southside B-B-Q
60 Ocean St., South Portland, 207/767-7119

Best Breakfast
Becky's
390 Commercial St., 207/773-7070

Best Brunch
Seamen's Club Restaurant
1 Exchange St., 207/772-7311

Best Burgers
Rosie's
330 Fore St., 207/772-5656
Stone Coast Brewery
14 York St., 207/773-2337

Best Casual Dining
David's Restaurant
164 Middle St., 207/773-4340

Best Coffee
Green Mountain Coffee Roasters
  15 Temple St., 207/773-4475
Java Joe's
  13 Exchange St., 207/761-5637

Best Desserts
Pate Aschou
  25 Pearl, 207/773-3334

Best Family Restaurants
Village Cafe
  112 Newbury St., 207/772-5320
Newark's Seafood Restaurant
  740 Broadway, South Portland, 207/799-3090

Best Health-Conscious Menu
Mesa Verde
  618 Congress St., 207/774-6089

Best Homestyle Food
Katahdin Restaurant
  106 High St., 207/774-1740

Best Italian Food
G'vanni's
  37 Wharf St., 207/775-9061
Perfetto
  28 Exchange St., 207/828-0001

Best Microbreweries
Stone Coast Brewery
  14 York St., 207/773-2337
Shipyard Brewery
  86 Newbury St., 207/761-0807
Gritty McDuff's
  396 Fore St., 207/772-2739

Best Outdoor Dining
Lobster Shack
  225 Two Lights Rd., Cape Elizabeth, 207/799-1677

Best Pizza
Ricetta's Brick Oven Pizzeria
  29 Western Ave., South Portland, 207/775-7400

Best Places to Eat When Someone Else Is Buying
Walter's
  15 Exchange St., 207/871-9258
Cafe Always
  47 Middle St., 207/774-9399

Best Regional Food
Lobster Shack
  225 Two Lights Rd., Cape Elizabeth, 207/799-1677
Gilbert's Chowder House
  92 Commercial St., 207/871-5636

Best Salad/Salad Bar
David's Restaurant
  164 Middle St., 207/773-4340

Best Sandwiches
Della's Catessen
  9 Deering Ave., 207/773-2624

M

Best Seafood
Newark's Seafood Restaurant
  740 Broadway, South Portland, 207/799-3090
Street and Company
  33 Wharf St., 207/775-0887

Best Steaks
F. Parker Reidy's
  83 Exchange St., 207/773-4731

Best Tea Room
Sweet Annie's Tea Shop
  93 India St., 207/773-3353

Best Thai Food
Sala Thai Restaurant
  1363 Washington Ave., 207/797-0871

Best View While Dining
Lobster Shack
  225 Two Lights Rd., Cape Elizabeth, 207/799-1677

Best Wine Selection
Walter's
  15 Exchange St., 207/871-9258
David's Restaurant
  164 Middle St., 207/773-4340

Standbys
Ben and Jerry's
  97A Exchange St., 207/773-3222

M

SANFORD, ME

Best Breakfast
Jerry's Restaurant
  2 Lebanon St., 207/324-0909
Jean's Bakery
  20 School St., 207/324-9827

Best Brunch
Mousam Falls Tavern
  Riverside Ave., 207/324-5430

Best Desserts
Shain's
  Wells Rd. S., 207/324-1449

Best Diner
Jerry's Restaurant
  2 Lebanon St., 207/324-0909

Best Family Restaurants
Le Beau's Pub and Grille
  277 Main St. Rear, 207/324-5664
The Falls Restaurant
  Riverside Ave., 207/324-5430
Weathervane Restaurant
  Rural Route 109, 207/324-0084

Best Ice Cream/Yogurt
Shain's
  Wells Rd. S., 207/324-1449

Best Pizza
House of Pizza
  270 Main St., 207/324-3161

Best Sandwiches
Moe's Italian Sandwiches
   4 School St., 207/490-0088

Best Seafood
Le Beau's Pub and Grille
   277 Main St., Rear, 207/324-5664

Best Steaks
The Falls Restaurant
   Riverside Ave., 207/324-5430

Standbys
Bonanza
   473 Main St., 207/324-6121
Dunkin' Donuts
   269 Main St., 207/324-8663

WATERVILLE, ME

Best Asian Restaurants
Jade Island Restaurant
   99 W. River Rd., 207/873-7181
Mei Lam Lau Restaurant
   John F. Kennedy Mall, 207/873-6378

Best Atmosphere
Last Unicorn
   8 Silver St., 207/873-6378
Silver Street Tavern
   2 Silver St., 207/873-2277

Best Brunch
Governor's
   356 Main St., 207/872-0677

Best Coffee
Jorgensen's
   103 Main St., 207/872-8711
   113 Main St., 207/872-8711
Main Street Cafe
   45 Main St., 207/872-8748

Best Desserts
Governor's
   356 Main St., 207/872-0677
Jorgensen's
   103 Main St., 207/872-8711
   113 Main St., 207/872-8711
Main Street Cafe
   45 Main St., 207/872-8748

Best Family Restaurants
Governor's
   356 Main St., 207/872-0677
Villager's Restaurant
   40 W. Concourse, 207/872-6231
Weathervane Seafoods
   470 Kennedy Memorial Dr., 207/873-4522

Best Ice Cream/Yogurt
Gifford's Ice Cream
   170 Silver St., 207/872-6631

M

Best Italian Food
Steve's Restaurant
  14 Silver St., 207/872-9887

Best Mexican Food
Sombrero's
  475 Kennedy Memorial Dr., 207/872-8226

Best Seafood
Weathervane Seafoods
  470 Kennedy Memorial Dr., 207/873-4522

Best Steaks
Steve's Restaurant
  14 Silver St., 207/872-9887

M

Maryland

Best Family Restaurant
The Olive Tree
  1005 Beards Hill Rd., 410/272-6217

Best Homestyle Food
New Ideal Diner
  104 S. Philadelphia Blvd., 410/272-1880

Best Ice Cream/Yogurt
Carvel
  951 Beards Hill Rd., Ste. 1, 410/272-0808

Best Italian Food
The Olive Tree
  1005 Beards Hill Rd., 410/272-6217

Best Pizza
Frank's Pizza
  37 W. Bel Air Ave., 410/272-2878

Best Sandwiches
Frank's Pizza
  37 W. Bel Air Ave., 410/272-2878

Best Seafood
Tidewater Grille
  300 Franklin St., Havre De Grace, 410/939-3313

Best Steaks
Colonel's Choice
  Carol Ave. at Rte. 40, 410/272-6500
Towne House Restaurant
  705 S. Philadelphia Blvd., 410/272-4404

Standbys
Golden Corral Family Steak House
  991 Beards Hill Rd., 410/272-0668

Best American Food
Northwood's
  609 Melvin Ave., 410/268-2609

M

Best Bar
Middleton Tavern
  2 Market Space, 410/263-3323

Best Brunch
Maryland Inn
  16 Church Circle, 410/263-2641

Best Burgers
McGarvey's Saloon
  8 Market Space, 410/263-5700

Best French Food
Cafe Normandie
  185 Main St., 410/263-3382

Best Greek/Mediterranean Food
Scirrocco Mediterranean Grill
  2552 Riva Rd., 410/573-0970

Best Indian Food
India Palace
  186 Main St., 410/263-7900

Best Italian Food
Scirrocco Mediterranean Grill
  2552 Riva Rd., 410/573-0970

Best Mexican Food
Caliente Restaurant
  50 West St., 410/268-8548

Best Seafood
Carrol's Creek Cafe
  410 Severn Ave., 410/263-8102
O'Leary's Seafood Restaurant
  310 Third St., 410/263-0884

Best Steaks
McGarvey's Saloon
  8 Market Space, 410/263-5700
Lewne's Steakhouse
  401 Fourth St., 410/263-1617

BALTIMORE, MD

Best Restaurant in Town
Orchard Market and Cafe
  8815 Orchard Tree Ln., 410/339-7700

Best Bagels
Joan and Gary's Original Bagel Company, Inc.
  1496 Reisterstown Rd., Pikesville, 410/484-9102
Sam's Bagels
  500 W. Cold Spring Ln., 410/243-1774
  915 Light St., 410/837-5774

Best Bars
Henninger's Tavern
  1812 Bank St., 410/342-2172
Peter's Inn
  504 S. Ann St., 410/675-7313

Best Breakfast
The Bridge
  353 Calvert St., 410/727-8858

Jimmy's Restaurant
  801 S. Broadway, 410/327-3273
Morning Edition Cafe
  153 N. Patterson Park Ave., 410/732-5133
Rallo's
  838 E. Fort Ave., 410/727-7067

Best Brunch
Sfuzzi
  100 E. Pratt St., 410/576-8500
The Hyatt
  300 Light St., 410/528-1234
Morning Edition Cafe
  153 N. Patterson Park Ave., 410/732-5133
Louie's Bookstore Cafe and Bakery
  518 N. Charles St., 410/962-1224

Best Burgers
Jerry D's Carry-Out
  7812 Harford Rd., Parkville, 410/665-9004
Alonso's Restaurant and Lounge
  415 W. Cold Spring Ln., 410/235-3433

Best Casual Dining
Jilly's
  1012 Reisterstown Rd., Pikesville, 410/653-0610

Best Cheap Meal
Nice and Easy Restaurant
  700 S. Broadway, 410/732-8821
Cafe Hon
  1009 W. 36th St., 410/243-1230

Best Chinese Food
Szechuan Restaurant
  1125 S. Charles St., 410/752-8409
Uncle Lee's
  3317 Greenmount Ave., 410/366-3333
  44 South St., 410/727-6666

Best Coffee
The Coffee Cafe
  6303 York Rd., 410/435-3040
The Daily Grind
  1726 Thames St., 410/558-0399
Donna's Coffee Bar
  Multiple Locations
City Cafe
  1001 Cathedral St., 410/539-4252

Best Coffeehouse
Funk's Democratic Coffee Spot
  1818 Eastern Ave., 410/276-3865

Best Delicatessen
Attman's Delicatessen
  1019 E. Lombard St., 410/563-2666

Best Desserts
Spike and Charlie's
  1225 Cathedral St., 410/752-8144
Vaccaro's Italian Pastry Shop
  222 Albemarle St., 410/685-4905

M

Gemelli Desserts
  25 Allegheny Ave., 410/321-8800

Best Diners
Double T Diner
  6300 Baltimore National Pike, 410/744-4151
Paper Moon Diner
  227 W. 29th St., 410/889-4444

Best Family Restaurant
Mick's
  425 York Rd., 410/825-0071

Best French Food
Cafe Troia
  28 W. Allegheny Ave., 410/337-0133

Best Happy-Hour Snacks
Sfuzzi
  100 E. Pratt St., 410/576-8500

Best Health-Conscious Menu
Harvey's of Green Spring Station
  2350 W. Joppa Rd., 410/296-9526

Best Homestyle Food
Black-Eyed Pea
  7939 S. Ritchie Hwy, Glen Burnie, 410/761-5572
  8335 Benson Dr., Columbia, 410/290-1522
Silver Diner
  825 Dulaney Valley Rd., 410/823-5566

Best Ice Cream/Yogurt
Scoops Ice Cream Parlor
  63 Shipping Pl., 410/288-2257

Best Indian Food
Akbar
  823 N. Charles St., 410/539-0944
  3541 Brenbrook Dr., Randallstown, 410/655-1600
Mughal Garden
  920 N. Charles St., 410/547-0001

Best Italian Food
Mamma Lucia
  9616 Reisterstown Rd., Owings Mills, 410/363-0496
Sabatino's Italian Restaurant
  901 Fawn St., 410/727-9414
Giuseppe's
  248 Albemarle St., 410/685-1859

Best Japanese Food
Matsuri Restaurant
  1105 S. Charles St., 410/752-8561
Kawasaki Japanese Food
  413 N. Charles St., 410/659-7600

Best Korean Food
Nam Kang
  2126 Maryland Ave., 410/685-6237
Kimmy's Restaurant and Carryout
  5016 Sinclair Ln., 410/483-0085
New No Da Ji Restaurant
  2501 N. Charles St., 410/235-4846

Best Late-Night Food
Paper Moon Diner
227 W. 29th St., 410/889-4444
Sip and Bite
2200 Boston St., 410/675-7077
Casa Mia's
40 York Rd., 410/321-8707

Best Mexican Food
Loco Hombre
413 W. Cold Spring Ln., 410/889-2233
Lista's
1637 Thames St., 410/327-0040

Best Microbrewery
The Wharf Rat Brew Pub and Restaurant
206 W. Pratt St., 410/244-8900

Best Neighborhood Bars
Alonso's Restaurant and Lounge
415 W. Cold Spring Ln., 410/235-3433
The Rendezvous Lounge
203 W. 25th St., 410/467-3860

Best Other Ethnic Food
The Helmand (Afghan)
806 N. Charles St., 410/752-0311
Braznell's Caribbean Kitchen (Caribbean)
1623 E. Baltimore St., 410/327-2445
Orchard Market and Cafe (Persian)
8815 Orchard Tree Ln., Towson, 410/339-7700

Best Outdoor Dining
Gypsy's Cafe
1103 Hollins St., 410/625-9310

Best Pizza
Al Pacino Cafe
900 Cathedral St., 410/962-8859
609 S. Broadway, 410/327-0005
542 E. Belvedere Ave., 410/323-7060
513 Baltimore Pike, Bel Air, 410/638-8057
Pizzeria Uno Restaurant and Bar
201 E. Pratt St., 410/625-5900
435 York Rd., 410/823-5566

Best Place to Be "Seen"
Hersh's Orchard Inn
1528 E. Joppa Rd., 410/823-0384

Best Place to Eat Alone
Borders Bookstore
415 York Rd., 410/296-0791

Best Places to Eat When Someone Else Is Buying
Polo Grill
4 W. University Pkwy., 410/235-8200
Tio Pepe Restaurant
10 E. Franklin St., 410/539-4675

Best Place to Take Guests
Pierpoint
1822 Aliceanna St., 410/675-2080

Best Place to Take the Kids
Irina's Cafe
· 3200 Barclay St., 410/889-1502

Best Regional Food
Koco's Pub
4301 Harford Rd., 410/426-3519
Angelina's Restaurant
7135 Harford Rd., 410/444-5545
Ransome's Harbor Hill Cafe
1032 Riverside Ave., 410/576-9720

Best Salad/Salad Bar
Produce Galore
5430 Lynx Lane, 410/730-1937
Paolo's Italian Restaurant
301 Light St., 410/539-7060
1 W. Pennsylvania Ave., 410/321-7000

Best Seafood
The Crab Shanty Restaurant
3410 Plumtree Dr., Ellicott City, 410/465-9660
Fisherman's Wharf Restaurant
826 Dulaney Valley Rd., 410/337-2909

Best Soul Food
Ree Bee's Place
1690B Annapolis Rd., Odenton, 410/674-2336

Best Sports Bar
Balls
200 W. Pratt St., 410/576-0721

Best Steaks
McCafferty's
1501 Sulgrave Ave., 410/664-2200

Best Thai Food
Thai Landing
1207 N. Charles St., 410/727-1234
The Bangkok Place
5230 York Rd., 410/433-0040
Thai Restaurant
3316 Greenmount Ave., 410/889-7303

Best Vegetarian Food
Live It Not Diet Natural Food
3803 Woodbine Ave., 410/542-7355

Best Vietnamese Food
Saigon Restaurant
3345 Bel Air Rd., 410/276-0055

Standbys
Chuck E. Cheese Pizza
809 Goucher Blvd., 410/823-1756
Ruth's Chris Steak House
34 Market Pl., 410/783-0033
600 Water St., 410/783-0033

BOWIE, MD

Best Restaurant in Town
Mare e Monti Ristorante
15554B Annapolis Rd., 301/262-9179

Best American Food
Rip's Country Inn
3809 N. Crane Hwy., 301/805-5901

Best Breakfast
Rick's American Grill
1334 Defense Hwy., Gambrills, 410/721-3500

Best Homestyle Food
Rick's American Grill
1334 Defense Hwy., Gambrills, 410/721-3500

Best Italian Food
Mare e Monti Ristorante
15554B Annapolis Rd., 301/262-9179

Best Lunch
Jasper's Restaurant
1651 Rte. 3, Crofton, 301/261-3505

Best Salad/Salad Bar
Jasper's Restaurant
1651 Rte. 3, Crofton, 301/261-3505

Best Seafood
Sly Horse Tavern
1678 Village Green, Crofton, 410/721-4550

Best Steaks
Rip's Country Inn
3809 N. Crane Hwy., 301/805-5901

M

CAMBRIDGE, MD

Best Atmosphere
McGuigan's Pub
411 Muir St., 410/228-7110

Best Breakfast
English's Family Restaurant
Rural Route 50, 410/228-4344

Best Burgers
Snapper's
112 Commerce St., 410/228-0112

Best Desserts
McGuigan's Pub
411 Muir St., 410/228-7110

Best Family Restaurant
Old Salty's Restaurant
2560 Hooper's Island Rd., Fishing Creek,
410/397-3752

Best Health-Conscious Menu
McGuigan's Pub
411 Muir St., 410/228-7110

Best Ice Cream/Yogurt
Hyser's Old Time Soda Fountain
824 Locust St., 410/228-3465

Best Italian Food
Rusticana Pizza
Shoal Creek Mall, 410/228-1515

Best Other Ethnic Food
McGuigan's Pub (English)
  411 Muir St., 410/228-7110

Best Outdoor Dining
Snapper's
  112 Commerce St., 410/228-0112

Best Pizza
Hyser's Old Time Soda Fountain
  824 Locust St., 410/228-3465
Rusticana Pizza
  Shoal Creek Mall, 410/228-1515

Best Places to Take the Kids
High Spot
  303 High St., 410/228-3410
Spicer's Seafood Restaurant
  802 Wood Rd., 410/221-0222

Best Sandwiches
Creek Deli
  106 Market Square, 410/228-1161
Pleez Stop Deli
  501 Maryland Ave., 410/228-7301

Best Seafood
Snapper's
  112 Commerce St., 410/228-0112
Spicer's Seafood Restaurant
  802 Wood Rd., 410/221-0222

Best Southwestern Food
Snapper's
  112 Commerce St., 410/228-0112

Best Steaks
High Spot
  303 High St., 410/228-3410

Best View While Dining
Snapper's
  112 Commerce St., 410/228-0112
Old Salty's Restaurant
  2560 Hooper's Island Rd., Fishing Creek,
    410/397-3752

CUMBERLAND, MD

Best Restaurant in Town
L'Osteria
  I-68, 301/777-3553

Best American Food
Harrigan's
  100 S. George St., 301/724-8800

Best Breakfast
D'Atri's Restaurant
  1118 National Hwy., 301/729-2774

Best Chinese Food
Peking Palace Chinese Restaurant
  1209 National Hwy., 301/729-1400

Best Italian Food
L'Osteria
I-68, 301/777-3553

Best Seafood
When Pigs Fly
18 Valley St., 301/722-7447

Best Steaks
Carmichael's
209 N. Mechanic St., 301/777-2523
J.B. Steak Cellar
I-68, Exit 46E, 301/722-6155

FREDERICK, MD

Best Restaurant in Town
Tauraso's Ristorante
4 East St., 301/663-6600

Best All-You-Can-Eat Buffets
Dan-Dee Motel and Country Inn
7817 Baltimore National Pike, 301/473-8282
Cozy Family Restaurant
103 Frederick Rd., 301/271-7373

Best Bar
Red Horse Restaurant
996 W. Patrick St., 301/663-3030

Best Breakfast
Beans and Bagels
49 E. Patrick St., 301/620-2165

Best Brunch
Old South Mountain Inn
6132 Old National Pike, 301/432-6155

Best Business Lunch
Deli Restaurant
57 E. Patrick St., 301/663-8122
Jennifer's
207 W. Patrick St., 301/662-0373

Best Coffee
Beans and Bagels
49 E. Patrick St., 301/620-2165

Best Family Restaurants
Dan-Dee Motel
7817 Baltimore National Pike, 301/473-8282
Cozy Family Restaurant
103 Frederick Rd., 301/271-7373

Best Health-Conscious Menu
Orchard Restaurant
48 E. Patrick St., 301/663-4912

Best Italian Food
Nido Italiano
111 E. Patrick St., 301/694-5939
Ernie's Italian Kitchen
1818 Rosemont Ave., 301/662-1287
Tauraso's Ristorante
4 East St., 301/663-6600

M

Best Mexican Food
La Paz Mexican Restaurant
  18 Market Space, 301/694-8980

Best Sandwiches
Jennifer's Restaurant
  207 W. Patrick St., 301/662-0373
Griff's Landing
  43 S. Market St., 301/694-8696

Best Seafood
Dutch's Daughters
  5901 Old National Pike, 301/663-0297
Quail Ridge Inn
  Rte. 27, 301/829-9040

Best Vegetarian Food
Orchard Restaurant
  48 E. Patrick St., 301/663-4912

GAITHERSBURG, MD

Best All-You-Can-Eat Buffet
Village Park Cafe
  2 Montgomery Village Ave., 301/948-8900

Best Barbecue/Ribs
Bare Bones
  617 S. Frederick Ave., 301/948-4344

Best Burgers
Hamburger Hamlet
  9811 Washington Blvd., 301/417-0773

Best Casual Dining
Olde Towne Tavern
  227 E. Diamond Ave., 301/948-4200

Best Chinese Food
Wok Express Chinese Restaurant
  9615 Lost Knife Rd., 301/948-8788

Best Dinner
Gentleman Jim's Restaurant
  18917 Earhart Ct., 301/963-7778
Golden Bull Grand Cafe
  7 Dalamar St., 301/948-3666

Best French Food
Lesparadis
  347 Muddy Branch Rd., 301/208-9493

Best Lunch
Gallagher's III
  16533 S. Frederick Ave., 301/977-9000
Muldoon's and JJ
  16143 Shady Grove Rd., 301/258-8866

Best Microbrewery
Olde Towne Tavern
  227 E. Diamond Ave., 301/948-4200

Best Outdoor Dining
Village Grill and Cafe
  18749 N. Frederick Ave., 301/948-5228

M

Best Salad/Salad Bar
Village Grill
18749 N. Frederick Ave., 301/948-5228
Gallagher's III
16533 S. Frederick Ave., 301/977-9000

Best Sandwiches
Roy's Place
2 E. Diamond Ave., 301/948-5548

Best Seafood
Fegan's Seafood
9811 Washington Blvd., 301/948-0900

Best Sports Bar
Chris' Restaurant
201 E. Diamond Ave., 301/869-6116

Best Steaks
Chris' Restaurant
201 E. Diamond Ave., 301/869-6116
Bugaboo Creek Steakhouse
15710 Shady Grove Rd., 301/548-9200

Best Thai Food
Thai Sa Mai Restaurant
8369 Snouffers School Rd., 301/963-1800

M

GLEN BURNIE, MD

Best Breakfast
Breakfast Shoppe
360 Ritchie Hwy., Severna Park, 410/544-8599
Honey Bee Drive-In
7346 Ritchie Hwy., 410/761-0477

Best Chinese Food
Ying's Restaurant
6619 Ritchie Hwy., 410/760-3131

Best Dinner
Sunset Restaurant
625 Greenway Rd. SE, 410/768-1417

Best Italian Food
Trattoria Alberto
1660 Crain Hwy. S., 410/761-0922

Best Place to Eat When Someone Else Is Buying
Trattoria Alberto
1660 Crain Hwy. S., 410/761-0922

Best Seafood
Seaside Seafood and Crab Shack
224 N. Crain Hwy., 410/760-2200

Best Thai Food
Bangkok Oriental
8043F Richie Hwy., 410/766-0973

Standbys
Sizzler
7142 Richie Hwy., 410/761-6044

HAGERSTOWN, MD

Best Restaurants in Town
Bavarian Inn and Lodge
  Rte. 1, Shepherdstown, 304/876-2551
Old South Mountain Inn
  6132 Old National Pike, Boonsboro, 301/432-6155
Mealey's Restaurant
  8 Main St., New Market, 301/865-5488

Best All-You-Can-Eat Buffet
Cozy Kitchen
  29 S. Potomoc St., 301/797-4922

Best Brunch
Old South Mountain Inn
  6132 Old National Pike, Boonsboro, 301/432-6155

Best German Food
Schmankerl Stube
  58 S. Potomoc St., 301/797-3354

Best Health-Conscious Menu
Grill at the Park Circle
  325 Virginia Ave., 301/797-9100

Best Japanese Food
House of Kobe
  757 Dual Hwy., 301/797-6979

Best Seafood
Nick's Airport Inn
  Rte. 11N, 301/733-8560

OCEAN CITY, MD

Best Restaurants in Town
Adolfo's Italian Family Restaurant
  806 S. Baltimore Ave., 410/289-4001
The Atlantic Hotel Restaurant
  2 N. Main St., Berlin, 410/641-0189

Best All-You-Can-Eat Buffet
Phillip's Crab House
  2004 N. Philadelphia Ave., 410/289-6821

Best Cheap Meal
Happy Chinese Restaurant
  9936 Stephen Decatur Hwy., 410/213-2663

Best Chinese Food
Charlie Chiang's Restaurant
  5401 Coastal Hwy., 410/723-4600

Best Italian Food
Adolfo's Italian
  806 S. Baltimore Ave., 410/289-4001

Best Mexican Food
Tio Gringo's
  5309 Ocean Hwy., 410/524-6244

Best Place to Eat When Someone Else Is Buying
The Atlantic Hotel Restaurant
  2 N. Main St., Berlin, 410/641-0189

Best Romantic Dining
The Atlantic Hotel Restaurant
   2 N. Main St., Berlin, 410/641-0189

Best Seafood
Phillip's by the Sea
   Oceanfront and Thirteenth St., 410/289-9121

Best Takeout Restaurant
Happy Chinese Restaurant
   9936 Stephen Decatur Hwy., 410/213-2663

ROCKVILLE, MD

Best Asian Restaurant
House of Chinese Chicken
   12710 Twinbrook Pkwy., 301/881-4500

Best Casual Dining
Tasty Diner
   11806 Rockville Pike, 301/770-0333

Best Diner
Tastee Diner
   8516 Georgia Ave., Silver Spring, 301/589-8171

Best Dinner
Houston's Restaurant
   12256 Rockville Pike, 301/468-3535

Best German Food
Wurzburg-Haus Restaurant
   7236 Muncaster Mill Rd., 301/330-0402

Best Italian Food
Il Pizzico
   15209 Frederick Rd., 301/309-0610

Best Pizza
Paolo's
   1801 Rockville Pike, 301/984-2211

Best Seafood
O'Donnell's
   8301 Wisconsin Ave., Bethesda, 301/654-5753

Best Vietnamese Food
Taste of Saigon
   410 Hungerford Dr., 301/424-7222

SALISBURY, MD

Best Barbecue/Ribs
Adam's, The Place for Ribs
   219 N. Fruitland St., 410/749-6961

Best Breakfast
Dayton's Chicken and Seafood
   909 Snow Hill Rd., 410/548-2272

Best Burgers
Good Ole Days
   733 S. Salisbury Blvd., 410/546-5701

Best Cheap Meal
Nacho Pete's
   717 Roland St., 410/546-0779

Best Chinese Food
Imperial Gallery Restaurant
  32B Civic Ave., 410/546-3103

Best Family Restaurant
English's Family Restaurant
  735 S. Salisbury Blvd., 410/742-8182
  1123 S. Division St., 410/742-8183

Best Italian Food
Zia's Pastaria
  2408 N. Salisbury Blvd., 410/543-9118

Best Sports Bar
Montana's Steak House and Sports Bar
  810 Beaglin Park Dr., 410/543-4415

Best Steaks
Montana's Steak House and Sports Bar
  810 Beaglin Park Dr., 410/543-4415

TOWSON, MD

Best Bars
Palermo's Grille
  106 W. Padonia Rd., Timonium, 410/252-0600
Michael's Cafe
  2119 York Rd., Timonium, 410/252-2022

Best Brunch
Peerce's Plantation
  12450 Dulaney Valley Rd., Phoenix, 410/252-3100

Best Casual Dining
Vito's Cafe
  10249 York Rd., Cockeysville, 410/666-3100

Best Cheap Meal
Sona's Cafe
  414 York Rd., 410/337-3837

Best Chinese Food
Hunt Valley Szechuan
  9 Schilling Rd., Hunt Valley, 410/527-1818

Best Diner
Ralphie's Diner
  9690 Deereco Rd., Timonium, 410/252-3990

Best Eclectic Menu
Pacific Rim
  9726 York Rd., Cockeysville, 410/666-2336

Best Italian Food
Liberatore's Ristorante
  9515 Deereco Rd., Timonium, 410/561-3300

Best Late-Night Food
Casa Mia's
  8601 Honeygo Blvd., 410/931-0200

Best Mexican Food
Saguaro's
  2 W. Pennsylvania Ave., 410/339-7774

Best Romantic Dining
The Milton Inn
  14833 York Rd., Sparks Glencoe, 410/771-4366

Best Sandwiches
Donna's Coffee Bar
  Multiple Locations

Best Seafood
Gibby's Seafood Restaurant
  22 W. Padonia Rd., Timonium, 410/560-0703
Ocean Pride Restaurant
  1534 York Rd., Lutherville, 410/321-7744

WALDORF, MD

Best Barbecue/Ribs
Lefty's Bar-B-Que Unlimited
  2064 Crain Hwy., 301/870-8998

Best Burgers
Flamers Charburgers
  5000 Hwy. 301, 301/870-7995

Best Chinese Food
Aloha
  175 Smallwood Village Ctr., 301/645-8907

Best Homestyle Food
Marie's Family Restaurant
  6325 Crain Hwy., La Plata, 301/932-6884

Best Pizza
Uno Chicago Bar and Grill
  11215 Mall Circle, 301/705-8420

Best Seafood
Captain Billy's Crab House
  Popes Creek Rd., La Plata, 301/932-4323

Standbys
Baskin-Robbins
  3261 Crain Hwy., 301/645-1108
Chuck E. Cheese Pizza
  4824 Festival Way, 301/932-4640
Haagen-Dazs
  1090 Smallwood Dr., 301/870-6612
International House of Pancakes
  2190 Crain Hwy., 301/843-1233
Outback Steakhouse
  3020 Crain Hwy., 301/645-4120
The Olive Garden
  3620 Crain Hwy., 301/374-9311
Old Country Buffet
  2916 Festival Way, 301/645-9161
Ruby Tuesday
  5000 Hwy. 301, 301/843-4020

M

Massachusetts

Best Breakfast
Daisy's
1185 N. Pleasant St., 413/549-6643

Best Chinese Food
Amherst Chinese Food
62 Main St., 413/253-7835

Best Desserts
Judie's
51 N. Pleasant St., 413/253-3491

Best Dinner
Seasons Restaurant
529 Belchertown Rd., 413/253-9909

Best Health-Conscious Menu
Judie's
51 N. Pleasant St., 413/253-3491

Best Italian Food
Melina's Trattoria
21 Center St., Northampton, 413/586-8900

Best Lunch
Antonio's Pizza
31 N. Pleasant St., 413/253-0808

Best Pizza
Antonio's Pizza
31 N. Pleasant St., 413/253-0808

Best Place to Eat When Someone Else Is Buying
Seasons Restaurant
529 Belchertown Rd., 413/253-9909

Best Seafood
East Side Grill
19 Strong Ave., Northampton, 413/586-3347

Best Thai Food
Amber Waves
31 Boltwood Walk, 413/253-9200

M

ANDOVER, MA

Best Restaurant in Town
Eighteen Elm Street
  18 Elm St., 508/470-1606

Best Breakfast
Shawsheen Luncheonette
  3 Lowell St., 508/475-9750

Best Continental Food
Backstreet Restaurant
  19 Essex St., 508/475-4411

Best Dinner
Eighteen Elm Street
  18 Elm St., 508/470-1606

Best Italian Food
Vincenzo's
  12 Main St., 508/475-7711

Best Lunch
Ninety-Nine Restaurant
  464 Lowell St., 508/475-8033
Bertucci's
  90 Main St., 508/470-3939

Best Pizza
Bertucci's
  90 Main St., 508/470-3939

M

ATHOL, MA

Best All-You-Can-Eat Buffet
Homestead Fine Foods and Spirits
  47 Daniel Shays Hwy., Orange, 508/544-8949

Best Atmosphere
Homestead Fine Foods and Spirits
  47 Daniel Shays Hwy., Orange, 508/544-8949

Best Breakfast
Cinnamon's Restaurant
  491 Main St., 508/249-6033

Best Burgers
Udder Place
  475 E. Main St., Orange, 508/544-8689

Best Chinese Food
King Sing Restaurant
  46 W. Main St., Orange, 508/544-8853

Best Ice Cream/Yogurt
Scoops Dairy Bar
  32 Freedom St., 508/249-9952
Udder Place
  475 E. Main St., Orange, 508/544-8689

Best Pizza
Athol House of Pizza Restaurant
  522 Main St., 508/249-3762

Best Sandwiches
Deli Patch
  131 S. Main St., 508/249-9956

Best Steaks
Athol Steak House
  14 Grove St., 508/249-2624
King Phillip Restaurant
  35 State Rd., Phillipston, 508/249-6300

ATTLEBORO, MA

Best Restaurant in Town
Ann's Place
  48 Bay Rd., Norton, 508/285-9766

Best American Food
Old Grist Mill Tavern
  390 Fall River Ave., Seekonk, 508/336-8460

Best Delicatessen
Bagels and Cream
  5 Bank St., 508/222-1318

Best Diner
Morin's Diner
  16 S. Main St., 508/222-9875

Best Dinner
Union Station
  88 Union St., 508/222-3760
Williams Restaurant
  16 S. Main St., 508/222-8834
Ann's Place
  48 Bay Rd., Norton, 508/285-9766

Best Family Restaurant
Morin's Diner
  16 S. Main St., 508/222-9875

Best Pizza
Eli's Pizza
  99 County St., 508/222-1824

Best Place to Eat When Someone Else Is Buying
Ann's Place
  48 Bay Rd., Norton, 508/285-9766

Best Seafood
Old Grist Mill
  390 Fall River Ave., Seekonk, 508/336-8460

Best Steaks
Bugaboo Creek Steak House
  1125 Fall River Ave., Seekonk, 508/336-2200

BEVERLY, MA

Best Atmosphere
Beverly Depot Restaurant
  10 Park St., 508/927-5402
Roscoe's Restaurant
  208 Rantoul St., 508/927-2028

Best Breakfast
Brothers Restaurant and Deli
  446 Rantoul St., 508/927-8535
Omelette Headquarters
  218 Cabot St., 508/922-8126

Best Eclectic Menu
Tapas Corner
  284 Cabot St., 508/927-9983

Best Greek/Mediterranean Food
Brothers Restaurant and Deli
  446 Rantoul St., 508/927-8535

Best Italian Food
Bella Venezia
  150 Cabot St., 508/927-2365

Best Mexican Food
Casa De Lucca
  146 Rantoul St., 508/922-7660

Best Romantic Dining
Chianti Cafe and Grill
  285 Cabot St., 508/921-9343

Best Salad/Salad Bar
Beverly Depot Restaurant
  10 Park St., 508/927-5402

Best Seafood
Cabot Place Restaurant
  256 Cabot St., 508/927-3920

Best Steaks
Roscoe's Restaurant
  208 Rantoul St., 508/927-2028

M

BOSTON, MA

Best Restaurants in Town
Aujourd'hui
  Four Seasons Hotel, 200 Boylston St., 617/338-4400
Biba
  272 Boylston St., 617/426-7878
Olive's
  10 City Sq., Charlestown, 617/242-1999
Rosalie's
  20 Sewall St., Marblehead, 617/631-5353
La Paloma
  1037 Main St., Weymouth, 617/335-1773
  195 Newport Ave., Quincy, 617/773-0512
Tosca
  14 North St., Hingham, 617/740-0080
Caffe Bella
  19 Warren St., Randolph, 617/961-7729
Rosalie's
  18 Sewall St., Marblehead, 617/631-5353
White Rainbow
  65 Main St., Gloucester, 617/281-0017
Appetito
  761 Beacon St., Newton, 617/244-9881
  1 Appleton St., 617/338-6777
Tuscan Grill
  361 Moody St., Waltham, 617/891-5486
Caprico
  53 Prospect St., Waltham, 617/ 894-2234
Pillar House
  26 Quinobequin Rd., Newton, 617/969-6500

Best American Food
Grill 23 and Bar
  161 Berkeley St., 617/542-2255
Joe's American Bar and Grill
  279 Dartmouth St., 617/536-4200
Biba
  272 Boylston St., 617/426-7878
Capital Grille
  359 Newbury St., 617/ 262-8900
Olive's
  10 City Sq., Charlestown, 617/242-1999

Best Barbecue/Ribs
East Coast Grill
  1271 Cambridge St., Cambridge, 617/350-7777
Redbones
  55 Chester St., Somerville, 617/628-2200
Village Smokehouse
  6 Harvard Sq., Brookline, 617/566-3782
East Coast Grill
  1271 Cambridge St., Cambridge, 617/491-6568

Best Beer Selection
Boston Beer Works
  61 Brookline Ave., 617/536-2337
Commonwealth Brewing Company
  138 Portland St., 617/523-8383
John Harvard's Brew House
  33 Dunster St., Cambridge, 617/868-3585
Sunset Grill and Tap
  130 Brighton Ave., Allyston, 617/254-1331

Best Breakfast
Charlie's Sandwich Shoppe
  429 Columbus Ave., 617/536-7669
Geoffrey's Cafe Bar
  578 Tremont St., 617/266-1122
  651 Boylston St., 617/437-6400
Sonsie
  327 Newbury St., 617/351-2500
Blue Diner
  178 Kneeland St., 617/338-4639

Best Brunch
Cafe Fleuri
  Hotel Meridien, 250 Franklin St., 617/451-1900
Ritz-Carlton Dining Room
  Ritz-Carlton Hotel, 15 Arlington St., 617/536-5700
Rowes Wharf Restaurant
  Boston Harbor Hotel, 70 Rowes Wharf, 617/439-3995

Best Burgers
Division Sixteen
  955 Boylston St., 617/353-0870
Casey's
  171 Broadway, Somerville, 617/625-5195
Mr. Bartley's Burger Cottage
  1246 Massachusetts Ave., Cambridge, 617/354-6559
Charley's Eating and Drinking Saloon
  284 Newbury St., 617/266-3000

M

Best Chinese Food
Golden Temple
  1651 Beacon St., Brookline, 617/277-9722
Grand Chau Chow
  52 Beach St., 617/426-6266
Kowloon
  948 Broadway, Saugus, 617/233-0077
Joyce Chen
  115 Stuart St., 617/720-1331
  390 Rindge Ave., Cambridge, 617/492-7373
Mr. Leung
  545 Boylston St., 617/236-4040

Best Clam Chowder
Turner Fisheries
  Westin Hotel, 10 Huntington Ave., 617/424-7425
Union Oyster House
  41 Union St., 617/227-2750
Boston Sail Loft Cafe and Bar
  1 Memorial Dr., Cambridge, 617/225-2222
  80 Atlantic Ave., 617/227-7280
No-Name Restaurant
  15 1/2 Fish Pier, 617/423-2705

Best Coffeehouses
Caffe Vittoria
  296 Hanover St., 617/227-7606
The Coffee Connection
  Multiple Locations

Best Delicatessens
B and D Deli
  1653 Beacon St., Brookline, 617/232-3727
KJ's Deli and Restaurant
  335 Harvard St., Brookline, 617/738-3354
S and S Restaurant
  1334 Cambridge St., Cambridge, 617/354-0777

Best Desserts
Ambrosia on Huntington
  116 Huntington Ave., 617/247-2400
Biba
  272 Boylston St., 617/426-7878
Olive's
  10 City Sq., Charlestown, 617/242-1999
Aujourd'hui
  Four Seasons Hotel, 200 Boylston St., 617/338-4400

Best Dim Sum
China Pearl
  9 Tyler St., 617/426-4338
Dynasty
  33 Edinboro St., 617/350-7777
Imperial Seafood
  70 Beach St., 617/426-8439

Best Eclectic Menu
Ambrosia on Huntington
  116 Huntington Ave., 617/247-2400
Cafe Eurosia
  Park Plaza Hotel, 54 Arlington St., 617/542-1616

Wild Ginger Bistro
  95 Massachusetts Ave., 617/267-2868

Best Family Restaurants
Mount Vernon Restaurant
  14 Broadway, Somerville, 617/666-3830
Paddock Lounge and Pizza
  249 Pearl St., Somerville, 617/628-6525

Best French Food
Julien
  Hotel Meridien, 250 Franklin St., 617/422-5194
L'Espalier
  30 Gloucester St., 617/262-3023
Robert Maison
  45 School St., 617/227-3370

Best Greek/Mediterranean Food
Averof Restaurant
  1924 Massachusetts Ave., Cambridge, 617/354-4500
Omonia Greek
  75 Charles St., 617/426-4310
Steve's Restaurant
  316 Newbury St., 617/267-1817
Dali
  415 Washington St., Somerville, 617/661-3254
Mediterraneo Bistro
  323 Turnpike Rd., Canton, 617/821-8881
Rialto
  The Charles Hotel, 1 Bennett St., Cambridge,
    617/864-1200

Best Homestyle Food
Mount Vernon Restaurant
  14 Broadway, Somerville, 617/666-3830

Best Indian Food
Bombay Bistro
  1353B Beacon St., Brookline, 617/734-2879
Bombay Club
  57 John F. Kennedy St., Cambridge, 617/661-8100
Kashmir
  279 Newbury St., 617/536-1695

Best Italian Food
Mama Maria's
  118 Bunker Hill St., Charlestown, 617/242-4687
  3 North Sq., 617/523-0077
Ristorante Toscano
  100 Condor St., 617/567-7600
  41 Charles St., 617/723-4090
Trattoria Il Panino
  11 Parmenter St., 617/720-1336
  310 Franklin St., 617/338-1000
Rialto
  Charles Hotel, 1 Bennett St., Cambridge,
    617/864-1200
The Chateau Restaurant
  195 School St., Waltham, 617/894-3339

Best Japanese Food
Gyuhama
  827 Boylston St., 617/437-0188

Cafe and Grill
.0 Columbus Ave., 617/421-9405
.281 Cambridge St., Cambridge, 617/497-8380
iyako
279A Newbury St., 617/236-0222
Kyoto Japanese Steak House and Sushi Bar
201 Stuart St., 617/542-1168

Best Late-Night Food
Blue Diner
150 Kneeland St., 617/426-7878
Rocco's
5 Charles St. S., 617/723-6800
Sonsie
327 Newbury St., 617/351-2500

Best Mexican Food
Border Cafe
32 Church St., Cambridge, 617/864-6100
817 Broadway, Saugus, 617/233-5308
Rudy's Cafe
248 Holland St., Somerville, 617/623-9201
Casa Romero
30 Gloucester St., 617/536-4341
La Paloma
1037 Main St., Weymouth, 617/335-1773
195 Newport Ave., Quincy, 617/773-0512
Sol Azteca
914A Beacon St., 617/262-0909

Best Middle Eastern Food
Cafe Jaffa
48 Gloucester St., 617/536-0230
Karoun
261 Walnut St., Newtonville, 617/964-3400
Middle East
472 Massachusetts Ave., Cambridge, 617/354-8238

Best Pizza
California Pizza Kitchen
800 Boylston St., 617/247-0888
Figs
67 Main St., Charlestown, 617/524-9016
Paddock Lounge and Pizza
249 Pearl St., Somerville, 617/628-6525
Mona Lisa Pizza
57 Fairmont Ave., Hyde Park, 617/361-6258
Pizzeria Regina
11 1/2 Thatcher, Hyde Park, 617/227-0765
Pizzeria Uno
Canal Park, Cambridge, 617/225-0330
1230 Commonwealth Ave., Allston, 617/739-0034
Copley Square, 617/267-8554
Faneuil Hall, 617/523-5722
280 Huntington Ave., 617/424-1697
Kenmore Square, 617/262-4911
Newton Corner, 617/964-2296
Porter Square, Cambridge, 617/497-1530

Best Regional Food
Durgin Park
  5 Faneuil Hall Market Pl., 617/227-2038
Legal Sea Foods
  Multiple Locations

Best Romantic Dining
Bay Tower Room
  60 State St., 33rd Fl., 617/723-1666
Cafe Budapest
  Copley Square Hotel, 90 Exeter St., 617/734-3388
Hungry I
  71 1/2 Charles St., 617/227-3524
L'Espalier
  30 Gloucester St., 617/ 262-3023

Best Salad/Salad Bar
Victor's Meat and Deli
  710 Broadway, Somerville, 617/625-3076

Best Seafood
Legal Sea Foods
  Multiple Locations
Skipjack's Fish House
  2 Brookline Pl., Brookline, 617/739-6428
  500 Boylston St., 617/536-3500
Turner Fisheries
  Westin Hotel, 10 Huntington Ave., 617/424-7425
Mount Vernon Restaurant
  14 Broadway, Somerville, 617/666-3830
Jimmy's Harborside Restaurant
  248 Northern Ave., 617/423-1000

Best Southwestern Food
Border Cafe
  32 Church St., Cambridge, 617/864-6100
  817 Broadway, 617/233-5308
Cottonwood Cafe
  1815 Massachusetts Ave., Cambridge, 617/661-7440
  222 Berkeley St., 617/247-2225
Zuma's Tex Mex Cafe
  7 Faneuil Hall Market Pl., 617/367-9114

Best Steaks
Capital Grille
  359 Newbury St., 617/262-8900
Hilltop Steak House
  855 Broadway, Saugus, 617/324-9200
Morton's of Chicago
  1 Exeter Plz., 617/266-5858
Mount Vernon Restaurant
  14 Broadway, Somerville, 617/666-3830

Best Thai Food
Amarin of Thailand
  287 Centre St., Newton Corner, 617/527-5255
Jae's Cafe and Grill
  520 Columbus Ave., 617/421-9405
  1281 Cambridge St., Cambridge, 617/497-8380
King and I
  145 Charles St., 617/227-3320
  259 Newbury St., 617/437-9611

M

...t Undiscovered Restaurants
...endel's Den
  89 Winthrop St., Cambridge, 617/491-1160
On the Park
  315 Shawmut Ave., 617/426-0862
Union Square Bistro
  16 Bow St., Somerville, 617/628-3344
Anchovies
  433 Columbus Ave., 617/266-5088
Uva
  1418 Commonwealth Ave., Brighton, 617/566-5670

Best Vegetarian Food
Country Life Vegetarian Buffet
  200 High St., 617/951-2462
Five Seasons
  669A Centre St., Jamaica Plain, 617/524-9016
The Small Planet Bar and Grill
  565 Boylston St., 617/536-4477
Buddha's Delight
  5 Beach St., 617/451-2395
Jae's Cafe and Grill
  1281 Cambridge St., Cambridge, 617/497-8380
  520 Columbus Avenue, 617/421-9405

Best Vietnamese Food
Elephant Walk
  70 Union Sq., Somerville, 617/623-9939
  900 Beacon St., 617/247-1500
Jae's Cafe and Grill
  520 Columbus Ave., 617/421-9405
  1281 Cambridge St., Cambridge, 617/497-8380
Pho Pasteur
  137 Brighton Ave., Allston, 617/783-2340
  682 Washington St., 617/482-7467
Ba Dat
  28 Harrison Ave., 617/426-8838
Amarin of Thailand
  287 Centre St., Newton Corner, 617/527-5255
King and I
  145 Charles St., 617/227-3320
  259 Newbury St., 617/437-9611

Best Wine Selection
Biba
  272 Boylston St., 617/426-7878
Capital Grille
  359 Newbury St., 617/262-8900
Ritz-Carlton Dining Room
  Ritz-Carlton Hotel, 15 Arlington St., 617/536-5700
Michael's Waterfront
  85 Atlantic Ave., 617/367-6425

BROCKTON, MA

Best American Food
Cape Cod Cafe
  979 Main St., 508/583-9420
George's Cafe
  228 Belmont St., 508/588-4231

Best Bar
Sidelines Sports Bar and Pub
232 E. Ashland St., 508/587-5511

Best Breakfast
Dew Drop Inn
610 N. Main St., 508/588-4147
Dorothy Lou Pastry Shop
605 Belmont St., 508/583-7035

Best Business Lunch
Chang Feng Restaurant
379 Belmont St., 508/587-5993
George's Cafe
228 Belmont St., 508/588-4231

Best Casual Dining
Sidelines Sports Bar and Pub
232 E. Ashland St., 508/587-5511

Best Chinese Food
Chang Feng Restaurant
379 Belmont St., 508/587-5993

Best Dinner
Cape Cod Cafe
979 Main St., 508/583-9420
Christo's
782 Crescent St., 508/588-4200

Best Family Restaurant
Italian Kitchen
1071 Main St., 508/586-2100

Best Greek/Mediterranean Food
Christo's
782 Crescent St., 508/588-4200

Best Homestyle Food
Dew Drop Inn
610 N. Main St., 508/588-4147

Best Italian Food
George's Cafe
228 Belmont St., 508/588-4231
Italian Kitchen
1071 Main St., 508/586-2100

Best Pastries
Dorothy Lou Pastry Shop
605 Belmont St., 508/583-7035

Best Salad/Salad Bar
Christo's
782 Crescent St., 508/588-4200

Best Thai Food
Chaophraya
165 Westgate Dr., 508/586-8530

M

CAPE COD, MA

Best Restaurants in Town
The Paddock Restaurant
20 Scudder Ave., Hyannis, 508/775-7677
Guido Murphy's
615 Main St., Hyannis, 508/775-7242

ars

Ho

e. 6A, Orleans, 508/255-5165

hael Patrick's Publick House
435 Main St., Dennis Port, 508/398-1620

Fat Jack's Cafe
335 Commercial St., Provincetown, 508/487-4822

Bobby Byrne's Pub
Mashpee Commons, Mashpee, 508/477-0600

Best Barbecue/Ribs
Mitchell's Steak and Rib House
451 Iyanough Rd., Hyannis, 508/775-6700

Best Breakfast
Bonatt's Bakery
537 Rte. 28, Harwichport, 508/432-7199
Hearth and Kettle
23 Richardson Rd., Centerville, 508/775-8878
Lori's Family Restaurant
Town Center Shopping Plaza, North Eastham,
508/255-4803
Marshland
109 Rte. 6A, Sandwich, 508/888-9824
Christine's Restaurant
581 Main St., West Dennis, 508/394-7333
Daggett House
59 North Water St., Edgartown, 508/627-4600
Jared Coffin House
29 Broad St., Nantucket, 508/228-2400

Best Brunch
L'Etoile
27 S. Summer St., Edgartown, 508/627-5187
Jared Coffin House
29 Broad St., Nantucket, 508/228-2400

Best Chinese Food
Golden Fountain Restaurant
203 W. Main St., Hyannis, 508/771-3332

Best Chowder
The Squire Restaurant
487 Main St., Chatham, 508/945-0945
Mildred's Chowder House
290 Iyanough Rd., Hyannis, 508/775-1045
Friendly Fisherman
Rte. 6, North Eastham, 508/255-6770
P-J's Dari-Burger
Rte. 6, Wellfleet, 508/349-2126
The Flume
Lake Avenue, Mashpee, 508/477-1456
The Navigator Restaurant
2 Main St., Edgartown, 508/627-4320

Best Delicatessens
Edgartown Deli
Main Street, Edgartown, 508/627-4789
Provisions
Straight Wharf, Nantucket, 508/228-3258

Best Desserts
D'Olimpio's New York Deli
   55 Iyanough Rd., Hyannis, 508/771-3220

Best Family Restaurants
Lobster Claw
   Rte. 6A, Orleans, 508/255-1800
Oliver's
   Bray Farm Rd. at Rte. 6A, Yarmouth Port,
      508/362-6062
Lobster Pot
   321 Commercial St., Provincetown, 508/487-0842
Beehive Restaurant
   406 Rte. 6A, Sandwich, 508/833-1184
Home Port Restaurant
   North Rd., Menemsha, 508/645-2679
The Hearth
   South Beach St., Nantucket, 508/228-1500

Best Ice Cream/Yogurt
Emack and Bolio Ice Cream
   Rte. 6A, Orleans, 508/255-5844
Sundae School
   387 Lower County Rd., Dennis Port, 508/394-9122
Four Seas Ice Cream
   360 South Main St., Centerville, 508/775-1394
Whistle Stop
   854 Rte. 28A, West Falmouth, 508/540-7585
Mad Martha's
   117 Circuit Ave., Oak Bluffs, 508/693-9151
   8 Union St., Vineyard Haven, 508/693-9764
The Juice Bar
   12 Broad St., Nantucket, 508/228-5799

Best Italian Food
Nauset Beach Club
   Main St., East Orleans, 508/255-8547
Alberto's Ristorante
   360 Main St., Hyannis, 508/778-1770

Best Lunch
Impudent Oyster
   15 Chatham Bars Ave., Chatham, 508/945-3545
Red Cottage
   36 Old Bass River Rd., South Dennis, 508/394-2923
Box Lunch
   Rte. 6, Eastham, 508/255-0799
Quarterdeck
   164 Main St., Falmouth, 508/548-9900

Best Mexican Food
Sam Diego's
   950 Iyanough Rd., Hyannis, 508/771-8816
Tacos Tacos
   Broad St., Nantucket, 508/228-5418

Best Outdoor Dining
Kadees Lobster and Clam Bar
   212 Main St., East Orleans, 508/255-6184
Tugboats
   21 Arlington St., Hyannis, 508/775-6433

M

Cafe Blase
   328 Commercial St., Provincetown, 508/487-9465
Flying Bridge
   220 Scranton Ave., Falmouth, 508/548-2700

Best Pizza
Binnacle Tavern
   Rte. 20, Orleans, 508/255-7901
Craigville Pizza and Mexican
   618 Craigville Beach Rd., West Hyannisport,
      508/775-2267
Upper Crust Pizza
   90 Commercial St., Wellfleet, 508/349-9562
Paul's Pizza and Seafood
   14 Benham Rd., Falmouth, 508/548-5838
Papa's Pizza
   158 Circuit Ave., Oak Bluffs, 508/693-1400
Vincent's Italian Restaurant
   21 S. Water St., Nantucket, 508/228-0189

Best Places to Eat When Someone Else Is Buying
Chillingsworth
   Rte. 6A, Brewster, 508/896-3640
The Regatta of Cotuit
   4631 Falmouth Rd. (Rte. 28), Cotuit, 508/428-5715
Whitman House
   Rte. 6, Truro, 508/487-1740
Dan'l Webster Inn
   149 Main St., Sandwich, 508/888-3622
Savoir Faire
   14 Church St., Edgartown, 508/627-9864
Twenty-One Federal
   21 Federal St., Nantucket, 508/228-2121

Best Restaurants Reachable by Boat
Brax Landing
   Rte. 28, Harwich Port, 508/432-5515
Baxter's Boathouse Club and Fish-N-Chips
   177 Pleasant St., Hyannis, 508/775-4490
Sal's Place
   99 Commercial St., Provincetown, 508/487-1279
Chart Room
   1 Shore Rd., Bourne, 508/563-5350
Black Dog Tavern
   Beach Street Extension, Vineyard Haven,
      508/693-9223

Best Romantic Dining
Captain Linnell House
   137 Skaket Beach Rd., Orleans, 508/255-3400
Alberto's Ristorante
   9 Ocean St., Hyannis, 508/778-1770
Aesop's Tables
   Main St., Wellfleet, 508/349-6450
Coonamessett Inn
   Jones Rd., Falmouth, 508/548-2300
Outermost Inn
   Lighthouse Rd., Gay Head, 508/645-2679
The Woodbox Inn
   29 Fair St., Nantucket, 508/228-0587

Best Seafood
Thompson's Clam Bar
  23 Snow Inn Rd., Harwich Port, 508/432-3595
Napi's
  7 Freeman St., Provincetown, 508/487-1145
Cooke's Seafood
  Rte. 28, Orleans, 508/255-5518
Kream and Kone
  527 Main St., Dennis Port, 508/394-0808
Lobster Pool
  Rte. 6, North Eastham, 508/255-9706
Clam Shack
  227 Clinton Ave., Falmouth, 508/540-7758
Popponesset Marketplace Raw Bar
  Rock Landing Rd., Mashpee, 508/477-9111
The Oyster Bar
  162 Circuit Ave., Oak Bluffs, 508/693-3300
Topper's at the Wauwinet
  120 Wauwinet Rd., Nantucket, 508/228-8768

Best Southwestern Food
Sweetwater's Grille
  644 Main St., Hyannis, 508/775-3323

Best View While Dining
Thompson's Clam Bar
  23 Snow Inn Rd., Harwichport, 508/432-3595
Mattakeese Wharf
  271 Mill Way, Barnstable, 508/362-4511
The Mews
  359 Commercial St., Provincetown, 508/487-1500
Regatta of Falmouth By-The-Sea
  Falmouth Harbor entrance, end of Scranton Ave.,
    Falmouth, 508/548-5400
Black Dog Tavern
  Beach Street Extension, Vineyard Haven,
    508/693-9223
Ropewalk
  Straight Wharf, Nantucket, 508/228-8886

Standbys
Ben and Jerry's
  Brackett Rd. at Rte. 6A, North Eastham,
    508/255-2817

CHELMSFORD, MA

Best Restaurant in Town
Vincenzo's Restaurant
  170 Concord Rd., 508/256-1250

Best American Food
Bainbridge's
  75 Princeton St., North Chelmsford, 508/251-8670

Best Bar
Glenview Pub
  248 Princeton St., North Chelmsford, 508/251-3591

Best Breakfast
Town Meeting Restaurant
  88 Chelmsford St., 508/250-1550

Best Burgers
Ground Round
185 Chelmsford St., 508/256-0051

Best Casual Dining
Glenview Pub
248 Princeton St., North Chelmsford, 508/251-3591

Best Chinese Food
Szechuan Chef
6 Vinal Sq., North Chelmsford, 508/251-9888

Best Family Restaurant
Skip's Restaurant
116 Chelmsford St., 508/256-2631

Best Italian Food
Vincenzo's Restaurant
170 Concord Rd., 508/256-1250

Best Pizza
Ciro's Pizzeria
170 Concord Rd., 508/256-6008
Bertucci's
14E Littleton Rd., 508/250-8800

Best Restaurant Meal Value
Skip's Restaurant
116 Chelmsford St., 508/256-2631

M

FITCHBURG, MA

Best Restaurant in Town
Cornerstone Restaurant
616 Central St., Leominster, 508/537-1991

Best Burgers
Red Checker Restaurant
192 Hamilton St., 508/534-5117

Best Chinese Food
Fitchburg Jade Chinese Restaurant
447 Main St., 508/343-0287

Best Delicatessen
Dagwood's Deli
490 Main St., 508/345-2141

Best Place to Eat When Someone Else Is Buying
Rendezvous Restaurant
100 Franklin Rd., 508/343-9624

Best Sandwiches
Dagwood's Deli
490 Main St., 508/345-2141

Best Seafood
S.S. Lobster Ltd.
691 River St., 508/342-6135

Best Sports Bar
Slatterly's Back Room
106 Lunenburg St., 508/342-8880

Standbys
Friendly's
464 John Fitch Hwy., 508/343-7965

FRAMINGHAM, MA

Best American Food
Finally Michael's
1280 Worcester Rd., 508/879-7345

Best Chinese Food
Lotus Flower Chinese Restaurant
341 Cochituate Rd., 508/872-6005
Uncle Chung's
266 Worcester Rd., 508/872-9200

Best Greek/Mediterranean Food
Aegean Restaurant
47 Beacon St., 508/879-8424

Best Japanese Food
Chef Orient
1538 Worcester Rd., 508/628-9227

Best Mexican Food
La Cantina Restaurant
911 Waverley St., 508/879-7874

Best Pizza
Pizzeria Uno
71 Worcester Rd., 508/620-1816
Bertucci's Brick Oven Pizzeria
150 Worcester Rd., 508/879-9161

Best Sandwiches
D'Angelo's Sandwich Shop
290 Worcester Rd., 508/626-0028

Best Seafood
Legal Sea Foods
1400 Worcester Rd., 508/820-1115
The Dolphin
10 Adams, Natick, 508/650-3474
7 South Ave., Natick, 508/655-0669

Best Steaks
Chef Orient
1538 Worcester Rd., 508/628-9227

Best Thai Food
Bangkok Oriental Thai Restaurant
50 Worcester Rd., 508/879-6001

GARDNER, MA

Best Restaurants in Town
The Old Mill Restaurant
Rte. 2A, Westminster, 508/874-5941
Sully's Eating and Drinking Place
74 Parker St., 508/632-7457

Best Steaks
Athol Steak House
14 Grove St., 508/249-2624

GLOUCESTER, MA

Best Restaurants in Town
Gull Restaurant
75 Essex St., 508/283-6565

531

Patio Restaurant of Magnolia
12 Lexington Ave., 508/525-3230

Best American Food
Cameron's Restaurant
206 Main St., 508/281-1331

Best Breakfast
Magnolia Breakfast Nook
16 Lexington Ave., 508/525-3895

Best Cheap Meal
Magnolia Breakfast Nook
16 Lexington Ave., 508/525-3895

Best Dinner
MT's Lobster House
25 Rogers, 508/582-0950
Patio Restaurant of Magnolia
12 Lexington Ave., 508/525-3230

Best Family Restaurant
Cameron's Restaurant
206 Main St., 508/281-1331

Best Italian Food
Il Porto
40 Railroad Ave., 508/282-4606

Best Seafood
Gull Restaurant
75 Essex St., 508/283-6565

GREENFIELD, MA

Best Atmosphere
Andiamo Restaurant
Huckle Hill Rd., Bernardston, 413/648-9107
Sienna
6B Elm, South Deerfield, 413/665-0215

Best Burgers
Brickers
184 Shelburne Rd., 413/774-2857

Best Casual Dining
Taylor's Tavern
238 Main St., 413/773-8313

Best Chinese Food
New Fortune China Restaurant
249 Mohawk Trail, 413/772-0838
Royal Panda
10 Fiske Ave., 413/772-2531

Best Coffee
Timberhill Coffee House
233 Main St., 413/772-0201

Best Family Restaurants
Bill's Restaurant
30 Federal St., 413/773-9230
Turnbull's Restaurant
242 Mohawk Trail, 413/773-8203

Best Italian Food
Andiamo Restaurant
Huckle Hill Rd., Bernardston, 413/648-9107

Sienna
6B Elm, South Deerfield, 413/665-0215

Best Place to Eat When Someone Else Is Buying
Deerfield Inn
81 Old Main St., Deerfield, 413/774-5587

Best Sandwiches
Brickers
184 Shelburne Rd., 413/774-2857

Best Seafood
Herm's
91 Main St., 413/772-6300
Pete's Fish Market and Seafood
54 School St., 413/772-2153

Best Steaks
Herm's
91 Main St., 413/772-6300

Best View While Dining
Andiamo Restaurant
Huckle Hill Rd., Bernardston, 413/648-9107

HAVERHILL, MA

Best Restaurant in Town
The Cobblestones
130 Washington St., 508/373-2410

Best Brunch
Jimmy's Restaurant III
2 Essex St., 508/372-8822

Best Casual Dining
Al's Place
251 Primrose St., 508/374-9846

Best Chinese Food
Oriental Garden
400 Lowell Ave., 508/373-5626

Best Delicatessen
A-1 Deli
92 Merrimack St., 508/372-7951

Best Dinner
The Cobblestones
130 Washington St., 508/373-2410

Best Family Restaurant
Al's Place
251 Primrose St., 508/374-9846

Best Lunch
Jimmy's Restaurant III
2 Essex St., 508/372-8822

Best Pizza
Sal's
95 Winter St., 508/521-7575

Best Sandwiches
Bagel Express
35 Railroad Sq., 508/521-4333

M

LAWRENCE, MA

Best American Food
Cedar Crest Restaurant
  187 Broadway St., 508/685-5722

Best Burgers
Lawton's Famous Frankfurters
  606 Canal St., 508/686-9603

Best Chinese Food
Beijing Restaurant
  1250 Osgood St., North Andover, 508/689-9500

Best Dinner
Capricornio Restaurant
  216 Hampshire St., 5087/688-2444
Beijing Restaurant
  1250 Osgood St., North Andover, 508/689-9500

Best Fast Food
Lawton's Famous Frankfurters
  606 Canal St., 508/686-9603

Best Lunch
Brother's Pizza
  145 Lawrence St., 508/688-7039

Best Middle Eastern Food
Bishop's Restaurant
  99 Hampshire St., 508/683-7143

Best Pizza
Brother's Pizza
  145 Lawrence St., 508/688-7039

Best Salad/Salad Bar
Brother's Pizza
  145 Lawrence St., 508/688-7039

Best Spanish Food
Capricornio Restaurant
  216 Hampshire St., 5087/688-2444

LOWELL, MA

Best American Food
Bel Gusto's D'Italia
  50 Warren St., 508/937-9447
Cobblestones
  91 Dutton St., 508/970-2282

Best Bar
The Office Pub
  660 Rogers, 508/441-9040

Best Burgers
Brewhouse Cafe and Grill
  201 Cabot St., 508/937-2690

Best Business Lunch
Old Worthen
  147 Worthen St., 508/441-3189

Best Casual Dining
Brewhouse Cafe and Grill
  201 Cabot St., 508/937-2690

Best Coffee
Mill City Coffee Shoppe
  5 Merrimack St., 508/452-8176

Best Delicatessen
Deli King
  885 Main, Tewksbury, 508/858-3855

Best Dinner
Cobblestones
  91 Dutton St., 508/970-2282

Best French Food
La Boniche Restaurant
  110 Gorham St., 508/458-9473

Best Greek/Mediterranean Food
Olympia Restaurant
  453 Market St., 508/452-8092

Best Indian Food
Bombay Mahal Restaurant
  45 Middle St., 508/441-2222

Best Italian Food
Bel Gusto's D'Italia
  50 Warren St., 508/937-9447

Best Lunch
Salads Plus
  14 Kearney Sq., 508/458-3003

Best Microbrewery
Brewhouse Cafe and Grill
  201 Cabot St., 508/937-2690

Best Other Ethnic Food
Mill City Coffee Shoppe (Portuguese)
  5 Merrimack St., 508/452-8176

Best Pizza
Queen's Pizza
  287 Chelmsford St., 508/452-8606

Best Salad/Salad Bar
Salads Plus
  14 Kearney Sq., 508/458-3003

Best Sandwiches
Deli King
  885 Main, Tewksbury, 508/858-3855

M

MANSFIELD, MA

Best Restaurants in Town
Ladonna's
  131 Copeland Dr., 508/261-7000
Jimmy's Pub
  141 N. Main St., 508/339-7167

Best American Food
Jimmy's Pub
  141 N. Main St., 508/339-7167

Best Breakfast
Old Colony Diner
  16 Old Colony Rd., 508/339-4983

Best Cheap Meal
Bernie's Limited
14 S. Main St., 508/339-6719

Best Italian Food
Ladonna's
131 Copeland Dr., 508/261-7000

Best Lunch
Bernie's Limited
14 S. Main St., 508/339-6719

Best Pizza
House of Pizza
175 N. Main St., 508/339-6400

Best Sandwiches
Bagel Train
351 N. Main St., 508/339-1800

MARLBOROUGH, MA

Best Bars
Kennedy's Pub
247A Maple St., 508/485-5800
Pastimes Bar and Grill
277 Main St., 508/485-0098

Best Burgers
Boston Market
185 Boston Post Rd., 508/229-2525

Best Chinese Food
Royal Mandarin
350 E. Main St., 508/485-8366

Best Coffee
Starbucks
189 Boston Post Rd., 508/485-8223

Best Ice Cream/Yogurt
Trombetta's Tee-Rarium
655 Farm Rd., 508/485-6429

Best Italian Food
Rocco's Restaurant and Pub
127 Lakeside Ave., 508/485-7717
The Oxford
109 Lakeside Ave., 508/485-0077

Best Pizza
Papa Gino's
205 E. Main St., 508/481-5245
Bertucci's Brick Oven Pizzeria
388 Boston Post Rd., 508/460-0911

Best Sandwiches
D'Angelo's Sandwich Shop
28 Boston Post Rd. E., 508/485-2363
JD Craig's Fine Food To Go
241 Boston Post Rd. W., 508/485-1588

Best Seafood
American Lobster
19 Northboro Rd., 508/481-9898

M

Best Steaks
Wildwood
189 Boston Post Rd., 508/481-2021

Best Thai Food
Chez Siam Restaurant
280 E. Main St., 508/485-3880

MARSHFIELD, MA

Best Restaurant in Town
Fairview
133 Ocean St., Brant Rock, 617/834-9144

Best Breakfast
Arthur and Pat's Restaurant
239 Ocean St., 617/834-9755

Best Chinese Food
Hung's Chinese Cuisine
43 Careswell St., 617/837-4440

Best Dinner
Fairview
133 Ocean St., Brant Rock, 617/834-9144

Best Family Restaurant
Bridgeway Inn
1289 Ferry St., 617/834-6505

Best Italian Food
Bertucci's
90 Derby, Hingham, 617/740-4405

Best Lunch
Hung's Chinese Cuisine
43 Careswell St., 617/837-4440

Best Pizza
American Pie
25 Webster Sq., 617/837-5211

METHUEN, MA

Best Atmosphere
Eighteen Fifty-Nine House
16 Hampshire St., 508/682-1859

Best Breakfast
Mamma Mary's
322 Merrimack St., 508/682-6299

Best Burgers
Eighteen Fifty-Nine House
16 Hampshire St., 508/682-1859

Best Coffee
Green Mountain Coffee
Flicks Video Center, 234 Pleasant St., 508/794-0068

Best Desserts
Hampstead Manor
251 Hampstead St., 508/687-9876

Best Family Restaurant
Mamma Mary's
322 Merrimack St., 508/682-6299

Best Health-Conscious Menu
Fit As A Fiddle
　90 Pleasant Valley St., 508/687-9630
Jackson's Restaurant
　478 Lowell St., 508/688-5021

Best Homestyle Food
1859 House
　16 Hampshire St., 508/682-1859

Best Ice Cream/Yogurt
Jay Gee's Ice Cream
　602 1/2 Lowell Blvd., 508/689-0456

Best Italian Food
Mamma Mary's
　322 Merrimack St., 508/682-6299

Best Other Ethnic Food
Shadi's Restaurant (Lebanese)
　58 Osgood St., 508/687-9698

Best Pizza
Theo's Pizza
　26 Hampshire Cir., 508/686-8288

Best Place to Take the Kids
Stagger Lee's
　114 Cross St., 508/688-9600

M

Best Seafood
Jackson's Restaurant
　478 Lowell St., 508/688-5021

Best Steaks
Jimmy's Restaurant II
　106 Lowell Blvd., 508/682-5542

Best View While Dining
Jackson's Restaurant
　478 Lowell St., 508/688-5021
Jimmy's Restaurant II
　106 Lowell Blvd., 508/682-5542

MILFORD, MA

Best Restaurants in Town
The Redwood Drive-Inn
　Rte. 16, Mendon, 508/473-2125
Pete's Bluebird
　85 Mendon St., Bellingham, 508/966-9717
The Caravan Restaurant
　500 W. Central St., Franklin, 508/528-9894

Best Asian Restaurant
The Milford Mandarin
　Quarry Square, 196 E. Main St. (Rte. 16) at Rte. 109,
　　508/478-8893

Best Italian Food
Fernando's Italian Villa
　90 Mendon St., Bellingham, 508/966-1500

Best Breakfast
What's Cookin'
942 Great Plain Ave., 617/444-9600
Bergson's Ice Cream Shop
1077 Great Plain Ave., 617/444-6997

Best Cheap Meal
What's Cookin'
942 Great Plain Ave., 617/444-9600

Best Chinese Food
The Joy Luck Club
1037 Great Plain Ave., 617/455-8908

Best Coffee
Bergson's Ice Cream Shop
1077 Great Plain Ave., 617/444-6997

Best Greek/Mediterranean Food
Four Stars Restaurant
1430 Highland Ave., 617/444-1011

Best Italian Food
Oggi's Ristorante
105 Chapel St., 617/444-0310

Best Pizza
Mom and Pop's Pizza
315 Chestnut St., 617/449-2255

Best Seafood
Four Stars Restaurant
1430 Highland Ave., 617/444-1011

Best Thai Food
Bai Thong
1257 Highland Ave., 617/433-0272

M

Best American Food
Miguel's Restaurant
253 Union St., 508/990-8781

Best Barbecue/Ribs
Skewers
142 Huttleston Ave., Fairhaven, 508/996-3303

Best Breakfast
Newport Creamery Restaurant
1071 Kempton St., 508/997-8383
950 Kings Hwy., 508/998-5323

Best Business Lunch
Manny's Cafe Restaurant
175 Sawyer St., 508/999-9804

Best Casual Dining
Not Your Average Joe's
61 State Rd., North Dartmouth, 508/992-5637

Best Chinese Food
China Lantern
116 Nauset St., 508/997-4474

Best Diner
Shawmut Diner
943 Shawmut Ave., 508/993-3073

Best Family Restaurant
Spearfield's
1 Johnny Cake Hill, 508/993-4848

Best Homestyle Food
Shawmut Diner
943 Shawmut Ave., 508/993-3073

Best Italian Food
Pa Raffa's Italian Restaurant
2857 Acushnet Ave., 508/995-7711
Pasta House Company
100 Alden Rd., Fairhaven, 508/993-9913

Best Lunch
Trevor's Place
562 Pleasant St., 508/979-5810

Best Other Ethnic Food
Portuguese Shanty (Portuguese)
2980 Acushnet Ave., 508/998-2645
Miguel's Restaurant (Portuguese)
253 Union St., 508/990-8781

Best Pizza
Riccardi's Italian Restaurant
901 Hathaway Rd., 508/996-3921
Not Your Average Joe's
61 State Rd., North Dartmouth, 508/992-5637
Fay's Knotty Pine Kitchen
2164 Acushnet Ave., 508/995-9838

Best Sandwiches
Spearfields
1 Johnny Cake Hill, 508/993-4848
Manny's Cafe Restaurant
175 Sawyer St., 508/999-9804
Three Flags
894 Purchase St., 508/997-6212

Best Seafood
Davy's Locker
1480 E. Rodney French Blvd., 508/992-7359
Three Flags
894 Purchase St., 508/997-6212

NORTHAMPTON, MA

Best Restaurant in Town
Spoleto Restaurant
50 Main St., 413/586-6313

Best Brunch
Sylvester's Restaurant
111 Pleasant St., 413/586-5343

Best Cajun/Creole Food
Eastside Grill
19 Strong Ave., 413/586-3347

Best Cheap Meal
Miss Florence Diner
  99 Main St., 413/584-3137
Blue Bonnet Diner
  324 King St., 413/584-3333

Best Chinese Food
Hunan Gourmet Chinese Restaurant
  261 King St., 413/585-0202

Best Desserts
Bananarama
  186 Main St., 413/586-9659

Best Diner
Miss Florence Diner
  99 Main St., 413/584-3137

Best Italian Food
Spoleto Restaurant
  50 Main St., 413/586-6313

Best Indian Food
India House
  45 State St., 413/586-6344

Best Lunch
Blue Bonnet Diner
  324 King St., 413/584-3333

Best Mexican Food
La Veracruzana
  31 Main St., 413/586-7181

Best Pizza
Geraldine's
  86 Green St., 413/586-5443

Best Seafood
Penguin Fish Market
  29 Union St., Easthampton, 413/527-7480

Best Steaks
Aqua Vitae
  37 Russell St., Hadley, 413/584-9892

Best Vegetarian Food
Paul and Elizabeth's
  150 Main St., 413/584-4832

PITTSFIELD, MA

Best Restaurant in Town
Truffles and Such
  Allendale Shopping Ctr., 413/442-0151

Best Breakfast
Court Square
  95 E St., 413/442-9896

Best Cheap Meal
Country Charm Restaurant
  Rte. 8, Cheshire, 413/743-1445

Best Coffeehouse
Sip of Seattle
  216 Elm St., 413/445-5143

Best Dinner
Sweet Basil Grille
306 Pittsfield Lenox Rd., 413/637-1270

Best Homestyle Food
Country Charm Restaurant
Rte. 8, Cheshire, 413/743-1445

Best Italian Food
Sweet Basil Grill
306 Pittsfield Lenox Rd., 413/637-1270

Best Pizza
Elizabeth's Restaurant
1264 E St., 413/448-8244

Best Place to Eat When Someone Else Is Buying
Truffles and Such
Allendale Shopping Ctr., 413/442-0151

Best Salad/Salad Bar
Dakota's Restaurant
1035 South St., 413/499-7900

Best Seafood
Sweet Basil Grille
306 Pittsfield Lenox Rd., 413/637-1270

Best Steaks
Dakota's Restaurant
1035 South St., 413/499-7900

M

PLYMOUTH, MA

Best Restaurant in Town
Handlebar Harry's
3 Cordage Park Mall, 508/747-1922
Run of the Mill Tavern
6 Spring Ln., 508/830-1262

Best American Food
The Colonial Restaurant
39 Main St., 508/746-0838

Best Seafood
Souza's Seafood Restaurant
Town Wharf, 508/746-5354
Wood's Seafood
Town Wharf, 508/746-0261

SALEM, MA

Best Restaurants in Town
Chase House
Pickering Wharf, 508/744-0000
Victoria Station
86 Wharf St., 508/745-3400

Best American Food
Blue Point Roast Beef and Seafood
100 Boston St., 508/741-3479

Best Breakfast
Red's Sandwich Shop
15 Central St., 508/745-3527

Best Italian Food
Bertini's
    284 Canal St., 508/744-1436

Best Japanese Food
Asahi Restaurant
    21 Congress St., 508/744-5376

Best Pizza
Mandee's Pizza
    408 Essex St., 508/745-6400

Best Sandwiches
Red's Sandwich Shop
    15 Central St., 508/745-3527

Best Seafood
Chase House
    Pickering Wharf, 508/744-0000
Dube's
    317 Jefferson Ave., 508/744-9531

Best Steaks
Chase House
    Pickering Wharf, 508/744-0000

SOUTHBRIDGE, MA

Best Atmosphere
The Harvest at Wells Farm
    425 Eastford Rd., 508/764-4546
Publick House
    Rte. 131, Sturbridge, 508/347-3313
Salem Cross Inn
    260 Main St., West Brookfield, 508/867-2345
    Rte. 9, West Brookfield, 508/867-8337

Best Breakfast
Elm Centre Coffee Shop
    39 Elm St., 508/764-7288
Annie's Country Kitchen
    140 Main St., Sturbridge, 508/347-2320

Best Burgers
Elm Centre Coffee Shop
    39 Elm St., 508/764-7288

Best Family Restaurant
Hook and Ladder Restaurant
    177 Elm St., 508/764-8405

Best French Food
Le Bearn Restaurant
    12 Cedar St., 508/347-5800

Best Greek/Mediterranean Food
Golden Greek Restaurant
    6 Sandersdale Rd., 508/765-0211

Best Health-Conscious Menu
Margaux's Deli and Catering
    33 Crystal St., 508/765-0954

Best Ice Cream/Yogurt
Coop's Scoops
    204 Worcester St., 508/764-3043

M

Best Italian Food
Mario's Restaurant
  274 Main St., 508/765-5338

Best Pizza
Central Pizza
  57 Central St., 508/764-2541
Great Oak Pizza
  922 Main St., 508/765-2929

Best Place to Eat When Someone Else Is Buying
The Harvest at Wells Farm
  425 Eastford Rd., 508/764-4546

Best Sandwiches
Margaux's Deli and Catering
  33 Crystal St., 508/765-0954

SPRINGFIELD, MA

Best Restaurants in Town
Deerfield Inn
  81 Old Main St., Deerfield, 413/774-5587
Delaney House
  1 Country Club Rd., Holyoke, 413/532-1800

Best Breakfast
Route 66 Diner
  950 Bay St., 413/737-4921

Best Business Lunch
Mexitalia Cafe
  1441 Main St., 413/781-6101

Best Chinese Food
Golden Dragon
  2223 Northampton St., Holyoke, 413/536-4299

Best Diner
Route 66 Diner
  950 Bay St., 413/737-4921

Best German Food
Student Prince and The Fort
  8 Fort St., 413/734-7475

Best Greek/Mediterranean Food
Mykonos European Restaurant
  1060 Wilbraham Rd., 413/783-6333

Best Indian Food
Sitar Restaurant
  1688 Main St., 413/732-8011

Best Italian Food
Lido Restaurant
  555 Worthington St., 413/736-9433
Silvano's Restaurant
  680 Worthington St., 413/734-9774

Best Lunch
Cafe Manhattan
  301 Bridge St., 413/737-7913

Best Pizza
Buona Pizza
  1441 Main St., 413/731-0881

M

Best Seafood
Tilly's Restaurant
    1390 Main St., 413/732-3613
Delaney House
    1 Country Club Rd., Holyoke, 413/532-1800
Deerfield Inn
    81 Old Main St., Deerfield, 413/774-5587

TAUNTON, MA

Best Restaurants in Town
Benjamin's Restaurant
    698 Bay St., 508/824-6313
Gary's Restaurant
    115 S. Main St., West Bridgewater, 508/584-4444

Best Chinese Food
The Big Wong
    1 Washington St., 508/880-0668

WESTFIELD, MA

Best American Food
Point East Lounge
    The Sheraton, 485 E. Main St., 413/568-1315

Best Breakfast
Farmer's Daughter
    36 Elm St., 413/568-5888

Best Chinese Food
China Star
    36 Southwick Rd., 413/568-9698

Best Delicatessen
Farmer's Daughter
    36 Elm St., 413/568-5888

Best Dinner
Sheraton Inn
    880 Russell Rd., 413/562-6505

Best Greek/Mediterranean Food
Davio's Restaurant
    198 Elm St., 413/562-5033
Cafe Santorini
    930 South Hampton Rd., 413/572-1022

Best Lunch
Davio's Restaurant
    198 Elm St., 413/562-5033
Point East Lounge
    The Sheraton, 485 E. Main St., 413/568-1315

Best Pizza
Daniele's Pizza
    1029 North Rd., 413/533-7400

WEST SPRINGFIELD, MA

Best Breakfast
Bickford's Family Restaurant
    1296 Riverdale St., 413/733-6055

Best Dinner
Blue Star Family Restaurant
    261 Union St., 413/781-1325

M

Best Italian Food
Patsy's Restaurant and Lounge
673 Main St., 413/734-2239
Blue Star Family Restaurant
261 Union St., 413/781-1325

Best Pizza
Mamma Mia's Pizzeria
60 Park Ave., 413/732-0400
Liquori's Pizza
589 Westfield St., 413/737-9690

Best Seafood
Patsy's Restaurant and Lounge
673 Main St., 413/734-2239

Best Steaks
Take Five
944 Springfield Rd., Feeding Hills, 413/786-0962

Best 24-Hour Restaurant
Bickford's Family Restaurant
1296 Riverdale St., 413/733-6055

WOBURN, MA

Best Restaurant in Town
J.C. Hillary's
311 Mishawum Rd., 617/935-7200

M

Best Bar
Ninety-Nine Restaurant
291 Mishawum Rd., 617/935-7210
194 Cambridge Rd., 617/938-8999

Best Eclectic Menu
Bistro O'Colemain
390 Main St., 617/937-9085

Best Family Restaurant
Ninety-Nine Restaurant
291 Mishawum Rd., 617/935-7210
194 Cambridge Rd., 617/938-8999

Best Place to Eat When Someone Else Is Buying
Cafe Escadrille
26 Cambridge Rd., Burlington, 617/273-1916

WORCESTER, MA

Best American Food
Webster House
1 Webster St., 508/757-7208

Best Bagels
Bagel Time
194B Park Ave., 508/798-0440

Best Barbecue/Ribs
Cactus Pete's
400 Park Ave., 508/752-3038

Best Beer Selection
O'Connor's Restaurant and Bar
1160 W. Boylston St., 508/853-0789

Best Brunch
Club Maxine's
Maxwell-Silverman's Toolhouse, 25 Union St.,
508/755-0961

Best Chinese Food
Ping's Garden
500 Madison St., 508/791-9577

Best Coffeehouses
Cafe Dolce
154 Shrewsbury St., 508/754-3761
Coffee Kingdom
2 Richmond Ave., 508/755-8936

Best Desserts
Cafe Dolce
154 Shrewsbury St., 508/754-3761

Best Diner
The Parkway
148 Shrewsbury St., 508/753-9968

Best Ice Cream/Yogurt
Pinecroft Dairy
555 Prospect St., West Boylston, 508/853-0717

Best Indian Food
Sweetheart Restaurant
270 Shrewsbury St., 508/752-3700
House of India
439 Park Ave., 508/752-1330

Best Italian Food
Dino's Ristorante
13 Lord St., 508/753-9978

Best Japanese Restaurant
Sakura Tokyo
640 Park Ave., 508/792-1078

Best Late-Night Food
Acapulco Mexican Restaurant
107 Highland St., 508/791-1746
Eleni's Midnite Cafe
630 Franklin St., 508/754-0996
Kenmore Diner
250 Franklin St., 508/753-9541

Best Mexican Food
Acapulco Mexican Restaurant
107 Highland St., 508/791-1746
Taco Amigo
976B Main St., 508/793-8226

Best New Restaurant
O'Flaherty's Piano Pub
1541 Main St., 508/799-4600

Best Other Ethnic Food
El Morocco (Lebanese)
100 Wall St., 508/756-7117
Caribbean Cuisine (Caribbean)
5 E. Mountain St., 508/856-9199
O'Connor's Restaurant and Bar (Irish/European)
1160 West Boylston St., 508/853-0789

M

Best Outdoor Dining
Tarragon's
  455 Park Ave., 508/799-6962

Best Pizza
Darooshi's Pizza
  91 Pleasant St., 508/799-9999
Papa Gino's
  Multiple Locations
Wonder Bar
  121 Shrewsbury St., 508/ 752-9909

Best Restaurant Meal Value
Webster House
  1 Webster St., 508/757-7208

Best Romantic Dining
Castle Restaurant
  1230 Main St., Leicester, 508/892-9090
Tiano's
  108 Grove St., 508/752-8901

Best Salad/Salad Bar
Abdow's Big Boy
  3 Stafford St., 508/755-3104
  442 Southbridge St., Auburn, 508/832-3229
  54 Lincoln St., 508/852-3940
  Westborough Shopping Ctr., 9 Lyman St.,
    Westborough, 508/366-7414

Best Sandwiches
Elsa's Bushel and Peck
  17 East Mountain St., 508/856-0516
  358 Main St., 508/752-9001
Regatta Deli
  28 Lake Ave., 508/756-6916

Best Seafood
Sole Proprietor
  118 Highland St., 508/798-3474

Best Steaks
Cactus Pete's
  400 Park Ave., 508/752-3038
Chuck's Steak House
  10 Prospect St., Auburn, 508/832-2553

Best Thai Food
Thai Orchid
  144 Commercial St., 508/792-9701

Best Vegetarian Food
The Living Earth
  232 Chandler St., 508/753-1896

Best Vietnamese Food
Da-Lat Restaurant
  425 Park Ave., 508/753-6036

Best Wine Selection
Castle Restaurant
  1230 Main St., Leicester, 508/892-9090

Standbys
Chuck E. Cheese Pizza
  50 Southwest Cutoff, 508/754-5151

Michigan

Best Restaurants in Town
The Golden Nugget
7305 Hwy. 12, Onsted, 517/467-2190
The Hathaway House
424 W. Adrian St., Blissfield, 517/486-2141

Best American Food
The Hathaway House
424 W. Adrian St., Blissfield, 517/486-2141
Bauer Manor
1280 W. Hwy. 12, Tipton, 517/431-2506

Best Atmosphere
The Golden Nuggett Saloon
7305 Hwy. 12, Onsted, 517/467-2190

Best Breakfast
Main Stop Restaurant
1003 N. Main St., 517/263-9873

Best Burgers
Ray's Tavern
114 S. Main St., 517/283-2665

Best Chinese Food
China Chef
124 S. Main St., 517/264-6868

Best Dinner
Brass Lantern
1853 W. Maumee St., 517/263-0411

Best Family Restaurant
Miller's Family Restaurant
1545 W. Maumee St., 517/265-7170

Best Italian Food
Cusumano's
1106 W. Chicago Blvd., Tecumseh, 517/423-7980

Best Mexican Food
CC Margarita and Company
521 S. Meridian Rd., Hudson, 517/448-7111

M

Espo's Mexican Grill
1416 S. Main St., 517/265-9099

ANN ARBOR, MI

Best Restaurant in Town
Bella Ciao Trattoria
118 W. Liberty St., 313/995-2107

Best All-You-Can-Eat Buffets
Afternoon Delight
251 E. Liberty St., 313/665-7513
Mongolian Barbecue
310 S. Main St., Royal Oak, 810/398-7755

Best American Food
Dominick's
812 Monroe St., 313/662-5414

Best Bar
Brown Jug Restaurant
1204 S. University Ave., 313/761-3355

Best Burgers
Brown Jug Restaurant
1204 S. University Ave., 313/761-3355

Best Business Lunch
Afternoon Delight
251 E. Liberty St., 313/665-7513
Maude's Restaurant
314 S. Fourth Ave., 313/662-8485

Best Casual Dining
Dominick's
812 Monroe St., 313/662-5414

Best Chinese Food
China Gate
1201 S. University Ave., 313/668-2445
Old China Restaurant
505 W. Cross St., Ypsilanti, 313/482-8333

Best Diner
Fleetwood Diner
300 S. Ashley St., 313/995-5502

Best Dinner
Argiero's Italian Restaurant
300 Detroit St., 313/665-0444

Best French Food
Earle
121 W. Washington St., 313/994-0211
Moveable Feast
326 W. Liberty St., 313/663-3278

Best German Food
Heidelberg Restaurant
215 N. Main St., 313/663-7758

Best Health-Conscious Menu
Seva Restaurant and Market
314 E. Liberty St., 313/662-1111

Best Homestyle Food
Fleetwood Diner
300 S. Ashley St., 313/995-5502

Best Italian Food
Argiero's Italian Restaurant
  300 Detroit St., 313/665-0444
Earle
  121 W. Washington St., 313/994-0211

Best Mexican Food
Prickly Pear Southwest Cafe
  328 S. Main St., 313/930-0047

Best Pizza
Brown Jug Restaurant
  1204 S. University Ave., 313/761-3355

Best Place to Eat When Someone Else Is Buying
Escoffier
  300 S. Thayer St., 313/995-3800

Best Salad/Salad Bar
Maude's Restaurant
  314 S. Fourth Ave., 313/662-8485

Best Seafood
Lord Fox
  5400 Plymouth Rd., 313/662-1647

Best Vegetarian Food
Maude's Restaurant
  314 S. Fourth Ave., 313/662-8485
Seva Restaurant and Market
  314 E. Liberty St., 313/662-1111

Best Wine Selection
Lord Fox
  5400 Plymouth Rd., 313/662-1647

BATTLE CREEK, MI

Best Atmosphere
Clara's on the River
  44 McCamly St. N., 616/963-0966

Best Barbecue/Ribs
Sam's Joint
  1600 State Rte. 66, Athens, 616/729-5010
Moonraker Lounge and Restaurant
  14490 Beadle Lake Rd., 616/962-7779

Best Brunch
Clara's on the River
  44 McCamly St. N., 616/963-0966

Best Burgers
Moonraker Lounge and Restaurant
  14490 Beadle Lake Rd., 616/962-7779

Best Chinese Food
Golden Dragon Restaurant
  906 Capital Ave. NE, 616/968-7159
Tony's Chop Suey
  215 Michigan Ave. W., 616/964-8138
Hong Kong Restaurant
  174 Columbia Ave. E., 616/965-4848

Best Coffee
Coffee Emporium
  34 W. Michigan St., 616/965-6220

Best Desserts
Piccadilly Grille
35 Jackson St. W., 616/962-9133

Best Homestyle Food
Homespun Restaurant
210 Columbia Ave. E., 616/962-5323

Best Ice Cream/Yogurt
Pastamazoo
55 Twentieth St. S., 616/963-1177

Best Italian Food
Roma Cafe and Spaghetti Factory
217 Michigan Ave. W., 616/968-6377

Best Mexican Food
Oye Amigos
307 E. Michigan Ave., Marshall, 616/781-7770
Bit O'Mexico
605 North Ave., 616/964-6100

Best Pizza
Mancino's Pizza
5285 Beckley Rd., 616/979-3100
Pennfield Pizza
1432 Capital Ave. NE, 616/964-9465

Best Sandwiches
Schlotzsky's Deli
14 W. Michigan Mall, 616/963-2526

Best Steaks
Finley's American Restaurant
140 Columbia Ave. E., 616/968-3938

BAY CITY, MI

Best Breakfast
Krzysiak House
1605 Michigan Ave., 517/894-5531

Best Burgers
Steamer's Pub
108 N. Linn St., 517/895-8559
Mulligan's Pub
109 Center Ave., 517/893-4555
O'Hare's
608 E. Midland, 517/893-5181

Best Chinese Food
Mandarin House Chinese Restaurant
1415 W. Center Rd., Essexville, 517/893-9499

Best Coffee
Espresso Express
916 N. Water St., 517/893-8898

Best Desserts
Grampa Tony's Restaurant
1108 Columbus Ave., 517/893-4795

Best Family Restaurants
Grampa Tony's Restaurant
1108 Columbus Ave., 517/893-4795
Krzysiak House
1605 Michigan Ave., 517/894-5531

Best Homestyle Food
Krzysiak House
1605 Michigan Ave., 517/894-5531

Best Ice Cream/Yogurt
Jamie's Dairies
3383 W. North Union Rd., 517/686-7804
1309 S. Farragut St., 517/893-7841
603 Columbus Ave., 517/893-7849
110 N. Madison Ave., 517/893-7871
1023 Broadway St., 517/893-7862

Best Italian Food
Grampa Tony's Restaurant
1108 Columbus Ave., 517/893-4795
O Sole Mio Restaurant
1005 Saginaw St., 517/893-3496

Best Seafood
Wagner's Steak and Seafood
807 N. Henry St., 517/686-1670

Best Steaks
Wagner's Steak and Seafood
807 N. Henry St., 517/686-1670

COLDWATER, MI

Best Atmosphere
Clairmont House
32 Rail Rd., 517/278-5257

Best Chinese Food
Charlie's II Restaurant
599 E. Chicago St., 517/278-2982

Best Coffee
Dutch Uncle Donuts
58 E. Chicago St., 517/278-8965

Best Family Restaurant
Coldwater Gardens
432 E. Chicago St., 517/278-3172

Best Greek/Mediterranean Food
Coldwater Gardens
432 E. Chicago St., 517/278-3172

Best Mexican Food
Crispito's Mexican and American Restaurant
494 Marshall St., 517/279-8477

Best Pizza
Mancino's Pizza
510 E. Chicago Rd., 517/278-2127

Best Sandwiches
B and K Root Beer Drive-In
378 W. Chicago Rd., 517/279-9048
Irma's Restaurant
14 W. Chicago St., 517/279-9965

Best Steaks
Monroe Street Station
19 S. Monroe St., 517/278-3149
Narrows
191 Narrows Rd., 517/278-5088

Standbys
Bob Evans
 24 N. Willowbrook Rd., 517/279-2101
TCBY
 407 E. Chicago St., 517/278-7820

DEARBORN, MI

Best American Food
M and M Cafe
 13355 Michigan Ave., 313/581-5775
Golden Feather Restaurant
 29633 Ford Rd., Garden City, 313/421-2114

Best Barbecue/Ribs
Golden Feather Restaurant
 29633 Ford Rd., Garden City, 313/421-2114

Best Breakfast
Andoni's Family Dining
 1620 N. Telegraph Rd., 313/278-9100
Dimitri's Fine Food
 2424 S. Telegraph Rd., 313/565-7066

Best Business Lunch
La Shish
 12918 Michigan Ave., 313/584-4477

Best Chinese Food
New Peking Restaurant
 29105 Ford Rd., Garden City, 313/425-2230

Best Delicatessen
Matti's on Monroe
 1842 Monroe St., 313/277-3253

Best Family Restaurant
Andoni's Family Dining
 1620 N. Telegraph Rd., 313/278-9100

Best Homestyle Food
Dimitri's Fine Food
 2424 S. Telegraph Rd., 313/565-7066

Best Italian Food
Giovanni's Ristorante
 330 S. Oakwood, 313/841-0122
Peppina's Italian Restaurant
 1128 Dix Hwy., Lincoln Park, 313/928-5523

Best Lunch
Lile's Sandwich Shop
 13800 Michigan Ave., 313/581-2821

Best Mexican Food
Xochimilco Restaurant
 3409 Bagley St., 313/843-0179

Best Middle Eastern Food
La Shish
 12918 Michigan Ave., 313/584-4477
M and M Cafe
 13355 Michigan Ave., 313/581-5775

Best Salad/Salad Bar
Salad Bar
 22023 Michigan Ave., 313/274-7520

Best Sandwiches
Lile's Sandwich Shop
13800 Michigan Ave., 313/581-2821
Noah's Sandwich Factory
14500 Michigan Ave., 313/582-8361

DETROIT, MI

Best Restaurants in Town
Daniel's
209 W. Sixth St., Royal Oak, 810/541-8050
Vintage Bistro
18450 Mack Ave., Grosse Pointe Farms, 313/886-9950
Rugby Grille
Townsend Hotel, 100 Townsend, Birmingham,
810/642-5999
Kyla's
214 W. Sixth St., Royal Oak, 810/548-7430
Rattlesnake Club
300 River Place at Joseph Campau, 313/567-4400

Best All-You-Can-Eat Buffet
Mongolian Barbecue
310 S. Main St., Royal Oak, 810/398-7755

Best Barbecue/Ribs
Mitchell's Barbecue and Grill
1824 W. Fourteen Mile Rd., Royal Oak, 810/280-0050

Best Breakfast
Jumps
63 Kercheval, Grosse Pointe Farms, 313/882-9555

Best Business Breakfast
Mesquite Creek
222 W. Jefferson, 313/964-5500

Best Cheap Meal
National Coney Island
19019 Mack Ave., Grosse Pointe, 313/881-5509

Best Chinese Food
Mon Jin Lau
1515 E. Maple Rd., Troy, 810/689-2332
East Winds
19160 Ten Mile Rd., Roseville, 810/771-7420

Best Coffeehouse
Lonestar Coffeehouse
207 S. Woodward, Birmingham, 810/642-2233

Best Delicatessen
Amer's Mediterranean Deli
312 S. State St., Ann Arbor, 313/761-6000
611 Church St., Ann Arbor, 313/769-1210

Best Desserts
Traffic Jam and Snug
4268 Second Ave., 313/831-9470
The Rattlesnake Club
300 River Place at Joseph Campau, 313/567-4400

Best Greek/Mediterranean Food
Pegasus in the Fisher
3011 W. Grand Blvd., 313/875-7400

Best Ice Cream/Yogurt
Ray's Ice Cream
 4233 Coolidge Hwy., Royal Oak, 810/549-5256

Best Indian Food
Peacock Tandoori
 4045 Maple St., Dearborn, 313/582-2344

Best Italian Food
Lelli's Inn
 7618 Woodward Ave., 313/871-1590

Best Japanese Food
Kyoto Japanese Steak House
 1985 W. Big Beaver Rd., 810/649-6340

Best Mexican Food
Xochimilco
 3409 Bagley St., 313/843-0179

Best Middle Eastern Food
La-Shish
 12918 Michigan Ave., Dearborn, 313/584-4477

Best Other Ethnic Food
Annabel's Catering (Brazilian)
 20097 W. Twelve Mile Rd., Southfield, 810/354-6155
Under the Eagle (Polish)
 9000 Joseph Campau St., Hamtramck, 313/875-5905

Best Pizza
Buddy's Rendezvous Pizza
 17125 Conant St., 313/892-9001
 19163 Mack Ave., 313/884-7400

Best Sandwiches
Bruschetta Cafe
 Oakland Mall, Troy, 810/589-2900

Best Seafood
Joe Muer's
 2000 Gratiot Ave., 313/567-1088
Big Fish
 700 Town Center Dr., Dearborn, 313/336-6350
Big Fish Too
 1111 W. Fourteen Mile Rd., Madison Heights,
  810/585-9533

Best Soul Food
Steve's Soul Food
 8443 Grand River Ave., 313/894-5560

Best Thai Food
Thai House
 4254 N. Woodward Ave., Royal Oak, 810/776-3660

Best Vegetarian Food
Inn Season Natural Food Cafe
 500 E. Fourth St., Royal Oak, 810/547-7916

Best Vietnamese Food
Mini
 475 University, Windsor, 519/254-2221

Best Wine Selection
The Whitney
 4421 Woodward Ave., 313/832-5700

Standbys
Fuddruckers
  43150 Grand River, Novi, 810/380-8787
Outback Steakhouse
  42871 Ford Rd., Canton, 313/981-4144

FLINT, MI

Best American Food
Broadstreet
  103 E. Broad St., Linden, 810/735-5844
White Horse Tavern
  621 W. Court St., 810/234-3811
Danny's
  4070 S. Saginaw St., 810/743-8970
Holly Hotel
  110 Battle Alley, Holly, 810/852-3720

Best Atmosphere
Holly Hotel
  110 Battle Alley, Holly, 810/852-3720

Best Breakfast
Balkan Bakery
  1325 W. Dayton St., 810/235-3431

Best Burgers
Bill Thomas' Halo Burger
  800 S. Saginaw St., 810/238-4015

Best Business Lunch
Red Rooster Makuch's Restaurant
  3302 Davison Rd., 810/742-9310

Best Continental Food
Broadstreet
  103 E. Broad St., Linden, 810/735-5844
City Lights Restaurant
  432 N. Saginaw St., Twelfth Fl., 810/232-8888

Best Diner
The Diner
  522 W. Broad St., Linden, 810/735-9741

Best Dinner
White Horse Tavern
  621 W. Court St., 810/234-3811

Best Fast Food
Angelo's Coney Island and Grill
  1816 Davison Rd., 810/238-3761
Bill Thomas' Halo Burger
  800 S. Saginaw St., 810/238-4015

Best Greek/Mediterranean Food
Angelo's Coney Island and Grill
  1816 Davison Rd., 810/238-3761

Best Homestyle Food
The Diner
  522 W. Broad St., Linden, 810/735-9741

Best Italian Food
Danny's
  4070 S. Saginaw St., 810/743-8970

M

talia Gardens
  401 W. Court St., 810/233-4112

Best Lunch
Angelo's Coney Island and Grill
  1816 Davison Rd., 810/238-3761

Best Pizza
Ruggero's
  2107 S. Linden Rd., 810/733-7633
  303 S. Saginaw St., 810/232-1411
  877 E. Fifth Ave., 810/234-0041
  1422 N. Chevrolet Ave., 810/233-4812

Best Romantic Dining
City Lights Restaurant
  432 N. Saginaw St., Twelfth Fl., 810/232-8888

Best Seafood
Whitey's Restaurant
  109 S. State Rd., 810/653-6666

Best View While Dining
City Lights Restaurant
  432 N. Saginaw St., Twelfth Fl., 810/232-8888

GRAND RAPIDS, MI

Best Restaurants in Town
The 1913 Room
  Amway Grand Plaza Hotel, 187 Monroe Ave. NW,
    616/774-2000
Gibson's
  1033 Lake Dr. SE, 616/774-8535
Sandpiper
  2225 South Shore, Macatawa, 616/335-5866
San Chez Bistro
  38 W. Fulton St., 616/774-8272

Best Bagels
Ada Bagel Cafe
  6250 28th St. SE, 616/954-1400
Barry Bagels
  28th St. near E. Paris Ave., 616/957-2300

Best Barbecue/Ribs
Damon's
  4515 28th St. SE, Kentwood, 616/956-1211
Sam's Joint
  4312 S. Division Ave., 616/538-9601
  107 E. Main, Caledonia, 616/891-1128
  15520 48th Ave., Coopersville, 616/837-8558
  19 N. Main St., Rockford, 616/866-3324
  6618 Old Grand Haven Rd., Norton Shores,
    616/798-7155
  7449 68th St., Alaska, 616/698-1833
Sam's Other Joint
  2412 Briggs Rd., Yankee Springs, 616/795-3695

Best Beer Selection
Flanagan's
  139 Pearl NW, 616/454-7852

Tootsie's: The Downtown Saloon
  Amway Grand Plaza Hotel, 187 Monroe Ave. NW,
    616/776-6495

Best Breakfast
Wolfgang's Just Breakfast
  1530 Wealthy SE, 616/454-5776
Red Geranium Cafe
  352 Michigan NE, 616/235-4680

Best Burgers
Cottage Bar and Restaurant
  18 La Grave Ave. SE, 616/454-9088

Best Business Lunch
Teazer's
  819 Ottawa NW, 616/459-2481
Hong Kong Inn
  121 Monroe Center, 616/451-3835

Best Casual Dining
Arnie's Bakery-Restaurant
  1960 Breton SE, 616/949-3801
  Eastbrook Mall, 3561 28th St., 616/956-7901
  710 Leonard NW, 616/454-3098
Grand River Saloon
  151 Ottawa Ave. NW, 616/458-2229
Honey Creek Inn
  8025 Cannonsburg Rd., 616/874-7849
Rose's
  550 Lakeside Dr. SE, 616/458-1122

Best Chinese Food
First Wok
  2301 44th St., 616/281-0681
  3509 Alpine Ave. NW, 616/784-1616
Hong Kong Inn
  121 Monroe Center, 616/451-3835
Yen Ching
  57 Monroe Center, 616/235-6969

Best Coffee
Kava House
  1445 Lake Dr. SE, 616/451-8600

Best Continental Food
Alpen Rose
  4 East 8th St., 616/393-2111
Pagano's
  9948 Cherry Valley Ave. SE, Caledonia, 616/891-0160

Best Delicatessen
Eastown Deli
  3730 28th St., 616/458-5439
Solomon's Deli
  221 Michigan NE, 616/774-0272

Best Desserts
Arnie's Bakery-Restaurant
  1960 Breton SE, 616/949-3801
  Eastbrook Mall, 3561 28th St., 616/959-7901
  710 Leonard NW, 616/454-3098
  127 E. Bridge St., Plainwell, 616/685-9495

The Gathering Place
  6886 Cascade Rd. SE, 616/949-3188

Best Diner
Brandywine
  1345 Lake Dr. SE, 616/774-8641

Best Family Restaurants
Bono's Italian Restaurant
  1418 Plainfield NE, 616/451-0010
Finley's American Restaurants
  1420 28th St. SW, 616/538-8600
  1950 44th St. SE, 616/455-9640
  2630 E. Beltline SE, 616/949-1560
  3495 Alpine NW, 616/784-6085
  4095 Plainfield NE, 616/364-0058

Best Fast Food
Mustard's Last Stand
  98 Monroe Center, 616/774-8143

Best German Food
Schnitzelbank
  342 Jefferson SE, 616/459-9527

Best Health-Conscious Menu
Gas Light Inn
  2162 Wealthy, 616/451-8611

Best Homestyle Food
Teazer's
  819 Ottawa NW, 616/459-2481
Fingers Restaurant
  4981 Plainfield, 616/363-3836
Red Geranium Cafe
  352 Michigan NE, 616/235-4680

Best Italian Food
Johnny Noto's Italian Ristorante
  4259 Lake Michigan Dr. NW, 616/791-0092
Florentine Pizzeria Restaurant
  4301 Kalamazoo St. SE, 616/455-2230
Pietro's Ristorante
  2780 Birchcrest off 28th St. SE, 616/452-3228
Vitale's
  834 Leonard NE, 616/458-3766

Best Japanese Food
Tokyo Grill and Sushi
  4478 Breton Rd. SE, Kentwood, 616/455-3433

Best Korean Food
Seoul Garden
  2409 E. Beltline SE, 616/956-1522

Best Mexican Food
Alma Latina
  45 S. Division, 616/454-6790
Jose Babushka's
  1820 44th St. SW, 616/534-0704
Texas Cafe
  956 E. Fulton, 616/451-0976

Best Other Ethnic Food
Osta's (Lebanese)
  2228 Wealthy St. SE, 616/456-8999
Wisla Shop (Polish)
  644 Stocking NW, 616/458-2903

Best Pizza
Pietro's
  2780 Birchcrest off 28th St. SE, 616/452-3228
Fricano's Pizza
  1400 Fulton, Grand Haven, 616/842-8640
Pallino's
  Gaslight Village, 2224 Wealthy SE, 616/458-4646

Best Places to Eat When Someone Else Is Buying
The 1913 Room
  Amway Grand Plaza Hotel, 187 Monroe Ave. NW,
    616/774-2000
Cygnus
  Amway Grand Plaza Hotel, 187 Monroe Ave. NW,
    616/776-6425
Gibson's
  1033 Lake Dr. SE, 616/774-8535

Best Regional Food
Sandpiper
  2225 South Shore, Macatawa, 616/335-5866
Thornapple Village Inn
  445 Thornapple Village Dr., Ada, 616/676-1233

Best Romantic Dining
Bay Pointe
  11456 Marsh Rd., Shelbyville, 616/672-5202
Rembrandt's
  333 Bridge St. NW, 616/459-8900
Thornapple Village Inn
  445 Thornapple Village Dr., Ada, 616/676-1233

Best Sandwiches
Buddie's Delicatessen and Bagelry
  2150 Wealthy SE, 616/235-3354
Eastown Deli
  3730 28th St., 616/458-5439
Ski's Sub Shop
  96 Monroe Center, 616/451-9504

Best Seafood
Arboreal Inn
  18191 174th Ave., Spring Lake, 616/842-3800
Charley's Crab
  63 Market St. SW, 616/459-2500

Best Southwestern Food
Beltline Bar
  16 28th St. SE, 616/245-0494

Best Spanish Food
San Chez Bistro
  38 W. Fulton, 616/774-8272

Best Sports Bar
Cheddar's Restaurant
  4284 28th SE, Kentwood, 616/940-1837

M

Best Steaks
Brann's Steak and Seafood
5080 Alpine NW, 616/784-2100
401 Leonard NW, 616/454-9368
4157 S. Division, 616/534-5421
Duck's Restaurant and Lounge
740 Michigan NE, 616/451-2767
Mountain Jack's
3600 28th St. SE, Kentwood, 616/949-9033

Best Thai Food
Thai House Restaurant
6447 28th St. SE, Cascade, 616/285-9944

Best Vegetarian Food
Down to Earth
10025 Belding Rd. NE, 616/691-7288

Standbys
Friday's
3345 28th St. SE, Kentwood, 616/957-3911
Fuddruckers
4061 28th St. SE, 616/940-8170
The Olive Garden
3030 Alpine NW, 616/785-0087
3883 28th St. SE, 616/940-1632
Ground Round
825 28th St. SE, 616/452-5210
Outback Steakhouse
3650 28th St. SE, 616/957-7932

M

HOLLAND, MI

Best Restaurant in Town
Sandpiper Restaurant
2225 S. Shore Rd., Macatawa, 616/335-5866

Best American Food
Queen's Inn Restaurant
12350 James St., 616/393-0310

Best Bread
Till Midnight
208 College Ave., 616/392-6883

Best Breakfast
Russ' Restaurant
1060 Lincoln Ave., 616/396-4036
210 N. River Ave., 616/392-6300
361 E. Eighth St., 616/396-2348

Best Business Lunch
Eighth Street Grill
20 W. Eighth St., 616/392-5888

Best Casual Dining
The Auburn
478 E. Sixteenth, 616/392-3017
Calypso's
Holland Holiday Inn, 650 E. 24th off Hwy. 31,
616/394-0111

Best Chinese Food
China Inn
  2863 W. Shore Dr., Ste. 105, 616/786-9230
  457 E. 32nd St., 616/395-8383

Best Continental Food
Sandpiper Restaurant
  2225 S. Shore Rd., Macatawa, 616/335-5866
Alpen Rose
  4 E. Eighth St., 616/393-2111
Pereddie's Bakery Deli
  447 Washington Sq., 616/394-3061

Best Dinner
Prime Tyme Restaurant
  1080 Lincoln Ave., 616/396-1071

Best Health-Conscious Menu
Till Midnight
  208 College Ave., 616/392-6883

Best Homestyle Food
Pereddie's Bakery Deli
  447 Washington Ave., 616/394-3061

Best Ice Cream/Yogurt
Captain Sundae
  365 Douglas Ave., 616/396-5938

Best Italian Food
Mancino's
  12465 James St., 616/786-0600
Eighty-Four East
  84 E. Eighth St., 616/396-8484
Pereddie's Bakery Deli
  447 Washington Ave., 616/394-3061

Best Mexican Food
Cantu's Mexican Restaurant
  380 W. Sixteenth St., 616/396-6622
Jose Babushka's
  12420 Felch, 616/392-9900

Best Other Ethnic Food
Queen's Inn Restaurant (Dutch)
  12350 James St., 616/393-0310

Best Pastries
Alpen Rose
  4 E. Eighth St., 616/393-2111

Best Pizza
Mancino's
  12465 James St., 616/786-0600

Best Romantic Dining
Till Midnight
  208 College Ave., 616/392-6883

Best Salad/Salad Bar
Pereddie's Bakery Deli
  447 Washington Ave., 616/394-3061

Best Sandwiches
Eighth Street Grill
  20 W. Eighth St., 616/392-5888

M

Best Seafood
Sandpiper Restaurant
2225 S. Shore Rd., Macatawa, 616/335-5866

Best Steaks
Prime Tyme Restaurant
1080 Lincoln Ave., 616/396-1071

Best View While Dining
Sandpiper Restaurant
2225 S. Shore Rd., Macatawa, 616/335-5866

JACKSON, MI

Best Barbecue/Ribs
West Texas Barbeque Company
2190 Brooklyn Rd., 517/784-0510

Best Breakfast
Ye Old Steakhouse
1319 E. Michigan Ave., 517/784-6744

Best Burgers
Kelly's Lunch
640 E. Michigan Ave., 517/787-9010
Eagle's Nest
1200 Eagle Point Rd., Clarklake, 517/529-9121
Schlenkers Sandwich Shop
1104 E. Ganson St., 517/783-1667

Best Ice Cream/Yogurt
Jackson All Star Dairy
1401 Daniel Rd., 517/782-7141

Best Pizza
Jaxon Pizza Factory
800 N. Waterloo St., 517/788-8366

Best Sandwiches
Brandywine Pub and Food
2125 Horton Rd., 517/783-2777

Best Seafood
Brandywine Pub and Food
2125 Horton Rd., 517/783-2777
Eagle's Nest
1200 Eagle Point Rd., Clarklake, 517/529-9121

Best Steaks
Brandywine Pub and Food
2125 Horton Rd., 517/783-2777
Ye Old Steakhouse
1319 E. Michigan Ave., 517/784-6744
Gilbert's Steak House
2323 Shirley Dr., 517/782-7135

Standbys
Cracker Barrel
2494 Airport Rd., 517/783-5300
Ground Round
1051 Boardman Rd., 517/782-3330

M

KALAMAZOO, MI

Best All-You-Can-Eat Buffet
Dane's Buffet
    4217 Portage St., 616/343-4264

Best Bars
Main Street Pub
    4574 W. Main St., 616/342-9710
Carlos Murphy's
    5650 W. Main St., 616/343-0330

Best Breakfast
Holly's Family Restaurant
    645 W. Michigan Ave., 616/343-4444
Food Dance Cafe
    161 E. Michigan Ave., 616/382-1888
Maggie's Bakery and Cafe
    2715 W. Michigan Ave., 616/381-1312

Best Brunch
Webster's
    100 W. Michigan Ave., 616/343-4444
Mountain Jack's Restaurant
    6701 S. Westnedge Ave., 616/327-6797

Best Burgers
Burdick's
    100 W. Michigan Ave., 616/343-3333
McGinnis Landing Restaurant
    5031 W. Main St., 616/388-9911

Best Business Lunch
Burdick's
    100 W. Michigan Ave., 616/343-3333
Damon's
    3124 S. Westnedge Ave., 616/342-4753

Best Casual Dining
Finley's American Restaurant
    6301 S. Westnedge Ave., 616/323-1104
    5160 W. Main St., 616/342-4360
McGinnis Landing Restaurant
    5031 W. Main St., 616/388-9911

Best Cheap Meal
Holly's Family Restaurant
    645 W. Michigan Ave., 616/343-4444
Mancino's Pizza
    3911 Gull Rd., 616/383-0066
    10100 Shaver Rd., 616/327-5121
    5363 S. Westnedge Ave., 616/382-2527

Best Chinese Food
Great Wall of China
    3025 S. Westnedge Ave., 616/343-9888

Best Coffee
Water Street Coffee Joint
    315 E. Water St., 616/373-2840

Best Desserts
McGinnis Landing Restaurant
    5031 W. Main St., 616/388-9911

M

Webster's
  100 W. Michigan Ave., 616/343-4444
Hawthorne Restaurant and Cafe
  9110 Portage Rd., 616/323-1327

Best Diner
Maggie's Bakery and Cafe
  2715 W. Michigan Ave., 616/381-1312

Best Family Restaurant
Finley's American Restaurant
  6301 S. Westnedge Ave., 616/323-1104
  5160 W. Main St., 616/342-4360

Best Health-Conscious Menu
Food Dance Cafe
  161 E. Michigan Ave., 616/382-1888
Hawthorne Restaurant and Cafe
  9110 Portage Rd., 616/323-1327

Best Homestyle Food
Bill Knapp's
  4315 W. Main St., 616/342-0227
  513 Portage Rd., 616/345-8655

Best Ice Cream/Yogurt
Carousel Ice Cream
  1710 W. Main St., 616/342-8746
  819 S. Westnedge Ave., 616/343-8493

Best Late-Night Food
McGinnis Landing Restaurant
  5031 W. Main St., 616/388-9911

Best Mexican Food
Carlos Murphy's
  5650 W. Main St., 616/343-0330
Mi Ranchito
  3806 S. Westnedge Ave., 616/343-7262
  3112 S. Ninth St., 616/375-5861

Best Pizza
Mancino's Pizza
  3911 Gull Rd., 616/383-0066
  10100 Shaver Rd., 616/327-5121
  5363 S. Westnedge Ave., 616/382-2527

Best Places to Be "Seen"
Hawthorne Restaurant and Cafe
  9110 Portage Rd., 616/323-1327
Webster's
  100 W. Michigan Ave., 616/343-4444

Best Place to Eat Alone
Damon's
  3124 S. Westnedge Ave., 616/342-4753

Best Places to Eat When Someone Else Is Buying
Hawthorne Restaurant and Cafe
  9110 Portage Rd., 616/323-1327
Webster's
  100 W. Michigan Ave., 616/343-4444
Great Lakes Shipping Company
  4525 W. KL Ave., 616/375-3650

Best Place to Take the Kids
The Pizza Parlor
  3301 W. Michigan Ave., Battle Creek, 616/962-8061

Best Romantic Dining
Hawthorne Restaurant and Cafe
  9110 Portage Rd., 616/323-1327
Webster's
  100 W. Michigan Ave., 616/343-4444

Best Sandwiches
Burdick's
  100 W. Michigan Ave., 616/343-3333
Mancino's Pizza
  3911 Gull Rd., 616/383-0066
  10100 Shaver Rd., 616/327-5121
  5363 S. Westnedge Ave., 616/382-2527

Best Steaks
Great Lakes Shipping Company
  4525 W. KL Ave., 616/575-3650
Mountain Jack's Restaurant
  6701 S. Westnedge Ave., 616/327-6797

Best Vegetarian Food
Burdick's
  100 W. Michigan Ave., 616/343-3333

Best Other Restaurant
Clara's on the River
  44 McCamly Station., Battle Creek, 616/963-0966

Standbys
Old Country Buffet
  6749 S. Westnedge Rd., 616/323-9669
Ryan's Family Steak House
  7141 S. Westnedge Ave., 616/327-0909
TCBY
  6404 S. Westnedge Ave., 616/329-7570
The Olive Garden
  6700 S. Westnedge Ave., 616/327-5001
Chi Chi's
  5609 W. Main St., 616/382-4055
Red Lobster
  6535 S. Westnedge Ave., 616/323-1329

LANSING, MI

Best Restaurant in Town
Dusty's Cellar
  1839 W. Grand River Ave., Okemos, 517/349-8680

Best Bar
Deluca's Restaurant
  2006 W. Willow St., 517/487-6087

Best Burgers
USA Cafe
  4750 Hagadorn Rd., East Lansing, 517/332-3660

Best Casual Dining
Deluca's Restaurant
  2006 W. Willow St., 517/487-6087
Blue Coyote
  113 Pere Marquette, 517/485-2583

Best Chinese Food
Gourmet Village
    4790 S. Hagadorn Rd., 517/333-6666

Best Continental Food
Dusty's Cellar
    1839 W. Grand River Ave., Okemos, 517/349-8680

Best Diner
USA Cafe
    4750 Hagadorn Rd., East Lansing, 517/332-3660

Best Dinner
Golden Rose Restaurant
    3056 Okemos Rd., Mason, 517/349-9500
Dusty's English Inn
    728 S. Michigan Rd., Eaton Rapids, 517/663-2500

Best Italian Food
Michelangelo's Restaurant
    213 E. Grand River Ave., East Lansing, 517/332-4825

Best Lunch
Clara's
    637 E. Michigan Ave., 517/372-7120

Best Mexican Food
Clara's
    637 E. Michigan Ave., 517/372-7120
El Azteco
    1016 W. Saginaw St., 517/485-4589

Best Microbrewery
Blue Coyote
    113 Pere Marquette, 517/485-2583

Best Other Ethnic Food
Sultan's (Middle Eastern/Mediterranean)
    4790 S. Hagadorn Rd., 517/333-4444

Best Pizza
Deluca's Restaurant
    2006 W. Willow St., 517/487-6087

Best Salad/Salad Bar
Clara's
    637 E. Michigan Ave., 517/372-7120

Best Wine Selection
Michelangelo's Restaurant
    213 E. Grand River Ave., East Lansing, 517/332-4825
Dusty's Cellar
    1839 W. Grand River Ave., Okemos, 517/349-8680

LIVONIA, MI

Best American Food
D. Dennison's
    37716 Six Mile Rd., 313/464-9030
Cafe Bon Homme
    844 Penniman Ave., 313/453-6260
Mountain Jack's Restaurant
    31501 Schoolcraft Rd., 313/458-7333

Best Breakfast
Golden Lantern
    33251 Five Mile Rd., 313/421-1012

Best Burgers
Bill Knapp's
  16995 Laurel Park Dr., 313/464-6363
  32955 Plymouth Rd., 313/427-0511
Max and Erma's
  37714 Six Mile Rd., 313/462-9870

Best Casual Dining
D. Dennison's
  37716 Six Mile Rd., 313/464-9030

Best Chinese Food
Szechuan Empire
  29215 Five Mile Rd., 313/458-7160
  37097 Six Mile Rd., 313/591-1901

Best Continental Food
Cafe Bon Homme
  844 Penniman Ave., 313/453-6260

Best Homestyle Food
Bill Knapp's
  16995 Laurel Park Dr., 313/464-6363
  32955 Plymouth Rd., 313/427-0511

Best Italian Food
DePalma's Dining
  31735 Plymouth Rd., 313/261-2430
Fonte D'Amore Ristorante
  32030 Plymouth Rd., 313/422-0770

Best Pizza
Buddy's Rendezvous Pizza
  33605 Plymouth Rd., 313/261-3550

Best Salad/Salad Bar
Buddy's Rendezvous Pizza
  33605 Plymouth Rd., 313/261-3550
D. Dennison's
  37716 Six Mile Rd., 313/464-9030

Best Sandwiches
Max and Erma's
  37714 Six Mile Rd., 313/462-9870

Best Seafood
D. Dennison's
  37716 Six Mile Rd., 313/464-9030

Best Steaks
Mountain Jack's
  31501 Schoolcraft Rd., 313/458-7333

Standbys
The Olive Garden
  14000 Middlebelt Rd., 313/458-5100

MARQUETTE, MI

Best Restaurants in Town
Northwoods Supper Club
  260 Northwoods Rd., 906/228-4343
The Vierling Saloon and Samplery
  119 S. Front St., 906/228-3533

Best Health-Conscious Menu
Sweetwater Cafe
517 N. Third St., 906/226-7009

Best Italian Food
Villa Capri Italian Cuisine
155 Bayou Rd., 906/225-1153

Best Mexican Food
Entre Amigos
142 W. Washington St., 906/228-4531

Best Sports Bar
Whiskers Sports Bar and Eatery
1700 Presque Isle Ave., 906/228-9038

MIDLAND, MI

Best Bar
One Hundred One Main Street Food and Spirits
101 E. Main St., 517/839-2896

Best Breakfast
Texan Family Restaurant
2008 N. Saginaw Rd., 517/631-4600
Big Boy Restaurant
1513 S. Saginaw Rd., 517/631-1059
Shirlene's Cuisine
1716 W. Wakerly Rd., 517/631-8750

Best Chinese Food
Bamboo Garden
2600 N. Saginaw Rd., 517/832-7967

Best Desserts
Sweet Onion
1415 S. Saginaw Rd., 517/631-2062

Best Place to Eat When Someone Else Is Buying
Ashman Court Hotel
111 W. Main St., 517/839-0500

Best Sandwiches
One Hundred One Main Street Food and Spirits
101 E. Main St., 517/839-2896

Best Seafood
Cafe Edward
5010 Bay City Rd., 517/496-3012

Best Steaks
Corky's
5100 Bay City Rd., 517/839-2896
Cafe Edward
5010 Bay City Rd., 517/496-3012

Standbys
Chi Chi's
6640 Eastman Ave., 517/832-4999
Baskin-Robbins
2311 Washington St., 517/832-3181

MONROE, MI

Best Breakfast
Ernie's Gathering Place
15425 S. Dixie Hwy., 313/242-2330

Monroe Diner
546 S. Telegraph Rd., 313/242-4077

Best Burgers
McGeady's Town Pub
39 S. Monroe St., 313/243-1220

Best Ice Cream/Yogurt
Independent Dairy
126 N. Telegraph Rd., 313/241-6016
7373 Bluebush Rd., 313/587-2112

Best Italian Food
Dominic's Italian Restaurant
15215 S. Dixie Hwy., 313/242-6300

Best Mexican Food
Carl's Hide-A-Way
2838 Lewis Ave., Ida, 313/269-9265

Best Pizza
Detroit Beach Restaurant
2630 N. Dixie Hwy., 313/289-3122

Best Regional Food
Ernie's Gathering Place
15425 S. Dixie Hwy., 313/242-2330

Best Seafood
Francesco's Pier House
6975 Laplaisance St., 313/242-6470
Quatro's
1295 Stewart Rd., 313/242-6788

Best Steaks
Quatro's
1295 Stewart Rd., 313/242-6788

M

MT. PLEASANT, MI

Best Breakfast
Big Boy Restaurant
1623 S. Mission St., 517/772-2476

Best Burgers
Brass Saloon
128 S. Main St., 517/772-0864

Best Coffee
Max and Emily's Bakery Cafe
125 E. Broadway St., 517/772-7460

Best Desserts
Sweet Onion
102 N. Mission St., 517/772-0801
The Lemon Grass
437 S. Mission, 517/772-0895

Best Family Restaurant
J.W. Filmore's
903 N. Mission St., 517/772-5950

Best Homestyle Food
J.W. Filmore's
903 N. Mission St., 517/772-5950
'tanley's Famous Restaurant
'20 E. Broadway St., 517/773-3259

e Cream/Yogurt
's
0 E. Pickard, 517/772-2332

st Italian Food
alian Oven
2336 S. Mission, 517/773-6836

Best Mexican Food
La Senorita Mexican Restaurant
1516 S. Mission St., 517/772-1331

Best Place to Eat When Someone Else Is Buying
Embers
1217 S. Mission St., 517/773-5007

Best Sandwiches
Max and Emily's Bakery Cafe
125 E. Broadway St., 517/772-7460

Best Seafood
Packard's Grill
Holiday Inn, 5665 E. Pickard St., 517/772-2905
Embers
1217 S. Mission St., 517/773-5007

Standbys
Pizza Hut
1216 S. Mission St., 517/773-6161

M **MUSKEGON, MI**

Best Restaurants in Town
Chesapeake Crab House
939 Third St., 616/728-2204
Rafferty's
601 Terrace Point Rd., 616/722-4461

Best American Food
Rafferty's
601 Terrace Point Rd., 616/722-4461

Best Breakfast
Hearthstone
3350 Glade St., 616/733-1056
Goober's Bakery
4165 Grand Haven Rd., 616/798-1213
Papa Bear's
2280 E. Apple Ave., 616/773-2067

Best Chinese Food
House of Chan
375 Gin Chan Ave., 616/733-9624

Best Coffee
Anton's Bakery
927 W. Laketon Ave., 616/759-7676

Best Dinner
Carmen's Cafe
315 W. Clay Ave., 616/726-6317
USA Cafe
2020 Lakeshore Dr., 616/755-7454

Best Family Restaurant
Cherokee Restaurant
1971 W. Sherman Blvd., 616/759-7006

Best Fast Food
G and L Chili Dogs
885 Jefferson St., 616/722-9119
771 W. Sherman Blvd., 616/733-1505

Best Homestyle Food
Cherokee Restaurant
1971 W. Sherman Blvd., 616/759-7006
Papa Bear's
2280 E. Apple Ave., 616/773-2067

Best Italian Food
Tony's Club
785 W. Broadway Ave., 616/739-7196

Best Lunch
Carmen's Cafe
315 W. Clay Ave., 616/726-6317
G and L Chili Dogs
885 Jefferson St., 616/722-9119
771 W. Sherman Blvd., 616/733-1505

Best Mexican Food
Flamingo II
1163 E. Laketon Ave., 616/722-1679

Best Place to Take the Kids
Cherokee Restaurant
1971 W. Sherman Blvd., 616/759-7006

Best Romantic Dining
Rafferty's
601 Terrace Blvd., 616/722-4461

Best Sandwiches
Hearthstone
3350 Glade St., 616/733-1056

Best Seafood
Chesapeake Crab House
939 Third St., 616/728-2204
Tony's Club
785 W. Broadway Ave., 616/739-7196

Best Steaks
Tony's Club
785 W. Broadway Ave., 616/739-7196

PETOSKEY, MI

Best Restaurant in Town
Andante
321 Bay St., 616/348-3321

Best Breakfast
Americana The Pancake House
Hwy. 31, 616/347-5530

Best Brunch
Perry Hotel
Bay St. at Lewis St., 616/347-4000

Best Burgers
Elias Brothers
751 Spring, 616/347-2931
Mitchell Street Pub
426 E. Mitchell St., 616/347-1801

Best Chinese Food
Peng Chinese Restaurant
29 N. U.S. 31, 616/347-2542

Best Coffee
Roast and Toast
309 E. Lake, 616/347-7767

Best Desserts
Perry Hotel
Bay St. at Lewis St., 616/347-4000

Best Ice Cream/Yogurt
Kilwin Chocolates
355 N. Division Rd., 616/347-3800

Best Italian Food
Villa Ristorante Italiano
Hwy. 131S, 616/347-1440

Best Mexican Food
La Senorita
1285 N. U.S. 31, 616/347-7750

Best Pizza
Mighty Fine Pizza
222 E. Mitchell St., 616/347-3255

Best Steaks
Schelde's
1315 N. U.S. 31, 616/347-7747

Standbys
Pizza Hut
1254 N. U.S. 31, 616/347-6230

PONTIAC, MI

Best Bar
Industry
15 S. Saginaw St., 810/334-1999

Best Barbecue/Ribs
Beale Street Blues
8 N. Saginaw St., 810/334-7900

Best Breakfast
Stadium Coney Island
101 N. Saginaw St., 810/338-2797

Best Burgers
Coyote Club
1 N. Saginaw St., 810/332-4695
Griff's Grill
49 N. Saginaw St., 810/334-9292

Best Coffee
Gargoyle's Coffeehouse
7 N. Saginaw St., 810/745-9790

Best Desserts
Chuck's Coney and Soul Food
370 Martin Luther King Jr. Blvd. N., 810/334-7624

Best Homestyle Food
Chuck's Coney and Soul Food
370 Martin Luther King Jr. Blvd. N., 810/334-7624

Best Ice Cream/Yogurt
Leeon Restaurant
 1252 N. Perry St., 810/334-1929

Best Italian Food
Allegro's
 1 N. Saginaw St., 810/338-7337

Best Mexican Food
Tenuta's Villa Rio
 454 W. Huron St., 810/338-9639
El Taco Loco
 143 S. Telegraph Rd., 810/334-9933

Best Sandwiches
Griff's Grill
 49 N. Saginaw St., 810/334-9292
Maya's Delicatessen
 22 N. Saginaw St., 810/332-8787
Pete's Coney Island
 839 W. Huron St., 810/334-5050

Best Seafood
Pike Street Restaurant
 18 W. Pike St., 810/334-7878

Best Soul Food
Chuck's Coney and Soul Food
 370 Martin Luther King Jr. Blvd. N., 810/334-7624

Best Steaks
Wide Track Diner
 1551 W. Wide Track, 810/332-4097

M

PORT HURON, MI

Best Breakfast
Thomas Edison Inn
 500 Thomas Edison Pkwy., 810/984-8000

Best Brunch
Thomas Edison Inn
 500 Thomas Edison Pkwy., 810/984-8000

Best Burgers
Koney Island Inn
 Birchwood Mall, Ste.714, 810/385-9492
Huron Athletic Club
 321 Huron Ave., 810/984-2299

Best Desserts
Thomas Edison Inn
 500 Thomas Edison Pkwy., 810/984-8000

Best Homestyle Food
Loxton's Family Restaurant
 3535 Lapeer Rd., 810/982-7771

Best Ice Cream/Yogurt
London Dairy
 2136 Pine Grove Ave., 810/984-5111

Best Italian Food
Tuttobene
 3812 Pine Grove Rd., 810/987-4900

Best Place to Eat When Someone Else Is Buying
Victorian Inn
  1229 Seventh St., 810/984-1437

Best Sandwiches
Main Street Deli
  902 Military, 810/984-2940

Best Seafood
River Crab Restaurant
  1337 N. River Rd., St. Clair, 810/329-2261
Fogcutter Restaurant
  511 Fort St., 810/897-3300

Best Steaks
Fogcutter Restaurant
  511 Fort St., 810/897-3300

ROCHESTER, MI

Best Bars
Deacon Brodie's Tavern
  75 Macomb Pl., Mt. Clemens, 810/954-3202
Mr. B's Food and Spirits
  423 S. Main St., 810/651-6534

Best Breakfast
Petker's Food and Spirits
  161 S. Livernois Rd., 810/652-0114

Best Brunch
Petker's Food and Spirits
  161 S. Livernois Rd., 810/652-0114

Best Burgers
Bill Knapp's
  3010 Walton Blvd., 810/375-1515

Best Business Lunch
Murdock's
  2086 Crooks Rd., 810/852-0550
Kruse and Muer on Main
  327 S. Main St., 810/652-9400

Best Casual Dining
Max and Erma's
  70 N. Adams Rd., 810/375-1535

Best Chinese Food
Pearl City North Restaurant
  2601 S. Rochester Rd., 810/852-0170

Best Coffee
Coffee Beanery
  Multiple Locations
Coffee Exchange
  6915 Orchard Lake Rd., West Bloomfield,
    810/737-1600

Best Desserts
Rochester Chop House and Bar
  306 N. Main St., 810/651-2266

Best Diner
Bill Knapp's
  3010 Walton Blvd., 810/375-1515

Best Family Restaurant
Max and Erma's Restaurant
 70 N. Adams Rd., 810/375-1535

Best Health-Conscious Menu
Elias Brothers
 3756 Rochester Rd., 810/852-5540

Best Homestyle Food
Rochester Cafe and Family Dining
 630 N. Main St., 810/652-0820

Best Ice Cream/Yogurt
Ray's Ice Cream
 4233 Coolidge Hwy., Royal Oak, 810/549-5256

Best Italian Food
Lino's
 50 W. Tienken Rd., 810/652-9002
Alfoccino of Rochester
 2091 S. Rochester Rd., 810/853-6633
Eastside Mario's
 2273 Crooks Rd., Rochester Hills, 810/853-9622

Best Late-Night Food
Rochester Chop House and Bar
 306 N. Main St., 810/651-2266

Best Mexican Food
El Nibble Nook Restaurant
 27725 Eight Mile Rd., Livonia, 810/474-0755

Best Pizza
Hungry Howie's Pizza and Subs
 606 N. Main St., 810/652-2010

Best Place to Be "Seen"
Rochester Chop House and Bar
 306 N. Main St., 810/651-2266

Best Place to Eat Alone
Paint Creek Tavern
 4480 Orion Rd., 810/651-8361

Best Place to Eat When Someone Else Is Buying
Scallops
 1002 N. Main St., 810/656-2525

Best Place to Take the Kids
Family Buggy Restaurant
 870 S. Rochester Rd., 810/656-0850

Best Romantic Dining
Rochester Chop House and Bar
 306 N. Main St., 810/651-2266

Best Salad/Salad Bar
Max and Erma's
 70 N. Adams Rd., 810/375-1535

Best Sandwiches
Pic-A-Deli
 3134 Walton Blvd., 810/375-1330

Best Seafood
Rochester Chop House and Bar
 306 N. Main St., 810/651-2266

M

Best Steaks
Mountain Jack's Restaurant
  2262 S. Telegraph Rd., Bloomfield Hills, 810/334-4694

Best Vegetarian Food
The Sheik
  543 Main St., 810/650-1392

Standbys
Chili's
  2735 S. Rochester Rd., Rochester Hills, 810/299-5281

SAGINAW, MI

Best Bar
Hamilton Street Pub
  308 Hamilton St., 517/790-2670

Best Breakfast
Sullivan's
  3475 Bay Rd., 517/799-8430
  2701 E. Genesee Ave., 517/754-7880
  5235 Gratiot Rd., 517/799-1940

Best Business Lunch
Sullivan's
  3475 Bay Rd., 517/799-8430
  2701 E. Genesee Ave., 517/754-7880
  5235 Gratiot Rd., 517/799-1940
Treasure Island
  924 N. Niagara St., 517/755-6577
Holly's Landing
  1134 N. Niagara St., 517/754-4461

Best Chinese Food
East Wind
  3747 East St., 517/754-3031
Hunan Chinese Restaurant
  3109 Bay Plaza Rd., 517/792-0303
Panda House
  1010 N. Niagara St., 517/755-5394

Best Family Restaurants
Sullivan's
  3475 Bay Rd., 517/799-8430
  2701 E. Genesee Ave., 517/754-7880
  5235 Gratiot Rd., 517/799-1940
Tony's Original Restaurant
  1029 Gratiot Rd., 517/792-1113
  2525 E. Genesee Ave., 517/753-4321
  1205 Lapeer Ave., 517/754-6001
  2612 State St., 517/793-1801

Best Health-Conscious Menu
Heart House Inn
  419 N. Michigan Ave., 517/753-3145

Best Homestyle Food
Sullivan's
  3475 Bay Rd., 517/799-8430
  2701 E. Genesco Ave., 517/754-7880
  5235 Gratiot Rd., 517/799-1940
Bill Knapp's
  4600 State St., 517/793-2150

Best Ice Cream/Yogurt
Mooney Ice Cream Store
  812 Williams St., 517/754-6641

Best Mexican Food
El Farolito Restaurant
  1346 N. Washington Ave., 517/771-9460
  115 N. Hamilton St., 517/799-8959
La Senorita
  3823 Bay Rd., 519/793-6312

Best Pizza
Guido's
  116 N. Michigan Ave., 517/790-1000

Best Place to Be "Seen"
Levi's Saloon
  6407 State St., 517/790-3538
  5212 Bay Rd., 517/793-6670

Best Place to Eat Alone
Cafe Suz
  6099 Gogg Gratiot Rd., 517/791-2343

Best Place to Eat When Someone Else Is Buying
The Montague Inn
  1581 S. Washington Ave., 517/752-3939

Best Romantic Dining
Delphine's
  4960 Towne Center Rd., 517/790-5050
Treasure Island
  924 N. Niagara St., 517/755-6577

M

Best Sandwiches
Wally's Old Fashioned Sandwich Shop
  216 S. Washington Ave., 517/752-8877
Intermission Deli
  2128 Bay St., 517/790-6777

Standbys
Ryan's Family Steak House
  3210 Bay Rd., 517/791-2472
Old Country Buffet
  4695 Bay Rd., 517/790-6523
Red Lobster
  4141 Bay Rd., 517/793-5250
The Olive Garden
  3630 Bay Rd., 517/796-2288
Outback Steakhouse
  2468 Tittadawasee Rd., 517/797-2319
Chi Chi's
  4837 Bay Rd., 517/790-2854
Chuck E. Cheese Pizza
  5105 Bay Rd., 517/791-1116

SOUTHGATE, MI

Best Restaurant in Town
Ramada Heritage Vertical Restaurant
  17201 N. Line St., 313/283-4400

Best Mexican Food
Mexican Gardens Restaurant
  15950 Eureka Rd., 313/282-5633

Mi Casa
12950 N. Line St., 313/282-0527

Best Other Ethnic Food
The Hungarian Rhapsody Restaurant (Hungarian)
14315 N. Line St., 313/283-9622

Best Pizza
Roma Pizzeria
13020 Eureka Rd., 313/282-4900

Best 24-Hour Restaurants
Louie's Family Dining
12119 Fort St., 313/283-3055
Antonia's Family Restaurant
14993 Dix Toledo Rd., 313/284-1040

TRAVERSE CITY, MI

Best Restaurants in Town
La Becasse Restaurant
9001 S. Dunns Farm Rd., Maple City, 616/334-3944
Rowe Inn Restaurant
6303 C48 Rd., Ellsworth, 616/588-7351
Tapawingo
9502 Lake St., Ellsworth, 616/588-7971

Best Breakfast
Mabel's Restaurant
472 Munson Ave., 616/947-0252
Omelette Shoppe and Bakery
124 S. Cass St., 616/946-0912
1209 E. Front St., 616/946-0590

Best Brunch
Reflections Restaurant
2061 N. Hwy. 31N, 616/938-2321

Best Burgers
Dill's Olde Towne Saloon
423 S. Union St., 616/947-7534
2030 N. Hwy. 31N, 616/938-1860

Best Chinese Food
Hunan Chinese Restaurant
1425 S. Airport Rd. W., 616/947-1388

Best Desserts
Windows
7677 W. Bay Shore Dr., 616/941-0100

Best Family Restaurants
Bowers Harbor Inn
13512 Peninsula Dr., 616/223-4222
Bowery
13512 Peninsula Dr., 616/223-4333

Best Health-Conscious Menu
Cousin Jenny's Gourmet Cornish
129 S. Union St., 616/941-7821
Mabel's Restaurant
472 Munson Ave., 616/947-0252
Omelette Shoppe and Bakery
124 S. Cass St., 616/946-0912
1209 E. Front St., 616/946-0590

M

Best Ice Cream/Yogurt
Kilwin Chocolates
129 E. Front St., 616/946-2403

Best Italian Food
Giovanni's Restaurant
9205 Hwy. 31S, Interlochen, 616/276-6244
Auntie Pasta's
2030 S. Airport Rd. W., 616/941-8147

Best Mexican Food
La Senorita
1245 S. Garfield Ave., 616/947-8820

Best Other Ethnic Food
Reflections Restaurant (Caribbean)
2061 N. Hwy. 31N, 616/938-2321

Best Pizza
Upper Crust
720 W. Front St., 616/946-5252

Best Seafood
Hattie's Restaurant
111 N. Saint Josephs, Suttons Bay, 616/271-6222
Reflections Restaurant
2061 N. Hwy. 31N, 616/938-2321

Best Steaks
Boone's Long Lake Inn
7208 Secor Rd., 616/946-3991

WARREN, MI

Best Bar
Mac and Ray's
30675 N. River Rd., Harrison Township, 810/463-9660

Best Breakfast
Bi-Centennial Family Restaurant
11747 E. Thirteen Mile Rd., 810/939-6580

Best Brunch
Arriva Italia Ristorante
6880 E. 12 Mile Rd., 810/573-8100

Best Burgers
Loon River Cafe
34911 Van Dyke Ave., Sterling Heights, 810/979-1420
Teddy's Tavern
7231 Chicago Rd., 810/268-7070

Best Coffee
Chocolate Gallery Cafe
3672 Chicago Rd., 810/979-1140
Deebe's Coffee Bar
29200 Hoover Rd., 810/558-3290
Lilli's in the Park
31800 Van Dyke Ave., 810/939-2991

Best Desserts
Chocolate Gallery Cafe
3672 Chicago Rd., 810/979-1140
Michelles Restaurant
31920 Van Dyke Ave., 810/795-1665

Lilli's in the Park
31800 Van Dyke Ave., 810/939-2991

Best Homestyle Food
Bi-Centennial Family Restaurant
11747 E. Thirteen Mile Rd., 810/939-6580

Best Ice Cream/Yogurt
Savino Sorbet
3255 W. Long Lake Rd., West Bloomfield,
810/539-1990
Leason's Dairy Bar and Grille
11475 E. Thirteen Mile Rd., 810/977-2680

Best Italian Food
Andiamo Italia
7096 E. 14 Mile Rd., 810/268-3200
Juliano's Restaurant
27380 Van Dyke Ave., 810/754-8383
Arriva Italia Ristorante
6880 E. 12 Mile Rd., 810/573-8100

Best Other Ethnic Food
La Shish (Lebanese)
32401 Van Dyke Ave., 810/977-2177
Ike's Family Dining (Middle Eastern)
39064 Van Dyke Ave., Sterling Heights, 810/979-4460

Best Pizza
Buddy's Rendezvous Pizzeria
14156 E. 12 Mile Rd., 810/774-3400
8100 E. Thirteen Mile Rd., 810/574-9200
Juliano's Restaurant
27380 Van Dyke Ave., 810/754-8383

Best Salad/Salad Bar
National Coney Island
30140 Van Dyke Ave., 810/751-7700
28628 Dequindre Rd., 810/558-9180

Best Sandwiches
Chocolate Gallery Cafe
3672 Chicago Rd., 810/979-1140
Lilli's in the Park
31800 Van Dyke Ave., 810/939-2991

Best Seafood
Mac and Ray's
30675 N. River Rd., Harrison Township, 810/463-9660

Best Steaks
Loon River Cafe
34911 Van Dyke Ave., Sterling Heights, 810/979-1420
L-Bow Room
28655 Schoenherr Rd., 810/558-9393

Best Thai Food
Empire Szechuan Gourmet
4203 E. 8 Mile Rd., 810/757-4040

Standbys
Bob Evans
7601 Chicago Rd., 810/979-9040
25700 Dequindre Rd., 810/754-9076
Lone Star Steakhouse
13785 Lakeside Cir., 810/566-4800

YPSILANTI, MI

Best Burgers
Boomba's Beer and Burgers
23 N. Washington St., 313/481-0101
The Sidetrack
56 E. Cross St., 313/483-1035

Best Delicatessen
Max's Delicatessen
6 W. Michigan Ave., 313/485-4610

Best Homestyle Food
Aubree's Saloon
39 E. Cross St., 313/483-1870

Best Italian Food
Cady's Grill
36 E. Cross Rd., 313/483-2800
Cottage Inn Cafe
1531 Washtenaw, 313/487-1515

Best Mexican Food
Aubree's Saloon
39 E. Cross St., 313/483-1870

Best Other Ethnic Food
Louis Cafe (Greek/Italian)
205 W. Michigan Ave., 313/486-5544

Best Seafood
Cady's Grill
36 E. Cross Rd., 313/483-2800

Best Steaks
Haab's Restaurant
18 W. Michigan Ave., 313/483-8200

M

Minnesota

Best All-You-Can-Eat Buffet
Days Inn
2306 E. Main St., 507/373-6471

Best Breakfast
Cafe Don'l
1701 W. Main St., 507/373-3420
2510 Bridge Ave., 507/377-8831

Best Brunch
Days Inn
2306 E. Main St., 507/373-6471

Best Burgers
Elbow Room
310 E. Eighth St., 507/373-1836
Office II
1119 S. Broadway Ave., 507/373-1536

Best Chinese Food
China Restaurant
805 E. Main St., 507/377-8888
Chinese Tea House
126 W. William St., 507/377-1899
Hong Kong Restaurant
212 E. Clark St., 507/373-1044

Best Coffee
Kaffe Hus
522 S. Broadway Ave., 507/377-2951

Best Desserts
Trumble's Restaurant
1811 E. Main St., 507/373-2638

Best Mexican Food
Casa Zamora Restaurant
2006 E. Main St., 507/373-6475

Best Pizza
A Taste of the Big Apple
105 N. Broadway Ave., 507/373-2666

M

Best Sandwiches
Trumble's Restaurant
  1811 E. Main St., 507/373-2638
Nelson's Super Value
  1619 W. Main St., 507/373-7357
Hy-Vee Food Store
  2708 N. Bridge Ave., 507/377-2257

Best Steaks
Philly's Bar and Grill
  804 E. Main St., 507/373-2450

Standbys
Dairy Queen
  1701 W. Main St., 507/373-3922
  2510 Bridge Ave., 507/373-7030
  504 N. Broadway Ave., 507/373-1021
Golden Corral Family Steak House
  1604 E. Main St., 507/373-7283
Perkins
  2215 E. Main St., 507/377-1624

AUSTIN, MN

Best Barbecue/Ribs
Old Mill Restaurant
  Rural Route 1, 507/437-2076

Best Breakfast
Watts Cooking
  1509 Tenth Pl. NE, 507/433-2633

Best Burgers
Oak Grill
  307 W. Oakland Ave., 507/437-4135

Best Chinese Food
China Wok
  323 Main St. N., 507/433-8360

Best Desserts
Jerry's Other Place
  1207 N. Main St., 507/433-2331
Oak Leaf
  208 S. Main St., 507/437-8555
Plaza Dining
  123 Third Ave. NE, 507/433-7271

Best Italian Food
Ciola's Ristorante
  123 Third Ave. NE, 507/433-7271

Best Pizza
Godfather's Pizza
  600 W. Oakland Ave., 507/437-8269
Steve's Pizza
  215 Second Ave. NE, 507/437-3249

Best Salad/Salad Bar
Oak Grill
  307 W. Oakland Ave., 507/437-4135

Best Steaks
Old Mill Restaurant
  Rural Route 1, 507/437-2076

M

Tolly's Time Out Restaurant
  100 Fourteenth St. SW, 507/437-6078

BEMIDJI, MN

Best Bars
Back Yard
  Hwy. 2W, 218/751-7853
Stats Sports Bar
  101 First St. W., 218/751-0441

Best Breakfast
Clementine's
  205 Second St. NW, 218/751-9063

Best Burgers
Classic Burgers
  701 Paul Bunyan Dr. NW, 218/751-1212

Best Coffee
Clementine's
  205 Second St. NW, 218/751-9063
Griffy's Eating Establishment
  319 Minnesota Ave. NW, 218/751-3609

Best Desserts
Union Station
  128 First St. NW, 218/751-9261

Best Mexican Food
T. Juan's Restaurante and Cantina
  305 Park Ave. SW, 218/751-6879

Best Other Ethnic Food
Che-Wa-Ka-E-Gon Restaurant (Native American)
  Hwy. 2E, Cass Lake, 218/335-8378

Best Pizza
Luigi's Pizza
  300 Beltrami Ave. NW, 218/751-1316

Best Salad/Salad Bar
Griffy's Eating Establishment
  319 Minnesota Ave. NW, 218/751-3609

Best Sandwiches
Griffy's Eating Establishment
  319 Minnesota Ave. NW, 218/751-3609

Best Seafood
Northern Inn
  3600 Moberg Dr., 218/751-9500
Stats Sports Bar
  101 First St. W., 218/751-0441

Best Steaks
Union Station
  128 First St. NW, 218/751-9261

Standbys
Dairy Queen
  1201 Paul Bunyan Dr. NW, 218/751-0977
  255 Paul Bunyan Dr., 218/751-4274
  700 Paul Bunyan Dr. SW, 218/751-2108
Perkins
  1120 Paul Bunyan Dr. NW, 218/751-7850

M

BLOOMINGTON, MN

Best Restaurant in Town
Kincaid's Steak, Chop, And Fish House
8400 Normandale Lake Blvd., 612/921-2255

Best Bread
Cafe Royale
Hotel Sofitel, 5601 W. 78th St., 612/835-1900

Best Chinese Food
Szechuan Express
9818 Aldrich Ave. S., 612/881-8068

Best Desserts
Cafe Royale
Hotel Sofitel, 5601 W. 78th St., 612/835-1900

Best French Food
Cafe Royale
Hotel Sofitel, 5601 W. 78th St., 612/835-1900

Best Happy Hour Snacks
Kincaid's
8400 Normandale Lake Blvd., 612/921-2255

Best Middle Eastern Food
Da-Afghan
929 W. Eighth St., 612/888-5824

Best Pizza
Edwardo's Natural Pizza
2633 Southtown Dr., 612/884-8400

Best Place to Eat When Someone Else Is Buying
Kincaid's Steak, Chop, And Fish House
8400 Normadale Lake Blvd., 612/921-2255

Best Seafood
Kincaid's Steak, Chop, and Fish House
8400 Normandale Lake Blvd., 612/921-2255

Best Wine Selection
Napa Valley Grille
Mall of America, 612/858-9934

Standbys
Tony Roma's
8301 Normandale Blvd., 612/835-3333
Mall of America, 612/854-7940

DULUTH, MN

Best Brunch
The Library
1410 Tower Ave., Superior, 715/392-4821

Best Burgers
Main Restaurant and Cocktail Lounge
20 N. Third Ave. W., 218/722-5921

Best Business Lunch
Pickwick
508 E. Superior St., 218/727-8901
Porter's
200 W. Superior St., 218/727-6746

Best Casual Dining
Grandma's Saloon and Deli
2202 Maple Grove Rd., 218/722-9313
Grandma's Sports Garden
425 S. Lake Ave., 218/722-4722

Best Chinese Food
Taste of Saigon
394 S. Lake Ave., 218/727-1598

Best Coffee
Barnes and Noble
615 W. Central Ave., 218/727-0191

Best Family Restaurants
Grandma's Saloon and Deli
2202 Maple Grove Rd., 218/722-9313
Grandma's Sports Garden
425 S. Lake Ave., 218/722-4722

Best Health-Conscious Menu
Porter's
200 W. Superior St., 218/727-6746

Best Ice Cream/Yogurt
Bridgeman's Restaurant
2202 Mountain Shadow Dr., 218/727-0196
Zona Rosa Mexican Restaurant
1410 Tower Ave., Ste. 300, Superior, 715/392-4161

Best Pizza
Godfather's Pizza
5515 Ramsey St., 218/628-0361
1725 Miller Trunk Hwy., 218/722-0360
1623 London Rd., 218/728-3631
Grandma's Saloon and Deli
2202 Maple Grove Rd., 218/722-9313

Best Place to Be "Seen"
Pickwick
508 E. Superior St., 218/727-8901

Best Place to Eat Alone
Porter's
200 W. Superior St., 218/727-6746

Best Place to Eat When Someone Else Is Buying
Pickwick
508 E. Superior St., 218/727-8901

Best Place to Take the Kids
Grandma's Saloon and Deli
2202 Maple Grove Rd., 218/722-9313

Best Romantic Dining
Porter's
200 W. Superior St., 218/727-6746

Best Sandwiches
Sir Benedict's by the Lake
805 E. Superior St., 218/728-1192

Best Seafood
Pickwick
508 E. Superior St., 218/727-8901

Best Steaks
Pickwick
508 E. Superior St., 218/727-8901

Standbys
Old Country Buffet
1600 Miller Trunk Hwy., 218/722-3599
Perkins
1302 Miller Trunk Hwy., 218/727-4188
2005 W. Michigan St., 218/628-1038
2502 London Rd., 218/728-3619
Chi Chi's
600 E. Superior St., 218/727-9079
Applebee's
Miller Hall Mall, 1600 Miller Trunk Hwy.,
218/723-1253
Ponderosa
1722 Miller Trunk Hwy., 218/722-9231
Red Lobster
301 S. Lake Ave., 218/722-7192

GRAND RAPIDS, MN

Best Atmosphere
Rutger's Sugarlake Lodge
1000 Otis Ln., Cohasset, 218/327-1462

Best Breakfast
Forest Lake Restaurant
1201 NW Fourth St., 218/326-3423

Best Burgers
Burl's Chicken-N-Burgers
973 NE Fourth St., 218/327-3504
Jack Pine Junction
11851 Hwy. 38, 218/326-9854

Best Chinese Food
Hong Kong Garden Restaurant
220 NE Second St., 218/327-1131

Best Coffee
First Grade
10 NW Fifth St., 218/326-9361

Best Desserts
First Grade
10 NW Fifth St., 218/326-9361

Best Homestyle Food
Whalen's Cafe
18 NW Fourth St., 218/326-8646

Best Pizza
Beno's Pizza and Video
324 NE Fourth St., 218/327-1400

Best Seafood
Captain Hook's Supper Club
29 Crystal Springs Rd., 218/326-0235
Cedars Dining Room
Sawmill Inn, 2301 S. Pokegama Ave., 218/326-8501

Best Steaks
Forest Lake Restaurant
1201 NW Fourth St., 218/326-3423

Cedars Dining Room
  Sawmill Inn, 2301 S. Pokegama Ave., 218/326-8501

Standbys
Dairy Queen
  615 NE Fourth St., 218/326-4906

HIBBING, MN

Best Bar
Mr. Nick's Corner Bar
  2001 First Ave., 218/262-1639

Best Barbecue/Ribs
Open Pit
  11406 Hwy. 37, 218/263-9994

Best Breakfast
Country Kitchen
  Hwy. 169 at 25th St., 218/263-3689

Best Burgers
Atrium Restaurant/Zimmy's Downtown Bar and Grill
  531 E. Howard St., 218/262-6145

Best Coffee
Java Caffe
  Irongate Mall, 218/262-2168
Androy Coffee Shop
  502 E. Howard St., 218/263-5917

Best Desserts
Sunrise Bakery
  1813 Third Ave. E., 218/263-4985

Best Homestyle Food
Old Howard Saloon and Eatery
  413 E. Howard St., 218/262-1031

Best Ice Cream/Yogurt
Cookies and Cream
  Hwy. 169 at Neuberg Rd., 218/262-5060

Best Italian Food
Valentini's Supper Club
  31 W. Lake St., Chisholm, 218/254-2607

Best Pizza
Sammy's Pizza and Restaurant
  106 E. Howard St., 218/263-7574

Best Sandwiches
Sunrise Deli-Lybba
  2135 First Ave., 218/263-5713

Best Seafood
Main Street Supper Club
  408 E. Hward St., 218/262-4815
Riverside Inn
  7477 Hwy. 5, Side Lake, 218/254-2322

Best Steaks
Bil-Mars Supper Club
  2114 Hwy. 73, 218/262-6201
Riverside Inn
  7477 Hwy. 5, Side Lake, 218/254-2322
Old Howard Saloon and Eatery
  413 E. Howard St., 218/262-1031

M

Main Street Supper Club
   408 E. Howard St., 218/262-4815

MANKATO, MN

Best Barbecue/Ribs
Lone Wolf BBQ
   802 Carney Ave., 507/386-7427

Best Breakfast
Happy Chef Restaurant
   1210 E. Madison Ave., 507/387-6780

Best Brunch
Applewood
   Rural Route 6, 507/625-4105

Best Burgers
Ruttle's 50's Grill
   1270 E. Madison Ave., 507/345-1950
   1850 Adams St., 507/625-1955
Eagle's Nest
   100 N. Second St., Eagle Lake, 507/257-9996

Best Chinese Food
Tonni's Restaurant
   625 E. Madison Ave., 507/388-7475

Best Coffee
Coffee Hag
   329 N. Riverfront Dr., 507/387-5533
Barnes and Noble
   1857 Adams St., 507/386-0110

Best Desserts
Baker's Square Restaurant
   1861 E. Madison Ave., 507/345-4240

Best French Food
Meray's
   113 E. Hickory St., 507/625-9217

Best Greek/Mediterranean Food
Massad's
   River Hills Mall, 1850 Adams St., 507/387-7111

Best Homestyle Food
Adrian's Eatery and Saloon
   1812 S. Riverfront Dr., 507/625-6776
Charley's Restaurant
   920 E. Madison Ave., 507/388-6845
Maggie's Cafe and Saloon
   1600 Monks Ave., 507/625-2659

Best Ice Cream/Yogurt
Old Corner Malt Shoppe
   1628 S. Riverfront Dr., 507/625-1680

Best Mexican Food
Mexican Village Restaurant
   1630 E. Madison Ave., 507/387-4455

Best Pizza
Jake's Stadium Pizza
   1614 Monks Ave., 507/345-5420
Pagliai's Pizza
   524 S. Front St., 507/345-6080

M

Best Sandwiches
Old Corner Malt Shoppe
  1628 S. Riverfront Dr., 507/625 1680
Stoney's Restaurant
  900 N. Riverfront Dr., 507/387-4813

Best Seafood
Applewood
  Rural Route 6, 507/625-4105
Westwood Bar and Restaurant
  1351 Squirrel's Nest Rd., Kasota, 507/243-9998
Country Pub
  Rural Route 1, Kasota, 507/931-5888

Best Steaks
Applewood
  Rural Route 6, 507/625-4105
Country Pub
  Rural Route 1, Kasota, 507/931-5888
Charley's Steakery
  River Hills Mall, 1850 Adams St., 507/387-1555

Standbys
Perkins
  1123 Range St., 507/345-5021

MINNEAPOLIS, MN

Best Restaurants in Town
Goodfellow's
  800 Nicollet Mall, 612/332-4800
Palomino Euro-Metro Bistro
  825 Hennepin Ave., 612/339-3800
W. A. Frost and Company
  374 Selby Ave., St. Paul, 612/224-5715
Buca
  11 S. Twelfth St., 612/332-2739
  2728 Gannon Rd., St. Paul, 612/772-4388

Best All-You-Can-Eat Buffet
Odaa Ethiopian Restaurant
  408 Cedar Ave. S., 612/338-4459

Best American Food
J.D. Hoyt's
  301 Washington Ave., 612/338-1560
Market Bar-B-Que
  1414 Nicollet Ave., 612/872-1111
  15320 Wayzata Blvd., Minnetonka, 612/475-1770

Best Bagels
Gelpe's Napoleon Bakery and Cafe
  2447 Hennepin Ave., 612/377-1870
Bruegger's
  319 Fourteenth Ave. SE, 612/623-9522
  1920 Portland Ave., 612/871-8379
  4953 Penn Ave. S., 612/929-6634
  1500 W. Lake St., 612/823-2756
  1100 Nicollet Mall, 612/338-3142
  800 Washington Ave. SE, 612/378-2145
  1433 E. Franklin Ave., Ste. 3B, 612/871-3948

Best Barbecue/Ribs
Market Bar-B-Que
 1414 Nicollet Ave., 612/372-1111
 15320 Wayzata Blvd., Minnetonka, 612/475-1700
Ted Cook's Nineteenth Hole Barbecue
 2814 E. 38th St., 612/721-2023
Rudolph's Bar-B-Que
 815 Hennepin Ave., 612/623-3671
 1933 Lyndale Ave. S., 612/871-8969

Best Bistro
Cafe Un Deux Trois
 114 S. Ninth St., 612/673-0686

Best Bread
Francesca's
 33 W. Seventh St., St. Paul, 612/292-0027
Cafe Latte
 850 Grand Ave., St. Paul, 612/ 224-5687
Muffuletta in the Park
 2260 Como Ave., St. Paul, 612/644-9116

Best Breakfast
Keys Cafe
 1007 Nicollet Mall, 612/339-6399
The Egg and I
 2704 S. Lyndale Ave., 612/872-7282
 2550 University Ave., St. Paul, 612/647-1292
Uptown Bar and Grill
 3018 Hennepin Ave., 612/823-5704
A and J Gem Cafe
 2827 1/2 Hennepin Ave., 612/874-1225
Rick's Ol' Time Cafe
 3756 Grand Ave. S., 612/827-8948

Best Brunch
Jax Cafe
 1928 University Ave. NE, 612/789-7297
Soba's
 2558 Lyndale Ave. S., 612/871-6631

Best Burgers
Matt's
 3500 Cedar Ave. S., 612/722-7072

Best Cafeteria
Giorgio's on the Lake
 1601 W. Lake St., 612/822-7071

Best Cheap Meal
Gallery Eight
 725 Vineland Place, 612/374-3701
Bryant-Lake Bowl
 810 W. Lake St., 612/825-3737

Best Chinese Food
Leeann Chin Chinese Cuisine
 900 Second Ave. S., 612/338-8488
Yangtze Restaurant
 St. Louis Park, 5625 Wayzata Blvd., 612/541-9469
Village Wok
 610 SE Washington Ave., 612/331-9041

Szechuan Express
  2650 Hennepin Ave. S., 612/374-1535
Ping's Szechuan Bar and Grill
  1401 Nicollet Ave., 612/874-9404
Rainbow Chinese Restaurant
  2750 Nicollet Ave., 612/870-7084

Best Coffee
The Prairie Star
  119 N. First St., 612/341-3526

Best Coffeehouses
Cafe Latte
  850 Grand Ave., St. Paul, 612/224-5687
Caribou Coffee
  Multiple Locations
Dunn Bros.
  Multiple Locations
Starbucks
  Multiple Locations

Best Delicatessens
Kramarczuk Sausage Company
  215 E. Hennepin Ave., 612/379-3018
Cecil's Deli
  651 Cleveland Ave. S., St. Paul, 612/698-6276

Best Desserts
Cafe Latte
  850 Grand Ave., St. Paul, 612/224-5687
Dixie's Bar and Grill
  695 Grand Ave., St. Paul, 612/222-7345
W.A. Frost and Company
  374 Selby Ave., St. Paul, 612/224-5715
Bakers Square
  Multiple Locations

Best Diner
Convention Grille
  308 Prince St., St. Paul, 612/290-2718
  3912 Sunnyside Rd., Edina, 612/290-2718

Best French Food
The New French Cafe
  128 N. Fourth St., 612/339-3790
Azur
  Gavidae Common, 651 Nicollet Mall, 612/342-2500
Cafe Un Deux Trois
  114 S. Ninth St., 612/673-0686

Best German Food
Black Forest Inn
  1 E. 26th St., 612/872-0812
Gasthaus Bavarian Hunter
  8390 Lofton Ave., Stillwater, 612/439-7128
Gasthof zur Gemutlichkeit
  2300 University Ave. NE, 612/781-3860

Best Greek/Mediterranean Food
It's Greek To Me
  626 W. Lake St., 612/825-9922
Christo's
  2632 Nicollet Ave. S., 612/871-2111

M

Nicklow's
3516 N. Lilac Dr., Crystal, 612/529-7751

Best Happy Hour Snacks
Champps Sports Bar
100 N. Sixth St., 612/335-5050
Palomino Euro-Metro Bistro
825 Hennepin Ave., 612/339-3800
Runyon's
107 N. Washington Ave., 612/332-7158
St. Paul Grill
350 Market St., St. Paul, 612/224-7455

Best Ice Cream/Yogurt
Sebastian Joe's
1007 Franklin Ave. W., 612/870-0065
4321 Upton Ave. S., 612/926-7916
Crema Cafe
3403 Lyndale Ave. S., 612/824-3868

Best Indian Food
Fair Oaks Restaurant
2335 Third Ave. S., 612/872-1181
Sri-Lanka Curry House
2821 Hennepin Ave., 612/871-2400
Taste of India
1745 Cope Ave. E., Maplewood, 612/773-5477

Best Italian Food
Giorgio
2451 Hennepin Ave., 612/374-5131
Broder's Cucina Italiana
2308 W. 59th St., Edina, 612/925-3113
Ristorante Luci
470 Cleveland Ave. S., St. Paul, 612/699-8258
Buca
11 S. Twelfth St., 612/332-2739
2728 Gannon Rd., St. Paul, 612/772-4388
Pronto Ristorante and Caffe
Hyatt Regency, 1300 Nicollet Mall, 612/333-4414
D'Amico Cucina
100 N. Sixth, Ste. 160, 612/338-2401

Best Japanese Food
Origami
30 N. First St., 612/333-8430
Saji-Ya
695 Grand Ave., St. Paul, 612/292-0444
Ichiban Japanese Steak House
1333 Nicollet Mall, 612/339-0540
Kikugawa
43 SE Main St., 612/378-3006
Samurai Japanese Steak and Seafood
850 Louisiana Ave., Golden Valley, 612/542-9922

Best Late-Night Food
Pizza Luce
119 N. Fourth St., 612/333-7359
Rogue
10 S. Fifth St., 612/371-1893
Village Wok
610 Washington Ave. SE, 612/331-9041

Best Mexican Food
La Corvina
  1570 Selby Ave., St. Paul, 612/645-5288
Pepito's
  4820 Chicago Ave., 612/822-2104
La Cucaracha
  36 S. Dale St., St. Paul, 612/221-9682
  315 First Ave. N., 612/339-1161
Boca Chica Restaurante
  11 Concord St. W., 612/222-8499

Best Microbrewery
Rock Bottom Brewery
  825 Hennepin Ave., 612/332-2739

Best Middle Eastern Food
Jerusalem's
  1518 Nicollet Ave., 612/871-8883
Caravan Serai
  2175 Ford Pkwy., St. Paul, 612/690-1935
Emily's Lebanese Delicatessen
  641 University Ave. NE, 612/379-4069

Best Other Ethnic Food
Machu Picchu (Peruvian/Latin)
  2940 Lyndale Ave. S., 612/822-2125
Chez Bananas (Caribbean)
  129 N. Fourth St., 612/340-0032

Best Outdoor Dining
W.A. Frost and Company
  374 Selby Ave., 612/224-5715
Black Forest Inn
  1 E. 26th St., 612/872-0812
Rock Bottom Brewery
  825 Hennepin Ave., 612/332-2739

Best Pizza
Sidney's Pizza Cafe
  15600 Hwy. 7, Minnetonka, 612/933-1000
  2120 S. Hennepin Ave., 612/870-7000
Green Mill
  Multiple Locations
Table of Contents
  1648 Grand Ave., St. Paul, 612/699-6595
Uptown Express
  1409 W. Lake St., 612/822-7400
  5 N. Seventh St., 612/338-4814
Pizza Luce
  119 N. Fourth St., 612/333-7359
Edwardo's Natural Pizza
  1125 Marquette Ave., 612/339-9700
Broadway Pizza
  Multiple Locations
Grampa Tony's
  631 Snelling Ave. S., St. Paul, 612/690-3297
D'Amico and Sons
  2210 Hennepin Ave. S., 612/374-1858
  2724 W. 43rd St., 612/920-2646
Leaning Tower
  2324 Lyndale Ave. S., 612/337-3532

M

American Pie
   Grant St. at LaSalle St., 612/871-1669
   514 Nicollet Mall, 612/332-6428
   2728 Gannon Rd., St. Paul, 612/772-4388

Best Place to Eat Alone
Moose and Sadie's
   212 Third Ave. N., 612/371-0464

Best Places to Eat When Someone Else Is Buying
Morton's of Chicago
   555 Nicollet Mall, 612/673-9700
The 510 Restaurant
   510 Groveland Ave., 612/874-6440
Goodfellow's
   800 Nicollet Mall, 612/332-4800
St. Paul Grill
   350 Market St., St. Paul, 612/224-7455

Best Restaurant Meal Value
Palomino Euro-Metro Bistro
   825 Hennepin Ave., 612/339-3800

Best Romantic Dining
Forepaugh's
   276 S. Exchange St., St. Paul, 612/224-5606
W. A. Frost and Company
   374 Selby Ave., St. Paul, 612/224-5715
Goodfellow's
   The Conservatory, Fourth Level, 800 Nicollet Mall,
      612/332-4800
Ristorante Luci
   470 Cleveland Ave. S., St. Paul, 612/699-8258
Gustino's
   30 S. Seventh St., 612/349-4075
D'Amico Cucina
   100 N. Sixth St., Ste. 160, 612/338-2401
Tour Cafe
   4924 France Ave. S., Edina, 612/929-1010

Best Salad/Salad Bar
Q Cumbers
   7465 France Ave. S., Edina, 612/831-0235
Linguini and Bob
   100 N. Sixth St., 612/332-1600
Nikki's Cafe
   107 Third Ave. N., 612/340-9098

Best Sandwiches
Cossetta's Italian Market and Pizzeria
   211 W. Seventh St., St. Paul, 612/222-3476
Monte Carlo Bar and Cafe
   219 Third Ave. N., 612/335-5900

Best Seafood
The Anchorage Restaurant and Lounge
   1330 Industrial Blvd., 612/379-4444

Best Soul Food
Arnellia's
   1183 University Ave., St. Paul, 612/642-5975

Best Steaks
Lindey's Prime Steak House
  3610 Snelling Ave. N., Arden Hills, 612/633-9813
Cherokee Sirloin Room
  886 Smith Ave. S., St. Paul, 612/457-2729
Murray's
  26 S. Sixth St., 612/339-0909
Manny's Steak House
  1300 Nicollet Mall, 612/339-9900

Best Sushi
Saji-Ya
  695 Grand Ave., St. Paul, 612/292-0444

Best Thai Food
Royal Orchid
  1835 Nicollet Ave. S., 612/872-1938
Ruam Mit Thai Cafe
  544 St. Peter St., St. Paul, 612/290-0067
Sawatdee
  607 Washington Ave. S., 612/338-6451
  118 N. Fourth St., 612/373-0840
  289 Fifth St. E., 612/222-5859

Best Vegetarian Food
Cafe Brenda
  300 First Ave. N., 612/342-9230
Good Earth Restaurant
  3460 W. 70th St., 612/925-1001
  3001 Hennepin Ave., 612/824-8533
Mud Pie Vegetarian Restaurant
  2549 S. Lyndale Ave., 612/872-9435

Best Vietnamese Food
August Moon
  5340 Wayzata Blvd., Golden Valley, 612/544-7017
Lotus Vietnamese Cuisine
  3037 Hennepin Ave., 612/825-2263
  113 W. Grant St., 612/870-1218
  313 Oak St. SE, 612/331-1781
White Lily Restaurant
  758 Grand Ave., St. Paul, 612/293-9124
Que Viet
  1272 Town Centre Dr., Eagan, 612/452-5018
  2211 NE Johnson St., 612/781-4744

Best Wine Selection
Goodfellow's
  800 Nicollet Mall, 612/332-4800
Manny's Steakhouse
  1300 Nicollet Mall, 612/339-9900
The St. Paul Grill
  350 Market St., St. Paul, 612/224-7455

Standbys
Fuddruckers
  3801 Minnesota Dr., Edina, 612/835-3833
Ruth's Chris Steak House
  920 Second Ave. S., 612/672-9000

M

MOORHEAD, MN

Best Atmosphere
Speak Easy Restaurant
   1001 30th Ave. S., 218/233-1326

Best Chinese Food
Golden Phoenix
   816 30th Ave. S., 218/236-7089

Best Coffee
Atomic Coffee
   15 Fourth St. S., 218/299-6161

Best Desserts
Treetop Restaurant
   403 Center Ave., Seventh Fl., 218/233-1393

Best Family Restaurant
Speak Easy Restaurant
   1001 30th Ave. S., 218/233-1326

Best Homestyle Food
Peggy's Pantry
   28 Fourth St. N., 218/233-8795

Best Italian Food
Speak Easy Restaurant
   1001 30th Ave. S., 218/233-1326

Best Mexican Food
Torero's Mexican Restaurant
   808 30th Ave. S., 218/233-2320

Best Pizza
Duane's House of Pizza
   1024 Center Ave., 218/236-0550
   402 Main Ave., 218/241-9000

Best Sandwiches
Moorhead Host
   Moorhead Center Mall, 218/236-8805
Hi-Ho Tavern
   10 Center Ave. E., Dilworth, 218/287-2975
Atomic Coffee
   15 Fourth St. S., 218/299-6161

Standbys
Dairy Queen
   24 Eighth St. S., 218/233-3221

ROCHESTER, MN

Best Restaurants in Town
Chardonnay
   732 Second St. SW, 507/252-1310
The Meadows
   Radisson Plaza, 150 S. Broadway, 507/281-8000

Best Bar
Smiling Moose Bar and Grill
   1829 Hwy. 52N, 507/289-1689

Best Breakfast
Bakers Square
   3539 22nd Ave. NW, 507/289-2468

Grandma's Kitchen
  1514 Broadway, 507/289-0331

Best Brunch
Legends
  Rochester Athletic Club, 3100 Nineteenth St. NW,
    507/287-9333

Best Burgers
Smiling Moose Bar and Grill
  1829 Hwy. 52N, 507/289-1689

Best Business Lunch
Michael's Restaurant and Lounge
  15 S. Broadway, 507/288-2020

Best Cheap Meal
Cheap Charlie's
  11 Fifth St. NW, 507/289-9591

Best Chinese Food
China Dynasty
  701 S. Broadway, 507/289-2333

Best Coffee
Barnes and Noble
  15 First St. SW, 507/288-3848

Best Diner
Cheap Charlie's
  11 Fifth St. NW, 507/289-9591

Best Family Restaurant
Smiling Moose Bar and Grill
  1829 Hwy. 52N, 507/289-1689

Best French Food
Victoria House French Restaurant
  709 Parkway Ave. S, 507/467-3457

Best Health-Conscious Menu
Zorba's Greek Restaurant
  924 Seventh St. NW, 507/281-1540

Best Homestyle Food
Cheap Charlie's
  11 Fifth St. NW, 507/289-9591

Best Ice Cream/Yogurt
McCormick's
  Radisson Plaza, 150 S. Broadway, 507/281-8000

Best Late-Night Food
The Greenhouse
  Kahler Hotel, 20 Second Ave. SW, 507/282-2581

Best Mexican Food
Fiesta Mexicana
  301 Seventeenth Ave. SW, 507/288-1116

Best Pizza
Redwood Room
  Broadstreet Cafe, 300 First Ave. NW, 507/281-2451

Best Place to Be "Seen"
The Meadows
  Radisson Plaza, 150 S. Broadway, 507/281-8000

M

Best Place to Eat Alone
Daube German Restaurant
  14 Historic Third St. SW, 507/280-6446

Best Places to Eat When Someone Else Is Buying
Chardonnay
  732 Second St. SW, 507/252-1310
The Meadows
  Radisson Plaza, 150 S. Broadway, 507/281-8000

Best Romantic Dining
Elizabethan Room
  Kahler Hotel, 20 Second Ave. SW, 507/282-2581

Best Salad/Salad Bar
John Barleycorn
  2804 S. Broadway, 507/285-0178

Best Sandwiches
Nelson Cheese Factory
  210 N. Broadway, 507/288-1888

Best Seafood
Hunan Garden
  1120 Seventh St. NW, 507/285-1438
Fisherman's Inn
  8 Fisherman Dr. NW, Oronoco, 507/367-4567

Best Steaks
Michael's Restaurant and Lounge
  15 S. Broadway, 507/288-2020

Best Tea Room
Chickadee Cottage Tearoom
  317 N. Lakeshore Dr., Lake City, 612/345-5155

Best Vegetarian Food
The Open Table
  16 S. Broadway, 507/287-8939

Best Other Restaurant
Henry Wellington
  216 First Ave. SW, 507/289-1949

Standbys
Old Country Buffet
  1300 Salem Rd. SW, 507/289-4586
Friday's
  300 Hwy. 52N, 507/281-2020
Applebee's
  333 Apache Mall, 507/252-0155

ST. CLOUD, MN

Best Bar
O'Hara Brothers Pub
  3308 Third St. N., 320/251-9877

Best Breakfast
McMillan's Restaurant
  3219 W. Division St., 320/252-7115

Best Burgers
O'Hara Brothers Pub
  3308 Third St. N., 320/251-9877

Best Chinese Food
Dong Khanh Chinese Restaurant
  810 W. Saint Germain St., 320/251-0656
Phoenix Too Chinese Cuisine
  660 Mall Germain, 320/654-8655
  4101 Division St., 320/251-3588
Hong Kong Restaurant
  37 33rd Ave. N., 320/251-5907

Best Coffee
Sano's Coffee and Tea House
  419 W. Saint Germain St., 320/253-6811

Best Desserts
D.B. Searle's
  18 Fifth Ave. S., 320/253-0655

Best Health-Conscious Menu
Good Earth Food Co-Op
  2010 Eighth St. N., 320/253-9290

Best Homestyle Food
Alvie's Family Restaurant
  451 E. Saint Germain St., 320/251-7575
  42 32nd Ave. S., 320/252-0955

Best Italian Food
Ciatti's Italian Restaurant
  660 Germain Mall, 320/251-5255

Best Mexican Food
Bravo Burritos Mexicatessen
  68 33rd Ave. S., 320/654-1269
  26 Fifth Ave. S., 320/252-5441

Best Pizza
House of Pizza
  19 Fifth Ave. S., 320/252-9300

Best Sandwiches
Anton's
  2001 W. Division St., 320/253-3611
O'Hara Brothers Pub
  3308 Third St. N., 320/251-9877
Bo Diddley's Deli
  129 25th Ave. S., 320/252-9475
  1501 Northway Dr., 320/255-1500

Best Seafood
Anton's
  2001 W. Division St., 320/253-3611
Angus McGee's
  139 S. Second Ave., 320/255-1207

Best Steaks
Anton's
  2001 W. Division St., 320/253-3611
O'Hara Brothers Pub
  3308 Third St. N., 320/251-9877
Angus McGee's
  139 S. Second Ave., 320/255-1207

M

ST. PAUL, MN

Best Restaurants in Town
W. A. Frost and Company
    374 Selby Ave., 612/224-5715
Buca
    11 S. Twelfth St., Minneapolis, 612/332-2739
    2728 Gannon Rd., 612/772-4388

Best Bread
Francesca's
    33 W. Seventh St., 612/292-0027
Cafe Latte
    850 Grand Ave., 612/ 224-5687
Muffuletta in the Park
    2260 Como Ave., 612/644-9116
    2704 S. Lyndale Ave., Minneapolis, 612/872-7282

Best Breakfast
The Egg and I
    2550 University Ave., 612/647-1292
    2704 Lyndale Ave., Minneapolis, 612/578-7282

Best Coffeehouse
Cafe Latte
    850 Grand Ave., 612/224-5687

Best Delicatessen
Cecil's Deli
    651 Cleveland Ave. S., 612/698-6276

Best Desserts
Cafe Latte
    850 Grand Ave., 612/224-5687
Dixie's Bar and Grill
    695 Grand Ave., 612/222-7345
W.A. Frost and Company
    374 Selby Ave., 612/224-5715

Best Diner
Convention Grille
    308 Prince St., 612/290-2718
    3912 Sunnyside Rd., Edina, 612/290-2718

Best Italian Food
Ristorante Luci
    470 Cleveland Ave. S., 612/699-8258
Buca
    11 S. Twelfth St., Minneapolis, 612/332-2739
    2728 Gannon Rd., 612/772-4388

Best Mexican Food
La Corvina
    1570 Selby Ave., 612/645-5288

Best Middle Eastern Food
Caravan Serai
    2175 Ford Pkwy., 612/690-1935

Best Pizza
Table of Contents
    1648 Grand Ave., 612/699-6595
Grampa Tony's
    631 Snelling Ave. S., 612/690-3297

American Pie
2728 Gannon Rd., 612/772-4388
Grant St. at La Salle St., Minneapolis, 612/871-1669
514 Nicollet Mall, Minneapolis, 612/332-6428

Best Place to Eat When Someone Else Is Buying
St. Paul Grill
350 Market St., 612/224-7455

Best Romantic Dining
Forepaugh's
276 S. Exchange St., 612/224-5606
W. A. Frost and Company
374 Selby Ave., 612/224-5715
Ristorante Luci
470 Cleveland Ave. S., 612/699-8258

Best Sandwiches
Cossetta's Italian Market and Pizzeria
211 West Seventh St., 612/222-3476

Best Soul Food
Arnellia's
1183 University Ave., 612/642-5975

Best Steaks
Cherokee Sirloin Room
886 Smith Ave. S., 612/457-2729

Best Sushi
Saji-Ya
695 Grand Ave., 612/292-0444

Best Thai Food
Ruam Mit Thai Cafe
544 St. Peter St., 612/290-0067

Best Vietnamese Food
White Lily Restaurant
758 Grand Ave., 612/293-9124

Best Wine Selection
The St. Paul Grill
350 Market St., 612/224-7455

WINONA, MN

Best Breakfast
Shorty's Cafe and Bar
528 Center St., 507/452-2622

Best Burgers
Jefferson Pub and Grill
57 Center St., 507/452-2718

Best Chinese Food
Great Hunan Restaurant
111 W. Third St., 507/452-1556

Best Coffee
Natural Habitat Coffeehouse
451 Huff St., 507/452-7020

Best Health-Conscious Menu
Natural Habitat Coffeehouse
451 Huff St., 507/452-7020

Best Homestyle Food
Happy Chef Restaurant
1476 Gilmore Ave., 507/454-5652

Best Sandwiches
Jefferson Pub and Grill
57 Center St., 507/452-2718

Best Steaks
Finn and Sawyers Bar and Restaurant
Walnut St. at Levee Park Dr., 507/452-3104

Standbys
Dairy Queen
1440 W. Broadway St., 507/452-6090
Pizza Hut
1630 W. Service Dr., 507/454-5193
617 Huff St., 507/454-5100

WORTHINGTON, MN

Best All-You-Can-Eat Buffet
Brandywine
Holiday Inn, 2015 N. Humiston Ave., 507/372-2991

Best Breakfast
Gobbler by the Mall
1861 Oxford St., 507/372-2200

Best Brunch
Brandywine
Holiday Inn, 2015 N. Humiston Ave., 507/372-2991

Best Chinese Food
Panda House Chinese Restaurant
913 Fourth Ave., 507/372-5155

Best Desserts
Ruttle's 50's Grill
1709 N. Humiston Ave., 507/376-1955
W.T. Berrie Ice Cream
1635 Oxford St., 507/376-9220

Best Family Restaurant
Michael's
1305 Spring Ave., 507/376-3187

Best Homestyle Food
Windmill Cafe
609 Kragness Ave. N., 507/376-5223

Best Ice Cream/Yogurt
W.T. Berrie Ice Cream
1635 Oxford St., 507/376-9220

Best Pizza
Godfather's Pizza
1635 Oxford St., 507/372-7391

Best Sandwiches
W.T. Berrie Ice Cream
1635 Oxford St., 507/376-9220

Best Seafood
Brandywine
Holiday Inn, 2015 N. Humiston Ave., 507/372-2991

Best Steaks
Michael's
1305 Spring Ave., 507/376-3187

Best Thai Food
Bangkok Cuisine
1719 East Ave., 507/376-9009

Standbys
Perkins
1445 Darling Dr., 507/372-7761
Pizza Hut
1551 N. Humiston Ave., 507/372-5512

M

Mississippi

Best Restaurant in Town
Germaine's Restaurant
  1203 Bienville Blvd., Ocean Springs, 601/875-4426

Best Casual Dining
Port-O-Call Seafood Restaurant
  15200 Lemoyne Blvd., 601/392-0335

Best Late-Night Food
Anthony's Under the Oaks
  1217 Washington Ave., 601/872-4564

Best Place to Eat Alone
McElroy's Harbor House
  695 Beach Blvd., 601/435-5001

Best Place to Eat When Someone Else Is Buying
Germaine's Restaurant
  1203 Bienville Blvd., Ocean Springs, 601/875-4426

Best Romantic Dining
Germaine's Restaurant
  1203 Bienville Blvd., Ocean Springs, 601/875-4426

Best Seafood
Aunt Jenny's Catfish Restaurant
  1217 Washington Ave., Ocean Springs, 601/875-9201
McElroy's Harbor House
  695 Beach Blvd., 601/435-5001

Best Tea Room
House of Chin
  2040 Beach Blvd., 601/388-1331

Standbys
Hardee's
  2600 Beach Blvd., 601/388-7052
  10324 Diberville Rd., 601/392-2666
Ryan's Family Steak House
  2300 E. Beach Dr., 601/896-5211

COLUMBUS, MS

Best All-You-Can-Eat Buffet
Country Kitchen
142 S. McCreary Rd., 601/327-9207

Best American Food
Harvey's
200 Main St., 601/327-1639

Best Barbecue/Ribs
Miz Lou's
903 Waterworks Rd., 601/327-2281

Best Breakfast
Pete's Restaurant
2123 Main St., 601/328-9861

Best Chinese Food
Gold Star Chinese Restaurant
1205 Hwy. 45N, 601/329-5247

Best Dinner
Brown's Downtown
509 Main St., 601/327-8880

Best Homestyle Food
Country Kitchen
142 S. McCreary Rd., 601/327-9207

Best Seafood
Brown's Downtown
509 Main St., 601/327-8880

Best Steaks
Brown's Downtown
509 Main St., 601/327-8880
Old Hickory Steakhouse
1301 Hwy. 45N, 601/328-9793

GREENVILLE, MS

Best Restaurants in Town
Fermo's
700 Hwy. 1S, 601/334-9934
Doe's Eat Place Too
502 Nelson St., 601/334-3315

Best Barbecue/Ribs
Nick's Barbecue
1847 Hwy. 82E, 601/335-2272

Best Homestyle Food
Jim's Cafe
314 Washington Ave., 601/332-5951

Best Italian Food
Fermo's
700 Hwy. 1S, 601/334-9934

Best Salad/Salad Bar
Sherman's Restaurant
1400 S. Main St., 601/332-6924

Best Seafood
Sherman's Restaurant
1400 S. Main St., 601/332-6924

Best Steaks
Doe's Eat Place Too
502 Nelson St., 601/334-3315

GULFPORT, MS

Best American Food
Boardwalk Restaurant
4128 W. Beach Blvd., 601/868-9262

Best Breakfast
Helen's Coffee Shop
2313 Fourteenth St., 601/863-8788

Best Casual Dining
Li'l Ray's Po-Boys
500A Courthouse Rd., 601/896-9601

Best Dinner
Vrazel's Fine Food Restaurant
3206 W. Beach Blvd., 601/863-2229

Best Homestyle Food
Cafe Reef
439 Hwy. 90, Waveland, 601/467-7333

Best Seafood
Chappy's Seafood Restaurant
624 E. Beach Blvd., 601/865-9755

Best Steaks
Blow-Fly Inn
1201 Washington Ave., 601/896-9812

M

HATTIESBURG, MS

Best Brunch
Purple Parrot
3810 Hardy St., 601/264-0656

Best Chinese Food
Mandarin House
4400 Hardy St., Ste. A7, 601/264-5511

Best Pasta
Crescent City Grill
3810 Hardy St., 601/264-0657

Best Sandwiches
Robby's Seafood and Etc.
6168 Hwy. 49N, 601/584-6150

Best Seafood
Crescent City Grill
3810 Hardy St., 601/264-0657

Best Steaks
Conestoga
6313 Hwy. 49N, 601/264-8816
Dennon's
3951 Hwy. 589, Sumrall, 601/758-4941

HOLLY SPRINGS, MS

Best Barbecue/Ribs
Pete's Bar-B-Q
540 Hwy. 7N, 601/252-9879

Best Breakfast
City Cafe
135A E. Van Dorn Ave., 601/252-9895

Best Brunch
Holly Inn Restaurant
350 Hwy. 78W, 601/252-1870

Best Burgers
Phillips Grocery
541 E. Van Dorn Ave., 601/252-4671

Best Chinese Food
Canton Chinese Restaurant
152 E. College Ave., 601/252-1589

Best Coffee
City Cafe
135A E. Van Dorn Ave., 601/252-9895
Johnnie Mae's Restaurant
133A E. Van Dorn Ave., 601/252-4298

Best Family Restaurant
Holly Inn Restaurant
350 Hwy. 78W, 601/252-1870

Best Homestyle Food
Johnnie Mae's Restaurant
133A E. Van Dorn Ave., 601/252-4298

Best Ice Cream/Yogurt
Tyson's Drugstore
145 E. Van Dorn Ave., 601/252-2321

Best Place to Take the Kids
Phillips Grocery
541 E. Van Dorn Ave., 601/252-4671

JACKSON, MS

Best American Food
Dennery's Restaurant
330 Greymont Ave., 601/354-2527

Best Atmosphere
Dennery's Restaurant
330 Greymont Ave., 601/354-2527

Best Barbecue/Ribs
Chimneyville BBQ Smoke House
970 High St., 601/354-4665

Best Brunch
Edison Walthall Hotel
225 E. Capitol St., 601/948-6161

Best Business Lunch
Keifer's Restaurant
120 N. Congress St., 601/353-4976
1395 Metrocenter Mall, 601/354-0760
705 Poplar Blvd., 601/355-6825

Best Chinese Food
Peking Chinese Restaurant
53151 I-55N, 601/362-7000

Best Continental Food
Dennery's Restaurant
330 Greymont Ave., 601/354-2527

Best Dinner
Kyoto Japanese Restaurant
6800 Old Canton Rd., Ridgeland, 601/956-8268
Ralph and Kacoo's Restaurant
100 Dyess St., Ridgeland, 601/957-0702
Edison Walthall Hotel
225 E. Capitol St., 601/948-6161

Best Greek/Mediterranean Food
Keifer's Restaurant
120 N. Congress St., 601/353-4976
1395 Metrocenter Mall, 601/354-0760
705 Poplar Blvd., 601/355-6825

Best Homestyle Food
Cock of the Walk Restaurant
141 Madison Landing Circle, 601/856-5500
Elite Restaurant
141 E. Capitol St., 601/352-5606

Best Japanese Food
Kyoto Japanese Restaurant
6800 Old Canton Rd., Ridgeland, 601/956-8268

Best Lunch
Elite Restaurant
141 E. Capitol St., 601/352-5606

Best Seafood
Ralph and Kacoo's Restaurant
100 Dyess St., Ridgeland, 601/957-0702
Dennery's Restaurant
330 Greymont Ave., 601/354-2527
Iron Horse Grill
320 W. Pearl St., 601/355-8419

Best Soul Food
Cock of the Walk Restaurant
141 Madison Landing Circle, 601/856-5500

Best Southwestern Food
Iron Horse Grill
320 W. Pearl St., 601/355-8419

Best Steaks
Kyoto Japanese Restaurant
6800 Old Canton Rd., Ridgeland, 601/956-8268
Dennery's Restaurant
330 Greymont Ave., 601/354-2527
Iron Horse Grill
320 W. Pearl St., 601/355-8419

Standbys
Tony Roma's
5402 I-55N, 601/957-6867

MERIDIAN, MS

Best Restaurant in Town
Hollybrook Fine Dining
1200 22nd Ave., 601/693-7584

Best Chinese Food
China Palace
College Park Shopping Ctr., 601/483-5082

Best Homestyle Food
Weidmann's
210 22nd Ave., 601/693-1751

Best Mexican Food
San Marcos Mexican Restaurant
826 Hwy. 19N, 601/693-6683

Best Place to Eat When Someone Else Is Buying
Hollybrook Fine Dining
1200 22nd Ave., 601/693-7584

Best Seafood
Weidmann's
210 22nd Ave., 601/693-1751

Best Steaks
Rustler Steakhouse
5915 Hwy. 80W, 601/693-6499

NATCHEZ, MS

Best Restaurant in Town
West Bank Eatery
710 Levee Rd., Vidalia, 318/336-9669

Best Burgers
Scrooge's Old English Pub
315 Main St., 601/446-9922

Best Homestyle Food
Cock of the Walk Restaurant
200 N. Broadway St., 601/446-8920

Best Salad/Salad Bar
Clara Nell's Downtown Deli
609 Franklin St., 601/445-7799

Best Sandwiches
Clara Nell's Downtown Deli
609 Franklin St., 601/445-7799

Best Seafood
Sandbar Restaurant
106 Carter St., Vidalia, 318/336-5173

Best Steaks
Scrooge's Old English Pub
315 Main St., 601/446-9922

Best View While Dining
West Bank Eatery
710 Levee Rd., Vidalia, 318/336-9669

Standbys
Shoney's
26 Seargent Prentiss Dr., 601/442-3761

OXFORD, MS

Best Atmosphere
Gin Restaurant
Harrison St., 601/234-0024

Best All-You-Can-Eat Buffets
Abbeville Catfish Restaurant
 Hwy. 7N, 601/234-8898
Cobb's Seafood and Steaks
 Hwy. 6W, 601/236-6380

Best Barbecue/Ribs
Dixie Creek Meat Market
 2304 Jackson Ave. W., 601/236-4100
Handy Andy Grocery
 800 N. Lamar Blvd., 601/234-4621

Best Breakfast
Bottletree Bakery
 923 Van Buren Ave., 601/236-5000

Best Burgers
Proud Larry's
 211 S. Lamar Blvd., 601/236-0050

Best Chinese Food
Ruby Chinese Restaurant
 2301 Jackson Ave. W., 601/234-8811

Best Coffee
Bottletree Bakery
 923 Van Buren Ave., 601/236-5000
Square Books
 160 Courthouse Sq., 601/236-2262
Smitty's
 208 S. Lamar Blvd., 601/234-9111

Best Desserts
Downtown Grill Restaurant
 110 Courthouse Sq., 601/234-2659
Hoka Theatre and Restaurant
 304 S. Fourteenth St., 601/234-3057

Best Eclectic Menu
City Grocery Reservation Line
 1118 Van Buren Ave., 601/232-8080

Best Family Restaurants
Beacon Restaurant
 1200 N. Lamar Blvd., 601/234-5041
Legends Bar and Grill
 1111 Jackson Ave., 601/236-4333
Cedars
 1007 College Hill Rd., 601/234-3855

Best Greek/Mediterranean Food
Kalo's Restaurant
 1414 W. Jackson Ave., 601/236-0026

Best Health-Conscious Menu
Harvest Cafe and Bakery
 1112 Van Buren Ave., 601/236-3757

Best Homestyle Food
Ruth and Jimmy's
 Hwy. 7 at Business District, 601/234-4312

Best Ice Cream/Yogurt
Square Books
 160 Courthouse Sq., 601/236-2262

M

Best Italian Food
Dino's Pizza Restaurant
  1420 Jackson Ave. W., 601/234-6777

Best Mexican Food
El Charro
  1908 W. Jackson Ave., 601/236-0058

Best Other Ethnic Food
Marie's Cafe and Shoppe (Lebanese)
  1006 Jackson Ave. E., 601/236-7502

Best Pizza
Dino's Pizza Restaurant
  1420 Jackson Ave. W., 601/234-6777
Proud Larry's
  211 S. Lamar Blvd., 601/236-0050

Best Place to Take the Kids
Legends Bar and Grill
  1111 Jackson Ave., 601/236-4333

Best Regional Food
Downtown Grill Restaurant
  110 Courthouse Sq., 601/234-2659

Best Romantic Dining
City Grocery Reservation Line
  1118 Van Buren Ave., 601/232-8080
Downtown Grill Restaurant
  110 Courthouse Sq., 601/234-2659

Best Salad/Salad Bar
Danver's International
  1107 Jackson Ave. W., 601/236-3225

Best Sandwiches
Hoka Theatre and Restaurant
  304 S. Fourteenth St., 601/234-3057
Proud Larry's
  211 S. Lamar Blvd., 601/236-0050

Best Seafood
City Grocery
  1118 Van Buren Ave., 601/232-8080
Downtown Grill Restaurant
  110 Courthouse Sq., 601/234-2659
Cobb's Seafood and Steaks
  Hwy. 6W, 601/236-6380

Best Steaks
Oxford Steak Company
  302 S. Eleventh St., 601/236-6460

Best Vegetarian Food
Harvest Cafe and Bakery
  1112 Van Buren Ave., 601/236-3757

PASCAGOULA, MS

Best Chinese Food
China Garden Restaurant
  3141 Denny Ave., 601/762-6186

Best Desserts
La Font Inn
  2703 Denny Ave., 601/762-7111

Best Italian Food
Marguerite's Italian Village
  2318 Ingalls Ave., 601/762-7464

Best Lunch
Fillet's Family Restaurant
  1911 Denny Ave., 601/769-0280

Best Seafood
River Docks Seafood Pier
  525 Denny Ave., 601/762-0570

Best Steaks
La Font Inn
  2703 Denny Ave., 601/762-7111

Standbys
Quincy's
  6706 Hwy. 63, Moss Point, 601/475-2666

STARKVILLE, MS

Best Barbecue/Ribs
Little Dooey
  100 Fellowship St., 601/323-6094

Best Burgers
Christy's Hamburger
  446 Hwy. 12W, 601/323-6497

Best Chinese Food
Peking Chinese Restaurant
  840 Hwy. 12W, 601/324-0555

Best Desserts
Harvey's
  406 Hwy. 12E, 601/323-1639

Best Homestyle Food
Little Dooey
  100 Fellowship St., 601/323-6094

Best Mexican Food
Mexico Tipico
  123 Hwy. 12, 601/323-2117

Best Pizza
CJ's Pizza
  600 Hwy. 12E, 601/323-8897

Best Sandwiches
Starkville Cafe
  211 University Dr., 601/323-1665

Standbys
Applebee's
  814 Hwy. 12W, 601/324-3459
Baskin-Robbins
  127 Hwy. 12W, 601/323-0331
Quincy's
  409 Hwy. 12E, 601/324-0053
Shoney's
  203 Hwy. 12W, 601/323-2211

M

TUPELO, MS

Best Barbecue/Ribs
Johnnie's Drive-In
  908 E. Main St., 601/842-6748
Rib Cage
  206 Troy St., 601/840-5400
Omar's Ranch House
  712 S. Gloster St., 601/840-1009

Best Breakfast
Shockley's
  Hwy. 45S, 601/842-6036

Best Burgers
Harvey's
  424 S. Gloster St., 601/842-6763
Jefferson Place Dining Room
  823 W. Jefferson St., 601/844-8696

Best Chinese Food
China Capital
  530 N. Gloster St., 601/841-0484
Sun-Kai Chinese Restaurant
  775 E. Main St., 601/844-7047
  726 S. Gloster St., 601/680-8888

Best Homestyle Food
Shockley's
  Hwy. 45S, 601/842-6036
Skip's Fine Foods
  Chesterville Rd., 601/844-0187

Best Ice Cream/Yogurt
Dairy Kream
  796 E. Main St., 601/842-7838
Yummy Yogurt
  105D Rankin Blvd., 601/841-1133
Finney's Sandwich and Soda Shop
  1009 W. Main St., 601/842-1746

Best Mexican Food
Casa Monterrey
  722 S. Gloster St., 601/844-1477

Best Pizza
Pizza Doctor
  2200 W. Main St., 601/844-2600
Vanelli's Restaurant
  1302 N. Gloster St., 601/844-4410

Best Sandwiches
Finney's Sandwich and Soda Shop
  1009 W. Main St., 601/842-1746

Best Seafood
Front Porch
  2827 Cliff Gookin Blvd., 601/842-1591
Woody's Restaurant
  619 N. Gloster St., 601/840-0460

Best Steaks
Gloster 205
  205 N. Gloster St., 601/842-7205

M

VICKSBURG, MS

Best American Food
Beechwood Restaurant and Lounge
4451 Clay St., 601/636-3761

Best Barbecue/Ribs
Goldie's Trail Bar-B-Q
4127 S. Washington St., 601/636-9839

Best Breakfast
The Adolph Rose
717 Clay St., 601/638-0468

Best Chinese Food
Sun Koon
3535 I-20 Frontage Rd., 601/638-4941

Best Homestyle Food
Walnut Hills
1214 Adams St., 601/638-4910

Best Sandwiches
The Adolph Rose
717 Clay St., 601/638-0468

Best Steaks
Maxwell's Restaurant
4207 E. Clay St., 601/636-1344

WAYNESBORO, MS

M

Best All-You-Can-Eat Buffets
Carol's Roundtable
103 Mississippi Dr., 601/735-2819
Magnolia Restaurant
109 Turner St., 601/735-5231

Best Burgers
McCool's
Herberts Mart Shopping Ctr., 601/735-3435

Best Chinese Food
Golden China
503 Azalea Dr., 601/735-9966

Best Coffee
McCool's
Herberts Mart Shopping Ctr., 601/735-3435

Best Desserts
McCool's
Herberts Mart Shopping Ctr., 601/735-3435

Best Family Restaurants
Carol's Roundtable
103 Mississippi Dr., 601/735-2819
Magnolia Restaurant
109 Turner St., 601/735-5231

Best Ice Cream/Yogurt
McCool's
Herberts Mart Shopping Ctr., 601/735-3435

Best Sandwiches
McCool's
Herberts Mart Shopping Ctr., 601/735-3435

Best Seafood
Overstreet's Catfish House
  Hwy. 84W, 601/735-9796

Standbys
Pizza Hut
  Hwy. 45N, 601/735-4315
Western Sizzlin
  Hwy. 45N, 601/735-1162
Pizza Inn
  902 Mississippi Dr., 601/735-5600

M

Missouri

Best Barbecue/Ribs
Zarda Bar-B-Q
214 N. State Rte. 7, 816/229-9999

Best Chinese Food
Jade Garden Chinese Restaurant
756 W. Hwy. 40, 816/224-0248

Best Homestyle Food
Betty's Family Dining
1428 W. Hwy. 40, 816/229-2260

Best Mexican Food
Jose Miguel's
1130 S. Outer Rd., 816/228-6606

Best Seafood
Nader's Steak House
1605 S. State Rte. 7, 816/229-9040
Marina Grog and Galley
22A Northshore Dr., 816/578-4400

Best Steaks
Nader's Steak House
1605 S. State Rte. 7, 816/229-9040
Marina Grog and Galley
22A Northshore Dr., 816/578-4400

Standbys
Dairy Queen
110 S. State Rte. 7, 816/229-1069
Perkins
3316 S. Outer Rd., 816/229-7977
Pizza Hut
1512 N. Woods Chapel Rd., 816/228-1840
100 S. State Rte. 7, 816/229-9175

Best Breakfast
Country Kitchen
1029 S. Washington St., 816/646-6500

Best Brunch
Willows Restaurant
  606 W. Old Hwy. 36, 816/646-6590

Best Burgers
Hick's Hometown Drive-In
  1311 Washington St., 816/646-1008

Best Chinese Food
Beijing Chinese Restaurant
  327 Washington St., 816/646-4112

Best Desserts
Harlow's Dining and Lounging
  609 Jackson St., 816/646-6812
Willows Restaurant
  606 W. Old Hwy. 36, 816/646-6590
Francine's Ice Cream and Bakery
  1007 Bryan St., 816/646-3333

Best Homestyle Food
Country Kitchen
  1029 S. Washington St., 816/646-6500

Best Ice Cream/Yogurt
Francine's Ice Cream and Bakery
  1007 Bryan St., 816/646-3333

Best Pizza
Royal Inn Pizza
  411 Park Ln., 816/646-5990

Best Seafood
Catfish Place
  Hwy. 36E, 816/646-5085
Washington Street
  1100 Washington St., 816/646-4058

Best Steaks
Harlow's Dining and Lounging
  609 Jackson St., 816/646-6812

Standbys
Golden Corral Family Steak House
  719 S. Washington St., 816/646-0047
Subway
  416 S. Washington St., 816/646-1110

CLINTON, MO

Best Barbecue/Ribs
Win-Mill Restaurant
  219 NW State Rte. 7, 816/885-8434

Best Breakfast
Uchie's Fine Foods
  127 W. Franklin St., 816/885-3262
Win-Mill Restaurant
  219 NW State Rte. 7, 816/885-8434

Best Burgers
Uchie's Fine Foods
  127 W. Franklin St., 816/885-3262
Win-Mill Restaurant
  219 NW State Rte. 7, 816/885-8434

Best Chinese Food
Egg Roll King Chinese Restaurant
701 N. Third St., 816/885-6547

Best Homestyle Food
Uchie's Fine Foods
127 W. Franklin St., 816/885-3262

Best Korean Food
Happy Garden
1407 E. Ohio St., 816/885-8940

Best Mexican Food
El Sambre Restaurant
1107 S. Second St., 816/885-4333
Cancun
1502 N. Second St., 816/885-4550

Best Pizza
Pizza Glen
205 E. Rives Rd., 816/885-8021

Standbys
Dairy Queen
Hwy. 7 at Hwy. 13N, 816/885-2062
Golden Corral Family Steak House
1520 E. Ohio St., 816/885-6545

COLUMBIA, MO

Best Breakfast

M

St. Louis Bread Company
Columbia Mall, 2300 Bernadette Dr., 573/446-7374
102 S. Ninth St., 573/442-4455
Heidelberg Restaurant
410 S. Ninth St., 573/449-6927

Best Brunch
Boone Tavern and Restaurant
811 E. Walnut St., 573/442-5123

Best Burgers
Harpo's Bar and Grill
29 S. Tenth St., 573/443-5418

Best Chinese Food
Peking Chinese Restaurant
122 S. Ninth St., 573/449-3716

Best Coffee
Lakota Coffee Company
24 S. Ninth St., 573/874-2852

Best Homestyle Food
Mediterranean Cafe
1104 Locust St., 573/443-6424

Best Italian Food
Trattoria Strada Nova
21 N. Ninth St., 573/442-8992
Bambino's
203 Hitt St., 573/443-4473

Best Mexican Food
Cafe Ole
15 S. Sixth St., 573/874-7097

Los Bandidos Mexican Restaurant
  220 S. Eighth St., 573/443-2419

Best Pizza
Shakespeare's Pizza
  225 S. Ninth St., 573/449-2454
Rome Pizzeria
  1101 E. Broadway, 573/449-3104

Best Sandwiches
St. Louis Bread Company
  Columbia Mall, 2300 Bernadette Dr., 573/446-7374
  102 S. Ninth St., 573/442-4455
Ninth Street Deli
  28 N. Ninth St., 573/875-8890

Best Seafood
Glenn's Cafe
  29 S. Ninth St., 573/443-3094

Best Steaks
Jack's Gourmet Restaurant
  1903 Business Loop 70E, 573/449-3927

Best Thai Food
Bangkok Gardens
  26 N. Ninth St., 573/874-3284

Standbys
Outback Steakhouse
  SW I-70, 573/815-0800

M

FLORISSANT, MO

Best American Food
Jordan's Restaurant
  12908 New Halls Ferry Rd., 314/838-1155

Best Italian Food
Canolli's
  462 N. Hwy. 67, 314/839-5988

Best Place to Eat When Someone Else Is Buying
Yacovelli's Restaurant
  407 Dunn Rd., 314/839-1000

INDEPENDENCE, MO

Best All-You-Can-Eat Buffet
Furr's Cafeteria
  16202 E. Hwy. 24, 816/257-1258

Best American Food
Montana Steak Company
  12712 E. Hwy. 40, 816/373-8777
Stephenson's Old Apple Farm
  16401 E. Hwy. 40, 816/373-5405

Best Atmosphere
Stephenson's Old Apple Farm
  16401 E. Hwy. 40, 816/373-5405

Best Business Lunch
Courthouse Exchange Restaurant
  113 W. Lexington Ave., 816/252-0344

Best Chinese Food
Magic Wok
3681 S. Noland Rd., 816/461-0218

Best Delicatessen
Tommy's Deli
121 W. Lexington Ave., 816/252-9900

Best Dinner
Montana Steak Company
12712 E. Hwy. 40, 816/373-8777

Best Family Restaurant
Furr's Cafeteria
16202 E. Hwy. 24, 816/257-1258

Best German Food
Rheinland
208 N. Main St., 816/461-5383

Best Homestyle Food
Stephenson's Old Apple Farm
16401 E. Hwy. 40, 816/373-5405

Best Ice Cream/Yogurt
Tommy's Deli
121 W. Lexington Ave., 816/252-9900

Best Italian Food
V's Italiano Ristorante
10819 E. Hwy. 40, 816/353-1241

Best Sandwiches
Courthouse Exchange Restaurant
113 W. Lexington Ave., 816/252-0344
Clinton's Soda Fountain and Gifts
100 W. Maple Ave., 816/833-2625

Best Steaks
Montana Steak Company
12712 E. Hwy. 40, 816/373-8777

Standbys
Old Country Buffet
13720 E. Hwy. 40, 816/478-1012

JOPLIN, MO

Best Barbecue/Ribs
Butcher's Block
2412 S. Main St., 417/624-1000
Jim Bob's Steaks and Ribs
2040 S. Range Line Rd., 417/781-3300

Best Burgers
Jim Bob's Steaks and Ribs
2040 S. Range Line Rd., 417/781-3300
Kitchen Pass Restaurant
1212 S. Main St., 417/624-9095

Best Italian Food
Travetti's Restaurante and Bar
3010 E. Twentieth St., 417/781-4344

Best Mexican Food
Casa Montez Restaurant
2324 S. Range Line Rd., 417/781-3610

Raphael's Mexican Restaurant
2601 S. Range Line Rd., 417/782-5008

Best Salad/Salad Bar
Kitchen Pass Restaurant
1212 S. Main St., 417/624-9095

Best Seafood
Crabby's Seafood Bar and Grill
815 W. Seventh St., 417/782-7372

Best Steaks
Jim Bob's Steaks and Ribs
2040 S. Range Line Rd., 417/781-3300
Kitchen Pass Restaurant
1212 S. Main St., 417/624-9095

Standbys
Shoney's
2127 S. Range Line Rd., 417/781-0667
Bob Evans
3607 S. Range Line Rd., 417/624-5445
Red Lobster
3131 S. Range Line Rd., 417/782-2199

KANSAS CITY, MO

Best Restaurants in Town
Cafe Allegro
1815 W. 39th St., 816/561-3663
The American Restaurant
2450 Grand Ave., 816/426-1133

Best Asian Restaurant
Double Dragon
5031 Main St., 816/531-5778

Best Barbecue/Ribs
Gates Bar-B-Q
1221 Brooklyn Ave., 816/483-3880
411 Swope Pkwy., 816/921-0409
4707 Paseo Blvd., 816/923-0900

Best Beer Selection
Charlie Hooper's
12 W. 63rd St., 816/361-8841

Best Breakfast
First Watch
1022 Westport Rd., 816/931-4401

Best Brunch
Tomfooleries
612 W. 47th St., 816/753-0555
Bristol Bar and Grill
4740 Jefferson St., 816/756-0606

Best Burgers
Westport Flea Market
817 Westport Rd., 816/931-1986

Best Business Lunch
Grand Street Cafe
4740 Grand Ave., 816/561-8000
Plaza III: The Steakhouse
4749 Pennsylvania St., 816/753-0000

Best Cafeteria
Furr's Cafeteria
　5407 NE Antioch Rd., 816/452-6400
　5600 E. Bannister Rd., 816/765-3110

Best Cajun/Creole Food
Jazz
　1823 W. 39th St., 816/531-5556
Kiki's Bon Ton Maison
　1515 Westport Rd., 816/931-9417

Best Chinese Food
Bo Ling's
　4800 Main St., 816/753-1718

Best Coffee
Latte Land
　318 W. 47th St., 816/931-7477

Best Coffeehouses
Fifty-First Street Coffeehouse
　318 E. 51st St., 816/756-3121
Broadway Cafe
　4106 Broadway St., 816/531-2432

Best Delicatessen
D'Bronx
　3904 Bell St., 816/531-0550

Best Desserts
Tippin's
　5080 N. Oak Trafficway, 816/459-7550
　9145 Hillcrest Rd., 816/761-3966

Best Diners
Chubby's
　1835 Independence Ave., 816/842-2482
The Corner
　4059 Broadway St., 816/931-6630

Best Dinner
The American Restaurant
　2450 Grand Ave., 816/426-1133
Ponak's
　2856 Southwest Blvd., 816/756-3850
Plaza III: The Steakhouse
　4749 Pennsylvania, 816/753-0000

Best French Food
La Mediterranean
　9058B Metcalf Ave., Overland Park, 913/341-9595
Tatsu's French Restaurant
　4603 W. 90th St., Shawnee Mission, 913/383-9801

Best German Food
Berliner Bear
　7815 Wornall Rd., 816/444-2828
Emile's European Deli and Restaurant
　302 Nichols Rd., 816/333-2132

Best Greek/Mediterranean Food
Tasso's
　211 W. 75th St., 816/363-4776
Boulevard Cafe
　703 Southwest Blvd., 816/642-6984

M

Best Indian Food
Mother India
9036 Metcalf Ave., Shawnee Mission, 913/341-0415

Best Italian Food
Garozzo's Ristorante
526 Harrison St., 816/221-2455

Best Japanese Food
Gojo Japanese Steakhouse
4163 Broadway St., 816/561-2501

Best Late-Night Food
Chubby's
1835 Independence Ave., 816/842-2482
Velvet Dog
400 E. 31st St., 816/753-9990
Chubby's on Broadway
3623 Broadway, 816/531-2483
Nichol's Lunch
SW Trafficway at 39th St., 816/561-5200
Antonio's Pizza
3834 Main St., 816/561-1988
1100 Main St., 816/421-4888
915 E. 85th St., 816/361-1988

Best Mexican Food
Margarita's
2829 Southwest Blvd., 816/931-4849

Best Middle Eastern Food
Jerusalem Cafe
431 Westport Rd., 816/756-2770

Best New Restaurant
YaYas Euro Bistro
4701 W. 119th St., 816/345-1111

Best Outdoor Dining
The Classic Cup Cafe
301 W. 47th St., 816/753-1840
4130 Pennsylvania Ave., 816/756-0771

Best Pizza
D'Bronx
3904 Bell St., 816/531-0550

Best Place to Be "Seen"
Parkway 600
600 Ward Pkwy., 816/435-4199

Best Restaurant Meal Value
Saigon 39
1806 1/2 W. 39th St., 816/531-4447

Best Romantic Dining
Skies
Hyatt Regency Ctr., 2345 McGee St., 816/435-4199
Peppercorn Duck Club
Hyatt Regency Ctr., 2345 McGee St., 816/435-4199

Best Salad/Salad Bar
Soup Exchange
11885 W. 95th St., Overland Park, 913/599-4999

Best Sandwiches
D'Bronx
  3904 Bell St., 816/531-0550

Best Seafood
Bristol Bar and Grill
  4740 Jefferson St., 816/756-0606
Savoy
  219 W. Ninth St., 816/842-3890

Best Soul Food
Ruby's
  1506 Brooklyn Ave., 816/221-2370

Best Southwestern Food
Coyote Grill
  4843 Johnson Dr., Mission, 913/362-3333

Best Steaks
Hereford House
  2 E. Twentieth St., 816/842-1080

Best Sushi
Jun's Authentic Japanese Restaurant
  7660 State Line Rd., Shawnee Mission, 913/341-4924

Best Thai Food
Thai Orchid
  5504 Mertway Dr., Mission, 913/384-2800
Bangkok Pavilion
  7249 W. 97th St., Overland Park, 913/341-3005

Best Vegetarian Food
Daily Bread
  645 E. 59th St., 816/531-1452
Jerusalem Cafe
  431 Westport Rd., 816/756-2770

Best Vietnamese Food
Saigon 39
  1806 1/2 W. 39th St., 816/531-4447

Best Wine Selection
Joe D's
  6227 Brookside Plz., 816/333-6116
Harry Starker's
  200 Nichols Rd., 816/756-2770

Standbys
Old Country Buffet
  8350 N. Broadway St., 816/436-5045

KIRKSVILLE, MO

Best Atmosphere
Pagliai's Pizza
  101 W. Washington St., 816/665-6678

Best Breakfast
Pancake City
  2101 N. Baltimore St., 816/665-6002

Best Chinese Food
China Palace Restaurant
  124 N. Franklin St., 816/627-8888
Minn's Tea House
  102 S. Elson St., 816/665-9610

Best Homestyle Food
Country Kitchen
2700 S. Baltimore St., 816/627-4555

Best Ice Cream/Yogurt
De Rosear Flowers and Gifts
108 W. Harrison St., 816/665-2818

Best Italian Food
Wooden Nickel
114 S. Elson St., 816/665-2760

Best Pizza
Pagliai's Pizza
101 W. Washington St., 816/665-6678

Best Place to Eat When Someone Else Is Buying
Minn's Cuisine
216 N. Franklin St., 816/665-2842

Best Steaks
Thousand Hills Dining Lodge
Rural Route 3, 816/665-7119

Best View While Dining
Thousand Hills Dining Lodge
Rural Route 3, 816/665-7119

MOBERLY, MO

Best All-You-Can-Eat Buffet
Ramada Inn
Hwy. 24 at Hwy. 63, 816/263-6540

Best Breakfast
Country Kitchen
530 E. Hwy. 24, 816/263-3191

Best Brunch
Ramada Inn
Hwy. 24 at Hwy. 63, 816/263-6540

Best Chinese Food
Chinese Chef
721 N. Morley St., 816/269-8221
Hunan Chinese Restaurant
537 W. Reed St., 816/263-6803

Best Desserts
First Class Catering and Cafe
2108 Silva Ln., 816/263-3704

Best Family Restaurant
Country Kitchen
530 E. Hwy. 24, 816/263-3191

Best Mexican Food
Nelly's Someplace Else
407 Urbandale, 816/263-7720

Best Pizza
Pizza Works
319 N. Morley St., 816/263-8102

Best Salad/Salad Bar
Nelly's Someplace Else
407 Urbandale, 816/263-7720

Best Sandwiches
First Class Catering and Cafe
  2108 Silva Ln., 816/263-3704

Best Seafood
CC Sawyers Restaurant
  104 W. Wrightman St., 816/263-7744

Best Steaks
CC Sawyers Restaurant
  104 W. Wrightman St., 816/263-7744
Richard's Steak House
  1633 S. Morley St., 816/263-2221

Standbys
Dairy Queen
  1714 N. Morley St., 816/263-4957
Golden Corral Family Steak House
  2038 Silva Ln., 816/263-7806
Pizza Hut
  520 E. Hwy. 24, 816/263-1511

ST. JOSEPH, MO

Best Barbecue/Ribs
The Quarter House
  520 S. Belt Hwy., 816/232-4767

Best Chinese Food
Chu's
  1521 St. Joseph Ave., 816/232-9968

Best Desserts
Jerre Anne Cafeteria and Bakery
  2640 Mitchell Ave., 816/232-6585

Best Homestyle Food
Jerre Anne Cafeteria and Bakery
  2640 Mitchell Ave., 816/232-6585
Common Ground
  614 Francis, 816/279-4577

Best Italian Food
Fazoli's
  504 N. Belt Hwy., 816/387-9539

Best Mexican Food
Barbosa's Castillo
  906 Sylvanie St., 816/233-4970
  4804 Frederick Ave., 816/232-0221
Palma's Authentic Mexican Restaurant
  2715 N. Belt Hwy., 816/279-9445

Best Sandwiches
Maid-Rite
  522 Felix St., 816/279-8382
Common Ground
  614 Francis, 816/279-4577

Best Seafood
Black Angus
  102 S. Third St., 816/279-8000

Best Steaks
D and G Restaurant
  1918 Frederick Ave., 816/232-7170

Frederick Inn Steakhouse
  1627 Frederick Ave., 816/364-5151
Hoof and Horn Steak House
  429 Illinois Ave., 816/238-0742
Black Angus
  102 S. Third St., 816/279-8000

Standbys
Baskin-Robbins
  2307 N. Belt Hwy., 816/232-3100
Red Lobster
  4101 Frederick Ave., 816/232-5011
Dairy Queen
  3203 St. Joseph Ave., 816/233-5495

ST. LOUIS, MO

Best Restaurants in Town
Tony's
  410 Market St., 314/231-7007
Blueberry Hill
  6504 Delmar, 314/727-0880

Best Asian Restaurants
Mai Lee
  8440 Delmar Blvd., 314/993-3754
Pho Grand
  3191 S. Grand Blvd., 314/664-7435

M

Best Bagels
Basically Bagels
  32 N. Euclid Ave., 314/454-3003

Best Bar
McGurk's
  1200 Russell Blvd., 314/776-8309

Best Barbecue/Ribs
K.C. Masterpiece
  611 N. Lindbergh Blvd., 314/991-5811

Best Beer Selection
Blueberry Hill
  6504 Delmar, 314/727-0880

Best Breakfast
Uncle Bill's
  3427 S. Kingshighway Blvd., 314/832-1973

Best Brunch
Adam's Mark
  315 Chestnut St., 314/241-7400

Best Burgers
Blueberry Hill
  6504 Delmar Blvd., 314/727-0880

Best Business Lunch
Cardwell's
  8100 Maryland, Clayton, 314/726-5055

Best Cafeteria
Miss Sheri's
  5406 Southfield Center Dr., 314/849-1141
  6607 Chippewa St., 314/644-6063

Best Cajun/Creole Food
Broussard's
  4301 S. Broadway, 314/353-5586

Best Casual Dining
Piccolo's Mediterranean Cafe
  1 Metropolitan Sq., 314/421-2887

Best Chinese Food
Yen Ching
  1012 Brentwood Blvd., 314/721-7507

Best Coffeehouses
Aesop's
  6611 Clayton Rd., 314/727-0809
Blue Moon Coffee House
  3710 Gravois Ave., 314/771-0260
Brandt's
  6525 Delmar Blvd., 314/727-3663
Ibid's
  6687 Delmar Blvd., 314/862-2233
Meshuggah
  565 Melville Ave., 314/726-5662
MoKaBe's
  124 W. Jefferson Ave., 314/822-1895
Oasis
  8130 Big Bend Blvd., 314/968-3038

Best Delicatessen
Kopperman's
  386 N. Euclid Ave., 314/361-0100

Best Desserts
Tippin's Restaurant and Pie Pantry
  10 Galleria, 314/721-3880
  11440 Olive St. Rd., 314/567-5694
  7331 Watson Rd., 314/352-0759

Best Diner
Eat-Rite Diner
  622 Chouteau St., 314/621-9621

Best Eclectic Menu
Piccolo's Mediterranean Cafe
  1 Metropolitan Sq., 314/421-2887

Best French Food
Cafe de France
  410 Olive St., 314/231-2204

Best German Food
Bevo Mill
  4749 Gravois Ave., 314/481-2626

Best Greek/Mediterranean Food
Spiro's
  3122 Watson Rd., 314/645-8383
  8406 Natural Bridge, 314/382-8074

Best Ice Cream/Yogurt
Crown Candy Kitchen
  1401 St. Louis Ave., 314/621-9650
Fritz's Frozen Custard
  1055 St. Catherine St., Florissant, 314/839-4100
  506 Jungermann Rd., St. Peters, 314/928-2606

M

Iggy's Frozen Yogurt
  10118 W. Florissant Ave., 314/867-5737
  1669 Pattern Dr., 314/653-1580
Lix Frozen Custard
  12808A Olive St. Rd., Creve Coeur, 314/576-7227
  16043 Manchester Rd., Ballwin, 314/230-8202
Maggie Moo's Creamery
  8853 Ladue Rd., 314/862-6651
  9051 Watson Rd., 314/963-0033
Nuberry's
  2 Maryland Plz., 314/454-0000
Ted Drewe's Frozen Custard
  4224 S. Grand Blvd., 314/352-7376
  6726 Chippewa St., 314/481-2652
Victoria's Kitchen and Ice Creamery
  4533 Pershing Pl., 314/361-8127
  6935 S. Lindbergh Blvd., 314/892-7711
  710 Second St., 314/231-5084

Best Indian Food
Bombay Indian Cuisine
  8501 Delmar Blvd., University City, 314/567-6850
Star of India
  4569 Laclede Ave., 314/361-6911

Best Italian Food
Kemoli's
  1 Metropolitan Sq., 314/421-0555
Pasta House Company
  Multiple Locations

Best Japanese Food
Robata of Japan
  111 Westport Plz., Twelfth Fl., 314/434-1007

Best Kosher Food
Kopperman's
  386 N. Euclid Ave., 314/361-0100

Best Late-Night Food
White Castle
  1111 Macklind Ave., 314/535-7430

Best Mexican Food
Casa Gallardo Mexican Restaurant
  11185 S. Towne Sq., 314/487-4121
  12796 Manchester Rd., 314/821-14403
  1821 N. Market St., 314/421-6766
  462 Westport Plz., 314/434-7755

Best Middle Eastern Food
Saleem's
  6501 Delmar Blvd., 314/721-7947

Best New Restaurants
Painted Plates
  6235 Delmar Blvd., 314/725-6565
Portabella
  15 N. Central Ave., 314/725-6588

Best Outdoor Dining
Busch's Grove
  9160 Clayton Rd., 314/993-0011

Best Pizza
Imo's
Multiple Locations
California Pizza Kitchen
1493 Saint Louis Galleria, 314/863-4500

Best Place to Be "Seen"
Cafe Balaban
405 N. Euclid St., 314/361-8085

Best Restaurant Meal Value
Hodak's
2100 Gravois Ave., 314/776-7292

Best Romantic Dining
Tony's
410 Market St., 314/231-7007

Best Salad/Salad Bar
Pasta House Company
Multiple Locations

Best Sandwiches
St. Louis Bread Company
Multiple Locations

Best Seafood
Blue Water Grill
2607 Hampton, 314/645-0707
Nantucket Cove
40 N. Kingshighway Blvd., 314/361-0625

Best Soul Food
London and Sons Wing House
3740 Dr. Martin Luther King Dr., 314/371-4925
4739 Goodfellow Blvd., 314/389-8328
6731 Page Ave., 314/725-4710

Best Southwestern Food
Casa Grill
1491 Galleria, 314/727-2223

Best Sports Bar
Ozzie's Restaurant and Sports Bar
645 Westport Plz., 314/434-1000

Best Sushi
Nobu's
8643 Olive Blvd., 314/997-2303

Best Thai Food
King and I
3157 S. Grand Blvd., 314/771-1777

Best Vegetarian Food
Sunshine Inn
8 1/2 S. Euclid Ave., 314/367-1413

Best Vietnamese Food
Pho Grand
3191 S. Grand Blvd., 314/664-7435

Best Wine Selection
Riddle's Penultimate
6307 Delmar Blvd., 314/725-6985

Standbys
Chuck E. Cheese Pizza
  2805 Target Dr., 314/741-8001
  7499 S. Lindbergh Blvd., 314/487-6707
Old Country Buffet
  7289 Watson Rd., 314/351-4524
  7597 S. Lindbergh Blvd., 314/894-3473
Red Lobster
  5733 S. Lindbergh Blvd., 314/487-7744
  9838 Watson Rd., 314/822-0433
Ruth's Chris Steak House
  101 S. Eleventh St., 314/241-7711

SIKESTON, MO

Best All-You-Can-Eat Buffet
China Pearl
  2301 E. Malone Ave., 573/472-1552

Best Atmosphere
Dumplin's
  100 Outlet Dr., 573/471-1550
  112 E. Center St., 573/471-8550
Lambert's Cafe
  2515 E. Malone Ave., 573/471-4261

Best Barbecue/Ribs
Bo's Pit Bar BQ
  1609 E. Malone Ave., 573/471-9927

Best Brunch
Dumplin's
  100 Outlet Dr., 573/471-1550
  112 E. Center St., 573/471-8550

Best Burgers
Kirby's Sandwich Shop
  109 N. Kingshighway St., 573/471-1318

Best Business Lunch
Ramada Inn
  I-55 at Hwy. 62, 573/471-4700

Best Chinese Food
China Pearl
  2301 E. Malone Ave., 573/472-1552

Best Coffee
Cheryl's Coffee and Cream
  211 River Birch Mall, 573/472-2211

Best Desserts
Dumplin's
  100 Outlet Dr., 573/471-1550
  112 E. Center St., 573/471-8550

Best Homestyle Food
Lambert's Cafe
  2515 E. Malone Ave., 573/471-4261

Best Italian Food
Fabian's
  803 S. Kingshighway St., 573/472-0060

Best Pizza
Mazzio's Pizza
  1511 E. Malone Ave., 573/471-7120

Best Sandwiches
Rochester's Deli
  400 N. Main St., 573/471-2139

Best Seafood
Fisherman's Net
  915 Kingsway Plaza Mall, 573/471-8102

Best Steaks
JD's Steakhouse and Saloon
  4 N. Interstate Dr., 573/471-4431

Standbys
Golden Corral Family Steak House
  945 S. Kingshighway St., 573/472-0286
Baskin-Robbins
  120 N. Main St., 573/471-0031

SPRINGFIELD, MO

Best All-You-Can-Eat Buffets
Heritage Cafeteria
  1310 S. Glenstone Ave., 417/881-7770
  1364 E. Battlefield St., 417/883-3033
  210 E. Sunshine St., 417/883-1626
McGuffy's
  2101 W. Chesterfield Blvd., 417/882-2484

M

Best American Food
Diamond Head Restaurant
  2734 S. Campbell Ave., 417/883-9581

Best Breakfast
Anton's Coffee Shop
  937 S. Glenstone Ave., 417/869-7681

Best Burgers
Taylor's Drive-In
  139 Memorial Plz., 417/862-3278

Best Business Lunch
Leong's Tea House
  1036 W. Sunshine St., 417/869-4444

Best Chinese Food
Leong's Tea House
  1036 W. Sunshine St., 417/869-4444
Diamond Head Restaurant
  2734 S. Campbell Ave., 417/883-9581

Best Delicatessen
Nearly Famous Deli and Pasta
  1828 S. Kentwood Ave., 417/883-3403

Best Dinner
Hamby's Steak House
  901 N. Boonville Ave., 417/869-7615

Best Family Restaurant
McGuffy's
  2101 W. Chesterfield Blvd., 417/882-2484

Best Greek/Mediterranean Food
Sophia's Cafe
3522 N. National Ave., 417/883-3367

Best Health-Conscious Menu
Nearly Famous Deli and Pasta
1828 S. Kentwood Ave., 417/883-3403

Best Homestyle Food
Anton's Coffee Shop
937 S. Glenstone Ave., 417/869-7681
Taylor's Drive-In
139 Memorial Plz., 417/862-3278

Best Italian Food
J. Parrino's Pasta House and Bar
1550L E. Battlefield Rd., 417/882-1808

Best Lunch
Sophia's Cafe
3522 N. National Ave., 417/883-3367

Best Mexican Food
Mexican Villa
316 W. Kearney St., 417/869-4340
1408 S. National Ave., 417/869-4459
434 S. Glenstone Ave., 417/831-6196
1337 E. Sunshine St., 417/887-1010
2122 W. Division St., 417/864-8551
1100 W. Sunshine St., 417/866-7292

Best Pizza
J. Parrino's Pasta House and Bar
1550L E. Battlefield Rd., 417/882-1808

Best Salad/Salad Bar
Nearly Famous Deli and Pasta
1828 S. Kentwood Ave., 417/883-3403

Best Steaks
Hamby's Steak House
901 N. Boonville Ave., 417/869-7615

Standbys
The Olive Garden
3105 S. Glenstone Ave., 417/886-3188

WEST PLAINS, MO

Best American Food
The Depot
1717 Terra Dr., 417/257-2880

Best Breakfast
Kenny's Walleye and Catfish House
612 Porter Wagoner Blvd., 417/256-1538

Best Burgers
TJ's Hickory House
W. Hwy. 160, 417/257-7614

Best Chinese Food
Diamond Head Restaurant
1214 Porter Wagoner Blvd., 417/256-4888

Best Coffee
Cornucopia Fine Foods
  Court Square, 417/256-0689
Yellow House Coffeehouse
  209 W. Cleveland, 417/256-3554

Best Homestyle Food
Ozark Cafe
  104 Washington Ave., 417/256-3340

Best Pizza
Simple Simon's Pizza
  1836 Porter Wagoner Blvd., 417/257-7700

Best Steaks
TJ's Hickory House
  W. Hwy. 160, 417/257-7614

Standbys
Pizza Hut
  1211 W. Porter Wagoner Blvd., 417/256-8157

M

Montana

Best Restaurants in Town
Rex Hotel
  2401 Montana Ave., 406/245-7477
Walker's Grill
  301 N. 27th St., 406/245-9291

Best American Food
Granary Restaurant
  1500 Poly Dr., 406/259-3488

Best Bread
Stella's Kitchen and Bakery
  110 N. 29th St., 406/248-3060

Best Breakfast
Kit Kat Cafe
  633 Main St., 406/259-9154

Best Burgers
King's Hat
  633 Main St., 406/259-4746
Casey's Golden Pheasant
  109 N. Broadway, 406/256-5200

Best Casual Dining
Bruno's Italian Specialties
  1002 First Ave. N., 406/248-4146
  1523 Broadwater Ave., 406/252-1616

Best Chinese Food
Golden Phoenix Chinese Restaurant
  79 Swords Ln., 406/256-0319

Best Coffee
Todd's Plantation Gourmet Coffee
  115 N. 29th St., 406/245-2720

Best Family Restaurant
Bruno's Italian Specialties
  1002 First Ave. N., 406/248-4146
  1523 Broadwater Ave., 406/252-1616

M

Best Fast Food
King's Hat
633 Main St., 406/259-4746

Best Italian Food
Vinnie's Italian Kitchen
119 N. Broadway, 406/256-8484
Bruno's Italian Specialties
1002 First Ave. N., 406/248-4146
1523 Broadwater Ave., 406/252-1616

Best Lunch
Stella's Kitchen and Bakery
110 N. 29th St., 406/248-3060

Best Pizza
Village Inn Pizza Parlor
2048 Grand Ave., 406/656-6706

Best Place to Eat When Someone Else Is Buying
Rex Hotel
2401 Montana Ave., 406/245-7477

Best Romantic Dining
Rex Hotel
2401 Montana Ave., 406/245-7477

Best Sandwiches
Pug Mahon's
3011 First Ave. N., 406/259-4190

Best Seafood
Windmill Club
3921 First Ave. S., 406/252-8100

Best Steaks
Walker's Grill
301 N. 27th St., 406/245-9291
Windmill Club
3921 First Ave. S., 406/252-8100

Best Thai Food
Thai Orchid Restaurant
2926 Second Ave., 406/256-2206

Standbys
The Olive Garden
2201 Grant Rd., 406/652-1395

BOZEMAN, MT

Best American Food
O'Brien's Restaurant
312 E. Main St., 406/587-3973

Best Barbecue/Ribs
Fred's Mesquite Diner
451 E. Main St., 406/585-8558

Best Chinese Food
Wong's Restaurant
125 W. Main St., 406/587-1686

Best Eclectic Menu
John Bozeman's Bistro
242 E. Main St., 406/587-4100

Best Place to Eat When Someone Else Is Buying
The Gallatin Gateway Inn
76405 Gallatin Rd., Gallatin Gateway, 406/763-4672

BUTTE, MT

Best American Food
Lydia's
5 Mile Harrison Ave., 406/494-2000

Best Burgers
The M and M Bar and Cafe
9 N. Main St., 406/723-7612

Best Chinese Food
Ming's Chinese Restaurant
116 W. Park St., 406/782-7058

Best Coffee
Columbia Garden Espresso
20 N. Main St., 406/782-8808

Best Health-Conscious Menu
The Uptown Cafe
47 E. Broadway St., 406/723-4735

Best Italian Food
Spaghettini's
101 Broadway, 406/782-8855

Best Salad/Salad Bar
Columbia Garden Espresso
20 N. Main St., 406/782-8808

Best Sandwiches
Columbia Garden Espresso
20 N. Main St., 406/782-8808

CUT BANK, MT

Best Breakfast
C and L Country Cafe
112 N. Central Ave., 406/873-5335

Best Burgers
Point Drive Inn
1119 E. Main St., 406/873-2431

Best Coffee
C and L Country Cafe
112 N. Central Ave., 406/873-5335

Best Family Restaurants
Glacier Motor Inn
15 First Ave. SW, 406/873-4022
C and L Country Cafe
112 N. Central Ave., 406/873-5335
Golden Harvest Cafe
109 W. Main St., 406/873-4010
JR's
918 E. Main St., 406/873-4401

Best Homestyle Food
C and L Country Cafe
112 N. Central Ave., 406/873-5335

Best Ice Cream/Yogurt
R Place
Northern Village Shopping Ctr., 406/873-4786

Best Pizza
Maxie's
1159 E. Railroad St., 406/873-4220

Best Places to Take the Kids
Point Drive Inn
1119 E. Main St., 406/873-2431
R Place
Northern Village Shopping Ctr., 406/873-4786

Best Salad/Salad Bar
JR's
918 E. Main St., 406/873-4401

Best Sandwiches
Golden Harvest Cafe
109 W. Main St., 406/873-4010

Best Seafood
Glacier Motor Inn
15 First Ave. SW, 406/873-4022
JR's
918 E. Main St., 406/873-4401

Best Steaks
Glacier Motor Inn
15 First Ave. SW, 406/873-4022
JR's
918 E. Main St., 406/873-4401

M

DILLON, MT

Best Atmosphere
Centennial Inn
122 S. Washington, 406/683-4454

Best Breakfast
Klondike Inn
23 N. Idaho St., 406/683-2141
Longhorn Saloon
8 N. Montana St., 406/683-6839
Anna's Oven
120 S. Montana St., 406/683-5766

Best Burgers
Papa T's
10 N. Montana St., 406/683-6432

Best Chinese Food
Western Wok
17 E. Bannack St., 406/683-2356

Best Coffee
Sweetwater Coffee
23 N. Idaho, 406/683-4141

Best Desserts
Anna's Oven
120 S. Montana St., 406/683-5766
Centennial Inn
122 S. Washington, 406/683-4454

Best Family Restaurants

Klondike Inn
23 N. Idaho St., 406/683-2141
Longhorn Saloon
8 N. Montana St., 406/683-6839
Lion's Den
725 N. Montana St., 406/683-2051

Best Homestyle Food
Longhorn Saloon
8 N. Montana St., 406/683-6839
Anna's Oven
120 S. Montana St., 406/683-5766

Best Ice Cream/Yogurt
Arctic Circle
135 S. Atlantic St., 406/683-4146
Peppermint Stick
39 N. Idaho, 406/683-6662

Best Pizza
Papa T's
10 N. Montana St., 406/683-6432

Best Sandwiches
Anna's Oven
120 S. Montana St., 406/683-5766
Sweetwater Coffee
23 N. Idaho, 406/683-4141

Best Seafood
Lion's Den
725 N. Montana St., 406/683-2051

Best Steaks
Lion's Den
725 N. Montana St., 406/683-2051

M

GLENDIVE, MT

Best Breakfast
Twilite Dining
209 N. Merrill Ave., 406/365-8705

Best Burgers
Doc and Eddy's
1515 W. Bell St., 406/365-6782

Best Coffee
Hill-A-Beans
102 S. Merrill Ave., 406/365-2415

Best Desserts
Bacio's
302 W. Town St., 406/365-9664

Best Family Restaurant
Best Western Inn
222 N. Kendrick Ave., 406/365-5655

Best Italian Food
Bacio's
302 W. Towne St., 406/365-9664

Best Pizza
Greg's Silver Dollar Casino
1101 W. Towne St., 406/365-2074

Best Sandwiches
Gust-Hauf
 300 W. Bell St., 406/365-4451
Hill-A-Beans
 102 S. Merrill Ave., 406/365-2415
Beer Jug
 313 N. Merrill Ave., 406/359-9986

Best Steaks
Best Western Inn
 222 N. Kendrick Ave., 406/365-5655

Standbys
Dairy Queen
 611 N. Merrill Ave., 406/365-6140

HAMILTON, MT

Best All-You-Can-Eat Buffet
Porter's Place
 Second St. at Market St., Corvallis, 406/961-4471

Best Barbecue/Ribs
Bad Bubba's BBQ
 105 N. Second St., 406/363-7427

Best Breakfast
BJ's Restaurant
 900 N. First St., 406/363-4650

Best Burgers
Nap's Grill
 220 N. Second St., 406/363-0136

Best Chinese Food
Far East Village
 610 N. First St., 406/363-6976

Best Coffee
Coffee Cup Cafe
 500 S. First St., 406/363-3822

Best Desserts
Sundance Cafe
 900 S. First St., 406/363-2810

Best Family Restaurant
Four B's Restaurant
 1105 N. First St., 406/363-4620

Best Homestyle Food
Coffee Cup Cafe
 500 S. First St., 406/363-3822

Best Ice Cream/Yogurt
Coffee Cup Cafe
 500 S. First St., 406/363-3822

Best Italian Food
La Trattoria
 315 S. Third St., 406/363-5030

Best Mexican Food
Sundance Cafe
 900 S. First St., 406/363-2810

Best Pizza
BJ's Restaurant
900 N. First St., 406/363-4650

Best Sandwiches
Back Door Deli
105 S. Third St., 406/363-4480

Best Steaks
Nap's Grill
220 N. Second St., 406/363-0136

HELENA, MT

Best Atmosphere
On Broadway
106 E. Broadway St., 406/443-1929
Windbag Saloon
19 S. Last Chance Gulch St., 406/443-9669
Stonehouse Restaurant
120 Reeders Alley, 406/449-2552

Best Breakfast
Park Plaza Hotel
22 N. Last Chance Gulch St., 406/443-2200

Best Brunch
Park Plaza Hotel
22 N. Last Chance Gulch St., 406/443-2200

Best Burgers
Overland Express
2250 Eleventh Ave., 406/449-2635

Best Business Lunch
Bert and Ernie's Saloon
361 N. Last Chance Gulch St., 406/443-5680

Best Chinese Food
Jade Gardens
3128 N. Montana Ave., 406/443-8899

Best Desserts
Queen City Cafe
42 S. Park Ave., 406/442-3354

Best Family Restaurant
Windbag Saloon
19 S. Last Chance Gulch St., 406/443-9669

Best Homestyle Food
Dearborn Country Inn
4 Cooper Dr., 406/468-2838

Best Ice Cream/Yogurt
On Broadway
106 E. Broadway St., 406/443-1929

Best Italian Food
Pasta Pantry
1218 Eleventh Ave., 406/442-1074

Best Lunch
On Broadway
106 E. Broadway St., 406/443-1929

M

Best Pizza
Godfather's Pizza
2216 N. Montana Ave., 406/443-7050

Best Place to Take the Kids
Windbag Saloon
19 S. Last Chance Gulch St., 406/443-9669

Best Sandwiches
Dagwood's
2101 N. Main St., 406/449-8200
601 Euclid St., 406/449-8100

Best Seafood
On Broadway
106 E. Broadway St., 406/443-1929
Queen City Cafe
42 S. Park Ave., 406/442-3354

Best Steaks
Gilly's Casino
920 E. Lyndale Ave., 406/442-6449

Standbys
Subway
1350 Cedar St., 406/443-5443

KALISPELL, MT

Best Breakfast
Finnegan's
660 E. Idaho St., 406/755-0322

Best Burgers
Norm's
34 Main St., 406/752-4092

Best Coffee
Sykes' Grocery and Market Restaurant
202 Second Ave. W., 406/257-4304

Best Desserts
Lighterside Restaurant
221 Main St., 406/752-3668

Best Family Restaurants
Four Seasons Restaurant
350 N. Main St., 406/755-1374
Fred's Family Restaurant
1600 Hwy. 93S, 406/257-8666

Best Homestyle Food
Four Seasons Restaurant
350 N. Main St., 406/755-1374
Fred's Family Restaurant
1600 Hwy. 93S, 406/257-8666

Best Ice Cream/Yogurt
Alpine Frozen Yogurt
20 N. Main St., 406/752-4610

Best Italian Food
Rocco's
3796 Hwy. 2E, 406/756-5834

Best Mexican Food
Dos Amigos Mexican Restaurant

25 Second Ave. W., 406/752-2711
El Oso Chico
2316 Hwy. 2E, 406/752-4772

Best Pizza
Stageline Pizza
211 Second St. W., 406/755-4444

Best Sandwiches
Lighterside Restaurant
221 Main St., 406/752-3668
Fresh Attitude
238 E. Center St., 406/257-1435
Stageline Pizza
211 Second St. W., 406/755-4444
Norm's
34 Main St., 406/752-4092

Best Seafood
Rocco's
3796 Hwy. 2E, 406/756-5834
Montana Grill
5480 Hwy. 93S, Somers, 406/857-3889

Best Steaks
First Avenue West
139 First Ave. W., 406/755-4441
Montana Grill
5480 Hwy. 93S, Somers, 406/857-3889
Hennessy's Restaurant
1701 Hwy. 93S, 406/755-6100

Best Vietnamese Food
Alley Connection Restaurant
22 First St. W., 406/752-7077

LEWISTOWN, MT

Best Atmosphere
Yogo Garden Restaurant
211 E. Main St., 406/538-8721

Best Burgers
Pete's Drive Inn
1308 W. Main St., 406/538-9400
Four Aces Casino and Restaurant
508 First Ave. N., 406/538-9744
Sportsman Restaurant
1660 W. Main St., 406/538-9053

Best Coffee
Six Eighteen Coffee
618 W. Main St., 406/538-3233
Shanny Shack
409 E. Main St., 406/538-6666

Best Family Restaurants
Empire Cafe
214 W. Main St., 406/538-9912
Sportsman Restaurant
1660 W. Main St., 406/538-9053
Yogo Garden Restaurant
211 E. Main St., 406/538-8721
Snow White Cafe
122 W. Main St., 406/538-3666

Best Homestyle Food
Empire Cafe
214 W. Main St., 406/538-9912
Snow White Cafe
122 W. Main St., 406/538-3666

Best Pizza
Howard's Pizza
116 Sixth Ave. N., 406/538-2164
Little Big Men Pizza
630 NE Main St., 406/538-2433

Best Salad/Salad Bar
Yogo Garden Restaurant
211 E. Main St., 406/538-8721

Best Sandwiches
Simply Divine
301 W. Broadway St., 406/538-7069
Whole Famdamily Restaurant
206 W. Main St., 406/538-5161

Best Seafood
Sportsman Restaurant
1660 W. Main St., 406/538-9053

Best Southwestern Food
Poor Man's Southwestern Cafe
413 W. Main St., 406/538-4277

Best Steaks
Bar Nineteen
Fairgrounds Rd., 406/538-3250

Standbys
Dairy Queen
104 E. Main St., 406/538-8429

MILES CITY, MT

Best All-You-Can-Eat Buffet
New Hunan Chinese and American Restaurant
716 N. Earling Ave., 406/232-3338

Best Breakfast
Cellar Casino
5 N. Eighth St., 406/232-5611
Four B's Restaurant
1406 S. Haynes Ave., 406/232-5772

Best Burgers
Cellar Casino
5 N. Eighth St., 406/232-5611

Best Chinese Food
New Hunan Chinese and American Restaurant
716 N. Earling Ave., 406/232-3338

Best Desserts
Club 519
519 Main St., 406/232-5133

Best Family Restaurants
Four B's Restaurant
1406 S. Haynes Ave., 406/232-5772
Gallagher's Family Restaurant
1215 S. Haynes Ave., 406/232-0099

Munchies
    1219 S. Haynes Ave., 406/232-1334
Club 519
    519 Main St., 406/232-5133

Best Sandwiches
Big Al's Sandwich Joint
    14 N. Eighth St., 406/232-1919

Best Seafood
Club 519
    519 Main St., 406/232-5133

Best Steaks
Club 519
    519 Main St., 406/232-5133
Cellar Casino
    5 N. Eighth St., 406/232-5611

Standbys
Dairy Queen
    Miles City Plz., Valley Dr. E., 406/232-2685
Pizza Hut
    905 S. Haynes Ave., 406/232-6130

MISSOULA, MT

Best Restaurant in Town
Alleycat Grill
    125 1/2 W. Main St., 406/728-3535

Best All-You-Can-Eat Buffet
Country Harvest Buffet
    Southgate, 2901 Brooks Ave., 406/728-6040

Best American Food
Del's Place
    400 E. Broadway, 406/728-0090

Best Asian Restaurant
The Mustard Seed
    419 W. Front St., 406/728-7825

Best Atmosphere
Shadows Keep
    102 Ben Hogan Dr., 406/728-5132

Best Bar
Depot Restaurant and Bar
    201 Railroad St. W., 406/728-9742

Best Barbecue/Ribs
Old Town Cafe
    127 W. Alder St., 406/728-9742

Best Breakfast
Old Town Cafe
    127 W. Alder St., 406/728-9742

Best Brunch
The Edgewater
    Village Red Lion, 100 Madison St., 406/728-3100

Best Burgers
Missoula Club
    139 W. Main St., 406/728-3740

M

Best Business Lunch
New Pacific Grill
   100 Railroad St. W., 406/542-3353

Best Casual Dining
Nine Mile House
   28030 Hwy. 10W, Huson, 406/626-5668

Best Cheap Meal
Thai Spicy
   206 W. Main St., 406/543-0260

Best Chinese Food
Mings
   1049 W. Central Ave., 406/728-9000

Best Coffee
Break Espresso
   432 N. Higgins Ave., 406/728-7300

Best Coffeehouse
Food for Thought
   540 Daly Ave., 406/721-6033

Best Desserts
Alleycat Grill
   125 1/2 W. Main St., 406/728-3535

Best Diner
Uptown Diner
   120 N. Higgins Ave., 406/542-2449

Best Fast Food
Del's Place
   400 E. Broadway, 406/728-0090

Best French Food
Lily Restaurant
   515 S. Higgins Ave., 406/542-0002

Best Greek/Mediterranean Food
Zorba's Greek Cuisine
   420 S. Orange St., 406/728-6076

Best Ice Cream/Yogurt
Big Dipper Ice Cream
   602 Myrtle, 406/543-5722

Best Italian Food
Zimorino's Banquet and Catering
   424 N. Higgins Ave., 406/728-6686

Best Mexican Food
Casa Pablo's
   147 W. Broadway St., 406/721-3854

Best Microbrewery
Iron Horse Brew Pub
   100 Railroad St. W., 406/728-8866

Best Pastries
Mammyth Bakery Cafe
   131 W. Main St., 406/549-5542

Best Pizza
Zimorino's Banquet and Catering
   424 N. Higgins Ave., 406/728-6686

Best Place to Eat When Someone Else Is Buying
New Pacific Grill
   100 Railroad St. W., 406/542-3353

Best Place to Take the Kids
Skipper's Seafood and Chowder
   3109 Brooks St., 406/721-1866

Best Quick Lunch
Doc's Gourmet Sandwich Shop
   214 N. Higgins Ave., 406/542-7414

Best Romantic Dining
Alleycat Grill
   125 1/2 W. Main St., 406/728-3535

Best Southwestern Food
Old Post Pub and Pasta Parlor
   103 W. Spruce St., 406/721-7399

Best Sports Bar
Press Box Casino
   835 E. Broadway St., 406/721-1212

Best Steaks
Guy's Cold Creek Steak House
   6600 Hwy. 12W, 406/273-2622

Best Thai Food
Thai Spicy
   206 W. Main St., 406/543-0260

Best Wine Selection
Alleycat Grill
   125 1/2 W. Main St., 406/728-3535

M

Nebraska

Best Restaurant in Town
Black Crow
  405 Court St., 402/228-7200

Best Breakfast
Beatrice Inn Motel Restaurant
  3500 N. Sixth St., 402/223-4074

Best Burgers
Michael J's Bar and Grill
  831 W. Court St., 402/228-9892

Best Chinese Food
Mar's Fine Foods
  2205 N. Sixth St., 402/223-2965

Best Continental Food
Black Crow
  405 Court St., 402/228-7200

Best Desserts
Black Crow
  405 Court St., 402/228-7200

Best Family Restaurant
Valentino's
  701 Court St., 402/223-3573

Best Ice Cream/Yogurt
Goodrich Dairy
  817 Court St., 402/228-3677

Best Italian Food
Valentino's
  701 Court St., 402/223-3573

Best Salad/Salad Bar
Black Crow
  405 Court St., 402/228-7200

Best Sandwiches
Black Crow
  405 Court St., 402/228-7200

N

Best Steaks
Courtyard Square
500 Fourth St., Fairbury, 402/729-3388

BROKEN BOW, NE

Best All-You-Can-Eat Buffet
Tumbleweed Cafe
850 E. South E St., 308/872-5454

Best Atmosphere
Lobby Restaurant
509 South E St., 308/872-3363

Best Barbecue/Ribs
Lobby Restaurant
509 South E St., 308/872-3363

Best Coffee
Tumbleweed Cafe
850 E. South E St., 308/872-5454

Best Desserts
Lobby Restaurant
509 South E St., 308/872-3363

Best Family Restaurant
Tumbleweed Cafe
850 E. South E St., 308/872-5454

Best Homestyle Food
Tumbleweed Cafe
850 E. South E St., 308/872-5454

Best Ice Cream/Yogurt
Dairy Corner Restaurant
551 South E St., 308/872-5950

Best Pizza
Casey's General Store
125 South E St., 308/872-9308

Best Place to Take the Kids
Tumbleweed Cafe
850 E. South E St., 308/872-5454

Best Sandwiches
Tumbleweed Cafe
850 E. South E St., 308/872-5454

Best Seafood
Lobby Restaurant
509 South E St., 308/872-3363

Best Steaks
Lobby Restaurant
509 South E St., 308/872-3363

Standbys
Pizza Hut
329 E. South E St., 308/872-6472
Subway
148 E. South E St., 308/872-3317

FREMONT, NE

Best Restaurant in Town
KC's Cafe and Bar
  631 N. Park Ave., 402/721-3353

Best American Food
Nick's Main Street Grill
  439 N. Main St., 402/727-9600

Best Chinese Food
Happy Inn Restaurant
  1035 E. 23rd St., 402/721-4711

Best Mexican Food
Sananna Lounge
  700 E. 23rd St., 402/727-9897

Best Pizza
Sananna Lounge
  700 E. 23rd St., 402/727-9897

Best Sandwiches
Irv's Deli and More
  35 W. Sixth St., 402/721-2015

GRAND ISLAND, NE

Best All-You-Can-Eat Buffet
Valentino's
  2245 N. Webb Rd., 308/382-7711

Best Breakfast
Country Kitchen
  3404 W. Thirteenth St., 308/382-7022
Tommy's Restaurant
  1325 S. Locust St., 308/381-0440

Best Chinese Food
Hunan Chinese Restaurant
  2249 N. Webb Rd., 308/384-6964
Yen Ching Chinese Restaurant
  2623 S. Locust St., 308/384-8298
  610 W. Second St., 308/384-3020

Best Homestyle Food
Conoco Motel Cafe
  2109 W. Second St., 308/382-9621

Best Italian Food
Nonna's Palazzo Restaurant
  820 W. Second St., 308/384-3029

Best Mexican Food
Dos Hermanos
  3311 W. Stolley Park Rd., 308/382-1080
El Tapatio
  2610 S. Locust St., 308/381-4511

Best Pizza
Valentino's
  2245 N. Webb Rd., 308/382-7711

Best Salad/Salad Bar
Valentino's
  2245 N. Webb Rd., 308/382-7711

N

Western Charloin Steak
1201 S. Locust St., 308/382-9011

Best Sandwiches
Schlotzsky's
3337 W. State St., 308/389-6141

Best Seafood
Dreisbach's
1137 S. Locust St., 308/382-5450

Best Steaks
Dreisbach's
1137 S. Locust St., 308/382-5450
Library Restaurant
2530 Saint Patrick Ave., 308/381-1115

Standbys
TCBY
2010 Lawrence Ln., 308/382-8514
Baskin-Robbins
1904 N. Dires Ave., 308/381-7222
Red Lobster
3430 W. Thirteenth St., 308/382-8879
Godfather's Pizza
1201 S. Locust St., 308/384-9090

HASTINGS, NE

Best Restaurants in Town
Barrel Bar Lounge
1200 E. South St., 402/463-9158
Bernardo's Steakhouse and Lounge
1109 S. Baltimore Ave., 402/463-4666
Big Dally's Deli
801 W. Second St., 402/463-7666
Old Fashioned Garden Cafe
2201 N. Old Hwy. 281, 402/463-8387
Lo Rayne's Restaurant and Lounge
1216 W. J St., 402/463-2784
Murphy's Wagon Wheel
107 N. Lincoln Ave., 402/463-3011
OK Cafe
806 W. Sixteenth St., 402/461-4663
Taylor's Steakhouse
1609 N. Kansas Ave., 402/462-8000
Back Rib Lounge
2727 W. Second St., Ste. 440, 402/463-0546

Best Chinese Food
Hunan Chinese Restaurant
2727 W. Second St., Ste. 302, 402/463-4040

Best Mexican Food
La Mejicana
627 W. First St., 402/463-0606

KEARNEY, NE

Best Restaurants in Town
The Cellar Bar and Lounge
3901 Second Ave., 308/236-6541

Habitat Restaurant
   121 W. 46th St., 308/237-2405
Alley Rose
   2013 Central Ave., 308/234-1261
French Cafe
   2202 Central Ave., 308/234-6808
Captain's Table
   Ramada Inn, 110 S. Second St., 308/237-5971

LINCOLN, NE

Best All-You-Can-Eat Buffets
Valentino's
   3457 Holdrege St., 402/467-3611
   3920 W. Kearney St., 402/470-3800
Bishop's Buffet
   6100 O St., 402/464-6346

Best Bagels
Bagels and Joe
   4701E Old Cheney Rd., 402/423-7797
   1339 O St., 402/477-6266

Best Breakfast
Village Inn
   2949 N. 27th St., 402/466-8408
   111 S. 29th St., 402/476-6525
   5001 Van Dorn St., 402/488-2424
   6555 O St., 402/489-8829
Garden Cafe
   6891 A St., 402/434-3750
Hy-Vee Food Stores
   2343 N. 48th St., 402/467-5505
   1401 Superior St., 402/477-4764
   3800 Old Cheney Rd., 402/421-2462
   6919 O St., 402/483-7707

Best Brunch
Legionnaire Club
   5730 O St., 402/467-1184
Grandmother's Restaurant and Lounge
   6940 A St., 402/483-7855
Valentino's
   3457 Holdrege St., 402/467-3611
   3920 W. Kearney St., 402/470-3800

Best Coffee
Mill
   800 P St., 402/475-5522
Bagels and Joe
   4701 Old Cheney Rd., Ste. E, 402/423-7797
   1339 O St., 402/477-6266

Best Chinese Food
Imperial Palace
   701 N. 27th St., 402/474-2688
House of Hunan Restaurant
   4900 O St., 402/467-2393
   5601 S. 56th St., 402/423-8079
Mr. Panda
   2900 N. 70th St., 402/464-8818

N

Best Desserts
Garden Cafe
   6891 A St., 402/434-3750
Grandmother's Restaurant and Lounge
   6940 A St., 402/483-7855

Best Dinner
Legionnaire Club
   5730 O St., 402/467-1184
Lazlo's Brewery and Grill
   710 P St., 402/474-2337

Best Greek/Mediterranean Food
Pappa John's Family Restaurant
   114 S. Fourteenth St., 402/477-7657
George's Gyros
   905 N. Sixteenth St., 402/438-2262
   1200 N. St., 402/476-2589
Kuhl's Restaurant
   1038 O St., 402/476-1311

Best Ice Cream/Yogurt
Goodrich Dairy
   1126 South St., 402/477-6864
   5501 Holdrege St., 402/466-1755
   5820 Fremont St., 402/464-8442
   2510 Randolph St., 402/475-3730
   4240 S. 48th St., 402/489-0149
   6900 O St., Ste. 121, 402/466-2888
I Can't Believe It's Yogurt
   101 N. Fourteenth St., 402/475-9117
   6940 Van Dorn St., Ste. 107, 402/489-9116
Colby Ridge Popcorn and Yogurt
   1401 Superior St., Ste. 5, 402/476-6822
   233 N. 48th St., 402/467-5811
   5440 South St., 402/483-5900
   3201 Pioneers Blvd., 402/489-9141

Best Italian Food
Grisanti's Casual Italian Restaurant
   6820 O St., 402/464-8444
Valentino's
   3457 Holdrege St., 402/467-3611
   3920 W. Kearney St., 402/470-3800

Best Lunch
Garden Cafe
   6891 A St., 402/434-3750
Lazlo's Brewery and Grill
   710 P St., 402/474-2337
Valentino's
   3457 Holdrege St., 402/467-3611
   3920 W. Kearney St., 402/470-3800
Bum Steer Steaks
   6440 O St., 402/467-5110

Best Mexican Food
Amigo's
   Multiple Locations
Tico's
   317 S. Seventeenth St., 402/475-1048

N

La Paz Mexican Restaurant
  321 N. Cotner Blvd., 402/466-9111

Best Pizza
Valentino's
  3457 Holdrege St., 402/467-3611
  3920 W. Kearney St., 402/470-3800

Best Seafood
Inn Harms Way
  201 N. Seventh St., 402/438-3033

Best Sports Bars
Bleachers
  5601 S. 56th St., Ste. 21, 402/423-5381
Brewsky's Food and Spirits
  1602 South St., 402/438-2739
Sportscasters Bar and Grill
  3048 N. 70th St., 402/466-6679

Best Steaks
The Steak House
  3441 Adams St., 402/466-2472
Misty's Restaurant and Lounge
  6235 Havelock Ave., 402/466-8424
  5508 S. 56th St., Ste. 5, 402/423-2288

Standbys
Old Country Buffet
  2241 O St., Ste. 1, 402/435-2727
Lone Star Steakhouse
  200 N. 70th St., 402/489-2100
Perkins
  2900 NW Twelfth St., 402/474-6162
  121 N. 48th St., 402/467-2674
Applebee's
  3730 Village Dr., 402/420-1182
Dairy Queen
  4130 S. 48th St., 402/488-1559
  760 W. O St., 402/475-3406
  1447 N. 27th St., 402/474-4331
  614 N. 66th St., 402/464-4240
Baskin-Robbins
  820 N. 70th St., 402/467-2947
TCBY
  6450 O St., 402/464-7766
  2437 S. 48th St., 402/421-8228
  5400 S. 56th St., Ste. 5, 402/421-8228
The Olive Garden
  6100 O St., 402/464-1910
Red Lobster
  6540 O St., 402/466-8397

NORFOLK, NE

Best Restaurants in Town
Prenger's Restaurant
  First and Norfolk Ave., 402/379-1900
The Uptown Eating Establishment
  326 Norfolk Ave., 402/371-7171
Norfolk Country Inn
  1201 S. Thirteenth St., 402/371-4430

Country Kitchen
1221 Omaha Ave., 402/371-0477
Village Inn
1915 Krenzien Dr., 402/371-8486
Mary's Restaurant
801 E. Norfolk Ave., 402/371-5525
Valentino's
1025 S. Thirteenth St., 402/379-2500

Standbys
Golden Corral Family Steak House
1021 S. Thirteenth St., 402/371-8210

NORTH PLATTE, NE

Best Restaurants in Town
The Depot
520 N. Jeffers St., 308/534-7844
Stockman Inn
1402 S. Jeffers St., 308/534-3630
Airport Inn
Lee Bird Field, 308/534-4340
Camino Inn
2102 S. Jeffers St., 308/532-9090
The Brick Wall
507 N. Dewey St., 308/532-7545
Merrick's Ranch House
1220 E. Fourth St., 308/532-8200

Best American Food
Hobb'E's
217 E. Sixth St., 308/534-9998

Best Chinese Food
Golden Dragon
120 W. Leota St., 308/532-8200
House of Oriental Food
508 N. Jeffers St., 308/534-0422

Best Mexican Food
La Casita Cafe
1911 E. Fourth St., 308/534-8077

OMAHA, NE

Best American Food
Bohemian Cafe
1406 S. Thirteenth St., 402/342-9838
Jams Bar and Grill
7814 Dodge St., 402/399-8300
M's Pub
422 S. Eleventh St., 402/342-2550
Old Chicago
13110 Birch Dr., 402/445-9393
Upstream Brewing Company
514 S. Eleventh St., 402/344-0200

Best Appetizers
Pipeline Tavern
1300 S. 72nd St., 402/399-8774

Best Asian Food
Chez Chong
   1015 S. Tenth St., 402/346-3635

Best Breakfast
Garden Cafe
   3321 S. 72nd St., 402/397-3384
   11040 Oak St., 402/393-0252
   1224 S. 103rd St., 402/397-1991
   14330 U St., 402/895-5938
   1212 Harney St., 402/422-1574
Market Basket
   911 S. 87th Ave., 402/397-1100

Best Brunch
Chardonnay
   Marriott Regency at 10220 Regency Cir.,
     402/399-9000
Maxine's Restaurant
   1616 Dodge St., 402/346-7600

Best Burgers
Coyote's
   1217 Howard St., 402/345-2047
Goldberg's
   2936 S. 132nd St., 402/333-1086
   5008 Dodge St., 402/556-2006

Best Chinese Food
House of Hunan
   2405 S. 132nd St., 402/334-5382
Imperial Palace
   11200 Davenport St., 402/330-3888
Imperial Palace Express
   10000 California St., 402/391-3885

Best Coffee
Garden Cafe
   11040 Oak St., 402/393-0252
   1224 S. 103rd St., 402/397-1991
   1212 Harney St., 402/422-1574
   14330 U St., 402/895-5938
   3321 S. 72nd St., 402/397-3384
MJ Java
   1200 Landmark Ctr., 402/342-5282

Best Continental Cuisine
French Cafe
   1017 Howard St., 402/341-3547
La Strada 72
   3125 S. 72nd St., 402/397-8389
V. Mertz
   1022 Howard St., 402/345-8980

Best Dinner
Gorat's Steak House
   4917 Center St., 402/551-3733
ams Bar and Grill
   7814 Dodge St, 402/399-8300
e Drover
   21 S. 73rd St., 402/391-7440

N

Best Homestyle Food
Bohemian Cafe
 1406 S. Thirteenth St., 402/342-9838
Garden Cafe
 11040 Oak St., 402/393-0252
 3321 S. 72nd St., 402/397-3384
 14330 U St., 402/895-5938
 1212 Harney St., 402/422-1574
 1224 S. 103rd St., 402/397-1991

Best Italian Food
Cafe Di Coppia
 120 Regency Pkwy., 402/392-2806
Lo Sole Mio Ristorante Italiano
 3001 S. 32nd Ave., 402/345-5656
Pasta Amore
 11027 Prairie Brook Rd., 402/391-2585
Vincenzo's Ristorante
 1818 N. 144th St., 402/498-3889
Vivace
 1110 Howard St., 402/342-2050

Best Mexican Food
Buena Vida
 7635 Cass St., 402/392-1021
El Alamo
 4917 S. 24th St., 402/731-8969
Fernando's
 380 N. 114th St, 402/330-5707
Julio's
 13043 Arbor St., 402/330-2110
 5402 N. 90th St., 402/572-5223
 510 S. Thirteenth St., 402/345-6921
 7555 Pacific St., 402/399-8059
O.J.'s
 9201 N. 30th St., 402/451-3266
Trini's
 1020 Howard St., 402/346-8400

Best Pizza
Big Fred's
 1301 S. 119th St., 402/333-4414
La Casa Pizzeria
 4432 Leavenworth St., 402/536-6464
 8216 Grover St., 402/391-6300
Zio's Pizzeria
 13463 W. Center Rd., 402/330-1444
 1213 Howard St., 402/344-2222
 7924 W. Dodge Rd., 402/391-1881

Best Romantic Dining
Amadeus at the Aquila
 1615 Howard St., 402/231-6019
Bistro at the Market
 406 S. Twelfth St., 402/346-4060
French Cafe
 1017 Howard St., 402/341-3547
Maxine's Restaurant
 1616 Dodge St., 402/346-7600

Best Steaks
Austins Steaks and Saloon
  11224 W. Dodge Rd., 402/498-8502
  12020 Anne St., 402/896-5373
  1101 Harney St., 402/344-3585
  1414 S. 72nd St., 402/397-0751
Brother Sebastian's
  1350 S. 119th St., 402/330-0300
Johnny's Cafe
  4702 S. 27th St., 402/731-4774
Lone Star
  3040 S. 143rd Plz., 402/333-1563
  655 N. 114th St., 402/493-1331
Omaha Prime Restaurant
  415 S. Eleventh St., 402/341-7040

Best View While Dining
Charlie's on the Lake
  4150 S. 144th St., 402/894-9411
Maxine's Restaurant
  Red Lion Hotel, 1616 Dodge St., 402/346-7600

SCOTTSBLUFF, NE

Best All-You-Can-Eat Buffet
Buffalo Steakhouse
  1901 21st Ave., 308/635-3111

Best Bar
O'Hara's Restaurant
  2302 Frontage Rd., 308/635-0050

Best Breakfast
Grampy's Pancake House
  1802 E. Twentieth Pl., 308/632-6906
Country Kitchen
  3485 Tenth St., Gering, 308/635-3800

Best Chinese Food
Oriental House
  1502 E. Twentieth St., 308/632-3922
Peking Garden
  802 W. 27th St., 308/635-3478

Best Coffee
Java Hut
  1813 Avenue A, 308/632-1522

Best Family Restaurant
Woodshed
  18 E. Sixteenth St., 308/635-3684

Best Homestyle Food
Country Kitchen
  3485 Tenth St., Gering, 308/635-3800

Best Italian Food
Scalora's Restaurant
  417 1/2 Box Butte Ave., Alliance, 308/762-1744

Best Sandwiches
Woodshed
  18 E. Sixteenth St., 308/635-3684

N

Best Steaks
Gaslight Restaurant
 3315 Tenth St., Gering, 308/632-7315

Standbys
Dairy Queen
 714 W. 27th St., 308/632-3663
Pizza Hut
 726 W. 27th St., 308/632-3022
TCBY
 2621 Fifth Ave., Ste. 3, 308/632-8000

VALENTINE, NE

Best Breakfast
Home Cafe
 101 W. Hwy. 20, 402/376-3222

Best Coffee
Ambrosia Garden
 105 N. Main St., 402/376-1927
Town Square
 269 N. Main St., 402/376-1424

Best Homestyle Food
Home Cafe
 101 W. Hwy. 20, 402/376-3222

Best Ice Cream/Yogurt
Ambrosia Garden
 105 N. Main St., 402/376-1927

Best Sandwiches
Ambrosia Garden
 105 N. Main St., 402/376-1927

Best Seafood
Jordan's Cafe
 E. Hwy. 20, 402/376-1255

Best Steaks
Jordan's Cafe
 E. Hwy. 20, 402/376-1255
Peppermill Restaurant
 112 N. Main St., 402/376-1440

Standbys
Pizza Hut
 E. Hwy. 20, 402/376-3303
Subway
 224 S. Main St., 402/376-2112

N

Nevada

Best Restaurants in Town
Station Grill and Rotisserie
  1105 S. Carson St., 702/883-8400
Wild Scallion
  318 N. Carson St., 702/883-8826

Best American Food
Bodine's
  5650 S. Carson St., 702/885-0303

Best Barbecue/Ribs
Pop's Barbecue
  224 S. Carson St., 702/884-4411

Best Italian Food
Garibaldi's
  301 N. Carson St., 702/884-4574
Panache's
  1750 S. Roop St., 702/882-1488

Best Place to Eat When Someone Else Is Buying
The Bonanza Restaurant
  3700 N. Carson St., 702/883-9696

Best Salad/Salad Bar
Carson Depot
  111 E. Telegraph Rd., 702/884-4546

Best Bar
Mattie's
  2525 Mountain City Hwy., 702/753-3877

Best Breakfast
Commercial Hotel and Casino
  345 Fourth St., 702/738-3181
Stockmen's Motor Hotel
  340 Commercial St., 702/738-5141

Best Brunch
Commercial Hotel and Casino
  345 Fourth St., 702/738-3181

N

Red Lion Inn and Casino
   2065 Idaho St., 702/738-2111

Best Burgers
Cimarron West Family Restaurant
   673 Cimarron Way, 702/753-8328

Best Cheap Meal
Golden Dragon
   1900 Idaho St., Ste. 101, 702/753-8415
Elko Dinner Station
   1430 Idaho St., 702/738-8528

Best Chinese Food
Golden Dragon
   1900 Idaho St., Ste. 101, 702/753-8415

Best Coffee
Coffee Mug
   1309 Idaho St., 702/738-5999
Cowboy Joe
   376 Fifth St., 702/753-5612

Best Desserts
Coffee Mug
   1309 Idaho St., 702/738-5999
Commercial Hotel and Casino
   345 Fourth St., 702/738-3181
D'Orazio Italian Gardens
   217 Idaho St., 702/738-7088

Best Family Restaurants
Nevada Dinner House
   351 Silver St., 702/738-8485
Star Hotel
   246 Silver St., 702/753-8696

Best Homestyle Food
Mattie's
   2525 Mountain City Hwy., 702/753-3877

Best Italian Food
D'Orazio Italian Gardens
   217 Idaho St., 702/738-7088

Best Other Ethnic Food
Nevada Dinner House (Basque)
   351 Silver St., 702/738-8485
Star Hotel (Basque)
   246 Silver St., 702/753-8696

Best Place to Take the Kids
Cimarron West Family Restaurant
   673 Cimarron Way, 702/753-8328

Best Salad/Salad Bar
Cimarron West Family Restaurant
   673 Cimarron Way, 702/753-8328

Best Sandwiches
Machi's
   778 Commercial St., 702/738-9772
Cowboy Joe
   376 Fifth St., 702/753-5612

Best Seafood
Pine Lodge
Main St., Lamoille, 702/753-6363

Best Steaks
Pine Lodge
Main St., Lamoille, 702/753-6363

ELY, NV

Best Breakfast
Kountry Kitchen Restaurant
940 Avenue F, 702/289-8854
Cell Block Dining Room
Jail House Motel and Casino, 211 Fifth St.,
702/289-3033

Best Burgers
Jerry's Restaurant
2160 Aultman St., 702/289-3905

Best Chinese Food
Good Friends Chinese Restaurant
1455 Aultman St., 702/289-4888
Orient Express
562 Aultman St., 702/289-3431

Best Coffee
Flower Basket
566 Aultman St., 702/289-2828

Best Family Restaurants
Evah's Copper Queen Restaurant
701 Avenue I, 702/289-4271
Cell Block Dining Room
Jail House Motel and Casino, 211 Fifth St.,
702/289-3033

Best Homestyle Food
Kountry Kitchen Restaurant
940 Avenue F, 702/289-8854
Cell Block Dining Room
Jail House Motel and Casino, 211 Fifth St.,
702/289-3033

Best Ice Cream/Yogurt
Ice Cream Fantasy
301 Aultman St., 702/289-2585
Economy Drug
696 Aultman St., 702/289-4929
Steptoe Drug
504 Aultman St., 702/289-2671

Best Pizza
Shy Simon's Pizza
905 Avenue F, 702/289-4162

Best Salad/Salad Bar
Evah's Copper Queen Restaurant
701 Avenue I, 702/289-4271

Best Seafood
Nevada Hotel
501 Aultman St., 702/289-6665

N

Best Steaks
Evah's Copper Queen Restaurant
  701 Avenue I, 702/289-4271
Nevada Hotel
  501 Aultman St., 702/289-6665

HENDERSON, NV

Best Restaurant in Town
Renata's
  4451 E. Sunset Rd., Ste. 1, 702/435-4000

Best Homestyle Food
Linda's Country Kitchen
  Mecca Rd. at Hwy. 373, Amargosa Valley,
    702/372-1200

Standbys
The Olive Garden
  4400 E. Sunset Rd., 702/451-5133
Outback Steakhouse
  4423 E. Sunset Rd., 702/451-7808

LAS VEGAS, NV

Best American Food
Country Inn
  2425 E. Desert Inn Rd., 702/731-5035
  1401 S. Rainbow Blvd., 702/254-0520

Best Bagels
Bagel Oasis
  9134 W. Sahara Ave., 702/363-0811

Best Barbecue/Ribs
Gates Bar-B-Que
  2710 E. Desert Inn Rd., 702/369-8010

Best Beer Selection
Der Baron's
  4300 Meadows Ln., 702/870-7788
  3455 E. Flamingo Rd., 702/382-5075
Mad Dogs and Englishmen Pub
  515 Las Vegas Blvd. S., 702/382-5075
  4755 Spring Mountain Rd., 702/362-0074

Best Breakfast
Hash House
  6000 W. Spring Mountain Rd., 702/873-9479

Best Brunch
Marie Callender's
  4875 W. Flamingo Rd., 702/365-6226
Alias Smith and Jones
  541 E. Twain Ave., 702/732-7401

Best Burgers
In-N-Out Burger
  1195 E. Desert Inn Rd., 702/791-3601
Fatburger
  3765 Las Vegas Blvd. S., 702/736-4733
  4851 W. Charleston Blvd., 702/870-4933

Best Chinese Food
Emperor's Table
  4670 S. Decatur Blvd., 702/876-9588

N

Full Ho
240 N. Jones Blvd., 702/878-2378

Best Coffee
Jitters
2457 E. Tropicana Ave., 702/898-0056
Cathay House
5300 W. Spring Mountain Rd., 702/876-3838

Best Delicatessen
Celebrity Deli
4055 S. Maryland Pkwy., 702/733-7827

Best Desserts
Marie Callender's
4875 W. Flamingo Rd., 702/365-6226
Cadillac Grille
2801 N. Tenaya Way, 702/255-5555

Best Family Restaurants
Country Inn Restaurant
2425 E. Desert Inn Rd., 702/731-5035
1401 S. Rainbow Blvd., 702/254-0520
Hush Puppy
7185 W. Charleston Blvd., 702/363-5988
7400 Las Vegas Blvd. S., 702/263-0013

Best French Food
Andre's
401 S. Sixth St., 702/385-5016

Best Happy Hour Snacks
Big Dog's
6390 W. Sahara Ave., 702/876-3647

N

Best Homestyle Food
Cousin's Cafe
3331 E. Tropicana Ave., 702/451-5440
N'Orleans
4725 W. Spring Mountain Rd., 702/364-8863

Best Ice Cream/Yogurt
Luv-It Frozen Custard
505 E. Oakley Blvd., 702/384-6452

Best Italian Food
North Beach Cafe
2605 S. Decatur Blvd., 702/247-9530

Best Japanese Food
Hamada of Japan
598 E. Flamingo Rd., 702/733-3005
Kabuki
1150 E. Twain Ave., 702/733-0066

Best Late-Night Food
Port Tack
3190 W. Sahara Ave., 702/873-3345
Play It Again Sam
4120 Spring Mountain Rd., 702/876-1550

Best Mexican Food
Viva Mercado
6182 W. Flamingo Rd., 702/871-8826

Ricardo's
   4300 Meadows Ln., 702/870-1088
   2380 E. Tropicana Ave., 702/798-4515
   4930 W. Flamingo Rd., 702/871-7119
Z Tejas Grill
   3824 S. Paradise, 702/732-1660

Best Other Ethnic Food
Red Sea (African)
   2226 Paradise Rd., 702/893-1740

Best Outdoor Dining
Cafe Michelle
   1350 E. Flamingo Rd., 702/735-8686
Cafe Nicolle
   4760 W. Sahara Ave., 702/870-7675

Best Pizza
Fasolini's Pizza Cafe
   222 S. Decatur Blvd., 702/877-0071

Best Place to Take the Kids
Blueberry Hill
   3790 E. Flamingo Rd., 702/433-9999
   5000 E. Bonanza Rd., 702/435-5555
   1280 S. Decatur Blvd., 702/877-8867
   1723 E. Charleston Blvd., 702/382-3330
   4601 Spring Mountain Rd., 702/876-0006

Best Romantic Dining
Tillerman
   2245 E. Flamingo Rd., 702/731-4036
Pistol Pete's
   710 S. Decatur Blvd., 702/877-8873
   3430 E. Tropicana Ave., 702/454-6366
   2401 E. Lake Mead Blvd., 702/399-1115
   350 N. Nellis Blvd., 702/459-1200
Andre's
   401 S. Sixth St., 702/385-5016
Kiefer's Atop The Carriage House
   105 E. Harmon Ave., 702/739-8000

Best Sandwiches
Capriotti's
   324 W. Sahara Ave., 702/474-0229

Best Seafood
Tillerman
   2245 E. Flamingo Rd., 702/731-4036

Best Steaks
Hungry Hunter
   2380 S. Rainbow Blvd., 702/873-0433

Best Thai Food
Thai Spice
   4433 W. Flamingo Rd., 702/362-5308
Lotus of Siam
   953 E. Sahara Ave., 702/735-4463

Best Vegetarian Food
Kathy's Ranch Market
   3455 E. Flamingo Rd., 702/434-8115
   6720 W. Sahara Ave., 702/253-7050

Standbys
Tony Roma's
620 E. Sahara Ave., 702/733-9914
200 Fremont St., 702/385-6257
International House of Pancakes
3111 W. Tropicana Ave., 702/736-3488
2210 Las Vegas Blvd. S., 702/384-6412
2490 Fremont St., 702/384-7881
3780 S. Maryland Pkwy., 702/737-0375
3595 S. Rainbow Blvd., 702/365-1004
6870 W. Cheyenne Ave., 702/656-3220
The Olive Garden
1545 E. Flamingo Rd., 702/735-0082
6850 W. Cheyenne Ave., 702/658-2144
1361 S. Decatur Blvd., 702/258-3453
Sizzler
2390 E. Bonanza Rd., 702/384-0038
307 S. Decatur Blvd., 702/878-1223
4901 S. Eastern Ave., 702/736-3120
3553 S. Rainbow Blvd., 702/227-0131
Red Lobster
200 S. Decatur Blvd., 702/877-0212
2325 E. Flamingo Rd., 702/731-0119
Ruth's Chris Steak House
3900 Paradise Rd., 702/791-7011
4561 W. Flamingo Rd., 702/248-7011

RENO, NV

Best Restaurant in Town
Christmas Tree Shops
20007 Mount Rose Hwy., 702/849-0127

Best All-You-Can-Eat Buffets
Silver Club Hotel and Casino
1040 Victorian Ave., Sparks, 702/358-4771
Clarion Hotel and Casino
3800 S. Virginia St., 702/825-4700
Eldorado Hotel
345 N. Virginia St., 702/786-5700

Best Atmosphere
Christmas Tree Shops
20007 Mount Rose Hwy., 702/849-0127

Best Breakfast
Sierra Sid Casino
200 N. McCarran Blvd., 702/359-0550

Best Burgers
Scooper's Drive-In
1356 Prater Way, Sparks, 702/331-6221
Juicy's Giant Hamburgers
301 S. Wells Ave., 702/322-2600
2900 Clearacre Ln., 702/329-5800

Best Casual Dining
Brew Brothers
Eldorado Hotel, 345 N. Virginia St., 702/786-5700

Best Fast Food
Scooper's Drive-In
1356 Prater Way, Sparks, 702/331-6221

Best Homestyle Food
Scooper's Drive-In
1356 Prater Way, Sparks, 702/331-6221

Best Italian Food
Two Guys From Italy
3501 S. Virginia St., 702/826-3700

Best Mexican Food
Mi Casa Too
2205 W. Fourth St., 702/323-6466
Pancho's Mexican Food
4550 S. Maryland Pkwy., 702/597-1515
3720 E. Sunset Rd., 702/898-8488

Best Microbrewery
Brew Brothers
Eldorado Hotel, 345 N. Virginia St., 702/786-5700

Best Salad/Salad Bar
Clarion Hotel and Casino
3800 S. Virginia St., 702/825-4700

Best Seafood
Clarion Hotel and Casino
3800 S. Virginia St., 702/825-4700

Best Steaks
Silver Club Hotel and Casino
1040 Victorian Ave., Sparks, 702/358-4771
Christmas Tree Shops
20007 Mount Rose Hwy., 702/849-0127

Best View While Dining
Eagle's Nest
472 Needlepeak Rd., Gardnerville, 702/588-6492
Christmas Tree Shops
20007 Mount Rose Hwy., 702/849-0127

SPARKS, NV

Best All-You-Can-Eat Buffet
Garden Buffet
Hwy. 50 at Stateline, Stateline, 702/588-2411

Best Breakfast
Craig's
430 N. McCarran Blvd., 702/331-2224

Best Burgers
Western Village Inn and Casino
815 Nichols Blvd., 702/331-1069

Best Cheap Meal
Plantation Station Casino
2121 Victorian Ave., 702/359-9440

Best Chinese Food
Rice Bowl Restaurant
950 Glendale Ave., 702/358-2198

Best Coffee
Western Village Inn and Casino
815 Nichols Blvd., 702/331-1069

Best Desserts
Garden Buffet
  Hwy. 50 at Stateline, Stateline, 702/588-2411
John Ascuaga's Nugget
  1100 Nugget Ave., 702/356-3300

Best Family Restaurant
Craig's
  430 N. McCarran Blvd., 702/331-2224

Best Homestyle Food
Craig's
  430 N. McCarran Blvd., 702/331-2224
Hugo's Rotisserie
  111 Country Club Dr., 702/832-3250
T's Rotisserie
  901 Tahoe Blvd., 702/831-2832

Best Places to Be "Seen"
John Ascuaga's Nugget
  1100 Nugget Ave., 702/356-3300
Trader Dick's
  Sparks Nugget Casino, 1100 Nugget Ave.,
    702/356-3300

Best Place to Eat When Someone Else Is Buying
Garden Buffet
  Hwy. 50 at Stateline, Stateline, 702/588-2411

Best Romantic Dining
Trader Dick's
  Sparks Nugget Casino, 1100 Nugget Ave.,
    702/356-3300

Best Seafood
Skipper's Seafood and Chowder
  2258 Oddie Blvd., 702/359-3474

Best Steaks
Garden Buffet
  Hwy. 50 at Stateline, Stateline, 702/588-2411
John Ascuaga's Nugget
  1100 Nugget Ave., 702/356-3300

Standbys
Sizzler
  615 E. Prater Way, 702/356-3969
Applebee's
  693 N. McCarran Blvd., 702/358-5811

WINNEMUCCA, NV

Best Barbecue/Ribs
Flyin' Pig Barbeque
  1100 W. Winnemucca Blvd., 702/623-4104

Best Breakfast
Griddle
  460 W. Winnemucca Blvd., 702/623-2977

Best Burgers
Dave's Dugout
  329 E. Winnemucca Blvd., 702/623-2763

Best Chinese Food
Chinese Garden
1061 W. Fourth St., 702/623-6777

Best Other Ethnic Food
Martin Hotel (Basque)
Melarkey and W. Railroad, 702/623-3197
Restaurante San Fermin (Basque)
485 W. Winnemucca Blvd., 702/625-2555

Best Seafood
Ormachea's Dinner House
180 Melarkey St., 702/623-3455

Best Steaks
Ormachea's Dinner House
180 Melarkey St., 702/623-3455
Winnemucca Hotel
95 N. Bridge St., 702/623-2908

Standbys
Pizza Hut
1692 W. Winnemucca Blvd., 702/623-5157
Subway
936 W. Winnemucca Blvd., 702/623-5515

N

New Hampshire

Best All-You-Can-Eat Buffet
Balsam's Grand Resort Hotel
 Rte. 26, Colebrook, 603/255-3400

Best Atmosphere
Birches
 128 Main St., Gorham, 603/466-5424
Balsam's Grand Resort Hotel
 Rte. 26, Colebrook, 603/255-3400

Best Breakfast
Wilford's
 117 Main St., Gorham, 603/466-2380
Loaf Around Bakery
 19 Exchange St., Gorham, 603/466-2706

Best Burgers
Mill Yard
 207 E. Mason St., 603/752-6430

Best Chinese Food
China Wok
 161 Main St., 603/752-1058

Best Desserts
Wilford's
 117 Main St., Gorham, 603/466-2380
Balsam's Grand Resort Hotel
 Rte. 26, Colebrook, 603/255-3400

Best Health-Conscious Menu
Loaf Around Bakery
 19 Exchange St., Gorham, 603/466-2706

Best Homestyle Food
Wilford's
 117 Main St., Gorham, 603/466-2380

Best Ice Cream/Yogurt
Northland Dairy Bar and Restaurant
 1808 Riverside Dr., 603/752-6210

Best Italian Food
La Bottega Saladino
 152 Main St., Gorham, 603/466-2520

N

Best Japanese Food
Yokohama Restaurant
  288 Main St., Gorham, 603/466-2501

Best Pizza
Mary's Pizza House
  9 Cascade Flat, Gorham, 603/752-6150

Best Place to Take the Kids
Northland Dairy Bar and Restaurant
  1808 Riverside Dr., 603/752-6210

Best Seafood
Northland Dairy Bar and Restaurant
  1808 Riverside Dr., 603/752-6210
Balsam's Grand Resort Hotel
  Rte. 26, Colebrook, 603/255-3400

Best Steaks
Town and Country Motor Inn
  Rte. 2, Gorham, 603/466-3315

CONCORD, NH

Best Cheap Meal
Capital City Diner
  25 Water St., 603/228-3463
Zeano's
  142 Loudon Rd., 603/224-2400

Best Chinese Food
Tea Garden Restaurant
  184 N. Main St., 603/228-4420

Best Diner
Capital City Diner
  25 Water St., 603/228-3463

Best Italian Food
Zeano's
  142 Loudon Rd., 603/224-2400

Best Mexican Food
Hermano's Cocina Mexicana
  6 Pleasant St. Ext., 603/224-5669

Best Pizza
Foodee's
  2 S. Main St., 603/224-2400

DOVER, NH

Best Restaurant in Town
Weathervane Restaurant
  2 Dover Point Rd., 603/749-2341

Best Breakfast
Charlotte's Copper Kettle
  499 Central Ave., 603/749-9383

Best Dinner
Weathervane Restaurant
  2 Dover Point Rd., 603/749-2341
Sixteen Third Street Restaurant
  16 Third St., 603/743-3767

Best Lunch
Ron's Place
2 Locust St., 603/749-4673

Best Place to Eat When Someone Else Is Buying
Ron's Place
2 Locust St., 603/749-4673

Best Seafood
Sixteen Third Street Restaurant
16 Third St., 603/743-3767

Best Sports Bar
Kick-Off
20 1/2 Chesnutt, 603/749-2890

Best Steaks
Woodsky's
887 Central Ave., 603/743-1811

KEENE, NH

Best Breakfast
Keene Bagel Works
120 Main St., 603/357-7751

Best Chinese Food
Imperial China
149 Emerald St., 603/357-0619

Best Coffee
Keene Bagel Works
120 Main St., 603/357-7751

Best Eclectic Menu
Mangos and Manners
39 Central Square, 603/357-1041

Best Family Restaurant
Papa Gino's
333 Winchester St., 603/352-9321

Best Ice Cream/Yogurt
Piazza
149 Main St., 603/352-5133

Best Italian Food
Martino's Spaghetti House
276 West St., 603/357-0859
Papa Gino's
333 Winchester St., 603/352-9321

Best Sandwiches
Brando's Deli
34 Washington St., 603/352-2434

LACONIA, NH

Best Atmosphere
B Mae's Eating and Drinking Establishment
Rural Route 11, Gilford, 603/293-4351
Mame's
Plymouth St., Meredith, 603/279-4631

Best Bars
B Mae's Eating and Drinking Establishment
Rural Route 11, Gilford, 603/293-4351

Mame's
  Plymouth St., Meredith, 603/279-4631

Best Barbecue/Ribs
JT's Bar-B-Q
  Rte. 3, 603/366-7322

Best Breakfast
Soda Shoppe
  Laconia Mall, 603/524-2366
Sunshine Coffee Shop
  311 Court St., 603/528-2277
Between the Bagel
  653 N. Main, 603/524-0193

Best Brunch
American Gourmet
  1429 Lake Shore Rd., Gilford, 603/524-5525
B Mae's Eating and Drinking Establishment
  Rural Route 11, Gilford, 603/293-4351

Best Burgers
JT's Bar-B-Q
  Rte. 3, 603/366-7322

Best Desserts
Fratello's Ristorante Italiano
  799 Union Ave., 603/528-2022
American Gourmet
  1429 Lake Shore Rd., Gilford, 603/524-5525

Best Family Restaurant
Mulligan's Restaurant
  Rural Route 3, Tilton, 603/528-4588

Best German Food
William Tell Inn
  Rural Route 11, 603/293-8803

Best Homestyle Food
Mulligan's Restaurant
  Rural Route 3, Tilton, 603/528-4588

Best Ice Cream/Yogurt
Soda Shoppe
  Laconia Mall, 603/524-2366
Sawyer's Dairy Bar
  Rte. 11, Gilford, 603/293-4422
Weeks Restaurant
  331 S. Main St., 603/524-4100

Best Italian Food
Fratello's Ristorante Italiano
  799 Union Ave., 603/528-2022

Best Pizza
Pizza Express
  4 Country Club Rd., 603/528-4200
Giuseppe's Show Time Pizzeria
  Rural Route 13, Daniel Webster Hwy., Meredith,
    603/279-3313

Best Romantic Dining
Oliver's Bakery and Restaurant
  Rural Route 3, Tilton, 603/286-7379

Best Salad/Salad Bar
Between the Bagel
653 N. Main, 603/524-0193

Best Sandwiches
Water Street Cafe
141 Water St., 603/524-4144

Best Seafood
Rigione's Galley
405 Union Ave., 603/524-0001
Weirs Veach Lobster Pound
Rural Route 3, 603/366-5713

Best Steaks
Blackstone's
76 Lake St., 603/524-7060
Hector's Fine Food and Spirits
Beacon St., 603/524-1009
Mame's
Plymouth St., Meredith, 603/279-4631

LEBANON, NH

Best Breakfast
Lou's Restaurant
30 S. Main St., Hanover, 603/643-3321

Best Chinese Food
Good Fortune Chinese Restaurant
45 Hanover St., 603/448-3888

Best Coffee
Bean Gallery
On the mall, 603/448-7302

Best Family Restaurants
Jesse's Restaurant
Lebanon Rd., Hanover, 603/643-4111
Riverside Grill Restaurant
65 Riverside Dr., 603/448-2571

Best Italian Food
Sweet Tomatoes Trattoria
1 Court St., 603/448-1711

Best Mexican Food
Shorty's Mexican Roadhouse
10 Benning St., Ste. 1, West Lebanon, 603/298-7200

Best Pizza
Lebanon Village Pizza
24 Hanover St., 603/448-2772

Best Sandwiches
Lebanon Village Pizza
24 Hanover St., 603/448-2772

Best Seafood
Weathervane Seafoods
Rte. 12A, West Lebanon, 603/298-7805

Best Steaks
Jesse's Restaurant
Lebanon Rd., Hanover, 603/643-4111

N

Standbys
Friendly's
Rte. 12A, West Lebanon, 603/298-7855

LITTLETON, NH

Best Restaurants in Town
Grand Depot Cafe
62 Cottage St., 603/444-5303
Tim-Bir Alley
Bethlehem Rd., Bethlehem, 603/444-6142

Best Atmosphere
Grand Depot Cafe
62 Cottage St., 603/444-5303
Tim-Bir Alley
Bethlehem Rd., Bethlehem, 603/444-6142

Best Breakfast
Coffee Pot
35 Main St., 603/444-5722

Best Coffee
Sunshine Bagel
19 Main St., 603/444-4090

Best Diners
Coffee Pot
35 Main St., 603/444-5722
Littleton Diner
170 Main St., 603/444-3994

Best Health-Conscious Menu
Cafe Munchies
Libson Rd., 603/444-1222

Best Homestyle Food
Littleton Diner
170 Main St., 603/444-3994

Best Ice Cream/Yogurt
Bishop's Ice Cream Shoppe
78 Cottage St., 603/444-6039

Best Pizza
Gold House of Pizza
84 Main St., 603/444-6190

Best Sandwiches
Cafe Munchies
Libson Rd., 603/444-1222

Best Seafood
Clam Shell Restaurant
Dells Rd., 603/444-6445

Best Steaks
Clam Shell Restaurant
Dells Rd., 603/444-6445

MANCHESTER, NH

Best Restaurant in Town
Yard Restaurant
S. Willow St., 603/623-3545

Best All-You-Can-Eat Buffet
Yard Restaurant
  S. Willow St., 603/623-3545

Best American Food
Back Room Restaurant
  245 Hooksett Rd., 603/669-6890
High Five Restaurant
  555 Canal St., 603/626-0555

Best Bagels
Bagel Works
  581 Second St., 603/647-6560

Best Breakfast
Yard Restaurant
  S. Willow St., 603/623-3545
Albee's on Amherst
  36 Amherst St., 603/623-6907
  15 Pearl St., 603/622-9015

Best Brunch
Yard Restaurant
  S. Willow St., 603/623-3545

Best Business Lunch
Aloha Restaurant
  901 Hanover St., 603/647-2100

Best Chinese Food
Aloha Restaurant
  901 Hanover St., 603/647-2100
Chen Yang Li
  124 S. River Rd., Bedford, 603/641-6922

Best Delicatessen
Albee's on Amherst
  36 Amherst St., 603/623-6907
  15 Pearl St., 603/622-9015

Best Dinner
Back Room Restaurant
  245 Hooksett Rd., 603/669-6890

Best Health-Conscious Menu
Sassafras
  90 Dow St., 603/641-1862

Best Italian Food
Cafe Pavone
  75 Arms Park Dr., 603/622-5488

Best Lunch
High Five Restaurant
  555 Canal St., 603/626-0555

Best Pizza
Luisa's Italian Pizzeria
  313 Lincoln St., 603/644-5559
  673 Hooksett Rd., 603/625-1331

Best Salad/Salad Bar
Yard Restaurant
  S. Willow St., 603/623-3545
Sassafras
  90 Dow St., 603/641-1862

N

Best Sandwiches
Albee's on Amherst
  36 Amherst St., 603/623-6907
  15 Pearl St., 603/622-9015

Best Seafood
Homestead
  176 Mammoth Rd., Londonderry, 603/437-2022

Best Steaks
Yard Restaurant
  S. Willow St., 603/623-3545
Homestead
  176 Mammoth Rd., Londonderry, 603/437-2022
Back Room Restaurant
  245 Hooksett Rd., 603/669-6890

PORTSMOUTH, NH

Best Atmosphere
Dunfey's Aboard the John Wannamaker
  1 Harbor Pl., 603/433-3111

Best Breakfast
Golden Egg
  967 Sagamore Ave., 603/436-0519

Best Brunch
Molly Malone's Restaurant
  177 State St., 603/433-7233

Best Burgers
Blue Mermaid
  The Hill, 603/427-2583

Best Health-Conscious Menu
Belle Peppers
  41 Congress, 603/427-2504
Stockpot
  53 Bow St., 603/431-1851

Best Other Ethnic Food
Blue Mermaid (Caribbean)
  The Hill, 603/427-2583

Best Pizza
Portsmouth Gas Light Company
  64 Market St., 603/430-9122

Best Salad/Salad Bar
Belle Peppers
  41 Congress, 603/427-2504

Best Sandwiches
Belle Peppers
  41 Congress, 603/427-2504

Best Seafood
Old Ferry Landing
  10 Ceres St., 603/431-5510
Ron's Beach House
  965 Ocean Blvd., Hampton, 603/926-1870

Best Steaks
Hurricane Restaurant
  Perkins Cove, Ogunquit, 207/646-6348

Ron's Beach House
  965 Ocean Blvd., Hampton, 603/926-1870

Best Vegetarian Food
Stockpot
  53 Bow St., 603/431-1851

Best View While Dining
Dunfey's Aboard the John Wannamaker
  1 Harbor Pl., 603/433-3111

Standbys
Ben and Jerry's
  367 Ocean Blvd., Hampton Beach, 603/926-8023
Friendly's
  2456 Lafayette Rd., 603/436-0324

SALEM, NH

Best Atmosphere
Millstone Manor
  43 Pelham Rd., 603/898-1918

Best Breakfast
Archie's Drive-In
  416 Emerson Ave., Hampstead, 603/329-5337

Best Brunch
Samantha's Restaurant
  122 Main St., 603/898-2283

Best Burgers
Archie's Drive-In
  416 Emerson Ave., Hampstead, 603/329-5337

Best Cheap Meal
Archie's Drive-In
  416 Emerson Ave., Hampstead, 603/329-5337

Best Coffee
Barnes and Noble
  125 S. Broadway, 603/898-1930
AntiquiTeas
  88 N. Broadway, 603/893-7337

Best Continental Food
Promises To Keep
  199 Rockingham Rd., Derry, 603/432-1559

Best Desserts
Millstone Manor
  43 Pelham Rd., 603/898-1918
AntiquiTeas
  88 N. Broadway, 603/893-7337

Best Health-Conscious Menu
Willow Tree
  327 S. Broadway, 603/898-5206

Best Ice Cream/Yogurt
Findeisen's Ice Cream
  125B S. Broadway, 603/898-5411

Best Middle Eastern Food
Samantha's Restaurant
  122 Main St., 603/898-2283

N

683

Best Pizza
Salem House of Pizza
  115A Main St., 603/893-5250

Best Places to Eat When Someone Else Is Buying
Promises To Keep
  199 Rockingham Rd., Derry, 603/432-1559
Millstone Manor
  43 Pelham Rd., 603/898-1918

Best Seafood
Weathervane Seafoods
  41 S. Broadway, 603/893-6269

Best Steaks
T-Bones Great American Eatery
  311 S. Broadway, 603/893-3444

N

New Jersey

Best Bagels
Lox, Stock and Bagels
  6433 Ventnor Ave., Ventnor, 609/822-8621

Best Bars
Deauville Inn
  Willard Dr. at Bay Dr., Strathmere, 609/263-2080
Gregory's
  900 Shore Rd., Somers Point, 609/927-6665
Irish Pub
  164 S. St. James Pl., 609/344-9063
Maynard's
  9306 Amherst Ave., Margate, 609/822-8423
The Oceanfront
  1400 Ocean Ave., Brigantine, 609/266-7731

Best Barbecue/Ribs
H.I. Rib and Company
  6613 Black Horse Pike, Pleasantville, 609/272-0885

Best Burgers
Point Pub
  Somers Point Shopping Ctr., Rte. 9, Somers Point,
    609/927-1522

Best Casual Dining
Dino's Subs and Pizza
  8016 Ventnor Ave., Margate, 609/822-6602

Best Chinese Food
Billy Ho's Imperial East
  7800 Ventnor Ave., Margate, 609/487-1040

Best Delicatessen
Downbeach Deli
  9210 Ventnor Ave., Margate, 609/823-7310

Best Diner
Shore Diner
  1140 Tilton Rd., Pleasantville, 609/641-3669

Best Eclectic Menu
Melissa's Bistro Fare
  9307 Ventnor Ave., Margate, 609/823-1414

N

Best German Food
Dutchman's Brauhaus
2500 E. Bay Ave., Beach Haven, 609/494-6910

Best Ice Cream/Yogurt
Tory's
3308 Ashbury Ave., Ocean City, 609/391-7933

Best Late-Night Food
Tony's Baltimore Grille
2800 Atlantic Ave., 609/345-5766

Best New Restaurant
Casa Bari
Central Square, Linwood, 609/653-6800

Best Pizza
Mack and Manco
758 Boardwalk, Ocean City, 609/399-2738
920 Boardwalk, Ocean City, 609/398-0720
Tom Quirk's
7309 Ventnor Ave., Ventnor, 609/822-6656

Best Romantic Dining
Green Gables
212 Centre St., Beach Haven, 609/492-3553
Hatteras Coastal Cuisine
801 Bay Ave., Somers Point, 609/926-3326

Best Sandwiches
Atlantic City Sub Shops
4 Heather Croft Sq., Pleasantville, 609/646-7799
Rte. 9 at Bethel Rd., Somers Point, 609/653-8181
307 N. Dorset Ave., Ventnor City, 609/823-9393
The Cheese Board
23 Central Sq., Linwood, 609/653-8088
White House Sub Shop
2301 Arctic Ave., 609/345-1564

Best Sushi
Tokyo Palace
135 Somers Point Blvd., Longport, 609/927-8650

Best Wine Selection
Angeloni's II
2400 Arctic Ave., 609/344-7875

BRIDGETON, NJ

Best Restaurants in Town
Benjamin's Restaurant
101 Commerce St. E., 609/451-6449
Ship John Inn
Pier at Market St., Greenwich, 609/451-1444

Best American Food
Benjamin's Restaurant
101 Commerce St. E., 609/451-6449

Best Bar
The Coach Room
59 Broad St. W., 609/451-0041

Best Breakfast
Westwood Restaurant
4 Townsend Ave., 609/451-6904

Best Greek/Mediterranean Food
Golden Pigeon
36 Landis Ave., 609/451-0940

Best Italian Food
Vito's Restaurant
2 West Ave., 609/451-2007

Best Lunch
Country Rose Restaurant
97 Trench Rd., 609/455-9294

Best Mexican Food
La Movida
125 E. Commerce, 609/453-0943

Best Seafood
Tinker's Seafood
17 Landis Ave., 609/455-1700
Ship John Inn
Pier at Market St., Greenwich, 609/451-1444

BRIDGEWATER, NJ

Best Bar
Green Knoll Grill
645 Hwy. 202-206N, 908/526-7090

Best Delicatessen
Steck's
325 Hwy. 202/206, 908/685-9587

Best Italian Food
La Cuchina
125 W. Main, Summerville, 908/526-4907
La Veranda
701 Lincoln Blvd., Middlesex, 908/302-1333

Standbys
Friday's
395 Hwy. 202/206, 908/707-1991
Lone Star Steakhouse
970 Hwy. 22, 908/526-8177

CHERRY HILL, NJ

Best Burgers
Champs Americana
25 Rte. 73 S, Marlton, 609/985-9333

Best Chinese Food
China Jade
450 E. Hwy. 70, 609/795-6668
Empress of China
1871 Rte. 70E, 609/424-4223

Best Coffee
Viennese Cafe and Pastry Shop
1442 Marlton Pike E., 609/795-0172

Best Continental Food
Viennese Cafe and Pastry Shop
1442 Marlton Pike E., 609/795-0172

Best Desserts
Viennese Cafe and Pastry Shop
1442 Marlton Pike E., 609/795-0172

N

Best Greek/Mediterranean Food
Athens Cafe Restaurant
1030 Marlton Pike W., 609/429-1061

Best Italian Food
Pastavino
124 E. Kings Hwy., Maple Shade, 609/727-1001
Lamberti Restaurant
1491 Brace Rd., 609/354-1157
Italian Bistro
1008 Astoria Blvd., 609/751-3300

Best Pizza
King of Pizza
2300 Rte. 70W, 609/665-9688

Best Sandwiches
Lou and Ann's Delicatessen
257 Rte. 70E, 609/795-2307
Chick's Deli
906 Township Ln., 609/429-2022

Best Seafood
Hideaway
63 Kresson Rd., 609/428-7379
Ponzio's Kingsway Diner
7 Rte. 70W, 609/428-4808
Steak 38 Cafe and Raw Bar
515 Rte. 38, 609/665-4090

Best Steaks
Ponzio's Kingsway Diner
7 Rte. 70W, 609/428-4808
Steak 38 Cafe and Raw Bar
515 Rte. 38, 609/665-4090

CRANFORD, NJ

Best Restaurant in Town
Cranford Hotel
1 S. Union Ave., 908/276-2121

Best Breakfast
Cranford Restaurant
7 North Ave. E., 908/272-2800

Best Burgers
The Office
1-7 South Ave., 908/272-3888

Best Dinner
Coach and Four Restaurant
24 North Ave. E., 908/276-3664

Best Homestyle Food
Margie's Place
27 N. Union Ave., 908/272-6336

Best Italian Food
Cortina Restaurant
28 North Ave., 908/276-5749

Best Lunch
Cranford Hotel
1 S. Union Ave., 908/276-2121

Best Seafood
Dennis Foy's Townsquare
6 Roosevelt Ave., Chatham, 201/701-0303

Best Steaks
The Office
1-7 South Ave., 908/272-3888

EAST BRUNSWICK, NJ

Best Restaurant in Town
La Fontana Restaurant
120 Albany St., New Brunswick, 908/249-7500

Best Breakfast
Colonial Diner
560 State Rte. 18, 908/254-4858

Best Business Lunch
Stuff Yer Face
1050 State Rte. 18, 908/257-2666

Best Cajun/Creole Food
Old Bay Restaurant
61 Church St., New Brunswick, 908/246-3114

Best Casual Dining
Colonial Diner
560 State Rte. 18, 908/254-4858

Best Diner
Colonial Diner
560 State Rte. 18, 908/254-4858

Best Italian Food
La Fontana Restaurant
120 Albany St., New Brunswick, 908/249-7500
Trattoria Moderna
593 State Rte. 18, 908/651-7737

Best Japanese Food
Sapporo Sushi and Steak House
375 George St., New Brunswick, 908/828-3888

Best Salad/Salad Bar
Stuff Yer Face
1050 State Rte. 18, 908/257-2666

Best Sandwiches
Stuff Yer Face
1050 State Rte. 18, 908/257-2666

Standbys
Outback Steakhouse
481 Hwy. 1, Edison, 908/819-0990
Red Lobster
750 State Rte. 18, 908/238-4810

ENGLEWOOD, NJ

Best Burgers
Midway Tavern
250 N. Washington Ave., Bergenfield, 201/385-8556

Best Chinese Food
Sally Ling's
1636 Palisade Ave., Fort Lee, 201/346-1282

N

Best Continental Food
Jamie's
574 Sylvan Ave., Englewood Cliffs, 201/568-4244
Wagon Wheel Restaurant
16 S. Front St., Bergenfield, 201/384-9464

Best Diner
Matthews Colonial Diner
430 S. Washington Ave., Bergenfield, 201/385-9496

Best Dinner
Cellar Bar and Grill
47 Legion Dr., Bergenfield, 201/385-5781

Best French Food
Chez Madeleine Restaurant
4 Bedford Ave., Bergenfield, 201/384-7637
La Petite Auberge
44 E. Madison Ave., Cresskill, 201/569-2270

Best Italian Food
Marcello and Dino Roman Cafe
12 Tappan Rd., Harrington Park, 201/767-4245
Michel's Ristorante
126 Engle St., Englewood, 201/871-1133
Villa Cortina
18 Piermont Rd., Tenafly, 201/567-6477
Wagon Wheel Restaurant
16 S. Front St., Bergenfield, 201/384-9464

Best Japanese Food
Alpine Shinwa
385 Rte. 9W, Alpine, 201/767-6322

Best Mexican Food
Mexicali Blues
665 Cedar Ln., Teaneck, 201/836-7161

Best Other Ethnic Food
Sam's Restaurant (Provencal)
41 Union Ave., Cresskill, 201/569-0556

Best Pizza
Nick's Pizza
44 W. Main St., Bergenfield, 201/385-9240

Best Spanish Food
Meson Madrid
343 Bergen Blvd., Palisades Park, 201/947-1038

Best Sports Bar
A's Rock and Sport Club
260 S. Washington Ave., Bergenfield, 201/384-3040

HILLSIDE, NJ

Best Restaurant in Town
New Blue Ribbon Restaurant
256 Hollywood Ave., 908/965-0300

Best American Food
New Blue Ribbon Restaurant
256 Hollywood Ave., 908/965-0300

Best Breakfast
Bagel Masters
1147 Liberty Ave., 908/527-8433

Best Italian Food
Alfonso's Seafood and Steak
   310 Hillside Ave., 908/688-8919

Best Pizza
M and M II Pizzeria
   1271 Liberty Ave., 201/923-0800

Best Seafood
Chenille's Seafood House
   114 Liberty Ave., 908/352-5234

HOBOKEN, NJ

Best Restaurant in Town
Baja Mexican Cuisine
   104 Fourteenth St., 201/653-0610

Best American Food
Lady Jane's Restaurant
   51 Fourteenth St., 201/659-9390
Park Cafe
   746 Park Ave., 201/659-0144
Onieal's Restaurant and Bar
   341 Park Ave., 201/653-9388
The Supper Club
   2 Hudson Pl., 201/222-6500
O'Donoghue's on First
   205 First St., 201/798-7711

Best Bars
Moran's
   501 Garden St., 201/795-2025
O'Donoghue's on First
   205 First St., 201/798-7711
Onieal's Restaurant and Bar
   341 Park Ave., 201/653-9388

Best Casual Dining
Benny Tudino's Pizzeria
   622 Washington St., 201/792-4132

Best Chinese Food
Front Page Chinese Cuisine
   1120 Washington St., 201/653-5676

Best Continental Food
Baja Mexican Cuisine
   104 Fourteenth St., 201/653-0610
Lady Jane's Restaurant
   51 Fourteenth St., 201/659-9390

Best Dinner
Baja Mexican Cuisine
   104 Fourteenth St., 201/653-0610
Onieal's Restaurant and Bar
   341 Park Ave., 201/653-9388

Best Family Restaurant
Leo's Grandevous
   200 Grand St., 201/659-9467

Best Italian Food
M and P Bianca Mano
   1116 Washington St., 201/795-0274

N

Leo's Grandevous
  200 Grand St., 201/659-9467
Ricco's Ristorante
  1024 Washington St., 201/792-5956

Best Mexican Food
Baja Mexican Cuisine
  104 Fourteenth St., 201/653-0610

Best Pizza
Benny Tudino's Pizzeria
  622 Washington St., 201/792-4132

Best Seafood
Onieal's Restaurant and Bar
  341 Park Ave., 201/653-9388

JERSEY CITY, NJ

Best Restaurant in Town
Casino-in-the-Park
  Lincoln Park, 201/333-1045

Best American Food
Casino-in-the-Park
  Lincoln Park, 201/333-1045
Moochie's Bistro
  516 Jersey Ave., 201/333-8343
VIP Diner Restaurant
  175 Sip Ave., 201/792-1400

Best Bar
Moochie's Bistro
  516 Jersey Ave., 201/333-8343

Best Breakfast
Colonette Restaurant
  405 State Rte. 440, 201/432-8222

Best Business Lunch
Rosie Radigan's
  10 Exchange Pl., 201/451-5566
VIP Diner Restaurant
  175 Sip Ave., 201/792-1400

Best Casual Dining
Moochie's Bistro
  516 Jersey Ave., 201/333-8343

Best Cheap Meal
Laico's Restaurant
  67 Terhune Ave., 201/434-4115

Best Chinese Food
Canton Tea Garden
  920 Bergen Ave., 201/653-4728

Best Diner
Colonette Restaurant
  405 State Rte. 440, 201/432-8222

Best Dinner
Lisbon Restaurant
  256 Warren St., 201/432-9222
VIP Diner Restaurant
  175 Sip Ave., 201/792-1400

Best Italian Food
Casa Dante Restaurant
737 Newark Ave., 201/795-2750
Laico's Restaurant
67 Terhune Ave., 201/434-4115
Puccini's Restaurant
1064 W. Side Ave., 201/432-4111

Best Seafood
Lincoln Inn
13 Lincoln St., 201/659-8686

Best Spanish Food
Lisbon Restaurant
256 Warren St., 201/432-9222

Best Steaks
Lincoln Inn
13 Lincoln St., 201/659-8686

KEARNY, NJ

Best Restaurant in Town
Torremolino's Restaurant
188 Midland Ave., 201/991-1849

Best Diner
Top's Diner
500 Passaic Ave., Harrison, 201/481-0490
Arlington Diner
1 River Rd., North Arlington, 201/998-6262

Best Family Restaurant
Eagan's Restaurant
440 Belleville Turnpike, North Arlington,
201/991-8167

Best Other Ethnic Food
Argyle Fish and Chip Restaurant (English)
212 Kearny Ave., 201/991-3900
Torremolino's Restaurant (Portuguese)
188 Midland Ave., 201/991-1849

Best Pizza
Pete's Place
934 Passaic Ave., 201/998-0488

LIVINGSTON, NJ

Best American Food
Don's Restaurant
650 S. Orange Ave., 201/992-4010

Best Breakfast
Ritz Diner
72 E. Mount Pleasant Ave., 201/533-1213

Best Burgers
Don's Restaurant
650 S. Orange Ave., 201/992-4010

Best Chinese Food
North Sea Village Cuisine
28 N. Livingston Ave., 201/992-7056

N

Best Diner
Ritz Diner
72 E. Mount Pleasant Ave., 201/533-1213

Best Family Restaurant
Don's Restaurant
650 S. Orange Ave., 201/992-4010

Best Italian Food
Nero's Restaurant and Lounge
618 S. Livingston Ave., 201/994-1410
Porto Bella
62 W. Mount Pleasant Ave., 201/992-1185

Best Pizza
Panevino Ristorante
637 W. Mount Pleasant Ave., 201/535-6160

LONG BRANCH, NJ

Best Barbecue/Ribs
Memphis Pig Out
67 First Ave., Atlantic Highlands, 908/291-5533

Best Brunch
Pleasure Bay
1 Ocean Blvd., 908/571-4000

Best Burgers
Sitting Duck
104 Myrtle Ave., 908/229-5566
Pour House
640 Shrewsbury Ave., Red Bank, 908/842-4337

Best Coffee
No Ordinary Joe
51 Broad St., Red Bank, 908/530-4040
Inkwell
665 Second Ave., 908/222-6886

Best Desserts
Pleasure Bay
1 Ocean Blvd., 908/571-4000

Best Ice Cream/Yogurt
Scoops Old Fashioned Ice Cream
50 Monmouth Rd., Oakhurst, 908/229-6266

Best Italian Food
Tuzzio's Italian Cuisine
224 Westwood Ave., 908/222-9614

Best Mexican Food
Casa Comida Mexican Restaurant
336 Branchport Ave., 908/229-7774

Best Pizza
Tony's
228 Morris Ave., 908/222-3535
Bertucci's Brick Oven Pizzeria
1910 State Hwy. 35, Ocean, 908/663-0200
Guidetti's Pizzeria and Subs
15 Memorial Pkwy., 908/222-0504
Freddie's Pizzeria
563 Broadway, 908/222-0931

Best Place to Eat When Someone Else Is Buying
Mumford Restaurant
    45 Atlantic Ave., 908/222-2657

Best Sandwiches
Primavera's Italian Specialty
    140 Brighton Ave., 908/229-1518

Best Seafood
Pleasure Bay
    1 Ocean Blvd., 908/571-4000
Doris and Ed's Seafood Restaurant
    348 Shore Dr., Highlands, 908/872-1565

Best Steaks
What's Your Beef
    21 W. River Rd., Rumson, 908/842-6205

Standbys
Perkins
    444 Ursula Plaza Shopping Ctr., 908/222-1206

MAYS LANDING, NJ

Best Happy Hour Snacks
Great American Pub and Grille
    Hamilton Shopping Center, 4403 W. Black Horse
        Pike, Ste. 165, 609/625-9500

Best Italian Food
Maplewood II
    6126 Black Horse Pike, 609/625-1181

Best Romantic Dining
Cousin's Country House
    3373 Bargaintown Rd., Egg Harbor Township,
        609/927-5777
Inn at Sugar Hill
    5704 Somers Point Rd., 609/625-2226

N

MONTCLAIR, NJ

Best French Food
Yves
    30 S. Fullerton Ave., 201/744-8282

Best Italian Food
Angelo's
    263 Ridge Rd., Rte. 17S, Lyndhurst, 201/939-1922
Il Tulipano
    1131 Pompton Ave., Cedar Grove, 201/256-9300
La Fontanella Ristorante
    1640 Broad St., Bloomfield, 201/893-0188

NEWARK, NJ

Best Restaurant in Town
Il Tulipano Restaurant
    1131 Pompton Ave., Cedar Grove, 201/256-9300

Best All-You-Can-Eat Buffet
Manor
    111 Prospect Ave., West Orange, 201/731-2360

American Food

ta
te. 17S, Woodridge, 201/939-5409
ayfair Farms
481 Eagle Rock Ave., West Orange, 201/731-4300

Best Asian Restaurant
Lee's Hawaiian Islander
768 Stuyvesant Ave., Lyndhurst, 201/939-3777

Best Chinese Food
Jade Fountain Restaurant
602 Ridge Rd., North Arlington, 201/991-5377

Best Dinner
Mayfair Farms
481 Eagle Rock Ave., West Orange, 201/731-4300
Michael Angelo's Restaurant
544 Bloomfield Ave., 201/485-9057
Pal's Cabin Restaurant
265 Prospect Ave., West Orange, 201/731-4000
La Riviera Trattoria
421 Piaget Ave., Clifton, 201/478-4181

Best French Food
Yves
30 S. Fullerton Ave., Montclair, 201/744-8282

Best Italian Food
Giovanni's Place
537 Bloomfield Ave., 201/484-0894
Michael Angelo's Restaurant
544 Bloomfield Ave., 201/485-9057
Michelle Restaurant
694 Summer Ave., 201/268-1144
Vesuvius Restaurant
501 Bloomfield Ave., 201/485-2878
La Riviera Trattoria
421 Piaget Ave., Clifton, 201/478-4181

Best Lunch
Pal's Cabin Restaurant
265 Prospect Ave., West Orange, 201/731-4000

Best Seafood
Manor
111 Prospect Ave., West Orange, 201/731-2360

NEW BRUNSWICK, NJ

Best Restaurants in Town
Panico's
103 Church St., 908/545-6100
Stage Left, An American Cafe
5 Livingston Ave., 908/828-4444

Best Bar
Old Man Rafferty's
106 Albany St., 908/846-6153

Best Business Lunch
Zia Grill
19 Dennis St., 908/249-1551
Two Albany Restaurant
2 Albany St., 908/873-6600

Old Bay Restaurant
  61 Church St., 908/246-3114

Best Cajun/Creole Food
Old Bay Restaurant
  61 Church St., 908/246-3114

Best Casual Dining
Church Street Trattoria
  94 Church St., 908/828-4355
Stuff Yer Face
  49 Easton Ave., 908/247-1727
Old Man Rafferty's
  106 Albany St., 908/846-6153

Best Continental Food
Frog and the Peach
  29 Dennis St., 908/846-3216

Best Eclectic Menu
Frog and the Peach
  29 Dennis St., 908/846-3216
Stage Left, An American Cafe
  5 Livingston Ave., 908/828-4444

Best Italian Food
Church Street Trattoria
  94 Church St., 908/828-4355
Panico's
  103 Church St., 908/545-6100
La Fontana Restaurant
  120 Albany St., 908/249-7500

Best Japanese Food
Sapporo Sushi and Steak House
  375 George St., 908/828-3888

Best Other Ethnic Food
JP Lee's Restaurant (Mongolian)
  1 Penn Plz., 908/828-3337

Best Pizza
Stuff Yer Face
  49 Easton Ave., 908/247-1727

Best Places to Eat When Someone Else Is Buying
La Fontana Restaurant
  120 Albany St., 908/249-7500
Stage Left, An American Cafe
  5 Livingston Ave., 908/828-4444

Best Southwestern Food
Zia Grill
  19 Dennis St., 908/249-1551

NORTH BERGEN, NJ

Best American Food
Amanda's
  908 Washington St., Hoboken, 201/798-0101

Best Chinese Food
Phoenix Garden Too
  88 Rte. 46W, Ridgefield, 201/313-0088

N

Best French Food
Cafe de Paris
555 Anderson Ave., Cliffside Park, 201/945-6998

Best Other Ethnic Food
Il Villaggio (Neapolitan)
651 Rte. 17S, Carlstadt, 201/935-7733

Best Seafood
Arthur's Landing
Port Imperial at Pershing Circle, Weehawken,
201/867-0777
River Palm Terrace
1416 River Rd., Edgewater, 201/224-2013

Best Spanish Food
Segovia
150 Moonachie Rd., Moonachie, 201/641-4266

Best Steaks
River Palm Terrace
1416 River Rd., Edgewater, 201/224-2013

PARAMUS, NJ

Best Restaurant in Town
The Office
3234 Chestnut St., Ridgewood, 201/652-1070

Best American Food
Freelance Cafe and Wine Bar
506 Piermont Ave., Piermont, 914/365-3250
Smith Brothers Dining Saloon
51 N. Broad St., Ridgewood, 201/444-8111

Best Bar
The Office
3234 Chestnut St., Ridgewood, 201/652-1070

Best Breakfast
Daily Treat Restaurant
177 E. Ridgewood Ave., Ridgewood, 201/652-9113

Best Chinese Food
Mai Wei
306 Saddle River Rd., Monsey, 914/356-5522

Best Family Restaurant
Daily Treat Restaurant
177 E. Ridgewood Ave., Ridgewood, 201/652-9113

Best French Food
Saddle River Inn
2 Barnstable Ct., Saddle River, 201/825-4016

Best Indian Food
Kailash Indo-Thai Cuisine
22 Oak St., Ridgewood, 201/251-9693

Best Italian Food
Fratelli's
119 E. Ridgewood Ave., Ridgewood, 201/447-9377
Natalie's
20 E. Ridgewood Ave., Ridgewood, 201/444-7887
Tuscany in the Park
650 From Rd., 201/986-0200

Valentino's
103 Spring Valley Rd., Ridgewood, 201/391-2230

Best Korean Food
Koreana
Mall at IV, Rte. 4W, 201/487-8558

Best Seafood
Pier 17
464 Rte. 17N, 201/967-1079

Best Thai Food
Kailash Indo-Thai Cuisine
22 Oak St., Ridgewood, 201/251-9693

PASSAIC, NJ

Best American Food
Mario's Restaurant and Pizzeria
710 Van Houten Ave., Clifton, 201/777-1559

Best Asian Restaurant
Lee's Hawaiian Islander
635 Lexington Ave., Clifton, 201/578-1977

Best Breakfast
Oasis Restaurant
683 Main Ave., 201/773-7474
Lenny Cohen's Deli
210 Washington Pl., 201/779-1403
Tick-Tock Diner
281 Allwood Rd., Clifton, 201/777-0511

Best Burgers
White Castle
1341 Main Ave., Clifton, 201/772-0335

Best Chinese Food
Chin See Gardens
603 Main Ave., 201/773-8627
China Garden Restaurant
306 Main Ave., Clifton, 201/773-7633

Best Delicatessen
Lenny Cohen's Deli
210 Washington Pl., 201/779-1403

Best Diners
Oasis Restaurant
683 Main Ave., 201/773-7474
Candlewood Diner
179 Patterson Ave., East Rutherford, 201/933-4446

Best Homestyle Food
Oasis Restaurant
683 Main Ave., 201/773-7474

Best Italian Food
Mario's Restaurant and Pizzeria
710 Van Houten Ave., Clifton, 201/777-1559
El Rodeo Restaurant
570 Main Ave., 201/773-4676

Best Lunch
Tick-Tock Diner
281 Allwood Rd., Clifton, 201/777-0511

N

Best Pizza
Bruno's Pizza and Restaurant
  1006 Hwy. 46, Clifton, 201/473-3339

Best Sandwiches
Lenny Cohen's Deli
  210 Washington Pl., 201/779-1403

Best Seafood
Sevilla Restaurant
  505 Main Ave., 201/777-5827
North American Lobster Company
  1555 Hwy. 46, Parsippany, 201/263-5500

Best Spanish Food
Sevilla Restaurant
  505 Main Ave., 201/777-5827
El Rodeo Restaurant
  570 Main Ave., 201/773-4676

Standbys
Friendly's
  156 Main Ave., 201/778-2553

PATERSON, NJ

Best Restaurants in Town
Branda's Restaurant
  6-09 Fair Lawn Ave., Fair Lawn, 201/797-6767
Good Fellas Ristorante and Bar
  661 Midland Ave., Garfield, 201/478-4000

Best American Food
Firehouse Family Restaurant
  42 Plauderville Ave., Garfield, 201/478-8900
Rosemary and Sage
  26 Hamburg Turnpike, Riverdale, 201/616-0606

Best Atmosphere
Firehouse Family Restaurant
  42 Plauderville Ave., Garfield, 201/478-8900

Best Breakfast
Empress Restaurant of Fair Lawn
  13-48 River Rd., Fair Lawn, 201/791-2895

Best Casual Dining
Sidewinder's
  279 Passaic St., Garfield, 201/778-7500

Best Continental Food
Branda's Restaurant
  6-09 Fair Lawn Ave., Fair Lawn, 201/797-6767

Best Diners
Empress Restaurant of Fair Lawn
  13-48 River Rd., Fair Lawn, 201/791-2895
Land and Sea Restaurant
  20-12 Fair Lawn Ave., Fair Lawn, 201/794-7240
  39-10 Broadway, Fair Lawn, 201/791-1936

Best Dinner
River Palm Terrace
  41-11 Rte. 4, Fair Lawn, 201/703-3500

Best Family Restaurants
Firehouse Family Restaurant
    42 Plauderville Ave., Garfield, 201/478-8900
Rivara's Grill House
    6-18 Maple Ave., Fair Lawn, 201/797-4878

Best Fast Food
Jimmy Jim's Grill
    399 Midland Ave., Garfield, 201/772-6953

Best French Food
Claude's Ho-Ho-Kus Inn
    E. Franklin Turnpike at Sheridan Ave., Ho-Ho-Kus,
        201/445-4115
Porquois Pas?
    6 Sycamore Ave., Ho-Ho-Kus, 201/251-8008

Best Italian Food
Aldo's
    393 Franklin Ave., Wyckoff, 201/891-2618
Barcelona's
    38 Harrison Ave., Garfield, 201/772-6960
Benedetto's
    4 Garfield Ave., Hawthorne, 201/423-0044
La Gardenia
    2410 Hamburg Turnpike, Wayne, 201/835-3585
Michele's Italian Restaurant
    32 Passaic St., Garfield, 201/365-9660
The Picola Italia
    14-13 Plaza Rd., Fair Lawn, 201/797-2510
Branda's Restaurant
    6-09 Fair Lawn Ave., Fair Lawn, 201/797-6767
Pip's
    226 McArthur Ave., Garfield, 201/478-0414
Via Forcella
    5 Sicomac Rd., North Haledon, 201/423-4420

Best Lunch
New Your Place
    7-07 Fair Lawn Ave., Fair Lawn, 201/796-8523

Best Other Ethnic Food
Pescador Restaurant (Spanish/Portuguese)
    1 Passaic St., Garfield, 201/472-0503

Best Place to Eat When Someone Else Is Buying
Good Fellas Ristorante and Bar
    661 Midland Ave., Garfield, 201/478-4000

Best Seafood
Sea Shack
    293 Polifly Rd., 201/489-7232

Best Southwestern Food
Sidewinder's
    279 Passaic St., Garfield, 201/478-0414

PRINCETON, NJ

Best Bar
Triumph's Brewery
    138 Nassau St., 609/924-7855
Annex Restaurant
    128 1/2 Nassau St., 609/921-7555

Best Breakfast
Carousel Luncheonette
  260 N. Nassau St., 609/924-2677
P.J.'s Pancake House Restaurant
  154 Nassau St., 609/924-1353
Harry's Luncheonette
  16 1/2 Witherspoon St., 609/921-9769

Best Burgers
J.B. Winberie Restaurant and Bar
  1 Palmer Sq., 609/921-0700

Best Chinese Food
Sunny Garden
  15 Farber Rd., West Windsor, 609/520-1881
Y.Y. Doodles
  260 Nassau St., 609/252-0663

Best Coffee
Small World Coffee
  14 Witherspoon Ln., 609/924-4377

Best Diner
Harry's Luncheonette
  16 1/2 Witherspoon St., 609/921-9769

Best Eclectic Menu
Le Plumet Royal Peacock Inn
  20 Bayard Ln., 609/921-0050

Best French Food
Lahiere's Restaurant
  5 Witherspoon St., 609/921-2798
Le Plumet Royal
  Peacock Inn, 20 Bayard Ln., 609/921-0050

Best Homestyle Food
Downtown Deluxe
  48 Leigh Ave., 609/921-3052

Best Ice Cream/Yogurt
Thomas Sweet Ice Cream
  179 Nassau St., 609/683-8720
  33 W. Palmer Sq., 609/683-1655
  183 Nassau St., 609/924-7222

Best Indian Food
Palace of Asia
  3371 Hwy. 1, Ste. 400, Lawrenceville, 609/987-0606

Best Italian Food
Casabona
  47A Hwy. 206, 609/252-0940
Teresa's Pizzetta Caffe
  21 E. Palmer Sq., 609/921-1974

Best Pizza
Pizza Colari
  124 Nassau, 609/924-0777
Pizza Star
  301 N. Harrison St., 609/921-7422

Best Sandwiches
Hoagie Haven
  242 Nassau St., 609/921-7723

SOMERVILLE, NJ

Best Bar
Newsroom
150 W. Main St., 908/231-1919

Best Breakfast
Country Fresh Pancake and Grill
145 W. Main St., 908/231-8090

Best Homestyle Food
Buffalo Bill's Texas Weiners
24 W. Main St., 908/725-9558

Best Italian Food
Ferraro's Restaurant and Pizza
18 W. Main St., 908/707-0029
Italy, Italy Pasta and Pizza
117 N. Gaston Ave., 908/725-9500

Best Lunch
Buffalo Bill's Texas Weiners
24 W. Main St., 908/725-9558

Best Pizza
Central Pizzeria and Pizza
122 W. Main St., 908/722-8272

Best Seafood
Scampi's Fish Market and Restaurant
198 W. Main St., 908/231-1919

TOMS RIVER, NJ

Best Burgers
Elk's Lodge
600 Washington St., 908/341-9863
Office Lounge and Restaurant
820 N. Main St., 908/349-0800

Best Coffee
Java Joint
73 Main St., 908/240-2123

Best Ice Cream/Yogurt
Rich's Ice Cream
Rte. 37 at King Rd., 908/349-3459

Best Italian Food
Bella Di Notte
247 Mantoloking Rd., Brick, 908/920-9158
Palumbo's Restaurant and Pizza
Rte. 9, Old Bridge, 908/727-0970
Neil's Restaurant
1450 Rte. 88, Brick, 908/458-5411
Pier One Restaurant
3430 Rte. 37E, 908/270-0914

Best Japanese Food
Hana Japanese Restaurant
927 Rte. 166, 908/286-4465

Best Pizza
Vergona's Pizzeria and Restaurant
K-Mart Shopping Plz., 213 Rte. 37E, 908/244-6616

N

Best Sandwiches
Java Joint
　73 Main St., 908/240-2123
Jersey Mike's Submarines
　1501 Rte. 37E, 908/929-0222

Best Seafood
Old Time Tavern
　Rte. 166 at N. Main St., 908/349-8778
Jack Baker's Lobster Shanty
　4 Robbins Pkwy., 908/240-4800
Water's Edge
　Bayview Ave., Bayville, 908/269-3000
Krone's Lavallette Inn
　1307 Grand Central Ave., 908/830-5200
Bum Rogers Tavern
　23rd Ave., Seaside Park, 908/830-2770
Pier One Restaurant
　3430 Rte. 37E, 908/270-0914

Best Steaks
Old Time Tavern
　Rte. 166 at N. Main St., 908/349-8778
Office Lounge and Restaurant
　820 N. Main St., 908/349-0800
Elk's Lodge
　600 Washington St., 908/341-9863
Pier One Restaurant
　3430 Rte. 37E, 908/270-0914

N

TRENTON, NJ

Best Atmosphere
Diamond's Store
　132 Kent St., 609/393-1000

Best Bar
Office Cafe
　2 Elmwood Ave., 609/586-8600

Best Breakfast
Mastoris Diner-Restaurant
　144 Hwy. 130, Bordentown, 609/298-4650

Best Burgers
Rossi's Bar and Grill
　501 Morris Ave., 609/394-9089

Best Desserts
Roebling Pub
　801 S. Clinton Ave., 609/396-9411

Best Diner
Mastoris Diner-Restaurant
　144 Hwy. 130, Bordentown, 609/298-4650

Best Ice Cream/Yogurt
Thomas Sweet Ice Cream
　179 Nassau St., Princeton, 609/683-8720
　33 W. Palmer Sq., Princeton, 609/683-1655
　183 Nassau St., Princeton, 609/924-7222

Best Italian Food
Amici's Restaurant
　600 Chestnut Ave., 609/396-6300

Chianti's
701 Whittaker Ave., 609/695-0011

Best Late-Night Food
Sal Deforte's Ristorante
200 Fulton St., 609/396-6856

Best Places to Eat When Someone Else Is Buying
Amici's Restaurant
600 Chestnut Ave., 609/396-6300
Diamond's Store
132 Kent St., 609/393-1000
Chianti's
701 Whittaker Ave., 609/695-0011

Best Romantic Dining
Sal Deforte's Ristorante
200 Fulton St., 609/396-6856

Best Sandwiches
Good Times Tavern
160 Ashmore Ave., 609/695-5067

Best Seafood
John Henry Seafood Restaurant
2 Mifflin St., 609/396-3083

Best Spanish Food
Malaga Spanish Restaurant
511 Lalor St., 609/396-8878

Best Steaks
De Lorenzo Pizza
1120 S. Broad St., 609/599-2251
Lorenzo's Cafe
66 S. Clinton Ave., 609/695-6868

N

VINELAND, NJ

Best Breakfast
Brewster Villa
2615 E. Chestnut Ave., 609/692-2022
Larry's II Restaurant
907 N. Main Rd., 609/692-9001

Best Brunch
Brewster Villa
2615 E. Chestnut Ave., 609/692-2022

Best Coffee
Coffee Time
Cumberland Mall, 609/327-6300

Best Greek/Mediterranean Food
Greek Island Restaurant
3513 S. Delsea Dr., 609/327-9462

Best Ice Cream/Yogurt
Ice Cream Palace
205 S. Delsea Dr., 609/692-9416

Best Italian Food
Brewster Villa
2615 E. Chestnut Ave., 609/692-2022
Di Donato's Villa Restaurant
376 E. Wheat Rd., 609/697-2900

Best Other Ethnic Food
Norma's Kitchen (Jamaican)
7 S. Sixth St., 609/691-5411

Best Pizza
Pizza Pizzazz
484 S. Brewster Rd., 609/692-7007

Best Sandwiches
Hello Deli
2 La Salle Plz., 609/691-3354

Best Seafood
Pegasus II Restaurant
251 S. Lincoln Ave., 609/692-6333
Midway Inn
Harding Hwy., Buena, 609/697-0001

Best Steaks
Pegasus II Restaurant
251 S. Lincoln Ave., 609/692-6333

WASHINGTON, NJ

Best Bar
Sports Scene Restaurant
State Hwy. 31, 908/689-0310

Best Breakfast
Kelly's Corner Restaurant
150 State Rte. 13N, 908/689-7486
Washington Diner Restaurant
State Hwy. 31 at State Hwy. 57, 908/689-3059

Best Diner
Kelly's Corner Restaurant
150 State Rte. 13N, 908/689-7486
Washington Diner Restaurant
State Hwy. 31 at State Hwy. 57, 908/689-3059

Best Homestyle Food
Kountry Kitchen
31 W. Washington Ave., 908/689-9732

Best Italian Food
Villa Scotto
314 State Rte. 31N, 908/689-8900

Best Pizza
Sal's Pizza
1 W. Washington Ave., 908/689-6336

Best Seafood
Backstage
301 W. Washington Ave., 908/689-4071

Best Steaks
Backstage
301 W. Washington Ave., 908/689-4071

Standbys
Dairy Queen
State Hwy. 31, 908/689-0619

WESTFIELD, NJ

Best American Food
B.G. Fields Restaurant
560 Springfield Ave., 908/233-2260
Jolly Trolley Saloon
411 North Ave. W., 908/232-1207
Westfield Diner
309 North Ave. E., 908/233-5200
Towne House Restaurant
114 Central Ave., 908/232-4517

Best Breakfast
Vicki's Place
110 E. Broad St., 908/233-6887

Best Chinese Food
China Light
102 E. Broad St., 908/654-7797

Best Italian Food
Ferraro's Italian Restaurant
14 Elm St., 908/232-1105
La Florentina Pizzeria
338 South Ave. E., 908/654-7220
Northside Trattoria
16 Prospect St., 908/232-7320
Theresa's Restaurant
47 Elm St., 908/233-9133

Best Japanese Food
Kotobuki Japanese Restaurant
110 Central Ave., 908/233-6547

Best Pizza
Cosimo's Pizza
118E E. Broad St., 908/654-8787
Buona Pizza
243 South Ave. E., 908/232-2066
Sorrento's Restaurant and Pizzeria
631 Central Ave., 908/232-2642

Best Seafood
Wyckoff's Steak House
932 South Ave. W., 908/654-9700

Best Steaks
Wyckoff's Steak House
932 South Ave. W., 908/654-9700

WILLINGBORO, NJ

Best Restaurant in Town
Pirate's Inn
Moorestown Centerton Rd., Mt. Laurel, 609/235-5737

Best Breakfast
Edgewater Queen
2614 Hwy. 130S, Beverly, 609/871-5228
Prince Inn Diner
Rte. 130 at Beverly Rd., Burlington, 609/386-5522

Best Diners
Edgewater Queen
2614 Hwy. 130S, Beverly, 609/871-5228

Prince Inn Diner
  Rte. 130 at Beverly Rd., Burlington, 609/386-5522
Golden Dawn Diner
  2020 Rte. 130S, Burlington, 609/877-2236

Best Seafood
Pirate's Inn
  Moorestown Centerton Rd., Mt. Laurel, 609/235-5737

Best Steaks
Arthur's House of Fine Foods
  630 E. Rte. 130, Burlington, 609/387-2334
Charlie Brown's Restaurant
  Rte. 541 at Burrs Rd., 609/265-1100
Gaetano's Steaks and Subs
  3131 Rte. 38, Mt. Laurel, 609/234-2255
  Beverly Rancocas Rd. at JFK Way, 609/871-5588
  7 Pennypacker Dr., 609/871-6861

N

New Mexico

Best Restaurants in Town
Our Lady of Mt. Carmel Restaurant
915 Texas Ave., 505/434-0722
Cottonwood Restaurant
2010 Pecan St., 505/434-8864

Best Bar
Keg's Brewery
817 Scenic Dr., 505/434-5654

Best Breakfast
Our Lady of Mt. Carmel Restaurant
915 Texas Ave., 505/434-0722

Best Brunch
Inn of the Mountain Gods
Carrizo Canyon Rd., Ruidoso, 505/257-5141

Best Casual Dining
Eagle's Nest Restaurant
905 S. White Sands Blvd., 505/437-8644

Best Chinese Food
Taiwan Kitchen
110 N. White Sands Blvd., 505/434-4337

Best Coffee
Mastroddi's Espresso Cafe
804 N. New York Ave., 505/437-2323

Best Desserts
Our Lady of Mt. Carmel Restaurant
915 Texas Ave., 505/434-0722

Best French Food
Chez Astrid Continental Food
1201 New York Ave., 505/434-1644

Best German Food
Bavarian House
1200 N. White Sands Blvd., 505/439-5920

Best Health-Conscious Menu
Our Lady of Mt. Carmel Restaurant
915 Texas Ave., 505/434-0722

Best Mexican Food
Alfredo's Mexican Kitchen
801 Delaware Ave., 505/437-1745

Best Pizza
Peter Piper Pizza
101 S. White Sands Blvd., 505/434-1828

Best Place to Eat When Someone Else Is Buying
Rebecca's at the Lodge in Cloudcroft
601 Corona Pl., Cloudcroft, 505/682-3131

Best Romantic Dining
Rebecca's at the Lodge in Cloudcroft
601 Corona Pl., Cloudcroft, 505/682-3131

Best Steaks
Eagle's Nest Restaurant
905 S. White Sands Blvd., 505/437-8644
Paul's Family Steakhouse
504 First St., 505/437-5592
Cattleman's Steak House
2904 N. White Sands Blvd., 505/434-5252

Standbys
Golden Corral Family Restaurant
261 Panorama Blvd., 505/439-8359
Western Sizzlin
1010 S. White Sands Blvd., 505/437-8233

ALBUQUERQUE, NM

Best Restaurant in Town
Romano's Macaroni Grill
2100 Louisiana Blvd. NE, 505/881-3400

Best All-You-Can-Eat Buffet
Tomato Cafe Pizza and Pasta Bar
1930 Juan Tabo Blvd. NE, 505/293-5100
5901 Wyoming Blvd. NE, 505/821-9300

Best Bar
Gecko's Gallery and Grill
3500 Central Ave. SE, 505/262-1848

Best Breakfast
Frontier Restaurant
2400 Central Ave. SE, 505/266-0550

Best Brunch
McGrath's
Hyatt Regency, 330 Tijeras Ave. NW, 505/766-6700

Best Burgers
Owl Cafe
800 Eubank Blvd. NE, 505/291-4900
Blake's Lotta Burger
Multiple Locations

Best Business Lunch
Weck's For Breakfast and Lunch
7200A Montgomery Blvd. NE, 505/881-0019

Best Casual Dining
Garduno's of Mexico
10551 Montgomery Blvd. NE, 505/298-5000
5400 Academy Rd. NE, 505/821-3030

2100 Louisiana Blvd. NE, 505/880-0055
8806 Fourth St. NW, 505/898-2772

Best Cheap Meal
Frontier Restaurant
2400 Central Ave. SE, 505/266-0550

Best Chinese Food
Bamboo House Chinese Restaurant
1745 Juan Tabo Blvd. NE, 505/293-0183

Best Coffee
Double Rainbow Bakery and Cafe
3416 Central Ave. SE, 505/255-6633

Best Desserts
Cafe Zurich
3513 Central Ave. NE, 505/265-2556

Best Diner
Scalo Northern Italian Grill
3500 Central Ave. SE, 505/255-8781

Best Family Restaurant
Black-Eyed Pea
4701 San Mateo Blvd. NE, 505/880-8733

Best French Food
Le Marmiton
5415B Academy Rd. NE, 505/821-6279

Best Health-Conscious Menu
Souper Salad
4411 San Mateo Blvd. NE, 505/255-8781
2225 Wyoming Blvd. NE, 505/294-7585
1606 Central Ave. SE, 505/243-9751

Best Homestyle Food
Black-Eyed Pea
4701 San Mateo Blvd. NE, 505/880-8733

Best Ice Cream/Yogurt
Marble Cow
3500 Central Ave. SE, 505/255-0300

Best Italian Food
Capo's Hide Away
8938 Fourth St. NW, 505/898-2002
Scalo Northern Italian Grill
3500 Central Ave. SE, 505/255-8781

Best Late-Night Food
Monte Vista Fire Station
3201 Central Ave. NE, 505/255-2424

Best Mexican Food
El Patio de Albuquerque
142 Harvard Dr. SE, 505/268-4245

Best Pizza
Il Vicino Pizzeria
3403 Central Ave. NE, 505/266-7855

Best Place to Be "Seen"
Stephen's
1311 Tijeras Ave. NW, 505/842-1773

N

Best Place to Eat Alone
Double Rainbow Bakery and Cafe
  3416 Central Ave. SE, 505/255-6633

Best Place to Eat When Someone Else Is Buying
Prairie Star Restaurant
  255 Prairie Star Rd., Bernalillo, 505/867-3327

Best Romantic Dining
Musashino Japanese Restaurant
  6205B Montgomery Blvd. NE, 505/880-0008

Best Salad/Salad Bar
Souper Salad
  4411 San Mateo Blvd. NE, 505/255-8781
  2225 Wyoming Blvd. NE, 505/294-7585
  5600 Wyoming Blvd. NE, 505/822-8370
  1606 Central Ave. SE, 505/243-9751

Best Sandwiches
Woody's Cafe and Coffee Bar
  11200 Montgomery Blvd. NE, 505/292-6800

Best Seafood
Cafe Oceana
  1414 Central Ave. SE, 505/247-2233

Best Steaks
Paul's Monterey Inn
  1000 Juan Tabo Blvd. NE, 505/294-1461

Best Vegetarian Food
Wild Oats
  6300A San Mateo Blvd. NE, 505/823-1933

Best Other Restaurant
Conrad's Downtown
  125 Second St. NW, 505/242-9090

CARLSBAD, NM

Best Barbecue/Ribs
The Red Chimney Pit Bar-B-Q
  817 N. Canal St., 505/885-8744

Best Burgers
Queen Cafe
  3670 Queens Hwy., 505/981-2439

Best Chinese Food
Kwan's Kitchen
  1511 S. Canal St., 505/887-5145

Best Mexican Food
Lucy's Mexicali Restaurant
  701 S. Canal St., 505/887-7714
Spanish Inn
  805 W. Mermod St., 505/885-3489
Cortez Cafe
  508 S. Canal St., 505/885-4747

Best Pizza
Pizza Mill and Sub Factory
  312 W. Church St., 505/887-5098

Best Seafood
Beaver's Restaurant
 1620 S. Canal St., 505/885-4515

Best Steaks
Sirloin Stockade
 710 S. Canal St., 505/887-7211

CLOVIS, NM

Best Barbecue/Ribs
Ben's BBQ
 2900 Mabry Dr., 505/762-4065
 1421 N. Prince St., 505/763-4241

Best Burgers
Bill's Jumbo Burgers
 501 N. Main St., 505/762-6300

Best Chinese Food
China Star
 1221 N. Main St., 505/762-8489

Best Japanese Food
Shogun Steak House
 600 Pyle St., 505/762-8577

Best Mexican Food
Leal's Mexican Food Restaurant
 3100 Mabry Dr., 505/763-4075
Juanito's Mexican Restaurant
 1608 Mabry Dr., 505/762-7822
Guadalajara Restaurant
 916 W. First St., 505/769-9965

Best Steaks
Poor Boy's Steak House
 2115 N. Prince St., 505/763-5222
K-Bob's Steak House
 1600 Mabry Dr., 505/763-4443
Ranchers and Farmers Steak House
 816 Lexington Rd., 505/763-6335

FARMINGTON, NM

Best American Food
Clancy's Pub
 2703 E. Twentieth St., 505/325-8176

Best Mexican Food
Senor Peppers
 1400 W. Navajo St., 505/327-0436
Paddock
 315 N. Auburn Ave., 505/327-3566
Anasazi Inn
 903 W. Main St., 505/325-4564
Los Hermanitos
 5915 E. Main, 505/326-5664

Best Seafood
The Trough
 Hwy. 550, Flora Vista, 505/334-6176
K.B. Dillon's
 101 W. Broadway, 505/325-0222

N

Five Seasons Restaurant
  1100 W. Broadway Ave., Bloomfield, 505/632-1196

Best Steaks
The Trough
  Hwy. 550, Flora Vista, 505/334-6176
K.B. Dillon's
  101 W. Broadway, 505/325-0222
Five Seasons Restaurant
  1100 W. Broadway Ave., Bloomfield, 505/632-1196

Standbys
Red Lobster
  3451 E. Main St., 505/325-5222

HOBBS, NM

Best Restaurant in Town
Cattle Baron Steak and Seafood Grill
  1930 N. Grimes St., 505/393-2800

Best All-You-Can-Eat Buffet
North Forty Restaurant
  408 W. Bender Blvd., 505/392-8178

Best American Food
Wallace's
  1403 E. Broadway St., 505/393-9025

Best Breakfast
Casey's
  209 W. Broadway St., 505/393-0308

Best Burgers
Casey's
  209 W. Broadway St., 505/393-0308
Saturday's
  312 W. Bender Blvd., 505/392-3651

Best Business Lunch
Furr's Cafeteria
  Broadmoore Mall, 726 E. Michigan Ave.,
    505/397-3211

Best Cheap Meal
Furr's Cafeteria
  Broadmoore Mall, 726 E. Michigan Ave.,
    505/397-3211
Casey's
  209 W. Broadway St., 505/393-0308

Best Chinese Food
Mi Won
  1518 E. Marland St., 505/393-7644
Peking Restaurant
  2404 N. Grimes St., 505/392-2411

Best Coffee
North Forty Restaurant
  408 W. Bender Blvd., 505/392-8178

Best Family Restaurants
Furr's Cafeteria
  Broadmoore Mall, 726 E. Michigan Ave.,
    505/397-3211

Kettle Restaurant
505 N. Marland Blvd., 505/397-0663

Best Homestyle Food
Prairie Rose
2004 N. Turner St., 505/393-9373
Grandy's Restaurant
1917 N. Turner St., 505/397-2219

Best Ice Cream/Yogurt
Saturday's
312 W. Bender Blvd., 505/392-3651

Best Mexican Food
Dan's Mexican Foods
921 S. Dal Paso St., 505/397-0097
Goncho's Restaurant
801 W. Bender Blvd., 505/397-3551
La Fiesta Restaurant
604 E. Broadway St., 505/397-1235
La Fondita
509 W. Broadway St., 505/397-0909

Best Place to Take the Kids
Sirloin Stockade
1406 E. Broadway St., 505/393-0306

Best Salad/Salad Bar
Cattle Baron Steak and Seafood
1930 N. Grimes St., 505/393-2800

Best Steaks
Cattle Baron Steak and Seafood
1930 N. Grimes St., 505/393-2800
Sirloin Stockade
1406 E. Broadway St., 505/393-0306

Standbys
Western Sizzlin
2022 N. Turner St., 505/393-7608

N

LAS CRUCES, NM

Best Bistro
Brass Cactus Bistro
1800 Avenida de'Mesilla, 505/527-4656

Best Desserts
Brass Cactus Bistro
1800 Avenida de'Mesilla, 505/527-4656

Best Eclectic Menu
Brass Cactus Bistro
1800 Avenida de'Mesilla, 505/527-4656

Best Mexican Food
Little Nellie's Chili Factory
939 N. Main St., 505/523-9911
Nellie's Cafe
1226 W. Hadley Ave., 505/524-9982
Roberto's Mexican Food
908 E. Amador Ave., 505/523-1851
Tatsu
930 El Paseo St., 505/526-7144

Best Middle Eastern Food
Casbah
2404 S. Locust, 505/522-8530

ROSWELL, NM

Best American Food
Peppers Grill
500 N. Main St., 505/623-1700

Best Italian Food
Pasta Cafe
4501 N. Main St., 505/624-1111
Mario's
200 E. Second St., 505/623-1740

Best Mexican Food
Martin's Capitol Cafe
110 W. Fourth St., 505/624-2111

Best Seafood
The Mason Jar Restaurant
3601 N. Main St., 505/623-7466
Cattleman's Steak House
1113 N. Main St., 505/622-2465

Best Steaks
Cattleman's Steak House
1113 N. Main St., 505/622-2465
The Mason Jar Restaurant
3601 N. Main St., 505/623-7466

SANTA FE, NM

Best Restaurant in Town
Santacafe
231 W. Washington Ave., 505/984-1788

Best All-You-Can-Eat Buffet
Furr's Cafeteria
522 W. Cordova Rd., 505/982-3816
De Vargas Shopping Mall, 564 Paseo de Peralta,
505/988-4431

Best Bar
El Farol Restaurant and Lounge
808 Canyon Rd., 505/983-9912

Best Breakfast
Tia Sophia's
210 W. San Francisco St., 505/983-9880

Best Brunch
Eldorado Hotel
309 W. San Francisco St., 505/988-4455

Best Burgers
San Francisco Bar and Grill
114 W. San Francisco St., 505/982-2044

Best Business Lunch
Pranzo Italian Grill
540 Montezuma Ave., 505/984-2645

Best Casual Dining
Tomasita's Cafe
500 S. Guadalupe St., 505/983-5721

Best Cheap Meal
Burrito Company
111 W. Washington Ave., 505/982-4453

Best Chinese Food
Imperial Wok Oriental Gourmet
731 Canyon Rd., 505/988-7100

Best Coffee
Downtown Subscriptions
376 Garcia St., 505/983-3085

Best Desserts
Zia Diner
326 S. Guadalupe St., 505/988-7008

Best Diner
Zia Diner
326 S. Guadalupe St., 505/988-7008

Best Family Restaurant
Garduno's of Santa Fe
130 Lincoln Ave., 505/983-9797

Best Health-Conscious Menu
Natural Cafe
1494 Cerrillos Rd., 505/983-1411

Best Homestyle Food
Bobcat Bite Restaurant
Old Las Vegas Hwy., 505/983-5319

Best Italian Food
Pranzo Italian Grill
500 Montezuma Ave., 505/988-3886
540 Montezuma Ave., 505/984-2645

Best Mexican Food
Shed
113 1/2 E. Palace Ave., 505/982-9030

Best Place to Be "Seen"
Cafe Escalera
130 Lincoln Ave., 505/989-8188

Best Place to Eat Alone
French Pastry Shop
100 E. San Francisco St., 505/983-6697

Best Place to Eat When Someone Else Is Buying
Coyote Cafe
132 W. Water St., 505/983-1615

Best Place to Take the Kids
Furr's Cafeteria
522 W. Cordova Rd., 505/982-3816
De Vargas Shopping Mall, 564 Paseo de Peralta,
505/988-4431

Best Romantic Dining
Casa Sena Restaurant
125 E. Palace Ave., 505/988-9232

Best Salad/Salad Bar
Souper Salad
2428 Cerrillos Rd., 505/473-1211

Best Sandwiches
Noon Whistle
451 W. Alameda St., 505/988-2636

Best Seafood
Anthony's at the Delta
228 Paseo de Onate, Espanola, 505/753-4511

Best Steaks
Steaksmith at El Gancho
Old Las Vegas Hwy., 505/988-3333

Best Tea Room
St. Francis Hotel
210 Don Gaspar Ave., 505/983-5700

Best Vegetarian Food
Healthy David's Cafe
418 Cerrillos Rd., 505/982-4147

Best Other Restaurant
Whistling Moon Cafe
402 N. Guadalupe St., 505/983-3093

Standbys
Denny's
3004 Cerrillos Rd., 505/471-2152
Haagen-Dazs
56 E. San Francisco St., 505/988-3858

SILVER CITY, NM

Best Breakfast
Drifter Motel
Hwy. 180E, 505/538-2916

Best Burgers
Fifty's Cafe
1874 Hwy. 180E, 505/538-3900

Best Chinese Food
Chinese Palace Restaurant
1608 N. Durango St., 505/538-9300

Best Pizza
R and R Pizza Express
1602 Silver Heights Blvd., 505/388-3600

Best Sandwiches
Grinder Mill
403 W. College Ave., 505/538-3366

Best Steaks
Buckhorn Saloon and Opera House
Hwy. 15, 505/538-9911

TAOS, NM

Best Breakfast
Ricky's Restaurant
Santa Fe Rd. S., 505/758-3589

Best Burgers
Ogelvie's Bar and Grille
103I E. Plaza, 505/758-8866

Best Business Lunch
Trading Post Cafe
  4179 State 68 Rd., Ranchos de Taos, 505/758-2042

Best Coffee
Taos Coffee Company
  18 S. Santa Fe Rd., 505/758-3331

Best Family Restaurant
Michael's Kitchen
  304 Paseo Del Pueblo Norte, 505/758-4178

Best French Food
La Folie
  122 Dona Luz, 505/758-8800

Best Health-Conscious Menu
Amigo's Natural Grocery
  326 Pueblo Sur, 505/758-8493
Apple Tree
  123 Bent St., 505/758-1900

Best Ice Cream/Yogurt
Taos Cow Ice Cream
  591 Arroyo Seco/Hondo Rd., Arroyo Seco,
    505/776-5640

Best Pizza
Outback Pizza
  712 Paseo Del Pueblo Norte, 505/758-3112

Best Place to Take the Kids
Michael's Kitchen
  304 Paseo Del Pueblo Norte, 505/758-4178

Best Sandwiches
Amigo's Natural Grocery
  326 Pueblo Sur, 505/758-8493

Best Spanish Food
Jacquelina's
  1541 Paseo Del Pueblo Sur, 505/751-0399

Best Steaks
Stakeout
  Hwy. 68, Ranchos De Taos, 505/758-2042

New York

Best Restaurants in Town
La Serre
  14 Green St., 518/463-6056
Cape House
  254 Broadway, 518/274-0167

Best American Food
Justin's
  301 Lark St., 518/436-7008
Barnsider
  480 Sand Creek Rd., Colonie, 518/869-2448
The Buzz Saw Restaurant and Lounge
  421 Water Ave. NE, 503/928-0642
Flinn's Parlor
  222 First Ave. SW, 503/928-9638

Best Bagels
Bagel Bite
  544 Delaware Ave., 518/449-1214
Cafe Manhattan Bagel Shoppe
  1814 Central Ave., 518/464-0573

Best Brunch
Qualters' Restaurant
  1108 Madison Ave., 518/489-8859

Best Burgers
Beff's Tavern
  15 Watervliet Ave., 518/482-2333
Sutter's Mill and Mining Company
  1200 Western Ave., 518/489-4910

Best Chinese Food
Silver Pavilion
  260 Wolf Rd., Colonie, 518/869-8686
Emperor Palace
  423 Madison Ave., 518/465-3124
Dumpling House
  120 Everett Rd., 518/458-7044
Amazing Wok
  267 Lark St., 518/434-3946

Peking
1100 Madison Ave., 518/435-0621

Best Coffeehouses
The Daily Grind
204 Lark St., 518/427-0464
Barnes and Noble
20 Wolf Rd., Colonie, 518/459-8183
Borders Books and Music
59 Wolf Rd., Colonie, 518/482-5800

Best Continental Food
Flinn's Parlor
222 First Ave. SW, 503/928-9638

Best Delicatessen
The Wine Depot and Deli
300 Second Ave. SW, 503/967-9499

Best Diner
Miss Albany Diner
893 Broadway, 518/465-9148
Quintessence
11 New Scotland Ave., 518/434-8186

Best French Food
Nicole's Bistro at L'Auberge
351 Broadway, 518/465-1111
L'Ecole Encore
44 Fuller Rd., 518/437-1234
La Serre
14 Green St., 518/463-6056

Best Happy-Hour Snacks
Beff's
15 Watervliet Ave., 518/482-2333

Best Ice Cream/Yogurt
Kurver Kreme
1349 Central Ave., Colonie, 518/459-4120

Best Indian Food
Sitar
1929 Central Ave., Colonie, 518/456-6670
Shalimar
31 Central Ave., 518/434-0890

Best Italian Food
Nicole's Ristorante
556 Delaware Ave., 518/436-4952
Lombardo's
121 Madison Ave., 518/462-9180
Cavaleri's
334 Second Ave., 518/463-4320
Cafe Capriccio
49 Grand St., 518/4650439
Pastabilities
250 Broadalvin St. SW, 503/924-9235

Best Japanese Food
Hiro's
1933 Central Ave., Colonie, 518/456-1180
Arita
192 N. Allen St., 518/482-1080

Best Late-Night Food
Cottage Diner
  4 New Scotland Ave., 518/426-7158

Best Mexican Food
El Loco Mexican Cafe
  465 Madison Ave., 518/436-1855
Garcia's
  1673 Central Ave., Colonie, 518/456-4116
Cactus Jack's
  455 Sand Creek Rd., Colonie, 518/482-5297

Best Middle Eastern Food
Mamoun's Falafel
  206 Washington Ave., 518/434-3901
BFS Catering and Imports
  1754 Western Ave., 518/452-6342

Best Other Ethnic Food
Novak's Hungarian Paprikas (Hungarian)
  2835 Santiam Hwy. SE, 503/967-9488

Best Outdoor Dining
Cranberry Bog
  56 Wolf Rd., Colonie, 518/459-5110
Cafe Hollywood
  275 Lark St., 518/472-9043

Best Pizza
Jeff's Pizzeria
  1038 Madison Ave., 518/489-2000
Sovrana
  63 N. Lake Ave., 518/434-8468
Fountain
  283 New Scotland Ave., 518/482-9898

Best Places To Eat Alone
Justin's
  301 Lark St., 518/436-7008
Quintessence
  11 New Scotland Ave., 518/434-8186

Best Places to Eat When Someone Else Is Buying
Yono's
  289 Hamilton St., 518/436-7747
La Serre
  14 Green St., 518/463-6056

Best Salad/Salad Bar
Justin's
  310 Lark St., 518/436-7008

Best Sandwiches
Debbie's Kitchen
  290 Lark St., 518/463-3829

Best Seafood
Real Seafood Company
  195 Wolf Rd., Colonie, 518/458-2068
Jack's Oyster House
  42 State St., 518/465-8854
Scrimshaw Restaurant
  660 Albany Shaker Rd., 518/452-5801
Depot Cafe
  822 Lyon St. S., 503/926-7326

N

Best Soul Food
Big John's
  51 Elizabeth St., 518/463-5972

Best Steaks
Barnsider
  480 Sand Creek Rd., Colonie, 518/869-2448
Butcher Block
  1632A Central Ave., Colonie, 518/456-1653

Best Thai Food
Bangkok Thai
  8 Wolf Rd., 518/435-1027

Best Vegetarian Food
Nepenthe
  154 Madison Ave., 518/436-0329
Dahlia's
  858 Madison Ave., 518/482-0931
Mother Earth's Cafe
  217 Western Ave., 518/434-0944

Best Vietnamese Food
My Linh's
  137-139 Madison Ave., 518/434-6884

Best Wine Selection
The Ginger Man
  234 Western Ave., 518/427-5963
Justin's
  301 Lark St., 518/436-7008

N **Standbys**
Ben and Jerry's
  Multiple Locations
Friday's
  Stuyvesant Plaza, 518/489-1661
Chuck E. Cheese Pizza
  1440 Central Ave., 518/459-2886
Red Lobster
  1557 Central Ave., Colonie, 518/869-7506

AMSTERDAM, NY

Best Breakfast
Briella's
  379 W. Main St., 518/842-2381

Best Diner
Windmill Diner
  4790 State Hwy. 30N, 518/842-0087

Best Dinner
Raindancer Steak Parlour
  4582 State Hwy. 30, 518/842-2606

Best Family Restaurant
Amsterdam Diner
  Rte. 30S, 518/842-9975

Best Italian Food
Lorenzo's Restaurant
  25 Union St., 518/842-9854

Best Pizza
Crystal Bar and Restaurant
  72 Lyon St., 518/842-9050

Best Steaks
Raindancer Steak Parlour
  4582 State Hwy. 30, 518/842-2606

AUBURN, NY

Best Restaurants in Town
Cassidy's Cafe and Restaurant
  135 Grant Ave., 315/252-6162
Lasca's
  252 Grant Ave., 315/253-4885

Best Brunch
Springside Inn
  41 Lake Rd., 315/252-7247

Best Coffee
Vermont Green Mountain Specialty Company
  50 E. Genesee St., Skaneateles, 315/685-1500
Phoenix Cafe
  2 South St., 315/258-8681

Best Desserts
Lasca's
  252 Grant Ave., 315/253-4885
Vermont Green Mountain Specialty Company
  50 E. Genesee St., Skaneateles, 315/685-1500

Best Homestyle Food
Auburn Family Restaurant
  161 Genesee St., 315/253-2274

N

Best Italian Food
Curley's Restaurant
  96 State St., 315/252-5224
Rosalie's Cucina
  841 W. Genesee St., Skaneateles, 315/685-2200

Best Pizza
Curley's Restaurant
  96 State St., 315/252-5224

Best Place to Eat When Someone Else Is Buying
Rosalie's Cucina
  841 W. Genesee St., Skaneateles, 315/685-2200

Best Sandwiches
Downtown Deli
  119 Genesee St., 315/255-1919

Best Seafood
Doug's Fish Fry
  8 Jordan St., Skaneateles, 315/685-3288

Best Steaks
Lasca's
  252 Grant Ave., 315/253-4885
Sunset Restaurant
  87 N. Division St., 315/252-9765

Best Vegetarian Food
Phoenix Cafe
  2 South St., 315/258-8681

BINGHAMTON, NY

Best Bar
Uncle Tony's
79 State St., 607/723-4488

Best Barbecue/Ribs
Niko's Char Pit
526 Court St., 607/724-2427
Theo's Restaurant
11 Main St., Johnson City, 607/797-0088

Best Breakfast
Silo Restaurant
Rte. 3 at Moran Rd., Greene, 607/656-4377

Best Brunch
Silo Restaurant
Rte. 3 at Moran Rd., Greene, 607/656-4377

Best Burgers
Uncle Tony's
79 State St., 607/723-4488

Best Coffee
Java Joe's
81 State St., 607/774-0966
Copper Cricket Cafe
266 Main St., 607/729-5620

Best Desserts
Copper Cricket Cafe
266 Main St., 607/729-5620

Best Family Restaurant
Cortese Restaurant
117 Robinson St., 607/723-6477

Best Ice Cream/Yogurt
Pat Mitchell's Ice Cream
1167 Vestal Ave., 607/722-4549

Best Italian Food
Orlando's
105-107 W. Main St., Endicott, 607/757-9276
Marinelli's Pizzeria
122 State St., 607/722-5251
Cortese Restaurant
117 Robinson St., 607/723-6477

Best Japanese Food
Kampai Japanese Steak House
Jensen Rd. at Vestal Pkwy. E., Vestal, 607/798-7521

Best Pizza
Consol Family Kitchen
101 Oak Hill Ave., Endicott, 607/754-7437
Marinelli's Pizzeria
122 State St., 607/722-5251
Cortese Restaurant
117 Robinson St., 607/723-6477

Best Place to Eat When Someone Else Is Buying
Number Five Restaurant
33 S. Washington St., 607/723-0555

Best Sandwiches
Old World Delicatessen
27 Court St., 607/722-5265
3908 Vestal Pkwy. E., Vestal, 607/798-7312

Best Seafood
Copper Cricket Cafe
266 Main St., 607/729-5620

Best Vietnamese Food
Mekong Vietnamese Restaurant
29 Willow St., Johnson City, 607/770-9628

Standbys
Red Lobster
1200 Vestal Pkwy. E., 607/754-3787

BRONX, NY

Best Atmosphere
Dominick's Restaurant
2335 Arthur Ave., 718/733-2807
2356 Westchester Ave., 718/822-8810

Best Brunch
Cafe Fifty Seven
312 W. 57th St., New York, 212/489-9767

Best Chinese Food
Lee Xing Chinese Restaurant
3207 Westchester Ave., 718/829-7945
Meiya Kitchen
858 Gerard Ave., 718/993-7710

Best Coffee
Unity Coffee Shop
58 E. 161st St., 718/665-6180

Best Delicatessen
Gianluca's Salumeria
1044 Morris Park Ave., 718/892-3080

Best Diners
Riverdale Diner
3657 Kingsbridge Ave., 718/884-6050
Unity Coffee Shop
58 E. 161st St., 718/665-6180

Best Homestyle Food
Dominick's Restaurant
2335 Arthur Ave., 718/733-2807
2356 Westchester Ave., 718/822-8810

Best Italian Food
Ann and Tony's Restaurant
2407 Arthur Ave., 718/364-8250
Venice Restaurant and Pizzeria
772 E. 149th St., 718/585-5164
Bella Vista Pizzeria
904A Hunts Point, 718/617-3939
354 E. Gun Hill Rd., 718/653-0314
Pasquale Rogoletto Restaurant
2311 Arthur Ave., 718/365-6644
Giovanni's Pizza and Restaurant
579 Grand Concourse, 718/402-6996

N

Dominick's Restaurant
  2335 Arthur Ave., 718/733-2807
  2356 Westchester Ave., 718/822-8810

Best Japanese Food
Sakura Delight Japanese Restaurant
  1 Riverdale Ave., 718/549-2606

Best Lunch
Balsam Luncheonette
  197 McClellan St., 718/590-9330
Unity Coffee Shop
  58 E. 161st St., 718/665-6180
Riverdale Diner
  3657 Kingsbridge Ave., 718/884-6050
Mary's Luncheonette
  1339 Oakpoint Ave., 718/542-5656

Best Pizza
Emilio's Pizza
  3843 E. Tremont Ave., 718/409-0929
Peppino's Pizza
  934 Morris Ave., 718/681-3879
Mario's Restaurant
  2342 Arthur Ave., 718/584-1188

Best Sandwiches
Balsam Luncheonette
  197 McClellan St., 718/590-9330
Gianluca's Salumeria
  1044 Morris Park Ave., 718/892-3080
Mary's Luncheonette
  1339 Oakpoint Ave., 718/542-5656

Best Seafood
Crab Shanty One
  361 City Island Ave., 718/885-1810
Land and Sea Restaurant
  5535 Broadway, 718/543-3423

Best Spanish Food
Lebanon Restaurant
  555 E. 169th St., 718/293-5681

Best Steaks
Frank's Soup Bowl
  3580 Bronxwood Ave., 718/519-9277
Land and Sea Restaurant
  5535 Broadway, 718/543-3423

BROOKLYN, NY

Best Restaurants in Town
La Bouillabaisse
  145 Atlantic Ave., 718/522-8275
Moustache Mid Eastern Pitza
  405 Atlantic Ave., 718/852-5555
Patsy's Pizza
  19 Old Fulton St., 718/858-4300
Cucina
  256 Fifth Ave., 718/230-0711

Best American Food
Chadwick's Restaurant
  8822 Third Ave., 718/833-9855

Best Atmosphere
River Cafe
  1 Water St., 718/522-5200
Milano Restaurant
  7514 Eighteenth Ave., 718/259-4300
Areo Restaurant
  8424 Third Ave., 718/238-0079

Best Brunch
River Cafe
  1 Water St., 718/522-5200

Best Chinese Food
Mr. Tang of Nostrand Avenue
  3344 Nostrand Ave., 718/769-6633
Mr. Tang of Third Avenue
  7523 Third Ave., 718/748-0400
Ocean Restaurant
  4911 Avenue D, 718/629-2255
Oriental Palace Restaurant
  5609 Eighth Ave., 718/633-6688

Best Coffee
Carini Pastry Shop
  3801 Thirteenth Ave., 718/438-9216

Best Delicatessens
Monte's Deli and Catering
  156 Avenue O, 718/259-1500
Once Upon A Sundae
  7701 Third Ave., 718/748-3412

Best Diner
Vegas Diner
  1619 86th St., 718/331-2221

Best Homestyle Food
Two Toms Restaurant
  255 Third Ave., 718/875-8689

Best Italian Food
Salvi Restaurant
  4220 Quentin Rd., 718/252-3030
Two Toms Restaurant
  255 Third Ave., 718/875-8689
Milano Restaurant
  7514 Eighteenth Ave., 718/259-4300
Areo Restaurant
  8424 Third Ave., 718/238-0079

Best Lunch
Once Upon A Sundae
  7701 Third Ave., 718/748-3412
Vegas Diner
  1619 86th St., 718/331-2221
Two Toms Restaurant
  255 Third Ave., 718/875-8689

Best Mexican Food
Ignacio's
  2147 Mill Ave., 718/968-1111

Best Pastries
Carini Pastry Shop
 3801 Thirteenth Ave., 718/438-9216

Best Pizza
Lento's
 7003 Third Ave. at Ovington St., 718/745-9197

Best Sandwiches
Monte's Deli and Catering
 156 Avenue O, 718/259-1500

Best Steaks
Peter Luger Steak House
 178 Broadway, 718/387-7400

Best Thai Food
Planet Thailand
 184 Bedford Ave., 718/599-5758

BUFFALO, NY

Best American Food
Oliver's Restaurant
 2095 Delaware Ave., 716/877-9662

Best Breakfast
Ambrosia Restaurant
 467 Elmwood Ave., 716/881-2196
Original Pancake House
 5479 Main St., Williamsville, 716/634-5515

Best Brunch
Panache
 Marriott Hotels, 1340 Millersport Hwy., Williamsville,
  716/689-6900

Best Business Lunch
Hourglass Restaurant
 981 Kenmore Ave., 716/877-8788

Best Casual Dining
Jimmy Mac's
 555 Elmwood Ave., 716/886-9112

Best Chinese Food
Chang's Garden
 938 Maple Rd., Williamsville, 716/689-3355

Best Family Restaurants
Park Lane Restaurant
 1360 Delaware Ave., 716/883-3344
 33 Gates Circle, 716/883-3344
Dandelions Restaurant
 1340 N. Forest Rd., Williamsville, 716/688-9714

Best French Food
Rue Franklin West
 341 Franklin St., 716/852-4416

Best Homestyle Food
Asa Ransom House Country Inn
 10529 Main St., Clarence, 716/759-2315

Best Ice Cream/Yogurt
Sweet Jenny's
 5590 Main St., 716/631-2424

Carvel Ice Cream Bakery
3410 Delaware Ave., 716/876-6141
3712 Harlem Rd., 716/837-9725

Best Italian Food
Little Talia Trattoria
1458 Hertel Ave., 716/833-8667
Chef's Restaurant
291 Seneca St., 716/856-9187
Siena Restaurant
4516 Main St., Amherst, 716/839-3108

Best Mexican Food
Garcia's Mexican Restaurant
3755 Union Rd., 716/681-9595
Mexican Joe's
1300 N. Forest Rd., 716/632-4530

Best Microbrewery
Buffalo Brew Pub
6861 Main St., Williamsville, 716/632-0552

Best Pizza
La Nova Pizzeria
371 W. Ferry St., 716/881-3303

Best Place to Eat Alone
Red Carpet Restaurant
5507 Main St., Williamsville, 716/634-1968

Best Places to Eat When Someone Else Is Buying
E.B. Green's Steakhouse
Hyatt Hotel, 2 Fountain Plz., 716/856-1234
Oliver's Restaurant
2095 Delaware Ave., 716/877-9662

Best Salad/Salad Bar
Oliver's Restaurant
2095 Delaware Ave., 716/877-9662

Best Sandwiches
Vito Fish and Chicken
900 William St., 716/854-2442

Best Seafood
Jerry's Seafood Restaurant
1226 Hertel Ave., 716/876-4138

Best Steaks
E.B. Green's Steakhouse
Hyatt Hotel, 2 Fountain Plz., 716/856-1234
Oliver's Restaurant
2095 Delaware Ave., 716/877-9662

Best Vegetarian Food
Rutabaga's Vegetarian Cuisine
177 Hodge Ave., 716/882-2909

Standbys
Perkins
2200 Sheridan Dr., 716/876-0808
2208 Delaware Ave., 716/877-7308
3601 Union Rd., 716/681-4120
Denny's
2215 Delaware Ave., Ste. 1344, 716/877-5398
2343 Union Rd., 716/668-6624
4610 Genesee St., 716/631-9297

731

Fuddruckers
  4300 Maple Rd., 716/836-3683
Friday's
  601 Main St., 716/854-7172
Red Lobster
  1000 McKinley Mall, 716/823-2901

ELMIRA, NY

Best Restaurants in Town
Pierce's 1894 Restaurant
  228 Oakwood Ave., Elmira Heights, 607/734-2022
The Hill Top Inn
  Jerusalem Hill Rd., 607/732-6728

Best American Food
Moretti's Restaurant
  800 Hatch St., 607/734-1535

Best Italian Food
Moretti's Restaurant
  800 Hatch St., 607/734-1535

ITHACA, NY

Best Restaurant in Town
Taughannock Farms Inn
  Rte. 89 at Taughannock Falls State Park,
    607/387-7711

Best Bar
The Rongovian Embassy
  1 W. Main St., Trumansburg, 607/387-3334

Best Breakfast
State Diner of Ithaca
  428 W. State St., 607/272-6189

Best Casual Dining
Antlers
  1159 Dryden Rd., 607/273-9725

Best Chinese Food
Main Moon Chinese Buffet
  401 Elmira Rd., 607/277-3399

Best Continental Food
Renee's American Bistro
  202 E. Falls St., 607/272-0656

Best Italian Food
Centini's Coddington Restaurant
  124 Coddington Rd., 607/273-0802
Joe's Restaurant
  602 W. Buffalo St., 607/273-2693
Lucatelli's Ristorante
  205 Elmire Rd., 607/273-0777

Best Mexican Food
The Rongovian Embassy
  1 W. Main St., Trumansburg, 607/387-3334

Best Other Ethnic Food
Dano's on Cayuga (East European)
  113 S. Cayuga St., 607/277-8942

Best Pizza
The Nines
311 College Ave., 607/272-1888
Little Joe's Restaurant
410 Eddy St., 607/273-2771

Best Steaks
Antlers
1159 Dryden Rd., 607/273-9725
Station Restaurant
806 W. Buffalo St., 607/272-2609

Best Thai Food
Thai Cuisine
501 S. Meadow St., 607/273-2031

Best 24-Hour Restaurant
State Diner of Ithaca
428 W. State St., 607/272-6189

Best Vegetarian Food
The Moosewood Restaurant
215 N. Cayuga St., 607/273-9610

Best View While Dining
Taughannock Farms Inn
Rte. 89 at Taughannock Falls State Park,
607/387-7711

JAMESTOWN, NY

Best Restaurant in Town
Hare and Hounds Inn
64 Lakeside Dr., Bemus Point, 716/386-2181

Best American Food
Ironstone Restaurant
516 W. Fourth St., 716/487-1516

Best Bistro
Stage Left
114 E. Third St., 716/664-5246

Best Breakfast
Good Morning Farm
2 Hadley Bay Rd., Stow, 716/763-1773

Best Continental Food
Ironstone Restaurant
516 W. Fourth St., 716/487-1516

Best Dinner
Hare and Hounds Inn
64 Lakeside Dr., Bemus Point, 716/386-2181
Vullo's Restaurant Veal House
Rte. 430, Greenhurst, 716/487-9568
Ironstone Restaurant
516 W. Fourth St., 716/487-1516

Best Homestyle Food
Ramsey's
Rte. 430, Greenhurst, 716/488-3503
Grainery Restaurant
Thornton Rd., Cherry Creek, 716/287-3500

733

Best Italian Food
The House of Petillo
382 Hunt Rd., 716/664-7457
La Scala
Rd. 1, Fluvanna Ave., 716/664-7534

Best Lunch
Colonnade
150 W. Fourth St., 716/664-3400

Best Seafood
Vullo's Restaurant Veal House
Rte. 430, Greenhurst, 716/487-9568
Grainery Restaurant
Thornton Rd., Cherry Creek, 716/287-3500
Davidson's Restaurant
398 E. Fairmount Ave., Lakewood, 716/763-9135

Best Steaks
Grainery Restaurant
Thornton Rd., Cherry Creek, 716/287-3500

Best Wine Selection
MacDuff's Restaurant
317 Pine St., 716/664-9414

KINGSTON, NY

Best American Food
Hoffman House Tavern
94 N. Front St., 914/338-2626

Best Bagels
Mr. Bagel
730 Ulster Ave., 914/338-3080

Best Bar
Foster's Coach House Tavern
22 Montgomery St., Rhinebeck, 914/876-8052

Best Bistro
Le Petit Bistro
8 East Market St., Rhinebeck, 914/876-7400

Best Breakfast
Deising's Bakery and Coffee Shop
111 N. Front St., 914/338-7503
584 Broadway, 914/338-1580

Best Brunch
The Beekman Arms 1776 Tavern
4 Mill St., Rhinebeck, 914/871-1766

Best Business Dinner
The Beekman Arms 1766 Tavern
4 Mill St., Rhinebeck, 914/871-1766

Best Casual Dining
Ship to Shore
15 W. Strand St., 914/331-7034

Best Cheap Meal
Rolling Rock Cafe
46 Rte. 9N, Rhinebeck, 914/876-7655

Best Chinese Food
Rondout Golden Duck
11 Broadway, 914/331-3221

Best Japanese Food
Golden Ginza
  24 Broadway, 914/339-8132

Best Late-Night Food
Rolling Rock Cafe
  46 Hwy. 9N, Rhinebeck, 914/876-7655

Best Mexican Food
Armadillo Bar and Grill
  97 Abeel St., 914/339-1550

Best Microbrewery
Woodstock Brewing Company
  20 St. James, 914/331-2810

Best Outdoor Dining
Hoffman House Tavern
  94 N. Front St., 914/338-2626

Best Pizza
C.J.'s Pizza North
  Rte. 9G at Old Post Rd., Rhinebeck, 914/876-7711

Best Restaurant Meal Value
Ship to Shore
  15 W. Strand St., 914/331-7034

Best Seafood
Ship to Shore
  15 W. Strand St., 914/331-7034

Best Steaks
Skytop Steak and Seafood Restaurant
  Onteora Trail, 914/338-6161

N

Best Vegetarian Food
Ambrosia Natural Foods
  276 Fair St., 914/338-2886

LACKAWANNA, NY

Best Restaurants in Town
Victoria Square Family Restaurant
  717 Ridge Rd., 716/825-6627
Mansford Inn
  3365 Abbott Rd., Archer Park, 716/828-1115

Best American Food
Crean's
  1245 Abbott Rd., 716/823-1255

Best Breakfast
First Ward Steel City Diner
  93 Ridge Rd., 716/824-4607

Best Casual Dining
Curly's Bar and Grill
  647 Ridge Rd., 716/824-9716

Best Diner
First Ward Steel City Diner
  93 Ridge Rd., 716/824-4607

Best Italian Food
Illio di Paolo's Restaurant
  3785 S. Park Ave., Blasdell, 716/825-3675

Pizza
dway Bobby's Pizzeria
35 Ridge Rd., 716/827-8750
cobi's Restaurant
1404 Abbott Rd., 716/825-5544

Best Sandwiches
Steve's Pig and Ox Roast
951 Ridge Rd., 716/824-8601

LOCKPORT, NY

Best Restaurants in Town
Garlock's Restaurant
35 S. Transit St., 716/433-5595
La Port's Pine Restaurant
48 Pine St., 716/433-9756
Shamus Restaurant
98 West Ave., 716/433-9809
Danny Sheehan's Steak House
491 West Ave., 716/433-4666

LONG ISLAND, NY

Best Restaurants in Town
Jessica's
54 Lincoln Ave., Rockville Centre, 516/536-6022
Due Torri Italian Restaurant
330 Motor Pkwy., Hauppauge, 516/435-8664
Jonathan's
3000 Jericho Turnpike, Garden City Park,
516/742-7300
Piping Rock Restaurant
130 Post Ave., Mineola, 516/333-5555
Calamari Kitchen
4 N. Cove Plz., Oyster Bay, 516/922-2999

Best American Food
Millie's Place
2014 Northern Blvd., Manhasset, 516/365-4344
The Birchwood
512 Pulaski, Riverhead, 516/727-4449
J.P. Michael's
307 Griffing Ave., Riverhead, 516/727-9010

Best Atmosphere
George Martin Restaurant
65 N. Park Ave., Rockville Centre, 516/678-7272

Best Bars
Finn MacCool's
205 Main St., Port Washington, 516/944-3439
Alias Smith and Jones Restaurant
2863 Woods Ave., Oceanside, 516/678-5888

Best Barbecue/Ribs
Raay-Nor's Cabin
550 Sunrise Hwy., Baldwin, 516/223-4886
Rib Roost
110 Shore Rd., Port Washington, 516/944-3272
Route 66
33 W. Sunrise Hwy., Merrick, 516/623-7866

Best Breakfast
Friend of a Farmer
1382 Old Northern Blvd., Roslyn, 516/625-3808
Stop 20 Diner
1336 Hempstead Turnpike, Elmont, 516/358-7142
The Riverhead Grill
85 E. Main St., Riverhead, 516/727-8495
Merrick Townhouse Diner
2160 Sunrise Hwy. E., Merrick, 516/546-2664
Imperial Diner
63 W. Merrick Rd., Freeport, 516/868-0303

Best Brunch
The Library
541 Port Washington Ave., Port Washington,
516/883-3122

Best Burgers
Alias Smith and Jones Restaurant
2863 Woods Ave., Oceanside, 516/678-5888
The Birchwood
512 Pulaski, Riverhead, 516/727-4449

Best Business Lunch
George Martin Restaurant
65 N. Park Ave., Rockville Centre, 516/678-7272

Best Casual Dining
Millie's Place
2014 Northern Blvd., Manhasset, 516/365-4344
Dodici's
12 N. Park Ave., Rockville Centre, 516/764-3000

Best Cheap Meal
Meson Ole
2055 Middle Country Rd., Centereach, 516/277-7798
Pazzo
179 Main St., Port Washington, 516/767-7117

Best Chinese Food
Szechuan Delight
24011 Linden Blvd., Elmont, 516/285-6088
Chef Tai's Chinese Restaurant
84 Old Shore Rd., Port Washington, 516/767-5111
Hunan Palace
129 W. Sunrise Hwy., Freeport, 516/868-8899
Hyting Restaurant
54 W. Main St., Riverhead, 516/727-1557

Best Coffee
International Delight Cafe
241 Sunrise Hwy., Rockville Centre, 516/766-7557

Best Continental Food
Di Benardo's Italian Cuisine
6300 Jericho Turnpike, Commack, 516/462-0800
The Harbor Side
503 E. Main St., Patchogue, 516/654-9290

Best Delicatessen
Ben's Kosher Deli and Restaurant
140 Wheatley Plz., Greenvale, 516/621-3340

N

Best Desserts
La Piccola Liguria
   47 Shore Rd., Port Washington, 516/767-6490

Best Diners
Suffolk Diner
   2101 Middle Country Rd., Centereach, 516/981-9855
Stop 20 Diner
   1336 Hempstead Turnpike, Elmont, 516/358-7142
Merrick Townhouse Diner
   2160 Sunrise Hwy. E., Merrick, 516/546-2664
Marybill Diner
   14 Merrick Ave. N., Merrick, 516/378-9715

Best Family Restaurants
Landmark Diner
   1023 Northern Blvd., Roslyn, 516/627-9635
Sparerib
   2098 Jericho Pike, Commack, 516/543-5050

Best Greek/Mediterranean Food
Shish-Kebab Restaurant
   283 Main St., Port Washington, 516/883-9309

Best Health-Conscious Menu
Friend of a Farmer
   1382 Old Northern Blvd., Roslyn, 516/625-3808

Best Homestyle Food
Publican's
   550 Plandome Rd., Manhasset, 516/627-7722
Marybill Diner
   14 Merrick Ave. N., Merrick, 516/378-9715

Best Indian Food
Diwan Restaurant
   37 Shore Rd., Port Washington, 516/767-7878
Indian Oven Restaurant
   67-71A Old Country Rd., Hicksville, 516/681-7070

Best Italian Food
La Vigna Restaurant
   63 Glen Cove Rd., Greenvale, 516/621-8440
Mamma Maria Cuchina Italian
   1525 Rte. 9, Clifton Park, 518/371-2106
Di Benardo's Italian Cuisine
   6300 Jericho Turnpike, Commack, 516/462-0800
Dockside Restaurant
   507 Guy Lombardo Ave., Freeport, 516/378-5544

Best Japanese Food
Gasho of Japan
   356 Vanderbilt Motor Pkwy., Hauppauge,
      516/231-3400
Restaurant Yamaguchi
   63 Main St., Port Washington, 516/883-3500

Best Lunch
International Delight Cafe
   241 Sunrise Hwy., Rockville Centre, 516/766-7557
Trotter's Tavern
   197 Mineola Blvd., Mineola, 516/746-9393
Lantern Restaurant
   564 Hempstead Pike, West Hampstead, 516/481-1434

Digger O'Dell's
58 W. Main St., Riverhead, 516/369-3200

Best Mexican Food
Amigo's Mexican Restaurant
52 Main St., Port Washington, 516/883-1315

Best Other Ethnic Food
Little Portugal (Portuguese)
241 Mineola Blvd., Mineola, 516/742-9797
The Birchwood (Polish-American)
512 Pulaski, Riverhead, 516/727-4449

Best Outdoor Dining
Sparerib
2098 Jericho Pike, Commack, 516/543-5050

Best Pizza
King Umberto
1339 Hempstead Turnpike, Elmont, 516/352-8391
Dodici's
12 N. Park Ave., Rockville Centre, 516/764-3000
Primo's
1091 Rte. 58, Riverhead, 516/727-8763

Best Place to Eat When Someone Else Is Buying
Bryant and Cooper Steak House
2 Middleneck Rd., Roslyn, 516/627-7270
Due Torri Italian Restaurant
330 Motor Pkwy., Hauppauge, 516/435-8664
Jessica's
54 Lincoln Ave., Rockville Centre, 516/536-6022

Best Place to Take the Kids
Shish-Kebab Restaurant
283 Main St., Port Washington, 516/883-9309

Best Restaurant Meal Value
Alpine Garden
Franklin Sq., 11 Franklin Ave., Elmont, 516/354-5770
P.G. Steakhouse
1745 E. Jericho Turnpike, Huntington, 516/499-1005

Best Salad/Salad Bar
Club House
987 Port Washington Blvd., Port Washington,
516/767-1112

Best Sandwiches
Modern Snackbar
Rte. 25, Aquebogue, 516/722-3655
Bagel Lover's
136 E. Main, Riverhead, 516/727-5080
Cooperage Inn
Sound Ave., Baiting Hollow, 516/727-8994

Best Seafood
Original Schooner
115 W. Broadway, Port Jefferson, 516/473-1220
Bellport Chowder House
19 Bellport Ln., Bellport, 516/286-2343
Louie's Shore Restaurant
395 Main St., Port Washington, 516/883-4242
Pier 95
95 Hudson Ave., Freeport, 516/867-9632

ay Seafood Bar and Grill
0 Willis Ave., Williston Park, 516/742-9191

st Southwestern Food
ute 66
33 W. Sunrise Hwy., Merrick, 516/623-7866

Best Spanish Food
House of Spain
2008 Merrick Rd., Merrick, 516/378-8777

Best Steaks
The Good Steer
Rte. 45, Ronkonkoma, 516/585-8212
Bryant and Cooper Steak House
2 Middleneck Rd., Roslyn, 516/627-7270
The Rendezvous
313 E. Main St., Riverhead, 516/727-6880
Nautilus Cafe
46 Woodcleft Ave., Freeport, 516/379-2566
Peppercorn's
25 E. Marie St., Hicksville, 516/931-4002

Best 24-Hour Restaurant
Landmark Diner
1023 Northern Blvd., Roslyn, 516/627-9635

Best View While Dining
Mamma Maria Cuchina Italian
1525 Rte. 9, Clifton Park, 518/371-2106

Best Wine Selection
Cottabella Ristorante
45A Shore Rd., Port Washington, 516/883-4920

MIDDLETOWN, NY

Best Atmosphere
Cafe Allegro
21 W. Main St., 914/343-4567

Best Breakfast
Colonial Diner
8 Dolson Ave., 914/342-3500

Best Diner
Middletown Forum Diner
229 Wickham Ave., 914/342-5155

Best Italian Food
Orrio's Restaurant
Ingrassia Rd., 914/343-9447

Best Japanese Food
Hana Restaurant and Sushi Bar
339 Rte. 211E, 914/342-6634

Best Lunch
Middletown Forum Diner
229 Wickham Ave., 914/342-5155

Best Pizza
Cafe Allegro
21 W. Main St., 914/343-4567

Best Seafood
Hunters Lodge
Rte. 6 at 17M, 914/342-4777

Best Steaks
Hunters Lodge
  Rte. 6 at 17M, 914/342-4777

NEW YORK, NY

Best Restaurants in Town
Hasaki
  210 E. Ninth St., 212/473-3327
Elio's
  Second Ave. at 84th, 212/772-2242
Cucina Della Fontana
  368 Bleecker St., 212/242-0636
Osteria al Doge
  142 W. 44th St., 212/944-3643
Water Club
  500 E. 30th St., 212/683-3333
Cottage East
  713 Second Ave., 212/286-8811
Kom Tang Soot Bul House
  32 W. 32nd St., 212/947-8482
Manhattan Cafe
  1161 First Ave., 212/888-6556
Bridge Cafe
  279 Water St., 212/227-3344
Cafe Andrusha
  1742 Second Ave., 212/360-1128
Seven A
  109 Ave. A, 212/475-9001
Vietnam Restaurant
  11 Doyers St., 212/693-0725
Arizona 206 and Cafe
  206 E. 60th St., 212/838-0440
Arturo's Pizzeria
  106 W. Houston, 212/475-9828
Jules
  65 St. Mark's Place, 212/477-5560
Bell Caffe
  310 Spring St., 212/334-2355
Capsuoto Freres
  451 Washington St., 212/966-4900
Mezzogiorno
  195 Spring St., 212/334-2112
Patrissy's
  98 Kenmare St., 212/226-8509
Anglers and Writers
  420 Hudson St., 212/675-0810
Cent' Anni
  50 Carmine St., 212/989-9494
Nine Jones Street
  9 Jones St., 212/989-1220
Chiam
  160 E. 48th St., 212/371-2323
Dojo
  14 W. Fourth St., 212/505-8934
Bouley Restaurant
  165 Duane St., 212/608/3852
Dok Suni
  119 First Ave., 212/477-9506

24 Chambers St., 212/227-7074

…isine De Saigon
154 W. Thirteenth St., 212/255-6003

El Parador Cafe
325 E. 34th St., 212/679-6812

Est Est Est
64 Carmine St., 212/255-6294

Fannie's Oyster Bar
765 Washington St., 212/255-5101

Follonico
6 W. 24th St., 212/691-6359

Great Shanghai
27 Division St., 212/966-7663

Hakata
224 W. 47th St., 212/730-6863

Chin Chin
216 E. 49th St., 212/888-4555

Boca Chica
13 First Ave., 212/473-0108

Hudson River Club
250 Vesey St., 212/786-1500

Il Cantinori
32 E. Tenth St., 212/673-6044

Triple Eight Palace
78 E. Broadway, 212/941-8886

Fiorello's
1900 Broadway, 212/595-5330

Il Mulino
86 W. Third St., 212/673-3783

Jai-Ya Thai
396 Third Ave., 212/889-1330

Kin Khao
171 Spring St., 212/966-3939

Havana NY
27 W. 38th St., 212/840-3035

Les Halles
411 Park Ave. S., 212/679-4111

Mappamondo
11 Abingdon Sq., 212/675-3100

Mesa Grill
102 Fifth Ave., 212/807-7400

Il Monello
1460 Second Ave., 212/535-9310

Mi Cocina
57 Jane St., 212/627-8273

N
33 Crosby St., 212/219-8856

Nobu
105 Hudson St., 212/219-0500

Noho Star
330 Lafayette St., 212/925-0070

Old Town Bar and Restaurant
45 E. Eighteenth St., 212/529-6732

The Posthouse
28 E. 63rd St., 212/935-2888

Le Madri
168 W. Eighteenth St., 212/727-8022

Two-Eleven Restaurant and Bar
  211 W. Broadway, 212/925-7202
Pedro Paramo
  430 E. Fourteenth St., 212/475-4581
Periyali
  35 W. Twentieth St., 212/463-7890
Primavera
  1578 First Ave., 212/861-8608
Rectangle's
  159 Second Ave., 212/677-8410
Regional Thai Taste
  208 Seventh Ave., 212/807-9872
Riverrun
  176 Franklin St., 212/966-3894
Roettele A.G.
  126 E. Seventh St., 212/674-4140
Rose Cafe
  24 Fifth Ave., 212/260-4118
Shanghai 1933
  209 E. 49th St., 212/486-1802
Sidewalkers
  12 W. 72nd St., 212/799-6070
Telephone Bar and Grill
  149 Second Ave., 212/529-5000
Walker's
  16 N. Moore St., 212/941-0142
Tropica
  200 Park Ave., 212/867-6767
Da Silvano
  260 Sixth Ave., 212/982-0090
Woo Lae Oak
  77 W. 46th St., 212/869-9958
Coldwater's
  988 Second Ave., 212/888-2122

Best American Food
Aureole Restaurant
  34 E. 61st St., 212/319-1660
Union Square Cafe
  21 E. Sixteenth St., 212/243-4020
The Grange Hall
  50 Commerce St., 212/924-5246
Gotham Bar and Grill
  12 E. Twelfth St., 212/620-4020
Mustang Grill
  1633 Second Ave., 212/744-9194
Tivoli Restaurant
  515 Third Ave., 212/532-3300
The Saloon
  1920 Broadway, 212/874-1500

Best Asian Restaurants
Lucky Chang's
  24 First Ave., 212/473-0516
Cottage East Restaurant
  713 Second Ave., 212/286-8811
Hop Lee
  16 Mott St., 212/962-6475

Best Atmosphere
Blue Ribbon Brasserie
  97 Sullivan St., 212/274-0404
Kin Khao Restaurant
  171 Spring St., 212/966-3939
The Markham
  59 Fifth Ave., 212/647-9391
Barole Restaurant
  398 W. Broadway, 212/226-1102
The Oak Room
  Algonquin Hotel, 59 W. 44th St., 212/840-6800
Lucky Chang's
  24 First Ave., 212/473-0516
Water Club
  500 E. 30th St., 212/683-3333
Halcyon Restaurant
  151 W. 54th St., 212/247-0670

Best Bagels
H and H
  639 W. 46th St., 212/595-8000
  1551 Second Ave., 212/734-7441
Ess-a-Bagel
  359 First Ave. at 21st St., 212/260-2252
  831 Third Ave. near 51st St., 212/980-1010

Best Bars
King Cole Room
  St. Regis Hotel, 2 E. 55th St., 212/753-4500
Bar 6
  502 Sixth Ave., 212/645-2439
Fanelli's Cafe
  94 Prince St., 212/226-9412
Churchill's Restaurant
  1277 Third Ave., 212/650-1618
McSorley's Ale House
  15 E. Seventh St., 212/473-9148
Donahue's Pub
  770 Second Ave., 212/883-1193
White Horse Tavern
  567 Hudson St., 212/989-3956

Best Barbecue/Ribs
Dallas Jones BBQ
  622 Broadway, 212/228-6400
  315 Sixth Ave., 212/741-7390
Virgil's Real Barbeque
  152 W. 44th St., 212/921-9494
Brother's Bar-B-Q
  228 W. Houston St., 212/727-2775
BBQ Restaurant
  21 University Pl., 212/674-4450
  132 Second Ave., 212/777-5574
Wylie's Ribs
  891 First Ave., 212/751-0700

Best Beer Selection
Chumley's
  86 Bedford St., 212/675-4449

Brewksy's
41 E. Seventh between Second and Third Aves.,
212/420-0671

Best Bistro
Pigalle
111 E. 29th St. between Lexington and Park Aves.,
212/779-7830

Best Bottomless Cup of Coffee
Caffe Lure
169 Sullivan St., 212/473-2642

Best Bread
Bouley Restaurant
165 Duane St., 212/608/3852
Park Avenue Cafe
100 E. 63rd St., 212/644-1900
Shark Bar
307 Amsterdam Ave. near 74th St., 212/874-8500
Ukrainian East Village Restaurant
140 Second Ave. between St. Marks Pl. and Ninth St.,
212/529-5024
Friend of a Farmer
77 Irving Pl., 212/477-2188
The Grange Hall
50 Commerce St., 212/924-5246
Chart House Restaurant
Foot of High Street, Dobbs Ferry, 914/693-4130
Cucina Della Fontana Restaurant
368 Bleecker St., 212/242-0636

Best Breakfast
Aggie's
146 W. Houston St. at MacDougal St., 212/673-8994
Kiev
117 Second Ave., 212/674-4040
Eisenberg's
174 Fifth Ave. near 22nd St., 212/675-5096
Bubby's
120 Hudson St., 212/219-0666
Royal Canadian Pancake House
2286 Broadway, 212/873-6052
1004 Second Ave., 212/980-4131
Caffe Lure
169 Sullivan St., 212/473-2642
Chock Full O'Nuts
370 Lexington Ave., 212/532-0300
Regency Hotel
540 Park Ave., 212/759-4100

Best Brunch
Zoe
90 Prince St. between Broadway and Mercer St.,
212/966-6722
Nadine's
99 Bank St., 212/924-3165
Cafe Botanica
160 Central Park S., 212/484-5120
Sign of the Dove
1110 Third Ave., 212/861-8080

Cornelia Street Cafe
  29 Cornelia St., 212/989-9318
Museum Cafe
  366 Columbus Ave., 212/799-0150
Oak Room and Bar
  The Plaza Hotel, 768 Fifth Ave., 212/759-3000
Cucina Della Fontana Restaurant
  368 Bleecker St., 212/242-0636
Tivoli Restaurant
  515 Third Ave., 212/532-3300

Best Burgers
Fanelli's
  94 Prince St. at Mercer St., 212/226-9412
Corner Bistro
  331 W. Fourth St., 212/242-9502
McHale's
  750 Eighth Ave. at 46th St., 212/246-8948
Broome Street Bar
  363 W. Broadway, 212/925-2086
Houlihan's
  Multiple Locations
Jackson Hole Wyoming Burgers
  232 E. 64th St., 212/371-7187
  1611 Second Ave., 212/737-8788
  521 Third Ave., 212/679-3264
Chelsea Grill
  135 Eighth Ave., 212/929-9766

Best Business Breakfast
Regency Hotel
  540 Park Ave., 212/759-4100
Berger's Delicatessen Restaurant
  44 W. 47th St., 212/719-4173

Best Business Lunch
Nobu
  105 Hudson St. at Franklin St., 212/219-0500
Four Seasons
  99 E. 52nd St., 212/754-9494

Best Cajun/Creole Food
Louisiana Community Bar and Grill
  622 Broadway, 212/460-9633

Best Casual Dining
Carmine's
  200 W. 44th St., 212/221-3800
La Spaghetteria
  178 Second Ave., 212/995-0900
Tivoli Restaurant
  515 Third Ave., 212/532-3300
Patrick Conway's
  40 E. 43rd St., 212/286-1873

Best Cheap Meal
Ruppert's Restaurant
  269 Columbus Ave. between 72nd and 73rd Sts.,
    212/873-9400
Carmine's
  200 W. 44th St., 212/221-3800

Trattoria Spaghetto
  232 Bleecker St., 212/255-6752
Cucina Della Fontana (early bird special)
  368 Bleecker St., 212/242-0636

Best Chelsea Bar
Chelsea Commons
  24th St. at Tenth Ave., 212/929-9424

Best Chinese Food
Canton
  45 Division St. between Bowery and Market St.,
    212/226-4441
Hong Fat
  1461 Amsterdam Ave., 212/862-9322
Shun Lee Palace East
  155 E. 55th St., 212/371-8844
Cottage East
  713 Second Ave., 212/286-8811
Hop Lee
  16 Mott St., 212/962-6475

Best Coffee
Starbucks
  2379 Broadway at 87th St., 212/875-8470

Best Coffeehouses
Philip's Coffee Company
  155 W. 56th St., 212/582-7347
Cafe Tina
  184 Prince St., 212/925-9387
Cafe Figaro
  184 Bleecker St., 212/677-1100
Caffe Dante
  81 MacDougal St., 212/982-5275

N

Best Continental Food
Tri-Beca Grill
  375 Greenwich St., 212/941-3900
Knickerbocker Bar and Grill
  33 University Pl., 212/228-8490
Le Madri
  168 W. Eighteenth St., 212/727-8022
An American Cafe
  2 Park Ave., 212/684-2122
Delegates Dining Room
  1 United Nations Plz., 212/963-7626

Best Delicatessens
Carnegie Delicatessen and Restaurant
  854 Seventh Ave., 212/757-2245
Katz Delicatessen
  205 E. Houston St., 212/254-2246
Stage Deli and Restaurant
  834 Seventh Ave., 212/245-7850
Lee and Elle
  336 Madison Ave., 212/867-5322
Second Avenue Kosher Deli
  156 Second Ave., 212/677-0606

Best Desserts
Cascabel
  218 Lafayette St. near Spring St., 212/431-7300

La Cote Basque
5 E. 55th St., 212/688-6525
Veniero Pasticceria
342 E. Eleventh St., 212/674-7264
Home
20 Cornelia St. between Bleecker and W. Fourth Sts.,
212/243-9578
La Spaghetteria
178 Second Ave., 212/995-0900
Planet Hollywood
140 W. 57th St., 212/333-7827

Best Diner
Market Diner
572 Eleventh Ave. at 43rd St., 212/695-0415
Cheyenne Diner
411 Ninth Ave. at 33rd St., 212/465-8750
Munson Diner
600 W. 49th St., 212/246-0964
Ellen's Stardust Diner
44 W. 63rd St., 212/977-4356
1377 Avenue of the Americas, 212/307-7575
Aggie's Diner
20 Second Ave., 212/473-0660

Best East Village Bar
Blanche's Ludwika Tavern
135 Avenue A between Eighth and Ninth Sts.,
212/673-3824

Best Eclectic Menu
Blue Ribbon Brasserie
97 Sullivan St., 212/274-0404
Cafe Des Artistes
1 W. 67th St., 212/877-3500
Sammy's Restaurant
157 Chrystie St., 212/475-9131

Best Family Restaurants
Knickerbocker Bar and Grill
33 University Pl., 212/228-8490
Tivoli Restaurant
515 Third Ave., 212/532-3300

Best French Food
Bouley
165 Duane St. between Greenwich and Hudson Sts.,
212/608-3852
Demarchelier
50 E. 86th St. between Park and Madison Aves.,
212/249-6300
Cafe Le Gamin
50 MacDougal St. between Houston and Prince Sts.,
212/254-4678
Lespinasse
2 E. 55th St., 212/339-6719
CT Restaurant
111 E. 22nd St., 212/995-8500
Trois Jean Restaurant
154 E. 79th St., 212/988-4858

Chez Jacqueline Restaurant
72 MacDougal St., 212/505-0727
Le Cirque
58 E. 65th St., 212/794-9292
La Reserve
4 W. 49th St., 212/247-2993
Le Perigord
405 E. 52nd St., 212/755-6244
La Caravelle
33 W. 55th St., 212/586-4252

Best German Food
Silver Swan
41 E. Twentieth St., 212/254-3611

Best Greek/Mediterranean Food
Uncle Nick's Greek Cuisine
402 W. 51st St., 212/245-7992
Avgerino's Greek Restaurant
153 E. 53rd St., 212/688-8828
Sirtaki Souvlaki
111 MacDougal St., 212/533-4950

Best Happy Hour Snacks
McBell's
359 Sixth Ave. between Washington Pl. and W.
Fourth, 212/675-6260
Shelburne-Murray Hill Hotel
303 Lexington Ave., 212/689-5200

Best Health-Conscious Menu
Quantum Leap
88 W. Third St. between Sullivan and Thompson Sts.,
212/677-8050
Zen Palate Restaurant
663 Ninth Ave., 212/582-1669
Do-Jo's
24 St. Marks Place, 212/674-9821

Best Homestyle Food
Jezebel
630 Ninth Ave., 212/582-1045

Best Ice Cream/Yogurt
Peppermint Park
1225 First Ave., 212/288-5054

Best Indian Food
Dawat
210 E. 58th St. between Second and Third Aves.,
212/355-7555
Haveli
100 Second Ave., 212/982-0533
Darbar Indian Restaurant
44 W. 56th St., 212/432-7227
Mitoli Restaurant
334 E. Sixth St., 212/533-2508
Akbar India Restaurant
475 Park Ave., 212/838-1717
Maurya
129 E. 27th St. at Lexington Ave., 212/689-7925

Best Italian Food
Cafe Trevi
  1570 First Ave. between 81st and 82nd Sts.,
    212/249-0040
Il Mulino
  86 W. Third St., 212/673-3783
Osteria al Doge
  142 W. 44th St., 212/944-3643
Da Umberto's Restaurant
  107 W. Seventeenth St., 212/989-0303
John's
  302 E. Twelfth St., 212/475-9531
  823 Second Ave., 212/867-4955
Trattoria Spaghetto
  232 Bleecker St. at Carmine St., 212/255-6752
Barolo Restaurant
  398 W. Broadway, 212/226-1102
Bello Restaurant
  863 Ninth Ave., 212/246-6773
Cucina Della Fontana
  368 Bleecker St., 212/242-0630
Forlini's Restaurant
  93 Baxter St., 212/349-6779

Best Japanese Food
Honmura An
  170 Mercer St. at Houston St., 212/334-5253
Hasaki
  210 E. Ninth St., 212/473-3327
Sushisay Restaurant
  38 E. 51st St., 212/755-1780
Japonica Restaurant
  100 University Pl., 212/243-7752
Tokubei 86
  314 E. 86th St., 212/628-5334
Totoya Restaurant
  1144 First Ave., 212/751-6123
Benihana of Tokyo
  120 E. 65th St., 212/593-1627
  47 W. 56th St., 212/581-0930
La Maison Japanese Restaurant
  125 E. 39th St., 212/682-7375

Best Korean Food
Pyung Chang Korean and Japanese Restaurant
  6025 Broadway between 242nd and 243rd St., Bronx,
    718/884-2134

Best Late-Night Food
Florent
  69 Gansevoort St., 212/989-5779
Odeon
  145 W. Broadway, 212/233-0507
The Cub Room
  183 Prince St., 212/777-0030
Blue Ribbon Brasserie
  97 Sullivan St., 212/274-0404
Elaine's Restaurant
  1703 Second Ave., 212/534-8103

Tivoli Restaurant
515 Third Ave., 212/532-3300
Kiev Restaurant
117 Second Ave., 212/674-4040

Best Mexican Food
Mi Cocina
57 Jane St. at Hudson St., 212/627-8273
Mary Ann's Chelsea Mexican Restaurant
116 Eighth Ave., 212/633-0877
Rosa Mexicano Restaurant
1063 First Ave., 212/753-7407
Lupe's East L.A. Kitchen
110 Avenue of the Americas, 212/966-1326
Zona Rosa Mexican Restaurant
211 E. 59th St., 212/759-4444
Alamo Restaurant
304 E. 48th St., 212/759-0590

Best Microbreweries
Harbor Ale
Staten Island, 718/370-0551
Zip City Brewing
3 W. Eighteenth St., 212/366-6333

Best Middle Eastern Food
The Magic Carpet
54 Carmine St., 212/627-9019

Best Neighborhood Restaurant
Campagnola Restaurant
1382 First Ave., 212/861-1102

Best Other Ethnic Food
Caribe (Caribbean)
117 Perry St. at Greenwich St., 212/255-9191
Kwanzaa (Caribbean)
19 Cleveland Pl. at Kenmare St., 212/941-6095
The Blue Nile (Ethiopian)
103 W. 77th St. at Columbus Ave., 212/580-3232
Brannigan's (Irish)
104 Greenwich St., 212/267-4646
Pamir (Afghan)
1437 Second Ave., 212/734-3791
1065 First Ave., 212/644-9258
Ariana Afghan Kabab Restaurant (Afghan)
787 Ninth Ave., 212/262-2323
Ukrainian East Village Restaurant (Ukrainian)
140 Second Ave., 212/529-5029

Best Outdoor Dining
Barolo
398 W. Broadway between Spring and Broome Sts.,
212/226-1102
Miracle Grill
112 First Ave., 212/254-2353

Best Pizza
Stromboli Pizza
112 University Pl. between Twelfth and Thirteenth
Sts., 212/255-0812
Sal and Carmine's
4671 Broadway, 212/663-7651

N

Two Boots
  37 Avenue A, 212/505-2276
Le Madri
  168 W. Eighteenth St. at Seventh Ave., 212/727-8022
John's Pizzeria
  278 Bleecker St., 212/243-1680
Arturo's Pizza
  1610 York Ave., 212/288-2430
Famous Ray's Original Pizza
  465 Sixth Ave., 212/243-2253
Sal's Pizzeria
  766 Second Ave., 212/986-1234

Best Places to Be "Seen"
Time Cafe
  380 Lafayette St., 212/533-7000
Gramercy Tavern
  42 E. Twentieth St., 212/477-0777
Twenty-One Club
  21 W. 52nd St., 212/582-7200
Mad 61
  10 E. 61st St., 212/833-2200
Cub Room
  183 Prince St., 212/777-0030
Four Seasons
  99 E. 52nd St., 212/754-9494
Tribeca Bar and Grill
  375 Greenwich St., 212/941-3900
Elaine's Restaurant
  1703 Second Ave., 212/534-8103
The Play-By-Play
  4 Penn Plaza, 212/465-5888

Best Places to Eat Alone
Mondo Cane Blues Club
  205 Thompson St., 212/254-5166
Cottage East
  713 Second Ave., 212/286-8811
Elephant and Castle
  68 Greenwich Ave., 212/243-1400

Best Place to Eat Before or After the Show
Cafe Luxembourg
  200 W. 70th St. between Amsterdam and West End
    Aves., 212/873-7411

Best Places to Eat When Someone Else Is Buying
Daniel
  20 E. 76th St., 212/288-0033
Smith and Wollensky
  201 E. 49th St., 212/753-1530
Petrossian Restaurant
  182 W. 58th St., 212/245-2214
Le Cirque Restaurant
  58 E. 65th St., 212/794-9292
Cafe Des Artistes
  1 W. 67th St., 212/877-3500
Box Tree
  250 E. 49th St., 212/593-9810

Water Club
  500 E. 30th St., 212/683-3333
Palm Restaurant
  837 Second Ave., 212/687-2953
Tavern on the Green
  Central Park West at 65th St., 212/873-3200

Best Place to Take the Kids
Hard Rock Cafe
  221 W. 57th St., 212/459-9320

Best Quick-Dinner-Before-the-Movie
La Spaghetteria
  178 Second Ave., 212/995-0900
Famous Ray's Original Pizza
  465 Sixth Ave., 212/243-2253

Best Quick Lunch
Baci Deli
  22 E. 47th St., 212/697-7664
Cottage East
  713 Second Ave., 212/286-8811
Mary Ann's Chelsea Mexican Restaurant
  116 Eighth Ave., 212/633-0877

Best Rice and Beans
La Taza De Oro
  96 Eighth Ave., 212/243-9946
Zarela
  953 Second Ave. between 50th and 51st St.,
    212/644-6740
Bayamo
  704 Broadway between Fourth St. and Washington
    Pl., 212/475-5151

Best Romantic Dining
Savoy
  940 Second Ave., 212/355-5132
Cafe Des Artistes
  1 W. 67th St., 212/877-3500
The Terrace
  400 W. 119th St., 212/666-9490
Ermina Italian Restaurant
  250 E. 83rd St., 212/879-4284
La Cote Basque
  5 E. 55th St., 212/688-6525
Water Club
  500 E. 30th St., 212/683-3333
Tavern on the Green
  Central Park West at W. 67th St., 212/873-3200
Cucina Della Fontana
  368 Bleecker St., 212/242-0636
Rainbow Room
  30 Rockefeller Plz., 212/632-5000

Best Salad/Salad Bar
Elephant and Castle
  68 Greenwich Ave. between Seventh Ave. and
    Eleventh, 212/243-1400
Healthy Pleasures
  93 University Pl. between Eleventh and Twelfth Sts.,
    212/353-3663

Time Cafe
  380 Lafayette St. between Great Jones and E. Fourth,
    212/533-7000
China Grill
  60 W. 53rd St., 212/333-7788

Best Sandwiches
Melampo
  105 Sullivan St. between Spring and Prince Sts.,
    212/334-8530
Katz Deli
  205 E. Houston St. at Ludlow St., 212/254-2248
Mangia
  16 E. 48th St., 212/754-7600
  54 W. 57th St., 212/582-3061
Barocco Restaurant
  301 Church St., 212/431-1445
Second Avenue Kosher Deli
  156 Second Ave., 212/677-0606
Paradise Muffin Company
  141 Eighth Ave., 212/647-0066

Best Schmooze Bars
China Grill
  60 W. 53rd St., 212/333-7788
Monkey Bar
  60 E. 54th St., 212/838-2600
Four Seasons
  99 E. 52nd St., 212/754-9494
Shelby Restaurant
  967 Lexington Ave., 212/988-4624
Cub Room
  183 Prince St., 212/777-0030
Royalton Hotel
  44 W. 44th St., 212/869-4400

Best Seafood
Manhattan Ocean Club
  57 W. 58th St., 212/371-7777
Pisces Restaurant
  95 Avenue A, 212/260-6660
Oyster Bar and Restaurant
  89 E. 42nd St., 212/490-6650
Dock's Restaurant
  2427 Broadway, 212/724-5588
  633 Third Ave., 212/986-8080

Best Soul Food
The Shark Bar
  307 Amsterdam Ave., 212/874-8500
Pink Teacup
  42 Grove St., 212/807-6755
Sylvia's Restaurant
  328 Lenox Ave., 212/996-0660

Best Southwestern Food
Mesa Grill
  102 Fifth Ave., 212/807-7400
Arizona 206
  206 E. 60th St., 212/421-4450

El Quijote Bar and Restaurant
226 W. 23rd St., 212/929-1855
El Rio Grande Restaurant
160 E. 38th St., 212/867-0922

Best Spanish Food
Bolo
23 E. 22nd St., 212/228-2200
El Quijote Bar and Restaurant
226 W. 23rd St., 212/929-1855
El Castillo De Jagua Restauarnt
113 Rivington St., 212/982-6412

Best Sports Bars
Scores
333 E. Sixtieth St., 212/421-3600
Mickey Mantle's Restaurant
42 Central Park S., 212/688-7777
Overtime
412 Eighth Ave., 212/465-8326
Polo Grounds Bar and Grill
1472 Third Ave., 212/570-5590

Best Steaks
Smith and Wollensky Steak House
201 E. 49th St., 212/753-1530
El Castillo De Jagua Restaurant
113 Rivington St., 212/982-6412
Manhattan Cafe
1161 First Ave., 212/888-6556

Best Sushi
Hasaki
210 E. Ninth St., 212/473-3327
Yama
49 Irving Pl. at Seventeenth St., 212/475-0969
Avenue A
105 Avenue A, 212/982-8109
Fujiyama Mama
467 Columbus Ave., 212/769-1144
Japonica Restaurant
100 University Pl., 212/243-7752

Best Tea Rooms
Russian Tea Room
150 W. 57th St., 212/265-0947
T Salon Cafe and Tea Emporium
142 Mercer St., 212/925-3700

Best Thai Food
Thai Cafe
925 Manhattan Ave. at Kent St., Greenpoint,
718/383-3562
Gingertoon
417 Bleecker St., 212/924-6420
Jai Ya
396 Third Ave. near 28th St., 212/889-1330
Vong
200 E. 54th St., 212/486-9592
Kin Khao Restaurant
171 Spring St., 212/966-3939

N

Thai House Cafe
151 Hudson St., 212/334-1085

Best 24-Hour Restaurants
Kiev Restaurant
117 Second Ave., 212/674-4040
Tivoli Restaurant
515 Third Ave., 212/532-3300
Wo-Hop Restaurant
17 Mott St., 212/267-2536

Best Undiscovered Restaurants
Verbena
124 W. 24th St., 212/255-6780
Savoy Restaurant
70 Prince St., 212/219-8570
Coming or Going Fifty-Eight Street
38 E. 58th St., 212/980-5858
La Spaghetteria
178 Second Ave., 212/995-0900
Kiev Restaurant
117 Second Ave., 212/674-4040
Nadine's Restaurant
99 Bank St., 212/924-3165

Best Upper West Side Bar
Dublin House
225 W. 79th St. between Broadway and
Amsterdam Ave., 212/874-9528
Main Street
446 Columbus Ave., 212/873-5025

Best Vegetarian Food
Souen Soho
210 Sixth Ave. at Prince St., 212/807-7421
Zen Palate
663 Ninth Ave., 212/582-1669
The Markham
59 Fifth Ave. between Twelfth and Thirteenth Sts.,
212/647-9391
Luma Restaurant
200 Ninth Ave., 212/633-8033
Nosmo King
54 Varick St., 212/966-1239
Zen Palate Restaurant
663 Ninth Ave., 212/582-1669
Do-Jo's
24 St. Marks Place, 212/674-9821

Best Village Restaurant
Caffe Dell'Artista
46 Greenwich Ave. between Charles and Perry Sts.,
212/645-4431

Best West Village Bars
Corner Bistro
331 W. Fourth St. at Jane St., 212/242-9502
White Horse
567 Hudson St., 212/989-3956

Best Wine Selection
Gramercy Tavern
42 E. Twentieth St., 212/477-0777

Oyster Bar and Restaurant
89 E. 42nd St., 212/490-6650
Michael's Restaurant
24 W. 55th St., 212/767-0555
Montrachet Restaurant
239 W. Broadway, 212/219-2777
Aureole Restaurant
34 E. 61st St., 212/319-1660
Water Club
500 E. 30th St., 212/683-3333

NIAGARA FALLS, NY

Best American Food
Burgundy's On The River
Best Western Inn, 7001 Buffalo Ave., 716/283-7612

Best Chinese Food
Chu's Dining Lounge
1019 Main St., 716/285-7278

Best Coffeehouse
Mom's Coffee Shop and Restaurant
8430 Niagara Falls Blvd., 716/297-6031

Best Family Restaurant
Goose's Roost
10158 Niagara Falls Blvd., 716/297-7497
343 Fourth St., 716/282-6255

Best Italian Food
Como Restaurant
2220 Pine Ave., 716/285-9341
La Hacienda
3019 Pine Ave., 716/285-2536

Best Mexican Food
La Casa Cardenas
921 Main St., 716/282-0231

Best Seafood
Riverside Inn
115 S. Water St., Lewiston, 716/754-8206

Best Steaks
Burgundy's On The River
Best Western Inn, 7001 Buffalo Ave., 716/283-7612
Pete's Market House Restaurant
1701 Pine Ave., 716/282-7225

Best View While Dining
Burgundy's On The River
Best Western Inn, 7001 Buffalo Ave., 716/283-7612
Riverside Inn
115 S. Water St., Lewiston, 716/754-8206

Standbys
Old Country Buffet
8215 Niagara Falls Blvd., 716/283-4910
Applebee's
1608 Military Rd., 716/298-1085
Dairy Queen
2301 Military Rd., 716/297-0526
2432 Niagara St., 716/285-1873
10051 Niagara Falls Blvd., 716/297-1911

N

Haagen-Dazs
302 Rainbow Blvd. N., 716/285-9016
Red Lobster
1900 Military Rd., 716/298-4273

NORTH TONAWANDA, NY

Best Restaurant in Town
Pane's Pizzeria and Restaurant
984 Payne Ave., 716/692-7076

Best American Food
Classic V
2443 Niagara Falls Blvd., Amherst, 716/691-4585

Best Breakfast
Country Kitchen
2043 Kennsington, Amherst, 716/839-0290

Best Dinner
Sassafras
Holiday Inn, 1881 Niagara Falls Blvd., Amherst,
716/691-8181

Best Homestyle Food
Nestor's Texas Red Hots
102 Webster St., 716/695-3596

Best Italian Food
Pane's Pizzeria and Restaurant
984 Payne Ave., 716/692-7076

Best Lunch
Nestor's Texas Red Hots
102 Webster St., 716/695-3596

Best Pizza
J.V.'s Pizza and Pasta House
354 Oliver St., 716/692-2796
Frank's Pizza Shack
452 Oliver St., 716/692-7984

PLATTSBURGH, NY

Best Restaurant in Town
Anthony's Restaurant
620 Upper Cornelia St., 518/561-6420

Best Breakfast
Beaver's Place
83 Margaret St., 518/561-5085

Best Casual Dining
Arnie's Restaurant
22 Margaret St., 518/563-3003

Best Dinner
Port of Call
Holiday Inn, I-87 at Rural Route 3, 518/561-5000

Best Italian Food
Anthony's Restaurant
620 Upper Cornelia St., 518/561-6420
Arnie's Restaurant
22 Margaret St., 518/563-3003

Best Lunch
Zachary's Lounge
　86 Margaret St., 518/561-8876

Best Pizza
Zachary's Lounge
　86 Margaret St., 518/561-8876

Best Seafood
Butcher Block
　16A Mounted Rte. 3, 518/563-0920

Best Steaks
Butcher Block
　16A Mounted Rte. 3, 518/563-0920

POUGHKEEPSIE, NY

Best Restaurant in Town
Christos Restaurant
　155 Wilbur Blvd., 914/471-3400

Best Chinese Food
Mill House Panda
　289 Mill St., 914/454-2530

Best Coffeehouse
Cappuccino by Coppola's
　568 South Rd., 914/462-4545

Best Diner
Palace Diner
　194 Washington St., 914/473-1576

Best Italian Food
Milanese Restaurant
　115 Main St., 914/471-9533
Coppola's of Poughkeepsie
　825 Main St., 914/452-3040

Best Japanese Food
O'Sho Fine Japanese Restaurant
　763 South Rd., 914/297-0540

Best Lunch
Dickens Restaurant
　796 Main St., 914/454-7322

Best Mexican Food
Spanky's Restaurant
　85 Main St., 914/485-2294

Best Seafood
River Station Restaurant
　25 Main St., 914/452-9207

Best Steaks
River Station Restaurant
　25 Main St., 914/452-9207

Best Sushi
O'Sho Japanese Steak House
　763 South Rd., 914/297-0540

N

QUEENS, NY

Best American Food
Sidetracks
45-12 Queens Blvd., Sunnyside, 718/786-3570

Best Burgers
P.J. Horgan's
42-17 Queens Blvd., Sunnyside, 718/729-9584

Best Cheap Meal
Goody's Chinese Restaurant
94-03B 63rd Dr., Flushing, 718/896-7159

Best Chinese Food
Joe's Shanghai Restaurant
136-21 37th Ave., Flushing, 718/539-3838

Best Continental Food
First Edition
41-08 Bell Blvd., Flushing, 718/428-8522
Sidetracks
45-12 Queens Blvd., Sunnyside, 718/786-3570

Best Delicatessen
Pastrami King Kosher Restaurant
124-24 Queens Blvd., Jamaica, 718/263-1717

Best Diner
Georgia Diner
86-55 Queens Blvd., Flushing, 718/651-4687

Best Greek/Mediterranean Food
Telly's Taverna
28-13 23rd Ave., Astoria, 718/728-9056

Best Ice Cream/Yogurt
Jahn's Since 1897
81-04 37th Ave., Flushing, 718/651-0700

Best Italian Food
Parkside Restaurant
107-01 51st Ave., Flushing, 718/271-9871
Piccola Venezia Restaurant
42-01 28th Ave., Astoria, 718/721-8470

Best Japanese Food
Ariyoshi
42-15 Queens Blvd., Sunnyside, 718/937-3288

Best Sandwiches
Ben's Best Kosher Deli
96-40 Queens Blvd., Flushing, 718/897-1700

Best Steaks
Kate Cassidy's Restaurant
6398 Woodhaven Blvd., Flushing, 718/894-6200

Best Vegetarian Food
Bamboo Garden Restaurant
4128 Main St., Flushing, 718/463-9240

ROCHESTER, NY

Best Restaurant in Town
Lock, Stock and Barrel
Market Place Mall, 716/424-6592

Best Bagels
Bruegger's
Multiple Locations

Best Beer Selection
Beers of the World
300 Winton Pl., 716/427-2852

Best Brunch
Charlie's Frog Pond
652 Park Ave., 716/271-1970

Best Burgers
Highland Park Diner
960 South Clinton, 716/461-5040

Best Cheap Meal
Aladdin's Natural Eatery
141 State St., 716/546-5000
646 Monroe Ave., 716/442-5000

Best Chinese Food
House of Poon
2185 Monroe Ave., 716/271-7371

Best Coffeehouses
Java Joe's
16 Gibbs St., 716/232-5282
Nancy's Coffee Collection
Irondequoit Mall, 716/338-7260
Marketplace Mall, 716/424-1630

Best Desserts
Creme de la Creme
295 Alexander St., 716/263-3580

N

Best Ice Cream/Yogurt
Abbott's Frozen Custard
Multiple Locations

Best Indian Food
India House
998 S. Clinton Ave., 716/244-9210

Best Japanese Food
The Plum House
686 Monroe Ave., 716/442-0778

Best Late-Night Food
Gitsis Texas Hots
600 Monroe Ave., 716/271-8260

Best Other Ethnic Food
Mamasan's Restaurant (Thai/Vietnamese)
309 University Ave., 716/546-3910

Best Pizza
Chester Cab Pizza
73 Fairport Rd., 716/381-9390
707 Park Ave., 716/244-8211

Best Romantic Dining
Edward's
13 South Fitzhugh St., 716/423-0140

Best Sports Bars
Bathtub Billy's
630 West Ridge Rd., 716/865-6510

The Distillery
1142 Mount Hope Ave., 716/271-4105

Best Steaks
Rick's Prime Rib House
788 Howard Rd., 716/235-2900
The Scotch and Sirloin
3450 Winton Place, 716/427-0808

ROME, NY

Best Restaurant in Town
Teddy's Restaurant
851 Black River Blvd. N., 315/336-7839

Best Atmosphere
Aquino's Restaurant
416 N. James St., 315/337-7440

Best Bar
Aquino's Restaurant
416 N. James St., 315/337-7440

Best Breakfast
The Iron Kettle Coffee Shoppe
215 E. Dominick St., 315/336-9543

Best Family Restaurant
Teddy's Restaurant
851 Black River Blvd. N., 315/336-7839

Best Italian Food
Savoy
255 E. Dominick St., 315/339-3166

Best Pizza
La Roma Pizzeria
600 Floyd Ave., 315/336-1113

Best Seafood
Coalyard Charlie's
100 Depeyster St., 315/336-9940

SCHENECTADY, NY

Best Restaurant in Town
Brandywine Diner
970 Emmett St., 518/372-6030

Best American Food
Union Hall Inn
2 Union Place, Johnstown, 518/762-3210
Stone Ends
Rte. 9W, Glenmont, 518/449-5181

Best Bagels
Cafe Manhattan Bagel Shoppe
123 Saratoga Rd., Scotia, 518/399-3877

Best Bread
Perreca's
33 North Jay St., 518/372-1875

Best Burgers
Jumpin' Jack's Drive-In
5 Schonowee Ave., Scotia, 518/393-6101

Best Coffeehouse
Caffe Dolce
142 Jay St., 518/347-2334

Best Delicatessen
Gershon's Deli
1600 Union St., 518/393-0617

Best Diners
Blue Ribbon Diner
1801 State St., 518/393-2600
Ruby's Silver Diner
167 Erie Blvd., 518/382-9741

Best French Food
Chez Pierre
Rte. 9, Wilton, 518/793-3550

Best Italian Food
D'Raymond's
269 Osborne Rd., Loudonville, 518/459-6364

Best Other Ethnic Food
Rene's Mountain View House (Swiss/French)
White Schoolhouse Rd., Chestertown, 518/494-2904

Best Outdoor Dining
Jumpin' Jack's Drive-In
5 Schonowee Ave., Scotia, 518/393-6101

Best Place to Eat When Someone Else Is Buying
Glen Sanders Mansion
1 Glen Ave., Scotia, 518/374-7262

Best Sandwiches
Maurice's Readi-Foods
268 State St., 518/377-7200

N

STATEN ISLAND, NY

Best Bars
Choir Loft
12 Cross St., 718/442-9615

Best Breakfast
A Old Bermuda Inn
2512 Arthur Kill Rd., 718/948-7600

Best Cheap Meal
Cosmo's
4115 Hylan Blvd., 718/356-6565

Best Chinese Food
Loon Chuan
85 Page Ave., 718/967-9819

Best Coffee
Colonnade Diner
2001 Hylan Blvd., 718/351-2900

Best Desserts
Andrew's Bakery
61 New Dorp Plz., 718/667-9696
Alfonso's Pastry Shoppe
1899 Victory Blvd., 718/273-8802

Best Diner
Front Page
  75 Page Ave., 718/966-7882

Best Dinner
MJ Supper Club
  4864 Arthur Kill Rd., 718/948-9503

Best Italian Food
La Strada Restaurant
  139 New Dorp Ln., 718/667-4040

Best Pizza
Cosmo's
  4115 Hylan Blvd., 718/356-6565

Best Romantic Dining
Brittany's
  7324 Amboy Rd., 718/948-7530
Forest Inn Restaurant
  843 Forest Ave., 718/727-6060

SYRACUSE, NY

Best Barbecue/Ribs
Dinosaur Bar-B-Q Express
  246 W. Willow St., 315/476-4937

Best Breakfast
Anna Marie's Restaurant
  3900 New Court Ave., 315/463-9371

Best Brunch
Arid Evans Inn
  7206 Genesee St., Fayetteville, 315/637-2020

Best Business Lunch
Empire Brewing Company
  120 Walton St., 315/475-2337

Best Cheap Meal
Dominick's Restaurant
  1370 Burnet Ave., 315/471-4262

Best Chinese Food
China Pavilion Chinese Restaurant
  22102 W. Genesee St., 315/488-2828

Best Coffeehouse
Nancy's Coffee Cafe
  Carousel Center Dr., 315/466-0185
  290 W. Jefferson St., 315/476-6550

Best Delicatessen
Brooklyn Pickle
  1600 W. Genesee St., 315/487-8000
  2222 Burnet Ave., 315/463-6220

Best Desserts
Happy Endings
  317 S. Clinton St., 315/475-1853

Best Diner
Anna Marie's Restaurant
  3900 New Court Ave., 315/463-9371

Best Family Restaurants
Saratoga Steaks and Seafood
  200 Waring Rd., 315/445-1976
Rosie O'Grady's
  103 Hamilton St., 315/488-0881

Best Italian Food
Fred Grimaldi's Ristorante
  2950 Erie Blvd. E., 315/445-0012

Best Mexican Food
La Bamba Mexican and American Deli
  1305 Milton Ave., 315/488-0576

Best Microbrewery
Empire Brewing Company
  120 Walton St., 315/475-2337

Best Pizza
Twin Trees
  1029 Milton Ave., 315/487-9638

Best Place to Eat When Someone Else Is Buying
Pascale Wine Bar and Restaurant
  204 W. Fayette St., 315/471-3040

Best Places to Take the Kids
Doug's Fish Fry Too
  3939 Milton Ave., 315/487-1507
Spaghetti Warehouse
  689 N. Clinton St., 315/475-1807

Best Salad/Salad Bar
Provisions Fine Baking and Catering
  216 Walton St., 315/472-3475

Best Sandwiches
Brooklyn Pickle
  1600 W. Genesee St., 315/487-8000
  2222 Burnet Ave., 315/463-6220

Best Seafood
Captain Ahab's Seafood and Steak
  3449 Erie Blvd. E., 315/446-3272

Best Steaks
The Scotch and Sirloin
  Shopping Town Mall, 3687 Erie Blvd. E., DeWitt,
    315/446-1771

Best Thai Food
Ling Ling Restaurant
  218 W. Genesee St., 315/422-2800

Best Wine Selection
Pascale Wine Bar and Restaurant
  204 W. Fayette St., 315/471-3040

Standbys
Baskin-Robbins
  101 Marshall St., 315/479-5194
  4051 Milton Ave., 315/468-0086

TROY, NY

Best American Food
River Street Cafe
  429 River St., 518/273-2740

Best Atmosphere
Troy Pub and Brewery
  417-419 River St., 518/273-2337

Best Bar
Smith's Restaurant of Cohoes
  171 Remsen St., Cohoes, 518/237-9809

Best Beer Selection
Holmes and Watson
  450 Broadway, 518/273-8526

Best Burgers
Troy Pub and Brewery
  417-419 River St., 518/273-2337

Best Chinese Food
China Inn
  4 Northern Dr., 518/237-0031

Best Diners
Brunswick Diner
  855 Hoosick Rd., 518/279-1932
Colonial Restaurant and Coffee
  880 Second Ave., 518/237-9384

Best Family Restaurant
Casey's East
  120 Hoosick St., 518/274-8485

Best Italian Food
Testo's Restaurant and Pizza Parlor
  Fourth Ave. at 124th St., North Troy, 518/235-0444
Verdile's Restaurant
  572 Second Ave., 518/235-8879
Nicole's Ristorante
  95 Ferry St., 518/274-5358
Italia Restaurant
  24 Fourth St., 518/273-8773

Best Microbreweries
Brown and Moran Brewing Company
  417-419 River St., 518/273-2337
Troy Pub and Brewery
  417-419 River St., 518/273-2337

Best Pizza
Purple Pub
  50 Cohoes Rd., Watervliet, 518/273-9646
De Fazio's Pizzeria
  266 Fourth St., 518/271-1111
Dante's Pizzeria
  70 Jefferson St., 518/272-4533
Verdile's Restaurant
  572 Second Ave., 518/235-8879

Best Place to Take the Kids
Casey's East
  120 Hoosick St., 518/274-8485

Best Sandwiches
Brown and Moran Brewing Company
  417 River St., 518/273-2337
Holmes and Watson
  450 Broadway, 518/273-8526

Best Seafood
Old Daley Inn
  499 Second Ave., 518/235-2656
Cape House
  254 Broadway, 518/274-0167

Best Steaks
Old Daley Inn
  499 Second Ave., 518/235-2656

UTICA, NY

Best Breakfast
Bagel Grove
  7 Burrstone Rd., 315/724-8015
Breakfast at Tiffany's
  40 Seneca Turnpike, Clinton, 315/853-8093

Best Burgers
Babe's Macaroni Grill and Bar
  80 N. Genesee St., 315/735-0777

Best Coffee
Bagel Grove
  7 Burrstone Rd., 315/724-8015

Best Desserts
Joey's Restaurant
  815 Mohawk St., 315/724-9769
Kirby's American Restaurant
  4982 Commercial Dr., Yorkville, 315/736-4141
Symeon's Greek Restaurant
  4941 Commercial Dr., Yorkville, 315/736-4074

Best Greek/Mediterranean Food
Symeon's Greek Restaurant
  4941 Commercial Dr., Yorkville, 315/736-4074

Best Homestyle Food
Tiny's Grill
  1014 State St., 315/732-9497
Hartford Queen Diner
  4784 Commercial Dr., New Hartford, 315/736-0312

Best Italian Food
Chesterfield Restaurant
  1713 Bleecker St., 315/732-9356
Joey's Restaurant
  815 Mohawk St., 315/724-9769

Best Pizza
Franco's Pizza Pasta Cafe
  2002 Genesee St., 315/724-4526
Sunset Pizza and Sub
  1428 Sunset Ave., 315/732-9000

Best Sandwiches
Columbia
  500 Columbia St., 315/732-1596
Tiny's Grill
  1014 State St., 315/732-9497

Best Seafood
Chesterfield Restaurant
  1713 Bleecker St., 315/732-9356

N

Jack Appleseed's Tavern
   151 N. Genesee St., 315/797-7979
Hook Line and Sinker Pub
   90 Seneca Turnpike, New Hartford, 315/732-3636

Best Steaks
Jack Appleseed's Tavern
   151 N. Genesee St., 315/797-7979
Kirby's American Restaurant
   4982 Commercial Dr., Yorkville, 315/736-4141
Raleigh Room
   Ramada Inn, 141 New Hartford St., New Hartford,
   315/735-3392

WATERTOWN, NY

Best Restaurant in Town
Carriage House Restaurant
   300 Washington St., 315/782-8000

Best All-You-Can-Eat Buffets
Carriage House Restaurant
   300 Washington St., 315/782-8000
Partridge Berry Inn
   Black River Rd., 315/788-4610

Best Atmosphere
Partridge Berry Inn
   Black River Rd., 315/788-4610

Best Chinese Food
Fung Hing Chinese Restaurant
   225 State St., 315/785-9688

Best Diner
Longway's Diner
   Theresa Rd., 315/782-1131

Best Family Restaurants
Art's Jug
   820 Huntington St., 315/782-9764
Giovanni's Ristorante
   616 Leray St., 315/788-6830

Best Homestyle Food
Longway's Diner
   Theresa Rd., 315/782-1131

Best Italian Food
Art's Jug
   820 Huntington St., 315/782-9764
Sboro's Restaurant
   836 Coffeen St., 315/788-1728
Giovanni's Ristorante
   616 Leray St., 315/788-6830

Best Lunch
Clubhouse
   5795 Washington Street Rd., 315/788-5234

Best Pizza
Art's Jug
   820 Huntington St., 315/782-9764

Best Sandwiches
Clubhouse
5795 Washington Street Rd., 315/788-5234

Best Steaks
Pete's Restaurant
111 Breen Ave., 315/782-6640

WHITE PLAINS, NY

Best American Food
Ashley's
51 Mamaroneck Ave., 914/683-5999

Best Burgers
Mr. Greenjeans Restaurant
100 Main St., 914/997-8122

Best Chinese Food
Hunan Ritz II
731 N. Broadway, 914/946-5010
White Plains Imperial Wok
736 N. Broadway, 914/686-2700

Best Continental Food
Sweetwaters Restaurant
577 N. Broadway, 914/328-8918

Best Desserts
My Favorite Muffin
100 Main St., 914/948-2136
Sweet Dreams Bake Shop
333 Mamaroneck Ave., 914/448-9535

Best French Food
La Panetiere
530 Milton Rd., Rye, 914/967-8140

Best Health-Conscious Menu
Sweetwaters Restaurant
577 N. Broadway, 914/328-8918

Best Italian Food
Mulino's of Westchester
99 Court St., 914/761-1818

Best Japanese Food
Noda's Japanese Steakhouse
200 Hamilton Ave., 914/949-0990

Best Mexican Food
Cactus Jack's
210 Saw Mill River Rd., Elmsford, 914/345-3334

Best Pizza
Ernesto Restaurant
130 W. Post Rd., 914/421-1414
Gianfranco Pizzeria
88 Virginia Rd., 914/682-5655

Best Sandwiches
P and P Delicatessen
670 N. Broadway, 914/683-8606

Best Seafood
Sam's of Gedney Way
52 Gedney Way, 914/949-0978

N

Crystal Bay Seafood and Company
5 John Walsh Blvd., Peekskill, 914/737-8332

Best Steaks
Oliver's Restaurant
15 S. Broadway, 914/761-6111
Willet House
20 Willett Ave., Port Chester, 914/939-7500

YONKERS, NY

Best Atmosphere
Argonaut Restaurant and Diner
1084 Yonkers Ave., 914/237-1445
Charlie Brown's
1820 Central Park Ave., 914/779-7227

Best Barbecue/Ribs
Texas Grill
Cross County Mall, 1 Xavier Cross County Rd.,
914/963-7427

Best Breakfast
Argonaut Restaurant and Diner
1084 Yonkers Ave., 914/237-1445

Best Chinese Food
Golden Wok
2250 Central Park Ave., 914/779-8438

Best Delicatessen
Epstein's Kosher Delicatessen
2369 Central Park Ave., 914/793-3131

Best Diner
Argonaut Restaurant and Diner
1084 Yonkers Ave., 914/237-1445

Best Greek/Mediterranean Food
Argonaut Restaurant and Diner
1084 Yonkers Ave., 914/237-1445

Best Homestyle Food
Kenny Rogers Roasters
1801 Central Park Ave., 914/793-9310

Best Ice Cream/Yogurt
Carvel Ice Cream Bakery
Multiple Locations

Best Italian Food
Luciano's Italian Restaurant
2192 Central Park Ave., 914/961-5550

Best Mexican Food
Corridos Mexicanos
1771 Central Park Ave., 914/779-0990

Best Pizza
Bene Bene Italian Restaurant
2500 Central Park Ave., 914/961-3795
Luciano's Italian Restaurant
2192 Central Park Ave., 914/961-5550

Best Place to Eat When Someone Else Is Buying
Danielle's
292 Columbus Ave., Tuckahoe, 914/337-1883

Best Sandwiches
Epstein's Kosher Delicatessen
  2369 Central Park Ave., 914/793-3131

Best Seafood
East Harbor Seafood Restaurant
  1560 Central Park Ave., 914/961-0100

Best Steaks
Charlie Brown's
  1820 Central Park Ave., 914/779-7227

Standbys
Sizzler
  1 East Dr., 914/376-9000
  2368 Central Park Ave., 914/793-4000
Friday's
  825 Central Park Ave., Scarsdale, 914/722-4088
  240 White Plains Rd., Tarrytown, 914/332-0960

N

North Carolina

Best All-You-Can-Eat Buffet
Grove Park Inn Resort
 290 Macon Ave., 704/252-2711

Best Bagels
Harry's Bagels
 333B Merrimon Ave., 704/254-2345

Best Bar
Barley's Pub
 42 Biltmore Ave., 704/255-0504

Best Barbecue/Ribs
Little Pigs
 1916 Hendersonville Rd., 704/684-0500
 384 McDowell St., 704/254-4253

Best Breakfast
J and S Cafeteria
 800 Fairview Rd., 704/684-3415

Best Brunch
Uptown Cafe
 22 Battery Park Ave., 704/684-3415
Grove Park Inn
 290 Macon Ave., 704/252-2711

Best Burgers
Westside Grill
 1190 Patton Ave., 704/252-9605

Best Business Lunch
Cafe on the Square
 1 Biltmore Ave., 704/251-5565

Best Cheap Meal
Apollo Flame Pizza
 485 Hendersonville Rd., 704/274-3582

Best Chinese Food
China Inn
 777 Biltmore Ave., 704/252-6129
China Palace
 4 S. Tunnel Rd., 704/298-7098

Best Coffee
Bean Street
3 Broadway, 704/255-8180

Best Continental Food
The Market Place
20 Wall St., 704/252-4162

Best Desserts
Grovewood Cafe
111 Grovewood Rd., 704/258-8956
Cafe on the Square
1 Biltmore Ave., 704/251-5565
The Hop Ice Cream Shop
507 Merrimon Ave., 704/252-8362

Best Diner
Tastee Diner
575 Haywood Rd., 704/252-9644

Best Family Restaurant
J and S Cafeteria
800 Fairview Rd., 704/684-3415

Best Greek/Mediterranean Food
Apollo Flame
485 Hendersonville Rd., 704/274-3582

Best Health-Conscious Menu
McGuffey's Restaurant
13 Kenilworth Knoll, 704/252-0956

Best Homestyle Food
Westside Grill
1190 Patton Ave., 704/252-9605
The Moose Cafe
570 Brevard Rd., 704/255-0920

Best Ice Cream/Yogurt
Biltmore Dairy Bar
115 Hendersonville Rd., 704/274-2370
800 Brevard Rd., 704/667-0213

Best Italian Food
Boston Pizza
501 Merrimon Ave., 704/252-9474
La Caterina
5 Pack Sq., 704/254-1148
Windmill European Grill
85 Tunnel Rd., 704/253-5285
Ristorante da Vincenzo's
10 N. Market St., 704/254-4698

Best Late-Night Food
New French Bar
1 Battery Park Ave., 704/252-3685
Hot Shot Cafe
7 Lodge St., 704/274-2170

Best Mexican Food
El Chapala
1435 Merrimon Ave., 704/258-0899
1455 Patton Ave., 704/258-3730
La Paz
10 Biltmore Plaza, 704/277-8779

Salsa's
  6 Patton Ave., 704/252-9805

Best Outdoor Dining
Max's Celebrity Deli, Grill and Bar
  130 College St., 704/258-1162

Best Pizza
Barley's Pub
  42 Biltmore Ave., 704/255-0504

Best Place to Be "Seen"
Cafe on the Square
  1 Biltmore Ave., 704/251-5565

Best Place to Eat Alone
Malaprop's Bookstore/Cafe
  61 Haywood St., 704/254-6734

Best Places to Eat When Someone Else Is Buying
Gabrielle's
  Richmond Hill Inn, 87 Richmond Hill Dr.,
    704/252-7313
Windmill European Grill
  85 Tunnel Rd., 704/253-5285

Best Romantic Dining
Horizons
  Grove Park Inn, 290 Macon Ave., 704/252-2711

Best Sandwiches
New French Bar
  1 Battery Park Ave., 704/252-3685
Bean Street
  3 Broadway, 704/255-8180
Blue Moon Bakery
  60 Biltmore Ave., 704/252-6063
Superette's
  78 Patton Ave., 704/254-0255
Two Guys Original Olde Style Hoagies
  235 Merrimon Ave., 704/254-9955
Max and Rosie's
  25 N. Lexington Ave., 704/254-5342

Best Seafood
Greenery Restaurant
  148 Tunnel Rd., 704/253-2809
Crabby Bill's
  Hwy. 74, Bat Cave, 704/625-1302

Best Tea Room
Tassels
  25 Ranking Ave., 704/252-6082

Best Vegetarian Food
Laughing Seed
  40 Wall St., 704/252-3445

Best View While Dining
Grove Park Inn
  290 Macon Ave., 704/252-2711

Best Other Restaurant
23 Page Restaurant
  1 Battery Park Ave., 704/252-3685

Standbys
Shoney's
  102 Tunnel Rd., 704/252-2982
  230 Hendersonville Rd., 704/274-1248
  25 Fury Dr., 704/258-3788
  Hwy. 70E, 704/298-3922
Fuddruckers
  130 Charlotte St., 704/254-2161
The Olive Garden
  121 Tunnel Rd., 704/255-9887
Chuck E. Cheese Pizza
  34 Tunnel Rd., 704/252-3883
Ryan's Family Steak House
  1053 Patton Ave., 704/258-3761
Red Lobster
  139 Tunnel Rd., 704/253-1617
Outback Steakhouse
  30 Tunnel Rd., 704/252-4510

BURLINGTON, NC

Best Coffee
Ham's Restaurant
  1610 S. Church St., 910/570-3099

Best Diner
Blue Ribbon Diner
  2465 S. Church St., 910/570-1120

Best Dinner
Cutting Board
  2619 Alamance Rd., 910/226-0291

Best Homestyle Food
Blue Ribbon Diner
  2465 S. Church St., 910/570-1120

Best Sandwiches
Ham's Restaurant
  1610 S. Church St., 910/570-3099

Best Steaks
Cutting Board
  2619 Alamance Rd., 910/226-0291

CARY, NC

Best Restaurant in Town
Fox and Hound Restaurant and Pub
  107 Edinburgh Dr. S., Ste. 119, 919/380-0080

Best Breakfast
Courtney's Restaurant
  685 Cary Towne Blvd., 919/469-8410

Best Coffee
G and M Gaulart and Maliclet French Cafe
  957 N. Harrison Ave., 919/469-2288

Best Desserts
Rebecca's Gourmet Bakery
  115G W. Chatham St., 919/469-2516

Best Family Restaurant
Jasper's
4300 Cary Pkwy., 919/319-3400

Best Ice Cream/Yogurt
Goodberry Creamery
1146 Kildaire Farm Rd., 919/467-2386

Best Italian Food
Fiore's
107 Edinburgh Dr., Ste. 135, 919/467-6028

Best Mexican Food
Coyote Cafe
1014 Ryan Rd., 919/469-5253

Best Other Ethnic Food
Ben's Jamaican Cuisine (Jamaican)
8306 Chapel Hill Rd., 919/380-1818

Best Pizza
Maximillian's Pasta Grille
1284 Buck Jones Rd., Raleigh, 919/460-6299

Best Place to Eat Alone
G and M Gaulart and Maliclet French Cafe
957 N. Harrison Ave., 919/469-2288

Best Romantic Dining
Seldom Blues Cafe
206B New Waverly Pl., 919/859-2583

Best Sandwiches
D'Nardy's
1259 Kildaire Farm Rd., 919/481-3381

Best Steaks
Vinnie's Steakhouse and Tavern
107 Edinburgh Dr. S., 919/380-8210

CHAPEL HILL, NC

Best Beer Selection
Rathskeller
157A E. Franklin St., 919/942-5158

Best Breakfast
Breadmen's Restaurant
324 W. Rosemary St., 919/967-7110
Elmo's Diner
200 N. Greensboro St., Carrboro, 919/929-2909

Best Chinese Food
Oriental Garden Gourmet Restaurant
503 W. Rosemary St., 919/967-8818

Best Greek/Mediterranean Food
Mariakakis Restaurant and Bakery
1 Mariakakis Plz., 919/942-1453

Best Italian Food
Four Eleven West Italian Cafe
411 W. Franklin St., 919/967-2782
Mariakakis Restaurant and Bakery
1 Mariakakis Plz., 919/942-1453

Best Mexican Food
Flying Burrito Mexican Restaurant
746 1/2 Airport Rd., 919/967-7744

Best Seafood
Squid's Restaurant
1201 Hwy. 15-501, 919/942-8757

Best Thai Food
Oriental Garden Gourmet Restaurant
503 W. Rosemary St., 919/967-8818

Standbys
Ben and Jerry's
102 W. Franklin St., 919/967-9068

CHARLOTTE, NC

Best Restaurants in Town
Hotel Charlotte
705 S. Sharon Amity Rd., 704/364-8755
Townhouse
1011 Providence Rd., 704/335-1546

Best American Food
Fifth Street Cafe
118 W. Fifth St., 704/358-8334
What's Cooking? Cafe and Catering
20700 N. Main St., Cornelius, 704/892-3800
Palatable Pleasures
2000 South Blvd., 704/377-9717

Best Asian Restaurants
Fortune Garden
809 E. Arrowood Rd., 704/523-2828
Tsing Tao
1600 Montford Dr., 704/525-5803

Best Bagels
Essex Street Bagel
1961 E. Seventh St., 704/377-3978
9315 Monroe Rd., 704/849-2799
8706 Pineville Matthews Rd., Pineville, 704/543-1543

Best Barbecue/Ribs
Carolina Country Barbecue
2501 Crownpoint Executive Dr., 704/847-4520

Best Breakfast
Landmark
4429 Central Ave., 704/532-1153
Original Pancake House
4736 Sharon Rd., 704/332-3224

Best Brunch
Bistro 100
100 N. Tryon St., 704/344-0515
Village Tavern
Rotunda Bldg., South Park, 704/552-9983

Best Burgers
Lupie's
2718 Monroe Rd., 704/374-1232

Best Business Lunch
Providence Cafe
  110 Perrin Pl., 704/376-2008

Best Cajun/Creole Food
Hotel Charlotte
  705 S. Sharon Amity Rd., 704/364-8755

Best Cheap Meal
Lupie's
  2718 Monroe Rd., 704/374-1232
New Big Village
  1537 Camden Rd., 704/332-3366

Best Chinese Food
Baoding
  4722F Sharon Rd., 704/552-8899
Wan Fu
  10719 Kettering Dr., 704/541-1688

Best Coffeehouses
Jackson's Java
  8544 University City Blvd., 704/548-1133
Jeremiah's Coffee and Tea Company
  1408BB East Blvd., 704/377-1680
Queen City Coffee Roasters
  8502 Park Rd., 704/556-9771

Best Continental Food
Valentino's
  3014 E. Independence Blvd., 704/375-9200

Best Delicatessens
Dikadee's Deli
  112 S. Tryon St., 704/347-3400
  1419 East Blvd., 704/333-3354
Chris' Deli Restaurant
  3619 E. Independence Blvd., 704/536-2670
Rusty's Deli
  320 S. Tryon St., 704/374-1140
  Quail Corners Shopping Ctr., 8512 Park Rd.,
    704/554-9012
  I-77 at Tyvola Rd., 704/527-2650
  Providence Commons, 704/845-8505

Best Desserts
Dikadee's Deli
  112 S. Tryon St., 704/347-3400
  1419 East Blvd., 704/333-3354
Red Rocks
  4223 Providence Rd., 704/364-0402

Best French Food
Bistro 100
  100 N. Tryon St., 704/344-0515

Best German Food
Rheinland Haus
  2418 Park Rd., 704/376-3836

Best Greek/Mediterranean Food
Grapevine Cafe
  540 Brandywine Rd., 704/523-5600

Akropolis
  Town Ctr. Plaza, 8500 University City Blvd.,
    704/548-8584
  8200 Providence Rd., Ste. 800, 704/541-5099

Best Health-Conscious Menu
Palatable Pleasures
  2000 South Blvd., 704/377-9717

Best Homestyle Food
All R's Cafe
  5660D Providence Square Shopping Ctr.,
    704/367-0067
Carvers Creek
  131 E. Woodlawn Rd., 704/525-0333
  6720 E. Independence Blvd., 704/535-3361
The Country Inn of Matthews
  341 Ames St., Matthews, 704/847-1447
Diamond
  1901 Commonwealth Ave., 704/375-8959
Feniwick's
  511 Providence Rd., 704/333-2750
  108 Sharon Amity Rd., 704/364-1719
Italian Isles
  5542 N. Tryon St., 704/596-4681
Liberty East
  5112 E. Independence Blvd., 704/568-8640
Simmons Fourth Ward Restaurant
  516 N. Graham St., 704/334-6640
Soul Shack
  3418 Tuckaseegee Rd., 704/391-9636

Best Italian Food
Mama Lena's
  5135 Albemarle Rd., 704/568-0000
Conte's Ristorante Italiano
  2839D Selwyn Ave., 704/344-1110
Mama Ricotta's
  901 S. Kings Dr., 704/343-0148
Si!
  8418 Park Rd., 704/556-0914

Best Japanese Food
Restaurant Tokyo
  4603 South Blvd., 704/527-8787

Best Mexican Food
El Gringo
  3735 Monroe Rd., 704/347-4241
La Paz
  523 Fenton Pl., 704/372-4168
Azteca
  116 E. Woodlawn Rd., 704/525-5110

Best Middle Eastern Food
Middle East Deli
  4508 E. Independence Blvd., 704/536-9847
Ali Baba
  4113A Monroe Rd., 704/376-0750

Best Outdoor Dining
Rocky Mountain Cafe
  1801 Scott Ave., 704/376-6983
Village Tavern
  Rotunda Bldg., South Park, 704/552-9983

Best Pizza
Wolfman Pizza
  2839A Selwyn Ave., 704/377-4695
  8318 Pineville Matthews Rd., Pineville, 704/543-9653
  106 S. Sharon Amity Rd., 704/366-3666
Luisa's Brick Oven
  1730 Abbey Pl., 704/522-8782
PizZarrelli's
  200 E. Boulevard, Dilworth, 704/335-7200
  9101 Pineville Matthews Rd., Pineville, 704/543-0647
Southend Brewery and Smokehouse
  2100 South Blvd., 704/358-4077
Zepeddie's Pizzeria
  200D W. Woodlawn Rd., 704/522-7772

Best Places to Eat When Someone Else Is Buying
Townhouse
  1011 Providence Rd., 704/335-1546
Mimosa Grill
  2 First Union Bldg., 327 S. Tryon St., 704/343-0700
Hotel Charlotte
  705 S. Sharon Amity Rd., 704/364-8755

Best Place to Take the Kids
Italian Oven
  10420 Centrum Pkwy., Pineville, 704/541-6760

Best Romantic Dining
The Lamplighter
  1065 E. Morehead St., 704/372-5343
Tokyo
  4603 South Blvd., 704/527-8787

Best Seafood
Blue Marlin
  2518 Sardis Rd. N., 704/847-1212
What's Cooking? Cafe and Catering
  20700 N. Main St., Cornelius, 704/892-3800
The Fishmarket
  6631 Morrison Blvd., 704/365-0883

Best Spanish Food
Ole Ole
  709 S. Kings Dr., 704/358-1102
Tio Montero
  207 Johnston Dr., Pineville, 704/889-2258

Best Steaks
University Place Restaurant
  9005 University Pl., 704/547-1985

Best Sushi
Tokyo
  4603 South Blvd., 704/527-8787
Tsukiji
  8320 Pineville Matthews Rd., Pineville, 704/543-4081

Best Thai Food
Thai House
 3210 N. Sharon Amity Rd., 704/532-6868
Thai Orchid
 4223 Providence Rd., 704/364-1134

Best Vegetarian Food
Harper's
 301 E. Woodlawn Rd., 704/522-8376
 320 S. Tryon St., Ste. 202, 704/375-9715
 6518 Fairview Rd., 704/366-6688
Ali Baba
 4113 Monroe Rd., 704/376-0750
Talley's
 1408 East Blvd., 704/334-9200

Best Vietnamese Food
Lang Van
 3019 Shamrock Dr., 704/531-9525
Cafe Saigon
 8418 Park Rd., 704/556-9911

Best Wine Selection
Slug's
 301 S. Tryon St., Ste. 300, 704/372-7778
 9005 J.M. Keynes Dr., 704/547-1985
Sonoma
 280 Charlotte Plaza, 704/375-2004

Standbys
Chuck E. Cheese Pizza
 5612 Albemarle Rd., 704/532-9570
 7701 Pineville Matthews Rd., Pineville, 704/541-0106
Long Horn Steakhouse
 700 E. Morehead St., 704/332-2300

N

CONCORD, NC

Best Breakfast
Troutman's Bar-B-Q
 Hwy. 601 at Hwy. 49, 704/786-9714
 362 Church St. N., 704/786-5213

Best Cafeteria
K and W Cafeteria
 1480 Hwy. 29N, 704/786-6151

Best Dinner
Meric's Restaurant
 11 Union St. S., Ste. 108, 704/784-4209

Best Italian Food
Villa Maria Italian Restaurant
 1445 Hwy. 29N, 704/788-1903

Standbys
Ryan's Family Steak House
 3000 Cloverleaf Pkwy., 704/784-2105

DURHAM, NC

Best Barbecue/Ribs
Bullock's Bar B Cue
 3330 Wortham St., 919/383-3211

Grady's American Grill
  4010 Chapel Hill Blvd., 919/419-7022
Damon's, The Place for Ribs
  3019 Auto Dr., 919/492-2574

Best Burgers
Grady's American Grill
  4010 Chapel Hill Blvd., 919/419-7022

Best Casual Dining
Sassy's Restaurant
  1821 Hillandale Rd., 919/383-0244

Best Coffee
Francesca's Dessert Caffe
  706B Ninth St., 919/286-4177

Best Desserts
Francesca's Dessert Caffe
  706B Ninth St., 919/286-4177

Best Family Restaurant
Bullock's Bar B Cue
  3330 Wortham St., 919/383-3211

Best Greek/Mediterranean Food
Spartacus Restaurant
  4139 Chapel Hill Blvd., 919/489-2848

Best Homestyle Food
Bullock's Bar B Cue
  3330 Wortham St., 919/383-3211

Best Ice Cream/Yogurt
Francesca's Dessert Caffe
  706B Ninth St., 919/286-4177

Best Italian Food
Romano's Macaroni Grill
  4020 Chapel Hill Blvd., 919/489-0313

Best Outdoor Dining
Jasper's
  4300 NW Cary Pkwy., Cary, 919/319-3400

Best Steaks
Grady's American Grill
  4010 Chapel Hill Blvd., 919/419-7022

Standbys
Chuck E. Cheese Pizza
  3724 Mayfair St., 919/493-6084
Applebee's
  3400 Westgate Dr., 919/489-7775

FAYETTEVILLE, NC

Best Burgers
Suds and Spuds
  102 S. Eastern Blvd., 910/485-7770

Best Business Lunch
Suds and Spuds
  102 S. Eastern Blvd., 910/485-7770

Best Cheap Meal
The Haymount Grill
  1304 Morgantown Rd., 910/484-0261

Suds and Spuds
102 S. Eastern Blvd., 910/485-7770

Best Chinese Food
Great Wall Chinese Restaurant
3411 Murchison Rd., 910/630-1500

Best Coffee
The Reading Room
319 Cross Creek Mall, 910/867-8988

Best Desserts
Mozart Cafe
Cross Pointe Ctr., 5075 Morgantown Rd.,
910/864-2920

Best Italian Food
Trio Cafe
201 S. McPherson Church Rd., Ste. 108, 910/868-2443

Best Pizza
Garo's Pizza
2805 1/2 Raeford Rd., 910/484-6336

Best Place to Be "Seen"
The Old Mill
1825 Johnson Mill Rd., 910/904-0470

Best Places to Eat When Someone Else Is Buying
La Terrace
270 SW Broad St., Southern Pines, 910/692-5622
The Old Mill
1825 Johnson Mill Rd., 910/904-0470

Best Romantic Dining
De Lafayette
6112 Cliffdale Rd., 910/868-4600
The Old Mill
1825 Johnson Mill Rd., 910/904-0470

Best Salad/Salad Bar
Boston Chicken
1909 Skibo Rd., 910/864-1666

Best Sandwiches
Dogwood Deli
315 N. Eastern Blvd., 910/484-9047

Best Tea Rooms
The Reading Room
319 Cross Creek Mall, 910/867-8988
Baskets and Bows
308 N. McPherson Church Rd., 910/864-7948

Best Thai Food
Tai Sho Restaurant
4565 Yadkin Rd., 910/864-5550
Bangkok Restaurant
5000 Yadkin Rd., 910/868-6901

Standbys
Ryan's Family Steak House
3613 Raeford Dr., 910/433-2962
Shoney's
Westwood Shopping Ctr., 910/868-6113
1945 Cedar Creek Rd., 910/323-9325

International House of Pancakes
  1424 Bragg Blvd., 910/485-1477
Baskin-Robbins
  2916 Bragg Blvd., 910/484-3831
  306 Owen Dr., 910/864-3131
Lone Star Steakhouse
  1800 Skibo Rd., 910/867-2222

GASTONIA, NC

Best All-You-Can-Eat Buffet
Jackson's Cafeteria
  401 Cox Rd., 704/868-4181

Best American Food
Billie Jean's Grasshopper Farm
  911 Union Rd., 704/853-8661

Best Atmosphere
Jigger's Drive-Inn
  1002 Gastonia Hwy., Bessemer City, 704/629-5050

Best Barbecue/Ribs
Black's Barbecue
  2902 York Hwy., 704/867-0941
Carolina Country Barbecue
  1101 Union Rd., 704/867-2481
  246 N. New Hope Rd., 704/865-2416

Best Burgers
Jigger's Drive-Inn
  1002 Gastonia Hwy., Bessemer City, 704/629-5050

Best Casual Dining
Billie Jean's Grasshopper Farm
  911 Union Rd., 704/853-8661

Best Chinese Food
Peking Chinese Restaurant
  1007 Union Rd., 704/864-6113
  3078 E. Franklin Blvd., 704/867-6600

Best Coffeehouse
Coffee, Tea and Thee
  3044 E. Franklin Blvd., 704/867-2026

Best Family Restaurant
Jackson's Cafeteria
  401 Cox Rd., 704/868-4181

Best Homestyle Food
Firestone Grill
  908 W. Franklin Blvd., 704/868-3117
Jackson's Cafeteria
  401 Cox Rd., 704/868-4181

Best Ice Cream/Yogurt
Tony's Ice Cream Company
  604 E. Franklin Blvd., 704/867-7085

Best Italian Food
Angie's Spaghetti House
  1404 S. Marietta St., 704/864-0302
Benn-Benn's Italian Kitchen
  617 E. Garrison Blvd., 704/867-1446

N

Best Mexican Food
La Fuenete Bar and Grill
    3070 E. Franklin Blvd., 704/866-7744

Best Pizza
Milano's Italian Restaurant
    904 S. New Hope Rd., 704/854-3946

Best Salad/Salad Bar
Chantilly's Tea Room
    1003 Union Rd., 704/868-9500

Best Seafood
Lineberger Fish Fry
    4253 S. New Hope Rd., 704/824-1587

Best Tea Room
Chantilly's Tea Room
    1003 Union Rd., 704/868-9500

GOLDSBORO, NC

Best Restaurants in Town
The Lantern Inn
    2201 E. Ash St., 919/734-5915
O'Riley's Restaurant and Pub
    2512 E. Ash St., 919/736-7757
Billy's Backstreet Restaurant
    620 N. Madison Ave., 919/736-4406

Best All-You-Can-Eat Buffet
K and W Cafeteria
    621 N. Berkeley Blvd., 919/751-1866

Best Asian Restaurant
Oriental Jade
    2102 Hwy. 117 Bypass N., 919/735-2125

Best Barbecue/Ribs
Wilber's Barbecue
    4172 E. Hwy. 70, 919/778-5218
McCall's Barbecue and Seafood
    139 Millers Chapel Rd., 919/751-0072

Best German Food
Cafe Edelweiss
    1809 N. Berkeley Blvd., 919/778-4446

Best Homestyle Food
Michelle's Restaurant
    1709 E. Ash St., 919/735-4128
K and W Cafeteria
    621 N. Berkeley Blvd., 919/751-1866

Best Italian Food
Mimmo's Italian Restaurant
    2215 E. Ash St., 919/734-2228
Katlyn's Restaurant
    335 N. Spence Ave., 919/778-9113

Best Lunch
Michelle's Restaurant
    1709 E. Ash St., 919/735-4128

Best Mexican Food
Mazatlan
    11 N. Berkeley Blvd., 919/751-9722

Best Seafood
Madison's Prime Rib and Steak
  413 E. New Hope Rd., 919/751-2009
Captain Bob's Seafood
  430 N. Berkeley Blvd., 919/778-8332

GREENSBORO, NC

Best Barbecue/Ribs
Jed's Bar-B-Que
  2416 Randleman Rd., 910/274-2145

Best Burgers
Spring Garden Bar and Grill
  1205 Spring Garden St., 910/379-0308
  5804 Hunt Club Rd., 910/292-8156
Steak-Out
  1609B W. Friendly Ave., 910/271-0855

Best Cheap Meal
K and W Cafeteria
  3000 Northline Ave., 910/292-2864
  3710 S. Holden Rd., 910/852-1661
  4310 Big Tree Way, 910/852-8957

Best Chinese Food
Mr. Wonton
  3220 Randleman Rd., 910/230-2222
  3709E Battleground Ave., 910/282-0044
  5710H High Point Rd., 910/632-8700

Best Coffee
Stocks and Buns
  220 N. Elm St., 910/273-3941

Best Delicatessen
Jay's Delicatessen
  627 Friendly Center Rd., 910/292-0741

Best Desserts
Ganache Baking Company
  2109A New Garden Rd., 910/545-9199

Best Family Restaurant
Western Steer Steakhouse
  3833 High Point Rd., 910/294-0046

Best Ice Cream/Yogurt
Swensen's Ice Cream
  3124 Kathleen Ave., 910/299-2707

Best Italian Food
Anton's Italian Cafe
  1628 Battleground Ave., 910/273-1386
Ragazzi's Restaurant
  2629 Battleground Ave., 910/288-4065

Best Mexican Food
Tijuana Fats
  360 Federal Pl., 910/272-1262

Best Outdoor Dining
Paisley's
  200 N. Davie St., 910/272-3222

N

Best Place to Take the Kids
Elizabeth's Pizza
    2116 Lawndale Dr., 910/370-0800
    4516 High Point Rd., 910/852-7377
    5605E W. Friendly Ave., 910/299-1772
    918 Summit Ave., 910/274-3638

Best Sandwiches
Jay's Delicatessen
    627 Friendly Center Rd., 910/292-0741

Best Seafood
Mahi's
    4721 Lawndale Dr., 910/282-8112
The Blue Marlin
    3017 High Point Rd., 910/854-5696

Best Steaks
Western Steer Steakhouse
    3833 High Point Rd., 910/294-0046

Standbys
Chuck E. Cheese Pizza
    702 Pembroke Rd., 910/855-0234
Outback Steakhouse
    1611 Westover Terrace, 910/282-6283

GREENVILLE, NC

Best Dinner
Christine's Fine Dining
    207 W. Greenville Blvd., 919/355-9500

Best Family Restaurant
K and W Cafeteria
    135 Carolina East Ctr., 919/756-7577

Best Homestyle Food
K and W Cafeteria
    135 Carolina East Ctr., 919/756-7577

Best Place to Take Guests
Christine's Fine Dining
    207 W. Greenville Blvd., 919/355-9500

Standbys
Red Lobster
    3501 S. Memorial Dr., 919/756-4000
Lone Star Steakhouse
    500 W. Greenville Blvd., 919/321-4900

HICKORY, NC

Best American Food
Vintage House Restaurant
    271 Third Ave. NW, 704/324-1210

Best Breakfast
Joel's Kitchen
    2145 N. Center St., 704/327-4816
Snack Bar
    1346 First Ave. SW, 704/322-5432

Best Burgers
Circus Hall of Cream
  First Ave. at 22nd St. SW, 704/328-4214
  1710 N. Center St., 704/322-2630

Best Chinese Food
Panda Inn Chinese Restaurant
  755 Fourth St. SW, 704/322-8822

Best Dinner
Hickory Station Restaurant
  232 Government Ave. SW, 704/322-1904

Best Family Restaurant
Village Inn Pizza Parlor
  326 Hwy. 70SE, 704/328-3010

Best Pizza
Village Inn Pizza Parlor
  326 Hwy. 70SE, 704/328-3010

Best Place to Take the Kids
Village Inn Pizza Parlor
  326 Hwy. 70SE, 704/328-3010

Best Seafood
Jones Fish Camp
  2410 Springs Rd. NE, 704/256-8441

HIGH POINT, NC

Best Restaurant in Town
Atrium Cafe
  430 S. Main St., 910/889-9934

N

Best Barbecue/Ribs
Henry James Bar-B-Que
  1701 Westchester Dr., 910/886-5315
  2201 S. Main St., 910/882-8057

Best Cheap Meal
K and W Cafeteria
  1661 Westchester Dr., 910/886-4422

Best Chinese Food
Hunan Chinese Restaurant
  1539 N. Main St., 910/885-6577

Best Coffee
Coffee Connection
  1345 N. Main St., 910/886-1746

Best Desserts
Coffee Connection
  1345 N. Main St., 910/886-1746

Best Family Restaurant
Rainbow Family Restaurant
  2116 Westchester Dr., 910/889-3133

Best French Food
J. Basul Noble's Restaurant
  114 S. Main St., 910/889-3354

Best Homestyle Food
Rainbow Family Restaurant
  2116 Westchester Dr., 910/889-3133

st Ice Cream/Yogurt
ogurt Shoppe
1677 Westchester Dr., 910/889-6289
215 E. Lexington Ave., 910/885-6602

Best Pizza
Elizabeth's Pizza
2505 Westchester Dr., 910/889-4030

Standbys
Outback Steakhouse
260 E. Paris Ave., 910/885-5176
Quincy's
200 Westchester Dr., 910/869-2015
2814 S. Main St., 910/434-1554
Golden Corral Family Steak House
1080 Mall Loop Rd., 910/884-1655
Applebee's
2001 N. Main St., 910/886-8450
Longhorn Steakhouse
1540 N. Main St., 910/883-7373

JACKSONVILLE, NC

Best All-You-Can-Eat Buffets
Piccadilly Cafeteria
361 Jacksonville Mall, 910/577-2195
Fisherman's Wharf
100 S. Marine Blvd., 910/455-5200

Best Chinese Food
Mai Tai Restaurant
109 Henderson Dr., 910/346-5382

Best Dinner
Santa Fe
2109 N. Marine Blvd., 910/346-4223

Best Homestyle Food
Helen's Kitchen
2405B N. Marine Blvd., 910/455-9882

Best Mexican Food
El Cerro Grande
505 N. Marine Blvd., 910/347-1307

Best Pizza
Tony's Pizza and Restaurant
Western Blvd., 910/353-8666

KANNAPOLIS, NC

Best American Food
Oak's Restaurant
1776 S. Cannon Blvd., 704/932-3900

Best Breakfast
Grandma Shattley's
1414 S. Main St., 704/932-7766
Bojangles' Restaurant
1301 Cannon Blvd., 704/932-5415

Best Cheap Meal
Grandma Shatley's
1414 S. Main St., 704/932-7766

Best Homestyle Food
K and W Cafeteria
310 Oak Ave., 704/938-9116

Best Steaks
Western Steer Steakhouse
803 N. Cannon Blvd., 704/932-8017

Standbys
Pizza Hut
901 N. Cannon Blvd., 704/932-4191
252 Oak Ave., 704/932-3125

KINSTON, NC

Best All-You-Can-Eat Buffet
Abbott's Country Buffet
3700 W. Vernon Ave., 919/527-5613

Best Barbecue/Ribs
King's Restaurant
409 E. New Bern Rd., 919/527-2101
602 N. McLewean St., 919/527-1661
2404 N. Queen St., 919/523-3303
Barbecue Lodge
Hwy. 70W, 919/522-3021

Best Breakfast
Lovick's Quick Lunch
320 N. Heritage St., 919/523-6854

Best Cafeteria
Christopher's
217 N. Queen St., 919/527-3716

Best Chinese Food
China King
2000 W. Vernon Ave., 919/527-7750

Best Fast Food
Billy's Drive-In
2010 N. Queen St., 919/523-3754

Best Pizza
Pizza Villa
1400 W. Vernon Ave., 919/527-2260

Best Place to Eat When Someone Else Is Buying
Seth Houston's
Frenchman Creek Shopping Ctr., Hwy. 70E,
919/523-2230

Best Sandwiches
Supreme Deli and Subs
106 E. Vernon Ave., 919/523-2230

Best Soul Food
Hanzie's Grill
206 N. East St., 919/523-4202

Best Steaks
Baron and Beef
Hwy. 70E, 919/527-6787

N

NEW BERN, NC

Best All-You-Can-Eat Buffet
Latitude 35
　Sheraton Hotel, 1 Bicentennial Park, 919/638-3585

Best Barbecue/Ribs
Moore's Barbecue
　15061 Hwy. 17S, 919/638-3937
Ruby's Barbecue and Ribs
　245 Hwy. 70E, 919/638-5395

Best Burgers
Charburger
　1906 Clarendon Blvd., 919/633-4067

Best Chinese Food
Great Wall of China
　2007 S. Glenburnie Rd., 919/638-1188

Best Coffee
Trent River Coffee Company
　208 Craven St., 919/514-2030

Best Homestyle Food
Billy's Ham and Eggs
　1300 S. Glenburnie Rd., 919/633-5498

Best Italian Food
Scalzo Italian Restaurant
　415 Broad St., 919/633-9898
Ragazzi's
　425 Hotel Dr., 919/637-5090

Best Pizza
Franco's Pizza
　1226 S. Glenburnie Rd., 919/633-9711

Best Places to Eat When Someone Else Is Buying
Henderson House
　216 Pollock St., 919/637-4784
Harvey Mansion Restaurant
　221 Tryton Palace Dr., 919/638-3205

Best Sandwiches
Fred and Claire's Restaurant
　247 Craven St., 919/638-5426
Pollock Street Delicatessen
　208 Pollock St., 919/637-2480

RALEIGH, NC

Best Restaurants in Town
The Angus Barn
　9401 Glenwood Ave., 919/683-1399
Crook's Corner
　610 W. Franklin St., Chapel Hill, 919/929-7643
Irregardless
　901 W. Morgan St., 919/833-9920
Vinnie's
　7440 Six Forks Rd., 919/847-7319
Fox and Hound
　107 Edinburgh Dr. S., Ste. 119, Cary, 919/380-0080
Seldom Blues Cafe
　206B New Waverly Pl., 919/859-2583

Four Eleven West Italian Cafe
   411 W. Franklin Rd., Chapel Hill, 919/967-2782
Pyewacket
   431 W. Franklin St., Chapel Hill, 919/929-0297
Magnolia Grill
   1002 Ninth St., Durham, 919/286-3609
Nana's
   2514 University Dr., Durham, 919/493-8545
Claudio's
   6300 Creedmoor Rd., 919/847-0083

Best Bagels
Big Apple Bagels/Bakery-Cafe
   112 Fayetteville St. Mall, 919/828-8228
Bruegger's Bagel Bakery
   Multiple Locations
Horwitz's Delicatessen
   107 Edenburg St., Cary, 919/467-2007
Manhattan Bagels
   2430 Hillsborough St., 919/828-2610
   7909121 Bent Tree Plz., 919/848-1310
New York Deli
   109 S. Wilmington St., 919/832-3554

Best Barbecue/Ribs
Barbecue Lodge
   4600 Capital Blvd., 919/872-4755
Cooper's Barbecue
   109 E. Davie St., 919/832-7614
Don Murray's
   2751 Capital Blvd., 919/872-6270

Best Beer Selection
Greenshields Brewery and Pub
   214 E. Martin St., 919/829-0214
Mr. Dunderbak's Old World Deli
   4325 Glenwood Ave., 919/781-7075

Best Brunch
Courtney's Restaurant
   2300 Gorman St., 919/859-3830
   407 E. Six Forks Rd., 919/834-3613
   685 Cary Towne Blvd., Cary, 919/469-8410
Gregory's
   7420 Six Forks Rd., 919/847-6230
Irregardless
   901 W. Morgan St., 919/833-9920
The Upper Crust
   8831 Six Forks Rd., 919/847-8088

Best Burgers
Char-Grill
   3211 Edwards Mill Rd., 919/781-2945
   4617 Atlantic Ave., 919/954-9556
   618 Hillsborough St., 919/821-7636
Fat Daddy's
   6201 Glenwood Ave., 919/787-3773
Spanky's
   101 E. Franklin St., Chapel Hill, 919/967-2678

N

Best Business Lunch
Angus Barn
  9401 Glenwood Ave., 919/683-1398
Claudio's
  6300 Creedmoor Rd., 919/847-0083
Vinnie's
  7440 Six Forks Rd., Cary, 919/847-7319

Best Cajun/Creole Food
Cajun Charlie's
  607 Glenwood Ave., 919/836-1919
New Orleans Cookery
  401 W. Franklin St., Chapel Hill, 919/929-3192

Best Coffee
Barista Java
  205 Wolfe St., 919/832-2201
  300 Parham St., 919/834-3350
Bruegger's Bagel Bakery
  Multiple Locations
Cup-A-Joe
  3100 Hillsborough St., 919/828-9665
The Third Place
  1811 Glenwood Ave., 919/834-6566

Best Delicatessens
Boars Head
  6282 Glenwood Ave., 919/781-5544
  8323 Creedmoor Rd., 919/846-1222
Horwitz's Delicatessen
  107 Edenburg St., Cary, 919/467-2007
New York Deli
  109 S. Wilmington, 919/832-3354

Best Desserts
The Angus Barn
  9401 Glenwood Ave., 919/683-1398
Claudio's Ristorante
  6300 Creedmoor Rd., 919/847-0083
La Residence
  202 W. Rosemary St., Chapel Hill, 919/967-2506
Winston's
  6401 Falls of Neuse Rd., 919/790-0700

Best Diners
Oak City Diner
  2305 Wake Forest Rd., 919/821-8020
Owens 501 Diner
  1500 N. Fordham Blvd., Chapel Hill, 919/933-3505

Best Homestyle Food
Big Ed's
  220 Wolfe St., 919/836-9909
Dip's Country Kitchen
  405 W. Rosemary St., Chapel Hill, 919/942-5837
Griffin's
  1604 N. Market Dr., 919/876-0125

Best Ice Cream/Yogurt
Goodberry's Creamery
  2421 Spring Forest Rd., 919/878-8159

Best Late-Night Food
Raleighwood Cinema Grille
  6609 Falls of Neuse Rd., 919/847-0326
Vinnie's
  7440 Six Forks Rd., 919/847-7319

Best Microbreweries
Carolina Brewery
  460 W. Franklin St., Chapel Hill, 919/942-1800
Greenshields
  214 E. Martin St., 919/829-0214

Best Pizza
Andy's Pizza
  1302 Millbrook Rd., 919/872-0797
  4217 Six Forks Rd., 919/781-9043
Brother's Pizza
  132 Kilmayne Dr., Cary, 919/481-0883
  2508 1/2 Hillsborough St., 919/832-3664
  4112 Pleasant Valley Rd., 919/881-0883
Lilly's
  1813 Glenwood Ave., 919/833-0226
Piccola Italia
  423 Woodburn Rd., 919/833-6888
  6325 Falls of Neuse Rd., Ste. 17, 919/872-1131

Best Places to Eat When Someone Else Is Buying
Angus Barn
  9400 Glenwood Ave., 919/683-1398
Fearrington House
  2000 Fearrington Village, Pittsboro, 919/542-2121
Magnolia Grill
  1002 Ninth St., Durham, 919/286-3609

Best Romantic Dining
Fearrington House
  2000 Fearrington Village Ctr., Pittsboro, 919/542-2121
La Residence
  202 W. Rosemary St., Chapel Hill, 919/967-2506
Margaux's
  8111-111 Creedmoor Rd., 919/846-9846

Best Salad/Salad Bar
Sam's Restaurant and Wine Bar
  8050 Wake Forest Rd., 919/876-4056

Best Seafood
42nd Street Oyster Bar
  508 W. Jones St., 919/831-2811

Best Steaks
The Angus Barn
  9400 Glenwood Ave., 919/683-1398
Vinnie's
  107 Edinburgh Dr. S., Cary, 919/380-8210
  7440 Six Forks Rd., 919/847-7319

Best Vegetarian Food
Irregardless
  901 W. Morgan St., 919/833-9920
Rathskeller
  2412 Hillsborough St., 919/821-5342

N

Best Wine Selection
A Southern Season
  1808 E. Franklin St., Chapel Hill, 919/929-7133
The Angus Barn
  9400 Glenwood Ave., 919/683-1398

Standbys
International House of Pancakes
  1313 Hillsborough St., 919/821-2242
Perkins
  2657 Appliance Ct., 919/828-7375
Golden Corral Family Steak House
  Multiple Locations
Ruby Tuesday
  1058 W. Club Blvd., Durham, 919/286-5100
  4325 Glenwood Ave., 919/420-0109
Ryan's Family Steak House
  Multiple Locations
Red Lobster
  4408 Old Wake Forest Rd., 919/872-5608
  4416 Chapel Hill Blvd., Durham, 919/493-3566
  5900 Glenwood Ave., 919/782-7314
Lone Star Steakhouse
  3630 Chapel Hill Blvd., Durham, 919/489-0030
  4215 Wake Forest Rd., 919/872-2333
  6515 Glenwood Ave., 919/781-8400
Outback Steakhouse
  3500 Mt. Moriah Rd., 919/493-2202
  7500 Creedmoor Rd., 919/846-3848

N

ROCKY MOUNT, NC

Best American Food
Carleton House
  213 N. Church St., 919/977-6576

Best Barbecue/Ribs
Gardner's Barbecue
  1331 N. Wesleyan Blvd., 919/442-0531
  841 N. Fairview Rd., 919/442-5522
  738 Raleigh Rd., 919/442-1761
  3627 Sunset Ave., 919/443-3996
Bob Melton's Barbecue
  631 E. Ridge St., 919/446-8513

Best Cheap Meal
K and W Cafeteria
  2320 Sunset Ave., 919/443-1179

Best Dinner
Texas Steakhouse
  711 Sutter Creek Blvd., 919/443-3888

Best Fast Food
Central Cafe
  132 S. Church St., 919/446-8568

Best Place to Eat When Someone Else Is Buying
Carleton House
  213 N. Church St., 919/977-6576

Best Steaks
Carleton House
213 N. Church St., 919/977-6576

Standbys
Waffle House
301 Bypass, 919/442-9466

Best Barbecue/Ribs
Jim's Barbecue
1624 W. Innes St., 704/633-1094
Wink's Barbecue
1532 E. Innes St., 704/637-2410

Best Breakfast
Jim's Barbecue
1624 W. Innes St., 704/633-1094

Best Dinner
Jasmine's
520 Jake Alexander Blvd. S., 704/637-3100

Best Family Restaurant
The Farmhouse
1602 Jake Alexander Blvd. S., 704/633-3276

Best Lunch
Bogart's
2128 Statesville Blvd., 704/637-2227

Best Seafood
Blue Bay Seafood Restaurant
8850 Statesville Blvd., 704/278-2226
2050 Statesville Blvd., 704/639-9500

Best Bars
A Fish Called Wally
4 Marina St., Wrightsville Beach, 910/256-8500
Ice House
115 S. Water St., 910/763-2264
Barbary Coast
116 S. Front St., 910/762-8996
Wave Hog Saloon
12 Dock St., 910/762-2827

Best Barbecue/Ribs
Jackson's Big Oak Barbecue
920 S. Kerr Ave., 910/799-1581

Best Breakfast
Jimbo's Grill
4900 Womack Rd., Sanford, 919/774-9634
White Front Breakfast House
1518 Market St., 910/762-5672

Best Brunch
Crook's-by-the-River
138 S. Front St., 910/762-8898

Best Burgers
The Dockside
1306 Airlie Rd., 910/256-2752

N

P.T.'s Olde Fashioned Grille
4544 Fountain Dr., 910/392-2293

Best Business Lunch
Elijah's Restaurant
2 Ann St., 910/343-1448
Salt Works
6301 Oleander Dr., 910/350-0018
4001 Wrightsville Ave., 910/392-1241

Best Casual Dining
Caffe Phoenix
9 S. Front St., 910/343-1395

Best Cheap Meal
Jackson's Big Oak Barbecue
920 S. Kerr Ave., 910/799-1581
K and W Cafeteria
3501 Oleander Dr., 910/762-7011

Best Chinese Food
Wings Chinese Restaurant
4002 Oleander Dr., 910/799-8178
New China Restaurant
3913 Oleander Dr., 910/799-3750
Szechuan Chinese Restaurant
419 S. College Rd., 910/799-1426

Best Coffee
Fontana Caffe
4555 Fountain Dr., 910/313-0227

Best Desserts
Oceanic Restaurant and Grill
703 S. Lumina Ave., Wrightsville Beach, 910/256-5551
Elijah's Restaurant
2 Ann St., 910/343-1448
The Pilot House
2 Ann St., 901/343-0200

Best Diner
Jimbo's Grill
4900 Womack Rd., Sanford, 919/774-9634

Best Family Restaurant
K and W Cafeteria
3501 Oleander Dr., 910/762-7011

Best Homestyle Food
Salt Works
6301 Oleander Dr., 910/350-0018
4001 Wrightsville Ave., 910/392-1241

Best Ice Cream/Yogurt
Swensen's Ice Cream
620 S. College Rd., 910/395-6740

Best Italian Food
Eddie Romanelli's Restaurant
5400 Oleander Dr., 910/799-7000
Etrusca Restaurant
530 Causeway Dr., Wrightsville Beach, 910/256-5077

Best Late-Night Food
Crook's-by-the-River
138 S. Front St., 910/762-8898

Best Mexican Food
El Cerro Grande
  7 Wayne Dr., 910/343-9181
Burrito Bob's Mexican Restaurant
  5901 Wrightsville Ave., 910/392-6520

Best Pizza
Incredible Pizza
  3600A S. College Rd., 910/791-7080
Gumby's Pizza
  1414D South College Rd., 910/313-0072

Best Places to Be "Seen"
Caffe Phoenix
  9 S. Front St., 910/343-1395
The Dockside
  1306 Airlie Rd., 910/256-2752

Best Places to Eat When Someone Else Is Buying
Trail's End Steak House
  Trails End Rd., 910/791-2034
Gardenia's
  7105 Wrightsville Ave., Wrightsville Beach,
    910/256-2421

Best Romantic Dining
Oceanic Restaurant and Grill
  703 S. Lumina Ave., Wrightsville Beach, 910/256-5551
Trail's End Steak House
  Trails End Rd., 910/791-2034
Roy's Riverboat Landing
  2 Market St., 910/763-7227

Best Salad/Salad Bar
Annabelle's
  4106 Oleander Dr., 910/791-4955

Best Sandwiches
Schlotzsky's
  3810 Oleander Dr., 910/395-0077
Swensen's Ice Cream
  620 S. College Rd., 910/395-6740
Deli Downtown
  110 S. Front St., 910/762-6995
Sandwich Factory
  123 Princess St., 910/762-0100

Best Seafood
Oceanic Restaurant and Grill
  703 S. Lumina Ave., Wrightsville Beach, 910/256-5551
Bridge Tender
  1414 Airlie Rd., Wrightsville Beach, 910/256-4519
Elijah's Restaurant
  2 Ann St., 910/343-1448

Best Steaks
Trail's End Steak House
  Trails End Rd., 910/791-2034

Best Vegetarian Food
Annabelle's
  4106 Oleander Dr., 910/791-4955
Sahara Pitas and Subs
  6706 Market St., 910/392-4070

N

Standbys
Golden Corral Family Steak House
  5130 New Centre Dr., 910/392-1983
Shoney's
  149 S. College Rd., 910/392-2830
  4107 Oleander Dr., 910/799-7254
Outback Steakhouse
  302 S. College Rd., 910/791-5335
Baskin-Robbins
  3809 Oleander Dr., 910/791-7192
TCBY
  343 S. College Rd., 910/395-2251
Pizza Hut
  2402 S. Seventeenth St., 910/392-0180
  4016 Oleander Dr., 910/799-3650
Chuck E. Cheese Pizza
  4389 Oleander Dr., 910/392-1234
Fuddruckers
  4107 Oleander Dr., 910/791-6900

WILSON, NC

Best Barbecue/Ribs
Parker's Barbecue
  Hwy. 301S, 919/237-0972
Bill's Barbecue
  3007 Downing St. SW, 919/237-4372

Best Breakfast
Country Restaurant
  4600 Nash Rd. W., 919/237-8723

Best Coffeehouse
Green River Coffee Company
  103 Ward Blvd. N., 919/243-6101

Best Desserts
Priscilla's
  2101 Tarboro St., 919/243-4944

Best Dinner
The Legacy
  301 E. Main St., Elm City, 919/236-3432

Best Seafood
Silver Lake Restaurant
  Hwy. 58N, 919/243-2034

Best Steaks
Griff's Steak Barn
  Hwy. 301S, 919/237-5935

WINSTON-SALEM, NC

Best Restaurant in Town
Ryan's Restaurant
  719 Coliseum Dr., 910/724-6132

Best Barbecue/Ribs
Mr. Barbecue
  1318 Peters Creek Pkwy., 910/725-7827

Best Cheap Meal
Mayflower Seafood Restaurant
  850 Peters Creek Pkwy., 910/725-3261

Best Family Restaurant
Ronni's Restaurant
  3656 Reynolds Rd., 910/924-1666

Best Southwestern Food
South by Southwest
  241 S. Marshall St., 910/727-0800

North Dakota

Best Restaurants in Town
Seven Seas
  2611 Old Red Trail., Mandan, 701/663-7401
Caspar's East Forty
  1401 Interchange Ave., 701/258-7222

Best All-You-Can-Eat Buffets
Royal Fork Buffet Restaurant
  1065 E. Interstate Ave., 701/222-0501
Midtowner
  111 Collins Ave., Mandan, 701/663-4459
Drumstick
  307 N. Third St., 701/223-8449

Best Brunch
Radisson Inn
  800 S. Third St., 701/258-7700
Peacock Alley Bar and Grill
  422 E. Main Ave., 701/255-7917
Drumstick
  307 N. Third St., 701/223-8449

Best Burgers
Wood House
  1825 N. Thirteenth St., 701/255-3654
It's Burger Time
  1320 E. Main Ave., 701/222-2458

Best Business Lunch
Peacock Alley Bar and Grill
  422 E. Main Ave., 701/255-7917
Caspar's East Forty
  1401 Interchange Ave., 701/258-7222
Drumstick
  307 N. Third St., 701/223-8449

Best Casual Dining
Speedway Restaurant
  Rural Route 2, Minot, 701/838-0649

N

Best Chinese Food
Jade Garden Restaurant
  431 S. Third St., 701/222-8615
Hong Kong Restaurant
  1055 E. Interstate Ave., 701/223-2130

Best Coffee
The Prairie Peddler
  Kirkwood Mall, Ste. 622, 701/223-1066
Green Earth Cafe
  208 E. Broadway Ave., 701/223-8646

Best Desserts
Green Earth Cafe
  208 E. Broadway Ave., 701/223-8646

Best Diners
Drumstick
  307 N. Third St., 701/223-8449
Little Cottage Cafe
  2513 E. Main Ave., 701/223-4949
Kroll's Kitchen
  1915 E. Main Ave., 701/255-3850

Best Health-Conscious Menu
Green Earth Cafe
  208 E. Broadway Ave., 701/223-8646
The International Restaurant
  Hwy. 83 at I-94, 701/258-6442

Best Homestyle Food
Drumstick
  307 N. Third St., 701/223-8449
Kroll's Kitchen
  1915 E. Main Ave., 701/255-3850
Dakota Farms Family Restaurant
  1301 E. Main Ave., 701/258-0559
Cary's Kitchen
  1307 Interchange Ave., 701/258-3470

Best Ice Cream/Yogurt
Lindy Sue's Third Street Emporium
  120 N. Third St., 701/224-1170

Best Italian Food
Captain Meriwether's Landing
  1700 River Rd., 701/224-0455
Doublewood Inn
  1400 Interchange Ave., 701/258-7000

Best Late-Night Food
Drumstick
  307 N. Third St., 701/223-8449

Best Mexican Food
Fiesta Villa
  411 E. Main Ave., 701/222-8075
Paradiso Mexican Restaurant
  2620 State St., 701/224-1111
Los Amigos Mexican Restaurant
  1010 Boundary Rd. NW, 701/663-1958

N

Best Pizza
A and B Pizza
  1017 E. Interstate Ave., 701/258-6002
  311 S. Seventh St., 701/222-3108

Best Places to be "Seen"
Peacock Alley Bar and Grill
  422 E. Main Ave., 701/255-7917
Fiesta Villa
  411 E. Main Ave., 701/222-8075

Best Place to Eat Alone
Green Earth Cafe
  208 E. Broadway Ave., 701/223-8646

Best Romantic Dining
Caspar's East Forty
  1401 Interchange Ave., 701/258-7222
Seven Seas
  2611 Old Red Trail, Mandan, 701/663-7401
Peacock Alley Bar and Grill
  422 E. Main Ave., 701/255-7917

Best Salad/Salad Bar
Royal Fork Buffet Restaurant
  1065 E. Interstate Ave., 701/222-0501
Caspar's East Forty
  1401 Interchange Ave., 701/258-7222

Best Sandwiches
Green Earth Cafe and One World
  208 E. Broadway Ave., 701/223-8646

Best Steaks
Seven Seas
  2611 Old Red Trail, Mandan, 701/663-7401
Speedway Restaurant
  Rural Route 2, Minot, 701/838-0649
Caspar's East Forty
  1401 Interchange Ave., 701/258-7222

Standbys
Ground Round
  526 S. Third St., 701/223-0000
Bonanza
  2000 N. Twelfth St., 701/223-1107
Perkins
  111 E. Interstate Ave., 701/222-0625
Denny's
  405 S. Seventh St., 701/223-2015
Applebee's
  434 S. Third St., 701/222-1018
TCBY
  500 E. Front Ave., 701/258-1864
Dairy Queen
  230 W. Broadway Ave., 701/223-0548
  103 W. Avenue A, 701/258-4438
Pizza Hut
  Hwy. 83N at Capital Ave., 701/258-1100
  413 E. Bismarck Expwy., 701/224-1047
  825 E. Broadway Ave., 701/223-2300

Little Caesar's
625 S. Washington St., 701/258-8888
1929 N. Washington St., 701/255-0000
Subway
221 S. Seventh St., 701/224-0049
301 S. Third St., 701/224-1169
2700 State St., 701/224-9294
2006 N. Twelfth St., 701/224-0030

DICKINSON, ND

Best Barbecue/Ribs
Jack's Family Restaurant
1406 W. Villard St., 701/225-5905

Best Breakfast
Rose Dakota Restaurant
Hospitality Inn, 532 Fifteenth St. W., 701/227-1853

Best Burgers
Rattlesnake Creek Brewery and Grill
2 Villard St. W., 701/225-9518

Best Chinese Food
China Wok
1173 Third Ave. W., 701/227-8889

Best Family Restaurants
Jack's Family Restaurant
1406 W. Villard St., 701/225-5905
German Hungarian Lodge
20 E. Broadway St., 701/225-3311

Best Homestyle Food
George's and the Owl
Hwy. 85 at Main St., Amidon, 701/879-6289

Best Sandwiches
Rattlesnake Creek Brewery and Grill
2 Villard St. W., 701/225-9518

Best Steaks
German Hungarian Lodge
20 E. Broadway St., 701/225-3311

Standbys
Dairy Queen
339 E. Villard St., 701/225-5971
Perkins
188 W. Museum Dr., 701/227-3001
Pizza Hut
1011 W. Broadway St., 701/225-8000

FARGO, ND

Best All-You-Can-Eat Buffet
Royal Fork Buffet Restaurant
4325 Thirteenth Ave. SW, 701/282-9539

Best Atmosphere
Great Northern Brewing Company
425 Broadway, 701/235-9707

Best Bar
The Rock
  901 40th St. SW, 701/282-3986

Best Breakfast
Fryin' Pan Family Restaurant
  302 Main Ave., 701/293-9952

Best Burgers
Fifties Cafe
  13 Eighth St. S., 701/298-0347

Best Chinese Food
Pearl Restaurant
  921 Fourth Ave. N., 701/232-1777

Best Desserts
Pannekoeken Griddle and Grille
  3340 Thirteenth Ave. SW, 701/237-3559

Best Family Restaurant
Embers Restaurant
  3838 Main Ave., 701/282-6330

Best Greek/Mediterranean Food
Santa Lucia Family Restaurant
  3111 Thirteenth Ave. SW, 701/298-3676

Best Ice Cream/Yogurt
Creamery
  3902 Thirteenth Ave. S., 701/282-3313

Best Late-Night Food
Conservatory Restaurant
  613 First Ave. N., 701/241-7080

Best Mexican Food
Mexican Village
  814 Main Ave., 701/293-0120
Paradiso Mexican Restaurant
  801 38th St. SW, 701/282-5747

Best Microbreweries
Great Northern Brewing Company
  425 Broadway, 701/235-9707
The Trader and Trapper Brewing Company
  617 Center Ave., Moorhead, 218/236-0202

Best Other Ethnic Food
Pannekoeken Griddle and Grille (Dutch)
  3340 Thirteenth Ave. SW, 701/237-3559

Best Pizza
Godfather's Pizza
  1439 S. University Dr., 701/280-2644
  4340 Thirteenth Ave. SW, 701/277-1666
Sammy's Pizza and Restaurant
  301 Broadway, 701/235-5331

Best Place to Eat When Someone Else Is Buying
Seasons at Rose Creek
  1500 Rose Creek Pkwy. E., 701/235-5000

Best Romantic Dining
Victoria's Restaurant
  101 First St., Wolverton, 218/995-2000

Best Salad/Salad Bar
The Trader and Trapper Brewing Company
617 Center Ave., Moorhead, 218/236-0202

Best Sandwiches
Grandma's Saloon and Grill
4201 Thirteenth Ave. S., 701/282-5439

Best View While Dining
The Treetop
403 Center Ave., Moorhead, 218/233-1393

Standbys
Perkins
1220 36th St. S., 701/232-2441
Friday's
4100 Thirteenth Ave. SW, 701/281-3030
Ground Round
2902 Thirteenth Ave. SW, 701/280-2288
Baskin-Robbins
1501 S. University Dr., 701/293-6611
The Olive Garden
4339 Thirteenth Ave. SW, 701/277-1241
Chuck E. Cheese Pizza
1202 Nodak Dr., 701/232-7967
Red Lobster
4215 Thirteenth Ave. S., 701/282-8983
Lone Star Steakhouse
4328 Thirteenth Ave. SW, 701/282-6642

N **GRAND FORKS, ND**

Best Restaurant in Town
Sanders 1907
312 Kittson Ave., 701/746-8970

Best All-You-Can-Eat Buffet
Royal Fork Buffet
Columbia Mall Shopping Ctr., 2800 S. Columbia Rd.,
701/746-0869

Best Bar
John Barleycorn
Columbia Mall Shopping Ctr., 2800 S. Columbia Rd.,
701/775-0501

Best Breakfast
Village Inn
3555 Gateway Dr., 701/746-5469
2451 S. Columbia Rd., 701/772-7241

Best Brunch
River Bend Supper Club
Hwy. 2, East Grand Forks, 218/773-2493

Best Burgers
Bronze Boot Steak House
1804 N. Washington St., 701/746-5433

Best Business Lunch
Town House
710 First Ave., 701/746-5411

Best Cheap Meal
Highway Host
3615 Gateway Dr., 701/775-3141

Best Chinese Food
Hunan Chinese Restaurant
  Columbia Mall Shopping Ctr., 2100 S. Columbia Rd.,
    701/772-0556

Best Coffee
The Coffee Company
  Columbia Mall Shopping Ctr., 2100 S. Columbia Rd.,
    701/772-1992

Best Desserts
Sanders 1907
  312 Kittson Ave., 701/746-8970

Best Diner
Noel's Cuisine
  309 Demers St., 701/772-8263

Best French Food
French Connection
  1726W S. Washington St., 701/746-8333
  414 Demers Ave., 701/780-9357

Best Health-Conscious Menu
Peartree Restaurant
  1210 N. 43rd St., 701/772-7131

Best Homestyle Food
Del's Coffee Shop
  1828 S. Washington St., 701/772-3311

Best Italian Food
Big Al's Pasta Parlor
  Hwy. 2W, 701/775-5341

Best Late-Night Food
Jeannie's Restaurant
  1106 S. Washington St., 701/772-6966

Best Pizza
Italian Moon Pizza and Mexican
  810 S. Washington St., 701/772-7277

Best Place to Be "Seen"
Sanders 1907
  312 Kittson Ave., 701/746-8970

Best Place to Eat Alone
Ramada Inn
  1205 N. 43rd St., 701/775-3951

Best Place to Eat When Someone Else Is Buying
Sanders 1907
  312 Kittson Ave., 701/746-8970

Best Romantic Dining
Ramada Inn
  1205 N. 43rd St., 701/775-3951

Best Sandwiches
Blue Moose
  East Grand Forks, 218/773-6516

Best Steaks
Whitey's
  109 Demers Ave., East Grand Forks, 218/773-1831
Grand Forks Good Ribs Steakhouse
  4223 Twelfth Ave. N., 701/746-7115

Best Tea Room
La Brasa
    2500 S. Washington St., 701/746-4871

Best Vegetarian Food
The Garden Vegetarian Foods
    420 Demers Ave., 701/746-5920

Standbys
Applebee's
    2851 S. Columbia Rd., 701/795-5688
Ground Round
    2800 32nd Ave., 701/775-4646
TCBY
    2400 S. Washington St., 701/746-5004
Chi Chi's
    3000 32nd Ave. S., 701/746-9431
Ponderosa
    2717 S. Columbia Rd., 701/746-1301
Red Lobster
    2675 32nd Ave. S., 701/772-8770

MINOT, ND

Best Restaurants in Town
Homesteader's Restaurant
    2501 Hwy. 2 at 52 Bypass W., 701/838-2274
Jake's Spice and Spirit
    1910 S. Broadway, 701/852-8355
The Speedway Restaurant
    Rural Route 2, 701/838-0649
Embassy Food and Drink
    112 Second Ave. SW, 701/852-4343
Sammy's Pizza Palace
    400 N. Broadway, 701/852-4486
Roll-N-Pin
    2145 N. Broadway, 701/839-8774

Best Seafood
Field and Stream
    1711 Seventh St. NW, 701/852-3663

Best Steaks
Field and Stream
    1711 Seventh St. NW, 701/852-3663

WILLISTON, ND

Best All-You-Can-Eat Buffet
El Rancho Motor Hotel
    1623 Second Ave. W., 701/572-6321

Best Breakfast
El Rancho Motor Hotel
    1623 Second Ave. W., 701/572-6321
Main Street Diner
    216 Main St., 701/774-0383

Best Burgers
Burger Queen and Pizza
    2516 Second Ave. W., 701/572-1840

Best Chinese Food
Hunan Restaurant
  1804 Second Ave. W., 701/572-3388
Ming Garden Restaurant
  302 Fourteenth St. W., 701/774-1940

Best Coffee
Gramma Sharon's Cafe
  4201 Second Ave. W., 701/572-1412

Best Diner
Main Street Diner
  216 Main St., 701/774-0383

Best Family Restaurants
Dakota Farms Family Restaurant
  1906 Second Ave. W., 701/572-4480
The Brickyard
  6 W. 25th St., 701/572-3848

Best Pizza
Burger Queen and Pizza
  2516 Second Ave. W., 701/572-1840

Best Sandwiches
Kettle Restaurant
  3901 Second Ave. W., 701/774-2831
The Brickyard
  6 W. 25th St., 701/572-3848

Best Steaks
Jerry's Fireside Dining
  1002 Second St. W., 701/572-0677
Pierce's Steak House
  408 First Ave. E., 701/572-4751

Standbys
Bonanza
  1501 Sixteenth St., 701/572-4814
Dairy Queen
  1620 Second Ave. W., 701/572-6474

N

Ohio

Best All-You-Can-Eat Buffet
Cathedral Buffet
  2690 State Rd., Cuyahoga Falls, 330/922-0467

Best Barbecue/Ribs
Damon's, The Place for Ribs
  150 Montrose West Ave., 330/665-5552

Best Breakfast
Country Kitchen
  1245 E. Waterloo Rd., 330/724-9357
  610 E. Cuyahoga Falls Ave., 330/928-1026

Best Burgers
Coach's Cafe
  1537 S. Main St., 330/773-1724

Best Casual Dining
Guy's Party Center
  500 E. Waterloo Rd., 330/724-3272

Best Cheap Meal
Bialy's at the Lake
  493 Portage Lakes Dr., 330/644-7177
Parasson's Italian Restaurant
  501 N. Main St., 330/376-2117
  959 E. Waterloo Rd., 330/724-9375

Best Chinese Food
House of Hunan
  2717 W. Market St., 330/864-8215
  376 E. Waterloo Rd., 330/773-1888

Best Coffee
Two Sisters Cafe and Catering
  380 S. Main St., 330/535-4480

Best Desserts
Cathedral Buffet
  2690 State Rd., Cuyahoga Falls, 330/922-0467

Best Eclectic Menu
Tangier Restaurant and Cabaret
  532 W. Market St., 330/376-7171

Best Family Restaurant
Bialy's at the Lake
  493 Portage Lakes Dr., 330/644-7177

Best Greek/Mediterranean Food
Gus' Chalet
  938 E. Tallmadge Ave., 330/633-2322

Best Ice Cream/Yogurt
Strickland's Frozen Custard II
  2420 Wedgewood Dr., 330/733-0133

Best Italian Food
Pazzzo Ristorante
  2855 W. Market St., 330/867-3644
Fontano White Pine
  566 White Pine Dr., 330/864-3050

Best Late-Night Food
Lamp Post
  2081 E. Market St., 330/784-1027

Best Mexican Food
Don Pablo's Mexican Kitchen
  145 Montrose West Ave., 330/666-0239

Best Other Ethnic Food
Playwright's (Irish)
  1603 Home Ave., 330/630-1677

Best Outdoor Dining
Pelican Cove
  3720 S. Main St., 330/645-0635

Best Pizza
Emidio and Sons Italian Restaurant
  636 N. Main St., 330/253-4777
Mama Rosa's
  184 East Tallmadge Ave., 330/253-8400
  1115 Brown St., 330/773-8235

Best Place to Eat When Someone Else Is Buying
Gus' Chalet
  938 E. Tallmadge Ave., 330/633-2322

Best Place to Take the Kids
East Side Mario's
  581 Howe Ave., 330/928-7288

Best Sandwiches
Louie's Bar and Grille
  739 E. Glenwood Ave., 330/535-5030

Best Steaks
Bialy's at the Lake
  493 Portage Lakes Dr., 330/644-7177
Young's Restaurant
  2744 Manchester Rd., 330/745-6116
Guy's Party Center
  500 E. Waterloo Rd., 330/724-3272

Best View While Dining
Harbour
  562 Portage Lakes Dr., 330/644-1664

Standbys
Applebee's
  508 Howe Ave., 330/928-1500

Bob Evans
  3211 S. Arlington Rd., 330/644-4811
  4076 Medina Rd., 330/666-2992
Chi Chi's
  1770 Brittain Rd., 330/630-2335
The Olive Garden
  3924 Medina Rd., 330/666-5313
Red Lobster
  3901 Medina Rd., 330/666-0727
Friendly's
  1700 W. Exchange St., 330/867-6922
  2400 Romig Rd., 330/753-1159
  2934 S. Arlington Rd., 330/644-0115
  3265 W. Market St., 330/867-7412
  3921 Medina Rd., 330/666-1088

ALLIANCE, OH

Best American Food
Polinori's Palm Garden Inn
  1441 S. Liberty Ave., 330/821-2680

Best Bar
Roadhouse Charlie Pizza
  2239 W. State St., 330/823-0578

Best Breakfast
Shaffer's Diner
  40 N. Park Ave., 330/823-0006

Best Casual Dining
Roadhouse Charlie Pizza
  2239 W. State St., 330/823-0578

Best Chinese Food
China House
  251 Hester Ave., 330/823-7669

Best Dinner
Taster's Choice Cafe
  1908 S. Union Ave., 330/821-6666

Best Diner
Shaffer's Diner
  40 N. Park Ave., 330/823-0006

Best Health-Conscious Menu
Taster's Choice Cafe
  1908 S. Union Ave., 330/821-6666

Best Homestyle Food
Shaffer's Diner
  40 N. Park Ave., 330/823-0006

Best Italian Food
Polinori's Palm Garden Inn
  1441 S. Liberty Ave., 330/821-2680

Best Mexican Food
Don Pancho's Fiesta Villa
  9 S. Union Ave., 330/823-4390

Best Pizza
Pisanello's Pizza
  344 W. State St., 330/823-7271

ASHLAND, OH

Best Restaurant in Town
Oak Park Tavern
2919 Park Ave. E., Mansfield, 419/589-2637

Best Breakfast
Lyn-Way Restaurant
1320 Cleveland Ave., 419/281-8911

Best Chinese Food
Great Dragon
1983 Baney Rd. S., 419/289-1688

Best Delicatessen
Kelly's Deli and Restaurant
622 Claremont Ave., 419/281-1313

Best Family Restaurants
Olde Keyes
1 N. Main St., Savannah, 419/962-4610
Lyn-Way Restaurant
1320 Cleveland Ave., 419/281-8911

Best Homestyle Food
Olde Keyes
1 N. Main St., Savannah, 419/962-4610

Best Sandwiches
Kelly's Deli and Restaurant
622 Claremont Ave., 419/281-1313

Best Seafood
Cabin
2106 State Rte. 603, 419/368-4457

Best Steaks
Cabin
2106 State Rte. 603, 419/368-4457

ASHTABULA, OH

Best Restaurant in Town
Hulbert's Restaurant
1033 Bridge St., 216/964-2594

Best American Food
Kork and Kettle
4618 Main Ave., 216/992-3013

Best Family Restaurant
Hil-Mak Sea Food Restaurant
449 Lake Ave., 216/964-3222

Best Italian Food
Caruso's Pizza and Spaghetti
2313 West Ave., 216/964-2646

Best Seafood
Hil-Mak Sea Food Restaurant
449 Lake Ave., 216/964-3222

Best Steaks
Lou's Stagecoach
5205 Lake Rd. W., 216/964-7930

Standbys
Perkins
1601 E. Prospect Rd., 216/993-8296

ATHENS, OH

Best Restaurants in Town
Sylvia's
 4 Depot St., 614/594-3484
Casa Nueva
 4 W. State St., 614/592-2016

Best Atmosphere
Seven Sauces
 66 N. Court St., 614/592-5555

Best Burgers
The Pub
 39 N. Court St., 614/592-9967

Best Business Lunch
Albert's
 23 W. Union St., 614/594-2233
Lam's Garden
 120 W. Union St., 614/592-1955
 934 E. State St., 614/594-4424
Casa Nueva
 4 W. State St., 614/592-2016

Best Chinese Food
Lam's Garden
 120 W. Union St., 614/592-1955
 934 E. State St., 614/594-4424

Best Coffee
Another Fool's Cafe
 24 1/2 E. State St., 614/593-3969
Front Room
 Ohio University, 20 Chubb Hall, 614/593-4141

Best Delicatessens
Zachary's
 30 N. Court St., 614/592-2000
Bagel Street Deli
 27 S. Court, 614/593-3838

Best Greek/Mediterranean Food
Souvlaki Sandwich Shop
 9 W. State St., 614/592-4131

Best Mexican Food
Casa Nueva
 4 W. State St., 614/592-2016

Best New Restaurants
Lui Lui's
 8 Station St., 614/594-8905
Gary's Family Restaurant
 230 Columbus Rd., 614/594-2892

Best Pizza
Late Night Pizza
 122 W. Union St., 614/592-2008

Best Vegetarian Food
Casa Nueva
 4 W. State St., 614/592-2016
Purple Chopstix
 371 1/2 Richland Ave., 614/592-4798

Zachary's Deli
  30 N. Court St., 614/592-2000

Standbys
Bob Evans
  357 E. State St., 614/592-3842
Papa John's
  433 E. State St., 614/594-7272
Pizza Hut
  394 Richland Ave., 614/594-4040
  803 E. State St., 614/593-3697
Ponderosa
  741 E. State St., 614/593-5758
Wendy's
  380 Richland Ave., 614/592-2545
  40 S. Court, 614/592-5200
Sonic Drive-In
  922 E. State St., 614/592-4575

BARBERTON, OH

Best American Food
Nancy's 562 Cafe
  562 W. Tuscarawas, 330/753-7733

Best Breakfast
Nancy's 562 Cafe
  562 W. Tuscarawas, 330/753-7733

Best Burgers
Wink's Drive-In
  75 Fifth St. SE, 330/745-4141

Best Italian Food
La Spaghetteria
  576 W. Tuscarawas, 330/753-7733

Best Lunch
Wink's Drive-In
  75 Fifth St. SE, 330/745-4141

Best Other Ethnic Food
Mickey J's (Slovenian)
  545 W. Tuscarawas, 330/753-7733

Best Pizza
Parasson's Italian Restaurant
  234 Wooster Rd. N., 330/753-2264

BEAVERCREEK, OH

Best American Food
Field's Restaurant
  3347 E. Patterson Rd., 513/426-6625

Best Breakfast
Debra Lee's
  3321 Dayton-Xenia, 513/429-3033

Best Burgers
Bellefair Restaurant
  1490 N. Fairfield Rd., 513/426-0788

Best Lunch
Fairfield Inn Restaurant
  1375 N. Fairfield Rd., 513/426-4536

Best Mexican Food
Don Pablo's
2745 Fairfield Commons, 513/320-1777

Best Steaks
Grub Steak
2220 State Rte. 35, Alpha, 513/429-3033
Max and Erma's
2739 Fairfield Commons, 513/320-2255

BOWLING GREEN, OH

Best American Food
Kaufman's
163 S. Main St., 419/352-2595
1628 E. Wooster St., 419/354-2535

Best Bar
Sam B's
146 N. Main St., 419/353-2277

Best Coffee
Cosmo's Cafe
126 E. Wooster St., 419/354-5282

Best Desserts
Cosmo's Cafe
126 E. Wooster St., 419/354-5282

Best Pizza
Pollyeyes Campus
440 E. Court St., 419/352-9638

Best Steaks
Kaufman's
163 S. Main St., 419/352-2595
1628 E. Wooster St., 419/354-2535

CANTON, OH

Best Atmosphere
Bender's Tavern
137 Court Ave. SW, 330/453-8424

Best Barbecue/Ribs
Damon's International
4220 Belden Village St. NW, 330/492-2413

Best Breakfast
Ashley's Restaurant
320 Market Ave. S., 330/454-5000

Best Burgers
Rumours Cafe
725 30th St. NE, 330/452-0442

Best Chinese Food
Genghis Khan Restaurant
4631 Everhard Rd. NW, 330/499-8887
Ricky Ly's Chinese Gourmet
4725 Dressler Rd. NW, 330/492-5909
Panda Garden Restaurant
3619 Cleveland Ave. NW, 330/492-2108

Best Coffee
Susan's Coffee and Tea
4740 Dressler Rd. NW, 330/493-0550

O

Best Family Restaurant
Desert Inn
300 Twelfth St. NW, 330/456-1766
John's Bar and Grille
2749 Cleveland Ave. NW, 330/454-1259

Best Ice Cream/Yogurt
Taggart's Ice Cream Parlor
1401 Fulton Rd. NW, 330/452-6844

Best Italian Food
Lolli's Restaurant
4801 Dressler Rd. NW, 330/492-6846

Best Mexican Food
Don Pancho's Fiesta Villa
9 S. Union Ave., Alliance, 330/823-4390

Best Pizza
Kraus Pizza Company
5440 Fulton Dr. NW, 330/494-7722
Pizza Oven
3314 Lesh St. NE, 330/454-1481
1601 30th St. NE, 330/453-1437
4000 Cleveland Ave. NW, 330/492-4333
4990 Dressler Rd. NW, 330/493-0090
3655 Cleveland Ave. SW, 330/484-2518
3153 Tuscarawas St. W., 330/452-8801
Pizza Plus
1909 Whipple Ave. NW, 330/478-5700

Best Place to Eat Alone
Bender's Tavern
137 Court Ave. SW, 330/453-8424

Best Place to Eat When Someone Else Is Buying
Lolli's Restaurant
4801 Dressler Rd. NW, 330/492-6846

Best Romantic Dining
Mozart Restaurant
3522 Cleveland Ave. NW, 330/493-8664

Best Seafood
Bender's Tavern
137 Court Ave. SW, 330/453-8424

Best Steaks
Baker's Cafe
1927 Stark Ave. SW, 330/454-0528
Lolli's Restaurant
4801 Dressler Rd. NW, 330/492-6846

CHILLICOTHE, OH

Best Barbecue/Ribs
Damon's International
10 N. Plaza Blvd., 614/775-8383

Best Breakfast
J.R. Valentine's Restaurant
787 N. Bridge St., 614/774-2471

Best Chinese Food
Diamond Head Restaurant
33 N. Paint St., 614/773-8585

Best Diner
Carl's Town House
95 S. Paint St., 614/773-1660

Best Homestyle Food
Carl's Town House
95 S. Paint St., 614/773-1660

Best Pizza
Poppa Dino's Pizzeria
45 E. Water St., 614/773-1114

Best Steaks
Richard's House of Beef and Seafood
1641 N. Bridge St., 614/775-7099

Best Thai Food
Bangkok Palace
870 N. Bridge St., 614/773-8424

CINCINNATI, OH

Best Bagels
Bagel Stop
621 Walnut St., 513/723-1903

Best Beer Selection
Allyn's Cafe
3538 Columbia Pkwy., 513/871-5779

Best Breakfast
First Watch
8118 Montgomery Rd., 513/891-0088
Anchor Grill
438 Pike St., Covington, 606/431-9498
Inn the Wood
277 Calhoun St., 513/221-3044

Best Cheap Meal
Stone Mill Bread Company
265 Hosea Ave., Clifton, 513/751-5050
3012 Madison Rd., Oakley, 513/631-8383
8 West Fourth St., 513/651-0030
Courtyard Cafe
1211 Main St., 513/723-1119
Rally's Hamburgers
Multiple Locations

Best Chinese Food
Blue Gibbon Chinese Restaurant
1231 Tennessee Ave., 513/641-4100
China Gourmet
3340 Erie Ave., 513/871-6612

Best Coffee
Awakenings Tea and Coffee
2734 Erie Ave., Hyde Park, 513/321-2525

Best Desserts
Petersen's
1111 St. Gregory St., 513/651-4777
Take the Cake
1437 Main St., 513/241-2772

Best Family Restaurant
Stone's Restaurant
3605 Harrison Ave., 513/661-6849

Best Happy Hour Snacks
Brick Yard
  2038 Madison Rd., O'Bryanville, 513/321-3953

Best Pizza
Pomidor's Pizza
  121 McMillan St., 513/861-0080
Pizzeria Uno
  324 Ludlow Ave., 513/281-8667
  7500 Beechmont Ave., 513/231-8667

Best Salad/Salad Bar
Celestial
  1071 Celestial St., 513/241-4455

Best Soul Food
Ernie's Catering
  869 Lincoln Ave., 513/961-8460

Best Steaks
Morton's of Chicago
  Tower Place, Ste. 105, 28 W. Fourth St., 513/241-4104
The Precinct
  311 Delta Ave., 513/321-5454

Best Thai Food
Bangkok Thai Cuisine
  1055 Main St., Rte. 22, Milford, 513/248-4853

Best Vegetarian Food
Mullane's Parkside Cafe
  723 Race St., 513/381-1331
Carol's Corner Cafe
  825 Main St., 513/651-2667

CLEVELAND, OH

Best American Food
Wards' Inn
  34105 Chagrin Blvd., 216/595-1954

Best Barbecue/Ribs
Winking Lizard
  25380 Miles Rd., 216/831-3488

Best Beer Selection
Harbor Inn
  1219 Main Ave., 216/241-3232

Best Breakfast
Yours Truly
  13228 Shaker Sq., 216/751-8646
  25300 Chagrin Blvd., 216/464-4848

Best Brunch
Fagan's
  996 Old River Rd., 216/241-6116
Pier W
  12700 Lake Ave. at Winston Place, Lakewood,
    216/228-2250

Best Burgers
Heck's Cafe
  11201 Detroit Ave., 216/221-8084
  2927 Bridge Ave., 216/861-5464

Best Business Lunch
Roxy Cafe
  National City Ctr., E. Ninth at Euclid, 216/523-5580

Best Casual Dining
Pastabilities
  13915 Cedar Rd., 216/321-8600

Best Chili
Skyline Chili
  4752 Ridge Rd., 216/351-7632
  5706 Mayfield Rd., 216/953-5929

Best Chinese Food
Bo Loong
  3922 Saint Clair Ave. NE, 216/391-3113

Best Coffee
Arabica Coffee Houses
  Multiple Locations

Best Delicatessen
Max's Deli and Restaurant
  19337 Detroit Rd., Rocky River, 216/356-2226

Best Desserts
Max's Deli and Restaurant
  19337 Detroit Rd., Rocky River, 216/356-2226

Best French Food
Sans Souci
  Stouffer Tower Plaza, 24 Public Sq., 216/696-5600

Best German Food
Hofbrau Haus
  1400 E. 55th St., 216/881-7773

Best Greek/Mediterranean Food
The Mad Greek Restaurant
  2466 Fairmount Blvd., 216/421-3333

Best Health-Conscious Menu
Calorie Gallery
  3710 Carnegie Ave., 216/431-1410

Best Ice Cream/Yogurt
Malley's Chocolates
  Multiple Locations

Best Indian Food
Saffron Patch
  20600 Chagrin Blvd., 216/295-0400

Best Italian Food
Pastabilities
  13915 Cedar Rd., 216/321-8600
Piccolo Mondo
  1352 W. Sixth St., 216/241-1300

Best Japanese Food
Otani
  6420 Mayfield Rd., Ste. 1625, 216/442-7098

Best Late-Night Food
Clifton Lunch
  11637 Clifton Blvd., 216/521-5003

Best Mexican Food
Lopez y Gonzalez
2066 Lee Rd., 216/371-7611
Luchita's
3456 W. 117th St., 216/252-1169

Best New Restaurant
Wards' Inn
34105 Chagrin Blvd., Moreland Hills, 216/595-1954

Best Other Ethnic Food
Empress Taytu Ethiopian Restaurant (Ethiopian)
6125 St. Clair Ave., 216/736-9400

Best Outdoor Dining
Gamekeeper's Taverne
87 West St., Chagrin Falls, 216/247-7744

Best Pizza
Mama Santa
12305 Mayfield Rd., 216/231-9567
Player's Pizza and Pasta
14527 Madison Ave., 216/226-5200

Best Place to Eat When Someone Else Is Buying
Classics
Omni Hotel, Carnegie at E. 96th St., 216/791-1300

Best Place to Take Guests
Top of the Town
1301 E. Ninth St., 216/771-1600

Best Place to Take the Kids
The Great Lakes Brewing Company
2516 Market St., 216/771-4404

Best Sandwiches
Grum's Sub Shoppe
1776 Coventry Rd., 216/321-4781
3427 Lee Rd., 216/751-4786
Max's Deli and Restaurant
19337 Detroit Rd., Rocky River, 216/356-2226

Best Seafood
Pier W
12700 Lake Ave. at Winston Place, Lakewood,
216/228-2250

Best Steaks
Hyde Park Grille
1825 Coventry Rd., Cleveland Heights, 216/321-6444
Morton's of Chicago
The Avenue at Tower City Ctr., 1600 W. Second St.,
215/621-6200
Jim's Steak House
1800 Scranton Rd., 216/241-6343
Diamond Grille
77 W. Market St., 216/253-0041

Best Vegetarian Food
Tommy's
1824 Coventry Rd., Cleveland Heights, 216/321-7757
Hunan by the Falls
508 E. Washington St., Chagrin Falls, 216/247-0808

Best Romantic Dining
Classics
  Omni Hotel, Carnegie at E. 96th St., 216/791-1300

Best Schmooze Bar
Piccolo Mondo
  1352 W. Sixth St., Warehouse District, 216/241-1300
Roxy Cafe
  National City Ctr., E. Ninth at Short Vincent,
    216/523-5580

Best Thai Food
Paul's Siam Cuisine
  1918 Lee Rd., 216/371-9575

Best Vegetarian Food
Tommy's
  1824 Coventry Rd., 216/321-7757

Best View While Dining
Top of the Town
  1301 E. Ninth St., 216/771-1600

Best Wine Selection
Wards' Inn
  34105 Chagrin Blvd., Moreland Hills, 216/595-1954

COLUMBUS, OH

Best Restaurants in Town
Fifty-Five Crosswoods
  55 Hutchinson Ave., Worthington, 614/846-5555
Handke's Cuisine
  520 S. Front St., 614/621-2500

Best Asian Restaurants
China Dynasty
  1930 E. Dublin-Granville Rd., 614/523-2009
Hunan Lion
  2000 Bethel Rd., 614/459-3933
Imperial Garden
  2950 Hayden Rd., 614/799-8655
Lai Lai Restaurant
  5125 E. Main St., 614/759-6868
Restaurant Japan
  1140 Kenny Ctr., 614/451-5411
Sapporo Wind
  6188 Cleveland Ave., 614/895-7575
Windchimes
  5742 Frantz Rd., 614/792-0990

Best Bistros
Lindey's
  169 E. Beck St., German Village, 614/228-4343
Pierre's Bistro
  1788 W. Fifth Ave., 614/481-9463

Best Brunch
Cameron's
  2185 W. Dublin-Granville Rd., Worthington,
    614/885-3663

Best Cajun/Creole Food
Gloria Cafe
  2092 W. Henderson Rd., 614/538-1822

Best Casual Dining
Bravo! Cucina Italiana
3000 Hayden Rd., 614/791-1022
Butch's Italian Cafe
4720 E. Main St., 614/864-7300
Cameron's
2185 W. Dublin-Granville Rd., Worthington,
614/885-3663
Christopher's
Riff Ctr., 31st Fl., 77 S. High St., 614/224-4100
Figlio
1369 Grandview Ave., 614/481-0745
Frezno Eclectic Kitchen
782 N. High St., 614/298-0031
Gloria Cafe
2092 W. Henderson Rd., 614/538-1822
Market Stand Cafe
Hyatt Regency, 350 N. High St., 614/463-1234
Pierre's Bistro
1788 W. Fifth Ave., 614/481-9463

Best Delicatessens
Au Bon Pain
20 S. Third St., 614/224-1922
Bermuda Onion
660 N. High St., 50 W. Broad, 614/228-8646
Brown Bag Deli
898 Mohawk St., 614/443-4214
Carfagna's
1045 E. Dublin-Granville Rd., 614/846-6340
Firdous Deli and Cafe
1538 N. High St., 614/299-1844
Katzinger's Delicatessen
475 S. Third St., 614/228-3354
Michael's Finest Market
771 Bethel Rd., 614/457-5000
Nazareth Deli
5663 Emporium Sq., 614/899-1177
Park Side Grabit and Go
641 N. High St., Short North, 614/621-9463
Vincenzo's Convenient Elegance
6363 Sawmill Rd., 614/792-1010

Best French Food
L'Antibes
772 N. High St., 614/291-1666

Best Indian Food
Flavors of India
29 Spruce St., 614/621-3223

Best Italian Food
Bravo!
3000 Hayden Rd., 614/791-1022
Butch's Italian Cafe
4720 E. Main St., 614/864-7300
Da Vinci's Ristorante
4740 Reed Rd., 614/451-5147
La Plaia
5766 Columbus Sq., 614/890-2070

Pasta Amore
  18 Dillmont Dr., 614/848-3636
Pastabilities
  1644 E. Dublin-Granville Rd., 614/891-8891
Pasta Petite
  6096 Boardwalk St., 614/436-4066
Scali Ristorante and Deli
  Rear of Livingston Ctr., 1901 Rte. 256, 614/759-7764
Tony's Italian Ristorante
  16 W. Beck St., 614/224-8669
Trattoria Roma
  1270 Morse Rd., 614/888-6686

Best Middle Eastern Food
Firdous Deli and Cafe
  1538 N. High St., 614/299-1844

Best Other Ethnic Food
Galaxy Cafe (Cuban/Mexican/Caribbean)
  33 Beech Ridge Dr., 614/846-7776
Gold Gate (Eastern European)
  1395 S. Hamilton Rd., 614/237-4151
Blue Nile Restaurant (Ethiopian)
  3686 E. Main St., 614/238-0591

Best Pizza
Figlio
  1369 Grandview Ave., 614/481-0745

Best Places to Eat When Someone Else Is Buying
Bexley's Monk
  2232 E. Main St., Bexley, 614/239-6665
Carolyn's
  489 City Park, 614/221-8100
Handke's Cuisine
  520 S. Front St., 614/621-2500
L'Antibes
  772 N. High St., 614/291-1666
Lindey's
  169 E. Beck St., 614/228-4343
Merlot
  5252 Norwich St., 614/529-1995
Sapporo Wind
  6188 Cleveland Ave., 614/895-7575
The Refectory
  1092 Bethel Rd., 614/451-9774
Rigsby's Cuisine Volatile
  698 N. High St., 614/461-7888
Bistro Roti
  1693 W. Lane Ave., 614/481-7684

Best Seafood
Fifty-Five on the Boulevard
  55 Nationwide Blvd., 614/228-5555

Best Spanish Food
Spain Restaurant
  3777 Sullivant Ave., 614/272-6363

Best Steaks
Morton's of Chicago
  2 Nationwide Plz., 614/464-4442

The Clarmont
  684 S. High St., 614/443-1125
Hyde Parke Grille
  1615 Old Henderson Rd., 614/442-3310
The Top
  2891 E. Main St., 614/231-8238

Best Southwestern Food
Nacho Mama's
  5277 High St., 614/548-5655

Best Thai Food
Thai Orchid
  7654 Sawmill Rd., 614/792-1112

Best Vietnamese Food
Saigon Palace
  114 N. Front St., 614/464-3325
Vietnam Restaurant
  2548 Bethel Rd., 614/459-1909

Best Wine Selection
The Refectory
  1092 Bethel Rd., 614/451-9774

DAYTON, OH

Best Barbecue/Ribs
Damon's, The Place for Ribs
  262 E. Stroop Rd., 513/294-7427

Best Brunch
Parmizzano's
  Marriott Hotel, 1414 S. Patterson Blvd., 513/223-1000
Lincoln Park Grill
  580 Lincoln Park Blvd., 513/293-6293

Best Burgers
Bill Knapp's
  2619 Miamisburg Centerville Rd., 513/435-1393
  4465 Indian Ripple Rd., 513/429-1020
  6460 Far Hills Ave., 513/433-4455
Rally's Hamburgers
  Multiple Locations

Best Chinese Food
Keeng Wha Restaurant and Lounge
  2221 Wagoner Ford Rd., 513/278-8889
Mark Pi's Ancient Wok
  5200 Salem Ave., 513/854-0705
  1875 Needmore Rd., 513/898-1466

Best Desserts
Four River Place
  4 River Pl., 513/224-0535

Best French Food
L'Auberge
  4120 Far Hills Ave., 513/299-5536

Best Homestyle Food
Bill Knapp's
   2619 Miamisburg Centerville Rd., 513/435-1393
   4465 Indian Ripple Rd., 513/429-1020
   6460 Far Hills Ave., 513/433-4455

Best Italian Food
Dominic's Restaurant
   1066 S. Main St., 513/222-4801
Spaghetti Warehouse
   36 W. Fifth St., 513/461-3913

Best Mexican Food
Pepito's
   3618 Wilmington Pike, 513/293-3777
   4904 Airway Rd., 513/252-5131
   2412 Catalpa Dr., 513/277-1476

Best Pizza
Donato's Pizza
   3375 Dayton Xenia Rd., 513/427-5880

Best Romantic Dining
Four River Place
   4 River Pl., 513/224-0535

Best Sandwiches
Izzy's
   117 S. Main St., 513/224-4444
Upper Krust
   1919 N. Main St., 513/277-7200
   6 N. Main St., 513/226-1339
   6149 Far Hills Ave., 513/435-9464
Max and Erma's
   8901 Kingsridge Dr., 513/433-6200
Cadillac Jack's
   1156 Kauffman Rd., Fairborn, 513/754-1061

Best Seafood
Jay's Kitchen Door
   225 E. Sixth St., 513/222-2892

Best Steaks
Oakwood Club
   2414 Far Hills Ave., 513/293-6973
Paragon Club
   797 Miamisburg Centerville Rd., 513/433-1234
Pine Club
   1926 Brown St., 513/288-7463

Best View While Dining
Four River Place
   4 River Pl., 513/224-0535

Standbys
Ryan's Family Steak House
   1136 Miamisburg Centerville Rd., 513/435-1934
   1760 E. Stroop Rd., 513/296-0528
   4111 Little York Rd., 513/890-5104
Bob Evans
   1285 Woodman Dr., 513/256-0040
   1850 E. Dorothy Ln., 513/293-3222
   1929 Harshman Rd., 513/233-8729

5571 Merily Way, 513/236-7707
7115 Far Hills Ave., 513/434-1366
7400 Miller Ln., 513/890-5333
Perkins
4090 Wilmington Pike, 513/299-3867
Friday's
2022 Miamisburg Centerville Rd., 513/439-3744
Applebee's
105 N. Springboro Pike, Ste. 301, 513/436-3222
8331 Old Troy Pike, 513/233-9973
The Olive Garden
2789 Miamisburg Centerville Rd., 513/435-0885
7500 Poe Ave., 513/454-0336
Chi Chi's
2925 Miamisburg Centerville Rd., 813/435-6264
Red Lobster
2803 N. Fairfield Rd., 513/429-1800
3908 Wilmington Pike, 513/293-6969
4520 Salem Ave., 513/276-5297
7615 Poe Ave., 513/898-0686

DELAWARE, OH

Best American Food
Bun's Restaurant
6 W. Winter St., 614/363-3731

Best Barbecue/Ribs
Damon's
1159 Columbus Pk., 614/369-7427

Best Homestyle Food
Heartland Cafe and Grille
19 E. Winter St., 614/363-0860

Best Italian Food
Sumeno's Ristorante
1812 Columbus Pk., 614/363-0939

Best Pizza
Tominilli's Pizza and Spaghetti
26 Sandusky St., 614/369-5184

Standbys
Friendly's
219 S. Sandusky St., 614/369-7711

ELYRIA, OH

Best Atmosphere
Tavern on the Mall
529 Midway Blvd., 216/324-3155

Best Bar
Moss' Prime Rib Restaurant
209 Broad St., 216/322-8611

Best Breakfast
Lunchbreak Cafe
353 Broad St., 216/322-3221

Best Casual Dining
Tavern on the Mall
529 Midway Blvd., 216/324-3155

Best Chinese Food
Hunan King
1537 W. River Rd., 216/324-4095

Best Desserts
Lunchbreak Cafe
353 Broad St., 216/322-3221

Best Diners
Hazel's Family Restaurant
615 Cleveland St., 216/365-3513
Mid Way Oh Boy Restaurant
6620 Lake Ave., 216/324-3711

Best Eclectic Menu
Grassie's Wayside Inn
447 Oberlin Rd., 216/322-0690

Best Family Restaurant
Hazel's Family Restaurant
615 Cleveland St., 216/365-3513

Best Other Ethnic Food
Mongo's (Tibetan)
36040 Sugar Ridge Rd., 216/327-2155

Best Pizza
East of Chicago Pizza Company
515E Abbe Rd. N., 216/365-6005

Best Salad/Salad Bar
Grassie's Wayside Inn
447 Oberlin Rd., 216/322-0690

Best Steaks
Moss' Prime Rib Restaurant
209 Broad St., 216/322-8611
Mountain Jack's Restaurant
1845 Lorain Blvd., 216/324-7700

Standbys
Applebee's
1540 W. River Rd., 216/324-1700
Red Lobster
6935 Midway Mall, 216/324-2244
Old Country Buffet
1565 W. River Rd., 216/324-2177
Ground Round
1524 W. River Rd., 216/324-3300

FAIRBORN, OH

Best Mexican Food
Don Pablo's
2745 Fairfield Commons, Beavercreek, 513/320-1777

Best Sandwiches
Cadillac Jack's
1156 Kauffman Rd., 513/754-1061

Best Sports Bar
Cold Beer and Cheeseburgers
2638 Colonel Glenn Hwy., 513/427-2337

Best Steaks
Max and Erma's
2739 Fairfield Commons, Beavercreek, 513/320-2255

Standbys
Bob Evans
  2648 Colonel Glenn Hwy., 513/427-0442

FINDLAY, OH

Best Bar
Rocking U Restaurant
  318 W. Main Cross St., 419/423-4471

Best Breakfast
Miller's Luncheonette
  203 N. Main St., 419/422-3081

Best Burgers
Wilson's Sandwich Shop
  600 S. Main St., 419/422-5051

Best Dinner
Rena's Restaurant
  321 S. Main St., 419/422-0808

Best Greek/Mediterranean Food
Rena's Restaurant
  321 S. Main St., 419/422-0808

Best Homestyle Food
Miller's Luncheonette
  203 N. Main St., 419/422-3081

Best Japanese Food
Japan West
  406 S. Main St., 419/424-1007

Best Mexican Food
Oler's Bar and Grill
  708 Lima Ave., 419/423-2846

Best Sandwiches
Rocking U Restaurant
  318 W. Main Cross St., 419/423-4471

GALLIPOLIS, OH

Best All-You-Can-Eat Buffet
Dale's Smorgasbord
  Silverbridge Plz., 614/446-0399

Best Family Restaurants
McClure's Family Restaurant
  820 Jackson Pike, 614/446-3837
Red Rooster Restaurant
  218 Jackson Pike, 614/446-6635
Lollipop Candy Store
  44 State St., 614/446-1199
Shake Shoppe
  383 Jackson Pike, 614/446-1611
  901 Second Ave., 614/446-2682

Best Place to Take the Kids
Lollipop Candy Store
  44 State St., 614/446-1199

Best Salad/Salad Bar
Mogie's
  39 Court St., 614/446-6647

Best Sandwiches
Mogie's
  39 Court St., 614/446-6647

Best Seafood
Holiday Inn
  577 State Rte. 7N, 614/446-0090

Best Steaks
Holiday Inn
  577 State Rte. 7N, 614/446-0090

Standbys
Bob Evans
  315 Upper River Rd., 614/446-6369
Dairy Queen
  169 Upper River Rd., 614/446-3278
Pizza Hut
  1308 Eastern Ave., 614/446-7622
Ponderosa
  215 Upper River Rd., 614/446-1101
Subway
  303 Upper River Rd., 614/446-6483

HAMILTON, OH

Best Bar
Scooter's Pub
  1483 Millville Ave., 513/887-9779

Best Breakfast
Frisch's
  2949 Dixie Hwy., 513/863-6159
  5570 Liberty Fairfield Rd., 513/737-1209
  1225 Main St., 513/863-6075

Best Burgers
Frisch's
  2949 Dixie Hwy., 513/863-6159
  5570 Liberty Fairfield Rd., 513/737-1209
  1225 Main St., 513/863-6075

Best Cajun/Creole Food
Jake's
  622 Riegart Sq., 513/868-8492

Best Desserts
Hyde's Restaurant
  130 S. Erie Hwy., 513/892-1287
Jake's
  622 Riegart Sq., 513/868-8492

Best Family Restaurant
Boston Market
  725 Nilles Rd., 513/829-1282

Best Homestyle Food
Boston Market
  725 Nilles Rd., 513/829-1282
Mamaw's Home Cooking
  1479 Millville Ave., 513/896-4600
Hyde's Restaurant
  130 S. Erie Hwy., 513/892-1287

Best Ice Cream/Yogurt
United Dairy Farmers
  11 N. Brookwood Ave., 513/863-1272

Best Late-Night Food
Dixie Hamburger
  2204 Dixie Hwy., 513/863-0015

Best Pizza
Richard's Pizza
  2343 Dixie Hwy., 513/894-3217
  417 Main St., 513/894-3296
Milillo's Fairfield Pizza
  680 Nilles Rd., 513/829-2200

Best Place to Eat Alone
Wolpert's Cafe
  1005 Eaton Cafe, 513/895-1377

Best Place to Eat When Someone Else Is Buying
Jake's
  622 Riegart Sq., 513/868-8492

Best Romantic Dining
Academy Restaurant
  343 N. Third St., 513/868-7171

Best Salad/Salad Bar
Frisch's
  2949 Dixie Hwy., 513/863-6159
  5570 Liberty Fairfield Rd., 513/737-1209
  1225 Main St., 513/863-6075
Jake's
  622 Riegart Sq., 513/868-8492

Best Sandwiches
Boston Market
  725 Nilles Rd., 513/829-1282
Frisch's
  2949 Dixie Hwy., 513/863-6159
  5570 Liberty Fairfield Rd., 513/737-1209
  1225 Main St., 513/863-6075
Deli Sandwich Shoppe
  23 N. Third St., 513/844-6500
Wolpert's Cafe
  1005 Eaton Cafe, 513/895-1377

Best Seafood
Academy Restaurant
  343 N. Third St., 513/868-7171

Best Steaks
Academy Restaurant
  343 N. Third St., 513/868-7171
Shady-Nook Restaurant
  879 Millville Oxford Rd., 513/863-4343

HILLSBORO, OH

Best Burgers
Magee's Snack Shop
  129 W. Main St., 513/393-2014

Best Desserts
Magee's Snack Shop
  129 W. Main St., 513/393-2014

Best Family Restaurant
Wooden Spoon Restaurant
1480 N. High St., 513/393-4956

Best Homestyle Food
Wooden Spoon Restaurant
1480 N. High St., 513/393-4956

Best Italian Food
Stephano's Pizza
145 Catherine St., 513/393-8500

Best Salad/Salad Bar
Stephano's Pizza
145 Catherine St., 513/393-8500

Best Sandwiches
Magee's Snack Shop
129 W. Main St., 513/393-2014

Best Seafood
Frontier Cattle Company
11145 N. Shore Dr., 513/393-6772

Best Steaks
Frontier Cattle Company
11145 N. Shore Dr., 513/393-6772

Standbys
Dairy Queen
1000 W. Main St., 513/393-2344

KENT, OH

Best Restaurant in Town
Pufferbelly
152 Franklin Ave., 216/673-1771

Best Breakfast
Ace's Restaurant
128 N. Water St., 216/673-3888
Susan Coffee and Tea
623 E. Main St., 216/677-0101

Best German Food
Henry Wahner's Restaurant
1609 E. Main St., 216/678-4055

Best Place to Eat When Someone Else Is Buying
Silver Pheasant
3085 Graham Rd., Stow, 216/678-2116

Best Steaks
Rusty Nail
7291 State Rte. 43, 216/673-2297

LANCASTER, OH

Best Breakfast
Snead's Restaurant
202 N. Cherry St., 614/654-1777

Best Burgers
White Cottage
525 N. High St., 614/654-9127

Best Coffee
Four Reasons
135 W. Main St., 614/654-2253

O

Best Desserts
Annie's Cheesecake and Tea Room
539 E. Main St., 614/654-3692

Best Homestyle Food
Snead's Restaurant
202 N. Cherry St., 614/654-1777

Best Lunch
Annie's Cheesecake and Tea Room
539 E. Main St., 614/654-3692

Best Pizza
Pink Cricket
929 E. Main St., 614/653-7300

Best Sandwiches
Four Reasons
135 W. Main St., 614/654-2253

Best Seafood
Mauger's Seafood Restaurant
512 E. Main St., 614/654-8237

LIMA, OH

Best All-You-Can-Eat Buffet
Old Barn Out Back
3175 W. Elm St., 419/991-3075

Best American Food
Burgundy's Restaurant
1365 N. Cable Rd., 419/224-5080

Best Burgers
Kewpee Hamburgers
2111 Allentown Rd., 419/227-9791
111 N. Elizabeth St., 419/228-1778
1350 Bellefontaine Ave., 419/229-1385

Best Family Restaurant
Huddle Fine Foods Restaurant
134 N. Metcalf St., 419/224-6851

Best Italian Food
Milano's
415 W. Market St., 419/225-4981

Best Steaks
Burgundy's Restaurant
1365 N. Cable Rd., 419/224-5080
Beef and Bourbon at Fireside
3801 Shawnee Rd., 419/999-1313

LORAIN, OH

Best Chinese Food
Hunan King Restaurant
3317 Oberlin Ave., 216/960-2162

Best Delicatessen
Louie's Deli and Restaurant
221 W. Fifth St., 216/245-5766

Best Homestyle Food
Chris' Restaurant
2812 W. Erie Ave., 216/245-5822

Best Pizza
Yala's Pizzeria
  3352 Oberlin Ave., 216/282-5169

Best Sandwiches
Louie's Deli and Restaurant
  221 W. Fifth St., 216/245-5766

Standbys
Bob Evans
  700 N. Leavitt Rd., Amherst, 216/988-8899
Ponderosa
  4743 Oberlin Ave., 216/282-4513
Chi Chi's
  128 Sheffield Ctr., 216/233-8830

MANSFIELD, OH

Best Chinese Food
China House
  1435 Park Ave. W., 419/529-9767

Best Coffee
Mr. T's Coffee Shop
  82 Park Ave. W., 419/522-2121

Best Desserts
Cheddar's Casual Cafe
  979 Lexington Springmill Rd., 419/747-9777

Best Ice Cream/Yogurt
Dairyland
  800 Springmill St., 419/525-2168

Best Pizza
East of Chicago
  1592 Park Ave. W., 419/529-8070
  614 Clairmont Ave., 419/289-0605

Best Place to Eat When Someone Else Is Buying
Cheddar's Casual Cafe
  979 Lexington Springmill Rd., 419/747-9777

Best Steaks
Cheddar's Casual Cafe
  979 Lexington Springmill Rd., 419/747-9777

Standbys
Ryan's Family Steak House
  994 Lexington Springmill Rd., 419/747-7926
Ponderosa
  2100 Worth St., 419/747-4292
Old Country Buffet
  1179 Park Ave. W., 419/529-8998
Applebee's
  1023 Lexington Springmill Rd., 419/747-5300
Bob Evans
  525 N. Trimble Rd., 419/529-2228
  30 W. Hanley Rd., 419/756-6031
The Olive Garden
  558 N. Lexington Springmill Rd., 419/529-5070
Chi Chi's
  2284 W. Fourth St., 419/747-6677
Red Lobster
  2322 W. Fourth St., 419/747-4700

O

MARIETTA, OH

Best Barbecue/Ribs
Damon's
  Comfort Inn, 700 Pike St., 614/373-6700

Best Burgers
Cone and Shake
  219 Pike St., 614/373-1067

Best Chinese Food
Hong Kong Restaurant
  90 Acme St., 614/374-7009

Best Family Restaurant
Damon's
  Comfort Inn, 700 Pike St., 614/373-6700

Best Health-Conscious Menu
Brighter Day Natural Foods
  10 Tiber Way, 614/374-2429

Best Ice Cream/Yogurt
Cone and Shake
  219 Pike St., 614/373-1067

Best Place to Take the Kids
Damon's
  Comfort Inn, 700 Pike St., 614/373-6700

Best Sandwiches
Third Street Deli
  343 Third St., 614/374-0003

Best Seafood
Becky Thatcher Restaurant
  237 Front St., 614/373-4130
Tally-Ho
  211 Second St., 614/374-5228

Best Steaks
Becky Thatcher Restaurant
  237 Front St., 614/373-4130
Damon's
  Comfort Inn, 700 Pike St., 614/373-6700
Tally-Ho
  211 Second St., 614/374-5228

Standbys
Bob Evans
  504 Pike St., 614/374-7474
Ryan's Family Steak House
  823 Pike St., 614/374-8062

MARION, OH

Best All-You-Can-Eat Buffet
Gateway Smorgasboard
  1348 Mount Vernon Ave., 614/389-4712

Best Bar
Maury's on Main
  138 S. Main St., 614/382-3019

Best Chinese Food
House of Hunan
  1583 Marion Waldo Rd., 614/387-0032

Best Lunch
Bucky's, An Extraordinary Eatery
1960 Marion Mount Gilead Rd., 614/389-5456

Best Pizza
OK Cafe
734 E. Center St., 614/387-6565

Best Sandwiches
Cafe George
131 S. Main St., 614/382-5281

Best Steaks
Michael's Steak House
1221 Delaware Ave., 614/382-6161

Standbys
Bob Evans
188 America Blvd., 614/389-4120

MASSILLON, OH

Best Restaurant in Town
Kurt's Inn
4104 Lincoln Way E., 330/478-2548

Best American Food
Padula's Restaurant
1328 First St. NE, 330/833-9984

Best Breakfast
Frank's Family Restaurant
1731 Lincoln Way E., 330/837-3232

Best Chinese Food
China Kitchen
2716 Lincoln Way E., 330/837-0188

Best Italian Food
Belleria Italian Restaurant
2484 Lincoln Way E., 330/832-4700

Best Lunch
Meldrum's
2144 Wale's Rd. NW, 330/833-4729

Best Pizza
Kraus' Pizza
915 Amherst Rd. NE, 330/832-2242

Best Sandwiches
Irish Exchange
8009 Hills and Dales Rd. NW, 330/833-5000

MIDDLETOWN, OH

Best All-You-Can-Eat Buffet
Stefano's Deli Cafe and Market
2200 Central Ave., 513/422-9922

Best American Food
Parrot Restaurant
100 S. Main St., 513/423-0191

Best Breakfast
Sun Shine Cafe
3131 S. Main St., 513/423-0022

Best Diner
Parrot Restaurant
100 S. Main St., 513/423-0191

Best Greek/Mediterranean Food
Grecian Delight
1300 Cincinnati Dayton Rd., 513/424-5411

Best Italian Food
Stefano's Deli Cafe and Market
2200 Central Ave., 513/422-9922

Best Pizza
Capozzi's
3530 Central Ave., 513/422-3882

Best Seafood
Manchester Inn
1027 Manchester Ave., 513/422-5481

Best Steaks
Manchester Inn
1027 Manchester Ave., 513/422-5481

NEWARK, OH

Best Burgers
Yesterday's Pub
78 Wilson St., 614/349-8009

Best Chinese Food
Imperial Palace China Garden
1225 W. Church St., 614/344-0361

Best Homestyle Food
Sparta Restaurant
16 W. Main St., 614/345-6040

Best Italian Food
A Taste of Italy
606 W. Church St., 614/344-1121

Best Salad/Salad Bar
A Taste of Italy
606 W. Church St., 614/344-1121

Best Steaks
Natoma Restaurant
10 N. Park Pl., 614/345-7260

NEW PHILADELPHIA, OH

Best Restaurant in Town
Zoar Tavern
1 Main St., 330/874-2170

Best Breakfast
Courthouse Cafe
110 S. Broadway, 330/343-7896

Best Dinner
Emanuela's Ristorante
413 N. Tuscarawas Ave., Dover, 330/364-6121

Best Italian Food
Uncle Primo's
435 Minnich Ave. NW, 330/364-2349

Best Other Ethnic Food
Dutch Valley (Amish)
State Hwy. 39, Sugarcreek, 330/852-4627

Best Seafood
Hangar Steak House and Lounge
1816 E. High Ave., 330/339-4011

Best Steaks
Leonard's Restaurant
719 S. Wooster Ave., Strasburg, 330/878-7772

PIQUA, OH

Best All-You-Can-Eat Buffet
Terry's Cafeteria
105 E. Greene St., 513/778-0566

Best Burgers
Checkers Food and Spirits
311 N. Main St., 513/773-6641

Best Casual Dining
Dave's Place
1106 Fisk St., 513/773-3373

Best Chinese Food
China East
1239 E. Ash St., 513/778-8688

Best Homestyle Food
Grandma's Kitchen
8262 W. State Rte. 41, Covington, 513/473-3031

Standbys
Bob Evans
999 E. Ash St., 513/773-7466

SANDUSKY, OH

Best Restaurant in Town
Bay Harbor Inn
Cedar Point Marina, 1 Cosway Dr., 419/625-6373

Best Breakfast
Berardi's Family Kitchen
1019 W. Perkins Ave., 419/626-4592

Best Brunch
Berardi's Family Kitchen
1019 W. Perkins Ave., 419/626-4592

Best Burgers
Plum Nilly
918 W. Perkins Ave., 419/625-8266

Best Italian Food
Cedar Villa Restaurant
1918 Cleveland Rd., 419/625-8487

Best Pizza
Cameo Pizza
702 W. Monroe St., 419/626-0187

Best Seafood
Bay Harbor
Cedar Point Marina, 1 Cosway Dr., 419/625-6373

841

Med's 800 Club Ol' Time Saloon
 1220 Sycamore Ln., 419/625-3776

Standbys
Chi Chi's
 4307 Milan Rd., 419/625-2744

SPRINGFIELD, OH

Best Brunch
Springfield Inn
 100 S. Fountain Ave., 513/322-3600

Best Business Lunch
Springfield Inn
 100 S. Fountain Ave., 513/322-3600

Best Cheap Meal
Hickory Inn
 652 N. Limestone St., 513/323-1702

Best Chinese Food
Hunan East
 1460 Upper Valley Pike, 513/322-5432
Mark Pi's China Gate
 2149 S. Limestone St., 513/322-0055
 1475 Upper Valley Pike, 513/325-1892

Best Delicatessen
Mike and Rosy's Deli
 330 W. McCreight Ave., 513/390-3511

Best Homestyle Food
Meadows Restaurant and Motel
 4105 E. National Rd., 513/323-0872

Best Italian Food
Fazoli's Restaurant
 2012 S. Limestone St., 513/323-9144
 2534 E. Main St., 513/322-9697

Best Romantic Dining
Springfield Inn
 100 S. Fountain Ave., 513/322-3600

Best Sandwiches
Mike and Rosy's Deli
 330 W. McCreight Ave., 513/390-3511

Best Seafood
Derr Road Inn
 4343 Derr Rd., 513/399-0822

Best Steaks
The Mill
 3404 W. National Rd., 513/324-4045

Best View While Dining
Derr Road Inn
 4343 Derr Rd., 513/399-0822

Standbys
Bob Evans
 1660 W. First St., 513/323-9151
 40 W. Leffel Ln., 513/324-0041
Perkins
 1170 Upper Valley Pike, 513/325-7073

2222 S. Limestone St., 513/325-9247
2531 E. Main St., 513/325-7394
Chi Chi's
1616 Upper Valley Pike, 513/325-5995
Chuck E. Cheese Pizza
2345 Valley Loop Rd., 513/324-4155

STEUBENVILLE, OH

Best American Food
Jaggin' Around Restaurant and Pub
501 Washington St., 614/282-1010

Best Breakfast
Damon's International
1350 University Blvd., 614/282-2745

Best Chinese Food
Hunan Chinese Restaurant
106 N. Fourth St., 614/282-8952

Best Greek/Mediterranean Food
Yorgo's Gyros/Potatos
127 North Fourth St., 614/282-9663

Best Italian Food
Naples Spaghetti House
329 North St., 614/283-3405

Best Steaks
Boots' Texas Roadhouse
4402 Sunset Blvd., 614/264-5599
Gas Lite Restaurant and Lounge
820 Canton Rd., 614/264-2225

STOW, OH

Best American Food
Triple Crown Restaurant
335 S. Main St., Monroe Falls, 330/633-5323

Best Breakfast
Cafe in Stow
4591 Darrow Rd., 330/688-0200

Best Desserts
Osman's Pies
4974 Darrow Rd., 330/655-2919

Best Homestyle Food
Charlie's Restaurant
3428 Darrow Rd., 330/688-3171

Best Ice Cream/Yogurt
Isaly's
3322 Kent Rd., 330/688-4269

Best Pizza
Rizzi's Pizzeria and Restaurant
4976 Darrow Rd., 330/655-2440

Best Seafood
Silver Pheasant
3085 Graham Rd., 330/678-2116

Best Steaks
Silver Pheasant
3085 Graham Rd., 330/678-2116

Best Breakfast
Original Pancake House
  3310 W. Central Ave., 419/535-5927

Best Burgers
Nick and Jimmy's Bar and Grill
  4956 Monroe St., 419/472-0756

Best Business Lunch
Christopher's Restaurant
  4210 Airport Hwy., 419/389-1777
Sky Line Club
  1 Seagate, Fl. 28, 419/247-1290
Timko's Soup and Such
  2500 W. Sylvania Ave., 419/475-4629

Best Casual Dining
Cooker Bar and Grill
  5700 Monroe St., 419/882-2222
  6658 Airport Hwy., 419/867-4994
J. Alexander's
  4315 Talmadge Rd., 419/474-8620

Best Chinese Food
Fu Yi's
  7130 Airport Hwy., 419/866-5262

Best Coffee
Sufficient Grounds
  3160 Markway Rd., 419/537-1988
Grasshopper Coffeehouse
  3053 W. Bancroft St., 419/534-3115

Best Coffeehouse
Grasshopper Coffeehouse
  3053 W. Bancroft St., 419/534-3115

Best Delicatessens
Grumpy's Deli
  11 N. Michigan St., 419/241-6728
Salad Galley
  1515 S. Byrne Rd., 419/534-3322
  3301 W. Central Ave., 419/534-3322
  611 Madison Ave., 419/243-3133
Sufficient Grounds
  3160 Markway Rd., 419/537-1988
Frisco Deli
  348 Secor Rd., 419/537-1777
  14019 Spring Metal Dr., 419/867-9500

Best Desserts
Grumpy's Deli
  11 N. Michigan St., 419/241-6728

Best Diner
Ralphie's
  1406 Reynolds Rd., 419/893-1212
  3005 Navarre Ave., 419/693-2500

Best Greek/Mediterranean Food
Theo's Taverna and Greek Restaurant
  823 N. Summit St., 419/242-8312

Best Homestyle Food
Alice Harvey's Place
  2521 Glendale Ave., 419/382-1011

Best Ice Cream/Yogurt
Pal's Ice Cream
  3333 Airport Hwy., 419/382-0615

Best Indian Food
Tandoor Cuisine of India
  2247 S. Reynolds Rd., 419/385-7467

Best Italian Food
Spaghetti Warehouse
  42 S. Superior St., 419/255-5038

Best Late-Night Food
Dominic's Italian Restaurant
  2121 S. Reynolds Rd., 419/381-8822
Georgio's Cafe
  426 N. Superior St., 419/242-2424

Best Mexican Food
El Matador Restaurant
  3309 N. Holland Sylvania Rd., 419/841-4434
  35 E. Alexis Rd., 419/476-2043
Loma Linda Restaurant
  10400 Airport Hwy., 419/865-5455

Best Pizza
Alexander's The Great Pizza
  1808 Arlington Ave., 419/389-1200
  3143 W. Central Ave., 419/531-2500
  3523 W. Alexis Rd., 419/473-2225
  819 N. Reynolds Rd., 419/531-4999

Best Places to Eat When Someone Else Is Buying
Fifi's Restaurant
  1423 Bernath Pkwy., 419/866-6777
Mancy's Restaurant
  953 Phillips Ave., 419/476-4154

Best Place to Take the Kids
Major Magic's All Star Pizza Revue
  5838 Monroe St., 419/885-1400

Best Romantic Dining
Fifi's Restaurant
  1423 Bernath Pkwy., 419/866-6777
Georgio's Cafe
  426 N. Superior St., 419/242-2424

Best Salad/Salad Bar
Salad Galley
  1515 S. Byrne Rd., 419/534-3322
  3301 W. Central Ave., 419/534-3322
  611 Madison Ave., 419/243-3133

Best Sandwiches
Grumpy's Deli
  11 N. Michigan St., 419/241-6728
Tony Packo's Cafe
  1902 Front St., 419/691-6054

Salad Galley
  1515 S. Byrne Rd., 419/534-3322
  3301 W. Central Ave., 419/534-3322
  611 Madison Ave., 419/243-3133
Frisco Deli
  348 Secor Rd., 419/537-1777
  14019 Spring Metal Dr., 419/867-9500
Sufficient Grounds
  3160 Markway Rd., 419/537-1988

Best Seafood
Muer's Seafood
  1435 Baronial Plaza Dr., 419/866-8877

Best Steaks
Mancy's Restaurant
  953 Phillips Ave., 419/476-4154

Best View While Dining
Aztec Grill and Bar
  1 Seagate, Ground Fl., 419/255-1116
Sky Line Club
  1 Seagate, 28th Fl., 419/247-1290

Standbys
Old Country Buffet
  5259 Airport Hwy., 419/382-9793
Friday's
  1334 Bernath Pkwy., 419/866-1798
Cracker Barrel
  27491 Helen Dr., 419/874-7481
The Olive Garden
  1919 S. Reynolds Rd., 419/389-1982
  5120 Monroe St., 419/885-3878
Chili's
  4801 Talmadge Rd., 419/472-7688
Friendly's
  1214 W. Alexis Rd., 419/476-4646
  2040 S. Reynolds Rd., Ste. 625, 419/865-8431
  2516 W. Sylvania Ave., 419/472-7402
  3301 W. Central Ave., 419/537-8623
  5307 Monroe St., 419/885-2717
  5957 W. Central Ave., 419/841-4842

WARREN, OH

Best Breakfast
Saratoga Restaurant
  129 E. Market St., 330/393-6646

Best Business Lunch
Jimmy Chieffo's Restaurant and Lounge
  3860 Youngstown Rd. SE, 330/369-6507
Alberini's Restaurant
  1201 Youngstown Warren Rd., Niles, 330/652-5895

Best Casual Dining
Mary M's Restaurant
  2940 Parkman Rd. NW, 330/898-3846

Best Coffee
Mocha House
  467 High St. NE, 330/392-3020

Best Desserts
Mocha House
467 High St. NE, 330/392-3020

Best Greek/Mediterranean Food
Saratoga Restaurant
129 E. Market St., 330/393-6646
Scrump-Deli-Icious
176 N. Park Ave., 330/393-9311

Best Ice Cream/Yogurt
Grandma's Real Ice Cream
199 Folsom St. NW, 330/847-6382
Webb's Ice Cream and Video
1913 Niles Cortland Rd., 330/856-3360

Best Italian Food
Jimmy Chieffo's Restaurant and Lounge
3860 Youngstown Rd. SE, 330/369-6507
Alberini's Restaurant
1201 Youngstown Warren Rd., Niles, 330/652-5895

Best Pizza
Sunrise Inn
510 E. Market St., 330/392-5176

Best Places to Eat When Someone Else Is Buying
Jimmy Chieffo's Restaurant and Lounge
3860 Youngstown Rd. SE, 330/369-6507
Alberini's Restaurant
1201 Youngstown Warren Rd., Niles, 330/652-5895

Best Romantic Dining
Alberini's Restaurant
1201 Youngstown Warren Rd., Niles, 330/652-5895

Best Sandwiches
Scrump-Deli-Icious
176 N. Park Ave., 330/393-9311

Best Seafood
Abruzzi's Cafe 422
4422 Youngstown Rd. SE, 330/369-2422

Best Steaks
Avalon Inn and Resort
9519 E. Market St., 330/856-1900

Standbys
Perkins
3870 Elm Rd. NE, 330/372-6660

WILLOUGHBY, OH

Best Brunch
Big Boy Restaurant
35441 Euclid Ave., 216/951-5040

Best Coffee
Thinker Coffeehouse
4148 Erie St., 216/942-5282

Best Desserts
Bakers Square Restaurant
28601 Chardon Rd., Wickliffe, 216/944-7777

Best Health-Conscious Menu
Thinker Coffeehouse
4148 Erie St., 216/942-5282

Best Italian Food
The Italian Oven
30170 Lake Shore Blvd., 216/585-0999

Best Mexican Food
Maximillian's
9080 Mentor Ave., 216/255-1720

Best Vegetarian Food
Thinker Coffeehouse
4148 Erie St., 216/942-5282

Standbys
Ponderosa
1485 E. 337th St., 216/942-2763
Perkins
6400 Center St., 216/255-3400
Denny's
34725 Euclid Ave., 216/942-0193
Friday's
7814 Reynolds Rd., 216/953-2400
Old Country Buffet
35085 Euclid Ave., 216/953-8912
Dairy Queen
4132 Erie St., 216/946-3690
34600 Euclid Ave., 216/946-6211
Pizza Hut
35050 Euclid Ave., 216/946-6444
34876 Vine St., 216/946-4446
Ground Round
30480 Lake Shore Blvd., Willowick, 216/944-7592

WOOSTER, OH

Best Restaurant in Town
Smithville Inn
109 W. Main St., Smithville, 330/669-2641

Best American Food
T.J.'s Restaurant
359 W. Liberty St., 330/264-6263

Best Breakfast
Parlor Restaurant
203 W. Liberty St., 330/262-4871

Best Family Restaurant
Smithville Inn
109 W. Main St., Smithville, 330/669-2641

Best Lunch
Abigail's Tea Room
146 S. Market St., 330/263-7755

Best Other Ethnic Food
Stagecoach Restaurant (Amish)
2179 E. Lincoln Way, 330/262-6582
Des Dutch Essenhaus (Amish)
176 N. Market St., Shreve, 330/567-2212

Best Salad/Salad Bar
The Barn
877 W. Main St., 330/669-2555

YOUNGSTOWN, OH

Best Atmosphere
Rachel's Steak and Seafood
169 S. Four Mile Run Rd., Austintown, 330/799-2800
Wick-Pollock Inn
603 Wick Ave., 330/746-1200

Best Barbecue/Ribs
Armadillo's Restaurant
3031 Mahoning Ave., 330/792-0662

Best Breakfast
Yankee Kitchen
6635 Market St., Boardman, 330/726-1300
484 Youngstown Kingsville SE, Vienna, 330/394-1116

Best Burgers
Coconut Grove
3229 South Ave., 330/788-0140

Best Business Lunch
Paonessa's
871 McKay Ct., 330/726-6001

Best Casual Dining
Paonessa's
871 McKay Ct., 330/726-6001

Best Cheap Meal
Cafe Roma
17 N. Champion St., 330/746-6900

Best Chinese Food
Imperial Palace
1212 Youngstown Warren Rd., Niles, 330/544-2388

Best Coffeehouses
Cherrypickers Coffee Cafe
7141 Tiffany Blvd., 330/629-2999
Beat Coffeehouse
215 Lincoln Ave., 330/743-4227

Best Delicatessen
Mr. P's Cafe and Bakery
7325 South Ave., 330/726-2442

Best Diner
Emerald Diner
825 N. Main St., 330/534-1441

Best Health-Conscious Menu
Crystal's Restaurant
1931 Belmont Ave., 330/743-5381

Best Homestyle Food
Elmton Inc.
584 Fifth Ave., 330/755-8511

Best Ice Cream/Yogurt
Handel's Homemade Ice Cream
310 Churchill Hubbard Rd., 330/759-1442
3622 Belmont Ave., 330/759-2417
3931 Handels Ct., 330/788-0356

Best Italian Food
Alberini's Restaurant
  1201 Youngstown Warren Rd., Niles, 330/652-5895

Best Late-Night Food
Boulevard Tavern
  3503 Southern Blvd., 330/788-0931
Splendid Restaurant and Lounge
  3330 South Ave., 330/782-3062

Best Mexican Food
La Fiesta
  1801 Midland Ave., 330/793-3967

Best Other Ethnic Food
Caribbean Delights (Caribbean)
  1746 Elm St., 330/744-2434

Best Pizza
Belleria Pizzeria
  1535 Logan Ave., 330/744-4085
Wedgewood Pizza Shop
  1622 S. Raccoon Rd., 330/799-2102
Elmton Inc.
  584 Fifth Ave., 330/755-8511

Best Place to Eat When Someone Else Is Buying
Alberini's Restaurant
  1201 Youngstown Warren Rd., Niles, 330/652-5895

Best Place to Take the Kids
Antone's Restaurant
  7424 Market St., 330/758-2218

Best Romantic Dining
Rachel's Steak and Seafood
  169 S. Four Mile Run Rd., Austintown, 330/799-2800
Wick-Pollock Inn
  603 Wick Ave., 330/746-1200

Best Steaks
Rachel's Steak and Seafood
  169 S. Four Mile Run Rd., Austintown, 330/799-2800

Best View While Dining
Moonraker
  1275 Boardman Poland Rd., 330/726-8841

Best Wine Selection
Alberini's Restaurant
  1201 Youngstown Warren Rd., Niles, 330/652-5895

ZANESVILLE, OH

Best Breakfast
Tee Jayes Country Place
  3315 Maple Ave., 614/450-7555

Best Chinese Food
Mark Pi's China Gate
  2502 Maple Ave., 614/453-6655

Best Italian Food
Maria Adornetto Restaurant
  953 Market St., 614/453-0643

Best Mexican Food
Zak's
   32 N. Fourth St., 614/453-2227

Best Pizza
Papa Chuck's
   375 Muskingum Ave., 614/452-6303
   3525 Maple Ave., 614/452-0368

Best Sandwiches
Adornetto's Pizzeria
   2224 Maple Ave., 614/453-0789
   2440 Maysville Pk., 216/454-6261

Best Steaks
Old Market House Inn
   424 Market St., 614/454-2555

O

Oklahoma

Best Restaurants in Town
Val's It's About Time
  800 N. Main St., 405/482-4580
Crystal's Restaurant
  2515 E. Broadway St., 405/477-3000
Eddie's Cafe
  1613 E. Broadway St., 405/482-1373
Furr's Cafeteria
  1400 N. Main St., Bldg. 163, 405/482-5823

Best Asian Restaurants
Polynesian Garden
  1700 Falcon Rd., 405/482-2831
The Fortune Cookie Restaurant
  119 S. Hudson St., 405/477-0775

Best Barbecue/Ribs
Woody's BBQ
  1100 N. Main St., 405/477-4756

Best Mexican Food
Bennie's
  1314 N. Main St., 405/482-8713

Standbys
Western Sizzlin
  3200 N. Main St., 405/477-1717
Golden Corral Family Steak House
  2011 N. Main St., 405/482-7125

Best Atmosphere
Cafe Alley
  107 E. Main St., 405/223-6413
Fireside Dining
  Hwy. 77, 405/226-4070

Best Barbecue/Ribs
Hick'ry House B-B-Q
  2200 S. Commerce St., 405/223-5855

Aub's Two Frogs Grill
  Hwy. 70, Lone Grove, 403/657-8645

Best Breakfast
Grandy's Restaurant
  819 N. Commerce St., 405/226-2051
Kettle Restaurant
  202 Holliday Dr., 405/226-8023

Best Burgers
Hamburger Inn
  27 N. Washington St., 405/223-7440

Best Chinese Food
Great Wall Chinese Restaurant
  2015 W. Broadway St., 405/226-4460

Best Coffee
Kimberly's By The Cup
  1200 N. Commerce St., 403/223-5297

Best Desserts
Cafe Alley
  107 E. Main St., 405/223-6413
Gourmet
  1606 McLish St., 405/223-0369

Best Dinner
Fireside Dining
  Hwy. 77, 405/226-4070

Best Ice Cream/Yogurt
Jenny's Ice Cream
  115 W. Main St., 405/226-6430

Best Mexican Food
El Chico Restaurant
  124 Holliday Dr., 405/226-3343
Polo's
  717 W. Broadway St., 405/226-7656

Best Salad/Salad Bar
Sirloin Stockade
  1217 N. Commerce St., 405/226-6281

Best Sandwiches
Cafe Alley
  107 E. Main St., 405/223-6413
Jenny's Ice Cream
  115 W. Main St., 405/226-6430

Best Seafood
Fireside Dining
  Hwy. 77, 405/226-4070
Aub's Two Frogs Grill
  Hwy. 70, Lone Grove, 403/657-8645

Best Steaks
Benson's
  110 Holliday Dr., 405/223-7848
Sirloin Stockade
  1217 N. Commerce St., 405/226-6281
Fireside Dining
  Hwy. 77, 405/226-4070

BARTLESVILLE, OK

Best Restaurant in Town
Sterling's Grille
2905 SE Frank Phillips Blvd., 918/335-0707

Best Barbecue/Ribs
Dink's Pit Bar-B-Que
2929 SE Frank Phillips Blvd., 918/335-0606

Best Burgers
Washington County Hamburger Store
412 S. Johnstone Ave., 918/336-4789
Murphy's Original Steak House
1625 SW Frank Phillips Blvd., 918/336-4789

Best Chinese Food
Szechuan Chinese Restaurant
516 SE Washington Blvd., 918/335-3945

Best Coffee
Java Bean Cafe
Eastland Mall, 572 SE Washington Blvd.,
918/335-9276

BROKEN ARROW, OK

Best Restaurant in Town
Cafe Savannah's
7501 E. Kenosha St., 918/357-2719

Best All-You-Can-Eat Buffet
China Palace Restaurant
113 N. Elm Pl., 918/258-6526

Best Bar
C.J. Moloney's
1849 S. Aspen Ave., 918/251-1973

Best Barbecue/Ribs
Robert's Bar BQ
9922 S. 241st East Ave., 918/451-0322

Best Breakfast
Midway Cafe
641 SE Washington Blvd., 918/335-1000

Best Brunch
Charlie Mitchell's Restaurant
605 S. Aspen Ave., 918/258-7681

Best Burgers
Goldie's Patio Grill
1912 S. Elm Pl., 918/455-6128

Best Business Lunch
Charlie Mitchell's Restaurant
605 S. Aspen Ave., 918/258-7681

Best Cheap Meal
Duffy's Restaurant
706 S. Elm Pl., 918/251-3285

Best Chinese Food
China Palace Restaurant
113 N. Elm Pl., 918/258-6526

Best Coffee
Golden Bagels
1009 N. Elm Pl., 918/258-1009

Best Desserts
Tea For Two
804 S. Main St., 918/251-8305

Best Diner
Duffy's Restaurant
706 S. Elm Pl., 918/251-3285

Best Family Restaurant
Delta Cafe
3806 S. Elm Pl., 918/455-1900

Best Homestyle Food
Midway Cafe
641 SE Washington Blvd., 918/335-1000

Best Ice Cream/Yogurt
Braum's Ice Cream and Dairy
4640 S. Elm Pl., 918/455-6464
804 N. Elm Pl., 918/258-2424
20200 E. 81st St., 918/251-4660

Best Italian Food
Zio's
7111 S. Domingo Rd., 918/250-5999

Best Late-Night Food
Charlie Mitchell's Restaurant
605 S. Aspen Ave., 918/258-7681

Best Pizza
All-Star Pizza
1921 S. Elm Pl., 918/451-7827

Best Place to Be "Seen"
Charlie Mitchell's Restaurant
605 S. Aspen Ave., 918/258-7681

Best Place to Eat Alone
Black Beans Bar-B-Q and Steaks
21914 E. 71st St., 918/355-2118

Best Place to Eat When Someone Else Is Buying
Hickory Hills Steak House
3600 W. Jaspar St., 918/451-2428

Best Romantic Dining
Cafe Savannah's
7501 E. Kenosha St., 918/357-2719
Petticoat Junction
25693 E. 71st St., 918/357-1967

Best Salad/Salad Bar
Sirloin Stockade
806 N. Aspen Ave., 918/258-1756

Best Sandwiches
C.J. Moloney's
1849 S. Aspen Ave., 918/251-1973

Best Seafood
Atlantic Sea Grill
8321A E. 61st St., 918/252-7966

Best Steaks
Hickory Hills Steak House
3600 W. Jaspar St., 918/451-2428

Best Tea Room
Tea For Two
804 S. Main St., 918/251-8305

Best Vegetarian Food
Delta Cafe
3806 S. Elm Pl., 918/455-1900

Standbys
Applebee's
3900 S. Elm Pl., 918/451-1715
El Chico
732 W. New Orleans St., 918/451-0633

DUNCAN, OK

Best Barbecue/Ribs
Hickies' BBQ
3325 N. Hwy. 81, 405/255-1551

Best Chinese Food
Peking Garden Chinese Restaurant
1203 S. Hwy. 81, 405/255-1806

Best Mexican Food
Don Jose's
3402 N. Hwy. 81, 405/252-5853
Eduardo's Mexican Restaurant
1304 N. Hwy. 81, 405/255-0781
El Palacio Mexican Restaurant
1209 Bois D'Arc, 405/252-1314

Best Seafood
Wright's Steak and Lobster House
905 E. Bois D'Arc Ave., 405/252-4363

Best Steaks
Wright's Steak and Lobster House
905 E. Bois D'Arc Ave., 405/252-4363

EDMOND, OK

Best Restaurant in Town
The Greystone Crab and Steakhouse
1 N. Sooner Rd., 405/340-4400

Best All-You-Can-Eat Buffet
Cici's Pizza
1520 E. Second, 405/341-1112

Best American Food
The Greystone Crab and Steakhouse
1 N. Sooner Rd., 405/340-4400
Johnnie's
3301 S. Boulevard St., 405/348-3214

Best Barbecue/Ribs
Bob's Bar-B-Que
257 S. Coltrane Rd., 405/348-4041

Best Breakfast
Around The Corner Restaurant
11 S. Broadway St., 405/341-5414

Best Brunch
The Greystone Crab and Steakhouse
  1 N. Sooner Rd., 405/340-4400

Best Burgers
Johnnie's Charcoal Broiler
  3301 S. Boulevard St., 405/348-3214

Best Business Lunch
Interurban Restaurant
  1301 E. Danforth Rd., 405/348-2792

Best Casual Dining
Cafe 501
  501 S. Boulevard St., 405/359-1501

Best Cheap Meal
Braum's Ice Cream and Dairy
  1612 S. Boulevard St., 405/341-3808
  3101 E. Memorial Rd., 405/478-4730
  1001 E. Danforth Rd., 405/348-7039

Best Chinese Food
Edmond Mandarin Chinese
  3412 S. Broadway St., 405/348-6300
Blue Moon
  1320 S. Broadway St., 405/340-3871

Best Coffee
Java Dave's
  9 S. Broadway St., 405/340-1693
  3331 S. Boulevard St., 405/348-3214

Best Delicatessen
New York Bagel Shop
  1700 S. Broadway St., 405/359-7722

Best Desserts
Twelve Oaks Restaurant
  6100 Midwest Blvd., 405/340-1002

Best Diner
Around The Corner Restaurant
  11 S. Broadway St., 405/341-5414

Best Family Restaurant
Johnnie's Charcoal Broiler
  3301 S. Boulevard St., 405/348-3214

Best French Food
Cafe 501
  501 S. Boulevard St., 405/359-1501

Best Health-Conscious Menu
Cafe 501
  501 S. Boulevard St., 405/359-1501
New York Bagel Shop
  1700 S. Broadway St., 405/359-7722

Best Homestyle Food
Hillbilly's Chicken
  206 E. Hwy. 66, 405/396-8177

Best Ice Cream/Yogurt
Braum's Ice Cream and Dairy
  1612 S. Boulevard St., 405/341-3808
  3101 E. Memorial Rd., 405/478-4730
  1001 E. Danforth Rd., 405/348-7039

Best Italian Food
Papa's Little Italy
    I35 and Hefner Rd., 405/478-4400

Best Late-Night Food
Nomad III
    2805 S. Broadway St., 405/340-4552

Best Mexican Food
Cocina De Mino
    3300 S. Broadway St., 405/348-7862

Best Pizza
Godfather's Pizza
    603 S. Broadway St., 405/348-7333

Best Place to Eat Alone
Hobby's Hoagies
    222 S. Santa Fe Ave., 405/348-2214

Best Place to Eat When Someone Else Is Buying
Twelve Oaks Restaurant
    6100 Midwest Blvd., 405/340-1002

Best Romantic Dining
The Greystone Crab and Steakhouse
    1 N. Sooner Rd., 405/340-4400

Best Steaks
The Greystone Crab and Steakhouse
    1 N. Sooner Rd., 405/340-4400

Best Tea Room
Diana's Tea Room
    108 S. Broadway St., 405/348-4789

Best Vegetarian Food
Edmond Mandarin Chinese
    3412 S. Broadway St., 405/348-6300

Best Other Restaurant
Pump's Restaurant
    617 S. Broadway St., 405/340-6107

Standbys
Outback Steakhouse
    3600 S. Broadway St., 405/359-7432

ELK CITY, OK

Best All-You-Can-Eat Buffet
The Gazebo
    Holiday Inn, 101 Meadowedge Dr., 405/225-6637

Best Breakfast
Flamingo Restaurant
    2010 W. Third St., 405/225-3412
Kettle Restaurant
    2700 E. Hwy. 66, 405/225-1071

Best Barbecue/Ribs
Bar-B-Que Shack
    611 S. Main St., 405/243-0787

Best Burgers
Flamingo Restaurant
    2010 W. Third St., 405/225-3412
Billie's
    210 N. Madison Ave., 405/225-3355

Best Coffee
Flamingo Restaurant
2010 W. Third St., 405/225-3412
Video Plus
901 W. Third St., 405/225-1000

Best Desserts
Flamingo Restaurant
2010 W. Third St., 405/225-3412
Country Dove Gifts and Tea Room
610 W. Third St., 405/225-7028

Best Homestyle Food
Flamingo Restaurant
2010 W. Third St., 405/225-3412

Best Italian Food
Sarah's Restaurant
108 Blue Ridge Dr., 405/225-7272

Best Ice Cream/Yogurt
Braum's Ice Cream
1111 W. Third St., 405/225-1011

Best Mexican Food
Lupe's Restaurant
905 N. Main St., 405/225-7109

Best Pizza
Mazzio's Pizza
103 Janets Way, 405/243-0000

Best Sandwiches
Cafe Elk City
107 W. Fifth St., 405/243-0801

Best Seafood
Simon's Catch
SW of City, 405/225-8400

Best Steaks
Simon's Catch
SW of City, 405/225-8400

Best Tea Room
Country Dove Gifts and Tea Room
610 W. Third St., 405/225-7028

ENID, OK

Best Bar
Toucan Harry's
210 N. Van Buren St., 405/234-2615

Best Brunch
Dutch Pantry
2818 S. Van Buren St., 405/242-7110

Best Business Lunch
Richill's Cafeteria
221 W. Randolph St., 405/237-4005

Best Casual Dining
Sneakers
1710 W. Willow Rd., 405/237-6325

Best Chinese Food
Combo King
 4125 W. Owen K. Garriott Rd., 405/242-7733
 923 S. Van Buren St., 405/242-7788

Best Coffee
Richard's Gourmet Coffee
 821 Commercial Cir., 405/237-6575

Best Family Restaurant
Cotton Patch Restaurant
 4901 W. Owen K. Garriott Rd., 405/242-8414

Best Health-Conscious Menu
Richill's Cafeteria
 221 W. Randolph St., 405/237-4005

Best Homestyle Food
Cotton Patch Restaurant
 4901 W. Owen Kay Garriott Rd., 405/242-8414

Best Ice Cream/Yogurt
Braum's Ice Cream and Dairy
 1119 E. Broadway Ave., 405/234-8253
 2709 W. Owen K. Garriott Rd., 405/234-8580
 1121 W. Willow Rd., 405/242-6152

Best Italian Food
Louisa's
 220 N. Independence, 405/233-8707

Best Late-Night Food
Taco Mayo
 913 W. Maple Ave., 405/233-5014

Best Pizza
Simple Simon's Pizza
 1402 E. Chestnut Ave., 405/233-8899

Best Place to Eat Alone
Richill's Cafeteria
 221 W. Randolph St., 405/237-4005

Best Place to Eat When Someone Else Is Buying
Toucan Harry's
 210 N. Van Buren St., 405/234-2615

Best Place to Take the Kids
Godfather's Pizza
 222 Sunset Plaza Shopping Ctr., 405/233-5766

Best Romantic Dining
Sage Room
 1927 S. Van Buren St., 405/233-1212

Best Sandwiches
Sneakers
 1710 W. Willow Rd., 405/237-6325

Best Steaks
The Sage Room
 1927 S. Van Buren St., 405/233-1212

Best Other Restaurant
City Boots
 800 W. Broadway Ave., 405/242-3663

Standbys
Western Sizzlin
4722 W. Owen K. Garriott Rd., 405/234-4121
Sonic Drive-In
4913 W. Owen K. Garriott Rd., 405/233-9100
905 W. Willow Rd., 405/233-8611
1617 S. Van Buren St., 405/234-2311
Baskin-Robbins
704 W. Maine Ave., 405/234-7416
El Chico
3710 W. Owen K. Garriott Rd., 405/234-1918
Red Lobster
4125 W. Owen K. Garriott Rd., 405/234-4200

LAWTON, OK

Best Breakfast
Victoria's
1125 E. Gore Blvd., 405/353-0200

Best Brunch
Rise and Shine Omelet Grill
201 SW Eleventh St., 405/355-3841
1529 NW Cache Rd., 405/353-8150
5239 NW Cache Rd., 405/353-4072

Best Burgers
Braum's Ice Cream and Dairy
608 NW Fort Sill Blvd., 405/353-5099
4435 NW Cache Rd., 405/353-5098
1211 SW Lee Blvd., 405/353-0764

Best Business Lunch
Bet's Country Ritz
529 SW Avenue C, 405/355-7200

Best Coffee
Forgotten Works Bookstore and Coffee Bar
603 SW Avenue E, 405/248-1575
Beans and Briar
200 SW Avenue C, Ste. 39, 405/357-2830

Best Desserts
French Market Caffe
1400B Sheridan Rd., 405/353-2323

Best Diner
Leo and Ken's Truck Stop
103 SE Lee Blvd., 405/357-8561

Best Family Restaurant
Calico County Restaurant
5203 NW Cache Rd., 405/353-7976

Best Health-Conscious Menu
Tea Room
213 SW Avenue C, 405/357-6116

Best Homestyle Food
Calico County Restaurant
5203 NW Cache Rd., 405/353-7976

Best Ice Cream/Yogurt
Braum's Ice Cream and Dairy
608 NW Fort Sill Blvd., 405/353-5099

4435 NW Cache Rd., 405/353-5098
1211 SW Lee Blvd., 405/353-0764

Best Italian Food
Pizano's Italian Restaurant
4512 SE Lee Blvd., 405/357-4033
Bianco's Italian Restaurant
113 NW Second St., 405/353-9543
Floridano's
300 NW Sheridan Rd., 405/353-5528

Best Mexican Food
El Zarape Restaurant
1015 SW Park Ave., 405/353-3610
Salas Authentic Mexican Foods
111 SW Lee Blvd., 405/357-1600

Best Place to Eat When Someone Else Is Buying
Martin's Restaurant
2107 NW Cache Rd., 405/355-0373

Best Romantic Dining
Martin's Restaurant
2107 NW Cache Rd., 405/355-0373
Pizano's Italian Restaurant
4512 SE Lee Blvd., 405/357-4033

Best Sandwiches
Harpo's
2502B NW Cache Rd., 405/357-3057
Schlotzsky's
3902 NW Cache Rd., 405/357-2867

Best Seafood
Fishermen's Cove
HC 32 Hwy. 49, 405/529-2672

Best Steaks
Old Plantation
Medicine Park, 405/529-9641

Best Tea Room
Tea Room
213 SW Avenue C, 405/357-6116

Best Other Restaurant
Crockett's Smokehouse
1508 W. Gore Blvd., 405/357-7427

Standbys
Golden Corral Family Steak House
4102 NW Cache Rd., 405/357-5113
Ryan's Family Steak House
2102 NW Cache Rd., 405/355-7926
Denny's
4020 NE Cache Rd., 405/353-4154
International House of Pancakes
1060 NW 38th St., 405/357-7464
Red Lobster
3112 NW Cache Rd., 405/248-4830

MCALESTER, OK

Best Barbecue/Ribs
Ball Hickory Pit Bar-B-Q
  319 W. Shawnee Ave., 918/423-4430

Best Breakfast
Meeting Place
  104 E. Choctaw Ave., 918/426-6416

Best Burgers
Ray's Grill
  215 E. Chickasaw Ave., 918/423-1444

Best Chinese Food
Hunan Chinese Restaurant
  733 S. George Nigh Expwy., 918/426-0481

Best Desserts
Janalynn's
  324 E. Carl Albert Pkwy., 918/423-4183
Marilyn's Restaurant
  1211 George Nigh Expwy., 918/426-1629

Best Health-Conscious Menu
Giacomo's Restaurant
  19 W. Comanche Ave., 918/423-2662
Pete's Place
  Hwy. 270E, Krebs, 918/423-2042

Best Homestyle Food
Marilyn's Restaurant
  1211 George Nigh Expwy., 918/426-1629

Best Ice Cream/Yogurt
Braum's Ice Cream
  1015 E. Carl Albert Pkwy., 918/426-0167

Best Italian Food
Giacomo's Restaurant
  19 W. Comanche Ave., 918/423-2662
Isle of Capri
  150 SW Seventh St., Krebs, 918/423-3062
Pete's Place
  Hwy. 270E, Krebs, 918/423-2042
Rosanna's
  205 E. Washington Ave., 918/423-2055

Best Mexican Food
Polo's of McAlester
  615 1/2 S. George Nigh Expwy., 918/423-7656

Best Sandwiches
East Gate Subs
  16 E. Choctaw Ave., 918/423-6272

Best Seafood
Trolley's Restaurant
  21 E. Monroe Ave., 918/423-2446

Best Steaks
Giacomo's Restaurant
  19 W. Comanche Ave., 918/423-2662

Standbys
Pizza Inn
  1746 E. Carl Albert Pkwy., 918/423-8280

MUSKOGEE, OK

Best American Food
Jasper's Restaurant
   1702 W. Okmulgee St., 918/682-7867

Best Barbecue/Ribs
Cowboy's Bar-B-Q
   401 N. York St., 918/682-0651
My Place Bar-B-Que
   4322 Okmulgee St., 918/683-5202
   1311 Gibson St., 918/683-2021
   501 N. Main St., 918/687-8524

Best Burgers
Ty's Hamburgers
   2406 Chandler Rd., 918/682-7599

Best Italian Food
Little Italy Fine Dining
   2432 N. 32nd St. W., 918/687-5699

Best Southwestern Food
Hamlin's El Toro East
   940 N. York St., 918/687-9982
Hamlin's El Toro West
   3620 W. Okmulgee St., 918/687-9194

Best Steaks
Okie's Restaurant
   219 S. 32nd St. W., 918/683-1056

NORMAN, OK

Best Restaurants in Town
Old Germany
   3750 West Robinson St., 405/321-6565
Norman Brewing Company
   102 W. Main St., 405/360-5726

Best Bar
The Deli
   309 White St., 405/360-6042

Best Breakfast
OK Diner
   213 E. Main St., 405/329-6642

Best Brunch
Pink's
   607 W. Boyd St., 405/366-7465

Best Burgers
Interurban
   105 W. Main St., 405/364-7942

Best Business Lunch
Interurban
   105 W. Main St., 405/364-7942

Best Casual Dining
Interurban
   105 W. Main St., 405/364-7942

Best Cheap Meal
OK Diner
   213 E. Main St., 405/329-6642

O

Best Chinese Food
Lai Lai Chinese Restaurant
   3720 W. Robinson St., 405/447-1555
Hunan Chinese Restaurant
   203 Hal Muldrow Dr.,405/360-0394
Orient Express
   722 Asp Ave., 405/364-2100

Best Coffee
New York Bagel Shop
   1150 W. Lindsey St., 405/360-4700
   301 W. Boyd St., 405/329-3000
La Baguette
   323 W. Boyd, 405/321-3424

Best Coffeehouse
Liquid Lounge
   114 W. Main St., 405/360-6791

Best Delicatessens
Breadworks
   1248 N. Interstate Dr., 405/321-3849
   211 E. Main St., 405/360-5778
   333 W. Boyd St., 405/360-5116
Lovelight Restaurant
   529 Buchanan Ave., 405/364-2073

Best Desserts
La Baguette
   323 W. Boyd St., 405/321-3424
   924 W. Main St., 405/329-5822

Best Diner
OK Diner
   213 E. Main St., 405/329-6642

Best Health-Conscious Menu
Lovelight Restaurant
   529 Buchanan Ave., 405/364-2073

Best Ice Cream/Yogurt
Braum's Ice Cream and Dairy
   400 E. Robinson St., 405/321-3431
   1320 E. Lindsey St., 405/360-2022
   1200 N. Interstate Dr., 405/364-7806
   1002 24th Ave. SW, 405/326-9155

Best Indian Food
Misal of India
   584 Buchanan Ave., 405/360-5888

Best Italian Food
Othello's Italian Restaurant
   434 Buchanan Ave., 405/360-2353
Jana's Restaurant
   1324 Interstate Dr., 405/447-7200

Best Late-Night Food
Kettle Restaurant
   1522 W. Lindsey St., 405/321-5236
   2520 W. Main St., 405/329-2263

Best Mexican Food
Cocina De Mino
   3750 W. Main St., 405/447-0330

Best New Restaurant
Norman Brewing Company
102 W. Main St., 405/360-5726

Best Pizza
Jana's Restaurant
1324 Interstate Dr., 405/447-7200

Best Place to Be "Seen"
The Mont
1300 Classen Blvd., 405/329-3330

Best Place to Eat Alone
Kettle Restaurant
1522 W. Lindsey St., 405/321-5236
2520 W. Main St., 405/329-2263

Best Place to Eat When Someone Else Is Buying
Old Germany
3750 West Robinson St., 405/321-6565

Best Romantic Dining
Victoria's Pasta Shop
327 White St., 405/329-0377

Best Sandwiches
The Deli
309 White St., 405/360-6042

Best Steaks
Indian Hills Restaurant and Club
6221 N. Interstate Dr., 405/364-7577

Best Vegetarian Food
Lovelight Restaurant
529 Buchanan Ave., 405/364-2073

Standbys
Golden Corral Family Steak House
2403 W. Main St., 405/364-2522
Cracker Barrel
800 N. Interstate Dr., 405/360-3117
Red Lobster
302 N. Interstate Dr., 405/364-6724

OKLAHOMA CITY, OK

Best Restaurants in Town
Bellini's Ristorante and Grill
6305 Waterford Blvd., Ste. 100, 405/848-1065
Coach House
6437 Avondale Dr., 405/842-1000
The Eagle's Nest
5700 United Founders Blvd., 405/840-5655

Best American Food
Black-Eyed Pea
13702 N. Pennsylvania Ave., 405/752-9744
1508 SW 74th St., 405/685-1000
6444 NW Expressway St., 405/721-2255
Charleston's
5907 NW Expressway St., 405/721-0060
Johnnie's
2652 W. Britton Rd., 405/751-2565
421 S.W. 74th St., 405/634-4681
6629 NW Expressway St., 405/721-9018

arsity Sports Grill
1140 NW 63rd St., 405/842-0898

Best Bars
Bricktown Brewery Restaurant and Pub
1 N. Oklahoma, 405/232-2739
Pearl's Oyster Bar
928 NW 63rd St., 405/848-8008
Flip's Wine Bar and Trattoria
5801 N. Western Ave., 405/843-1527
Full Moon Cafe
6714 N. Western Ave., 405/848-3070
Henry Hudson's Pub
13134 Pennsylvania Ave., 405/752-1444
401 SW 74th St., 405/631-0212
7500 SE Fifteenth St., 405/732-0232
3938 W. Reno Ave., 405/943-9080
3509 NW 58th St., 405/946-5771
VZD's
4200 N. Western, 405/524-4200
Varsity Sports Grill
1140 NW 63rd St., 405/842-0898

Best Barbecue/Ribs
County Line Restaurant
1226 NE 63rd St., 405/478-4955
Jack's Bar-B-Que
2724 W. Britton Rd., 405/755-7510
4418 NW 39th St., 405/946-1865
Leo's Barbecue and Catering
3631 N. Kelley, 405/427-3254
8014 N. Western, 405/843-7929
Piggy's Bar-B-Q
303 E. Sheridan Ave., 405/232-3912

Best Brunch
Classen Grill
5124 N. Classen Rd., 405/842-0428
Flip's Wine Bar and Trattoria
5801 N. Western, 405/843-1527
Harrigan's
2125 W. Memorial Rd., 405/751-7322
2203 SW 74th St., 405/686-1012
6420 NW Expressway St., 405/728-1329
Jimmy's Egg
2132 W. Britton Rd., 405/842-2944
1616 N. May Ave., 405/942-8710
5829 Melton Dr., 405/728-8343
308 S. Air Depot Blvd., 405/732-6433
2801 W. I-240 Service Rd.
Waterford Hotel
6300 Waterford Blvd., 405/848-4782

Best Chinese Food
Golden Palace
6308 E. Reno Ave., 405/737-7118
Grand House
1140 NW 24th St., 405/524-7333
Hunan Chinese Restaurant
1500 SW 74th St., 405/685-5288
9211 Pennsylvania Pl., 405/843-6233

Lido Restaurant
 2518 N. Military Ave., Ste. 101, 405/521-1902
Orient Express
 7311 N. MacArthur Blvd., 405/721-0882

Best Coffeehouses
Java Dave's
 10 NE Tenth St., 405/236-0272
 101 N. Broadway Ave., 405/232-5728
 7936 N. May Ave., 405/840-9949
Medina's Coffee House and Gallery
 3004 N. Paseo St., 405/524-7949
New Orleans Cafe
 3009 N. Classen Blvd., 405/557-1102
Yippee Yi-Yo Cafe
 4723 N. Western Ave., 405/524-5282

Best Delicatessens
Breadworks
 7300 N. Western Ave., 405/842-7571
City Bites
 4646 N. Santa Fe Ave., 405/528-6797
 7309 S. Western Ave., 405/632-6655
 12058 N. May Ave., 405/752-1771
 6001 N. May Ave., 405/842-3355
New York Bagel Shop
 211 N. Robinson Ave., 405/235-3700
 9235 Pennsylvania Pl., 405/848-3366
Someplace Else
 2310 N. Western Ave., 405/524-0887

Best German Food
Helga's German Restaurant
 4900 N. May Ave., 405/948-8216
Ingrid's Kitchen
 3701 N. Youngs Blvd., 405/946-8444
Old Germany
 15920 SE 29th St., Choctaw, 405/390-8647
Royal Bavaria
 3401 S. Sooner Rd., Moore, 405/799-7666

Best Health-Conscious Menu
City Bites
 4646 N. Santa Fe Ave., 405/528-6797
 7309 S. Western Ave., 405/632-6655
 12058 N. May Ave., 405/752-1771
 6001 N. May Ave., 405/842-3355
Good Eats Cafe
 3000 W. Britton Rd., 405/751-3287
New York Bagel Shop
 211 N. Robinson Ave., 405/235-3700
 9235 Pennsylvania Pl., 405/848-3366
Stefanie's Meals for Every Lifestyle
 351 N. Air Depot Blvd., 405/733-4922
 7301 N. Classen Blvd., 405/848-0805
 5583 NW Expressway St., 405/722-3118
 7636 N. Western Ave., 405/848-0321
Tulio's
 3325 S. Robinson Ave., 405/634-6571

O

st Indian Food
anta
  11919 N. Pennsylvania Ave., 405/752-5283
Gopuram Taste of India
  4559 NW 23rd St., 405/948-7373

Best Italian Food
Bellini's Ristorante and Grill
  6305 Waterford Blvd., Ste. 100, 405/848-1065
Flip's Wine Bar and Trattoria
  5801 N. Western Ave., 405/843-1527
Portobello Ristorante
  5418 N. Western Ave., 405/848-7678
Spaghetti Warehouse
  101 E. Sheridan Ave., 405/235-0402
Tony's Italian Specialties
  2824 N. Pennsylvania Ave., 405/524-7705

Best Mexican Food
Chelino's Mexican Restaurant
  15 E. California Ave., Bricktown, 405/235-3533
  4221 S. Robinson Ave., 405/636-1548
  427 SW 36th St., 405/636-1110
Cocina De Mino
  20 N. Broadway Ave., 405/232-6466
  12325 N. May Ave., 405/749-8800
  3840 N. MacArthur Blvd., 405/495-6789
  325 SE 29th St., 405/632-1036
  6000 NW Second St., 405/495-0411
La Roca Mexican Restaurant
  409 W. Reno Ave., 405/235-9596
  412 S. Walker Ave., 405/235-8646
  7550 W. May Ave., 405/840-1968

Best New Restaurants
Chelino's Mexican Restaurant
  15 E. California Ave., Bricktown, 405/235-3533
Ground Floor Cafe
  6430 Avondale Dr., 405/842-2233
Scooter's
  303 NW 62nd St., 405/840-2453
Trapper's Fish Camp
  4300 W. Reno Ave., 405/943-9111

Best Seafood
Der Dutchman Seafood Restaurant
  6201 NW Expressway St., 405/721-1313
Fishkie's Seafood Restaurant
  6816 N. Western, 405/840-3474
Pearl's Oyster Bar
  2125 NW I-240 Service Rd., 405/682-1500
  928 NW 63rd St., 405/848-8008
Trapper's Fish Camp
  4300 W. Reno Ave., 405/943-9111

Best Steaks
Cattlemen's Steak House
  1309 S. Agnew, 405/236-0416
Junior's
  2601 NW Expressway St., 405/848-5597

UR Cook's Steakhouse
  6444 NW Expressway St., 405/722-6500

Standbys
Chili's
  1704 S. Meridian Ave., 405/682-2453
  5501 NW Expressway St., 405/728-7444
Steak and Ale
  13601 N. May Ave., 405/752-0944
  500 S. Meridian Ave., 405/943-1406
  5500 N. Brookline Ave., 405/947-1601
  920 SW 74th St., 405/631-3349
Outback Steakhouse
  2219 SW 74th St., 405/686-0918
  316 S. Meridian Ave., 405/942-4564
Red Lobster
  1000 W. I-240 Service Rd., 405/634-3395
  2625 W. Memorial Rd., 405/755-1390
  4243 NW Expressway St., 405/842-1453
The Olive Garden
  2321 SW 74th St., 405/685-0781
  2639 W. Memorial Rd., 405/749-8188

PONCA CITY, OK

Best American Food
Blue Moon
  1418 E. South Ave., 405/762-2425

Best Bar
Crown and Rose
  731 N. Fourteenth St., 405/762-8489

Best Barbecue/Ribs
Head Country Bar-B-Q Restaurant
  1217 E. Prospect Ave., 405/767-8304
Blue Moon
  1418 E. South Ave., 405/762-2425

Best Delicatessen
Fat and Skinnie's Buffet Catering
  120 N. Third St., 405/765-9243

Best Family Restaurants
Nottingham's Grand Cafe
  423 E. Grand Ave., 405/762-2310
Cobb's Cafe
  801 S. First St., 405/762-2434

Best Italian Food
Ristorante Bravo
  200 N. Second St., 405/762-7280

Best Steaks
The Rusty Barrel
  2005 N. Fourteenth St., 405/765-6689
Pauline's Supper Club
  114 La Cann Dr., 405/765-5460

Standbys
El Chico
  900 E. Prospect St., 405/765-2224

SALLISAW, OK

Best Barbecue/Ribs
Wild Horse Mountain Bar-B-Que
  Hwy. 61, 918/775-9960

Best Breakfast
Dana's Restaurant
  Hwy. 59 at I-40, 918/775-4921

Best Burgers
Peggy's Cafe
  126 E. Cherokee St., 918/775-3148

Best Cheap Meal
Golden Wu Restaurant
  702 E. Cherokee St., 918/776-0808
Peggy's Cafe
  126 E. Cherokee St., 918/775-3148

Best Chinese Food
Full Moon
  122 W. Cherokee St., 918/775-8580
Golden Wu Restaurant
  702 E. Cherokee St., 918/776-0808

Best Ice Cream/Yogurt
Braum's Ice Cream
  615 S. Kerr Blvd., 918/775-9965

Best Pizza
Peggy's Cafe
  126 E. Cherokee St., 918/775-3148

Best Place to Take the Kids
Simple Simon's Pizza
  2401 E. Cherokee St., 918/775-5511

Standbys
Pizza Hut
  Hwy. 64E, 918/775-5509
Subway
  1900F E. Cherokee St., 918/775-6965
Western Sizzlin
  815 S. Kerr Blvd., 918/775-6268

SHAWNEE, OK

Best American Food
Garfield's Restaurant and Pub
  4901 N. Kickapoo St., Ste. 1660, 405/273-3301

Best Barbecue/Ribs
Van's Pig Stand
  717 E. Highland St., 405/273-8704

Best Chinese Food
Sunrise Chinese Restaurant
  1814 N. Harrison St., 405/275-7271

Best Mexican Food
Amigo's Mexican Restaurant
  1718 N. Kickapoo St., 405/275-5552

Best Steaks
Jay's Classic Steakhouse
  37808 Old 270 Hwy., 405/275-6867

Standbys
Red Lobster
435 Shawnee Mall Rd., 405/273-6215

STILLWATER, OK

Best Restaurants in Town
Eskimo Joe's
501 W. Elm Ave., 405/377-0799
Hideaway
230 S. Knoblock St., 405/372-4777

Best Mexican Food
Mexico Joe's
311 E. Hall of Fame Ave., 405/372-1169
Bobo's Mexican Restaurante
5020 W. Sixth Ave., 405/372-9353

Best Seafood
Stillwater Bay
501 W. Elm Ave., 405/743-2780

Best Steaks
Stillwater Bay
501 W. Elm Ave., 405/743-2780
Sirloin Stockade
208 N. Perkins Rd., 405/624-1681

TULSA, OK

Best Atmosphere
Royal Dragon
7837 E. 51st St., 918/664-2245
Warren Duck Club
6110 S. Yale Ave., 918/495-1000

Best Barbecue/Ribs
Rib Crib
1607 S. Harvard Ave., 918/742-6327
5025 S. Sheridan Rd., 918/663-4295

Best Breakfast
Brookside by Day
3313 S. Peoria Ave., 918/745-9989

Best Burgers
Burger Street
2107 S. Harvard Ave., 918/747-3711
4919 S. Peoria Ave., 918/744-0427
6151 E. 51st St., 918/664-1774
7445 E. Admiral Pl., 918/838-7605
Cherry Street Brewery
1516 S. Quaker Ave., 918/582-2739

Best Cheap Meal
Hideaway Pizza
1503 E. Fifteenth St., 918/582-4777
Jason's Deli
8321 E. 61st St., 918/252-9999

Best Chinese Food
Bamboo Garden
3922 S. Hudson Ave., 918/622-6227
Royal Dragon
7837 E. 51st St., 918/664-2245

Great Wall Restaurant
7105 S. Yale Ave., 918/494-8652

Best Coffee
Java Dave's Coffee
1326 E. Fifteenth St., 918/592-3317
3310 S. Peoria Ave., 918/744-5317
427 S. Boston Ave., 918/587-3317
6239 E. Fifteenth St., 918/836-7317
8013D S. Sheridan Rd., 918/492-8317

Best Delicatessen
Boston Deli
6231 E. 61st St., 918/492-4747
708 S. Boston Ave., 918/582-3353

Best Desserts
Spaghetti Warehouse
221 E. Brady St., 918/587-4440

Best Health-Conscious Menu
Big Al's Subs and Health Foods
3303 E. Fifteenth St., 918/744-5085

Best Homestyle Food
Betty Ann's Restaurant
4401 S. Memorial Dr., 918/663-8269
Black-Eyed Pea
3118 S. Garnett Rd., 918/665-7435
8040 S. Yale Ave., 918/493-6318
Wanda J's Restaurant
5001 N. Peoria Ave., 918/425-3651

Best Ice Cream/Yogurt
I Can't Believe It's Yogurt
1 Williams Ctr., Ste. 107, 918/599-8226
3807A S. Peoria Ave., 918/744-5056
Braum's Ice Cream and Dairy
Multiple Locations

Best Indian Food
India Palace
6963 S. Lewis Ave., 918/492-8040

Best Italian Food
Mondo's Italian Restaurant
6000 N. Lewis Ave., 918/749-2233
6746 S. Memorial Dr., 918/254-7778

Best Late-Night Food
Hoffbrau Bar and Grill
1738 S. Boston Ave., 918/583-9520

Best Mexican Food
Mexicali Border Cafe
14 W. Brady St., 918/582-3383
7104 S. Sheridan Rd., Ste. 9, 918/481-1114

Best Outdoor Dining
Full Moon Cafe
1525 E. Fifteenth St., 918/583-6666

Best Pizza
Hideaway Pizza
1503 E. Fifteenth St., 918/582-4777

Best Romantic Dining
Atlantic Sea Grill
  8321A E. 61st St., 918/252-7966

Best Salad/Salad Bar
Spaghetti Warehouse
  221 E. Brady St., 918/587-4440
Jason's Deli
  8321 E. 61st St., 918/252-9999

Best Sandwiches
Big Al's Subs and Health Foods
  3303 E. Fifteenth St., 918/744-5085
Boston Deli
  6231 E. 61st St., 918/492-4747
  708 S. Boston Ave., 918/582-3353

Best Seafood
Atlantic Sea Grill
  8321A E. 61st St., 918/252-7966
Landry's Seafood House
  7646 E. 61st St., 918/252-1010
S and J Oyster Company
  3301 S. Peoria Ave., 918/744-4440

Best Steaks
Silver Flame Steak and Seafood
  6526 E. 51st St., 918/664-9224

Best View While Dining
Cherry Street Brewery
  1516 S. Quaker Ave., 918/582-2739
Full Moon Cafe
  1525 E. Fifteenth St., 918/583-6666

Standbys
Po' Folks
  5111 S. Peoria Ave., 918/749-6606

O

WOODWARD, OK

Best Atmosphere
Polly Anna Cafe
  902 Main St., 405/256-9037

Best Barbecue/Ribs
Rib Ranch
  2424 Williams Ave., 405/256-6081

Best Breakfast
Polly Anna Cafe
  902 Main St., 405/256-9037

Best Burgers
JB Steakhouse
  225 E. Main St., 405/256-4845
West Side Restaurant
  2329 Oklahoma Ave., 405/256-6992

Best Desserts
Polly Anna Cafe
  902 Main St., 405/256-9037

Best Family Restaurant
Rib Ranch
  2424 Williams Ave., 405/256-6081

Best Homestyle Food
Polly Anna Cafe
902 Main St., 405/256-9037

Best Ice Cream/Yogurt
Braum's Ice Cream and Dairy
2403 Williams Ave., 405/256-4630

Best Sandwiches
Chicken Roscoe's
1023 Main St., 405/254-2149

Best Steaks
JB Steakhouse
225 E. Main St., 405/256-4845

Oregon

Best American Food
The Buzz Saw Restaurant and Lounge
   421 Water Ave. NE, 541/928-0642
Flinn's Parlor
   222 First Ave. SW, 541/928-9638

Best Continental Food
Flinn's Parlor
   222 First Ave. SW, 541/928-9638

Best Delicatessen
The Wine Depot and Deli
   300 Second Ave. SW, 541/967-9499

Best Italian Food
Capriccio's Ristorante
   442 W. First St., 541/924-9932
Pastabilities
   250 Broadalvin St. SW, 541/924-9235

Best Other Ethnic Food
Novak's Hungarian Paprikas (Hungarian)
   2835 Santiam Hwy. SE, 541/967-9488

Best Seafood
Depot Cafe
   822 Lyon St. S., 541/926-7326

Best Sandwiches
Victoria Dahl's
   2921 Marine Dr., 503/325-7109

Best Seafood
The Ship Inn
   1 Second St., 503/325-0033

Best View While Dining
Pier 11 Feedstore Restaurant
   7711 Eleventh St., 503/325-0279

BANDON, OR

Best Breakfast
Minute Cafe
  145 N. Second St., 541/347-2707

Best Brunch
Bandon Boatworks Restaurant
  275 Lincoln Ave. SW, 541/347-2111
Lord Bennett's Restaurant
  1695 Beach Loop Rd., 541/347-3663

Best French Food
Christophe at Face Rock
  3225 Beach Loop Dr., 541/347-3261

Best Lunch
Bandon Boatworks Restaurant
  275 Lincoln Ave. SW, 541/347-2111
Lord Bennett's Restaurant
  1695 Beach Loop Rd., 541/347-3663

Best Restaurant Meal Value
Harp's Restaurant
  130 Chicago Ave. SE, 541/347-9057
Sea Star Guesthouse
  370 First St., 541/347-9632

Best Seafood
Bandon Boatworks Restaurant
  275 Lincoln Ave. SW, 541/347-2111
Harp's Restaurant
  130 Chicago Ave. SE, 541/347-9057

Best View While Dining
Lord Bennett's Restaurant
  1695 Beach Loop Rd., 541/347-3663

BEND, OR

Best Atmosphere
Royal Blend Coffee
  1075 NW Newport Ave., 541/383-0873
  1289 NE Second St., 541/382-6349
Deschutes Brewery
  1044 NW Bond St., 541/382-9242

Best Breakfast
Pilot Butte Drive In
  917 NE Greenwood Ave., 541/382-2972

Best Chinese Food
Eddie's Canton
  909 NW Bond St., 541/389-5154

Best Coffee
Royal Blend Coffee
  1075 NW Newport Ave., 541/383-0873
  1289 NE Second St., 541/382-6349

Best Continental Food
Pine Tavern Restaurant
  967 NW Brooks St., 541/382-5581

Best Desserts
Broken Top
  61999 Broken Top Dr., 541/383-8210
Scanlon's
  61615 Mount Bachelor Dr., 541/382-8769

Best Health-Conscious Menu
Baja Norte
  801 NW Wall St., 541/385-0611

Best Ice Cream/Yogurt
Sweeney's Family Creamery and Eatery
  61470 S. Hwy. 97, 541/388-0012

Best Japanese Food
Yoko's Japanese Restaurant
  1028 NW Bond St., 541/382-2999

Best Mexican Food
Baja Norte
  801 NW Wall St., 541/385-0611
Mexicali Rose
  301 NE Franklin Ave., 541/389-0149

Best Microbrewery
Deschutes Brewery
  1044 NW Bond St., 541/382-9242

Best Pizza
John Dough's Pizza
  34 SW Fourteenth St., 541/382-3645

Best Seafood
Kayo's
  61363 S. Hwy. 97, 541/389-1400
McKenzie's Restaurant
  1033 NW Bond St., 541/388-3891

Best Thai Food
Toomie's
  119 NW Minnesota Ave., 541/388-5590

BROOKINGS, OR

Best Casual Dining
Wharfside Seafood Restaurant
  16362 Lower Harbor Rd., Harbor, 541/469-7316

Best Desserts
Hog Wild
  16160 Hwy. 10S, 541/469-8869

Best Mexican Food
Los Amigos
  541 Chetco Ave., Ste. 1, 541/469-4102

Best Sandwiches
The Tea Room
  434 Redwood St., 541/469-7240

BURNS, OR

Best Atmosphere
Burns Power House Restaurant
  305 E. Monroe St., 541/573-9060

Best Bar
Palace Cafe
  260 N. Broadway Ave., 541/573-6636

Best Breakfast
Ye Olde Castle
  186 W. Monroe St., 541/573-6601
Jerry's Restaurant
  937 Oregon Ave., 541/573-7000

Best Chinese Food
Hilander Restaurant
  195 N. Broadway Ave., 541/573-2111

Best Homestyle Food
Steen's Mountain Cafe
  195 N. Alder Ave., 541/573-7226

Best Mexican Food
Mazatlan
  239 N. Broadway, 541/573-1829

Best Other Ethnic Food
Steen's Mountain Cafe (Basque)
  195 N. Alder Ave., 541/573-7226

Best Pizza
Windmill Pizza Company
  673 W. Monroe St., 541/573-5421
Central Pastime
  211 N. Broadway Ave., 541/573-6261

Best Sandwiches
Wayside Delicatessen
  530 N. Broadway Ave., 541/573-7020

Best Seafood
Burns Power House Restaurant
  305 E. Monroe St., 541/573-9060
Pine Room Cafe
  543 W. Monroe St., 541/573-6631

Best Steaks
Burns Power House Restaurant
  305 E. Monroe St., 541/573-9060
Pine Room Cafe
  543 W. Monroe St., 541/573-6631

Standbys
Dairy Queen
  State Hwy. 20W, 541/573-2203

COOS BAY, OR

Best Beer Selection
Blue Heron Bistro
  100 Commercial Ave., 541/267-3933

Best Breakfast
Pancake Mill Restaurant
  23900 Tremont St., North Bend, 541/756-2751

Best Burgers
Bay Burger Inn
  1175 Newmark Ave., 541/888-3688
Leon's
  1120 Virginia Ave., North Bend, 541/756-1914

Best Chinese Food
Kum-Yon's
  835 S. Broadway, 541/269-2662
Ming Palace
  3480 Tremont St., North Bend, 541/756-2537

Best Coffee
Kaffe 101
  134 S. Broadway, 541/267-4894

Best Desserts
Red Lion Inn
  1313 N. Bayshore Dr., 541/267-4141

Best Family Restaurants
Virginia Street Diner
  1430 Virginia Ave., North Bend, 541/269-9700
Sea Basket
  4579 Small Boat Basin, 541/888-5711
Pony Village Lodge
  Pony Village, North Bend, 541/756-3191
Timber Inn Restaurant
  1001 N. Bayshore Dr., 541/267-4622
Little Richard's
  581 N. Bayshore Dr., 541/267-7711

Best Italian Food
Benetti's Italian Restaurant
  260 S. Broadway, 541/267-6066

Best Mexican Food
Playa del Sol
  525 Newport Hwy. 101, 541/469-4102
Puerto Vallarta
  230 S. Second St., 541/269-0919

Best Pizza
Papa Murphy's
  880 Ingersoll, 541/269-9700
Gino's Pizza Inn
  1324 Virginia Ave., 541/756-5000

Best Restaurant Meal Value
Playa del Sol
  525 Newport Hwy. 101, 541/469-4102

Best Sandwiches
Blue Heron Bistro
  100 Commercial Ave., 541/267-3933
Back Alley
  North Bend Lanes Bowling Ctr., 1225 Virginia Ave.,
    North Bend, 541/756-0571

Best Seafood
Portside Restaurant
  Charleston Boat Basin, 541/888-5544
Cheryn's Seafood
  5102 Cape Arago Hwy., Charleston, 541/888-3251

Best Steaks
Hilltop House
  166 N. Bay Dr., North Bend, 541/756-4160

CORVALLIS, OR

Best Restaurants in Town
Michael's Landing
603 NW Second St., 541/754-6141
Bombs Away Cafe
2527 NW Monroe Ave., 541/757-7221
China Delight
325 NW Fifteenth St., 541/753-0791

Best Delicatessen
Old World Deli
341 SW Second St., 541/752-8549

Best Pizza
Woodstock's Pizza Parlor
1045 NW Kings Blvd., 541/752-5151

Best Seafood
The Gables Restaurant
1121 NW Ninth St., 541/752-3364
McGrath's Fish House
350 NE Circle Blvd., 541/752-3474

Best Vegetarian Food
Nearly Normal's
109 NW Fifteenth St., 541/753-0791

EUGENE, OR

Best All-You-Can-Eat Buffet
Izzy's Pizza Restaurant
210 Division Ave., 541/689-6443
730 E. Broadway, 541/484-2919

Best Atmosphere
Piccolo's Eurobistro
Downtown Athletic Club, 999 Willamette St.,
541/484-4011

Best Barbecue/Ribs
West Brothers BBQ
844 Olive St., 541/345-8489

Best Breakfast
Original Pancake House
659 E. Broadway, 541/343-7523
French Horn Cafe and Bakery
1591 Williamette St., 541/343-7473

Best Chinese Food
Ocean Sky
1601 Chambers St., 541/342-4848

Best Coffee
Full City Coffee Roasters
842 Pearl St., 541/344-0475

Best Continental Food
Valley River Inn
1000 Valley River Way, 541/341-3462

Best Delicatessens
Hawthorne's Cafe and Deli
153 E. Broadway, 541/683-0783
Rosewater's Deli and Catering
44 W. Broadway, 541/485-4342

Best French Food
Chanterelle
   207 E. Fifth Ave., 541/484-4065

Best Greek/Mediterranean Food
Mekala's
   296 E. Fifth Ave., 541/342-4872

Best Ice Cream/Yogurt
Prince Puckler's Homemade Ice Cream
   10 Van Buren St., 541/687-8785
   1605 E. Nineteenth Ave., 541/344-4418
   861 Willamette St., 541/343-2621

Best Italian Food
Mazzi's Italian Food
   3377 E. Amazon Dr., 541/687-2252
   2495 Hilyard St., 541/344-9291
Original Joe's Restaurant
   21 W. Sixth Ave., 541/485-4820

Best Mexican Food
Tres Hermanos
   99 W. Broadway, 541/342-4058

Best Microbreweries
Steelhead Brewery and Cafe
   199 E. Fifth Ave., 541/686-2739
Field's Restaurant and Brew Pub
   1290 Oak St., 541/341-6599

Best Pizza
Izzy's Pizza Restaurant
   210 Division Ave., 541/689-6443
   730 E. Broadway, 541/484-2919
Mona Lizza Pasta, Pool and Pizza
   830 Olive St., 541/345-1072
Pegasus Smokehouse Pizza
   790 E. Fourteenth Ave., 541/344-4471

Best Sandwiches
Hawthorne's Cafe and Deli
   153 E. Broadway, 541/683-0783
Rosewater's Deli and Catering
   44 W. Broadway, 541/485-4342

Best Seafood
Oscar's Garden Cafe
   Hilton Hotel, 66 E. Sixth Ave., 541/342-2000

Best Steaks
Oregon Electric Station
   27 E. Fifth Ave., 541/485-4444

Best View While Dining
Vistas
   Hilton Hotel, 66 E. Sixth Ave., 541/342-6655

FLORENCE, OR

Best Bread
Blue Hen Cafe
   1675 Hwy. 101, 541/997-3907

Best Breakfast
Blue Hen Cafe
  1675 Hwy. 101, 541/997-3907

Best Burgers
Blue Hen Cafe
  1675 Hwy. 101, 541/997-3907
Florence In and Out Hamburgers
  586 Hwy. 101, 541/997-8322

Best Casual Dining
Traveler's Cove
  1362 Bay St., 541/997-6845

Best Desserts
Blue Hen Cafe
  1675 Hwy. 101, 541/997-3907
Traveler's Cove
  1362 Bay St., 541/997-6845

Best View While Dining
Surfside Restaurant and Lounge
  88416 First Ave., 541/997-8263

GRANTS PASS, OR

Best Restaurants in Town
The Yankee Pot Roast
  720 NW Sixth St., 541/476-0551
Charlie W's
  201 SW G St., 541/474-2096
Paradise Ranch Inn
  7000 Monument Dr., 541/479-4333
The Wolf Creek Inn
  100 Front St., Wolf Creek, 541/866-2474

Best French Food
Legrand's Bakery
  323 NE E St., 541/471-1554

KLAMATH FALLS, OR

Best French Food
Chez Nous
  3927 S. Sixth St., 541/883-8719

Best Italian Food
Fiorella's Italian Restaurant
  6139 Simmers Ave., 541/882-1878

Best Mexican Food
Maria's of Keno
  2424 Shasta Way, 541/884-0787
Sergio's Mexican Restaurant
  4650 S. Sixth St., 541/885-6885

LA GRANDE, OR

Best Barbecue/Ribs
Smokehouse Restaurant
  2208 Adams Ave., 541/963-9692

Best Breakfast
Smokehouse Restaurant
  2208 Adams Ave., 541/963-9692

Best Burgers
Scotty's
809 Adams Ave., 541/963-8266

Best Coffee
Highway 30 Coffee Company
1102 Washington Ave., 541/963-6821

Best Family Restaurant
Farm House Family Restaurant
401 Adams Ave., 541/963-9318

Best Homestyle Food
Farm House Family Restaurant
401 Adams Ave., 541/963-9318

Best Italian Food
Luigi's
1011 Adams Ave., 541/963-0613

Best Mexican Food
Mamacita's
110 Depot St., 541/963-6223

Best Pizza
Klondike Pizza
2104 Island Ave., 541/963-0994
2610 Bearco, 541/963-4949

Best Sandwiches
Cock and Bull Villa Roma
1414 Adams Ave., 541/963-0573

Best Seafood
Ten Depot Street
10 Depot St., 541/963-8766

Best Steaks
Wrangler Steakhouse
1914 Adams Ave., 541/963-3131

O

LINCOLN CITY, OR

Best Bread
Whale Cove Inn
2345 SW Hwy. 101, Depoe Bay, 541/765-2255

Best Casual Dining
Surfrider Resort
3115 NW Hwy. 101, Depoe Bay, 541/764-2311

Best Desserts
Bay House
5911 SW Hwy. 101, 541/996-3222

Best French Food
Chez Jeannette
7150 Old Hwy. 101, Gleneden Beach, 541/764-3434

Best Seafood
Bay House
5911 SW Hwy. 101, 541/996-3222
Shilo Restaurant and Lounge
1501 NW 40th St., 541/994-5255
Surfrider Resort
3115 NW Hwy. 101, Depoe Bay, 541/764-2311

Tidal Raves
279 NW Hwy. 101, Depoe Bay, 541/765-2995

Best Vegetarian Food
The Noodle
2185 NW Hwy. 101, 541/994-8800

Best View While Dining
The Inn at Spanish Head
4009 SW Hwy. 101, 541/996-2161
Whale Cove Inn
2345 SW Hwy. 101, Depoe Bay, 541/765-2255
Chez Jeannette
7150 Old Hwy. 101, Gleneden Beach, 541/764-3434
Tidal Raves
279 NW Hwy. 101, Depoe Bay, 541/765-2995

Best Wine Selection
Bay House
5911 SW Hwy. 101, 541/996-3222
Salishan Lodge
7760 Hwy. 101N, Gleneden Beach, 541/764-2371

MEDFORD, OR

Best Restaurants in Town
Bel Di's
Hwy. 62, Shady Cove, 541/878-2010
Genessee Place
203 Genessee St., 541/772-5581
Jacksonville Inn
175 E. California St., Jacksonville, 541/889-1900
Primavera
First St. at Hargadine St., Ashland, 541/488-1994
Winchester Inn
35 S. Second St., Ashland, 541/488-1115

Best French Food
Chateaulin
50 E. Main St., Ashland, 541/482-2264

Best Wine Selection
Jacksonville Inn
175 E. California St., Jacksonville, 541/889-1900

NEWPORT, OR

Best Asian Restaurant
Kum-Yon's
1006 SW Coast Hwy., 541/265-5330

Best Bread
Whale's Tale
452 SW Bay Blvd., 541/265-8660

Best Beer Selection
Bayfront Brewery and Public House
748 SW Bay Blvd., 541/265-3188

Best Breakfast
Whale's Tale
452 SW Bay Blvd., 541/265-8660

Best Brunch
Canyon Way Bookstore and Restaurant
  1216 SW Canyon Way, 541/265-8319
Champagne Patio
  1630 N. Coast Hwy. 101, 541/265-3044

Best Casual Dining
Canyon Way Bookstore and Restaurant
  1216 SW Canyon Way, 541/265-8319

Best Lunch
Canyon Way Bookstore and Restaurant
  1216 SW Canyon Way, 541/265-8319
Champagne Patio
  1630 N. Coast Hwy. 101, 541/265-3044

Best Pizza
At's A Pizza
  352 SW Ninth St., 541/265-6000
Izzy's Pizza Restaurant
  5251 N. Coast Hwy., 541/265-3636

Best Restaurant Meal Value
Izzy's Pizza Restaurant
  5251 N. Coast Hwy., 541/265-3636

Best Salad/Salad Bar
Izzy's Pizza Restaurant
  5251 N. Coast Hwy., 541/265-3636

Best Sandwiches
Champagne Patio
  1630 N. Coast Hwy. 101, 541/265-3044

Best Steaks
Canyon Way Bookstore and Restaurant
  1216 SW Canyon Way, 541/265-8319

Best Vegetarian Food
Whale's Tale
  452 SW Bay Blvd., 541/265-8660

Best View While Dining
Izzy's Pizza Restaurant
  5251 N. Coast Hwy., 541/265-3636

Best Wine Selection
Champagne Patio
  1630 N. Coast Hwy. 101, 541/265-3044

PENDLETON, OR

Best All-You-Can-Eat Buffet
King's Table Buffet
  210 SW Seventeenth St., 541/276-2284

Best Barbecue/Ribs
Circle S Barbecue
  210 SE Fifth St., 541/276-9637

Best Breakfast
Kopper Kitchen Restaurant
  319 SE Nye Ave., 541/278-0678

Best Burgers
A and R Burger Island
  912 SE Emigrant Ave., 541/276-3352

Best Cheap Meal
King's Table Buffet
  210 SW Seventeenth St., 541/276-2284

Best Chinese Food
Golden Fountain
  437 S. Main St., 541/276-6130
Lee's Cafe
  502 SW Emigrant Ave., 541/276-5819

Best Dinner
Raphael's Restaurant
  233 SE Fourth St., 541/276-8500

Best Family Restaurant
King's Table Buffet
  210 SW Seventeenth St., 541/276-2284

Best Homestyle Food
Circle S Barbecue
  210 SE Fifth St., 541/276-9637

Best Pizza
Big John's Hometown Pizza
  225 SW Ninth St., 541/276-0550

Best Place to Eat When Someone Else Is Buying
Raphael's Restaurant
  233 SE Fourth St., 541/276-8500

Best Sandwiches
USA Subs
  1004 SW Court Ave., 541/278-7827

Best Steaks
Cimmiyotti's
  137 S. Main St., 541/276-4314

Standbys
Dairy Queen
  1415 SW Court Ave., 541/276-1472
Denny's
  610 SW 23rd St., 541/276-0215
Sizzler
  1515 Southgate, 541/278-2663

PORTLAND, OR

Best Atmosphere
Ron Paul Catering
  1441 NE Broadway St., 503/284-5347
  6141 SW Macadam Ave., 503/977-0313

Best Bread
Bread and Ink Cafe
  3610 SW Hawthorne Blvd., 503/239-4756

Best Breakfast
Bread and Ink Cafe
  3610 SW Hawthorne Blvd., 503/239-4756
Original Pancake House
  8600 SW Barbur Blvd., 503/246-9007

Best Burgers
Bread and Ink Cafe
  3610 SW Hawthorne Blvd., 503/239-4756

Hamburger Mary's
840 SW Park Ave., 503/223-0900
Kupie Cone Drive-In
3835 SE Holgate Blvd., 503/775-3890

Best Business Lunch
Atwater's Restaurant and Lounge
111 SW Fifth Ave., 30th Fl., 503/275-3600

Best Casual Dining
Hawthorne Street Cafe
3354 SE Hawthorne Blvd., 503/232-4982

Best Cheap Meal
Saigon Kitchen
3829 SE Division St., 503/236-2312
835 NE Broadway St., 503/281-3669

Best Coffee
Papaccino's
4441 SE Woodstock Blvd., 503/771-2825
8421 SW Terwilliger Blvd., 503/452-8859

Best Continental Food
Avalon Grill
4630 SW Macadam Ave., 503/227-4630
Bread and Ink Cafe
3610 SW Hawthorne Blvd., 503/239-4756

Best Delicatessen
Woodstock Wine and Deli
4030 SE Woodstock St., 503/777-2208

Best Desserts
Papa Haydn
5829 SW Milwaukee Ave., 503/232-9440
701 NW 23rd Ave., 503/228-7317

Best Health-Conscious Menu
Old Wives' Tale Restaurant
1300 E. Burnside St., 503/238-0470

Best Ice Cream/Yogurt
Simply Irresistible
1620 SE Bybee Blvd., 503/231-2960
Coffee People
Multiple Locations

Best Italian Food
Alessandro's
301 SW Morrison St., 503/242-2515
Pazzo Ristorante
627 SW Washington St., 503/228-1515
Rustica
1700 NE Broadway St., 503/288-0990

Best Mexican Food
El Palenque Mexican Restaurant
8324 SE Seventeenth Ave., 503/231-5140

Best Other Ethnic Food
Jarra's Ethiopian Restaurant (Ethiopian)
1435 SE Hawthorne Blvd., 503/230-8990
Marrakesh Moroccan Restaurant (Moroccan)
121 NW 23rd Ave., 503/248-9442

Best Pizza
Old Town Pizza
226 NW Davis St., 503/222-9999
Oasis Cafe
3701 Hawthorne Blvd., 503/231-0901

Best Place to Eat When Someone Else Is Buying
Genoa Restaurant
2832 SE Belmont St., 503/238-1464

Best Romantic Dining
Higgins Restaurant
1239 SW Broadway, 503/222-9070

Best Salad/Salad Bar
Ron Paul Catering
1441 NE Broadway St., 503/284-5347
6141 SW Macadam Ave., 503/977-0313

Best Sandwiches
Woodstock Wine and Deli
4030 SE Woodstock St., 503/777-2208

Best Seafood
Jake's Famous Crawfish
401 SW Twelfth Ave., 503/226-1419

Best Steaks
McCormick and Schmick's
235 SW First Ave., 503/224-7522

Best Vietnamese Food
Saigon Kitchen
3829 SE Division St., 503/236-2312
835 NE Broadway St., 503/281-3669

Best View While Dining
Avalon Grill
4630 SW Macadam Ave., 503/227-4630
Old Spaghetti Factory
715 SW Bancroft St., 503/222-5375
Old Wives' Tale Restaurant
1300 E. Burnside St., 503/238-0470

Best Wine Selection
Woodstock Wine and Deli
4030 SE Woodstock St., 503/777-2208

ROSEBURG, OR

Best Restaurants in Town
Chubby's
1350 NE Stephens St., Ste. 10, 541/440-2779
Del Rey Cafe
5669 Murphy Stevens Rd., 541/672-1522
The Owl Restaurant
2011 NE Stephens St., 541/672-3904
Poochie's
413 SE Jackson St., 541/672-6978
Sandpiper Restaurant
1450 NW Mulholland Dr., 541/672-8633
Between the Buns Sandwich Shop
214 SE Jackson St., 541/672-8633
250 NE Garden Valley Blvd., Ste. 18, 541/672-0342

Rumors-Kowloon Restaurant
  2686 NE Diamond Lake Blvd., 541/673-0095

Best Breakfast
Old Town Cafe
  527 SE Jackson, 541/440-4901
Sandpiper Restaurant
  1450 NW Mulholland Dr., 541/673-0021

Best Burgers
Jersey Lilly
  1430 NE Dee St., 541/672-9131

Best Chinese Food
China Palace
  968 NE Stephens St., 541/672-8899
Rumors-Kowloon Restaurant
  2686 NE Diamond Lake Blvd., 541/673-0095

Best Coffee
Cafe Espresso
  368 SE Jackson St., 541/672-1859

Best Desserts
Gallery Restaurant
  809 SE Main St., 541/673-6357

Best German Food
Teske's Germania
  647 SE Jackson St., 541/672-5401

Best Ice Cream/Yogurt
Gay 90's Ice Cream Parlor Deli
  925 W. Harvard Blvd., 541/672-5679

Best Mexican Food
Los Dos Amigos
  537 SE Jackson St., 541/673-1351

Best Microbrewery
Umpqua Brewing Company
  328 SE Jackson St., 541/672-0452

Best Pizza
Round Table Pizza
  2040 NW Stewart Pkwy., 541/673-2047

Best Sandwiches
Between the Buns Sandwich Shop
  214 SE Jackson St., 541/672-8633
  250 NE Garden Valley Blvd., Ste. 18, 541/672-0342

Best Steaks
Beef and Brew
  2060 Stewart Pkwy., 541/673-8030

Best Tea Room
Victoria's Pantry
  9029 Old Hwy. 99S, Dillard, 541/679-4524

Best Thai Food
House of Siam
  2521 W. Harvard Blvd., 541/673-8357

SALEM, OR

Best Atmosphere
Inn at Orchard Heights
695 Orchard Heights Rd. NW, 503/378-1780

Best Barbecue/Ribs
Jackie's Ribs
3404 Commercial St. SE, 503/399-7464

Best Breakfast
Original Pancake House
4656 Commercial St. SE, 503/378-0431
4685 Portland Rd. NE, 503/393-9124

Best Burgers
Tropical Beach Cafe
2653 Commercial St. SE, 503/362-1100

Best Cheap Meal
Golden Crown Restaurant
365 Liberty St. NE, 503/362-9560

Best Coffee
Starbucks
3411 Commercial St. SE, 503/391-7193
399 Court St. NE, 503/375-2156

Best Delicatessen
Lunch Box
135 Liberty St. NE, 503/364-9862

Best Desserts
Gerry Frank's Konditorei
310 Kearney St. SE, 503/585-7070

Best Indian Food
India Palace
377 Court St. NE, 503/371-4808

Best Italian Food
Alessandro's
325 High St. E., 503/370-9951

Best Microbrewery
Cascade Microbrewery
3529 Fairview Industrial Dr. SE, 503/378-0737

Best Outdoor Dining
Ram Border Cafe and Sports Bar
515 Twelfth St. SE, 503/363-1904

Best Pizza
Izzy's Pizza Restaurant
2205 Lancaster Dr. NE, 503/399-0915
2990 Commercial St. SE, 503/581-9831
3400 River Rd. N., 503/390-5002
Locomotion Pizza
4550 Commercial St. SE, 503/364-3004

Best Place to Take the Kids
Locomotion Pizza
4550 Commercial St. SE, 503/364-3004

Best Romantic Dining
Night Deposit
195 Commercial St. NE, 503/585-5588

Best Sandwiches
Lunch Box
135 Liberty St. NE, 503/364-9862

Best Seafood
McGrath's Fish House
350 Chemeketa St. NE, 503/362-0736
831 Lancaster Dr. NE, 503/362-6729

Best Steaks
Holly House
2025 Golf Course Rd. S., 503/399-0449
Night Deposit
195 Commercial St. NE, 503/585-5588

Best View While Dining
Eola Inn
4250 Dallas Hwy. NW, 503/378-7521

YACHATS, OR

Best Burgers
Big Wheel Drive-In
965 S. Crestline Dr., Waldport, 541/563-3640

Best Pizza
At's A Pizza
235 SW Arrow St., Waldport, 541/563-3232

Best Restaurant Meal Value
Synnove's
280 SW Arrow St., Waldport, 541/563-4433

Best Salad/Salad Bar
The Adobe Motel and Restaurant
1555 Hwy. 101, 541/547-3141

Best Sandwiches
Yankee Clipper Sandwich Company
125 Ocean Dr., 541/547-4004

Best Seafood
La Serre Restaurant
Second at Beach St., 541/547-3420

Best Steaks
The Adobe Motel and Restaurant
1555 Hwy. 101, 541/547-3141

Best View While Dining
The Adobe Motel and Restaurant
1555 Hwy. 101, 541/547-3141

Best Wine Selection
La Serre Restaurant
Second at Beach St., 541/547-3420

O

893

Pennsylvania

Best Atmosphere
Village Inn
    4140 W. Tilghman St., 610/395-2017

Best Bar
T.K.'s Corral
    801 N. Fifteenth St., 610/437-3970

Best Breakfast
Brass Rail Restaurant
    1137 W. Hamilton St., 610/434-9383
    3015 Lehigh St., 610/797-1927

Best Casual Dining
Finley's American Restaurant
    3400 Lehigh St., 610/965-8447

Best Chinese Food
China House
    4783 W. Tilghman St., 610/395-1855
Mandarin House South
    3025 W. Emmaus Ave., 610/791-2000

Best Family Restaurant
Your Place Restaurant
    2035 Downyflake Ln., 610/791-4819

Best Ice Cream/Yogurt
Ice Cream World
    3512 Hamilton Blvd., 610/439-8591

Best Italian Food
Original Carmen's Restaurant
    1125 Third St., Catasauqua, 610/266-2626

Best Mexican Food
Pancho and Sonny's
    2073 31st St. SW, 610/797-9300

Best Middle Eastern Food
Beirut Restaurant
    651 Union Blvd., 610/437-4023

P

Elias Sweet Spoon
101 W. Tilghman St., 610/820-5660

Best Pizza
Dino's Pizza Restaurant
3300 Lehigh St., 610/791-5107
Vito's Italian Delights
704 W. Emmaus Ave., 610/791-9111

Best Place to Eat When Someone Else Is Buying
Ambassador Restaurant
3750 Hamilton Blvd., 610/432-2025

Best Sandwiches
Wally's Deli
711 N. Seventeenth St., 610/435-7177

Best Seafood
Shanty Restaurant
617 N. Nineteenth St., 610/398-1760

Standbys
Denny's
2149 Lehigh St., 610/797-2176
1871 Catasauqua Rd., 610/264-8063
Lone Star Steakhouse
1410 Grape St., Whitehall, 610/432-0939
Outback Steakhouse
3100 W. Tilghman St., 610/437-7117
Red Lobster
800 Grape St., Whitehall, 610/264-5541
Friendly's
2952 Lehigh St., 610/797-7050

ALTOONA, PA

Best All-You-Can-Eat Buffet
Hoss's Steak and Sea House
621 Valley View Blvd., 814/946-5715

Best Breakfast
Granny's Restaurant
613 Valley View Blvd., 814/942-0491

Best Burgers
Hoss's Steak and Sea House
621 Valley View Blvd., 814/946-5715

Best Casual Dining
Hoss's Steak and Sea House
621 Valley View Blvd., 814/946-5715

Best Cheap Meal
Tasty Tacos Inc.
220 E. Plank Rd., 814/942-9789

Best Chinese Food
House of Chang Peking II
601 Logan Blvd., 814/942-3322

Best Desserts
Hoss's Steak and Sea House
621 Valley View Blvd., 814/946-5715
Allegro Restaurant
3926 Broad Ave., 814/946-5216

Best Family Restaurant
Hoss's Steak and Sea House
  621 Valley View Blvd., 814/946-5715

Best Homestyle Food
Granny's Restaurant
  613 Valley View Blvd., 814/942-0491

Best Late-Night Food
Original Italian Pizza
  709 Fourth Ave., Juniata, 814/942-9770

Best Pizza
Brother's Pizza
  1600 Ninth Ave., 814/942-7444

Best Place to Eat Alone
Lena's Cafe
  2000 Eighth Ave., 814/943-9655

Best Place to Eat When Someone Else Is Buying
Allegro Restaurant
  3926 Broad Ave., 814/946-5216

Best Romantic Dining
The Laurel Room
  Ramada Inn, 1 Sheraton Dr., 814/946-1631

Best Sandwiches
Original Italian Pizza
  709 Fourth Ave., Juniata, 814/942-9770

Best Steaks
Hoss's Steak and Sea House
  621 Valley View Blvd., 814/946-5715

Standbys
Baskin-Robbins
  31 Logan Blvd., 814/943-7807
Chi Chi's
  100 W. Plank Rd., 814/942-9080
Chuck E. Cheese Pizza
  3415 Pleasant Valley Blvd., 814/942-2410
The Olive Garden
  3315 Pleasant Valley Blvd., 814/949-9540

BEAVER, PA

Best Restaurant in Town
Wooden Angel
  100 Leopard Ln., 412/774-7880

Best Breakfast
Pappan's Family Restaurant
  1635 Third St., 412/775-5914
  1198 Mulberry St., 412/774-7711

Best Burgers
Bert's Wooden Indian Bar-B-Que
  Sharon Rd. at Leopard's Ln., West Bridgewater,
    412/774-7992

Best Casual Dining
Bert's Wooden Indian Bar-B-Que
  Sharon Rd. at Leopard's Ln., West Bridgewater,
    412/774-7992

P

Best Diner
Campbell and Family Restaurant
518 Third St., 412/774-5453

Best Family Restaurant
Campbell and Family Restaurant
518 Third St., 412/774-5453

Best Lunch
Boston Beanery
500 Market St., Bridgewater, 412/774-7071

BETHLEHEM, PA

Best Breakfast
Hack's
59 E. Broad St., 610/868-9997

Best Brunch
The Pioneer Room
Hotel Bethlehem, 437 Main St., 610/867-3711

Best Burgers
New Street Bridge Works
Fourth and New St., 610/868-1313

Best Coffee
Confetti Cafe
462 Main St., 610/861-7484

Best Desserts
Cafe
221 W. Broad St., 610/866-1686
Viennese Pastries Cafe
500 Main St., 610/866-0112

Best Italian Food
Giovanni's Italian American Restaurant
16 W. Broad St., 610/861-9246

Best Mexican Food
Vicky's Fonda
13 E. Broad St., 610/691-2888

Best Pizza
Penn Pizza
554 N. New St., 610/866-3532

Best Salad/Salad Bar
New Street Bridge Works
Fourth St. at New St., 610/868-1313

Best Sandwiches
Confetti Cafe
462 Main St., 610/861-7484

Best Seafood
The Pioneer Room
Hotel Bethlehem, 437 Main St., 610/867-3711
New Street Bridge Works
Fourth St. at New St., 610/868-1313
Minsi Trail Inn
626 Stefko Blvd., 610/691-5613

Best Steaks
Candlelight Inn
4431 Easton Ave., 610/691-7777

Minsi Trail Inn
  626 Stefko Blvd., 610/691-5613

Best Thai Food
Cafe
  221 W. Broad St., 610/866-1686

EASTON, PA

Best Restaurants in Town
Alan's Stockyard
  1600 N. Delaware, 610/253-9371
Candlelight Inn
  4431 Easton Ave., Bethlehem, 610/691-7777

Best Breakfast
City Diner
  25th St. at Freemansburg Ave., 610/258-5526
H.W. Crossings
  3701 Nazareth Rd., 610/258-7599

Best Casual Dining
Supreme Court
  683 Walnut St., 610/258-5812

Best Homestyle Food
City Diner
  25th St. at Freemansburg Ave., 610/258-5526

Best Ice Cream/Yogurt
Hartman's Two Family Restaurant
  5920 Sullivan Trail, Nazareth, 610/759-5217

Best Italian Food
Apollo Pizza Restaurant
  900 Walnut St., 610/258-6955
Hilltop Italian American
  204 W. Madison St., 610/253-9903

Best Seafood
Alan's Stockyard
  1600 N. Delaware, 610/253-9371

Best Steaks
Keystone Steakhouse
  1200 Northampton St., 610/253-4640

ELIZABETHTOWN, PA

Best Bar
Mookie's Tavern and Eatery
  800 Mount Gretna Rd., 717/367-5544

Best Chinese Food
Chan's Garden
  17 W. High St., 717/361-8411

Best Regional Food
Elizabethtown Inn
  28 S. Market St., 717/367-7907

ERIE, PA

Best American Food
Pufferbelly Restaurant and Bar
  414 French St., 814/454-1557

Best Barbecue/Ribs
Red Neck BBQ
  1301 Parade St., 814/456-5864

Best Breakfast
Pie in the Sky Cafe
  463 W. Eighth St., 814/459-8638

Best Brunch
Pufferbelly Restaurant and Bar
  414 French St., 814/454-1557
Maxi's
  Bel Aire Hotel Complex, 2800 W. Eighth St.,
    814/833-1116

Best Burgers
Plymouth Tavern
  1109 State St., 814/453-6454

Best Cheap Meal
Plymouth Tavern
  1109 State St., 814/453-6454

Best Delicatessens
Peppers Deli
  1022 State St., 814/453-3468
Tickles Deli
  17 W. Fourth St., 814/455-5718
  3602 W. Lake Rd., 814/838-0579

Best Diner
Beaners
  26 N. Park Row, 814/455-4600

Best Ice Cream/Yogurt
Kaley's Korner Ice Cream
  1537 W. 38th St., 814/864-2772

Best Indian Food
Oasis Restaurant
  3 N. Park Row, 814/452-6111

Best Italian Food
Martucci's Tavern
  2641 Myrtle St., 814/455-6564

Best Late-Night Dining
Dominick's Restaurant
  123 E. Twelfth St., 814/459-5781

Best Outdoor Dining
Elephant Bar and Restaurant
  2826 W. Eighth St., 814/838-3613
Pufferbelly Restaurant and Bar
  414 French St., 814/454-1557
Smugglers' Wharf
  3 State St., 814/459-4273

Best Pizza
Valerio's Italian Restaurant
  3205 Pittsburgh Ave., 814/833-2959

Best Place to Eat Alone
Dominick's Restaurant
  123 E. Twelfth St., 814/459-5781

Best Place to Eat When Someone Else Is Buying
Erie Club
    524 Peach St., 814/455-1328

Best Romantic Dining
Stonehouse Inn
    4753 W. Lake Rd., 814/838-9296
Erie Club
    524 Peach St., 814/455-1328

Best Sandwiches
Peppers Deli
    1022 State St., 814/453-3468

Best Steaks
Marketplace Grill
    319 State St., 814/455-7272

Best View While Dining
Smugglers' Wharf
    3 State St., 814/459-4273
Waterfront Seafood and Steak House
    4 State St., 814/459-0606

GLENOLDEN, PA

Best Breakfast
MacDade Diner
    1030 MacDade Blvd., Collingdale, 610/583-0391

Best Delicatessen
Anna's
    303 Sutton Ave., Folsom, 610/534-9289

Best Diner
Gateway Diner
    2215 MacDade Blvd., Holmes, 610/532-2825

Best Dinner
Erin's Pub
    36 W. Winona Ave., Norwood, 610/461-0991

Best Italian Food
Italian Village
    902 MacDade Blvd., Millmont Park, 610/237-0200

Best Pizza
Imperial Pizza
    615 South Ave., Primos Secane, 610/543-9393

Best Sandwiches
New London Pizza
    1016 Lincoln Ave., Prospect Park, 610/461-9330

GREENSBURG, PA

Best All-You-Can-Eat Buffet
Vista Plateau Dining Room
    Four Points Sheraton Hotel, 100 Sheraton Dr.,
        412/836-6060

Best American Food
Mountain View Inn
    1001 Village Dr., 412/834-5300

Best Barbecue/Ribs
Bar-B-Que and Ale
    Rte. 30E, Latrobe, 412/539-7427

P

Best Breakfast
Valley Dairy
  11 Eastgate Shopping Plz., 412/832-1545

Best Brunch
Vista Plateau Dining Room
  Four Points Sheraton Hotel, 100 Sheraton Dr.,
    412/836-6060

Best Business Lunch
Vista Plateau Dining Room
  Four Points Sheraton Hotel, 100 Sheraton Dr.,
    412/836-6060

Best Italian Food
Ernie Vallozzi's Restaurant
  Rte. 30E, 412/836-7663
Rizzo's Malabar Inn
  Keener Dr., Crabtree, 412/836-4323

Best Pizza
Jioio's Italian Takeout and Sit Down
  939 Carbon Rd., 412/836-6676
Rizzo's Malabar Inn
  Keener Dr., Crabtree, 412/836-4323

Best Seafood
Mountain View Inn
  1001 Village Dr., 412/834-5300
Ernie Vallozzi's Restaurant
  Rte. 30E, 412/836-7663

Best Steaks
Ernie Vallozzi's Restaurant
  Rte. 30E, 412/836-7663

Standbys
Ground Round
  960 E. Pittsburgh St., 412/836-1550
TCBY
  133 Donahue Rd., 412/836-8229
Chi Chi's
  830 E. Pittsburgh St., 412/834-7880

P

HARRISBURG, PA

Best Atmosphere
Kosta's
  451 N. 21st St., Camp Hill, 717/761-1118
Al Mediterraneo
  288 E. Main St., Hummelstown, 717/566-5086

Best Bar
Rod's Road House Cafe
  1031 Eisenhower Blvd., 717/939-9915

Best Barbecue/Ribs
Red Rabbit Drive-In
  Rural Route 4, Duncannon, 717/834-4696

Best Breakfast
Arches
  4125 N. Front St., 717/233-5891

Best Brunch
Circular Dining Room
  Hotel Hershey, Hotel Rd., Hershey, 717/533-2171

Best Burgers
Colonial Park Diner
  4301 Jonestown Rd., 717/541-9794
Harris House Tavern
  16 N. Third St., 717/236-0861

Best Business Lunch
Arches
  4125 N. Front St., 717/233-5891

Best Cheap Meal
Zephyr Express
  400 N. Second St., 717/257-1328

Best Chinese Food
The Bloom
  204 Walnut St., 717/238-8355

Best Coffee
Gingerbread Man
  12 E. Park Ctr., 717/564-4078

Best Continental Food
Maverick
  1851 Arsenal Blvd., 717/233-7688

Best Diner
Colonial Park Diner
  4301 Jonestown Rd., 717/541-9794

Best Greek/Mediterranean Food
Al Mediterraneo
  288 E. Main St., Hummelstown, 717/566-5086

Best Health-Conscious Menu
Isaac's Restaurant and Deli
  Oakhurst Square, 2900 Singletown Rd., 717/541-1111

P

Best Ice Cream/Yogurt
Colonial Park Diner
  4301 Jonestown Rd., 717/541-9794

Best Indian Food
Passage to India
  525 S. Front St., 717/233-1202

Best Late-Night Food
Zephyr Express
  400 N. Second St., 717/257-1328

Best Mexican Food
Casa Chico
  451 Swatara St., Steelton, 717/939-4907

Best Pizza
Zephyr Express
  400 N. Second St., 717/257-1328

Best Place to Eat When Someone Else Is Buying
Circular Dining Room
  Hotel Hershey, Hotel Rd., Hershey, 717/533-2171

Best Romantic Dining
Golden Sheaf
  1 N. Second St., 717/237-6400

Best Sandwiches
Sandwich Man
111 N. Second St., 717/236-7171
5640 Allentown Blvd., 717/540-1818

Best Seafood
Kosta's
451 N. 21st St., Camp Hill, 717/761-1118

Best Steaks
Glass Lounge
4745 N. Front St., 717/255-9919
Maverick
1851 Arsenal Blvd., 717/233-7688

HAVERTOWN, PA

Best Restaurant in Town
Nais Cuisine
13 W. Benedict Ave., 610/789-5983

Best Bar
Westgate Pub
1021 W. Chester Pk., 610/446-3030

Best Chinese Restaurant
Sampan Inn
8 Brookline Blvd., 610/446-2188

Best Diner
Llanerch Diner
Township Line Rd., Upper Darby, [no telephone]

Best French Food
Nais Cuisine
13 W. Benedict Ave., 610/789-5983

Best Homestyle Food
Llanerch Diner
Township Line Rd., Upper Darby, [no telephone]

Best Italian Food
Lamplighter Tavern
8 Campbell Ave., 610/446-2733

Best Seafood
Quarry Inn
300 W. Chester Pk., 610/789-1414

HAZLETON, PA

Best Atmosphere
Powerhouse Eatery
Powerhouse Rd., White Haven, 717/443-4480

Best Barbecue/Ribs
Knotty Pines
26th St. at N. First St., 717/455-3211

Best Breakfast
Dubatto's Family Restaurant
615 E. Broad St., 717/454-7676
Ferdinand's Family Restaurant
1000 W. Fifteenth St., 717/454-6397

Best Chinese Food
Five Star Chinese Restaurant
Rte. 93 at Airport Rd., Ste. C1, 717/455-3478

Best Desserts
Ovalon Restaurant
  254 N. Wyoming St., 717/454-0853
Scatton's Restaurant
  1008 N. Vine St., 717/455-6630

Best Ice Cream/Yogurt
Scooper's Ice Cream
  32nd St. at Church St., 717/450-6543

Best Italian Food
Library Lounge
  615 E. Broad St., 717/455-3920
Scatton's Restaurant
  1008 N. Vine St., 717/455-6630
Ovalon Restaurant
  254 N. Wyoming St., 717/454-0853

Best Pizza
Pasquale's Pizzeria
  41 E. Diamond Ave., 717/459-5085
Senape's Tavern Pizza
  835 N. Vine St., 717/454-9168
Georgio's Sub and Pizza
  25 N. Laurel St., 717/459-1818

Best Sandwiches
Georgio's Sub and Pizza
  25 N. Laurel St., 717/459-1818
Senape's Tavern Pizza
  835 N. Vine St., 717/454-9168

Best Seafood
Library Lounge
  615 E. Broad St., 717/455-3920
Scatton's Restaurant
  1008 N. Vine St., 717/455-6630
Ovalon Restaurant
  254 N. Wyoming St., 717/454-0853

Best Steaks
Library Lounge
  615 E. Broad St., 717/455-3920
Ovalon Restaurant
  254 N. Wyoming St., 717/454-0853
Scatton's Restaurant
  1008 N. Vine St., 717/455-6630

JOHNSTOWN, PA

Best Bar
Johnnie's Restaurant and Lounge
  415 Main St., 814/536-9309

Best Breakfast
Eat N Park Restaurant
  1461 Scalp Ave., 814/266-5714
  1900 Minno Dr., 814/255-7711

Best Casual Dining
Johnnie's Restaurant and Lounge
  415 Main St., 814/536-9309

Best Chinese Food
Szechuan Chinese Restaurant
124 Main St., 814/535-8845

Best Dinner
Encore Restaurant and Lounge
3100 Elton Rd., 814/269-3431

Best Pizza
Santo's Pizza
1749 Goucher St., 814/255-7138

Best Seafood
Surf and Turf Inn
100 Valley Pk., 814/536-9250

Best Steaks
Surf and Turf Inn
100 Valley Pk., 814/536-9250

LANCASTER, PA

Best Breakfast
Red Rose Luncheonette
101 E. King St., 717/392-8620
Zimmerman's Family Restaurant
66 N. Queen St., 717/394-6977

Best Brunch
Eden Resort Inn
222 Eden Rd., 717/560-8400

Best Burgers
Lancaster Dispensing Company
33 N. Market St., 717/299-4602

Best Chinese Food
China Garden Restaurant
1254 Millersville Pike, 717/397-1327
Hong Kong Garden
1807 Columbia Ave., 717/394-4336

Best Continental Food
Log Cabin Restaurant
11 Lehoy Forest Dr., Leola, 717/626-1181

Best Desserts
Gallo Rosso
337 N. Queen St., 717/392-5616

Best Homestyle Food
Good and Plenty Restaurant
Rte. 896, Smoketown, 717/394-7111

Best Ice Cream/Yogurt
Oregon Dairy Farm Market
2900 Oregon Pike, Lititz, 717/656-2856

Best Indian Food
Kiran Palace
1358 Columbia Ave., 717/295-9508

Best Italian Food
Gallo Rosso
337 N. Queen St., 717/392-5616

Portofino Italian Ristorante
254 E. Frederick St., 717/394-1635

Best Late-Night Food
McFly's
10 S. Prince, 717/299-3456

Best Mexican Food
Carlos and Charlie's Bar
915 N. Plum St., 717/293-8704
2309 Columbia Ave., 717/399-1912

Best Pizza
House of Pizza
23 W. Chestnut St., 717/393-1747
Sam's Pizza
710 Columbia Ave., 717/299-7391

Best Places to Eat When Someone Else Is Buying
Stock Yard Inn
1147 Lititz Pike, 717/394-3481
Restaurant at Doneckers
333 N. State St., Ephrata, 717/738-9508

Best Place to Take the Kids
Garfield's Restaurant
222 Eden Rd., 717/569-5454

Best Sandwiches
Press Room
26-28 W. King, 717/399-5400

Best Seafood
Kegel's Seafood Restaurant
551 W. King St., 717/397-2832
Monk's Tunic
18 W. Orange St., 717/399-9121
Oyster Bay Restaurant
37 E. Orange St., 717/392-1828

Best Steaks
Loft Restaurant
201 W. Orange St., 717/299-0661
Monk's Tunic
18 W. Orange St., 717/399-9121

LEBANON, PA

Best American Food
Fenwick Tavern and Restaurant
2200 Cumberland St., 717/272-9280

Best Atmosphere
Lantern Lodge
411 N. College, Myerstown, 717/866-6536

Best Breakfast
Kreider's Dairy Farm Restaurant
2221 W. Cumberland St., 717/272-1084

Best Business Lunch
Fenwick Tavern and Restaurant
2200 Cumberland St., 717/272-9280

Best Casual Dining
Eli's
1010 W. Crestview Dr., 717/273-7777

Best Continental Food
Lantern Lodge
411 N. College, Myerstown, 717/866-6536

Best German Food
Little Corner of Germany Cafe
3050 Lebanon Rd. (Rte. 72), Manheim, 717/665-7641

Best Lunch
Eli's
1010 W. Crestview Dr., 717/273-7777

Best Outdoor Dining
Tap Room Restaurant
502 E. Lehman St., 717/272-0713

LOCK HAVEN, PA

Best All-You-Can-Eat Buffet
Big Wrangler Family Restaurant
Rural Route 2, Mill Hall, 717/748-9671

Best Breakfast
Blue Chimney Restaurant
Rte. 150, Mill Hall, 717/726-6420
Aungst Family Restaurant
Rte. 150, Mill Hall, 717/726-6233

Best Business Lunch
Dutch Haven Restaurant
201 E. Bald Eagle St., 717/748-7444
Fox's Market House Restaurant
142 E. Church St., 717/748-4000

Best Family Restaurant
Black Forest Inn
15 Black Forest Dr., 717/769-7203
Old Kingsley Inn
Third St. at Huron Ave., Renovo, 717/923-2642

Best Homestyle Food
Kathy's Kitchen
201 Logan Ave., 717/748-7977

Best Ice Cream/Yogurt
Overdorf's Drive-In
835 Woodward Ave., 717/748-6118
Schon's Restaurant
241 Allegheny St., Jersey Shore, 717/398-7095

Best Italian Food
Santino's Italian Cuisine
100 S. Main St., Jersey Shore, 717/398-4484

Best Pizza
Original Italian Pizza
136 E. Main St., 717/748-8027
Santino's Italian Cuisine
100 S. Main St., Jersey Shore, 717/398-4484

Best Sandwiches
Jeff's Place
225 E. Main St., 717/748-2234

Best Seafood
Bell Springs
Rural Route 1, Mill Hall, 717/726-7570

Best Steaks
Big Wrangler Family Restaurant
Rural Route 2, Mill Hall, 717/748-9671

MONROEVILLE, PA

Best Breakfast
Eat N Park Restaurant
805 Lysle Blvd., McKeesport, 412/664-9148

Best Chinese Food
China Jade Restaurant
4313 Walnut St., McKeesport, 412/751-8213

Best Italian Food
Italian Oven
2644 Mosside Blvd., 412/373-6836

Best Sandwiches
Rudy's Submarines
3942 William Penn Hwy., 412/372-9738
1794 Golden Mile Hwy., 412/327-9721

Best Seafood
Gold Rush Restaurant
1205 Mosside Blvd., 412/372-1699

Best Steaks
Gold Rush Restaurant
1205 Mosside Blvd., 412/372-1699

Standbys
Pizza Hut
4320 Northern Pk., 412/372-7110
3936 Monroeville Blvd., 412/373-4700

NEW CASTLE, PA

Best Restaurant in Town
Olde Library Inn
106 E. North St., 412/656-1090

Best American Food
Frengel's
1245 W. State St., 412/654-6491

Best Breakfast
Hazel's Restaurant
119 N. Mercer St., 412/654-2621

Best Homestyle Food
Hazel's Restaurant
119 N. Mercer St., 412/654-2621

Best Italian Food
Medure's Restaurant
2001 E. Washington St., 412/658-1103

Best Other Ethnic Food
Shad Hanna's (Syrian)
1046 Butler Ave., 412/654-0133
1245 W. State St., 412/654-6491

Best Steaks
Olde Library Inn
106 E. North St., 412/656-1090

P

NORRISTOWN, PA

Best Bar
A.J.'s Pub
22 W. Main St., 610/270-9580

Best Chinese Food
88 Chinese Kitchen
32 W. Main St., 610/278-6711

Best Italian Food
Giacamo's Restaurant
368 E. Main St., 610/277-7277

Best Lunch
A.J.'s Pub
22 W. Main St., 610/270-9580

Best Pizza
Sala's Pizza
12 W. Main St., 610/277-3776

Best Sandwiches
The Peanut Gallery
1832 Markley St., 610/275-4777

PHILADELPHIA, PA

Best Restaurants in Town
Fountain
Four Seasons Hotel, 1 Logan Sq., 215/963-1500
Dante and Luigi's
762 S. Tenth St., 215/922-9501

Best Atmosphere
Tutto Misto
605 S. Third St., 215/923-7220

Best Bagels
Delancey Street
50 E. Wynnewood Rd., Wynnewood, 610/896-8837

Best Bread
Sarcone's
758 S. Ninth St., 215/922-0445
Baker Street
8009 Germantown Ave., Chestnut Hill, 215/248-2500
Suburban Square, Ardmore, 610/649-8842

Best Breakfast
Down Home Diner
1100 Arch St., 215/627-1955
Emil's
1800 S. Broad St., 215/468-4474
Nifty Fifties
1356 E. Passyunk Ave., 215/468-1950
2451 Grant Ave., 215/676-1950
Continental Diner
138 Market St., 215/922-2344
Fairmount Bagel Institute (FBI)
2501 Olive St., 215/235-2245
267 S. Nineteenth St., 215/735-2222
Savoy Diner
232 S. Eleventh St., 215/923-2348

Best Brunch
Jake's
　4365 Main St., Manayunk, 215/483-0444
Radnor Hotel
　591 E. Lancaster Ave., St. Davids, 610/341-3500
Museum of American Art of the Pennsylvania Academy
of the Fine Arts
　118 N. Broad St., 215/972-7600
Hotel Du Pont
　100 W. Eleventh St., Wilmington, 302/594-3100
Cafe Nola
　328 South St., 215/627-2590
Rosebud's Cafe
　8201 Germantown Ave., 215/849-4382
Fountain
　Four Seasons Hotel, 1 Logan Sq., 215/963-1500
White Dog Cafe
　3420 Sansom St., 215/386-9224

Best Burgers
Fireworks
　Twelfth St. at Filbert St., 215/925-3499
Ishkabibble's
　337 South St., 215/923-4337
Roosevelt's
　8011 E. Roosevelt Blvd., 215/332-1440
Fat Edna's Pub
　146 Vassar St., Roxborough, 215/482-3208
Sassafras
　48 S. Second St., 215/925-2317

Best Business Breakfast
Pyramid Club
　Mellon Bank Tower, 1753 Market St., 215/567-6510

Best Business Lunch
Pennsylvania General Store
　Reading Terminal, Twelfth St. at Arch St.,
　　215/592-9772
Thai Singha House
　3939 Chestnut St., 215/382-8001
White Dog Cafe
　3420 Sansom St., 215/386-9224

Best Casual Dining
Primavera
　146 South St., 215/925-7832
　384 W. Lancaster Ave., Wayne, 610/254-0200

Best Cheesesteaks
Jim's Steaks
　400 South St., 215/928-1911
　431 N. 62nd St., 215/747-6615
Pat's King of Steaks
　1237 E. Passyunk Ave., 215/468-1546
Tony Luke's
　39 E. Oregon Ave., 215/551-5725
Dalessandro's
　600 Wendover St., Roxborough, 215/482-5407

Best Cheap Meal
Roosevelt's Pub
  23rd St. at Walnut St., 215/636-9722
East Junior
  1625 Chestnut St., Ste. 13F, 215/567-2477
Le Bus
  1100 Filbert St., 215/592-0422
  220 Krams Ave., 215/930-0255
  3402 Sansom St., 215/387-3800
Momi
  526 S. Fourth St., 215/625-0370
Taco House
  1218 Pine St., 215/735-1880

Best Chinese Food
Yangming
  1051 Conestoga Rd., Bryn Mawr, 610/527-3200
Imperial Inn
  146 N. Tenth St., 215/627-2299
Joe's Peking Duck House
  925 Race St., 215/922-3277
Charles Plaza
  234-36 North Tenth St., 215/829-4383

Best Coffeehouses
Last Drop
  1300 Pine St., 215/893-0434
Millenium
  212 S. Twelfth St., 215/731-9798
PQ's
  129 S. Sixteenth St., 215/564-6950
Quarry Street Cafe
  147 N. Third St., 215/413-1360

Best Delicatessens
Famous Fourth Street
  Reading Terminal, Twelfth St. at Arch St.,
    215/629-5990
Koch's
  4309 Locust St., 215/222-8662
Latimer
  255 S. Fifteenth St., 215/545-9244

Best Desserts
Striped Bass
  1500 Walnut St., 215/732-4444
Treetops
  Rittenhouse Hotel, 210 W. Rittenhouse Sq.,
    215/790-2533
Panorama
  14 N. Front St., 215/922-7800
Pink Rose Pastry Shop
  630 S. Fourth St., 215/592-0565
White Dog Cafe
  3420 Sansom St., 215/386-9224
Mick's
  200 S. Broad St., 215/732-7997
Coffee Stop
  130 S. Seventeenth St., 215/988-0061

Best Diners
American Diner
  4201 Chestnut St., 215/387-1451
  435 Spring Garden St., 215/592-8838
Diner on the Square
  275 S. Nineteenth St., 215/735-5787
Melrose Diner
  1501 Snyder Ave., 215/467-6644
Silk City Diner
  435 Spring Garden St., 215/592-8838

Best Happy Hour Snacks
London Grill
  2301 Fairmount Ave., 215/978-454

Best Homestyle Food
Country Club Restaurant and Pastry Shop
  1717 Cottman Ave., 215/722-0500
Momi
  526 S. Fourth St., 215/625-0370
Milano's Italian Kitchen
  2001 Market St., 215/851-8722

Best Ice Cream/Yogurt
Alaska
  100 Chestnut St., 215/592-8800
Hillary's Gourmet Ice Cream
  2006 Chestnut St., 215/561-6962
  3401 Walnut St., 215/387-8837
  437 South St., 215/922-4931
  8500 Henry Ave., 215/487-2777
More Than Just Ice Cream
  1141 Pine St., 215/574-0586

Best Indian Food
Rajbhog
  738 Tabor Ave., 215/537-1937

Best Italian Food
Marabella's
  1420 Locust St., 215/545-1845
  1700 Benjamin Franklin Pkwy., 215/981-5555
Ralph's
  760 S. Ninth St., 215/627-6011
Saloon Restaurant
  750 S. Seventh St., 215/627-1811

Best Late-Night Food
Diner on the Square
  275 S. Nineteenth St., 215/735-5787
Bar 17
  Latham Hotel, 135 S. Seventeenth St., 215/563-7474
Melrose Diner
  1501 Snyder Ave., 215/467-6644
South Street Diner
  140 South St., 215/627-5258

Best Lunch
Little Pete's
  219 S. Seventeenth St., 215/545-5508
Magnolia
  1602 Locust St., 215/546-4180

P

Tony Luke's
39 E. Oregon Ave., 215/551-5725

Best Mexican Food
Tequila's
1511 Locust St., 215/546-0181
Zocalo
3600 Lancaster Ave., 215/895-0139

Best New Restaurants
Circa
1518 Walnut St., 215/545-6800
Pamplona
225 S. Twelfth St., 215/627-9059
Striped Bass
1500 Walnut St., 215/732-4444

Best Other Ethnic Food
Tierra Columbiana (Cuban)
4535 N. Fifth St., 215/324-6086

Best Pizza
Bertucci's
1515 Locust St., 215/731-1400
Joe's King of Pizzas
111 S. Thirteenth St., 215/627-1615
Pine Street Pizza
1138 Pine St., 215/922-2526
Upscale Pizza Joint
4120 Main, Manayunk, 215/482-9000
Celebre's
15th St. at Packer Ave., 215/467-3255
Primavera Pizza Kitchen
7 E. Lancaster Ave., Ardmore, 610/642-8000
Upstairs at Varalli
1345 Locust St., 215/546-4200
Savas
1547 Spring Garden St., 215/564-1910

Best Places to Be "Seen"
Carolina's
333 Belrose Ln., Radnor, 610/687-2801
Steinboy's Famous Deli
9359 Krewstown Rd., 215/673-6000

Best Quick Lunch
Dean and DeLuca
1601 Market St., 215/563-7755
Bravo Bistro
175 King of Prussia Rd., Radnor, 610/293-9521

Best Places to Eat When Someone Else Is Buying
The Fountain
1 Logan Sq., 215/963-1500
Le Bec-Fin
1523 Walnut St., 215/567-1000
Striped Bass
1500 Walnut St., 215/732-4444

Best Romantic Dining
Bridgid's
726 N. 24th St., 215/232-3232

Astral Plane
  1708 Lombard St., 215/546-6230
The Garden
  1617 Spruce St., 215/546-4455
Monte Carlo Living Room
  150 South St., 215/925-2220
Spring Mill Cafe
  164 Barren Hill Rd., Conshohocken, 610/828-2550

Best Salad/Salad Bar
Marathon Grill
  121 S. Sixteenth St., 215/569-3278
  1617 JF Kennedy Blvd., 215/564-4745
Pollo Rosso
  8229 Germantown Ave., Chestnut Hill, 215/248-9338
Goat Hollow
  300 W. Mount Pleasant Ave., 215/242-4710

Best Sandwiches
Rocco's at the Bellevue
  650 South St., 215/755-9550
Salumeria
  3000 Market St., 215/222-7444
  Reading Terminal, Twelfth St. at Arch St.,
    215/592-8150
Tony Luke's
  39 E. Oregon Ave., 215/551-5725
Slack's Hoagie Shack
  8439 Frankford Ave., 215/338-6777
Inky's
  602 South St., 215/627-6214

Best Seafood
Bookbinder's
  215 S. Fifteenth St., 215/545-1137
Seafood Unlimited
  270 S. Twentieth St., 215/732-9012
Striped Bass
  1500 Walnut St., 215/732-4444
Palm
  200 S. Broad St., 215/546-7256

Best Steaks
Kansas City Prime
  4417 Main St., 215/482-3700

Best Sushi
Aoi
  1210 Walnut St., 215/985-1838
Genji
  4002 Spruce St., 215/387-1583
Hikaru
  108 S. Eighteenth St., 215/496-9950
Sagami
  37 Crescent Blvd. at Rte. 30, Collingswood,
    609/854-9773

Best Thai Food
Sabai Thai
  831 Baltimore Ave., East Lansing, 610/622-9878
My Thai
  2200 South St., 215/985-1878

Best Undiscovered Restaurant
Chanterelle's
1312 Spruce St., 215/735-7551

Best Vegetarian Food
Mary's
400 Roxborough Ave., Roxborough, 215/487-2249
Cherry Street Vegetarian
1010 Cherry St., 215/922-8987
Essene Cafe
719 Fourth St., 215/928-3722
Harmony Vegetarian
135 N. Ninth St., 215/627-4520

Best Vietnamese Food
Vietnam
211 N. Eleventh St., 215/592-1163

Best Wine Selection
Le Bec Fin
1523 Walnut St., 215/567-1000
Panorama
14 N. Front St., 215/922-7800
Zanzibar Blue
305 S. Eleventh St., 215/829-0300

PITTSBURGH, PA

Best Restaurants in Town
Cafe Allegro
51 S. Twelfth St., 412/481-7788
The Carlton
1 Mellon Bank Ctr., 412/391-4099
Wooden Nickel
219 Market St., Millersburg, 717/692-3003
Hyeholde Restaurant
190 Hyeholde Dr., Coraopolis, 412/264-3116
Wooden Angel
100 Leopard Ln., Beaver, 412/774-7880
Cafe Georgio
24 Donati Rd., 412/833-7000
Rico's
1 Rico Ln., 412/931-1989

Best All-You-Can-Eat Buffet
Eat N Park
2874 W. Liberty Ave., 412/561-4944
4596 William Penn Hwy., Murrysville, 412/327-7270
5143 Rte. 8, Gibsonia, 412/443-7280
Sheffield Rd. at 21st St., Aliquippa, 412/378-4400
Twelfth St. at Seventh Ave., Beaver Falls,
412/843-3750

Best American Food
Siena
430 Market St., 412/338-0900

Best Atmosphere
Rico's
1 Rico Ln., 412/931-1989
Stone Mansion
1600 Stone Mansion Dr., Wexford, 412/934-3000

Cafe Allegro
   51 S. Twelfth St., 412/481-7788
Cafe Azure
   317 S. Craig St., 412/681-3533

Best Bagels
Bruegger's Bagel Bakery
   1719 Murray Ave., 412/422-2814
   1720 Washington Rd., 412/833-7996
   3714 Forbes Ave., 412/682-6360
   413 Market St., 412/471-3972
Schwartz's Bagels
   1317 E. Carson St., 412/431-0915
   1743 Fifth Ave., 412/566-9007
   800 E. Warrington Ave., 412/488-6700
Bageland Restaurant
   2120 Murray Ave., 412/521-2111

Best Barbecue/Ribs
Bobby Rubino's
   10 Commerce Ave., 412/642-7427
Tessaro's
   4601 Liberty Ave., 412/682-6809
Damon's
   855 Freeport Rd., 412/782-3750
Wilson's Bar-B-Q
   700 N. Taylor Ave., 412/322-7427

Best Beer Selection
Seventh Street Grille
   137 Seventh St., 412/338-0303
Mad Mex
   370 Atwood St., 412/681-5656
   7905 McKnight Rd., 366-5656
Chiodo's Tavern
   107 W. Eighth St., 412/461-3113

Best Breakfast
Jo Jo's Restaurant
   110 S. Twentieth St., 412/261-0280
Pamela's
   3703 Forbes Ave., 412/683-4066
   5813 Forbes Ave., 412/422-9457
   5527 Walnut St., 412/683-1003
Ritter's Diner
   5221 Baum Blvd., 412/682-4852
DeLuca's Restaurant
   2015 E. Penn Ave., 412/566-2195

Best Brunch
Grand Concourse Restaurant
   1 Station Sq., 412/261-1717
Sheraton Station Square
   Sheraton Hotel, 7 Station Square Dr., 412/261-2000

Best Burgers
Jergel's
   3385 Babcock Blvd., 412/364-9902
Tessaro's
   4601 Liberty Ave., 412/682-6809

P

Best Chinese Food
Chan's Tea House
  1009 W. View Park Dr., 412/931-0134
Jimmy Tsang's Chinese Restaurant
  5700 Centre Ave., 412/661-4226
Mark Pi's China Gate
  1500 Washington Rd., Ste. 3, Mt. Lebanon,
    412/341-8890
Sichuan House Chinese Restaurant
  1717 Cochran Rd., 412/563-5252
  1335 Freeport Rd., 412/967-0789
  1900 Murray Ave., 412/422-2700

Best Coffeehouses
Arabica
  733 Copeland St., 412/621-4401
  5887 Forbes Ave., 412/422-2226
  1501 E. Carson St., 412/381-8330
The Beehive Coffeehouse
  1327 E. Carson St., 412/488-4483
Sip
  238 Shady Ave., 412/361-4478
The Strip Bar
  1413 Penn Ave., 412/471-1043

Best Continental Food
Mallorca Restaurant
  2228 E. Carson St., 412/488-1818
Cafe Allegro
  51 S. Twelfth St., 412/481-7788
Le Pommier
  2104 E. Carson St., 412/682-2620
Cafe Azure
  317 S. Craig St., 412/681-3533

Best Delicatessens
Brown Bag Deli
  Multiple Locations
Pittsburgh Deli Company
  728 Copeland St., 412/682-3354
Rhoda's Deli Restaurant
  2201 Murray Ave., 412/521-4555

Best Desserts
Mitchell's Ice Cream
  3123 Babcock Blvd., 412/364-9988
Gullifty's
  1922 Murray Ave., 415/521-8222
Houlihan's
  1741 Washington Rd., 412/831-9797
  15 Station Sq., 412/232-0302
King's Family Restaurant
  Multiple Locations

Best Diners
Jo Jo's Restaurant
  110 S. Twentieth St., 412/261-0280
Ritter's Diner
  5221 Baum Blvd., 412/682-4852
Tom's Diner
  2937 W. Liberty Ave., 412/531-2350

Best Family Restaurants
Eat N Park
2874 W. Liberty Ave., 412/561-4944
4596 William Penn Hwy., Murrysville, 412/327-7270
5143 Rte. 8, Gibsonia, 412/443-7280
Sheffield Rd. at 21st St., Aliquippa, 412/378-4400
Twelfth St. at Seventh Ave., Beaver Falls,
412/843-3750
Hoss's Steak and Sea House
Multiple Locations

Best Health-Conscious Menu
Shadyside Balcony
5520 Walnut St., 412/687-0110
Coral Garden Chinese Restaurant
1621 S. Braddock Ave., Swiss Vale, 412/731-1101
Sweet Basil
5882 Forbes Ave., 412/421-9958

Best Ice Cream/Yogurt
Bruster's Old Fashion Ice Cream
2569 Brandt School Rd., Wexford, 412/934-0840
4070 Beechwood Blvd., 412/422-9555
Riverside Dr. at Rte. 51, Beaver, 412/774-4155
Dave and Andy's Homemade Ice Cream
207 Atwood St., 412/681-9906
Shadyside Scoops
5418 Walnut St., 412/681-8880

Best Indian Food
India Garden
328 Atwood St., 412/682-3000
Star of India
412 S. Craig St., 412/681-5700

Best Italian Food
Davio
2100 Broadway Ave., 412/531-7422
Pasta Piatto
736 Bellefonte St., 412/621-5547
Piccolo Piccolo Restaurant
Wood St., 412/261-7234
DiPietro's
10500 Perry Hwy., Wexford, 412/934-1050

Best Japanese Food
Kiku Japanese Restaurant
Station Square, 412/765-3200

Best Late-Night Food
Eat N Park
2874 W. Liberty Ave., 412/561-4944
4596 William Penn Hwy., Murrysville, 412/327-7270
5143 Rte. 8, Gibsonia, 412/443-7280
Sheffield Rd. at 21st St., Aliquippa, 412/378-4400
Twelfth St. at Seventh Ave., Beaver Falls,
412/843-3750
Primanti Brothers
3803 Forbes Ave., 412/621-4444
46 Eighteenth St., 412/263-2142
11 Cherry Way, 412/566-8051

P

Best Mexican Food
Franklin Inn
  2313 Rochester Rd., 412/366-4140
Cozumel Restaurante Mexicano
  1145 E. Pittsburgh St., Greenburg, 412/836-2653
Mad Mex
  370 Atwood St, 412/681-5656
  7905 McKnight Rd., 412/366-5656

Best Microbrewery
Penn Brewery
  800 Vinial, 412/237-9400

Best Middle Eastern Food
Ali Baba
  404 S. Craig St., 412/682-2829
Amel's Restaurant
  435 McNeilly Rd., 412/563-3466

Best New Restaurants
Mad Mex
  370 Atwood St., 412/681-5656
  7905 McKnight Rd., 412/366-5656
Oakland's Spice Island Teahouse
  253 Atwood St., 412/687-8821
The Classroom
  133 Camp Ln., 412/942-4878

Best Outdoor Dining
J. Harris' Grill
  5747 Ellsworth Ave., 412/363-0833

Best Pizza
PaPa J's Pizza and Pasta
  638 Washington Rd., 412/343-7272
DiPietro's
  10500 Perry Hwy., Wexford, 412/934-1050
Caruso's Pizza
  656 Washington Rd., 412/343-1722
Mineo's Pizza House
  2128 Murray Ave., 412/521-9864

Best Places to Take the Kids
Eat N Park
  2874 W. Liberty Ave., 412/561-4944
  4596 William Penn Hwy., Murrysville, 412/327-7270
  5143 Rte. 8, Gibsonia, 412/443-7280
  Sheffield Rd. at 21st St., Aliquippa, 412/378-4400
  Twelfth St. at Seventh Ave., Beaver Falls,
    412/843-3750
King's Family Restaurant
  Multiple Locations

Best Restaurant Meal Value
Armstrong's Restaurant
  1136 N. Thorn Run Ext., Coraopolis, 412/262-9355
Asian Palace
  3500 William Penn Hwy., 412/823-2121

Best Romantic Dining
Rico's
  1 Rico Ln., 412/931-1989

920

Stone Mansion
  1600 Stone Mansion Dr., Wexford, 412/934-3000

Best Salad/Salad Bar
Blarney Stone
  30 Grant Ave., 412/781-1666

Best Sandwiches
Peppi's
  12 Smithfield St., 412/281-1510
  927 Western Ave., 412/231-9009
  1721 Penn Ave., 412/562-0125
Primanti Brothers
  3803 Forbes Ave., 412/621-4444
  46 Eighteenth St., 412/263-2142
  11 Cherry Way, 412/566-8051
Wexford Post Office Deli
  120 Wexford Bayne Rd., Wexford, 412/935-3354

Best Seafood
Poli's Seafood Restaurant
  2607 Murray Ave., 412/521-6400
Rodi Grille House
  204 Rodi Rd., 412/241-1730
Robert Wholley's Fish Market
  1711 Penn Ave., 412/261-3693
Wright's Seafood Inn
  1837 Washington St., Carnegie, 412/423-1255

Best Sports Bar
Hi-Tops Sports Bar
  1130 Perry Hwy., 412/782-3760

Best Steaks
Colony
  Greentree at Cochran Rd., 412/341-3060
Mardi Gras Steak and Seafood
  634 Camp Home Rd., 412/369-9916

Best Vegetarian Food
East End Food Co-Op
  7516 Meade St., 412/242-3598
Himalayan Tibetan Restaurant
  3531 Forbes Ave., 412/687-6550
Janet's Cafe
  901 E. Carson St., 412/381-5308
Mad Mex
  370 Atwood St., 412/681-5656
  7905 McKnight Rd., 412/366-5656

Best Wine Selection
The Carlton
  1 Mellon Bank Ctr., 412/391-4099
Le Mont Restaurant
  1114 Grandview, 412/431-3100
Le Pommier
  2104 E. Carson St., 412/682-2620
Wooden Angel
  100 Leopard Ln., Beaver, 412/774-7880

P

Standbys
Chi Chi's
   1598 Washington Rd., 412/833-8886
   7201 McKnight Rd., 412/364-2414
   1165 McKinney Ln., 412/937-0818
Chili's
   7404 McKnight Rd., 412/364-5678
Chuck E. Cheese Pizza
   249 N. Craig St., 412/655-8840
Friday's
   5300 Corporate Dr., 412/367-1101
Lone Star Steak House
   Multiple Locations
Old Country Buffet
   1155 Washington Pike, Bridgeville, 412/257-8640
   4801 McKnight Rd., 412/369-8801
   591 Clairton Blvd., Pleasant Hills, 412/653-0732
Ruth's Chris Steak House
   6 PPG Pl., Third St. at Market St., 412/391-4800
The Ground Round
   2000 Greentree Rd., 412/561-2187
   1600 Washington Rd., 412/833-7580

POTTSTOWN, PA

Best Restaurants in Town
Sunnybrook Ballroom and Convention Center
   E. High St. at Sunnybrook Rd., 610/326-6400
Lakeside Inn
   594 Westridge Pike, Limrick, 610/495-6222

Best American Food
Sunnybrook Ballroom and Convention Center
   E. High St. at Sunnybrook Rd., 610/326-6400

Best Brunch
Gables Inn
   3373 Westridge Pike, 610/495-5777

Best Chinese Food
Panda Heaven Chinese Restaurant
   11A Coventry Square Mall, 610/970-6999

Best Continental Food
Coventry Forge Inn
   3360 Coventryville Rd., 610/469-6222

Best Italian Food
Cutillo's Restaurant
   2688 E. High St., 610/327-2910

Best Lunch
Coventry Tea Room
   Rte. 23, 610/469-9134

READING, PA

Best All-You-Can-Eat Buffet
Chef Alan's Restaurant and Lounge
   525 Penn Ave., 610/375-4012

Best Atmosphere
Stokesay Castle
   Hill Rd. at Spook Ln., 610/375-4588

Widow Finney's Restaurant
30 S. Fourth St., 610/378-1776

Best Bar
Peanut Bar
332 Penn St., 610/376-8500

Best Barbecue/Ribs
Wild Wings Cafe
Reading Regional Airport Rd., 610/478-1747

Best Breakfast
Arner's Family Restaurant
1714 State Hill Rd., 610/372-6101
4643 Pottsville Pike, 610/926-9002
Deluxe Restaurant
415 Lancaster Pike W., 610/775-2577
Butler's Pantry
348 Penn St., 610/373-7555

Best Chinese Food
China Penn Restaurant
4203A Perkiomen Ave., 610/779-9754
1816 Bern Rd., West Lawn, 610/374-5656

Best Coffee
Coffee Shop Book House
643 Penn Ave., 610/375-1311
Salon Salon
600 Penn Ave., 610/372-3705

Best Desserts
Arner's Family Restaurant
1714 State Hill Rd., 610/372-6101
4643 Pottsville Pike, 610/926-9002
Chef Alan's Restaurant and Lounge
525 Penn Ave., 610/375-4012

Best Eclectic Menu
Dan's Restaurant
1049 Penn St., 610/373-2075
Cafe Unicorn
116 Lafayette St., 610/929-9992

Best French Food
Green Hills Inn
2444 Morgantown Rd., 610/777-9611

Best German Food
Alpenhof Restaurant
903 Morgantown Rd., 610/373-1624

Best Health-Conscious Menu
California Bar and Grill
699 Mountain View Rd., 610/777-7224
Sahara Restaurant
334 Penn St., 610/374-8500

Best Homestyle Food
Lantern Lodge Motor Inn
411 N. College St., Myerstown, 717/866-6536

Best Ice Cream/Yogurt
Bresler's Ice Cream and Yogurt
3050 N. Fifth Street Hwy., 610/929-3317

P

Best Italian Food
Bravo
  1160 Buttonwood St., 610/378-9200
Pachuilo's Italian Restaurant
  850 N. Eighth St., 610/376-2717

Best Mexican Food
El Tapatio
  801 Walnut St., 610/373-8872

Best Middle Eastern Food
Sahara Restaurant
  334 Penn St., 610/374-8500

Best Pizza
Paolo's Pizza Restaurant
  1200 Lancaster Pike W., 610/775-3500
Santino's Family Restaurant
  1 Wellington Blvd., 610/670-2052

Best Places to Eat When Someone Else Is Buying
Joe's Restaurant
  450 S. Seventh St., 610/373-6794
Stokesay Castle
  Hill Rd. at Spook Ln., 610/375-4588

Best Regional Food
Dutch Country Kitchen
  Fairground Market, 610/929-3016
Reeser Wegman's Restaurant
  4401 Pottsville Pike, 610/929-2538

Best Salad/Salad Bar
Butler's Pantry
  348 Penn St., 610/373-7555

Best Sandwiches
Butler's Pantry
  348 Penn St., 610/373-7555
Dave's New York Style Deli
  850 Moss St., 610/374-6880

Best Seafood
Crab Barn
  2613 Hampden Blvd., 610/921-8922

Best Steaks
Inn at Reading
  1040 N. Park Rd., Wyomissing, 610/372-7811

Best Thai Food
Thai Cuisine
  153 N. Eighth St., 610/375-6685

SCRANTON, PA

Best Restaurant in Town
Cooper's Seafood House
  701 N. Washington Ave., 717/346-6883

Best Bar
Fresno's Restaurant
  Rte. 6, Scranton Carbondale Hwy., 717/383-9400

Best Burgers
Jim Dandy's
  Mark Plaza, Edwardsville, 717/288-3500

Best Chinese Food
House of China
1137 Moosic St., 717/343-8118

Best Family Restaurant
Carmella's
140 Erie St., 717/961-3070

Best Greek/Mediterranean Food
Aegean II Restaurant and Bar
134 N. Main Ave., 717/969-6080

Best Late-Night Food
Fresno's Restaurant
Rte. 6, Scranton Carbondale Hwy., 717/383-9400

Best Pizza
Calabria Pizza and Restaurant
531 Pittston Ave., 717/969-6200

Best Quick Lunch
Lackawanna Station
700 Lackawanna Ave., 717/342-8300

Best 24-Hour Restaurant
Waffle Shop and Family Restaurant
917 Wyoming Ave., 717/344-2288

Best Other Restaurant
Marvelous Mugs
Montage Mountain Rd. at Davis St., 717/961-1551

Standbys
Friendly's
708 N. Blakely St., 717/961-1565
Denny's
410 Scranton Carbondale Hwy., 717/346-8006
TCBY
217 Scranton Carbondale Hwy., 717/961-3033

P

STATE COLLEGE, PA

Best American Food
Corner Room
100 W. College Ave., 814/237-3051

Best Breakfast
Waffle Shop
364 E. College Ave., 814/237-9741
1229 N. Atherton St., 814/238-7460

Best Desserts
University Creamery
Pennsylvania State College, Shortledge St. at
Curtin St., 814/865-7535

Best Dinner
Tavern Restaurant
220 E. College Ave., 814/238-6116

Best Ice Cream/Yogurt
University Creamery
Pennsylvania State College, Shortledge St. at
Curtin St., 814/865-7535

Best Italian Food
Mario and Luigi's
113 S. Garner St., 814/237-0374
1272 N. Atherton St., 814/234-4273

Best Lunch
Waffle Shop
364 E. College Ave., 814/237-9741
1229 N. Atherton St., 814/238-7460

Best Pizza
Hi-Way Pizza Pubs
340 E. College Ave., 814/237-5718
1688 N. Atherton St., 814/237-0375
428 Westerly Parkway Plz., 814/237-1074

Best Steaks
Hoss's Steak and Sea House
1450 N. Atherton St., 814/234-4009

SWARTHMORE, PA

Best Restaurant in Town
American Bistro
Rte. 420 at Morton Ave., Morton, 610/543-3033

Best Atmosphere
Ingleneuk Tea House and Catering
120 Park Ave., 610/543-4569

Best French Food
American Bistro
Rte. 420 at Morton Ave., Morton, 610/543-3033

Best Lunch
Occasionally Yours
10 Park Ave., 610/328-9360

Best Salad/Salad Bar
Occasionally Yours
10 Park Ave., 610/328-9360

Best Sandwiches
Cheese Court
1 Park Ave., 610/328-4140

UNIONTOWN, PA

Best All-You-Can-Eat Buffet
Sun Porch
Rte. 40E, Hopwood, 412/439-5734

Best Bar
Bud Murphy's
718 McCormick Ave., Connellsville, 412/628-4827

Best Breakfast
Herring's
Rte. 40, Hopwood, 412/438-9823
Lone Star
Rural Rte. 40, Markleysburg, 412/329-5631

Best Burgers
Ruse's Roost
Rte. 40E, Hopwood, 412/437-2796

Best Diner
Herring's
Rte. 40, Hopwood, 412/438-9823
Glisan's Restaurant
Rural Rte. 1, Markleysburg, 412/329-4636

Best Family Restaurant
Coal Baron Restaurant
Rte. 40W, 412/439-0111

Best French Food
Chez Gerard
Rte. 40, Hopwood, 412/437-9001

Best Ice Cream/Yogurt
Ruse's Roost
Rte. 40E, Hopwood, 412/437-2796

Best Italian Food
Fabrizi's Italian Take-Outs
56 Lebanon Ave., 412/438-7737
The Stonehouse Hotel and Restaurant
Rural Route 2, Farmington, 412/329-8876
Luigi's Italian Restaurant
Rte. 119S, Connellsville, 412/626-0422

Best Middle Eastern Food
Sam's Restaurant
208 Morgantown St., 412/438-7050

Best Pizza
Mom Maruca's Pizza Shop
265 N. Gallatin Ave., 412/438-9066
Bud Murphy's
718 McCormick Ave., Connellsville, 412/628-4827

Best Sandwiches
Ruse's Roost
Rte. 40E, Hopwood, 412/437-2796
Bud Murphy's
718 McCormick Ave., Connellsville, 412/628-4827

Best Seafood
The Golden Trout
Nemacolin Woodlands, Rte. 40E, Farmington,
412/329-8555
Watering Trough
National Pike E., Hopwood, 412/438-9716

Best Steaks
Watering Trough
National Pike E., Hopwood, 412/438-9716

WARREN, PA

Best Barbecue/Ribs
Jefferson House and Pub
119 Market St., 814/723-2268

Best Breakfast
Plaza Restaurant
328 Pennsylvania Ave. W., 814/723-5660

Best Burgers
Plaza Restaurant
328 Pennsylvania Ave. W., 814/723-5660

P

Best Coffee
Roy's Texas Lunch
214 Pennsylvania Ave. W., 814/723-5292

Best Diners
Plaza Restaurant
328 Pennsylvania Ave. W., 814/723-5660
Roy's Texas Lunch
214 Pennsylvania Ave. W., 814/723-5292

Best Family Restaurants
Allegheny River Hotel
2101 Pennsylvania Ave. E., 814/723-4104
Mineral Well
Rural Route 1, Clarendon, 814/723-9840

Best Ice Cream/Yogurt
V and J Pizza and Sub Shop
601 Pennsylvania Ave. E., 814/723-3406

Best Italian Food
Mineral Well
Rural Route 1, Clarendon, 814/723-9840

Best Sandwiches
V and J Pizza and Sub Shop
601 Pennsylvania Ave. E., 814/723-3406

Best Steaks
Busy Bee Restaurant
229 Pennsylvania Ave. W., 814/723-9868

WILKES-BARRE, PA

Best Breakfast
Holiday Pancake House
116 Wilkes Barre Township Blvd., 717/824-4927
152 Hill St., 717/829-5931

Best Coffee
Bakers Inn
6 S. Main St., 717/823-8580

Best Desserts
Bakers Inn
6 S. Main St., 717/823-8580

Best Italian Food
Perugino's
205 S. Main St., 717/825-6803

Best Japanese Food
Katana
41 S. Main St., 717/825-9080

Best Pizza
Serpico Pizza
220 East End Ctr., 717/824-4477

Best Sandwiches
Bakers Inn
6 S. Main St., 717/823-8580

Standbys
Chi Chi's
20 East End Ctr. 717/824-8887

P

Denny's
488 Kidder St., 717/825-5208
Friday's
800 Kidder St., 717/823-9923
Old Country Buffet
26 East End Ctr., 717/822-1332
Red Lobster
10 East End Ctr., 717/825-6122

WILLIAMSPORT, PA

Best Restaurants in Town
Tag's Bar and Grill
1254 Memorial Ave., 717/322-9288
Bridge Tavern
222 Market St., 717/323-8839
The Villa
2016 E. Third St., 717/323-5533

Standbys
Chi Chi's
2502 E. Third St., 717/321-9208
Red Lobster
1951 E. Third St., 717/323-0423

YORK, PA

Best Restaurants in Town
Village Green Family Restaurant
2300 E. Market St., 717/755-9839
Roosevelt Tavern
400 W. Philadelphia St., 717/854-7725
Boulevard Spirits and Provisions
2500 E. Market St., 717/757-3663

Best Brunch
Commonwealth Room
Yorktown Hotel, 48 E. Market, 717/848-1111

Best Business Lunch
Autographs
Yorktown Hotel, 48 E. Market, 717/848-1111

Best Cheap Meal
Uncle's Place
13 N. Duke St., 717/854-1827

Best Chinese Food
Peter Chang Chinese
907 Loucks Rd., 717/845-8138
Shangrila Chinese Restaurant
2149 White St., 717/854-3333

Best Family Restaurant
Alexander's Family Restaurant
840 Carlisle Rd., 717/846-1041

Best Homestyle Food
Alexander's Family Restaurant
840 Carlisle Rd., 717/846-1041

Best Italian Food
Anthony's
801 Loucks Rd., 717/843-0063

P

Alberto's Restaurant and Pizza
2736 S. Queen St., 717/741-3854
2530 W. Market St., 717/792-4602

Best Mexican Food
El Serrano Restaurant
3410 E. Market St., 717/757-4963

Best Pizza
Marcello Pizza
713 Arsenal Rd., 717/755-9760
17 W. Market St., 717/854-7811

Best Place to Eat When Someone Else Is Buying
Accomac Inn
Accomac Rd., Wrightsville, 717/252-1521

Best Sandwiches
Isaac's Restaurant and Deli
2960 Whiteford Rd., 717/751-0515
Jim and Nena's Pizzeria
35 W. Market St., 717/854-0241

Best Seafood
Mr. Bill's Quarterdeck Seafood
2600 Keyway Dr., 717/741-0872
Lamotte's Restaurant
7 E. Franklin St., New Freedom, 717/235-2295

Best Tea Room
Isaac's West
2159 White St., Ste. A101, 717/854-2292

Best Vegetarian Food
Blue Moon Cafe
361 W. Market St., 717/854-6664

Best Other Restaurant
The Left Bank Restaurant and Bar
120 N. George St., 717/843-8010

Standbys
Lone Star Steakhouse
922 Loucks Rd., 717/848-2588
Old Country Buffet
905 Loucks Rd., 717/845-4367

930

Rhode Island

Best Restaurants in Town
Redlefsen's Rotisserie and Grill
425 Hope St., 401/254-1188
S.S. Dion
520 Thames St., 401/253-2884

Best Breakfast
Hope Diner
742 Hope St., 401/253-1759

Best Diner
Hope Diner
742 Hope St., 401/253-1759

Best Regional Food
The Lobster Pot
119 Hope St., 401/253-9100

Best Restaurant Meal Value
Tweet's
180 Mount Hope Ave., 401/253-9811

Best Seafood
The Lobster Pot
119 Hope St., 401/253-9100

Best Asian Restaurant
Galaxie Restaurant
957 Reservoir Ave., 401/946-9464

Best Breakfast
Bickford's Family Restaurant
860 Reservoir Ave., 401/943-6004
Mike's Kitchen
170 Randall St., 401/946-5320

Best Burgers
Chelo's Beef Hearth
1275 Reservoir Ave., 401/942-7666

Best Coffee
Caffe-Bonami
1082 Park Ave., 401/943-8400

R

Cafe Luna
10 Midway Rd., 401/944-1438
Ocean Coffee Roasters
110 Waterman Ave., 401/331-5282

Best Ice Cream/Yogurt
Newport Creamery
51 Baldwin Orchard Dr., Ste. 178, 401/821-7789
150 Midway Rd., 401/944-3397
Dear Hearts Ice Cream
2218 Broad St., 401/941-5167

Best Italian Food
Caffe Itri
1686 Cranston St., 401/942-1970
Twin Oaks Restaurant
100 Sabra St., 401/781-9693

Best Mexican Food
Spain Restaurant
1073 Reservoir Ave., 401/946-8686

Best Pizza
Tony's Pizza and Restaurant
548 Pontiac Ave., 401/781-1334
Calvitto's Pizza and Bakery
1391 Park Ave., 401/944-3737

Best Restaurant Meal Value
Mike's Kitchen
170 Randall St., 401/946-5320
Silver Palace
623 Reservoir Ave., 401/467-0077

Best Steaks
Twin Oaks Restaurant
100 Sabra St., 401/781-9693

EAST PROVIDENCE, RI

Best Barbecue/Ribs
Bugaboo Creek Steak House
1275 Wampanoag Trail, Riverside, 401/433-5500

Best Breakfast
Wampanoag Diner
2800 Pawtucket Ave., 401/434-9880
Roast House
40 Newport Ave., 401/435-3054

Best Brunch
Audrey's
State Rte. 114A at State Rte. 44, Seekonk,
508/336-4636

Best Chinese Food
Imperial Villa Restaurant
3348 Pawtucket Ave., Riverside, 401/434-1150

Best Desserts
Gregg's Restaurant
1940 Pawtucket Ave., 401/438-5700

Best Diner
Wampanoag Diner
2800 Pawtucket Ave., 401/434-9880

Best Family Restaurants
Gregg's Restaurant
  1940 Pawtucket Ave., 401/438-5700
Joseph's Family Restaurant
  315 Waterman Ave., 401/438-5250

Best Homestyle Food
Joseph's Family Restaurant
  315 Waterman Ave., 401/438-5250

Best Ice Cream/Yogurt
Sunshine Creamery
  305 N. Broadway, Rumford, 401/431-2828

Best Italian Food
Cafe Gianni
  335 Newport Ave., Rumford, 401/438-2226

Best Pizza
Uncle Tony's Pizza and Pasta
  141 Newport Ave., Rumford, 401/438-4646

Best Place to Take the Kids
Bugaboo Creek Steak House
  1275 Wampanoag Trail, Riverside, 401/433-5500

Best Sandwiches
Waterman Avenue Deli
  97 Waterman Ave., 401/434-4964

Best Seafood
Old Grist Mill Tavern
  390 Fall River Ave., Seekonk, 508/336-8460
Old Oyster House Restaurant
  28 Water St., 401/431-1133
One Hundred Thirty-Three Club
  29 Warren Ave., 401/438-1330

Best Steaks
Old Grist Mill Tavern
  390 Fall River Ave., Seekonk, 508/336-8460
Bugaboo Creek Steak House
  1275 Wampanoag Trail, Riverside, 401/433-5500
One Hundred Thirty-Three Club
  29 Warren Ave., 401/438-1330

R

NARRAGANSETT, RI

Best Bar
Coast Guard House
  40 Ocean Rd., 401/789-0700

Best Breakfast
Breakfast Nook
  6130 Post Rd., North Kingston, 401/884-6108

Best Brunch
Coast Guard House
  40 Ocean Rd., 401/789-0700

Best Chinese Food
Chen's Restaurant
  60 Old Tower Hill Rd., Wakefield, 401/783-8516

Best Coffee
Coffee Bean
  20 Woodruff Ave., 401/782-6226

Best Delicatessen
Brown Street Cafe
  85 Brown St., North Kingston, 401/294-1150

Best Ice Cream/Yogurt
Heffie's
  1820 Boston Neck Rd., North Kingston, 401/295-1414

Best Italian Food
Casa Rossi
  90 Point Judith Rd., 401/789-6385

Best Regional Food
George's of Galilee
  250 Sand Hill Cove Rd., 401/783-2306

Best Restaurant Meal Value
Walt's Roast Beef
  6660 Post Rd., North Kingston, 401/884-9719

Best Seafood
Aunt Carrie's
  1240 Ocean Rd., 401/783-7930
Harborside
  68 Brown St., North Kingston, 401/295-0444
Captain Jack's
  706 Succotash Rd., Wakefield, 401/789-4556

Best Steaks
Red Rooster Tavern
  7385 Post Rd., North Kingston, 401/295-8804

NEWPORT, RI

Best Restaurants in Town
The Brick Alley Pub and Restaurant
  140 Thames St., 401/849-6334
Via Via Cafe
  112 Williams St., 401/846-4074
Clarke Cooke House
  3 Bannister's Wharf, 401/849-2900

R

Best American Food
Yesterday's
  28 Washington Sq., 401/847-0116

Best Bars
The White Horse Tavern
  16 Farewell St., 401/849-3600
The Brick Alley Pub and Restaurant
  140 Thames St., 401/849-6334

Best Barbecue/Ribs
Music Hall Cafe
  250 Thames St., 401/848-2330

Best Breakfast
Coffee Corner
  283 Broadway, 401/849-2902
Muriel's
  58 Spring St., 401/849-7780

Best Burgers
The Brick Alley Pub and Restaurant
  140 Thames St., 401/849-6334

Best Chinese Food
Batik Garden
  99 E. Main Rd., 401/848-0663

Best Chowder
The Black Pearl
  Bannister's Wharf, 401/846-5264

Best Coffee
Ocean Coffee Roasters
  22 Washington Sq., 401/846-6060

Best Delicatessens
Cappuccino's
  92 William St., 401/846-7145
Sig's Market and Caterers
  7 Carroll Ave., 401/847-9668

Best Diner
Fourth Street Diner
  184 Admiral Kalbfus Rd., 401/847-2069

Best French Food
Courtyard La Petit Auberge
  19 Charles St., 401/849-6669

Best Italian Food
Puerini's
  24 Memorial Blvd. W., 401/847-5506

Best Old Favorite Restaurant
The White Horse Tavern
  16 Farewell St., 401/849-3600

Best Other Ethnic Food
Sea Shai (Japanese/Korean)
  747 Aquidneck Ave., Ste. 1B, Middletown,
    401/849-5180

Best Pizza
Nikola's
  38 Memorial Blvd. W., 401/849-6611
Via Via
  112 Williams St., 401/846-4074
  372 Thames St., 401/848-0880

Best Restaurant Meal Value
Salas'
  343 Thames St., 401/849-7895

Best Romantic Dining
Canfield House
  5 Memorial Blvd., 401/847-0416
Inn at Castle Hill
  Ocean Ave., 401/899-3800

Best Sandwiches
Newport Creamery
  49 Long Wharf Mall, 401/849-8469
  18 Bellevue Ave., 401/846-6332

Best Seafood
The Mooring
  Newport Yacht Center, Sayers Wharf, 401/846-2260
Christie's
  351 Thames St., 401/847-5400

R

Canfield House
  5 Memorial Blvd., 401/847-0416

Best Steaks
Chart House
  22 Bowens Wharf, 401/849-7555
The Brick Alley Pub and Restaurant
  140 Thames St., 401/849-6334

Best Tea Room
Hammett Room
  505 Thames St., 401/842-0428

Best Wine Selection
The Place at Yesterdays
  28 Washington Sq., 401/847-0116

Standbys
Baskin-Robbins
  270 Bellevue Ave., 401/846-9337
Ben and Jerry's
  10 Perry Mill Wharf, 401/846-2663

PAWTUCKET, RI

Best Barbecue/Ribs
Wes' Ribs
  38 Dike St., Providence, 401/421-9090
Sticki Fingers
  137 Douglas Ave., 401/272-7427
Coachmen's Lodge
  273 Wrentham Rd., Bellingham, 508/883-9888

Best Breakfast
Bill's Restaurant
  844 Newport Ave., 401/726-9265
Kip's
  826 Newport Ave., 401/726-9882
Modern Diner
  364 East Ave., 401/726-8390

Best Brunch
Holiday Inn
  800 Greenwich Ave., Warwick, 401/732-6000
L.A. Roberts
  6900 Post Rd., North Kingston, 401/885-0575

Best Burgers
Stanley's
  534 Dexter St., Central Falls, 401/726-9689
Local Hero
  101 Higginson Ave., Lincoln, 401/724-0230
  4 Power Rd., 401/727-3459

Best Chinese Food
Food Super Dragon
  805 Broadway, 401/723-3960
Tin Tin
  223 Newport Ave., 401/725-8118
China Inn
  285 Main St., 401/723-3960

Best Coffee
Honey Dew
  1515 Newport Ave., 401/723-5580

Tyler's
  196 Division St., 401/728-5750
Local Hero
  4 Power Rd., 401/727-3459

Best Delicatessens
Local Hero
  101 Higginson Ave., Lincoln, 401/724-0230
Jim's Deli
  1702 Mendon Rd., Cumberland, 401/334-1011
Shaw's Meats
  435 Power Rd., 401/728-8120
Barney's
  727 East Ave., 401/727-1010

Best Diner
Modern Diner
  364 East Ave., 401/726-8390

Best Ice Cream/Yogurt
Dot's Dairy Bar
  1476 Newport Ave., 401/724-9150
Newport Creamery
  100 Main St., 401/724-4630
  665 Central Ave., 401/724-3170
Ice Cream Machine
  4288 Diamond Hill Rd., 401/333-5053

Best Japanese Food
Oki Japanese Steakhouse
  1270 Mineral Spring Ave., North Providence,
    401/728-7970

Best Other Ethnic Food
Hot Pockets (Lebanese/Middle Eastern)
  285 Thayer St., 401/751-3251
Lisbon at Night (Portuguese)
  17 Exchange St., 401/723-2030
Estrella's (Portuguese)
  736 N. Broadway, East Providence, 401/434-5130
Madeira (Portuguese)
  288 Warren Ave., East Providence, 401/431-1322

Best Pizza
House of Pizza
  206 Division St., 401/725-9433
Twins Pizza
  1000 Mineral Spring Ave., North Providence,
    401/726-0549
Ronzio Pizzeria
  727 East Ave., 401/722-5330
Toti's Pizza Palace
  622 Central Ave., 401/728-9797

Best Regional Food
Local Hero
  4 Power Rd., 401/727-3459
  101 Higginson Ave., Lincoln, 401/724-0230

Best Restaurant Meal Value
Local Hero
  4 Power Rd., 401/727-3459
  101 Higginson Ave., Lincoln, 401/724-0230

R

Best Salad/Salad Bar
Grist Mill
390 Fall River Ave., Seekonk, 508/336-8460

Standbys
Ponderosa
562 Washington St., South Attleboro, 508/399-6138

PROVIDENCE, RI

Best Restaurant in Town
Twin Oaks
100 Sabra St., Cranston, 401/781-9693

Best Bagels
Bagels East
135 Elmgrove Ave., 401/331-6195
Cafe Such a Bagel
1245 Putnam Pike, Smithfield, 401/233-0100

Best Barbecue/Ribs
Wes' Rib House
38 Dike St., 401/421-9090

Best Bread
Downcity Diner
151 Weybosset St., 401/331-9217

Best Breakfast
Wampanoag Diner
2800 Pawtucket Ave., East Providence, 401/434-9880
Leon's
166 Broadway, 401/273-1055
Downcity Diner
151 Weybosset St., 401/331-9217
Roast House
8 Louisquisset Pike, North Smithfield, 401/765-0919
Plaza Grille
64 De Pasquale Ave., 401/274-8684
Seaplane Diner
307 Allens Ave., 401/941-9547

Best Brunch
Kountry Kitchen Restaurant
10 Smith Ave., Greenville, 401/949-0840
Audrey's Cafe
315 Main St., 401/884-4441
Leon's
166 Broadway, 401/273-1055
Biltmore
11 Dorrance St., 401/421-0700
Four Corners Family Restaurant
3841 Main Rd., 401/625-1307
Marriott
Charles St. at Orms St., 401/272-2400

Best Burgers
Stanley's
535 Dexter St., Central Falls, 401/726-9689
Bugaboo Creek Steak House
1275 Wampanoag Trail, Riverside, 401/433-5500
Chelo's
Multiple Locations

R

Best Chinese Food
China Inn
  6 The Arcade, 401/331-1717
Dragon Express
  82 Broadway, 401/847-1686
Little Chopsticks
  495 Smith St., 401/351-4290

Best Delicatessens
Schroeder's
  204 Willett Ave., Riverside, 401/437-1610
Geoff's
  163 Benefit St., 401/751-2248
  178 Angell St., 401/751-9214
  239 Westminster St., 401/751-0240

Best Desserts
Audrey's Cafe
  315 Main St., 401/884-4441
Gregg's Restaurant
  1303 N. Main St., 401/831-5700
Newport Doubletree
  1 Goat Island, 401/849-2600
Meeting Street Cafe
  220 Meeting St., 401/273-1066

Best Diners
Wampanoag Diner
  2800 Pawtucket Ave., East Providence, 401/434-9880
Downcity Diner
  151 Weybosset St., 401/331-9217

Best Family Restaurant
Wright's Farm
  84 Inman Rd., 401/769-2856

Best Health-Conscious Menu
D'Angelo's
  Multiple Locations
Gregg's Restaurant
  1303 N. Main St., 401/831-5700
Little Chopsticks
  495 Smith St., 401/351-4290

Best Ice Cream/Yogurt
Newport Creamery
  Multiple Locations
Helger's Ice Cream Shoppe
  2475 Main Rd., 401/624-4560

Best Italian Food
Camille's Roman Garden
  71 Bradford St., 401/751-4812
Tortilla Flats
  355 Hope St., 401/751-6777

Best Pizza
Uncle Tony's Pizza and Pasta
  Multiple Locations
Caserta Pizzeria
  121 Spruce St., 401/272-3618
Adesso
  161 Cushing St., 401/521-0770

R

Bob and Timmy's
57 De Pasquale Ave., 401/453-2221
Sammy's House of Pizza
1370 Middle Spring St., 401/353-7827

Best Place to Eat When Someone Else Is Buying
Capital Grille
1 Cookson Pl., 401/521-5600

Best Regional Food
Chelo's
Multiple Locations
Hemenway's
1 Old Stone Sq., 401/351-8570
Aunt Carrie's
1240 Ocean Rd., 401/783-7930
Rocky Point
1759 Post Rd., 401/739-4222
Chopmist Hill Inn
1315 Chopmist Hill Rd., North Scituate, 401/647-2388

Best Restaurant Meal Value
Angelo's Civita Farnese
141 Atwells Ave., 401/621-8171
Cheap Eats
999 W. Main Rd., 401/849-8181
Little Inn
103 Putnam Pl., Johnston, 401/231-0570
Marchetti's
1463 Park Ave., 401/943-7649

Best Romantic Dining
Blue Grotto
210 Atwells Ave., 401/272-9030
Clark Cooke House
3 Bannisters Wharf, 401/849-2900
Country Harvest
67 W. Main Rd., 401/635-4579
La France Restaurant
960 Hope St., 401/331-9233
Pot Au Feu
44 Custom House St., 401/273-8953

Best Salad/Salad Bar
Pot Au Feu
44 Custom House St., 401/273-8953
Leo's
99 Chestnut St., 401/274-3541

Best Sandwiches
Meeting Street Cafe
220 Meeting St., 401/273-1066
Leon's
166 Broadway, 401/273-1055

Best Schmooze Bar
Leo's
99 Chestnut St., 401/274-3541

Best Seafood
Hemenway's
1 Old Stone Sq., 401/351-8570

Monterey
  1910 Post Rd., 401/738-3407

Best Steaks
Club 44
  355 Putnam Pl., Smithfield, 401/231-2240
Capital Grille
  1 Cookson Pl., 401/521-5600

Best Tea Room
Bushberry
  466 Putnam Pike, Greenville, 401/949-5230

WARWICK, RI

Best Atmosphere
Sardo's Hospitality and Fine Dining
  100 Folly Landing, 401/884-9499

Best Bar
Dave's Bar and Grill
  2339 Post Rd., 401/739-7444

Best Barbecue/Ribs
Bugaboo Creek Steak House
  30 Jefferson Blvd., 401/781-1400

Best Breakfast
Bickford's Family Restaurant
  969 Bald Hill Rd., 401/828-2080
  20 Jefferson Blvd., 401/785-9660

Best Brunch
Remington's
  Holiday Inn at the Crossings, 800 Greenwich Ave.,
    401/732-6000

Best Burgers
Chelo's of Warwick
  2225 Post Rd., 401/737-7299
Bugaboo Creek Steak House
  30 Jefferson Blvd., 401/781-1400

Best Chinese Food
Islander Restaurant
  2318 W. Shore Rd., 401/738-9861
Panda Island
  300 Quaker Ln., 401/821-5553
China Inn
  1557 Bald Hill Rd., 401/823-3355

Best Delicatessens
Ricotti's
  1639 Warwick Ave., 401/737-9847
  27 Post Rd., 401/737-9580
The Food Chalet
  874 Post Rd., 401/467-9169

Best Desserts
Chelo's of Warwick
  2225 Post Rd., 401/737-7299
Gregg's Restaurant
  1359 Post Rd., 401/467-5700

R

Best Family Restaurant
Bugaboo Creek Steak House
  30 Jefferson Blvd., 401/781-1400

Best Ice Cream/Yogurt
Carvel Ice Cream Bakery
  1775 Post Rd., 401/738-0495
I Can't Believe It's Yogurt
  300 Quaker Ln., 401/823-3609

Best Italian Food
Portofino
  897 Post Rd., 401/461-8920

Best Pizza
Bertucci's Brick Oven Pizzeria
  1946 Post Rd., 401/732-4343
Pizza King
  1356 Greenwich Ave., 401/732-1338
Uno Pizzerio
  399 Bald Hill Rd., 401/738-5610

Best Regional Food
Crow's Nest
  288 Arnolds Neck Dr., 401/732-6575

Best Restaurant Meal Value
Walt's Roast Beef
  1800 Post Rd., 401/732-0374
Dave's Bar and Grill
  2339 Post Rd., 401/739-7444

Best Salad/Salad Bar
Monterey Steakhouse
  1910 Post Rd., 401/738-3407

Best Sandwiches
Ricotti's
  1639 Warwick Ave., 401/737-9847
  27 Post Rd., 401/737-9580

Best Seafood
Crow's Nest
  288 Arnolds Neck Dr., 401/732-6575

Best Steaks
Bugaboo Creek Steak House
  30 Jefferson Blvd., 401/781-1400

Best View While Dining
Crow's Nest
  288 Arnolds Neck Dr., 401/732-6575
Sardo's Hospitality and Fine Dining
  100 Folly Landing, 401/884-9499

Standbys
Chili's
  1276 Bald Hill Rd., 401/821-0310
HomeTown Buffet
  1245 Bald Hill Rd., 401/826-4494
Shoney's
  1000 Bald Hill Rd., 401/781-1400
The Olive Garden
  31A Universal Blvd., 401/821-732

Best Restaurant in Town
West Valley Inn
4 Blossom St., 401/822-2834

Best Breakfast
A.J.'s Restaurant
1365 Main St., 401/828-4160

Best Cheap Meal
Mr. Taco
49 Providence St., 401/828-7573

Best Chinese Food
House of Wu
52 Providence St., 401/828-7720

Best Delicatessen
Pinelli's
701 Quaker Ln., 401/821-8828

Best Dinner
Cowesett Inn
226 Cowesett Ave., 401/828-4726

Best Italian Food
Evelyn's Villa
272 Cowesett Ave., 401/821-0060

Best Lunch
Stephen's Backyard
11 Curson St., 401/821-0030

Best Mexican Food
Mr. Taco
49 Providence St., 401/828-7573

Best American Food
Flood Tide Restaurant
Rte. 1 at 27, Mystic, 203/536-8140

Best Bagels
Woody's Cafe
43 Broad St., 401/596-1991

Best Barbecue/Ribs
W.B. Cody's
265 Post Rd., 401/322-4070
Dave's Bar and Grill
2339 Post Rd., 401/739-7444

Best Chinese Food
China Pavillion
148 Granite St., 401/596-9888

Best Delicatessen
Fortuna's
140 Franklin St., 401/596-1883

Best Health-Conscious Menu
Bravo Cafe
20 E. Main St., Mystic, 203/536-3604

Best Lunch
Brick Oven
209 Main St., Ashaway, 401/377-2230

R

Best Outdoor Dining
Hitching Post
5400 Post Rd., Charlestown, 401/364-7495
Best Pizza
Pizza Lady
271 Post Rd., 401/322-0221
2 Prospect St., Pawcatuck, 203/599-1113

Best Seafood
Hitching Post [summers only]
5400 Post Rd., Charlestown, 401/364-7495

WOONSOCKET, RI

Best Restaurant in Town
Vermette's Restaurant
1347 Diamond Hill Rd., 401/769-0429

Best American Food
Union House Pub
18 Bridge St., Blackstone, 508/883-5353

Best Breakfast
Coffee and Cream
Victory Hwy., Rte. 102, North Smithfield,
401/767-5566
4 Greenville Rd., North Smithfield, 401/762-4352
Roast House
116 Washington Hwy., Lincoln, 401/333-2450
Gisele's Kitchen
479 Great Rd., Lincoln, 401/722-8737

Best Brunch
Breakfast Nook
190 Front St., Lincoln, 401/727-2704

Best Chinese Food
Chan's
267 Main St., 401/765-1900

Best Coffee
Local Hero
101 Higginson Ave., Lincoln, 401/724-0230

Best Delicatessen
Jim's Deli
1702 Mendon Rd., Cumberland, 401/334-1011

Best Diner
Kennedy's Lunch
673 Saint Paul St., North Smithfield, 401/762-9211
Asia
Lincoln Mall, Lincoln, 401/334-3200

Best Dinner
Vermette's Restaurant
1347 Diamond Hill Rd., 401/769-0429

Best Health-Conscious Menu
Local Hero
101 Higginson Ave., Lincoln, 401/724-0230

Best Italian Food
Savini's Restaurant
476 Rathbun St., 401/762-5114

Bocce Club
   226 St. Louis Ave., 401/762-0155

Best Lunch
Box Seat
   350 River St., 401/762-0900
Cafe Binelli
   1800 Mendon Rd., Cumberland, 401/333-3444

Best Pizza
Arnold Pizza
   260 Arnold St., 401/762-5662
Mezza Luna
   7 Park Sq., 401/769-7654

Best Seafood
El Dorado
   401 Clinton St., 401/767-1961

Best Sports Bar
Box Seat
   350 River St., 401/762-0900

Best Steaks
King's Inn
   629 Washington Hwy., Lincoln, 401/333-0900

R

South Carolina

Best Atmosphere
No. 10 Downing Street
  241 Laurens St. SW, 803/642-9062
Willcox Inn
  100 Colleton Ave. SW, 803/649-1377

Best Barbecue/Ribs
Bobby's Bar-B-Q Buffet
  1897 Jefferson Davis Hwy., Warrenville, 803/593-5900
Whiskey Road Bar-B-Q
  4248 Whiskey Rd., 803/649-4260

Best Breakfast
Alvanos Restaurant
  122 Laurens St. NW, 803/643-9710
Track Kitchen
  420 Mead Ave., 803/641-9628

Best Brunch
No. 10 Downing Street
  241 Laurens St. SW, 803/642-9062
New Moon Cafe
  116 Laurens St. NW, 803/643-7088

Best Burgers
Alvanos Restaurant
  122 Laurens St. NW, 803/643-9710

Best Chinese Food
China Palace Restaurant
  1368 Whiskey Rd., 803/642-9270

Best Coffee
New Moon Cafe
  116 Laurens St. NW, 803/643-7088

Best Desserts
Stoplight Deli
  119 Laurens St. NW, 803/642-3354
Olive Oils Italian Cuisine
  223 Chesterfield St. S., 803/649-3726

S

Best Health-Conscious Menu
Stoplight Deli
119 Laurens St. NW, 803/642-3354
Carolina Bistro
117 Newberry St., 803/648-3700
New Moon Cafe
116 Laurens St., 803/643-7088

Best Homestyle Food
Blue Top Grill
212 Aiken Rd., Graniteville, 803/663-3971
Alvanos Restaurant
122 Laurens St. NW, 803/643-9710
Chick-N-Snack
102 Breezy Hill Rd., Graniteville, 803/663-9395
Ford's Lunch
406 Main St., Graniteville, 803/663-3251

Best Italian Food
Olive Oils Italian Cuisine
223 Chesterfield St. S., 803/649-3726

Best Other Ethnic Food
Mango's (Caribbean)
149 Laurens St., 803/643-0620

Best Pizza
Ferrando's Italian Pizzeria
3032 Augusta Rd., Warrenville, 803/593-6400
Acropolis Pizza Restaurant
1647 Richland Ave. E., 803/649-7601

Best Place to Take the Kids
Stoplight Deli
119 Laurens St. NW, 803/642-3354

Best Romantic Dining
No. 10 Downing Street
241 Laurens St. SW, 803/642-9062
Olive Oils Italian Cuisine
223 Chesterfield St. S., 803/649-3726

Best Sandwiches
Stoplight Deli
119 Laurens St. NW, 803/642-3354

Best Seafood
Captain Bill's Seafood
258 Pleasure Rd., Gloverville, 803/593-8313
Bowery West Side
151 Bee Ln., 803/648-2900
Up Your Alley Restaurant
222 The Alley, 803/649-2603

Best Steaks
Bowery West Side
151 Bee Ln., 803/648-2900
Up Your Alley Restaurant
222 The Alley, 803/649-2603
Variety Restaurant
921 York St. NE, 803/648-6987

Standbys
Baskin-Robbins
Kalmia Plaza Shopping, 803/649-3131

ANDERSON, SC

Best Bar
TJ Whispers Live Entertainment
3434 Cinema Ctr., 864/224-7300

Best Breakfast
Butterbean's
206 Concord Rd., 864/261-3198

Best Business Lunch
Towne House Restaurant
125 N. Main St., 864/225-9791
O'Charley's of Anderson
3132 Clemson Blvd., 864/224-1417

Best Cheap Meal
Mama Penn's Family Dining
2935 N. Main St., 864/224-2402

Best Chinese Food
Dragon Den Chinese Restaurant
3323 Clemson Blvd., 864/224-7135

Best Coffee
Grace's Coffeehouse and Restaurant
1510 N. Murray Ave., 864/231-6739

Best Desserts
Friends Foods with a Flair
112 N. Main St., 864/231-0663

Best Family Restaurant
Mama Penn's Family Dining
2935 N. Main St., 864/224-2402

Best Italian Food
Capri's Italian
2407 N. Main St., 864/224-5405
Tomato Rumba's
3730 Clemson Blvd., 864/375-1696

Best Mexican Food
Monterrey Mexican Restaurant
3191 N. Main St., 864/225-1316

Best Pizza
Pizza Inn
3420 Clemson Blvd., 864/226-6215

Best Places to Be "Seen"
Stone's Throw Restaurant
3450 Cinema Ctr., 864/231-774
Eleven Hundred Nine South Main
1109 S. Main St., 864/225-1109

Best Place to Eat When Someone Else Is Buying
Eleven Hundred Nine South Main
1109 S. Main St., 864/225-1109

Best Regional Food
Liberty Hall Inn
621 S. Mechanic St., 864/646-7500

Best Romantic Dining
Doni's Under the Trees
3422 Clemson Blvd., 864/224-7107

S

Best Salad/Salad Bar
Daddy Rabbit's
603 E. Greenville St., 864/225-5555
3501 Clemson Blvd., 864/226-8888

Best Sandwiches
Grace's Coffeehouse and Restaurant
1510 N. Murray Ave., 864/231-6739

Best Seafood
Doni's Under the Trees
3422 Clemson Blvd., 864/224-7107
RJ T-Bone's
1017 123 Bypass, Seneca, 864/882-1017

Standbys
Applebee's
3441 Clemson Blvd., 864/225-4752
Baskin-Robbins
3501 Clemson Blvd., 864/225-8197
Outback Steakhouse
110 Interstate Blvd., 864/261-6283

BEAUFORT, SC

Best Barbecue/Ribs
Duke's Barbecue
3166 Boundary St., 803/524-1128
Sergeant White's Restaurant
1908 Boundary St., 803/522-2029

Best Breakfast
Blackstone's Groceries
915 Bay St., 803/524-4330

Best Brunch
Gadsby Tavern
822 Bay St., 803/525-1800
Beaufort Inn and Fine Dining
809 Port Republic St., 803/521-9000

Best Burgers
Captain Stewbee's Cafe
1 Landing Dr., Port Royal, 803/525-6768
Steamer
168 Sea Island Pkwy., 803/522-0210
Bananas
910 Bay St., 803/522-0910

Best Casual Dining
Plum's
904 1/2 Bay St., 803/525-1946

Best Coffee
Firehouse Books
706 Craven St., 803/522-2665

Best Desserts
Emily's
906 Port Republic St., 803/522-1866

Best Homestyle Food
Backstreet Cafe
813 Port Republic St., 803/524-2100

Best Ice Cream/Yogurt
Bresler's
  Beaufort Plaza, 803/524-9228
Fitzripple's
  Oaks Shopping Ctr., 803/521-0072
Plum's
  904 1/2 Bay St., 803/525-1946

Best Pizza
Dad's Place
  2611 Boundary St., 803/522-3237
Upper Crust
  Hwy. 21, 803/521-1999
Cinelli Pizzeria
  Hwy. 280 at Hwy. 802, Burton, 803/525-0910

Best Sandwiches
Bananas
  910 Bay St., 803/522-0910
Plum's
  904 1/2 Bay St., 803/525-1946

Best Seafood
Dockside Restaurant
  1699 Eleventh St. W., Port Royal, 803/524-7433
Factory Creek Landing
  67 Sea Island Pkwy., 803/525-1165

Best Steaks
Dockside Restaurant
  1699 Eleventh St. W., Port Royal, 803/524-7433

CHARLESTON, SC

Best All-You-Can-Eat Buffet
Trotter's Restaurant
  I-26 at Hwy. 56, Clinton, 803/833-4900

Best Bars
Henry's
  54 N. Market St., 803/723-4363
East Bay Trading Company
  161 E. Bay St., 803/722-0722

Best Breakfast
Baker's Cafe
  214 King St., 803/577-2694
Bear E. Patch Cafe
  801 Folly Rd., 803/762-6555

Best Burgers
Jack's Cafe
  41 George St., 803/723-5237

Best Cheap Meal
Pinckney Cafe and Espresso
  18 Pinckney St., 803/577-0961

Best Chinese Food
Emperor's Garden Chinese
  874 Orleans Dr., 803/556-7212

Best Coffee
Cafe Rainbow
  282 King St., 803/853-9777

S

Best Desserts
Kaminsky's Most Excellent Cafe
78 N. Market St., 803/853-8270
Mint Julep
68 Queen St., 803/853-6468

Best Family Restaurant
Sticky Fingers
341 Johnnie Dodds Blvd., Mt. Pleasant, 803/856-9840

Best French Food
Market East Bistro
14 N. Market St., 803/577-5080

Best Health-Conscious Menu
Sermet's Grill
630 Skylark Dr., 803/769-4433

Best Homestyle Food
Sticky Fingers
341 Johnnie Dodds Blvd., Mt. Pleasant, 803/856-9840

Best Ice Cream/Yogurt
Kaminsky's Most Excellent Cafe
78 N. Market St., 803/853-8270
Bear E. Patch Cafe
801 Folly Rd., 803/762-6555

Best Italian Food
Vincenzo's
232 Meeting St., 803/577-7953

Best Late-Night Food
T-Bone's Texas Style Steak House
1668 Hwy. 171, 803/769-0350
Fannie's Twenty-Four Hour
137 Market St., 803/723-7121

Best Mexican Food
Juanita Greenberg
75 1/2 Wentworth St., 803/577-2877

Best Pizza
Andolini's Pizza
82 Wentworth St., 803/722-7437

Best Place to Eat Alone
Pinckney Cafe and Espresso
18 Pinckney St., 803/577-0961

Best Place to Eat When Someone Else Is Buying
Magnolia's
185 E. Bay St., 803/722-6150

Best Place to Take the Kids
Sticky Fingers
341 Johnnie Dodds Blvd., Mt. Pleasant, 803/856-9840

Best Romantic Dining
Blossom Cafe
171 E. Bay St., 803/722-9200
Fulton Five
5 Fulton St., 803/853-5555

Best Sandwiches
Lewis' Charleston Grill
224 King St., 803/577-4522

Best Seafood
Crawdaddys Seafood Restaurant
  1600 Peas Island Rd., 803/762-4336

Best Steaks
Arizona Bar and Grill
  14 Chapel St., 803/577-5090

Best Tea Room
Patio Tea Room
  41 Bogard St., 803/722-8117

Best Vegetarian Food
Sermet's Grill
  630 Skylark Dr., 803/769-4433

Best Other Restaurant
Woodlands Resort
  329 Old Postern Rd., Summerville, 803/875-2600

COLUMBIA, SC

Best Bar
Yesterdays
  2030 Devinc St., 803/799-0196
  612 Saint Andrews Rd., 803/731-9626

Best Business Lunch
Dixie Seafood Company
  902B Gervais St., 803/771-6753
One Two Three
  7001 Saint Andrews Rd., 803/781-0118

Best Chinese Food
Eggroll Chen
  715 Crowson Rd., 803/787-6820

Best Desserts
Spinnaker's Restaurant
  100 Columbiana Circle, 803/781-0701

Best Homestyle Food
Lizard's Thicket Restaurant
  Multiple Locations

Best Ice Cream/Yogurt
Immaculate Consumption
  933 Main St., 803/799-9053
Freshens Premium Yogurt
  100 Columbiana Circle, Ste. 1254, 803/781-8464

Best Italian Food
Garibaldi's of Columbia
  2013 Greene St., 803/771-8888
Capri's
  7467 Saint Andrews Rd., 803/781-0302

Best Mexican Food
San Jose Mexican Restaurant
  4722 Forest Dr., 803/790-0678
  559 Saint Andrews Rd., 803/772-4251

Best Place to Be "Seen"
Garibaldi's of Columbia
  2013 Greene St., 803/771-8888

S

Best Place to Eat When Someone Else Is Buying
Garibaldi's of Columbia
2013 Greene St., 803/771-8888

Best Romantic Dining
Garibaldi's of Columbia
2013 Greene St., 803/771-8888

Best Sandwiches
Beulah's Bar and Grill
902 Gervais St., 803/779-4655

Best Seafood
Dixie Seafood Company
902B Gervais St., 803/771-6753
Dee's on the River
701 Alexander Rd., 803/926-8173

Standbys
International House of Pancakes
4467 Devine St., 803/782-9646
Applebee's
2344 Broad River Rd., 803/731-2853
245 O'Neil Ct., 803/736-6104
4505 Devine St., 803/787-4687
Chili's
280 Harbison Blvd., 803/732-2911
Outback Steakhouse
252F Harbison Blvd., 803/732-3771
Friday's
3400 Forest Dr., Ste. 1024, 803/787-9085
El Chico Mexican Restaurant
1728 Bush River Rd., 803/772-0770

FLORENCE, SC

Best Restaurants in Town
P.A.'s Restaurant
1534 S. Irby St., 803/665-0846
Percy and Willie's
2401 David H. McCloud Blvd., 803/669-1620

Best Breakfast
Canterbury Coffeehouse
320 S. Dargan, 803/673-9282
Venus Pancake House
471 W. Palmetto St., 803/669-9977

Best Coffee
Canterbury Coffeehouse
320 S. Dargan, 803/673-9282

Best Desserts
Grotto Italian Restaurant
1749 S. Irby St., 803/667-8651
Red Bone Alley Restaurant
1903 W. Palmetto St., 803/673-0035

Best Family Restaurant
Venus Pancake House
471 W. Palmetto St., 803/669-9977

Best Greek/Mediterranean Food
Niko's Greek Restaurant
1931 Second Loop Rd., 803/664-9190

Best Health-Conscious Menu
Red Bone Alley Restaurant
1903 W. Palmetto St., 803/673-0035

Best Italian Food
Grotto Italian Restaurant
1749 S. Irby St., 803/667-8651

Best Lunch
P.A.'s Restaurant
1534 S. Irby St., 803/665-0846

Best Mexican Food
Corona Mexican Restaurant
2029 W. Evans St., 803/665-6508

Best Salad/Salad Bar
P.A.'s Restaurant
1534 S. Irby St., 803/665-0846

GEORGETOWN, SC

Best Breakfast
Lafayette Restaurant
711 Church St., 803/546-5033

Best Burgers
Lands End Restaurant
1 Marina Dr., 803/527-1376
River Room Restaurant
801 Front St., 803/527-4110

Best Desserts
Kudzu Bakery
714 Front St., 803/546-1847

Best Family Restaurants
Lafayette Restaurant
711 Church St., 803/546-5033
Lands End Restaurant
1 Marina Dr., 803/527-1376

Best Ice Cream/Yogurt
JR Yogurt and Ice Cream
1063 N. Fraser St., 803/546-1623

Best Lunch
Pink Magnolia
719 Front St., 803/527-6506

Best Pizza
Tony's Famous Pizza
415 N. Fraser St., 803/546-1612

Best Salad/Salad Bar
Daniel's Waterfront Eatery
713 Front St., 803/546-4377
River Room Restaurant
801 Front St., 803/527-4110

Best Sandwiches
Daniel's Waterfront Eatery
713 Front St., 803/546-4377
River Room Restaurant
801 Front St., 803/527-4110

S

Best Seafood
River Room Restaurant
  801 Front St., 803/527-4110

Best Steaks
Nanna's Steakhouse and Kitchen
  Hwy. 17N, 803/527-0077

Standbys
Quincy's
  219 Church St., 803/546-9510
Shoney's
  208 Church St., 803/546-4112

GREENVILLE, SC

Best Atmosphere
Seven Oaks Restaurant
  104 Broadus Ave., 864/232-1895
The Terrace
  100 Villa Rd., 864/242-3804

Best Breakfast
Stax's Omega Diner
  72 W. Orchard Park Dr., 864/297-6639

Best Burgers
Como's Restaurant
  1611 Augusta St., 864/233-1385
Beacon Drive-In
  255 Reidville Rd., Spartanburg, 864/585-9387

Best Business Lunch
Eight Five Eight
  18 E. North St., 864/242-8883

Best Casual Dining
Stax's Peppermill
  30 W. Orchard Park Dr., 864/288-9320

Best Chinese Food
Dragon Den Chinese Restaurant
  420 N. Pleasantburg Dr., 864/242-1777

Best Coffee
Stax's Omega Diner
  72 W. Orchard Park Dr., 864/297-6639

Best Diner
Stax's Omega Diner
  72 W. Orchard Park Dr., 864/297-6639

Best Health-Conscious Menu
Annie's Natural Cafe
  121 S. Main St., 864/271-4872

Best Ice Cream/Yogurt
Swensen's Ice Cream
  2025 Wade Hampton Blvd., 864/268-7945

Best Italian Food
Capri's Italian Restaurant
  500 E. Stone Ave., 864/235-4552
  1130 Woodruff Rd., 864/288-5884
Vince's
  1 E. Antrim Dr., 864/233-1621

Best Mexican Food
Monterrey Mexican Restaurant
   1813 Laurens Rd., 864/271-2561
   2801 Poinsett Hwy., 864/271-3625
   2716 Wade Hampton Blvd., 864/268-5277

Best Place to Be "Seen"
Vince's
   1 E. Antrim Dr., 864/233-1621

Best Places to Eat When Someone Else Is Buying
Seven Oaks Restaurant
   104 Broadus Ave., 864/232-1895
The Terrace
   100 Villa Rd., 864/242-3804

Best Romantic Dining
Harry's on Morgan Square
   116 Magnolia St., Spartanburg, 864/583-8121

Best Sandwiches
Schlotzsky's
   2121 Augusta St., 864/232-7229

Best Seafood
Peddler Steak House
   2000 Poinsett Hwy., 864/235-7192

Best Steaks
Peddler Steak House
   2000 Poinsett Hwy., 864/235-7192

Standbys
Papa John's
   3795 E. North St., 864/370-2500
Fuddruckers
   1147 Woodruff Rd., 864/234-7528
   221 N. Main St., 864/235-6400

GREENWOOD, SC

Best Restaurants in Town
Ranch House Restaurant
   1213 Bypass 72NE, 864/223-5905
Inn on the Square
   104 Court St., 864/223-4488

Best All-You-Can-Eat Buffet
Yoder's Dutch Kitchen
   Hwy. 72E, Abbeville, 864/459-5556

Best Bar
Rosie O'Malley's
   248 Birchtree Dr., 864/229-4040

Best Chinese Food
China Garden
   421 Montague Ave., 864/223-2999

Best Family Restaurant
Rosie O'Malley's
   248 Birchtree Dr., 864/229-4040

Best Homestyle Food
Yoder's Dutch Kitchen
   Hwy. 72E, Abbeville, 864/459-5556

S

Best Italian Food
Fazoli's
3432 Clemson Blvd., Anderson, 864/225-7918
Capri's Italian
1704 Bypass 72NE, 864/223-0367

Best Lunch
Fatz Cafe
3123 S. Hwy. 14, 864/288-1929
225 S. Pleasantburg Dr., Greenville, 864/467-9542

Best Sandwiches
T-Bone's
110 Phoenix St., 864/227-1300

Best Steaks
Rosie O'Malley's
248 Birchtree Dr., 864/229-4040

HILTON HEAD, SC

Best Restaurants in Town
Golden Rose Seafood Restaurant
78 Beach City Rd., 803/681-2717
Abe Grant's
650 William Hills Pkwy., 803/785-3675
Hilton Head Diner
6 Marina Side Dr., Hwy. 278, 803/686-2400
Riley's
Port Royal Plaza, 803/681-4153

Best Barbecue/Ribs
Jodie's
6 Polk Ave., 803/785-2464

Best Place to Eat When Someone Else Is Buying
Charlie's E'toile Verte
1000 Plantation Center, 803/785-9277

MYRTLE BEACH, SC

Best Restaurant in Town
Thoroughbreds Restaurant
9706 Hwy. 17N, 803/497-2636

Best All-You-Can-Eat Buffet
K and W Cafeteria
2001 S. Kings Hwy., 803/448-1669
79th Ave. at Hwy. 17, 803/449-1442

Best Sandwiches
Dagwood's
400 Eleventh Ave. N., 803/448-0100
Miami Subs
2703 N. Kings Hwy., 803/444-0268

Best Seafood
Chesapeake House
9918 Hwy. 17N, 803/449-3231

Standbys
The Olive Garden
1405 N. Kings Hwy., 803/626-8856
Outback Steakhouse
7025 N. Kings Hwy., 803/449-5888

S

ORANGEBURG, SC

Best Barbecue/Ribs
Earl Duke's Barbecue
1878 Charleston Hwy., 803/534-4493

Best Breakfast
Biddie Banquet
1575 John C. Calhoun Dr. SE, 803/534-0488

Best Burgers
Central Park USA
168 John C. Calhoun Dr. SE, 803/531-3444
Dairy O
504 Russell St. SE, 803/536-4205

Best Chinese Food
China Palace
1045 Five Chop Rd. SE, 803/536-4676

Best Homestyle Food
Biddie Banquet
1575 John C. Calhoun Dr. SE, 803/534-0488
Crossroads Restaurant
1680 Neeses Hwy., 803/531-4064

Best Ice Cream/Yogurt
Dairy O
504 Russell St. SE, 803/536-4205

Best Sandwiches
Chestnut Grill
1455 Chestnut St. NE, 803/531-1747
Schlotzsky's
1208 Saint Matthews Rd. NE, 803/536-5628

Best Seafood
Fisherman's Catch
603 Bleakley St. SE, 803/531-1033

Standbys
Quincy's
780 John C. Calhoun Dr. SE, 803/534-7560
Red Lobster
2347 Chestnut St. NE, 803/533-7676
Ryan's Family Steak House
2580 North Rd. NE, 803/534-6605

PAWLEYS ISLAND, SC

Best Bar
Litchfield Beach Fish House
Hwy. 17, 803/237-3949

Best Italian Food
Deniro's Italian Ristorante
105 Hwy. 17, 803/237-1397

Best Romantic Dining
Deniro's Italian Ristorante
105 Hwy. 17, 803/237-1397

Best Seafood
Litchfield Beach Fish House
Hwy. 17, 803/237-3949

S

ROCK HILL, SC

Best American Food
Anna J's Restaurant
  1025 Camden Ave., 803/327-9943
Thursdays Too
  147 Herlong Ave., 803/366-6117
White Horse Ltd.
  617 Cherry Rd., 803/328-2172

Best Atmosphere
Thursdays Too
  147 Herlong Ave., 803/366-6117

Best Breakfast
The Little Cafe
  1533 Woodhaven Rd., 803/329-1440
Watkins Grill
  123 Elk Ave., 803/327-4923

Best Burgers
Checkers
  2615 Cherry Rd., 803/324-7538
Sagebrush Steakhouse and Saloon
  2445 Cherry Rd., 803/366-8331

Best Cafeteria
Jackson's Cafeteria
  Village Square, 1734 Ebenezer Rd., 803/366-6860

Best Casual Dining
Sagebrush Steakhouse and Saloon
  2445 Cherry Rd., 803/366-8331

Best Homestyle Food
Watkins Grill
  123 Elk Ave., 803/327-4923
Sagebrush Steakhouse and Saloon
  2445 Cherry Rd., 803/366-8331

Best Lunch
Thursdays Too
  147 Herlong Ave., 803/366-6117
Watkins Grill
  123 Elk Ave., 803/327-4923

Best Mexican Food
El Cancun
  1244 Cherry Rd., 803/366-6996

Best Other Ethnic Food
Tropical Escape Cafe (Pacific Rim cuisine)
  590 N. Anderson Rd., Hwy. 21 Bypass, 803/366-3888

Best Sandwiches
For What It's Worth
  122 E. Main St., 803/327-1450

Best Seafood
Tam's Tavern
  1027 W. Oakland Ave., 803/329-2226
Tropical Escape Cafe
  590 N. Anderson Rd., Hwy. 21 Bypass, 803/366-3888

Best Steaks
Sagebrush Steakhouse and Saloon
  2445 Cherry Rd., 803/366-8331

S

Tropical Escape Cafe
590 N. Anderson Rd., Hwy. 21 Bypass, 803/366-3888

Standbys
Cracker Barrel
2140 Manna Ct., Exit 79, 803/327-6141
Subway
2349 Cherry Rd., 803/324-7929
119 Herlong, 803/366-7827
1240 E. Main St., 803/328-1990

SPARTANBURG, SC

Best Breakfast
Papa Sam's Breakfast Nook
191 E. Saint John St., 864/582-6655
Skillet Restaurant
435 E. Main St., 864/582-3206

Best Burgers
Beacon Drive-In
255 Reidville Rd., 864/585-9387
Sugar and Spice Drive-In Restaurant
212 S. Pine St., 864/585-3991

Best Business Lunch
As You Like It
401 E. Kennedy St., 864/573-6633

Best Cheap Meal
The Sandwich Factory
112 Main St., 864/585-8506

Best Chinese Food
Great Wall 2
1120 Asheville Hwy., 864/583-4668
Shanghai Restaurant
240 W. Blackstone Rd., 864/574-1300

Best Coffee
The Sandwich Factory
112 Main St., 864/585-8506

Best Desserts
Harry's on Morgan Square
116 Magnolia St., 864/583-8121
Spice of Life Gourmet Market
100 Wood Row, 864/585-3737

Best Diner
Skillet Restaurant
435 E. Main St., 864/582-3206

Best Family Restaurant
Wade's Restaurant
1000 N. Pine St., 864/582-3800

Best German Food
Gerhard's Cafe
1200 E. Main St., 864/591-1920

Best Homestyle Food
Woodward's Cafe
438 Stevens St., 864/585-5986

S

Best Ice Cream/Yogurt
Ice Creams and Coffee Beans
  551 E. Main St., 864/597-1510
  1735 Reidville Rd., 864/574-2252
Mainstreet Cafe
  930 E. Main St., 864/583-0464

Best Italian Food
Capri's Italian Restaurant
  299 E. Wood St., 864/583-7811
  1600 Reidville Rd., 864/576-4152
Dante Italian Restaurant
  456 Oak Grove Rd., 864/576-2107
Renato's Italian Restaurant
  221 E. Kennedy St., 864/585-7027
Stefano's Restaurant
  1560 Union St., 864/591-1941

Best Mexican Food
Zapata's Cafe Gallery and Bongo Bar
  146 N. Church St., 864/948-1661

Best Place to Eat Alone
Mimi's Uptown
  180 E. Main St., 864/585-8332

Best Places to Eat When Someone Else Is Buying
Harry's on Morgan Square
  116 Magnolia St., 864/583-8121
Spice of Life Gourmet Market
  100 Wood Row, 864/585-3737

Best Romantic Dining
Harry's on Morgan Square
  116 Magnolia St., 864/583-8121

Best Sandwiches
As You Like It
  401 E. Kennedy St., 864/573-6633
Ice Creams and Coffee Beans
  551 E. Main St., 864/597-1510
  1735 Reidville Rd., 864/574-2252
The Sandwich Factory
  112 Main St., 864/585-8506

Best Seafood
Walnut Grove Seafood Restaurant
  Hwy. 221 at I-26, 864/574-7777

Best Steaks
Le Baron Restaurant
  2600 E. Main St., 864/579-3111
Peddler Steak House
  464 E. Main St., 864/583-5874
Piedmont Steak House
  276 Magnolia St., 864/582-4380

Best Tea Rooms
Grapevine Shoppe and Tea Room
  113 Wall St., 864/573-1484
Piazza Tea Room
  571 E. Main St., 864/582-5861

Standbys
Fuddruckers
   1509 Reidville Rd., 864/576-8329

SUMTER, SC

Best Barbecue/Ribs
Ward's
   416 E. Liberty St., 803/775-2490
   1087 Alice Dr., 803/775-0008

Best Chinese Food
The Dragon Restaurant
   236 S. Pike W., 803/778-1807

Best Italian Food
Sambino's Italian Restaurant
   4742 Broad St., 803/494-9494

Best Wine Selection
Lilfred's of Camden
   Hwy. 521, Rembert, 803/432-7063

S

South Dakota

Best Restaurants in Town
Refuge Lounge
715 Lancelot Dr., 605/229-2681
Flame Restaurant and Lounge
25 Main St., 605/225-2082
Helen's California Kitchen
Melgaard Rd., 605/225-9286

Best Breakfast
Country Kitchen
2221 Sixth St., 605/692-6968
Dakota Inn Restaurant
1441 Sixth St., 605/692-9320

Best Burgers
Nick's Hamburger Shop
427 Main Ave., 605/692-4324

Best Coffee
Moxie Java
Village Square, 605/692-1740
Joe House
311 Third St., 605/692-5777

Best Desserts
Casper's Cafe
420 Main Ave., 605/692-7240
Ram Pub
327 Main Ave., 605/692-2485

Best Family Restaurants
Cook's Kitchen
304 Main Ave., 605/692-1303
Country Kitchen
2221 Sixth St., 605/692-6968

Best Greek/Mediterranean Food
George's Pizza and Steak House
311 Main Ave., 605/692-6610

S

Best Homestyle Food
Cook's Kitchen
  304 Main Ave., 605/692-1303
Granmoo's Kitchen and Gordon's Meats
  417 Main Ave., 605/692-1290
Dakota Inn Restaurant
  1441 Sixth St., 605/692-9320

Best Pizza
George's Pizza and Steak House
  311 Main Ave., 605/692-6610

Best Sandwiches
Granmoo's Kitchen and Gordon's Meats
  417 Main Ave., 605/692-1290
Mad Jack's Brown Baggers
  805 Medary Ave., 605/692-2878

Best Seafood
Casper's Cafe
  420 Main Ave., 605/692-7240
Ram Pub
  327 Main Ave., 605/692-2485

Best Steaks
Casper's Cafe
  420 Main Ave., 605/692-7240
Pheasant Restaurant
  726 Main Ave. S., 605/692-4723
Steak and Buffet
  1815 Sixth St., 605/692-1740

Standbys
Dairy Queen
  122 Sixth St. W., 605/692-2021
  520 22nd Ave., 605/692-1364

HOT SPRINGS, SD

Best American Food
Al's Cafe
  333 S. Chicago St., 605/745-6588

Best Bar
Yogi's Den
  625 N. River St., 605/745-5949

Best Breakfast
Cascade Restaurant
  800 Mammouth St., 605/745-3878
Dakota Rose Restaurant
  E. Hwy. 79, 605/745-6447
Maverick Restaurant
  Hwy. 18-385 at Hwy. 79, 605/745-4215

Best Burgers
Yogi's Den
  625 N. River St., 605/745-5949

Best Chinese Food
Al's Cafe
  333 S. Chicago St., 605/745-6588

S

Best Coffee
Katz Cafe
  603 N. River St., 605/745-6005

Best Family Restaurants
Cascade Restaurant
  800 Mammouth St., 605/745-3878
Dakota Rose Restaurant
  E. Hwy. 79, 605/745-6447
Maverick Restaurant
  Hwy. 18-385 at Hwy. 79, 605/745-4215

Best Homestyle Food
Black Hills Family Restaurant
  745 Battle Mountain Ave., 605/745-3737

Best Ice Cream/Yogurt
Katz Cafe
  603 N. River St., 605/745-6005

Best Salad/Salad Bar
Katz Cafe
  603 N. River St., 605/745-6005

Best Sandwiches
Katz Cafe
  603 N. River St., 605/745-6005

Best Steaks
Cascade Restaurant
  800 Mammouth St., 605/745-3878
Dakota Rose Restaurant
  E. Hwy. 79, 605/745-6447
Maverick Restaurant
  Hwy. 18-385 at Hwy. 79, 605/745-4215

Standbys
Pizza Hut
  Hwy. 385, 605/745-5443

HURON, SD

Best All-You-Can-Eat Buffet
Barn Restaurant
  S. Hwy. 37, 605/352-9238

Best Breakfast
The Festivals
  Crossroads Hotel and Convention Center, 100 Fourth
    St. SW, 605/352-3204

Best Burgers
The Festivals
  Crossroads Hotel and Convention Center, 100 Fourth
    St. SW, 605/352-3204

Best Cheap Meal
Sid's Lunch
  340 Kansas Ave. SE, 605/352-5300
Scoreboard
  315 N. Main St., Mitchell, 605/996-9488

Best Chinese Food
Prom Oriental Kitchen
  149 Dakota Ave. S., 605/352-1844

S

Best Coffee
Coffee Tree
  110 Third St., 605/352-6401

Best Family Restaurant
Barn Restaurant
  S. Hwy. 37, 605/352-9238
The Festivals
  Crossroads Hotel and Convention Center, 100 Fourth
    St. SW, 605/352-3204
Country Kitchen
  2050 Dakota Ave., 605/353-1955

Best Homestyle Food
Sid's Lunch
  340 Kansas Ave. SE, 605/352-5300
Country Kitchen
  2050 Dakota Ave., 605/353-1955
Scoreboard
  315 N. Main St., Mitchell, 605/996-9488

Best Steaks
Prime Time Tavern
  2110 Dakota Ave. S., 605/352-9906
Shenanigan's Pub and Cafe
  1000 Eighteenth St. SW, 605/352-4617

Standbys
Subway
  875 Dakota Ave. S., 605/352-2010
Dairy Queen
  165 Lincoln Ave. SW, 605/352-5097

PIERRE, SD

Best Bar
Shenanigans
  602 W. Sioux Ave., 605/224-5657

Best Breakfast
Country Kitchen
  221 E. Pleasant Dr., 605/224-8431

Best Burgers
Point After Sports Bar
  620 S. Cleveland Ave., 605/224-8326

Best Desserts
Kozy Korner Family Restaurant
  217 E. Dakota Ave., 605/224-9547

Best Family Restaurants
Country Kitchen
  221 E. Pleasant Dr., 605/224-8431
Kozy Korner Family Restaurant
  217 E. Dakota Ave., 605/224-9547

Best Health-Conscious Menu
Classy's
  1615 N. Harrison Ave., 605/224-5857

Best Homestyle Food
Town and Country Restaurant
  808 W. Sioux Ave., 605/224-7183

Best Pizza
Gator's Pizza
  1615 N. Harrison Ave., 605/224-6262
Pizza Ranch
  1610 N. Hwy. 83, Fort Pierre, 605/223-9114

Best Salad/Salad Bar
Classy's
  1615 N. Harrison Ave., 605/224-5857

Best Sandwiches
Gator's Pizza
  1615 N. Harrison Ave., 605/224-6262

Best Sports Bar
Point After Sports Bar
  620 S. Cleveland Ave., 605/224-8326

Best Steaks
Cattleman's Club
  29608 South Dakota Hwy. 34, 605/224-9774

Standbys
Dairy Queen
  519 W. Sioux Ave., 605/224-1200

RAPID CITY, SD

Best Restaurants in Town
Firehouse Brewing Company
  610 Main St., 605/348-1915
Elk Creek Steakhouse
  I-90 at Elk Creek Rd., Exit 46, Piedmont,
  605/787-6349

Best Chinese Food
Golden Phoenix
  2421 W. Main St., 605/348-4195

Best Pizza
B.J.'s Grinder King
  902 Main St., 605/348-3166

Best Romantic Dining
Fireside Inn
  Rural Route 8, 605/342-3900

Best Sandwiches
Uptown Grill
  615 Main St., 605/343-1942

S

SIOUX FALLS, SC

Best Restaurant in Town
Minerva's Cafe and Bar
  301 S. Phillips Ave., 605/334-0386

Best All-You-Can-Eat Buffet
Royal Fork Buffet Restaurant
  4610 W. Empire Pl., 605/361-1094

Best Bar
Sioux Falls Brewing Company
  431 N. Phillips Ave., 605/332-4847

Best Breakfast
Minerva's 26th Street Market
  1716 S. Western Ave., 605/334-7491

Best Brunch
Royal Fork Buffet Restaurant
 4610 W. Empire Pl., 605/361-1094

Best Burgers
Dillinger's Diner
 300 N. Dakota Ave., 605/339-2888
 1316 S. Cliff Ave., 605/334-0444

Best Business Lunch
Minerva's Cafe and Bar
 301 S. Phillips Ave., 605/334-0386

Best Casual Dining
Minerva's 26th Street Market
 1716 S. Western Ave., 605/334-7491

Best Cheap Meal
Roll 'N Pin Restaurant
 3015 W. Russell St., 605/339-9190

Best Chinese Food
Szechwan Chinese Restaurant
 415 N. Minnesota Ave., 605/332-2010
 2821 W. 41st St., 605/336-9488
 423 S. Phillips Ave., 605/339-4116

Best Coffee
Barnes and Noble
 3800 S. Louise Ave., 605/361-9244

Best Diner
Di's Place
 Park Ridge Rexall Drug, 1600 S. Western Ave.,
 605/336-3612

Best Family Restaurant
Roll 'N Pin Restaurant
 3015 W. Russell St., 605/339-9190

Best French Food
Theo's
 601 W. 33rd St., 605/338-6801

Best Health-Conscious Menu
Minerva's 26th Street Market
 1716 S. Western Ave., 605/334-7491

Best Homestyle Food
Roll 'N Pin Restaurant
 3015 W. Russell St., 605/339-9190

Best Pizza
Pizza Ranch
 945 S. Marion Rd., 605/334-4820

Best Places to Be "Seen"
Theo's
 601 W. 33rd St., 605/338-6801
Sioux Falls Brewing Company
 431 N. Phillips Ave., 605/332-4847

Best Place to Eat When Someone Else Is Buying
Theo's
 601 W. 33rd St., 605/338-6801

Best Place to Take the Kids
Valentino's
2000 W. 41st St., 605/339-9900

Best Romantic Dining
Kristina's
334 S. Phillips Ave., 605/331-4860

Best Salad/Salad Bar
Valentino's
2000 W. 41st St., 605/339-9900

Best Sandwiches
Kristina's
334 S. Phillips Ave., 605/331-4860

Best Steaks
Tea Steakhouse
215 S. Main St., Tea, 605/368-9667

Best Tea Room
Parsonage
3915 S. Hawthorn Ave., 605/334-8838

Best Vegetarian Food
Kristina's
334 S. Phillips Ave., 605/331-4860

Standbys
TCBY
3400 W. 49th St., 605/361-7778
1006 W. Eighteenth St., 605/339-2633
4001 W. 41st St., Ste. 204, 605/361-7452
The Olive Garden
3121 W. 41st St., 605/333-0290
Applebee's
3800 S. Louise Ave., 605/362-1926
Chi-Chi's
4301 W. 41st St., 605/361-9900
Perkins
5304 N. Cliff Ave., 605/335-7918
2604 W. 41st. St., 605/339-1310
3400 S. Gateway Blvd., 605/361-7525
Red Lobster
3901 W. 41st St., 605/361-6952

S

STURGIS, SD

Best All-You-Can-Eat Buffets
Boulder Canyon Restaurant
Hwy. 14A at Boulder Canyon Route, 605/347-3787
Country Kitchen
620 E. Jackson Blvd., Spearfish, 605/642-4200

Best Burgers
Mom's
2214 Junction Ave., 605/347-3709

Best Coffee
Bob's Family Restaurant
1039 Main St., 605/347-2930

Best Desserts
Ranch House Cafe
1223 Fulton St., 605/347-5503

Best Family Restaurant
Bob's Family Restaurant
1039 Main St., 605/347-2930

Best Homestyle Food
Country Kitchen
620 E. Jackson Blvd., Spearfish, 605/642-4200

Best Ice Cream/Yogurt
Mom's
2214 Junction Ave., 605/347-3709

Best Pizza
Gold Pan Pizza
1102 Main St., 605/347-5221

Best Sandwiches
Bob's Family Restaurant
1039 Main St., 605/347-2930
G-Meister's Cafe
I-90 Exit 30, 605/347-9240

Best Steaks
Elk Creek Steakhouse
I-90 at Elk Creek Rd., Exit 46, Piedmont,
605/787-6349

VERMILLION, SD

Best All-You-Can-Eat Buffet
Becky's
102 E. Cherry St., 605/624-4720

Best Breakfast
Becky's
102 E. Cherry St., 605/624-4720

Best Brunch
Becky's
102 E. Cherry St., 605/624-4720

Best Burgers
Bimbo's Burger Bar
918 E. Cherry St., 605/624-4791

Best Coffee
Coffee Shop Gallery
108 E. Main St., Bldg. B, 605/624-2945

Best Desserts
Recuerdo De Mexico
112 E. Main St., 605/624-6445
Silver Dollar Saloon and Eatery
1216 E. Cherry St., 605/624-4830

Best Family Restaurant
Cowboy Family Restaurant
1122 E. Cherry St., 605/624-8879

Best Greasy Spoon
Whimp's Place
Main St., Burbank, 605/624-9973

Best Health-Conscious Menu
Emma's Kitchen
13 W. Main St., 605/624-9337

Best Homestyle Food
Ida Mae's
    8 Center St., 605/624-4003

Best Ice Cream/Yogurt
R-Pizza
    2 W. Main St., 605/624-6757

Best Korean Food
Chae's Restaurant
    8 W. Main St., 605/624-2294

Best Mexican Food
Recuerdo De Mexico
    112 E. Main St., 605/624-6445

Best Sandwiches
Emma's Kitchen
    13 W. Main St., 605/624-9337

WATERTOWN, SD

Best All-You-Can-Eat Buffet
Steak and Buffet
    710 Tenth St. SW, 605/886-4822

Best Barbecue/Ribs
Second Street Station
    15 Second St. SW, 605/886-8304

Best Breakfast
Grainery
    I-29 at Hwy. 212, 605/882-3950
Country Kitchen
    Hwy. 10, Sisseton, 605/698-3077
Wheel Inn
    Fourth Ave. at Hwy. 20, 605/886-4649

Best Burgers
Drake Motor Inn
    Hwy. 81 at Hwy. 212, 605/886-8411

Best Coffee
Java House
    1002 Fourteenth St. SE, 605/882-2000

Best Desserts
Country Kitchen
    Hwy. 10, Sisseton, 605/698-3077

Best Family Restaurants
Grainery
    I-29 at Hwy. 212, 605/882-3950
Steak and Buffet
    710 Tenth St. SW, 605/886-4822
Country Kitchen
    Hwy. 10, Sisseton, 605/698-3077

Best Ice Cream/Yogurt
Little Dipper
    1300 Ninth Ave., SE, 605/886-9114

Best Pizza
Godfather's Pizza
    1300 Ninth Ave. SE, 605/882-1232

S

Best Salad/Salad Bar
Drake Motor Inn
  Hwy. 81 at Hwy. 212, 605/886-8411
Country Kitchen
  Hwy. 10, Sisseton, 605/698-3077

Best Sandwiches
Dagwood's
  23 Fifth St. NE, 605/886-6568

Best Seafood
Lakeshore
  100 N. Lake Dr., 605/882-3422

Best Steaks
Second Street Station
  15 Second St. SW, 605/886-8304

S

Tennessee

Best Barbecue/Ribs
Pardner's
5444 Hwy. 11E, Piney Flats, 423/538-5539

Best Burgers
Pal's
960 Volunteer Pkwy., 423/652-2291

Best Cheap Meal
Pal's
960 Volunteer Pkwy., 423/652-2291

Best Dinner
Athens Steakhouse
329 Eighth St., 423/652-2202
105 Goodson St., 703/466-8271

Best Fast Food
Acme Hot Dog
1030 Broad St., 423/764-2263

Best Ice Cream/Yogurt
Kay's Ice Cream
9 Pennsylvania Ave., 423/968-9974

Best Lunch
The Feed Room
620 State St., 423/764-0545

Best Mexican Food
La Carreta
530 Volunteer Pkwy., 423/989-3361

Best Steaks
Athens Steakhouse
329 Eighth St., 423/652-2202
105 Goodson St., 703/466-8271

Best Restaurant in Town
The Loft
328 Cherokee Blvd., 423/266-3601

975

Best Bar
Yesterday's Restaurant
820 Georgia Ave., 423/756-1978

Best Burgers
Armando's Brownie Burgers
3943 St. Elmo Ave., 423/825-1840

Best Business Lunch
Town and Country Restaurant
110 N. Market St., 423/267-8544

Best Chinese Food
New Peking Mandarin House
1801 Dayton Blvd., 423/870-9915

Best Coffee
Mudpie Coffeehouse
12 Frazier Ave., 423/267-9043

Best Desserts
The Loft
328 Cherokee Blvd., 423/266-3601

Best French Food
La Cabriole
1341 Burgess Rd., 423/821-0350

Best Health-Conscious Menu
Country Life Vegetarian Restaurant
3748 Ringgold Rd., 423/622-2451

Best Homestyle Food
Country Place Restaurant
5025 Dayton Blvd., 423/875-0741
7320 Shallowford Rd., 423/855-1392

Best Ice Cream/Yogurt
Mr. T's Delivery and Ice Cream
3912 Tennessee Ave., 423/821-5084

Best Italian Food
Provino's Italian Restaurant
5084 South Terrace, 423/899-2559

Best Late-Night Food
Steak N Shake
2296 Gunbarrel Rd., 423/892-2993

Best Mexican Food
Las Margaritas Mexican Restaurant and Cantina
1101 Hixson Pike, 423/756-3332

Best Pizza
Brickoven Grill
5437 Hwy. 153, 423/875-4454

Best Place to Be "Seen"
Station House Restaurant
Holiday Inn, 1400 Market St., 423/266-5000

Best Place to Eat When Someone Else Is Buying
Daryl's Sandwich Shop
9 W. Eighth St., 423/267-6819

Best Romantic Dining
The Loft
328 Cherokee Blvd., 423/266-3601

Best Salad/Salad Bar
Fifth Quarter Steak House
 5501 Brainerd Rd., 423/899-0181

Best Vegetarian Food
Country Life Vegetarian Restaurant
 3748 Ringgold Rd., 423/622-2451

Best Other Restaurant
Southside Grill
 1400 Cowart St., 423/266-6511

Standbys
Old Country Buffet
 2020 Gunbarrel Rd., 423/499-0814
Cracker Barrel
 1460 N. Mack Smith Rd.,423/899-5729
 2346 Shallowford Village Dr., 423/892-0977
Friday's
 2215 Hamilton Place Blvd., 423/855-8443
 2 Market St., 423/752-8443
Red Lobster
 8 Office Park, 423/870-2371
 5709 Lee Hwy., 423/894-5846
Outback Steakhouse
 2120 Hamilton Blvd., 423/899-2600
Ryan's Family Steak House
 5104 Hixson Pike, 423/875-8135
 5326 Ringgold Rd., 423/894-0592

CLARKSVILLE, TN

Best Bar
Franklin Street Pub
 132 Franklin St., 615/552-3726

Best Barbecue/Ribs
Mayfield's Barbecue
 247 Hwy. 149, 615/647-6237

Best Burgers
Buffalo Brady's Wooden Nickel
 1009 S. Riverside Dr., 615/552-1401
Johnny's Burgers and Pizza
 428 College St., 615/647-4545

Best Chinese Food
China Star Restaurant
 804 S. Riverside Dr., 615/648-4405

Best Coffee
Briar and Bean
 Governor's Square Mall, 2801 Wilma Rudolph Blvd.,
 615/552-6465

Best Desserts
Sweet Shoppe
 135 Franklin St., 615/551-8580

Best Homestyle Food
Wilson's Catfish
 2560 Wilma Rudolph Blvd., 615/552-2342
Mayfield's Barbecue
 247 Hwy. 149, 615/647-6237

T

Best Mexican Food
Acapulco Mexican Restaurant
  1148 College St., 615/645-2193
Cancun Mexican Restaurant
  1820 Madison St., 615/647-1493

Best Pizza
Mr. Gatti's Pizza
  1209 Fort Campbell Blvd., 615/6472612
  1807 Madison St., 615/647-7728
Scotto Pizza
  Governor's Square Mall, 2801 Wilma Rudolph Blvd.,
    615/552-6977

Best Sandwiches
Buffalo Brady's Wooden Nickel
  1009 S. Riverside Dr., 615/552-1401

Best Seafood
Wilson's Catfish
  2560 Wilma Rudolph Blvd., 615/5522342

Best Steaks
Logan's Roadhouse
  3072 Wilma Rudolph Blvd., 615/6458333

CLEVELAND, TN

Best Restaurant in Town
J. Steven's Fine Food Restaurant
  220 N. Ocoee St., 423/478-5544

Best Breakfast
Rebel North
  2502 Ocoee St. N., 423/472-6524

Best Chinese Food
China Hall
  145 Stuart Rd. NE, 423/479-6666

Best Italian Food
Gondolier Pizza
  3300 Keith St. NW, 423/472-4998

Best Lunch
Jenkins Deli
  88 Mouse Creek Rd. NW, 423/4795315

Best Mexican Food
Monterrey Mexican Restaurant
  3055 Keith St. NW, 423/339-5700

Best Pizza
Gondolier Pizza
  3300 Keith St. NW, 423/472-4998

Best Sandwiches
Jenkins Deli
  88 Mouse Creek Rd. NW, 423/4795315

Best Steaks
Roblyn's Steak House
  1422 25th St. NW, 423/476-8808

COLUMBIA, TN

Best Restaurant in Town
Legends Restaurant
2401 Pulaski Pike, 615/380-1888

Best Breakfast
Legends Restaurant
2401 Pulaski Pike, 615/380-1888

Best Chinese Food
Chinese Panda Restaurant
100 Berrywood Dr., 615/381-7733

Best Homestyle Food
Harlan House
104 W. Sixth St., 615/388-6868

COOKEVILLE, TN

Best Restaurant in Town
Scarecrow Country Inn
644 Whitson Chapel Rd., 615/526-3431

Best Barbecue/Ribs
Bobby Q's
1070 N. Washington Ave., 615/526-1024

Best Burgers
Dipsy Doodle Drive-In
1442 W. Broad St., 615/526-2986

Best Chinese Food
China Garden Restaurant
831 S. Jefferson Ave., 615/526-4120

Best Diner
Algood Diner
340 W. Main St., Algood, 615/537-3153

Best Homestyle Food
Algood Diner
340 W. Main St., Algood, 615/537-3153
City Square Cafe
453 E. Broad St., 615/528-9120
Dipsy Doodle Drive-In
1442 W. Broad St., 615/526-2986

Best Lunch
Diner on First
120 W. First St., 615/520-0173
O'Charley's
1401 Interstate Dr., 615/520-1898

Best Seafood
Blue Harbor Restaurant
1814 Salem Rd., 615/372-8748

Standbys
Little Caesar's
122 S. Willow Ave., 615/526-7710
Outback Steakhouse
1390 Interstate Dr., 615/372-2145

T

DYERSBURG, TN

Best All-You-Can-Eat Buffet
Mom's
  Lake Dr. on Reelfoot Lake, 901/253-7303

Best American Food
Catfish Corner
  1910 Upper Finley Rd., 901/285-6428

Best Bar
Chequers
  110 Main Ave. S., 901/285-0515

Best Barbecue/Ribs
Neil's Barbeque and Grill
  470 Mall Blvd., Bldg. A, 901/287-8400

Best Bread
Plaza Restaurant
  Hwy. 51 Bypass, 901/287-7893

Best Breakfast
Cozy Kitchen
  100 Church Ave. N., 901/285-1054

Best Chinese Food
New China
  506 Hwy. 51 Bypass, 901/285-1573

Best Coffeehouse
Old Hickory House
  Hwy. 51N, 901/285-2702

Best Desserts
Mom's
  Lake Dr. on Reelfoot Lake, 901/253-7303
Plaza Restaurant
  Hwy. 51N, 901/287-7893

Best Happy Hour Snacks
Terrace Restaurant
  Holiday Inn, Hwy. 78 at Hwy. 51, 901/285-8601

Best Homestyle Food
Mom's
  Lake Dr. on Reelfoot Lake, 901/253-7303

Best Place to Be "Seen"
Terrace Restaurant
  Holiday Inn, Hwy. 78 at Hwy. 51, 901/285-8601

Best Place to Eat When Someone Else Is Buying
Neil's Barbeque and Grill
  470 Mall Blvd., Bldg. A, 901/287-8400

Best Romantic Dining
Daddy Jack's Steak and Seafood
  835 Hwy. 51N Bypass, 901/286-6744

Best Salad/Salad Bar
Grecian Steak House
  2265 St. John Ave., 901/286-6842

Best Seafood
Daddy Jack's Steak and Seafood
  835 Hwy. 51N Bypass, 901/286-6744

Best Steaks
Tennessee Rib Eye
   1130 Henry St., 901/285-4648

Standbys
Dairy Queen
   832 Main Ave. S., 901/285-1111
Domino's Pizza
   304 W. Court St., 901/285-3030

JACKSON, TN

Best Restaurant in Town
Dixie Castle
   215 E. Baltimore St., 901/423-3359

Best Breakfast
Old Country Store on the Square
   110 S. Liberty St., 901/423-8696

Best Homestyle Food
Dumplin's of Jackson
   31C Wiley Parker Rd., 901/664-4959

Best Italian Food
Baudo's Restaurant
   559 Wiley Parker Rd., 901/668-1447
Old Town Spaghetti Store
   550 Carriage House Dr., 901/668-4937

Best Mexican Food
Los Portales
   1652 S. Highland Ave., 901/424-2484
   127 Old Hickory Blvd., 901/664-6217
   19B Stonebrook Pl., 901/661-9041

Best Seafood
Catfish Cabin
   1290 S. Highland Ave., 901/422-1001

Best Steaks
Dixie Castle
   215 E. Baltimore St., 901/423-3359

Standbys
Ryan's Family Steakhouse
   71 Stonebrook Pl., 901/668-7472
Subway
   660 Carriage House Dr., 901/668-1678
   955C N. Parkway, 901/424-9297

JOHNSON CITY, TN

Best American Food
Cheers Restaurant
   1905 N. Roan St., 423/929-1023

Best Atmosphere
Fuji House
   1804 N. Eastman Rd., Ste. 4, Kingsport, 423/247-1688

Best Casual Dining
Cheers Restaurant
   1905 N. Roan St., 423/929-1023
Down Home
   300 W. Main St., 423/929-9822

T

Best Chinese Food
Golden Dragon
  1735 W. State of Franklin Rd., 423/928-5068
Fuji House
  1804 N. Eastman Rd., Ste. 4, Kingsport, 423/247-1688

Best Italian Food
Italian Garden Pizza
  750 Gray Station Rd., 423/477-5823

Best Lunch
Mingle's Delicatessen and Pizza
  2100 N. Greenwood Dr., 423/928-8609

Best Pizza
Crazy Tomato Pizza Pasta
  203 Princeton Rd., 423/283-0211

Best Sandwiches
Poor Richard's Deli
  825 W. Walnut St., 423/926-8611
  106 Mountcastle Dr., 423/282-8711

Standbys
Lone Star Steakhouse
  1805 N. Roan St., 423/929-3136

KINGSPORT, TN

Best Brunch
Eugene's
  Ramada Inn, 2005 Lamasa Dr., 423/245-0271

Best Steaks
Skoby's Restaurant
  1001 Konnarock Rd., 423/245-2761

Best Takeout Restaurant
Pal's
  4224 Fort Henry Dr., 423/239-3442
  1316 Lynn Garden Dr., 423/245-2871
  1120 E. Stone Dr., 423/246-2309

Standbys
Pizza Hut
  807 Lynn Garden Dr., 423/245-6659
  1616 E. Stone Dr., 423/245-8181
  4500 University Blvd., 423/247-2791
  1901 Fort Henry Dr., 423/245-1951

KNOXVILLE, TN

Best Restaurants in Town
Naples Italian Restaurant
  5500 Kingston Pike, 423/584-5033
The Orangery
  5412 Kingston Pike, 423/588-2964
Regas
  318 N. Gay St., 423/637-9805

Best All-You-Can-Eat Buffet
Mandarin House
  8111 Gleason Rd., 423/694-0350

Best American Food
Litton's Diner
  1612 Downtown W., 423/690-2345

Best Appetizers
Copper Cellar
  1807 Cumberland Ave., 423/673-3411
  3001 Industrial Pkwy. E., 423/5223500
  7316 Kingston Pike, 423/673-3422

Best Asian Restaurants
China Inn
  6450 Kingston Pike, 423/588-7815
Mandarin House
  8111 Gleason Rd., 423/694-0350
Stir Fry Cafe
  7240 Kingston Pike, 423/588-7815
Malaysia
  6761 Clinton Hwy., 423/947-3333

Best Atmosphere
King Tut's Grill
  4123 Martin Mill Pike, 423/573-6021

Best Bar
Ivory's
  4705 Old Kingston Pike, 423/588-6023

Best Barbecue/Ribs
Buddy's
  3700 E. Magnolia Ave., 423/523-3550
  4401 Chapman Hwy., 423/579-1747
  4500 N. Broadway St., 423/687-2959
  5806 Kingston Pike, 423/584-1924
  8402 Kingston Pike, 423/691-0088
Calhoun's
  10020 Kingston Pike, 423/673-3444
  400 Neyland Dr., 423/673-3355
Corky's
  260 N. Peters Rd., 423/690-3137

Best Beer Selection
Smoky Mountain Brewing Company
  424 S. Gay St., 423/673-8400

Best Bread
The Big Easy
  125 E. Jackson Ave., 423/523-7711

Best Brunch
Copper Cellar
  1807 Cumberland Ave., 423/673-3411
  3001 Industrial Pkwy. E., 423/5223500
  7316 Kingston Pike, 423/673-3422
Darryl's
  5616 Merchants Center Blvd., 423/688-1792
  6604 Kingston Pike, 423/584-1879
Country Garden
  Hyatt Regency, 500 Hill Ave., 423/637-1234
Chesapeake's
  500 Henley St., 423/673-3433

Best Burgers
Litton's Diner
  2803 Essary Rd., 423/688-0429
  2813 Essary Rd., 423/687-8788
Bel Air Grill
  9117 Executive Park Dr., 423/694-0606

Best Business Lunch
Regas
  318 N. Gay St., 423/637-9805

Best Cafeterias
Morrison's
  7600 Kingston Pike, 423/693-0383
  East Town Mall, Ste. 3052, 423/522-5952
Sand's
  4808 Kingston Pike, 423/584-5191
  9379 Kingston Pike, 423/694-6005

Best Cajun/Creole Food
The Big Easy
  125 E. Jackson Ave., 423/523-7711

Best Cheap Meal
King Tut's Grill
  4123 Martin Mill Pike, 423/573-6021
Little Italy Subs and Pizza
  5104A Kingston Pike, 423/584-1204
Malaysia
  6761 Clinton Hwy., 423/947-3333

Best Coffeehouse
Java
  109 1/2 S. Central St., 423/525-1600

Best Continental Food
The Orangery
  5412 Kingston Pike, 423/588-2964

Best Delicatessens
Harold's Kosher Deli
  131 S. Gay St., 423/523-5315
New York Bagel and Deli
  4622 Kingston Pike, 423/588-1364

Best Desserts
Smokey Mountain Brewing Company
  424 S. Gay St., 423/673-8400

Best Diners
Sutherland Deli
  2011 Euclid Ave., 423/524-6272
Summit Diner
  137 S. Central St., 423/546-8301

Best Eclectic Menu
The Sunspot
  1909 Cumberland Ave., 423/524-3380

Best Family Restaurant
The Silver Spoon Cafe
  7240 Kingston Pike, 423/584-1066

Best French Food
The Orangery
  5412 Kingston Pike, 423/588-2964

Best Health-Conscious Menu
The Sunspot
  1909 Cumberland Ave., 423/524-3380

Best Indian Food
The Elephant Room
  102 S. Central, 423/637-4002

Best Italian Food
Italian Market and Grill
  9648 Kingston Pike, 423/690-2600
Naples Italian Restaurant
  5500 Kingston Pike, 423/584-5033

Best Late-Night Food
Vic and Bill's
  1501 White Ave., 423/524-9863

Best Mexican Food
Cancun
  4409 Chapman Hwy., 423/577-8881
  4829 N. Broadway St., 423/688-4030
Garcia's
  1516 Downtown West Blvd., 423/690-9910
La Paz
  8025 Kingston Pike, 423/690-5250
La Carretta
  411 Broadway St., 423/689-4631

Best Middle Eastern Food
King Tut's Grill
  4123 Martin Mill Pike, 423/573-6021

Best Other Ethnic Food
Dad's Cafe and Restaurant (Lebanese)
  5032 Whitaker Dr., 615/584-2143

Best Pizza
Stefano's
  11531 Kingston Pike, 423/671-0500
  1937 Cumberland Ave., 423/522-4151
  7213 Kingston Pike, 423/588-1841
  9111 Executive Park Dr., Ste. 5C, 423/539-0033
Tomato Head
  12 Market Square Mall, 423/637-4067

Best Place to Be "Seen"
Michael's
  7049 Kingston Pike, 423/588-2455

Best Place to Eat Alone
Little Italian Subs and Pizza
  5104A Kingston Pike, 423/584-1204

Best Places to Eat When Someone Else Is Buying
The Orangery
  5412 Kingston Pike, 423/588-2964
The Painted Table
  9000 Kingston Pike, 423/470-2286

Best Quick Lunch
Little Italian Subs and Pizza
  5104A Kingston Pike, 423/584-1204

Best Romantic Dining
Italian Market and Grill
  9648 Kingston Pike, 423/690-2600
Naples Italian Restaurant
  5500 Kingston Pike, 423/584-5033
The Orangery
  5412 Kingston Pike, 423/588-2964
The Melting Pot
  111 N. Central, 423/971-5400

Best Salad/Salad Bar
Grady's
  318 N. Peters Rd., 423/694-4663
  6739A Kingston Pike, 423/584-4663
Silver Spoon Cafe
  7240 Kingston Pike, 423/584-1066
Tomato Head
  12 Market Square Mall, 423/637-4067

Best Sandwiches
Harold's Kosher Deli
  131 S. Gay St., 423/523-5315
New York Bagel and Deli
  4622 Kingston Pike, 423/588-1364
Sam and Andy's
  717 Eighteenth St., 423/524-9527
Vic and Bill's
  1501 White Ave., 423/524-9863

Best Seafood
Chesapeake's
  500 Henley St., 423/673-3433
Shrimp Shack
  8027 Kingston Pike, 423/539-1700

Best Schmooze Bar
Michael's
  7049 Kingston Pike, 423/588-2455

Best Sports Bar
Hooray's
  106 S. Central St., 423/546-6729

Best Steaks
Chop House
  9700 Kingston Pike, 423/531-2677
Regas
  318 N. Gay St., 423/637-9805
Ye Olde Steak House
  6838 Chapman Hwy., 423/577-9328
Vic and Bill's
  1501 White Ave., 423/524-9863

Best Vegetarian Food
Falafel Hut
  601 Fifteenth St., 423/522-4963
The Sunspot
  1909 Cumberland Ave., 423/524-3380
Tjaarda's
  118 S. Central, 423/637-8702
China Inn
  6450 Kingston Pike, 423/588-7815

Best Wine Selection
The Orangery
  5412 Kingston Pike, 423/588-2964

MARYVILLE, TN

Best Breakfast
Four-Eleven Restaurant
  2635 Hwy. 11S, 423/982-7346

Best Chinese Food
Panda Garden
  2129 E. Broadway Ave., 423/981-4900

Best Delicatessen
All American Deli
  245 Calderwood Hwy., 423/982-3139

Best Homestyle Food
Four-Eleven Restaurant
  2635 Hwy. 11S, 423/982-7346

Best Italian Food
Alexandro's Ristorante
  218 S. Calderwood St., 423/984-2539

Best Lunch
Morningside Inn
  1406 Wilkinson Pike, 423/982-1735

Best Mexican Food
Los Amigos
  409 N. Cusick St., 423/983-6022

Best Sandwiches
Ham and Goody's
  227 W. Broadway Ave., 423/983-2680

MEMPHIS, TN

Best Asian Restaurants
Ping's Garden
  3700 Ridgeway, 901/365-9898
Saigon Le
  51 N. Cleveland, 901/276-5326

Best Barbecue/Ribs
Cozy Corner
  745 North Parkway, 901/527-9158
Interstate Bar-B-Q
  2265 S. Third, 901/775-2921
John Wills
  5101 Sanderlin, 901/761-5101
Neely's
  5700 Mt. Moriah, 901/795-4177
  670 Jefferson, 901/521-9798

Best Bistros
Bistro 122
  5101 Sanderlin, 901/761-0663
Lulu Grille
  565 Erin Dr., 901/763-3677

Best Burgers
Automatic Slim's
  83 S. Second, 901/525-7948

T

Belmont Grill
  4970 Poplar, 901/767-0305
Fox Ridge Pizza
  5950 Knight Arnold, 901/794-8876
Huey's
  1927 Madison Ave., 901/726-4372
  2858 Hickory Hill Rd., 901/375-4373

Best Business Lunch
Bistro 122
  5101 Sanderlin Ave., 901/761-0663
Cafe Society
  212 N. Evergreen, 901/722-2177

Best Greek/Mediterranean Food
Melos Taverna
  2021 Madison, 901/725-1863

Best Homestyle Food
Buntyn
  3070 Southern Ave., 901/458-8776
The Cupboard
  1495 Union, 901/276-8015
Ferguson's
  2794 Coleman, 901/383-1101
  3171 Summer, 901/458-2728
Yellow Rose Cafe
  56 N. Main, 901/527-5692

Best Indian Food
Delhi Palace
  6100 Macon Rd., 901/386-3600

Best Italian Food
The Original Grisanti's
  1489 Airways Blvd., 901/458-2648
Romano's Macaroni Grill
  6705 Poplar Ave., 901/753-6588

Best Japanese Food
Sekisui of Japan
  50 Humphreys Blvd., 901/747-0001

Best Mexican Food
Acapulco
  3681 Jackson, 901/386-1199
El Jardin
  1607 Getwell Rd., 901/743-0594
Molly's La Casita
  2006 Madison Ave., 901/726-1873
  4972 Park Ave., 901/685-1616

Best Other Ethnic Food
Automatic Slim's (Caribbean)
  83 S. Second St., 901/525-7948
In Limbo (Caribbean)
  928 S. Cooper, 901/726-4999
Lupe and Bea's (Cuban)
  394 N. Watkins, 901/726-9877

Best Pizza
Bosco's Pizza Kitchen and Brewery
  2250 West St., Germantown, 901/7567310

Broadway Pizza
  2581 Broad Ave., 901/454-7930
Pete and Sam's
  3886 Park Ave., 901/458-0694

Best Soul Food
Fourway Grill
  998 Mississippi Blvd., 901/775-2351
Miss Ellen's
  601 South Parkway E., 901/942-4888

Best Steaks
Jim's Place East
  5560 Shelby Oaks Dr., 901/388-7200
Pete and Sam's
  3886 Park Ave., 901/458-0694

MORRISTOWN, TN

Best Restaurant in Town
Angelo's
  3614 W. Andrew Johnson Hwy., 423/581-4882

Best All-You-Can-Eat Buffet
Luby's Cafeteria
  College Square Mall, 2550 E. Morris Blvd.,
  423/587-1966

Best Atmosphere
Angelo's
  3614 W. Andrew Johnson Hwy., 423/581-4882

Best Barbecue/Ribs
Richey's Bar-B-Que Shoppe
  1414 W. Andrew Johnson Hwy., 423/586-3665

Best Homestyle Food
Mountain Woods Cookin'
  1336 W. Andrew Johnson Hwy., 423/586-4070

Best Mexican Food
Mexico Lindo
  3351 W. Andrew Johnson Hwy., 423/587-9754

Best Salad/Salad Bar
Justin's Restaurant
  1825 W. Andrew Johnson Hwy., 423/581-8343

Best Sandwiches
Mustard Seed Cafe
  333 E. Main St., Oak Ridge, 423/4829952

Best Steaks
Little Dutch Restaurant
  115 S. Cumberland St., 423/581-1441

Standbys
Quincy's
  1114 W. First North St., 423/587-2850
Shoney's
  1933 W. Andrew Johnson Hwy., 423/581-0800

T

MURFREESBORO, TN

Best Restaurants in Town
Chesney's
  1695 Memorial Blvd., 615/896-5588
City Cafe
  113 E. Main St., 615/893-1303

Best American Food
Demo's Steak and Spaghetti House
  1115 NW Broad St., 615/895-3701
Front Porch Cafe
  114 E. College St., 615/896-6771
H.R.H. Dumplin's
  107 E. Main St., 615/895-1776

Best Barbecue/Ribs
Bar-B-Cutie
  905 Old Fort Pkwy., 615/980-9470

Best Chinese Food
Hunan Chinese Restaurant
  2112 S. Church St., 615/893-7008

Best Homestyle Food
Clearview Restaurant
  222 S. Highland Ave., 615/896-0520

Best Lunch
City Cafe
  113 E. Main St., 615/373-5555
Clearview Restaurant
  222 S. Highland Ave., 615/896-0520

Best Mexican Food
Camino Real
  301 NW Broad St., 615/890-1412

Best Pizza
Mazzio's Pizza
  1624 Memorial Blvd., 615/895-8646

Best Steaks
Logan's Roadhouse
  740 NW Broad St., 615/895-4419

NASHVILLE, TN

T

Best Restaurants in Town
Cakewalk
  3001 West End Ave., 615/320-7778
Capitol Grill
  Hermitage Hotel, Sixth at Union, 615/244-3121
Bound'ry
  911 Twentieth Ave. S., 615/321-3043
Houston's
  3000 West End Ave., 615/269-3481
The Mad Platter
  1239 Sixth Ave. N., 615/242-2563
Sunset Grill
  2001 Belcourt Ave., 615/386-3663
Antonio's
  7097 Old Harding Pike, 615/646-9166
Choices
  108 Fourth Ave. S., Franklin, 615/7948696

Green Hills Grille
  2122 Hillsboro Dr., 615/383-6444

Best All-You-Can-Eat Buffets
New Orleans Manor
  1400 Murfreesboro Rd., 615/367-2777
Golden Dragon
  81 White Bridge Rd., 615/356-1110
  1795 Gallatin Rd. N., Madison, 615/865-6854
  104 Saunders Ferry Rd., Hendersonville,
    615/264-2126
  4115 Lebanon Rd., Hermitage, 615/889-9577
Evergreen Restaurant
  1141 Bell Rd., 615/731-2777
Opryland Buffet
  Opryland Hotel, 2800 Opryland Dr., 615/871-6848

Best Atmosphere
Cafe One Two Three
  123 Twelfth Avenue N., 615/255-2233
Twelfth and Porter
  114 Twelfth Ave. N., 615/254-7236

Best Bars
O'Charley's
  1108 Murfreesboro Rd., 615/361-3651
  17 White Bridge Rd., 615/356-1344
  5500 Old Hickory Blvd., 615/883-6993
Rio Bravo
  3015 West End Ave., 615/329-1745

Best Barbecue/Ribs
Bar-B-Cutie
  501 Donelson Pike, 615/872-0207
  5221 Nolensville Pike, 615/834-6556
Calhoun's
  2001 Gallatin Rd. N., 615/859-1050
  96 White Bridge Rd., 615/356-0855
Corky's
  100 Franklin Rd., Brentwood, 615/3731020
Houston's
  300 West End Ave., 615/269-3481
Whitt's Barbecue
  5310 Harding Road, 615/356-3435
  3621 Nolensville Road, 615/831-0309
  5211 Alabama Ave., 615/385-1553
  2535 Lebanon Road, 615/883-6907
  1800 Antioch Pike, 615/331-5936
  4601A Andrew Jackson Pkwy., Hermitage,
    615/885-4146

Best Breakfast
Loveless Cafe
  Loveless Motel, 8400 Hwy. 100, 615/646-9700
Pancake Pantry
  1724 21st Ave. S., 615/383-9333

Best Brunch
Mere Bulles
  152 Second Ave. N., 615/256-2582
Cakewalk
  3001 West End Ave., 615/320-7778

T

Nashville Country Club
　1811 Broadway, 615/321-0066
O'Charley's
　1108 Murfreesboro Rd., 615/361-3651
　17 White Bridge Rd., 615/356-1344
　5500 Old Hickory Blvd., 615/883-6993
Opryland Hotel
　2800 Opryland Dr., 615/889-1000

Best Burgers
Brown's Diner
　2102 Blair Blvd., 615/269-5509
Rotier's
　2413 Elliston Pl., 615/327-9892
Fat Mo's
　946 Richards Rd., 615/781-1830
　2620 Franklin Rd., 615/298-1111

Best Business Lunch
Houston's
　300 West End Ave., 615/269-3481
The Merchants
　401 Broadway, 615/254-1892
Mere Bulles
　152 Second Ave. N., 615/256-2582
Jules Dining Hall and Bar Car
　209 Tenth Ave. S., 615/259-4875
Sunset Grill
　2001 Belcourt Ave., 615/386-3663
Satsuma Tea Room
　417 Union Ave., 615/256-0760
Midtown Cafe
　102 Nineteenth Ave. S., 615/320-7176
Nashville Country Club
　1811 Broadway, 615/321-0066
Wild Boar
　2014 Broadway, 615/329-1313
Granite Falls
　2000 Broadway, 615/327-9250

Best Catfish
Cock of the Walk
　2624 Music Valley Dr., 615/889-1930
Sportsman's Grille
　5405 Harding Pike, 615/356-6206
Uncle Bud's
　1214 Lakeview Dr., 615/790-1234
　714 Stewarts Ferry Pike, 615/872-7700

Best Cheap Meal
Arnold's Country Kitchen
　605 Eighth Ave. S., 615/256-4455
Elliston Place Soda Shop
　2111 Elliston Pl., 615/327-1090
August Moon
　7075 Hwy. 70S, 615/646-5333
　4004 Hillsboro Rd., 615/298-9999
　116 Wilson Pike, 615/371-1999
International Market and Restaurant
　2010B Belmont Blvd., 615/297-4453

Best Chinese Food
August Moon
  7075 Hwy. 70S, 615/646-5333
  4004 Hillsboro Rd., 615/298-9999
  116 Wilson Pike, 615/371-1999
Golden Dragon
  81 White Bridge Rd., 615/356-1110
  1795 Gallatin Rd. N., Madison, 615/865-6854
  104 Saunders Ferry Rd., Hendersonville,
    615/264-2126
  115 Lebanon Rd., Hermitage, 615/889-9577

Best Coffeehouses
Bongo Java
  2007 Belmont Blvd., 615/385-5282
Cafe Elliston
  10 Louise Ave., 615/329-0024
Bean Central
  817 West End Ave., 615/321-8530
Cafe Milano
  176 Third Ave. N., 615/255-0073

Best Diner
Brown's Diner
  2102 Blair Blvd., 615/269-5509

Best Desserts
Cakewalk
  3001 West End Ave., 615/320-7778
Sunset Grill
  2001 Belcourt Ave., 615/386-3663
The Cooker Bar and Grille
  1211 Murfreesboro Rd., 615/361-4747
  2609 West End Ave., 615/327-2925
  317 Bluebird Dr., Goodlettsville, 615/859-2756
  4770 Lebanon Rd., Hermitage, 615/883-9700
Sylvan Park Restaurant
  2201 Bandywood Dr., 615/292-6449
  221 Sixth Ave. N., 615/255-1562
  4502 Murphy Rd., 615/292-9275
  5207 Nolensville Rd., 615/781-3077

Best Eclectic Menu
Cafe One Two Three
  123 Twelfth Ave. N., 615/255-2233
Twelfth and Porter
  114 Twelfth Ave. N., 615/254-7236
Jules Dining Hall and Bar Car
  209 Tenth Ave. S., 615/259-4875

Best Greek/Mediterranean Food
Demetri's
  3415 West End Ave., 615/385-1929
Tabouli's
  2015 Belmont Blvd., 615/386-0106

Best Health-Conscious Menu
Country Life Vegetarian Restaurant
  1917-19 Division St., 615/327-3695
Garden Allegro
  1805 Church St., 615/327-3834

T

Slice of Life
  1811 Division St., 615/329-2525
Green Hills Grille
  2122 Hillsboro Dr., 615/383-6444

Best Homestyle Food
Arnold's Country Kitchen
  605 Eighth Ave. S., 615/256-4455
Rotier's
  2413 Elliston Pl., 615/327-9892
Hap Townes Restaurant
  493 Humphreys, 615/242-7035
Elliston Place Soda Shop
  2111 Elliston Pl., 615/327-1090
Sylvan Park Restaurant
  2201 Bandywood Dr., 615/292-6449
  221 Sixth Ave. N., 615/255-1562
  4502 Murphy Rd., 615/292-9275
  5207 Nolensville Rd., 615/781-307
Mack's Cafe
  2009 Broadway, 615/327-0700
Belle Meade Buffet
  4534 Harding Rd., 615/615/298-5571

Best Indian Food
Sitar
  116 21st Ave. N., 615/321-8888
Shalimar
  4111 Hillsboro Rd., 615/269-8577

Best Italian Food
Sole Mio
  94 Peabody St., 615/256-4013
Amerigo
  1920 West End Ave., 615/320-1740
Finezza Trattoria
  5404 Harding Pike, 615/356-9398
Caesar's
  88 White Bridge Rd., 615/352-3661
Romano's Macaroni Grill
  1712 Galleria Blvd., Franklin, 615/771-7002

Best Japanese Food
Goten Japanese Restaurant
  110 21st Ave. S., 615/321-4537

Best Mexican Food
La Paz
  3808 Cleghorn Ave., 615/383-5200
Las Palmas
  1400 Antioch Pike, 615/831-0863
  5511 Charlotte Pike, 615/352-0313
  803 Two Mile Pkwy., 615/851-7315
Rio Bravo
  3015 West End Ave., 615/329-1745
Camino Real
  548 Alexander Plaza, Franklin, 615/790-3104

Best Microbreweries
Blackstone
  1918 West End Ave., 615/327-9969

The Gerst Haus
  228 Woodland St., 615/256-9760
Big River Grille and Brewing Works
  111 Broadway, 615/251-4677
Market Street Brewery
  134 Second Ave. N., 615/259-9611

Best Outdoor Dining
Rio Bravo
  3015 West End Ave., 615/329-1745
Granite Falls
  2000 Broadway, 615/327-9250
San Antonio Taco Company
  208 Commerce St., 615/259-4413
  416 21st Ave. S., 615/327-4322
Sunset Grill
  2001 Belcourt Ave., 615/386-3663

Best Pizza
DaVinci's
  1812 Hayes St., 615/329-8098
Obie's Flying Tomato
  2217 Elliston Pl., 615/327-4772
Pizza Perfect
  1602 21st Ave. S., 615/329-2757
  4002 Granny White Pike, 615/2970345

Best Places to Eat When Someone Else Is Buying
Capitol Grill
  Hermitage Hotel, Sixth at Union, 615/244-3121
Mario's Italian Restaurant
  2005 Broadway, 615/327-3232
The Mad Platter
  1239 Sixth Ave. N., 615/242-2563
Morton's of Chicago
  625 Church St., 615/259-4558
Cakewalk
  3001 West End Ave., 615/320-7778
Arthur's
  Union Station Hotel, 1001 Broadway, 615/255-1494

Best Place to Take the Kids
Dalt's
  38 White Bridge Rd., 615/352-8121

Best Romantic Dining
Arthur's
  1001 Broadway, 615/255-1494
F. Scott's
  2210 Crestmoor Rd., 615/269-5861
Cafe One Two Three
  123 Twelfth Ave. N., 615-255-2233
Capitol Grill
  Hermitage Hotel, Sixth at Union, 615/244-3121
The Mad Platter
  1239 Sixth Ave. N., 615/242-2563

Best Salad/Salad Bar
Houston's
  3000 West End Ave., 615/269-3481

T

J. Alexander's
  1721 Galleria Blvd., Franklin, 615/771-7779
  73 White Bridge Rd., 615/352-0981
Cooker Bar and Grille
  1211 Murfreesboro Rd., 615/361-4747
  2609 West End Ave., 615/327-2925
  317 Bluebird Dr., Goodlettsville, 615/859-2756
  4770 Lebanon Rd., Hermitage, 615/883-9700

Best Sandwiches
Jonathan's Village Cafe
  1803 21st Ave. S., 615/385-9301
Pizza Perfect
  1602 21st Ave. S., 615/329-2757
  4002 Granny White Pike, 615/297-0345
Mosko's Muncheonette
  2204 Elliston Pl., 615/327-2658
Sub Stop
  1701 Broadway, 615/255-6482

Best Schmooze Bars
Ace of Clubs
  114 Second Ave. S., 615/254-2237
Big Daddy's
  1204 Murfreesboro Pike, 615/361-9922
Club Mere Bulles
  152 Second Ave. N., 615/256-2582

Best Seafood
Florida Seafood Kitchen
  3798 Nolensville Pike, 615/832-5081
Laurell's Second Avenue Oyster Bar
  176 Second Ave. N., 615/256-1026
New Orleans Manor
  1400 Murfreesboro Rd., 615/367-2777

Best Sports Bars
Box Seat
  2221 Bandywood Dr., 615/383-8018
Jonathan's Village Cafe
  1803 21st Ave. S., 615/385-9301
Sportsman's Grille
  1601 21st Ave. S., 615/320-1633
  5405 Harding Pl., 615/356-6206

Best Steaks
Jimmy Kelly's
  217 Louise Ave., 615/329-4349
Logan's Roadhouse
  5300 Hickory Hollow Ln., 615/731-4022
  1715 Gallatin Pike N., Goodlettsville, 615/860-9220
Morton's of Chicago
  625 Church St., 615/259-4558

Best Tea Rooms
The Towne House Tea Room
  165 Eighth Ave. N., 615/254-1277
Satsuma Tea Room
  417 Union Ave., 615/256-0760

Best Thai Food
The Orchid
  73 White Bridge Rd., 615/353-9411

Siam Cafe
  316 McCall St., 615/834-3181

Best Vegetarian Food
Country Life Vegetarian Restaurant
  1917-19 Division St., 615/327-3695
Garden Allegro
  1805 Church St., 615/327-3834
Slice of Life
  1811 Division St., 615/329-2525

Best Wine Selection
Mario's Italian Restaurant
  2005 Broadway, 615/327-3232
Capitol Grill
  Hermitage Hotel, Sixth at Union, 615/244-3121

OAK RIDGE, TN

Best Restaurant in Town
Bleu Hound Grill
  80 E. Tennessee Ave., 423/481-6101

Best American Food
Simply Divine
  213 Jackson Sq., 423/482-0077

Best Breakfast
Daily Grind
  221 Jackson Sq., 423/483-9200

Best Chinese Food
Magic Wok
  202 Tyler Rd., 423/482-6628

Best Coffee
Daily Grind
  221 Jackson Sq., 423/483-9200

Best Continental Food
Bleu Hound Grill
  80 E. Tennessee Ave., 423/481-6101

Best Homestyle Food
Village Restaurant
  123 Central Ave., 423/483-1675

Best Pasta
Simply Divine
  213 Jackson Sq., 423/482-0077

Best Pizza
Time-Out Deli
  138 Randolph Rd., 423/483-7349

Best Sandwiches
Time-Out Deli
  138 Randolph Rd., 423/483-7349

PULASKI, TN

Best Atmosphere
Heritage House Restaurant
  219 S. Third St., 615/363-2313
Legends Restaurant
  1030 W. College St., 615/363-5612

T

Best Barbecue/Ribs
Lawler's Barbecue
  Hwy. 64, 615/363-3515
Reed's Barbecue
  821 Mill St., 615/363-0320
Legends Restaurant
  1030 W. College St., 615/363-5612

Best Breakfast
Jim's Diner
  425 S. First St., 615/363-9120
Reeves Drug Store
  125 N. First St., 615/363-2561

Best Burgers
Jim's Diner
  425 S. First St., 615/363-9120
Lawler's Barbecue
  Hwy. 64, 615/363-3515

Best Coffee
Bluebird Cafe
  124 S. First St., 615/363-4681
Reeves Drug Store
  125 N. First St., 615/363-2561

Best Desserts
Green Valley General Store
  Hurricane Creek Rd., 615/363-6562

Best Homestyle Food
Heritage House Restaurant
  219 S. Third St., 615/363-2313
Tater Patch
  1665 W. College St., 615/363-4224

Best Ice Cream/Yogurt
Reeves Drug Store
  125 N. First St., 615/363-2561
Green Valley General Store
  Hurricane Creek Rd., 615/363-6562

Best Pizza
Jeb's
  108 S. Second St., 615/424-8038

Best Sandwiches
Tater Patch
  1665 W. College St., 615/363-4224

Best Steaks
Legends Restaurant
  1030 W. College St., 615/363-5612
Sarge's Shack
  Hwy. 64 at Hwy. 65 Exit 14, 615/363-1310

UNION CITY, TN

Best All-You-Can-Eat Buffet
Dixie Barn
  1315 N. Old Troy Rd., 901/885-3663

Best Barbecue/Ribs
Corner Bar B-Q
  1425 E. Reelfoot Ave., 901/885-9924

Best Burgers
P.V.'s Hut
   209 E. Florida St., 901/885-5737

Best Chinese Food
New Jade Chinese Restaurant
   1413 S. First St., 901/885-9999

Best Desserts
Dumplin's
   206 E. Reelfoot Ave., Ste. 3, 901/885-9028

Best Homestyle Food
Dixie Barn
   1315 N. Old Troy Rd., 901/885-3663
Searcy's Cafeteria
   306 S. First St., 901/885-0332
Dumplin's
   206 E. Reelfoot Ave., Ste. 3, 901/885-9028

Best Pizza
Olympia Pizza and Steak House
   1705 W. Reelfoot Ave., 901/885-3611
Snappy Tomato
   509 First St., 901/885-7627

Best Steaks
Olympia Pizza and Steak House
   1705 W. Reelfoot Ave., 901/885-3611

Standbys
Dairy Queen
   100 S. Miles Ave., 901/885-1001
Shoney's
   Hwy. 51N, 901/885-7754

T

Texas

Best Atmosphere
Perini Ranch Steak House
   Hwy. 89, Buffalo Gap, 915/572-3339

Best Barbecue/Ribs
Joe Allen's Pit Bar-B-Que
   1233 S. Treadway Blvd., 915/672-6082

Best Breakfast
Kettle Restaurant
   1750 E. I-20, 915/672-4545
   3374 Turner Plz., 915/692-4280

Best Burgers
Tucson's Family Bar and Grill
   3370 N. First St., 915/676-8279
Georgia B's Diner
   3905 S. First St., 915/675-5170

Best Business Lunch
Tucson's Family Bar and Grill
   3370 N. First St., 915/676-8279

Best Chinese Food
China Star
   3601 S. First St., 915/677-2000

Best Coffee
McLemore-Bass
   2136 Pine St., 915/673-8882

Best Diner
Georgia B's Diner
   3905 S. First St., 915/675-5170

Best Family Restaurants
Furr's Cafeteria
   3350 S. Clack St., 915/692-8330
Tucson's Family Bar and Grill
   3370 N. First St., 915/676-8279
Luby's Cafeteria
   4310 Buffalo Gap Rd., Ste. 1184, 915/695-2000

T

st Homestyle Food
etty Rose's
2402 S. Seventh St., 915/673-5809

Best Japanese Food
Shogun Japanese Steak House
3130 S. Clack St., 915/695-6660

Best Mexican Food
Dos Amigos
3650 N. Sixth St., 915/672-2992

Best Outdoor Dining
Perini Ranch Steak House
Hwy. 89, Buffalo Gap, 915/572-3339

Best Pizza
Crystal's Pizza and Spaghetti
2201 S. First St., 915/672-5616
Cici's Pizza
3366 Turner Plz., 915/692-1660

Best Places to Eat When Someone Else Is Buying
Outpost
3126 S. Clack St., 915/692-3595
Perini Ranch Steak House
Hwy. 89, Buffalo Gap, 915/572-3339

Best Place to Take the Kids
Mr. Gatti's Pizza
2665 Buffalo Gap Rd., 915/692-6326

Best Romantic Dining
Perini Ranch Steak House
Hwy. 89, Buffalo Gap, 915/572-3339

Best Salad/Salad Bar
Greenjeans Salad Bar Plus
4646 S. Fourteenth St., 915/692-1772

Best Seafood
Cahoots Catfish and Oyster Bar
301 S. Eleventh St., 915/672-6540
Perini Ranch Steak House
Hwy. 89, Buffalo Gap, 915/572-3339

Best Tea Room
Hickory Street Cafe
644 Hickory St., 915/675-0465

Best View While Dining
The Petroleum Club of Abilene
500 Chestnut St., 915/677-5218

Standbys
Chili's
4302 S. Clack St., 915/698-1660
International House of Pancakes
3750 S. Clack St., 915/695-2432
Golden Corral Family Steak House
4101 S. Danville Dr., 915/692-4592
Baskin-Robbins
3510 N. First St., 915/675-0431
4102 Buffalo Gap Rd., 915/698-9031
The Olive Garden
3210 S. Clack St., 915/691-0388

El Chico
  4310 Buffalo Gap Rd., 915/695-2875
Western Sizzlin'
  1802 S. Clack St., 915/698-4340
Red Lobster
  1280 S. Clack St., 915/695-1191

AMARILLO, TX

Best Barbecue/Ribs
Cattle Call
  Westgate Mall, 7701 W. I-40, Ste. 398, 806/353-1227

Best Breakfast
Carrow's Restaurant
  2116 S. Georgia St., 806/359-9162

Best Burgers
Whataburger
  4111 W. 45th Ave., 806/355-9244
  3401 Coulter Dr., 806/358-8573
  2424 S. Georgia St., 806/359-5472
  734 N. Pierce St., 806/373-8875

Best Business Lunch
Harrigan's Restaurant
  3311 Olsen Blvd., 806/358-8901

Best Casual Dining
Marty's
  2740 Westhaven Village, 806/353-3523

Best Cheap Meal
Mr. Gatti's Pizza
  34th at Western St., 806/355-5601

Best Chinese Food
Peking Chinese Restaurant
  2511 Paramount Blvd., 806/353-9179

Best Coffee
Roasters Coffee and Tea
  2620 Wolflin Village, 806/359-7099

Best Health-Conscious Menu
Bless Your Heart
  2203 Paramount Blvd., 806/351-0055

Best Homestyle Food
All the Fixin's Restaurant
  3333 S. Coulter St., 806/358-7444

Best Ice Cream/Yogurt
Braum's Ice Cream and Dairy
  1700 S. Western St., 806/359-7363
  801 E. Amarillo Blvd., 806/372-3626
  4629 S. Western St., 806/359-7412
  7401 W. 34th Ave., 806/356-9030

Best Late-Night Food
Bennigan's
  3401 W. I-40, 806/358-7409

Best Mexican Food
Los Insurgentes
  3521 W. Fifteenth Ave., 806/353-5361

T

Santa Fe Restaurant and Bar
3333 Coulter Dr., 806/358-8333

Best Pizza
Mr. Gatti's Pizza
34th at Western St., 806/355-5601

Best Place to Eat When Someone Else Is Buying
Harrigan's Restaurant
3311 Olsen Blvd., 806/358-8901

Best Place to Take the Kids
Mr. Gatti's Pizza
34th at Western St., 806/355-5601

Best Regional Food
El Patio
5619 Amarillo Blvd. E., 806/383-8438

Best Seafood
David's Steaks and Seafood
2721 Virginia Circle, 806/355-8171

Best Steaks
Big Texan Steak Ranch
7701 I-40E, 806/273-6000

Best Tea Room
Back Porch Restaurant
3440 Bell St., 806/358-8871

Best Thai Food
Thai Star
3800 Amarillo Blvd. E., 806/383-4727

Standbys
The Olive Garden
4121 W. I-40, 806/355-9973
Steak and Ale
2915 W. I-40, 806/359-1631
Chili's
3810 W. I-40, 806/379-6118

ARLINGTON, TX

Best Atmosphere
Piccolo Mondo Italian Restaurant
829 E. Lamar Blvd., 817/265-09174

Best Bar
J. Gilligan's Bar and Grill
407 E. South St., 817/274-8561

Best Barbecue/Ribs
Spring Creek Barbecue
3608 S. Cooper St., 817/465-0553

Best Bistro
Bistro Bagatelle
406 W. Abram St., 817/261-0488

Best Breakfast
Country Kitchen
1409 N. Collins St., 817/261-5663

Best Burgers
Al's Hamburgers
1001 NE Green Oaks Blvd., Ste. 103, 817/275-8918

Best Business Lunch
Harrigan's Restaurant
944 E. Copeland Rd., 817/277-2400
5900 I-20W, 817/483-9103

Best Cajun/Creole Food
Atchafalaya River Cafe
1520 Stadium Dr. W., 817/261-4696

Best Casual Dining
Mac's Bar and Grill
6077 I-20W, 817/572-0541

Best Chinese Food
China Cafe
3415 S. Cooper St., 817/468-2727

Best Desserts
Tippin's Restaurant and Pie
3321 S. Cooper St., 817/467-7437

Best Family Restaurant
Black-Eyed Pea
1400 N. Collins St., 817/275-8973
3808 S. Cooper St., 817/467-9555

Best French Food
Cacharel
221 E. Lamar Blvd., Ste. 910, 817/640-9981

Best Health-Conscious Menu
Jason's Deli
780 Road to Six Flags E., 817/860-2888

Best Homestyle Food
Hatch's Corner
6950 Forest Hill Dr., Ft. Worth, 817/293-8295

Best Ice Cream/Yogurt
Marble Slab Creamery
780 Road to Six Flags W., 817/277-3363
4261 W. Green Oaks Blvd., 817/483-9960

Best Indian Food
Tandoor The Indian Restaurant
532 Fielder North Plz., 817/261-6604

Best Italian Food
Italian Villa
6033 I-20W, 817/561-2226
Romano's Macaroni Grill
1670 I-20W, 817/784-1197

Best Late-Night Food
Cheddar's Restaurant
4820 Little Rd., 817/572-2966
812 Six Flags Dr., 817/640-6073

Best Microbrewery
Humperdink's Bar and Grill
700 Six Flags Dr., 817/640-8553

T

Best Outdoor Dining
Don Pablo's Restaurant
  3765 S. Cooper St., 817/472-5533
On The Border Cafe
  2011 E. Copeland Rd., 817/261-3598

Best Pizza
Mama's Pizza
  4201 W. Green Oaks Blvd., 817/478-5757

Best Place to Eat Alone
Jason's Deli
  780 Road to Six Flags E., 817/860-2888

Best Place to Eat When Someone Else Is Buying
Cacharel
  221 E. Lamar Blvd., Ste. 910, 817/640-9981

Best Romantic Dining
Cacharel
  221 E. Lamar Blvd., Ste. 910, 817/640-9981

Best Salad/Salad Bar
Souper Salad Restaurant
  1325 I-20W, 817/557-9738

Best Sandwiches
Jason's Deli
  780 Road to Six Flags E., 817/860-2888

Best Sandwiches
Boo Boo's Food Shop
  1130 S. Bowen Rd., 817/274-3641

Best Steaks
Arlington Steak House
  1724 W. Division St., 817/275-7881

Standbys
Golden Corral Family Steak House
  2340 S. Cooper St., 817/557-0018
International House of Pancakes
  701 W. Abram St., 817/275-5602
Cracker Barrel
  4300 S. Bowen Rd., 817/465-9583
  1251 N. Watson Rd., 817/633-5477
Chuck E. Cheese Pizza
  3200 Justiss Dr., 817/649-2933
  2216 S. Fielder Rd., 817/861-1561

T

AUSTIN, TX

Best Restaurants in Town
Mars Restaurant and Bar
  1610 San Antonio, 512/472-3901
Jeffrey's Restaurant
  1204 W. Lynn St., 512/477-5584
Chez Nous
  510 Neches, 512/4732413
Chuy's Restaurant
  10520 N. Lamar Blvd., 512/836-3218
  1728 Barton Springs Rd., 512/474-4452
Mezzaluna
  310 Colorado St., 512/472-6770

Best All-You-Can-Eat Buffets
Hickory Street Bar and Grill
  800 Congress Ave., 512/477-8968
Fonda San Miguel
  2330 W. North Loop Blvd., 512/459-4121
The Cafe at the Four Seasons Hotel
  99 San Jacinto Blvd., 512/478-4500

Best American Food
Threadgill's
  6416 N. Lamar Blvd., 512/451-5440
Good Eats Cafe
  10508 N. Lamar Blvd., 512/832-8291
Hut's
  807 W. Sixth, 512/472-0693

Best Atmosphere
Chuy's Restaurant
  1728 Barton Springs Rd., 512/474-4452

Best Bagels
Hot Jumbo Bagel
  307 W. Fifth St., 512/477-1137
The Bagelry
  13376 N. Hwy. 183, 512/918-9822
  183 Research Blvd., 512/918-9822
  8127 Mesa Dr., Ste. B-202, 512/502-9222
Katz's Deli
  618 W. Sixth St., 512/472-2037

Best Barbecue/Ribs
County Line on the Lake
  5204 Rural Route 2222, 512/346-3664
Ruby's Barbecue and Catering Company
  512 W. 29th St., Ste. A12, 512/477-1651
County Line on the Hill
  6500 Bee Caves Rd., 512/327-1742

Best Beer Selection
Dog and Duck Pub
  406 W. Seventeenth St., 512/479-0598
Maggie Mae's
  512 Trinity St., 512/478-8541
Double Dave's Pizzaworks
  9608 N. Lamar Blvd., 512/476-3283

Best Bread
Texas French Bread
  3213 Red River St., 512/478-8794
  3500 Jefferson St., 512/451-0118
  2330 S. Lamar Blvd., 512/443-9866
  1722 S. Congress Ave., 512/440-1122
  416 Congress Ave., 512/477-8046
  3112A Windsor Rd., 512/478-8845
  2900 Rio Grande St., 512/499-0544
Sweetish Hill Bakery
  98 San Jacinto Blvd., 512/472-2411
  1120 W. Sixth St., 512/472-1347
  922 Congress Ave., 512/477-2442

Best Breakfast
Kerbey Lane Cafe
  3704 Kerbey Ln., 512/451-1436

T

2111 Dixon St., Ste. 10, 512/443-3696
2700 S. Lamar Blvd., 512/445-4451
12602 Research Blvd., 512/258-7757
El Zarape
2103 E. Cesar Chavez, 512/320-0308
Joe's Bakery and Coffee Shop
2305 E. Seventh St., 512/472-0017

Best Brunch
Fonda San Miguel
2330 W. North Loop Blvd., 512/459-4121
The Cafe at the Four Seasons Hotel
99 San Jacinto Blvd., 512/478-4500

Best Burgers
Dan's Hamburgers
1822 S. Congress Ave., 512/444-5738
Dirty's
2808 Guadalupe St., 512/477-3173
Mad Dog and Beans
512 W. 24th, 512/472-2676

Best Cajun/Creole Food
Pappadeaux's Seafood Kitchen
6319 I-35N, 512/452-9363

Best Cheap Meal
Hut's
807 W. Sixth St., 512/472-0693
Rosie's Tamale House
2701 S. Congress Ave., 512/462-9484
13776 Research Blvd., 512/219-7793
13436 Hwy. 7W, 512/263-5245
Dot's Place Cafeteria
13805 Orchid Ln., 512/255-7288

Best Chinese Food
Chinatown
2712 Bee Caves Rd., 512/327-6588
3407 Greystone Dr., 512/343-9307
Suzi's Chinese Kitchen
1152 S. Lamar Blvd., 512/441-8400
Tien Hong
8301 Burnet Rd., 512/458-2263

Best Coffee
Ruta Maya Coffee House
218 W. Fourth St., 512/472-9637
Captain Quackenbush's Cafe
2120 Guadalupe St., 512/472-4477

Best Continental Food
Jeffrey's
1204 W. Lynn St., 512/477-5584

Best Delicatessens
Jason's Deli
9722 Great Hills Trail, 512/345-9586
3300 Bee Caves Rd., 512/328-0200
Katz's Deli
618 W. Sixth St., 512/472-2037
Phoenicia Bakery and Deli
2912 S. Lamar Blvd., 512/447-4444

Best Desserts
Chez Fred
  9070 Research Blvd. at Burnet Rd., Crossroads,
    512/451-6494
  1014 Walsh Tarlton at Bee Caves Rd., Westlake,
    512/451-6494
Dr. Chocolate
  4001 N. Lamar, 512/454-0555
Z Tejas Grill
  1110 W. Sixth St., 512/478-5355

Best Family Restaurants
Jeff's Marina Cafe
  2219 Westlake Dr., 512/327-9500
Hangtown
  29th St. at Rio Grande, 512/476-8696

Best Fast Food
HEB Food Court
  Hancock Center, 40th at Red River, 512/458-1517
Short Stop
  1144A Airport Blvd., 512/928-1010
  5609 Adams Ave., 512/453-7839
  2217 E. Seventh St., 512/469-0607
  3710 Airport Blvd., 512/469-0731
  3811A I-35N, 512/459-9949
  3001 W. Anderson Ln., 512/458-6104
  9414 Parkfield Dr., 512/835-7074
  6603 Berkman Dr., 512/926-1925

Best French Food
Chez Nous
  510 Neches St., 512/473-2413

Best German Food
Gunther's
  11606 I-35N, 512/834-0474
Acorn Cafe
  2602 Guadalupe St., 512/472-2816

Best Greek/Mediterranean Food
Ted's Greek Corner
  417 Congress Ave., 512/472-4494

Best Health-Conscious Menu
Martin Brothers Cafe
  2815 Guadalupe St., 512/478-9001
Casa de Luz
  1701 Toomey Dr., 512/476-2535
Good Eats Cafe
  1530 Barton Springs Rd., 512/476-8141
  6801 Burnet Rd., 512/451-2560
  10508 N. Lamar Blvd., 512/832-8291

Best Homestyle Food
Threadgill's Restaurant
  6416 N. Lamar Blvd., 512/451-5440
Dirty's
  2808 Guadalupe St., 512/477-3173

Best Ice Cream/Yogurt
Amy's Ice Cream
  3403 Guadalupe St., 512/458-6895

T

10000 Research Blvd., 512/345-1006
1012B W. Sixth St., 512/480-0673
2308B Lake Austin Blvd., 512/479-8830

Best Indian Food
Taj Palace
4141 Capital of Texas Hwy., 512/447-1997
6700 Middle Fiskville Rd., 512/452-9959
Star of India
2900 W. Anderson, Ste. 12D, Northwood Plaza,
512/452-8199

Best Italian Food
Mezzaluna
310 Colorado St., 512/472-6770
Basil's Restaurant
900 W. Tenth St., 512/477-5576
Romeo's
1500 Barton Springs Rd., 512/476-1090

Best Late-Night Food
Kerbey Lane Cafe
3704 Kerbey Ln., 512/451-1436
2111 Dixon St., Ste. 10, 512/443-3696
2700 S. Lamar Blvd., 512/445-4451
12602 Research Blvd., 512/258-7757
Ruby's Barbecue and Catering Company
29th at Guadalupe St., 512/477-1651

Best Mexican Food
Fonda San Miguel
2330 W. North Loop Blvd., 512/459-4121
Manuel's
310 Congress Ave., 512/472-7555
El Rinconcito Cucina Mexicana
1014E N. Lamar Blvd., 512/476-5277
Guero's
1412 S. Congress Ave., 512/707-8232

Best Microbreweries
Waterloo Brewing Company
401 Guadalupe St., 512/477-1836
Dog and Duck Pub
406 W. Seventeenth St., 512/479-0598

Best Middle Eastern Food
Armen's Mediterranean Restaurant
12196 N. MoPac Expwy., 512/835-8888
2222 Rio Grande St., 512/474-2068

Best Outdoor Dining
Shady Grove
1624 Barton Springs Rd., 512/474-9991

Best Pastries
Upper Crust
4508 Burnet Rd., 512/467-0102
La Madeleine
35th St. at N. Lamar Blvd., 512/302-1485

Best Pizza
Pizza Nizza
1608 Barton Springs Rd., 512/474-7470

Conan's Pizza
1912 Smith Rd., 512/385-5914
603 W. 29th St., 512/478-5712

Best Place to Eat Alone
Kerbey Lane Cafe
3704 Kerbey Ln., 512/451-1436
2111 Dixon St., Ste. 10, 512/443-3696
2700 S. Lamar Blvd., 512/445-4451
12602 Research Blvd., 512/258-7757

Best Places to Eat When Someone Else Is Buying
Castle Hill Cafe
1101 W. Fifth St., 512/476-0728
Mezzaluna
310 Colorado St., 512/472-6770
Jeffrey's Restaurant
1204 W. Lynn St., 512/477-5584

Best Places to Take the Kids
Celebration Station
4525 I-35S, 512/448-3533
Matt's El Rancho
2613 S. Lamar Blvd., 512/462-9333
Spaghetti Warehouse
117 W. Fourth St., 512/476-4059

Best Regional Food
El Rancho
2613 S. Lamar Pl., 512/462-9333
Hudson's on the Bend
3509 Ranch Rd. N., 512/266-1369

Best Romantic Dining
Jeffrey's Restaurant
1204 W. Lynn St., 512/477-5584
Castle Hill Cafe
1101 W. Fifth St., 512/476-0728
Hudson's on the Bend
3509 Hwy. 620N, 512/266-1369

Best Salad/Salad Bar
Eastside Cafe
2113 Manor Rd., 214/476-5858
Souper Salad
6201 Middle Fiskville Rd., 512/459-9967
10710 Research Blvd., 512/343-0807
4211 S. Lamar Blvd., 512/441-6958
2438 W. Anderson Ln., 512/451-9320
6700 Middle Fiskville Rd., 512/453-7687
Bitter End
311 Colorado St., 512/478-2337

Best Sandwiches
Delaware Subs
6266 W. Hwy. 290, 512/892-0463
8105 Mesa Dr., 512/345-3816
Hyde Park Bar and Grill
4206 Duval St., 512/458-3168
Thundercloud Subs
Multiple Locations

T

Best Seafood
Pappadeaux's Seafood Kitchen
6319 I-35N, 512/452-9363
Gilligan's Seafood and Oyster Bar
407 Colorado St., 512/474-7474

Best Soul Food
Soul Kitchen
2931 E. Twelfth St., 512/478-0251

Best Southwestern Food
Z Tejas Grill
1110 W. Sixth St., 512/478-5355
Chuy's Restaurant
10520 N. Lamar Blvd., 512/836-3218
1728 Barton Springs Rd., 512/474-4452
El Mercado
1302 S. First St., 512/447-7445
7414 Burnet Rd., 512/454-2500

Best Steaks
Dan McKlusky's Restaurant
301 E. Sixth St., 512/473-8924
10000 Research Blvd., 512/346-0780
Hoffbrau
613 W. Sixth St., 512/472-0822
Austin Land and Cattle Company
1205 N. Lamar, 512/472-1813

Best Sushi
Osaka
13492 Research Blvd., Ste. 160, 512/948-8012
Musashino
3407 Greystone Dr., 512/795-8593
Sushi Dokoro
3407 Greystone, 512/795-8593

Best Tea Room
Mozart's Inc.
3826 Lake Austin Blvd., 512/477-2900

Best Thai Food
Thai Kitchen
803 E. William Cannon, 512/445-4844
3437 Bee Caves Rd., 512/327-3528
Satay
3202 W. Anderson Ln., 512/467-6731

Best Vegetarian Food
West Lynn Cafe
1110 W. Lynn St., 512/482-0950
Mother's Cafe and Garden
4215 Duval St., 512/451-3994
Acorn Cafe
2602 Guadalupe St., 512/472-2816

Best Vietnamese Food
Fortune Pho 75
5501 N. Lamar Blvd., 512/458-1792

Best View While Dining
Oasis
6550 Comanche Trail, 512/266-2441

Best Wine Selection
Mezzaluna
310 Colorado St., 512/472-6770
Louie's 106
106 E. Sixth St., 512/476-2010
Jeffrey's Restaurant
1204 W. Lynn St., 512/477-5584

Standbys
Baskin-Robbins
2219 E. Riverside Dr., 512/441-5438
8756 Research Blvd., 512/459-4479
5503 Balcones Dr., 512/452-0777
3616 Far West Blvd., 512/338-4148
The Olive Garden
8833 Burnett Rd., 512/459-0701
3940 S. Lamar Blvd., 512/474-7470
Chuck E. Cheese Pizza
502 W. Ben White Blvd., 512/441-9681
8038 Burnet Rd., 512/451-0296
Fuddrucker's
2700 W. Anderson Ln., 512/458-6268
4024 S. Lamar Blvd., 512/444-8202
Subway
1705D S. Lakeshore Blvd., 512/448-3363
2021 Guadalupe St., 512/482-0599
6705 W. Hwy. 290, 512/892-3240
3724 N. Lamar Blvd., 512/459-7233
5400 Brodie Ln., 512/891-9022
4201 S. Congress Ave., 512/447-4111
Red Lobster
3815 S. Lamar Blvd., 512/447-1824
109 W. Anderson Ln., 512/451-6404

BAYTOWN, TX

Best Atmosphere
Rooster's Steak House
6 W. Texas Ave., 281/428-8222

Best Bar
Speakeasy
1800 W. Main St., 281/428-8955

Best Barbecue/Ribs
Going's Barbecue Company
1007 N. Main St., 281/422-4600

Best Breakfast
Kettle Restaurant
4915 E. I-10, 281/421-1656

Best Cheap Meal
Pancho's Mexican Restaurant
220 Gulf Freeway S., 281/332-4499

Best Chinese Food
Lee Palace Restaurant
6942 Garth Rd., 281/421-1203
Dong Hwa Chinese Restaurant
4529 Garth Rd., 281/420-2781

T

Best Delicatessen
Doyle's Deli
1504 San Jacinto Mall, 281/421-1643

Best Health-Conscious Menu
The Health Way
407 W. Baker Rd., 281/427-9000

Best Homestyle Food
Murray's Family Restaurant
1001 Memorial Dr., 281/422-5386

Best Ice Cream/Yogurt
Sportyballs
423 W. Texas Ave., 281/428-2485

Best Lunch
Luna's Mexican Restaurant
4539 Garth Rd., 281/422-9090

Best Mexican Food
Tia Maria's Mexican Restaurant
1711 Garth Rd., 281/427-8666

Best Place to Eat Alone
Sportyballs
423 W. Texas Ave., 281/428-2485

Best Seafood
Baytown Seafood
709 W. Main St., 281/427-2478
Crab House
317 Toddville Rd., Seabrook, 281/474-5836

Best Steaks
Rooster's Steak House
6 W. Texas Ave., 281/428-8222

Best Other Restaurant
Glass Onion Cafe
214 W. Texas Ave., 281/420-1750

Standbys
Ryan's Family Steak House
3703 Garth Rd., 281/420-1491
International House of Pancakes
8911 1/2 Hwy. 146, Mont Belvieu, 281/576-5684

T

BEAUMONT, TX

Best Barbecue/Ribs
Broussard's Links Plus Ribs
2930 S. Eleventh St., 409/842-1221

Best Breakfast
Pig Stand
612 Washington Blvd., 409/835-5153
3695 College St., 409/835-9394
1595 Calder St., 409/835-9702

Best Burgers
Novrozsky Hamburgers
458 N. Eighth St., 409/832-3113
4230 Calder Ave., 409/898-8688
4438 Dowlen Rd., 409/899-4076

Best Cajun/Creole Food
Cajun Cookery
2505 McArthur Dr., Orange, 409/886-0990

Best Cheap Meal
Black-Eyed Pea
6455 Phelan Blvd., 409/866-2617

Best Chinese Food
Mandarin Restaurant
4415 Calder Ave., 409/899-4344

Best Delicatessen
Jason's Deli
112 Gateway St., 409/833-5914
414 Dowlen Rd., 409/866-9015

Best Desserts
Patrizi's Restaurant
2050 I-10S, 409/842-5151
Marble Slab Creamery
6626 Phelan Blvd., 409/866-4740

Best Family Restaurant
Black-Eyed Pea
6455 Phelan Blvd., 409/866-2617

Best Italian Food
Carlo's Restaurant and Bar
2570 Calder St., 409/833-0108

Best Mexican Food
Elena's
1865 College St., 409/832-1203

Best Pizza
Mazzio's Pizza
5025 Eastex Freeway, 409/899-1400

Best Place to Take Guests
David's Upstairs
745 N. Eleventh St., 409/898-0214

Best Regional Food
Tamale Company
6025 Phelan Blvd., 409/769-3300

Best Romantic Dining
Carlo's Restaurant and Bar
2570 Calder St., 409/833-0108

Best Sandwiches
Jason's Deli
112 Gateway St., 409/833-5914
414 Dowlen Rd., 409/866-9015

Best Seafood
Don's Seafood and Steak House
2290 I-10S, 409/842-0686
Gulf Port Restaurant
3950 I-10S, 409/842-5995

Best Steaks
Hoffbrau Steaks
2310 N. Eleventh St., 409/892-6911

T

Best Tea Room
Green Beanery Cafe
2121 McFaddin St., 409/833-5913

Standbys
International House of Pancakes
3830 College St., 409/833-5510
Golden Corral Family Steak House
4145 College St., 409/842-2441

BIG SPRING, TX

Best Barbecue/Ribs
Al's and Sons Bar-B-Q
1810 S. Gregg St., 915/267-8921

Best Breakfast
Mary Jo's Country Kitchen
109 E. Second St., 915/264-6343
Country Fare Restaurant
I-20W at Hwy. 87, 915/264-4444

Best Burgers
Al's and Sons Bar-B-Q
1810 S. Gregg St., 915/267-8921

Best Coffee
Spanky's Coffee and Company
1909A Gregg St., 915/264-6747

Best Desserts
Red Mesa Grill
2401 S. Gregg St., 915/263-2205

Best Homestyle Food
Mary Jo's Country Kitchen
109 E. Second St., 915/264-6343

Best Mexican Food
Spanish Inn Restaurant
200 NW Third St., 915/267-9340
Carlos' Restaurant and Bar
308 NW Third St., 915/267-9141
Alberto's Crystal Cafe
120 E. Second St., 915/267-9024

Best Sandwiches
Red Mesa Grill
2401 S. Gregg St., 915/263-2205

Best Seafood
Mel's Catch of the Day Fish
504 S. Gregg St., 915/267-6266

Best Steaks
Casey's Steak and Seafood
N. Service Rd. at I-20W, 915/263-1651
Brandin' Iron Inn
Hwy. 87S, 915/267-7661

Standbys
Baskin-Robbins
2110 S. Gregg St., 915/267-3131

BROWNSVILLE, TX

Best All-You-Can-Eat Buffet
Kettle Pancake House
  854 N. Expressway, 210/542-2731

Best Bar
Vermillion
  115 Paredes Line Rd., 210/542-9893

Best Barbecue/Ribs
La Hacienda
  804 Paredes Line Rd., 210/550-0055

Best Breakfast
Kettle Pancake House
  854 N. Expressway, 210/542-2731

Best Burgers
Vermillion
  115 Paredes Line Rd., 210/542-9893
Whataburger
  2021 International Blvd., 210/542-0963
  2290 N. Expressway, 210/546-2572
  2419 Boca Chica Blvd., 210/546-2361

Best Casual Dining
Palm Court Restaurant
  2235 Boca Chica Blvd., 210/542-3575

Best Chinese Food
Lotus Court Restaurant
  1774 E. Price Rd., 210/544-3331
Lotus Inn
  905 N. Expressway, 210/542-5715

Best Coffee
Toddle Inn
  1740 Central Blvd., 210/542-8838

Best Desserts
Palm Court Restaurant
  2235 Boca Chica Blvd., 210/542-3575

Best Italian Food
Gio Villa Italian Food
  2325 Central Blvd., 210/542-9057

Best Mexican Food
Antonio's Mexican Village
  2921 Boca Chica Blvd., 210/542-6504
Jesse's Cantina and Restaurant
  2700 Padre Blvd., South Padre Island, 210/761-4500

Best Pizza
Gio Villa Italian Food
  2325 Central Blvd., 210/542-9057
D'Pizza Joint
  2413 Padre Blvd., South Padre Island, 210/761-7995

Best Sandwiches
Vermillion
  115 Paredes Line Rd., 210/542-9893

Best Seafood
Beacon Harbor
  3505 Boca Chica Blvd., 210/542-9143

T

Best Steaks
La Hacienda
  804 Paredes Line Rd., 210/550-0055

Standbys
Applebee's
  2960 Boca Chica Blvd., 210/542-7474
TCBY
  2921 Boca Chica Blvd., 210/542-6669
  1191 E. Ruben M. Torres Blvd., 210/541-6499
Shoney's
  2355 N. Expressway, 210/504-1500

BRYAN/COLLEGE STATION, TX

Best Restaurant in Town
Tom's Barbecue and Steak House
  2001 Texas Ave. S., College Station, 409/696-2076
  3610 S. College Ave., Bryan, 409/846-4275

Best Bar
Dixie Chicken
  307 University Dr., College Station, 409/846-2322

Best Burgers
Whataburger
  906 S. Texas Ave., Bryan, 409/822-0624

Best Business Lunch
Ken Martin's Steak House
  3231 E. 29th St., Bryan, 409/776-7500

Best Chinese Food
Chinese Garden
  2901 S. Texas Ave., Bryan, 409/823-2818

Best Family Restaurant
Ken Martin's Steak House
  3231 E. 29th St., Bryan, 409/776-7500

Best Late-Night Food
Arby's
  3501 E. 29th St., Bryan, 409/260-2729

Best Mexican Food
Jose's Restaurant
  3824 Texas Ave. S., College Station, 409/268-0036

Best Place to Be "Seen"
Bennigan's
  1505A Texas Ave. S., College Station, 409/696-9066

Best Place to Eat Alone
Chicken Oil Company
  3600 S. College Ave., Bryan, 409/463-3306

Best Place to Eat When Someone Else Is Buying
Oxford Street Restaurant and Pub
  1710 Briarcrest Dr., Bryan, 409/268-0792

Best Salad/Salad Bar
Oxford Street Restaurant and Pub
  1710 Briarcrest Dr., Bryan, 409/268-0792

Best Steaks
Oxford Street Restaurant and Pub
  1710 Briarcrest Dr., Bryan, 409/268-0792

Standbys
Old Country Buffet
  2402D Texas Ave. S., College Station, 409/696-4477
Applebee's
  200 Texas Ave., College Station, 409/260-3003
Little Caesar's
  1775 Briarcrest Dr., Bryan, 409/776-7171
Subway
  2500 S. Texas Ave., Bryan, 409/823-7827
Red Lobster
  813 Texas Ave. S., College Station, 409/764-9310

CONROE, TX

Best Barbecue/Ribs
Read's BBQ
  1202 N. Frazier St., 409/539-2322

Best Burgers
Burger Boy
  217 E. Davis St., 409/756-3440

Best Chinese Food
Hunan Village Restaurant
  1402A Loop 336W, 409/539-6811
Imperial Garden
  3708E W. Davis St., 409/539-1566

Best Desserts
Kuntry Katfish
  Hwy. 105W, 409/760-3386

Best Health-Conscious Menu
Garden Cafe
  1406A Loop 336W, 409/539-9663

Best Homestyle Food
Kuntry Katfish
  Hwy. 105W, 409/760-3386

Best Ice Cream/Yogurt
I Can't Believe It's Yogurt
  1422 Loop 336W, 409/539-1109

Best Italian Food
Villa Italia
  6035 Hwy. 105W, 409/539-5599
  203 Simonton, 409/539-1915

Best Mexican Food
El Pollino
  201 N. Frazier St., 409/756-2614

Best Sandwiches
Garden Cafe
  1406A Loop 336W, 409/539-9663

Best Seafood
Kuntry Katfish
  Hwy. 105W, 409/760-3386

Best Steaks
Hofbrau Steaks
  2031 Plantation Dr., 409/756-1554

T

Best Tea Room
Garden Cafe
1406A Loop 336W, 409/539-9663

CORPUS CHRISTI, TX

Best Atmosphere
Roadhouse Inn
11223 Up River Rd., 512/241-0621

Best Barbecue/Ribs
Bar-B-Q Man
4932 I-37, 512/888-4248
County Line Barbecue
6102 Ocean Dr., 512/991-7427

Best Breakfast
Kettle Restaurant
6301 I-37, 512/289-5622
4001 S. Padre Island Dr., 512/855-4778
5015 Ayers St., 512/852-7818

Best Burgers
EZ's Pizzas and Burgers
5425 S. Padre Island Dr., 512/992-1292
Whataburger
Multiple Locations

Best Business Lunch
Water Street Oyster Bar
309 N. Water St., 512/881-9448

Best Cajun/Creole Food
Country Cajun
3741 S. Alameda St., 512/851-8514

Best Chinese Food
Golden Crown Chinese Restaurant
6601 Everhart Rd., Ste. B7, 512/854-5506
2739 S. Staples St., 512/853-8886
Mao-Tai Chinese Restaurant
4601 S. Padre Island Dr., 512/852-8877

Best Delicatessen
Jason's Deli
Gulfway Shopping Ctr., 1416 Airline Dr., 512/992-4649

Best Desserts
Ultimate Cheesecake Factory
22 Lamar Park Ctr., 512/852-4159
4210 S. Alameda St., 512/991-7892

Best Diner
Elmo's City Diner and Bar
622 N. Water St., 512/883-1643

Best Health-Conscious Menu
Lighthouse Restaurant
444 N. Shoreline Blvd., 512/881-8210

Best Homestyle Food
Elmo's City Diner and Bar
622 N. Water St., 512/883-1643
Roadhouse Inn
11223 Up River Rd., 512/241-0621

Best Italian Food
Mama Mia's
128 N. Mesquite St., 512/883-3773

Best Mexican Food
Old Mexico Restaurant
3329 Leopard St., 512/883-6461
Pepe's Mexican Cafe
15 Gaslight Sq., 512/888-7373

Best Pizza
Cici's Pizza
4102A S. Staples St., 512/814-2424

Best Romantic Dining
Lighthouse Restaurant
444 N. Shoreline Blvd., 512/881-8210
Window on the Bay
Howard Johnson's, 300 N. Shoreline Blvd.,
512/887-1645

Best Salad/Salad Bar
Mama Mia's
128 N. Mesquite St., 512/883-3773
Salads Etc.
5702 S. Staples St., 512/985-0428

Best Seafood
Catfish Charlie's
5830 McArdle Rd., 512/993-0363

Best Sushi
Origami
1220 Airline Blvd., 512/993-3966

Best Tea Room
Jeron's Tea Room
1521 N. Chaparral St., 512/882-1939

Best Vegetarian Food
Salads Etc.
5702 S. Staples St., 512/985-0428

Best Vietnamese Food
Vietnam
4501 S. Padre Island Dr., 512/853-2682

Best View While Dining
Window on the Bay
Howard Johnson's, 300 N. Shoreline Blvd.,
512/887-1645

Standbys
Old Country Buffet
4839 S. Staples St., 512/985-1762
Denny's
5165 I-37, 512/884-2579
4918 S. Padre Island Dr., 512/992-4332
6201 S. Padre Island Dr., 512/991-1314
Golden Corral Family Steak House
5274 S. Staples St., 512/992-8667
Baskin-Robbins
4773 Padre Island Dr., 512/852-0945
1444 Airline Rd., 512/991-2691

Chuck E. Cheese Pizza
5118 Staples St., 512/993-8824
Longhorn Steaks
4535 S. Padre Island Dr., Ste. 33, 512/853-5664

DALLAS, TX

Best Restaurant in Town
Star Canyon
3102 Oak Lawn (in the Centrum), 214/520-7827

Best Bagels
Bagel Boulevard Cafe
Promenade Shopping Ctr., 770 Coit Rd., Ste. 2403,
214/437-4313

Best Barbecue/Ribs
Baker's Ribs
2724 Commerce St., 214/748-5433
4844 Greenville, 214/373-0082
Sonny Bryan's
2202 Inwood, 214/357-7120
Harry's American Bar-B-Que
3910 Maple, 214/522-4433
Red Hot and Blue
9810 N. Central Expwy. at Walnut Hill, 214/368-7427
Carter's
1621 S. Oakland, 214/428-9461
Rudy's B-B-Q
3707 Lemmon Ave., 214/526-0188

Best Biscuits
Barbec's
8949 Garland Rd., 214/321-5597
1625 S. Buckner Blvd., 214/391-4482

Best Bistros
L'Ancestral
4514 Travis St., 214/528-1081
Le Chardonnay
500 Crescent Crt., Ste. 165, 214/922-4555
Watel's
1923 McKinney Ave., 214/720-0323

Best Breakfast
Mecca Restaurant
10422 Harry Hines, 214/352-0051

Best Burgers
Theo's Diner
111 Hall St., 214/747-6936
Chip's
4501 N. Central Expwy., 214/526-1092
Snuffer's
8330 Meadow Rd., Ste. 220, 214/696-6393
14910 Midway Rd., 214/991-8811
3526 Greenville Ave., 214/826-6850

Best Cheap Meal
Queen of Sheba
3527 McKinney, 214/521-0491

Best Chinese Food
Cafe Panda
  7919 Inwood, 214/902-9500
Tong's House
  1910 Promenade Center, 214/231-8858
Chin Big Wong Chinese Seafood
  2121 Greenville Ave., 214/821-4198
China Blossom
  3107 W. Camp Wisdom Rd., 214/330-4303

Best Coffee
Sixteen Eighty-Three The Coffee House
  8220B Westchester Dr., 214/368-4188
Cafe Brazil
  2221 Abrams Rd., 214/826-9522
  6420 N. Central Expwy., 214/691-7791
Cafe Society
  4514 Travis, 214/528-6543

Best Desserts
Quadrangle Grille
  2800 Routh St., 214/979-9022
Basha
  2217 Greenville, 214/824-7794

Best French Food
Calluaud
  5405 Lovers Ln., 214/352-1997
Juniper
  2917 Fairmount, 214/855-0700

Best German Food
Kuby's
  6601 Snider Plz., 214/363-2261

Best Homestyle Food
Mama's Daughter's Diner
  2014 Irving Blvd., 214/742-8646
Black-Eyed Pea
  Multiple Locations
Celebration
  4503 W. Lovers Ln., 214/351-5681

Best Indian Food
Bombay Cricket Club
  2508 Maple, 214/871-1333

Best Italian Food
Pomodoro
  2520 Cedar Springs, 214/871-1924
Ruggieri's
  2911 Routh St., 214/871-7377
Piccola Cucina
  1030 Northpark Ctr., Ste. 330, 214/691-0488
Campisi's Restaurant
  5610 E. Mockingbird, 214/827-0355
Mi Piacci
  14854 Montfort, Addison, 214/934-8424
Terilli's
  2815 Greenville Ave., 214/827-3993

T

Best Late-Night Food
The Metro Diner No.4
  3309 Gaston, 214/828-2190
Cafe Brazil
  6420 N. Central Expwy., 214/691-7791

Best Lunch
Treebeards
  Plaza of the Americas, 700 N. Pearl, 214/871-7477

Best Other Ethnic Food
Gloria's (Salvadoran)
  4140 Lemmon Ave., 214/521-7576

Best Outdoor Dining
The Green Room
  2715 Elm, 214/748-7666
Terilli's
  2815 Greenville Ave., 214/827-3993
Tejano in Oak Cliff
  110 W. Davis, 214/943-8610

Best Pizza
Arcodoro
  2520 Cedar Springs, 214/871-1924
Cafe Italica
  4152 Travis, 214/559-6106
Olympic
  7568 Greenville Ave., 214/692-5861
  2907 W. Northwest Hwy., 214/358-4111
Al's Pizzeria
  159 Walnut Hill Village, 214/350-2714

Best Regional Food
El Arroyo
  7402 Greenville Ave., 214/363-4464
Taos Southwest Cafe
  6330 Gaston Ave., 214/827-2423

Best Restaurant Meal Value
St. Pete's Dancing Marlin
  2730 Commerce St., 214/698-1511

Best Romantic Dining
York Street
  6047 Lewis St., 214/826-0968
The French Room
  Adolphus Hotel, 1321 Commerce St., 214/742-8200
The Grape
  2808 Greenville Ave., 214/828-1981

Best Salad/Salad Bar
Parigi
  3311 Oak Lawn, 214/521-0295
La Madeleine
  13355 Noel Rd., 214/991-7788
Bluebonnet Cafe
  Whole Foods Market, 2218 Greenville, 214/828-0052
Souper Salads
  3401 Airport Freeway, Irving, 214/255-9526

Best Seafood
Daddy Jack's
  1916 Greenville Ave., 214/826-4910

Galveston Island Seafood
  9551 Fair Oaks Ave., 214/348-8844
Newport's
  In the Brewery, 703 McKinney Ave., 214/954-0220

Best Steaks
Del Frisco's
  5251 Spring Valley Rd., 214/490-9000

Best Thai Food
Toy's Cafe
  4422 Lemmon Ave., 214/528-7233
Thai Soon
  2018 Greenville Ave., 214/821-7666
Thailanna
  4315 Bryan St., 214/827-6478

Best Vegetarian Food
Thai Soon
  2018 Greenville Ave., 214/821-7666
Kalachandji's
  5430 Gurley Ave., 214/821-1048
Cade's Bowl of Beans
  2332 S. Good, Latimer, 214/421-5850
Cosmic Cup
  2912 Oak Lawn Ave., 214/521-6157

Best Vietnamese Food
Arc-en-Ciel
  3555 W. Walnut Park Cir., Garland, 214/272-2188

Standbys
Haagen-Dazs
  73 Highland Park Shopping Village, 214/559-3757

DEL RIO, TX

Best Restaurants in Town
Don Marcelino Restaurant
  1110 Avenue F, 210/775-6242
Cripple Creek Saloon
  Hwy. 90W, 210/775-0153
The Windmill
  1811 Avenue F, 210/774-7003
Memo's
  804 E. Loyosa St., 210/775-8104

Best Thai Food
Jitra Thai Cuisine
  801 Gibbs St., 210/775-7553

DENISON, TX

Best Restaurant in Town
Old Italian Depot
  101 E. Main St., 903/463-2145

Best Barbecue/Ribs
Carter Red
  2001 S. Austin Ave., 903/465-8337

Best Chinese Food
China Inn
  505 S. Armstrong Ave. 903/465-6622

T

Best Italian Food
Old Italian Depot
101 E. Main St., 903/463-2145

Best Mexican Food
Garcia's Mexican Cafe
119 W. Main St., 903/463-1624
2900 Woodlawn Blvd., 903/463-4414

Best Steaks
Carter Red
2001 S. Austin Ave., 903/465-8337

DENTON, TX

Best Breakfast
Homestead
401 S. Locust St., Ste. 101, 817/566-3240
Jim's Diner
110 Fry St., 817/382-4442

Best Burgers
Ranchman's Cafe
110 W. Bailey, Ponder, 817/479-2221

Best Chinese Food
Red Pepper's Chinese Restaurant
2412 S. I-35E, 817/387-1688

Best Coffee
Cappucino Cafe
707 Sunset, 817/565-1808

Best Desserts
Cappucino Cafe
707 Sunset, 817/565-1808

Best Greek/Mediterranean Food
Arcadia's
314 W. University Dr., 817/591-8489

Best Homestyle Food
Jim's Diner
110 Fry St., 817/382-4442

Best Ice Cream/Yogurt
Braum's
301 W. University Dr., 817/382-2710

Best Italian Food
Milano Restaurant
911A Avenue C, 817/383-2021

Best Late-Night Food
Jim's Diner
110 Fry St., 817/382-4442

Best Mexican Food
Mazatlan Restaurant
1928 N. Ruddell St., 817/566-1718

Best Salad/Salad Bar
Rama's Courtyard
222 W. Hickory, 817/383-8491

Best Steaks
Ranchman's Cafe
110 W. Bailey, Ponder, 817/479-2221

Best Vegetarian Food
Kharma
103 Avenue A, 817/382-5858

EDINBURG, TX

Best All-You-Can-Eat Buffet
Grand View
Echo Motor Hotel, 1903 S. Closner Blvd.,
210/383-3823

Best Breakfast
El Taco Place
620 S. Closner Blvd., 210/381-5452
Hec and Bec Restaurant
317 E. University Dr., 210/383-8592

Best Brunch
Gourmet Shop
1410 W. University Dr., 210/381-8303

Best Burgers
Hamburger King
524 E. University Dr., 210/383-9091

Best Desserts
Shea-Martin Cafe and Catering
217 S. Closner Blvd., 210/380-0401

Best Family Restaurants
Las Brasas Restaurant
1701 W. University Dr., 210/380-6624
La Casa Del Taco
321 W. University Dr., 210/383-0521

Best Homestyle Food
Kuntry Kitchen
2207 S. Hwy. 281, 210/380-0521

Best Italian Food
The Ripe Olive
1328 N. Closner Blvd., 210/383-0474

Best Mexican Food
La Casa Del Taco
321 W. University Dr., 210/383-0521
Las Brasas
1701 W. University Dr., 210/380-6624

Best Pizza
Peter Piper Pizza
1009 S. Closner Blvd., 210/380-6666

Best Place to Take the Kids
Peter Piper Pizza
1009 S. Closner Blvd., 210/380-6666

Best Salad/Salad Bar
Shea-Martin Cafe and Catering
217 S. Closner Blvd., 210/380-0401

Best Seafood
La Jaiba
524 W. University Dr., 210/316-3474

T

Best Steaks
Grand View
Echo Motor Hotel, 1903 S. Closner Blvd.,
210/383-3823

EL PASO, TX

Best All-You-Can-Eat Buffet
K-Bob's Steakhouse
10059 Dyer St., 915/751-8100
7597 N. Mesa St., 915/581-8780
9530 Viscount Blvd., 915/598-1266

Best Atmosphere
Carlos and Mickey's Restaurant
1310 Magruder St., 915/778-3323

Best Bar
Kiki's Restaurant and Bar
2719 N. Piedras St., 915/565-6713

Best Barbecue/Ribs
The Brisket Bar-B-Q
11420 Rojas Dr., Ste. 5, 915/595-0114

Best Chinese Food
Uncle Bao's Restaurant
5668 N. Mesa St., 915/585-1818
9515 Gateway Blvd. W., 915/592-1101

Best Coffee
Barnes and Noble
9521 Viscount Blvd., 915/590-1932
705 Sumland Park Dr., 915/581-5353

Best Desserts
Marie Callender's
10501 Gateway Blvd. W., 915/592-6920

Best Family Restaurants
Cafe Rio
Camino Real Paso del Norte Hotel, 501 S. El Paso Dr.,
915/534-3020
Great American Land and Cattle
2220 N. Yarborough Dr., 915/595-1772
7600 Alabama St., 915/751-5300

Best Greek/Mediterranean Food
Tassos Greek and Seafood Restaurant
1850 Trawood Dr., 915/590-5584

Best Health-Conscious Menu
Eating with Grace
6110 N. Mesa St., 915/585-9099

Best Homestyle Food
Black-Eyed Pea
1420 N. Lee Trevino Dr., 915/595-0055
760 Sunland Park Dr., 915/584-9888

Best Italian Food
Acquarello
7500 N. Mesa St., 915/587-5995
Dominic's
717 E. San Antonio Ave., 915/544-0011

Best Japanese Food
Samurai
7040 N. Mesa St., 915/585-8848

Best Mexican Food
Amigos
2000 Montana Ave., 915/533-0155
Kiki's Restaurant and Bar
2719 N. Piedras St., 915/565-6713

Best Pizza
Cici's Pizza
11335 Montwood Dr., 915/857-3355
7500 N. Mesa St., 915/833-4900

Best Place to Take the Kids
Peter Piper Pizza
Multiple Locations

Best Romantic Dining
Carlos and Mickey's Restaurant
1310 Magruder St., 915/778-3323

Best Salad/Salad Bar
K-Bob's Steakhouse
10059 Dyer St., 915/751-8100
7597 N. Mesa St., 915/581-8780
9530 Viscount Blvd., 915/598-1266

Best Seafood
Tassos Greek and Seafood Restaurant
1850 Trawood Dr., 915/590-5584

Best Spanish Food
Barcelona
3130 N. Lee Trevino Dr., 915/595-6600

Best Steaks
Cattlemen's Steakhouse
3045 S. Carlsbad Rd., 915/764-2283

Best Tea Room
La Jolla Tea Room
5411 N. Mesa St., 915/587-6020

Standbys
Shoney's
7501 N. Mesa St., 915/587-7504
Baskin-Robbins
9574 Dyer St., 915/755-3132
Red Lobster
7111 N. Mesa St., 915/581-1051
9201 Gateway Blvd. W., 915/591-8108

T

FT. STOCKTON, TX

Best All-You-Can-Eat Buffet
Brazen Bean
350 W. Dickinson Blvd., 915/336-3070

Best Barbecue/Ribs
K-Bob's Steakhouse
2800 W. Dickinson Blvd., 915/336-6233

Best Burgers
Burrito Inn
805 N. Alamo St., 915/336-3141

Best Coffee
Linda's Cards and Gifts
119 N. Main St., 915/336-7674

Best Homestyle Food
Brazen Bean
350 W. Dickinson Blvd., 915/336-3070

Best Mexican Food
Burrito Inn
805 N. Alamo St., 915/336-3141
Mi Casita
405 E. Dickinson Blvd., 915/336-5368

Best Salad/Salad Bar
Brazen Bean
350 W. Dickinson Blvd., 915/336-3070

Best Steaks
K-Bob's Steakhouse
2800 W. Dickinson Blvd., 915/336-6233

Standbys
Pizza Hut
911 W. Dickinson Blvd., 915/336-5264
Subway
2005 W. Dickinson Blvd., 915/336-8722

FT. WORTH, TX

Best Asian Restaurants
China Coast
4840 SW Loop 820, 817/738-3272
Szechuan Chinese Restaurant
5712 Locke Ave., 817/738-7300

Best Atmosphere
Seventh Street Cafe
3500 W. Seventh St., 817/870-1672

Best Barbecue/Ribs
Angelo's
2533 White Settlement Rd., 817/332-0357
Cousin's Pit Barbecue
6262 McCart Ave., 817/346-2511
Railhead Smokehouse
5518 W. Vickery Blvd., 817/738-9808

Best Beer Selection
Billy Miner's Saloon
150 W. Third St., 817/877-3301
Garfield Restaurant and Pub
3811 S. Cooper, Arlington, 817/467-7773
Pig and Whistle Pub
5731 Locke Ave., 817/731-4938

Best Breakfast
La Madeleine French Bakery
6140 Camp Bowie Blvd., 817/654-0471
2101 N. Collins St., Arlington, 817/459-1327
Paris Coffee Shop
700 W. Magnolia Ave., 817/335-2041

Best Brunch
Uncle Julio's Fine Mexican
5301 Camp Bowie Blvd., 817/377-2777

Best Burgers
B.J. Keefer's
909 W. Magnolia Ave., 817/921-0889
Billy Miner's Saloon
150 W. Third St., 817/877-3301
Kinkaid's
4901 Camp Bowie Blvd., 817/732-2881

Best Cajun/Creole Food
Razzoo's Cajun Cafe
318 Main St., 817/429-7009

Best Cheap Meal
Cici's Pizza
Multiple Locations
Razzoo's Cajun Cafe
318 Main St., 817/429-7009

Best Chinese Food
Bamboo Garden
6415 McCart Ave., 817/292-9655
China Coast
4840 SW Loop 820, 817/738-3272
7536 Grapevine Hwy., 817/595-4395
Szechuan Chinese Restaurant
5712 Locke Ave., 817/738-7300
Wan Fu
6399 Camp Bowie Blvd., 817/731-2388

Best Coffeehouses
Borders Books and Music Espresso Bar
4613 S. Hulen St., 817/370-9473
The Coffee Haus
478 Lincoln Sq., Ste. 302, Arlington, 817/274-0006
Brix End
3408 Camp Bowie Blvd., 817/338-1638
La Madeleine
2101 N. Collins St., Arlington, 817/459-1327
6140 Camp Bowie Blvd., 817/654-0471
Four Star Coffee Bar
3324 W. Seventh St., 817/336-5555

Best Delicatessens
Jason's Deli
6244 Camp Bowie Blvd., 817/738-7144
5443 S. Hulen St., 817/370-9187
Carshon's Delicatessen
3133 Cleburne Rd., 817/923-1907

Best Desserts
Carshon's Delicatessen
3133 Cleburne Rd., 817/923-1907
Swiss Pastry Shop
3936 W. Vickery Blvd., 817/732-5661
Tippin's Restaurant and Pie Pantry
3321 S. Cooper St., Arlington, 817/467-7437
5209 Rufe Snow Dr., North Richland Hills,
817/577-0777

Best Eclectic Menu
Seventh Street Cafe
3500 W. Seventh St., 817/870-1672

T

Best French Food
Saint-Emillion Restaurant
3617 W. Seventh St., 817/737-2781

Best German Food
Edelweiss German Restaurant
3801A Southwest Blvd., 817/738-5934

Best Homestyle Food
Black-Eyed Pea
1400 N. Collins St., Arlington, 817/275-8973
3808 S. Cooper St., Arlington, 817/467-9555
6001 SW Loop 820, 817/370-9701
6357 Camp Bowie Blvd., Ste. 200, 817/737-6142
800 E. Loop 820, 817/496-0213
900 Airport Freeway, Hurst, 817/428-1096
Celebration Restaurant
4600 Dexter Ave., 817/731-6272
Paris Coffee Shop
700 W. Magnolia Ave., 817/335-2041

Best Indian Food
Maharaja
6308 Hulen Bend Blvd., 817/263-7156

Best Italian Food
On Broadway Ristorante
6306 Hulen Bend Blvd., 817/346-8841
Romano's Macaroni Grill
1670 I-20W, Arlington, 817/784-1197
Sardine's Ristorante Italiano
3410 Camp Bowie Blvd., 817/332-9937
Spaghetti Warehouse
600 E. Exchange Ave., 817/625-4171
La Piazza
3431 W. Seventh St., 817/334-0000
Ol' South Pancake House
1507 S. University Dr., 817/336-0311
5148 E. Belknap St., 817/834-1291

Best Mexican Food
El Rancho Grande
1400 N. Main St., 817/624-9206
Joe T. Garcia's
2140 N. Main St., 817/626-5770
2201 N. Commerce St., 817/626-4356
Mercado Juarez
1651 E. Northside Dr., 817/838-8285
2222 Miller Rd., Arlington, 817/649-3324
Uncle Julio's Fine Mexican
5301 Camp Bowie Blvd., 817/377-2777

Best Middle Eastern Food
Hedary's Lebanese Restaurant
3308 Fairfield Ave., 817/731-6961

Best Other Ethnic Food
Papi's Restaurant (Puerto Rican)
5336 Birchman Ave., 817/763-8442

Best Outdoor Dining
Joe T. Garcia's
  2140 N. Main St., 817/626-5770
  2201 N. Commerce St., 817/626-4356
On The Border Cafe
  2011 E. Copeland Rd., Arlington, 817/261-3598
Uncle Julio's
  5301 Camp Bowie Blvd., 817/377-2777

Best Pizza
Mama's Pizza
  1316 S. Cooper St., Arlington, 817/277-1011
  1813 W. Berry St., 817/923-3541
  3130 E. Rosedale St., 817/535-8421
  4201 W. Green Oaks Blvd., Arlington, 817/478-5757
  4801 Camp Bowie Blvd., 817/731-2451
Pizzeria Uno
  1301 N. Collins St., Ste. 201, Arlington, 817/277-1080
  300 Houston St., 817/885-8667

Best Place to Eat When Someone Else Is Buying
Reflections
  Worthington Hotel, 200 Main St., 817/870-1000

Best Places to Take the Kids
Black-Eyed Pea
  1400 N. Collins St., Arlington, 817/275-8973
  3808 S. Cooper St., Arlington, 817/467-9555
  6001 SW Loop 820, 817/370-9701
  6357 Camp Bowie Blvd., Ste. 200, 817/737-6142
  800 E. Loop 820, 817/496-0213
  900 Airport Freeway, Hurst, 817/428-1096
Cici's Pizza
  3401 Alta Mesa Blvd., 817/370-6292

Best Places to Take Guests
The Balcony of Ridglea
  6100 Camp Bowie Blvd., 817/332-9937
Celebration Restaurant
  4600 Dexter Ave., 817/731-6272
Le Chardonnay
  2443 Forest Park Blvd., 817/926-5622
Worthington Hotel
  200 Main St., 817/870-1000

Best Quick Lunch
Pizzeria Uno
  300 Houston St., 817/885-8667

Best Romantic Dining
The Balcony of Ridglea
  6100 Camp Bowie Blvd., 817/731-3719
Italian Inn Ridglea
  6323B Camp Bowie Blvd., 817/737-0123
Sardine's Ristorante Italiano
  3410 Camp Bowie Blvd., 817/332-9937

Best Seafood
Pappadeaux's Seafood Kitchen
  1304 Copeland Rd., Arlington, 817/543-0544
Water Street Seafood Company
  1540 S. University Dr., 817/877-3474

T

Best Steaks
Cattlemen's Steakhouse
 2458 N. Main St., 817/624-3945
The Keg Rodeo Steakhouse
 1309 Calhoun St., 817/332-1288

Best Vegetarian Food
Black-Eyed Pea
 1400 N. Collins St., Arlington, 817/275-8973
 3808 S. Cooper St., Arlington, 817/467-9555
 6001 SW Loop 820, 817/370-9701
 6357 Camp Bowie Blvd., Ste. 200, 817/737-6142
 800 E. Loop 820, 817/496-0213
 900 Airport Freeway, Hurst, 817/428-1096
King Tut
 1512 W. Magnolia Ave., 817/335-3051
Luby's Cafeteria
 1200 Bridgewood Dr., 817/457-5200
 251 University Dr., 817/870-9875
 3252 SE Loop 820, 817/293-0060
 4800 S. Hulen St., 817/292-5014
 7624 Grapevine Hwy., 817/284-4758

Best Vietnamese Food
Kim Hai
 2420 E. Arkansas Ln., Arlington, 817/275-2449
Phuong Cafe
 4045 E. Belknap St., 817/831-2010
Tu Hai
 3909 E. Bayonet, Haltom City, 817/834-6473

Standbys
International House of Pancakes
 308 E. Seminary, 817/926-7551
 3700 Alta Mesa, 817/292-6508
 5920 Quebec St., 817/237-2894
The Olive Garden
 1400 E. Copeland Rd., Arlington, 817/861-8877
 4604 S. Cooper St., 817/472-9733
 4700 SW Loop 820, 817/377-8091
 8020 Bedford Euless Rd., North Richland Hills,
  817/581-9511
 925 Alta Mere Dr., 817/732-0618
Denny's
 4400 South Freeway, 817/924-2431
 6048 S. Hulen St., 817/370-7188
 6737 Camp Bowie Blvd., 817/737-6551
Outback Steakhouse
 1151 I-20W, Arlington, 817/557-5959
 2102 N. Collins St., 817/265-9381
 4608 Bryant Irvin Rd., 817/370-7800
 701 Airport Freeway, Hurst, 817/285-0004

GALVESTON, TX

Best Bar
M and M Bar and Grill
 2401 Church St., 409/762-2230

Best Breakfast
El Nopalito
  614 42nd St., 409/763-9815

Best Brunch
Spoonbill
  San Luis Hotel, 5222 Seawall Blvd., 409/744-1500

Best Cheap Meal
Happy Buddha
  2827 61st St., 409/744-5774

Best Chinese Food
Happy Buddha
  2827 61st St., 409/744-5774

Best Coffee
Rock and Java
  213 Tremont, 409/762-8083

Best Family Restaurant
Nash D'Amico's Pasta and Clam
  2328 Strand St., 409/763-6500

Best Greek/Mediterranean Food
Mikonos Pub and Deli
  2101 Post Office St., 409/762-3985

Best Health-Conscious Menu
Yaga's Tropical Cafe
  2314 Strand St., 409/762-6676

Best Homestyle Food
Schutte's Corner
  8021 Post Office St., 409/763-8111

Best Ice Cream/Yogurt
Marble Slab Creamery
  2705 61st St., 409/744-6215

Best Italian Food
Nash D'Amico's Pasta and Clam
  2328 Strand St., 409/763-6500

Best Late-Night Food
Wentletrap, A Restaurant
  2301 Strand St., 409/765-5545

Best Mexican Food
La Mixteca
  1818 Mechanic Rd., 409/762-2235
Marco's Mexican Restaurant
  2705 61st St., 409/740-2024

Best Pizza
Mario's Flying Pizza Restaurant
  2202 61st St., 409/744-2975

Best Place to Eat Alone
Mikonos Pub and Deli
  2101 Post Office St., 409/762-3985

Best Place to Eat When Someone Else Is Buying
Clary's Restaurant
  8509 Teichman Rd., 409/740-0771
  1002 Commodore Dr., 409/740-1103

T

Best Romantic Dining
Gaido's Seaside Inn
  3800 Seawall Blvd., 409/762-9625

Best Salad/Salad Bar
Mikonos Pub and Deli
  2101 Post Office St., 409/762-3985

Best Sandwiches
Paul's Sandwich Shop
  706 Holiday Dr., 409/763-9256
  412 20th St., 409/765-8319

Best Seafood
Clary's Restaurant
  8509 Teichman Rd., 409/740-0771
  1002 Commodore Dr., 409/740-1103
Gaido's
  3800 Seawall Blvd., 409/762-9625

Best Steaks
Clary's Restaurant
  8509 Teichman Rd., 409/740-0771
  1002 Commodore Dr., 409/740-1103

GREENVILLE, TX

Best Barbecue/Ribs
Spare Rib
  7818 Wesley St., 903/455-0219

Best Burgers
Lee Street Hamburger Company
  2500 Lee St., 903/454-0001

Best Chinese Food
Yen Jing Chinese Restaurant
  5113 S. Wesley St., 903/454-7413

Best Desserts
Puddin' Hill Store
  4007 I-30 (Exit 95), 903/455-6931
Bob Whitworth's Cafe and Patio
  8119 Wesley St., 903/455-3440

Best Ice Cream/Yogurt
Braum's Ice Cream and Dairy
  4206 Wesley St., 903/454-1158

Best Mexican Food
Molina's Mexican Cuisine
  4207 Wesley St., 903/455-4043

Best Sandwiches
Puddin' Hill Store
  4007 I-30 (Exit 95), 903/455-6931

Best Seafood
Bob Whitworth's Cafe and Patio
  8119 Wesley St., 903/455-3440

Best Steaks
Bob Whitworth's Cafe and Patio
  8119 Wesley St., 903/455-3440

HOUSTON, TX

Best Restaurants in Town
The Ruggles Grill
   903 Westheimer Rd., 713/524-3839
America's
   1800 Post Oak Blvd., 713/961-1492

Best Barbecue/Ribs
Goode Company Barbecue
   5109 Kirby Dr., 713/522-2530
   8911 Katy Freeway, 713/464-1901
Williams Smokehouse
   5903 Wheatley, 713/592-9448

Best Beer Selection
The Gingerman
   5607 1/2 Morningside Dr., 713/526-2770
Richmond Avenue Arms
   5920 Richmond Ave., 713/784-7722

Best Bread
La Madeleine French Bakery and Cafe
   600 Travis St., 713/225-6715
   6205 Kirby Dr., 713/942-7797
   10001 Westheimer Rd., 713/266-7674
   4002 Westheimer Rd., 713/623-0644
Le Moulin European Bakery
   5645 Beechnut St., 713/779-1618
Empire Baking Company
   1616 Post Oak Blvd., 713/871-9779

Best Breakfast
Buffalo Grille
   3116 Bissonnet St., 713/661-3663
Cafe Artiste
   1601 W. Main, 713/528-3704

Best Brunch
La Strada
   322 Westheimer Rd., 713/523-1014
Ritz-Carlton
   1919 Briar Oaks Lane, 713/840-7600
Pavani Madras Cuisine
   12403 Scarsdale Blvd., 713/484-7476

Best Burgers
Becks Prime
   11000 Westheimer Rd., 713/952-2325
   2615 Augusta Dr., 713/266-9901
   2902 Kirby Dr., 713/524-7085
Goode Company Hamburgers and Taqueria
   4902 Kirby Dr., 713/520-9153
Otto's Hamburgers
   5502 Memorial, 713/864-8526
Burger Joint
   8013 John Ralston Rd., 713/458-6774

Best Cafeteria
Dimassi's
   5064 Richmond Ave., 713/439-7481

T

Best Cheap Meal
Jimmy's Taco Shack
213 E. Main, League City, 713/332-6706

Best Chinese Food
Chinese Cafe
5092 Richmond Ave., 713/621-2888
Dong Ting
611 Stuart St., 713/527-0005
Kim Son
2001 Jefferson St., 713/222-2461

Best Coffeehouses
Empire Cafe
1732 Westheimer Rd., 713/528-5282
Mientje's
2470 Times, 713/523-8724

Best Desserts
Empire Cafe
1732 Westheimer Rd., 713/528-5282
Nielsen's Delicatessen
4500 Richmond Ave., 713/963-8005

Best Dim Sum
Imperial Palace
9160 Bellaire, 713/773-3838
2001 Jefferson, 713/222-2461
8200 Wilcrest, 713/498-7841

Best Enchiladas
Ninfa's Mexican Restaurant
Multiple Locations
Irma's
22 N. Chenevert, 713/222-0767
Cafe Annie
1728 Post Oak Blvd., 713/840-1111

Best Fast Food
Zuzu Handmade Mexican Food
5462 FM 1960 W., 713/537-1777
10001 Westheimer Rd., 713/974-4403

Best Homestyle Food
Mom's Cookin'
905 Taft, 713/522-4500
Backstreet Cafe
1103 S. Shepherd Dr., 713/521-2239

Best Ice Cream/Yogurt
Amy's Ice Creams and Coffees
3816 Farnham, 713/526-2697
Woodway Grill
5055 Woodway, 713/623-0788

Best Indian Food
Khyber
2510 Richmond Ave., 713/942-9424

Best Italian Food
Baci
2441 University Blvd., 713/524-1266

Best Japanese Food
Japon
  2444 Times Blvd., 713/526-2100

Best Late-Night Food
House of Pies
  4444 FM 1960 Rd. W., 713/890-7437
  6142 Westheimer Rd., 713/782-1290
  6314 Antoine Dr., 713/680-1641
  3112 Kirby Dr., 713/528-3816
Droubi's Bakery
  3233 Hilcroft, 713/782-6160
  7333 Hilcroft, 713/988-5897
Spanish Flower Mexican Restaurant
  4701 N. Main, 713/869-1706

Best Microbrewery
Houston Brewery
  6224 Richmond Ave., 713/953-0101

Best Mexican Food
Irma's
  22 N. Chenevert St., 713/222-0767
Ninfa's Mexican Restaurant
  Multiple Locations

Best Mom-and-Pop Restaurants
Cafe Lili
  5757 Westheimer Rd., 713/952-6969
Barnaby's Cafe
  604 Fairview, 713/522-0106

Best New Restaurant
L'Aventure
  1811 S. Shepherd, 713/527-9800

Best Outdoor Dining
River Cafe
  3615 Montrose, 713/529-0088
Cafe Noche
  2409 Montrose, 713/529-2409
Backstreet Cafe
  1103 S. Shepherd, 713/521-2239
Patrenella's
  813 Jackson Hill St., 713/863-8223
Yakov's Deli
  3925 Richmond Ave., 713/621-3308

Best Pasta
Carraba's Italian Restaurant
  502 W. Bay Area Blvd., Webster, 713/338-0574
  2335 Hwy. 6, Sugarland, 713/980-4433
Boulevard Bistro
  4319 Montrose, 713/524-6922

Best Pesto
Cafe Express
  1422 W. Gray, 713/522-3100
  1800 Post Oak Blvd., 713/963-9222
  3200 Kirby Dr., 713/522-3994

Best Pizza
Star Pizza
  2111 Norfolk, 713/523-0800

Collina's
  3933 Richmond Ave., 713/621-8844
Mia Pizza
  11148 Westheimer Rd., 713/977-1003
Fuzzy's Pizza
  823 Antoine Dr., 713/682-8836

Best Place to Be "Seen"
Empire Cafe
  1732 Westheimer Rd., 713/528-5282

Best Places to Eat When Someone Else Is Buying
Cafe Annie
  1728 Post Oak Blvd., 713/840-1111
Anthony's
  4007 Westheimer Rd., 713/961-0552

Best Place to Take the Kids
Skeeter's Mesquite Grill
  5529 Wesleyan St., 713/660-7090

Best Salad/Salad Bar
Houston's
  4848 Kirby Dr., 713/529-2385
  5888 Westheimer Rd., 713/975-1947

Best Sandwiches
Backstreet Cafe
  1103 S. Shepherd, 713/521-2239
Ouisie's Table
  3939 San Felipe, 713/528-2264
Jason's Deli
  2611 S. Shepherd Dr., Ste. 100, 713/520-6728
  2530 University Blvd., 713/522-2660
  5403D FM 1960 Rd. W., 713/444-7515
  10321A Katy Freeway, 713/467-2007
  5860 Westheimer Rd., 713/975-7878

Best Seafood
Pappadeaux Seafood Kitchen
  Multiple Locations
Denis Seafood
  12109 Westheimer Rd., 713/497-1110
Los Andes
  3700 Richmond Ave., 713/622-2686
Captain Benny's Half Shell Oyster Bar
  8506 S. Main, 713/666-5469
  8018 Katy Freeway, 713/683-1042
Goode Company Seafood
  2621 Westpark Dr., 713/523-7154

Best Soul Food
Brennan's
  3300 Smith, 713/522-9711

Best Steaks
Brenner's
  10911 Katy Freeway, 713/465-2901

Best Sushi
Miyako
  2910 Kirby Dr., 713/520-9797
  6345 Westheimer Rd., 713/781-6300

Best Thai Food
Tubtim
  6488 FM 1960 W., 713/893-8889

Best Vegetarian Food
A Moveable Feast
  2202 W. Alabama St., 713/528-3585
Yildizlar
  3419 Kirby Dr., 713/524-7735
Dimassi's
  5064 Richmond Ave., 713/439-7481
Wonderful Vegetarian
  7549 Westheimer Rd., 713/977-3137

Standbys
Ruth's Chris Steak House
  6213 Richmond Ave., 713/789-2333

HUNTSVILLE, TX

Best Chinese Food
Imperial Garden
  3708E W. Davis St., 409/539-1566

Best Homestyle Food
The Texan Cafe
  1120 Sam Houston Ave., 409/295-2381

Best Mexican Food
Casa Tomas Mexican Restaurant
  3315 I-45, 409/291-0752

Best Seafood
Junction Steak and Seafood
  2641 Eleventh St., 409/291-2183

Best Steaks
Junction Steak and Seafood
  2641 Eleventh St., 409/291-2183

KILLEEN, TX

Best Restaurant in Town
Henderson's Family Restaurant
  405 Avenue A, 817/554-8505

Best All-You-Can-Eat Buffet
Pancho's Mexican Buffet
  1502 E. Central Texas Expwy., 817/634-4590

Best Barbecue/Ribs
Sam's Barbecue
  1414 S. Fort Hood St., 817/526-8087

Best Burgers
Grid Iron Pro Style Burgers
  1303 E. Rancier Ave., 817/628-8959

Best Brunch
NCO Officer's Club
  37th St., Ft. Hood, 817/532-3317

Best Business Lunch
Henderson's Family Restaurant
  405 Avenue A, 817/554-8505

T

Best Catfish
Ches's Restaurant
413 E. Hwy. 190, Copperas Cove, 817/547-3877

Best Cheap Meal
Ches's Restaurant
413 E. Hwy. 190, Copperas Cove, 817/547-3877

Best Chinese Food
China Star
910 E. Central Texas Expwy., 817/634-8100

Best Desserts
Henderson's Family Restaurant
405 Avenue A, 817/554-8505

Best German Food
Munchner Kind'l German Restaurant
1519 Florence Rd., 817/634-1818

Best Homestyle Food
Ches's Restaurant
413 E. Hwy. 190, Copperas Cove, 817/547-3877

Best Italian Food
Divino's Italian Restorante
2100 SW S. Young, 817/680-3383

Best Mexican Food
Casa Castillo
129 W. Veterans Memorial Blvd., 817/634-1191
Pancho's Mexican Buffet
1502 E. Central Texas Expwy., 817/634-4590

Best Place to Be "Seen"
Remington's Restaurant
1721 E. Central Texas Expwy., 817/634-1555

Best Place to Eat Alone
Luby's Cafeteria
1705 E. Central Texas Expwy., 817/628-8500

Best Place to Take the Kids
Pistol Pete's Pizza
100 Hwy. 190, 817/526-5559

Best Romantic Dining
Remington's Restaurant
1721 E. Central Texas Expwy., 817/634-1555

Best Steaks
Henderson's Family Restaurant
405 Avenue A, 817/554-8505

Standbys
Denny's
1108 S. Fort Hood St., 817/634-8616
Sonic Drive-In
2701 E. Rancier Ave., 817/526-9999
Applebee's
2700 E. Central Texas Expwy., 817/526-9711
TCBY
1801 E. Central Texas Expwy., 817/690-4300
Red Lobster
1001 E. Central Texas Expwy., 817/526-7335

Western Sizzlin
  1001 W. Hallmark Ave., 817/628-8601
Subway
  3301 E. Rancier Ave., 817/699-7827
  1100 Old FM 440 Rd., 817/628-7827
  612 N. Fort Hood St., 817/634-7827

LAREDO, TX

Best Breakfast
Tacoi Palenque
  4515 San Bernardo Ave., Ste.725, 210/725-9898

Best Burgers
Santa Maria Party House
  1909 Santa Maria Ave., 210/724-6969

Best Business Lunch
La Posada Hotel Suites
  1000 Zaragoza St., 210/722-1701

Best French Food
Chez Mauricette
  500 Flores Ave., 210/726-9453

Best Indian Food
Bombay Bar and Grill
  201 W. Del Mar Blvd., 210/717-1003

Best Late-Night Food
Tacoi Palenque
  4515 San Bernardo Ave., Ste.725, 210/725-9898

Best Mexican Food
Tacoi Palenque
  4515 San Bernardo Ave., Ste.725, 210/725-9898
Unicorn Restaurant and Pegasus
  3810 San Bernardo Ave., 210/727-4663

Best Other Ethnic Food
Kon-Tiki Polynesian (Polynesian)
  4803B San Bernardo Ave., 210/727-4962

Best Outdoor Dining
Tacoi Palenque
  4515 San Bernardo Ave., Ste.725, 210/725-9898

Best Pizza
Pistol Pete's Pizza
  3615 McDonell Ave., 210/725-2508
  4600 San Dario Ave., 210/725-2508

Best Place to Take the Kids
Tacoi Palenque
  4515 San Bernardo Ave., Ste.725, 210/725-9898

Best Seafood
Mariscos El Pescador
  3919 San Dario Ave., 210/724-8958
Pelican's Wharf
  619 Chicago St., 210/727-5070

Best Steaks
Unicorn Restaurant and Pegasus
  3810 San Bernardo Ave., 210/727-4663

T

Standbys
Golden Corral Family Restaurant
  5930 San Bernardo Ave., 210/791-3373
Baskin-Robbins
  4803 San Bernardo Ave., 210/724-2541

LEWISVILLE, TX

Best Restaurant in Town
The Pantry
  1288 W. Main St., 214/221-0608

Best Italian Food
Salerno's
  3407 Long Prairie Rd., 214/539-9534

Best Mexican Food
Tamayo's Mexican Food
  501 S. Stemmons Freeway, 214/221-5276

Best Steaks
The Grotto
  2300 Highland Village Rd., Ste. 500, 214/318-0515

LONGVIEW, TX

Best Bar
Bentley's Comedy Club
  310 Spur 63, 903/753-3766

Best Burgers
Butcher Shop
  102 Lehigh St., 903/758-6066

Best Chinese Food
Hupei Chinese Restaurant
  501 N. Spur 63, 903/757-6261

Best Desserts
Oxford Street Restaurant
  421 N. Spur 63, 903/758-9130

Best Family Restaurant
Armadillo Willie's
  102 E. Tyler St., 903/236-4970

Best Health-Conscious Menu
Jack's Natural Food
  1614 Judson Rd., 903/753-4800
  2199 Gilmer Rd., 903/759-4262

Best Homestyle Food
Cotton Patch Cafe
  1228 McCann Rd., 903/236-4009

Best Italian Food
Monjuni's
  212 E. Marshall Ave., 903/236-8541

Best Mexican Food
Posados
  110 Triple Creek, 903/234-9115

Best Pizza
Pizza King
  1100 E. Marshall Ave., 903/753-0912

T

Best Place to Be "Seen"
Armadillo Willie's
102 E. Tyler St., 903/236-4970

Best Place to Eat Alone
Jason's Deli
103 W. Loop 281, 903/663-5161

Best Romantic Dining
Summit Club
211 E. Tyler St., Ste. 918, 903/753-0331

Best Sandwiches
Jason's Deli
103 W. Loop 281, 903/663-5161

Best Seafood
Cace's Seafood and Steak House
1501 E. Marshall Ave., 903/753-7691

Best Steaks
Oxford Street Restaurant
421 N. Spur 63, 903/758-9130

Best Tea Room
Annie's Tea Room
107 N. Tyler St., Big Sandy, 903/636-4952

Best Vegetarian Food
Jack's Natural Food
1614 Judson Rd., 903/753-4800
2199 Gilmer Rd., 903/759-4262

Standbys
Golden Corral Family Steak House
440 W. Loop 281, 903/757-8779
Ryan's Family Steak House
301 E. Loop 281, 903/236-7926
Shoney's
203 W. Loop 281, 903/665-5488
Sonic Drive-In
1611 Judson Rd., 903/758-7961
2106 Gilmer Rd., 903/297-6868
1307 S. High St., 903/758-5944
TCBY
2601 Justin Rd., 903/234-2808
Chili's
2800 Judson Rd., 903/663-2221
Red Lobster
3515 McCann Rd., 903/757-6939

T

LUBBOCK, TX

Best Barbecue/Ribs
Stubb's Bar-B-Q
620 Nineteenth St., 806/747-4777
County Line
Rural Route 3, Box 308, 806/763-6001

Best Breakfast
Mesquite's
2419 Broadway St., 806/763-1159

Best Burgers
Pete's Drive-In
1002 Avenue Q, 806/765-8419

118th at S. University, 806/745-4662
529 34th St., 806/762-8995
4156 34th St., 806/792-2806

Best Cajun/Creole Food
Jazz, A Louisiana Kitchen
3703C Nineteenth St., 806/799-2124

Best Cheap Meal
Bryan's Steaks
1212 50th St., 806/744-5491

Best Desserts
Harrigan's Restaurant
3801 50th St., 806/792-4648

Best Family Restaurant
County Line
Rural Route 3, Box 308, 806/763-6001

Best French Food
Chez Suzette
4423 50th St., 806/795-6796

Best German Food
Schnitzel Haus
FM 835 near Buffalo Springs Lake, 806/763-3223

Best Health-Conscious Menu
Bless Your Heart Restaurant
3701 Nineteenth St., 806/791-2211
Orlando's Italian Restaurant
2402 Avenue Q, 806/747-5998
6951 Indiana Ave., 806/797-8646

Best Indian Food
Delhi Palace Indian Restaurant
5401 Aberdeen Ave., 806/799-6772

Best Italian Food
Orlando's Italian Restaurant
2402 Avenue Q, 806/747-5998
6951 Indiana Ave., 806/797-8646

Best Mexican Food
Juan in a Million
1324 E. 50th St., 806/741-1852

Best Microbrewery
Hub City Brewery
1807 Avenue H, 806/747-1535

Best Salad/Salad Bar
Bless Your Heart Restaurant
3701 Nineteenth St., 806/791-2211

Best Seafood
River Smith's Catering
1602 Main St., 806/744-3474
322 Avenue U, 806/765-8164
Shogun
4520 50th St., 806/797-6044
Cattle Baron Steak and Seafood
8201 Quaker Ave., 806/798-7033

Best Steaks
Depot's Restaurant and Bar
   1801 Avenue G, 806/747-1646

Best Thai Food
Choochai Thai Cuisine
   2330 Nineteenth St., 806/747-1767

Best View While Dining
County Line
   Rural Route 3, Box 308, 806/763-6001

Standbys
Baskin-Robbins
   2902 50th St., 806/793-2240
   315 University Ave., 806/762-8509
   3408 82nd St., 806/797-5008
   4902 34th St., 806/795-1545

LUFKIN, TX

Best Desserts
The Lunch Box
   1422 N. Timberland Dr., 409/639-6334

Best German Food
The Wurst Haus
   4105 Ted Trout Dr., 409/875-2205

Best Homestyle Food
Fuller's Buffet
   1124 S. First St., 409/632-8200

MARSHALL, TX

Best Restaurants in Town
The Hungry Potter
   4901 Elysian Fields Ave., 903/935-1227
Annie Skinner's Riverboat Club
   107 W. Austin St., Jefferson, 903/665-7121
Big Pines
   Pine Island Rd., Karnack, 903/679-3466
Galley Pub
   121 Austin St., Jefferson, 903/665-3641

Best French Food
The Taylor House
   212 W. Bowie St., 903/938-8549

Best Italian Food
Gucci's
   1300 Pinecrest Rd., 903/938-3841

MCALLEN, TX

Best Restaurants in Town
Pepper's Restaurant
   4800 N. Tenth St., 210/631-2082
The Mill
   4105 N. Tenth St., 210/686-6847

Best Bar
Pepper's Restaurant
   4800 N. Tenth St., 210/631-2082

T

Best Barbecue/Ribs
Red Barn BBQ
   4701 N. McColl Rd., 210/631-8332

Best Burgers
Pepper's Restaurant
   4800 N. Tenth St., 210/631-2082

Best Business Lunch
Pepper's Restaurant
   4800 N. Tenth St., 210/631-2082

Best Cheap Meal
El Pato Mexican Food
   3019 N. Tenth St., 210/682-1576
   1121 W. Hwy. 83, 210/687-8269
   2263 Pecan Blvd., 210/682-3176
   1300 E. Tamarack Ave., 210/687-5227

Best Chinese Food
Royal China Restaurant
   1020 Nolana St., 210/631-9009

Best Coffee
Kafecito's
   400 Nolana Loop, 210/664-2464

Best Desserts
Irma's Sweete Shoppe
   120 E. Park Ave., Pharr, 210/787-7131

Best Health-Conscious Menu
Yogurt, Etc.
   2901K N. Tenth St., 210/682-8737

Best Homestyle Food
Luby's Cafeteria
   1215 S. Tenth St., 210/682-3115
   4901 N. Tenth St., 210/687-9568

Best Italian Food
Iannelli Ristorante Italiano
   2316 N. Tenth St., 210/631-0666
La Pasta Italian Restaurant
   3713 N. Tenth St., 210/631-0342

Best Late-Night Food
Taco Cabana
   1010 S. Tenth St., 210/630-2888

Best Mexican Food
Casa Del Taco
   1100 Houston St., 210/631-8193
   600 S. Tenth St., 210/682-1255
Tequila Charlie's
   1114 S. Chance St., 210/664-0065
La Mexicano
   4019 N. Tenth St., 210/631-8191
Johnny's Mexican
   1010 W. Houston Ave., 210/686-9061
La Terraza
   Doubletree Club Hotel, 101 N. Main St., 210/631-1101
La Mexicana
   709 Hwy. 83 W., Pharr, 210/787-7884

Best Place to Be "Seen"
Pepper's Restaurant
  4800 N. Tenth St., 210/631-2082

Best Place to Eat When Someone Else Is Buying
Oyster Bar III
  600 N. Tenth St., 210/686-9924

Best Romantic Dining
Alex's Restaurant and Bar
  2901 N. Tenth St., 210/686-2132

Best Sandwiches
Schlotzsky's
  2616 N. Tenth St., 210/687-6566

Best Seafood
Oyster Bar III
  600 N. Tenth St., 210/686-9924

Best Steaks
Alex's Restaurant and Bar
  2901 N. Tenth St., 210/686-2132
Santa Fe Steakhouse
  1918 S. Tenth St., 210/630-2331

Best Tea Room
Kafecito's
  400 Nolana Loop, 210/664-2464

Standbys
Applebee's
  514 E. Expwy. 83, 210/686-8484

MCKINNEY, TX

Best Restaurant in Town
Bill Smith Cafe
  1510 W. University Dr., 214/542-5331

Best German Food
Rhineland Haus
  1330 N. MacDonald, 214/562-0124

Best Mexican Food
San Miguel Grill
  506 W. University Dr., 214/548-2345

MESQUITE, TX

T

Best Restaurant in Town
Grady's American Grill
  3811 Pavillion Ct., 214/686-1919

Best All-You-Can-Eat Buffet
Memories
  2015 N. Galloway Ave., 214/288-9359

Best Breakfast
Circle Grill
  3701 N. Buckner Blvd., Dallas, 214/324-4140

Best Brunch
Benedict's Restaurant
  4800 Belt Line Rd., Dallas, 214/490-0500

Best Burgers
The Feed Bag
  3600 Gus Thomasson Rd., Ste. 100, 214/270-0852

Best Casual Dining
Don Pablo's
3900 Pavillion Rd., 214/613-7832

Best Cheap Meal
Burger Street
6424 Greenville Ave., Dallas, 214/890-7913
13612 Preston Rd., Dallas, 214/392-3282
9180 Skillman St., Dallas, 214/348-3127

Best Chinese Food
Chi's Wok
1111 N. Town East Blvd., Ste. 10, 214/279-1088
China Coast Restaurant
4000 Towne Crossing Blvd., 214/613-9929

Best Desserts
Braum's Ice Cream and Dairy
219 N. Galloway Ave., 214/285-6066
4645 Gus Thomasson Rd., 214/279-2661

Best Diner
Owen's Family Restaurant
3919 Pavillion Ct., 214/613-8690

Best Family Restaurant
Donna's Kitchen
3600 Gus Thomasson Rd., 214/613-3651

Best Health-Conscious Menu
Boston Market
1230 N. Town East Blvd., 214/681-0600

Best Homestyle Food
Luby's Cafeteria
3301 Gus Thomasson Rd., 214/279-6169

Best Ice Cream/Yogurt
Braum's Ice Cream and Dairy
219 N. Galloway Ave., 214/285-6066
4645 Gus Thomasson Rd., 214/279-2661

Best Italian Food
Calzone's Pizza and Italian
2411 N. Galloway Ave., 214/686-8905

Best Indian Food
Ranjini Indian Cuisine
1813B N. Galloway Ave., 214/329-1599

Best Late-Night Food
Kettle Restaurant
1125 Gross Rd., 214/289-8946

Best Mexican Food
Martinez Restaurant
810 W. Kearney St., 214/288-7772

Best Pizza
Cici's Pizza
3330 N. Galloway Ave., 214/686-1700

Best Sandwiches
Grady's American Grill
3811 Pavillion Ct., 214/686-1919
Donna's Kitchen
3600 Gus Thomasson Rd., 214/613-3651

Best Steaks
Trail Dust Steak House
  21717 Lyndon B. Johnson Freeway, 214/289-5457

Best Tea Room
Lady Primrose's Thatched Pantry
  500 Crescent Ct., Dallas, 214/871-8334

Best Vegetarian Food
Macrobiotic Center of Dallas
  850 S. Greenville Ave., Dallas, 214/669-8323

Standbys
Subway
  12350 Lake June Rd., 214/286-4200
  3522 Gus Thomasson Rd., 214/270-0268
  2063 Town East Shopping Ctr., 214/613-9898
  1704 Military Pkwy., 214/289-7827
  2411 N. Galloway Ave., 214/613-7374
Ryan's Family Steak House
  909 Tripp Rd., 214/613-8826
Red Lobster
  3906 Towne Crossing Blvd., 214/613-1444
Outback Steakhouse
  3903 Towne Crossing Blvd., 214/686-0555
El Chico
  2028 Town East Mall, 214/270-7727

MIDLAND, TX

Best Bar
Bennigan's
  4517 N. Midkiff Rd., 915/697-3237

Best Business Lunch
Abuelo's Mexican Restaurant
  4610 N. Garfield St., 915/685-3335

Best Chinese Food
Hunan Garden
  4410 N. Midkiff Rd., Ste. A-10, 915/697-9818

Best Italian Food
Luigi's Italian Restaurant
  111 N. Big Spring St., 915/683-6363

Best Late-Night Food
Bennigan's
  4517 N. Midkiff Rd., 915/697-3237

Best Mexican Food
Abuelo's Mexican Restaurant
  4610 N. Garfield St., 915/685-3335

Best Place to Be "Seen"
Abuelo's Mexican Restaurant
  4610 N. Garfield St., 915/685-3335

Best Place to Eat When Someone Else Is Buying
Abuelo's Mexican Restaurant
  4610 N. Garfield St., 915/685-3335

Best Place to Take the Kids
Luby's Cafeteria
  2510 W. Louisiana Ave., 915/682-6256

T

Best Romantic Dining
Venezia Restaurant
  20 Plaza Ctr., 915/687-0900

Best Sandwiches
Murray's Deli
  3211 W. Wadley St., Ste. 24, 915/697-3433

Best Steaks
Cattlemen's Restaurant
  3300 N. Big Spring St., 915/682-5668

Standbys
Golden Corral Family Steak House
  4709 N. Midkiff Rd., 915/689-7706
Denny's
  3701 W. Wall St., 915/697-3237
Chili's
  2100 W. Loop 250N, 915/687-3744
El Chico
  2101 W. Wadley St., Ste. 45, 915/683-4311
Baskin-Robbins
  2101 W. Wadley Ave., Ste. 4, 915/682-7131
Pizza Hut
  4320 Andrews Hwy., 915/697-5581
  427 Andrews Hwy., 915/686-1888
  2200 W. Wadley Ave., 915/683-2240
  4400 N. Midland Dr., 915/694-7225
Red Lobster
  2319 W. Loop 250N, 915/687-1945

NACOGDOCHES, TX

Best Barbecue/Ribs
Smokehouse
  2709 Westward Dr., 409/560-6714

Best Breakfast
Hot Biscuit
  3227 South St., 409/560-3555

Best Burgers
Butcher Boy's Meats and Deli
  900 N. Mound St., 409/560-1137
Smokehouse
  2709 Westward Dr., 409/560-6714

Best Chinese Food
Szechuan Chinese Restaurant
  3205 N. University Dr., 409/569-2266

Best Homestyle Food
Cotton Patch Cafe
  3117 North St., Ste. 1, 409/569-6926

Best Mexican Food
La Carreta
  3000 North St., 409/569-2800

Best Seafood
Californian
  342 N. University Dr., 409/560-1985

T

NEW BRAUNFELS, TX

Best Restaurant in Town
The Grist Mill
  1287 Gruene Rd., 210/625-0684

Best American Food
Plaza Diner
  367 Main Plaza, 210/620-7070

Best Burgers
Molly Joe's
  1153 Oasis St., 210/620-1234

Best German Food
Krause's Cafe
  148 S. Castell Ave., 210/625-7581

Best Mexican Food
Molly Joe's
  1153 Oasis St., 210/620-1234
Adobe Cafe
  124 W. Hwy. 81, 210/620-4433

Best Seafood
Clear Springs Restaurant
  1692 Hwy. 46S, 210/629-3775

ODESSA, TX

Best Burgers
Texas Burger
  1507 John Ben Shepperd Pkwy., 915/367-9584
  5200 Andrews Hwy., 915/366-3801
  7546 W. University Blvd., 915/381-7593

Best Business Lunch
Harrigan's Restaurant
  2701 John Ben Shepperd Pkwy., 915/367-4185

Best Cheap Meal
Mr. Gatti's Pizza
  2750 N. Grandview, 915/368-4488

Best Chinese Food
Sakura Restaurant
  4555 E. University Blvd., 915/367-6332

Best Health-Conscious Menu
Calico Cafe
  2931 E. Hwy. 80, 915/334-6899

Best Italian Food
Sorento's
  4019 John Ben Shepperd Pkwy., 915/550-8434

Best Mexican Food
Al's Mexican Food
  4651 N. Grandview Ave., 915/362-5571

Best Pizza
Mr. Gatti's Pizza
  2750 N. Grandview, 915/368-4488

Best Place to Eat Alone
Harrigan's Restaurant
  2701 John Ben Shepperd Pkwy., 915/367-4185

T

Best Romantic Dining
Zucchi's
1541 John Ben Shepperd Pkwy., Ste. 18,
915/550-7443

Best Steaks
Barn Door Restaurant
2140 N. Grant Ave., 915/337-4142
Cattlemen's Restaurant
3300 N. Big Spring St., 915/682-5668

Best Vegetarian Food
Calico Cafe
2931 E. Hwy. 80, 915/334-6899

Standbys
Golden Corral Family Steak House
4037 E. 42nd St., 915/363-8705
International House of Pancakes
2973 John Ben Shepperd Pkwy., 915/363-8742
Baskin-Robbins
1400 N. Country Rd. W., 915/332-3831
2618A N. Grandview Ave., 915/366-6031
The Olive Garden
2705 W. Loop 250, 915/687-4400
Red Lobster
4536 E. University Blvd., 915/367-8926
Subway
3830 Andrews Hwy., 915/363-9626
2633 N. Country Rd. W., 915/332-4517
2720 N. Grandview Ave., 915/363-0770
604 E. Eighth St., 915/580-3314

PARIS, TX

Best Barbecue/Ribs
Tommy's Barbecue
6825 Lamar Ave., 903/785-2808

Best Breakfast
McKee's 24-Hour Family Restaurant
1355 N. Collegiate Dr., 903/785-0002

Best Burgers
McKee's 24-Hour Family Restaurant
1355 N. Collegiate Dr., 903/785-0002

Best Chinese Food
China Star
1810 Lamar Ave., 903/785-8872

Best Homestyle Food
McKee's 24-Hour Family Restaurant
1355 N. Collegiate Dr., 903/785-0002

Best Ice Cream/Yogurt
Braum's Ice Cream
2160 Lamar Ave., 903/784-0214
2035 Bonham St., 903/784-2142

Best Mexican Food
Papacita's Mexican Restaurant
3015 Loop 286, 903/785-7797

Best Seafood
Fish Fry
3500 NE Loop 286, 903/785-6144

Best Steaks
Sirloin Stockade
1167 Lamar Ave., 903/785-0319

Standbys
Pizza Hut
1610 Clarksville St., 903/784-5051

PASADENA, TX

Best All-You-Can-Eat Buffet
China River Buffet
3807 Spencer Hwy., 713/910-8899

Best Bar
Clearlake Beach Club
3813 NASA Roadway, Kemah, 713/326-3066

Best Barbecue/Ribs
Feed Lot Barbecue
1920 Richey St., 713/477-1531

Best Burgers
Joe's Texan Burger
2406 Preston Ave., 713/472-5001

Best Casual Dining
Kettle Restaurant
3002 Pasadena Hwy., 713/472-5270
6926 Spencer Hwy., 713/479-0988

Best Chinese Food
China River Buffet
3807 Spencer Hwy., 713/910-8899

Best Family Restaurant
Black-Eyed Pea
3800A Spencer Hwy., 713/947-2776

Best Late-Night Food
Kettle Restaurant
3002 Pasadena Hwy., 713/472-5270
6926 Spencer Hwy., 713/479-0988

Best Mexican Food
Marco's Mexican Restaurant
1860 E. Beltway 8, 713/472-1919
Tortillas
9602 Spencer Hwy., La Porte, 713/479-1710

Best Outdoor Dining
On the Border Cafe
4608 Westheimer Rd., Houston, 713/961-4494

Best Pizza
Mitchelo's Pizza, Pasta and More
1900A Strawberry Rd., 713/473-8200

Best Place to Eat When Someone Else Is Buying
On the Border Cafe
4608 Westheimer Rd., Houston, 713/961-4494

Best Romantic Dining
Monument Inn
4406 Battleground Rd., La Porte, 713/479-1521

T

Best Sandwiches
Schlotzsky's Deli
   1221 S. Main and Southmore, 713/473-3930
   3830 Spencer Hwy., 713/946-2034

Best Seafood
Monument Inn
   4406 Battleground Rd., La Porte, 713/479-1521

Best View While Dining
Monument Inn
   4406 Battleground Rd., La Porte, 713/479-1521

PLAINVIEW, TX

Best Barbecue/Ribs
Chuckwagon Bar-B-Q
   2105 Dimmit Rd., 806/296-9907

Best Breakfast
Spudnut Shop
   1806 W. Fifth St., 806/296-9198

Best Chinese Food
Far East Restaurant
   910 S. I-27, 806/296-6812

Best Coffee
Spudnut Shop
   1806 W. Fifth St., 806/296-9198

Best Family Restaurant
Kettle Restaurant
   700 N. I-27, 806/293-1423

Best Homestyle Food
Cotton Patch Cafe
   3314 Olton Rd., 806/293-5522

Best Ice Cream/Yogurt
Roaring 50's Sandwich Shop
   600 Quincy St., 806/293-4264

Best Mexican Food
Leal's Mexican Restaurant
   3311 Olton Rd., 806/293-5355

Best Sandwiches
Fieldhouse Sandwich Shop
   3402B Olton Rd., 806/293-5092
Roaring 50's Sandwich Shop
   600 Quincy St., 806/293-4264

Best Tea Room
Bridal House by Fleur-De-Lis
   212 W. Ninth St., 806/296-9444

Standbys
Pizza Hut
   2909 Olton Rd., 806/293-5000

PLANO, TX

Best American Food
Jack Astor's Bar and Grill
   2901 N. Central Expwy., 214/423-0533

Best Bar
Humperdink's Restaurant
  1601 N. Central Expwy., Richardson, 214/690-4867

Best Barbecue/Ribs
Dickey's Barbecue Pit
  1211 Fourteenth St., 214/423-9960
  1441A Coit Rd., 214/867-2901

Best Breakfast
Poor Richard's Cafe
  2442 K Avenue, 214/423-1524

Best Brunch
Plaza Cafe
  Dallas Grand Hotel, 1914 Commerce St., Dallas,
    214/747-7000

Best Burgers
Chuck's Restaurant
  3308 Preston Rd., 214/596-4211

Best Casual Dining
Jack Astor's Bar and Grill
  2901 N. Central Expwy., 214/423-0533

Best Chinese Food
Wang's Chinese Restaurant
  3033 W. Parker Rd., 214/985-9099

Best Coffee
Starbucks
  2201 Preston Rd., 214/964-7020
  801 W. Fifteenth St., 214/422-5003

Best Desserts
Patrizio North
  1900 Preston Rd., 214/964-2200

Best Family Restaurant
Black-Eyed Pea
  1915 N. Central Expwy., 214/423-5565
  1932 Preston Park Blvd., 214/964-1353

Best Health-Conscious Menu
Souper Salad
  1017 N. Central Expwy., 214/422-7022

Best Homestyle Food
Good Eats Cafe
  1101 N. Central Expwy., 214/516/3287

Best Ice Cream/Yogurt
Braum's Ice Cream and Dairy
  1401 Independence Pkwy., 214/596-1404
  1718 Fourteenth St., 214/424-8767
  2005 W. Parker Rd., 214/596-3358
  600 E. Fifteenth St., 214/423-2801

Best Italian Food
Picasso's
  3948 Legacy Dr., 214/618-4143
La Riviera Trattoria
  421 Piaget Ave., Clifton, 201/478-4181

Best Late-Night Food
Humperdink's Restaurant
  1601 N. Central Expwy., Richardson, 214/690-4867

T

Best Mexican Food
Tino's Mexican Restaurant
 811 N. Central Expwy., 214/424-2572
Tino's Too
 1585 K Avenue, 214/881-9226

Best Pastries
Patrizio North
 1900 Preston Rd., 214/964-2200

Best Pizza
Mr. Jim's Pizzeria
 2357 Jupiter Rd., 214/422-1953

Best Place to Eat Alone
La Riviera Trattoria
 421 Piaget Ave., Clifton, 201/478-4181

Best Place to Eat When Someone Else Is Buying
Plaza Cafe
 Dallas Grand Hotel, 1914 Commerce St., Dallas,
 214/747-7000

Best Place to Take the Kids
Cici's Pizza
 2011 W. Spring Creek Pkwy., 214/517-8004
 2220 Coit Rd., 214/964-0061
 3611 Fourteenth St., 214/423-0240

Best Salad/Salad Bar
Souper Salad
 1017 N. Central Expwy., 214/422-7022

Best Steaks
Hoffbrau Steaks
 3310 N. Central Expwy., 214/423-4475

PORT ARTHUR, TX

Best Brunch
Holiday Inn
 2929 Jimmy Johnson Blvd., 409/724-5000

Best Business Lunch
Port Arthur Club
 441 Austin Ave., 409/982-2011

Best Casual Dining
Schooner
 1507 Hwy. 69, 409/722-2323

Best Chinese Food
New China Restaurant
 2600 Memorial Blvd., 409/983-4937

Best Desserts
Pieface
 2525 Jefferson Dr., 409/962-4443

Best Diner
Pigstands
 3695 College St., Beaumont, 409/835-9394
 1595 Calder St., Beaumont, 409/835-9702

Best Health-Conscious Menu
Bennigan's
 325 I-10N, Beaumont, 409/833-2648

Best Homestyle Food
French Quarter
  533 Twin City Hwy., 409/962-6326
Dorothy's Front Porch
  1001 Holmes Rd., Nederland, 409/722-1472

Best Ice Cream/Yogurt
Marble Slab Creamery
  6626 Phelan Blvd., Beaumont, 409/866-4740

Best Italian Food
Patrizi's Restaurant
  2050 I-10S, Beaumont, 409/842-5151

Best Late-Night Food
Bennigan's
  325 I-10N, Beaumont, 409/833-2648

Best Mexican Food
Guadalajara Restaurant
  1600 Ninth Ave., 409/983-9173

Best Pizza
Peter Piper Pizza
  3647 N. Twin City Hwy., 409/962-5522

Best Place to Be "Seen"
Pompano Club
  330 Twin City Hwy., Port Neches, 409/727-3111

Best Place to Eat Alone
Casa Ole Mexican Restaurant
  3100 Hwy. 365, 409/727-5377
  4801 N. Twin City Hwy., 409/963-0185

Best Place to Eat When Someone Else Is Buying
Sartin's
  6725 Eastex Freeway, Beaumont, 409/892-6771

Best Place to Take the Kids
Pancho's Mexican Buffet
  850 S. Eleventh St., Beaumont, 409/835-0289

Best Romantic Dining
Sartin's
  6725 Eastex Freeway, Beaumont, 409/892-6771

Best Sandwiches
Jason's Deli
  170 Central Mall Shopping Ctr., 409/727-6420

Best Seafood
Dorothy's Front Porch
  1001 Holmes Rd., Nederland, 409/722-1472

Best Vegetarian Food
Luby's Cafeteria
  745 N. Eleventh St., Beaumont, 409/892-4181

Standbys
International House of Pancakes
  3830 College St., Beaumont, 409/833-5510
Golden Corral Family Steak House
  4145 College St., Beaumont, 409/842-2441
The Olive Garden
  585 I-10N, Beaumont, 409/832-9058

Outback Steakhouse
  2060 I-10S, 409/842-6699
Waffle House
  2940 75th St., 409/724-2141

ROSENBERG, TX

Best Restaurant in Town
Hill's Cafe
  1011 FM 359 Rd., 281/341-0030

Best Chinese Food
Hunan Garden Restaurant
  4601 Avenue H, Ste. 7, 281/342-7279

Best Mexican Food
Larry's Original Mexican
  116 E. Hwy. 60A, Richmond, 281/342-2881

Best Steaks
Western Steakhouse
  3614 Avenue I, 281/342-9602

Best 24-Hour Restaurant
The Texas Grill Restaurant
  1210 Avenue H, 281/342-4775

SAN ANGELO, TX

Best Bar
Santa Fe Junction
  1524 S. Bryant Blvd., 915/658-5068

Best Burgers
Charcoal House
  1616 S. Bryant Blvd., 915/653-6666
  1205 N. Chadbourne St., 915/657-2931

Best Business Lunch
Michael's
  Cactus Hotel, 36 E. Twohig Ave., 915/658-6373

Best Cheap Meal
Mr. T's Grocery and Market
  900 W. Avenue J, 915/655-6944

Best Chinese Food
China Garden Restaurant
  4217 S. College Hills Blvd., 915/949-2838

Best Coffee
Cactus Coffee and Tea
  Cactus Hotel, 36 E. Twohig Ave., 915/659-1470

Best Desserts
Cactus Coffee and Tea
  Cactus Hotel, 36 E. Twohig Ave., 915/659-1470

Best Diner
Dixie Diner
  102 N. Bryant Blvd., 915/655-6279

Best Family Restaurant
Shakey's Pizza Parlor
  20 Howard St., 915/944-7611

Best Homestyle Food
Peasant Village
  23 S. Park, 915/655-4811

Best Italian Food
Spaghetti Western
  2307 Loop 306, 915/944-8082
Taste of Italy
  3520 Knickerbocker Rd., 915/944-3290

Best Late-Night Food
Kettle Restaurant
  1811 S. Bryant Blvd., 915/655-5542

Best Mexican Food
Fuentes Cafe Downtown
  101 S. Chadbourne St., 915/658-2430
Better Than Nothing
  1911 S. Bryant Blvd., 915/655-3553
La Casa Blanca
  3020 N. Chadbourne St., 915/653-1058
Little Mexico Restaurant
  4248 Sherwood Way, 915/949-5570
Henry's Diner
  3015 Sherwood Way, 915/944-3245

Best Pizza
Pinocchio's Pizza
  4241 Southwest Blvd., 915/949-6666

Best Place to Be "Seen"
China Garden Restaurant
  4217 S. College Hills Blvd., 915/949-2838

Best Place to Eat Alone
Taste of Italy
  3520 Knickerbocker Rd., 915/944-3290

Best Place to Eat When Someone Else Is Buying
Twin Mountains Steakhouse
  6534 Hwy. 67S, 915/949-4239

Best Place to Take the Kids
Shakey's Pizza Parlor
  20 Howard St., 915/944-7611

Best Romantic Dining
Taste of Italy
  3520 Knickerbocker Rd., 915/944-3290

Best Sandwiches
Concho Confetti
  42 E. Concho Rd., 915/655-3962

Best Seafood
Wharf
  2302 W. Loop 306, 915/944-3414

Best Steaks
Zentner's Steak House
  1901 Knickerbocker Rd., 915/949-2821
  2715 Sherwood Way, 915/942-8631
Twin Mountain Steakhouse
  6534 Hwy. 67S, 915/949-4239

T

Best Tea Room
Jabberwocky's
33 E. Concho St., 915/659-6903

Standbys
Golden Corral Family Steak House
1801 Knickerbocker Rd., 915/949-2554
Baskin-Robbins
3524 Knickerbocker Rd., 915/944-8646
Red Lobster
3909 Sunset Dr., 915/942-6711

SAN ANTONIO, TX

Best American Food
Restaurant Biga
206 E. Locust, 210/255-0722

Best Barbecue/Ribs
The County Line
111 W. Crockett, 210/229-1941
606 W. Afton Oaks Blvd., 210/496-0011
Big Buck's A-1 Bar-B-Q
120 W. Commerce St., 210/212-3895

Best Bistros
Bistro Time
5137 Fredericksburg Rd., 210/344-6626
Boardwalk Bistro
4011 Broadway St., 210/824-0100

Best Burgers
Chris Madrid's Nachos and Burgers
1900 Blanco, 210/735-3552

Best Business Lunch
Paesano's
1715 McCullough, 210/226-9541

Best Cajun/Creole Food
Pappadeaux's Seafood Kitchen
76 NE Loop 410, 210/340-7143

Best Chinese Food
Hung Fong
3624 Broadway, 210/822-9211
Gin's Chinese Restaurant
5337 Glen Ridge Dr., 210/684-7008

Best Coffeehouse
Rock and Java
502 Embassy Oaks, Ste. 142, 210/494-5282

Best Continental Food
Boardwalk Bistro
4011 Broadway, 210/824-0100

Best Delicatessen
Jason's Deli
9933 W. I-10, 210/690-3354
Pavillion North Shopping Ctr., Loop 410 at
McCullough, 210/524-9288

Best French Food
La Madeleine
4820 Broadway, 210/829-7271

Best German Food
Nadler's
7053 San Pedro Ave., 210/340-1021

Best Greek/Mediterranean Food
Babylon
901 S. Alamo, 210/229-9335

Best Happy Hour Snacks
Houlihan's
120 North Star Mall, 210/340-6062

Best Health-Conscious Menu
Cafe Lite and Bakery
459 McCarty Rd., 210/342-3336
8498 Fredericksburg Rd., 210/614-2600
999 E. Basse Rd., 210/824-0027

Best Indian Food
Simi's
4535 Fredricksburg Rd., 210/737-3166

Best Italian Food
Paesano's
1715 McCullough, 210/226-9541
Little Italy
824 Afterglow St., 210/349-2060

Best Japanese Food
Koi Kawa
4051 Broadway St., 210/805-8111

Best Mexican Food
Los Barrios
4223 Blanco, 210/732-6017
Nacho Mama's
24057 Old Fredericksburg Rd., 210/698-0020
El Mirador
722 S. St. Mary's St., 210/225-9444

Best New Restaurant
Pappadeaux's Seafood Kitchen
76 NE Loop 410, 210/340-7143

Best Pizza
EZ's
5720 Bandera Rd., 210/681-2222
734 W. Bitters, 210/490-6666
8498 N. New Braunfels, 210/828-1111

Best Regional Food
Cascabel Restaurant and Bar
Sheraton Fiesta Hotel, 37 NE Loop 410, 210/366-2424

Best River Walk Restaurant
Boudro's
421 E. Commerce, 210/224-8484

Best Salad/Salad Bar
Souper Salad
Multiple Locations

Best Seafood
Sea Island Shrimp House
10141 Wurzbach, 210/558-8989
322 W. Rector, 210/342-7771

T

Best Thai Food
Dang's Thai
1146 Austin Hwy., 210/829-7345

Best Vietnamese Food
Saigon Dynasty
9226 Wurzbach, 210/614-6799

Standbys
Ruth's Chris Steak House
7720 Jones Maltsberger, 210/821-5051

SAN MARCOS, TX

Best Atmosphere
Texas Red's Steakhouse and Saloon
120 W. Grove St., 512/754-8808

Best Barbecue/Ribs
Kreuz Market
208 S. Commerce St., Lockhart, 512/398-2361
Salt Lick BBQ
1826 Fram Market Rd., Dripping Springs,
512/858-4959

Best Breakfast
Herbert's Taco Hut
419 Riverside Dr., 512/353-9323
Wesray's
215 N. LBJ Dr., 512/353-3663

Best Burgers
Grins Restaurant
802 N. LBJ Dr., 512/392-4746

Best Cheap Meal
Herbert's Taco Hut
419 Riverside Dr., 512/353-9323

Best Chinese Food
Hong Kong Restaurant
812 S. Guadalupe St., 512/392-5665
Imperial Garden Chinese Restaurant
1104L Thorpe Ln., 512/353-3355

Best Coffee
Wesray's
215 N. LBJ Dr., 512/353-3663

Best Desserts
Cottage Kitchen
400 E. Hopkins St., 512/392-4295
Palmer's Restaurant and Bar
218 Moore St., 512/353-3500

Best Health-Conscious Menu
Grins Restaurant
802 N. LBJ Dr., 512/392-4746

Best Homestyle Food
Cottage Kitchen
400 E. Hopkins St., 512/392-4295

Best Mexican Food
Herbert's Taco Hut
419 Riverside Dr., 512/353-9323

Best Pizza
Schlotzsky's
909 Hwy. 80, 512/353-3354

Best Sandwiches
Schlotzsky's
909 Hwy. 80, 512/353-3354

Best Steaks
Texas Reds Steakhouse and Saloon
120 W. Grove St., 512/754-8808

SHERMAN, TX

Best Barbecue/Ribs
Clark's Outpost Bar-B-Q
Hwy. 377 at Gene Autry Dr., Tioga, 817/437-2414
Don's Barbeque
1250 W. Dallas Ave., Cooper, 903/395-2977

Best Breakfast
Kettle Restaurant
2100 Texoma Pkwy., 903/868-2395

Best Chinese Food
Gourmet China
4909 N. Hwy. 75, 903/892-3882

Best Coffee
Not Just Coffee
1924 N. Grand, 903/892-9788

Best Desserts
Sue Conrad's Pies
219 N. Travis St., 903/893-5053

Best Health-Conscious Menu
Tiffin Shop
221 Sunset Blvd., 903/893-4737

Best Homestyle Food
City Limits
4521 Texoma Pkwy., 903/893-9117

Best Ice Cream/Yogurt
Braum's
600 N. Travis St., 903/893-2421

Best Indian Food
Tiffin Shop
221 Sunset Blvd., 903/893-4737

Best Italian Food
Old Italian Depot
101 E. Main St., Denison, 903/463-2145

Best Mexican Food
Garcia's Mexican Cafe
106B Sunset Blvd., 903/893-8388
119 W. Main St., Denison, 903/463-1624
2900 Woodlawn Blvd., Denison, 903/463-4414

Best Sandwiches
Sandwich Shop
110 E. Houston St., 903/892-9305
Vitina's Deli Delights
1001 N. Travis St., 903/892-6480

T

Best Seafood
Tiffin Shop
221 Sunset Blvd., 903/893-4737

Best Soul Food
Hunter's Kitchen
1703 N. Woods, 903/870-039

TEMPLE, TX

Best Barbecue/Ribs
Cyclone Corral Bar B-Q
Rural Route 1, 817/985-2317

Best Breakfast
Blue Bonnet Cafe
705 S. 25th St., 817/773-6654

Best Burgers
Jody's Family Restaurant
1307 S. First St., 817/774-7999

Best Homestyle Food
Blue Bonnet Cafe
705 S. 25th St., 817/773-6654

Best Italian Food
Sorge's
1323 S. 57th St., 817/899-1492

Best Mexican Food
Casa Salgado
715 S. First St., 817/770-1313
Las Casas Restaurante
2907 S. General Bruce Dr., 817/774-7476

Best Seafood
Frank's Lakeview Inn and Anchor Club
2207 Lake Rd., Belton, 817/939-5771

TEXARKANA, TX

Best Restaurants in Town
Park Place
2905 Arkansas Blvd., 501/772-2201
Doc Alexander's
4900 Texas Blvd., 903/792-7925

Best Homestyle Food
Bryce's Cafeteria
2021 Mall Dr., 903/792-1611

TEXAS CITY, TX

Best Barbecue/Ribs
Grand Prize Barbeque
2223 Palmer Hwy., 409/948-6501

Best Breakfast
Kelly's
4604 Gulf Freeway, Lamarque, 409/935-3131
Busy Bee Cafe
3440 Palmer Hwy., 409/945-8444
2008 Texas Ave., 409/943-4007

Best Chinese Food
Fortune Chinese Restaurant
3118 Palmer Hwy., 409/945-3134

Best Homestyle Food
Kelly's
4604 Gulf Freeway, Lamarque, 409/935-3131

Best Mexican Food
Marco's Mexican Restaurant
1020 W. NASA Rd. 1, Webster, 713/338-1247

Best Pizza
Cici's Pizza
3506 Palmer Hwy., 409/945-2021

Best Seafood
Gus' Restaurant
911 Eleventh Ave. N., 409/948-8004

Best Steaks
Gus' Restaurant
911 Eleventh Ave. N., 409/948-8004

Standbys
The Olive Garden
10212 Emmette F. Lowry Expwy., 409/986-7471
Baskin-Robbins
2802 Palmer Hwy., 409/948-2182

TYLER, TX

Best Restaurants in Town
Fuller's Fine Foods
601 E. Front St., 903/593-3572
Mansion on the Hill
3324 Old Anderson Hwy., 903/533-1628

Best Bar
Rick's
104 W. Erwin St., 903/531-2415

Best Breakfast
D's Royal Coffee Shop
710 E. Front St., 903/597-3653

Best Brunch
Broadway South
5701 S. Broadway Ave., 903/561-5800

Best Burgers
J.W. Finn's Cafe
2324 S. Southeast Loop 323, 903/592-2833

Best Business Lunch
Oxford Street
3300 Troup Hwy., 903/593-2655

Best Casual Dining
Jason's Deli
4740 S. Broadway Ave., 903/561-5380

Best Cheap Meal
Bruno's Pizza
1400 S. Vine Ave., 903/595-1676

Best Chinese Food
Hunan Chinese Restaurant
1610 S. Vine Ave., 903/595-6677
Liang's Chinese Restaurant
1828 E. Southeast Loop 323, 903/593-7883

Best Coffee
Tyler Square Antiques and Tea Room
117 S. Broadway Ave., 903/593-6888
Country Coffee House
4200 Old Bullard Rd., 903/581-4641

Best Desserts
Chez Bazan French Bakery
5930 Old Bullard Rd., 903/561-9644

Best Diner
Fuller's Fine Foods
601 E. Front St., 903/595-1676
Cox's Grill
706 W. Front St., 903/593-8940

Best Family Restaurant
Pauline's Country Buffet
3040 W. Gentry Pkwy., 903/592-1955

Best French Food
Currents Restaurant
1121 E. Second St., 903/597-3771

Best Health-Conscious Menu
Honey Tree
211 Shelley Dr., 903/561-5329
Cace's Seafood
7011 S. Broadway Ave., 903/581-0744
Szechuan Chinese Restaurant
6421 S. Broadway Ave., 903/581-4310
Liang's Chinese Restaurant
1828 E. Southeast Loop 323, 903/593-7883

Best Homestyle Food
Pauline's Country Buffet
3040 W. Gentry Pkwy., 903/592-1955

Best Ice Cream/Yogurt
La Yogurt
322 E. Southeast Loop 323, 903/561-9977

Best Italian Food
Giuseppe's
212 Grande Blvd., 903/534-0265

Best Mexican Food
Papacita's Mexican Restaurant
6704 S. Broadway Ave., 903/581-7433

Best Pizza
Bruno's Pizza
1400 S. Vine St., 903/595-1676

Best Places to Be "Seen"
Fuller's Fine Foods
601 E. Front St., 903/593-3572
Mansion on the Hill
3324 Old Anderson Hwy., 903/533-1628

Best Romantic Dining
Mansion on the Hill
  3324 Old Anderson Hwy., 903/533-1628

Best Sandwiches
Jason's Deli
  4740 S. Broadway Ave., 903/561-5380
Schlotzsky's
  709 S. Beckham Ave., 903/592-8390
  4500 S. Broadway Ave., 903/561-2650

Best Seafood
Cace's Seafood
  7011 S. Broadway Ave., 903/581-0744

Best Steaks
Allen's Steakhouse
  4111 Tupe Hwy., 903/509-2535

Best Tea Rooms
Tyler Square Antiques and Tea Room
  117 S. Broadway Ave., 903/593-6888
Annie's Tea Room
  107 N. Tyler St., Big Sandy, 903/636-4952

Best Vegetarian Food
Honey Tree
  211 Shelley Dr., 903/561-5329

VICTORIA, TX

Best Breakfast
Village Inn
  2301 N. Ben Jordan St., 512/572-0770

Best Cajun/Creole Food
Boudreaux
  2507 Port Lavaca Dr., 512/578-9192

Best Chinese Food
Dragon Palace
  5223 Hallettsville Hwy., 512/573-1342
Great Wall Chinese Restaurant
  2902 Houston Hwy., 512/572-3788
China Inn
  3602 Houston Hwy., 512/573-0609

Best Italian Food
Olde Victoria Restaurant
  207 N. Navarro St., 512/572-8840

Best Mexican Food
Tejas Cafe and Bar
  2902 N. Navarro St., 512/572-9433
Taqueria Victoria
  209 S. Main St., 512/572-8226
Del Lago Restaurant
  1002 N. Navarro St., 512/572-3846

Best Sandwiches
Fossati's
  302 S. Main St., 512/576-3354

Best Other Restaurant
Plaza Club
  1 O'Connor Plz., Twelfth Fl., 512/578-1881

T

WACO, TX

Best Atmosphere
Buzzard Billy's
  208 S. University Parks Dr., 817/753-2778
Chelsea Street Pub
  6001 W. Waco Dr., Ste. 103, 817/772-1830

Best Bar
Chelsea Street Pub
  6001 W. Waco Dr., Ste. 103, 817/772-1830

Best Burgers
Whataburger Restaurant
  100 S. Loop 340, 817/772-0642
  420 N. Valley Mills Dr., 817/772-5822
  928 S. Seventh St., 817/753-0389
  950 N. Loop 340, 817/799-0267

Best Cajun/Creole Food
Buzzard Billy's
  208 S. University Parks Dr., 817/753-2778

Best Family Restaurant
Black-Eyed Pea
  5501 Bosque Blvd., 817/772-9771

Best Japanese Food
Samurai Japanese Steak House
  347 Parkdale Ctr., 817/776-5197

Best Mexican Food
Trujillo's Comedor Y Cantina
  2612 La Salle Ave., 817/756-1331

Best Pizza
Poppa Rollo's Pizza
  703 N. Valley Mills Dr., 817/776-6776

Best Place to Take the Kids
Mr. Gatti's Pizza
  1300 N. Valley Mills Dr., 817/772-6821
  1725 S. Valley Mills Dr., 817/753-7452
  1845 Lake Shore Dr., 817/756-6636

Best Seafood
Buzzard Billy's
  208 S. University Parks Dr., 817/753-2778

Best Southwestern Food
Diamond Back's
  217 Mary St., 817/757-2871

Best Thai Food
Thai Orchid Restaurant
  1017 N. University Parks Dr., 817/752-3555

Best Vietnamese Food
Ly-Le's Vietnamese Food
  331 W. Hwy. 6, 817/776-0489

Standbys
International House of Pancakes
  1000 S. Fourth St., 817/754-3001
Shoney's
  901 S. University Parks Dr., 817/753-6828
The Olive Garden
  5921 W. Waco Dr., 817/751-1667

Baskin-Robbins
    1019 S. University Parks Dr., 817/752-9430
    5301 Bosque Blvd., Ste. 103E, 817/776-6155
Golden Corral Family Steak House
    618 N. Valley Mills Dr., 817/751-9088
Red Lobster
    4900 Bosque Blvd., 817/776-7810

WICHITA FALLS, TX

Best Barbecue/Ribs
Stanley's
    2703 Avenue U, 817/692-8561

Best Brunch
Bennigan's
    4521 Kemp Blvd., 817/692-8844

Best Burgers
Whataburger Restaurant
    1040 Central Freeway, 817/723-1019
    1111A Holliday St., 817/723-8532
    2725 Southwest Pkwy., 817/692-0015
    311 Midwestern Pkwy., 817/691-3101
    3404 McNiel Ave., 817/696-2201
    3900 Sheppard Access Rd., 817/855-4411

Best Chinese Food
Hunan Chinese Restaurant
    3916 Kemp Blvd., 817/691-3900

Best Coffee
Kiwi Koast Bagel and Coffee Company
    2611 Plaza Pkwy., 817/696-5494

Best Delicatessen
Bogart's Deli
    2708 Southwest Pkwy., 817/692-4242
    813 Broad St., 817/767-3354

Best Desserts
Bogart's Deli
    2708 Southwest Pkwy., 817/692-4242
    813 Broad St., 817/767-3354

Best Homestyle Food
Pioneer Restaurant
    1100 Sheppard Access Rd., 817/723-8146
    1400 Tenth St., 817/322-9461
    812 Holliday St., 817/723-8512

Best Ice Cream/Yogurt
Braum's
    2304 Kemp Blvd., 817/766-0789
    3808 Jacksboro Hwy., 817/322-6317
    4711 Southwest Pkwy., 817/691-4251

Best Italian Food
Lalani's Restaurant and Grill
    1111B Holliday St., 817/322-5252
    2301 Midwestern Pkwy., 817/692-4754

Best Japanese Food
Japanese Steak House Samurai
    2611 Plaza Pkwy., 817/696-2626

T

Best Late-Night Food
Bennigan's
4521 Kemp Blvd., 817/692-8844
Bogart's Deli
2708 Southwest Pkwy., 817/692-4242
813 Broad St., 817/767-3354

Best Mexican Food
La Familia Hernandez
1912 Elmwood Ave. N., 817/696-3457

Best Pizza
Cici's Pizza
2710 Southwest Pkwy., 817/691-6060

Best Place to Eat When Someone Else Is Buying
Fat McBride's Steaks
4537 Maplewood Ave., 817/696-0250

Best Place to Take the Kids
Cici's Pizza
2710 Southwest Pkwy., 817/691-6060

Best Romantic Dining
Lalani's Restaurant and Grill
1111B Holliday St., 817/322-5252
2301 Midwestern Pkwy., 817/692-4754

Best Salad/Salad Bar
Bogart's Deli
2708 Southwest Pkwy., 817/692-4242
813 Broad St., 817/767-3354

Best Sandwiches
Bogart's Deli
2708 Southwest Pkwy., 817/692-4242
813 Broad St., 817/767-3354

Best Steaks
Fat McBride's Steaks
4537 Maplewood Ave., 817/696-0250

Standbys
International House of Pancakes
1004 Broad St., 817/322-4555
The Olive Garden
3916 Kemp Blvd., 817/692-4714
Golden Corral Family Steak House
3812 Kemp Blvd., 817/691-1818
Red Lobster
4401 Kemp Blvd., 817/691-2531

T

Utah

Best Breakfast
Sullivan's Cafe
86 S. Main St., 801/586-6761

Best Burgers
Brad's Food Hut
546 N. Main St., 801/586-6358
Top Spot Drive Inn
650 S. Main St., 801/586-9661
Hermie's
294 N. Main St., 801/865-0612

Best Casual Dining
Rusty's Ranch House
2275 E. Hwy. 14, 801/586-3839

Best Chinese Food
China Garden Restaurant
64 N. Main St., 801/586-6042
Hunan Chinese Restaurant
501 S. Main St., 801/586-8952

Best Coffee
Dog and Duck
50 W. Center St., 801/586-0355

Best Desserts
Dog and Duck
50 W. Center St., 801/586-0355

Best Family Restaurants
Pancho and Lefty's
2107 N. Main St., 801/586-7501
Boomer's
5 N. Main St., 801/865-9665
La Fiesta Mexican Restaurant
890 N. Main St., 801/586-4646

Best Homestyle Food
Brad's Food Hut
546 N. Main St., 801/586-6358
Hermie's
294 N. Main St., 801/865-0612

U

Best Mexican Food
Pancho and Lefty's
2107 N. Main St., 801/586-7501
La Fiesta Mexican Restaurant
890 N. Main St., 801/586-4646

Best Places to Eat When Someone Else Is Buying
Adriana's
164 S. 100W, 801/865-1234
Milt's Stage Stop
Hwy. 14, 801/586-9344

Best Sandwiches
Dog and Duck
50 W. Center St., 801/586-0355
Top Spot Drive Inn
650 S. Main St., 801/586-9661

Best Seafood
Milt's Stage Stop
Hwy. 14, 801/586-9344
Rusty's Ranch House
2275 E. Hwy 14, 801/586-3839

Best Steaks
Milt's Stage Stop
Hwy. 14, 801/586-9344
Rusty's Ranch House
2275 E. Hwy. 14, 801/586-3839

LOGAN, UT

Best Restaurant in Town
Grape Vine Restaurant
129 N. Hwy. 100E, 801/752-1977

Best Atmosphere
The Zanavoo Lodge
4880 E. Hwy. 89, 801/752-0085

Best Coffee
Straw Ibis Market Cafe
52 Federal Ave., 801/753-4777

Best Family Restaurant
Frontier Pies Restaurant
43 E. 1400N, 801/752-9280

MURRAY, UT

U

Best Barbecue/Ribs
Buffalo Joe's
5927 S. State, 801/261-3537

Best Breakfast
Village Inn
5941 S. State, 801/268-1292

Best Burgers
Red Robin
316 E. 6400 S., 801/266-9410

Best Desserts
Buffalo Joe's
5927 S. State, 801/261-3537

Village Inn
5941 S. State, 801/268-1292

Best Health-Conscious Menu
Leslie's Guiltless Grill
65 E. Fifth Ave., 801/266-4430

Best Homestyle Food
Galaxy Diner
6099 S. State, 801/262-8262

Best Mexican Food
Restaurant Morelia
6098 S. State St., 801/265-8790

Best Pizza
Godfather's Pizza
5456 S. Ninth E., 801/266-8105

Best Steaks
Chuck-A-Rama Buffet
4150 S. Redwood Rd., 801/967-0300
Buffalo Joe's
5927 S. State, 801/261-3537

Standbys
The Olive Garden
6305 S. State St., 801/269-8138
Pizza Hut
5905 S. State St., 801/262-4055
Red Lobster
298 E. Winchester St., 801/288-2940

OGDEN, UT

Best Breakfast
Galaxy Diner
4250 Harrison Blvd., 801/621-2161

Best Business Lunch
Good Time Spaghetti Company
373 31st St., 801/627-4181

Best Cheap Meal
Andy's Chuck Wagon Buffet
3684 Wall Ave., 801/393-2911

Best Chinese Food
Utah Noodle
3019 Washington Blvd., 801/392-6002

Best Desserts
Galaxy Diner
4250 Harrison Blvd., 801/621-2161

Best Diner
Galaxy Diner
4250 Harrison Blvd., 801/621-2161

Best Family Restaurant
Frontier Pies Restaurant
4137 Riverdale Rd., 801/399-4411

Best German Food
Bavarian Chalet German Restaurant
4387 Harrison Blvd., 801/479-7561

U

Best Health-Conscious Menu
Edible Art's
  1462 Washington Blvd., 801/621-4477

Best Ice Cream/Yogurt
Farr's Ice Cream
  286 21st St., 801/393-8629

Best Late-Night Food
Galaxy Diner
  4250 Harrison Blvd., 801/621-2161

Best Mexican Food
El Matador
  2564 Ogden Ave., 801/393-3151

Best Pizza
Ligori's Pizza and Pasta
  4421 Harrison Blvd., 801/476-0476

Best Place to Be "Seen"
Prairie Schooner Steak House
  445 Park Blvd., 801/392-2712

Best Place to Eat When Someone Else Is Buying
Frontier Pies Restaurant
  4137 Riverdale Rd., 801/399-4411

Best Romantic Dining
The Roof
  15 E. South Temple, Salt Lake City, 801/539-1911

Best Salad/Salad Bar
Andy's Chuck Wagon Buffet
  3684 Wall Ave., 801/393-2911

Best Sandwiches
Training Table Restaurant
  4510 Harrison Blvd., 801/399-5050

Best Steaks
Prairie Schooner Steak House
  445 Park Blvd., 801/392-2712

Standbys
The Olive Garden
  675 Ring Rd., Layton, 801/546-1447

OREM, UT

Best Burgers
Howie's Premium Root Beer
  365 N. State St., 801/222-9595

Best Business Lunch
Magleby's
  1675 N. Hwy. 200W, Provo, 801/374-6249

Best Cheap Meal
Howie's Premium Root Beer
  365 N. State St., 801/222-9595

Best Chinese Food
Great China Restaurant
  380 E. Hwy. 1300S, 801/224-2238

Best Family Restaurants
Prestwich Farms Restaurant
  289 E. Hwy. 1300S, 801/226-7437

U

Chuck-A-Rama Buffet
  1408 S. State St., 801/225-9300

Best Homestyle Food
Prestwich Farms Restaurant
  289 E. Hwy. 1300S, 801/226-7437

Best Ice Cream/Yogurt
Carousel Ice Cream Parlor
  168 S. Hwy. 1200W, 801/235-9139

Best Italian Food
The Brick Oven
  111 E. Hwy. 800N, 801/374-8800

Best Late-Night Food
El Azteca Mexican Takeout
  46 W. Hwy. 430N, 801/375-9690

Best Pizza
Godfather's Pizza
  333 E. Hwy. 1300S, 801/226-2040

Best Place to Eat When Someone Else Is Buying
Magleby's
  1675 N. Hwy. 200W, Provo, 801/374-6249

Best Salad/Salad Bar
The Brickoven
  111 E. Hwy. 800N, 801/374-8800

Best Steaks
Chuck-A-Rama Buffet
  1408 S. State St., 801/225-9300

Standbys
Golden Corral Family Steak House
  225 W. Hwy. 1300S, 801/225-6299
Wendy's
  1444 S. State St., 801/226-3018
Sizzler
  1240 S. State St., 801/224-1615
The Olive Garden
  504 W. Hwy. 2230N, Provo, 801/377-0062

PRICE, UT

Best Burgers
JB's
  715 E. Main St., 801/637-1840

Best Desserts
JB's
  715 E. Main St., 801/637-1840

Best Family Restaurant
Ricardo's Restaurant
  655 E. Main St., 801/637-2020

Best Greek/Mediterranean Food
Greek Streak
  84 S. Carbon Ave., 801/637-1930

Best Italian Food
Farlaino's Cafe
  87 W. Main St., 801/637-9217

U

Best Mexican Food
Ricardo's Restaurant
  655 E. Main St., 801/637-2020

Standbys
Baskin-Robbins
  1191 E. Main St., 801/637-3631
Pizza Hut
  212 S. Hwy. 55, 801/637-6410

PROVO, UT

Best Restaurants in Town
Magleby's Restaurant
  1675 N. Hwy. 200W, 801/374-6249
Sundance Tree Room
  North Fork Provo Canyon, 801/225-4107

Best Breakfast
Keith's Lunch
  190 W. Hwy. 100S, 801/375-3505

Best Burgers
The T-Bone Restaurant
  9695 S. State St., Springville, 801/489-7920

Best Business Lunch
Gandolfo's
  18 N. University, 801/375-3354

Best Cheap Meal
Underground Company
  65 N. University Ave., 801/377-5044

Best Chinese Food
China Lilly
  98 W. Center St., 801/371-8888

Best Family Restaurant
Viva Spaghetti
  1718 N. University Pkwy., 801/374-5906

Best Homestyle Food
Keith's Lunch
  190 W. Hwy. 100S, 801/375-3505

Best Italian Food
La Dolce Vita
  61 N. Hwy. 100E, 801/373-8482

Best Mexican Food
El Azteca
  746 E. Hwy. 820N, 801/373-9312
Los Hermanos
  16 W. Center St., 801/375-5732

Best Pizza
Brick Oven
  111 E. Hwy. 800N, 801/374-8800

Best Place to Eat When Someone Else Is Buying
Sundance Tree Room
  North Fork Provo Canyon, 801/225-4107

Best Place to Take the Kids
Viva Spaghetti
  1718 N. University Pkwy., 801/374-5906

Best Salad/Salad Bar
Gandolfo's
   18 N. University, 801/375-3354

Best Sandwiches
Gandolfo's
   18 N. University, 801/375-3354

Best Steaks
Ruby River
   969 S. State St., Springville, 801/489-7920

ST. GEORGE, UT

Best American Food
The Palms Restaurant
   850 S. Bluff St., 801/628-4235

Best Chinese Food
Hong Kong Dynasty
   635 E. Saint George Blvd., 801/968-0929

Best Greek/Mediterranean Food
Basila's Greek and Italian Cafe
   2 W. Saint George Blvd., 801/673-7671

Best Pizza
The Pizza Factory
   2 W. Saint George Blvd., 801/628-1234
   490 W. Saint George Blvd., Ste. 2, 801/634-1234

Best Sandwiches
Charlie's Malts and Ice Cream
   287 W. Saint George Blvd., 801/628-6304

Best Steaks
Brandin' Iron Steakhouse
   939 E. Main St., Pine Valley, 801/574-2261

SALT LAKE CITY, UT

Best All-You-Can-Eat Buffet
Chuck-A-Rama Buffet
   2960 Highland Dr., 801/487-0879
   744 E. 400S, 801/531-0995

Best Atmosphere
Fuggles
   367 W. 200S, 801/363-7000

Best Bar
New Yorker Club
   60 Market St., 801/363-0166

Best Burgers
Hires Big H
   2900 W. 4700S, 801/965-1010
   425 S. 700E, 801/364-4582

Best Continental Food
Dodo
   680 S. 900E, 801/328-9348

Best Desserts
Dodo
   680 S. 900E, 801/328-9348

U

Best Greek/Mediterranean Food
Greek Souvlaki No.1 Original
    404 E. 300S, 801/322-2062
    1446 S. State St., 801/487-3481

Best Ice Cream/Yogurt
Snelgrove Ice Cream
    850 E. 2100S, 801/486-4457
    65 W. South Temple, 801/534-0246
Red's Frozen Yogurt
    300 S. Main St., 801/363-6935
    366 S. 500E, 801/363-6907
    870 S. 900E, 801/359-8111

Best Italian Food
Al Forno's Ristorante
    239 S. 500E, 801/359-6040

Best Japanese Food
Hashi Japanese Restaurant
    1352 S. 2100E, 801/583-5701
Shogun Restaurant
    321 S. Main St., 801/364-7142

Best Mexican Food
La Frontera
    1236 W. 400S, 801/532-3158
Rio Grande Cafe
    270 Rio Grande St., 801/364-3302

Best Microbrewery
Fuggles
    367 W. 200S, 801/363-7000

Best Pizza
Deloretto's Pizzeria
    2010 S. State St., 801/485-6615
Godfather's Pizza
    5456 S. 900E, 801/268-4478

Best Place to Eat When Someone Else Is Buying
New Yorker Club
    60 Market St., 801/363-0166

Best Romantic Dining
New Yorker Club
    60 Market St., 801/363-0166

Best Seafood
La Caille
    956 Wasatch Blvd., 801/942-1751

Best Steaks
La Caille
    956 Wasatch Blvd., 801/942-1751

Best Vietnamese Food
East West Connection
    14 S. Foothill Dr., 801/581-1128

Standbys
Chuck E. Cheese Pizza
    4425 S. State St., 801/261 2888

VERNAL, UT

Best Barbecue/Ribs
Seven Eleven Cafe
   77 E. Main St., 801/789-1170

Best Breakfast
JB's Family Restaurant
   475 W. Main St., 801/789-4547
Weston Lamplighter
   120 E. Main St., 801/789-0312

Best Burgers
Skillet East
   251 E. Main St., 801/789-3641

Best Chinese Food
Mea Palace
   2539 N. Vernal Ave., 801/789-7703

Best Coffee
Spoof's Coffee and Tea Shop
   38 E. Main St., 801/789-1154

Best Homestyle Food
Seven Eleven Cafe
   77 E. Main St., 801/789-1170

Best Italian Food
Pizza Barn
   831 W. Main St., 801/789-2030

Best Mexican Food
Casa Rios
   2015 W. Hwy. 40, 801/789-0103
La Cabana
   56 W. Main St., 801/789-3151

Best Sandwiches
Great American Cafe
   13 S. Vernal Ave., 801/789-1115

Best Steaks
Bud's Steakhouse
   65 S. Vernal Ave., 801/789-9963

Standbys
Golden Corral Family Steak House
   1096 W. Hwy. 40, 801/789-7268

U

Vermont

Best Restaurants in Town
The Country House Restaurant
   276 N. Main St., 802/476-4282
Soup-n-Greens
   321 N. Main St., 802/479-9862
The Hilltop Restaurant
   Quarry Hill Rd., 802/479-2129
Northeast Culinary Institute Restaurant
   250 Main St., Montpelier, 802/223-6324
Chef's Table
   118 Main St., Montpelier, 802/229-9202
The Wayside Restaurant
   Barre Rd., Montpelier, 802/223-6611

Best Italian Food
Sarducci's
   3 Main St., Montpelier, 802/223-0229

Best Restaurants in Town
Blue Ben Diner
   102 Hunt St., 802/442-5140
Bennington Station
   150 Depot St., 802/447-1080
Alldays and Onions
   519 Main St., 802/447-0043

V

Best Atmosphere
Latchis Grille and Windham Brewery
   6 Flat St., 802/254-4747
Marina Restaurant
   28 Springtree Rd., 802/257-7563
TJ Buckley's
   132 Elliot St., 802/257-4922

Best Breakfast
Chelsea Royal Diner
  Rte. 9, 802/254-8399
Riverview Restaurant
  9 Bridge St., 802/254-9841

Best Burgers
Marina Restaurant
  28 Springtree Rd., 802/257-7563

Best Chinese Food
Jade Wah Chinese-American
  40 Main St., 802/254-2392
Panda North Chinese Restaurant
  Putney Rd., Ste. 1, 802/257-4578

Best Coffee
Cafe Beyond
  29 High St., 802/258-4900
Coffee Country
  1 Harmony Pl., 802/257-0032
Mocha Joe's
  82 Main St., 802/257-7794

Best Family Restaurant
Picnics
  Putney Rd., 802/254-9675

Best Health-Conscious Menu
Common Ground
  25 Elliot St., 802/257-0855

Best Indian Food
India Palace
  69 Elliot Terrace, 802/254-6143

Best Korean Food
Shin-La Restaurant
  57 Main St., 802/257-5226

Best Microbreweries
McNeil's
  90 Elliott St., 802/254-2553
Latchis Grille and Windham Brewery
  6 Flat St., 802/254-4747

Best Pizza
Frankie's Pizzeria
  Harmony Pl., 802/254-2420
Vermont Inn Pizza
  228 Canal St., 802/254-6264

Best Places to Eat When Someone Else Is Buying
Four Columns Inn and Restaurant
  230 West St., Newfane, 802/365-7713
TJ Buckley's
  132 Elliot St., 802/257-4922
Peter Havens
  32 Elliot St., 802/257-3333

Best Place to Take the Kids
Kidsplace
  20 Elliott St., 802/254-5212

Best Seafood
Marina Restaurant
28 Springtree Rd., 802/257-7563

Best Steaks
Jolly Butcher's Tavern
Rte. 9 Marlboro Rd., 802/254-6043
Steak Out
Putney Rd., 802/257-1333

Best View While Dining
Skyline Restaurant
Rte. 9, Marlboro, 802/464-3536
Marina Restaurant
28 Springtree Rd., 802/257-7563

Standbys
Friendly's
Putney Rd., 802/257-4004

BURLINGTON, VT

Best Barbecue/Ribs
Pepper's Memphis BBQ
95 Saint Paul St., 802/863-4740

Best Bistro
Leunig's Old World Cafe
115 Church St., 802/863-3759

Best Breakfast
Sneakers
36 Main St., Winooski, 802/655-9081

Best Brunch
Sneakers
36 Main St., Winooski, 802/655-9081

Best Burgers
Sneakers
36 Main St., Winooski, 802/655-9081

Best Cajun/Creole Food
Bourbon Street Grill
213 College St., 802/865-2800

Best Coffee
Java Blues
197 College St., 802/860-5060
Muddy Waters
184 Main St., 802/658-0466

Best Eclectic Menu
Daily Planet
15 Center St., 802/862-9647

Best French Food
Leunig's Old World Cafe
115 Church St., 802/863-3759
Cafe Shelburne Francais
Rte. 7, Shelburne, 802/985-3939

Best Health-Conscious Menu
Five Spice Cafe
175 Church St., 802/864-4045

V

Best Indian Food
India House Restaurant
207 Colchester Ave., 802/862-7800

Best Italian Food
Buono Appetito Italian Restaurant
1963 Shelburne Rd., Shelburne, 802/985-2232

Best Japanese Food
Sakura Japanese Restaurant
2 Church St., 802/863-1988

Best Pizza
Buono Appetito Italian Restaurant
1963 Shelburne Rd., Shelburne, 802/985-2232

Best Sandwiches
Red Onion Restaurant
140 1/2 Church St., 802/865-2563
310 Pine St., 802/863-2788

Best Seafood
Dockside
209 Battery St., 802/864-5266
Ray's Seafood Market
7 Pinecrest Dr., Essex Junction, 802/879-3611

Best Steaks
Sirloin Saloon
1908 Shelburne Rd., Shelburne, 802/985-2200

Best Thai Food
Parima
185 Pearl St., 802/864-7917

Best Vietnamese Food
Sai-Gon Cafe
133-135 Bank St., 802/863-5637

Standbys
Ben and Jerry's
169 Cherry St., 802/862-9620

MIDDLEBURY, VT

Best American Food
Middlebury Inn
Rte. 7, 802/388-4961

Best Atmosphere
Woody's Restaurant
5 Bakery Ln., 802/388-4182
Waybury Inn
Rte. 125, East Middlebury, 802/388-4015

Best Bar
Amigo's Restaurant
4 Merchants Row, 802/388-3624

Best Breakfast
Rosie's Restaurant
Rte. 7, 802/388-7052

Best Burgers
Steve's Park Diner
12 Merchants Row, 802/388-3297

Best Business Lunch
Middlebury Inn
Rte. 7, 802/388-4961

Best Chinese Food
Panda House
2 Maple St., 802/388-3101

Best Coffee
Storm Cafe
3 Mill St., Frog Hollow Mill, 802/388-1063

Best Desserts
Angela's
86 Main St., 802/388-0002
Fire and Ice Restaurant
26 Seymour St., 802/388-7166

Best French Food
Roland's Place
Rte. 7 off Rte. 17 Interchange, New Haven,
802/453-6309

Best Italian Food
Amigo's Restaurant
4 Merchants Row, 802/388-3624
Vermont Pasta Restaurant
3 Green St., Vergennes, 802/877-3413
Angela's
86 Main St., 802/388-0002

Best Mexican Food
Amigo's Restaurant
4 Merchants Row, 802/388-3624

Best Pizza
Green Peppers Restaurant
11 Washington St., 802/388-3164

Best Place to Take the Kids
Rosie's Restaurant
Rte. 7, 802/388-7052

Best Sandwiches
Green Peppers Restaurant
11 Washington St., 802/388-3164
Mister Ups
Bakery Ln., 802/388-6724

Best Seafood
Fire and Ice Restaurant
26 Seymour St., 802/388-7166

Best Steaks
Fire and Ice Restaurant
26 Seymour St., 802/388-7166

Best View While Dining
Mister Ups
Bakery Ln., 802/388-6724
Woody's Restaurant
5 Bakery Ln., 802/388-4182

Standbys
Ben and Jerry's
Rte. 4, Killington, 802/773-2221

V

MONTPELIER, VT

Best Breakfast
Burlington Bagel Bakery
  89 Main St., 802/223-0533

Best Chinese Food
China Star Chinese Restaurant
  15 Main St., 802/223-0808

Best Coffee
Crump's Coffee House
  11 Main St., 802/229-1019

Best Italian Food
Sarducci's
  3 Main St., 802/223-0229

Best Mexican Food
Julio's
  44 Main St., 802/229-9348

Best Pizza
Angeleno's Pizza
  15 Barre St., 802/229-5721

Best Steaks
Main Street Bar and Grill
  118 Main St., 802/223-3188

Standbys
Ben and Jerry's
  89 Main St., 802/223-5530

NEWPORT, VT

Best Atmosphere
Heermansmith Farm
  Heermansmith Farm Rd., Coventry, 802/754-8866
The Corner
  27 Main St., 802/334-1336

Best Breakfast
Brown Cow
  990 E. Main St., 802/334-7887
Miss Newport Diner
  E. Main St., 802/334-7742

Best Burgers
East Side Restaurant
  25 Lake St., 802/334-2340

Best Casual Dining
East Side Restaurant
  25 Lake St., 802/334-2340

Best Coffee
East Side Restaurant
  25 Lake St., 802/334-2340

Best Desserts
East Side Restaurant
  25 Lake St., 802/334-2340
Heermansmith Farm
  Heermansmith Farm Rd., Coventry, 802/754-8866

V

Best Family Restaurants
Brown Cow
 990 E. Main St., 802/334-7887
Long Branch Restaurant
 Derby Rd., 802/334-6430

Best German Food
Forsthaus Restaurant
 Rte. 14, Newport Center, 802/334-7294

Best Italian Food
The Corner
 27 Main St., 802/334-1336
Buon Amici
 Railroad St., North Troy, 802/988-2299

Best Pizza
Village Pizza
 E. Main St., 802/334-7929

Best Sandwiches
Long Branch Restaurant
 Derby Rd., 802/334-6430

Best Seafood
East Side Restaurant
 25 Lake St., 802/334-2340
Long Branch Restaurant
 Derby Rd., 802/334-6430
The Corner
 27 Main St., 802/334-1336

Best Steaks
East Side Restaurant
 25 Lake St., 802/334-2340
Long Branch Restaurant
 Derby Rd., 802/334-6430

RUTLAND, VT

Best Restaurants in Town
Rutland Restaurant
 57 Merchants Row, 802/775-7447
Clem's Country Kitchen
 51 Wales St., 802/775-6104
Season's Circle Coffee House
 24 Wales St., 802/773-3701

Best Chinese Food
Kong Chow Restaurant
 48 Center St., 802/775-5244

WHITE RIVER JUNCTION, VT

V

Best Breakfast
Polka Dot
 1 Main St., 802/295-9722

Best Dinner
Cashie's at the Coolidge
 17 S. Main St., 802/295-3118
AJ's Steakhouse
 2 Bowling Ln., 802/295-3071

Best Health-Conscious Menu
Itasca Vermont Ltd.
  2 N. Main St., 802/295-1025

Best Homestyle Food
Polka Dot
  1 Main St., 802/295-9722

Best Lunch
Cashie's at the Coolidge
  17 S. Main St., 802/295-3118
Del Roma Restaurant
  16 Gates St., 802/295-9705
Wildflowers Restaurant
  Rural Route 4, Quechee, 802/295-7051
William Tally House
  Sykes Ave., 802/295-3835

Best Pizza
Pizza Chef of Quechee
  Rt. 4 E., Quechee, 802/296-6669

Best Sandwiches
Gondola Deli and Sub Shop
  2 Maple St., 802/295-9070
Than Wheeler Coaches Corner
  15 N. Main St., 802/295-4847

Best Sports Bar
Than Wheeler Coaches Corner
  15 N. Main St., 802/295-4847

Best Steaks
AJ's Steakhouse
  2 Bowling Ln., 802/295-3071

Best Vegetarian Food
Itasca Vermont Ltd.
  2 N. Main St., 802/295-1025

V

Virginia

Best Barbecue/Ribs
Pardner's
5444 Hwy. 11E, Piney Flats, 423/538-5539

Best Burgers
Pal's
960 Volunteer Pkwy., 423/652-2291

Best Cheap Meal
Pal's
960 Volunteer Pkwy., 423/652-2291

Best Dinner
Athens Steakhouse
329 Eighth St., 423/652-2202
105 Goodson St., 540/466-8271

Best Fast Food
Acme Hot Dog
1030 Broad St., 423/764-2263

Best Ice Cream/Yogurt
Kay's Ice Cream
9 Pennsylvania Ave., 423/968-9974

Best Lunch
The Feed Room
620 State St., 423/764-0545

Best Mexican Food
La Carreta
530 Volunteer Pkwy., 423/989-3361

Best Steaks
Athens Steakhouse
329 Eighth St., 423/652-2202
105 Goodson St., 540/466-8271

V

Best Restaurant in Town
Oregano Joe's
1252 Emmet St. N., 804/971-9308

Best Breakfast
Tavern
  1140 Emmet St. N., 804/295-0404
  Rte. 250W, 804/972-2231
Spudnut Shop
  309 Avon St., 804/296-0590

Best Cajun/Creole Food
Southern Culture
  633 W. Main St., 804/979-1990

Best Greek/Mediterranean Food
Cafe Europa
  1331 W. Main St., 804/294-4040

Best Italian Food
Oregano Joe's
  1252 Emmet St. N., 804/971-9308
Rococo's
  2001 Commonwealth Dr., 804/971-7371

Best Lunch
Blue Bird Cafe
  625 W. Main St., 804/295-1166

Best Place to Eat When Someone Else Is Buying
Silver Thatch Inn
  3001 Hollymead Dr., 804/978-4686

Best Sandwiches
Bodo's Bagel Bakery
  505 Preston Ave., 804/293-5224
  1418 Emmet St. N., 804/977-9598

CHESAPEAKE, VA

Best Barbecue/Ribs
Mr. Pig's Bar-B-Q
  445 Battlefield Blvd. N., 804/547-5171
Billy's Bar-BQ
  1642 Sparrow Rd., 804/420-3233

Best Business Lunch
Van Beek's Deli
  1101 Eden Way, 804/547-1668

Best Casual Dining
Pargo's Restaurant
  1436 Greenbrier Pkwy., 804/420-1900

Best Chinese Food
China Coast
  230 Jarman Rd., 804/420-2393
  4108 Portsmouth Blvd., 804/488-7334

Best Family Restaurant
Frankie's Place for Ribs
  146 S. Battlefield Blvd., 804/546-0030

Best Homestyle Food
Black-Eyed Pea
  1432 Greenbrier Pkwy., 804/523-5977

Best Outdoor Dining
Cara's Restaurant
  123 Battlefield Blvd. N., 804/436-2754

V

Best Place to Eat When Someone Else Is Buying
Locks Pointe Restaurant
  136 Battlefield Blvd. N., 804/547-9618

Best Romantic Dining
Locks Pointe Restaurant
  136 Battlefield Blvd. N., 804/547-9618

Best Sandwiches
Cheers Unlimited Cafe and Tavern
  1405 Greenbrier Pkwy., 804/424-4665

Best Steaks
Carvers Creek
  1020 Eden Way N., 804/523-6188

Best View While Dining
Cara's Restaurant
  123 Battlefield Blvd. N., 804/436-2754
Locks Pointe Restaurant
  136 Battlefield Blvd. N., 804/547-9618

Standbys
Old Country Buffet
  1412 Greenbrier Pkwy., 804/366-5586
  4300 Portsmouth Blvd., 804/488-4373
International House of Pancakes
  641 Battlefield Blvd. N., 804/549-0030
Fuddruckers
  1105 Merchants Way, 804/549-1670
Ruby Tuesday
  1412 Greenbrier Pkwy., 804/366-0739
  4200 Portsmouth Blvd., 804/465-1054
The Olive Garden
  1631 Ring Rd., 804/424-4758
  4117 Chesapeake Square Blvd., 804/465-2139

DANVILLE, VA

Best All-You-Can-Eat Buffet
Stratford Inn and Restaurant
  2500 Riverside Dr., 804/793-2500

Best Barbecue/Ribs
Short Sugar's Bar-B-Q
  2215 Riverside Dr., 804/793-4800

Best Breakfast
Stratford Inn and Restaurant
  2500 Riverside Dr., 804/793-2500

Best Burgers
Sir Richard's Steak House
  1513 S. Boston Rd., 804/822-6444

Best Chinese Food
Long River Restaurant
  2835 Riverside Dr., 804/799-6770

Best Coffee
Main Street Coffee Emporium
  435 Main St., 804/792-4252

Best Desserts
Baron's
  671 Woodlawn Dr., 804/822-0120

V

Stratford Inn and Restaurant
2500 Riverside Dr., 804/793-2500

Best Homestyle Food
Danview Restaurant
116 Danview Dr., 804/793-3552
Mary's Diner
1203 Piney Forest Rd., 804/836-5034

Best Italian Food
Joe and Mimma's Italian Pizza
3232 Riverside, Ste. 3336, 804/799-5763

Best Pizza
Joe and Mimma's Italian Pizza
3232 Riverside, Ste. 3336, 804/799-5763

Best Sandwiches
Rock Ola Cafe
140 Crown Dr., 804/793-1848
Yesterday's Cafe
443 Main St., 804/793-2629

Best Seafood
Baron's
671 Woodlawn Dr., 804/822-0120
Stratford Inn and Restaurant
2500 Riverside Dr., 804/793-2500
King Of The Sea Restaurant
1799 Memorial Dr., 804/793-0331
Mayflower Seafood Restaurant
2320 Riverside Dr., 804/792-8817
Libby Hill Seafood Restaurant
2105 Riverside Dr., 804/791-4680

Best Steaks
Baron's
671 Woodlawn Dr., 804/822-0120
Sir Richard's Steak House
1513 S. Boston Rd., 804/822-6444
Stratford Inn and Restaurant
2500 Riverside Dr., 804/793-2500

Standbys
Baskin-Robbins
208 Collins Dr., 804/791-4741

FAIRFAX, VA

Best Bagels
Manhattan Bagel Company
1032 Willard Way, 703/591-2525

Best Breakfast
Le Peep Restaurant
3922 Old Lee Hwy., 703/273-7337
Manhattan Bagel Company
1032 Willard Way, 703/591-2525

Best Chinese Food
House of Lions
11180 Main St., 703/273-3998
Hunan Eatery
4008 University Dr., 703/352-2888
9412 Main St., 703/764-3040

Best Coffee
Kiari's Coffee Source
10380 Willard Way, 703/352-0884

Best Desserts
Amphora Restaurant
377 Maple Ave. W., 703/938-7877

Best Family Restaurant
Black-Eyed Pea
3971 Chain Bridge Rd., 703/352-0588

Best French Food
Hermitage Inn
7134 Main St., Clifton, 703/266-1623

Best Homestyle Food
Black-Eyed Pea
3971 Chain Bridge Rd., 703/352-0588

Best Italian Food
Cafe Italia II
10515 Main St., 703/385-6767

Best Mexican Food
Carlos O'Kelly's Mexican Cafe
9959 Main St., 703/591-7113

Best Pizza
Tony's New York Pizza
Fairlake Shopping Ctr., 13087 Fairlake Dr.,
703/502-0808

Best Place to Eat When Someone Else Is Buying
Hermitage Inn
7134 Main St., Clifton, 703/266-1623

Best Place to Take the Kids
Black-Eyed Pea
3971 Chain Bridge Rd., 703/352-0588

Best Sandwiches
Kiari's Coffee Source
10380 Willard Way, 703/352-0884

Best View While Dining
House of Lions
11180 Main St., 703/273-3998

Standbys
Sizzler
Rural Route 50, 703/273-3583
Baskin-Robbins
10400 Lee Hwy., 703/273-3131
9547 Braddock Rd., 703/425-5131

V

HARRISONBURG, VA

Best All-You-Can-Eat Buffet
Carrie's Cafeteria
111 S. Carlton St., 540/433-2365

Best Bar
Blue Foxx Cafe
2061 S. Evelyn Bird Ave., 540/432-3699

Best Breakfast
Mr. J's Bagels and Deli
   1635 E. Market St., 540/564-0416

Best Brunch
Sheraton
   1400 E. Market St., 540/433-2521

Best Delicatessen
Brooklyn's Delicatessen
   2035 E. Market St., 540/433-4090

Best Diners
Jess's Lunch
   22 S. Main St., 540/434-8282
Downtown Grill
   62 S. Main St., 540/433-2047

Best Fast Food
Little Grill
   621 N. Main St., 540/434-3594

Best Greek/Mediterranean Food
Gus' Taverna
   95 S. Main St., 540/564-1487

Best Italian Food
L'Italia Restaurant
   815 E. Market St., 540/433-0961

Best Lunch
Jess' Lunch
   22 S. Main St., 540/434-8282
Downtown Grill
   62 S. Main St., 540/433-2047
Spanky's Delicatessen
   60 W. Water St., 540/434-7647

Best Mexican Food
El Charro Mexican Restaurant
   1570 E. Market St., 540/564-0386

Best Place to Eat When Someone Else Is Buying
Joshua Wilton House
   412 S. Main St., 540/434-4464

HOPEWELL, VA

Best All-You-Can-Eat Buffet
Broadway Cafeteria
   120 E. City Point Rd., 804/458-1700

Best Barbecue/Ribs
K and L Barbecue
   1410 Maple St., 804/458-4241
City Point Rib Company
   208 E. Cawson St., 804/458-2331

Best Burgers
Burger Fair
   2510 Oaklawn Blvd., 804/458-9921

Best Chinese Food
China Inn
   2703C Oaklawn Blvd., 804/458-5748

Best Italian Food
Rosa's Pizza Restaurant
    4108 Oaklawn Blvd., 804/458-8744

Best Pizza
Luisa's Pizza
    323 Cavalier Sq., 804/458-8000

Best Seafood
Captain's Cove Seafood Restaurant
    910 N. 21st Ave., 804/452-1368

Standbys
Hardee's
    2915 Oaklawn Blvd., 804/458-0360
    310 W. Randolph Rd., 804/458-0184

LYNCHBURG, VA

Best All-You-Can-Eat Buffet
Country Cookin'
    2323 Memorial Ave., 804/528-5931
    8686 Timberlake Rd., 804/239-1996

Best Breakfast
Myrt's Hot Dogs
    2810 Candlers Mountain Rd., 804/237-6124

Best Business Lunch
Shaker's Restaurant
    3401 Candlers Mountain Rd., 804/847-7425
    2095 Langhorne Rd., 804/847-0234

Best Chinese Food
China Garden
    21 Wadsworth St., 804/528-2855

Best Desserts
Billie Joe's
    4915 Fort Ave., 804/237-7825

Best Diner
Home Cookin'
    2034 Lakeside Dr., 804/385-7352

Best Family Restaurant
Country Cookin'
    8686 Timberlake Rd., 804/239-1996

Best Homestyle Food
Country Cookin'
    8686 Timberlake Rd., 804/239-1996
Home Cookin'
    2034 Lakeside Dr., 804/385-7352

Best Ice Cream/Yogurt
Billie Joe's
    4915 Fort Ave., 804/237-7825

Best Italian Food
Fazoli's
    2629 Wards Rd., 804/832-1200

Best Place to Take the Kids
Billy Bob's Pizza
    312 Border St., 804/237-0682

V

Best Romantic Dining
Crown Sterling Steaks
  6120 Fort Ave., 804/239-7744

Best Sandwiches
Westside Delicatessen
  7701 Timberlake Rd., 804/239-6304

Best Seafood
Harbor Inn Seafood
  3220 Old Forest Rd., 804/385-6888

Best Tea Room
Texas Inn
  422 Main St., 804/846-3823

Standbys
Applebee's
  3624 Candlers Mountain Rd., 804/528-2626
Shoney's
  2245 Langhorne Rd., 804/845-7242
  5515 Fort Ave., 804/239-1770
TCBY
  2300 Wards Rd., 804/237-4773
  9516 Timberlake Rd., 804/237-8259
Ground Round
  2819 Candlers Mountain Rd., 804/237-1692
Pizza Hut
  2413 Memorial Ave., 804/845-1433
  4901 Fort Ave., 804/239-9557
  9607F Timberlake Dr., 804/237-5222
  3025 Old Forest Rd., 804/385-7713
Golden Corral Family Steak House
  6201 Fort Ave., 804/237-5189

MANASSAS, VA

Best Italian Food
Carmelio's
  9108 Center St., 703/368-5522

Best Microbrewery
Hero's American Restaurant
  9412 Main St., 703/330-1534

Best Thai Food
Thai Secret Restaurant
  9114 Center St., 703/361-2500

MCLEAN, VA

Best American Food
Clyde's of Tysons Corner
  8332 Leesburg Pk., 703/734-1900

Best Atmosphere
Il Borgo Restaurante II
  1381A Beverly Rd., 703/893-1400
J.R.'s Stockyards Inn
  8130 Watson St., 703/893-3390
Kazan Restaurant
  6813 Redmond Dr., 703/734-1960

V

Best Barbecue/Ribs
Three Pigs
  1394 Chain Bridge Rd., 703/356-1700

Best Chinese Food
Wok and Roll
  1371 Beverly Rd., 703/556-8811

Best Delicatessen
Italian Deli
  6813 Elm St., 703/506-1136

Best Desserts
Il Borgo Restaurante II
  1381A Beverly Rd., 703/893-1400

Best Family Restaurants
Evans Farm Inn
  1696 Chain Bridge Rd., 703/356-8000
J.R.'s Stockyards Inn
  8130 Watson St., 703/893-3390
Pulcinella
  6852 Old Dominion Dr., 703/893-7777

Best French Food
La Mirabelle
  6645 Old Dominion Dr., 703/893-8484

Best Greek/Mediterranean Food
Greek Taverna
  6828 Old Dominion Dr., 703/556-0788

Best Italian Food
Il Borgo Restaurante II
  1381A Beverly Rd., 703/893-1400
Pulcinella
  6852 Old Dominion Dr., 703/893-7777

Best Other Ethnic Food
Kazan Restaurant (Turkish)
  6813 Redmond Dr., 703/734-1960

Best Outdoor Dining
Tertulia Restaurant
  6710B Old Dominion Dr., 703/448-7787

Best Pizza
Pulcinella
  6852 Old Dominion Dr., 703/893-7777

Best Place to Take the Kids
Pulcinella
  6852 Old Dominion Dr., 703/893-7777

Best Sandwiches
Italian Deli
  6813 Elm St., 703/506-1136

Best Steaks
J.R.'s Stockyards Inn
  8130 Watson St., 703/893-3390

Best View While Dining
Ritz-Carlton Tysons Corner
  1700 Tysons Blvd., 703/506-4300

V

Standbys
Baskin-Robbins
6833 Redmond Dr., 703/356-3185
Pizza Hut
6643 Old Dominion Dr., 703/356-9714
8119 Watson St., 703/734-5744

NEWPORT NEWS, VA

Best Restaurants in Town
The Kitchen at Powhatan Plantation
3601 Ironbound Rd., James City County,
804/220-1200
Fire and Ice
2040 Coliseum Dr., Hampton, 804/826-6698
Via Via Cafe
112 Williams St., 401/846-4074
Clarke Cooke House
3 Bannisters Wharf, 401/849-2900

Best American Food
Garden of the Heart
49 W. Queen's Way, Hampton, 804/722-5022
The Grate Steak
1934 Coliseum Dr., Hampton, 804/827-1886
Mike's Place
458 Warwick Village Shopping Center, 804/599-5500
Surrey House Restaurant
Rte. 31E, Surry, 804/294-3389

Best Atmosphere
Coach House Tavern
Off Rte. 5 at Berkeley Plantation, Charles City
County, 804/829-6003

Best Barbecue/Ribs
Bodine's Hickory Smoked Bar-B-Que
754 J. Clyde Morris Blvd., 804/596-7427
Pierce's Pitt Bar-B-Que
333 Waterside Dr., Norfolk, 804/622-0758
447 Rochambeau Dr., Williamsburg, 804/565-2955

Best Breakfast
Belgian Waffle and Family Steak House
621 J. Clyde Morris Blvd., 804/591-8563
Warwick Restaurant
12306 Warwick Blvd., 804/595-0231

Best Brunch
Chamberlin Hotel
Fort Monroe, Hampton, 804/723-6511

Best Burgers
Mike's Place
458 Warwick Village Shopping Center, 804/599-5500

Best Chinese Food
Good Fortune Chinese Restaurant
Willow Oaks Shopping Center, 225D-1 Fox Hill Rd.,
Hampton, 804/851-6888
Ming Gate Restaurant
3509 Kecoughtan Rd., Hampton, 804/723-9572

Port Arthur Restaurant
11137 Warwick Blvd., 804/599-6474

Best Coffee
Coffee Beanery
12300 Jefferson Ave., 804/249-9226
Warwick Restaurant
12306 Warwick Blvd., 804/595-0231

Best Continental Food
Seawell's Ordinary
Rte. 17, Ordinary, 804/642-3635

Best Delicatessens
Danny's Deli Restaurant
10838 Warwick Blvd., 804/595-0252
Mark's Delicatessen
12720 McManus Blvd., 804/886-6610

Best Eclectic Menu
Bray Dining Room
Kingsmill Resort, James City County, 804/253-3900

Best Family Restaurants
Sammy and Nick's Family Restaurants
11834 Canon Blvd., 804/873-8738
Belgian Waffle and Family Steak House
621 J. Clyde Morris Blvd., 804/591-8563
Warwick Restaurant
12306 Warwick Blvd., 804/595-0231

Best French Food
Bon Appetit
11710 Jefferson Ave., 804/873-0644
Courtyard La Petit Auberge
19 Charles St., 401/849-6669

Best German Food
Das Waldcafe
12529 Warwick Blvd., 804/930-1781

Best Homestyle Food
Welcome South
8558 Richmond Rd., Toano, 804/556-8255
C.W. Cowling's Restaurant and Lounge
1278 Smithfield Shopping Plaza, Smithfield,
804/357-0044

Best Italian Food
Carmela's Homestyle Italian Cuisine
14501 Warwick Blvd., 804/874-8421
Joe and Mimma's Italian Pizza Restaurant
826 J. Clyde Morris Blvd., 804/596-6664
Mulberry Inn
16890 Warwick Blvd., 804/887-3000

Best Japanese Food
Kappo Nara Seafood and Sushi Restaurant
550 Oyster Point Rd., 804/249-5395
Nara of Japan
10608 Warwick Blvd., 804/595-7399

Best Mexican Food
El Mariachi Mexican Restaurante
660 J. Clyde Morris Blvd., 804/596-4933

V

Mi Paseo
3326 W. Mercury Blvd., Hampton, 804/825-2482

Best Old Favorite Restaurant
The White Horse Tavern
16 Farewell St., 401/849-3600

Best Outdoor Dining
Second Street Restaurant and Tavern
132 E. Queen St., Hampton, 804/722-6811

Best Pizza
Anna's Italian Pizza
9708 Warwick Blvd., 804/595-0723
Joe and Mimma's Italian Pizza Restaurant
862 J. Clyde Morris Blvd., 804/596-6664

Best Salad/Salad Bar
Sammy and Nick's Family Restaurant
11834 Canon Blvd., 804/873-8738

Best Sandwiches
Newport Creamery
49 Long Wharf Mall, 401/849-8469
18 Bellevue Ave., 401/846-6332
Mike's Place
458 Warwick Village Shopping Center, 804/599-5500

Best Seafood
Bill's Seafood House
10900 Warwick Blvd., 804/595-4320
Captain George's
2710 W. Mercury Blvd., Hampton, 804/826-1436
Harpoon Larry's Oyster Bar
2000 N. Armistead Ave., Hampton, 804/827-0600
Nick's Seafood Pavilion
Water Street,Yorktown, 804/887-5269

Best Steaks
The Grate Steak
1934 Coliseum Dr., Hampton, 804/827-1886
Sammy and Nick's Family Restaurants
11834 Canon Blvd., 804/873-8738
Steve's Steak House
11847 Jefferson Ave., 804/595-9483

Best Vegetarian Food
Fire and Ice
2040 Coliseum Dr., Hampton, 804/826-6698
Upper Crust
2123 Coliseum Dr., Hampton, 804/838-8006

Best Vietnamese Food
Mai Vietnamese Restaurant
Denbigh Village Center, 14346 Warwick Blvd.,
Ste. 356, 804/874-2700
Chez Trinh
157 Monticello Ave., Williamsburg, 804/253-1888

Standbys
The Olive Garden
1049 W. Mercury Blvd., Hampton, 804/825-8874
Red Lobster
1046 W. Mercury Blvd., Hampton, 804/838-6062

Ryan's Family Steak House
  11883 Jefferson Ave., 804/930-4400
Papa John's
  15507 Warwick Blvd., 804/888-0008
Chi-Chi's
  12755 Jefferson Ave., 804/886-1493
Old Country Buffet
  14346 Warwick Blvd., 804/874-2556
Dunkin' Donuts
  12753 Jefferson Ave., 804/874-8670
Outback Steakhouse
  1255 Fordham Dr., Kemps River Crossing, Virginia
    Beach, 804/523-4832
  12558 Jefferson Ave., 804/249-3637
Ruby Tuesday
  12300 Jefferson Ave., 804/249-1828
Steak and Ale Restaurant
  2031 Coliseum Dr., Hampton, 804/838-7123
International House of Pancakes
  11745 Jefferson Ave., 804/591-0388
Shoney's
  10158 Jefferson Ave., 804/596-0871
  557A Denbigh Blvd., 804/874-0013

NORFOLK, VA

Best Restaurant in Town
Dumbwaiter
  128 College Pl., 804/623-3663

Best All-You-Can-Eat Buffet
The Bait Shack
  333 Waterside Dr., 804/622-3654

Best American Food
Dumbwaiter
  128 College Pl., 804/623-3663
Elliot's Restaurant
  1421 Colley Ave., 804/625-0259
Freemason Abbey
  209 W. Freemason St., 804/622-3966
The Grate Steak
  235 N. Military Hwy., 804/461-5501
Magnolia Steak
  Colley Ave. at Princess Anne Rd., 804/625-0400
The Bienville Grill
  723 W. 21st St., 804/625-5427
Bistro!
  210 W. York St., 804/622-3210
Cafe 21
  742G 21st St., 804/625-4218
Crackers
  821 W. 21st. St., 804/640-0200

Best Atmosphere
Freemason Abbey Restaurant
  209 W. Freemason St., 804/622-3966

Best Bars
All-Star Bar and Grill
  333 Waterside Dr., 804/625-5483

V

Legends of Norfolk
  333 Waterside Dr., 804/625-5483

Best Barbecue/Ribs
J.P.'s Smokehouse
  Selden Arcade, 804/623-7111
Pierce's Barbecue
  333 Waterside Dr., 804/622-0738
Wooden Nickel
  1455 N. Military Hwy., 804/461-5522

Best Breakfast
Charlie's Breakfast and Lunch
  1800A Granby St., 804/625-0824

Best Brunch
Freemason Abbey
  209 W. Freemason St., 804/622-3966
Riverwalk Restaurant
  777 Waterside Dr., 804/622-2868

Best Burgers
Elliot's Restaurant
  1421 Colley Ave., 804/625-0259
Kelly's Tavern
  1408 Colley Ave., 804/623-3216

Best Business Lunch
Freemason Abbey Restaurant
  209 W. Freemason St., 804/622-3966
Phillips Waterside
  333 Waterside Dr., 804/627-6600

Best Casual Dining
Morrison's Cafeteria
  530 N. Military Hwy., 804/461-2477

Best Cheap Meal
The Bait Shack
  333 Waterside Dr., 804/622-3654

Best Coffee
First Colony Coffee House
  132 E. Little Creek Rd., 804/480-1225
  2000 Colonial Ave., 804/622-0149
Prince Books and Coffee Shoppe
  109 E. Main St., 804/622-9223

Best Coffeehouses
First Colony Coffee House
  132 E. Little Creek Rd., 804/480-1225
  2000 Colonial Ave., 804/622-0149
Prince Books and Coffee Shoppe
  109 E. Main St., 804/622-9223

Best Continental Food
Norfolk Waterside Marriott Dining Room
  253 E. Main St., 804/627-4200
Monastery Restaurant
  443 Granby St., 804/625-8193

Best Delicatessen
Schlotzsky's
  246 E. Main St., 804/627-2867
  700 N. Military Hwy., 804/455-2867

V

Best Diner
Charlie's Breakfast and Lunch
  1800A Granby St., 804/625-0824

Best Family Restaurant
Darryl's Restaurant and Bar 1930
  1020 N. Military Hwy., 804/466-1930

Best Greek/Mediterranean Food
Orapax Inn
  1300 Redgate Ave., 804/627-8041

Best Homestyle Food
The Bait Shack
  333 Waterside Dr., 804/622-3654

Best Ice Cream/Yogurt
High's Ice Cream Store
  7862 Tidewater Dr., 804/588-9002

Best Indian Food
Nawab Indian Cuisine
  888 N. Military Hwy., 804/455-8080

Best Italian Food
Adante Cafe and Gourmet Market
  417 N. Military Hwy., 804/466-1888
Il Porto
  323 Waterside Dr., 804/627-4400
Fellini's
  3910 Colley Ave., 804/625-3000

Best Late-Night Food
Bienville Grill
  723 W. 21st St., 804/625-5427

Best Mexican Food
El Rodeo Autentico Restaurante
  5834 E. Virginia Beach Blvd., 804/466-9077

Best Outdoor Dining
Phillips Waterside
  333 Waterside Dr., 804/627-6600

Best Pizza
Chanello's Pizza
  105 Greenbrier Ave., 804/440-5858
  3201 E. Ocean View Ave., 804/588-2200
  4820 Hampton Blvd., 804/440-0800
  6213 Chesapeake Blvd., 804/858-4000
Orapax Inn
  1300 Redgate Ave., 804/627-8041
La Galleria Ristorante
  120 College Pl., 804/623-3939

Best Place to Eat When Someone Else Is Buying
Ship's Cabin Seafood Restaurant
  4110 E. Ocean View Ave., 804/362-4659

Best Place to Take the Kids
Darryl's Restaurant and Bar 1930
  1020 N. Military Hwy., 804/466-1930

Best Romantic Dining
Ship's Cabin Seafood Restaurant
  4110 E. Ocean View Ave., 804/362-4659

V

Best Salad/Salad Bar
Green Trees
  112 Bank St., 804/625-2455

Best Sandwiches
Famous Uncle Al's
  200 Plume St., 804/625-8319

Best Seafood
Phillips Waterside
  333 Waterside Dr., 804/627-6600
Ship's Cabin Seafood Restaurant
  4110 E. Ocean View Ave., 804/362-4659
Fisherman's Wharf
  1571 Bayville St., 804/480-3113

Best Sports Bar
Stormy's Sports Pub
  235 E. Main St., 804/627-4200

Best Steaks
Grate Steak
  235 N. Military Hwy., 804/461-5501

Best Vegetarian Food
Green Trees
  112 Bank St., 804/625-2455

Standbys
International House of Pancakes
  1153 N. Military Hwy., 804/461-5604
Shoney's
  114 E. 21st St., 804/625-6510
  2437 E. Little Creek Rd., 804/583-5143
  6667 E. Virginia Beach Blvd., 804/461-4068

PETERSBURG, VA

Best Bar
Annabelle's
  2733 Park Ave., 804/732-0997

Best Barbecue/Ribs
King's Barbecue
  2910 S. Crater Rd., 804/732-0975
  3221 W. Washington St., 804/732-5861

Best Burgers
Aunt Sarah's Pancake House
  403 E. Washington St., 804/732-5411

Best Chinese Food
Hunan Palace Restaurant
  405 E. Washington St., 804/732-2331
Lee's Express
  21 W. Washington St., 804/732-5337

Best Ice Cream/Yogurt
High's Mayberry Ice Cream
  2004 S. Sycamore St., 804/733-9575

Best Italian Food
Roma's Restaurant
  2447 County Dr., 804/861-0414

V

Best Pizza
Roma's Restaurant
  2447 County Dr., 804/861-0414

Best Place to Eat When Someone Else Is Buying
Annabelle's
  2733 Park Ave., 804/732-0997

Best Romantic Dining
Annabelle's
  2733 Park Ave., 804/732-0997

Best Seafood
Captain Tom's Seafood
  1717 Boulevard, Colonial Heights, 804/526-0005

Best View While Dining
Captain Tom's Seafood
  1717 Boulevard, Colonial Heights, 804/526-0005

Standbys
Old Country Buffet
  1829 Southpark Blvd., Colonial Heights,
    804/520-5117
Shoney's
  2535 S. Crater Rd., 804/732-3454
Dairy Queen
  101 S. Crater Rd., 804/861-1169
Western Sizzlin
  5107 Oaklawn Blvd., 804/458-7880
Chi Chi's
  2001 Southpark Blvd., Colonial Heights,
    804/526-3588
Golden Corral Family Steak House
  2501 Conduit Rd., Colonial Heights, 804/520-4581
Subway
  3219 S. Crater Rd., 804/732-2860
Applebee's
  449 Southpark Cir., Colonial Heights, 804/526-6038
Red Lobster
  119 Temple Lake Dr., Colonial Heights, 804/520-6820
Steak and Ale
  500 E. Wythe St., 804/861-5993

PORTSMOUTH, VA

Best Barbecue/Ribs
Rodman's Bones and Buddies
  3526 Western Branch Blvd., 804/397-3900
  5917 Churchland Blvd., 804/483-2000

Best Breakfast
Waffle Town USA
  3110 High St., 804/399-6612

Best Burgers
Circle Seafood Restaurant
  3010 High St., 804/397-8196

Best Chinese Food
Dragon Town Chinese Restaurant
  4748 W. Norfolk Rd., 804/483-9189

V

Best Continental Food
Cafe Europa
319 High St., 804/399-6652

Best Delicatessen
Mom's Best Deli
340 Broad St., 804/399-1199

Best Homestyle Food
Jones' Restaurant
5811 W. Norfolk Rd., 804/484-1996

Best Ice Cream/Yogurt
High's Ice Cream Store
5792 Churchland Blvd., 804/483-0731

Best Italian Food
Mario's Pizza and Restaurant
611 Airline Blvd., 804/399-8970

Best Mexican Food
La Tolteca
6031 High St. W., 804/484-8043

Best Outdoor Dining
Max
425 Water St., 804/397-1866

Best Pizza
Mario's Pizza and Restaurant
611 Airline Blvd., 804/399-8970

Best Sandwiches
Mom's Best Deli
340 Broad St., 804/399-1199

Best Seafood
Amory's Seafood Restaurant
5909 High St. W., 804/483-1518
Amory's Wharf
10 Crawford Pkwy., 804/399-0991
Circle Seafood Restaurant
3010 High St., 804/397-8196

Best Steaks
Circle Seafood Restaurant
3010 High St., 804/397-8196

Best View While Dining
Scale O' De Whale
3515 Shipwright St., 804/483-2772

Standbys
Golden Corral Family Steak House
3269 Western Branch Blvd., 804/483-1621

V

RESTON, VA

Best Restaurant in Town
Clyde's of Reston
11905 Market St., 703/742-6081

Best American Food
Clyde's of Reston
11905 Market St., 703/787-6601

Best Barbecue/Ribs
Pepper's Texas Bar-B-Q
  1810 Michael Faraday Dr., 703/435-9696

Best Burgers
Clyde's of Reston
  11905 Market St., 703/787-6601

Best Chinese Food
China Star
  1800 Michael Faraday Ct., 703/435-8666
China Town
  1771 Library St., 703/435-4260

Best Coffee
Starbucks
  1444 Northpoint Village Ctr., 703/787-9341

Best Desserts
Jasmine Cafe
  1633A Washington Plaza N., 703/471-9114

Best Dim Sum
Fortune of Reston
  1428 Northpoint Village Ctr., 703/318-8898

Best Family Restaurant
The Melting Pot
  11400 Commerce Park Dr., 703/264-0900

Best French Food
Jasmine Cafe
  1633A Washington Plaza N., 703/471-9114
Chez Francois L'Auberge
  332 Springvale Rd., Great Falls, 703/759-3800

Best Greek/Mediterranean Food
Marie's Restaurant
  11130M S. Lakes Dr., 703/620-6555

Best Ice Cream/Yogurt
Lee's Ice Cream
  11917 Freedom Dr., 703/471-8902

Best Italian Food
Il Cigno Restaurant
  1617 Washington Plaza N., 703/471-0121
Paolo's
  11898 Market St., 703/318-8920

Best Late-Night Food
Paolo's
  11898 Market St., 703/318-8920

Best Mexican Food
Rio Grande Cafe
  1827 Library St., 703/904-0703

Best Pizza
Paolo's
  11898 Market St., 703/318-8920
Pizzeria Uno Restaurant and Bar
  11948 Market St., 703/742-8667

Best Places to Eat When Someone Else Is Buying
Clyde's of Reston
  11905 Market St., 703/787-6601

V

Market Street Bar and Grill
1800 Presidents St., 703/709-6262

Best Place to Take the Kids
Roy Rogers Restaurant
11170 S. Lakes Dr., 703/620-2249
11850 Sunrise Valley Dr., 703/860-2292

Best Romantic Dining
Chez Francois L'Auberge
332 Springvale Rd., Great Falls, 703/759-3800

Best Seafood
Clyde's of Reston
11905 Market St., 703/787-6601

Best Steaks
Market Street Bar and Grill
1800 Presidents St., 703/709-6262

Best View While Dining
Marie's Restaurant
11130M S. Lakes Dr., 703/620-6555

RICHMOND, VA

Best All-You-Can-Eat Buffet
Tobacco Restaurant
1201 E. Cary St., 804/782-9555

Best Atmosphere
Tobacco Restaurant
1201 E. Cary St., 804/782-9555

Best Bars
Castle Thunder Cafe
1726 E. Main St., 804/648-3038
Southern Culture Restaurant
2229 W. Main St., 804/355-6939

Best Barbecue/Ribs
Bill's Barbecue
11230 Midlothian Turnpike, 804/379-0899
3100 N. Boulevard, 804/355-9745
5805 W. Broad St., 804/288-9991
700 E. Main St., 804/643-9857
8820 W. Broad St., 804/270-9722
927 Myers St., 804/355-9905

Best Breakfast
Aunt Sarah's Pancake House
4205 W. Broad St., 804/358-8812
5100 S. Laburnum Ave., 804/222-2080
7927 W. Broad St., 804/747-8284
8201 Midlothian Turnpike, 804/323-0639
2126 Willis Rd., 804/271-1070

Best Brunch
T.J.'s
Jefferson Hotel, Franklin St. at Adams St.,
804/788-8000

Best Burgers
Strawberry Street Cafe
421 Strawberry St., 804/353-6860

Best Business Lunch
Bogart's Restaurant
  203 N. Lombardy St., 804/353-9280
  443 N. Ridge Rd., 804/285-1603

Best Casual Dining
Robin Inn
  2601 Park Ave., 804/353-0298
Slip at Shockoe
  11 S. Twelfth St., 804/643-3313

Best Chinese Food
Peking Chinese Restaurant
  5710 Grove Ave., 804/288-8371
  8904 W. Broad St., 804/270-9898

Best Coffee
Virginia Coffee and Tea Company
  1211 W. Main St., 804/355-2739

Best Family Restaurant
Black-Eyed Pea
  10201 Midlothian Turnpike, 804/560-3168

Best Greek/Mediterranean Food
Crazy Greek
  1903 Staples Mill Rd., 804/355-3786

Best Homestyle Food
Black-Eyed Pea
  10201 Midlothian Turnpike, 804/560-3168

Best Ice Cream/Yogurt
Gelati Celesti Ice Cream Makers
  8906A W. Broad St., 804/346-0038

Best Indian Food
Bombay Curry House
  4401 W. Broad St., 804/359-0054

Best Italian Food
Amici Ristorante
  3343 W. Cary St., 804/353-4700
Italian Oven
  10921 Midlothian Turnpike, 804/379-1400
  8932 Quioccasin Rd., 804/740-1400
Caffe Di Pagliacci
  214 N. Lombardy St., 804/353-3040

Best Mexican Food
La Siesta Mexican Restaurant
  9900 Midlothian Turnpike, 804/272-7333

Best Outdoor Dining
Du Jour
  5806 Grove Ave., 804/285-1301

Best Pizza
Mary Angela's Italian Subs
  3345 W. Cary St., 804/353-2333
Bottoms Up Pizza
  1700 Dock St., 804/644-4400

Best Place to Eat When Someone Else Is Buying
Tobacco Restaurant
  1201 E. Cary St., 804/782-9555

V

Best Salad/Salad Bar
Strawberry Street Cafe
   421 Strawberry St., 804/353-6860

Best Sandwiches
Mary Angela's Italian Subs
   3345 W. Cary St., 804/353-2333

Best Tea Room
Virginia Coffee and Tea Company
   1211 W. Main St., 804/355-2739

Standbys
Old Country Buffet
   7801 W. Broad St., 804/672-1185
Chuck E. Cheese Pizza
   10430 Midlothian Turnpike, 804/330-9865
Friday's
   10301 Midlothian Turnpike, 804/330-0203
   7023 W. Broad St., 804/672-9477
Ruth's Chris Steak House
   11500 Huguenot Rd., Midlothian, 804/378-0600

ROANOKE, VA

Best Restaurants in Town
Alexander's
   105 S. Jefferson St., 540/982-6983
Montano's
   3733 Franklin Rd., 540/344-8960
Roanoker
   2522 Colonial Ave. SW, 540/344-7746
Stephen's
   2926 Franklin Rd. SW, 540/344-7203

Best Bars
Awful Arthur's
   108 Campbell Ave., 540/344-2997
Charade's
   2801 Hershberger Rd. NW, 540/563-9300
Confeddy's
   32 Market Sq. SE, 540/343-9746

Best Beer Selection
Cheers
   1650 Braeburn Dr., Salem, 540/389-4600
Montano's
   3733 Franklin Rd., 540/344-8960
Valley Country
   3348 Salem Turnpike NW, 540/344-6510

V

Best Delicatessens
Five Boro Bagels
   2016 Electric Rd., Rte. 419, 540/989-5569
The New Yorker
   2802 Williamson Rd. NW, 540/366-0935
The Upper Crust
   1713 Riverview Dr., Salem, 540/389-7540

Best Happy Hour Snacks
Awful Arthur's
   108 Campbell Ave., 540/344-2997

Mac and Maggie's
    4202 Electric Rd., 540/774-7427
Montano's
    3733 Franklin Rd., 540/344-8960

Best Late-Night Food
Mac and Maggie's
    4202 Electric Rd., 540/774-7427
Texas Tavern
    114 Church Ave. W, 540/342-4825

Best Wine Selection
Chateau Morrisette
    Rural Route 1, Floyd, 540/593-2865
The Library
    3117 Franklin Rd. SW, 540/985-0811
Montano's
    3733 Franklin Rd., 540/344-8960

Standbys
Baskin-Robbins
    2121 Colonial Ave. SW, 540/343-5853
    4220 Williamson Rd. NE, 540/366-9724
Dairy Queen
    2350 Orange Ave. NE, 540/343-9556
    4802 Valley View Blvd. NW, 540/563-5788
Waffle House
    3606 Franklin Rd. SW, 540/345-3181
    6608 Thirlane Rd. NW, 540/366-2676

SALEM, VA

Best Restaurants in Town
Mac and Bob's
    316 E. Main St., 540/389-5999
Holiday Inn
    1671 Skyview Rd., 540/389-7061
Macado's
    211 E. Main St., 540/387-2686
Famous Anthony's
    176 W. Main St., 540/389-4502

SUFFOLK, VA

Best Barbecue/Ribs
Herb's Barbeque
    868 Carolina Rd., 804/539-9785

Best Breakfast
Bunny's Restaurant
    1901 Wilroy Rd., 804/538-2325
Dining Room
    510 E. Pinner St., 804/539-4265

Best Burgers
Herb's Barbeque
    868 Carolina Rd., 804/539-9785

Best Chinese Food
Big Won
    927 W. Constance Rd., 804/934-8676

V

Best Family Restaurants
Bunny's Restaurant
1901 Wilroy Rd., 804/538-2325
Dining Room
510 E. Pinner St., 804/539-4265

Best Homestyle Food
Bunny's Restaurant
1901 Wilroy Rd., 804/538-2325
Herb's Barbeque
868 Carolina Rd., 804/539-9785
Dining Room
510 E. Pinner St., 804/539-4265

Best Pizza
Maria's Pizza and Subs Shop
812 W. Constance Rd., 804/934-2641

Best Sandwiches
Maria's Pizza and Subs Shop
812 W. Constance Rd., 804/934-2641

Best Seafood
George's Steak House
1260 Holland Rd., 804/934-1726
Main Street Restaurant and Raw Bar
1467 N. Main St., 804/934-9235

Best Steaks
George's Steak House
1260 Holland Rd., 804/934-1726
Main Street Restaurant and Raw Bar
1467 N. Main St., 804/934-9235

Standbys
Dairy Queen
806 N. Main St., 804/539-4074
Applebee's
1206 N. Main St., 804/934-8676

VIRGINIA BEACH, VA

Best American Food
Cafe Society
1807 Mediterranean Ave., 804/422-8774
Five 01 City Grill
501 N. Birdneck Rd., 804/425-7195

Best Bar
Five Hundred and One City Grill
501 N. Birdneck Rd., 804/425-7195

Best Barbecue/Ribs
Frankie's Place for Ribs
5200 Fairfield Shopping Ctr., 804/495-7427
408 Laskin Rd., 804/428-7631

Best Breakfast
Village Inn
313 Independence Blvd., 804/499-5557

Best Brunch
T.K. Tripp's Restaurant
101 S. Independence Blvd., 804/490-4517

V

Best Burgers
Raven Restaurant
  1200 Atlantic Ave., 804/425-9556

Best Casual Dining
Annabelle's
  21 Pembroke Mall, Ste. 4586, 804/490-3888
Chick's Oyster Bar
  2143 Vista Cir., 804/481-5757

Best Cheap Meal
La Fogata
  3900 Bonney Rd., 804/463-6339

Best Chinese Food
Great Wall Chinese Restaurant
  1001 Providence Square Shopping Ctr., 804/467-4917
  875 S. Lynnhaven Pkwy., 804/468-1212
Szechuan Garden Restaurant
  2720 N. Mall Dr., 804/463-1680

Best Coffee
First Colony Coffee House
  1550 Laskin Rd., 804/428-2994

Best Coffeehouse
First Colony Coffee House
  1550 Laskin Rd., 804/428-2994

Best Desserts
Aldo's Ristorante
  1860 Laskin Rd., 804/491-1111
Cuisine and Company
  3004 Pacific Ave., 804/428-6700

Best French Food
Le Chambord
  324 N. Great Neck Rd., 804/498-1234
La Caravelle Restaurant
  1040 Laskin Rd., 804/428-2477

Best Health-Conscious Menu
Heritage Health Food Store
  314 Laskin Rd., 804/428-0500

Best Homestyle Food
Carolina Cookin' Family Restaurant
  6567 College Park Sq., 804/523-4529

Best Indian Food
India Restaurant
  5760 Northampton Blvd., 804/460-2100

Best Italian Food
Aldo's Ristorante
  1860 Laskin Rd., 804/491-1111
Il Giardino Ristorante
  910 Atlantic Ave., 804/422-6464
Pasta e Pani
  1065 Laskin Rd., 804/428-2299

Best Japanese Food
Shogun Japanese Steak House
  550 First Colonial Rd., 804/422-5150

V

Best Mexican Food
La Fogata
  3900 Bonney Rd., 804/463-6339
El Rodeo Mexican Restaurant
  5209 Providence Rd., 804/474-2698

Best Middle Eastern Food
Anatolia
  2158 Great Neck Sq., 804/496-9777

Best Outdoor Dining
Sandbridge Restaurant and Bar
  205 Sandbridge Rd., 804/426-2193

Best Place to Be "Seen"
Duck-In and Gazebo
  3324 Shore Dr., 804/481-0201

Best Place to Eat Alone
Gus' Mariner Restaurant
  57th St. at Atlantic Ave., 804/425-5699

Best Place to Eat When Someone Else Is Buying
Le Chambord
  324 N. Great Neck Rd., 804/498-1234

Best Romantic Dining
Alexander's on the Bay
  Fentress Ave., 804/464-4999
Tandom's
  2932 Virginia Beach Blvd., 804/340-5637

Best Salad/Salad Bar
Tandom's
  2932 Virginia Beach Blvd., 804/340-5637

Best Sandwiches
Jewish Mother
  3108 Pacific Ave., 804/422-5430
Taste Unlimited
  213 36th St., 804/425-0977
  4097 Shore Dr., 804/464-1566
  638 Hilltop West Shopping Ctr., 804/425-1858

Best Seafood
Chick's Oyster Bar
  2143 Vista Cir., 804/481-5757
Alexander's on the Bay
  Foot of Fentress St., 804/464-4999
Sandbridge Restaurant and Bar
  205 Sandbridge Rd., 804/426-2193
Coastal Grill
  1427 N. Great Neck Rd., 804/496-3348
Steinhilber's Thalia Acres Inn
  653 Thalia Rd., 804/340-1156
The Lucky Star
  1608 Pleasure House Rd., 804/363-8410
Henry's Seafood Restaurant
  3319 Shore Dr., 804/481-7300
Duck-In and Gazebo
  3324 Shore Dr., 804/481-0201

Best Steaks
Aberdeen Barn
  5805 Northampton Blvd., 804/464-1580

Best Vegetarian Food
Cafe Central
  5350 Kemps River Dr., 804/420-2561

Best View While Dining
Sandbridge Restaurant and Bar
  205 Sandbridge Rd., 804/426-2193

Standbys
Shoney's
  1620 Laskin Rd., 804/428-7948
  5668 Indian River Rd., 804/420-3773
Fuddruckers
  4625 Virginia Beach Blvd., 804/456-1118
TCBY
  140 Virginia Beach Blvd., 804/486-6720
  2150 N. Great Neck Rd., 804/481-4696
  5256A Providence Rd., 804/495-3777
  5386 Kemps River Dr., 804/523-1499
  717 Independence Blvd., 804/473-8183
  Timberlake Shopping Ctr., Ste. 728, 804/467-3853
Chi Chi's
  739 Lynnhaven Pkwy., 804/463-3550
Old Country Buffet
  1952 Laskin Rd., 804/428-3907

WILLIAMSBURG, VA

Best American Food
Christiana Campbell's Tavern
  Waller St., 804/229-2141
King's Arms Tavern
  Duke of Gloucester St., 804/229-1000
Regency Room
  Williamsburg Inn, Colonial Williamsburg,
    804/229-2141
Shields Tavern
  Duke of Gloucester St., 804/229-1000
Trellis Cafe, Restaurant and Grill
  Duke of Gloucester St., 804/229-8610
Victoria's Fire
  Festival Marketplace, 264AB McLaws Circle,
    804/220-2511

Best Asian Restaurant
Sakura Japanese Steak House
  601 Prince George St., 804/253-1233

Best Barbecue/Ribs
Pierce's Pitt Bar-B-Que
  447 Rochambeau Dr., 804/565-2955

Best Chinese Food
Dynasty Restaurant
  1621 Richmond Rd., 804/220-8888
Peking Restaurant
  122A Waller Mill Rd., 804/229-2288

Best French Food
Le Yaca
  Village Shops at Kingsmill, Rte. 60, 804/220-3616

V

Best Italian Food
Ristorante Primo
  1325 Jamestown Rd., 804/229-9212

Best Japanese Food
Sakura Japanese Steak and Seafood Restaurant
  601 Prince George St., 804/253-1233

Best Mexican Food
La Tolteca
  5351 Richmond Rd., 804/253-2939

Best Seafood
Berret's Restaurant-Raw Bar
  199 S. Boundary, 804/253-1847
The Whaling Company
  494 McLaws Circle, 804/229-0275

Best Steaks
The Aberdeen Barn
  1601 Richmond Rd., 804/229-6661

Best Vegetarian Food
The Trellis
  403 Duke of Gloucester St., 804/229-8610

Best Vietnamese Food
Chez Trinh Restaurant
  157 Monticello Ave., 804/253-1888

Standbys
Cracker Barrel
  200 Bypass Rd., 804/220-3384

V

Washington

Best Breakfast
Sidney's
512 W. Heron St., 360/533-6635

Best Burgers
Billy's Restaurant
322 E. Heron St., 360/533-7144

Best Chinese Food
Ocean Palace
212 E. Wishkah St., 360/533-6966

Best Coffee
Duffy's
1605 Simpson Ave., 360/532-3842

Best Desserts
Bridges Restaurant
112 N. G St., 360/532-6563

Best Dinner
Levee Street Restaurant
709 Levee St., Hoquiam, 360/532-1959

Best Family Restaurant
Duffy's
1605 Simpson Ave., 360/532-3842

Best Homestyle Food
Duffy's
1605 Simpson Ave., 360/532-3842

Best Italian Food
Parma Italian Restaurante
116 W. Heron St., 360/532-3166

Best Mexican Food
Mazatlan Restaurant
202 E. Wishkah St., 360/532-0940
Casa Mia
2936 Simpson Ave., Hoquiam, 360/533-2010

Best Sandwiches
Billy's Restaurant
322 E. Heron St., 360/533-7144

W

Best Seafood
Pelican Point Restaurant
  2681 Westhaven Dr., Westport, 360/268-1333

Best Steaks
Seven Hundred Seven Restaurant
  707 W. Curtis St., 360/533-2662
Bridges Restaurant
  112 N. G St., 360/532-6563

Standbys
Baskin-Robbins
  1014 E. Wishkah St., 360/533-5040

BELLEVUE, WA

Best Restaurant in Town
The New Jake O'Shaughnessey's
  401 Bellevue Sq., 206/455-5559

Best Barbecue/Ribs
Three Pigs Barbecue
  1044 116th Ave. NE, 206/453-0888

Best Breakfast
Red Lion Inn
  818 112th Ave. NE, 206/455-1515
Yankee Diner
  13856 Bel Red Rd., 206/643-1558

Best Burgers
Yankee Diner
  13856 Bel Red Rd., 206/643-1558

Best Chinese Food
Empress of China
  707 148th Ave. NE, 206/747-8700
Best Wok
  19 148th Ave. NE, 206/747-7031

Best Homestyle Food
Yankee Diner
  13856 Bel Red Rd., 206/643-1558

Best Indian
Raga Cuisine of India
  555 108th Ave. NE, 206/450-0336

Best Italian Food
Spazzo Mediterranean Grill
  10655 NE Fourth St., Ninth Fl., 206/454-8255
Cucina! Cucina! Italian Cafe
  800 Bellevue Way NE, Ste. 18, 206/637-1177

Best Mexican Food
Azteca Mexican Restaurants
  15100 SE 38th St., 206/641-5988

Best Middle Eastern Food
Ebru Mediterranean Deli
  15600 NE Eighth St., 206/641-4352

Best Other Ethnic Food
Pogacha Restaurant (Yugoslavian/Russian)
  119 106th Ave. NE, 206/455-5670
Russian Tea Room (Yugoslavian/Russian)
  10425 NE Eighth St., 206/451-3234

W

Best Pizza
Coyote Creek Pizza Company
228 Central Way, Kirkland, 206/822-2226

Best Sandwiches
Grand Central Bakery
138 107th Ave., 206/454-9661

Best Seafood
The New Jake O'Shaughnessey's
401 Bellevue Sq., 206/455-5559

Best Steaks
The New Jake O'Shaughnessey's
401 Bellevue Sq., 206/455-5559

Best Thai Food
Thai Kitchen Restaurant
14115 NE Twentieth St., 206/641-9166
King and I Restaurant
10509 Main St., 206/462-9337

BELLINGHAM, WA

Best Restaurants in Town
Mannino's Italian Restaurant
130 E. Champion St., 360/671-7955
Orchard Street Brewery
709 W. Orchard Dr., Ste. 1, 360/647-1614
Pacific Cafe
100 N. Commercial St., 360/647-0800

Best All-You-Can-Eat Buffet
Cathay House
950 Lincoln St., 360/676-9100

Best Bars
Archer Ale House
1212 Tenth St., 360/647-7002
Orchard Street Brewery
709 W. Orchard Dr., Ste. 1, 360/647-1614

Best Breakfast
Little Cheerful Cafe
133 E. Holly St., 360/738-8824

Best Brunch
Chuckanut Manor Restaurant
302 Chuckanut Dr., Bow, 360/766-6191

Best Burgers
Bullie's Restaurant and Oyster Bar
1200 Harris Ave., 360/734-2855

Best Business Lunch
Casino Bar and Grill
1224 Cornwall Ave., 360/733-3500
Colophon Cafe
1208 Eleventh St., 360/647-0092

Best Casual Dining
Boomer's Drive-In
310 N. Samish Way, 360/647-2666
Pacific Cafe
100 N. Commercial St., 360/647-0800

W

Best Cheap Meal
The Royal Inn Restaurant
  208 E. Holly St., 360/738-3701

Best Coffee
Starbucks
  2814 Merdian St., 360/647-8128
  1225 E. Sunset Dr., 360/734-0702
  210 36th St., 360/738-1402
  4285 Guide Meridian Rd., 360/650-0883

Best Desserts
La Patisserie
  3098 Northwest Ave., 360/671-3671
Colophon Cafe
  1208 Eleventh St., 360/647-0092

Best Diners
Carol's Coffee Cup
  5415 Mount Baker Hwy., Deming, 360/592-5641
Bullie's Restaurant and Oyster Bar
  1200 Harris Ave., 360/734-2855

Best Family Restaurant
Red Robin
  100 Telegraph Rd., 360/734-9991

Best French Food
La Belle Rose
  1801 Roeder Ave., 360/647-0833

Best Health-Conscious Menu
Old Town Cafe
  316 W. Holly St., 360/671-5522
Pepper Sisters
  1055 N. State St., 360/671-3414

Best Homestyle Food
Mitzel's American Kitchen
  241 Telegraph Rd., 360/671-5522

Best Ice Cream/Yogurt
The Ice Creamery
  1 Bellis Fair Pkwy., 360/734-7502

Best Italian Food
Mannino's Italian Restaurant
  130 E. Champion St., 360/671-7955
Il Fiasco Restaurant
  1309 Commercial St., 360/676-9136

Best Late-Night Food
Orchard Street Brewery
  709 W. Orchard Dr., Ste. 1, 360/647-1614

Best Mexican Food
La Pinata Mexican Restaurant
  1317 Commercial St., 360/647-1101

Best Microbrewery
Orchard Street Brewery
  709 W. Orchard Dr., Ste. 1, 360/647-1614

Best Pizza
Stanello's Restaurant
  1304 Twelfth St., 360/676-1304

W

Cicchitti's East Coast
 1230 N. State St., 360/671-8447

Best Place to Be "Seen"
Il Fiasco Restaurant
 1309 Commercial St., 360/676-9136

Best Place to Eat Alone
Swan Cafe
 1220 N. Forest St., 360/734-0542

Best Place to Eat When Someone Else Is Buying
Il Fiasco Restaurant
 1309 Commercial St., 360/676-9136

Best Place to Take the Kids
Red Robin
 100 Telegraph Rd., 360/734-9991

Best Romantic Dining
Pacific Cafe
 100 N. Commercial St., 360/647-0800

Best Salad/Salad Bar
Bob's Burgers
 1781 Main St., Ferndale, 360/384-1766

Best Sandwiches
Casino Bar and Grill
 1224 Cornwall Ave., 360/733-3500
The Bagelry
 1319 Railroad Ave., 360/676-5288

Best Seafood
Oyster Bar
 240 Chuckanut Dr., 360/766-6185
Pacific Cafe
 100 N. Commercial St., 360/647-0800

Best Steaks
Stuart Anderson's
 8413 Evergreen Way, 360/355-7400

Best Vegetarian Food
Pepper Sisters
 1055 N. State St., 360/671-3414

Best Other Restaurant
Innisfree Restaurant
 9393 Mount Baker Hwy., Deming, 360/599-2373

BREMERTON, WA

Best Restaurants in Town
Pleasant Beach Grill and Oyster House
 4738 Lynwood Center Rd. NE, Bainbridge Island,
  206/842-4347
The Boat Shed Restaurant
 101 Shore Dr., 206/377-2600
Jose's Flamingo Cafe
 18830 Front St. NE, Poulsbo, 206/779-7676

CENTRALIA, WA

Best Breakfast
Country Cousin
 1054 Harrison Ave., 360/736-2200

W

Alva's Place
227 SW Riverside Dr., Chehalis, 360/748-0877

Best Burgers
Burgerville USA
818 Harrison Ave., 360/736-5212

Best Chinese Food
Mandarin Chef
705 1/2 N. Tower Ave., 360/736-9326
Shanghai Restaurant
519 N. Tower Ave., 360/736-4539

Best Coffee
Madrid's Espresso
202 S. Tower Ave., 360/330-5464

Best Desserts
Antique Mall Cafe
201 S. Pearl St., 360/736-1183
Sweet Inspirations
514 N. Market Blvd., Chehalis, 360/748-7102

Best Family Restaurant
Country Cousin
1054 Harrison Ave., 360/736-2200

Best Homestyle Food
Country Cousin
1054 Harrison Ave., 360/736-2200
Alva's Place
227 SW Riverside Dr., Chehalis, 360/748-0877

Best Mexican Food
Azteca Mexican Restaurants
118 N. Tower Ave., 360/736-0973
Plaza Jalisco
1340 NW Maryland Ave., Chehalis, 360/748-4298

Best Pizza
Figaro's Italian Pizza
1704 S. Gold St., 360/736-3221
Pacific Pizza
309 W. Main St., 360/736-4400

Best Sandwiches
Antique Mall Cafe
201 S. Pearl St., 360/736-1183
Sweet Inspirations
514 N. Market Blvd., Chehalis, 360/748-7102

Best Steaks
Rib-Eye Restaurant
1336 Rush Rd., Chehalis, 360/748-0288

Standbys
Denny's
1052A Harrison Ave., 360/736-6917

W

EVERETT, WA

Best Restaurant in Town
Passport Restaurant
1509 Wall St., 206/259-5037

Best Barbecue/Ribs
Down Home Bar-B-Que
1409 Hewitt Ave., 206/258-6005

Best Breakfast
Sisters
2804 Grand Ave., 206/252-0480
Karl's Bakery and Coffee Shoppe
2814 Wetmore Ave., 206/252-1774
Totem Family Dining
4410 Rucker Ave., 206/252-3277

Best Burgers
Buck's American Cafe
2901 Hewitt Ave., 206/258-1351

Best Business Lunch
Passport Restaurant
1509 Wall St., 206/259-5037

Best Cheap Meal
Mom's Teriyaki
2934 Colby Ave., 206/339-5535

Best Desserts
Pave Specialty Bakery
2613 Colby Ave., 206/252-0250

Best Dinner
Passport Restaurant
1509 Wall St., 206/259-5037
Confetti's Restaurant
1722 W. Maine View Dr., 206/258-4000
Anthony's Homeport
1726 W. Marine View Dr., 206/252-3333

Best Greek/Mediterranean Food
Donato's
2609 Colby Ave., 206/258-2151

Best Health-Conscious Menu
Sisters
2804 Grand Ave., 206/252-0480

Best Indian Food
India's Palace
1405 Hewitt Ave., 206/252-8543

Best Italian Food
Anna's Italian Kitchen
2930 Colby Ave., 206/252-8225
Donato's
2609 Colby Ave., 206/258-2151
Bella Rosa Ristorante Italiano
2803 Colby Ave., 206/258-8028
Gianni's Ristorante Italiano
5030 Evergreen Way, 206/252-2435

Best Lunch
Sisters
2804 Grand Ave., 206/252-0480
Passport Restaurant
1509 Wall St., 206/259-5037
Anthony's Homeport
1726 W. Marine View Dr., 206/252-3333

W

Best Mexican Food
Tampico Mexican Restaurant
2303 Broadway, 206/339-2427

Best Pizza
Giorgio's Pizza House
9031 Evergreen Way, 206/347-1542

Best Place to Take the Kids
Alfy's Pizza
12720 Fourth Ave. W., 206/353-1776
2317 Broadway, 206/258-9333
7404 Evergreen Way, 206/355-1776
9620 Nineteenth Ave. SE, Silver Lake, 206/338-2577

Best Restaurant Meal Value
Sisters
2804 Grand Ave., 206/252-0480
India Palace
1405 Hewitt Ave., 206/252-8543
Alligator Soul
2013 1/2 Hewitt Ave., 206/259-6311

Best Romantic Dining
Passport Restaurant
1509 Wall St., 206/259-5037

Best Seafood
Anthony's Homeport
1726 W. Marine View Dr., 206/252-3333

Best Steaks
Anthony's Homeport
1726 W. Marine View Dr., 206/252-3333

Best View While Dining
Anthony's Homeport
1726 W. Marine View Dr., 206/252-3333
Confetti's Restaurant
1722 W. Maine View Dr., 206/258-4000

Standbys
Baskin-Robbins
1402 SE Everrett Mall Way, 206/355-3100
4019 Colby Ave., 206/259-6336
5802 Evergreen Way, 206/353-3444

FEDERAL WAY, WA

Best Restaurant in Town
Salty's
28201 Redondo Beach Dr. S., 206/946-0636

Best Breakfast
Coffee Crossing
2500B SW 336th St., 206/838-2742

W

Best Business Lunch
Diamond Jim's
1616 S. 235th St., 206/927-4045

Best Diner
Rose's Highway Inn
26915 Pacific Hwy. S., Kent, 206/839-7277

Best Family Restaurant
Rose's Highway Inn
  26915 Pacific Hwy. S., Kent, 206/839-7277

Best Italian Food
Giancarlo
  4624 SW 320th St., 206/838-1101
Verrazano's Italian-American
  28835 Pacific Hwy. S., 206/946-4122

Best Mexican Food
Azteca Mexican Restaurant
  31740 23rd Ave. S., 206/839-6693

Best Pizza
Milton Tavern
  7320 Pacific Hwy. E., Tacoma, 206/922-3340

Best Place to Eat When Someone Else Is Buying
Salty's
  28201 Redondo Beach Dr. S., 206/946-0636

Best Romantic Dining
Giancarlo
  4624 SW 320th St., 206/838-1101

Best Sandwiches
Diamond Jim's
  1616 S. 235th St., 206/927-4045

Best Seafood
Salty's
  28201 Redondo Beach Dr. S., 206/946-0636

Best Steaks
Diamond Jim's
  1616 S. 235th St., 206/927-4045

Best View While Dining
Giancarlo
  4624 SW 320th St., 206/838-1101

KENNEWICK, WA

Best All-You-Can-Eat Buffet
Granny's Buffet
  1621 Canal, 509/735-9887

Best Breakfast
Sterling's Famous Steak
  890 George Washington Way, Richland, 509/946-0681

Best Brunch
Red Lion Inn
  2525 N. Twentieth Ave., Pasco, 509/547-0701

Best Burgers
Red Robin
  1021 Columbia Center Blvd., 509/736-6008
  924 George Washington Way, Richland, 509/943-8484

Best Business Lunch
Henry's Restaurant
  3013 W. Clearwater Ave., 509/735-1996
  1435 George Washington Way, Richland,
    509/946-8706

W

Best Cheap Meal
Shari's of Kennewick
1200 N. Columbia Center Blvd., 509/735-7438
Shari's of Richland
1745 George Washington Way, Richland,
509/946-0681

Best Chinese Food
Chinese Garden
1520 N. Fourth Ave., Pasco, 509/545-6324

Best Family Restaurants
Shari's of Kennewick
1200 N. Columbia Center Blvd., 509/735-7438
Shari's of Richland
1745 George Washington Way, Richland,
509/946-0681

Best Homestyle Food
Country Gentlemen Company
1320 N. Twentieth Ave., Pasco, 509/547-6446
300 N. Ely St., 509/783-0128

Best Mexican Food
Casa Chapala
107 E. Columbia Dr., 509/586-4224

Best Pizza
Round Table Pizza
2230 W. Court St., Pasco, 509/545-1091

Best Sandwiches
Jennifer's Bakery
413B N. Kellogg, 509/783-6505

Best Steaks
T.S. Cattle Company Steakhouse
6515 W. Clearwater, Ste. 400, 509/783-8251

Standbys
Red Lobster
1120 N. Columbia Center Blvd., 509/735-1190

KENT, WA

Best Restaurants in Town
The Dinner House
24306 Roberts Dr., Black Diamond, 206/886-2524
Mirabella
1819 W. Meeker St., 206/854-0967

Best Breakfast
Black Diamond Bakery and Restaurant
32805 Railroad Ave., Black Diamond, 360/886-2741

Best Business Lunch
Bittersweet
211 First Ave. S., 206/854-0707

Best Casual Dining
Pasquale's
21609 84th Ave. S., 206/872-8258

Best Chinese Food
Tao Tao Restaurant
25664 104th Ave. SE, 206/852-8755

Spring City Chinese Cuisine
17615 SE 272nd St., 206/630-3638

Best Family Restaurant
Pasquale's
21609 84th Ave. S., 206/872-8258

Best Greek/Mediterranean Food
Spiro's
215 First Ave. S., 206/854-1030

Best Health-Conscious Menu
Bittersweet
211 First Ave. S., 206/854-0707

Best Italian Food
Pasquale's
21609 84th Ave. S., 206/872-8258
Mirabella
1819 W. Meeker St., 206/854-0967
Auguri Ristorante
13018 SE Kent-Kagley Rd., 206/631-8262

Best Romantic Dining
Dinner House
24306 Roberts Dr., Black Diamond, 206/886-2524

Best Salad/Salad Bar
Bittersweet
211 First Ave. S., 206/854-0707

Best Sandwiches
Granpa's Hickory Pit Barbecue
26708 180th Ave. SE, 206/631-8821

LONGVIEW, WA

Best Bar
Allen Street Cafe
108 Allen, Kelso, 360/414-5232

Best Breakfast
The Pantry
919 Fifteenth Ave., 360/425-8880
Pancake House
1425 California Way, 360/577-9966

Best Business Lunch
Henri's
4545 Ocean Beach Hwy., 360/425-7970

Best Casual Dining
Masthead Restaurant
1210 Ocean Beach Hwy., 360/577-7972
Trophies Sports Broiler
409 S. Pacific Ave., 360/577-6787

Best Chinese Food
Golden Palace
1245 Fourteenth Ave., 360/423-4261
Chiu's Mongolian Grill
970 Fourteenth Ave., 360/577-1597

Best Coffee
Apple-A-Day Restaurant
902 Fourteenth Ave., 360/423-9600

W

Best Desserts
Judy's Restaurant and Catering
  1036 Washington Way, 360/423-9262
Apple-A-Day Restaurant
  902 Fourteenth Ave., 360/423-9600

Best Family Restaurant
Spaghetti Works and Deli
  1339 Commerce, Main Fl., Ste. 111, 360/577-1136

Best Health-Conscious Menu
Apple-A-Day Restaurant
  902 Fourteenth Ave., 360/423-9600

Best Homestyle Food
Country Folks Deli
  1323 Commerce Ave., 360/425-2837

Best Italian Food
Spaghetti Works and Deli
  1339 Commerce, Main Fl., Ste. 111, 360/577-1136

Best Place to Be "Seen"
Henri's
  4545 Ocean Beach Hwy., 360/425-7970

Best Place to Eat Alone
Commerce Cafe
  1338 Commerce Ave., 360/577-0115

Best Romantic Dining
Rutherglen Mansion
  420 Rutherglen Rd., 360/425-5816

Best Salad/Salad Bar
Judy's
  1036 Washington Way, 360/423-9262
Bart's Restaurant
  1208 Washington Way, 360/425-2179

Best Steaks
Elmer's Restaurant
  804 Ocean Beach Hwy., 360/577-1990

Best Tea Room
Bookshop Cafe
  1203 Fourteenth Ave., 360/425-8707

Best Vegetarian Food
Country Village Cafe
  711 Vandercook Way, 360/425-8100

Standbys
Sizzler
  936 Ocean Beach Hwy., 360/577-0607

W

LYNNWOOD, WA

Best Restaurants in Town
Mario's Ristorante
  19226 Hwy. 99, 206/776-6525
Paparazzi
  184 33rd St., 206/776-9551
Red Robin
  18410 33rd Ave. W., 206/771-6492

Best Seafood
Arnie's Restaurant
300 Admiral Way, Ste. 211, Edmonds, 206/774-8661

Standbys
Tony Roma's
3828 196th St. SW, 206/771-3700
Applebee's
4626 196th St. SW, 206/672-2626
The Olive Garden
4221 196th St. SW, 206/670-2977
Red Lobster
4231 196th St. SW, 206/672-1137

MERCER ISLAND, WA

Best Restaurant in Town
Alpenland Delicatessen
2707 78th Ave. SE, 206/232-4780

Best Italian Food
Roberto's Family Restaurant
7619 SE 27th St., 206/232-7383

Best Mexican Food
M.I. Pueblo Grill
7811 SE 27th St., 206/232-8750

Best Thai Food
Thai on Mercer
7691 SE 27th St., 206/236-9990

MOSES LAKE, WA

Best Breakfast
Bob's Cafe at the Inn
1807 Kittleson Rd., 509/765-3211

Best Chinese Food
Lin's Restaurant
601 S. Pioneer Way, 509/766-4257

Best Homestyle Food
Bob's Cafe at the Inn
1807 Kittleson Rd., 509/765-3211

Best Japanese Food
Kiyoji's Sapporo
440 Melva Ln., 509/765-9314

Best Mexican Food
Inca Mexican Restaurant
404 E. Third Ave., 509/766-2426

Best Pizza
Chico's Pizza Parlor
917 S. Dahlia Dr., 509/765-4589

W

Best Sandwiches
Bob's Cafe at the Inn
1807 Kittleson Rd., 509/765-3211

OLYMPIA, WA

Best Atmosphere
Spar Restaurant
114 Fourth Ave. E., 360/357-6444

Best Bistro
Capitale Espresso Grill
609 Capitol Way S., 360/352-8007

Best Breakfast
San Francisco Street Bakery
1320 San Francisco St. NE, 360/753-8553

Best Casual Dining
Budd Bay Cafe
525 Columbus St. SW, 360/357-6963

Best Coffee
Dancing Goats Espresso Company
124 Fourth Ave. E., 360/754-8187

Best Desserts
Sweet Oasis Mediterranean Cafe
507A Capitol Way S., 360/956-0470

Best Family Restaurant
Falls Terrace Restaurant
106 Deschutes Way SW, 360/943-7830

Best Mexican Food
Saritas
909 Sleater Kinney Rd. SE, Lacey, 360/456-7269

Best Microbrewery
Fish Tale Ale
515 Jefferson St. SE, 360/943-6480

Best Pastries
Sweet Oasis Mediterranean Cafe
507A Capitol Way S., 360/956-0470

Best Pizza
Brewery City Pizza Company
2705 Limited Ln. NW, 360/754-7800
4353 Martin Way E., 360/491-6630
5150 Capitol Blvd. S., 360/754-6767

Best Salad/Salad Bar
Falls Terrace Restaurant
106 Deschutes Way SW, 360/943-7830

Best Seafood
Budd Bay Cafe
525 Columbus St. SW, 360/357-6963
Gardner's Seafood and Pasta
111 Thurston Ave. NW, 360/786-8466

Best Steaks
Falls Terrace Restaurant
106 Deschutes Way SW, 360/943-7830

Best Thai Food
Saigon Rendez-Vous Restaurant
117 Fifth Ave. SW, 360/352-1989

Best Vegetarian Food
Urban Onion Restaurant
116 Legion Way SE, 360/943-9242

Standbys
Sizzler
3315 Pacific Ave. SE, 360/459-8657

Baskin-Robbins
  3010 Harrison Ave. NW, 360/943-1231
  3431 Capitol Blvd. S., 360/786-0431
The Olive Garden
  2400 Capitol Mall Dr. SW, 360/754-6717

PORT TOWNSEND, WA

Best Atmosphere
Lanza's Ristorante and Pizzeria
  1020 Lawrence St., 360/385-6221
Lonnie's Restaurant
  2330 Washington St., 360/385-0700
Silverwater Cafe
  237 Taylor St., 360/385-6448
Manresa Castle
  Seventh at Sheridan, 360/385-5750

Best Breakfast
Landfall Restaurant
  412 Water St., 360/385-5814
Sea J's Cafe
  2501 Washington St., 360/385-6312
Salal Cafe
  634 Water St., 360/385-6532

Best Burgers
Erickson's Burger and Fish Bar
  600 W. Sims Way, 360/385-1467
Public House Grill
  1038 Water St., 360/385-9708
Lighthouse Cafe
  955 Water St., 360/385-1165

Best Chinese Food
Shanghai Restaurant
  Hudson Pt., 360/385-4810
Silver Place
  2001 Sims Way, 360/385-6175

Best Coffee
Elevated Ice Cream Company
  627 Water St., 360/385-1156
Uptown Oasis
  720 Tyler St., 360/385-2130
Bread and Roses
  230 Quincy St., 360/385-1004

Best Desserts
Silverwater Cafe
  237 Taylor St., 360/385-6448
Lonnie's Restaurant
  2330 Washington St., 360/385-0700

Best Family Restaurants
El Sarape Mexican Restaurant
  630 Water St., 360/379-9343
Silverwater Cafe
  237 Taylor St., 360/385-6448
Public House Grill
  1038 Water St., 360/385-9708

W

Manresa Castle
  Seventh and Sheridan, 360/385-5750
Landing Restaurant
  1433C W. Sims Way, 360/385-5964
Lanza's Ristorante and Pizzeria
  1020 Lawrence St., 360/385-6221

Best Health-Conscious Menu
Blackberries
  Fort Worden State Park, 360/385-9950
Silverwater Cafe
  237 Taylor St., 360/385-6448
Salal Cafe
  634 Water St., 360/385-6532
Lanza's Ristorante and Pizzeria
  1020 Lawrence St., 360/385-6221

Best Ice Cream/Yogurt
Elevated Ice Cream Company
  627 Water St., 360/385-1156

Best Mexican Food
El Sarape Mexican Restaurant
  630 Water St., 360/379-9343

Best Pizza
Waterfront Pizza
  951 Water St., 360/385-6629
Checkers Pizza
  1232 W. Sims Way, 360/385-5888

Best Place to Eat When Someone Else Is Buying
Lonnie's Restaurant
  2330 Washington St., 360/385-0700

Best Sandwiches
Bayview
  1539 Water St., 360/385-1461
Water Street Deli-Restaurant
  926 Water St., 360/385-2422

Best Seafood
Lanza's Ristorante and Pizzeria
  1020 Lawrence St., 360/385-6221
Silverwater Cafe
  237 Taylor St., 360/385-6448
Manresa Castle
  Seventh at Sheridan, 360/385-5750

Best Steaks
Public House Grill
  1038 Water St., 360/385-9708

Best Thai Food
Khu Larb Thai Restaurant
  225 Adams St., 360/385-5023

Best Vegetarian Food
Blackberries
  Fort Worden State Park, 360/385-9950

W

REDMOND, WA

Best Restaurants in Town
Red Robin
  2390 148th Ave. NE, 206/641-3810
Redmond Brown Bag Cafe
  8412 164th Ave. NE, 206/861-4099
Sweetwater
  7824 Leary Way NE, 206/883-9090

Best Chinese Food
Peking Restaurant
  16857 Redmond Way, 206/883-9090

Best Family Restaurant
Billy McHale's Restaurant
  15210 Redmond Way, 206/881-0316

Best Italian Food
Bizzaro Italian Cafe
  1307 N. 46th St., 206/545-7327
Franki's Pizza and Pasta
  16630 Redmond Way, 206/883-8407

Best Japanese Food
Kikya Restaurant
  8105 161st Ave. NE, 206/869-6131

Best Mexican Food
Azteca Mexican Restaurants
  22003 66th Ave. W., Mountlake Terrace, 206/672-0601

Best Thai Food
Redmond Thai Cuisine
  16421 Cleveland, 206/869-6131
Thai and Teriyaki Takeout
  4026 148th Ave. NE, 206/881-9700

SEATTLE, WA

Best Restaurants in Town
Fuller's
  1400 Sixth Ave., 206/447-5544
Palace Kitchen
  2030 Fifth Ave., 206/448-2001

Best Asian Restaurants
Wild Ginger Asian Restaurant
  1400 Western Ave., 206/623-4450
Saigon Bistro
  1032 S. Jackson St., 206/329-4939

Best Atmosphere
Palisade Waterfront Restaurant
  2601 W. Marina Pl., 206/285-1000

Best Bagels
Spot Bagel Bakery
  1815 N. 45th Ave., 206/633-7768
  7 Boston St., 206/284-6107

Best Breakfast
Julia's
  5410 Ballard Ave. NW, Ballard, 206/783-2033
  1714 N. 44th St., 206/633-1175

W

Best Brunch
Salish Lodge
  37807 SE Fall City, Snoqualmie, 206/888-2556

Best Burgers
Figuero's
  1010 Western Ave., 206/682-5799
Kidd Valley Hamburgers
  135 Fifteenth Ave. E., 206/328-8133
  14303 Aurora Ave. N., 206/364-8493
  531 Queen Anne Ave. N., 206/284-0184
  5502 25th Ave. NE, 206/522-0890
  4910 Green Lake Way N., 206/547-0121
Red Mill Burgers
  67th Ave. at Phinney Ave., 206/783-6362

Best Cheap Meal
Dick's Drive-In Restaurant
  4426 Second Ave. NE, 206/634-0300
  111 NE 45th St., 206/632-5125
  9208 Holman Rd. NW, 206/783-5233
  12325 30th Ave. NE, 206/363-7777
  500 Queen Anne Ave. N., 206/285-5155

Best Chinese Food
Snappy Dragon
  8917 Roosevelt Way, 206/528-5575

Best Coffeehouse
Still Life Coffeehouse
  709 N. 35th Ave., 206/547-9850

Best Desserts
Cafe Dilettante
  416 Broadway E., 206/329-6463

Best Eclectic Menu
Gravity Bar
  113 Virginia St., 206/448-8826

Best Family Restaurant
Yankee Diner
  5300 24th Ave. NW, 206/783-1999
  13859 Bel Red Rd., Bellevue, 206/643-1558
  4010 196th St. SW, Lynnwood, 206/775-5485

Best Health-Conscious Menu
Macheezmo Mouse
  701 Fifth Ave., 206/382-1730
  425 Queen Anne Ave. N., 206/282-9904
  1815 N. 45th St., Ste. 112, 206/545-0153
  211 Broadway E., 206/325-0072

Best Indian Food

Raga Cuisine of India
  555 108th Ave. NE, Bellevue, 206/450-0336
Chutney's
  519 First Ave. N., 206/284-6799

Best Italian Food
Saleh Al Lago
  6804 E. Green Lake Way N., 206/524-4044
Spazzo Mediterranean Grill
  10655 NE Fourth St., Ninth Fl., Bellevue,
    206/454-8255

Il Terrazzo Carmine
411 First Ave. S., 206/467-7797

Best Late-Night Food
Thirteen Coins Restaurant
125 Boren Ave. N., 206/682-2513

Best Lunch
McCormick and Schmick's
1103 First Ave., 206/623-5500
9404 E. Marginal Way S., 206/762-4418
Rattlers Grill
1823 Eastlake Ave. E., 206/325-7350

Best Mexican Food
Circo! Circo! Mexican Restaurant
12709 NE 124th Ave., Kirkland, 206/821-9405
Mama's Mexican Kitchen
2234 Second Ave., 206/728-6262
El Camino Restaurant
607 N. 35th Ave., Ballard, 206/632-7303

Best Microbreweries
Redhook Ale Brewery
3400 Phinney Ave. N., 206/548-8000
Pike Place Brewery
1432 Western Ave., 206/622-3373
Pike Pl. Public Market, 206/467-8465

Best Outdoor Dining
Ray's Boathouse
6049 Seaview Ave. NW, 206/789-3770

Best Pizza
Cucina! Cucina! Italian Cafe
800 Bellevue Way SE, Ste. 118, Bellevue,
206/637-1177
Pizzeria Pagliacci
4529 University Way NE, 206/726-1717
426 Broadway E., 206/324-0730
55 Queen Anne Ave. N., 206/285-1232

Best Place to Eat Alone
Sid's Deli
250 Fourth Ave., 206/443-5567

Best Place to Eat When Someone Else Is Buying
Canlis Restaurant
2576 Aurora Ave. N., 206/283-3313

Best Place to Take the Kids
Iron Horse
311 Third Ave. S., 206/223-9506

Best Romantic Dining
Adriatica Restaurant
1107 Dexter Ave. N., 206/285-5000

Best Salad/Salad Bar
Zoopa
393 Strander Blvd., 206/575-0500

Best Sandwiches
City Foods
2522 Fifth Ave., 206/441-3663

W

Best Seafood
Ray's Boathouse
  6049 Seaview Ave. NW, 206/789-3770
Anthony's Homeport
  6135 Seaview Ave. NW, 206/783-0780
Chandler's Crabhouse
  901 Fairview Ave. N., 206/223-2722

Best Southwestern Food
Cactus Restaurant
  4220 E. Madison St., 206/324-4140

Best Steaks
Metropolitan Grill
  820 Second Ave., 206/624-3287

Best Sushi
Nikko
  1900 Fifth Ave., 206/322-4641
Sanmi Sushi
  2601 W. Marina Pl., 206/283-9978

Best Thai Food
Thai Thai
  11205 Sixteenth Ave. SW, 206/246-2246

Best Undiscovered Restaurant
Pirosmani
  2220 Queen Anne Ave. N., 206/285-3360

Best Vegetarian Food
Cafe Flora
  2901 E. Madison St., 206/325-9100

Best Vietnamese Food
Cafe Loc
  407 Broad St., 206/441-6883
  305 Harrison St., 206/728-9292
Viet My Restaurant
  129 Prefontaine Pl. S., 206/382-9923
Saigon Bistro
  1032 S. Jackson St., 206/329-4939

Best Wine Selection
Ponti Seafood Grill
  3014 Third Ave. N., 206/284-3000
Ray's Boathouse
  6049 Seaview Ave. NW, 206/789-3770

SPOKANE, WA

Best Atmosphere
Patsy Clark's Mansion
  2208 W. Second Ave., 509/838-8300

W

Best Breakfast
Waffles and More
  41 W. Third Ave., 509/624-3353
  5312 N. Division St., 509/484-4049
  9425 E. Sprague Ave., 509/928-8055

Best Burgers
Red Robin
  9904 N. Newport Hwy., 509/467-3382

Best Chinese Food
Kay Lon Garden Restaurant
2819 N. Division St., 509/326-1333

Best Family Restaurant
Old Spaghetti Factory
152 S. Monroe St., 509/624-8916

Best Japanese Food
Mustard Seed
245 W. Spokane Falls Blvd., 509/747-2689
9806 E. Sprague Ave., 509/924-3194

Best Mexican Food
Chapala Restaurant
1801 N. Hamilton St., 509/484-4534
2820 E. 29th Ave., 509/534-7388
6315 N. Division St., 509/468-0209

Best Pizza
Pizza Pipeline
10220 N. Division St., 509/466-8080
1303 N. Washington St., 509/326-6412
13908 E. Sprague Ave., 509/921-0000
1724 W. Wellesley Ave., 509/328-1111
2823 E. 27th Ave., 509/534-2222

Best Place to Eat When Someone Else Is Buying
Patsy Clark's Mansion
2208 W. Second Ave., 509/838-8300

Best Places to Take the Kids
Cyrus O'Leary's
516 W. Main Ave., 509/624-9000
Tomato Brothers
6220 N. Division St., 509/484-4500

Best Sandwiches
Domini Sandwiches
703 W. Sprague Ave., 509/747-2324
Bruchi's
11101 E. Sprague Ave., 509/924-4139
4750 N. Division St., 509/482-4432
829 E. Indiana Ave., 509/483-5503
10406 N. Division St., 509/468-8518
2804 E. 20th Ave., 509/533-0935
1006 E. Francis Ave., 509/483-8429

Best Seafood
Clinkerdagger
621 W. Mallon Ave., 509/328-5965
Salty's
510 N. Lincoln St., 509/327-8888

Best Steaks
Arizona Steakhouse
333 W. Spokane Falls Blvd., 509/455-8206

Best Vegetarian Food
Onion
302 W. Riverside Ave., 509/747-3852
7522 N. Division St., 509/482-6100

W

Best View While Dining
Ankeny's
  515 W. Sprague Ave., 509/838-6311

Standbys
Old Country Buffet
  12209 E. Sprague Ave., 509/927-1002
Tony Roma's
  7640 N. Division St., 509/482-7180
Sizzler
  4320 N. Division St., 509/489-3700
  9707 E. Sprague Ave., 509/928-7300
Golden Corral Family Steak House
  7117 N. Division St., 509/468-1895
Baskin-Robbins
  1230 S. Grand Blvd., 509/747-0091
  12510 E. Sprague Ave., 509/924-3131
  1925 N. Monroe St., 509/327-1531
  4212 E. Sprague Ave., 509/536-0031
  4750 N. Division St., 509/487-5574
  9111 N. Country Homes Blvd., 509/467-5264
TCBY
  1318 S. Grand Blvd., 509/455-9673
  1902 W. Francis Ave., 509/327-3760

TACOMA, WA

Best Atmosphere
Tacoma Bar and Grill
  625 S. Commerce St., 206/572-4861

Best Bar
The Swiss
  1904 S. Jefferson Ave., 206/572-2821

Best Barbecue/Ribs
Bob's Barbecue Pit Too
  911 S. Eleventh St., 206/627-4899

Best Breakfast
Harvester Restaurant
  29 Tacoma Ave. N., 206/272-1193

Best Brunch
Winter Garden Cafe
  Sheraton Hotel, 1320 Broadway, 206/572-3200

Best Burgers
Frisko Freeze
  10404 S. Tacoma Way, 206/581-4800
  1201 Division Ave., 206/272-4800
  13720 Pacific Ave. S., 206/531-4800
  1902 65th Ave. W., 206/566-6843

Best Chinese Food
Great Wall of China Restaurant
  3121 S. 38th St., 206/473-2500

Best Coffee
Starbucks
  Multiple Locations

W

Best Greek/Mediterranean Food
It's Greek To Me
  1703 Sixth Ave., 206/272-1375

Best Homestyle Food
Southern Kitchen
  1716 Sixth Ave., 206/627-4282

Best Italian Food
Lorenzo's Restaurant
  2811 Sixth Ave., 206/272-3331

Best Mexican Food
Moctezuma's Mexican Restaurant
  4102 S. 56th St., 206/474-5593

Best Microbrewery
Engine House Number Nine
  611 N. Pine St., 206/272-3435

Best Outdoor Dining
C.I. Shenanigan's
  3017 N. Ruston Way, 206/752-8811

Best Pizza
Godfather's Pizza
  15709 Pacific Ave. S., 206/536-1488
  5114 Sixth Ave., 206/759-8332
  5605 Pacific Ave., 206/474-0543
  5927 Mount Tacoma Dr. SW, 206/584-4144
  7315 27th St. W., 206/565-7334

Best Place to Eat Alone
Tacoma Bar and Grill
  625 S. Commerce St., 206/572-4861

Best Place to Eat When Someone Else Is Buying
Stanley and Seafort's Steak Chop
  115 E. 34th St., 206/473-7300

Best Romantic Dining
Tacoma Bar and Grill
  625 S. Commerce St., 206/572-4861

Best Salad/Salad Bar
Keg Restaurant
  2212 Mildred St. W., 206/565-7300

Best Seafood
C.I. Shenanigan's
  3017 N. Ruston Way, 206/752-8811
Stanley and Seafort's Steak Chop
  115 E. 34th St., 206/473-7300

Best Steaks
Stanley and Seafort's Steak Chop
  115 E. 34th St., 206/473-7300

Best Tea Room
Grazie Ristorante
  2301 N. 30th St., 206/627-0231

Best View While Dining
C.I. Shenanigan's
  3017 N. Ruston Way, 206/752-8811
Stanley and Seafort's Steak Chop
  115 E. 34th St., 206/473-7300

W

Standbys
The Olive Garden
   1921 S. 72nd St., 206/475-1772

VANCOUVER, WA

Best Restaurants in Town
Pinot Ganache
   1004 Washington St., 360/695-7786
Sheldon's Cafe at the Grant House
   1101 Officers Row, 360/699-1213
Andrew's Restaurant and Catering
   611 W. Eleventh St., 360/693-3252
McMenamin's on the Columbia
   1801 SE Columbia River Dr., 360/699-1521

Best Atmosphere
Beaches
   1919 SE Columbia River Dr., 360/699-1592

Best Chinese Food
Great Wall Restaurant
   13503B SE Mill Plain Blvd., 360/256-6688

Best Mexican Food
Who Song and Larry's
   111 Columbia Way, 360/695-1198

WALLA WALLA, WA

Best Restaurants in Town
Patit Creek
   725 E. Dayton Ave., Dayton, 509/382-2625
The Homestead Restaurant
   1528 E. Isaacs Ave., 509/522-0345
Merchants, Ltd. French Bakery
   21 E. Main St., 509/525-0900
The Addition Restaurant and Catering
   16 S. Colville St., 509/525-5007
Rosita's
   1005 S. Ninth St., 509/525-5007
   201 E. Main, 509/525-6361

Best Bar
Blue Mountain Tavern
   2025 E. Isaacs Ave., 509/525-9941

Best Burgers
The Iceburg Drive-In
   616 Birch St., 509/529-1793

Best Coffee
Merchants, Ltd. French Bakery
   21 E. Main St., 509/525-0900

Best Fast Food
Outrageous Taco
   221 E. Main St., 509/529-5454

Best Ice Cream/Yogurt
Ice-Burg
   616 W. Burch St., 509/529-1793

Best Italian Food
Pastime Cafe
   215 W. Main St., 509/525-0873

Best Mexican Food
El Sombrero Mexican Restaurant
4 W. Oak St., 509/522-4984
La Casita
428 Ash St., 509/525-2598

Best Pizza
Pepe's Pizza
1533 E. Isaacs Ave., 509/529-2550

WENATCHEE, WA

Best Restaurants in Town
Steven's at Mission Square
218 N. Mission St., 509/663-6573
Andrea Keller's Restaurant
829 Front St., 509/548-6000

Best Seafood
Cougar Inn
23379 Hwy. 207, Leavenworth, 509/763-3354

Best Steaks
The Windmill
1501 N. Wenatchee Ave., 509/663-3478
Cougar Inn
23379 Hwy. 207, Leavenworth, 509/763-3354

YAKIMA, WA

Best Restaurant in Town
Greystone Restaurant
5 N. Front St., 509/248-9801

Best Bar
Grant's Brewery Pub
32 N. Front St., 509/575-2922

Best Breakfast
Twin Bridges Inn
1315 N. First St., 509/452-6352
Cafe European
3105 Summitview Ave., 509/248-5844

Best Burgers
Miner's Drive-In Restaurant
2415 First St., 509/457-8194

Best Casual Dining
Whistlin' Jack Lodge
20800 State Rte. 410, Naches, 509/658-2433

Best Chinese Food
George's Wok and Grill
1208 S. 80th Ave., 509/966-0933
China Star
14 N. Second St., 509/248-9992

Best Delicatessen
Fifth Avenue Deli
415 W. Walnut St., 509/452-2332

Best Desserts
Cafe European Coffee
3105 Summitview Ave., 509/248-5844

W

Best Health-Conscious Menu
Teriyaki Grille
   901B W. Yakima Ave., 509/575-4911

Best Mexican Food
Las Margaritas Mexican Restaurant
   1460 N. Sixteenth Ave., 509/575-1553
Santiago's Gourmet Mexican
   111 E. Yakima Ave., 509/453-1644

Best Place to Be "Seen"
Birchfield Manor
   2018 Birchfield Rd., 509/452-1960

Best Place to Eat Alone
Deli de Pasta
   7 N. Front St., 509/453-0571

Best Place to Eat When Someone Else Is Buying
Gasperetti's
   1013 N. First St., 509/248-0628

Best Steaks
Stuart Anderson's Restaurant
   501 N. Front St., 509/248-4540

Standbys
Red Lobster
   905 N. First St., 509/575-3640

W

Washington, DC

Best Restaurants in Town
L'Auberge Chez Francois
  332 Springvale Rd., 703/759-3800
Prime Rib
  2020 K St. NW, 202/466-8811
Sam and Harry's
  1200 Nineteenth St. NW, 202/296-4333
La Bergerie
  218 N. Lee St., Alexandria, 703/683-1007
Carlyle Grand Cafe
  4000 28th St. S., Arlington, 703/931-0777
Ristorante Mare e Monti
  15554 Annapolis Rd., Bowie, 301/262-9179

Best Asian Restaurants
Duangrat's
  5878 Leesburg Prk., Bailey's Cross Roads,
    703/820-5795
Mr. K's
  2121 K St. NW, 202/331-8868
Queen Bee
  3181 Wilson Blvd., Arlington, 703/527-3444

Best Cheap Meal
Red Hot and Blue
  1600 Wilson Blvd., Arlington, 703/276-7427
Rio Grande Cafe
  4919 Fairmont Ave., Bethesda, 301/656-2981
Hard Times Cafe
  1404 King St., Alexandria, 703/683-5340

Best French Food
L'Auberge Chez Francois
  332 Springvale Rd., 703/759-3800
Le Lion d'Or
  1150 Connecticut Ave. NW, 202/296-7672
Jean-Louis at the Watergate
  2650 Virginia Ave. NW, 202/298-4488

Best Italian Food
Galileo
  1110 21st St. NW, 202/293-7191

W

i Ricchi
1220 Nineteenth St. NW, 202/835-0459
Pines of Rome
4709 Hampden Ln., Bethesda, 301/657-8775

Best Late-Night Food
Bistro Francais
3128 M St. NW, 202/338-3830
Silver Diner
11806 Rockville Pk., Rockville, 301/770-0333
Tastee Diner
7731 Woodmont Ave., Bethesda, 301/652-3970

Best Mexican Food
Rio Grande Cafe
4919 Fairmont Ave., Bethesda, 301/656-2981
Cactus Cantina
3300 Wisconsin Ave. NW, 202/686-7222
Austin Grill
2404 Wisconsin Ave. NW, 202/337-8080

Best Other Ethnic Food
Panjshir Restaurant (Afghan)
924 W. Broad St., Falls Church, 703/536-4566
Afghan Kabob (Afghan)
3320 M St. NW, 202/337-0300
Zed's Ethiopian Cuisine (Ethiopian)
3318 M St. NW, 202/333-4710
Red Sea Ethiopian Restaurant (Ethiopian)
2463 Eighteenth St. NW, 202/483-5000
Marrakesh Restaurant (Moroccan)
617 New York Ave. NW, 202/393-9393

Best Restaurant Meal Value
L'Auberge Chez Francois
332 Springvale Rd., 703/759-3800
Music City Roadhouse
1050 30th St. NW, 202/337-4444
Rio Grande Cafe
4919 Fairmont Ave., Bethesda, 301/656-2981

Best Romantic Dining
L'Auberge Chez Francois
332 Springvale Rd., 703/759-3800
Inn at Little Washington
["Call for directions."], 703/675-3800

Best Seafood
Kinkead's
2000 Pennsylvania Ave. NW, 202/296-7900
Crisfield
8606 Colesville Rd., Silver Spring, 301/588-1572
O'Donnell's Restaurant
8301 Wisconsin Ave., Bethesda, 301/656-6200

Best Steaks
Morton's of Chicago
3251 Prospect St. NW, Georgetown, 202/342-6258
Prime Rib
2020 K St. NW, 202/466-8811

W

Best Vegetarian Food
Nora
　2132 Florida Ave. NW, 202/462-5143
Food for Thought
　1738 Connecticut Ave. NW, 202/797-1095

Best Vietnamese Food
Miss Saigon Restaurant
　1847 Columbia Rd. NW, 202/667-1900

Standbys
Ruth's Chris Steak House
　1801 Connecticut Ave. NW, 202/797-0033

W

West Virginia

Best Restaurant in Town
Char
  100 Char Dr., 304/253-1760

Best Italian Food
Giuseppe's Restaurant
  707 Main St., Mt. Hope, 304/877-5022

Best Seafood
The Lighthouse
  3166 Robert C. Byrd Dr., 304/252-7763

Best Steaks
Texas Steakhouse
  140 Harper Park Dr., 304/253-1436

Standbys
Pizza Hut
  1304 N. Valley Dr., 304/252-8686
  1912 Harper Rd., 304/255-0708

Best Restaurant in Town
Oak Supper Club
  HC 78 Box 47A, Pipestem, 304/466-4800

Best American Food
Oak Supper Club
  HC 78 Box 47A, Pipestem, 304/466-4800

Best Lunch
Peacock Cafe
  460 Plaza, Ste. 10, 304/327-2484

Best Seafood
Johnston's Inn and Restaurant
  Old Oakvale Rd., Princeton, 304/425-7591

Best Steaks
Johnston's Inn and Restaurant
  Old Oakvale Rd., Princeton, 304/425-7591

W

Standbys
Cracker Barrel
  161 Ambrose Ln., Princeton, 304/425-4003

CHARLESTON, WV

Best Barbecue/Ribs
Joey's Downtown
  115 Quarrier St., 304/343-4121

Best Burgers
Rally's Hamburgers
  1626 Washington St. E., 304/343-6432
  1667 Third Ave., 304/345-2808

Best Delicatessen
Deli-D-Lite
  6545 MacCorkle Ave. SE, 304/925-4642

Best Family Restaurant
Harding's Family Restaurant
  2772 Pennsylvania Ave., 304/344-5044

Best Homestyle Food
Diehl's Restaurant
  152 Main Ave., Nitro, 304/755-9353

Best Japanese Food
Hibachi Japanese Steak House
  741 Washington St. W., 304/342-7616

Best Salad/Salad Bar
Fifth Quarter Steakhouse
  201 Clendenin St., 304/345-2726

Best Sandwiches
Deli-D-Lite
  6545 MacCorkle Ave. SE, 304/925-4642

Best View While Dining
Holiday Inn Charleston House
  600 Kanawha Blvd. E., 304/344-4092

Standbys
Bob Evans
  450 Quarrier St., 304/342-9631
  6309 MacCorkle Ave. SE, 304/925-2223
Shoney's
  116 Kanawha Blvd. E., 304/346-9437
  3600 MacCorkle Ave. SE, 304/925-2127
The Olive Garden
  1061 Charleston Town Ctr., 304/344-4410
Baskin-Robbins
  4120 MacCorkle Ave. SE, 304/925-3013
Chi Chi's
  5515 MacCorkle Ave. SE, 304/925-2138
Red Lobster
  160 Court St., 304/345-1161
Outback Steakhouse
  1062 Charleston Town Ctr., 304/345-0440

CLARKSBURG, WV

Best Barbecue/Ribs
Damon's The Place for Ribs
  110 Emily Dr., 304/624-7427

Best Chinese Food
Peking Chinese Restaurant
　Rte. 50E at Old Bridgeport Hill, 304/623-5828

Best Coffee
Andrew and Ballard Book Cellar
　343 W. Main St., 304/623-0644

Best Italian Food
Victoria's
　Greenbriar Motel, 200 Buckhannon Pike,
　　304/624-5518
Phillip's Restaurant
　401 N. Fifth St., 304/624-1404

Best Pizza
Chunki's Pizza and Subs
　762 W. Pike St., 304/623-3100

Best Sandwiches
Chunki's Pizza and Subs
　762 W. Pike St., 304/623-3100

Best Seafood
Jim Reid's Restaurant
　1422 Buckhannon Pike, 304/623-4909

FAIRMONT, WV

Best Restaurant in Town
Tiffany's
　Bellview Blvd., 304/363-9651

Best Chinese Food
China Garden
　1406 Country Club Rd., 304/367-1994

Best Homestyle Food
Renaissance
　323 Adams, 304/367-9747
Say-Boy Steak House Restaurant
　905 Country Club Rd., 304/366-7252

Best Italian Food
Muriale's Restaurant
　1742 Fairmont Ave., 304/363-3190

Best Lunch
Renaissance
　323 Adams, 304/367-9747

Best Steaks
Say-Boy Steak House Restaurant
　905 Country Club Rd., 304/366-7252

HUNTINGTON, WV

Best Restaurant in Town
Rebels and Redcoats Tavern
　412 Seventh Ave., 304/523-8829

Best All-You-Can-Eat Buffet
Bailey's Cafeteria
　410 Ninth St., 304/522-3663

Best Bar
Damon's
　1001 Third Ave., 304/697-7427

W

Best Breakfast
Down Town Breakfast and Deli
625 Eighth St., 304/523-3542

Best Burgers
Heritage Station
15 Heritage Village, 304/523-6373

Best Chinese Food
China Garden
804 Sixth Ave., 304/697-5524
Happy Dragon
1238 Fourth Ave., 304/697-9061

Best Coffee
Renaissance Book Company and Coffee House
831 Fourth Ave., 304/529-7323

Best Italian Food
Rocco's Spaghetti House
252 Main St., Ceredo, 304/453-3000

Best Late-Night Food
Dwight's
823 Eighth St., 304/522-7441
601 First St., 304/525-3591

Best Mexican Food
Chili Willi's Mexican Cantina
841 Fourth Ave., 304/529-4857

Best Pizza
Evaroni's Pizza
914 Oak St., Kenova, 304/453-4355

Best Places to Be "Seen"
Oliver's
322 Tenth St., 304/522-2415
Calamity Cafe
1555 Third Ave., 304/525-4171

Best Place to Eat Alone
Oliver's
322 Tenth St., 304/522-2415

Best Place to Eat When Someone Else Is Buying
Rocco's Spaghetti House
252 Main St., Ceredo, 304/453-3000

Best Place to Take the Kids
Gino's Pizza and Spaghetti House
1401 Washington Ave., 304/529-3271
4448 Waverly Rd., 304/429-6711
1001 Third Ave., 304/529-2547
2501 Fifth Ave., 304/529-6086
146 Norway Ave., 304/522-9557
940 Fourth Ave., Ste. 418, 304/525-2943

Best Romantic Dining
Rocco's Spaghetti House
252 Main St., Ceredo, 304/453-3000

Best Sandwiches
Down Town Breakfast and Deli
625 Eighth St., 304/523-3542

Standbys
Bob Evans
  606 Third Ave., 304/525-6610
Chi Chi's
  952 Third Ave., 304/525-1076
Shoney's
  1720 Washington Ave., 304/429-2065
  5179 Hwy. 60, 304/736-3551
Red Lobster
  200 Tenth St., 304/529-4042

MARTINSBURG, WV

Best Burgers
Hoss's Steak and Sea House
  2200 Aikens Ctr., 304/267-2224
Peppermill
  141 S. Queen St., 304/263-3986

Best Chinese Food
Gateway Peking Restaurant
  100 W. Martin St., 304/263-6544

Best Desserts
American Deli
  315 W. Stephens St., 304/263-4656
Peppermill
  141 S. Queen St., 304/263-3986

Best Homestyle Food
Linda and Danny's Kitchen
  1161 Winchester Ave., 304/263-7821
Warm Springs Eatery
  Berkeley Plaza Shopping Ctr., 304/264-0410

Best Ice Cream/Yogurt
Rock Hill Creamery
  313 S. Queen St., 304/264-2373

Best Italian Food
Taste of Italy Restaurant
  240 Lutz Ave., 304/264-0231

Best Mexican Food
Rio Grande
  127 N. Queen St., 304/267-1684

Best Pizza
Ramon's Pizza and Sub Shop
  329 Winchester Ave., 304/263-2989

Best Sandwiches
American Deli
  315 W. Stephens St., 304/263-4656
Ramon's Pizza and Sub Shop
  329 Winchester Ave., 304/263-2989
Peppermill
  141 S. Queen St., 304/263-3986

Best Seafood
Heatherfield's Restaurant
  301 Foxcroft Ave., 304/267-8311
Market House
  100 N. Queen St., 304/263-7615

W

Hoss's Steak and Sea House
  2200 Aikens Ctr., 304/267-2224
Peppermill
  141 S. Queen St., 304/263-3986

Best Steaks
Heatherfield's Restaurant
  301 Foxcroft Ave., 304/267-8311
Market House
  100 N. Queen St., 304/263-7615
Hoss's Steak and Sea House
  2200 Aikens Ctr., 304/267-2224
Peppermill
  141 S. Queen St., 304/263-3986

Standbys
Bob Evans
  999 S. Foxcroft Ave., 304/263-7022
Denny's
  2003 Mid Atlantic Pkwy., 304/267-9400

MORGANTOWN, WV

Best Barbecue/Ribs
Buffalo Wild Wings and Weck (BW3)
  268 High St., 304/292-2999

Best Breakfast
Eat N Park Restaurant
  353 Patteson Dr., 304/598-0020

Best Family Restaurant
Boston Beanery
  321 High St., 304/292-0165
  383 Patterson Dr., 304/599-1870

Best Lunch
Boston Beanery
  321 High St., 304/292-0165
  383 Patterson Dr., 304/599-1870

Standbys
Western Sizzlin
  14 Commerce Dr., Westover, 304/296-5790
Shoney's
  3504 Monongahela Blvd., 304/599-9606

PARKERSBURG, WV

Best Breakfast
Mountaineer Family Restaurant
  Hwy. 50, 304/422-0101

Best Burgers
Yielky's Sandwich Shop
  2502 Camden Ave., 304/428-9195

Best Chinese Food
House of Hunan
  100 Lakeview Ctr., 304/422-1688

Best Diner
Belrock Country Diner
  1802 Washington Blvd., Belpre, 614/423-5233

W

Best Homestyle Food
Travelers Restaurant
 328 Seventh St., 304/428-9177

Best Italian Food
Jimmy Colombo's Restaurant
 1236 Seventh St., 304/428-5472

Best 24-Hour Restaurant
Mountaineer Family Restaurant
 Hwy. 50, 304/422-0101

WEIRTON, WV

Best Restaurant in Town
Annie's Restaurant and Lounge
 350 Three Springs Dr., 304/723-5522

Best Barbecue/Ribs
Happy's BBQ Ribs
 4075 Main St., 304/797-7427

Best Breakfast
Weirton Bus Terminal
 3075 Main St., 304/748-0750

Best Italian Food
Mario's Restaurant
 3806 Main St., 304/748-1179

Best Steaks
Dee Jay's
 1229 Penna Ave., 304/748-1150

WHEELING, WV

Best American Food
Blake's Family Restaurant
 800 Lafayette Ave., Moundsville, 304/845-7090

Best Breakfast
Blake's Family Restaurant
 800 Lafayette Ave., Moundsville, 304/845-7090

Best Business Lunch
Riverside Restaurant and Lounge
 949 Main St., 304/233-8507

Best Chinese Food
Panda Restaurant
 1133 Market St., 304/232-7572

Best German Food
Keg und Kraut
 167 Wood St., 304/232-5654

Best Homestyle Food
Mitchell's Restaurant
 1203 First St., Moundsville, 304/845-8440

W

Best Pizza
Pizza Outlet
 1127 Market St., 304/232-1100

Best Salad/Salad Bar
Riverside Restaurant and Lounge
 949 Main St., 304/233-8507

Wisconsin

Best Restaurant in Town
Trim B's Restaurant
201 S. Walnut St., 414/734-9204

Best Bar
Dos Bandidos Restaurant and Pub
1004 S. Olde Oneida St., 414/731-3322

Best Breakfast
Paper Valley Hotel and Conference Center
333 W. College Ave., 414/733-8000

Best Brunch
Paper Valley Hotel and Conference Center
333 W. College Ave., 414/733-8000

Best Burgers
Friar Tuck's
2120 W. College Ave., 414/730-1004

Best Chinese Food
Chef Chu's Chinese Cuisine
719 W. College Ave., 414/749-0330

Best Eclectic Menu
Hobnobbin'
710 W. Grove St., 414/733-5465

Best Health-Conscious Menu
Casbah Cafe
225 E. College Ave., 414/731-9977

Best Italian Food
Victoria's
503 W. College Ave., 414/730-9595

Best Mexican Food
Dos Bandidos Restaurant and Pub
1004 S. Olde Oneida St., 414/731-3322

Best Pizza
Knott's Landing
124 Main St., 414/725-7777

W

Best Sandwiches
Pizza King-Subs
   1326 N. Meade St., 414/731-6577
   1717 E. Calumet St., 414/731-3234
   1003 W. Northland Ave., 414/734-9996

Best Seafood
Cali Restaurant
   201 N. Appleton St., 414/830-0700

Best Steaks
George's Steak House
   2208 S. Memorial Dr., 414/733-4939

Best Vegetarian Food
Casbah Cafe
   225 E. College Ave., 414/731-9977

Standbys
The Olive Garden
   1275 N. Casaloma Dr., 414/954-8005

ASHLAND, WI

Best Breakfast
Michael's
   421 Main St. E., 715/682-8838

Best Burgers
Railyard Pub
   400 W. Third St., 715/682-9199

Best Coffee
Black Cat Coffeehouse
   211 Chapple Ave., 715/682-3680

Best Desserts
Black Cat Coffeehouse
   211 Chapple Ave., 715/682-3680

Best Health-Conscious Menu
Black Cat Coffeehouse
   211 Chapple Ave., 715/682-3680

Best Homestyle Food
Breakwater Cafe
   1808 Lake Shore Dr. E., 715/682-8388
The Restaurant
   2300 Lake Shore Dr. W., 715/682-9808

Best Italian Food
Paisano's Family Restaurant
   111 W. Main St., 715/682-5577

Best Pizza
Frankie's Pizza
   1315 Lake Shore Dr. E., 715/682-9980
Hugo's Pizza
   221 Sanborn Ave., 715/682-8202
Pizza Pub
   1402 Lake Shore Dr. E., 715/682-6641

Best Steaks
Ashland Depot
   400 Third St. W., 715/682-4200
Marine Supper Club
   Rural Route 3, 715/682-3298

W

BELOIT, WI

Best Barbecue/Ribs
Taasbag II
2683 Prairie Ave., 608/365-0999

Best Breakfast
Country Store East
1351 E. Grand Ave., 608/365-4023
202 Shirland Ave., 608/362-7750

Best Burgers
Hanson's Tavern
615 Cranston Rd., 608/362-8559

Best Chinese Food
Imperial Palace
302 S. Park Ave., South Beloit, 815/389-8844

Best Desserts
Manor
2102 Freeman Pkwy., 608/365-1608

Best Family Restaurant
Country Store East
1351 E. Grand Ave., 608/365-4023
202 Shirland Ave., 608/362-7750

Best Homestyle Food
Country Store East
1351 E. Grand Ave., 608/365-4023
202 Shirland Ave., 608/362-7750

Best Italian Food
Domenico Pizza and Restaurant
534 E. Grand Ave., 608/365-9489

Best Pizza
Domenico Pizza and Restaurant
534 E. Grand Ave., 608/365-9489

Best Sandwiches
Cousin's Submarines
2528 Hwy. 14, Janesville, 608/757-2733

Best Seafood
Manor
2102 Freeman Pkwy., 608/365-1608

Best Steaks
Manor
2102 Freeman Pkwy., 608/365-1608
Gun Club Restaurant
Rte. 1 at Colley Rd., 608/362-9900

EAU CLAIRE, WI

Best Restaurant in Town
Sweetwater's Restaurant
1104 W. Clairemont Ave., 715/834-577

Best Bars
Pioneer Tavern
401 Water St., 715/832-4455
She-Nannigan's and Peanuts
415 Water St., 715/832-5061

W

Best Breakfast
Pied Piper
  1527 S. Hastings Way, 715/834-8922

Best Brunch
Burgundy's
  Ramada Inn, 1202 W. Clairemont Ave., 715/834-3181

Best Burgers
Culver's
  2021 Brackett Ave., 715/831-1060

Best Business Lunch
Woo's Pagoda Restaurant
  1700 S. Hastings Way, 715/832-6431

Best Coffee
Country Kitchen
  2308 E. Clairemont Ave., 715/832-3677

Best Diner
Pied Piper Restaurant
  1527 S. Hastings Way, 715/834-8922

Best Family Restaurant
Cheese to Please
  2823 London Rd., 715/834-4444

Best Homestyle Food
Cheese to Please
  2823 London Rd., 715/834-4444

Best Ice Cream/Yogurt
Culver's
  2021 Brackett Ave., 715/831-1060

Best Italian Food
Draganettie's
  3120 Hillcrest Pkwy., 715/834-9234
Mona Lisa's
  428 Water St., 715/839-8969

Best Late-Night Food
Country Kitchen
  2308 E. Clairemont Ave., 715/832-3677

Best Place to Take the Kids
Cheese to Please
  2823 London Rd., 715/834-4444

Best Sandwiches
Erbert and Gerbert's Subs and Clubs
  405 Water St., 715/835-9995

Best Steaks
Sweetwater's Restaurant
  1104 W. Clairemont Ave., 715/834-577

W   **Standbys**
Old Country Buffet
  2613 E. Clairemont Ave., 715/834-9699
Pizza Hut
  2602 E. Clairemont Ave., 715/834-5346
  1242 W. Clairemont Ave., 715/834-1004
  405 S. Farwell St., 715/834-9391
  2225 Eddy Ln., 715/833-1222
Red Lobster
  1019 W. Clairemont Ave., 715/833-0184

FOND DU LAC, WI

Best Breakfast
Schreiner's Restaurant
  168 N. Pioneer Rd., 414/922-0590
Ransom's Restaurant
  245 N. Peters Ave., 414/923-4400

Best Brunch
Rosewood Room
  Ramada Inn, 1 N. Main St., 414/923-3000

Best Burgers
Scenario
  1000 S. Main St., 414/921-9922
Friar Tuck's
  570 W. Johnson St., 414/921-4027

Best Chinese Food
Chinatown Kitchen
  18 N. Main St., 414/923-9688

Best Homestyle Food
Oasis Family Restaurant
  339 N. Main St., 414/922-3345
Rolling Meadows Family Restaurant
  947 S. Rolling Meadows Dr., 414/922-9140

Best Ice Cream/Yogurt
Gilles Frozen Custard
  819 S. Main St., 414/922-4900

Best Italian Food
Tami's
  109 S. Main St., 414/922-6162

Best Mexican Food
Mazatlan
  237 S. Main St., 414/924-9012

Best Pizza
Pizza Ville Restaurant
  160 W. Scott St., 414/921-1700

Best Sandwiches
Scenario
  1000 S. Main St., 414/921-9922
Friar Tuck's
  570 W. Johnson St., 414/921-4027

Best Seafood
Sunset Supper Club
  N7364 Winnebago Dr., 414/922-4540
Jim and Linda's Lakeview Club
  W3496 County Trunk W., Malone, 414/795-4116

Best Steaks
Sunset Supper Club
  N7364 Winnebago Dr., 414/922-4540
Jim and Linda's Lakeview Club
  W3496 County Trunk W., Malone, 414/795-4116
Theo's
  24 N. Main St., 414/922-8899

W

GREEN BAY, WI

Best Bar
Gipper's Sports Bar and Grill
  1860 University Ave., 414/435-1515

Best Barbecue/Ribs
Wally's Spot Supper Club
  1979 Main St., 414/468-7924

Best Breakfast
Peyton's Restaurant
  780 Packer Dr., 414/499-3161

Best Brunch
Pepik's Restaurant
  333 Main St., 414/432-4555

Best Burgers
Settlement Inn
  3254 Bay Settlement Rd., 414/465-8415

Best Business Lunch
Wild Onion
  1632 Hwy. 41, De Pere, 414/336-2303

Best Casual Dining
Gipper's Sports Bar and Grill
  1860 University Ave., 414/435-1515

Best Chinese Food
Mandarin Garden Restaurant
  2394 S. Oneida St., 414/499-4459
Lee's Pandas Wok Restaurant
  2247 University Ave., 414/468-1370

Best Family Restaurant
Peyton's Restaurant
  780 Packer Dr., 414/499-3161

Best German Food
Lorelei Inn
  1412 S. Webster Ave., 414/432-5921

Best Ice Cream/Yogurt
Hansen's Dairy Stores
  1329 S. Webster Ave., 414/432-4712
  620 Gray St., 414/494-1090
  2180 S. Ridge Rd., 414/497-0480
  1689 E. Mason St., 414/465-1790
  2363 W. Mason St., 414/496-1036
  1742 University Ave., 414/437-0056

Best Italian Food
Victoria's
  2610 Bay Settlement Rd., 414/468-8070
Zimmani's Deli
  333 Main St., 414/436-2340
  2809 S. Oneida St., 414/499-3327

Best Mexican Food
Los Banditos
  1258 Main St., 414/432-9462
  2335 W. Mason St., 414/494-4505

W

Best Pizza
Jake's Pizza
1149 Main St., 414/432-8012
Green Bay Pizza Company
2229 University Ave., 414/465-9555

Best Sandwiches
Erbert and Gerbert's Subs and Clubs
227 N. Washington St., 414/435-7827

Best Seafood
Eagle's Nest Supper Club
3261 Nicolet Dr., 414/468-0976

Best Steaks
Kroll's East
1658 Main St., 414/468-4422
Kroll's West
1990 S. Ridge Rd., 414/497-1111
Settlement Inn
3254 Bay Settlement Rd., 414/465-8415

JANESVILLE, WI

Best Restaurant in Town
Campi's Restaurant and Lounge
4323 N. State Rd. 26, 608/758-0321

Best Bar
Looking Glass
18 N. Main St., 608/755-9828

Best Barbecue/Ribs
Harpo's West
5201 W. State Rd. 11, 608/752-8886

Best Burgers
Geri's Hamburgers
702 Center Ave., 608/754-0838
Cornerstone Restaurant and Lounge
2601 Morse St., 608/754-1919

Best Business Lunch
Looking Glass
18 N. Main St., 608/755-9828

Best Chinese Food
Yummy Wok
2600 E. Milwaukee Ave., 608/754-5535

Best Diner
Geri's Hamburgers
702 Center Ave., 608/754-0838

Best Italian Food
Frankie's on Main
54 S. Main St., 608/758-1888

Best Pizza
Lisa Pizzeria
1650 Center Ave., 608/756-1117

Best Seafood
The Ding-A-Ling Club
Race St. at Luccus St., Hanover, 608/879-9209

W

Best Steaks
Cherry's Steak and Prime
13 N. Franklin St., 608/754-9775

Standbys
Ground Round
2753 Milton Ave., 608/754-4466
Shoney's
3136 Hwy. 14E,.608/758-3200
TCBY
1724 Holiday Dr., 608/757-1978

KENOSHA, WI

Best Restaurants in Town
Ray Radigan's Restaurant
11712 Sheridan Rd., 414/694-0455
Hob Nob
277 Sheridan Rd., 414/552-8008
Mangia Trattoria Pizzeria
5717 Sheridan Rd., 414/652-4285

Best Breakfast
Taste of Wisconsin
7515 125th Ave., 414/857-9110

Best Brunch
Lake Geneva Inn
N. 2009 State Rd. 120, Lake Geneva, 414/248-5680

Best Burgers
Taste of Wisconsin
7515 125th Ave., 414/857-9110

Best Business Lunch
D'Carlo
5140 Sixth Ave., 414/654-3932

Best Cheap Meal
Taste of Wisconsin
7515 125th Ave., 414/857-9110

Best Chinese Food
China House
3450 52nd St., 414/652-8811

Best Desserts
Mangia Trattoria Pizzeria
5717 Sheridan Rd., 414/652-4285

Best Family Restaurant
Lake Geneva Inn
N. 2009 State Rd. 120, Lake Geneva, 414/248-5680

Best Homestyle Food
Taste of Wisconsin
7515 125th Ave., 414/857-9110

W

Best Italian Food
Mangia Trattoria Pizzeria
5717 Sheridan Rd., 414/652-4285
Pasta al Dente
3715 80th St., 414/694-884

Best Pizza
Ruffolos I
    4621 38th Ave., 414/656-0685
Ruffolos II
    3931 45th St., 414/656-0441
Ruffolos III
    11820 Sheridan Rd., 414/694-4003

Best Place to Take the Kids
Lake Geneva Inn
    N. 2009 State Rd. 120, Lake Geneva, 414/248-5680

Best Sandwiches
Big Apple Bagel
    5902 75th St., 414/694-2330

Best Steaks
Corner House
    1521 Washington Ave., Racine, 414/637-1295

LA CROSSE, WI

Best Restaurants in Town
Freight House Restaurant
    107 Vine St., 608/784-6211
Ed Sullivan's
    Sullivan Rd., Trempealeau, 608/534-7775

Best Bar
Howie's
    1128 La Crosse St., 608/784-7400

Best Barbecue/Ribs
Piggy's on Front
    328 Front St. S., 608/784-4877

Best Breakfast
Mr. D's Donut Shop and Restaurant
    1146 State St., 608/784-6737

Best Burgers
Howie's
    1128 La Crosse St., 608/784-7400

Best Business Lunch
Mr. D's Donut Shop and Restaurant
    1146 State St., 608/784-6737
Picasso's Cafe
    600 Third St. N., 608/784-4485

Best Chinese Food
Hunan Chinese Restaurant
    318 Fourth St. S., 608/784-7878

Best Desserts
Picasso's Cafe
    600 Third St. N., 608/784-4485

Best Health-Conscious Menu
Mr. D's Donut Shop and Restaurant
    1146 State St., 608/784-6737

Best Homestyle Food
Mr. D's Donut Shop and Restaurant
    1146 State St., 608/784-6737

W

Best Italian Food
Di Sciascio's Coon Creek Inn
110 Central Ave., Coon Valley, 608/452-3182

Best Mexican Food
Esteban's Mexican Restaurante
300 Third St. S., 608/785-2388

Best Pizza
Pizza King
2929 South Ave., 608/788-1926
Edwardo's Pizza Wagon
1930 Rose St., 608/783-8282
Big Al's Pizzeria
115 Third St. S., 608/782-7550

Best Salad/Salad Bar
Picasso's Cafe
600 Third St. N., 608/784-4485
Freight House Restaurant
107 Vine St., 608/784-6211
Ed Sullivan's
Sullivan Rd., Trempealeau, 608/534-7775

Best Sandwiches
Pizza King
2929 South Ave., 608/788-1926
Piggy's on Front
328 Front St. S., 608/784-4877

Best Seafood
Freight House Restaurant
107 Vine St., 608/784-6211
New Villa
2132 Ward Ave., 608/788-4400

Best Steaks
Freight House Restaurant
107 Vine St., 608/784-6211

Best Vegetarian Food
Mr. D's Donut Shop and Restaurant
1146 State St., 608/784-6737

MADISON, WI

Best Asian Restaurants
Imperial Garden
4214 E. Washington Ave., 608/249-0466
2039 Allen Blvd., Middleton, 608/238-6445
Red Pepper
1518 N. Stoughton Rd., 608/249-1373
Hong Kong Cafe
2 S. Mills St., 608/259-1668
Bahn Thai
2809 University Ave., 608/233-3900
944 Williamson St., 608/256-0202
Ruby's
900 W. Broadway, 608/221-9290

Best Bread
Mountain Jack's
4520 E. Towne Blvd., 608/244-4714
7315 W. Towne Way, 608/833-7383

W

Wild Iris
  1225 Regent St., 608/257-4747

Best Breakfast
Mickie's Dairy Bar
  1511 Monroe St., 608/256-9476
C's Bakery
  2622 Allen Blvd., Middleton, 608/836-4700
O'Malley's Greenhouse
  2254 Hwy. 22, Montello, 608/297-2266
Ovens of Brittany
  Multiple Locations •

Best Brunch
White Horse Inn
  202 N. Henry St., 608/255-9933
Dry Bean
  5264 Verona Rd., 608/274-2326
Ovens of Brittany
  Multiple Locations
The Fess
  123 E. Doty St., 608/256-0263
Nau-ti-Gal
  5360 Westport Rd., 608/246-3130

Best Burgers
Dotty Dumpling's Dowry
  116 N. Fairchild St., 608/255-3175
  2906 W. Beltline Hwy., Middleton, 608/836-5577
Oakcrest Tavern
  5371 Old Middleton Rd., 608/233-1243
Plaza Tavern
  319 N. Henry St., 608/255-6592
Culver's
  2906 W. Beltline Hwy., Middleton, 608/836-5577
Nau-ti-gal
  5360 Westport Rd., 608/246-3130

Best Business Lunch
Edgewater
  666 Wisconsin Ave., 608/256-9071
Botticelli's
  107 King St., 608/257-1110
Madison Club
  5 E. Wilson St., 608/255-4861
The Opera House
  126 S. Pinckney St., 608/284-8466

Best Coffeehouses
Canterbury Booksellers
  315 W. Gorham St., 608/258-9911
Steep and Brew
  855 E. Broadway, 608/223-0707
  2871 University Ave., 608/238-6878
  6656 Odana Rd., 608/833-6656
  544 State St., 608/256-2902
Victor Allen's
  401 State St., 608/255-0117
  5501 Odana Rd., 608/274-6166
  2858 University Ave., 608/231-3222
  1730 Fordem Ave.,608/241-1340

W

713 Post Rd., 608/274-4666
410 Donofrio Dr., 608/833-8501

Best Delicatessens
Ella's Deli
425 State St., 608/257-8611
2902 E. Washington Ave., 608/241-5291
Radical Rye
231 State St., 608/256-1200

Best Desserts
Michael's Frozen Custard
2531 Monroe St., 608/231-3500
3826 Atwood Ave., 608/222-4110
Canterbury Booksellers
315 W. Gorham St., 608/258-9911
Clasen's
7610 Donna Dr., Middleton, 608/831-2032
Ella's Deli
2902 E. Washington Ave., 608/241-5291
425 State St., 608/257-8611

Best Diners
Monty's Blue Plate
2089 Atwood Ave., 608/244-8505
Danny's Diner
7475 Mineral Point Rd., 608/833-9507

Best German Food
Essen Haus
514 E. Wilson St., 608/255-4674

Best Greasy Spoons
Bev's
2422 Winnebago St., 608/244-9618
Mickey's Tavern
1524 Williamson St., 608/251-9964
The Curve
653 S. Park St., 608/251-0311
Dotty Dumpling's Dowry
116 N. Fairchild St., 608/255-3175

Best Greek/Mediterranean Food
Kosta's
117 State St., 608/255-6671

Best Ice Cream/Yogurt
Michael's Frozen Custard
2531 Monroe St., 608/231-3500
3826 Atwood Ave., 608/222-4110
Babcock Hall Dairies
1605 Linden Dr., 608/262-3047
Chocolate Shoppe
468 State St., 608/255-5454
2221 Daniels St., 608/221-8640
1726 Fordem Ave., 608/241-2747
1 University Sq., 608/257-8949
702 N. Midvale Blvd., 608/233-5866
Freshens
237 E. Towne Mall, 608/244-3237
Yogurt Express
2315 W. Broadway, 608/222-7444
2701G University Ave., 608/233-4313

499 State St., 608/255-9876
7416 Mineral Point Rd., 608/833-7050

Best Italian Food
Portabella's
425 N. Francis, 608/256-3186
Antonio's
1109 S. Park St., 608/251-1412

Best Late-Night Food
Cafe Palms
636 W. Washington Ave., 608/256-0166

Best Lunch
Sunprint
704 S. Whitney Way, 608/274-7374
638 State St., 608/255-1555
Wild Iris
1225 Regent St., 608/257-4747

Best Mexican Food
Pasqual's
2098 Atwood Ave., 608/244-3142
2534 Monroe St., 608/238-4419
Pedro's
3555 E. Washington Ave., 608/241-8110

Best New Restaurants
Deb and Lola's
227 State St., 608/255-0820
Coyote Capers
1201 Williamson St., 608/251-1313
Kafe Kahoutek
640 W. Washington Ave., 608/255-0035
LaPaella
2784 S. Fish Hatchery Blvd., 608/273-2666
Pasta Per Tutti
2009 Atwood Ave., 608/242-1800
Sunprint West
638 State St., 608/255-1555
704 S. Whitney Way, 608/274-7374

Best Middle Eastern Food
Husnu's
547 State St., 608/256-0900
Lulu's
2524 University Ave., 608/233-2172

Best Pizza
Pizzeria Uno
222 W. Gorham St., 608/255-7722
7601 Mineral Point Rd., 608/833-7200
Pizza Extreme
605 E. Washington Ave., 608/259-1500
Paison's
University Square, 608/257-2832

Best Places to Eat When Someone Else Is Buying
Blue Marlin
101 N. Hamilton St., 608/255-2255
L'Escargot
2784 S. Fish Hatchery Rd., 608/273-2666

W

Peppino's
5518 University Ave., 608/233-2200
L'Etoile
25 N. Pinckney St., 608/251-0500

Best Place to Take the Kids
Ella's Deli
2902 E. Washington Ave., 608/241-5291
425 State St., 608/257-8611

Best Sandwiches
Ella's Deli
425 State St., 608/257-8611
2902 E. Washington Ave., 608/241-5291
Radical Rye
231 State St., 608/256-1200

Best Seafood
Blue Marlin
101 N. Hamilton St., 608/255-2255
Mariner's Inn
5339 Lighthouse Bay Dr., 608/246-3120
Captain Bill's
2701 Century Harbor Rd., 608/831-7327

Best Steaks
Prime Quarter
3520 E. Washington Ave., 608/244-3520
Delaney's Charcoal Steaks
449 Grand Canyon Dr., 608/833-7337
Smoky's Club
3005 University Ave., 608/233-2120
Mariner's Inn
5339 Lighthouse Bay Dr., 608/246-3120

Best Vegetarian Food
Savory Thymes
1146 Williamson St., 608/255-2292
Country Life Vegetarian Foods
2465 Perry St., 608/257-3286
Sunporch
2701 University Ave., 608/231-1111
638 State St., 608/255-1555
704 S. Whitney Way, 608/274-7374

Standbys
Perkins
1410 Damon Rd., 608/251-7550
4863 Hayes Rd., 608/241-9123
5237 University Ave., 608/238-5133
6601 Grand Teton Plz., 608/833-1223
Friday's
420 Gammon Pl., 608/833-8443
TCBY
6654 Odana Rd., 608/833-8474
The Olive Garden
4320 E. Towne Blvd., 608/249-0340
3826 Atwood Ave., 608/222-4110
Chi Chi's
414 Grand Canyon Dr., 608/251-4344
Chuck E. Cheese Pizza
438 Grand Canyon Dr., 608/829-2000

W

Red Lobster
418 S. Gammon Rd., 608/833-1991

MANITOWAC, WI

Best Breakfast
Dugout
4117 Broadway St., 414/684-1622
Four Seasons Family Restaurant
3950 Calumet Ave., 414/683-1444

Best Burgers
Dugout
4117 Broadway St., 414/684-1622
Penguin Drive-In Restaurant
3900 Calumet Ave., 414/684-6403

Best Chinese Food
Chinatown Kitchen
807 Buffalo St., 414/683-9330
Jade Palace
1103 S. Tenth St., 414/682-5352

Best Desserts
Machut's Supper Club
3911 Lincoln Ave., Two Rivers, 414/793-9432
Inn on Maritime Bay
101 Maritime Dr., 414/682-7000

Best Ice Cream/Yogurt
Cedar Crest Specialties
2000 S. Tenth St., 414/682-5577

Best Mexican Food
Carolina's Lone Star
901 Chicago St., 414/682-6300

Best Pizza
Luigi's Pizza Palace III
6124 Hwy. 151, 414/684-4200
Tony's Pizza
2204 Washington St., 414/682-8669

Best Sandwiches
Butch's Osman Oasis
10731 Hwy. 42, Newton, 414/726-4311
Four Seasons Family Restaurant
3950 Calumet Ave., 414/683-1444
Dugout
4117 Broadway St., 414/684-1622

Best Seafood
Stock's Dinner Club
8330 Center Rd., Newton, 414/726-4404
Machut's Supper Club
3911 Lincoln Ave., Two Rivers, 414/793-9432

Best Steaks
Stock's Dinner Club
8330 Center Rd., Newton, 414/726-4404
Machut's Supper Club
3911 Lincoln Ave., Two Rivers, 414/793-9432

W

MILWAUKEE, WI

Best Restaurants in Town
Grenadier's
    747 N. Broadway, 414/276-0747
English Room
    424 E. Wisconsin Ave., 414/273-8222
Pandl's in Bayside
    8825 N. Lake Dr., 414/352-7300
Fox and Hounds Restaurant
    1298 Friess Lake Rd., Hubertus, 414/251-4100

Best Bagels
Big Apple Bagels
    5710 S. 108th St., Hales Corner., 414/529-3050

Best Barbecue/Ribs
Saz's Grand Avenue
    275 W. Wisconsin Ave., 414/273-4404
Jerry's Old Town Inn
    N116 W15841 Main St., Germantown, 414/251-4455
Pitch's Kansas City Style
    11320 W. Bluemound Rd., 414/774-7180
Butler Inn
    12400 W. Hampton Ave., Butler, 414/783-5899

Best Brunch
Pandl's in Bayside
    8825 N. Lake Dr., 414/352-7300
Boder's on the River
    11919 N. River Rd., Mequon, 414/242-0335
Seven Seas
    1807 Nagawicka Rd., Hartland, 414/367-3903
La Par
    Silver Spring Country Club, N56 W21318 Silver
        Spring Rd., Menomonee Falls, 414/252-4994

Best Burgers
Barley Pop Pub
    N116 W16137 Main St., Germantown, 414/255-2086
Centennial Bar and Grille
    10352 N. Port Washington Rd., Mequon, 414/241-4353
First Precinct
    13995 W. National Ave., New Berlin, 414/785-0277
Solly's
    4629 N. Port Washington Rd., Glendale, 414/332-8808

Best Chinese Food
Yen Ching Restaurant
    7630 W. Good Hope Rd., 414/353-6677
East Garden Chinese Restaurant
    3600 N. Oakland Ave., 414/962-7460
Toy's Chinatown Restaurant
    830 N. Third St., 414/271-5166
Emperor of China
    1010 E. Brady St., 414/271-8889

Best French Food
Grenadier's
    747 N. Broadway, 414/276-0747
Mike and Anna's
    2000 S. Eighth St., 414/643-0072

Cream and Crepe Cafe
  N70 W6340 Bridge Rd., Cedarburg, 414/377-0900

Best German Food
Karl Ratzsch's Restaurant
  320 E. Mason St., 414/276-2720
John Ernst Restaurant
  600 E. Ogden Ave., 414/273-1878
Bavarian Wurst Haus Restaurant
  8310 W. Appleton Ave., 414/464-0060

Best Greek/Mediterranean Food
Oakland Gyros
  2867 N. Oakland Ave., 414/963-1393
Mykonos Restaurant
  8501 W. Capitol Dr., 414/438-1939

Best Italian Food
Maniaci's Cafe Siciliano
  6904 N. Santa Monica Blvd., 414/352-5757
Bartolotta's Restaurant
  7616 W. State St., 414/771-7910
Mimma's Cafe
  1307 E. Brady St., 414/271-7337
Giovanni's Restaurant
  1683 N. Van Buren St., 414/291-5600

Best Japanese Food
Seigo's Japanese Steak House
  5501 W. National Ave., 414/383-9777
Izumi's Fine Japanese Dining
  2178 N. Prospect Ave., 414/271-5278
Tokyo Japanese Restaurant
  12950 W. Bluemound Rd., Elm Grove, 414/797-7818

Best Late-Night Food
Elsa's on the Park
  833 N. Jefferson St., 414/765-0615
Red Mill
  1005 S. Elm Grove Rd., Brookfield, 414/782-8780
Eagan's on Water
  1030 N. Water St., 414/271-6900
Saz's Grand Avenue
  275 W. Wisconsin Ave., 414/273-4404

Best Mexican Food
Rudy's Mexican Restaurant
  631 S. Fifth St., 414/291-0296

Best Middle Eastern Food
Casablanca Med Eastern Cuisine
  3468 N. Oakland Ave., 414/961-8810

Best Other Ethnic Food
Old Town Serbian Gourmet House (Serbian)
  522 W. Lincoln Ave., 414/672-0206

W

Best Places to Eat When Someone Else Is Buying
Steven Wade's Cafe
  17001 W. Greenfield Ave., New Berlin, 414/784-0774
Grenadier's
  747 N. Broadway, 414/276-0747
Sanford Restaurant
  1547 N. Jackson St., 414/276-9608

English Room
424 E. Wisconsin Ave., 414/273-8222

Best Romantic Dining
Fox and Hounds Restaurant
1298 Friess Lake Rd., Hubertus, 414/251-4100
English Room
424 E. Wisconsin Ave., 414/273-8222
Heaven City Restaurant
591 W27850 National Ave., Mukwonago, 414/363-5191
Harold's Restaurant
4747 S. Howell Ave., 414/481-8000

Best Seafood
River Lane Inn
4313 West River Ln., 414/354-1995
Riversite
11120 Cedarburg Rd., Mequon, 414/242-6050
Nantucket Shores Restaurant
924 E. Juneau Ave., 414/278-8660
Anchorage Restaurant
4700 N. Port Washington Rd., 414/962-4710
Red Rock Cafe
4022 N. Oakland Ave., 414/962-4545

Best Steaks
Jake's
6030 W. North Ave., 414/771-0550
Sally's Meeting Place in Stone Bank
N67 W33525 County Trunk Hwy. K, Stone Bank,
414/367-1288
Clock Steak House
720 N. Plankinton Ave., 414/272-1278
Club Forest
4200 W. County Line Rd. 96N, Mequon, 414/238-0876
Di Miceli's Rafters
7228 S. 27th St., Oak Creek, 414/761-2222

Best Thai Food
King and I Thai Restaurant
7225 N. 76th St., 414/353-6069
823 N. Second St., 414/276-4181

OSHKOSH, WI

Best Restaurants in Town
Granary Restaurant
50 W. Sixth Ave., 414/233-3929
Butch's Anchor Inn
225 W. Twentieth Ave., 414/232-3742

Best Bar
Tony's Place
556 W. Seventh St., 414/235-4447

Best Breakfast
Annie's American Cafe
1930 Omro Rd., 414/233-7880

Best Business Lunch
B and B
686 N. Main St., 414/235-6421

Best Chinese Food
Great Wall Restaurant and Lounge
  700 N. Koeller St., 414/231-1828

Best Diner
Annie's American Cafe
  1930 Omro Rd., 414/233-7880

Best Homestyle Food
Annie's American Cafe
  1930 Omro Rd., 414/233-7880

Best Italian Food
Vitale's Italian Cuisine
  307 W. Murdock Ave., 414/426-0886
Victoria's
  1145 N. Wasburn, 414/426-9134

Best Salad/Salad Bar
B and B
  686 N. Main St., 414/235-6421

Best Seafood
Granary Restaurant
  50 W. Sixth Ave., 414/233-3929
Champs Food and Spirits
  527 W. Ninth Ave., 414/233-3474

Best Steaks
Granary Restaurant
  50 W. Sixth Ave., 414/233-3929

RACINE, WI

Best Burgers
Ritzy's Restaurant
  5821 Washington Ave., 414/886-3121

Best Business Lunch
Main Street Bistro
  340 S. Main St., 414/637-4340

Best Casual Dining
Chancery Pub and Restaurant
  6430 Washington Ave., 414/886-5600

Best Cheap Meal
Ritzy's Restaurant
  5821 Washington Ave., 414/886-3121
Infusino's Pizzeria
  3301 Washington Ave., 414/634-2727
Athan's Family Restaurant
  2100 Douglas Ave., 414/633-8060

Best Chinese Food
Great Wall Chinese Restaurant
  6025 Washington Ave., 414/886-9700

Best Desserts
Main Street Bistro
  340 S. Main St., 414/637-4340

Best Family Restaurant
Chancery Pub and Restaurant
  6430 Washington Ave., 414/886-5600

W

Best Italian Food
Infusino's Pizzeria
    3301 Washington Ave., 414/634-2727
Totero's
    2343 Mead St., 414/634-9488

Best Mexican Food
Tacos del Rey
    2207 Lathrop Ave., 414/632-6340

Best Pizza
Infusino's Pizzeria
    3301 Washington Ave., 414/634-2727
DeRango's Pizza Palace
    3840 Douglas Ave., 414/639-4112

Best Place to Eat When Someone Else Is Buying
Main Street Bistro
    340 S. Main St., 414/637-4340

Best Place to Take the Kids
Chancery Pub and Restaurant
    6430 Washington Ave., 414/886-5600

Best Romantic Dining
Valentyne's
    1675 Douglas Ave., 414/633-7500

Best Sandwiches
Chancery Pub and Restaurant
    6430 Washington Ave., 414/886-5600

Best Seafood
Chartroom
    209 Dodge St., 414/632-9901

Best Steaks
Corner House
    1521 Washington Ave., 414/637-1295

Best Other Restaurant
Docks Waterfront Restaurant
    2 Fourth St., 414/631-5555

Standbys
Denny's
    5501 Washington Ave., 414/637-9170
Chi Chi's
    5200 Durand Ave., 414/554-7200
Ground Round
    6300 Washington Ave., 414/886-1850

SHEBOYGAN, WI

Best Breakfast
Sy's Restaurant
    1735 Calumet Dr., 414/452-7850

Best Cheap Meal
Sy's Restaurant
    1735 Calumet Dr., 414/452-7850

Best Chinese Food
Imperial Palace
    2910 Kohler Memorial Dr., 414/452-2291

W

Best Coffee
Golden Palate Delicatessen
  632 N. Eighth St., 414/457-6565

Best Desserts
Randall's Frozen Custard
  3827 Superior Ave., 414/458-9699

Best Family Restaurant
Faye's Pizza
  1821 Calumet Dr., 414/458-4171

Best Ice Cream/Yogurt
Randall's Frozen Custard
  3827 Superior Ave., 414/458-9699

Best Italian Food
Trattoria Stefano
  522 S. Eighth St., 414/452-8455

Best Pizza
Faye's Pizza
  1821 Calumet Dr., 414/458-4171

Best Place to Eat Alone
Golden Palate Delicatessen
  632 N. Eighth St., 414/457-6565

Best Place to Eat When Someone Else Is Buying
Immigrant Room Restaurant and Winery
  407 Highland Dr., Kohler, 414/457-8888

Best Romantic Dining
Immigrant Room Restaurant and Winery
  407 Highland Dr., Kohler, 414/457-8888

Best Sandwiches
Ella's Dela Delicatessen
  1113 N. Eighth St., 414/457-3034
Golden Palate Delicatessen
  632 N. Eighth St., 414/457-6565

Best Steaks
Immigrant Room Restaurant and Winery
  407 Highland Dr., Kohler, 414/457-8888

STEVENS POINT, WI

Best Barbecue/Ribs
Mesquite Grill
  Hwy. 51, 715/341-1340
Silver Coach
  38 Park Ridge Dr., 715/341-6588

Best Cajun/Creole Food
Silver Coach
  38 Park Ridge Dr., 715/341-6588

Best Coffee
Supreme Bean
  1100 Main St., Ste. 1A, 715/344-0077

Best Continental Food
Bernard's Continental Restaurant
  710 Second St. N., 715/344-3365

W

Best Ice Cream/Yogurt
Sweet Treats
913 Main St., 715/341-4990

Best Italian Food
Pagliacci
1800 N. Point Dr., 715/346-6010

Best Place to Eat When Someone Else Is Buying
The Restaurant
1800 N. Point Dr., 715/346-6010

Best Seafood
Hot Fish Shop
1140 Clark St., 715/344-4252
Pagliacci
1800 N. Point Dr., 715/346-6010

Best Steaks
Mesquite Grill
Hwy. 51, 715/341-1340
Silver Coach
38 Park Ridge Dr., 715/341-6588

WAUKESHA, WI

Best Bar
Chancery Pub and Restaurant
2100 E. Moreland Blvd., 414/549-1720

Best Burgers
Red Rooster Inn
N14 W22032 Watertown Rd., 414/547-6668

Best Business Lunch
Chancery Pub and Restaurant
2100 E. Moreland Blvd., 414/549-1720

Best Casual Dining
Michael's Italian-American Restaurant
1400 S. Grand Ave., 414/549-0406
Louie's
319 Williams St., 414/549-2242

Best Chinese Food
Imperial House
1500 E. Moreland Blvd., 414/544-6267
Ching Hwa Restaurant
1947 E. Main St., 414/544-1983

Best Delicatessen
Strand Foods and Deli
1218 The Strand, 414/547-5835

Best Family Restaurant
Baker's Square Restaurant
1430 Moreland Blvd., 414/544-2023

Best German Food
Gasthaus
2720 N. Grandview Blvd., 414/544-4460

Best Greek/Mediterranean Food
Louie's
319 Williams St., 414/549-2242

W

1178

Best Ice Cream/Yogurt
Charlene Kaye's Ice Cream and Sandwich Shop
280 W. Broadway, 414/521-3250

Best Italian Food
Michael's Italian-American Restaurant
1400 S. Grand Ave., 414/549-0406

Best Mexican Food
Jalisco Restaurant
1120 Whiterock Ave., 414/521-1986

Best Pizza
Michael's Italian-American Restaurant
1400 S. Grand Ave., 414/549-0406

WAUSAU, WI

Best Barbecue/Ribs
Palms Supper Club
5912 Business Hwy. 51, Schofield, 715/359-2200

Best Breakfast
Tri City
525 Grand Ave., Schofield, 715/359-9596

Best Burgers
Wausau Mine Company
3904 W. Stewart Ave., 715/845-7304

Best Chinese Food
Peking Chinese and American Restaurant
221 Scott St., 715/842-8080

Best Desserts
Twenty-Five Hundred Ten Restaurant
2510 W. Stewart Ave., 715/845-2510

Best Homestyle Food
Bill's Fine Food and Lounge
932 S. Third Ave., 715/842-3669
George's Restaurant
1706 1/2 W. Stewart Ave., 715/845-7067

Best Ice Cream/Yogurt
Finnegan's Ice Cream Parlor
129 N. Third Ave., 715/842-8805

Best Mexican Food
Pedro's Mexican Restaurante
110 E. Kent St., 715/848-4048
Chico's
5704 State Hwy. 52, 715/842-9851

Best Pizza
Wausau Mine Company
3904 W. Stewart Ave., 715/845-7304

Best Seafood
Palms Supper Club
5912 Business Hwy. 51, Schofield, 715/359-2200
Twenty-Five Hundred Ten Restaurant
2510 W. Stewart Ave., 715/845-2510
Gulliver's Landing
2204 Rib Mountain Dr., 715/842-9098
Michael's Supper Club
2901 Rib Mountain Dr., 715/842-9856

W

Best Steaks
Palms Supper Club
  5912 Business Hwy. 51, Schofield, 715/359-2200
Twenty-Five Hundred Ten Restaurant
  2510 W. Stewart Ave., 715/845-2510
Captain's Restaurant
  1914 W. Stewart Ave., 715/842-2271
Michael's Supper Club
  2901 Rib Mountain Dr., 715/842-9856

WEST BEND, WI

Best Barbecue/Ribs
Walden Supper Club
  2472 Wallace Lake Rd., 414/334-4664

Best Breakfast
Carol's Kitchen
  157 N. Main St., Ste. 2, 414/334-7010

Best Burgers
Toucan Custard
  600 N. Main St., 414/338-8444
J.D. Tasha's
  147 N. Main St., 414/338-8200

Best Chinese Food
China Palace
  817 S. Main St., 414/334-5952

Best Coffee
Devon Delights
  102 N. Main St., 414/335-1811

Best Continental Food
Old Courthouse Inn
  518 Poplar St., 414/335-6302

Best Desserts
Cream and Crepe Cafe
  N70W6340 Bridge Rd., Cedarburg, 414/377-0900

Best Ice Cream/Yogurt
Toucan Custard
  600 N. Main St., 414/338-8444

Best Pizza
Dick's Pizzaria
  1750 W. Washington St., 414/334-2591

Best Steaks
Coachman House Supper Club
  1006 S. Main St., 414/334-9491
White Tail Inn
  5802 Hwy. 144N, 414/644-5553

W

Wyoming

Best Restaurant in Town
Goose Egg Inn
  10580 Goose Egg Rd., 307/473-8838

Best Breakfast
Casper's Good Cooking
  581 N. Poplar St., 307/237-3033

Best Business Lunch
Cafe Jose's
  1600 E. Second St., 307/235-6599

Best Chinese Food
South Sea Chinese Restaurant
  2025 E. Second St., 307/237-4777

Best Family Restaurant
L.B.M. Pizza
  3350 Cy Ave., 307/235-0786

Best Italian Food
Bosco's Italian Restaurant
  847 E. A St., 307/265-9658
Anthony's Upper Crust
  241 S. Center St., 307/234-3071

Best Mexican Food
El Jarro Restaurant
  500 W. F St., 307/577-0538
  621 SE Wyoming Blvd., 307/235-8500
Cafe Jose's
  1600 E. Second St., 307/235-6599

Best Sandwiches
Mountain View Sub Shop
  239 E. First St., 307/237-7999

Best Seafood
Goose Egg Inn
  10580 Goose Egg Rd., 307/473-8838

Best Steaks
Goose Egg Inn
  10580 Goose Egg Rd., 307/473-8838

W

Standbys
HomeTown Buffet
601 Wyoming Blvd., 307/577-5953
Pizza Hut
3738 Cy Ave., 307/265-0804
3741 E. Second St., 307/577-9112
515 E. Collins Dr., 307/237-8646

CHEYENNE, WY

Best Restaurant in Town
Poor Richard's
2233 E. Lincolnway, 307/635-5114

Best Bar
Medicine Bow Brewery
115 E. Seventeenth St., 307/778-2739

Best Brunch
Hitching Post Inn
1700 W. Lincolnway, 307/638-3301

Best Burgers
C and B Potts
1650 Dell Range Blvd., 307/632-8636

Best Business Lunch
Lexie's Cafe
216 E. Seventeenth St., 307/638-8712

Best Cheap Meal
Taco John's
3411 E. Pershing Blvd., 307/634-7430
2220 Carey Ave., 307/634-7853
101 S. Greeley Hwy., 307/634-1555
5410 Yellowstone Rd., 307/637-2863

Best Chinese Food
Twin Dragon
1809 Cary Ave., 307/637-6622

Best Coffee
Java Joint
1720 Capitol Ave., 307/638-7332

Best Homestyle Food
Owl Inn Restaurant
3919 Central Ave., 307/638-8578

Best Italian Food
Avanti Restaurant
4620 Grandview Ave., 307/634-3432

Best Mexican Food
Casa de Trujillo
122 W. Sixth St., 307/635-1227

Best Place to Eat When Someone Else Is Buying
Poor Richard's
2233 E. Lincolnway, 307/635-5114

Best Romantic Dining
Lexie's Cafe
216 E. Seventeenth St., 307/638-8712

Best Salad/Salad Bar
Little America Hotel and Resort
 2800 W. Lincolnway, 307/775-8400

Best Sandwiches
Little Philly
 1121 W. Lincolnway, 307/632-6824

Best Steaks
Little Bear Inn
 1700 Little Bear Rd., 307/634-3684

Best Other Restaurant
Cloud Nine Restaurant
 300 E. Eighth Ave., 307/635-1525

Standbys
Old Country Buffet
 1400 Dell Range Blvd., 307/632-5358
Perkins
 1730 Dell Range Blvd., 307/634-7577
Applebee's
 1401 Dell Range Blvd., 307/638-3434
Baskin-Robbins
 723 E. Sixteenth St., 307/635-2588
Pizza Hut
 2215 E. Lincolnway, 307/635-4151
 5320 Yellowstone Rd., 307/634-0854
Red Lobster
 1923 Dell Range Blvd., 307/778-2724

CODY, WY

Best Barbecue/Ribs
M's B Ribs
 103 W. Yellowstone Ave., 307/527-6373

Best Breakfast
Irma Hotel
 1192 Sheridan Ave., 307/587-4221

Best Burgers
Proud Cut Saloon
 1227 Sheridan Ave., 307/527-6905
Silver Dollar Bar and Grill
 1313 Sheridan Ave., 307/587-3554

Best Coffee
Cody Coffee Company
 1702 Sheridan Ave., 307/527-7879
Caffee Espresso
 1272 Sheridan Ave., 307/527-4444
Peter's Cafe Bakery
 1191 Sheridan Ave., 307/527-5040

Best Desserts
Maxwell's
 937 Sheridan Ave., 307/527-7749
Sunset House Restaurant
 1651 Eighth St., 307/587-2257

Best Family Restaurants
Cattleman's Cut
 225 Yellowstone Ave., 307/527-7432

W

Sunset House Restaurant
   1651 Eighth St., 307/587-2257

Best Health-Conscious Menu
Maxwell's
   937 Sheridan Ave., 307/527-7749

Best Homestyle Food
Our Place
   148 Yellowstone Ave., 307/527-4420

Best Ice Cream/Yogurt
Ice Cream Parlor
   1320 Sheridan Ave., 307/587-9084

Best Pizza
Pizza on the Run
   1453 Sheridan Ave., 307/527-7862

Best Salad/Salad Bar
Silver Dollar Bar and Grill
   1313 Sheridan Ave., 307/587-3554

Best Sandwiches
Peter's Cafe Bakery
   1191 Sheridan Ave., 307/527-5040

Best Seafood
Proud Cut Saloon
   1227 Sheridan Ave., 307/527-6905
Maxwell's
   937 Sheridan Ave., 307/527-7749

Best Steaks
Proud Cut Saloon
   1227 Sheridan Ave., 307/527-6905
Maxwell's
   937 Sheridan Ave., 307/527-7749

DOUGLAS, WY

Best All-You-Can-Eat Buffet
Clementine's
   1199 Mesa Dr., 307/358-5554

Best Atmosphere
Country Inn
   2341 Richards St., 307/358-3575
Shutes Restaurant and Lounge
   Best Western Douglas Inn, 1450 Riverbend Dr.,
      307/358-9790

Best Breakfast
Village Inn
   1840 Richards St., 307/358-5600

Best Brunch
La Bonte Inn
   206 E. Walnut St., 307/358-9856

Best Burgers
Clementine's
   1199 Mesa Dr., 307/358-5554

Best Casual Dining
Clementine's
   1199 Mesa Dr., 307/358-5554

Best Chinese Food
Four Seasons Chinese Restaurant
1120 Richards St., 307/358-5091

Best Coffee
Village Inn
1840 Richards St., 307/358-5600

Best Continental Food
Shutes Restaurant and Lounge
Best Western Douglas Inn, 1450 Riverbend Dr.,
307/358-9790

Best Desserts
Shutes Restaurant and Lounge
Best Western Douglas Inn, 1450 Riverbend Dr.,
307/358-9790

Best Greek/Mediterranean Food
Shutes Restaurant and Lounge
Best Western Douglas Inn, 1450 Riverbend Dr.,
307/358-9790

Best Health-Conscious Menu
Thru The Grapevine
301 Center St., 307/358-4567

Best Homestyle Food
La Bonte Inn
206 E. Walnut St., 307/358-9856

Best Ice Cream/Yogurt
Covered Wagon Drive Inn
1728 Richards St., 307/358-5085
How Sweet It Is
128 N. Second St., 307/358-4906

Best Mexican Food
Santa Fe Cafe
1954 Richards St., 307/358-5933

Best Seafood
Clementine's
1199 Mesa Dr., 307/358-5554

Best Steaks
Country Inn
2341 Richards St., 307/358-3575

GILLETTE, WY

Best Atmosphere
Humphrey's Bar and Grill
408 W. Juniper Ln., 307/682-0100

Best Bar
Las Margaritas
2107 S. Douglas Hwy., 307/682-6545

Best Breakfast
Bazel's
408 S. Douglas Hwy., 307/686-5149
Village Inn
806 E. Second St., 307/682-8823

Best Burgers
Bazel's
408 S. Douglas Hwy., 307/686-5149

W

Best Casual Dining
Humphrey's Bar and Grill
   408 W. Juniper Ln., 307/682-0100

Best Chinese Food
Hong Kong Restaurant
   1612 W. Second St., 307/682-5829

Best Coffee
Coffee Friends
   320 S. Gillette Ave., 307/686-6119

Best Family Restaurant
Village Inn
   806 E. Second St., 307/682-8823

Best Homestyle Food
Bazel's
   408 S. Douglas Hwy., 307/686-5149
Lula Belle Coffee Shop
   101 N. Gillette Ave., 307/682-9798

Best Ice Cream/Yogurt
Polar Bear Frozen Yogurt
   900 Camel Dr., Ste. GG, 307/682-3155

Best Mexican Food
Las Margaritas
   2107 S. Douglas Hwy., 307/682-6545

Best Pizza
Godfather's Pizza
   501 W. Lakeway Rd., 307/686-7777

Best Salad/Salad Bar
Bailey's Bar and Grill
   301 S. Gillette Ave., 307/686-7678

Best Sandwiches
Bailey's Bar and Grill
   301 S. Gillette Ave., 307/686-7678
Humphrey's Bar and Grill
   408 W. Juniper Ln., 307/682-0100

Best Sports Bar
Humphrey's Bar and Grill
   408 W. Juniper Ln., 307/682-0100

Best Steaks
Prime Rib Restaurant
   1205 S. Douglas Hwy., 307/682-2944

Standbys
Perkins
   2510 S. Douglas Hwy., 307/682-6887

JACKSON, WY

W

Best Atmosphere
Blue Lion
   160 N. Millward St., 307/733-3912
Cadillac Restaurant
   55 N. Cache St., 307/733-3279

Best Barbecue/Ribs
Bubba's Bar-B-Que Restaurant
   515 W. Broadway, 307/733-2288

Best Breakfast
Nora's Fishcreek Inn
  5600 W. Hwy. 22, Wilson, 307/733-8288
Jedediah's
  135 E. Broadway, 307/733-5671

Best Burgers
Billy's Burgers
  55 N. Cache St., 307/733-3279

Best Health-Conscious Menu
Sweetwater Restaurant
  85 Kings Hwy., 307/733-3553

Best Italian Food
Anthony's Italian Restaurant
  50 S. Glenwood, 307/733-3717

Best Pizza
Mountain High Pizza Pie
  120 W. Broadway, 307/733-3646

Best Places to Eat When Someone Else Is Buying
Snake River Grill
  84 E. Broadway, 307/733-0557
The Range
  225 N. Cache St., 307/733-5481

Best Sandwiches
Bunnery
  130 N. Cache St., 307/733-5474
Best Seafood
Louie's Steak and Seafood
  175 N. Center, 307/733-6803

Best Steaks
Gun Barrel Steakhouse
  862 W. Broadway, 307/733-3287

LARAMIE, WY

Best Restaurants in Town
The Old Corral
  2756 Hwy. 130, Centennial, 307/745-5918
The Cavalryman
  4425 N. Third St., 307/745-5551
Cafe Jacques
  216 Grand St., 307/742-5522
Jeffrey's Bistro
  123 E. Ivinson Ave., 307/742-7046
Overland Fine Eatery
  100 E. Ivinson Ave., 307/721-2800
Winger's
  3626 Grand St., 307/742-4999
The Library Restaurant and Brewery
  1622 E. Grand, 307/742-0500
Shari's of Laramie
  666 N. Third St., 307/721-4813
Cafe Ole
  519 Boswell Dr., 307/742-8383
El Conquistador
  110 E. Ivinson Ave., 307/742-2377

W

POWELL, WY

Best Breakfast
Hamilton House
    201 N. Hamilton St., 307/754-5703
Skyline Cafe
    141 E. Coulter Ave., 307/754-8052

Best Burgers
Bent Street Station
    117 S. Bent St., 307/754-3384
Hansel and Gretel's
    113 S. Bent St., 307/754-2191

Best Chinese Food
Chong Mia's
    151 E. Coulter Ave., 307/754-7924

Best Coffee
Raven's Wing Gallery
    109 N. Bent St., 307/754-9830

Best Ice Cream/Yogurt
Linda's Ice Cream
    119 N. Bent St., 307/754-9553

Best Mexican Food
El Tapatio
    112 N. Bent St., 307/754-8085

Best Steaks
Bent Street Station
    117 S. Bent St., 307/754-3384
Lamplighter Inn
    234 E. First St., 307/754-2226

RAWLINS, WY

Best American Food
Aspen House
    318 Fifth St., 307/324-4787

Best Bar
Peppermill Bar and Grill
    309 W. Cedar St., 307/324-8100

Best Breakfast
Country Kitchen
    1800 E. Cedar St., 307/324-7968
Golden Spike Restaurant
    1617 W. Spruce St., 307/324-2284
Pantry Restaurant
    221 W. Cedar St., 307/324-7860

Best Chinese Food
Aspen House
    318 Fifth St., 307/324-4787
China Panda
    1810 E. Cedar St., 307/324-2198
Ron and Mary's Golden Peacock Cafe
    1811 W. Spruce St., 307/324-8110

Best Coffee
Fifth Street Bistro
    112 Fifth St., 307/324-7246

W

Best Desserts
Frontier Pies
2300 W. Spruce St., 307/328-2181

Best Family Restaurant
Country Kitchen
1800 E. Cedar St., 307/324-7968

Best Mexican Food
Rosie's Lariat
410 E. Cedar St., 307/324-5261

Best Sandwiches
Fifth Street Bistro
112 Fifth St., 307/324-7246

ROCK SPRINGS, WY

Best Restaurants in Town
Red Feather Inn
211 E. Flaming Gorge Way, Green River, 307/875-6625
The Outlaw Inn
1630 Elk St., 307/362-6623
White Mountain Mining Company
West of Rock Springs, 307/382-5265

Best American Food
Cruel Jack's
8 Purple Sage Rd., 307/382-9018

Best Barbecue/Ribs
Log Inn Supper Club
112 Purple Sage Rd., 307/362-7166
E. Flaming Gorge, 307/362-7166

Best Italian Food
Park Grill and Lounge
19 Elk St., 307/362-3701

Best Seafood
Log Inn Supper Club
112 Purple Sage Rd., 307/362-7166
E. Flaming Gorge, 307/362-7166
T and J's North Park Dining
1501 Clubhouse Dr., 307/362-3950

Best Steaks
Log Inn Supper Club
112 Purple Sage Rd., 307/362-7166
E. Flaming Gorge, 307/362-7166
T and J's North Park Dining
1501 Clubhouse Dr., 307/362-3950
Ted's Supper Club
9 Purple Sage Rd., 307/362-7323

SHERIDAN, WY

W

Best Atmosphere
Sheridan Inn
856 Broadway St., 307/674-5049

Best Burgers
Sheridan Inn
856 Broadway St., 307/674-5049
Sanford's Grub and Pub
5 E. Alger, 307/674-1722

Best Chinese Food
Golden China Restaurant
  727 E. Brundage Ln., 307/674-7181

Best Coffee
Coffee House
  123 N. Main St., 307/674-8619

Best Ice Cream/Yogurt
  The stand at Sheridan Recreational District,
    Kendrick Park [no phone]

Best Italian Food
Ciao
  120 N. Main St., 307/672-2838

Best Pizza
Ole's Pizza and Spaghetti House
  1842 Coffeen Ave., Ste. 110, 307/672-3636

Best Sandwiches
Melinda's
  57 N. Main St., 307/674-9188
Sheridan Inn
  856 Broadway St., 307/674-5049

Best Steaks
Golden Steer
  2071 N. Main St., 307/674-9334

Standbys
Perkins
  1373 Coffeen Ave., 307/674-9336

WHEATLAND, WY

Best All-You-Can-Eat Buffet
Vimbo's
  203 Sixteenth St., 307/322-3725

Best Atmosphere
Maestro Espresso Bar
  962 Gilcrest, 307/322-4860

Best Breakfast
Breakfast Inn
  86 Sixteenth St., 307/322-9302

Best Burgers
Vimbo's
  203 Sixteenth St., 307/322-3725

Best Coffee
Maestro Espresso Bar
  962 Gilcrest, 307/322-4860

Best Ice Cream/Yogurt
Squaw Mountain Soda Fountain
  1501 Sixteenth St., 307/322-4932

Best Mexican Food
El Gringo's
  705 Tenth St., 307/322-4402

Best Seafood
Vimbo's
  203 Sixteenth St., 307/322-3725

W

Best Steaks
Vimbo's
    203 Sixteenth St., 307/322-3725

Standbys
Pizza Hut
    1801 Sixteenth St., 307/322-4001

W

Notes on Restaurants

City: _____
State: _____ Date of Visit: _____
Restaurant visited: _____
_____

Service: ❑ Satisfactory ❑ Good
         ❑ Excellent   ❑ Unsatisfactory

Food: ❑ Satisfactory ❑ Good
         ❑ Excellent   ❑ Unsatisfactory

Food/drink I especially enjoyed: _____
_____
_____
_____

Food/drink I did not like: _____
_____
_____
_____

Other notes: _____
_____
_____
_____
_____

City: _____
State: _____ Date of Visit: _____
Restaurant visited: _____
_____

Service: ❑ Satisfactory ❑ Good
         ❑ Excellent   ❑ Unsatisfactory

Food: ❑ Satisfactory ❑ Good
         ❑ Excellent   ❑ Unsatisfactory

Food/drink I especially enjoyed: _____
_____
_____
_____

Food/drink I did not like: _____
_____
_____
_____

Other notes: _____
_____
_____
_____
_____

City: _____
State: _____ Date of Visit: _____
Restaurant visited: _____

Service: ❑ Satisfactory   ❑ Good
          ❑ Excellent   ❑ Unsatisfactory

Food: ❑ Satisfactory   ❑ Good
          ❑ Excellent   ❑ Unsatisfactory

Food/drink I especially enjoyed: _____
_____
_____
_____

Food/drink I did not like: _____
_____
_____
_____

Other notes: _____
_____
_____
_____
_____

City: _____
State: _____ Date of Visit: _____
Restaurant visited: _____

Service: ❑ Satisfactory   ❑ Good
          ❑ Excellent   ❑ Unsatisfactory

Food: ❑ Satisfactory   ❑ Good
          ❑ Excellent   ❑ Unsatisfactory

Food/drink I especially enjoyed: _____
_____
_____
_____

Food/drink I did not like: _____
_____
_____
_____

Other notes: _____
_____
_____
_____
_____

City: _____
State: _____ Date of Visit: _____
Restaurant visited: _____

Service: ❑ Satisfactory ❑ Good
        ❑ Excellent ❑ Unsatisfactory

Food: ❑ Satisfactory ❑ Good
     ❑ Excellent ❑ Unsatisfactory

Food/drink I especially enjoyed: _____
_____
_____
_____

Food/drink I did not like: _____
_____
_____
_____

Other notes: _____
_____
_____
_____
_____

City: _____
State: _____ Date of Visit: _____
Restaurant visited: _____

Service: ❑ Satisfactory ❑ Good
        ❑ Excellent ❑ Unsatisfactory

Food: ❑ Satisfactory ❑ Good
     ❑ Excellent ❑ Unsatisfactory

Food/drink I especially enjoyed: _____
_____
_____
_____

Food/drink I did not like: _____
_____
_____
_____

Other notes: _____
_____
_____
_____
_____

City: _____
State: _____ Date of Visit: _____
Restaurant visited: _____
_____

Service: ❏ Satisfactory   ❏ Good
         ❏ Excellent   ❏ Unsatisfactory

Food: ❏ Satisfactory   ❏ Good
         ❏ Excellent   ❏ Unsatisfactory

Food/drink I especially enjoyed: _____
_____
_____
_____

Food/drink I did not like: _____
_____
_____
_____

Other notes: _____
_____
_____
_____
_____

City: _____
State: _____ Date of Visit: _____
Restaurant visited: _____
_____

Service: ❏ Satisfactory   ❏ Good
         ❏ Excellent   ❏ Unsatisfactory

Food: ❏ Satisfactory   ❏ Good
         ❏ Excellent   ❏ Unsatisfactory

Food/drink I especially enjoyed: _____
_____
_____
_____

Food/drink I did not like: _____
_____
_____
_____

Other notes: _____
_____
_____
_____
_____

City: _____
State: _____ Date of Visit: _____
Restaurant visited: _____
_____

Service: ❑ Satisfactory   ❑ Good
         ❑ Excellent   ❑ Unsatisfactory

Food: ❑ Satisfactory   ❑ Good
         ❑ Excellent   ❑ Unsatisfactory

Food/drink I especially enjoyed: _____
_____
_____
_____

Food/drink I did not like: _____
_____
_____
_____

Other notes: _____
_____
_____
_____
_____

City: _____
State: _____ Date of Visit: _____
Restaurant visited: _____

Service: ❑ Satisfactory   ❑ Good
         ❑ Excellent   ❑ Unsatisfactory

Food: ❑ Satisfactory   ❑ Good
         ❑ Excellent   ❑ Unsatisfactory

Food/drink I especially enjoyed: _____
_____
_____

Food/drink I did not like: _____
_____
_____
_____

Other notes: _____
_____
_____
_____
_____

Help make Where the Locals Eat *more accurate and useful— send us your comments and suggestions.*

The editors of this directory constantly strive to improve and update the information in **Where the Locals Eat.** Your views are important to us. If you have been a guest recently at one of the restaurants listed in our directory, we want your evaluation of it— good or bad. We hope that you will take a few moments to complete this short questionnaire—or a part of it— before returning it, in confidence, to us. Thank you!

A. Have you recently visited any of the restaurants included in *Where the Locals Eat*?
   If so, please let us know what you thought of them.

1. _____
   (name of restaurant)
in _____
   (city and state)

What was your opinion of this restaurant?

_____
_____
_____
_____
_____

2. _____
   (name of restaurant)
in _____
   (city and state)

What was your opinion of this restaurant?

_____
_____
_____
_____
_____

3. _____
   (name of restaurant)
in _____
   (city and state)

What was your opinion of this restaurant?

_____
_____
_____
_____
_____

B. Have you recently visited any restaurants that you believe should be included in the next edition of *Where the Locals Eat?*

If so, please tell us which restaurants you want us to consider. (We are especially interested in the restaurants in your area that are your favorites.)

_____
(name of restaurant)
in _____
(city and state)

_____
(name of restaurant)
in _____
(city and state)

_____
(name of restaurant)
in _____
(city and state)

C. How can we improve *Where the Locals Eat?* Your suggestions for improving our directory are welcome. If you have something to say about *Where the Locals Eat*—a comment, a correction, a compliment—please write your comments below. Thank you for your interest.

_____
_____
_____
_____
_____
_____
_____
_____
_____
_____
_____
_____

From:

_____
(name)

_____
(street address)

_____
(city, state, ZIP)

Return this questionnaire to: Lee Wilson, Editor, *Where the Locals Eat*, Magellan Press, Inc., P.O. Box 121075, Nashville, TN 37212. Photocopies will not be accepted.

Book Orders

Additional copies of **Where the Locals Eat** may be ordered directly from the publisher. Use the order blank below (or a photocopy) to place your order.

Please send **Where the Locals Eat** in the quantity indicated below.

Ship to:

_____
(name)

_____
(street address)

_____
(city, state, ZIP)

Number of Copies Ordered: _____

Amount enclosed: $_____

(Send $19.95 plus $2.00 shipping and handling *per copy ordered.* Make check payable to MAGELLAN PRESS, INC. Tennessee residents must include sales tax.)

Mail check and order blank to:

MAGELLAN PRESS, INC.
P.O. Box 121075
Nashville, TN 37212